T0134733

Lecture Notes in Computer Science 12710

More information about this subseries at http://www.springer.com/series/7410

Juan A. Garay (Ed.)

Public-Key Cryptography – PKC 2021

24th IACR International Conference on Practice and Theory of Public Key Cryptography Virtual Event, May 10–13, 2021 Proceedings, Part I

Editor
Juan A. Garay
Texas A&M University
College Station, TX, USA

ISSN 0302-9743 ISSN 1611-3349 (electronic)
Lecture Notes in Computer Science
ISBN 978-3-030-75244-6 ISBN 978-3-030-75245-3 (eBook)
https://doi.org/10.1007/978-3-030-75245-3

LNCS Sublibrary: SL4 – Security and Cryptology

This Springer imprint is published by the registered company Springer Nature Switzerland AG
The registered company address is: Gewerbestrasse 11, 6330 Cham, Switzerland

Preface

The 24th International Conference on Practice and Theory of Public-Key Cryptography (PKC 2021) was held virtually over Zoom from May 10th to May 13th, 2021. It was supposed to take place in Edinburgh, Scotland, but due to COVID-19 this was not possible. The conference is organized annually by the International Association for Cryptologic Research (IACR), and is the main annual conference with an explicit focus on public-key cryptography. Given NIST's efforts on standardization of post-quantum cryptography, this year constructions and cryptanalysis in this area were specially encouraged. These proceedings are comprised of two volumes and include the 52 papers that were selected by the Program Committee (PC), as well as a one-page abstract corresponding to one of the two invited talks, which reflect this year's focus.

The 52 accepted papers were selected out of a total of 156 received submissions. Submissions were assigned to at least three reviewers, while submissions by PC members received at least four reviews. Due to time constraints, the review period this year did not include a rebuttal step, where the authors get a chance to preview their papers' preliminary reviews. The review process, however, was fairly interactive, as in a large number of occasions reviewers posed questions to the authors. Six of the accepted papers were first conditionally accepted and received an additional round of reviewing; in addition, two of the papers were "soft merged" due to the similarity of results and shared one presentation slot.

Given the high number and quality of the submissions, the reviewing and paper selection process was a challenging task and I am deeply grateful to the members of the PC for their high dedication and thorough work. In addition to the PC members, many external reviewers joined the review process in their particular areas of expertise. We were fortunate to have this knowledgeable and energetic team of experts, and I am deeply grateful to all of them for their contributions. The submissions included two papers with which I had a conflict of interest (they were authored by current and/or close collaborators). For these two papers I abstained from the management of the discussion and delegated this task to a PC member. Many thanks to Hoeteck Wee and Vassilis Zikas, respectively, for their help in managing these two papers.

The paper submission, review and discussion processes were effectively and efficiently made possible by the Web-Submission-and-Review software, written by Shai Halevi, and hosted by the IACR. As always, many thanks to Shai for his assistance with the system's various features.

This year the program was further enriched by two invited talks by Léo Ducas (CWI, the Netherlands; "Lattices and Factoring") and Eike Kiltz (Ruhr-Universität Bochum, Germany; "How Provably Secure are (EC)DSA Signatures?"). My special thanks to Lèo and Eike for accepting the invitation and great presentations.

I am also grateful for their predisposition, availability, and efforts (unfortunately not fully realized when we decided to go virtual) to Markulf Kohlweiss and Petros Wallden, who served as General Co-chairs, and to Dimitris Karakostas (all from The

University of Edinburgh), who managed the conference's website. I finally thank all the authors who submitted papers to this conference, and all the conference attendees who made this event a truly intellectually stimulating one through their active (albeit remote) participation.

Next time, Edinburgh!

March 2021 Juan A. Garay

PKC 2021

The 24th International Conference on Practice and Theory of Public-Key Cryptography

Virtual Event
May 10–13, 2021

Organized in cooperation with IACR

General Chairs

Markulf Kohlweiss	The University of Edinburgh, UK
Petros Wallden	The University of Edinburgh, UK

Program Chair

Juan A. Garay	Texas A&M University, USA

Program Committee

Daniel Apon	NIST, USA
Christian Badertscher	IOHK, Switzerland
Saikrishna Badrinarayanan	Visa Research, USA
Manuel Barbosa	University of Porto, Portugal
Paulo Barreto	University of Washington-Tacoma, USA
Fabrice Benhamouda	Algorand Foundation, USA
Michele Ciampi	The University of Edinburgh, UK
Yi Deng	Chinese Academy of Sciences, China
Yfke Dulek	QuSoft and CWI, the Netherlands
Marc Joye	Zama, France
Shuichi Katsumata	AIST, Japan
Lisa Kohl	CWI, the Netherlands
Venkata Koppula	IIT Delhi, India
Changmin Lee	KIAS, South Korea
Feng-Hao Liu	Florida Atlantic University, USA
Vadim Lyubashevsky	IBM Research, Switzerland
Giulio Malavolta	Max Planck Institute, Germany
Mary Maller	Ethereum Foundation, UK
Takahiro Matsuda	AIST, Japan
Peihan Miao	University of Illinois at Chicago, USA
David Naccache	ENS, France
Adam O'Neill	University of Massachusetts Amherst, USA
Cristina Onete	University of Limoges and XLIM, France

Giorgos Panagiotakos	University of Athens, Greece
Alice Pellet-Mary	KUL, Belgium
Christophe Petit	University of Birmingham, UK
Bertram Poettering	IBM Research, Switzerland
Melissa Rossi	ANSSI, France
Olivier Sanders	Orange Labs, France
Berry Schoenmakers	TU Eindhoven, the Netherlands
Fang Song	Portland State University, USA
Akshayaram Srinivasan	Tata Institute of Fundamental Research, India
Qiang Tang	The University of Sydney, Australia
Hoeteck Wee	NTT Research and ENS, France
Vassilis Zikas	Purdue University, USA

Sponsoring Institutions

The Scottish Informatics and Computer Science Alliance (SICSA) Cyber Nexus
INPUT|OUTPUT
DFINITY

External Reviewers

Behzad Abdolmaleki
Ojaswi Acharya
Thomas Attema
Nuttapong Attrapadung
Reza Azarderakhsh
Karim Baghery
Shi Bai
James Bartusek
Andrea Basso
Carsten Baum
Ward Beullens
Olivier Blazy
Charlotte Bonte
Jonathan Bootle
Pedro Branco
Konstantinos Brazitikos
Xavier Bultel
Sèbastien Canard
Wouter Castryk
Jie Chen
Long Chen
Yu Chen
Benoit Chevallier-Mames
Wonhee Cho
Jérémy Chotard
Ran Cohen
Orel Cosseron
Geoffroy Couteau
Daniele Cozzo
Gareth Davies
Yi Deng
Jintai Ding
Ehsan Ebrahimi
Keita Emura
Thomas Espitau
Leo Fan
Antonio Faonio
Thibauld Feneuil
Hanwen Feng
Weiqi Feng
Luca De Feo
Rex Fernando
Ben Fisch
Boris Fouotsa
Pierre-Alain Fouque
Phillip Gajland
Chaya Ganesh
Rachit Garg
Romain Gay
Nicholas Genise
Riddhi Ghosal
Huijing Gong
Junqing Gong
Rishab Goyal
Vipul Goyal
François Gérard
Mohammad Hajiabadi
Shai Halevi
Mike Hamburg
Kyoohyung Han
Patrick Harasser
Brett Hemenway
Julia Hesse
Minki Hhan
Seungwan Hong
Yuncong Hu
Andreas Hlsing
Muhammad Ishaq
David Jao
Sam Jaques
Stanislaw Jarecki
Dingding Jia

Zhengzhong Jin
Daniel Jost
Bhavana Kanukurthi
Harish Karthikeyan
John Kelsey
Dongwoo Kim
Duhyeong Kim
Jiseung Kim
Fuyuki Kitagawa
Susumu Kiyoshima
Michael Klooss
Yashvanth Kondi
Brian Koziel
Hugo Krawczyk
Mukul Kulkarni
Nishant Kumar
Pèter Kutas
Fabien Laguillaumie
Qiqi Lai
Russel Lai
Anja Lehmann
Chengyu Lin
Xi Lin
Yanyan Liu
Chen-Da Liu-Zhang
George Lu
Steve Lu
Yun Lu
Zhenliang Lu
Fermi Ma
Shunli Ma
Gilles Macario-Rat
Christian Majenz
Nathan Manohar
Ange Martinelli
Simon-Philipp Merz
Romy Minko
Dustin Moody
Hiraku Morita
Michael Naehrig
Anderson Nascimento
Khoa Nguyen
Ngoc Khanh Nguyen
Anca Nitulescu
Martha Hovd Norberg
Hiroshi Onuki
Michele Orr
Jiaxin Pan
Bo Pang
Louiza Papachristodoulou
Sikhar Patranabis
Geovandro Pereira
Ray Perlner
Federico Pintore
Bernardo Portela
Youming Qiao
Tian Qiu
Willy Quach
Srinivasan Raghuraman
Divya Ravi
Lo Robert
Angela Robinson
Miruna Rosca
Paul Rösler
Yusuke Sakai
Dimitris Sakavalas
Peter Scholl
Jacob Schuldt
Rebecca Schwerdt
Toon Segers
Gregor Seiler
Yannick Seurin
Akash Shah
Sina Shiehian
Luisa Siniscalchi
Daniel Smith-Tone
Yongha Son
Yongsoo Song
Florian Speelman
Martijn Stam
Yiru Sun
Katsuyuki Takashima
Samuel Tap
Aravind Thyagarajan
Song Tian
Jacques Traoré
Yiannis Tselekounis
Bogdan Ursu
Prashant Vasudevan
Hendrik Waldner
Alexandre Wallet
Hailong Wang
Luping Wang
Yuyu Wang
Zhedong Wang
Charlotte Weitkämper
Weiqiang Wen
Benjamin Wesolowski
David Wu
Keita Xagawa
Tiancheng Xie
Anshu Yadav
Sophia Yakoubov
Shota Yamada
Takashi Yamakawa
Avishay Yanai
Kazuki Yoneyama
Aaram Yun
Thomas Zacharias
Mohammad Zaheri
Cong Zhang
Jiaheng Zhang
Kai Zhang
Yongjun Zhao

Contents – Part I

Post-Quantum Constructions and Cryptanalysis

Cryptographic Primitives and Schemes

Contents – Part II

Post-Quantum Constructions and Cryptanalysis

QCCA-Secure Generic Key Encapsulation Mechanism with Tighter Security in the Quantum Random Oracle Model

Xu Liu[1,2] and Mingqiang Wang[1,2](✉)

[1] School of Mathematics, Shandong University, Jinan, China
liuxu17@mail.sdu.edu.cn, wangmingqiang@sdu.edu.cn
[2] Key Laboratory of Cryptologic Technology and Information Security, Ministry of Education, Shandong University, Jinan, China

Abstract. Xagawa and Yamakawa (PQCrypto 2019) proved the transformation SXY can tightly turn DS secure PKEs into IND-qCCA secure KEMs in the quantum random oracle model (QROM). But transformations such as KC, TPunc that turn PKEs with standard security (OW-CPA or IND-CPA) into DS secure PKEs still suffer from quadratic security loss in the QROM. In this paper, we give a tighter security reduction for the transformation KC that turns OW-CPA secure deterministic PKEs into modified DS secure PKEs in the QROM. We use the Measure-Rewind-Measure One-Way to Hiding Lemma recently introduced by Kuchta et al. (EUROCRYPT 2020) to avoid the square-root advantage loss. Moreover, we extend it to the case that underlying PKEs are not perfectly correct. Combining with other transformations, we finally obtain a generic KEM from any IND-CPA secure PKE. Our security reduction has roughly the same tightness as the result of Kuchta et al. without any other assumptions and we achieve the stronger IND-qCCA security. We also give a similar result for another KEM transformation achieving the same security notion from any OW-CPA secure deterministic PKE.

Keywords: Key encapsulation mechanism · Quantum chosen ciphertext security · Quantum random oracle model

1 Introduction

Key encapsulation mechanism (KEM) is a foundational cryptography primitive. It can be used to construct efficient hybrid encryption using the KEM/DEM paradigm [8]. Indistinguishability under chosen ciphertext attacks (IND-CCA) is widely used as the desired security notion for KEM and public-key encryption (PKE). With the development of quantum computer, we need to develop cryptographic schemes that would be secure against both quantum and classical computers. In this paper, we consider the indistinguishability under quantum chosen ciphertext attacks (IND-qCCA) for KEM in the quantum random oracle model (QROM).

J. A. Garay (Ed.): PKC 2021, LNCS 12710, pp. 3–26, 2021.
https://doi.org/10.1007/978-3-030-75245-3_1

In the quantum world, one can deal with superposition states, which brings more capabilities to the adversaries. To achieve the security against quantum adversaries, we have to base our cryptographic constructions on quantum-resistant assumptions. But it is not sufficient if adversaries can interact with honest parties using quantum communication. Boneh et al. [6] argued that quantum random oracle model should be used instead of random oracle model (ROM) [4]. In the QROM, hash functions are modeled as public oracles similarly as ROM but with quantum access. Furthermore, Boneh and Zhandry [7] introduced the IND-qCCA security notion for PKE, where adversaries can make quantum queries to the decryption oracle. Their goal is to construct classical systems that remain secure even when implemented on a quantum computer, thereby potentially giving the attacker the ability to issue quantum queries. Following it, Xagawa and Yamakawa [22] considered the IND-qCCA security for KEM, where adversaries can make quantum queries to the decapsulation oracle. Note that different from PKE, there is no challenge messages queried by the adversary in the IND-CCA game for KEM. All interactions with the adversary use quantum communication. Therefore, the corresponding IND-qCCA security in the QROM is the security notion against fully quantum adversaries for KEM.

To achieve the IND-CCA security, generic transformations such as Fujisaki-Okamoto (FO) transformation [10,11] are usually used. They can transform a weakly secure (one-wayness under chosen plaintext attacks (OW-CPA) or indistinguishability under chosen plaintext attacks (IND-CPA)) PKE to a IND-CCA one. Dent [9] gave the KEM version of FO. Hofheinz, Hövelmanns and Kiltz [12] analyzed it in a modular way, decomposing it into two transformations named T and $\mathsf{U}^{\not\perp}$. They also introduced some variants of transformation $\mathsf{U}^{\not\perp}$ named $\mathsf{U}^{\not\perp}_m$, $\mathsf{U}^{\perp}$ and $\mathsf{U}^{\perp}_m$, and they gave a detailed result about them in the classical setting. Subsequent works [5,13,15–18] are devoted to the analysis in the quantum setting. The core tool used in these analysis is the One-Way to Hiding (O2H) Lemma [21] and its variants [2,5,12,18]. Roughly speaking, the O2H lemma can be used to construct a one-wayness adversary from a distinguisher.

Recently, Kuchta et al. [18] introduced a new O2H variant named Measure-Rewind-Measure One-Way to Hiding (MRM O2H) Lemma. It is the first variant to get rid of the square-root advantage loss, and using this lemma, they gave a security proof for FO from IND-CPA security to IND-CCA security without the square-root advantage loss for the first time. Their security proof is nearly tight for low query depth attacks. The case of (relatively) low query depth attacks tends to be of high practical interest, since it corresponds, for instance, to massively parallelized attacks, which are the standard approach to deal with high computation costs in practical cryptanalysis. However, their proof doesn't apply to the IND-qCCA security. As argued in [7,22], in order to be immune to quantum superposition attacks, quantum chosen ciphertext security is worth investigating. On the other hand, Saito, Xagawa and Yamakawa [20] introduced a new security notion named disjoint simulatability (DS). Intuitively, disjoint simulatability means that we can efficiently sample "fake ciphertexts" that are computationally indistinguishable from real ciphertexts ("simulatability"), while the set of possible fake ciphertexts is required to be (almost) disjoint from the set of real ciphertexts ("disjointness"). In addition, they gave a transformation named SXY which can tightly turn DS secure PKEs into IND-CCA secure KEMs. Furthermore, they find it can be easily extended to the stronger IND-qCCA security tightly also [22]. However, transformations KC and TPunc introduced in [20] from standard secure (OW-CPA or IND-CPA) PKEs to DS secure PKEs still suffer from quadratic security loss, so is the KEM combined with transformation SXY.

Our Contributions. In this paper, we analyze two generic KEMs and we prove that they achieve IND-qCCA security from standard security without quadratic security loss in the QROM. At the heart of our result is a tighter security reduction for the transformation KC. We modify the definition of DS and we use the MRM O2H lemma to prove that the transformation KC can transform a OW-CPA secure deterministic PKE (dPKE) into a modified DS secure PKE without the square-root advantage loss. Moreover, we don't require the underlying PKE to be perfectly correct as before.

The first KEM we analyzed is SXY $\circ$ KC $\circ$ T and the second KEM is SXY $\circ$ KC. We give an overview in Fig. 1. The upper part and the lower part of Fig. 1 are the two KEMs respectively. The second KEM is relatively simple, and it is the combination of transformation KC and transformation SXY. Xagawa and Yamakawa has already proved transformation SXY can tightly turn δ-correct DS secure dPKEs into IND-qCCA secure KEMs in the QROM (Lemma 5 [22]).

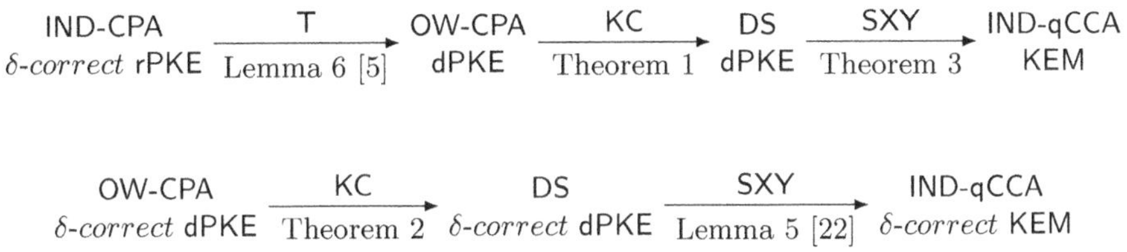

IND-CPA δ-*correct* rPKE	$\xrightarrow[\text{Lemma 6 [5]}]{\text{T}}$	OW-CPA dPKE	$\xrightarrow[\text{Theorem 1}]{\text{KC}}$	DS dPKE	$\xrightarrow[\text{Theorem 3}]{\text{SXY}}$	IND-qCCA KEM

OW-CPA δ-*correct* dPKE	$\xrightarrow[\text{Theorem 2}]{\text{KC}}$	DS δ-*correct* dPKE	$\xrightarrow[\text{Lemma 5 [22]}]{\text{SXY}}$	IND-qCCA δ-*correct* KEM

Fig. 1. Overview of KEMs.

In the previous security proofs of KC [17,20], some variants of O2H lemmas are used. However, they all incur a quadratic loss of security. The MRM O2H lemma doesn't suffer from it, but it requires the simulator can simulate both G and H. In our case, the simulator doesn't know the $m^* \in S$, however, the simulator can simulate G (or H) that should be reprogrammed at m^* by testing whether the queried m satisfies $\mathsf{Enc}(pk, m) = c^*$ or not instead. With a detailed analysis, the MRM O2H lemma can be applied to prove the second property of DS even if the underlying PKE is not perfectly correct. But it is difficult to satisfy the first requirement of DS with imperfectly correct underlying PKEs in KC. However, we find that the DS notion in [20] is slightly stronger, so we make a modification to its definition to relax the requirement. With this new DS notion, we get rid of the perfectly correctness requirement in KC. And finally we prove that the transformation KC can turn δ-correct OW-CPA secure dPKEs into δ-correct DS secure dPKEs without the square-root advantage loss in Theorem 2.[1]

The underlying PKE of above KEM is dPKE. If we want to let the underlying PKE be a rPKE (randomized PKE), we can apply the transformation T first. And this yields the first KEM. Although there exists results of transformation T that it can turn δ-correct IND-CPA secure rPKEs into OW-CPA secure dPKEs (Lemma 6 [5]), we cannot simply append it to the proof of the second KEM. The reason is that the concept of δ-correct doesn't apply to the resulting dPKE of T directly, though the resulting dPKE is not perfectly correct. So actually, Theorem 1 and Theorem 3 are different from corresponding Theorem 2 and Lemma 5 [22]. In the proof of Theorem 3, we use the method in [12,15] to deal with it. In the proof of Theorem 1, we make a direct analysis to get a better result. Specifically, we use a different Bad event than that in the proof of Theorem 2 to separate the case that a "bad" message is chosen.

Here we give a comparison of KEM transformations from IND-CPA secure PKEs in the QROM in Table 1. Kuchta et al.'s [18] proof of $\mathsf{FO}^{\not\perp}$ achieves the best known security bound of KEMs from IND-CPA security to IND-CCA security in the QROM. Xagawa and Yamakawa [22] gave the first KEM to achieve the stronger IND-qCCA security. And Jiang et al. [17] improved the security bound of Tpunc. But the security bound of the combination scheme is still larger than the first one in certain settings. Our proof of KEM := SXY ∘ KC ∘ T achieves the IND-qCCA security with tighter security bound than the second one, roughly the same as the first one. What's more, it doesn't need any other requirements.

Table 1. Comparison of KEM transformations from IND-CPA secure PKEs in the QROM. The "Security bound" column shows the dependence of the approximate upper bound on attacker's advantage $\mathsf{Adv}(\mathcal{A})$ against the KEM in terms of the attacker advantage ϵ against the underlying PKE, and $\mathcal{A}$'s total query number q or query depth d to quantum random oracles.

Transformation	Underlying security	Achieved security	Security bound	Other requirements
$\mathsf{FO}^{\not\perp} := \mathsf{U}^{\not\perp} \circ \mathsf{T}$[18]	IND-CPA	IND-CCA	$d^2\epsilon$	T[PKE, G] is η-injective.
SXY ∘ TPunc[17,22]	IND-CPA	IND-qCCA	$\sqrt{q\epsilon}$	PKE is perfectly correct.
SXY ∘ KC ∘ T [This work]	IND-CPA	IND-qCCA	$d^2\epsilon$	-

2 Preliminaries

2.1 Notation

For a finite set S, $|S|$ denotes the cardinality of S, and we denote the sampling of a uniformly random element x from S by $x \xleftarrow{\$} S$, while we denote the sampling

[1] In the main body of the paper, Theorem 2 actually follows Theorem 1. Here we reverse the order of introduction.

according to some distribution $\mathcal{D}$ by $x \leftarrow \mathcal{D}$. $\mathcal{U}_S$ denotes the uniform distribution over S. By $[\![B]\!]$ we denote the bit that is 1 if the Boolean statement B is true, and otherwise 0.

We denote deterministic computation of an algorithm A on input x by $y := \mathsf{A}(x)$. We denote algorithms with access to an oracle O by A^O. Unless stated otherwise, we assume all our algorithms to be probabilistic and denote the computation by $y \leftarrow \mathsf{A}(x)$. We also use the notation $y := \mathsf{A}(x; r)$ to make the randomness r explicit. By $\mathsf{Time}(\mathsf{A})$ we denote the running time of A.

Some algorithms such as Gen need a security parameter $\lambda \in \mathbb{N}$ as input. However, we usually omit it for simplicity. We say a function is *negligible* in λ if $f(\lambda) = \lambda^{-\omega(1)}$. PPT stands for probabilistic polynomial time.

2.2 Quantum Computation

We refer to [19] for basic of quantum computation. In this subsection we mainly present several useful lemmas.

Quantum Random Oracle Model. Following [3,6], we review a quantum oracle O as a mapping

$$|x\rangle |y\rangle \rightarrow |x\rangle |y \oplus O(x)\rangle,$$

where $O : \{0,1\}^n \rightarrow \{0,1\}^m, x \in \{0,1\}^n$ and $y \in \{0,1\}^m$. Roughly speaking, the quantum random oracle model (QROM) is an idealized model where a hash function is modeled as a publicly and quantumly accessible random oracle, while adversaries are only given classical oracle access in the classical random oracle model (ROM).

Lemma 1 ([20, Lemma 2.2]). *Let l be an integer. Let $\mathsf{H} : \{0,1\}^l \times X \rightarrow Y$ and $\mathsf{H}' : X \rightarrow Y$ be two independent random oracles. If an unbounded time quantum adversary $\mathcal{A}$ makes a query to H at most q_H times, then we have*

$$\left|\Pr[1 \leftarrow \mathcal{A}^{\mathsf{H},\mathsf{H}(s,\cdot)} | s \leftarrow \{0,1\}^l] - \Pr[1 \leftarrow \mathcal{A}^{\mathsf{H},\mathsf{H}'}]\right| \leq q_\mathsf{H} \cdot 2^{\frac{-l+1}{2}}$$

where all oracle accesses of $\mathcal{A}$ can be quantum.

Lemma 2 (Generic Distinguishing Problem with Bounded Probabilities [1,13,14]**).** *Let X be a finite set, and let $\lambda \in [0,1]$. $\mathsf{F}_1 : X \rightarrow \{0,1\}$ is the following function: For each $x \in X$, $\mathsf{F}_1(x) = 1$ with probability λ_x ($\lambda_x \leq \lambda$), and $\mathsf{F}_1(x) = 0$ else. F_2 is the constant zero function. Then, for any algorithm A issuing at most q quantum queries to F_1 or F_2, $|\Pr[1 \leftarrow \mathsf{A}^{\mathsf{F}_1}] - \Pr[1 \leftarrow \mathsf{A}^{\mathsf{F}_2}]| \leq 8q^2\lambda$.*

Lemma 3 (Measure-Rewind-Measure One-Way to Hiding [18, Lemma 3.3]**).** *Let $G, H : X \rightarrow Y$ be random functions, z be a random value, and $S \subseteq X$ be a random set such that $G(x) = H(x)$ for every $x \notin S$. The tuple (G, H, S, z) may have arbitrary joint distribution. Furthermore, let $\mathcal{A}^O$ be a quantum oracle* *algorithm which queries oracle O with query depth d. Then we can construct an algorithm* $\mathcal{D}^{G,H}(z)$ *such that* $\mathsf{Time}(\mathcal{D}^{G,H}) \approx 2 \cdot \mathsf{Time}(\mathcal{A}^O)^2$ *and*

$$\mathsf{Adv}(\mathcal{A}^O) \leq 4d \cdot \mathsf{Adv}(\mathcal{D}^{G,H}).$$

Here $\mathsf{Adv}(\mathcal{A}^O) := |P_{\mathsf{left}} - P_{\mathsf{right}}|$ *with*

$$P_{\mathsf{left}} := \Pr_{H,z}[1 \leftarrow \mathcal{A}^H(z)], \ P_{\mathsf{right}} := \Pr_{G,z}[1 \leftarrow \mathcal{A}^G(z)],$$

and

$$\mathsf{Adv}(\mathcal{D}^{G,H}) := \Pr_{G,H,S,z}[T \cap S \neq \varnothing | T \leftarrow \mathcal{D}^{G,H}(z)].$$

2.3 Public-Key Encryption

Definition 1 (PKE). *A* (randomized) *public-key encryption scheme* ((r)PKE) *is defined over a message space* $\mathcal{M}$, *a ciphertext space* $\mathcal{C}$, *a public key space* $\mathcal{PK}$ *and a secret key space* $\mathcal{SK}$. *It consists of a triple of algorithms* $\mathsf{PKE} = (\mathsf{Gen}, \mathsf{Enc}, \mathsf{Dec})$ *defined as follows.*

- $\mathsf{Gen} \to (pk, sk)$ *is a randomized algorithm that returns a public key* $pk \in \mathcal{PK}$ *and a secret key* $sk \in \mathcal{SK}$.
- $\mathsf{Enc}(pk, m) \to c$ *is a randomized algorithm that takes as input a public key* pk *and a message* $m \in \mathcal{M}$, *and outputs a ciphertext* $c \in \mathcal{C}$. *If necessary, we make the used randomness of* Enc *explicit by writing* $c := \mathsf{Enc}(pk, m; r)$, *where* $r \xleftarrow{\$} \mathcal{R}$ *and* $\mathcal{R}$ *is the randomness space.*
- $\mathsf{Dec}(sk, c) \to m/\perp$ *is a deterministic algorithm that takes as input a secret key* $sk \in \mathcal{SK}$ *and a ciphertext* $c \in \mathcal{C}$ *and returns either a message* $m \in \mathcal{M}$ *or a failure symbol* $\perp \notin \mathcal{M}$.

A deterministic *public-key encryption scheme* (dPKE) *is defined the same way, except that* Enc *is a deterministic algorithm.*

Definition 2 (Correctness [12]**).** *A public-key encryption scheme* PKE *is* δ-*correct if*

$$\mathrm{E}\left[\max_{m \in \mathcal{M}} \Pr[\mathsf{Dec}(sk, c) \neq m | c \leftarrow \mathsf{Enc}(pk, m)]\right] \leq \delta,$$

where the expectation is taken over $(pk, sk) \leftarrow \mathsf{Gen}$. *We say the* PKE *is perfectly correct if* $\delta = 0$.

Remark 1. Above correctness definition is in the standard model, there is no random oracle relative to the PKE. But we still use this definition in the random oracle model if random oracles have no effect on it.

[2] Actually, from the proof of lemma 3.2 and lemma 3.3 in [18], we have $\mathsf{Time}(\mathcal{D}^{G,H}) \approx \mathsf{Time}(\mathcal{B}_i^{G,H}) + \mathsf{Time}(\mathcal{C}_i^{G,H}) \approx \mathsf{Time}(\mathcal{B}_i^{G,H}) + \left(\mathsf{Time}(\mathcal{B}_i^{G,H}) + 2\left(\mathsf{Time}(\mathcal{A}_i^O) - \mathsf{Time}(\mathcal{B}_i^{G,H})\right)\right) \approx 2 \cdot \mathsf{Time}(\mathcal{A}^O)$.

Let $\mathsf{PKE} = (\mathsf{Gen}, \mathsf{Enc}, \mathsf{Dec})$ be a public-key encryption scheme with message space $\mathcal{M}$. We now define three security notions for it. We say the PKE is GOAL-ATK secure if $\mathsf{Adv}^{\mathsf{GOAL}\text{-}\mathsf{ATK}}_{\mathsf{PKE},\mathcal{A}}$ is negligible for any PPT adversary $\mathcal{A}$.

Definition 3 (OW-CPA). *The One-Wayness under Chosen Plaintext Attacks* (OW-CPA) *game for* PKE *is defined in Fig. 2, and the* OW-CPA *advantage of an adversary $\mathcal{A}$ against* PKE *is defined as* $\mathsf{Adv}^{\mathsf{OW}\text{-}\mathsf{CPA}}_{\mathsf{PKE},\mathcal{A}} := \Pr[\mathsf{OW}\text{-}\mathsf{CPA}^{\mathcal{A}}_{\mathsf{PKE}} \Rightarrow 1]$.

GAME $\mathsf{OW}\text{-}\mathsf{CPA}^{\mathcal{A}}_{\mathsf{PKE}}$	**GAME** $\mathsf{IND}\text{-}\mathsf{CPA}^{\mathcal{A}}_{\mathsf{PKE}}$
$(pk, sk) \leftarrow \mathsf{Gen}$	$(pk, sk) \leftarrow \mathsf{Gen}$
$m^* \xleftarrow{\$} \mathcal{M}$	$b \xleftarrow{\$} \{0, 1\}$
$c^* \leftarrow \mathsf{Enc}(pk, m^*)$	$(m_0^*, m_1^*, st) \leftarrow \mathcal{A}_1(pk)$
$m' \leftarrow \mathcal{A}(pk, c^*)$	$c^* \leftarrow \mathsf{Enc}(pk, m_b^*)$
return $[\![m' = m^*]\!]$	$b' \leftarrow \mathcal{A}_2(pk, c^*, st)$
	return $[\![b' = b]\!]$

Fig. 2. Games OW-CPA and IND-CPA for PKE.

Definition 4 (IND-CPA). *The Indistinguishability under Chosen Plaintext Attacks* (IND-CPA) *game for* PKE *is defined in Fig. 2, and the* IND-CPA *advantage of an adversary* $\mathcal{A} = (\mathcal{A}_1, \mathcal{A}_2)$ *against* PKE *is defined as* $\mathsf{Adv}^{\mathsf{IND}\text{-}\mathsf{CPA}}_{\mathsf{PKE},\mathcal{A}} := 2|\Pr[\mathsf{IND}\text{-}\mathsf{CPA}^{\mathcal{A}}_{\mathsf{PKE}} \Rightarrow 1] - 1/2|$.

Definition 5 (IND-qCCA [7]). *The Indistinguishability under quantum Chosen Ciphertext Attacks* (IND-qCCA) *game for* PKE *is defined in Fig. 3, and the* IND-qCCA *advantage of an adversary* $\mathcal{A} = (\mathcal{A}_1, \mathcal{A}_2)$ *against* PKE *is defined as* $\mathsf{Adv}^{\mathsf{IND}\text{-}\mathsf{qCCA}}_{\mathsf{PKE},\mathcal{A}} := |\Pr[\mathsf{IND}\text{-}\mathsf{qCCA}^{\mathcal{A}}_{\mathsf{PKE}} \Rightarrow 1] - 1/2|$.

GAME $\mathsf{IND}\text{-}\mathsf{qCCA}^{\mathcal{A}}_{\mathsf{PKE}}$	$\mathsf{Dec}_a(\sum_{c,m} \psi_{c,m} \lvert c, m\rangle)$
$(pk, sk) \leftarrow \mathsf{Gen}$	**return** $\sum_{c,m} \psi_{c,m} \lvert c, m \oplus f_a(c)\rangle$
$b \xleftarrow{\$} \{0, 1\}$	
$(m_0^*, m_1^*, st) \leftarrow \mathcal{A}_1^{\mathsf{Dec}_\perp}(pk)$	$f_a(c)$
$c^* \leftarrow \mathsf{Enc}(pk, m_b^*)$	**if** $c = a$
$b' \leftarrow \mathcal{A}_2^{\mathsf{Dec}_{c^*}}(pk, c^*, st)$	**return** $m' := \perp$
return $[\![b' = b]\!]$	**else return** $m' := \mathsf{Dec}(sk, c)$

Fig. 3. Game IND-qCCA for PKE.

Saito, Xagawa and Yamakawa [20] introduced a new security notion named DS for dPKE. Here we give a modified version and we keep the name unchanged in this paper.

Definition 6 (DS, modified from [20]). *Let $\mathcal{D}_{\mathcal{M}}$ denote an efficiently samplеable distribution on a set $\mathcal{M}$. A deterministic public-key encryption scheme* $\mathsf{PKE} = (\mathsf{Gen}, \mathsf{Enc}, \mathsf{Dec})$ *with plaintext and ciphertext spaces $\mathcal{M}$ and $\mathcal{C}$ is $\mathcal{D}_{\mathcal{M}}$-disjoint-simulatable* (DS) *if there exists a PPT algorithm $\mathcal{S}$ that satisfies the followings.*

- *Disjointness:*

$$\mathsf{Disj}_{\mathsf{PKE},\mathcal{S}} := \Pr[c^* \in \mathsf{Enc}(pk, \mathcal{M}) | (pk, sk) \leftarrow \mathsf{Gen}, c^* \leftarrow \mathcal{S}(pk)]$$

  is negligible.
- *Ciphertext-indistinguishability: For any PPT adversary $\mathcal{A}$,*

$$\mathsf{Adv}^{\mathsf{DS\text{-}IND}}_{\mathsf{PKE},\mathcal{D}_{\mathcal{M}},\mathcal{A},\mathcal{S}} :=$$

$$\left| \begin{array}{c} \Pr[1 \leftarrow \mathcal{A}(pk, c^*) | (pk, sk) \leftarrow \mathsf{Gen}, m^* \leftarrow \mathcal{D}_{\mathcal{M}}, c^* := \mathsf{Enc}(pk, m^*)] \\ - \Pr[1 \leftarrow \mathcal{A}(pk, c^*) | (pk, sk) \leftarrow \mathsf{Gen}, c^* \leftarrow \mathcal{S}(pk)] \end{array} \right|$$

  is negligible.

Remark 2. In the original definition of DS, the first condition is "statistical disjointness":

$$\mathsf{Disj}_{\mathsf{PKE},\mathcal{S}} := \max_{(pk,sk) \in \mathsf{Gen}(1^\lambda; \mathcal{R})} \Pr[c^* \in \mathsf{Enc}(pk, \mathcal{M}) | c^* \leftarrow \mathcal{S}(pk)]$$

is negligible, where λ is the security parameter and $\mathcal{R}$ denotes the randomness space for Gen. We relax this condition to "disjointness" as we find it is sufficient to prove those theorems we needed.

2.4 Key Encapsulation Mechanism

Definition 7 (KEM). *A key encapsulation mechanism* (KEM) *is defined over a key space $\mathcal{K}$, a ciphertext space $\mathcal{C}$, a public key space $\mathcal{PK}$ and a secret key space $\mathcal{SK}$. It consists of a triple of algorithms* $\mathsf{KEM} = (\mathsf{Gene}, \mathsf{Enca}, \mathsf{Deca})$ *defined as follows.*

- $\mathsf{Gene} \rightarrow (pk, sk)$ *is a randomized algorithm that returns a public key $pk \in \mathcal{PK}$ and a secret key $sk \in \mathcal{SK}$.*
- $\mathsf{Enca}(pk) \rightarrow (c, k)$ *is a randomized algorithm that takes as input a public key pk and outputs a ciphertext $c \in \mathcal{C}$ as well as a key $k \in \mathcal{K}$.*
- $\mathsf{Deca}(sk, c) \rightarrow k/\perp$ *is a deterministic algorithm that takes as input a secret key $sk \in \mathcal{SK}$ and a ciphertext $c \in \mathcal{C}$ and returns either a key $k \in \mathcal{K}$ or a failure symbol $\perp \notin \mathcal{K}$.*

Definition 8 (Correctness [12]). *A key encapsulation mechanism* KEM *is δ-correct if*

$$\Pr[\mathsf{Deca}(sk, c) \neq k | (pk, sk) \leftarrow \mathsf{Gene}, (c, k) \leftarrow \mathsf{Enca}(pk)] \leq \delta.$$

Let $\mathsf{KEM} = (\mathsf{Gene}, \mathsf{Enca}, \mathsf{Deca})$ be a key encapsulation mechanism with key space $\mathcal{K}$. Following the definition of IND-qCCA for PKE, the KEM version for it can be defined similarly. We say the KEM is IND-qCCA secure if $\mathsf{Adv}^{\mathsf{IND\text{-}qCCA}}_{\mathsf{KEM},\mathcal{A}}$ is negligible for any PPT adversary $\mathcal{A}$.

Definition 9 (IND-qCCA [22]). *The* IND-qCCA *game for* KEM *is defined in Fig. 4, and the* IND-qCCA *advantage of an adversary* $\mathcal{A}$ *against* KEM *is defined as* $\mathsf{Adv}^{\mathsf{IND\text{-}qCCA}}_{\mathsf{KEM},\mathcal{A}} := |\Pr[\mathsf{IND\text{-}qCCA}^{\mathcal{A}}_{\mathsf{KEM}} \Rightarrow 1] - 1/2|$.

GAME $\mathsf{IND\text{-}qCCA}^{\mathcal{A}}_{\mathsf{KEM}}$	$\mathsf{Deca}_a(\sum_{c,k} \psi_{c,k} \vert c, k\rangle)$
$(pk, sk) \leftarrow \mathsf{Gene}$	**return** $\sum_{c,k} \psi_{c,k} \vert c, k \oplus f_a(c)\rangle$
$b \xleftarrow{\$} \{0, 1\}$	
$(c^*, k_0^*) \leftarrow \mathsf{Enca}(pk)$	$\underline{f_a(c)}$
$k_1^* \xleftarrow{\$} \mathcal{K}$	**if** $c = a$
$b' \leftarrow \mathcal{A}^{\mathsf{Deca}_{c^*}}(pk, c^*, k_b^*)$	**return** $k' := \perp$
return $[\![b' = b]\!]$	**else return** $k' := \mathsf{Deca}(sk, c)$

Fig. 4. Game IND-qCCA for KEM.

3 Tighter Proofs for the Transformation KC

In this section, we give a tighter security reduction for the transformation KC [20] that transforms OW-CPA secure dPKEs into DS secure dPKEs without the perfect correctness requirement of underlying PKEs.

Transformation KC. To a deterministic public-key encryption scheme $\mathsf{PKE} = (\mathsf{Gen}, \mathsf{Enc}, \mathsf{Dec})$ with message space $\mathcal{M}$, and a hash function $\mathsf{H} : \mathcal{M} \to \{0, 1\}^n$, we associate $\mathsf{PKE}' := \mathsf{KC}[\mathsf{PKE}, \mathsf{H}]$. The algorithms of $\mathsf{PKE}' = (\mathsf{Gen}', \mathsf{Enc}', \mathsf{Dec}')$ are defined in Fig. 5.

$\underline{\mathsf{Gen}'}$	$\underline{\mathsf{Enc}'(pk, m)}$	$\underline{\mathsf{Dec}'(sk, (c, d))}$	$\underline{\mathcal{S}(pk)}$
$(pk, sk) \leftarrow \mathsf{Gen}$	$c := \mathsf{Enc}(pk, m)$	$m' := \mathsf{Dec}(sk, c)$	$m^* \leftarrow \mathcal{U}_{\mathcal{M}}$
return (pk, sk)	$d := \mathsf{H}(m)$	**if** $m' = \perp$ **or** $\mathsf{H}(m') \neq d$	$c^* := \mathsf{Enc}(pk, m^*)$
	return (c, d)	**return** $\perp$	$d^* \xleftarrow{\$} \{0, 1\}^n$
		else return m'	**return** (c^*, d^*)

Fig. 5. $\mathsf{PKE}' = (\mathsf{Gen}', \mathsf{Enc}', \mathsf{Dec}') := \mathsf{KC}[\mathsf{PKE}, \mathsf{H}]$ with simulator $\mathcal{S}$.

Before we prove the security of KC, we first review the transformation T introduced in [12].

Transformation T. To a public-key encryption scheme $\mathsf{PKE}_0 = (\mathsf{Gen}_0, \mathsf{Enc}_0, \mathsf{Dec}_0)$ with message space $\mathcal{M}$ and randomness space $\mathcal{R}$, and a hash function $\mathsf{G}: \mathcal{M} \to \mathcal{R}$, we associate $\mathsf{PKE} := \mathsf{T}[\mathsf{PKE}_0, \mathsf{G}]$. The algorithms of $\mathsf{PKE} = (\mathsf{Gen}, \mathsf{Enc}, \mathsf{Dec})$ are defined in Fig. 6.

$\underline{\mathsf{Gen}}$	$\underline{\mathsf{Enc}(pk, m)}$	$\underline{\mathsf{Dec}(sk, c)}$
$(pk, sk) \leftarrow \mathsf{Gen}_0$	$c := \mathsf{Enc}_0(pk, m; \mathsf{G}(m))$	$m' := \mathsf{Dec}_0(sk, c)$
return (pk, sk)	**return** c	**if** $m' = \perp$ **or** $\mathsf{Enc}_0(pk, m'; \mathsf{G}(m')) \neq c$
		return $\perp$
		else return m'

Fig. 6. $\mathsf{PKE} = (\mathsf{Gen}, \mathsf{Enc}, \mathsf{Dec}) := \mathsf{T}[\mathsf{PKE}_0, \mathsf{G}]$.

Next, we give a lemma related to the transformation T. It roughly speaks that there is a high probability the ciphertext corresponding to a randomly chosen message has only one preimage with regard to $\mathsf{PKE} := \mathsf{T}[\mathsf{PKE}_0, \mathsf{G}]$.

Lemma 4. *Let* $\mathsf{PKE}_0 = (\mathsf{Gen}_0, \mathsf{Enc}_0, \mathsf{Dec}_0)$ *be a* δ*-correct* rPKE *with message space* $\mathcal{M}$ *and randomness space* $\mathcal{R}$*. We define a set with respect to fixed* (pk, sk) *and* $\mathsf{G} \in \Omega_{\mathsf{G}}$:

$$S^{collision}_{(pk,sk),\mathsf{G}} := \{m \in \mathcal{M} | \exists m' \neq m, \mathsf{Enc}_0(pk, m'; \mathsf{G}(m')) = \mathsf{Enc}_0(pk, m; \mathsf{G}(m))\},$$

where Ω_{G} *denotes the set of all functions* $\mathsf{G}: \mathcal{M} \to \mathcal{R}$.

Then we have

$$\Pr[m \in S^{collision}_{(pk,sk),\mathsf{G}} | (pk, sk) \leftarrow \mathsf{Gen}_0, \mathsf{G} \xleftarrow{\$} \Omega_{\mathsf{G}}, m \xleftarrow{\$} \mathcal{M}] \leq 2\delta.$$

Proof. From the definition of δ-correct, we have

$$\underset{(pk,sk)\leftarrow\mathsf{Gen}_0}{\mathrm{E}} \left[\max_{m \in \mathcal{M}} \Pr[\mathsf{Dec}_0(sk, c) \neq m | c \leftarrow \mathsf{Enc}_0(pk, m)] \right] \leq \delta.$$

The inequality still holds when the m is chosen at random, i.e.,

$$\underset{(pk,sk)\leftarrow\mathsf{Gen}_0}{\mathrm{E}} \left[\underset{m \xleftarrow{\$} \mathcal{M}}{\mathrm{E}} \Pr[\mathsf{Dec}_0(sk, c) \neq m | c \leftarrow \mathsf{Enc}_0(pk, m)] \right] \leq \delta.$$

We represent above inequality in a different form with equivalent meaning:

$$\Pr[\mathsf{Dec}_0(sk, c) \neq m | (pk, sk) \leftarrow \mathsf{Gen}_0, m \xleftarrow{\$} \mathcal{M}, c \leftarrow \mathsf{Enc}_0(pk, m)] \leq \delta.$$

Then we make the randomness used by Enc_0 explicit:

$$\Pr[\mathsf{Dec}_0(sk, \mathsf{Enc}_0(pk, m; r)) \neq m | (pk, sk) \leftarrow \mathsf{Gen}_0, m \xleftarrow{\$} \mathcal{M}, r \xleftarrow{\$} \mathcal{R}] \leq \delta.$$

It equals that:

$$\Pr[\mathsf{Dec_0}(sk, \mathsf{Enc_0}(pk, m; \mathsf{G}(m))) \neq m | (pk, sk) \leftarrow \mathsf{Gen_0}, m \xleftarrow{\$} \mathcal{M}, \mathsf{G} \xleftarrow{\$} \Omega_{\mathsf{G}}] \leq \delta.$$

Here we define a set in which messages are incorrectly decrypted with respect to fixed (pk, sk) and G:

$$S^{error}_{(pk,sk),\mathsf{G}} := \{m \in \mathcal{M} | \mathsf{Dec_0}(sk, \mathsf{Enc_0}(pk, m; \mathsf{G}(m))) \neq m\}.$$

Finally, we have

$$\begin{aligned}
&\Pr[m \in S^{collision}_{(pk,sk),\mathsf{G}} | (pk, sk) \leftarrow \mathsf{Gen_0}, \mathsf{G} \xleftarrow{\$} \Omega_{\mathsf{G}}, m \xleftarrow{\$} \mathcal{M}] \\
&\leq 2 \Pr[m \in S^{collision}_{(pk,sk),\mathsf{G}} \cap S^{error}_{(pk,sk),\mathsf{G}} | (pk, sk) \leftarrow \mathsf{Gen_0}, \mathsf{G} \xleftarrow{\$} \Omega_{\mathsf{G}}, m \xleftarrow{\$} \mathcal{M}] \\
&\leq 2 \Pr[m \in S^{error}_{(pk,sk),\mathsf{G}} | (pk, sk) \leftarrow \mathsf{Gen_0}, \mathsf{G} \xleftarrow{\$} \Omega_{\mathsf{G}}, m \xleftarrow{\$} \mathcal{M}] \\
&= 2 \Pr[\mathsf{Dec_0}(sk, \mathsf{Enc_0}(pk, m; \mathsf{G}(m))) \neq m | (pk, sk) \leftarrow \mathsf{Gen_0}, m \xleftarrow{\$} \mathcal{M}, \mathsf{G} \xleftarrow{\$} \Omega_{\mathsf{G}}] \\
&\leq 2\delta,
\end{aligned}$$

where the first inequality follows from the fact that m is chosen randomly and $|S^{collision}_{(pk,sk),\mathsf{G}} \setminus S^{error}_{(pk,sk),\mathsf{G}}| \leq |S^{collision}_{(pk,sk),\mathsf{G}} \cap S^{error}_{(pk,sk),\mathsf{G}}|$ for fixed (pk, sk) and G. □

Now we are ready to prove the security of KC in the QROM. In particular, we prove it in two cases. The first case is that the underlying dPKE is derived from T, as opposed to a general δ-correct dPKE in the second case. In both cases, underlying PKEs don't need to be perfectly correct.

Previous proofs [17,20] use some variants of O2H lemma, but they all incur a quadratic loss of security. Kuchta et al. [18] recently introduced the MRM O2H lemma (Lemma 3) without the square-root advantage loss. We apply it to KC and we avoid the square-root advantage loss in the proof accordingly.

Theorem 1 (Security of KC in the QROM, Case 1). *Let PKE be a dPKE transformed from $\mathsf{PKE_0}$ by T, i.e., $\mathsf{PKE} := \mathsf{T}[\mathsf{PKE_0}, \mathsf{G}]$. $\mathsf{PKE_0}$ is a δ-correct rPKE with message space $\mathcal{M}$ and randomness space $\mathcal{R}$. Let $\mathsf{G} : \mathcal{M} \rightarrow \mathcal{R}$, $\mathsf{H} : \mathcal{M} \rightarrow \{0,1\}^n$ be hash functions modeled as quantum random oracles. $\mathsf{PKE}' := \mathsf{KC}[\mathsf{PKE}, \mathsf{H}]$ and $\mathcal{S}$ is the algorithm defined in Fig. 5. Then we have $\mathsf{Disj}_{\mathsf{PKE}',\mathcal{S}} \leq 2^{-n} + 2\delta$. Moreover, for any adversary $\mathcal{A}$ against the $\mathsf{DS\text{-}IND}$ security of PKE' issuing quantum queries to H with depth d_{H}, there exists an adversary $\mathcal{B}$ against the $\mathsf{OW\text{-}CPA}$ security of PKE such that*

$$\mathsf{Adv}^{\mathsf{DS\text{-}IND}}_{\mathsf{PKE}',\mathcal{U}_{\mathcal{M}},\mathcal{A},\mathcal{S}} \leq 4d_{\mathsf{H}} \cdot (\mathsf{Adv}^{\mathsf{OW\text{-}CPA}}_{\mathsf{PKE},\mathcal{B}} + 2\delta)$$

and $\mathsf{Time}(\mathcal{B}) \approx 2 \cdot \mathsf{Time}(\mathcal{A})$.

Proof. We first define two events:

$$\mathsf{Bad} := [m^* \in S^{collision}_{(pk,sk),\mathsf{G}} | (pk, sk) \leftarrow \mathsf{Gen}, \mathsf{G} \xleftarrow{\$} \Omega_{\mathsf{G}}, m^* \xleftarrow{\$} \mathcal{M}],$$

where $S^{collision}_{(pk,sk),\mathsf{G}}$ is defined in Lemma 4, and Lemma 4 says that $\Pr[\mathsf{Bad}] \leq 2\delta$ as Gen equals $\mathsf{Gen_0}$;

$$\mathsf{Disj} := [(c^*, d^*) \in \mathsf{Enc}'(pk, \mathcal{M}) | (pk, sk) \leftarrow \mathsf{Gen}', (c^*, d^*) \leftarrow \mathcal{S}(pk)].$$

Then, we have

$$\begin{aligned} \mathsf{Disj}_{\mathsf{PKE}',\mathcal{S}} &= \Pr[\mathsf{Disj}] \\ &= \Pr[\mathsf{Disj} \wedge \overline{\mathsf{Bad}}] + \Pr[\mathsf{Disj} \wedge \mathsf{Bad}] \\ &\leq \Pr[\mathsf{Disj} \wedge \overline{\mathsf{Bad}}] + \Pr[\mathsf{Bad}] \\ &\leq 2^{-n} + 2\delta, \end{aligned}$$

where the first equality follows from the definition of DS and the last inequality follows from the fact that if Bad doesn't happen, the only possibility that Disj happens is the second part d^* of the element returned by $\mathcal{S}$ collides with the unique value which is $\mathsf{H}(m^*)$. The probability of this is 2^{-n} as d^* is chosen uniformly at random.

To prove the rest of the theorem, we consider games in Fig. 7. From the definition of DS, we have

$$\mathsf{Adv}^{\mathsf{DS\text{-}IND}}_{\mathsf{PKE}',\mathcal{U}_{\mathcal{M}},\mathcal{A},\mathcal{S}} = |\Pr[G_0^{\mathcal{A}} \Rightarrow 1] - \Pr[G_1^{\mathcal{A}} \Rightarrow 1]|.$$

GAMES $G_0 - G_2$

$(pk, sk) \leftarrow \mathsf{Gen}$; $\mathsf{H} \xleftarrow{\$} \Omega_{\mathsf{H}}$
$\mathsf{G} \xleftarrow{\$} \Omega_{\mathsf{G}}$
$m^* \xleftarrow{\$} \mathcal{M}$
$c^* := \mathsf{Enc}(pk, m^*) = \mathsf{Enc_0}(pk, m^*; \mathsf{G}(m^*))$
$d^* := \mathsf{H}(m^*)$ $//G_0, G_2$
$d^* \xleftarrow{\$} \{0,1\}^n$ $//G_1$
$\mathsf{H}' := \mathsf{H}$; $S_{c^*} := \{m \in \mathcal{M} | \mathsf{Enc}(pk, m) = c^*\}$ $//G_2$
for each $m \in S_{c^*}$, $\mathsf{H}'(m) \xleftarrow{\$} \{0,1\}^n$ $//G_2$
$b \leftarrow \mathcal{A}^{\mathsf{H},\mathsf{G}}(pk, (c^*, d^*))$ $//G_0 - G_1$
$b \leftarrow \mathcal{A}^{\mathsf{H}',\mathsf{G}}(pk, (c^*, d^*))$ $//G_2$
return b

Fig. 7. Games $G_0 - G_2$ for the proof of Theorem 1.

Notice that H', d^* in game G_2 are randomly distributed as H, d^* in game G_1, and they are independent of each other and $\mathcal{A}$'s other view (G, pk, c^*) in both G_1 and G_2, that is, the environments of $\mathcal{A}$ in G_1 and G_2 have the same distribution. It follows that

$$\Pr[G_1^{\mathcal{A}} \Rightarrow 1] = \Pr[G_2^{\mathcal{A}} \Rightarrow 1].$$

The only difference between game G_0 and game G_2 is that $\mathcal{A}$ is interacted with H or H' respectively. Therefore, applying Lemma 3 with $X = \mathcal{M}, Y = \{0,1\}^n, G = \mathsf{H}, H = \mathsf{H}', S = S_{c^*}, z = (\mathsf{G}, pk, (c^*, d^*))^3$ and $\mathcal{A}$, we can construct algorithm $\mathcal{D}$, with run-time $\approx 2 \cdot \mathsf{Time}(\mathcal{A})$ and making oracle calls to H, H' and G in game G_3, such that

$$|\Pr[G_0^{\mathcal{A}} \Rightarrow 1] - \Pr[G_2^{\mathcal{A}} \Rightarrow 1]| \leq 4d_{\mathsf{H}} \cdot \Pr[T \cap S_{c^*} \neq \varnothing],$$

where T is the output of $\mathcal{D}$ and game G_3 is described in Fig. 8.

GAME G_3

$(pk, sk) \leftarrow \mathsf{Gen};\ \mathsf{H} \xleftarrow{\$} \Omega_{\mathsf{H}}$

$\mathsf{G} \xleftarrow{\$} \Omega_{\mathsf{G}}$

$m^* \xleftarrow{\$} \mathcal{M}$

$c^* := \mathsf{Enc}(pk, m^*) = \mathsf{Enc_0}(pk, m^*; \mathsf{G}(m^*))$

$d^* := \mathsf{H}(m^*)$

$\mathsf{H}' := \mathsf{H};\ S_{c^*} := \{m \in \mathcal{M} | \mathsf{Enc}(pk, m) = c^*\}$

for each $m \in S_{c^*},\ \mathsf{H}'(m) \xleftarrow{\$} \{0,1\}^n$

$T \leftarrow \mathcal{D}^{\mathsf{H},\mathsf{H}',\mathsf{G}}(pk, (c^*, d^*))$

if $T \cap S_{c^*} \neq \varnothing$

  $m' :=$ any element $\in T \cap S_{c^*}$

else $m' := \perp$

return $[\![m' = m^*]\!]$

Fig. 8. Game G_3 for the proof of Theorem 1.

The game G_3 actually can be seen as the $\mathsf{OW\text{-}CPA}$ game for PKE, in which an adversary $\mathcal{B}$ invokes the algorithm $\mathcal{D}$. More specifically, the $\mathsf{OW\text{-}CPA}$ game for PKE and the adversary $\mathcal{B}$ against PKE we construct are described in Fig. 9. We note that $\mathcal{B}$ cannot directly compute $\mathsf{H}(m^*)$ because m^* is unknown for $\mathcal{B}$, but $\mathcal{B}$ can choose a random value $d^* \in \{0,1\}^n$ as $\mathsf{H}(m^*)$ in advance and simulate H using it, i.e., $\mathcal{B}$ returns d^* if $\mathsf{Enc}(pk, m) = c^*$, else returns $\mathsf{H}(m)$, where m is $\mathcal{D}$'s query to H. Furthermore, if Bad doesn't happen, the set S_{c^*} has only one element, m^*, and the environments of $\mathcal{D}$ in game G_3 and game $\mathsf{OW\text{-}CPA}_{\mathsf{PKE}}^{\mathcal{B}}$ have the same distribution. In other words, $\mathcal{B}$ can simulate the environment for $\mathcal{D}$ as

[3] Like the note of [2, Theorem 1], if we want to consider an adversary $\mathcal{A}^{H,F}()$, we can instead write $\mathcal{A}^{H}(F)$ where F is a complete (exponential size) description of F since there is no assumption on the size of z. From another point of view, we can simply extend the Lemma 3 to cover this case explicitly by letting $\mathcal{D}$ forward $\mathcal{A}$'s queries to the additional oracles and send the replies back to $\mathcal{A}$.

in game G_3 perfectly in the case that Bad doesn't happen. Therefore, we have

$$\begin{aligned}\mathsf{Adv}^{\mathsf{OW\text{-}CPA}}_{\mathsf{PKE},\mathcal{B}} &= \Pr[\mathsf{OW\text{-}CPA}^{\mathcal{B}}_{\mathsf{PKE}} \Rightarrow 1] \\ &= \Pr[\mathcal{B} \Rightarrow m^*] \\ &\geq \Pr[\mathcal{B} \Rightarrow m^* \wedge \overline{\mathsf{Bad}}] \\ &= \Pr[T \cap S_{c^*} \neq \varnothing \wedge \overline{\mathsf{Bad}}],\end{aligned}$$

where the final equality holds for the same reason that if Bad doesn't happen, the set S_{c^*} has only one element, m^*.

GAME $\mathsf{OW\text{-}CPA}^{\mathcal{B}}_{\mathsf{PKE}}$	$\mathcal{B}^{\mathsf{G}}(pk, c^*)$
$(pk, sk) \leftarrow \mathsf{Gen}$	$\mathsf{H}' \xleftarrow{\$} \Omega_{\mathsf{H}};\ d^* \xleftarrow{\$} \{0,1\}^n$
$\mathsf{G} \xleftarrow{\$} \Omega_{\mathsf{G}}$	$\mathsf{H} := \mathsf{H}';\ S_{c^*} := \{m \in \mathcal{M} \mid \mathsf{Enc}(pk, m) = c^*\}$
$m^* \xleftarrow{\$} \mathcal{M}$	**for each** $m \in S_{c^*}$, $\mathsf{H}(m) := d^*$
$c^* := \mathsf{Enc}(pk, m^*)$	$T \leftarrow \mathcal{D}^{\mathsf{H},\mathsf{H}',\mathsf{G}}(pk, (c^*, d^*))$
$\quad = \mathsf{Enc}_0(pk, m^*; \mathsf{G}(m^*))$	**if** $T \cap S_{c^*} \neq \varnothing$
$m' \leftarrow \mathcal{B}^{\mathsf{G}}(pk, c^*)$	$\quad$ **return** any element $\in T \cap S_{c^*}$
return $[\![m' = m^*]\!]$	**else return** $\perp$

Fig. 9. Game $\mathsf{OW\text{-}CPA}^{\mathcal{B}}_{\mathsf{PKE}}$ for the proof of Theorem 1.

Combining above formulas with the following simple inequality:

$$\Pr[T \cap S_{c^*} \neq \varnothing] \leq \Pr[T \cap S_{c^*} \neq \varnothing \wedge \overline{\mathsf{Bad}}] + \Pr[\mathsf{Bad}],$$

we finally obtain

$$\begin{aligned}\mathsf{Adv}^{\mathsf{DS\text{-}IND}}_{\mathsf{PKE}',\mathcal{U}_{\mathcal{M}},\mathcal{A},\mathcal{S}} &= |\Pr[G_0^{\mathcal{A}} \Rightarrow 1] - \Pr[G_1^{\mathcal{A}} \Rightarrow 1]| \\ &= |\Pr[G_0^{\mathcal{A}} \Rightarrow 1] - \Pr[G_2^{\mathcal{A}} \Rightarrow 1]| \\ &\leq 4d_{\mathsf{H}} \cdot \Pr[T \cap S_{c^*} \neq \varnothing] \\ &\leq 4d_{\mathsf{H}} \cdot (\Pr[T \cap S_{c^*} \neq \varnothing \wedge \overline{\mathsf{Bad}}] + \Pr[\mathsf{Bad}]) \\ &\leq 4d_{\mathsf{H}} \cdot (\mathsf{Adv}^{\mathsf{OW\text{-}CPA}}_{\mathsf{PKE},\mathcal{B}} + 2\delta).\end{aligned}$$

□

Theorem 2 (Security of KC in the QROM, Case 2). *Let* PKE *be a* δ*-correct* dPKE *with message space* $\mathcal{M}$*. Let* $\mathsf{H} : \mathcal{M} \to \{0,1\}^n$ *be a hash function modeled as a quantum random oracle.* $\mathsf{PKE}' := \mathsf{KC}[\mathsf{PKE}, \mathsf{H}]$ *and* $\mathcal{S}$ *is the algorithm defined in Fig. 5. Then we have* $\mathsf{Disj}_{\mathsf{PKE}',\mathcal{S}} \leq 2^{-n} + \delta$*. Moreover, for any adversary* $\mathcal{A}$ *against the* DS-IND *security of* PKE′ *issuing quantum queries to* H *with depth* d_{H}*, there exists an adversary* $\mathcal{B}$ *against the* OW-CPA *security of* PKE *such that*

$$\mathsf{Adv}^{\mathsf{DS\text{-}IND}}_{\mathsf{PKE}',\mathcal{U}_{\mathcal{M}},\mathcal{A},\mathcal{S}} \leq 4d_{\mathsf{H}} \cdot (\mathsf{Adv}^{\mathsf{OW\text{-}CPA}}_{\mathsf{PKE},\mathcal{B}} + \delta)$$

and $\mathsf{Time}(\mathcal{B}) \approx 2 \cdot \mathsf{Time}(\mathcal{A})$.

Proof. The proof is essentially the same as Theorem 1's proof, except for the definition of Bad:

$$\mathsf{Bad} := [\exists m \in \mathcal{M},\ \mathsf{Dec}(sk, \mathsf{Enc}(pk, m)) \neq m | (pk, sk) \leftarrow \mathsf{Gen}].$$

From the fact that PKE is deterministic and the definition of δ-correct, we have

$$\Pr[\mathsf{Bad}] \leq \delta.$$

Then, we complete the proof. □

Remark 3. PKE' remains δ-correct.

4 QCCA-Secure Generic KEM in the QROM

In this section, we prove that DS secure dPKEs can be converted to IND-qCCA secure KEMs by transformation SXY [20] in the QROM. In particular, we also consider two cases corresponding to the two cases in Sect. 3. The first case is that the underlying dPKE is derived from $\mathsf{KC} \circ \mathsf{T}$[4], as opposed to a general δ-correct dPKE in the second case. In both cases, underlying PKEs don't need to be perfectly correct. Note that the second case was proved in [22], we present it here as a lemma.

At the end, we combine results in this paper and get two IND-qCCA secure generic KEMs without quadratic security loss in the QROM. One is based on rPKEs and the other is based on dPKEs.

Transformation SXY. To a deterministic public-key encryption scheme $\mathsf{PKE}' = (\mathsf{Gen}', \mathsf{Enc}', \mathsf{Dec}')$ with message space $\mathcal{M}$ and ciphertext space $\mathcal{C}$, and two hash functions $\mathsf{H}_1 : \mathcal{M} \to \mathcal{K}$, $\mathsf{H}_2 : \{0,1\}^l \times \mathcal{C} \to \mathcal{K}$, we associate $\mathsf{KEM} := \mathsf{SXY}[\mathsf{PKE}', \mathsf{H}_1, \mathsf{H}_2]$. The algorithms of $\mathsf{KEM} = (\mathsf{Gene}, \mathsf{Enca}, \mathsf{Deca})$ are defined in Fig. 10.

<u>Gene</u>	<u>Enca(pk)</u>	<u>Deca($(sk, s), c$)</u>
$(pk, sk) \leftarrow \mathsf{Gen}'$	$m \leftarrow \mathcal{D}_{\mathcal{M}}$	$m' := \mathsf{Dec}'(sk, c)$
$s \xleftarrow{\$} \{0,1\}^l$	$c := \mathsf{Enc}'(pk, m)$	**if** $m' = \perp$ **or** $\mathsf{Enc}'(pk, m') \neq c$
return $(pk, (sk, s))$	$k := \mathsf{H}_1(m)$	**return** $k' := \mathsf{H}_2(s, c)$
	return (c, k)	**else return** $k' := \mathsf{H}_1(m')$

Fig. 10. $\mathsf{KEM} = (\mathsf{Gene}, \mathsf{Enca}, \mathsf{Deca}) := \mathsf{SXY}[\mathsf{PKE}', \mathsf{H}_1, \mathsf{H}_2]$.

[4] T is the point and KC can be replaced by other suitable transformations.

Theorem 3 (IND-qCCA **Security of** SXY **in the QROM, Case 1**). *Let* PKE' *be a* dPKE *transformed from* PKE_0 *by* $\mathsf{KC} \circ \mathsf{T}$, *i.e.*, $\mathsf{PKE}' := \mathsf{KC}[\mathsf{T}[\mathsf{PKE}_0, \mathsf{G}], \mathsf{H}]$. PKE_0 *is a* δ*-correct* rPKE *with message space* $\mathcal{M}$, *ciphertext space* $\mathcal{C}$ *and randomness space* $\mathcal{R}$. *Let* $\mathsf{G} : \mathcal{M} \to \mathcal{R}$, $\mathsf{H} : \mathcal{M} \to \{0,1\}^n$, $\mathsf{H}_1 : \mathcal{M} \to \mathcal{K}$, $\mathsf{H}_2 : \{0,1\}^l \times \mathcal{C} \times \{0,1\}^n \to \mathcal{K}$ *be hash functions modeled as quantum random oracles. Suppose that* PKE' *is* $\mathcal{D}_{\mathcal{M}}$*-disjoint-simulatable with a simulator* $\mathcal{S}$. *Then for any adversary* $\mathcal{A}$ *against the* IND-qCCA *security of* $\mathsf{KEM} := \mathsf{SXY}[\mathsf{PKE}', \mathsf{H}_1, \mathsf{H}_2]$ *issuing* q_{G} *and* q_{H_2} *quantum queries to* G *and* H_2, *there exists an adversary* $\mathcal{B}$ *against the* DS-IND *security of* PKE' *such that*

$$\mathsf{Adv}_{\mathsf{KEM},\mathcal{A}}^{\mathsf{IND\text{-}qCCA}} \leq \mathsf{Adv}_{\mathsf{PKE}',\mathcal{D}_{\mathcal{M}},\mathcal{B},\mathcal{S}}^{\mathsf{DS\text{-}IND}} + \mathsf{Disj}_{\mathsf{PKE}',\mathcal{S}} + q_{\mathsf{H}_2} \cdot 2^{\frac{-l+1}{2}} + (16q_{\mathsf{G}}^2 + 2) \cdot \delta$$

and $\mathsf{Time}(\mathcal{B}) \approx \mathsf{Time}(\mathcal{A})$.

Proof. We use a game-hopping proof. The proof is essentially the same as the following Lemma 5 [22]'s proof, except for two more games. We insert game $G_{0.5}$ and $G_{3.5}$ into G_0, G_1 and G_3, G_4 respectively. Besides, we replace the event $\overline{\mathsf{Acc}}$ with another event Bad. The overview of all games is given in Table 2.

Table 2. Summary of games for the proof of Theorem 3.

Game	H_1	c^*	k_0^*	k_1^*	Decryption of valid c	Decryption of invalid c	G/G'	justification
G_0	$\mathsf{H}_1(\cdot)$	$\mathsf{Enc}'(pk, m^*)$	$\mathsf{H}_1(m^*)$	random	$\mathsf{H}_1(m)$	$\mathsf{H}_2(s, c)$	G	
$G_{0.5}$	$\mathsf{H}_1(\cdot)$	$\mathsf{Enc}'(pk, m^*)$	$\mathsf{H}_1(m^*)$	random	$\mathsf{H}_1(m)$	$\mathsf{H}_2(s, c)$	G'	Lemma 2
G_1	$\mathsf{H}_1(\cdot)$	$\mathsf{Enc}'(pk, m^*)$	$\mathsf{H}_1(m^*)$	random	$\mathsf{H}_1(m)$	$\mathsf{H}_q(c)$	G'	Lemma 1
$G_{1.5}$	$\mathsf{H}_q'(\mathsf{Enc}'(pk, \cdot))$	$\mathsf{Enc}'(pk, m^*)$	$\mathsf{H}_1(m^*)$	random	$\mathsf{H}_1(m)$	$\mathsf{H}_q(c)$	G'	$\overline{\mathsf{Bad}}$
G_2	$\mathsf{H}_q(\mathsf{Enc}'(pk, \cdot))$	$\mathsf{Enc}'(pk, m^*)$	$\mathsf{H}_1(m^*)$	random	$\mathsf{H}_1(m)$	$\mathsf{H}_q(c)$	G'	$\overline{\mathsf{Bad}}$
G_3	$\mathsf{H}_q(\mathsf{Enc}'(pk, \cdot))$	$\mathsf{Enc}'(pk, m^*)$	$\mathsf{H}_q(c^*)$	random	$\mathsf{H}_q(c)$	$\mathsf{H}_q(c)$	G'	Conceptual
$G_{3.5}$	$\mathsf{H}_q(\mathsf{Enc}'(pk, \cdot))$	$\mathsf{Enc}'(pk, m^*)$	$\mathsf{H}_q(c^*)$	random	$\mathsf{H}_q(c)$	$\mathsf{H}_q(c)$	G	Lemma 2
G_4	$\mathsf{H}_q(\mathsf{Enc}'(pk, \cdot))$	$\mathcal{S}(pk)$	$\mathsf{H}_q(c^*)$	random	$\mathsf{H}_q(c)$	$\mathsf{H}_q(c)$	G	DS-IND

GAME G_0: This is the original game, $\mathsf{IND\text{-}qCCA}_{\mathsf{KEM}}^{\mathcal{A}}$.

Let G' be a random function such that $\mathsf{G}'(m)$ is sampled according to the uniform distribution over $\mathcal{R}_{(pk,sk),m}^{good} := \{r \in \mathcal{R} | \mathsf{Dec}_0(sk, \mathsf{Enc}_0(pk, m; r)) = m\}$. Let $\Omega_{\mathsf{G}'}$ be the set of all functions G'. Define $\delta_{(pk,sk),m} = \frac{|\mathcal{R} \setminus \mathcal{R}_{(pk,sk),m}^{good}|}{|\mathcal{R}|}$ as the fraction of bad randomness and $\delta_{(pk,sk)} = \max_{m \in \mathcal{M}} \delta_{(pk,sk),m}$. With this notation $\delta = \mathrm{E}[\delta_{(pk,sk)}]$, where the expectation is taken over $(pk, sk) \leftarrow \mathsf{Gen}_0$.

GAME $G_{0.5}$: This game is the same as G_0 except that we replace G by G' that uniformly samples from "good" randomness at random, i.e., $\mathsf{G}' \xleftarrow{\$} \Omega_{\mathsf{G}'}$.

GAME G_1: This game is the same as $G_{0.5}$ except that $\mathsf{H}_2(s, c)$ in the decapsulation oracle is replaced with $\mathsf{H}_q(c)$ where $\mathsf{H}_q : \mathcal{C} \times \{0,1\}^n \to \mathcal{K}$ is another random oracle. We remark that $\mathcal{A}$ is not given direct access to H_q.

GAME $G_{1.5}$: This game is the same as G_1 except that the random oracle $\mathsf{H}_1(\cdot)$ is simulated by $\mathsf{H}_q'(\mathsf{Enc}'(pk, \cdot))$ where H_q' is yet another random oracle. We remark that the decapsulation oracle and generation of k_0^* also use $\mathsf{H}'_q(\mathsf{Enc}'(pk,\cdot))$ as $\mathsf{H}_1(\cdot)$ and that $\mathcal{A}$ is not given direct access to H'_q.

GAME G_2: This game is the same as $G_{1.5}$ except that the random oracle $\mathsf{H}_1(\cdot)$ is simulated by $\mathsf{H}_q(\mathsf{Enc}'(pk,\cdot))$ instead of $\mathsf{H}'_q(\mathsf{Enc}'(pk,\cdot))$. We remark that the decapsulation oracle and generation of k_0^* also use $\mathsf{H}_q(\mathsf{Enc}'(pk,\cdot))$ as $\mathsf{H}_1(\cdot)$.

GAME G_3: This game is the same as G_2 except that k_0^* is set as $\mathsf{H}_q(c^*)$ and the decapsulation oracle always returns $\mathsf{H}_q(c)$ as long as $c \neq c^*$. We denote the modified decapsulation oracle by Deca'.

GAME $G_{3.5}$: This game is the same as G_3 except that we switch G' back to the ideal random oracle G.

GAME G_4: This game is the same as $G_{3.5}$ except that c^* is set as $\mathcal{S}(pk)$.

The above completes the descriptions of games. We clearly have

$$\mathsf{Adv}^{\mathsf{IND\text{-}qCCA}}_{\mathsf{KEM},\mathcal{A}} = |\Pr[G_0 \Rightarrow 1] - 1/2|$$

by the definition. We bound this by the following claims.

Claim 1. *We have*

$$|\Pr[G_0 \Rightarrow 1] - \Pr[G_{0.5} \Rightarrow 1]| \leq 8q_{\mathsf{G}}^2\delta,$$

$$|\Pr[G_3 \Rightarrow 1] - \Pr[G_{3.5} \Rightarrow 1]| \leq 8q_{\mathsf{G}}^2\delta.$$

Proof. Following the same analysis as in the proof of [15, Theorem 1], we can show that the distinguishing problem between G_0 and $G_{0.5}$ is essentially the distinguishing problem between G and G', which can be converted into a distinguishing problem between F_1 and F_2, where F_1 is a function such that $\mathsf{F}_1(m)$ is sampled according to Bernoulli distribution $B_{\delta_{(pk,sk),m}}$, i.e., $\Pr[\mathsf{F}_1(m) = 1] = \delta_{(pk,sk),m}$ and $\Pr[\mathsf{F}_1(m) = 0] = 1 - \delta_{(pk,sk),m}$, and F_2 is a constant function that always outputs 0 for any input. Thus, conditioned on a fixed (pk, sk) we obtain by Lemma 2, $|\Pr[G_0 \Rightarrow 1|(pk,sk)] - \Pr[G_{0.5} \Rightarrow 1|(pk,sk)]| \leq 8q_{\mathsf{G}}^2\delta_{(pk,sk)}$. By averaging over $(pk,sk) \leftarrow \mathsf{Gen}_0$ we finally obtain

$$|\Pr[G_0 \Rightarrow 1] - \Pr[G_{0.5} \Rightarrow 1]| \leq 8q_{\mathsf{G}}^2\mathrm{E}[\delta_{(pk,sk)}] = 8q_{\mathsf{G}}^2\delta.$$

In the same way, we have

$$|\Pr[G_3 \Rightarrow 1] - \Pr[G_{3.5} \Rightarrow 1]| \leq 8q_{\mathsf{G}}^2\delta.$$

□

Claim 2. *We have*

$$|\Pr[G_{0.5} \Rightarrow 1] - \Pr[G_1 \Rightarrow 1]| \leq q_{\mathsf{H}_2} \cdot 2^{\frac{-l+1}{2}}.$$

Proof. This is obvious from Lemma 1. □

Claim 3. *We define an event:*

$$\mathsf{Bad} := [\exists m \in \mathcal{M}, \mathcal{R}^{good}_{(pk,sk),m} = \varnothing | (pk, sk) \leftarrow \mathsf{Gen}_0].$$

Then we have $\Pr[\mathsf{Bad}] \leq \delta$ *and*

$$|\Pr[G_1 \Rightarrow 1] - 1/2| \leq |\Pr[G_1 \Rightarrow 1 \wedge \overline{\mathsf{Bad}}] - 1/2| + \delta.$$

Proof. By the definition, we have

$$\begin{aligned}
&\Pr[\mathsf{Bad}]\\
&= \Pr[\exists m \in \mathcal{M}, \mathcal{R}^{good}_{(pk,sk),m} = \varnothing | (pk, sk) \leftarrow \mathsf{Gen}_0]\\
&= \Pr[\exists m \in \mathcal{M}, \delta_{(pk,sk),m} = 1 | (pk, sk) \leftarrow \mathsf{Gen}_0]\\
&= \Pr[\delta_{(pk,sk)} = 1 | (pk, sk) \leftarrow \mathsf{Gen}_0]\\
&\leq \mathrm{E}[\delta_{(pk,sk)}]\\
&= \delta.
\end{aligned}$$

Then we have

$$\begin{aligned}
&|\Pr[G_1 \Rightarrow 1] - 1/2|\\
&= |\Pr[G_1 \Rightarrow 1 \wedge \overline{\mathsf{Bad}}] + \Pr[G_1 \Rightarrow 1 \wedge \mathsf{Bad}] - 1/2|\\
&\leq |\Pr[G_1 \Rightarrow 1 \wedge \overline{\mathsf{Bad}}] - 1/2| + \Pr[G_1 \Rightarrow 1 \wedge \mathsf{Bad}]\\
&\leq |\Pr[G_1 \Rightarrow 1 \wedge \overline{\mathsf{Bad}}] - 1/2| + \Pr[\mathsf{Bad}]\\
&\leq |\Pr[G_1 \Rightarrow 1 \wedge \overline{\mathsf{Bad}}] - 1/2| + \delta
\end{aligned}$$

as we wanted. □

Claim 4. *We have*

$$\Pr[G_1 \Rightarrow 1 \wedge \overline{\mathsf{Bad}}] = \Pr[G_{1.5} \Rightarrow 1 \wedge \overline{\mathsf{Bad}}].$$

Proof. From the definition of G', if Bad doesn't happen, any message can be decrypted correctly for the PKE', i.e., $\mathsf{Dec}'(sk, \mathsf{Enc}'(pk, m)) = m$ for all $m \in \mathcal{M}$. Therefore, $\mathsf{Enc}'(pk, \cdot)$ is injective. And if $\mathsf{H}'_q(\cdot)$ is a random function, then $\mathsf{H}'_q(\mathsf{Enc}'(pk, \cdot))$ is also a random function. Remarking that access to H'_q is not given to $\mathcal{A}$, it causes no difference from the view of $\mathcal{A}$ if we replace $\mathsf{H}_1(\cdot)$ with $\mathsf{H}'_q(\mathsf{Enc}'(pk, \cdot))$. □

Claim 5. *We have*

$$\Pr[G_{1.5} \Rightarrow 1 \wedge \overline{\mathsf{Bad}}] = \Pr[G_2 \Rightarrow 1 \wedge \overline{\mathsf{Bad}}].$$

Proof. We say that a ciphertext c is valid if we have $\mathsf{Enc}'(pk, \mathsf{Dec}'(sk, c)) = c$ and invalid otherwise. We remark that H_q is used only for decrypting an invalid ciphertext c as $\mathsf{H}_q(c)$ in $G_{1.5}$. This means that a value of $\mathsf{H}_q(c)$ for a valid c is not used at all in $G_{1.5}$.

On the other hand, any output of $\mathsf{Enc}'(pk, \cdot)$ is valid if Bad doesn't happen. Since H'_q is only used for evaluating an output of $\mathsf{Enc}'(pk, \cdot)$, a value of $\mathsf{H}'_q(c)$ for an invalid c is not used at all in $G_{1.5}$.

Hence, it causes no difference from the view of $\mathcal{A}$ if we use the same random oracle H_q instead of two independent random oracles H_q and H'_q. □

Claim 6. *We have*

$$\Pr[G_2 \Rightarrow 1 \wedge \overline{\mathsf{Bad}}] = \Pr[G_3 \Rightarrow 1 \wedge \overline{\mathsf{Bad}}].$$

Proof. Since we set $\mathsf{H}_1(\cdot) := \mathsf{H}_q(\mathsf{Enc}'(pk, \cdot))$, for any valid c and $m := \mathsf{Dec}'(sk, c)$, we have $\mathsf{H}_1(m) = \mathsf{H}_q(\mathsf{Enc}'(pk, m)) = \mathsf{H}_q(c)$. Therefore, responses of the decapsulation oracle are unchanged. We also have $\mathsf{H}_1(m^*) = \mathsf{H}_q(c^*)$. □

Claim 7. *We have*

$$|\Pr[G_3 \Rightarrow 1 \wedge \overline{\mathsf{Bad}}] - 1/2| \leq |\Pr[G_3 \Rightarrow 1] - 1/2| + \delta.$$

Proof. We have

$$\begin{aligned}
&|\Pr[G_3 \Rightarrow 1 \wedge \overline{\mathsf{Bad}}] - 1/2| \\
&= |\Pr[G_3 \Rightarrow 1] - \Pr[G_3 \Rightarrow 1 \wedge \mathsf{Bad}] - 1/2| \\
&\leq |\Pr[G_3 \Rightarrow 1] - 1/2| + \Pr[G_3 \Rightarrow 1 \wedge \mathsf{Bad}] \\
&\leq |\Pr[G_3 \Rightarrow 1] - 1/2| + \Pr[\mathsf{Bad}] \\
&\leq |\Pr[G_3 \Rightarrow 1] - 1/2| + \delta.
\end{aligned}$$

□

Claim 8. *There exists a quantum adversary $\mathcal{B}$ such that*

$$|\Pr[G_{3.5} \Rightarrow 1] - \Pr[G_4 \Rightarrow 1]| = \mathsf{Adv}^{\mathsf{DS\text{-}IND}}_{\mathsf{PKE}', \mathcal{D}_{\mathcal{M}}, \mathcal{B}, \mathcal{S}}$$

and $\mathsf{Time}(\mathcal{B}) \approx \mathsf{Time}(\mathcal{A})$.

Proof. We construct an adversary $\mathcal{B}$, which is allowed to access two random oracles H_q and H_2, against the disjoint simulatability as follows.

$\mathcal{B}^{\mathsf{H}_q, \mathsf{H}_2}(pk, c^*)$: It picks $b \leftarrow \{0, 1\}$, sets $k_0^* := \mathsf{H}_q(c^*)$ and $k_1^* \xleftarrow{\$} \mathcal{K}$, and invokes $b' \leftarrow \mathcal{A}^{\mathsf{H}_1, \mathsf{H}_2, \mathsf{Deca}'}(pk, c^*, k_b^*)$ where $\mathcal{A}$'s oracles are simulated as follows.

- $\mathsf{H}_1(\cdot)$ is simulated by $\mathsf{H}_q(\mathsf{Enc}'(pk, \cdot))$.
- H_2 can be simulated because $\mathcal{B}$ has access to an oracle H_2.
- Deca' is simulated by filtering c^* and using $\mathsf{H}_q(\cdot)$, that is, on input $\sum_{c,k} \psi_{c,k} |c, k\rangle$, $\mathcal{B}$ returns $\sum_{c \neq c^*, k} \psi_{c,k} |c, k \oplus \mathsf{H}_q(c)\rangle + \sum_k \psi_{c^*,k} |c^*, k \oplus \bot\rangle$.

Finally, $\mathcal{B}$ returns $[\![b' = b]\!]$.

This completes the description of $\mathcal{B}$. It is easy to see that $\mathcal{B}$ perfectly simulates $G_{3.5}$ if $c^* = \mathsf{Enc}'(pk, m^*)$ and G_4 if $c^* = \mathcal{S}(pk)$. Therefore, we have

$$|\Pr[G_{3.5} \Rightarrow 1] - \Pr[G_4 \Rightarrow 1]| = \mathsf{Adv}^{\mathsf{DS\text{-}IND}}_{\mathsf{PKE}', \mathcal{D}_{\mathcal{M}}, \mathcal{B}, \mathcal{S}}$$

and $\mathsf{Time}(\mathcal{B}) \approx \mathsf{Time}(\mathcal{A})$. □

Claim 9. *We have*

$$|\Pr[G_4 \Rightarrow 1] - 1/2| \leq \mathsf{Disj}_{\mathsf{PKE}',\mathcal{S}}.$$

Proof. Let Bad' denote the event that c^* is in $\mathsf{Enc}'(pk, \mathcal{M})$ in G_4. Then we have

$$\Pr[\mathsf{Bad}'] = \mathsf{Disj}_{\mathsf{PKE}',\mathcal{S}}.$$

When Bad' does not occur, i.e., $c^* \notin \mathsf{Enc}'(pk, \mathcal{M})$, $\mathcal{A}$ obtains no information about $k_0^* = \mathsf{H}_q(c^*)$. This is because queries to H_1 only reveal $\mathsf{H}_q(c)$ for $c \in \mathsf{Enc}'(pk, \mathcal{M})$, and $\mathsf{Deca}'(c)$ returns $\perp$ if $c = c^*$. Therefore, we have

$$\Pr[G_4 \Rightarrow 1|\overline{\mathsf{Bad}'}] = 1/2.$$

Combining the above, we have

$$\begin{aligned}
&|\Pr[G_4 \Rightarrow 1] - 1/2| \\
&= |\Pr[\mathsf{Bad}'] \cdot (\Pr[G_4 \Rightarrow 1|\mathsf{Bad}'] - 1/2) + \Pr[\overline{\mathsf{Bad}'}] \cdot (\Pr[G_4 \Rightarrow 1|\overline{\mathsf{Bad}'}] - 1/2)| \\
&\leq \Pr[\mathsf{Bad}'] + |\Pr[G_4 \Rightarrow 1|\overline{\mathsf{Bad}'}] - 1/2| \\
&= \mathsf{Disj}_{\mathsf{PKE}',\mathcal{S}}
\end{aligned}$$

as we wanted. □

Combining all claims above, we obtain the following inequality:

$$\begin{aligned}
&\mathsf{Adv}_{\mathsf{KEM},\mathcal{A}}^{\mathsf{IND\text{-}qCCA}} \\
&= |\Pr[G_0 \Rightarrow 1] - 1/2| \\
&\leq |\Pr[G_{0.5} \Rightarrow 1] - 1/2| + 8q_{\mathsf{G}}^2\delta \\
&\leq |\Pr[G_1 \Rightarrow 1] - 1/2| + q_{\mathsf{H}_2} \cdot 2^{\frac{-l+1}{2}} + 8q_{\mathsf{G}}^2\delta \\
&\leq |\Pr[G_1 \Rightarrow 1 \wedge \overline{\mathsf{Bad}}] - 1/2| + \delta + q_{\mathsf{H}_2} \cdot 2^{\frac{-l+1}{2}} + 8q_{\mathsf{G}}^2\delta \\
&= |\Pr[G_{1.5} \Rightarrow 1 \wedge \overline{\mathsf{Bad}}] - 1/2| + \delta + q_{\mathsf{H}_2} \cdot 2^{\frac{-l+1}{2}} + 8q_{\mathsf{G}}^2\delta \\
&= |\Pr[G_2 \Rightarrow 1 \wedge \overline{\mathsf{Bad}}] - 1/2| + \delta + q_{\mathsf{H}_2} \cdot 2^{\frac{-l+1}{2}} + 8q_{\mathsf{G}}^2\delta \\
&= |\Pr[G_3 \Rightarrow 1 \wedge \overline{\mathsf{Bad}}] - 1/2| + \delta + q_{\mathsf{H}_2} \cdot 2^{\frac{-l+1}{2}} + 8q_{\mathsf{G}}^2\delta \\
&\leq |\Pr[G_3 \Rightarrow 1] - 1/2| + 2\delta + q_{\mathsf{H}_2} \cdot 2^{\frac{-l+1}{2}} + 8q_{\mathsf{G}}^2\delta \\
&\leq |\Pr[G_{3.5} \Rightarrow 1] - 1/2| + 2\delta + q_{\mathsf{H}_2} \cdot 2^{\frac{-l+1}{2}} + 16q_{\mathsf{G}}^2\delta \\
&\leq |\Pr[G_4 \Rightarrow 1] - 1/2| + \mathsf{Adv}_{\mathsf{PKE}',\mathcal{D}_{\mathcal{M}},\mathcal{B},\mathcal{S}}^{\mathsf{DS\text{-}IND}} + q_{\mathsf{H}_2} \cdot 2^{\frac{-l+1}{2}} + (16q_{\mathsf{G}}^2 + 2) \cdot \delta \\
&\leq \mathsf{Adv}_{\mathsf{PKE}',\mathcal{D}_{\mathcal{M}},\mathcal{B},\mathcal{S}}^{\mathsf{DS\text{-}IND}} + \mathsf{Disj}_{\mathsf{PKE}',\mathcal{S}} + q_{\mathsf{H}_2} \cdot 2^{\frac{-l+1}{2}} + (16q_{\mathsf{G}}^2 + 2) \cdot \delta.
\end{aligned}$$

□

Lemma 5 (IND-qCCA **Security of** SXY **in the QROM, Case 2** [22, Theorem 4.1]). *Let* PKE′ *be a* δ*-correct* dPKE *with message space* $\mathcal{M}$ *and ciphertext* *space* $\mathcal{C}$. *Let* $\mathsf{H}_1 : \mathcal{M} \to \mathcal{K}$, $\mathsf{H}_2 : \{0,1\}^l \times \mathcal{C} \to \mathcal{K}$ *be hash functions modeled as quantum random oracles. Suppose that* PKE' *is* $\mathcal{D}_{\mathcal{M}}$*-disjoint-simulatable with a simulator* $\mathcal{S}$. *Then for any adversary* $\mathcal{A}$ *against the* IND-qCCA *security of* $\mathsf{KEM} := \mathsf{SXY}[\mathsf{PKE}', \mathsf{H}_1, \mathsf{H}_2]$ *issuing* q_{H_2} *quantum queries to* H_2, *there exists an adversary* $\mathcal{B}$ *against the* DS-IND *security of* PKE' *such that*

$$\mathsf{Adv}_{\mathsf{KEM},\mathcal{A}}^{\mathsf{IND\text{-}qCCA}} \leq \mathsf{Adv}_{\mathsf{PKE}',\mathcal{D}_{\mathcal{M}},\mathcal{B},\mathcal{S}}^{\mathsf{DS\text{-}IND}} + \mathsf{Disj}_{\mathsf{PKE}',\mathcal{S}} + q_{\mathsf{H}_2} \cdot 2^{\frac{-l+1}{2}} + 2\delta$$

and $\mathsf{Time}(\mathcal{B}) \approx \mathsf{Time}(\mathcal{A})$.

Remark 4. Lemma 5 still holds with our modified definition of DS. The only thing that needs to be changed is "$\Pr[\mathsf{Bad}] \leq \mathsf{Disj}_{\mathsf{PKE}_1,\mathcal{S}}$" in [22, Lemma 4.8], which should be replaced with "$\Pr[\mathsf{Bad}] = \mathsf{Disj}_{\mathsf{PKE}_1,\mathcal{S}}$" as $(ek, dk) \leftarrow \mathsf{Gen}_1$ exactly in the proof.

Remark 5. KEM remains δ-correct.

We also need the following lemma about the security of transformation T. It is a version without the square-root advantage loss at the cost of stronger security requirement of the underlying PKE.

Lemma 6 (Security of T in the QROM [5, Theorem 1]**).** *Let* PKE_0 *be a* rPKE *with messages space* $\mathcal{M}$ *and random space* $\mathcal{R}$. *Let* $\mathsf{G} : \mathcal{M} \to \mathcal{R}$ *be a hash function modeled as a quantum random oracle. Then for any adversary* $\mathcal{A}$ *against the* OW-CPA *security of* $\mathsf{PKE} := \mathsf{T}[\mathsf{PKE}_0, \mathsf{G}]$ *issuing* q_{G} *quantum queries to* G *with depth* d_{G}, *there exists an adversary* $\mathcal{B}$ *against the* IND-CPA *security of* PKE_0 *such that*

$$\mathsf{Adv}_{\mathsf{PKE},\mathcal{A}}^{\mathsf{OW\text{-}CPA}} \leq (d_{\mathsf{G}} + 2) \cdot \left(\mathsf{Adv}_{\mathsf{PKE}_0,\mathcal{B}}^{\mathsf{IND\text{-}CPA}} + \frac{8(q_{\mathsf{G}} + 1)}{|\mathcal{M}|} \right)$$

and $\mathsf{Time}(\mathcal{B}) \approx \mathsf{Time}(\mathcal{A})$.

Finally, we can get the security results of the two KEMs. For simplicity, we assume the number of parallel queries is n_p for all oracle algorithms. And we use $\mathcal{A}^{\mathsf{P}}$ in the following proofs to denote the adversary against the scheme P.

Combining Lemma 6 with Theorem 1 and Theorem 3, we obtain the following result for the IND-qCCA security of $\mathsf{KEM} := \mathsf{SXY} \circ \mathsf{KC} \circ \mathsf{T}$ from the IND-CPA security of a δ-correct rPKE in the QROM.

Corollary 1 (IND-qCCA Security of $\mathsf{SXY} \circ \mathsf{KC} \circ \mathsf{T}$ in the QROM). *Let* PKE_0 *be a* δ*-correct* rPKE *with message space* $\mathcal{M}$, *ciphertext space* $\mathcal{C}$ *and randomness space* $\mathcal{R}$. *Let* $\mathsf{G} : \mathcal{M} \to \mathcal{R}$, $\mathsf{H} : \mathcal{M} \to \{0,1\}^n$, $\mathsf{H}_1 : \mathcal{M} \to \mathcal{K}$, $\mathsf{H}_2 : \{0,1\}^l \times \mathcal{C} \times \{0,1\}^n \to \mathcal{K}$ *be hash functions modeled as quantum random oracles. Then for any adversary* $\mathcal{A}$ *against the* IND-qCCA *security of* $\mathsf{KEM} := \mathsf{SXY}[\mathsf{KC}[\mathsf{T}[\mathsf{PKE}_0, \mathsf{G}], \mathsf{H}], \mathsf{H}_1, \mathsf{H}_2]$ *issuing* q_{G}, q_{H}, q_{H_1} *and* q_{H_2} *quantum queries to* G, H, H_1 *and* H_2 *with* *depth* d_{G}*,* d_{H}*,* d_{H_1} *and* d_{H_2}*, there exists an adversary* $\mathcal{B}$ *against the* IND-CPA *security of* PKE_0 *such that*

$$\mathsf{Adv}^{\mathsf{IND\text{-}qCCA}}_{\mathsf{KEM},\mathcal{A}} \leq 4d'_{\mathsf{H}}(d'_{\mathsf{G}}+2)\cdot\left(\mathsf{Adv}^{\mathsf{IND\text{-}CPA}}_{\mathsf{PKE}_0,\mathcal{B}} + \frac{8(q'_{\mathsf{G}}+1)}{|\mathcal{M}|}\right) + (16q^2_{\mathsf{G}} + 8d'_{\mathsf{H}} + 4)\cdot\delta + q_{\mathsf{H}_2}\cdot 2^{\frac{-l+1}{2}} + 2^{-n}$$

and $\mathsf{Time}(\mathcal{B}) \approx 2\cdot\mathsf{Time}(\mathcal{A})$*, where* $d'_{\mathsf{H}} := d_{\mathsf{H}} + d_{\mathsf{H}_1}$*,* $d'_{\mathsf{G}} := 2(d_{\mathsf{G}} + d_{\mathsf{H}} + 2d_{\mathsf{H}_1} + 1)$ *and* $q'_{\mathsf{G}} := 2(q_{\mathsf{G}} + q_{\mathsf{H}} + 2q_{\mathsf{H}_1} + n_p)$*.*

Proof. From the construction of $\mathcal{A}^{\mathsf{PKE}'}$ in the proof of Theorem 3, we can know that $\mathcal{A}^{\mathsf{PKE}'}$ issues $q_{\mathsf{G}}+q_{\mathsf{H}_1}$, $q_{\mathsf{H}}+q_{\mathsf{H}_1}$ queries to G, H with depth $d_{\mathsf{G}}+d_{\mathsf{H}_1}$, $d_{\mathsf{H}}+d_{\mathsf{H}_1}$. Furthermore, from the construction of $\mathcal{A}^{\mathsf{PKE}}$ in the proof of Theorem 1 and the construction of $\mathcal{D}$ in the proof of Lemma 3, we can know that $\mathcal{A}^{\mathsf{PKE}}$ issues at most $(q_{\mathsf{G}} + q_{\mathsf{H}_1}) \times 2 + (q_{\mathsf{H}} + q_{\mathsf{H}_1}) \times 2 + 2n_p$ queries to G with depth $(d_{\mathsf{G}} + d_{\mathsf{H}_1}) \times 2 + (d_{\mathsf{H}} + d_{\mathsf{H}_1}) \times 2 + 2$, where the first part comes from $\mathcal{D}$'s twice invocations to $\mathcal{A}^{\mathsf{PKE}'}$, the second part comes from $\mathcal{D}$'s queries to H and H', and the third part comes from $\mathcal{A}^{\mathsf{PKE}}$'s testing of the set T returned by $\mathcal{D}$. □

Combining Theorem 2 with Lemma 5, we obtain the following result for the IND-qCCA security of $\mathsf{KEM} := \mathsf{SXY} \circ \mathsf{KC}$ from the OW-CPA security of a δ-correct dPKE in the QROM.

Corollary 2 (IND-qCCA **Security of** $\mathsf{SXY} \circ \mathsf{KC}$ **in the QROM).** *Let* PKE *be a* δ*-correct* dPKE *with message space* $\mathcal{M}$ *and ciphertext space* $\mathcal{C}$*. Let* $\mathsf{H} : \mathcal{M} \to \{0,1\}^n$*,* $\mathsf{H}_1 : \mathcal{M} \to \mathcal{K}$*,* $\mathsf{H}_2 : \{0,1\}^l \times \mathcal{C} \times \{0,1\}^n \to \mathcal{K}$ *be hash functions modeled as quantum random oracles. Then for any adversary* $\mathcal{A}$ *against the* IND-qCCA *security of* $\mathsf{KEM} := \mathsf{SXY}[\mathsf{KC}[\mathsf{PKE},\mathsf{H}],\mathsf{H}_1,\mathsf{H}_2]$ *issuing* q_{H}*,* q_{H_1} *and* q_{H_2} *quantum queries to* H*,* H_1 *and* H_2 *with depth* d_{H}*,* d_{H_1} *and* d_{H_2}*, there exists an adversary* $\mathcal{B}$ *against the* OW-CPA *security of* PKE *such that*

$$\mathsf{Adv}^{\mathsf{IND\text{-}qCCA}}_{\mathsf{KEM},\mathcal{A}} \leq 4d'_{\mathsf{H}}\cdot\mathsf{Adv}^{\mathsf{OW\text{-}CPA}}_{\mathsf{PKE},\mathcal{B}} + (4d'_{\mathsf{H}}+3)\cdot\delta + q_{\mathsf{H}_2}\cdot 2^{\frac{-l+1}{2}} + 2^{-n}$$

and $\mathsf{Time}(\mathcal{B}) \approx 2\cdot\mathsf{Time}(\mathcal{A})$*, where* $d'_{\mathsf{H}} := d_{\mathsf{H}} + d_{\mathsf{H}_1}$*.*

Proof. From the construction of $\mathcal{A}^{\mathsf{PKE}'}$ in the proof of Lemma 5, we can know that $\mathcal{A}^{\mathsf{PKE}'}$ issues $q_{\mathsf{H}} + q_{\mathsf{H}_1}$ queries to H with depth $d_{\mathsf{H}} + d_{\mathsf{H}_1}$. □

Acknowledgements. We would like to thank the anonymous reviewers for pointing out proof gaps in a previous version of this paper and for their helpful suggestions. The authors are supported by the National Key Research and Development Program of China (Grant No. 2018YFA0704702), the National Natural Science Foundation of China (Grant No. 61832012) and the National Cryptography Development Fund (Grant No. MMJJ20180210).

References

1. Ambainis, A., Rosmanis, A., Unruh, D.: Quantum attacks on classical proof systems: the hardness of quantum rewinding. In: 2014 IEEE 55th Annual Symposium on Foundations of Computer Science, pp. 474–483, October 2014. https://doi.org/10.1109/FOCS.2014.57
2. Ambainis, A., Hamburg, M., Unruh, D.: Quantum security proofs using semi-classical oracles. In: Boldyreva, A., Micciancio, D. (eds.) CRYPTO 2019. LNCS, vol. 11693, pp. 269–295. Springer, Cham (2019). https://doi.org/10.1007/978-3-030-26951-7_10
3. Beals, R., Buhrman, H., Cleve, R., Mosca, M., de Wolf, R.: Quantum lower bounds by polynomials. J. ACM **48**(4), 778–797 (2001). https://doi.org/10.1145/502090.502097
4. Bellare, M., Rogaway, P.: Random oracles are practical: A paradigm for designing efficient protocols. In: Proceedings of the 1st ACM Conference on Computer and Communications Security. pp. 62–73. CCS '93, Association for Computing Machinery, New York (1993). https://doi.org/10.1145/168588.168596
5. Bindel, N., Hamburg, M., Hövelmanns, K., Hülsing, A., Persichetti, E.: Tighter proofs of CCA security in the quantum random oracle model. In: Hofheinz, D., Rosen, A. (eds.) TCC 2019. LNCS, vol. 11892, pp. 61–90. Springer, Cham (2019). https://doi.org/10.1007/978-3-030-36033-7_3
6. Boneh, D., Dagdelen, Ö., Fischlin, M., Lehmann, A., Schaffner, C., Zhandry, M.: Random Oracles in a quantum world. In: Lee, D.H., Wang, X. (eds.) ASIACRYPT 2011. LNCS, vol. 7073, pp. 41–69. Springer, Heidelberg (2011). https://doi.org/10.1007/978-3-642-25385-0_3
7. Boneh, D., Zhandry, M.: Secure signatures and chosen ciphertext security in a quantum computing world. In: Canetti, R., Garay, J.A. (eds.) CRYPTO 2013. LNCS, vol. 8043, pp. 361–379. Springer, Heidelberg (2013). https://doi.org/10.1007/978-3-642-40084-1_21
8. Cramer, R., Shoup, V.: Design and analysis of practical public-key encryption schemes secure against adaptive chosen ciphertext attack. SIAM J. Comput. **33**(1), 167–226 (2004). https://doi.org/10.1137/S0097539702403773
9. Dent, A.W.: A designer's guide to KEMs. In: Paterson, K.G. (ed.) Cryptography and Coding 2003. LNCS, vol. 2898, pp. 133–151. Springer, Heidelberg (2003). https://doi.org/10.1007/978-3-540-40974-8_12
10. Fujisaki, E., Okamoto, T.: Secure integration of asymmetric and symmetric encryption schemes. In: Wiener, M. (ed.) CRYPTO 1999. LNCS, vol. 1666, pp. 537–554. Springer, Heidelberg (1999). https://doi.org/10.1007/3-540-48405-1_34
11. Fujisaki, E., Okamoto, T.: Secure integration of asymmetric and symmetric encryption schemes. J. Cryptology **26**(1), 80–101 (Jan 2013). https://doi.org/10.1007/s00145-011-9114-1
12. Hofheinz, D., Hövelmanns, K., Kiltz, E.: A modular analysis of the fujisaki-okamoto transformation. In: Kalai, Y., Reyzin, L. (eds.) TCC 2017. LNCS, vol. 10677, pp. 341–371. Springer, Cham (2017). https://doi.org/10.1007/978-3-319-70500-2_12
13. Hövelmanns, K., Kiltz, E., Schäge, S., Unruh, D.: Generic authenticated key exchange in the quantum random Oracle model. In: Kiayias, A., Kohlweiss, M., Wallden, P., Zikas, V. (eds.) PKC 2020. LNCS, vol. 12111, pp. 389–422. Springer, Cham (2020). https://doi.org/10.1007/978-3-030-45388-6_14

14. Hülsing, A., Rijneveld, J., Song, F.: Mitigating multi-target attacks in hash-based signatures. In: Cheng, C.-M., Chung, K.-M., Persiano, G., Yang, B.-Y. (eds.) PKC 2016. LNCS, vol. 9614, pp. 387–416. Springer, Heidelberg (2016). https://doi.org/10.1007/978-3-662-49384-7_15
15. Jiang, H., Zhang, Z., Chen, L., Wang, H., Ma, Z.: IND-CCA-secure key encapsulation mechanism in the quantum random Oracle model, revisited. In: Shacham, H., Boldyreva, A. (eds.) CRYPTO 2018. LNCS, vol. 10993, pp. 96–125. Springer, Cham (2018). https://doi.org/10.1007/978-3-319-96878-0_4
16. Jiang, H., Zhang, Z., Ma, Z.: Key encapsulation mechanism with explicit rejection in the quantum random Oracle model. In: Lin, D., Sako, K. (eds.) PKC 2019. LNCS, vol. 11443, pp. 618–645. Springer, Cham (2019). https://doi.org/10.1007/978-3-030-17259-6_21
17. Jiang, H., Zhang, Z., Ma, Z.: Tighter security proofs for generic key encapsulation mechanism in the quantum random Oracle model. In: Ding, J., Steinwandt, R. (eds.) PQCrypto 2019. LNCS, vol. 11505, pp. 227–248. Springer, Cham (2019). https://doi.org/10.1007/978-3-030-25510-7_13
18. Kuchta, V., Sakzad, A., Stehlé, D., Steinfeld, R., Sun, S.-F.: Measure-rewind-measure: tighter quantum random Oracle model proofs for one-way to hiding and CCA Security. In: Canteaut, A., Ishai, Y. (eds.) EUROCRYPT 2020. LNCS, vol. 12107, pp. 703–728. Springer, Cham (2020). https://doi.org/10.1007/978-3-030-45727-3_24
19. Nielsen, M.A., Chuang, I.L.: Quantum Computation and Quantum Information: 10th Anniversary Edition, 10th edn. Cambridge University Press, USA (2011)
20. Saito, T., Xagawa, K., Yamakawa, T.: Tightly-secure key-encapsulation mechanism in the quantum random Oracle model. In: Nielsen, J.B., Rijmen, V. (eds.) EUROCRYPT 2018. LNCS, vol. 10822, pp. 520–551. Springer, Cham (2018). https://doi.org/10.1007/978-3-319-78372-7_17
21. Unruh, D.: Revocable quantum timed-release encryption. In: Nguyen, P.Q., Oswald, E. (eds.) EUROCRYPT 2014. LNCS, vol. 8441, pp. 129–146. Springer, Heidelberg (2014). https://doi.org/10.1007/978-3-642-55220-5_8
22. Xagawa, K., Yamakawa, T.: (Tightly) QCCA-secure key-encapsulation mechanism in the quantum random Oracle model. In: Ding, J., Steinwandt, R. (eds.) PQCrypto 2019. LNCS, vol. 11505, pp. 249–268. Springer, Cham (2019). https://doi.org/10.1007/978-3-030-25510-7_14

An Alternative Approach for SIDH Arithmetic

Cyril Bouvier(✉) and Laurent Imbert(✉)

LIRMM, Univ. Montpellier, CNRS, Montpellier, France
cyril.bouvier@lirmm.fr, laurent.imbert@lirmm.fr

Abstract. In this paper, we present new algorithms for the field arithmetic layers of supersingular isogeny Diffie-Hellman; one of the fifteen remaining candidates in the NIST post-quantum standardization process. Our approach uses a polynomial representation of the field elements together with mechanisms to keep the coefficients within bounds during the arithmetic operations. We present timings and comparisons for SIKEp503 and suggest a novel 736-bit prime that offers a 1.17× speedup compared to SIKEp751 for a similar level of security.

Keywords: Supersingular isogeny Diffie-Hellman · Polynomial Modular Number System · Efficient arithmetic

1 Introduction

Driven by recent advances in quantum computing and the potential threat on public-key cryptography [5,17], the National Institute of Standards and Technology (NIST) launched a post-quantum cryptography standardization process. Sixty-nine public-key encryption and signature algorithms entered the competition in 2017. After over a year of evaluation, NIST revealed a list of 26 candidates selected for a second round of evaluation. At the end of July 2020, a list of seven third-round finalists (4 encryption/KEMs, 3 digital signature schemes) together with eight alternate candidates (5 encryption/KEMs, 3 digital signature schemes) was made public.

One of the encryption/KEMs 3rd-round alternate candidate is based on the Supersingular Isogeny Diffie-Hellman (SIDH) scheme proposed in 2011 by Jao and De Feo [12]. Its security relies on the hardness of computing a smooth-degree isogeny between two supersingular elliptic curves. The resulting NIST proposal, called SIKE for Supersingular Isogeny Key encapsulation [11], includes various optimizations from recent works such as [7] and [8]. SIKE is the only candidate based on isogenies between elliptic curves. A noteworthy advantage of SIKE over the other candidates is its very small public key sizes – the smallest of all encryption and KEMs schemes – as well as very small cyphertexts. However, as pointed out in [1]: "The main drawback to SIKE is that its performance (measured in clock cycles) is roughly an order of magnitude worse than many of its

J. A. Garay (Ed.): PKC 2021, LNCS 12710, pp. 27–44, 2021.
https://doi.org/10.1007/978-3-030-75245-3_2

competitors. Much work has been done to optimize implementations, including the compressed-key version, and it is hoped that such optimizations continue."

This is exactly the purpose of the present work dedicated to the arithmetic of SIDH. The theoretical foundations of isogeny-based cryptography are beyond the scope of this paper. We refer the newcomer to this field of research to [6,9,10,18] to only cite a few.

SIDH requires intensive computations in a quadratic extension of the finite field $\mathbb{F}_p$, where p is a prime of the form $p = c \cdot p_A^{e_A} \cdot p_B^{e_B} \pm 1$ for some primes p_A, p_B and some small c. The smallest value between $p_A^{e_A}$ and $p_B^{e_B}$ dictates the security level of the protocol. The primes p_A and p_B are thus chosen so that $p_A^{e_A}$ and $p_B^{e_B}$ are roughly the same size; preferably $p_A^{e_A} \approx p_B^{e_B} \approx \sqrt{p}$.

SIKE targets four security levels. The NIST proposal contains two algorithms called SIKE.PKE for public-key encryption and SIKE.KEM for key encapsulation mechanism. Both are implemented with four sets of parameters denoted SIKEpxxx, where xxx $\in \{434, 503, 610, 751\}$ corresponds to the bitlength of p. For all of these primes, $c = 1$, $p_A = 2$, $p_B = 3$ and $p \equiv 3 \mod 4$. The quadratic extension $\mathbb{F}_{p^2}$ can thus be represented as $\mathbb{F}_p(i)$ with $i^2 = -1$. The arithmetic layers implemented in SIKE are already highly optimized. The field level notably makes use of a very efficient Montgomery reduction that benefits from the special form of p (see [4] for more details).

In this paper, we propose a new, efficient way to perform the arithmetic in $\mathbb{F}_{p^2}$ for these special SIDH primes. Our arithmetic relies on the concept of Polynomial Modular Number Systems (PMNS) proposed by Bajard, Imbert and Plantard [2] as an alternative approach for performing the arithmetic modulo N. In a PMNS, the elements are represented as polynomials of bounded degree, and the basic arithmetic operations are carried out using polynomial arithmetic. In Sect. 2, we extend the initial definition of PMNS to any finite field $\mathbb{F}_{p^k}$ and we present generic algorithms for the conversions from and into PMNS, and for the basic arithmetic operations. Ideally, we want the polynomial coefficients to be as small as possible. The main difficulty, only partially solved in [2], is to perform the arithmetic operations while keeping these coefficients small. In Sect. 3, we present a Montgomery-like coefficient reduction algorithm first suggested in [16] for prime fields $\mathbb{F}_p$, that can be used to solve this problem. In Algorithm 1, we give an extended generic version that works for any finite field $\mathbb{F}_{p^k}$. The principal contribution of this work is a special case of PMNS perfectly suited to the arithmetic of SIDH. We present optimized arithmetic algorithms and some implementation details in Sect. 4. Finally, we illustrate the efficiency of our approach with some experimental results and some comparisons with the SIKE parameters in Sect. 5. In particular, we suggest a new prime $p736$ which outperforms SIKEp751 by approximately 17% for a similar level of security. Our code is available at https://gitlab.inria.fr/ciao/pmns-for-sidh.

During the development of this work, a preprint posted on the IACR eprint archive [19] suggested a "new data representation", used to improve the arithmetic of SIDH. In reality, this "new" representation is a PMNS representation, which the authors did not seem to be aware of. Their coefficient reduction strategy is inspired by a modified Barrett algorithm from [13]. Unfortunately, their implementation is an order of magnitude slower than both the optimized version of SIKE and the present work.

2 PMNS for Finite Fields

The Polynomial Modular Number System (PMNS) [2] was introduced to perform arithmetic in rings $\mathbb{Z}/N\mathbb{Z}$, with N being any positive integer, using integer polynomial arithmetic. It was used, in particular, to perform arithmetic in prime fields. In this section, we will extend the definition of PMNS representation to include all finite fields.

Definition 1 (PMNS basis and γ-representation). *Let p be a prime, k a positive integer and $\mathbb{F}_{p^k}$ be the finite field with p^k elements. Moreover, let n be a positive integer and E a degree-n polynomial such that E has a root $\gamma \in \mathbb{F}_{p^k}$ of algebraic degree k. Let Γ denotes the minimal polynomial of γ.*

The tuple $\mathcal{B} = (p, k, n, \Gamma, E, \gamma)$ is called a PMNS basis for the field $\mathbb{F}_{p^k}$.

A polynomial $V \in \mathbb{Z}[X]$ of degree $< n$ such that $V(\gamma) = v$, with $v \in \mathbb{F}_{p^k}$, is called a γ-representation of v in the PMNS basis $\mathcal{B}$.

Note that, by definition of γ, the polynomial Γ has degree exactly k; and since Γ is the minimal polynomial of γ, we also have $k \leq n$. Thus, for all v in $\mathbb{F}_{p^k}$, the expansion of v in the basis $(1, \gamma, \ldots, \gamma^{k-1})$ of $\mathbb{F}_{p^k}$ is a trivial γ-representation for v. Therefore, every elements of $\mathbb{F}_{p^k}$ admits a γ-representation. However, an element of $\mathbb{F}_{p^k}$ may have multiple γ-representations. We say that two integer polynomials U and V are equivalent if they represent the same element in $\mathbb{F}_{p^k}$, i.e. if $U(\gamma) = V(\gamma)$.

Example 2. The parameters $p = 19$, $k = 1$, $n = 3$, $\Gamma = X - 7$, $E = X^3 - 1$, $\gamma = 7$ define a PMNS basis for the prime field $\mathbb{F}_{19}$. It is easy to verify that $\Gamma(\gamma) \equiv E(\gamma) \equiv 0 \pmod{19}$. In Table 1, we list all the γ-representations of the elements of $\mathbb{F}_{19}$ with coefficients in $\{-1, 0, 1\}$.

Example 3. The parameters $p = 5$, $k = 2$, $n = 4$, $\Gamma = X^2 - 2$, $E = X^4 + 1$, $\gamma = \sqrt{2}$ define a PMNS basis for the field $\mathbb{F}_{5^2}$. It is easy to verify that $\Gamma(\gamma) \equiv E(\gamma) = 0$ in $\mathbb{F}_{5^2}$. Considering this PMNS basis with coefficients bounded by 2 in absolute value, we can see that, for example, $3\sqrt{2}$ admits two γ-representations ($-X^3$ and $X^3 + X$) and $3 + \sqrt{2}$ admits four γ-representations ($X^3 - X^2 - X$, $-X^2 + X$, $X^3 + X^2 - X + 1$, $X^2 + X + 1$).

Although γ-representations always exist, in practice, we are interested in polynomials with small coefficients.

Definition 4 (reduced representations). *Let $\mathcal{B}$ be a PMNS basis and let ρ be a positive integer. A γ-representation V of $v \in \mathbb{F}_{p^k}$ is said to be ρ-reduced if all the coefficients of the polynomial V are less than ρ in absolute value, i.e. $|v_i| < \rho$, for $0 \leq i < n$. (In the rest of this article, we may simply use the term reduced when there is no ambiguity on ρ.)*

Table 1. γ-representations of the elements of $\mathbb{F}_{19}$ with coefficients in $\{-1, 0, 1\}$ in the PMNS basis $\mathcal{B} = (19, 1, 3, X - 7, X^3 - 1, 7)$.

$v \in \mathbb{F}_{19}$	γ-representations	$v \in \mathbb{F}_{19}$	γ-representations
0	$-X^2 - X - 1,\ 0,\ X^2 + X + 1$	10	$X^2 - 1$
1	$-X^2 - X,\ 1$	11	$-X - 1,\ X^2$
2	$-X^2 - X + 1$	12	$-X,\ X^2 + 1$
3	$X^2 - X - 1$	13	$-X + 1$
4	$X^2 - X$	14	$-X^2 + X - 1$
5	$X^2 - X + 1$	15	$-X^2 + X$
6	$X - 1$	16	$-X^2 + X + 1$
7	$-X^2 - 1, X$	17	$X^2 + X - 1$
8	$-X^2,\ X + 1$	18	$-1,\ X^2 + X$
9	$-X^2 + 1$		

In practice, we will work with ρ-reduced γ-representations, with well chosen values of ρ. If ρ is too small, it may happen that some elements of $\mathbb{F}_{p^k}$ have no ρ-reduced γ-representation. A lower bound on values ρ for which all elements of $\mathbb{F}_{p^k}$ have a ρ-reduced γ-representation can be computed by considering a particular lattice associated to the PMNS basis. For a PMNS basis $\mathcal{B}$, let $\mathcal{L}_\mathcal{B}$ denote the lattice over $\mathbb{Z}^n$ generated by the set of vectors corresponding to integer polynomials $Z \in \mathbb{Z}[X]$ of degree at most $n - 1$ such that $Z(\gamma) = 0$ in $\mathbb{F}_{p^k}$. An elementary basis of $\mathcal{L}_\mathcal{B}$ is given by the n polynomials $p, pX, \ldots, pX^{k-1}$, $X^k - \gamma^k$, $X^{k+1} - \gamma^k X, \ldots, X^{n-1} - \gamma^k X^{n-1-k}$, or equivalently by the following $n \times n$, integer row-matrix

$$\mathcal{L}_\mathcal{B} = \begin{pmatrix} p & 0 & \cdots & \cdots & \cdots\cdots\cdots & 0 \\ 0 & \ddots & & & & \vdots \\ \vdots & & \ddots & & & \vdots \\ 0 & \cdots & 0 & p & 0 \quad 0 \cdots & 0 \\ -\gamma^k & 0 & \cdots & 0 & 1 \quad 0 \cdots & 0 \\ 0 & \ddots & & & \ddots & \vdots \\ \vdots & & \ddots & & \ddots & 0 \\ 0 & \cdots & 0 & -\gamma^k & 0 \cdots 0 & 1 \end{pmatrix}. \tag{1}$$

Let A be the row-matrix of any basis of $\mathcal{L}_\mathcal{B}$ and let $||A||_1$ be its 1-norm, defined as $||A||_1 = \max\{\sum_{i=0}^{n} |a_{i,j}|,\ 0 \leq j < n\}$. Then, using [3, Theorem 2.2] we know that if $\rho > \frac{1}{2}||A||_1$, then there exist at least one ρ-reduced γ-representation for every element of $\mathbb{F}_{p^k}$. This result means that any lattice reduction algorithm (assuming n is not too large) such as LLL or BKZ can be used to determine a lower bound on the values of ρ that are valid to define a notion of reduction for a PMNS basis.

In the next sections, we present generic algorithms for the conversions from and into PMNS and for the basic arithmetic operations. As we shall see, the main and only stumbling block is to ensure that the output results have reduced coefficients.

2.1 Conversions and Basic Arithmetic Operations

From PMNS: Given a γ-representation $V \in \mathbb{Z}[X]$, computing the corresponding element in $\mathbb{F}_{p^k}$ is just a matter of evaluating V at γ, with arithmetic operations carried out in $\mathbb{F}_{p^k}$.

To PMNS: Given $v \in \mathbb{F}_{p^k}$, computing a γ-representation for v is equivalent to writing v in the basis $(1, \gamma, ..., \gamma^{k-1})$. However, in general, the obtained representation is not reduced.

Addition/Subtraction: A γ-representation of the sum $u+v$ (resp. difference $u-v$) is computed by adding (resp. subtracting) the corresponding polynomials U and V. Again, the resulting polynomial may not be reduced.

Multiplication: A γ-representation of the product uv can be computed in two steps. We first compute $W = U \times V$ so that $W(\gamma) = U(\gamma)V(\gamma) = uv$ in $\mathbb{F}_{p^k}$. Since $\deg W \leq 2n - 2$, we reduce the degree by computing $W' = W \bmod E$. We have $W' = W - QE$ for some polynomial Q, with $\deg W' < \deg E = n$. Since γ is a root of E, $W'(\gamma) = W(\gamma)$. Thus, W' is a γ-representation of uv. However, as for the addition, this representation is not reduced.

Note that the polynomial E can be freely chosen. In practice, we will often choose $E = X^n - e$, with $e \in \mathbb{Z}$, as it allows for faster algorithms. It is also easier to compute useful bounds in this case. For example, if U and V are both ρ-reduced γ-representations, then it is not difficult to see that the coefficients of $W' = UV \bmod (X^n - e)$ are bounded by $n|e|\rho^2$ in absolute value.

2.2 Coefficient Reduction

Let $\mathcal{B} = (p, n, k, \Gamma, E, \gamma)$ be a PMNS basis and $\mathcal{L}_\mathcal{B}$ be the associated lattice given in (1). According to [3], we know that if $\rho > \frac{1}{2}||A||_1$ for some basis A of $\mathcal{L}_\mathcal{B}$, then all the elements of $\mathbb{F}_{p^k}$ admit a ρ-reduced γ-representation. Computing a ρ-reduced γ-representation for $v \in \mathbb{F}_{p^k}$ from V, an equivalent non-reduced one, amounts to reducing the vector corresponding to the polynomial V modulo the lattice $\mathcal{L}_\mathcal{B}$. We thus need a way to efficiently find a lattice vector that is close enough to V. (In general we do not need to compute the closest vector to V.)

In [2], Bajard et al. suggested to perform this operation through lookup tables. A lattice vector close to V is retrieved from a precomputed table, using the most significant bits of the coefficients of V. The retrieved vector is then subtracted from V to obtain a reduced representation. The size of the precomputed table depends on the number of bits that need to be reduced. This approach may be appropriate for a very few bits, but becomes unpractical as the number of bits to reduce grows. In order to manage larger reductions, the authors of [2] present various strategy to reduce the size of the required tables at the cost of some extra arithmetic operations.

The next section presents an alternative approach that do not require any table. First suggested in [16] for prime fields $\mathbb{F}_p$, it naturally extends to any finite field $\mathbb{F}_{p^k}$. It is inspired by Montgomery multiplication/reduction [15]. Therefore, it is only stable in the so-called Montgomery representation, and can only be used after a multiplication. In Sect. 4.2, we detail our reduction strategy after an addition in the case of special PMNS basis for SIDH.

3 PMNS Coefficient Reduction à la Montgomery

Given a γ-representation C of some field element $c \in \mathbb{F}_{p^k}$, Algorithm 1 below computes a γ-representation of $c/2^\omega$ whose coefficients are approximately ω bits smaller than those of c. The value 2^ω plays the same role as the Montgomery constant. In practice ω is chosen according to the size of ρ; the smaller integer multiple of the word-size larger than ρ is a common choice. The algorithm also needs a γ-representation of zero, denoted M in Algorithm 1. Any representation of zero that is invertible in $(\mathbb{Z}/2^\omega\mathbb{Z})[X]/(E)$ is an acceptable choice for M.

Algorithm 1. (Generic) Montgomery coefficient reduction

Input: C a γ-representation of $c \in \mathbb{F}_{p^k}$, M a γ-representation of zero and M' the inverse of $-M$ in $(\mathbb{Z}/2^\omega\mathbb{Z})[X]/(E)$.
Output: R a γ-representation of $c/2^\omega$
1: $Q \leftarrow CM' \bmod E \bmod 2^\omega$
2: $R \leftarrow (C + QM \bmod E)/2^\omega$
3: **return** R

In order to prove the correctness of Algorithm 1, simply observe that in the ring $(\mathbb{Z}/2^\omega\mathbb{Z})[X]/(E)$, the polynomial $C + QM$ is zero, so the last division is exact. Moreover, since $M(\gamma) = 0$ in $\mathbb{F}_{p^k}$, we have $(C + QM)(\gamma) = C(\gamma)$ in $\mathbb{F}_{p^k}$ so that R is a γ-representation of $c/2^\omega$.

In general, it is difficult to derive useful bounds on the size of the output coefficients. However, in the case $E = X^n - e$, with $e \in \mathbb{Z}$, we can show that the size of the output coefficients are approximately ω bits smaller than those of the input. If we assume that M is ρ-reduced and that the coefficients of C are less than 2^t in absolute value, with t a positive integer, then the coefficients of

$C+QM \bmod E$ are less than $2^t+2^\omega n|e|\rho$ in absolute value. Thus, the coefficients of the output are less than $2^{t-\omega}+n|e|\rho$ in absolute value.

In the rest of this paper, we concentrate our attention on a special class of PMNS basis well suited to SIDH. In particular, we shall explain how this generic algorithm can be used to efficiently reduce the coefficients after a multiplication of two reduced γ-representations.

4 PMNS for SIDH

In SIDH, arithmetic operations are performed in $\mathbb{F}_{p^2}$ for a prime p of the form $c \cdot p_A^{e_A} \cdot p_B^{e_B} \pm 1$, where p_A, p_B are two distinct primes. For efficiency reasons, a common choice is to opt for $p_A = 2, p_B = 3, c = 1$. In this section, we will show that PMNS basis are very well-suited to SIDH. We will describe our *special PMNS basis for SIDH* in a slightly more general setting.

Definition 5. *Let p be an odd prime of the form $p = |\gamma^n/e - 1|$, where γ is an element of $\overline{\mathbb{F}_p}$ of algebraic order $k > 0$ such that γ^k is an integer; n is a positive integer; and e is an integer divisor of γ^k. Note that since p is an integer, we must have $k|n$. A PMNS basis for $\mathbb{F}_{p^k}$ of the form $(p, k, n, X^k - \gamma^k, X^n - e, \gamma)$ is called a* special PMNS basis for SIDH.

Proposition 6. *If $\mathcal{B} = (p, k, n, X^k - \gamma^k, X^n - e, \gamma)$ is a special PMNS basis for SIDH, then the polynomial $M = (\gamma^k/e)X^{n-k} - 1$ is a γ-representation of zero in $\mathcal{B}$.*

Proof. Simply observe that $M(\gamma) = \pm p$. □

In addition to being a representation of zero, the polynomial M is also very sparse, with exactly two nonzero coefficients. Moreover, since $\gamma^k \approx p^{k/n}$, these coefficients are "small". As will be explained in details in Sect. 4.3, these properties, which come from the special form of p, are essential for the efficiency of the Montgomery reduction algorithm.

Remark 7. Given $\mathcal{B}$ a special PMNS basis for SIDH, a small basis of the lattice $\mathcal{L}_\mathcal{B}$ associated to $\mathcal{B}$ (as defined in (1)) is given by the n vectors corresponding to the n polynomials M, XM, $\cdots$, $X^{k-1}M$, Γ, $X\Gamma$, $\cdots$, $X^{n-k-1}\Gamma$. The 1-norm of the columns of the corresponding matrix is either $|\gamma^k|+1$ or $|\gamma^k/e|+1$. Thus, the 1-norm of the matrix is $|\gamma^k|+1$ for all $e \in \mathbb{Z}$. Using [3, Th. 2.2], this implies that $(|\gamma^k|+1)/2$ is a lower bound for ρ. In other terms, it guarantees that if $\rho > (|\gamma^k|+1)/2$, then any $v \in \mathbb{F}_{p^k}$ admits a ρ-reduced γ-representation in $\mathcal{B}$.

Example 8. Let $p = 2^{250}3^{159} - 1$ be the prime called SIKEp503 in the SIKE [11] submission to the NIST post-quantum standardization process. Special PMNS basis for SIDH make it possible to represent the elements of $\mathbb{F}_p$, but also those of $\mathbb{F}_{p^2}$ directly.

- A special PMNS basis for SIDH for the prime field $\mathbb{F}_p$, may be obtained by writing $p = (2^{25}3^{16})^{10}/3 - 1$, i.e. $k = 1$, $n = 10$, $e = 3$, and $\gamma = 2^{25}3^{16}$. We have $\Gamma = X - 2^{25}3^{16}$ and $E = X^{10} - 3$. Any value ρ greater than the 50-bit integer $\gamma/2 = 2^{24}3^{16}$, can be used to define reduced representations. In particular, the polynomial $M = 2^{25}3^{15}X^9 - 1$ is a (ρ-reduced) γ-representation of zero. In this case, the extension field $\mathbb{F}_{p^2}$ may be defined as $\mathbb{F}_p(i)$ where $i^2 = -1$.
- Alternatively, a special PMNS basis for SIDH can be built directly for the quadratic extension $\mathbb{F}_{p^2}$ by writing $p = (2^{62}3^{40}\sqrt{-2})^4/3 - 1$, i.e. $k = 2$, $n = 4$, $e = 3$, and $\gamma = 2^{62}3^{40}\sqrt{-2}$. We have $\Gamma = X^2 + 2^{125}3^{80}$ and $E = X^4 - 3$. Any value ρ greater than the 252-bit integer $\gamma^2/2 = 2^{125}3^{80}$, can be used to define reduced representations. In particular, the polynomial $M = -2^{125}3^{79}X^2 - 1$ is a (ρ-reduced) γ-representation of zero.

4.1 Conversions from and into the Representation

Converting an element of $\mathbb{F}_{p^k}$ to a special PMNS basis for SIDH is done in two steps. First, we write the element in the basis $(1, \gamma, \cdots, \gamma^{k-1})$. This can be done with integer coefficients in $[0, p[$. Then, we need to write each integer coefficient in radix $|\gamma^k|$ (recall than γ^k is an integer) with integer digits in $[-|\gamma^k|/2, |\gamma^k|/2[$. Each coefficient has at most n/k digits. Hence, the output is a polynomial of degree less than n whose coefficients are less than or equal to $|\gamma^k|/2$ in absolute value. In other words, it is ρ-reduced for every possible ρ-value, according to Remark 7.

The reverse conversion, from a special PMNS basis for SIDH to an element of $\mathbb{F}_{p^k}$, is performed by evaluating the polynomial at γ.

4.2 Coefficients Reduction for Additions and Subtractions

The ability to quickly reduce the coefficients after the various arithmetic operations is crucial for the overall efficiency our approach.

Let us first consider the reduction of the coefficients after additions and subtractions that only increase the coefficients' size by a few bits.

The proposed reduction algorithm is presented in Algorithm 2. For the algorithm to work, we require ρ to be larger than $|\gamma^k|$, i.e. twice the lower bound given by remark 7. The operations in line 6 correspond to an euclidean division by ρ, with signed remainder. Since ρ can be freely chosen, it is judicious to pick a power of 2 that makes this operation very fast and easy to implement.

Theorem 9. *Let $\mathcal{B}$ be a special PMNS basis for SIDH, with $\rho > |\gamma^k|$, and let t a fixed positive integer. If* $\max|R| + |e|\max|Q| < \rho/2$, *then Algorithm 2 is correct.*

Proof. At the end of the algorithm, we have

$$V \equiv U + (X^k - \gamma^k)\sum_{i=0}^{n-1} c_i X^i \pmod{E}$$

which means that $V(\gamma) = U(\gamma)$ in $\mathbb{F}_{p^k}$. Hence U and V are equivalent in $\mathcal{B}$.

Algorithm 2. Coefficient reduction

Input: a special PMNS basis for SIDH $\mathcal{B} = (p, k, n, X^k - \gamma^k, X^n - e, \gamma)$; a positive integer t; and an element U of $\mathcal{B}$ of degree at most $n-1$ with $|u_i| < t\rho$ for $0 \leq i < n$.
Output: a reduced element V of $\mathcal{B}$ of degree at most $n-1$ with $|v_i| < \rho$ for $0 \leq i < n$, equivalent to U.

1: $Q[j] \leftarrow \lfloor j\rho/\gamma^k \rceil$ for $0 \leq j \leq t$ ▷ precomputations
2: $R[j] \leftarrow j\rho - \gamma^k Q[j]$ for $0 \leq j \leq t$ ▷ precomputations

3: **function** CoeffReduc(U)
4: $c_j \leftarrow 0$ for $-k \leq j < 0$
5: **for** $i = 0$ to $n-1$ **do**
6: Write u_i as $s_i \times u_{i,h} \times \rho + u_{i,\ell}$ with $s_i = \pm 1$, $u_{i,h} \geq 0$ and $|u_{i,\ell}| \leq \rho/2$
7: $v_i \leftarrow u_{i,\ell} + s_i \times R[u_{i,h}] + c_{i-k}$
8: $c_i \leftarrow s_i \times Q[u_{i,h}]$
9: $v_j \leftarrow v_j + e \times c_{n-k+j}$ for $0 \leq j < k$
10: **return** V

Now, for $0 \leq i < k$, we have $c_{i-k} = 0$, thus

$$\begin{aligned} v_i &= u_{i,\ell} + s_i \times R[u_{i,j}] + c_{i-k} + e \times c_{n-k+j} \\ &\leq \frac{\rho}{2} + \max|R| + e \times \max|C| < \rho \end{aligned}$$

And for $k \leq i < n$, $v_i = u_{i,\ell} + s_i \times R[u_{i,j}] + c_{i-k}$, and the same bound is achieved with the same arguments. □

In practice we will use this algorithm with $t = 2$ or $t = 4$, the precomputed tables will be of length 3 or 5. The elements of R are stored on as many bits as $|\gamma^k|$ and, if ρ is close to $|\gamma^k|$, the elements of Q are approximately t-bit long. For larger values of t, the precomputed tables would be too large, so, for example, Algorithm 2 cannot be used to perform the reduction after a multiplication.

Example 10. With the special PMNS basis for SIDH for SIKEp503 from Example 8: $\mathcal{B} = (\text{SIKEp503}, 1, 10, X - 2^{25}3^{16}, X^{10} - 3, 2^{25}3^{16})$, ρ will be chosen as the smallest power of 2 larger than γ, i.e. $\rho = 2^{51}$. The condition of Theorem 9 is satisfied for $t = 2$, $t = 4$, $t = 128$, and even for $t = 2^{20}$, but this later value is too large to be practical.

4.3 Montgomery Multiplication

Finally, we need to adapt the new Montgomery reduction algorithm described in Algorithm 1 in the case of a special PMNS basis for SIDH and show that it can be used after a multiplication to obtain a reduced representation.

Algorithm 1, requires a representation of zero that is invertible in the quotient ring $(\mathbb{Z}/2^\omega\mathbb{Z})[X]/(E)$. In the case of a special PMNS basis for SIDH, we exhibited the good candidate M for a representation of zero in Proposition 6. The next theorem demonstrates that M can indeed be used in the Montgomery reduction algorithm and also gives a explicit formula for its inverse.

Theorem 11. *Let $\mathcal{B} = (p, k, n, \Gamma, E, \gamma)$ be a special PMNS basis for SIDH and let $M = (\gamma^k/e)X^{n-k} - 1$ be the representative of zero in $\mathcal{B}$ introduced in Proposition 6. Let ω be a positive integer such that $\gamma^{n+k}/e^2 \equiv 0 \pmod{2^\omega}$, and let β be the largest integer such that $\gamma^{\beta k}/e \not\equiv 0 \pmod{2^\omega}$ (the assumption on ω implies that $\beta \leq n/k$). Then, the inverse of the polynomial $-M$ in $(\mathbb{Z}/2^\omega\mathbb{Z})[X]/(E)$ is given by:*

$$M' = 1 + \sum_{i=1}^{\beta} \frac{\gamma^{ik}}{e} X^{n-ik}$$

Proof. Let us show that $M \times M' = -1$ in $(\mathbb{Z}/2^\omega\mathbb{Z})[X]/(E)$.

$$\begin{aligned} M \times M' &= \left(\frac{\gamma^k}{e} X^{n-k} - 1\right) \times \left(1 + \sum_{i=1}^{\beta} \frac{\gamma^{ik}}{e} X^{n-ik}\right) \\ &= \frac{\gamma^k}{e} X^{n-k} + \sum_{i=1}^{\beta} \frac{\gamma^{(i+1)k}}{e^2} X^{2n-(i+1)k} - \sum_{i=1}^{\beta} \frac{\gamma^{ik}}{e} X^{n-ik} - 1 \\ &= \sum_{i=2}^{\beta+1} \frac{\gamma^{ik}}{e^2} X^{2n-ik} - \sum_{i=2}^{\beta} \frac{\gamma^{ik}}{e} X^{n-ik} - 1. \end{aligned}$$

Since $E = X^n - e$, we have $X^n \equiv e \pmod{E}$. Therefore

$$\begin{aligned} M \times M' &\equiv \sum_{i=2}^{\beta} \frac{\gamma^{ik}}{e} X^{n-ik} + \frac{\gamma^{(\beta+1)k}}{e^2} X^{2n-(\beta+1)k} - \sum_{i=2}^{\beta} \frac{\gamma^{ik}}{e} X^{n-ik} - 1 \pmod{E} \\ &\equiv \frac{\gamma^{(\beta+1)k}}{e^2} X^{2n-(\beta+1)k} - 1 \pmod{E}. \end{aligned}$$

If $2n - (\beta + 1)k \geq n$ (i.e. $\beta k < n$), then, after reduction by $E = X^n - e$, we have

$$M \times M' = \frac{\gamma^{(\beta+1)k}}{e} X^{n-(\beta+1)k} - 1$$

which is equal to -1 in $(\mathbb{Z}/2^\omega\mathbb{Z})[X]/(E)$ by definition of β. Finally, if $\beta k = n$, we conclude using the fact that $\gamma^{n+k}/e^2 \equiv 0 \bmod 2^\omega$. □

Note that for SIDH[1], the assumption $\gamma^{n+k}/e^2 \equiv 0 \pmod{2^\omega}$ is easy to satisfy as γ is divisible by a large power of 2. In practice, the choice of ω and the fact that 2^w is almost half the size of γ will often imply that β, which corresponds to the number of non-constant monomials of M' is 2.

Example 12. Let us consider again the special PMNS basis for SIDH for SIKEp503 from Example 8: $\mathcal{B} = (\text{SIKEp503}, 1, 10, X - 2^{25}3^{16}, X^{10} - 3, 2^{25}3^{16})$.

[1] With $p_A = 2$.

On a 64-bit architecture, we may want to use $\omega = 64$. The condition $\gamma^{n+k}/e^2 = 2^{275}3^{174} \equiv 0 \pmod{2^{64}}$ is easily satisfied. Since $\gamma^2 = 2^{50}3^{32} \not\equiv 0 \pmod{2^{64}}$ and $\gamma^3 = 2^{75}3^{48} \equiv 0 \pmod{2^{64}}$, we have $\beta = 2$. Thus

$$M' = \frac{\gamma}{e}X^9 + \frac{\gamma^2}{e}X^8 + 1.$$

Theorem 13. *Using the same notations as in Theorem 11. Let ρ be a bound on the coefficient size such that $\rho > |\gamma^k|$. Let C be an element of $\mathcal{B}$ with coefficients bounded by $2^\omega \rho$ in absolute value. Then, Algorithm 1 applied to C will return an element of $\mathcal{B}$ with coefficients bounded by 2ρ in absolute value.*

Proof. Considering that the coefficients of Q are bounded by 2^ω and taking into account the special form of M, the product $QM \mod E$ has its coefficients bounded by $2^\omega|\gamma^k| + 2^\omega$ in absolute value. So the coefficients of the polynomial returned by Algorithm 1 are bounded by

$$\frac{|c_i| + 2^\omega|\gamma^k| + 2^\omega}{2^\omega} < \frac{2^\omega\rho + 2^\omega|\gamma^k| + 2^\omega}{2^\omega} = \rho + |\gamma^k| + 1 \leq 2\rho.$$

□

4.4 Implementation Details of Montgomery Reduction

Theorem 14. *Let $(p, k, n, X^k - \gamma^k, X^n - e, \gamma)$ be a special PMNS basis for SIDH. Let ω, β, M and M' be defined as in Theorem 11. Let $C = \sum_{i=0}^{n-1} c_i X^i$ be a integer polynomial and $Q = \sum_{i=0}^{n-1} q_i X^i$ be the product $CM' \bmod E \bmod 2^\omega$ from line 1 of Algorithm 1. The coefficients of Q are given by:*

$$q_i = \begin{cases} c_i + \sum_{j=1}^{\beta} \frac{\gamma^{jk}}{e} c_{i+jk-n} \mod 2^\omega & \text{if } n-k \leq i < n \\ c_i + \gamma^k q_{i+k} \mod 2^\omega & \text{if } 0 \leq i < n-k \end{cases}$$

Moreover,

$$C + QM = \sum_{i=0}^{n-k-1} (c_i + \gamma^k q_{i+k} - q_i)X^i + \sum_{i=n-k}^{n-1} (c_i + \frac{\gamma^k}{e} q_{i-n+k} - q_i)X^i \mod E$$

Proof.

$$CM' = (\sum_{i=0}^{n-1} c_i X^i)(1 + \sum_{j=1}^{\beta} \frac{\gamma^{jk}}{e} X^{n-jk}) = \sum_{i=0}^{n-1} c_i X^i + \sum_{j=1}^{\beta}\sum_{i=0}^{n-1} \frac{\gamma^{jk}}{e} c_i X^{n-jk+i}$$

$$\equiv \sum_{i=0}^{n-1} c_i X^i + \sum_{j=1}^{\beta} \left(\sum_{i=0}^{jk-1} \frac{\gamma^{jk}}{e} c_i X^{n-jk+i} + \sum_{i=jk}^{n-1} \gamma^{jk} c_i X^{i-jk} \right) \pmod{E}$$

$$\equiv \sum_{i=0}^{n-1} c_i X^i + \sum_{j=1}^{\beta} \left(\sum_{i=n-jk}^{n-1} \frac{\gamma^{jk}}{e} c_{i-n+jk} X^i + \sum_{i=0}^{n-1-jk} \gamma^{jk} c_{jk+i} X^i \right)$$

$$\equiv \sum_{i=0}^{n-1} \left(c_i + \sum_{j=1}^{\min(\lfloor \frac{n-i-1}{k} \rfloor, \beta)} \gamma^{jk} c_{i+jk} + \sum_{j=\lfloor \frac{n-i-1}{k} \rfloor + 1}^{\beta} \frac{\gamma^{jk}}{e} c_{i+jk-n} \right) X^i$$

The formula for q_i in the case $n-k \le i < n$ is proven from the above formula by noticing that in this case $\lfloor (n-i-1)/k \rfloor = 0$.

To prove the formula in the case $0 \le i < n-k$, we need the two following facts: first that $\lfloor (n-(i+k)-1)/k \rfloor = \lfloor (n-i-1)/k \rfloor - 1$ and then that multiplying q_{i+k} by γ^k is equivalent to shifting the indexes in the sum. To conclude, it remains to use the fact that $\gamma^{(\beta+1)k}/e \equiv 0 \pmod{2^\omega}$.

The formula from $C+QM$ comes from a straightforward computation of the product $QM \bmod E$ using the particular form of $M = (\gamma^k/e)X^{n-k} - 1$. □

This theorem proves that Algorithm 3 is a correct adaption of Algorithm 1 in the case of a special PMNS basis for SIDH. It is more efficient as it performs only a linear number of multiplications: β multiplications modulo 2^ω per iteration in the first loop and 1 full multiplication per iteration for the second and third loops. The remaining operations are additions and shifts.

Algorithm 3. Montgomery reduction for special PMNS basis for SIDH

Input: as in Algorithm 1
Output: as in Algorithm 1

1: **for** $j = n-1$ down to $n-k$ **do**
2: $\quad q_j \leftarrow c_j + \sum_{i=1}^{\beta} (\gamma^{ik}/e) c_{j+ik-n} \mod 2^\omega$
3: **for** $j = n-k-1$ down to 0 **do**
4: $\quad t_j \leftarrow c_j + \gamma^k q_{j+k}$
5: $\quad (r_j, q_j) \leftarrow (\lfloor t_j/2^\omega \rfloor, t_j \bmod 2^\omega)$
6: **for** $j = n-1$ down to $n-k$ **do**
7: $\quad t_j \leftarrow c_j + (\gamma^k/e) q_{j-n+k}$
8: $\quad r_j \leftarrow \lfloor t_j/2^\omega \rfloor$
9: **return** R

Algorithm 3 compute the q_j's starting from q_{n-1} down to q_0. It first computes $q_{n-1}, \dots, q_{n-k}$ using the first case of the formula from Theorem 14. Then for j from $n-k-1$ to 0, it computes the full product $\gamma^k q_{j+k} + c_j$, uses it to compute the j-th coefficient of $(C+QM)/2^\omega$ and takes it modulo 2^ω to obtain q_j. Note that, while computing the j-th coefficient of $(C+QM)/2^\omega$, we do not need to subtract q_j before dividing by 2^ω as the two operands are equal modulo 2^ω.

5 Results

In this section we validate the efficiency of our novel arithmetic through two special PMNS basis for SIDH. We compare our implementation with the code available on the Github repository PQCrypto-SIDH [14][2], more precisely with the uncompressed, optimized x64 implementation. We implemented the PMNS arithmetic in assembly and did not make any changes to the code handling the elliptic operations nor the SIDH and SIKE functions. For our new prime $p736$, we generated the necessary sets of parameters as well as new optimized strategies for the isogeny computations using the specifications from [11].

The operations of conversions into and from PMNS are only computed once before and after communications between the parties as the protocol specifies the format of the exchange data. For the coordinates of the public generators points of the SIKE protocol, we replaced their value in the source code by a reduced PMNS representation.

As pointed out in the introduction, an approach similar to ours was independently proposed in [19]. We did not include their timings in our comparisons since their implementation is about ten times slower than both the optimized implementation of SIKE and the present work.

Note that the arithmetic of SIKE implemented in [14] is already highly optimized. For the quadratic extension field $\mathbb{F}_p(i)$, it uses a Karatsuba-like algorithm for the multiplication but only performs two modular reductions (instead of three). For the arithmetic in $\mathbb{F}_p$, it benefits from the special form of p. Indeed, for $p = 2^{e_2}3^{e_3} - 1$, the Montgomery modular reduction may be greatly optimized. First, because the multiplication by p may be replaced by a multiplication by $p + 1 = 2^{e_2}3^{e_3}$, which itself reduces to a multiplication by 3^{e_3} plus some shifts, followed by a subtraction. Second, because the inverse of p modulo the Montgomery constant R (chosen as the smallest multiple of the word-size larger than p) is equal to -1 modulo 2^w for $w = 32, 64$, which further reduces the overall number of word multiplications. More details are given in [4].

All comparisons were performed on a desktop computer with a 3.2 GHz Intel Core i7-8700 (Coffee Lake) processor with Hyper-Threading and TurboBoost disabled, running Ubuntu 18.04.5 and gcc 6.5.0. The compilation options used are identical to the ones in the Makefile provided by [14].

The code is available at https://gitlab.inria.fr/ciao/pmns-for-sidh. The current version of this article corresponds to commit `fc666429`.

[2] We use commit `4eb51ae0` (few commits after tag version 3.3).

5.1 SIKEp503

As a proof of concept, and for comparisons and compatibility purposes, we generated two different special PMNS basis for SIKEp503 $= 2^{250}3^{159} - 1$.

Our first special PMNS basis uses polynomials of degree 9 with coefficients on a single 64-bit word. We used the following parameters:

$$k = 1 \qquad n = 10 \qquad \gamma = 2^{25}3^{16}$$
$$\Gamma = X - \gamma \qquad E = X^{10} - 3 \qquad \rho = 2^{56}$$

In this case, we implemented Algorithm 3 with $\omega = 64$.

We also consider a second special PMNS basis with degree-2 polynomials and coefficients on three 64-bit words; hence a total of nine 64-bit words.

$$k = 1 \qquad n = 3 \qquad \gamma = 2^{84}3^{53}$$
$$\Gamma = X - \gamma \qquad E = X^3 - 4 \qquad \rho = 2^{170}$$

In this case, we implemented Algorithm 3 with $\omega = 192$.

In Table 2, we give the number of clock cycles for the main arithmetic operations in our two PMNS basis denoted 10×1 and 3×3 respectively and we compare them to the corresponding operations from the optimized reference implementation of SIKE [14]. We split the cost of a $\mathbb{F}_p$ multiplication into the actual multiple-precision or polynomial product, followed by the Montgomery reduction. In the PMNS cases, the product corresponds to the polynomial multiplication modulo E, and the Montgomery reduction corresponds to the coefficient reduction algorithm (Algorithm 3) presented in Sect. 4.4.

Table 2. SIKEp503: cost of field operations in number of clock cycles

	[14]	This work 10×1	Speedup	This work 3×3	Speedup
$\mathbb{F}_p$ Addition	19	22	0.86	19	1.00
$\mathbb{F}_p$ Multiplication	143	131	1.09	139	1.03
Product	72	113	0.64	108	0.67
Montgomery reduction	55	23	2.39	33	1.67
$\mathbb{F}_{p^2}$ Addition	35	41	0.85	35	1.00
$\mathbb{F}_{p^2}$ Multiplication	358	446	0.80	423	0.85
$\mathbb{F}_{p^2}$ Square	308	318	0.97	300	1.03

Despite a much faster Montgomery reduction, and a slightly faster multiplication in $\mathbb{F}_p$, our multiplication in $\mathbb{F}_{p^2}$ remains slower than that of SIKEp503. This is mainly due to the fact that our field elements are represented on two extra words for the 10×1 variant and one extra word for the 3×3 variant.

Therefore, our product requires more word-size multiplications. And since the multiplication in $\mathbb{F}_{p^2}$ uses 3 products but only two reductions, the overall performance of the original SIKE implementation is better. As can be seen in Table 3, these results translate immediately to the key exchange and key encapsulation schemes.

5.2 SIKEp751 Versus Our p736

The prime SIKEp751 $= 2^{372}3^{239} - 1$ in the NIST submission was proposed for the largest security level. For an equivalent level of security, we propose a new 736-bit prime, called p_{736} in the following. In order to build a special PMNS basis for the finite field $\mathbb{F}_p$ for $p = p_{736} = 2^{361}3^{236} - 1$, we used the following parameters:

$$k = 1 \qquad n = 4 \qquad \gamma = 2^{91}3^{59}$$
$$\Gamma = X - \gamma \qquad E = X^4 - 8 \qquad \rho = 2^{186}$$

Table 3. SIKEp503: cost of SIDH and SIKE operations in number of clock cycles

	[14]	This work 10 × 1	Speedup	This work 3 × 3	Speedup
Key exchange					
Alice's key generation	5322813	6584635	0.81	6188158	0.86
Bob's key generation	5927772	7254013	0.82	6781400	0.87
Alice's shared key computation	4361263	5324520	0.82	4988913	0.87
Bob's shared key computation	5036883	6182503	0.81	5695130	0.88
Kem					
Key generation	5946153	7297933	0.81	6784183	0.88
Encapsulation	9726092	11925016	0.82	11174206	0.87
Decapsulation	10359163	12688804	0.82	11877351	0.87

In this case, we implemented Algorithm 3 with $\omega = 192$. This PMNS basis uses degree-3 polynomials and coefficients on three 64-bit words; hence a total of twelve 64-bit words, the same number of words used for the arithmetic of SIKEp751.

For this prime, we choose to use 2^{360} instead of 2^{361} for Alice's subgroup order, in order to be able to use only 4-isogeny in the key computation.

As for SIKEp503 above, we compared the field arithmetic operations for both SIKEp751 and our p_{736}. The results presented in Table 4 exhibit a 10% speedup for the multiplication and 29% for the square in $\mathbb{F}_{p^2}$. And as a consequence, a 1.17× speedup factor for the key exchange and key encapsulation schemes (see Table 5).

Table 4. p_{736} and SIKEp751: cost of field operations in number of clock cycles

	[14] SIKEp751	This work p_{736}	Speedup
$\mathbb{F}_p$ Addition	29	22	1.32
$\mathbb{F}_p$ Multiplication	274	198	1.38
Product	140	162	0.86
Montgomery reduction	106	39	2.72
$\mathbb{F}_{p^2}$ Addition	54	40	1.35
$\mathbb{F}_{p^2}$ Multiplication	693	631	1.10
$\mathbb{F}_{p^2}$ Square	559	435	1.29

Table 5. p_{736} and SIKEp751: cost of SIDH and SIKE operations in number of clock cycles

	[14] SIKEp751	This work p_{736}	Speedup
Key exchange			
Alice's key generation	15836023	13625479	1.16
Bob's key generation	17945236	15609183	1.15
Alice's shared key computation	13040542	11140436	1.17
Bob's shared key computation	15368807	13326150	1.15
Kem			
Key generation	17975299	15609821	1.15
Encapsulation	28849145	24735564	1.17
Decapsulation	31317267	26879415	1.17

6 Conclusions

We presented new algorithms to perform the arithmetic for primes used in the context of SIDH. These algorithms uses a polynomial representation of the field elements based on the existing Polynomial Modular Number System. We proposed new techniques to control the size of the coefficients of those polynomial representations which are particularly effective for the primes used in the context of SIDH.

We show that our new approach is competitive with the optimized implementation accompanying the SIKE submission to the NIST post-quantum standardization process. For the largest security level, we proposed a new prime that offers a 1.17× speedup compared to SIKEp751.

As seen for SIKEp503, different PMNS basis can be constructed for a given prime. Playing with the polynomial degree and the coefficient's sizes offers many optimization options for implementing the field arithmetic operations that should be further investigated. Moreover, as explained in Example 8, PMNS can handle elements of $\mathbb{F}_{p^2}$ directly. This nice feature could make it possible to consider primes for SIDH that are congruent to 1 (mod 4). But, for SIDH primes of the form $p = c \cdot 2^{e_2} \cdot 3^{e_3} + 1$, square roots of integers of the form $\pm 2^a 3^b$ always exist in $\mathbb{F}_p$, which prevents us from using a γ^k of this form in Definition 5 to build a special PMNS basis for SIDH directly for $\mathbb{F}_{p^2}$ in this case. However, we believe that extra improvements and more primes of interest for SIDH are at hand.

Acknowledgements. In the submitted version of this work, the Montgomery-like coefficient reduction algorithm was presented as an original contribution. We are most grateful to thank Pascal Véron who pointed out Christophe Nègre and Thomas Plantard's paper [16] that actually contains the original algorithm.

This work was supported by the French *Agence Nationale de la Recherche, projet CIAO (ANR-19-CE48-0008).*

References

1. Alagic, G., et al.: Status report on the second round of the NIST post-quantum cryptography standardization process. Technical report NISTIR 8309, National Institute of Standards and Technology, U.S. Department of Commerce, July 2020. https://doi.org/10.6028/NIST.IR.8309
2. Bajard, J.-C., Imbert, L., Plantard, T.: Arithmetic operations in the polynomial modular number system. In: Proceedings of the 17th IEEE Symposium on Computer Arithmetic, ARITH17, pp. 206–213. IEEE Computer Society (2005). https://doi.org/10.1109/ARITH.2005.11
3. Bajard, J.-C., Marrez, J., Plantard, T., Véron, P.: On polynomial modular number systems over $\mathbb{Z}/p\mathbb{Z}$ (2020). https://hal.sorbonne-universite.fr/hal-02883341
4. Bos, J.W., Friedberger, S.: Faster modular arithmetic for isogeny-based crypto on embedded devices. J. Cryptogr. Eng. **10**(2), 97–109 (2020). https://doi.org/10.1007/s13389-019-00214-6
5. Buchanan, W., Woodward, A.: Will quantum computers be the end of public key encryption? J. Cyber Secur. Technol. **1**(1), 1–22 (2017). https://doi.org/10.1080/23742917.2016.1226650
6. Costello, C.: Supersingular isogeny key exchange for beginners. In: Paterson, K.G., Stebila, D. (eds.) SAC 2019. LNCS, vol. 11959, pp. 21–50. Springer, Cham (2020). https://doi.org/10.1007/978-3-030-38471-5_2
7. Costello, C., Longa, P., Naehrig, M.: Efficient algorithms for supersingular isogeny Diffie-Hellman. In: Robshaw, M., Katz, J. (eds.) CRYPTO 2016. LNCS, vol. 9814, pp. 572–601. Springer, Heidelberg (2016). https://doi.org/10.1007/978-3-662-53018-4_21
8. Faz-Hernández, A., López-Hernández, J.C., Ochoa-Jiménez, E., Rodríguez-Henríquez, F.: A faster software implementation of the supersingular isogeny diffie-hellman key exchange protocol. IEEE Trans. Comput. **67**(11), 1622–1636 (2018). https://doi.org/10.1109/TC.2017.2771535
9. De Feo, L.: Mathematics of isogeny based cryptography (2017)
10. Galbraith, S.D., Vercauteren, F.: Computational problems in supersingular elliptic curve isogenies. Cryptology ePrint Archive, Report 2017/774 (2017). https://eprint.iacr.org/2017/774

11. Jao, D., et al.: SIKE - supersingular isogeny key encapsulation. Submission to the NIST Post-Quantum Standardization project (2017), sike.org
12. Jao, D., De Feo, L.: Towards quantum-resistant cryptosystems from supersingular elliptic curve isogenies. In: Yang, B.-Y. (ed.) PQCrypto 2011. LNCS, vol. 7071, pp. 19–34. Springer, Heidelberg (2011). https://doi.org/10.1007/978-3-642-25405-5_2
13. Karmakar, A., Roy, S.S., Vercauteren, F., Verbauwhede, I.: Efficient finite field multiplication for isogeny based post quantum cryptography. In: Duquesne, S., Petkova-Nikova, S. (eds.) WAIFI 2016. LNCS, vol. 10064, pp. 193–207. Springer, Cham (2016). https://doi.org/10.1007/978-3-319-55227-9_14
14. Longa, P., et al.: PQCrypto-SIDH (2020). https://github.com/microsoft/PQCrypto-SIDH
15. Montgomery, P.L.: Modular multiplication without trial division. Math. Comput. **44**(170), 519–521 (1985)
16. Negre, C., Plantard, T.: Efficient modular arithmetic in adapted modular number system using Lagrange representation. In: Mu, Y., Susilo, W., Seberry, J. (eds.) ACISP 2008. LNCS, vol. 5107, pp. 463–477. Springer, Heidelberg (2008). https://doi.org/10.1007/978-3-540-70500-0_34
17. Shor, P.W.: Algorithms for quantum computation: discrete logarithms and factoring. In: Proceedings 35th Annual Symposium on Foundations of Computer Science, pp. 124–134 (1994). https://doi.org/10.1109/sfcs.1994.365700
18. Smith, B.: Pre- and post-quantum Diffie-Hellman from groups, actions, and isogenies. In: Budaghyan, L., Rodríguez-Henríquez, F. (eds.) WAIFI 2018. LNCS, vol. 11321, pp. 3–40. Springer, Cham (2018). https://doi.org/10.1007/978-3-030-05153-2_1
19. Tian, J., Wang, P., Liu, Z., Lin, J., Wang, Z., Großschadl, J.: Faster Software Implementation of the SIKE Protocol Based on A New Data Representation. Cryptology ePrint Archive, Report 2020/660 (2020). https://eprint.iacr.org/2020/660

The Convergence of Slide-Type Reductions

Michael Walter(✉)

IST Austria, Klosterneuburg, Austria
michael.walter@ist.ac.at

Abstract. In this work, we apply the dynamical systems analysis of Hanrot *et al.* (CRYPTO'11) to a class of lattice block reduction algorithms that includes (natural variants of) slide reduction and block-Rankin reduction. This implies sharper bounds on the polynomial running times (in the query model) for these algorithms and opens the door to faster practical variants of slide reduction. We give heuristic arguments showing that such variants can indeed speed up slide reduction significantly in practice. This is confirmed by experimental evidence, which also shows that our variants are competitive with state-of-the-art reduction algorithms.

1 Introduction

Lattice block reduction is a key tool in cryptanalysis, so understanding its potential and its limitations is essential for the security of many cryptosystems. The basic idea of lattice block reduction is to use an oracle that solves the shortest vector problem (SVP) on lattices with low dimension to find short vectors in lattices with larger dimension. Most work in lattice block reduction has focused on BKZ [Sch87, SE94] – the first generalization of the celebrated LLL [LLL82] algorithm, see e.g. [GN08b, HPS11, CN11, Wal15, ADH+19, AWHT16, ABF+20, LN20] to list just a few. Other reduction algorithms are known, like slide reduction [GN08a, ALNS20] and SDBKZ [MW16], which allow proving better bounds on the output quality, but in practice BKZ is still the go-to choice for finding short vectors. Block reduction algorithms are usually judged by the shortness of the vectors they are able to find within a given amount of time. The length of the vector found can be quantified in two different ways: by its ratio with either 1) the shortest non-zero vector of the lattice (the approximation factor) or 2) the (n-th root of the) volume/determinant of the lattice (the Hermite factor).

Slide Reduction. The focus of this work is slide reduction and, to some degree, its generalization to block-Rankin reduction [LN14]. When it was introduced, slide reduction provided the best-known bounds on the approximation and Hermite factor and was easily proved to terminate in a polynomial number of calls

Supported by the European Research Council, ERC consolidator grant (682815 - TOC-NeT).

J. A. Garay (Ed.): PKC 2021, LNCS 12710, pp. 45–67, 2021.
https://doi.org/10.1007/978-3-030-75245-3_3

to the SVP oracle. Other algorithms achieving the same Hermite factor and terminating in a (smaller) polynomial number of SVP calls are known at this point [MW16,Neu17], but to date, slide reduction still achieves the best bound on the approximation factor. The basic idea of slide reduction is simple: given a basis $\mathbf{B}$ for an n-dimensional lattice, a block size d that divides[1] n and an oracle that solves SVP in dimension d, apply the SVP oracle to the n/d disjoint (projected) blocks $\left(\mathbf{B}_{[id+1,(i+1)d]}\right)_i$ of the basis. Then apply the oracle to the *dual* of the blocks shifted by 1, i.e. to $\left(\widehat{\mathbf{B}}_{[id+2,(i+1)d+1]}\right)_i$. This results in "primal" and "dual" blocks that overlap by one index (and $d-1$ indices). This process is repeated until no more progress is made. The generalization to block-Rankin reduction works similarly, but it solves a more general problem and uses a more general tool. It approximates the densest sublattice problem (DSP) [DM13], which is itself a generalization of SVP, by relying on an oracle that solves the k-DSP in dimension d. (SVP corresponds to 1-DSP.) In this variant, the dual blocks are shifted by k resulting in overlaps of size k. The analysis of this algorithm is a straightforward adaptation of the one for slide reduction. Unfortunately, initial experimental evaluations of slide reduction [GN08a,GN08b] found it to be not competitive in practice with BKZ and so far there has been no research into practical variants of slide reduction and block-Rankin reduction to the best of our knowledge. This is despite the fact that it offers some trivial parallelization, since the disjoint blocks can be processed independently. This is not true for other reduction algorithms and could give slide reduction a considerable advantage in practice, especially because modern SVP solvers are hard to distribute.

Dynamical Systems Analyses. Inspired by the analysis of LLL, [GN08a,LN14] used an analysis based on a potential function to bound the number of oracle calls in slide reduction and block-Rankin reduction. Such an analysis does not work well for BKZ and for a long time it was open if the number of oracle calls in BKZ may be polynomially bounded. This changed when [HPS11] proposed an analysis based on dynamical systems to study BKZ and showed that one can put a polynomial bound on the number of oracle calls while preserving its output quality. Interestingly, this bound was much stronger than the one proven for slide reduction (and block-Rankin reduction) using the potential function. It was conjectured in [HPS11] that applying their approach to slide reduction may give much better bounds than the ones proven in [GN08a,LN14].

A similar analysis was later used to study another reduction algorithm, SDBKZ [MW16], where the analysis was simpler and cleaner. Unfortunately, [MW16] left a gap, where for certain parameterizations of the algorithm the bound on the number of oracle calls was not polynomial. The gap was closed later by [Neu17], using a seemingly different analysis: "simple (and sharper) induction arguments on a bound on the bit sizes". On closer inspection, it turns out that the analysis of [Neu17] can also be seen as an instance of the typical

[1] The restriction that $d \mid n$ is lifted in [ALNS20] by combining it with the algorithm of [MW16].

dynamical systems analysis, but with a small tweak. We make this tweak explicit in Sect. 5, which allows us to apply a similar tweak in our analysis of Slide-type reductions (see below).

1.1 Results

In this work, we consider a class of reduction algorithms that capture natural variants of slide reduction and block-Rankin reduction. We apply the dynamical systems analysis to the algorithms in this class and show that they converge quickly. This implies sharper polynomial-time running time bounds in the query model for slide reduction (when used to find short vectors in terms of the Hermite factor) and block-Rankin reduction.

Theorem 1 (Informal). *Let $\mathbf{B} \in \mathbb{R}^{m \times n}$ be an LLL-reduced lattice basis with $\det(\mathcal{L}(\mathbf{B})) = 1$ and $\epsilon > 0$ an arbitrary constant. After $O\left(\frac{n^3}{dk(d-k)} \ln\left(\frac{n}{\epsilon}\right)\right)$ calls to the (k,d)-DSP oracle, the output basis of block-Rankin reduction satisfies*

$$\det\left(\mathcal{L}\left(\mathbf{B}_{[1,k]}\right)\right)^{1/k} \lesssim (1+\epsilon)\gamma_{k,d}^{\frac{n-k}{2k(d-k)}}.$$

The best previous bound on the number of oracle queries proven in [LN14] is $O\left(\frac{n^3 \log \max_i \|\mathbf{b}_i\|}{\epsilon d^2}\right)$. For degenerate cases, $\max_i \|\mathbf{b}_i\|$ can be arbitrarily large (within the restriction that its logarithm is polynomial in the input size) even for LLL-reduced bases of lattices with determinant 1. (We focus on lattices with determinant 1 in this work for convenience. This is w.l.o.g. since one can always scale the lattice accordingly.) Theorem 1 confirms the conjecture of [HPS11]. Not only does it give a much stronger bound for slide reduction in case $k = 1$, it also gives a bound for block-Rankin reduction that depends on the overlap k and improves for increasing k. This can be viewed as formalizing the intuition that a larger overlap leads to faster propagation of information within the basis. Of course, solving the DSP for larger k is also harder and thus the complexity of the oracle itself will be larger and so will the overall running time.

In light of this it is natural to replace the DSP oracle by an oracle that approximates the DSP instead of solving it exactly. This suggests a variant, where the DSP problem is approximated using an HKZ oracle. We call this variant HKZ-slide reduction. It is inspired by recent observations in [ADH+19] that modern SVP solvers do not only find the shortest vector but approximately HKZ reduce the head of the basis essentially for free. Compared with slide reduction, increasing the overlap in HKZ-slide reduction decreases the running time at the cost of slightly increasing the length of the shortest vector found. We give heuristic arguments (Sect. 4.1) and experimental evidence (Sect. 4.2) that demonstrate that this trade-off can be very favorable in practice. A well chosen overlap yields a variant of slide reduction that we consider competitive with the state-of-the-art in lattice block reduction [ADH+19]. When interpreting this result, it should be kept in mind that we did not explore all options to fine-tune the oracle to our algorithm and that BKZ has received considerable research effort to arrive at the performance level it is at now. This is not the case for slide reduction. To the best of our knowledge, this work is the first attempt of improving the practical performance of slide reduction beyond speeding up the SVP oracle.

1.2 Techniques

We define a class of algorithms, which we call Slide-type reductions, and use the dynamical systems analysis introduced in [HPS11] to analyze their behavior by studying the properties of a system $\mathbf{x} \mapsto \mathbf{A}\mathbf{x} + \mathbf{b}$. Here, the variable $\mathbf{x}$ is a function of the current basis during the execution and $\mathbf{A}$ and $\mathbf{b}$ depend on the reduction algorithm (see Sect. 2.2 for details). The fixed point of the system determines the result of the reduction and the norm of $\mathbf{A}$ its running time. After modeling Slide-type reductions in this way, we confirm that the fixed point yields the expected output quality as was proven in previous work for algorithms that fall into the class of Slide-type reductions, but we are actually more interested in the convergence of the system. Accordingly, we wish to study the norm of $\mathbf{A}$, which in our case has the following form:

$$\mathbf{A} = \begin{pmatrix} 1-2\beta & \beta & & & \\ \beta & 1-2\beta & \beta & & \\ & & \cdots & & \\ & & & \beta & 1-2\beta \end{pmatrix}$$

for some $0 < \beta \leq 1/4$ that depends on the parameters of the algorithm. Our goal is to bound some norm (induced by some vector p-norm) of $\mathbf{A}$ away from 1, i.e. show that $\|\mathbf{A}\|_p \leq 1 - \epsilon$ for some large enough $\epsilon > 0$. Clearly, this does not work for the row or column sum norm ($p = \infty$ and $p = 1$, respectively), since they are 1. We conjecture that the spectral norm ($p = 2$) is in fact smaller than 1, but this seems hard to prove directly. Instead, we apply a trick implicitly used by Neumaier [Neu17] to analyze SDBKZ: we apply a change of variable. We make Neumaier's trick explicit in Sect. 5 and then apply a similar change to our system. This results in a new matrix, for which we can easily bound the row sum norm ($p = \infty$), which implies our results.

1.3 Open Problems

Our results show that slide reduction finds short vectors in terms of the Hermite factor much faster than was previously proven. By using a well-known reduction due to Lovász [Lov86], one can also find short vectors in terms of the approximation factor at the cost of calling slide reduction $O(n)$ times, increasing the running time by this factor. However, the resulting approximation factor is somewhat worse than what is proved in [GN08a]. An interesting open problem is whether one can prove that the approximation factor of [GN08a] can also be achieved with a number of oracle calls similar to our bound. Conversely, it might be that achieving this approximation factor does indeed require many more oracle calls.

We show in Sect. 4.2 that our variant of slide reduction is competitive with state-of-the-art reduction algorithms, but does not outperform them. However, given the lack of research into practical variants of slide reduction, we believe this might well be possible. We outline some avenues in Sect. 4.2 to improve our variant.

2 Preliminaries

Notation. Numbers and reals are denoted by lower case letters. For $n_1 \leq n_2 \in \mathbb{Z}$ we denote the set $\{n_1, \ldots, n_2\}$ by $[n_1, n_2]$. For vectors we use bold lower case letters and the i-th entry of a vector $\mathbf{v}$ is denoted by v_i. Let $\langle \mathbf{v}, \mathbf{w} \rangle = \sum_i v_i \cdot w_i$ be the scalar product of two vectors. If $p \geq 1$ the p norm of a vector $\mathbf{v}$ is $\|\mathbf{v}\|_p = (\sum |v_i|^p)^{1/p}$. We will only be concerned with the norms given by $p = 1$, 2, and ∞. Whenever we omit the subscript p, we mean the standard Euclidean norm, i.e. $p = 2$. Matrices are denoted by bold upper case letters. The i-th column of a matrix $\mathbf{B}$ is denoted by $\mathbf{b}_i$ and the entry in row i and column j by $\mathbf{B}_{i,j}$. For any matrix $\mathbf{B}$ and $p \geq 1$ we define the induced norm to be $\|\mathbf{B}\|_p = \max_{\|\mathbf{x}\|_p=1} (\|\mathbf{Bx}\|_p)$. For $p = 1$ (resp. ∞) this is often denoted by the column (row) sum norm, since $\|\mathbf{B}\|_1 = \max_j \sum_i |\mathbf{B}_{i,j}|$ and $\|\mathbf{B}\|_\infty = \max_i \sum_j |\mathbf{B}_{i,j}|$; for $p = 2$ this is also known as the spectral norm, i.e. the largest singular value of $\mathbf{B}$.

2.1 Lattices

A *lattice* Λ is a discrete subgroup of $\mathbb{R}^m$ and is generated by a matrix $\mathbf{B} \in \mathbb{R}^{m \times n}$, i.e. $\Lambda = \mathcal{L}(\mathbf{B}) = \{\mathbf{Bx} \colon \mathbf{x} \in \mathbb{Z}^n\}$. If $\mathbf{B}$ has full column rank, it is called a *basis* of Λ and $\dim(\Lambda) = n$ is the dimension (or rank) of Λ. Any lattice of dimension larger than 1 has infinitely many bases, which are related to each other by right-multiplication with unimodular matrices. We use the notion of projected subblocks $\mathbf{B}_{[i,j]}$ for $i < j < n$, i.e. $\mathbf{B}_{[i,j]}$ is the matrix consisting of the columns $\mathbf{b}_i, \mathbf{b}_{i+1}, \ldots, \mathbf{b}_j$ projected onto the space orthogonal to $\text{span}_{\mathbb{R}}(\mathbf{b}_1, \mathbf{b}_2, \ldots, \mathbf{b}_{i-1})$. We define the *Gram-Schmidt-Orthogonalization* (GSO) $\mathbf{B}^*$ of $\mathbf{B}$, where the i-th column $\mathbf{b}_i^*$ of $\mathbf{B}^*$ is defined as $\mathbf{b}_i^* = \mathbf{b}_i - \sum_{j<i} \mu_{i,j} \mathbf{b}_j^*$ and $\mu_{i,j} = \langle \mathbf{b}_i, \mathbf{b}_j^* \rangle / \|\mathbf{b}_j^*\|^2$ (and $\mathbf{b}_1^* = \mathbf{b}_1$). In other words, $\mathbf{b}_i^* = \mathbf{B}_{[i,i]}$. For every basis of a lattice with dimension larger than 1 there are infinitely many bases that have the same GSO vectors $\mathbf{b}_i^*$, among which there is a (not necessarily unique) basis that minimizes $\|\mathbf{b}_i\|$ for all i. Transforming a basis into this form is commonly known as *size-reduction* and is easily and efficiently done using a slight modification of the Gram-Schmidt process. In this work, we will implicitly assume all bases to be size-reduced. The reader can simply assume that any basis operation is followed by a size-reduction.

Every lattice Λ has invariants associated to it. One of them is its determinant $\det(\mathcal{L}(\mathbf{B})) = \prod_i \|\mathbf{b}_i^*\|$ for any basis $\mathbf{B}$. Note that this implies that for any two bases $\mathbf{B}$ and $\mathbf{B}'$ of the same lattice we have $\prod_i \|\mathbf{b}_i^*\| = \prod_i \|(\mathbf{b}_i')^*\|$ and the determinant is efficiently computable given any basis. Furthermore, for every lattice Λ we denote the length of its shortest non-zero vector (also known as its *first minimum*) by $\lambda_1(\Lambda)$, which is always well defined. We use the short-hand notations $\det(\mathbf{B}) = \det(\mathcal{L}(\mathbf{B}))$ and $\lambda_1(\mathbf{B}) = \lambda_1(\mathcal{L}(\mathbf{B}))$ if no confusion may arise.

Hermite's constant is defined as $\gamma_n = \sup_{\Lambda:\dim(\Lambda)=n} (\lambda_1(\Lambda) / \det(\Lambda))^2$. Minkowski's theorem is a classic result that shows that $\gamma_n \leq n$. Viewing a shortest vector as the basis of a 1-dimensional sublattice of Λ leads to a straightforward generalization of the first minimum to the densest k-dimensional sublattice $\mu_k(\Lambda) = \min_{\Lambda' \subset \Lambda:\dim(\Lambda')=k} \det(\Lambda')$. The corresponding generalization of Hermite's constant is known as Rankin's constant $\gamma_{k,n} = \sup_{\Lambda:\dim(\Lambda=n)} \left(\mu_k(\Lambda) / \det(\Lambda)^{k/n}\right)^2$.

There is a heuristic version of Minkowski's bound based on the Gaussian heuristic which states that most lattices that arise in practice satisfy $\lambda_1(\Lambda) \approx \sqrt{d/2\pi e} \det(\Lambda)^{1/n}$, unless there is an explicit reason to believe otherwise (e.g. an unusually short vector is planted in the lattice). We note that there is a theory of random lattices, which allows to turn this bound into a rigorous average-case version of Minkowski's bound, see e.g. [ALNS20] and references therein. For this work it is sufficient to know that the Gaussian heuristic is precise enough for lattices with dimension larger than 45 arising in lattice block reduction to predict its behavior in practice [CN11, GN08b, MW16].

Heuristic 1 [Gaussian Heuristic]. *For any lattice Λ with $\dim(\Lambda) \geq 45$ arising in lattice reduction we assume that $\lambda_1(\Lambda) \approx \sqrt{d/2\pi e} \det(\Lambda)^{1/n}$.*

For every lattice Λ, its *dual* is defined as $\hat{\Lambda} = \{\mathbf{w} \in \operatorname{span}_{\mathbb{R}}(\Lambda) \mid \langle \mathbf{w}, \mathbf{v} \rangle \in \mathbb{Z} \text{ for all } \mathbf{v} \in \Lambda\}$. It is a classical fact that $\det(\hat{\Lambda}) = \det(\Lambda)^{-1}$. For a lattice basis $\mathbf{B}$, let $\widehat{\mathbf{B}}$ be the unique matrix that satisfies $\operatorname{span}_{\mathbb{R}}(\mathbf{B}) = \operatorname{span}_{\mathbb{R}}(\widehat{\mathbf{B}})$ and $\mathbf{B}^T\widehat{\mathbf{B}} = \widehat{\mathbf{B}}^T\mathbf{B} = \mathbf{R}$, where $\mathbf{R}$ is the identity matrix with reversed columns (see Sect. 5). Then $\widehat{\mathcal{L}(\mathbf{B})} = \mathcal{L}(\widehat{\mathbf{B}})$ and we denote $\widehat{\mathbf{B}}$ as the *reversed dual basis* of $\mathbf{B}$. Note that $\widehat{\mathbf{B}_{[i,j]}} = \widehat{\mathbf{B}}_{[n+1-j,n+1-i]}$.

Definition 1. *Let $\mathbf{B} \in \mathbb{Z}^{m\times n}$ be a lattice basis. We call $\mathbf{B}$ k-partial HKZ reduced if $\|\mathbf{b}_i^*\| = \lambda_1(\mathbf{B}_{[i,n]})$ for all $i \in [1,k]$.*

An n-dimensional basis $\mathbf{B}$ is SVP reduced (HKZ reduced), if it is 1-partial (n-partial, resp.) HKZ reduced. The *root Hermite factor* achieved by $\mathbf{B}$ is defined as $(\|\mathbf{b}_1\| / \det(\mathbf{B})^{1/n})^{1/n}$.

We use some notation from [HS07]:

Definition 2. *For a lattice basis $\mathbf{B}$ we define $\pi_{[j,k]}(\mathbf{B}) = \left(\prod_{i=j}^{k} \|\mathbf{b}_i^*\|\right)^{1/(k-j+1)}$ and $\Gamma_n(k) = \prod_{i=d-k}^{d-1} \gamma_{i+1}^{\frac{1}{2i}}$. We sometimes omit $\mathbf{B}$ and simply write $\pi_{[j,k]}$ if $\mathbf{B}$ is clear from context.*

Using these definitions, [HS07] proves useful inequalities regarding the geometry of (k-partial) HKZ reduced bases. We will use the following:

Lemma 1 ([HS07]). *If* $\mathbf{B}$ *is* k*-partial HKZ reduced, then*

$$\pi_{[1,k]} \leq \Gamma_d(k)^{d/k} \pi_{k+1,d}.$$

The proof is pretty straightforward using Minkowski's bound and induction.

Definition 3. *A basis* $\mathbf{B} \in \mathbb{R}^{m \times n}$ *is called* LLL-reduced[2] *if* $\|\mathbf{b}_i^*\| = \lambda_1(\mathbf{B}_{[i,i+1]})$*, which implies* $\|\mathbf{b}_i^*\| \leq \gamma_2 \|\mathbf{b}_{i+1}^*\|$*, for all* $i \in [1, n-1]$.

We will need the following two facts about LLL.

Fact 1. *If* $\mathbf{B} \in \mathbb{R}^{m \times n}$ *is LLL-reduced, then we have*

$$\pi_{[1,i]} \leq \gamma_2^{\frac{n-i}{2}} \pi_{[1,n]}$$

for all $i \in [1, n]$.

See e.g. [PT09] for a proof.

Fact 2. *Let* $\mathbf{B} \in \mathbb{R}^{m \times n}$ *be a lattice basis and* $\mathbf{B}'$ *be the result of applying LLL to* $\mathbf{B}$. *Then we have*

$$\pi_{[1,i]}(\mathbf{B}') \leq \pi_{[1,i]}(\mathbf{B})$$

for all $i \in [1, n]$.

Fact 2 can be seen to be true from a similar argument to the one showing that the potential function used to analyze LLL may only decrease under the swaps that LLL performs. More specifically, LLL reduction only applies two types of operations: size-reduction, which does not change the value $\pi_{[1,i]}(\mathbf{B})$ for any i, and swapping consecutive vectors. Swapping vectors only affects the value $\pi_{[1,i]}(\mathbf{B})$ for exactly one i and the condition, under which such swaps are performed, ensures that this value can only decrease.

Finally, BKZ is a block-wise generalization of LLL.

Definition 4. *A basis* $\mathbf{B} \in \mathbb{R}^{m \times n}$ *is called* d-BKZ *reduced if* $\|\mathbf{b}_i^*\| = \lambda_1(\mathbf{B}_{[i,\ell]})$*, where* $\ell = \min(i+d, n)$*, for all* $i \in [1, n]$.

2.2 Discrete-Time Affine Dynamical Systems

Consider some dynamical system

$$\mathbf{x} \mapsto \mathbf{A}\mathbf{x} + \mathbf{b} \tag{1}$$

and assume that $\|\mathbf{A}\|_p < 1$ for some p. This implies two facts:

[2] Technically, LLL reduction also requires size-reduction and usually contains a slack factor in the inequality to guarantee termination in polynomial time. Neither of these additional requirements are important for this work, so we ignore it here for simplicity.

1. Equation (1) has at most one fixed point $\mathbf{x}^* = \mathbf{A}\mathbf{x}^* + \mathbf{b}$, and
2. if Eq. (1) has a fixed point $\mathbf{x}^*$ it converges to $\mathbf{x}^*$ exponentially fast in the number of iterations (with base $e^{-(1-\|\mathbf{A}\|_p)}$).

To see 1., note that two distinct fixed points $\mathbf{x}_1^* \neq \mathbf{x}_2^*$ would imply

$$0 \neq \|\mathbf{x}_1^* - \mathbf{x}_2^*\|_p = \|\mathbf{A}\left(\mathbf{x}_1^* - \mathbf{x}_2^*\right)\|_p \leq \|\mathbf{A}\|_p \|\mathbf{x}_1^* - \mathbf{x}_2^*\|_p < \|\mathbf{x}_1^* - \mathbf{x}_2^*\|_p$$

which is a contradiction. For 2., let $\mathbf{x}^*$ be the unique fixed point of Eq. (1). We can write any input $\mathbf{x}'$ as $\mathbf{x}' = \mathbf{x}^* + \mathbf{e}$ for some "error vector" $\mathbf{e}$. When applying the system to it, we get $\mathbf{x}' \mapsto \mathbf{A}\mathbf{x}' + \mathbf{b} = \mathbf{x}^* + \mathbf{A}\mathbf{e}$. So the error vector $\mathbf{e}$ is mapped to $\mathbf{A}\mathbf{e}$. Applying this ℓ times maps $\mathbf{e}$ to $\mathbf{A}^\ell\mathbf{e}$, which means after ℓ iterations the error vector has norm $\|\mathbf{A}^\ell\mathbf{e}\|_p \leq \|\mathbf{A}^\ell\|_p\|\mathbf{e}\|_p$. Let $\|\mathbf{A}\|_p \leq 1-\epsilon$ for some $\epsilon > 0$, then $\|\mathbf{A}^\ell\|_p \leq \|\mathbf{A}\|_p^\ell \leq (1-\epsilon)^\ell \leq e^{-\epsilon\ell}$, so the error vector will decay exponentially in ℓ with base $e^{-\epsilon}$ and the system converges to the fixed point $\mathbf{x}^*$.

Let $\mathbf{D}$ be an invertible matrix. We can use $\mathbf{D}$ for a change of variable to $\mathbf{y} = \mathbf{D}\mathbf{x}$, which allows to rewrite Eq. (1) to

$$\mathbf{y} = \mathbf{D}\mathbf{x} \mapsto \mathbf{D}\mathbf{A}\mathbf{D}^{-1}\mathbf{y} + \mathbf{D}\mathbf{b} \tag{2}$$

It is easy to see that for any fixed point $\mathbf{x}^*$ of Eq. (1), $\mathbf{y}^* = \mathbf{D}\mathbf{x}^*$ is a fixed point of Eq. (2). This can be useful as it is often more convenient to bound $\|\mathbf{D}\mathbf{A}\mathbf{D}^{-1}\|_p$ for some $\mathbf{D}$ and p than $\|\mathbf{A}\|_p$ (as we will see). If additionally the condition number $\kappa_p(\mathbf{D}) = \|\mathbf{D}\|_p\|\mathbf{D}^{-1}\|_p$ is small, then system (1) converges almost as quickly as system (2):

Fact 3. *Let $\mathbf{x}^\ell$ be a vector resulting from applying system (1) ℓ times to the input $\mathbf{x}^0$ and denote $\mathbf{e}^\ell = \mathbf{x}^\ell - \mathbf{x}^*$. Let $\mathbf{D}$ be an invertible matrix such that $\|\mathbf{D}\mathbf{A}\mathbf{D}^{-1}\|_p = 1-\epsilon$ for some $\epsilon > 0$. Then $\|\mathbf{e}^\ell\|_p \leq \exp(-\ell\epsilon)\,\kappa_p(\mathbf{D})\,\|\mathbf{e}^0\|_p$.*

Proof. Let $\mathbf{y}^0 = \mathbf{D}\mathbf{x}^0$ and $\mathbf{y}^{\ell+1} = \mathbf{D}\mathbf{A}\mathbf{D}^{-1}\mathbf{y}^\ell + \mathbf{D}\mathbf{b}$ for all $\ell > 0$. Induction shows that $\mathbf{y}^\ell = \mathbf{D}\mathbf{x}^\ell$. By above argument, we have $\|\mathbf{y}^\ell - \mathbf{y}^*\|_p \leq \exp(-\ell\epsilon)\,\|\mathbf{y}^0 - \mathbf{y}^*\|_p$. Now the result follows from

$$\begin{aligned}
\|\mathbf{e}^\ell\|_p &= \|\mathbf{x}^\ell - \mathbf{x}^*\|_p \\
&= \|\mathbf{D}^{-1}\mathbf{y}^\ell - \mathbf{D}^{-1}\mathbf{y}^*\|_p \\
&\leq \|\mathbf{D}^{-1}\|_p\|\mathbf{y}^\ell - \mathbf{y}^*\|_p \\
&\leq \exp(-\ell\epsilon)\,\|\mathbf{D}^{-1}\|_p\|\mathbf{y}^0 - \mathbf{y}^*\|_p \\
&\leq \exp(-\ell\epsilon)\,\|\mathbf{D}^{-1}\|_p\|\mathbf{D}\|_p\|\mathbf{e}^0\|_p.
\end{aligned}$$

□

Application to Lattice Reduction. Dynamical systems are a useful tool to study lattice reduction algorithms. As was first observed in [HPS11], for an iteration of some lattice reduction algorithm we can often show that $\mathbf{y} \leq \mathbf{A}\mathbf{x} + \mathbf{b}$, where $\mathbf{x}$ ($\mathbf{y}$) is some characterization of the input (output, resp.) basis for this iteration. If all entries in $\mathbf{A}$ are non-negative, we can iterate this inequality to derive inequalities for consecutive iterations. So the system $\mathbf{x} \mapsto \mathbf{A}\mathbf{x} + \mathbf{b}$ describes valid upper bounds for the vector $\mathbf{x}$ characterizing the current basis during the execution of the algorithm.

3 Slide-Type Reductions

Let $\mathsf{O}_{k,d}$ be an oracle that takes as input an n-dimensional basis $\mathbf{B}$ and an index $i < n - d$ and modifies $\mathbf{B}$ such that $\pi_{[i,i+k-1]} \leq \alpha \cdot \pi_{[i,i+d-1]}$ (and leaves the rest unchanged). In Algorithm 1, we present a class of algorithms which resemble slide reduction and are parameterized by such an oracle $\mathsf{O}_{k,d}$. The algorithm runs in primal and dual tours. During a primal tour, the n/d disjoint blocks of the basis are reduced using $\mathsf{O}_{k,d}$. Then the reversed dual basis is computed and $n/d - 1$ disjoint blocks are passed to the oracle. The blocks in the dual tour are chosen such that the corresponding primal blocks are shifted by k with respect to the blocks in the primal tour. Slide reduction itself (or rather a natural variant) can be recovered by instantiating $\mathsf{O}_{k,d}$ with an SVP oracle in dimension d, hence $k = 1$ and $\alpha = \sqrt{\gamma_d}$. Block-Rankin reduction corresponds to using a (k, d)-DSP oracle, in which case $\alpha = \gamma_{k,d}^{1/2k}$. Finally, we can also define a new algorithm by letting $\mathsf{O}_{k,d}$ be an algorithm that k-partial HKZ reduces a d-dimensional basis. In that case, Lemma 1 implies $\alpha = \Gamma_d(k)^{(d-k)/k}$.

Definition 5. *Let $\mathsf{O}_{k,d}$ be an algorithm that k-partial HKZ reduces a d-dimensional basis. We call Algorithm 1 instantiated with $\mathsf{O}_{k,d}$* (k, d)-HKZ-slide reduction.

Algorithm 1. Slide-type Reduction. $\mathsf{O}_{k,d}$ is an oracle that takes as input a basis $\mathbf{B}$ and an index i and modifies $\mathbf{B}$ such that $\pi_{[i,i+k-1]} \leq \alpha \cdot \pi_{[i,i+d-1]}$ (and leaves the rest unchanged.)

---

procedure SLIDE-TYPE REDUCTION($\mathbf{B}, \mathsf{O}_{k,d}(\cdot, \cdot)$)
  while progress is made **do**
    $\mathbf{B} \leftarrow \mathsf{O}_{k,d}(\mathbf{B}, id + 1)$ for all $i \in [0, n/d - 1]$
    $\mathbf{B} \leftarrow \widehat{\mathbf{B}}$
    $\mathbf{B} \leftarrow \mathsf{O}_{k,d}(\mathbf{B}, id - k)$ for all $i \in [1, n/d - 1]$
    $\mathbf{B} \leftarrow \widehat{\mathbf{B}}$
  end while
end procedure

We remark that it is customary in lattice reduction theory to apply LLL reduction in between the calls to the oracle. This is important to control the size of the numbers, which in turn allows to bound the complexity of the oracle itself. Since we focus on the number of calls to the oracle, we chose to present Algorithm 1 without any calls to LLL. Note that none of such calls will have any effect on our bounds due to Fact 2, since we will work with upper bounds on the subdeterminants $\pi_{[1,i]}$. These can only decrease during the application of LLL, so any upper bound that held before applying LLL also holds afterwards.

3.1 Convergence

The following theorem contains the main technical contribution of this work and the remainder of this subsection is devoted to proving it.

Theorem 2. *Let* $\mathbf{B} \in \mathbb{R}^{m \times n}$ *be a lattice basis with* $\det(\mathcal{L}(\mathbf{B})) = 1$*. Let* $k \leq d \in \mathbb{Z}$ *such that* $n = pd$ *for some* $d \in \mathbb{Z}$*,* $p \geq 2$ *and* $\mathsf{O}_{k,d}$ *be an oracle that on input a basis* $\mathbf{B}'$ *and index* $i < n - d$ *produces a basis* $\mathbf{C}$ *such that*

- $\pi_{[i,i+k-1]}(\mathbf{C}) \leq \alpha \cdot \pi_{[i,i+d-1]}(\mathbf{B}')$ *and*
- $\mathbf{c}_j = \mathbf{b}'_j$ *for all* $j \notin [i, i+d-1]$*.*

Let $\mu_i = i(p-i)\frac{d}{d-k}\ln\alpha$*,* $\mathbf{B}_\ell$ *the basis after the* ℓ*-th iteration and* $\epsilon_\ell = \max_{i\in[1,p]} |\ln(\pi_{[1,id]}(\mathbf{B}_\ell)) - \mu_i|$*. Then we have*

$$\epsilon_\ell \leq \exp\left(\frac{-4k(d-k)}{n^2}\ell\right)\frac{p^2}{4(p-1)}\epsilon_0$$

after ℓ *iterations of Slide-type reduction with oracle* $\mathsf{O}_{k,d}$*.*

Proof. During a primal tour, Slide-type reduction turns a basis $\mathbf{B}$ into a basis $\mathbf{B}'$ such that

$$\ln \pi_{[id+1,id+k]}(\mathbf{B}') \leq \ln \pi_{[id+1,id+d]}(\mathbf{B}) + \ln\alpha \tag{3}$$

for $i \in [0, p-1]$. Similarly, a dual tour yields

$$\ln \pi_{[id+1,id+k]}(\mathbf{B}') \geq \ln \pi_{[(i-1)d+2,id+1]}(\mathbf{B}) - \ln\alpha \tag{4}$$

We consider the leading subdeterminants corresponding to the blocks considered by Algorithm 1. Let $y_i = id \ln \pi_{[1,id]}(\mathbf{B})$ for $i \in [1, p-1]$. (Note that $y_p = 0$, since we assume that the lattice has unit determinant, so we may ignore this variable.) Now we apply a primal tour and denote $x_i = ((i-1)d + k)\ln \pi_{[1,(i-1)d+k]}(\mathbf{B}')$ for $i \in [1,p]$ after that tour. Then we have by Eq. (3)

$$x_i \leq \frac{d-k}{d} y_{i-1} + \frac{k}{d} y_i + k\ln\alpha$$

for $i \in [1,p]$, where we define $y_0 = y_p = 0$. In matrix form we have $\mathbf{x} \leq \mathbf{A}_p\mathbf{y} + \mathbf{b}_p$ with

$$\mathbf{A}_p = \begin{pmatrix} \frac{k}{d} & & & \\ \omega & \frac{k}{d} & & \\ & \omega & \frac{k}{d} & \\ & & \cdots & \\ & & & \frac{k}{d} \\ & & & \omega \end{pmatrix} \in \mathbb{R}^{p\times(p-1)}$$

where $\omega = \frac{d-k}{d}$ and $\mathbf{b}_p = k\ln\alpha \cdot \mathbf{1} \in \mathbb{R}^p$.

Now let y_i' as y_i above but after the next dual tour. From Eq. (4) we get

$$x_i - y_{i-1}' \geq \frac{k}{d}(x_i - x_{i-1}) - k \ln \alpha$$

or equivalently

$$y_i \leq \omega x_{i+1} + \frac{k}{d} x_i + k \ln \alpha$$

for $i \in [1, p-1]$. Again, in matrix form $\mathbf{y} \leq \mathbf{A}_d \mathbf{x} + \mathbf{b}_d$, where $\mathbf{b}_d = k \ln \alpha \cdot \mathbf{1} \in \mathbb{R}^{p-1}$ and

$$\mathbf{A}_d = \begin{pmatrix} \frac{k}{d} & \omega & & \\ & \frac{k}{d} & \omega & \\ & & \cdots & \\ & & & \frac{k}{d} \ \omega \end{pmatrix} = \mathbf{A}_p^T$$

By combining the two set of inequalities, we obtain:

$$\mathbf{y}' \leq \mathbf{A}_d \mathbf{x} + \mathbf{b}_d \leq \mathbf{A}_d (\mathbf{A}_p \mathbf{y} + \mathbf{b}_p) + \mathbf{b}_d = \mathbf{A}_p^T \mathbf{A}_p \mathbf{y} + \left(\mathbf{A}_p^T \mathbf{b}_p + \mathbf{b}_d\right)$$

Thus, the general matrix that characterizes a primal and dual tour is

$$\mathbf{A} = \mathbf{A}_p^T \mathbf{A}_p = \begin{pmatrix} \tilde{\omega} & \frac{k\omega}{d} & & \\ \frac{k\omega}{d} & \tilde{\omega} & \frac{k\omega}{d} & \\ & & \cdots & \\ & & \frac{k\omega}{d} & \tilde{\omega} \end{pmatrix} = \begin{pmatrix} 1-2\beta & \beta & & \\ \beta & 1-2\beta & \beta & \\ & & \cdots & \\ & & \beta & 1-2\beta \end{pmatrix} \in \mathbb{R}^{(p-1)\times(p-1)} \tag{5}$$

where $\tilde{\omega} = \omega^2 + (k/d)^2$ and $\beta = \frac{k(d-k)}{d^2}$. And with $\mathbf{b} = \mathbf{A}_p^T \mathbf{b}_p + \mathbf{b}_d = 2 \cdot \mathbf{b}_d$ the dynamical system we are interested in is

$$\mathbf{y} \mapsto \mathbf{A}\mathbf{y} + \mathbf{b}. \tag{6}$$

The theorem now follows from Lemma 2 and 3 below, in which we analyze the fixed point and the convergence of system (6), resp. □

Lemma 2. *For the system in Eq. (6) and the vector* $\mathbf{y}^* \in \mathbb{R}^{p-1}$ *with*

$$y_i^* = i(p-i) \frac{d^2}{d-k} \ln \alpha$$

we have $\mathbf{A}\mathbf{y}^* + \mathbf{b} = \mathbf{y}^*$.

Proof. Note that we can extend the definition of y_i^* to $i = 0$ and $i = p$, in which case we have $y_0^* = y_p^* = 0$. So the lemma follows if we can show that

$$\beta y_{i-1}^* + (1-2\beta) y_i^* + \beta y_{i+1}^* + 2k \ln \alpha = y_i^*$$

for all $i \in [1, p-1]$. This is equivalent to

$$\beta \left(y_{i-1}^* + y_{i+1}^* - 2y_i^*\right) + 2k \ln \alpha = 0$$

which is easily seen to be true by straightforward calculation. □

Lemma 3. *Let* **A** *as in Eq. (5). Then there exists an invertible matrix* **D** *with* $\kappa_\infty(\mathbf{D}) = \frac{p^2}{4(p-1)}$ *such that*

$$\|\mathbf{DAD}^{-1}\|_\infty \leq 1 - \frac{4k(d-k)}{n^2}$$

for any $p \geq 2$.

Proof. Let **D** be the diagonal matrix such that

$$\mathbf{D}^{-1} = \begin{pmatrix} p-1 & & & \\ & 2(p-2) & & \\ & & \cdots & \\ & & & p-1 \end{pmatrix}$$

We now analyze the matrix

$$\mathbf{DAD}^{-1} = \begin{pmatrix} 1-2\beta & \frac{2(p-2)}{p-1}\beta & & & \\ \frac{p-1}{2(p-2)}\beta & 1-2\beta & \frac{3(p-3)}{2(p-2)}\beta & & \\ & \frac{2(p-2)}{3(p-3)}\beta & 1-2\beta & \frac{4(p-4)}{3(p-3)}\beta & \\ & & & \cdots & \\ & & & \frac{(p-2)2}{p-1}\beta & 1-2\beta \end{pmatrix}$$

The sum of the i-th row is

$$\begin{aligned} S_i &= 1 - 2\beta + \beta\frac{(i-1)(p-i+1) + (i+1)(p-i-1)}{i(p-i)} \\ &= 1 - 2\beta\left(1 - \frac{ip - i^2 - 1}{ip - i^2}\right) \\ &= 1 - \frac{2\beta}{ip - i^2} \\ &\leq 1 - \frac{8\beta}{p^2} \\ &= 1 - \frac{8k(d-k)}{n^2} \end{aligned}$$

for $i \in [2, \ldots, p-2]$. Finally, we have

$$S_1 = S_{p-1} \leq 1 - \frac{2pk(d-k)}{n^2}$$

from which the lemma follows. □

3.2 Implications

We now show how Theorem 2 implies bounds for the running time of Slide-type reduction algorithms.

Corollary 1. *Let* $\mathbf{B} \in \mathbb{R}^{m \times n}$ *be an LLL-reduced lattice basis with* $\det(\mathcal{L}(\mathbf{B})) = 1$ *and* $\epsilon > 0$ *an arbitrary constant. After* $\ell \geq \frac{n^2}{4k(d-k)} \ln\left(\frac{\frac{n^2}{2d} + \frac{n^3}{4d^3}\ln\alpha}{\epsilon}\right)$ *tours of Slide-type reduction with oracle* $\mathsf{O}_{k,d}$ *such that* $\alpha \geq \gamma_2$*, the output basis satisfies*

$$\pi_{[1,d]} = \prod_{i=1}^{d} \|\mathbf{b}_i^*\|^{\frac{1}{d}} \leq \exp(\epsilon + \mu_1) \approx (1+\epsilon)\,\alpha^{\frac{n-d}{d-k}}.$$

Accordingly, the number of oracle queries is bounded by $\frac{n^3}{2dk(d-k)} \ln\left(\frac{\frac{n^2}{2d} + \frac{n^3}{4d^3}\ln\alpha}{\epsilon}\right)$.

Proof. Theorem 2 shows that in order to obtain $\epsilon_\ell \leq \epsilon$ for arbitrary $\epsilon > 0$, it is sufficient to set

$$\ell \geq \frac{n^2}{4k(d-k)} \ln\left(\frac{p^2 \epsilon_0}{4(p-1)\epsilon}\right).$$

By Fact 1 we have

$$\epsilon_0 = \max_{i \in [1,p]} |\ln \pi_{[1,id]}(\mathbf{B}) - \mu_i| \leq \frac{n-1}{2} \ln \gamma_2 + \frac{n^2}{4d(d-k)} \ln \alpha \leq n + \frac{n^2}{2d^2} \ln \alpha$$

where we assume that $k \leq d/2$. Finally, notice that $p^2/(4(p-1)) \leq p/2 = n/2d$ for all $p \geq 2$. □

Corollary 1 implies the following corollaries.

Corollary 2. *Let* $\mathbf{B} \in \mathbb{R}^{m \times n}$ *be an LLL-reduced lattice basis with* $\det(\mathcal{L}(\mathbf{B})) = 1$ *and* $\epsilon > 0$ *an arbitrary constant. After* $O\left(\frac{n^3}{dk(d-k)} \ln\left(\frac{n}{\epsilon}\right)\right)$ *calls to the* (k,d)*-DSP oracle, the output basis of block-Rankin reduction satisfies*

$$\pi_{[1,d]} = \prod_{i=1}^{d} \|\mathbf{b}_i^*\|^{\frac{1}{d}} \leq \exp(\epsilon + \mu_1) = \exp(\epsilon)\,\gamma_{k,d}^{\frac{n-d}{2k(d-k)}} \approx (1+\epsilon)\,\gamma_{k,d}^{\frac{n-d}{2k(d-k)}}.$$

One more call to the oracle yields

$$\pi_{[1,k]} \leq \exp(\epsilon)\,\gamma_{k,d}^{\frac{n-k}{2k(d-k)}} \approx (1+\epsilon)\,\gamma_{k,d}^{\frac{n-k}{2k(d-k)}}.$$

The case of slide reduction follows as a special case ($k = 1$) and we note that the number of SVP calls matches the one proven for other lattice reduction algorithms using this technique [HPS11, LN20, MW16]. Recall that the bound on the number of oracle queries proven in [LN14] is $O\left(\frac{n^3 \log \max_i \|\mathbf{b}_i\|}{\epsilon d^2}\right)$. For degenerate cases $\max_i \|\mathbf{b}_i\|$ can be arbitrarily large (within the restriction that its logarithm is polynomial in the input size) even for LLL-reduced bases of lattices with determinant 1. Similar to the recent work of [LN20], we are able to achieve a bound that is independent of $\max_i \|\mathbf{b}_i\|$ using the dynamical systems approach. The length of the vectors just contributes to the $\log n$ factor in our bound. ([HPS11] does not claim to achieve this but obtains a bound with a doubly logarithmic dependence on $\max_i \|\mathbf{b}_i\|$.) Furthermore, the dependence on ϵ is much tighter in two ways: 1) in [LN14] the slack factor in the output quality is $(1+\epsilon)^{(n-k)/(4(d-k))}$, while in Corollary 2 it is just $\exp(\epsilon) \approx (1+\epsilon)$. 2) The dependence of the bound on the number of oracle queries is linear in $1/\epsilon$, while in our bound it is only logarithmic. Finally, the remaining polynomial factor matches in the two bounds for small values of k, but our bound depends on k and actually decreases with growing k up to an improvement of $1/d$ for $k = d/2$. This seems to be a feature of the dynamical systems analysis as it is unclear if the LLL-style potential function analysis of [LN14] can be used to study the dependence of the number of calls on k.

Corollary 3. *Let* $\mathbf{B} \in \mathbb{R}^{m \times n}$ *be an LLL-reduced lattice basis with* $\det(\mathcal{L}(\mathbf{B})) = 1$ *and* $\epsilon > 0$ *an arbitrary constant. After* $O\left(\frac{n^3}{dk(d-k)} \ln\left(\frac{n}{\epsilon}\right)\right)$ *calls to the* k*-partial HKZ oracle, the output basis of* (k,d)*-HKZ-slide reduction satisfies*

$$\pi_{[1,d]} = \prod_{i=1}^{d} \|\mathbf{b}_i^*\|^{\frac{1}{d}} \leq \exp(\epsilon + \mu_1) = \exp(\epsilon)\, \Gamma_d(k)^{\frac{n-d}{k}} \approx (1+\epsilon)\, \Gamma_d(k)^{\frac{n-d}{k}}.$$

One more call to the oracle yields

$$\|\mathbf{b}_1\| \leq \exp(\epsilon) \sqrt{\gamma_d}\, \Gamma_d(k)^{\frac{n-d}{k}} \approx (1+\epsilon) \sqrt{\gamma_d}\, \Gamma_d(k)^{\frac{n-d}{k}}.$$

We can try to get bounds on the Hermite factor of (k,d)-HKZ-slide reduction in terms of γ_d by using some straightforward bounds on $\Gamma_d(k)$.

Lemma 4. *For a* (k,d)*-HKZ-slide reduced basis we have*

$$\|\mathbf{b}_1\| \leq \sqrt{d}^{\,1+\frac{n-d}{k}\log\frac{d}{d-k}} \det(\mathbf{B})^{\frac{1}{n}} \leq \sqrt{d}^{\,\frac{n-k}{d-k}} \det(\mathbf{B})^{\frac{1}{n}} \tag{7}$$

$$\|\mathbf{b}_1\| \leq \sqrt{\gamma_{d-k+1}}^{\,\frac{n-1}{d-k}} \det(\mathbf{B})^{\frac{1}{n}} \tag{8}$$

Proof. Both follow from Corollary 3. For Eq. (7) use the bound $\Gamma_d(k) \leq \sqrt{d}^{\log\frac{d}{d-k}}$ proven in [HS07] and $\log 1 + x \leq x$.

For Eq. (8), recall Mordell's inequality $\gamma_n^{\frac{1}{n-1}} \leq \gamma_k^{\frac{1}{k-1}}$, which shows that $\Gamma_d(k) \leq \sqrt{\gamma_{d-k+1}}^{\frac{k}{d-k}}$. So we have

$$\|\mathbf{b}_1\| \leq \sqrt{\gamma_d}\sqrt{\gamma_{d-k+1}}^{\,\frac{n-d}{d-k}} \det(\mathbf{B})^{\frac{1}{n}}.$$

Finally, use Mordell's inequality again to see that $\sqrt{\gamma_d} \leq \sqrt{\gamma_{d-k+1}}^{\frac{d-1}{d-k}}$ to conclude. □

The bound on the Hermite factor achieved by HKZ-slide reduction suggests that running (k,d)-HKZ-slide reduction is no better than running $(1, d-k+1)$-HKZ-slide reduction, i.e. vanilla slide reduction with block size $d-k+1$. Since solving SVP in dimension $d-k+1$ is easier by a factor $2^{\Omega(k)}$ than k-partial HKZ reduction in dimension d, it stands to reason that using $k=1$ is optimal. However, in the next sections we will make heuristic arguments and show experimental evidence that using larger k can be worthwhile in practice.

4 HKZ-Slide Reduction in Practice

In this section we give heuristic arguments (Sect. 4.1) and experimental evidence showing that HKZ-slide reduction can outperform slide reduction and yield a faster algorithm in practice.

4.1 Heuristic Analysis

Note that the convergence analysis in Sect. 3.1 is agnostic to the value α. So we can use the same analysis for a heuristic evaluation, but instead of using Minkowski's inequality, we use the Gaussian heuristic. So by defining $g_d = \sqrt{d/2\pi e}$ and $\alpha = G_d(k) = \prod_{i=d-k}^{d-1} g_{i+1}^{\frac{1}{i}}$ we can get a bound on the density of the first block of a (k, d)-HKZ-slide reduced basis based on Heuristic 1, which is

$$\pi_{[1,d]} \approx G_d(k)^{\frac{n-d}{k}} \det(\mathbf{B})^{\frac{1}{n}}$$

which implies

$$\|\mathbf{b}_1\| \approx g_d G_d(k)^{\frac{n-d}{k}} \det(\mathbf{B})^{\frac{1}{n}}.$$

Now we can compare the quality that we achieve by using different overlaps and block sizes. See Fig. 1 for an example. Running (k, d)-HKZ-slide reduction yields a better basis than running slide reduction with block size $k - d + 1$ (but also needs a partial HKZ oracle in larger dimension).

To estimate the practical behavior of HKZ-slide reduction and slide reduction, we make the following assumptions: 1) we assume that the dependence of the running time of (k, d)-HKZ-slide reduction on the overlap k is $1/k(d-k)$, and 2) that the complexity of the k-partial HKZ oracle is $2^{d/3+O(1)}$ and independent of k. The first assumption is supported by our analysis in Sect. 3.1. The second assumption is supported by the observation in [ADH+19] that SVP oracles in practice tend to not only find the shortest vector in a lattice, but additionally HKZ reduce the head of the basis "for free". The complexity of the oracle is a crude estimate of heuristic bounds on the complexity of sieving. More accurate estimates are a little smaller than what we assumed above. Adapting the following argument would thus provide slightly better results.

As a baseline for our comparison we select 90-slide reduction on a 270 dimensional lattice and analyze how reducing the block size to $90 - k'$ and increasing the overlap to k compare in terms of speed-up while ensuring that both yield similar output quality. Specifically, for every k we numerically compute $k' < k$ such that $(90-k')$-slide reduction achieves similar root Hermite factor as $(k, 90)$-HKZ-slide reduction. The speed-up of $(k, 90)$-HKZ-slide reduction over 90-slide reduction is $k(d-k)/(d-1)$ given our assumptions. The speed-up achieved by $(90 - k')$-slide reduction is $2^{k'/3}(d - k' + 1)/d$. (We ignore the issue of divisibility of block size and lattice dimension here for simplicity.) The ratio of the two quantities is given in Fig. 2. The figure suggests that $(k, 90)$-HKZ-slide reduction with a well-chosen overlap k can be up to 4 times faster than slide reduction with similar output quality.

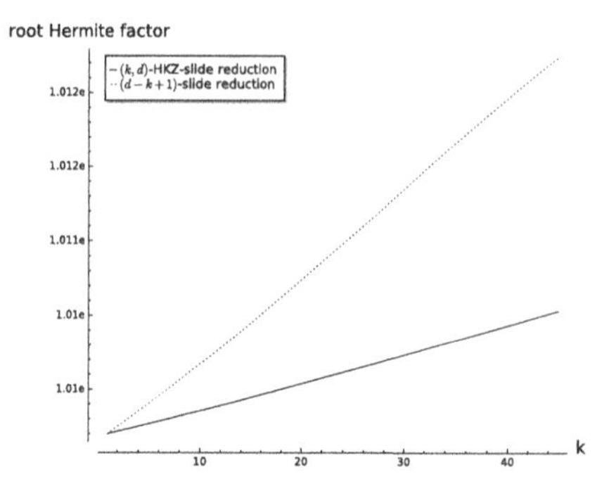

Fig. 1. Comparison of root Hermite factor for running $(k, 90)$-HKZ-slide reduction on a basis with dimension 270 vs $(90 - k)$-slide reduction

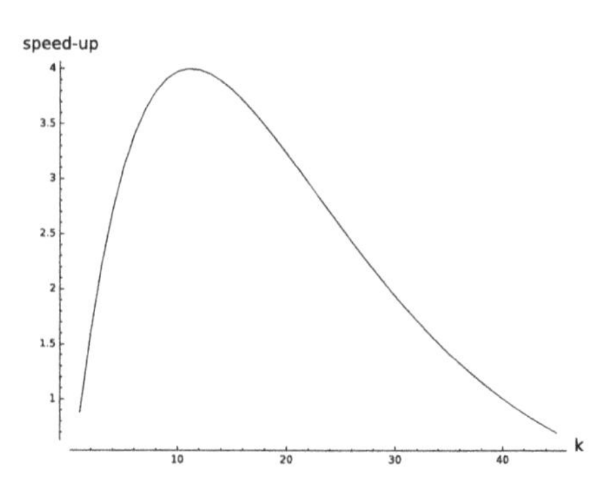

Fig. 2. Speed-up factor of running $(k, 90)$-HKZ-slide reduction on a basis with dimension 270 vs $(90 - k')$-slide reduction with comparable Hermite factor.

4.2 Experiments

We provide an implementation of HKZ-slide reduction[3] in the G6K framework of [ADH+19], which (among a lot of other things) provides an interface to an SVP algorithm based on sieving. The authors observe that, in fact, the output of this algorithm seems to approximate partial-HKZ reduction. Their work also shows that basic (called *naive* in [ADH+19]) BKZ based on sieving starts outperforming state-of-the-art enumeration based methods for block sizes below 80, and more carefully tuned variants well below 65.

For our implementation we treat the SVP algorithm of G6K as a k-partial-HKZ oracle for arbitrary $k \leq 15$, which seems justified by the observations made in [ADH+19]. To test the hypothesis of the previous section, we run (k, d)-HKZ-slide reduction for $k \in \{1, 5, 10, 15\}$ and $d \in \{60, 85\}$ on lattices from the lattice challenge [BLR08]. To avoid issues with block sizes not dividing the dimension we select the dimension as the largest integer multiple of d such that the algorithm does not run into numerical issues. For $d = 60$ and $d = 85$, this is $n = 180$ (i.e. $p = 3$ blocks) and $n = 170$ (i.e. $p = 2$ blocks), respectively. The results are shown in Figs. 3a and 3c. All data points are averaged (in both axes) over the same 10 lattices (challenge seeds 0 to 9), which are preprocessed using `fplll` [dt16] with block size 45 (for $d = 60$) and 60 (for $d = 85$).

Figure 3a demonstrates that for relatively small block sizes, the behavior of k-HKZ-slide reduction is actually better than expected: not only does a larger k lead to a faster convergence (which is expected), all of the tested k also lead to better output quality. This can at least in part be explained by the relatively small block size and the corresponding approximation error of the Gaussian heuristic. This is supported by Fig. 3c, where at least the overlaps $k = 5$ and

[3] Code available at: http://pub.ist.ac.at/~mwalter/publication/hkz_slide/hkz_slide.zip.

$k = 15$ behave as expected: faster convergence but poorer output quality. (Note though that the difference in output quality between overlaps 1 and 5 is minor.) However, the case of $k = 10$ seems to be a special case that behaves exceptionally well even for large block size. We cannot explain this phenomenon beyond baseless speculation at this point and leave an in-depth investigation to future work. In summary, we believe that the results give sufficient evidence that the trade-off achieved by HKZ-slide reduction can indeed be very favorable when considering overlaps larger than 1 (i.e. beyond slide reduction).

To put the results into context, we also compare HKZ-slide reduction with the BKZ variants implemented in G6K on the same lattices. For HKZ-slide reduction we chose $k = 10$. We compared to three "standard" variants of BKZ: 1) naive BKZ, which treats the SVP algorithm as a black box; 2) the "Pump and Jump" (PnJ) variant, which recycles computation done during previous calls to the SVP algorithm to save cost in later calls; 3) a progressive variant of the PnJ strategy, which starts with smaller block sizes and successively runs BKZ tours with increasing block size. We leave all parameters for the PnJ versions at their default. [ADH+19] reported that some fine-tuning can improve the PnJ variant further, but since our goal is only to demonstrate the competitiveness of HKZ-slide reduction rather than a fine-grained comparison, we do not believe such fine-tuning is necessary here. Naive BKZ and the PnJ variant is called with the same block size (on the same bases as HKZ-slide reduction) and the number of tours is chosen such that the running time is roughly in the ballpark of the HKZ-slide reduction experiments. For progressive PnJ, we run 1 tour of each block size starting from $d - 10$ up to $d + 5$, where d is the block size chosen for the other algorithms. The results are shown in Fig. 3b and 3d respectively. They show that HKZ-slide reduction can outperform the naive version of BKZ significantly, but it also seems to be better than PnJ. However, progressive PnJ seems to have the edge over HKZ-slide reduction, but we consider the latter at least competitive.

Caveats. We focus our attention in these experiments on the root Hermite factor that the different algorithms achieve in a given amount of time. This has been established as the main measure of output quality for lattice reduction, since they are usually used to find short vectors. When targeting a short vector, (HKZ-) slide reduction has the advantage that it focuses on improving a set of pivot points distributed across the basis, while BKZ attempts to improve the entire basis. This seems to result in a lower cost for slide reduction. But finding short vectors is not the only use case: often one is interested in a basis that is reduced according to a more global measure, e.g. one wants all basis vectors to be short or the GSO vectors should not drop off too quickly. In this case, BKZ seems to be the more natural choice.

Potential Improvements. We do not make any attempts to fine-tune the SVP oracle to HKZ-slide reduction and its parameters. The SVP-oracle itself has several parameters which potentially influence how well it performs as a k-partial-HKZ oracle. We leave such a fine-tuning as interesting future work.

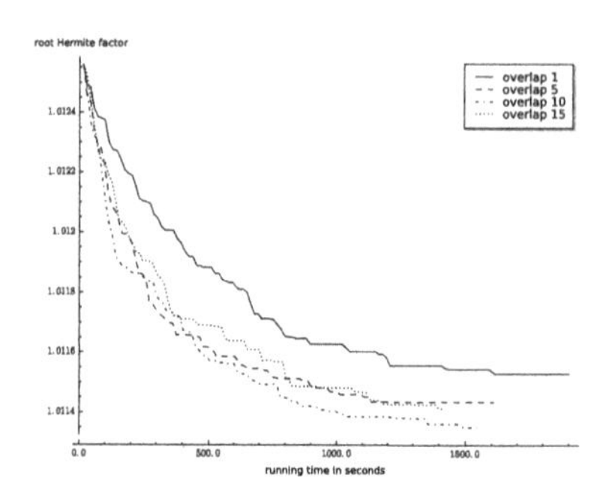

(a) HKZ-slide reduction on a lattice with dimension 180 and block size 60

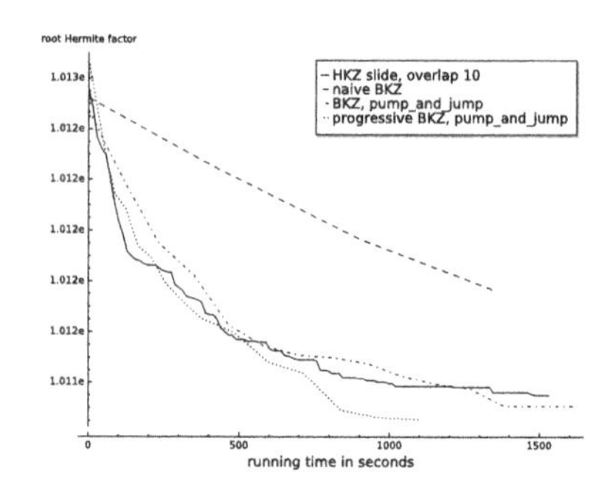

(b) Comparison of HKZ-slide reduction and BKZ on a lattice with dimension 180 and block size 60

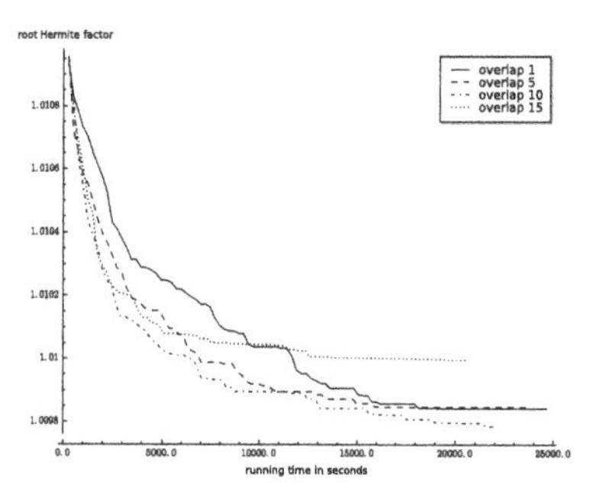

(c) HKZ-slide reduction on a lattice with dimension 170 and block size 85

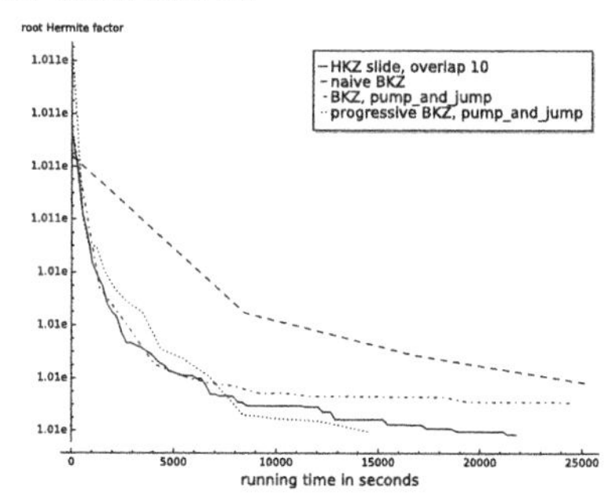

(d) Comparison of HKZ-slide reduction and BKZ on a lattice with dimension 170 and block size 85

Fig. 3. Comparison of HKZ-slide-reduction with different overlaps and with various BKZ variants

Furthermore, we note that applying BKZ/PnJ with increasing block sizes results in significant improvements. It stands to reason that including an element of "progressiveness" could significantly improve HKZ-slide reduction. However, the strength of HKZ-slide reduction of focusing its attention on pivot points instead of the entire basis could be a disadvantage here: it may not be as suitable as a preprocessing for other algorithms, possibly including itself. Still, finding an effective way of naturally progressing slide reduction might lead to improvements, but we believe simply increasing the block size is unlikely to be sufficient here. Finally, given the above observations, a natural approach seems to be to use progressive BKZ/PnJ as a preprocessing and only apply HKZ-slide reduction in the final step to find a short vector.

5 SDBKZ: Revisiting Neumaier's Analysis

We conclude this work by revisiting Neumaier's analysis [Neu17] of SDBKZ [MW16]. Using a change of variable allows us to recast it as a variant of the conventional dynamic analysis. The matrix used in Sect. 3 for the change of variable was inspired by this reformulation.

5.1 Reminders

We first give a brief description of the SDBKZ algorithm and the analysis from [MW16]. The algorithm can be viewed as iterating the following 2 steps:

1. perform a forward tour by applying the SVP oracle successively to the projected blocks of the basis (i.e. a truncated BKZ tour)
2. compute the reversed dual of the basis.

For convenience, the SDBKZ lattice reduction algorithm is provided as Algorithm 2.

Algorithm 2. SDBKZ. O_d is an oracle that takes as input a basis $\mathbf{B}$ and an index i and modifies $\mathbf{B}$ such that $\mathbf{B}_{[i,i+d-1]}$ is SVP reduced (and leaves the rest unchanged.)

procedure SDBKZ($\mathbf{B}, \mathsf{O}_d(\cdot,\cdot)$)
  while progress is made **do**
    $\mathbf{B} \leftarrow \mathsf{O}_d(\mathbf{B}, i)$ for all $i \in [0, n-d]$
    $\mathbf{B} \leftarrow \widehat{\mathbf{B}}$
  end while
end procedure

Let $\mathbf{B}$ be a lattice basis. In [MW16], the following variables were considered

$$\mathbf{x} = (\log\det(\mathbf{b}_1, \ldots, \mathbf{b}_{d+i-1}))_{1\le i\le n-d}.$$

When applying the two steps of SDBKZ to a lattice basis, [MW16] showed that for the output basis $\mathbf{B}'$ we have $\mathbf{x}' \le \mathbf{RAx} + \mathbf{Rb}$, where

$$\mathbf{b} = \alpha d \begin{bmatrix} 1-\omega \\ \vdots \\ 1-\omega^{n-d} \end{bmatrix} \quad \mathbf{A} = \frac{1}{d}\begin{bmatrix} 1 & & & \\ \omega & 1 & & \\ \vdots & \ddots & \ddots & \\ \omega^{n-d-1} & \cdots & \omega & 1 \end{bmatrix}$$

$$\mathbf{R} = \begin{bmatrix} & & & 1 \\ & & 1 & \\ & \cdot^{\cdot^{\cdot}} & & \\ 1 & & & \end{bmatrix}$$

$\alpha = \frac{1}{2}\log\gamma_d$ and $\omega = (1-\frac{1}{d})$. This lead to the analysis of the dynamical system

$$\mathbf{x} \mapsto \mathbf{RAx} + \mathbf{Rb}. \tag{9}$$

[MW16] showed that this system has exactly one fixed point $\mathbf{x}^*$ with

$$x_i^* = \frac{(d+i-1)(n-d-i+1)}{d-1}\alpha$$

which can be used to obtain bounds on the output quality of the algorithm. Here we are more interested in the convergence analysis. For this, note that

$$\|\mathbf{RA}\|_\infty = \|\mathbf{A}\|_\infty = 1 - \omega^{n-d}$$

which means that the number of tours required to achieve $\|\mathbf{e}\|_\infty \leq c$ for some constant c is proportional to $\exp((n-d)/d)$. This is polynomial as long as $d = \Omega(n)$, but for $d = o(n)$ this results in a superpolynomial bound.

5.2 Neumaier's Analysis

As stated above, Neumaier's analysis of SDBKZ [Neu17] can be viewed as a change of variable for $\mathbf{x}$. Neumaier implicitly chose the diagonal matrix

$$\mathbf{D}^{-1} = \begin{bmatrix} d(n-d) & & & \\ & (d+1)(n-d-1) & & \\ & & \ddots & \\ & & & n-1 \end{bmatrix}$$

which yields the new fixed point $\mathbf{y}^* = \frac{\alpha}{d-1}\mathbf{1}$ (cf. μ_s from [Neu17]). We now analyze the matrix $\mathbf{A}' = \mathbf{DRAD}^{-1}$: First, we observe that

$$\mathbf{A}_{ij} = \begin{cases} \frac{1}{d}\omega^{i-j} & i \geq j \\ 0 & i < j \end{cases}$$

and so

$$(\mathbf{RA})_{ij} = \begin{cases} \frac{1}{d}\omega^{(n-d+1-i)-j} & i+j \leq n-d+1 \\ 0 & i+j > n-d+1 \end{cases}$$

and finally

$$\mathbf{A}'_{ij} = (\mathbf{DRAD}^{-1})_{ij} = \begin{cases} \frac{(d+j-1)(n-d-j+1)}{d(d+i-1)(n-d-i+1)}\omega^{(n-d+1-i)-j} & i+j \leq n-d+1 \\ 0 & i+j > n-d+1 \end{cases} \quad (10)$$

Lemma 5. *Let* $\mathbf{A}'$ *as defined in Eq. (10). Then,* $\|\mathbf{A}'\|_\infty \leq 1 - \epsilon$*, where* $\epsilon = \left(1 + \frac{n^2}{4d(d-1)}\right)^{-1}$.

Proof. Let $S_i = \sum_j \mathbf{A}'_{ij}$ be the sum of every row in $\mathbf{A}'$. We have

$$\begin{aligned} S_i &= \frac{1}{d(d+i-1)(n-d-i+1)} \sum_{j=1}^{n-d-i+1} (d+j-1)(n-d-j+1)\omega^{n-d+1-i-j} \\ &= \frac{(d+i)(n-d-i)}{(d+i-1)(n-d-i+1)}\omega S_{i+1} + \frac{i(n-i)}{d(d+i-1)(n-d-i+1)} \end{aligned}$$

(where we set $S_{n-d+1} = 0$.) We now show by induction on i that $S_i \leq 1 - \epsilon$. Clearly, the bound holds for S_{n-d+1} since $\epsilon \leq 1$. So now we have

$$\begin{aligned} S_i &= \frac{(d+i)(n-d-i)}{(d+i-1)(n-d-i+1)}\omega S_{i+1} + \frac{i(n-i)}{d(d+i-1)(n-d-i+1)} \\ &\leq \frac{(d+i)(n-d-i)}{(d+i-1)(n-d-i+1)}\omega(1-\epsilon) + \frac{i(n-i)}{d(d+i-1)(n-d-i+1)} \\ &= \frac{(d-1)(d+i)(n-d-i)}{d(d+i-1)(n-d-i+1)}(1-\epsilon) + \frac{i(n-i)}{d(d+i-1)(n-d-i+1)} \end{aligned}$$

by assumption. Showing that the RHS is less than $1-\epsilon$ is equivalent to showing that

$$(d-1)(d+i)(n-d-i)(1-\epsilon) + i(n-i) \leq d(d+i-1)(n-d-i+1)(1-\epsilon)$$

which is equivalent to

$$i(n-i) \leq [d(d+i-1)(n-d-i+1) - (d-1)(d+i)(n-d-i)]\,(1-\epsilon).$$

It is straightforward (though a little tedious) to verify that

$$d(d+i-1)(n-d-i+1) - (d-1)(d+i)(n-d-i) = i(n-i) + d(d-1).$$

which yields the condition

$$i(n-i) \leq [i(n-i) + d(d-1)]\,(1-\epsilon)$$

which again is equivalent to

$$\epsilon\,[i(n-i) + d(d-1)] \leq d(d-1)$$

and thus $\epsilon \leq \left(1 + \frac{i(n-i)}{d(d-1)}\right)^{-1}$. We note this quantity is minimized for $i = n/2$ and thus by definition of ϵ, this condition holds. Since all our transformations were equivalences, this proves the bound on S_i. □

Readers familiar with Neumaier's work will recognize the calculations. It is easy to see that $\kappa(\mathbf{D}) = \frac{n^2}{4(n-1)}$, which is small enough so that the number of tours required for the algorithm is proportional to $1 + \frac{n^2}{4d(d-1)}$. This matches the bound obtained in [Neu17].

Acknowledgment. This work was initiated in discussions with Léo Ducas, when the author was visiting the *Simons Institute for the Theory of Computation* during the program "Lattices: Algorithms, Complexity, and Cryptography". We thank Thomas Espitau for pointing out a bug in a proof in an earlier version of this manuscript.

References

ABF+20. Albrecht, M.R., Bai, S., Fouque, P.-A., Kirchner, P., Stehlé, D., Wen, W.: Faster enumeration-based lattice reduction: root hermite factor $k^{1/(2k)}$ Time $k^{k/8+o(k)}$. In: Micciancio, D., Ristenpart, T. (eds.) CRYPTO 2020. LNCS, vol. 12171, pp. 186–212. Springer, Cham (2020). https://doi.org/10.1007/978-3-030-56880-1_7

ADH+19. Albrecht, M.R., Ducas, L., Herold, G., Kirshanova, E., Postlethwaite, E.W., Stevens, M.: The general sieve kernel and new records in lattice reduction. In: Ishai, Y., Rijmen, V. (eds.) EUROCRYPT 2019. LNCS, vol. 11477, pp. 717–746. Springer, Cham (2019). https://doi.org/10.1007/978-3-030-17656-3_25

ALNS20. Aggarwal, D., Li, J., Nguyen, P.Q., Stephens-Davidowitz, N.: Slide reduction, revisited—filling the gaps in SVP approximation. In: Micciancio, D., Ristenpart, T. (eds.) CRYPTO 2020. LNCS, vol. 12171, pp. 274–295. Springer, Cham (2020). https://doi.org/10.1007/978-3-030-56880-1_10

AWHT16. Aono, Y., Wang, Y., Hayashi, T., Takagi, T.: Improved progressive BKZ algorithms and their precise cost estimation by sharp simulator. In: Fischlin, M., Coron, J.-S. (eds.) EUROCRYPT 2016. LNCS, vol. 9665, pp. 789–819. Springer, Heidelberg (2016). https://doi.org/10.1007/978-3-662-49890-3_30

BLR08. Buchmann, J., Lindner, R., Rückert, M.: Explicit hard instances of the shortest vector problem. In: Buchmann, J., Ding, J. (eds.) PQCrypto 2008. LNCS, vol. 5299, pp. 79–94. Springer, Heidelberg (2008). https://doi.org/10.1007/978-3-540-88403-3_6

CN11. Chen, Y., Nguyen, P.Q.: BKZ 2.0: better lattice security estimates. In: Lee, D.H., Wang, X. (eds.) ASIACRYPT 2011. LNCS, vol. 7073, pp. 1–20. Springer, Heidelberg (2011). https://doi.org/10.1007/978-3-642-25385-0_1

DM13. Dadush, D., Micciancio, D.: Algorithms for the densest sub-lattice problem. In: Khanna, S., (ed.) 24th SODA, pp. 1103–1122. ACM-SIAM, January 2013

dt16. The FPLLL development team. fplll, a lattice reduction library (2016). https://github.com/fplll/fplll

GN08a. Gama, N., Nguyen, P.Q.: Finding short lattice vectors within Mordell's inequality. In: Ladner, R.E., Dwork, C., (eds.) 40th ACM STOC, pp. 207–216. ACM Press, May 2008

GN08b. Gama, N., Nguyen, P.Q.: Predicting lattice reduction. In: Smart, N. (ed.) EUROCRYPT 2008. LNCS, vol. 4965, pp. 31–51. Springer, Heidelberg (2008). https://doi.org/10.1007/978-3-540-78967-3_3

HPS11. Hanrot, G., Pujol, X., Stehlé, D.: Analyzing blockwise lattice algorithms using dynamical systems. In: Rogaway, P. (ed.) CRYPTO 2011. LNCS, vol. 6841, pp. 447–464. Springer, Heidelberg (2011). https://doi.org/10.1007/978-3-642-22792-9_25

HS07. Hanrot, G., Stehlé, D.: Improved analysis of Kannan's shortest lattice vector algorithm. In: Menezes, A. (ed.) CRYPTO 2007. LNCS, vol. 4622, pp. 170–186. Springer, Heidelberg (2007)

LLL82. Lenstra, A.K., Lenstra Jr., H.W., Lovász, L.: Factoring polynomials with rational coefficients. Mathematische Annalen **261**, 513–534 (1982)

LN14. Li, J., Nguyen, P.: Approximating the densest sublattice from rankin's inequality. LMS J. Comput. Math. [electronic only], **17**, 08 (2014)

LN20. Li, J., Nguyen, P.Q.: A complete analysis of the bkz lattice reduction algorithm. Cryptology ePrint Archive, Report 2020/1237 (2020). https://eprint.iacr.org/2020/1237

Lov86. Lovász, L.: An algorithmic theory of numbers, graphs and convexity, vol. 50. CBMS. SIAM (1986)

MW16. Micciancio, D., Walter, M.: Practical, predictable lattice basis reduction. In: Fischlin, M., Coron, J.-S. (eds.) EUROCRYPT 2016. LNCS, vol. 9665, pp. 820–849. Springer, Heidelberg (2016). https://doi.org/10.1007/978-3-662-49890-3_31

Neu17. Neumaier, A.: Bounding basis reduction properties. Des. Codes Cryptogr., **84**(1-2), 237–259 (2017)

PT09. Pataki, G., Tural, M.: Unifying lll inequalities (2009)

Sch87. Schnorr, C.-P.: A hierarchy of polynomial time lattice basis reduction algorithms. Theoret. Comput. Sci. **53**(2–3), 201–224 (1987)

SE94. Schnorr, C.-P., Euchner, M.: Lattice basis reduction: Improved practical algorithms and solving subset sum problems. Mathematical Programm. **66**(1–3), 181–199, August 1994. Preliminary version in FCT 1991

Wal15. Walter, M.: Lattice point enumeration on block reduced bases. In: Lehmann, A., Wolf, S. (eds.) ICITS 2015. LNCS, vol. 9063, pp. 269–282. Springer, Cham (2015). https://doi.org/10.1007/978-3-319-17470-9_16

On the Success Probability of Solving Unique SVP via BKZ

Eamonn W. Postlethwaite and Fernando Virdia(✉)

Information Security Group, Royal Holloway, University of London, Egham, UK
{eamonn.postlethwaite.2016,fernando.virdia.2016}@rhul.ac.uk

Abstract. As lattice-based key encapsulation, digital signature, and fully homomorphic encryption schemes near standardisation, ever more focus is being directed to the precise estimation of the security of these schemes. The primal attack reduces key recovery against such schemes to instances of the unique Shortest Vector Problem (uSVP). Dachman-Soled *et al.* (Crypto 2020) recently proposed a new approach for fine-grained estimation of the cost of the primal attack when using Progressive BKZ for lattice reduction. In this paper we review and extend their technique to BKZ 2.0 and provide extensive experimental evidence of its accuracy. Using this technique we also explain results from previous primal attack experiments by Albrecht *et al.* (Asiacrypt 2017) where attacks succeeded with smaller than expected block sizes. Finally, we use our simulators to reestimate the cost of attacking the three lattice KEM finalists of the NIST Post Quantum Standardisation Process.

Keywords: Cryptanalysis · Lattice-based cryptography · Lattice reduction

1 Introduction

In recent years, the popularity of lattice-based cryptography has greatly increased. Lattices have been used to design traditional cryptographic primitives such as one way functions, public key encryption, key exchange, digital signatures, as well as more advanced constructions such as identity and attribute based encryption, and fully homomorphic encryption.

One reason for this popularity is that lattice problems, e.g. the Shortest Vector Problem (SVP) and Bounded Distance Decoding (BDD), are believed to be hard also for quantum computers. Hence, schemes based on such problems are good candidates for providing quantum-safe public key cryptography. Indeed, 23

E. W. Postlethwaite and F. Virdia: This work was supported by the EPSRC and the UK government as part of the Centre for Doctoral Training in Cyber Security at Royal Holloway, University of London (EP/P009301/1).
E. W. Postlethwaite and F. Virdia: This work was carried out in part while the authors were visiting the Lattices: Algorithms, Complexity, and Cryptography program at the Simons Institute for the Theory of Computing.

J. A. Garay (Ed.): PKC 2021, LNCS 12710, pp. 68–98, 2021.
https://doi.org/10.1007/978-3-030-75245-3_4

of the original 69 *complete and proper* schemes submitted to the National Institute of Standards and Technology (NIST) as part of the Post Quantum Standardisation Process [NIS16] are based on various lattice problems with varying amounts of structure. Given the long shelf life of cryptographic standards and the high stakes of standardising primitives, the security of these schemes, and thus the concrete hardness of lattice problems, should be understood in detail.

Two popular problems chosen to design lattice-based schemes are the Learning With Errors (LWE) problem (with its ring and module variants) and the NTRU problem. A variety of attack strategies against these problems exist. Asymptotically, the best option is the approach of Arora–Ge [AG11], while, again asymptotically, in the case of binary secrets, BKW variants [KF15, GJS15] perform well. In practice however, the best attacks seem to be the *primal*, *dual* and *hybrid* attacks. All three rely on lattice reduction algorithms, such as BKZ [SE91, SE94, CN11], Progressive BKZ [AWHT16], Self-Dual BKZ [MW16], G6K [ADH+19] and Slide Reduction [GN08a], to find either a unique (up to sign) embedded shortest vector, or more generally a good lattice basis. In particular, the primal attack is often estimated as the cheapest option [ACD+18].

The primal attack against LWE and NTRU consists of using lattice reduction to solve an instance of the unique Shortest Vector Problem (uSVP). The most popular lattice reduction algorithm is BKZ. Current complexity estimates for solving uSVP directly depend on estimating the smallest block size β such that BKZ-β successfully recovers the unique shortest vector. This β is commonly found by following the methodology introduced in [ADPS16, §6.3], and experimentally investigated in [AGVW17].

In their experiments, Albrecht *et al.* [AGVW17] and Bai *et al.* [BMW19], report that smaller than expected block sizes can result in a non-negligible probability of solving uSVP instances arising from the primal attack, when using BKZ. Some concerns were raised [BCLv19] that this could indicate an overestimate of the complexity of the primal attack for cryptographically sized instances. Furthermore, the experiments carried out in 2017 [AGVW17] only focused on recovering a unique shortest vector sampled coefficientwise from a discrete Gaussian distribution. While [AGVW17] claims that the [ADPS16] methodology would also hold for binary and ternary distributions, the authors do not provide experimental evidence. Recent work [CCLS20] revisited the binary and ternary case in the small block size regime $\beta \leq 45$ and concluded that discrete Gaussian errors are more secure. We disagree, and discuss [CCLS20] further in Sect. 5.2.

Dachman-Soled *et al.* [DSDGR20] recently proposed an approach for estimating the complexity of the primal attack that makes use of probability distributions for the norms of particular projections of the unique shortest vector, rather than only expected values. This results in a new approach that allows one to better predict the behaviour of the attack when considering block sizes smaller than those expected to be successful by the [ADPS16] methodology. The authors of [DSDGR20] use this approach to develop a simulator that predicts the expected block size by which Progressive BKZ will solve an isotropic uSVP instance. In this work, we call such a simulator a *uSVP simulator*. They use this uSVP simulator in the setting of solving LWE instances with extra hints about the secret, and verify the accuracy of their predictions as the number of hints varies.

Our Contributions. Our first contribution is the implementation of a variant of the uSVP simulator for Progressive BKZ, and the development of a new uSVP simulator for BKZ 2.0. Rather than only returning the expected successful block size, we extract full probability mass functions for successful block sizes, which allow for a more direct comparison to experimental results. Our simulators are also faster than those in [DSDGR20], simulating success probabilities for Kyber1024 in 31 s against the 2 h of [DSDGR20]. This allows for potentially easier inclusion in parameter selection scripts, such as the LWE estimator [APS15]. We note that since the time of writing, the latest version of the simulator proposed in [DSDGR20] adopted the same speedup techniques.

Our second contribution is extensive experiments on the success probability of different block sizes for BKZ 2.0 and Progressive BKZ, on uSVP lattices generated from LWE instances with discrete Gaussian, binary or ternary secret and error distributions. Our experiments show that the uSVP simulators accurately predict the block sizes needed to solve uSVP instances via lattice reduction, for all distributions tested.

As a final contribution, we reestimate the security of the three lattice KEM finalists of the NIST PQC using our uSVP simulators. We compare the expected block sizes they suggest to those predicted by the original methodology of [ADPS16]. We note that our uSVP simulators estimate that a slightly larger average block size than predicted is required, meaning that [ADPS16] likely resulted in an underestimate of their security.[1] We also observe that this phenomenon can, in large part, be attributed to the original [ADPS16] methodology using the Geometric Series Assumption. Replacing this assumption with the output of the [CN11] BKZ simulator reduces the predictive gap between the [ADPS16] methodology and our uSVP simulators.

All of our code and data can be found at github.com/fvirdia/usvp-simulation.

Related Work. The Geometric Series Assumption (GSA), used to predict the output quality of lattice reduction, was introduced in [Sch03]. A simulator, specifically for the output quality of BKZ, was introduced in [CN11]. This simulator more accurately predicts the final, or *tail*, region of the basis profile of a BKZ reduced lattice, improving over the GSA. A refined BKZ simulator was presented in [BSW18], which improves over the [CN11] simulator in the first region, or *head*, of the basis profile. Alkim *et al.* [ADPS16] introduced a BKZ specific method for estimating the block size required to solve uSVP instances arising from the primal attack; its accuracy was investigated in [AGVW17, BMW19]. This method, combined with basis profile simulation after BKZ reduction and arguments about distributions describing the lengths of projections of the unique

[1] A similar phenomenon had also been observed in [DSDGR20] for NTRU-HPS.

short vector, is extended in [DSDGR20] to predict the expected block size by which Progressive BKZ will solve isotropic uSVP instances.

Paper Structure. In Sect. 2 we introduce the necessary preliminaries and notation regarding linear algebra, computational lattice problems, and lattice reduction. In Sect. 3 we review the original [ADPS16] methodology for predicting the expected required block sizes for solving uSVP instances. In Sect. 4 we review the approach of [DSDGR20] and use it to propose uSVP simulators for BKZ 2.0 and Progressive BKZ. In Sect. 5 we describe our experiments and results. In Sect. 6 we use our uSVP simulators to provide preliminary estimates of the block sizes required to successfully perform key recovery attacks on the three NIST PQC lattice KEM finalists, and compare this to predictions using the [ADPS16] methodology.

2 Preliminaries

Linear Algebra. The set $\{1, \ldots, n\}$ is denoted by $[n]$. We denote vectors by bold lowercase letters such as $\boldsymbol{v}$, and matrices by bold uppercase letters such as $\boldsymbol{M}$. We denote the $n \times n$ identity matrix as $\boldsymbol{I}_n$. Throughout, we use row vectors and count indices from 1. We represent a basis $\{\boldsymbol{b}_1, \ldots, \boldsymbol{b}_d\}$ of $\mathbb{R}^d$ as the matrix $\boldsymbol{B}$ having the basis vectors as rows. Given a basis $\boldsymbol{B}$, we can derive an orthogonal basis $\boldsymbol{B}^*$ via the Gram–Schmidt process. The rows of $\boldsymbol{B}^*$ are

$$\boldsymbol{b}_i^* = \boldsymbol{b}_i - \sum_{j<i} \mu_{i,j} \boldsymbol{b}_j^* \quad \text{for} \quad i \in [d], \quad \text{where} \quad \mu_{i,j} = \langle \boldsymbol{b}_i, \boldsymbol{b}_j^* \rangle / \|\boldsymbol{b}_j^*\|^2 \quad \text{for} \quad i > j.$$

We denote by $\text{span}_{\mathbb{R}}\left(\{\boldsymbol{v}_i\}_i\right) = \{\sum_i \lambda_i \boldsymbol{v}_i \colon \lambda_i \in \mathbb{R}\}$ the real span of a set of real vectors $\{\boldsymbol{v}_i\}_i$. Given a basis $\boldsymbol{B}$ of $\mathbb{R}^d$ we denote by $\pi_{\boldsymbol{B},k} \colon \mathbb{R}^d \to \mathbb{R}^d$ the linear operator projecting vectors orthogonally to the subspace $\text{span}_{\mathbb{R}}\left(\{\boldsymbol{b}_1, \ldots, \boldsymbol{b}_{k-1}\}\right)$. Note $\pi_{\boldsymbol{B},1}$ is the identity on $\mathbb{R}^d$. We write π_i when the basis is clear from context. Given a vector space $V = \text{span}_{\mathbb{R}}(\boldsymbol{B})$, its projective subspace $\pi_k(V)$ of dimension $d - k + 1$ has a basis $\{\pi_k(\boldsymbol{b}_k), \ldots, \pi_k(\boldsymbol{b}_d)\}$, where

$$\pi_k(\boldsymbol{b}_i) = \boldsymbol{b}_i - \sum_{j<k} \mu_{i,j} \boldsymbol{b}_j^* = \boldsymbol{b}_i^* + \sum_{k \le j < i} \mu_{i,j} \boldsymbol{b}_j^* \quad \text{for} \quad i \ge k.$$

By definition, this implies that $\pi_k(\boldsymbol{b}_k) = \boldsymbol{b}_k^*$, and that $\pi_j(\pi_k(\boldsymbol{v})) = \pi_k(\boldsymbol{v})$ for any $j \le k$. Given an orthogonal basis $\boldsymbol{B}^*$ and a vector $\boldsymbol{t} = t_1^* \boldsymbol{b}_1^* + \cdots + t_d^* \boldsymbol{b}_d^*$, its projections are given by $\pi_k(\boldsymbol{t}) = t_k^* \boldsymbol{b}_k^* + \cdots + t_d^* \boldsymbol{b}_d^*$. We abuse notation and write $\pi_i(\boldsymbol{B}[j:k])$ to mean the matrix with rows $\pi_i(\boldsymbol{b}_j), \ldots, \pi_i(\boldsymbol{b}_k)$.

Probability. Given a probability distribution D with support $S \subset \mathbb{R}$, we denote sampling an element $s \in S$ according to D as $s \leftarrow D$. For a finite support S, we denote the uniform distribution over S as $\mathcal{U}(S)$. We denote the mean and variance of D as $\mathbb{E}(s)$ or $\mathbb{E}(D)$, and $\mathbb{V}(s)$ or $\mathbb{V}(D)$, respectively. We sometimes use $\sqrt{\mathbb{V}}$

similarly to denote the standard deviation. Given a discrete (resp. continuous) probability distribution D, we denote its probability mass function (resp. probability density function) as f_D and its cumulative mass function (resp. cumulative density function) as F_D. Given $s \leftarrow D$, by definition $P[s \leq x] = F_D(x)$. We recall the conditional probability chain rule. If $E_1, \ldots, E_n$ are events, then $P[E_1 \cap \cdots \cap E_n] = P[E_1 | E_2 \cap \cdots \cap E_n] P[E_2 \cap \cdots \cap E_n]$. We denote by Γ the gamma function $\Gamma(x) = \int_0^\infty t^{x-1} e^{-t} dt$ for $x > 0$.

The Gaussian Distribution. We recall some properties of the continuous Gaussian distribution. We denote by $N(\mu, \sigma^2)$ the probability distribution over $\mathbb{R}$ of mean μ and standard deviation σ, variance σ^2, with density function

$$f_{N(\mu,\sigma^2)}(x) = \frac{1}{\sigma\sqrt{2\pi}} e^{-\frac{1}{2}\left(\frac{x-\mu}{\sigma}\right)^2}.$$

Given a random variable $X \sim N(\mu_X, \sigma_X^2)$ and a scalar $\lambda > 0$, the random variable $Y = \lambda \cdot X$ follows a distribution $N(\lambda\mu_X, \lambda^2\sigma_X^2)$. Given n independent and identically distributed random variables $X_i \sim N(0,1)$, the random variable $X_1^2 + \cdots + X_n^2$ follows a chi-squared distribution χ_n^2 over $\mathbb{R}_{\geq 0}$ of mean n and variance $2n$, with probability density function

$$f_{\chi_n^2}(x) = \frac{1}{2^{n/2}\Gamma(n/2)} x^{n/2-1} e^{-x/2}.$$

Given n independent and identically distributed random variables $Y_i \sim N(0, \sigma^2)$, the random variable $Y_1^2 + \cdots + Y_n^2$ follows a distribution $\sigma^2 \cdot \chi_n^2$ of mean $n\sigma^2$ and variance $2n\sigma^4$, that is, a chi-squared distribution where every sample is scaled by a factor of σ^2. We call this a *scaled* chi-squared distribution.

Discrete Gaussians. We denote by $D_{\mu,\sigma}$ the discrete Gaussian distribution over $\mathbb{Z}$ with mean $\mu \in \mathbb{R}$ and standard deviation $\sigma \in \mathbb{R}^+$. It has probability mass function $f_{D_{\mu,\sigma}} : \mathbb{Z} \to [0,1], x \mapsto f_{N(\mu,\sigma^2)}(x)/f_{N(\mu,\sigma^2)}(\mathbb{Z})$, where $f_{N(\mu,\sigma^2)}(\mathbb{Z}) = \sum_{x\in\mathbb{Z}} f_{N(\mu,\sigma^2)}(x)$. Discrete Gaussian distributions with $\mu = 0$, or the distributions these imply over $\mathbb{Z}_q$ for some modulus q, are widely used in lattice cryptography to sample entries of error and secret vectors from. In our analyses below, we work with vectors $\boldsymbol{t}$ sampled coefficientwise from a discrete Gaussian, and with their projections $\pi_i(\boldsymbol{t})$. We model the squared norms $\|\pi_i(\boldsymbol{t})\|^2$ as random variables following a scaled chi-squared distribution with the appropriate degrees of freedom. For example, for some vector $\boldsymbol{v} = (v_1, \ldots, v_d)$ with each $v_i \leftarrow D_{0,\sigma}$ sampled independently, we model $\|\pi_{\boldsymbol{B},i}(\boldsymbol{v})\|^2 \sim \sigma^2 \cdot \chi_{d-i+1}^2$, where $\boldsymbol{B}$ is a lattice basis being reduced.

Bounded Uniform Distributions. Given a finite subset $S \subset \mathbb{Z}$, we call the uniform distribution $\mathcal{U}(S)$ a *bounded uniform* distribution. Of particular interest in this work are the binary and ternary distributions, where $S = \{0, 1\}$

and $S = \{-1, 0, 1\}$. Similarly to the case of the discrete Gaussian, works using the [ADPS16] methodology for estimating the complexity of lattice reduction, such as the 'LWE estimator' [APS15], implicitly model $\|\pi_{\boldsymbol{B},i}(\boldsymbol{v})\|^2 \sim \sigma^2 \cdot \chi^2_{d-i+1}$ for vectors $\boldsymbol{v}$ sampled coefficientwise from a bounded uniform distribution having $\mathbb{E}(\mathcal{U}(S)) = 0$ and $\mathbb{V}(\mathcal{U}(S)) = \sigma^2$, and $\boldsymbol{B}$ a lattice basis being reduced.

Lattices. A real lattice of rank n and dimension d is the integer span of n linearly independent vectors $\boldsymbol{b}_1, \ldots, \boldsymbol{b}_n \in \mathbb{R}^d$, which we collect into a basis $\boldsymbol{B}$. The lattice generated by $\boldsymbol{B}$ is

$$\Lambda = \Lambda(\boldsymbol{B}) = \{x_1\boldsymbol{b}_1 + \cdots + x_n\boldsymbol{b}_n : x_i \in \mathbb{Z}\},$$

and is a discrete subgroup of $(\mathbb{R}^d, +)$. For $n \geq 2$ and $\Lambda = \Lambda(\boldsymbol{B})$, we have also $\Lambda = \Lambda(\boldsymbol{UB})$ for any $\boldsymbol{U} \in \mathrm{GL}_n(\mathbb{Z})$. Hence Λ has infinitely many bases. An invariant of a lattice is its volume.

Definition 1 (Lattice volume). *Given any basis $\boldsymbol{B}$ for a lattice Λ,*

$$\mathrm{vol}(\Lambda) = \sqrt{\det(\boldsymbol{B}^t\boldsymbol{B})} = \prod_{i=1}^{n} \|\boldsymbol{b}_i^*\|.$$

This quantity is exactly the volume of a fundamental parallelepiped of Λ, that is, the volume of the set $\{\boldsymbol{xB} : \boldsymbol{x} \in [0,1)^n\}$. Other properties of interest in lattices are their minima.

Definition 2 (Lattice minima). *Let $B_d(r)$ be the closed ball of radius r in $\mathbb{R}^d$ and $i \in [n]$. Define $\lambda_i(\Lambda)$, the ith minima of Λ,*

$$\lambda_i(\Lambda) = \min\left\{r \in \mathbb{R}^+ : \Lambda \cap B_d(r) \text{ contains } i \text{ linearly independent vectors}\right\}.$$

A lattice can be tessellated by centring a copy of the fundamental domain on each lattice point. This fact can be used to approximate the number of lattice points in some 'nice enough' measurable set. The Gaussian heuristic says that the number of lattice points in a measurable set S is approximately $\mathrm{vol}(S)/\mathrm{vol}(\Lambda)$. The Gaussian heuristic can be used to approximate the first minimum $\lambda_1(\Lambda)$.

Definition 3 (Gaussian heuristic for the shortest vector). *Given a rank n lattice Λ, the Gaussian heuristic approximates the smallest radius containing a lattice point as*

$$\mathrm{gh}(\Lambda) = \sqrt{\frac{n}{2\pi e}}\,\mathrm{vol}(\Lambda)^{1/n}.$$

Various computational problems can be defined using lattices. We focus on the following.

Definition 4 (Shortest Vector Problem (SVP)). *Given a lattice Λ find a vector $\boldsymbol{v} \in \Lambda$ of length $\lambda_1(\Lambda)$.*

Definition 5 (γ-unique Shortest Vector Problem (uSVP$_\gamma$)). *Given a lattice Λ such that $\lambda_2(\Lambda) > \gamma\lambda_1(\Lambda)$, find the unique (up to sign) $\boldsymbol{v} \in \Lambda$ of length $\lambda_1(\Lambda)$. Unless specified, $\gamma = 1$.*

Definition 6 (Learning With Errors (LWE) [Reg09]**).** *Let n, q be positive integers, χ be a probability distribution on $\mathbb{Z}_q$ and $\boldsymbol{s}$ be a secret vector in $\mathbb{Z}_q^n$. We denote by $L_{\boldsymbol{s},\chi}$ the probability distribution on $\mathbb{Z}_q^n \times \mathbb{Z}_q$ obtained by sampling $\boldsymbol{a} \leftarrow \mathcal{U}(\mathbb{Z}_q^n)$, $e \leftarrow \chi$, and returning $(\boldsymbol{a}, c) = (\mathbf{a}, \langle \mathbf{a}, \mathbf{s}\rangle + e) \in \mathbb{Z}_q^n \times \mathbb{Z}_q$.*
Decision LWE *is the problem of deciding whether pairs $(\mathbf{a}, c) \in \mathbb{Z}_q^n \times \mathbb{Z}_q$ are sampled according to $L_{\mathbf{s},\chi}$ or $\mathcal{U}(\mathbb{Z}_q^n \times \mathbb{Z}_q)$.*
Search LWE *is the problem of recovering $\boldsymbol{s}$ from pairs sampled according to $L_{\mathbf{s},\chi}$.*
For a given distribution $L_{\mathbf{s},\chi}$ and prime power modulus q, Decision LWE *and* Search LWE *are polynomial time equivalent [Reg09].*

We note that the distribution χ from which the error is drawn tends to encode some notion of *smallness*, which is usually required for functionality. Throughout this work, we assume m LWE samples $\{(\boldsymbol{a}_i, c_i) \leftarrow L_{\mathbf{s},\chi}\}_{i=1}^m$ are available. These can be written in matrix form as $(\boldsymbol{A}, \boldsymbol{c}) = (\boldsymbol{A}, \boldsymbol{s}\boldsymbol{A} + \boldsymbol{e}) \in \mathbb{Z}_q^{n\times m} \times \mathbb{Z}_q^{1\times m}$. In the original formulation, the LWE secret vector is sampled uniformly from $\mathbb{Z}_q^n$. A standard transformation [MR09, ACPS09] maps m samples from an LWE distribution $L_{\mathbf{s},\chi}$ with $\boldsymbol{s} \leftarrow \mathcal{U}(\mathbb{Z}_q^n)$ to $m - n$ samples from an LWE distribution $L_{\mathbf{s}',\chi}$ where the secret vector $\boldsymbol{s}'$ is sampled coefficientwise from χ. Such a distribution is said to be in *normal form*. In general, more efficient key exchange can be built from LWE distributions where the secret is sampled from a narrow distribution such as χ (*small secret* LWE) or from a distribution imposing or implying few non zero entries in $\boldsymbol{s}$ (*sparse secret* LWE). In this work χ_s (resp. χ_e) represents the distribution from which coefficients of $\boldsymbol{s}$ (resp. $\boldsymbol{e}$) are sampled. Note that with high probability any n samples $(\boldsymbol{A}, \boldsymbol{c})$ from an LWE distribution with prime modulus q with $\boldsymbol{s} \leftarrow \chi_s^n$ and $\boldsymbol{e} \leftarrow \chi_e^n$ can be turned into n LWE samples $(\boldsymbol{A}^{-1}, \boldsymbol{c}\boldsymbol{A}^{-1})$ where the roles of χ_e and χ_s are swapped. This can be useful for creating embedding lattices (see below) when choosing $m \leq n$.

Embedding Lattices. The primal attack transforms the Search LWE problem into a uSVP instance. This can always be achieved using Kannan's embedding [Kan87]. In the case of small secret LWE, the Bai–Galbraith embedding variant [BG14] can also exploit differences in χ_s and χ_e, whenever the former is small or sparse. In particular, given LWE samples $(\boldsymbol{A}, \boldsymbol{c})$ in such an instance, the primal attack starts by constructing the following embedding lattice basis

$$\boldsymbol{B} = \begin{pmatrix} \mathbf{0} & q\mathbf{I}_m & \mathbf{0} \\ \nu\mathbf{I}_n & -\boldsymbol{A} & \mathbf{0} \\ \mathbf{0} & \mathbf{c} & c \end{pmatrix} \tag{1}$$

and performs lattice reduction to recover the unique shortest vector $\boldsymbol{t} = (* \mid \boldsymbol{s} \mid 1) \cdot \boldsymbol{B} = (\nu\, \boldsymbol{s} \mid \boldsymbol{e} \mid c)$ for suitable values of $*$ and c, and a scalar ν that balances the contributions of $\boldsymbol{s}$ and $\boldsymbol{e}$ to the norm of $\boldsymbol{t}$. An alternative approach is to first reduce the $(n+m) \times (n+m)$ top left minor of $\boldsymbol{B}$ as a form of preprocessing (e.g. if $\boldsymbol{A}$ is a common reference string for multiple LWE distributions), and later append the last row to finish the search for a specific target vector [LN13]. While lattice reduction software that takes $\boldsymbol{B}$ as input often requires that $\nu \in \mathbb{Z}$, in the IACR ePrint version of this paper we discuss a standard way to construct variants of this embedding that allow us in practice to use any $\nu \in \mathbb{R}$, as well as to centre the χ_s and χ_e distributions. For example, applying these techniques to an LWE instance with a binary secret distribution results in an embedding where the first n coordinates of $\boldsymbol{t}$ are distributed uniformly in $\{-1, 1\}$.

Lattice Reduction. In general, lattice reduction is any algorithmic technique that takes as input a basis of a lattice and finds a basis of better quality. Many different notions of reduced basis exist, most of which can be intuitively captured by a basis being formed of short and close to orthogonal vectors. The celebrated LLL algorithm [LLL82] achieves the following.

Definition 7 (LLL reduced). *For $\delta \in (1/4, 1)$ a basis $\boldsymbol{B}$ is δ-LLL reduced if $|\mu_{i,j}| \leq 1/2$ for all $1 \leq j < i \leq d$ and $(\delta - \mu_{i,i-1}^2) \left\|\boldsymbol{b}_{i-1}^*\right\|^2 \leq \left\|\boldsymbol{b}_i^*\right\|^2$ for $i \in \{2, \ldots, d\}$.*

In this work we consider the performance of the BKZ algorithm [SE91,SE94], which achieves the following.

Definition 8 (BKZ- β reduced). *A basis $\boldsymbol{B}$ is BKZ-β reduced if it is LLL reduced and for all $i \in [d-1]$, $\|\boldsymbol{b}_i^*\| = \lambda_1\left(\pi_i(\boldsymbol{B}[i\colon \min(i+\beta-1, d)])\right)$.*

In order to do this, an oracle O_{SVP} is used, that, given a lattice, finds its shortest vector. BKZ repeatedly calls O_{SVP} on the projected sublattices, or *blocks*, $\pi_i(\boldsymbol{B}[i\colon \min(i+\beta-1, d)])$. If the output vector $\boldsymbol{v}$ is shorter than the current first vector in the block, it is inserted into the basis at the beginning of the block. Then LLL is run on the basis to remove linear dependencies introduced by this insertion. Throughout, we make use of the BKZ implementation in the FPLLL [dt16a] library, which sets $\delta = 0.99$ in its underlying calls to LLL.

In Algorithm 1, we present a description of the BKZ algorithm. In its original description, BKZ terminates after a full tour is executed without inserting. We follow algorithmic improvements and do not necessarily run tours until this point. In particular, the notion of *early abort* (called *auto-abort* in some implementations [dt16a]) was introduced as part of the BKZ 2.0 algorithm [CN11]. The idea is that the majority of improvement occurs in a few early tours, whereas many tours are required before convergence. Following experimental analysis of BKZ [Che13, Figure 4.6], [Alb17, §2.5], Albrecht [Alb17] identifies $\tau = 16$ as the number of tours after which little improvement is made to the basis quality. Furthermore, BKZ 2.0 integrates local block rerandomisation and preprocessing into the originally proposed O_{SVP} oracle, enumeration. We note that while recent advances in lattice sieving mean that enumeration O_{SVP} oracles are no longer the fastest in practice [ADH+19] for large SVP instances, our heuristic analysis

```
   Data: LLL reduced lattice basis B
   Data: block size β
 1 repeat                                                        /* tour */
 2 |  for i ← 1 to d do
 3 |  |  ℓ ← ||b*_i||
 4 |  |  j ← min(i + β − 1, d)
 5 |  |  v ← O_SVP(π_i(B[i : j]))
 6 |  |  if ||v|| ≤ ℓ then
 7 |  |  |  v' ← x_i b_i + ··· + x_j b_j where v = x_i π_i(b_i) + ··· + x_j π_i(b_j)
 8 |  |  |  extend B by inserting v' into B at index i
 9 |  |  |_ LLL on B to remove linear dependencies, drop 0 row
10 |  |_ if if no insertion was made then yield ⊤ else yield ⊥
11 |_ if ⊤ for all i then return
```

Algorithm 1: Simplified view of the BKZ Algorithm. The instructions inside the `repeat` context are called a BKZ *tour*.

is independent of the underlying O_{SVP} oracle, and for the block sizes we consider the enumeration of FPLLL is slightly faster than the sieves of [ADH+19].

In [AWHT16], Aono *et al.* introduce another variant of BKZ that they name Progressive BKZ. Here, the basis is reduced using increasingly larger block sizes β, running tours of BKZ-β each time. For the purposes of this paper, we define Progressive BKZ as in Algorithm 2, allowing an arbitrary number τ of tours to be run for each block size.

```
   Data: LLL reduced lattice basis B of rank d
   Data: τ ∈ Z+
 1 β ← 3
 2 while β ≤ d do                                                /* round */
 3 |  run τ tours of BKZ-β on basis B
 4 |_ β ← β + 1
```

Algorithm 2: Progressive BKZ Algorithm, as used in this work.

One consequence of lattice reduction is that it controls how quickly the lengths of the Gram–Schmidt vectors $\boldsymbol{b}_i^*$ (for an output basis $\boldsymbol{B}$) decay. In particular, the larger β is chosen in BKZ, the slower these lengths decay and the closer to orthogonal the basis vectors are. We call the lengths of the Gram–Schmidt vectors, the *basis profile*.

Definition 9 (Basis profile). *Given a basis $\boldsymbol{B}$ of a lattice of rank n, we define the profile of $\boldsymbol{B}$ as the set of squared norms of the orthogonal vectors $\{\|\boldsymbol{b}_i^*\|^2\}_{i=1}^n$.*

Remark 1. In our algorithms, we refer to exact or estimated values $\|\boldsymbol{b}_i^*\|^2$ for a basis as `profile`$[i]$.

Theoretical results exist about the output quality of BKZ-β [HPS11, ALNSD20], as well as heuristic assumptions, which better model average case performance when reducing random q-ary lattices.

Definition 10 (Geometric Series Assumption (GSA) [Sch03]**).** *Given a basis $\boldsymbol{B}$, the norms of the Gram-Schmidt vectors $\boldsymbol{b}_i^*$ after lattice reduction satisfy*

$$\|\boldsymbol{b}_i^*\| = \alpha^{i-1} \cdot \|\boldsymbol{b}_1\|, \text{ for some } 0 < \alpha < 1.$$

In the case of BKZ-β, α can be derived as a function of β, by combining an estimate for $\|\boldsymbol{b}_1\|$ returned by BKZ [Che13] and the (constancy of the) lattice volume. The GSA can be seen as a global view of a lattice basis, using only the constant volume of the full lattice Λ and an estimate for the length of the first basis vector to calculate α. However, the volume of local *blocks* is not constant as LLL or BKZ is run on a basis. Chen and Nguyen propose a *BKZ simulator* [CN11] that takes this intuition into account to improve on the GSA in the case of BKZ. It takes as *input* a profile $\{\|\boldsymbol{b}_i^*\|^2\}_i$ and simulates a tour of BKZ-β by calculating, block by block, the Gaussian heuristic of the current β dimensional block, 'inserting' a vector of that length at the beginning of said block, and redistributing the necessary length to the subsequent Gram–Schmidt vectors to keep $\text{vol}(\Lambda)$ constant. Since projected sublattices of small rank, e.g. $n \leq 45$, do not behave as random,[2] to simulate the profile for the final indices of the basis the BKZ simulator stops using the Gaussian heuristic and instead uses experimental averages over unit volume lattices (scaled appropriately). This design also allows for one to simulate a fixed number of tours, rather than assuming convergence, as in the GSA. The process can be made probabilistic by 'inserting' a vector with length drawn from a probability distribution centred on the length suggested by the Gaussian heuristic [BSW18]. The latter approach better captures a phenomenon of lattice reduction called the *head concavity*.

Throughout our work we make use of the Chen–Nguyen simulator as implemented in FPyLLL [dt16b]. In Algorithm 3 we define a BKZSim subroutine that returns a [CN11] simulation for an input basis profile. Here $\text{LWE}_{n,q,\chi,m}$ is a basis produced as in (1) with $c = 1$, assuming normal form so that $\nu = 1$ and $\chi = \chi_s = \chi_e$. To produce the profile of an LLL reduced LWE basis, we considered three options. In the case of the instances used in our experiments, which are described in Sect. 5, such a profile can be easily obtained by performing LLL on any particular embedding basis. However, this is not the case for cryptographically sized embeddings, where FPLLL's implementation of LLL can only run with high enough floating point precision by using MPFR [FHL+07], which becomes impractically slow. An alternative is to use a GSA slope corresponding to LLL reduction. This correctly predicts the slope of the main section of the profile, but does not account for the role played by the q-vectors in the embedding basis, which are short enough to not be affected by LLL [HG07]. The third option is to use a specific basis profile simulator for LLL that captures the effect of the q-vectors. We opt for the third option; a description of the Z-shape phenomenon and its simulation can be found in the IACR ePrint version of this paper.

[2] See e.g. [Che13, §2.3.2] for a formal introduction.

Input: (n, q, χ, m) or profile $\{\|b_i^*\|^2\}_i$
Input: β, τ
1 **if** $\{\|b_i^*\|^2\}_i$ *not provided as input* **then**
2 $\quad \{\|b_i^*\|^2\}_i \leftarrow$ simulated profile of LLL reduced $\mathrm{LWE}_{n,q,\chi,m}$ instance
3 $\{\|b_i^*\|^2\}_i \leftarrow$ [CN11] simulation of τ tours of BKZ-β on $\{\|b_i^*\|^2\}_i$
4 **return** $\{\|b_i^*\|^2\}_i$

Algorithm 3: BKZSim subroutine.

3 Choosing BKZ Block Sizes and the '2016 Estimate'

In this section we motivate and explain the approach introduced in [ADPS16] to predict the block size required to solve uSVP using lattice reduction.

The runtime of BKZ-β is dominated by that of the O_{SVP} subroutine. The latter is often implemented using lattice point enumeration with preprocessing, which has time complexity $\beta^{\Theta(\beta)}$, or lattice sieving, which has time and memory complexity $2^{\Theta(\beta)}$. Therefore, to estimate the complexity of solving uSVP using lattice reduction, it is crucial to estimate the smallest block size sufficient to recover the unique shortest vector $t \in \Lambda$.

The most successful approach for making such estimates was introduced in [ADPS16, §6.3] and is sometimes referred to in the literature as the '2016 estimate'. The idea is to estimate a block size β such that at some point during lattice reduction, O_{SVP} will return a projection of the uSVP solution as the shortest vector in a local projected sublattice. If the rank of this projected sublattice is large enough, subsequent cheap lattice reduction operations (usually, a single call to LLL [AGVW17]) will recover the full uSVP solution. Concretely, this approach consists of finding the smallest β such that in the final full sized block starting at index $d - \beta + 1$,

$$\|\pi_{d-\beta+1}(t)\| \le \left\|b_{d-\beta+1}^*\right\|, \tag{2}$$

resulting in O_{SVP} recovering the projection of t at index $d - \beta + 1$.

In [ADPS16], the authors consider normal form LWE, and assume the secret distribution χ to be centred around 0. The uSVP solution will be an embedded vector for which each entry is drawn i.i.d. from a distribution of standard deviation σ and mean $\mu = 0$, with the addition of one final, constant, entry c.[3] Using the Bai–Galbraith embedding, our target vector is $t = (s \mid e \mid c)$, of dimension $d = n + m + 1$. The squared norm $\|t\|^2$ may be modelled as a random variable following a scaled chi-squared distribution $\sigma^2 \cdot \chi^2_{d-1}$ with $d-1$ degrees of freedom, plus a fixed contribution from c, resulting in $\mathbb{E}(\|t\|^2) = (d-1)\sigma^2 + c^2$.

In [ADPS16], the authors approximate the left hand side of (2) as $\|\pi_{d-\beta+1}(t)\| \approx \mathbb{E}(\|t\|)\sqrt{\beta/d} \approx \sigma\sqrt{\beta}$, where they approximate $\mathbb{E}(\|t\|) \approx \sigma\sqrt{d}$. The approximation $\mathbb{E}(\|t\|) \approx \sigma\sqrt{d}$ replaces $(d-1)\sigma^2 + c^2$ with $d\sigma^2$, which for

[3] This constant c is often chosen as 1, which gives better attacks in practice [AFG13, BG14, AGVW17], though formally it should be chosen as σ [LM09].

large d or for $c \approx \sigma$ introduces little error, and assumes that $\mathbb{E}(\|\boldsymbol{t}\|) = \mathbb{E}(\|\boldsymbol{t}\|^2)^{1/2}$. The error in this assumption tends to 0 as $d \to \infty$, so we ignore it. An exact derivation can be found in the IACR ePrint version of this paper. This assumption can also be avoided altogether by working with squared lengths, as we do in our analysis.

To approximate the right hand side of (2), in [ADPS16, §6.3] the authors make use of the GSA. Assuming that BKZ-β returns a first basis vector of length $\ell_1(\beta)$ when called with the basis of a random q-ary lattice as input, this results in the following win condition that β must satisfy for solving uSVP using BKZ-β,

$$\sqrt{\beta}\sigma \approx \|\pi_{d-\beta+1}(\boldsymbol{t})\| \leq \left\|\boldsymbol{b}^*_{d-\beta+1}\right\| \approx \alpha(\beta)^{d-\beta} \cdot \ell_1(\beta). \tag{3}$$

At first glance the careful reader may notice an apparent contradiction in the methodology. Indeed, the GSA describes the basis profile produced by BKZ for a random lattice, and in [ADPS16] ℓ_1 is determined assuming this is the case. However, we are reducing a uSVP embedding lattice. While the embedding basis looks like that of a random q-ary lattice, the shortest vector will be shorter than $\ell_1(\beta)$. Yet, this shortest vector is hard to find. What (3) aims to capture is exactly the moment where BKZ is able to find this shortest vector, and hence distinguish our uSVP embedding lattice from a random q-ary lattice. The GSA and ℓ_1 are used to describe the status of the basis up until this moment, while it still looks like the basis of a random q-ary lattice.

In this model, (3) provides a clear cut answer to what is the smallest viable block size to solve uSVP. In practice, BKZ 2.0 is a randomised algorithm, working on a random uSVP instance. In [AGVW17], the authors verify the validity of this win condition, resulting in a success probability of approximately 90% when using β chosen by following (3). However, they also measure that somewhat smaller block sizes also present some relatively high success probabilities of solving uSVP.

4 Simulating Solving uSVP

In this section, we review and extend recent work on capturing the probabilistic nature of the described uSVP win condition. In [DSDGR20], Dachman-Soled *et al.* revisit the [ADPS16] heuristic methodology described in Sect. 3. The authors are concerned with accurately predicting the effects that introducing side channel information to their lattice embedding has on the success probability of solving uSVP using Progressive BKZ, while also maintaining accuracy in the small block size regime, $\beta \leq 45$. The authors describe a *uSVP simulator* (not to be confused with the BKZ simulator of [CN11]), designed to predict the success probability of Progressive BKZ solving an *isotropic* uSVP instance by a specific block size.[4] Using their uSVP simulator, they predict the expected successful block size for a series of experiments they run, and verify the accuracy of

[4] Any uSVP instance used in the primal attack can be made isotropic, where $\sigma = 1$.

their predictions. We start by simplifying the [DSDGR20] uSVP simulator for Progressive BKZ, and then develop a similar uSVP simulator for BKZ 2.0. We focus on the simulator as described in [DSDGR20] at the time of release. Since the time of writing, the latest version of the simulator proposed in [DSDGR20] adopted some of the techniques described below, for allowing $\tau > 1$ and faster simulations.

4.1 Progressive BKZ

The approach proposed in [DSDGR20] to estimate the required block size to solve a uSVP instance is to simulate the status of a lattice basis as it is being reduced, and with it the probability at each step of the lattice reduction algorithm that the target vector is recovered.

Input: d
1 $p_{\text{tot}} \leftarrow 0$, $\bar{\beta} \leftarrow 0$
2 `profile` $\leftarrow$ GSA profile of an LLL reduced, rank d, isotropic uSVP instance basis
3 **for** $\beta \leftarrow 3$ **to** d **do** /* round */
4   `profile` $\leftarrow$ BKZSim(`profile`, β, 1)
5     $p_{\text{lift}} \leftarrow P[\boldsymbol{t}$ recovered in $\lfloor d/\beta \rfloor$ rounds $\mid \pi_{d-\beta+1}(\boldsymbol{t})$ recovered this round$]$
6     $p_{\text{rec}} \leftarrow P[x \leftarrow \chi^2_\beta : x \leq \texttt{profile}[d-\beta+1]]$
7     $p_{\text{new}} \leftarrow (1 - p_{\text{tot}}) \cdot p_{\text{rec}} \cdot p_{\text{lift}}$
8     $\bar{\beta} \leftarrow \bar{\beta} + \beta \cdot p_{\text{new}}$
9     $p_{\text{tot}} \leftarrow p_{\text{tot}} + p_{\text{new}}$
10   **if** $p_{tot} \geq 0.999$ **then break**
11 **return** $\bar{\beta}$

Algorithm 4: Isotropic uSVP simulator for Progressive BKZ with $\tau = 1$, as proposed in [DSDGR20]. We omit the details of computing p_{lift} for simplicity and note that p_{rec} represents $P[\pi_{d-\beta+1}(\boldsymbol{t})$ recovered this round$]$. Returns the expected block size $\bar{\beta}$ required to solve uSVP.

Let W be the event of solving uSVP during the run of Progressive SVP, W_β the probability of being able to solve uSVP during the round with block size β, and $F_\beta = \neg W_\beta$. Following the notation in Algorithm 2, we assume $\tau = 1$, meaning that for each block size β exactly one tour of BKZ-β is run. They implicitly partition W as follows

$$P[W] = P[W_3] + P[W_4 \wedge F_3] + P[W_5 \wedge F_4 \wedge F_3] + \cdots = \sum_{\beta=3}^{d} P\left[W_\beta \wedge \bigwedge_{j=3}^{\beta-1} F_j\right].$$

Their computation of the expected winning block size $\bar{\beta}$ amounts to implicitly defining a probability mass function for a random variable B representing the *first viable* block size to solve the uSVP instance, and computing its expected value. In the case of Progressive BKZ, a block size β being the first viable means that it is the round of BKZ run with block size β (i.e. the tour of Line 3 of Algorithm 2 with block size β) and not any earlier round using a smaller block size, that will solve the uSVP instance. The resulting probability mass function for the distribution of B can be modelled as

$$P[B = \beta] = P\left[W_\beta \wedge \bigwedge_{j=3}^{\beta-1} F_j\right].$$

The probability $P[W_\beta]$ is itself modelled as the product of the probability of successfully recovering $\pi_{d-\beta+1}(\boldsymbol{t})$ by calling O_{SVP} on the last full size block,

$$P[\pi_{d-\beta+1}(\boldsymbol{t}) \text{ recovered using block size } \beta] \approx P[x \leftarrow \chi^2_\beta : x \leq \texttt{profile}[d-\beta+1]],$$

and the probability of successfully lifting the projection over subsequent rounds, p_{lift}. In their implementation of Algorithm 4, Dachman-Soled *et al.* use a chain of conditional probabilities to compute p_{lift}. Events W_i and F_j for $i \neq j$ are considered to be independent, therefore $P[B = \beta]$ is computed as the relevant product.

We introduce two simplifications to the above uSVP simulator. Firstly, we noticed experimentally that running BKZ with block sizes smaller than 40 will not solve instances for which the [ADPS16] approach predicts a winning block size of $\beta \gtrsim 60$, where most cryptographic applications (and our experiments) reside. Therefore, we skip probability computations for any block sizes smaller than 40. Furthermore, values of p_{lift} approach 1 quickly as β increases, such that one can simply assign $p_{\text{lift}} = 1$ for $\beta \geq 40$; a similar phenomenon is noted in [AGVW17]. Finally, by allowing multiple tours per block size, we define a uSVP simulator, Algorithm 5, for Progressive BKZ as described in Algorithm 2 where τ may be greater than 1. A comparison between the output of Algorithms 4 and 5 can be found in Fig. 1 for four isotropic LWE instances, where $\tau = 1$. To produce Fig. 1, we tweaked the original [DSDGR20] code in order to extract the implicit probability mass function $P[B = \beta]$. Our simplifications significantly speed up the simulation by avoiding the expensive computation of p_{lift}. In particular, our simulations for Kyber 512 (resp. 1024) take 4 s (resp. 31 s) against the 20 min (resp. 2 h) of [DSDGR20]. We can see that the output probabilities $P[B \leq \beta]$ and the expected successful block sizes differ only slightly, and optimistically for the attacker, on low dimensional instances, with this difference shrinking for cryptographically sized problems.

4.2 BKZ

Using the same approach as for Algorithm 4 and Algorithm 5, we implemented a uSVP simulator for BKZ, described in Algorithm 6. In this case, the basis profile after a number of tours of BKZ-β is simulated in one shot using the [CN11] simulator. Given that the block size is fixed, the probabilities are only accumulated over tours. It should be noted that the event of β being the first viable block size

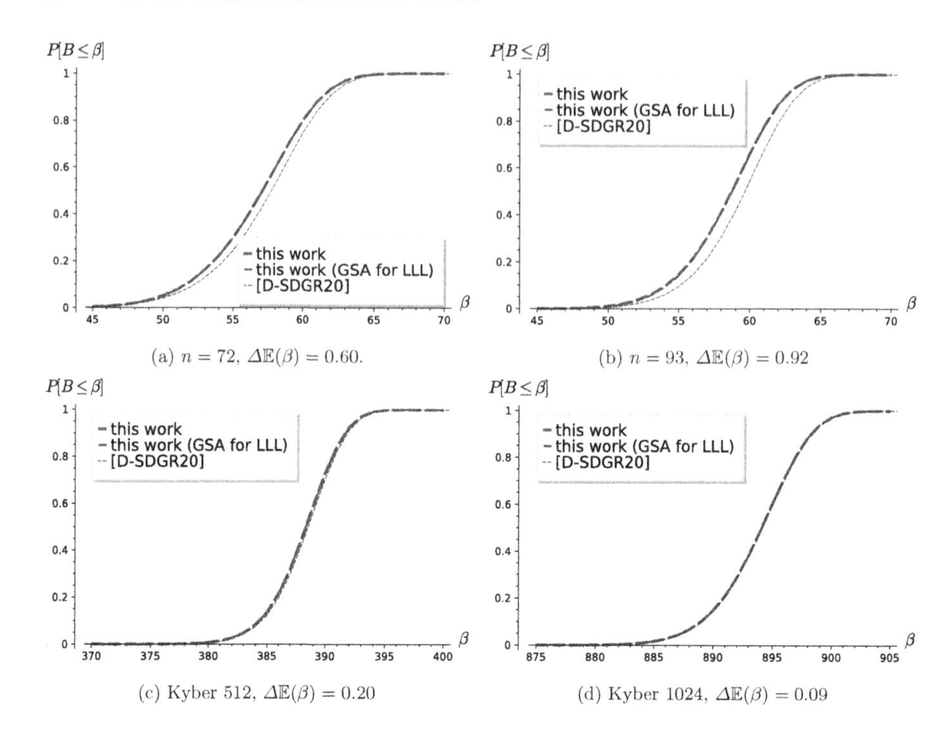

(a) $n = 72$, $\Delta\mathbb{E}(\beta) = 0.60$.

(b) $n = 93$, $\Delta\mathbb{E}(\beta) = 0.92$

(c) Kyber 512, $\Delta\mathbb{E}(\beta) = 0.20$

(d) Kyber 1024, $\Delta\mathbb{E}(\beta) = 0.09$

Fig. 1. Comparison between the output of Algorithm 4 [DSDGR20] and Algorithm 5 (this work) for isotropic parameters ($\sigma = 1$) from Table 1, and on Kyber 512 and 1024 [SAB+19]. The difference in predicted mean first viable block size between the two simulators is reported as $\Delta\mathbb{E}(\beta)$.

changes in the case of BKZ. In this case, no unsuccessful tours with a smaller block size are run by the algorithm. Instead, we consider β being first viable if running BKZ-$(\beta - 1)$ would not result in a solution to the uSVP instance but running BKZ-β would.

Algorithm 6 returns the probability that τ tours of BKZ-β will solve uSVP, but does not exclude the possibility of winning with a smaller block size. We assume in our model that if τ tours of BKZ-β solve a given uSVP instance, then τ tours of BKZ-β', for $\beta' > \beta$, also will. The values output by Algorithm 6 for a given instance can therefore be interpreted as a cumulative mass function for the first viable block size, i.e. $P[B \leq \beta]$. By running the simulator for increasing block sizes until it outputs probability 1, one may recover the probability mass function $P[B = \beta]$ as

$$P[B = \beta] = P[B \leq \beta] - P[B \leq \beta - 1].$$

```
    Input: (n, q, χ, m), τ
 1  p_tot ← 0, P ← {}, β ← 3
 2  d ← n + m + 1, σ^2 ← V(χ)
 3  profile ← simulated profile of LLL reduced LWE_{n,q,χ,m} instance
 4  while β < 40 do
 5  |   profile ← BKZSim(profile, β, τ)
 6  |_  β ← β + 1
 7  while β ≤ d do                                                   /* rounds */
 8  |   for tour ← 1 to τ do                                          /* tours */
 9  |   |   profile ← BKZSim(profile, β, 1)
10  |   |   p_new ← P[x ← σ^2 χ^2_β : x ≤ profile[d − β + 1]]
11  |   |   P[β] ← (1 − p_tot) · p_new
12  |   |   p_tot ← p_tot + P[β]
13  |   |_  if p_tot ≥ 0.999 then break
14  |_  β ← β + 1
15  return P
```

Algorithm 5: Unique-SVP success probability simulator running Progressive BKZ, running τ tours for each block size, then increasing the block size by 1. Returns the probability mass function $P[B = \beta]$ of solving uSVP in the round using block size β.

```
    Input: (n, q, χ, m), β, τ
 1  p_tot ← 0, σ^2 ← V(χ)
 2  d ← n + m + 1
 3  for tour ← 1 to τ do
 4  |   profile ← BKZSim((n, q, χ, m), β, tour)
 5  |   p_new ← P[x ← σ^2 χ^2_β : x ≤ profile[d − β + 1]]
 6  |_  p_tot ← p_tot + (1 − p_tot) · p_new
 7  return p_tot
```

Algorithm 6: Unique-SVP success probability estimator when running τ tours of BKZ-β. Returns the probability of solving the uSVP instance.

5 Experiments

In this section, we describe the experiments we run to check the accuracy of Algorithms 5 and 6, and discuss the results. We start by describing our original batch of experiments in Sect. 5.1. In Sect. 5.2 we make some observations about our experimental results, and describe further tweaked experiments that we run to verify our understanding of the results.

5.1 Initial Experiments

Our aim in this section is threefold: first, we want to provide experimental evidence for the accuracy of our BKZ and Progressive BKZ uSVP simulators when predicting the success probability of the primal attack against LWE with discrete Gaussian secret and error for different block sizes; second, we want to compare previous experiments [AGVW17] to our uSVP simulations; and finally, we want to explore the effect that binary or ternary distributions have on the primal attack. Throughout our experiments, we use BKZ 2.0 as implemented in FPyLLL [dt16b] version 0.5.1dev, writing our own Progressive BKZ script by using FPyLLL's BKZ 2.0 as a subroutine.

For our first goal, we choose three different parametrisations of the LWE problem, for which the [ADPS16] approach predicts an expected successful block size of either 60 or 61. We give the parameters in Table 1. All parameter sets in these batches use discrete Gaussian secret and error with $\mathbb{V}(\chi_s) = \mathbb{V}(\chi_e) = \sigma^2$. The number of LWE samples used, m, is determined by what the LWE estimator [APS15] predicts to be optimal, using (3). For each parameter set we generate 100 instances, and reduce them using either BKZ or Progressive BKZ. We then check whether lattice reduction positioned the embedded shortest target vector in the first index of the reduced basis.

In the case of BKZ, for each basis we run a number of tours of BKZ with block size $\beta = 45, \ldots, 65$. The number of tours, τ, takes the values $5, 10, 15, 20, 30$. This results in a total of 100 bases, reduced independently 21×5 times each, once for every combination of β and τ. For every set of 100 reductions, we record the success rate by counting the number of solved instances. We run a similar set of experiments using Progressive BKZ, allowing $\tau \geq 1$ tours per block size, in order to see at what point running extra tours per block size becomes redundant. For this reason, we reduce each basis 5 times, once per value of τ in $1, 5, 10, 15, 20$. After every call to the BKZ subroutine, we check whether the instance is solved. If not, we increase the block size by 1 and run a further tour of BKZ.

The resulting success rates for BKZ and Progressive BKZ (with $\tau = 1$) are plotted in Fig. 2, together with the output of our uSVP simulators, interpolated as curves. Figure 3 contains similar plots for Progressive BKZ with $\tau \geq 1$. In Fig. 5 we plot the measured difference between the average mean and standard deviation for the simulated and experimental probability distributions, for both Progressive BKZ and BKZ.

Table 1. List of LWE parameters used for testing our uSVP simulators. The instances are in normal form. We use the Bai–Galbraith embedding and the number of samples used, m_{2016}, is given by the LWE estimator (commit `428d6ea`).

n	q	σ	m_{2016}	β_{2016}
72	97	1	87	61
93	257	1	105	61
100	257	$\sqrt{2/3}$	104	60

For our second goal, we take the success probabilities reported in [AGVW17] for their experiments. In Fig. 4 we report their measured success rates at optimal and smaller than optimal block sizes, and we superimpose our BKZ success probability simulations.

Finally, for our third goal, we run Progressive BKZ experiments for τ in $1, 5, 10, 15, 20$ on three parameter sets using bounded uniform secrets. In particular, we pick the $n = 72$ and $n = 93$ parameters from Table 1 but sample secret $\boldsymbol{s}$ and error $\boldsymbol{e}$ coefficients uniformly from the set $\{-1, 1\}$, and the $n = 100$ parameters with secret and error coefficients sampled uniformly from $\{-1, 0, 1\}$. This preserves the same standard deviations as in Table 1, while adding more structure to the target vector. In the first case, the $\boldsymbol{s}$ and $\boldsymbol{e}$ are equivalent to those of a scaled and centred LWE instance with binary secret and error (see the IACR ePrint version of this paper), while in the second case, the problem is LWE with ternary $\boldsymbol{s}$ and $\boldsymbol{e}$. The resulting success probability plots can be found in Fig. 6.

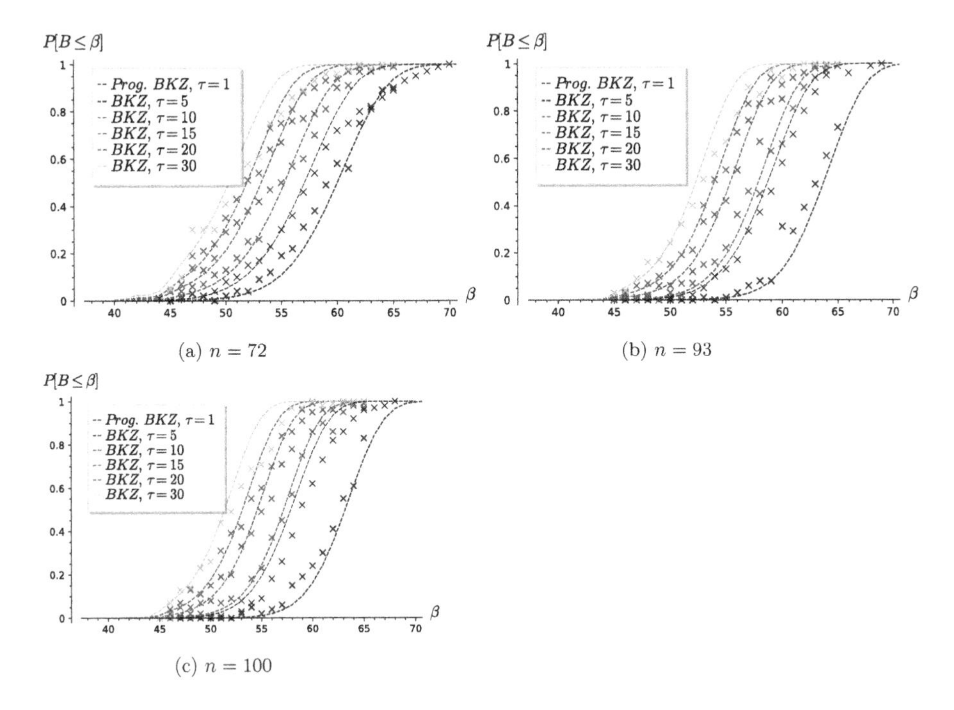

(a) $n = 72$

(b) $n = 93$

(c) $n = 100$

Fig. 2. Comparison of simulated success probabilities with experimental results for BKZ and Progressive BKZ (with $\tau = 1$). Dashed lines are simulations, crosses are experiments. In the case of Progressive BKZ, 100 total instances are reduced. In the case of BKZ, each experimental result is averaged over 100 instances, with experiments using up to block size 65.

5.2 Observations

Experimental success rates for both BKZ and Progressive BKZ are in line with the output of the simulators described in Sect. 4. Below, we look at the results.

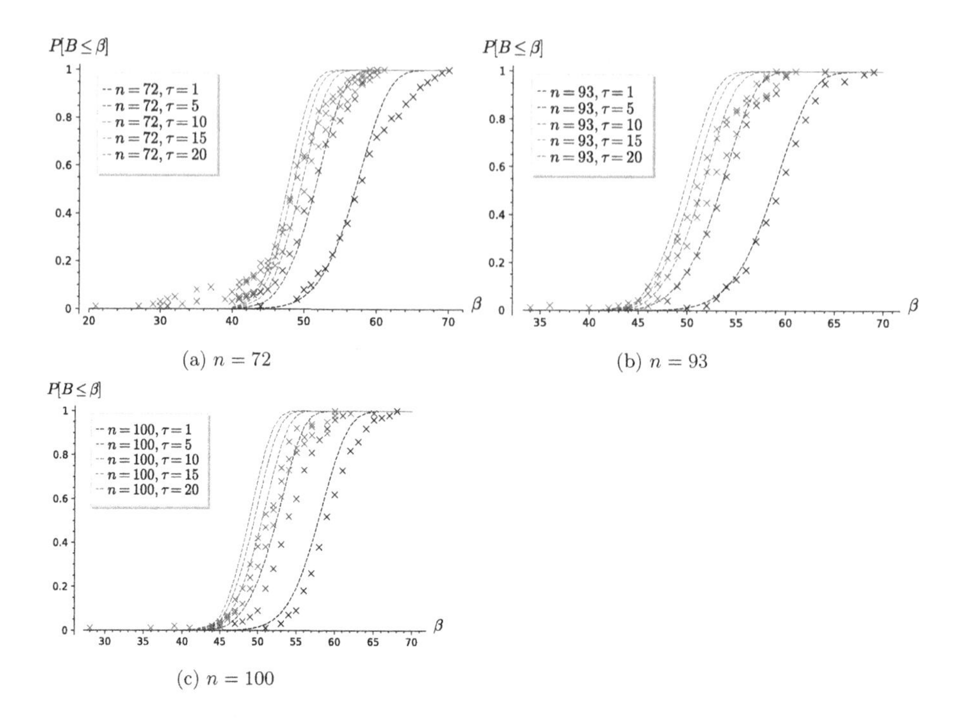

(a) $n = 72$

(b) $n = 93$

(c) $n = 100$

Fig. 3. Comparison of simulated success probabilities with experimental results for Progressive BKZ with $\tau \geq 1$. Dashed lines are simulations, crosses are experiments.

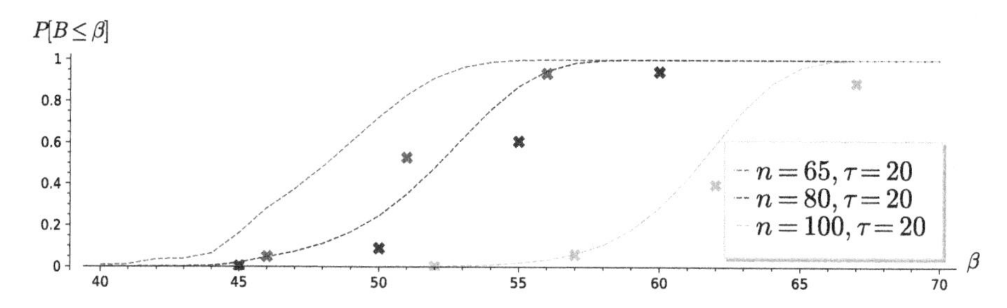

Fig. 4. Comparison of simulated BKZ success probabilities with experimental results reported in Table 1 of [AGVW17].

Progressive BKZ. In the case of Progressive BKZ, simulations seem to predict accurately the success probabilities for $\tau \leq 10$ and all secret and error distributions used. Throughout our experiments reported in Fig. 3, we observe two ways in which experiments slightly deviate from predictions.

Firstly, the success probability appears to stop significantly increasing for $\tau > 10$, even when the simulation does predict some improvement. We expect this to be a consequence of the large amount of lattice reduction being performed. Indeed, whenever the BKZ-β subroutine is called, the basis has already been reduced with τ tours of BKZ-$(\beta - j)$ for $j = 1, \ldots, \beta - 3$. This suggests that

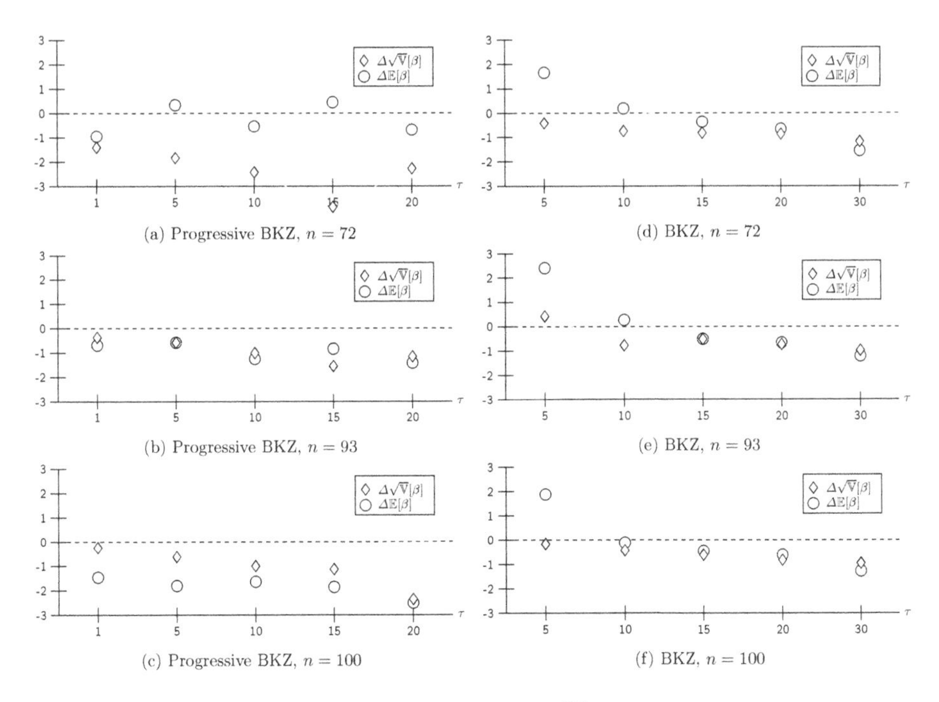

Fig. 5. The measured difference $\Delta\mathbb{E}[\beta]$ (resp. $\Delta\sqrt{\mathbb{V}}[\beta]$) between the simulated and experimental successful block size mean (resp. standard deviation), as τ grows. $\Delta\mathbb{E}[\beta] \geq 0$ (resp. $\Delta\mathbb{V}[\beta] \geq 0$) represents the simulated successful block size mean (resp. standard deviation) being greater than the experimentally measured value.

little progress on the basis profile can be made with each new tour of BKZ-β. In our experiments, we use FPyLLL's BKZ 2.0 implementation with auto-abort, which triggers by default after the slope of the basis profile does not improve for five tours, the slope being computed using a simple linear regression of the logarithm of the basis profile. This means that if it is the case that little progress can be made, fewer than τ tours will be run. To verify this, we rerun experiments while measuring the number of tours run by the BKZ subroutine. The data for the $n = 100$ experiments can be found in Fig. 7, and seems to confirm that auto-abort for $\beta > 20$ is much more frequently triggered for $\tau > 10$. This problem does not affect Progressive BKZ with $\tau = 1$ since, even with auto-abort, one tour is always run, and only slightly affects $\tau = 5$ and $\tau = 10$.[5] Predictions match experiments well in the $\tau \leq 10$ cases. We note that, even if we were to force all τ tours to be performed, once 'would be auto-abort' conditions are reached, very few (if any) alterations would likely be made to the basis by each new tour. This means that the last full block of the basis would not be being rerandomised

[5] Auto-abort will also not trigger for $\tau = 5$, however in this case sometimes the BKZ-β subroutine with $\beta \leq 10$ returns after only one tour due to not making any changes to the basis.

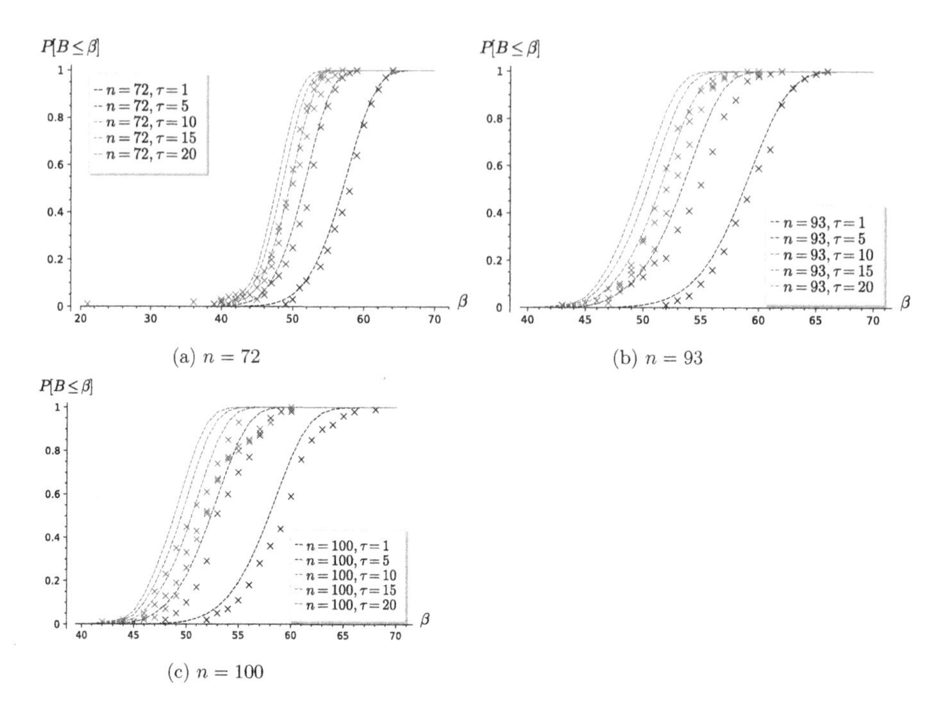

Fig. 6. Comparison of simulated success probabilities with experimental results for Progressive BKZ on LWE instances with scaled and centred binary secret and error (Figs. 6a and 6b), and ternary secret and error (Fig. 6c). Dashed lines are simulations, crosses are experiments. Each experimental result is averaged over 100 instances. No changes were made to the uSVP simulators.

enough for the event of recovering $\pi_{d-\beta+1}(\boldsymbol{t})$ at tour i to be independent from the event of recovering it at tour $i-1$, as our model assumes. For example, if the basis was not modified by the latest i-th tour and $\pi_{d-\beta+1}(\boldsymbol{t})$ was not recovered by O_{SVP} after tour $i-1$, it will also not be recovered after tour i.

The other phenomenon is the presence of a slight plateau in the probability plots as $P[B \leq \beta] \geq 0.8$. In the case of $n = 72$ we also see that smaller than predicted block sizes accumulate a significant success probability. Interestingly, this effect does not appear to be present in the case of binary secret and error LWE, see Figs. 6a and 6b. We expect that this phenomenon is caused by the slight variation in *sample variance* throughout our experiments. Indeed, if we think of our target vector $\boldsymbol{t} = (t_1, \ldots, t_d)$ as sampled coefficientwise from some distribution χ with variance σ^2, in practice the resulting sample variance for each particular LWE instance $s^2 := \frac{1}{d}\sum_{i=1}^{d}(t_i - \bar{t})^2$, with $\bar{t} := \frac{1}{d}\sum t_i$ the *sample mean*, will likely slightly deviate from σ^2. We would therefore expect $\|\pi_i(\boldsymbol{t})\|^2$ to follow a distribution slightly different to $\sigma^2 \cdot \chi^2_{d-i+1}$. However, in the case of $\chi = \mathcal{U}(\{-1, 1\})$, the distribution resulting from scaled and centred binary LWE

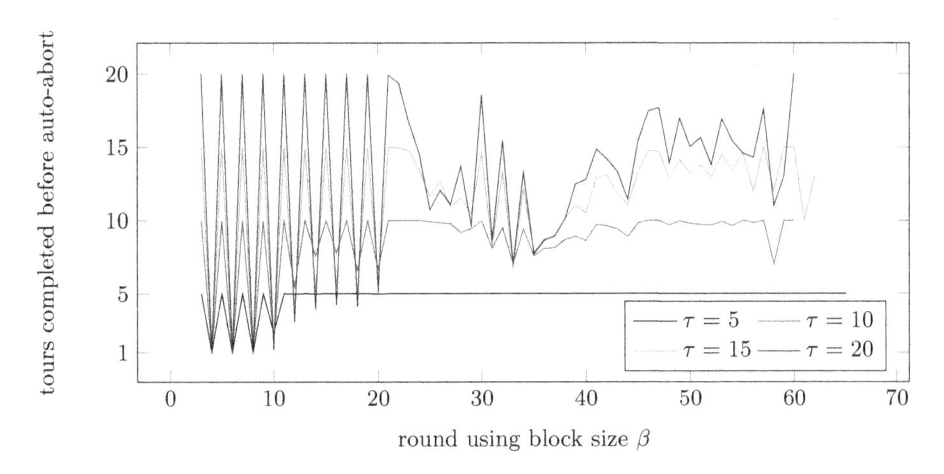

Fig. 7. Measured number of tours run by the BKZ 2.0 subroutine of Progressive BKZ with $\tau \geq 5$ for each round of reduction with block size β. Numbers are from experiments using the $n = 100$ parameters from Table 1, with discrete Gaussian secret and error. Values are averaged over 100 instances. Less than τ tours are run if either BKZ-β does not change the basis or auto-abort triggers.

embeddings, this distribution has a very small variance of s^2, i.e. $\mathbb{V}(s^2)$,[6] meaning that most sampled target vectors will have sample variance almost exactly $\mathbb{V}(\chi) = 1$. To verify this hypothesis, we run a set of $n = 72$ and $n = 100$ discrete Gaussian experiments from Table 1, where we resample each LWE instance until the target vector's sample variance is within a 2% error of σ^2, and then run Progressive BKZ with τ in $1, 5, 10$. The resulting experimental probability distributions, shown in Fig. 8, do not present plateaus (and in the case of $n = 72$, they also do not present the high success probability for small block sizes), supporting our hypothesis. In practice, this effect should not significantly affect cryptographic parameters, as $\mathbb{V}(s^2) \in O(\frac{1}{d})$ [KK51, Eq. 7.20], keeping the effect of fluctuations in $\|\pi_{d-\beta+1}(\boldsymbol{t})\|^2$ small as the embedding dimension d increases.

Our uSVP simulators output similarly accurate simulations for scaled and centred binary, and ternary, secret and errors, as seen in Fig. 6, without making any alterations. This is in line with the notion that the hardness of solving uSVP via lattice reduction depends on the standard deviation of the target vector's coefficients rather than their exact distribution. In recent work [CCLS20], Chen *et al.* run small block size ($\beta \leq 45$) experiments and from their results conclude that the [ADPS16] methodology may be overestimating the security of binary and ternary secret LWE instances, and that discrete Gaussian secrets offer 'greater security levels'. We believe their conclusions to be incorrect. First, their experiments are exclusively run in the small block size regime, where it

[6] Following [KK51,SR02], we compute $\mathbb{V}(s^2)$ as approximately 0.00995, 0.00112, and 0.00005 for a discrete Gaussian with $\sigma^2 = 1$, $\mathcal{U}(\{-1, 0, 1\})$ and $\mathcal{U}(\{-1, 1\})$ respectively, for sets of 200 ($\approx d$) samples.

is known that lattice heuristics often do not hold [GN08b, §4.2], [CN11, §6.1]. Second, their methodology does not take into account the norm of the embedded shortest vector. In their experiments they compare $\mathrm{LWE}_{n,q,\chi,m}$ instances where χ is swapped between several distributions with different variances. They use the [BG14] embedding, which results in target vectors whose expected norms grow with the variance of χ. This means instances with narrower χ will be easier to solve, something that can already be predicted by running the LWE estimator using the `secret_distribution` parameter. The estimator will also perform secret coefficient guessing, thus reducing the dimensionality of the problem. After this guessing has occurred, narrower χ giving rise to easier instances does not mean that Gaussian secrets offer 'greater security levels' than binary or ternary secrets, but rather that when fixing n, q, m, the larger the secret variance, the harder the instance. Gaussian secrets with variance smaller than 1/4 would result in lower security than binary secrets in such a setting. We think the experiments to determine whether discrete Gaussian secrets are more secure than binary or ternary secrets should therefore be to compare LWE instances with different secret distributions, but equal variances, as done in this section, and that parameter selection for small secret LWE should keep the secret's variance in consideration.

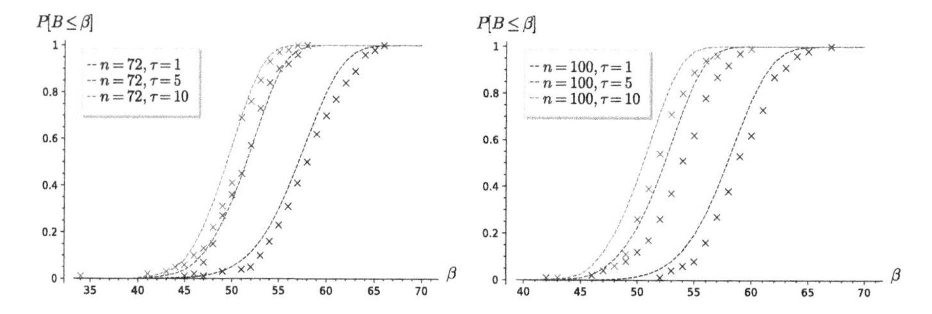

Fig. 8. Progressive BKZ success probability against LWE instances with discrete Gaussian secret and error and $(n, \sigma^2) \in \{(72, 1)(100, 2/3)\}$, such that their sample variance is within 2% of σ^2.

BKZ. In the case of BKZ, simulations seem to stay similarly accurate across all secret dimensions n, as reported in Fig. 2. It should be noted that, even though a larger gap than for Progressive BKZ can be seen between predictions and experiments in the case of $\tau = 5$, this predictive gap in expected block size of less than 3 corresponds to about 1 bit in a core-sieve cost model [ADPS16]. Furthermore, this gap narrows as τ increases. Following experimental results from [Che13, Figure 4.6] and [Alb17], designers often [ACD+18] consider it sufficient to reduce a basis using $\tau = 16$ tours of BKZ when specifying BKZ cost models, due to the basis quality not improving significantly after 16 tours. Our simulators seem accurate for values of τ in such a regime. Another observation is that Progressive BKZ with $\tau = 1$ outperforms BKZ with $\tau = 5$. Indeed, the earlier performs approximately β tours of increasing block size versus the latter's five tours of block size β. It seems therefore that for these lattice parameters Progressive BKZ applies 'more' lattice reduction. We do not attempt to give a closed formula for the minimum block size for which BKZ outperforms Progressive BKZ in output quality. We also see that the phenomenon of success probabilities not increasing when $\tau \geq 10$, as in the Progressive BKZ case, does not occur here. This is compatible with our understanding of this phenomenon in the case of Progressive BKZ. Indeed, BKZ-β will not auto-abort as often due to the input basis not having already been reduced with, for example, τ tours of BKZ-$(\beta - 1)$.

However, a different interesting phenomenon can be observed. Sometimes, as the block size is increased, the experimental success probability of BKZ lowers, see the BKZ experiments in Fig. 2. For example, this happens between block sizes 60 and 61 in Fig. 2a when running $\tau = 5$ tours of BKZ. Originally we believed this to be caused by the preprocessing strategies used in FPyLLL. Indeed, at the time of writing, preprocessing strategies for block size β (resp. $\beta + 1$) could include running BKZ-β' (resp. BKZ-β''), with $\beta' > \beta''$, resulting in inferior quality preprocessing for BKZ-$(\beta + 1)$ than for BKZ-β. We replaced the default preprocessing strategies with a custom one such that preprocessing block sizes are non decreasing as a function of β, however this did not remove the effect. A possible cause for this phenomenon could be that basis profiles output by the [CN11] simulator do not capture the possibility that Gram–Schmidt vector norms can be non decreasing as a function of their index. This means that one could have a BKZ-β reduced basis such that $\left\|\boldsymbol{b}^*_{d-\beta}\right\| < \left\|\boldsymbol{b}^*_{d-\beta+1}\right\|$. This event happening across instances or block sizes could be a potential cause for the phenomenon. The probabilistic BKZ simulator developed in [BSW18] seems to better capture this phenomenon, when run with a fixed PRNG seed. An example of the output of our uSVP simulator for BKZ, when replacing the [CN11] simulator with the [BSW18] simulator, can be found in Fig. 9. However, our experimental measurements are averaged over 100 runs. Running our uSVP simulator with the [BSW18] simulator, and averaging its output, results in a simulation with strictly increasing probabilities, unlike our measurements. In any case, the overall success probability predictions stay reasonably accurate.

Finally, looking at Fig. 4, it seems that our simulations are consistent with the measurements originally reported in [AGVW17, Table 1]. The simulators therefore seem to explain the reported success probabilities of lower than expected block sizes in that paper.

6 Simulations of Cryptographically Sized LWE Instances

In previous sections we developed simulators for the success probability of solving uSVP instances and tested them against uSVP embedding lattices generated from small LWE instances that could be solved in practice. An immediate application could be to use such simulators to estimate the behaviour of lattice reduction when used against cryptographically sized instances.

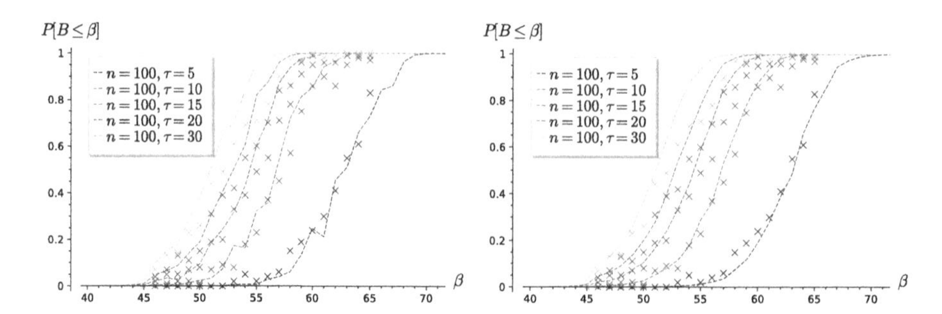

Fig. 9. Both figures show BKZ experiments and uSVP simulations for $n = 100$ instances with Gaussian secret and error, where the calls to the [CN11] simulator made in Algorithm 6 are replaced. The left plot shows simulations where the [BSW18] simulator is used with a fixed PRNG seed. The right plot shows the same experimental data with simulations obtained by averaging the output of the [BSW18] simulator over 10 different seeds.

Here we use the simulator to compute the expected first viable block sizes required to solve LWE and NTRU instances proposed for the NIST PQC standardisation process. In particular we look at the second round versions of the three lattice KEM finalists; Kyber [SAB+19], NTRU [ZCH+19], and Saber [DKRV19]. An interesting option would be to use the simulators to predict what block size is required to solve an instance with a target low success probability. However, as we discuss in Sect. 5.2, the simulations are not necessarily fully accurate for smaller or larger block sizes, due to the fluctuations in sample variance that an instance can have. While the effect should be minor for cryptographically sized instances, low probability attacks may also include combinatorial techniques not captured by our simulators. Therefore, extracting block sizes for low probability attacks from the simulated probabilities may not capture all of the necessary subtleties. Furthermore, we will see that the window of block sizes predicted to be first viable is relatively narrow, so that lower success probability attacks without combinatorial tricks should not be significantly cheaper than higher success probability attacks.

In Table 2, we look at parameter sets from the lattice KEM finalists in the third round of the NIST PQC standardisation process [NIS16], as specified during the second round. We provide expected first viable block sizes $\mathbb{E}(\beta)$ (and their standard deviations $\sqrt{\mathbb{V}}(\beta)$) when using 15 tours of BKZ, and Progressive BKZ with $\tau = 1$ or 5 (see Algorithm 2). We choose $\tau = 15$ for BKZ due to our experiments confirming the accuracy of our estimator for this value and its closeness to 16, which is commonly found in BKZ cost models. We choose $\tau = 1$ and $\tau = 5$ in the case of Progressive BKZ since our experiments suggest both cases are accurately predicted by the uSVP simulator; this allows us to see if running more tours in the BKZ subroutine has any effect on the complexity of cryptographically sized parameters.

Two clear disclaimers should be made. First, in Table 2 we list the expected block size required to solve uSVP instances for the primal attack. While in an aggressive cost model for these algorithms, such as core-SVP [ADPS16], one could be tempted to make direct cost comparisons between algorithms based only on β, in the case of BKZ we assume that τ tours of BKZ-β are run, while in the case of Progressive BKZ about $\tau\beta$ tours of varying block size are run. Second, for both algorithms we fixed the same number of samples m, chosen with the aid of the LWE estimator as the optimal number of samples when using the '2016 estimate' (except in the case of NTRU, where we assume $m = n$ samples). This is not necessarily the optimal number of samples for each specific block size when computed using a uSVP simulator. We therefore avoid making claims and comparisons regarding the exact cost of solving uSVP using the two algorithms, and propose our results as an intermediate step between using the current LWE estimator and finding a theoretically cheapest attack using our simulators.

6.1 Observations

In almost all cases the mean required block size $\mathbb{E}(\beta)$ is predicted to be larger than the LWE estimator currently suggests. Our results for using Progressive BKZ with $\tau = 1$ against NTRU-HPS are in line with what Dachman-Soled *et al.* [DSDGR20, Table 5] predict (NTRU-HPS being the only examined scheme in common). The increase in $\mathbb{E}(\beta)$ may seem counterintuitive. The Alkim *et al.* [ADPS16] methodology already aims to recover $\mathbb{E}(\beta)$, with the simulators described in Sect. 4 capturing the success probability of smaller block sizes, possibly reducing the value of $\mathbb{E}(\beta)$. Indeed, the increase seems to be mainly due to the use of the [CN11] simulator rather than the GSA for predicting the profile of a BKZ reduced basis (i.e. the right hand side of (3)). An illustrative example of this happening in the case of Kyber 512 can be see in Fig. 10. Indeed, patching the LWE estimator to partially[7] use the [CN11] simulator, we obtain $\mathbb{E}(\beta)$ of Kyber 512 (resp. Kyber 768, Kyber 1024) of 390 (resp. 636, 890), narrowing the gap with the predictions obtained in Table 2 by using our uSVP simulators. The small standard deviations reported in Table 2 suggest that the success probability of block sizes below $\mathbb{E}(\beta)$ decrease quickly.

[7] For simplicity, our patch uses the GSA to predict the required block size to perform lattice reduction and the optimal number of samples, as before. It uses the [CN11] simulator for the basis profile output by BKZ, and to predict the block size required to win by running O_{SVP} on the last basis block.

Table 2. Security estimates for some lattice schemes. The number of samples m used in the embedding for Kyber (LWE) and Saber (LWR) is chosen using the LWE estimator, to optimise the cost of the attack following the 2016 estimate for BKZ [ADPS16]. In the case of NTRU, the number of samples m is chosen equal to n. β_{2016} is the block size suggested by the LWE estimator. For BKZ and Progressive BKZ (PBKZ), $\mathbb{E}(\beta)$ and $\sqrt{\mathbb{V}}(\beta)$ are the mean and standard deviation of the distribution of first viable block sizes.

							BKZ 2.0, τ=15		PBKZ, τ=1		PBKZ, τ=5	
Scheme	n	q	σ_s	σ_e	β_{2016}	m	$\mathbb{E}(\beta)$	$\sqrt{\mathbb{V}}(\beta)$	$\mathbb{E}(\beta)$	$\sqrt{\mathbb{V}}(\beta)$	$\mathbb{E}(\beta)$	$\sqrt{\mathbb{V}}(\beta)$
Kyber 512	512	3329	1	1	381	484	386.06	2.56	389.53	2.88	385.70	2.32
Kyber 768	768	3329	1	1	623	681	634.41	2.96	638.23	3.30	634.00	2.66
Kyber 1024	1024	3329	1	1	873	860	891.13	3.31	895.24	3.66	890.63	2.96
LightSaber	512	8192	$\sqrt{5/2}$	$\sqrt{21}/2$	404	507	408.81	2.65	412.24	2.96	408.35	2.39
Saber	768	8192	$\sqrt{2}$	$\sqrt{21}/2$	648	736	659.36	3.00	663.10	3.32	658.85	2.68
FireSaber	1024	8192	$\sqrt{3/2}$	$\sqrt{21}/2$	890	891	907.76	3.34	911.78	3.68	907.16	2.97
ntruhps2048509	508	2048	$\sqrt{2/3}$	$\sqrt{1/2}$	374	508	375.93	2.58	379.56	2.92	375.71	2.36
ntruhps2048677	676	2048	$\sqrt{2/3}$	$\sqrt{\frac{127}{338}}$	521	676	522.78	2.82	526.77	3.18	522.67	2.57
ntruhps4096821	820	4096	$\sqrt{2/3}$	$\sqrt{\frac{51}{82}}$	621	820	628.78	2.83	632.54	3.17	628.43	2.55
ntruhrss701	700	8192	$\sqrt{2/3}$	$\sqrt{2/3}$	471	700	477.20	2.48	480.51	2.77	476.72	2.23

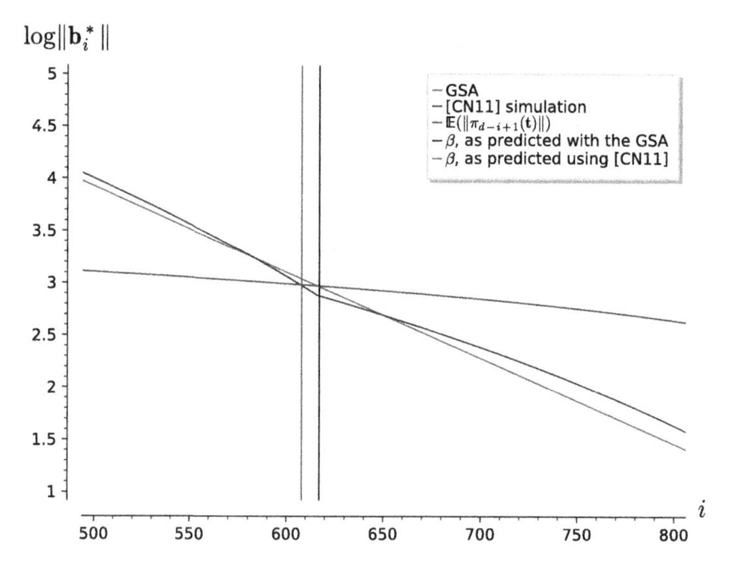

Fig. 10. Example plot showing the effect on the [ADPS16] methodology of using the [CN11] BKZ simulator rather than the GSA, in the case of Kyber 512. Due to the resulting higher basis profile, the GSA leads to picking a smaller block size. The required winning block size in the [ADPS16] methodology is the distance from the vertical line indicating the intersection to the final basis index d. Note that this plot is zoomed in ($d > 800$).

Conclusion. Overall, our data suggests that the experiments in Sect. 5 show that the techniques in Sect. 4 help to more accurately predict lattice reduction success probabilities for solving uSVP. It also suggests that in the case of short vectors sampled coefficientwise from bounded uniform distributions, it is the variance of the distribution, and not the exact probability mass function, that determines the hardness of the LWE instance. The uSVP simulators also seem to explain the success probability for smaller than expected block sizes reported in [AGVW17].

As part of our experiments, we also tested whether using Progressive BKZ with $\tau > 1$ could be beneficial for an attacker. This seems to be useful to some small degree from the point of view the of success probabilities, although BKZ seems to perform comparatively well. However, Progressive BKZ could be of interest to an attacker that wants to start performing lattice reduction as part of a long term attack, but initially has access to fewer resources[8] than necessary to run BKZ with the expected first viable block size. Progressive BKZ would then allow them to increase their resources as the attack progresses, with $\tau > 1$ allowing them to stop at an overall slightly smaller final block size.

We also note that our preliminary estimates for the success probabilities of lattice reduction on cryptographically sized instances result in higher block sizes than output by the LWE estimator [APS15]. This seems to be mostly due to our use of a BKZ simulator rather than the GSA. A patch to the LWE estimator substituting the GSA with a BKZ simulator could mitigate this effect.

Acknowledgements. We would like to thank Martin Albrecht and Léo Ducas for useful conversations, and for their help simulating the LLL output profile.

References

ACD+18. Albrecht, M.R., et al.: Estimate all the LWE, NTRU schemes! In: Catalano, D., De Prisco, R. (eds.) SCN 2018. LNCS, vol. 11035, pp. 351–367. Springer, Cham (2018). https://doi.org/10.1007/978-3-319-98113-0_19

ACPS09. Applebaum, B., Cash, D., Peikert, C., Sahai, A.: Fast cryptographic primitives and circular-secure encryption based on hard learning problems. In: Halevi, S. (ed.) CRYPTO 2009. LNCS, vol. 5677, pp. 595–618. Springer, Heidelberg (2009). https://doi.org/10.1007/978-3-642-03356-8_35

ADH+19. Albrecht, M.R., Ducas, L., Herold, G., Kirshanova, E., Postlethwaite, E.W., Stevens, M.: The general sieve kernel and new records in lattice reduction. In: Ishai, Y., Rijmen, V. (eds.) EUROCRYPT 2019. LNCS, vol. 11477, pp. 717–746. Springer, Cham (2019). https://doi.org/10.1007/978-3-030-17656-3_25

ADPS16. Alkim, E., Ducas, L., Pöppelmann, T., Schwabe, P.: Post-quantum key exchange–a new hope. In: USENIX (2016)

AFG13. Albrecht, M.R., Fitzpatrick, R., Göpfert, F.: On the efficacy of solving LWE by reduction to unique-SVP. In: Lee, H.-S., Han, D.-G. (eds.) ICISC 2013. LNCS, vol. 8565, pp. 293–310. Springer, Cham (2014). https://doi.org/10.1007/978-3-319-12160-4_18

[8] Say, memory if using lattice sieving to implement O_{SVP}.

AG11. Arora, S., Ge, R.: New algorithms for learning in presence of errors. In: Aceto, L., Henzinger, M., Sgall, J. (eds.) ICALP 2011. LNCS, vol. 6755, pp. 403–415. Springer, Heidelberg (2011). https://doi.org/10.1007/978-3-642-22006-7_34

AGVW17. Albrecht, M.R., Göpfert, F., Virdia, F., Wunderer, T.: Revisiting the expected cost of solving uSVP and applications to LWE. In: Takagi, T., Peyrin, T. (eds.) ASIACRYPT 2017. LNCS, vol. 10624, pp. 297–322. Springer, Cham (2017). https://doi.org/10.1007/978-3-319-70694-8_11

Alb17. Albrecht, M.R.: On dual lattice attacks against small-secret LWE and parameter choices in HElib and SEAL. In: Coron, J., Nielsen, J.B. (eds.) EUROCRYPT 2017. LNCS, vol. 10211, pp. 103–129. Springer, Cham (2017). https://doi.org/10.1007/978-3-319-56614-6_4

ALNSD20. Aggarwal, D., Li, J., Nguyen, P.Q., Stephens-Davidowitz, N.: Slide reduction, revisited—filling the gaps in SVP approximation. In: Micciancio, D., Ristenpart, T. (eds.) CRYPTO 2020. LNCS, vol. 12171, pp. 274–295. Springer, Cham (2020). https://doi.org/10.1007/978-3-030-56880-1_10

APS15. Albrecht, M.R., Player, R., Scott, S.: On the concrete hardness of learning with errors. JMC **9**(3), 169–203 (2015)

AWHT16. Aono, Y., Wang, Y., Hayashi, T., Takagi, T.: Improved progressive BKZ algorithms and their precise cost estimation by sharp simulator. In: Fischlin, M., Coron, J.-S. (eds.) EUROCRYPT 2016. LNCS, vol. 9665, pp. 789–819. Springer, Heidelberg (2016). https://doi.org/10.1007/978-3-662-49890-3_30

BCLv19. Bernstein, D.J., Chuengsatiansup, C., Lange, T., van Vredendaal, C.: NTRU Prime. Technical report, NIST (2019)

BG14. Bai, S., Galbraith, S.D.: Lattice decoding attacks on binary LWE. In: Susilo, W., Mu, Y. (eds.) ACISP 2014. LNCS, vol. 8544, pp. 322–337. Springer, Cham (2014). https://doi.org/10.1007/978-3-319-08344-5_21

BMW19. Bai, S., Miller, S., Wen, W.: A refined analysis of the cost for solving LWE via uSVP. In: Buchmann, J., Nitaj, A., Rachidi, T. (eds.) AFRICACRYPT 2019. LNCS, vol. 11627, pp. 181–205. Springer, Cham (2019). https://doi.org/10.1007/978-3-030-23696-0_10

BSW18. Bai, S., Stehlé, D., Wen, W.: Measuring, simulating and exploiting the head concavity phenomenon in BKZ. In: Peyrin, T., Galbraith, S. (eds.) ASIACRYPT 2018. LNCS, vol. 11272, pp. 369–404. Springer, Cham (2018). https://doi.org/10.1007/978-3-030-03326-2_13

CCLS20. Chen, H., Chua, L., Lauter, K.E., Song, Y.: On the concrete security of LWE with small secret. IACR ePrint # **2020**, 539 (2020)

Che13. Chen, Y.: Réduction de réseau et sécurité concrète du chiffrement complètement homomorphe. PhD thesis, Université Paris Diderot (2013)

CN11. Chen, Y., Nguyen, P.Q.: BKZ 2.0: better lattice security estimates. In: Lee, D.H., Wang, X. (eds.) ASIACRYPT 2011. LNCS, vol. 7073, pp. 1–20. Springer, Heidelberg (2011). https://doi.org/10.1007/978-3-642-25385-0_1

DKRV19. D'Anvers, J.-P., Karmakar, A., Roy, S.S., Vercauteren, F.: SABER. Technical report, NIST (2019)

DSDGR20. Dachman-Soled, D., Ducas, L., Gong, H., Rossi, M.: LWE with side information: attacks and concrete security estimation. In: Micciancio, D., Ristenpart, T. (eds.) CRYPTO 2020. LNCS, vol. 12171, pp. 329–358. Springer, Cham (2020). https://doi.org/10.1007/978-3-030-56880-1_12

dt16a. The FPLLL development team. fplll, a lattice reduction library (2016) dt16b. The FPyLLL development team. fpylll, a python interface for fplll (2016)

FHL+07. Fousse, L., Hanrot, G., Lefèvre, V., Pélissier, P., Zimmermann, P.: MPFR: a multiple-precision binary floating-point library with correct rounding. ACM Trans. Math. Softw. **33**(2), 13 (2007)

GJS15. Guo, Q., Johansson, T., Stankovski, P.: Coded-BKW: solving LWE using lattice codes. In: Gennaro, R., Robshaw, M. (eds.) CRYPTO 2015. LNCS, vol. 9215, pp. 23–42. Springer, Heidelberg (2015). https://doi.org/10.1007/978-3-662-47989-6_2

GN08a. Gama, N., Nguyen, P.Q.: Finding short lattice vectors within mordell's inequality. In: STOC (2008)

GN08b. Gama, N., Nguyen, P.Q.: Predicting lattice reduction. In: Smart, N. (ed.) EUROCRYPT 2008. LNCS, vol. 4965, pp. 31–51. Springer, Heidelberg (2008). https://doi.org/10.1007/978-3-540-78967-3_3

HG07. Howgrave-Graham, N.: A hybrid lattice-reduction and meet-in-the-middle attack against NTRU. In: Menezes, A. (ed.) CRYPTO 2007. LNCS, vol. 4622, pp. 150–169. Springer, Heidelberg (2007). https://doi.org/10.1007/978-3-540-74143-5_9

HPS11. Hanrot, G., Pujol, X., Stehlé, D.: Analyzing blockwise lattice algorithms using dynamical systems. In: Rogaway, P. (ed.) CRYPTO 2011. LNCS, vol. 6841, pp. 447–464. Springer, Heidelberg (2011). https://doi.org/10.1007/978-3-642-22792-9_25

Kan87. Kannan, R.: Minkowski's convex body theorem and integer programming. Math. Oper. Res. **12**(3), 415–440 (1987)

KF15. Kirchner, P., Fouque, P.-A.: An improved BKW algorithm for LWE with applications to cryptography and lattices. In: Gennaro, R., Robshaw, M. (eds.) CRYPTO 2015. LNCS, vol. 9215, pp. 43–62. Springer, Heidelberg (2015). https://doi.org/10.1007/978-3-662-47989-6_3

KK51. Kenney, J.F., Keeping, E.S.: Mathematics of Statistics. Van Nostrand, New York (1951)

LLL82. Lenstra, H.W.Jr., Lenstra, A.K., Lovász, L.: Factoring polynomials with rational coefficients. Math. Ann. **261**, 515–534 (1982)

LM09. Lyubashevsky, V., Micciancio, D.: On bounded distance decoding, unique shortest vectors, and the minimum distance problem. In: Halevi, S. (ed.) CRYPTO 2009. LNCS, vol. 5677, pp. 577–594. Springer, Heidelberg (2009). https://doi.org/10.1007/978-3-642-03356-8_34

LN13. Liu, M., Nguyen, P.Q.: Solving BDD by enumeration: an update. In: Dawson, Ed. (ed.) CT-RSA 2013. LNCS, vol. 7779, pp. 293–309. Springer, Heidelberg (2013). https://doi.org/10.1007/978-3-642-36095-4_19

MR09. Micciancio, D., Regev, O.: Lattice-based cryptography. In: Bernstein, D.J., Buchmann, J., Dahmen, E. (eds.) Post-Quantum Cryptography. Springer, Berlin Heidelberg (2009). https://doi.org/10.1007/978-3-540-88702-7_5

MW16. Micciancio, D., Walter, M.: Practical, predictable lattice basis reduction. In: Fischlin, M., Coron, J.-S. (eds.) EUROCRYPT 2016. LNCS, vol. 9665, pp. 820–849. Springer, Heidelberg (2016). https://doi.org/10.1007/978-3-662-49890-3_31

NIS16. NIST. Submission requirements and evaluation criteria for the Post-Quantum Cryptography standardization process (2016)

Reg09. Regev, O.: On lattices, learning with errors, random linear codes, and cryptography. J. ACM **56**(6), 1–40 (2009)

SAB+19. Schwabe, P., et al.: CRYSTALS-KYBER. Technical report, NIST (2019)

Sch03. Schnorr, C.P.: Lattice reduction by random sampling and birthday methods. In: Alt, H., Habib, M. (eds.) STACS 2003. LNCS, vol. 2607, pp. 145–156. Springer, Heidelberg (2003). https://doi.org/10.1007/3-540-36494-3_14

SE91. Schnorr, C.P., Euchner, M.: Lattice basis reduction: improved practical algorithms and solving subset sum problems. In: Budach, L. (ed.) FCT 1991. LNCS, vol. 529, pp. 68–85. Springer, Heidelberg (1991). https://doi.org/10.1007/3-540-54458-5_51

SE94. Schnorr, C.-P., Euchner, M.: Lattice basis reduction: improved practical algorithms and solving subset sum problems. Math. Program. **66**(1–3), 181–199 (1994)

SR02. Smith, M.D., Rose, C.: Mathematical Statistics with Mathematica®, p. 264. Springer, Berlin (2002)

ZCH+19. Zhang, Z., et al.: NTRUEncrypt. Technical report, NIST (2019)

Two-Round n-out-of-n and Multi-signatures and Trapdoor Commitment from Lattices

Ivan Damgård[1](✉), Claudio Orlandi[1], Akira Takahashi[1], and Mehdi Tibouchi[2]

[1] Department of Computer Science and DIGIT, Aarhus University, Aarhus, Denmark
{ivan,orlandi,takahashi}@cs.au.dk
[2] NTT Corporation, Tokyo, Japan
mehdi.tibouchi.br@hco.ntt.co.jp

Abstract. Although they have been studied for a long time, distributed signature protocols have garnered renewed interest in recent years in view of novel applications to topics like blockchains. Most recent works have focused on distributed versions of ECDSA or variants of Schnorr signatures, however, and in particular, little attention has been given to constructions based on post-quantum secure assumptions like the hardness of lattice problems. A few lattice-based threshold signature and multi-signatureschemes have been proposed in the literature, but they either rely on hash-and-sign lattice signatures (which tend to be comparatively inefficient), use expensive generic transformations, or only come with incomplete security proofs.

In this paper, we construct several lattice-based distributed signing protocols with low round complexity followingthe Fiat–Shamir with Aborts (FSwA) paradigm of Lyubashevsky (Asiacrypt 2009). Our protocols can be seen as distributed variants of the fast Dilithium-G signature scheme and the full security proof can be made assuming the hardness of module SIS and LWE problems. A key step to achieving security (unexplained in some earlier papers) is to prevent the leakage that can occur when parties abort after their first message—which can inevitably happen in the Fiat–Shamir with Aborts setting. We manage to do so using homomorphic commitments.

Exploiting the similarities between FSwA and Schnorr-style signatures, our approach makes the most of observations from recent advancements in the discrete log setting, such as Drijvers et al.'s seminal work on two-round multi-signatures (S&P 2019). In particular, we observe that the use of commitment not only resolves the subtle issue with aborts, but also makes it possible to realize secure *two-round n-out-of-n distributed signing* and *multi-signature in the plain public key model*, by equipping the commitment with a trapdoor feature. The construction of suitable trapdoor commitment from lattices is a side contribution of this paper.

1 Introduction

In recent years, distributed signing protocols have been actively researched, motivated by many new applications for instance in the blockchain domain. One of

J. A. Garay (Ed.): PKC 2021, LNCS 12710, pp. 99–130, 2021.
https://doi.org/10.1007/978-3-030-75245-3_5

the main motivations to construct a distributed signature is reducing the risk of compromising the secret key, which could occur in various ways, for instance as a result of attacks on cryptographic devices. In this paper, we study two similar classes of distributed signing protocols that can be constructed from standard lattice-based computational hardness assumptions, namely n-out-of-n distributed signature schemes and multi-signature schemes.

n-out-of-n Signature. An n-out-of-n signature is a special case of general t-out-of-n threshold signature. At a high level, the parties involved in n-out-of-n signature first invoke a key generation protocol in a way that each individual party P_j learns a share sk_j of the single signing key sk, but sk is unknown to anyone, and then they interact with each other to sign the message of interest. The required security property can be informally stated as follows: If all n parties agree to sign the message then they always produce a single signature that can be verified with a single public key pk; if at most $n-1$ parties are corrupted, it is not possible for them to generate a valid signature. Several recent works have studied threshold versions of ECDSA, arguably the most widely deployed signature scheme, both in the 2-out-of-2 variant [19,32,59] and in the more general t-out-of-n case [17,20,27,29,33,44,46–48,60]. However it is well known that ECDSA does not withstand quantum attacks since it is based on discrete log, and it is therefore important to study post-quantum alternatives which support threshold signing. Despite this, very few works have considered n-out-of-n (or t-out-of-n) lattice-based signatures. Bendlin et al. [10] proposed a threshold protocol to generate Gentry–Peikert–Vaikuntanathan signature [50]; Boneh et al. [15] developed a universal thresholdizer that turns any signature scheme into a non-interactive threshold one, at the cost of using relatively heavy threshold fully homomorphic encryption.

Fiat–Shamir with Aborts. Neither of the above previous papers investigated signatures following the *Fiat–Shamir with Aborts (FSwA)* paradigm due to Lyubashevsky [62,63], which was specifically designed for lattice-based signatures and is nowadays one of the most efficient and popular approaches to constructing such schemes. Recall that in standard Fiat-Shamir signatures, the scheme is based on an underlying 3-move Σ-protocol where transcripts are of form (w, c, z) and where c is a random challenge. This interactive protocol is then turned into a non-interactive signature scheme by choosing the challenge as the hash of the first message w and the message to be signed. The FSwA paradigm follows the same approach, with the important difference that the signer (prover) is allowed to abort the protocol after seeing the challenge. Only the non-aborting instances are used for signatures, and it turns out that this allows the signer to reduce the size of the randomness used and hence reduces signature size. This comes at the cost of marginally larger signing time because some (usually quite small) fraction of the protocol executions are lost due to aborts.

Examples of single-user schemes based on FSwA include Dilithium [65] and qTESLA [14], which are round-3 and round-2 candidates of the NIST Post-Quantum Cryptography Standardization process. Cozzo and Smart [26] recently estimated the concrete communication and computational costs required to build a distributed version of these schemes by computing Dilithium and qTESLA with generic multi-party computation. They pointed out inherent performance issue with MPC due to the mixture of both linear and non-linear operations within the FSwA framework. Given all this, an obvious open question is to construct secure n-out-of-n protocols specifically tailored to the FSwA, while also achieving small round complexity.

Multi-signature. A multi-signature protocol somewhat resembles n-out-of-n signature and allows a group of n parties holding a signing key $sk_1, \ldots, sk_n$ to collaboratively sign the same message to obtain a single signature. However, multi-signature protocols differ from n-out-of-n signing in the following ways: (1) there is no dedicated key generation protocol, and instead each party P_j locally generates its own key pair (pk_j, sk_j) and publish pk_j before signing (so-called the *plain public-key model* [9]), (2) the group of signing parties is usually not fixed, and each party can initiate the signing protocol with a dynamically chosen set of parties associated with $L = \{pk_1, \ldots, pk_n\}$, and (3) the verification algorithm usually doesn't take a single fixed public key, and instead takes a particular set of public keys L that involved in the signing protocol. Hence, roughly speaking, multi-signatures have more flexibility than n-out-of-n signatures in terms of the choice of co-signers, at the cost of larger joint public key size and verification time (unless more advanced feature like key aggregation [69] is supported).

Schnorr vs FSwA. There is a long line of research that starts from Schnorr's signature scheme [80] and follows the standard Fiat–Shamir paradigm to build distributed signatures [2,49,57,75,81] and multi-signatures [3,9,68–70,73,74,82]. In particular, Drijvers et al. [35] recently discovered a flaw of the existing *two-round* Schnorr-based multi-signatures, with a novel concurrent attack relying on the generalized birthday algorithm of Wagner [86]. They accordingly proposed mBCJ scheme, a provably secure variant of Bagherzhandi et al.'s BCJ scheme [3].

Unlike distributed n-out-of-n signatures, several *three* or *four-round* multi-signatures based on FSwA are already present in the literature. Bansarkhani and Sturm [4] extended Güneysu–Lyubashevsky–Pöppelmann (GLP) [53] signature and proposed the first multi-signature following the FSwA paradigm, which was recently followed by multiple similar variants [42,43,67,83,85]. Relying on the syntactic similarities between Schnorr and FSwA-style signatures, these protocols essentially borrow the ideas of Schnorr-based counterparts; for instance, [4] can be considered as a direct adaptation of Bellare and Neven's three-round Schnorr-like multi-signature [9]. However, as explained below, the security proofs of all these protocols are either incomplete or relying on a non-standard hardness assumption, where the underlying problem only emerges in the Fiat–Shamir *with aborts* setting. Therefore, we are also motivated to construct a provably secure multi-signature protocol within this paradigm, while making the most of useful observations from the discrete log setting.

Issue with "aborts". We first observe that there is an inherent issue when constructing distributed FSwA signatures. Just like earlier constructions in the discrete log setting [9,75] previous FSwA multi-signatures ask all parties to start doing what is essentially a single-user FSwA signature, and always reveal the first "commit" message of the underlying Σ-protocol. Then all these messages are added up and the sum is hashed, together with the message to be signed, in order to obtain the challenge. This means that all executions are revealed, whether they abort or not. An important issue with the FSwA approach is that, currently there is no known general way to prove the underlying Σ-protocol zero-knowledge in case of aborts [11, §3.2],[41, §4],[5,6],[64, p. 26]. As a result, the signer should not reveal any of the aborted executions since otherwise the scheme cannot be proved secure. This issue is not serious in a single-user scheme, since the Σ-protocol is made non-interactive in the random oracle model anyway and there is no reason why the signer would reveal aborted executions.

In an interactive setting, the standard approach to circumvent the issue is to send a commitment to the first Σ-protocol message and only reveal it if the rejection sampling is successful. However, the previous FSwA multi-signatures skipped this subtle step. Thus the concurrent work by Fukumitsu and Hasegawa [43] (who constructed a FSwA-style multi-signature proven secure in QROM) had to rely on an additional non-standard assumption (which they call "rejected LWE"), while publicly available security proofs of other similar constructions [4,42,67,83,85] do not explain how to simulate the aborted executions. Despite the lack of such discussion in the proofs there are no known concrete attacks against the existing schemes, and it may be that one could patch the problem by making additional non-standard assumptions, or by carefully choosing the parameter such that the additional assumptions hold unconditionally. Still, it is paramount to strive to find protocols which can be proven secure relying on well-established computational hardness assumptions like LWE and SIS.

1.1 Contributions

FSwA-Based Distributed Signatures with Full Security Proof. In this paper we construct FSwA-type n-out-of-n distributed and multi-signature protocols solely relying on the hardness of learning with errors (LWE) and short integer solution (SIS) problems. Our constructions can be seen as distributed variants of the fast Dilithium-G signature scheme [37]. As a first step, we circumvent the aborts issue mentioned above by utilizing Baum et al.'s *additively homomorphic* commitment scheme [7], which is currently the most efficient construction based on lattices and relies on the hardness of Module-LWE and Module-SIS problems. This results in a provably secure (in the classical random oracle model), three-round n-out-of-n signature protocol DS_3[1].

[1] It is still an open question whether the aborts issue can instead be resolved by careful parameter choice, allowing to simulate the rejected transcripts without any additional assumptions. But we are aware of on-going work in this direction. If the question is answered in the affirmative our three-round protocol could be proven secure even without a commitment. However, the use of homomorphic commitment is crucial for constructing our new two-round protocols, which is our main contribution.

First Two-Round Protocols. Previous FSwA-based multi-signatures required at least three rounds of interaction. On the other hand, as most recent discrete log-based solutions indicate [35,57,73,74], two rounds is a natural goal because this clearly seems to be minimal for a distributed signature protocol based on the Fiat-Shamir paradigm: we first need to determine what should be hashed in order to get the challenge in the underlying Σ-protocol. This must (for security) include randomness from several players and hence requires at least one round of interaction. After this we need to determine the prover's answer in the Σ-protocol. This cannot be computed until the challenge is known and must (for security) require contributions from several players, and we therefore need at least one more round.

In this paper, we show that the application of homomorphic commitment not only resolves the issue with aborts, but also makes it possible to reduce the round complexity to two rounds. We do this by adding a *trapdoor* feature to the commitment scheme (a separate contribution that we discuss in more detail below). This results in a two-round, n-out-of-n signature protocol DS_2 presented in Sect. 3. With a slight modification this n-out-of-n protocol can be also turned into a two-round multi-signature scheme in the plain public key model. We describe a multi-signature variant MS_2 in the full version of this paper [30].

Our main two-round result highlights several important similarities and differences which emerge when translating a discrete log-based protocol to lattice-based one. The approaches taken in our two-round protocols are highly inspired by mBCJ discrete log-based multi-signature by Drijvers et al. [35] In particular, we observe that it is crucial for two-round protocols to use message-dependent commitment keys (as in mBCJ) instead of a single fixed key for all signing attempts (as in the original BCJ [3]), because otherwise the proof doesn't go through. Drijvers et al. only presented a full security proof for the protocol in the *key verification model*, in which each co-signer has to submit a zero-knowledge proof of knowledge of the secret key. Our protocols confirm that a similar approach securely transfers to the lattice setting even under different security models: distributed n-out-of-n signature with dedicated key generation phase, and multi-signature in the plain public key model.

Lattice-Based Trapdoor Commitment. As mentioned above, we turn Baum et al.'s scheme into a trapdoor commitment in Sect. 4, so that the two-round protocols DS_2 and MS_2 are indeed instantiable with only lattice-based assumptions. We make use of the lattice trapdoor by Micciancio and Peikert [71] to generate a trapdoor commitment key in the ring setting. The only modification required is that the committer now samples randomness from the discrete Gaussian distribution instead of the uniform distribution. This way, the committer holding a trapdoor of the commitment key can equivocate a commitment to an arbitrary message by sampling a small randomness vector from the Gaussian distribution. Such randomness is indeed indistinguishable from the actual randomness used in the committing algorithm. Since only a limited number of lattice-based trapdoor commitment schemes are known [18,38,51,52,58] our technique may be of independent interest.

1.2 Technical Overview

Our protocols are based on Dilithium signature scheme, which works over rings $R = \mathbb{Z}[X]/(f(X))$ and $R_q = \mathbb{Z}_q[X]/(f(X))$ defined with an appropriate irreducible polynomial $f(X)$ (see preliminaries for more formal details). Here we go over the core ideas of our construction by considering simple 2-out-of-2 signing protocols. The protocols below can be generalized to an n-party setting in a straightforward manner. We assume that each party P_j for $j = 1, 2$ owns a secret signing key share $\mathbf{s}_j \in R^{\ell+k}$ which has small coefficients, and a public random matrix $\bar{\mathbf{A}} = [\mathbf{A}|\mathbf{I}] \in R_q^{k\times(\ell+k)}$. The joint public verification key is defined as $pk = (\mathbf{A}, \mathbf{t})$, where $\mathbf{t} = \bar{\mathbf{A}}(\mathbf{s}_1 + \mathbf{s}_2) \bmod q$. In the actual protocols pk also needs to be generated in a distributed way, but here we omit the key generation phase for brevity's sake.

Naive Approach. We first present a naive (insecure) way to construct a 2-party signing protocol from FSwA. If the reader is familiar with CoSi Schnorr multi-signature [82] this construction is essentially its lattice-based, 2-out-of-2 variant. In this protocol the parties P_j for $j = 1, 2$ involved in signing the message μ work as follows.

1. P_j samples a randomness $\mathbf{y}_j$ from some distribution $D^{\ell+k}$ defined over $R^{\ell+k}$ (which is typically the uniform distribution over a small range or discrete Gaussian), and then sends out the first message of FSwA $\mathbf{w}_j = \bar{\mathbf{A}}\mathbf{y}_j \bmod q$.
2. P_j locally derives a joint challenge $c \leftarrow \mathsf{H}(\mathbf{w}_1 + \mathbf{w}_2, \mu, pk)$ and performs the rejection sampling $\mathsf{RejSamp}(c\mathbf{s}_j, \mathbf{z}_j)$ with $\mathbf{z}_j = c\mathbf{s}_j + \mathbf{y}_j$; if the result of $\mathsf{RejSamp}(c\mathbf{s}_j, \mathbf{z}_j)$ is "reject" then P_j sets $\mathbf{z}_j := \perp$. After exchanging $\mathbf{z}_j$'s if $\mathbf{z}_1 = \perp$ or $\mathbf{z}_2 = \perp$ (i.e., either of the parties aborts), then the protocol restarts from the step 1.
3. Each party outputs $(\mathbf{w}, \mathbf{z}) := (\mathbf{w}_1 + \mathbf{w}_2, \mathbf{z}_1 + \mathbf{z}_2)$ as a signature on μ.

Note that the rejection sampling step is needed to make the distribution of $\mathbf{z}_j$ independent of a secret $\mathbf{s}_j$. The verification algorithm checks that the norm of $\mathbf{z}$ is small, and that $\bar{\mathbf{A}}\mathbf{z} - c\mathbf{t} = \mathbf{w} \pmod q$ holds, where the challenge is recomputed as $c \leftarrow \mathsf{H}(\mathbf{w}, \mu, pk)$. One can easily check that the signature generated as above satisfies correctness, thanks to the linearity of the SIS function $f_{\bar{\mathbf{A}}}(\mathbf{x}) = \bar{\mathbf{A}}\mathbf{x} \bmod q$. However, we observe that an attempt to give a security proof fails due to two problems. Suppose the first party $\widetilde{P_1}$ is corrupt and let us try to simulate the values returned by honest P_2, whenever queried by the adversary.

First, since the protocol reveals $\mathbf{w}_2$ whether P_2 aborts or not, the joint distribution of rejected transcript $(\mathbf{w}_2, c, \perp)$ has to be simulated. As mentioned earlier, there is no known way to simulate it; in fact, the honest verifier zero knowledge (HVZK) of FSwA is only proven for "non-aborting" cases in the original work by Lyubashevsky [62–64] and its successors. Note that the obvious fix where players hash the initial messages and only reveal them if there is no abort will not work here: the protocols need to *add* the initial messages together before obtaining the challenge c in order to reduce signature size, only the sum is included in the signature. So with this approach the initial messages must be known in the clear before the challenge can be generated.

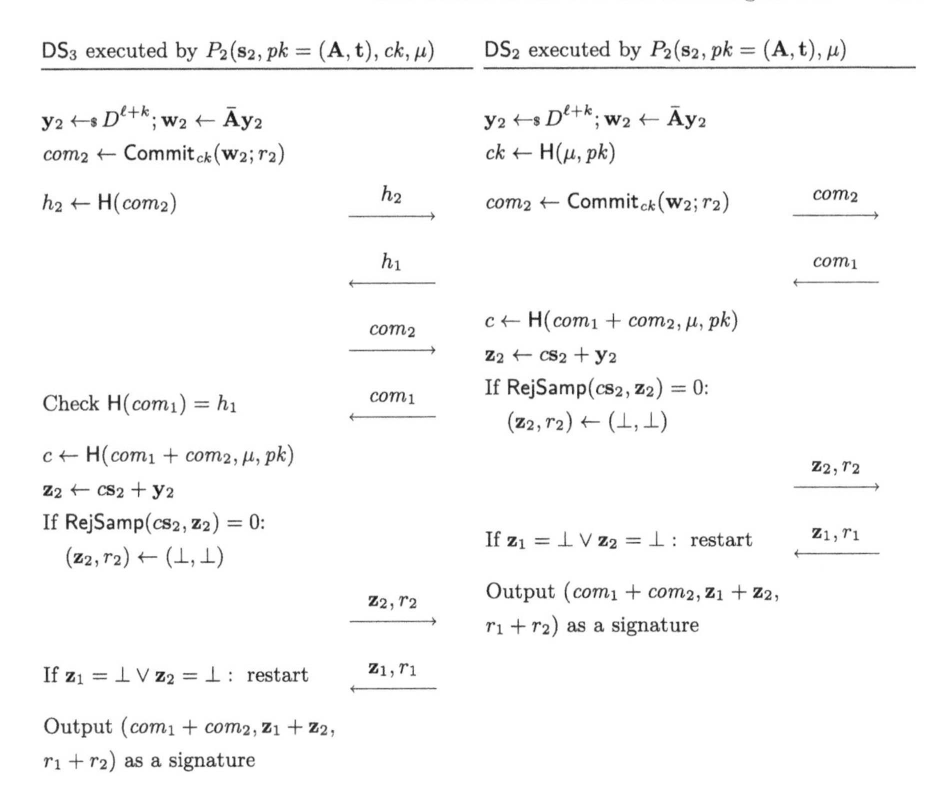

Fig. 1. Comparison of different instantiations of FSwA-based 2-party signing protocols

The second problem is more generic and could also occur in the standard Fiat–Shamir-style two party signing: if P_2 sends out $\mathbf{w}_2$ first, then the simulator does not know $\mathbf{w}_1$. In FS-style constructions, the usual strategy for signing oracle query simulation is to first sample a challenge c by itself, generate a simulated transcript $(\mathbf{w}_2, c, \mathbf{z}_2)$ by invoking a special HVZK simulator on c, and then program the random oracle H such that its output is fixed to a predefined challenge c. In the two-party setting, however, derivation of the *joint* challenge $c = \mathsf{H}(\mathbf{w}_1 + \mathbf{w}_2, \mu, pk)$ requires contribution from $\widetilde{P}_1$ and thus there is no way for the simulator to program H in advance. Not only the proof doesn't go through, but also this naive construction is amenable to a concrete attack, which allows malicious $\widetilde{P}_1$ to create a valid forgery by adaptively choosing $\mathbf{w}_1$ after seeing $\mathbf{w}_2$. In [30] we describe this attack relying on a variant of Wagner's generalized birthday problem [54,86].

Homomorphic Commitment to Simulate Aborts. We now present an intermediate provably secure protocol that circumvents the above issues. See DS_3 in Fig. 1. To address the first issue with aborts, each player P_j now commits to an initial Σ-protocol message $\mathbf{w}_j$ using an *additively homomorphic* commitment com_j. Thanks to the hiding property, each party leaks no useful information about $\mathbf{w}_j$ until the rejection sampling is successful, and thus it is now possible to simulate a rejected transcript $(com_j, c, \perp)$. Then P_j broadcasts a hash based commitment to com_j, to deal with the second issue. Once all parties have done this, com_j's are revealed in the next round and checked against the hashes. Once the com_j's are known, they can be added together in a meaningful way by the homomorphic property, and we then hash the sum and the message to get the challenge. The verification now receives a signature consisting of three elements $(com, \mathbf{z}, r)$ and simply checks that $\bar{\mathbf{A}}\mathbf{z} - c\mathbf{t} \pmod q$ and r form a correct opening to com, where the challenge is recomputed as $c \leftarrow \mathsf{H}(com, \mu, pk)$.

We note that the extra round for hash commitment is a standard technique, previously used in multiple three-round protocols, such as Nicolosi et al. [75] and Bellare and Neven [9] in the discrete log setting, and Bansarkhani and Sturm [4] in their FSwA-based instantiation. This way, the simulator for honest P_2 can successfully extract corrupt $\widetilde{P}_1$'s share com_1 by keeping track of incoming queries to H (when modeled as a random oracle), and program H such that $\mathsf{H}(com_1 + com_2, \mu, pk) := c$ before revealing com_2. For the completeness, in [30] we provide a formal security proof for DS_3 by showing a reduction to Module-LWE *without* relying on the forking lemma [9,79]. This is made possible by instantiating the construction with unconditionally binding commitment, which allows us to avoid rewinding the adversary and apply the *lossy identification* technique by Abdalla et al. [1].

One efficiency issue is, that the protocol has to be restarted until *all* parties pass the rejection sampling step simultaneously. All previous FSwA-based multi-signatures also had the same issues, but we can mitigate by running sufficiently many parallel executions of the protocol at once, or by carefully choosing the parameters for rejection sampling. To further reduce the number of aborts, we chose to instantiate the protocol with Dilithium-"G" [37] instead of the one submitted to NIST competition [65].

Trapdoor Commitment to Avoid the Extra Round. Although DS_3 is secure, the first round of interaction may seem redundant, since the parties are essentially "committing to a commitment". We show that the extra hash commitment round can be indeed dropped by adding a trapdoor feature to the commitment scheme, which allows the so-called *straight-line simulation* technique by Damgård [28]. We present our main two-round protocol DS_2 in Fig. 1. This way, the simulation of honest P_2 does not require the knowledge of corrupt $\widetilde{P}_1$'s commitment share; instead, the simulator can now simply send a commitment com_2 (to some random value) and then later equivocate to an arbitrary value using the known trapdoor td associated with a trapdoored commitment key tck. Concretely, the simulator need not program the random oracle this time, and instead derives a challenge $c \leftarrow \mathsf{H}(com_1 + com_2, \mu, pk)$ as the real honest party would do. Now the simulator invokes a (special) HVZK simulator with c as input, to obtain a transcript $(\mathbf{w}_2, c, \mathbf{z}_2)$. With some constant probability it equivocates com_2 to $\mathbf{w}_2$, or otherwise sends out $\perp$ to simulate aborts. We also stress that the *per-message commitment key* $ck \leftarrow \mathsf{H}(\mu, pk)$ is crucial in the two-round protocol; if a single ck is used across all signing attempts, then a concurrent attack similar to the one against the naive construction becomes applicable. Unlike the three-round protocol, we present a security proof relying on the forking lemma and we reduce the security to both Module-SIS and Module-LWE assumptions; since a trapdoor commitment can at most be computationally binding, we must extract from the adversary two different openings to the same commitment in order to be able to reduce security to the binding property. We leave for future work a tighter security proof, as well as a proof in the quantum random oracle model. We can now convert to a two-round multi-signature scheme in the plain public key model: following Bellare–Neven [9] the protocol now generates *per-user challenges* $c_j = \mathsf{H}(\mathbf{t}_j, \sum_j com_j, \mu, L)$ for each user's public key $\mathbf{t}_j \in L$, instead of interactively generating the fixed joint public key $\mathbf{t}$ in advance. The verification algorithm is adjusted accordingly: given $(com, \mathbf{z}, r)$ and a list of public keys L, the verifier checks that $\bar{\mathbf{A}}\mathbf{z} - \sum_j c_j \mathbf{t}_j \pmod q$ and r form a correct opening to com, where c_j's are recomputed as in the signing protocol.

1.3 Related Work

The FSwA paradigm was first proposed by Lyubashevsky [62,63] and many efficient signature schemes following this framework have been devised, such as GLP [53], BLISS [36], Dilithium [65] and qTESLA [14]. Bansarkhani and Sturm [4] extended GLP signature and proposed the first multi-signature following the FSwA paradigm. Since then several variants appeared in the literature: four-round protocol with public key aggregation [67], three-round protocol with tight security proof [42] and proof in QROM [43], ID-based blind multi-signature [85] and ID-based proxy multi-signature [83]. However, as mentioned earlier the security proofs for all these multi-signatures are either incomplete or rely on a non-standard heuristic assumption. Choi and Kim [22] proposed a linearly homomorphic multi-signature from lattices trapdoors. Kansal and Dutta [55] constructed a single-round multi-signature scheme relying on the hardness of SIS, which was soon after broken by Liu et al. [61]. Several lattice-based threshold *ring signatures* exist in the literature, such as Cayrel et al. [21], Bettaieb and Schrek [13], and Torres et al. [84]. Döroz et al. [34] devised lattice-based *aggregate signature schemes* relying on rejection sampling. Very recently, Esgin et al. [39] developed FSwA-based *adaptor signatures* with application to blockchains.

Our two-round protocols rely on trapdoor commitment to enable the straight-line simulation of ZK. The trick is originated in a concurrent ZK proof by Damgård [28] and similar ideas have been extensively used in the ZK literature [12,23–25], to turn honest verifier ZK proof into full-fledged ZK. Moreover, recent efficient lattice-based ZK proofs [16,31,40,41,87] also make use of Baum et al.'s additively homomorphic commitment. The issue of revealing the first "commit" message in the FSwA framework has been also discussed by Barthe et al. [5] in the context of masking countermeasure against side-channel attacks, and they used Baum et al.'s commitment to circumvent the issue. The homomorphic lattice-based trapdoor commitment could also be instantiated with

GSW-FHE [51], homomorphic trapdoor functions [52], Chameleon hash [18,38] or mercurial commitment [58].

Comparison with Bendlin et al. [10] An entirely different approach to constructing threshold signatures based on lattices relies not on the Fiat–Shamir with aborts paradigm, but on GPV hash-and-sign signatures [50]. This approach was introduced by Bendlin et al. in [10], who described how to implement Peikert's hash-and-sign signatures [78] in a multiparty setting. Compared to the approach in this paper, it has the advantage of realizing the same distributed signature scheme (e.g., with the same size bound for verification) independently of the number of parties, and in particular, signature size does not grow with the number of parties. Moreover, it supports more general access structure than the full threshold considered in this paper (although their protocol does not withstand dishonest majority for the sake of information-theoretic security, while our protocol does tolerate up to $n-1$ corrupt parties). Its main downside, however, is that the most expensive part of Peikert's signing algorithm, namely the offline lattice Gaussian sampling phase, is carried out using *generic multiparty computation* (this is the first step of the protocol π_{Perturb} described in [10, Fig. 23]). This makes it difficult to estimate the concrete efficiency of Bendlin et al.'s protocol, but since the Peikert signature scheme is fairly costly even in a single-user setting, the protocol is unlikely to be practical.

In contrast, while our protocols do use discrete Gaussian sampling, it is only carried out *locally by each party*, and it is Gaussian sampling over $\mathbb{Z}$ rather than a lattice, which is considerably less costly. Furthermore, while we also use lattice trapdoors as a proof technique in the trapdoor commitment scheme of our two-round protocol, trapdoor Gaussian sampling is never carried out in the actual protocol, only in the simulation (the actual protocol has no trapdoor). Thus, our protocols entirely avoid the expensive machinery present in Bendlin et al.'s scheme, and have a fully concrete instantiation (at the cost of signatures increasing in size with the number of parties).

2 Preliminaries

Notations. For positive integers a and b such that $a < b$ we use the integer interval notation $[a, b]$ to denote $\{a, a+1, \ldots, b\}$; we use $[b]$ as shorthand for $[1, b]$. If S is a set we write $s \leftarrow_\$ S$ to indicate sampling s from the uniform distribution defined over S; if D is a probability distribution we write $s \leftarrow_\$ D$ to indicate sampling s from the distribution D; if we are explicit about the set S over which the distribution D is defined then we write $D(S)$; if $\mathcal{A}$ is an algorithm we write $s \leftarrow \mathcal{A}$ to indicate assigning an output from $\mathcal{A}$ to s.

2.1 Polynomial Rings and Discrete Gaussian Distribution

In this paper most operations work over rings $R = \mathbb{Z}[X]/(f(X))$ and $R_q = \mathbb{Z}_q[X]/(f(X))$, where q is a modulus, N is a power of two defining the degree of $f(X)$, and $f(X) = X^N + 1$ is the $2N$-th cyclotomic polynomial. Following [37], we consider *centered modular reduction* mod $^{\pm}q$: for any $v \in \mathbb{Z}_q$, $v' = v \mod {}^{\pm}q$ is defined to be a unique integer in the range $[-\lfloor q/2 \rfloor, \lfloor q/2 \rfloor]$ such that $v' = v \mod q$. We define the norm of $v \in \mathbb{Z}_q$ such that $\|v\| := |v \mod {}^{\pm}q|$. Now we define the L^p-norm for a (vector of) ring element $\mathbf{v} = (\sum_{i=0}^{N-1} v_{i,1}X^i, \ldots, \sum_{i=0}^{N-1} v_{i,m}X^i)^T \in R^m$ as follows:

$$\|\mathbf{v}\|_p := \left\|(v_{0,1}, \ldots, v_{N-1,1}, \ldots, v_{0,m}, \ldots, v_{N-1,m})^T\right\|_p.$$

We rely on the following *key set* $S_\eta \subseteq R$ parameterized by $\eta \geq 0$ consisting of small polynomials: $S_\eta = \{x \in R : \|x\|_\infty \leq \eta\}$. Moreover the *challenge set* $C \subseteq R$ parameterized by $\kappa \geq 0$ consists of small and sparse polynomials, which will be used as the image of random oracle H_0: $C = \{c \in R : \|c\|_\infty = 1 \wedge \|c\|_1 = \kappa\}$. The discrete Gaussian distribution over R^m is defined as follows.

Definition 1 (Discrete Gaussian Distribution over R^m). *For* $\mathbf{x} \in R^m$*, let* $\rho_{\mathbf{v},s}(\mathbf{x}) = \exp\left(-\pi \|\mathbf{x} - \mathbf{v}\|_2^2 / s^2\right)$ *be a* Gaussian function *of parameters* $\mathbf{v} \in R^m$ *and* $s \in \mathbb{R}$*. The* discrete Gaussian distribution $D^m_{\mathbf{v},s}$ *centered at* $\mathbf{v}$ *is*

$$D^m_{\mathbf{v},s}(\mathbf{x}) := \rho_{\mathbf{v},s}(\mathbf{x}) / \rho_{\mathbf{v},s}(R^m)$$

where $\rho_{\mathbf{v},s}(R^m) = \sum_{\mathbf{x} \in R^m} \rho_{\mathbf{v},s}(\mathbf{x})$.

In what follows we omit the subscript $\mathbf{v}$ if $\mathbf{v} = \mathbf{0}$ and write D^m_s as a shorthand. When s exceeds the so-called *smoothing parameter* $\eta(R^m) \leq \omega(\sqrt{\log(mN)})$ of the ambient space, then the discrete Gaussians $D_{R^m - \mathbf{v},s} = D^m_{\mathbf{v},s} - \mathbf{v}$ supported on all cosets of R^m are statistically close, and hence D^m_s behaves qualitatively like a continuous Gaussian of standard deviation $\sigma = s/\sqrt{2\pi}$. The condition on s will be satisfied for all the discrete Gaussians in this paper, and hence $\sigma = s/\sqrt{2\pi}$ will be called the standard deviation (even though it technically holds only up to negligible error). For the same reason, we will always be in a setting where the following fact [72, Theorem 3.3][40, Lemma 9] holds.

Lemma 1 (Sum of Discrete Gaussian Samples). *Suppose s exceeds the smoothing parameter by a factor $\geq \sqrt{2}$. Let $\mathbf{x}_i$ for $i \in [n]$ be independent samples from the distribution D^m_s. Then the distribution of $\mathbf{x} = \sum_i \mathbf{x}_i$ is statistically close to $D^m_{s\sqrt{n}}$.*

2.2 Lattice Problems

Below we define two standard lattice problems over rings: module short integer solution (MSIS) and learning with errors (MLWE). We also call them MSIS/MLWE *assumption* if for any probabilistic polynomial-time adversaries the probability that they can solve a given problem is negligible.

Definition 2 ($\mathsf{MSIS}_{q,k,\ell,\beta}$ problem). *Given a random matrix* $\mathbf{A} \leftarrow_\$ R_q^{k \times \ell}$ *find a vector* $\mathbf{x} \in R_q^{\ell+k} \setminus \{\mathbf{0}\}$ *such that* $[\mathbf{A}|\mathbf{I}] \cdot \mathbf{x} = \mathbf{0}$ *and* $\|\mathbf{x}\|_2 \leq \beta$.

Definition 3 ($\mathsf{MLWE}_{q,k,\ell,\eta}$ problem). *Given a pair* $(\mathbf{A}, \mathbf{t}) \in R_q^{k \times \ell} \times R_q^k$ *decide whether it was generated uniformly at random from* $R_q^{k \times \ell} \times R_q^k$*, or it was generated in a way that* $\mathbf{A} \leftarrow_\$ R_q^{k \times \ell}, \mathbf{s} \leftarrow_\$ S_\eta^{\ell+k}$ *and* $\mathbf{t} := [\mathbf{A}|\mathbf{I}] \cdot \mathbf{s}$.

2.3 Fiat–Shamir with Aborts Framework and Dilithium-G

Algorithm 1. Key generation

Require: $pp = (R_q, k, \ell, \eta, B, s, M)$
Ensure: (sk, pk)
1: $\mathbf{A} \leftarrow_\$ R_q^{k\times\ell}$
2: $\bar{\mathbf{A}} := [\mathbf{A}|\mathbf{I}] \in R_q^{k\times(\ell+k)}$
3: $(\mathbf{s}_1, \mathbf{s}_2) \leftarrow_\$ S_\eta^\ell \times S_\eta^k; \mathbf{s} := \begin{bmatrix}\mathbf{s}_1\\ \mathbf{s}_2\end{bmatrix}$
4: $\mathbf{t} := \bar{\mathbf{A}}\mathbf{s}$
5: $sk := \mathbf{s}$
6: $pk := (\bar{\mathbf{A}}, \mathbf{t})$
7: **return** (sk, pk)

Algorithm 3. Signature generation

Require: $sk, \mu, pp = (R_q, k, \ell, \eta, B, s, M)$
Ensure: valid signature pair $(\mathbf{z}, \mathbf{c})$
1: $(\mathbf{y}_1, \mathbf{y}_2) \leftarrow_\$ D_s^\ell \times D_s^k; \mathbf{y} := \begin{bmatrix}\mathbf{y}_1\\ \mathbf{y}_2\end{bmatrix}$
2: $\mathbf{w} := \bar{\mathbf{A}}\mathbf{y}$
3: $c \leftarrow \mathsf{H}_0(\mathbf{w}, \mu, pk)$
4: $\mathbf{z} := c\mathbf{s} + \mathbf{y}$
5: With prob. $\min\left(1, D_s^{\ell+k}(\mathbf{z})/(M \cdot D_{c\mathbf{s},s}^{\ell+k}(\mathbf{z}))\right)$:
6:     **return** $(\mathbf{z}, c)$
7: Restart otherwise

Algorithm 2. Signature verification

Require: $pk, (\mathbf{z}, c), \mu, pp$
1: If $\|\mathbf{z}\|_2 \leq B$ and $c = \mathsf{H}_0(\bar{\mathbf{A}}\mathbf{z} - c\mathbf{t}, \mu, pk)$:
2:     **return** 1
3: Otherwise: **return** 0

Algorithm 4. $\mathsf{Trans}(sk, c)$

1: $\mathbf{y} \leftarrow_\$ D_s^{\ell+k}$
2: $\mathbf{w} := \bar{\mathbf{A}}\mathbf{y}$
3: $\mathbf{z} := c\mathbf{s} + \mathbf{y}$
4: With prob. $\min\left(1, D_s^{\ell+k}(\mathbf{z})/(M \cdot D_{c\mathbf{s},s}^{\ell+k}(\mathbf{z}))\right)$:
5:     **return** $(\mathbf{w}, c, \mathbf{z})$
6: Otherwise:
7:     **return** $(\perp, c, \perp)$

Algorithm 5. $\mathsf{SimTrans}(pk, c)$

1: $\mathbf{z} \leftarrow_\$ D_s^{\ell+k}$
2: $\mathbf{w} := \bar{\mathbf{A}}\mathbf{z} - c\mathbf{t}$
3: With prob. $1/M$:
4:     **return** $(\mathbf{w}, c, \mathbf{z})$
5: Otherwise:
6:     **return** $(\perp, c, \perp)$

We present a non-optimized version of Dilithium-G signature scheme in Algorithms 1 to 3, on which we base our distributed signing protocols. The random oracle is defined as $\mathsf{H}_0 : \{0,1\}^* \to C$. Due to [63, Lemma 4.4] we restate below, the maximum L^2-norm of the signature $\mathbf{z} \in R^{\ell+k}$ is set to $B = \gamma\sigma\sqrt{(\ell+k)N}$, where the parameter $\gamma > 1$ is chosen such that the probability $\gamma^{(\ell+k)N} e^{(\ell+k)N(1-\gamma^2)/2}$ is negligible.

Lemma 2. *For any* $\gamma > 1$, $\Pr[\|\mathbf{z}\|_2 > \gamma\sigma\sqrt{mN} : \mathbf{z} \leftarrow_\$ D_s^m] < \gamma^{mN} e^{mN(1-\gamma^2)/2}$.

The following claim by Lyubashevsky (adapted from [63, Lemma 4.5]) is crucial for the signing oracle of FSwA to be simulatable, and also to decide the standard deviation σ as well as the expected number of repetitions M. For instance, setting $\alpha = 11$ and $t = 12$ leads to $M \approx 3$. Although M is asymptotically superconstant, t increases very slowly in practice, and hence M behaves essentially like a constant for practical security parameters (in the literature, it is often taken as 12 to ensure $\epsilon < 2^{-100}$, thereby ensuring > 100 bits of security).

Lemma 3. *For* $V \subseteq R^m$ *let* $T = \max_{\mathbf{v}\in V} \|\mathbf{v}\|_2$. *Fix some* t *such that* $t = \omega(\sqrt{\log(mN)})$ *and* $t = o(\log(mN))$. *If* $\sigma = \alpha T$ *for any positive* α, *then*

$$\Pr[M \geq D_s^m(\mathbf{z})/D_{\mathbf{v},s}^m(\mathbf{z}) : \mathbf{z} \leftarrow_\$ D_s^m(\mathbf{z})] \geq 1 - \epsilon$$

where $M = e^{t/\alpha+1/(2\alpha^2)}$ *and* $\epsilon = 2e^{-t^2/2}$.

We now present a supporting lemma which is required for Dilithium-G to be UF-CMA secure. This is almost a direct consequence of Lemma 3 and a similar result appears in [56, Lemma 4.3] to prove the security of Dilithium signature instantiated with the uniform distribution. We remark that the simulator in Algorithm 5 can only simulate transcripts of non-abort executions in the underlying *interactive* Σ-protocol; in fact, if Trans output $\mathbf{w}$ in case of rejection as it's done in the interactive protocol then there is no known method to simulate the *joint distribution* of $(\mathbf{w}, c, \perp)$ [11,64] (without assuming some ad-hoc assumptions like rejection-DCK [5] or rejected-LWE [43]). We give a proof in the full version of this paper [30].

Lemma 4 (Non-abort Special Honest Verifier Zero Knowledge). *Let* $m = \ell+k$ *and* $T = \max_{c\in C,\mathbf{s}\in S_\eta^m} \|c\cdot\mathbf{s}\|_2$. *Fix some* t *such that* $t = \omega(\sqrt{\log(mN)})$ *and* $t = o(\log(mN))$. *If* $\sigma = \alpha T$ *for any positive* α, *then for any* $c \in C$ *and* $\mathbf{s} \in S_\eta^m$, *the output distribution of* $\mathsf{Trans}(sk, c)$ *(Algorithm 4) is within statistical distance* ϵ/M *of the output distribution of* $\mathsf{SimTrans}(pk, c)$ *(Algorithm 5), where* $M = e^{t/\alpha+1/(2\alpha^2)}$ *and* $\epsilon = 2e^{-t^2/2}$. *Moreover,* $\Pr[\mathsf{Trans}(\mathbf{s}, c) \neq (\perp, c, \perp)] \geq (1-\epsilon)/M$.

2.4 Trapdoor Homomorphic Commitment Scheme

Below we formally define a trapdoor commitment scheme. In [30] we also define standard security requirements like hiding and binding, as well as the two additional properties required by our protocols: additive homomorphism and uniform key. The lattice-based commitments described in Sect. 4 indeed satisfy all of them. The uniform property is required since our protocols rely on commitment key derivation via random oracles mapping to a key space S_{ck}, and thus its output distribution should look like the one from CGen. Many other standard schemes like Pedersen commitment [77] trivially satisfy this property. The additive homomorphism is also needed to preserve the algebraic structure of the first "commit" message of FSwA.

Definition 4 (Trapdoor Commitment Scheme). *A trapdoor commitment scheme* TCOM *consists of the following algorithms.*

- $\mathsf{CSetup}(1^\lambda) \to cpp$: *The setup algorithm outputs a public parameter* cpp *defining sets* $S_{ck}, S_{msg}, S_r, S_{com}$, *and* S_{td} *and the distribution* $D(S_r)$ *from which the randomness is sampled.*
- $\mathsf{CGen}(cpp) \to ck$: *The key generation algorithm that samples a commitment key from* S_{ck}.
- $\mathsf{Commit}_{ck}(msg; r) \to com$: *The committing algorithm that takes a message* $msg \in S_{msg}$ *and randomness* $r \in S_r$ *as input and outputs* $com \in S_{com}$. *We simply write* $\mathsf{Commit}_{ck}(msg)$ *when it uses* r *sampled from* $D(S_r)$.
- $\mathsf{Open}_{ck}(com, r, msg) \to b$: *The opening algorithm outputs* $b = 1$ *if the input tuple is valid, and* $b = 0$ *otherwise.*

- $\mathsf{TCGen}(cpp) \rightarrow (tck, td)$: *The trapdoor key generation algorithm that outputs* $tck \in S_{ck}$ *and the trapdoor* $td \in S_{td}$.
- $\mathsf{TCommit}_{tck}(td) \rightarrow com$: *The trapdoor committing algorithm that outputs a commitment* $com \in S_{com}$.
- $\mathsf{Eqv}_{tck}(td, com, msg) \rightarrow r$: *The equivocation algorithm that outputs randomness* $r \in S_r$.

A trapdoor commitment is said to be secure if it is unconditionally hiding, computationally binding, and for any $msg \in S_{msg}$, *the statistical distance* ϵ_{td} *between* (ck, msg, com, r) *and* (tck, msg, com', r') *is negligible in* λ, *where* $cpp \leftarrow \mathsf{CSetup}(1^\lambda); ck \leftarrow \mathsf{CGen}(cpp); r \leftarrow_\$ D(S_r); com \leftarrow \mathsf{Commit}_{ck}(msg; r)$ *and* $(tck, td) \leftarrow \mathsf{TCGen}(cpp); com' \leftarrow \mathsf{TCommit}_{tck}(td); r' \leftarrow \mathsf{Eqv}_{tck}(td, com', msg)$.

2.5 Security Notions for n-out-of-n Signature and Multi-signature

We first define the n-out-of-n distributed signature protocol and its security notion. The game-based security notion below is based on the one presented by Lindell [59] for two-party signing protocol. Our definition can be regarded as its generalization to n-party setting. Following Lindell, we assume that the key generation can be invoked only once, while many signing sessions can be executed concurrently. The main difference is that, in our protocols all players have the same role, and therefore we fix wlog the index of honest party and challenger to n, who has to send out the message first in each round of interaction. This way, we assume that the adversary $\mathcal{A}$ who corrupts $P_1, \ldots, P_{n-1}$ is *rushing* by default (i.e., $\mathcal{A}$ is allowed to choose their own messages based on P_n's message).

Definition 5 (Distributed Signature Protocol). *A distributed signature protocol* DS *consists of the following algorithms.*

- $\mathsf{Setup}(1^\lambda) \rightarrow pp$: *The set up algorithm that outputs public parameters* pp *on a security parameter* λ *as input.*
- $\mathsf{Gen}_j(pp) \rightarrow (sk_j, pk)$ *for every* $j \in [n]$: *The interactive key generation algorithm that is run by party* P_j. *Each* P_j *runs the protocol on public parameters* pp *as input. At the end of the protocol* P_j *obtains a secret key share* sk_j *and public key* pk.
- $\mathsf{Sign}_j(sid, sk_j, pk, \mu) \rightarrow \sigma$ *for every* $j \in [n]$: *The interactive signing algorithm that is run by party* P_j. *Each* P_j *runs the protocol on session ID* sid, *its signing key share* sk_j, *public key* pk, *and message to be signed* μ *as input. We also assume that the algorithm can use any state information obtained during the key generation phase. At the end of the protocol* P_j *obtains a signature* σ *as output.*
- $\mathsf{Ver}(\sigma, \mu, pk) \rightarrow b$: *The verification algorithm that takes a signature, message, and a single public key* pk *and outputs* $b = 1$ *if the signature is valid and otherwise* $b = 0$.

$\mathsf{Exp}^{\mathsf{DS\text{-}UF\text{-}CMA}}_{\mathsf{DS}}(\mathcal{A})$	$\mathsf{Exp}^{\mathsf{MS\text{-}UF\text{-}CMA}}_{\mathsf{MS}}(\mathcal{A})$
1 : $Mset \leftarrow \emptyset$	1 : $Mset \leftarrow \emptyset$
2 : $pp \leftarrow \mathsf{Setup}(1^\lambda)$	2 : $pp \leftarrow \mathsf{Setup}(1^\lambda)$
3 : $(\mu^*, \sigma^*) \leftarrow \mathcal{A}^{\mathcal{O}^{\mathsf{DS}}_n(\cdot,\cdot)}(pp)$	3 : $(sk, pk) \leftarrow \mathsf{Gen}(pp)$
4 : $b \leftarrow \mathsf{Ver}(\mu^*, \sigma^*, pk)$	4 : $(\mu^*, \sigma^*, L^*) \leftarrow \mathcal{A}^{\mathcal{O}^{\mathsf{MS}}(\cdot,\cdot)}(pk, pp)$
5 : **return** $(b = 1) \wedge \mu^* \notin Mset$	5 : $b \leftarrow \mathsf{Ver}(\mu^*, \sigma^*, L^*)$
	6 : **return** $(b = 1) \wedge pk \in L^* \wedge (\mu^*, L^*) \notin Mset$

Fig. 2. DS-UF-CMA and MS-UF-CMA experiments. The oracles $\mathcal{O}^{\mathsf{DS}}_n$ and $\mathcal{O}^{\mathsf{MS}}$ are described in Figs. 3 and 4. In the left (resp. right) experiment, $Mset$ is the set of all inputs μ (resp. (μ, L)) such that (sid, μ) (resp. $(sid, (\mu, L))$) was queried by $\mathcal{A}$ to its oracle as the first query with identifier $sid \neq 0$ (resp with any identifier sid). Note that pk in the left experiment is the public verification key output by P_n when it completes $\mathsf{Gen}_n(pp)$.

Oracle $\mathcal{O}^{\mathsf{DS}}_n(sid, m)$

The oracle is initialized with public parameters pp generated by Setup algorithm. The variable $flag$ is initially set to false.

Key Generation Upon receiving $(0, m)$, if $flag = \mathsf{true}$ then return $\perp$. Otherwise do the following:

- If the oracle is queried with $sid = 0$ for the first time then it initializes a machine $\mathcal{M}_0$ running the instructions of party P_n in the distributed key generation protocol $\mathsf{Gen}_n(pp)$. If P_n sends the first message in the key generation protocol, then this message is the oracle reply.
- If $\mathcal{M}_0$ has been already initialized then the oracle hands the machine $\mathcal{M}_0$ the next incoming message m and returns $\mathcal{M}_0$'s reply. If $\mathcal{M}_0$ concludes with local output (sk_n, pk), then set $flag = \mathsf{true}$.

Signature Generation Upon receiving (sid, m) with $sid \neq 0$, if $flag = \mathsf{false}$ then return $\perp$. Otherwise do the following:

- If the oracle is queried with sid for the first time then parse the incoming message m as μ. It initializes a machine $\mathcal{M}_{sid}$ running the instructions of party P_n in the distributed signing protocol $\mathsf{Sign}_n(sid, sk_n, pk, \mu)$. The machine $\mathcal{M}_{sid}$ is initialized with the key share and any state information stored by $\mathcal{M}_0$ at the end of the key generation phase. The message μ to be signed is included in $Mset$. If P_n sends the first message in the signing protocol, then this message is the oracle reply.
- If $\mathcal{M}_{sid}$ has been already initialized then the oracle hands the machine $\mathcal{M}_{sid}$ the next incoming message m and returns the next message sent by $\mathcal{M}_{sid}$. If $\mathcal{M}_{sid}$ concludes with local output σ, then the output obtained by $\mathcal{M}_{sid}$ is returned.

Fig. 3. Honest party oracle for the distributed signing protocol.

Definition 6. (DS-UF-CMA **Security**). *A distributed signature protocol* DS *is said to be* DS-UF-CMA *(distributed signature unforgeability against chosen message attacks) secure, if for any probabilistic polynomial time adversary $\mathcal{A}$, its advantage*

$$\mathbf{Adv}^{\mathsf{DS\text{-}UF\text{-}CMA}}_{\mathsf{DS}}(\mathcal{A}) := \Pr\left[\mathsf{Exp}^{\mathsf{DS\text{-}UF\text{-}CMA}}_{\mathsf{DS}}(\mathcal{A}) \rightarrow 1\right]$$

is negligible in λ, where $\mathsf{Exp}^{\mathsf{DS\text{-}UF\text{-}CMA}}_{\mathsf{DS}}(\mathcal{A})$ is described in Fig. 2.

Oracle $\mathcal{O}^{\mathsf{MS}}(sid, m)$

The oracle is initialized with public parameters pp generated by Setup algorithm.

Signature Generation Upon receiving (sid, m) do the following:

- If the oracle is queried with sid for the first time then parse the incoming message m as (μ, L). If $pk \notin L$ then it returns $\perp$. Otherwise it initializes a machine $\mathcal{M}_{sid}$ running the instructions of party P in the multi-signature protocol $\mathsf{Sign}(sid, sk, pk, \mu, L)$. The machine $\mathcal{M}_{sid}$ is initialized with the key pair (sk, pk) and any state information obtained during $\mathsf{Gen}(pp)$. The pair (μ, L) is included in $Mset$. If P sends the first message in the signing protocol, then this message is the oracle reply.
- If $\mathcal{M}_{sid}$ has been already initialized then the oracle hands the machine $\mathcal{M}_{sid}$ the next incoming message m and returns the next message sent by $\mathcal{M}_{sid}$. If $\mathcal{M}_{sid}$ concludes, then the output obtained by $\mathcal{M}_{sid}$ is returned.

Fig. 4. Honest party oracle for the multi-signature protocol.

Next we define the standard security notion of multi-signature protocol in the plain public-key model. The following definitions are adapted from [9], but the syntax is made consistent with n-out-of-n signing. The main difference from the distributed signature is, that there is no interactive key generation protocol and the adversary is not required to fix its key pair at the beginning of the game. Accordingly, the adversary can dynamically choose a set of public keys involving the challenger's key, and query the signing oracle to receive signatures. On the other hand, assuming that key aggregation is not always supported the verification algorithm takes a set of public keys, instead of a single combined public key as in the prior case. We also note that n is now the number of *maximum* number of parties involved in a single execution of signing protocol, since the size of L may vary depending on a protocol instance.

Definition 7 (Multi-signature Protocol). *A multisignature protocol* MS *consists of the following algorithms.*

- $\mathsf{Setup}(1^\lambda) \to pp$: *The set up algorithm that outputs a public parameter pp on a security parameter λ as input.*
- $\mathsf{Gen}(pp) \to (sk, pk)$: *The non-interactive key generation algorithm that outputs a key pair on a public parameter pp as input.*
- $\mathsf{Sign}(sid, sk, pk, \mu, L) \to \sigma$: *The interactive signing algorithm that is run by a party P holding a key pair (sk, pk). Each P runs the protocol on session ID sid, its signing key sk, public key pk, message to be signed μ, and a set of co-signers' public keys L as input. At the end of the protocol P obtains a signature σ as output.*
- $\mathsf{Ver}(\sigma, \mu, L) \to b$: *The verification algorithm that takes a signature, message, and a set of public keys and outputs $b = 1$ if the signature is valid and otherwise $b = 0$.*

Definition 8 (MS-UF-CMA Security). *A multisignature protocol* MS *is said to be* MS-UF-CMA *(multisignature unforgeability against chosen message attacks)* *secure, if for any probabilistic polynomial time adversary $\mathcal{A}$, its advantage*

$$\mathbf{Adv}_{\mathsf{MS}}^{\mathsf{MS\text{-}UF\text{-}CMA}}(\mathcal{A}) := \Pr\left[\mathsf{Exp}_{\mathsf{MS}}^{\mathsf{MS\text{-}UF\text{-}CMA}}(\mathcal{A}) \to 1\right]$$

is negligible in λ, where $\mathsf{Exp}_{\mathsf{MS}}^{\mathsf{MS\text{-}UF\text{-}CMA}}(\mathcal{A})$ is described in Fig. 2.

3 DS_2: Two-Round n-out-of-n Signing from Module-LWE and Module-SIS

3.1 Protocol Specification and Overview

This section presents our main construction: provably secure two-round n-out-of-n protocol $\mathsf{DS}_2 = (\mathsf{Setup}, (\mathsf{Gen}_j)_{j\in[n]}, (\mathsf{Sign}_j)_{j\in[n]}, \mathsf{Ver})$, formally specified in Fig. 5. As mentioned in Sect. 2.5 all players have the same role and hence we only present n-th player's behavior. The protocol is built on top of additively homomorphic trapdoor commitment scheme TCOM with uniform keys (see Definition 4 and [30] for the formal definitions), and we will describe concrete instances of TCOM later in Sect. 4. We go over high-level ideas for each step below.

Table 1. Parameters for our distributed signature protocols.

Parameter	Description
n	Number of parties
N	A power of two defining the degree of $f(X)$
$f(X) = X^N + 1$	The $2N$-th cyclotomic polynomial
q	Prime modulus
$R = \mathbb{Z}[X]/(f(X))$	Cyclotomic ring
$R_q = \mathbb{Z}_q[X]/(f(X))$	Ring
k	The height of random matrices $\mathbf{A}$
ℓ	The width of random matrices $\mathbf{A}$
γ	Parameter defining the tail-bound of Lemma 2
$B = \gamma\sigma\sqrt{N(\ell + k)}$	The maximum L^2-norm of signature share $\mathbf{z}_j \in R^{\ell+k}$ for $j \in [n]$
$B_n = \sqrt{n}B$	The maximum L^2-norm of combined signature $\mathbf{z} \in R^{\ell+k}$
κ	The maximum L^1-norm of challenge vector c
$C = \{c \in R : \|c\|_\infty = 1 \wedge \|c\|_1 = \kappa\}$	Challenge space where $\lvert C\rvert = \binom{N}{\kappa}2^\kappa$
$S_\eta = \{x \in R : \|x\|_\infty \leq \eta\}$	Set of small secrets
$T = \kappa\eta\sqrt{N(\ell + k)}$	Chosen such that Lemma 4 holds
α	Parameter defining σ and M
$\sigma = s/\sqrt{2\pi} = \alpha T$	Standard deviation of the Gaussian distribution
$t = \omega(\sqrt{\log(mN)}) \wedge t = o(\log(mN))$	Parameter defining M such that Lemma 3 holds
$M = e^{t/\alpha+1/(2\alpha^2)}$	The expected number of restarts until a single party can proceed
$M_n = M^n$	The expected number of restarts until all n parties proceed simultaneously
cpp	Parameters for commitment scheme honestly generated with CSetup
l_1, l_2, l_4	Output bit lengths of random oracles H_1, H_2 and H_4

Parameter Setup. We assume that a trusted party invokes $\mathsf{DS}_2.\mathsf{Setup}(1^\lambda)$ that outputs a set of public parameters described in Table 1 as well as the parameter for commitment scheme *cpp* (which is obtained by internally invoking $\mathsf{TCOM.CSetup}(1^\lambda)$). Most parameters commonly appear in the literature about the Fiat–Shamir with aborts paradigm (e.g. [37,63]) and we therefore omit the details here. The bit length l_1 and l_2 should be sufficiently long for the random oracle commitments to be secure. The only additional parameters are B_n and M_n, which we describe below in Sect. 3.2.

Key Generation. The key generation $\mathsf{DS}_2.\mathsf{Gen}_n$ essentially follows the approach by Nicolosi et al. [75] for two-party Schnorr signing. Upon receiving public parameters, all participants first interactively generate a random matrix $\mathbf{A} \in R_q^{k\times\ell}$, a part of Dilithium-G public key. This can be securely done with simple random oracle commitments[2]; as long as there is at least one honest party sampling a matrix share correctly, the resulting combined matrix is guaranteed to follow the uniform distribution. For the exact same reason, the exchange of $\mathbf{t}_j$'s is also carried with the random oracle. This way, we can prevent the adversary from choosing some malicious public key share depending on the honest party's share (the so-called *rogue key attack* [70]). Furthermore, the party's index j is concatenated with the values to be hashed for the sake of "domain separation" [8]. This way, we prevent rushing adversaries from simply sending back the hash coming from the honest party and claiming that they know the preimage after seeing the honest party's opening.

Signature Generation. The first crucial step of $\mathsf{DS}_2.\mathsf{Sign}_n$ in Fig. 5 is commitment key generation at **Inputs** 3; in fact, if instead some fixed key *ck* was used for all signing attempts, one could come up with a sub-exponential attack that outputs a valid forgery with respect to the joint public key $\mathbf{t}$. In [30] we sketch a variant of the concurrent attack due to Drijvers et al. [35]. The original attack was against two-round Schnorr multi-signatures including BCJ scheme [3], but due to the very similar structure of FSwA-based lattice signatures an attack would become feasible against a fixed-key variant of DS_2. This motivates us to derive a message-dependent commitment key, following the mBCJ scheme of Drijvers et al.

Then the signing protocol starts by exchanging the first "commit" messages of Σ-protocol, from which all parties derive a single joint challenge $c \in C$ via a random oracle. As we discussed earlier no participants are allowed to reveal $\mathbf{w}_j$ until the rejection sampling phase, and instead they send its commitment com_j, which is to be opened only if the signature share $\mathbf{z}_j$ passes the rejection sampling. Finally, the com_j's and r_j's are added together in a meaningful way, thanks to the homomorphic property of commitment scheme.

[2] We remark that the "commitments" generated by H_1 and H_2 in Fig. 5 are not randomized, and therefore they are not hiding. In our protocol, however, all committed values have high min-entropy and this is indeed sufficient for the security proof to hold. Alternatively, one could cheaply turn them into full-fledged secure and extractable commitments by additionally hashing random strings that are to be sent out during the opening phase [76].

Protocol $\mathsf{DS}_2.\mathsf{Gen}_n(pp)$

The protocol is parameterized by public parameters described in Table 1 and relies on the random oracles $\mathsf{H}_1 : \{0,1\}^* \to \{0,1\}^{l_1}$ and $\mathsf{H}_2 : \{0,1\}^* \to \{0,1\}^{l_2}$.

Matrix Generation

1. Sample a random matrix share $\mathbf{A}_n \leftarrow\!\!\$\, R_q^{k\times\ell}$ and generate a random oracle commitment $g_n \leftarrow \mathsf{H}_1(\mathbf{A}_n, n)$. Send out g_n.
2. Upon receiving g_j for all $j \in [n-1]$ send out $\mathbf{A}_n$.
3. Upon receiving $\mathbf{A}_j$ for all $j \in [n-1]$:
   a. If $\mathsf{H}_1(\mathbf{A}_j, j) \neq g_j$ for some j then send out ABORT.
   b. Otherwise set public random matrix $\bar{\mathbf{A}} := [\mathbf{A}|\mathbf{I}] \in R_q^{k\times(\ell+k)}$, where $\mathbf{A} := \sum_{j\in[n]} \mathbf{A}_j$.

Key Pair Generation

1. Sample a secret key share $\mathbf{s}_n \leftarrow\!\!\$\, S_\eta^{\ell+k}$ and compute a public key share $\mathbf{t}_n := \bar{\mathbf{A}}\mathbf{s}_n$, respectively, and generate a random oracle commitment $g'_n \leftarrow \mathsf{H}_2(\mathbf{t}_n, n)$. Send out g'_n.
2. Upon receiving g'_j for all $j \in [n-1]$ send out $\mathbf{t}_n$.
3. Upon receiving $\mathbf{t}_j$ for all $j \in [n-1]$:
   a. If $\mathsf{H}_2(\mathbf{t}_j, j) \neq g'_j$ for some j then send out ABORT.
   b. Otherwise set a combined public key $\mathbf{t} := \sum_{j\in[n]} \mathbf{t}_j$

If the protocol does not abort, P_n obtains $(sk_n, pk) = (\mathbf{s}_n, (\mathbf{A}, \mathbf{t}))$ as local output.

Protocol $\mathsf{DS}_2.\mathsf{Sign}_n(sid, sk_n, pk, \mu)$

The protocol is parameterized by public parameters described in Table 1 and relies on the random oracles $\mathsf{H}_0 : \{0,1\}^* \to C$ and $\mathsf{H}_3 : \{0,1\}^* \to S_{ck}$. The protocol assumes that $\mathsf{DS}_2.\mathsf{Gen}_n(pp)$ has been previously invoked. If a party halts with ABORT at any point, then all $\mathsf{Sign}_n(sid, sk_n, pk, \mu)$ executions are aborted.

Inputs

1. P_n receives a unique session ID sid, $sk_n = \mathbf{s}_n$, $pk = (\mathbf{A}, \mathbf{t})$ and message $\mu \in \{0,1\}^*$ as input.
2. P_n verifies that sid has not been used before (if it has been, the protocol is not executed).
3. P_n locally computes a per-message commitment key $ck \leftarrow \mathsf{H}_3(\mu, pk)$.

Signature Generation P_n works as follows:

1. Compute the first message as follows.
   a. Sample $\mathbf{y}_n \leftarrow\!\!\$\, D_s^{\ell+k}$ and compute $\mathbf{w}_n := \bar{\mathbf{A}}\mathbf{y}_n$.
   b. Compute $com_n \leftarrow \mathsf{Commit}_{ck}(\mathbf{w}_n; r_n)$ with $r_n \leftarrow\!\!\$\, D(S_r)$.
   c. Send out com_n.
2. Upon receiving com_j for all $j \in [n-1]$ compute the signature share as follows.
   a. Set $com := \sum_{j\in[n]} com_j$.
   b. Derive a challenge $c \leftarrow \mathsf{H}_0(com, \mu, pk)$.
   c. Computes a signature share $\mathbf{z}_n := c\mathbf{s}_n + \mathbf{y}_n$.
   d. Run the rejection sampling on input $(c\mathbf{s}_n, \mathbf{z}_n)$, i.e., with probability

$$\min\left(1, D_s^{\ell+k}(\mathbf{z}_n)/(M \cdot D_{c\mathbf{s}_n,s}^{\ell+k}(\mathbf{z}_n))\right)$$

   send out $(\mathbf{z}_n, r_n)$; otherwise send out RESTART and go to 1.
3. Upon receiving RESTART from some party go to 1. Otherwise upon receiving $(\mathbf{z}_j, r_j)$ for all $j \in [n-1]$ compute the combined signature as follows
   a. For each $j \in [n-1]$ reconstruct $\mathbf{w}_j := \bar{\mathbf{A}}\mathbf{z}_j - c\mathbf{t}_j$ and validate the signature share:

$$\|\mathbf{z}_j\|_2 \leq B \quad \text{and} \quad \mathsf{Open}_{ck}(com_j, r_j, \mathbf{w}_j) = 1.$$

   If the check fails for some j then send out ABORT.
   b. Compute $\mathbf{z} := \sum_{j\in[n]} \mathbf{z}_j$ and $r := \sum_{j\in[n]} r_j$.

If the protocol does not abort, P_n obtains a signature $(com, \mathbf{z}, r)$ as local output.

Algorithm $\mathsf{DS}_2.\mathsf{Ver}((com, \mathbf{z}, r), \mu, pk)$

Upon receiving a message μ, signature $(com, \mathbf{z}, r)$, and combined public key $pk = (\mathbf{A}, \mathbf{t})$, generate a commitment key $ck \leftarrow \mathsf{H}_3(\mu, pk)$, derive a challenge $c \leftarrow \mathsf{H}_0(com, \mu, pk)$ and reconstruct $\mathbf{w} := \bar{\mathbf{A}}\mathbf{z} - c\mathbf{t}$. Then accept if $\|\mathbf{z}\|_2 \leq B_n$ and $\mathsf{Open}_{ck}(com, r, \mathbf{w}) = 1$.

Fig. 5. Distributed n-out-of-n signature scheme.

Verification and Correctness. Thanks to the linearity of underlying scheme and homomorphism of the commitment, the verifier only needs to validate the sum of signature shares, commitments and randomness. Here the Euclidean-norm bound B_n is set according to Lemma 1; if all parties honestly follow the protocol then the sum of n Gaussian shares is only $\sqrt{n}$ times larger (while if we employed the plain Dilithium as a base scheme then the bound would grow almost linearly). Hence together with the tail-bound of Lemma 2 it is indeed sufficient to set $B_n = \sqrt{n}B$ for the correctness to hold with overwhelming probability. To guarantee perfect correctness, the bound check can be also carried out during the signing protocol so that it simply restarts when the generated signature is too large (which of course only happens with negligible probability and shouldn't matter in practice).

3.2 Asymptotic Efficiency Analysis

Number of Aborts and Signature Size. As indicated in Table 1 the probability that all participants simultaneously proceed is $1/M_n = 1/M^n$, where $1/M$ is the probability that each party asks to proceed. To make M_n reasonably small, say $M_n = 3$, we should set $\alpha \geq 11n$ [37], leading to $\sigma \geq 11nT$. This already increases the bound B of each signature share linearly compared to a non-distributed signature like Dilithium-G. In addition, we should set the bound B_n for combined signature to $\sqrt{n}B$ for the correctness to hold, and thus the SIS solution that we find in the security reduction grows by a factor of $n^{3/2}$.

This translates to a signature size increase of a factor of roughly[3] $O(\log n)$, so the scaling in terms of the number of parties is reasonable. In addition, when using the trapdoor commitment scheme of Sect. 4, one can substantially reduce the signature size by using the common Fiat–Shamir trick of expressing the signature as $(c, \mathbf{z}, r)$ instead of $(com, \mathbf{z}, r)$, and carrying out the verification by first recomputing the commitment using the randomness r, and then checking the consistency of the challenge: $c \stackrel{?}{=} \mathsf{H}_0(com, \mu, pk)$. This keeps signature size close to the original Dilithium-G, despite the relatively large size of commitments.

We expect that a number of further optimizations are possible to improve the efficiency of this protocol in both asymptotic and concrete terms (e.g., by relying on stronger assumptions like (Mod-)NTRU), although this is left for further work. Accordingly, we also leave for further work the question of providing concrete parameters for the protocol, since the methodology for setting parameters is currently a moving target (e.g., the original parameters for Dilithium-G

[3] To be more precise, since the verification bound scales as $n^{3/2}$, one should also increase q by the same bound to avoid arithmetic overflow. This makes the MSIS problem harder, but the MLWE easier if the dimension is kept unchanged. To keep the same security level, one should therefore also increase N by a factor of $1 + O(\frac{\log n}{\log q_0})$ where q_0 is the value of q in the single-user setting. Therefore, one could in principle argue that signature size actually scales as $O(\log^2 n)$. However, one typically chooses $q_0 > 2^{20}$, and therefore even in settings with billions of parties, $\frac{\log n}{\log q_0} < 2$. Thus, one can effectively regard N as independent of n.

are not considered up-to-date), there is arguably no good point of comparison in the literature (in particular, no previous lattice-based two-round protocol), and again, a concrete instantiation would likely rely on stronger assumptions to achieve better efficiency anyway.

Round Complexity. If this protocol is used as it is, it only outputs a signature after the three rounds with probability $1/M_n$ (which is 1/3 with the parameters above). As a result, to effectively compute a signature, it has to be repeated M_n times on average, and so the expected number of rounds is in fact larger than 2 ($2M_n = 6$ in this case). One can of course adjust the parameters to reduce M_n to any constant greater than 1, or even to $1 + o(1)$ by picking e.g. $\alpha = \Theta(n^{1+\epsilon})$; this results in an expected number of rounds arbitrarily close to 2. Alternatively, one can keep a 2-round protocol while ensuring that the parties output a signature with overwhelming probability, simply by running sufficiently many parallel executions of the protocol at once: $\lambda / \left(\log \frac{M_n}{M_n - 1}\right)$ parallel executions suffice if λ is the security parameter.

3.3 Security

Theorem 1. *Suppose the trapdoor commitment scheme* TCOM *is secure, additively homomorphic and has uniform keys. For any probabilistic polynomial-time adversary* $\mathcal{A}$ *that initiates a single key generation protocol by querying* $\mathcal{O}_n^{\mathsf{DS}_2}$ *with sid* $= 0$*, initiates* Q_s *signature generation protocols by querying* $\mathcal{O}_n^{\mathsf{DS}_2}$ *with sid* $\neq 0$*, and makes* Q_h *queries to the random oracle* $\mathsf{H}_0, \mathsf{H}_1, \mathsf{H}_2, \mathsf{H}_3$*, the protocol* DS_2 *of Fig. 5 is* $\mathsf{DS\text{-}UF\text{-}CMA}$ *secure under* $\mathsf{MSIS}_{q,k,\ell+1,\beta}$ *and* $\mathsf{MLWE}_{q,k,\ell,\eta}$ *assumptions, where* $\beta = 2\sqrt{B_n^2 + \kappa}$*.*

We give a sketch of the security proof. The full proof with concrete security bound is given in [30]. We also remark that its multi-signature variant MS_2 [30] can be proven secure relying on essentially the same idea. We show that given any efficient adversary $\mathcal{A}$ that creates a valid forgery with non-negligible probability, one can break either $\mathsf{MSIS}_{q,k,\ell+1,\beta}$ assumption or computational binding of TCOM.

Key Generation Simulation. For the key generation phase, since the public key share of the honest signer $\mathbf{t}_n$ is indistinguishable from the vector sampled from R_q^k uniformly at random due to $\mathsf{MLWE}_{q,k,\ell,\eta}$ assumption, the honest party oracle simulator can replace $\mathbf{t}_n$ with such a vector. Therefore, the distribution of combined public key $\mathbf{t} = \sum_{j \in [n]} \mathbf{t}_j$ is also indistinguishable from the uniform distribution. Thanks to the random oracle commitment, after the adversary has submitted g'_j for each $j \in [n-1]$ one can extract the adversary's public key share $\mathbf{t}_j$, with which the simulator sets its share a posteriori $\mathbf{t}_n := \mathbf{t} - \sum_{j \in [n-1]} \mathbf{t}_j$ and programs the random oracle accordingly $\mathsf{H}_2(\mathbf{t}_n, n) := g'_n$. Using the same argument, one can set a random matrix share $\mathbf{A}_n := \mathbf{A} - \sum_{j \in [n-1]} \mathbf{A}_j$ given a resulting random matrix $\mathbf{A} \leftarrow_{\$} R_q^{k \times \ell}$. Now we can embed an instance of $\mathsf{MSIS}_{q,k,\ell+1,\beta}$, which is denoted as $[\mathbf{A}'|\mathbf{I}]$ with $\mathbf{A}' \leftarrow_{\$} R_q^{k \times (\ell+1)}$. Due to the way we simulated the joint public key $(\mathbf{A}, \mathbf{t})$ is uniformly distributed in $R_q^{k\times\ell} \times R_q^k$, so replacing it with a $\mathsf{MSIS}_{q,k,\ell+1,\beta}$ instance doesn't change the view of adversary at all, if $\mathbf{A}'$ is regarded as $\mathbf{A}' = [\mathbf{A}|\mathbf{t}]$.

Signature Generation Simulation. The oracle simulation closely follows the one for mBCJ [35]. Concretely, the oracle simulator programs H_3 so that for each signing query it returns tck generated via $(tck, td) \leftarrow \mathsf{TCGen}(cpp)$, and for the specific crucial query that is used to create a forgery it returns an actual commitment key $ck \leftarrow \mathsf{CGen}(cpp)$, which has been received by the reduction algorithm as a problem instance of the binding game. This way, upon receiving signing queries the oracle simulator can send out a "fake" commitment $com_n \leftarrow \mathsf{TCommit}_{tck}(td)$ at the first round, and then the known trapdoor td allows to later equivocate to a simulated first message of the Σ-protocol *after* the joint random challenge $c \in C$ has been derived; formally, it samples a simulated signature share $\mathbf{z}_n \leftarrow_{\$} D_s^{\ell+k}$ and then derives randomness as $r_n \leftarrow \mathsf{Eqv}_{tck}(td, com_n, \mathbf{w}_n := \bar{\mathbf{A}}\mathbf{z}_n - c\mathbf{t}_n)$. On the other hand, when the reduction obtains two openings after applying the forking lemma it can indeed break the binding property with respect to a real commitment key ck.

Forking Lemma. Our proof is relying on the forking lemma [9,79]. This is mainly because we instantiated the protocol with a trapdoor commitment, which inevitably implies that the binding is only computational. Hence to construct a reduction that breaks binding, we do have to make the adversary submit two valid openings for a single commitment under the same key, which seems to require some kind of rewinding technique. After applying the forking lemma, the adversary submits two forgeries with distinct challenges $c^* \neq \hat{c}^*$, with which we can indeed find a solution to $\mathsf{MSIS}_{q,k,\ell+1,\beta}$, or otherwise break computational binding with respect to ck. Concretely, after invoking the forking lemma, we obtain two forgeries $(com^*, \mathbf{z}^*, r^*, \mu^*)$ and $(\hat{com}^*, \hat{\mathbf{z}}^*, \hat{r}^*, \hat{\mu}^*)$ such that $c^* = \mathsf{H}(com^*, \mu, pk) \neq \mathsf{H}(\hat{com}^*, \hat{\mu}^*, pk) = \hat{c}^*$, $com^* = \hat{com}^*$, $\mu^* = \hat{\mu}^*$, and $\mathsf{H}(\mu^*, pk) = \mathsf{H}(\hat{\mu}^*, pk) = ck$. Since both forgeries are verified, we have $\|\mathbf{z}^*\|_2 \leq B_n \wedge \|\hat{\mathbf{z}}^*\|_2 \leq B_n$, and

$$\mathsf{Open}_{ck}(com^*, r^*, \bar{\mathbf{A}}\mathbf{z}^* - c^*\mathbf{t}) = \mathsf{Open}_{ck}(com^*, \hat{r}^*, \bar{\mathbf{A}}\hat{\mathbf{z}}^* - \hat{c}^*\mathbf{t}) = 1.$$

If $\bar{\mathbf{A}}\mathbf{z}^* - c^*\mathbf{t} \neq \bar{\mathbf{A}}\hat{\mathbf{z}}^* - \hat{c}^*\mathbf{t}$ then it means that computational binding is broken with respect to a commitment key ck. Suppose $\bar{\mathbf{A}}\mathbf{z}^* - c^*\mathbf{t} = \bar{\mathbf{A}}\hat{\mathbf{z}}^* - \hat{c}^*\mathbf{t}$. Rearranging it leads to

$$[\mathbf{A}|\mathbf{I}|\mathbf{t}] \begin{bmatrix} \mathbf{z}^* - \hat{\mathbf{z}}^* \\ \hat{c}^* - c^* \end{bmatrix} = \mathbf{0}.$$

Recalling that $[\mathbf{A}'|\mathbf{I}] = [\mathbf{A}|\mathbf{t}|\mathbf{I}]$ is an instance of $\mathsf{MSIS}_{q,k,\ell+1,\beta}$ problem, we have found a valid solution if $\beta = \sqrt{(2B_n)^2 + 4\kappa}$, since $\|\mathbf{z}^* - \hat{\mathbf{z}}^*\|_2 \leq 2B_n$ and $0 < \|\hat{c}^* - c^*\|_2 \leq \sqrt{4\kappa}$.

4 Lattice-Based Commitments

In this section, we describe possible constructions for the lattice-based commitment schemes used in our protocols. The three-round protocol DS_3 requires a statistically binding, computationally hiding homomorphic commitment scheme, whereas the two-round protocol DS_2 of Sect. 3 needs a statistically hiding *trapdoor* homomorphic commitment scheme. We show that both types of commitments can be obtained using the techniques of Baum et al. [7]. More precisely, the first type of commitment scheme is a simple variant of the scheme of [7], in a parameter range that ensures statistical instead of just computational binding. The fact that such a parameter choice is possible is folklore, and does in fact appear in an earlier version of [7], so we do not claim any novelty in that regard.

The construction of a lattice-based trapdoor commitment scheme does not seem to appear in the literature, but we show that it is again possible by combining [7] with Micciancio–Peikert style trapdoors [71]. To prevent statistical learning attacks on the trapdoor sampling, however, it is important to sample the randomness in the commitment according to a discrete Gaussian distribution, in contrast with Baum et al.'s original scheme.

4.1 Statistically Binding Commitment Scheme

We first describe a statistically binding commitment scheme from lattices. The scheme, described in [30], is a simple variant of the scheme from [7], that mainly differs in the choice of parameter regime: we choose parameters so as to make the underlying SIS problem vacuously hard, and hence the scheme statistically binding. Another minor change is the reliance on discrete Gaussian distributions, for somewhat more standard and compact LWE parameters. The correctness and security properties, as well as the constraints on parameters, are obtained as follows.

Correctness. By construction. We select the bound B as $\Omega(s \cdot \sqrt{m' \cdot N})$. By [71, Lemma 2.9], this ensures that the probability to retry in the committing algorithm is negligible.

Statistically Binding. Suppose that an adversary can construct a commitment $\mathbf{f}$ on two distinct messages $x \neq x'$, with the associated randomness $\mathbf{r}, \mathbf{r}'$. Since $x \neq x'$, the correctness condition ensures that $\mathbf{r}$ and $\mathbf{r}'$ are distinct and of norm $\leq B$, and satisfy $\hat{\mathbf{A}}_1 \cdot (\mathbf{r} - \mathbf{r}') \equiv 0 \pmod{q}$. This means in particular that there are non zero elements in the Euclidean ball $B_{m'}(0, 2B)$ of radius $2B$ in $R_q^{m'}$ that map to $\mathbf{0}$ in R_q^m. But this happens with negligible probability on the choice of $\hat{\mathbf{A}}_1$ when $|B_{m'}(0, 2B)|/q^{mN} = 2^{-\Omega(N)}$. Now $|B_{m'}(0, 2B)| = o\big((2\pi e/m'N)^{m'N/2} \cdot (2B)^{m'N}\big)$. Hence, picking for example $m' = 2m$, we get:

$$\frac{|B_{m'}(0, 2B)|}{q^{mN}} \ll \left(\frac{4\pi e \cdot B^2}{mNq}\right)^{mN},$$

and the condition is satisfied for example with $q > 8\pi e B^2/mN$.

Computationally Hiding. The randomness $\mathbf{r}$ can be written in the form $[\mathbf{r}_1 \; \mathbf{r}_2 \; \mathbf{s}]^T$ where $\mathbf{r}_1 \in R_q^m$, $\mathbf{r}_2 \in R_q^k$, $\mathbf{s} \in R_q^{m'-m-k}$ are all sampled from discrete

Gaussians of parameter s. The commitment elements then become:

$$\mathbf{f}_1 = \mathbf{r}_1 + \hat{\mathbf{A}}'_1 \cdot \begin{bmatrix} \mathbf{r}_2 \\ \mathbf{s} \end{bmatrix} \qquad \mathbf{f}_2 = \mathbf{r}_2 + \hat{\mathbf{A}}'_2 \cdot \mathbf{s} + \mathbf{x},$$

and distinguishing those values from uniform are clearly instances of decision MLWE. Picking $k = m$, $m' = 2m$, $s = \Theta(\sqrt{mN})$, $B = \Theta(mN)$, $q = \Theta\big((mN)^{3/2}\big)$ yields a simple instatiation with essentially standard security parameters.

4.2 Trapdoor Commitment Scheme

We now turn to the construction of a trapdoor commitment scheme with suitable homomorphic properties for our purposes. Our proposed scheme is described in Fig. 6. It is presented as a commitment for a *single* ring element $x \in R_q$. It is straightforward to extend it to support a vector $\mathbf{x} \in R_q^k$, but the efficiency gain from doing so is limited compared to simply committing to each coefficient separately, so we omit the extension.

We briefly discuss the various correctness and security properties of the scheme, together with the constraints that the various parameters need to satisfy. In short, we need to pick the standard deviation of the coefficients of the trapdoor matrix $\mathbf{R}$ large enough to ensure that the trapdoor key is statistically close to a normal commitment key; then, the randomness $\mathbf{r}$ in commitments should have large enough standard deviation to make commitments statistically close to uniform (and in particular statistically hiding), and also be sampleable using the trapdoor. These are constraints on $\bar{s}$ and s respectively. Finally, the bound B for verification should be large enough to accommodate valid commitments, and small enough compared to q to still make the scheme computationally binding (which corresponds to the hardness of an underlying Ring-SIS problem). Let us now discuss the properties one by one.

Correctness. By construction. We select the bound B as $C \cdot s \cdot \sqrt{N}(\sqrt{\ell + 2w} + 1)$ where $C \approx 1/\sqrt{2\pi}$ is the constant in [71, Lemma 2.9]. By that lemma, this ensures that the probability to retry in the committing algorithm is negligible (and in particular, the distribution of $\mathbf{r}$ after the rejection sampling is statistically close to the original Gaussian).

Computationally Binding. Suppose that an adversary can construct a commitment $\mathbf{f}$ on two distinct messages $x \neq x'$, with the associated randomness $\mathbf{r}, \mathbf{r}'$. Since $x \neq x'$, the correctness condition ensures that $\mathbf{r}$ and $\mathbf{r}'$ are distinct and of norm $\leq B$, and satisfy $\hat{\mathbf{A}}_1 \cdot (\mathbf{r} - \mathbf{r}') \equiv 0 \pmod{q}$ where $\hat{\mathbf{A}}_1$ is the first row of $\hat{\mathbf{A}}$. Therefore, the vector $\mathbf{z} = \mathbf{r} - \mathbf{r}'$ is a solution of the Ring-SIS problem with bound $2B$ associated with $\hat{\mathbf{A}}_1$ (or equivalently, to the $\mathsf{MSIS}_{q,1,\ell+2w-1,2B}$ problem), and finding such a solution is hard.

Note that since the first entry of $\hat{\mathbf{A}}_1$ is invertible, one can put it in the form $[\mathbf{A}|\mathbf{I}]$ without loss of generality to express it directly as an MSIS problem in the sense of Definition 2. It also reduces tightly to standard Ring-SIS, because a random row vector in $R_q^{\ell+2w}$ contains an invertible entry except with probability at most $(N/q)^{\ell+2w} = 1/N^{\Omega(\log N)}$, which is negligible.

Statistically Hiding. It suffices to make sure that

$$\hat{\mathbf{A}} \cdot D_s^{\ell+2w} \approx_s U(R_q^2)$$

with high probability on the choice of $\hat{\mathbf{A}}$. This is addressed by [66, Corollary 7.5], which shows that it suffices to pick $s > 2N \cdot q^{(2+2/N)/(\ell+2w)}$.

Indistinguishability of the Trapdoor. To ensure that the commitment key $\hat{\mathbf{A}}$ generated by TCGen is indistinguishable from a regular commitment key, it suffices to ensure that $\bar{\mathbf{A}}\mathbf{R}$ is statistically close to uniform. Again by [66, Corollary 7.5], this is guaranteed for $\bar{s} > 2N \cdot q^{(2+2/N)/\ell}$. By setting $\ell = w = \lceil \log_2 q \rceil$, we can thus pick $\bar{s} = \Theta(N)$.

Equivocability. It is clear that an $\mathbf{r}$ sampled according to the given lattice coset discrete Gaussian is distributed as in the regular commitment algorithm (up to the negligible statistical distance due to rejection sampling). The only constraint is thus on the Gaussian parameter that can be achieved by the trapdoor Gaussian sampling algorithm. By [71, Sect. 5.4], the constraint on s is as follows:

$$s \geq \|\mathbf{R}\| \cdot \omega(\sqrt{\log N})$$

where $\|\mathbf{R}\| \leq C \cdot \bar{s}\sqrt{N}(\sqrt{\ell} + \sqrt{2w} + 1)$ by [71, Lemma 2.9]. Thus, one can pick $s = \Theta(N^{3/2} \log^2 N)$.

From the previous paragraphs, we can in particular see that the trapdoor commitment satisfies the security requirements of Definition 4. Thus, to summarize, we have proved the following theorem.

Theorem 2. *The trapdoor commitment scheme of Fig. 6, with the following choice of parameters:*

$$\bar{s} = \Theta(N) \qquad s = \Theta(N^{3/2} \log^2 N) \qquad B = \Theta(N^2 \log^3 N)$$
$$\ell = w = \lceil \log_2 q \rceil \qquad q = N^{2+\varepsilon} \qquad (\varepsilon > 0,\ q \text{ prime}).$$

is a secure trapdoor commitment scheme assuming that the $\mathsf{MSIS}_{q,1,\ell+2w-1,2B}$ *problem is hard.*

Note that we did not strive for optimality in the parameter selection; a finer analysis is likely to lead to a more compact scheme.

Furthermore, although the commitment has a linear structure that gives it homomorphic features, we need to increase parameters slightly to support additive homomorphism: this is because the standard deviation of the sum of n randomness vectors $\mathbf{v}$ is $\sqrt{n}$ times larger. Therefore, B (and accordingly q) should be increased by a factor of $\sqrt{n}$ to accomodate for n-party additive homomorphism. For constant n, of course, this does not affect the asymptotic efficiency.

Protocol Lattice-based Commitment Scheme

$\mathsf{CSetup}(1^\lambda)$ takes a security parameter and outputs $cpp = (N, q, \bar{s}, s, B, \ell, w)$.

$\mathsf{CGen}(cpp)$ takes a commitment parameter and samples $\hat{a}_{1,1} \leftarrow\!\!\$\, R_q^\times$ (a uniform invertible element of R_q) and $\hat{a}_{1,j} \leftarrow\!\!\$\, R_q$ for $j = 2, \ldots, \ell + 2w$, $\hat{a}_{2,j} \leftarrow\!\!\$\, R_q$ for $j = 3, \ldots, \ell + 2w$. It then outputs:

$$\hat{\mathbf{A}} = \begin{bmatrix} \hat{a}_{1,1} & \hat{a}_{1,2} & \hat{a}_{1,3} & \cdots & \hat{a}_{1,\ell+2w} \\ 0 & 1 & \hat{a}_{2,3} & \cdots & \hat{a}_{2,\ell+2w} \end{bmatrix}$$

as ck.

$\mathsf{Commit}_{ck}(x)$ takes $x \in R_q$ and samples a discrete Gaussian vector of randomness $\mathbf{r} \leftarrow\!\!\$\, D_s^{\ell+2w}$. It then outputs

$$\mathbf{f} = \hat{\mathbf{A}} \cdot \mathbf{r} + \begin{bmatrix} 0 \\ x \end{bmatrix} \in R_q^2.$$

To ensure perfect correctness, retry unless $\|\mathbf{r}\|_2 \leq B$.

$\mathsf{Open}_{ck}(\mathbf{f}, \mathbf{r}, x)$ takes commitments, randomness and message, and checks that

$$\mathbf{f} = \hat{\mathbf{A}} \cdot \mathbf{r} + \begin{bmatrix} 0 \\ x \end{bmatrix} \quad \text{and} \quad \|\mathbf{r}\|_2 \leq B.$$

$\mathsf{TCGen}(cpp)$ takes a commitment parameter and samples $\bar{\mathbf{A}} \in R_q^{2 \times \ell}$ of the form:

$$\bar{\mathbf{A}} = \begin{bmatrix} \bar{a}_{1,1} & \bar{a}_{1,2} & \bar{a}_{1,3} & \cdots & \bar{a}_{1,\ell} \\ 0 & 1 & \bar{a}_{2,3} & \cdots & \bar{a}_{2,\ell} \end{bmatrix}$$

where all the $\bar{a}_{i,j}$ are uniform in R_q, except $\bar{a}_{1,1}$ which is uniform in $R_q^\times$. It also samples $\mathbf{R} \leftarrow\!\!\$\, D_{\bar{s}}^{\ell \times 2w}$ with discrete Gaussian entries. It then outputs $\mathbf{R}$ as the trapdoor td and $\hat{\mathbf{A}} = [\bar{\mathbf{A}} | \mathbf{G} - \bar{\mathbf{A}}\mathbf{R}]$ as the commitment key tck, where $\mathbf{G}$ is given by:

$$\mathbf{G} = \begin{bmatrix} 1 & 2 & \cdots & 2^{w-1} & 0 & 0 & \cdots & 0 \\ 0 & 0 & \cdots & 0 & 1 & 2 & \cdots & 2^{w-1} \end{bmatrix} \in R^{2 \times 2w}.$$

$\mathsf{TCommit}_{tck}(td)$ simply returns a uniformly random commitment $\mathbf{f} \leftarrow\!\!\$\, R_q^{2 \times 1}$. There is no need to keep a state.

$\mathsf{Eqv}_{tck}(\mathbf{R}, \mathbf{f}, x)$ uses the trapdoor discrete Gaussian sampling algorithm of Micciancio–Peikert [71, Algorithm 3] (or faster variants such as the one described in [45]) to sample $\mathbf{r} \leftarrow\!\!\$\, D_{\Lambda_{\mathbf{u}}^{\perp}(\hat{\mathbf{A}}), s}$ according to the discrete Gaussian of parameter s supported on the lattice coset:

$$\Lambda_{\mathbf{u}}^{\perp}(\hat{\mathbf{A}}) = \left\{ \mathbf{z} \in R^{\ell+2w} \ : \ \hat{\mathbf{A}} \cdot \mathbf{z} \equiv \mathbf{u} \pmod{q} \right\} \quad \text{where} \quad \mathbf{u} = \mathbf{f} - \begin{bmatrix} 0 \\ x \end{bmatrix}.$$

Fig. 6. Equivocable variant of the commitment from [7].

Acknowledgment. This research was supported by: the Concordium Blockchain Research Center, Aarhus University, Denmark; the Carlsberg Foundation under the Semper Ardens Research Project CF18-112 (BCM); the European Research Council (ERC) under the European Unions's Horizon 2020 research and innovation programme under grant agreement No 803096 (SPEC); the Danish Independent Research Council under Grant-ID DFF-6108-00169 (FoCC). We thank Cecilia Boschini for her insightful comments on an early form of our two-round protocol. We are grateful for helpful suggestions by anonymous reviewers.

References

1. Abdalla, M., Fouque, P.A., Lyubashevsky, V., Tibouchi, M.: Tightly secure signatures from Lossy identification schemes. J. Cryptol. **29**(3), 597–631
2. Abe, M., Fehr, S.: Adaptively secure Feldman VSS and applications to universally-composable threshold cryptography. In: Franklin, M. (ed.) CRYPTO 2004. LNCS, vol. 3152, pp. 317–334. Springer, Heidelberg (2004). https://doi.org/10.1007/978-3-540-28628-8_20
3. Bagherzandi, A., Cheon, J.H., Jarecki, S.: Multisignatures secure under the discrete logarithm assumption and a generalized forking lemma. In: ACM CCS 2008, pp. 449–458. ACM Press (2008)
4. El Bansarkhani, R., Sturm, J.: An efficient lattice-based multisignature scheme with applications to bitcoins. In: Foresti, S., Persiano, G. (eds.) CANS 2016. LNCS, vol. 10052, pp. 140–155. Springer, Cham (2016). https://doi.org/10.1007/978-3-319-48965-0_9
5. Barthe, G., et al.: Masking the GLP lattice-based signature scheme at any order. In: Nielsen, J.B., Rijmen, V. (eds.) EUROCRYPT 2018. LNCS, vol. 10821, pp. 354–384. Springer, Cham (2018). https://doi.org/10.1007/978-3-319-78375-8_12
6. Barthe, G., Belaïd, S., Espitau, T., Fouque, P.A., Rossi, M., Tibouchi, M.: GALACTICS: Gaussian sampling for lattice-based constant- time implementation of cryptographic signatures, revisited. In: ACM CCS 2019, pp. 2147–2164. ACM Press (2019)
7. Baum, C., Damgård, I., Lyubashevsky, V., Oechsner, S., Peikert, C.: More efficient commitments from structured lattice assumptions. In: Catalano, D., De Prisco, R. (eds.) SCN 2018. LNCS, vol. 11035, pp. 368–385. Springer, Cham (2018). https://doi.org/10.1007/978-3-319-98113-0_20
8. Bellare, M., Davis, H., Günther, F.: Separate your domains: NIST PQC KEMs, oracle cloning and read-only indifferentiability. In: Canteaut, A., Ishai, Y. (eds.) EUROCRYPT 2020. LNCS, vol. 12106, pp. 3–32. Springer, Cham (2020). https://doi.org/10.1007/978-3-030-45724-2_1
9. Bellare, M., Neven, G.: Multi-signatures in the plain public-key model and a general forking lemma. In: ACM CCS 2006, pp. 390–399. ACM Press (2006)
10. Bendlin, R., Krehbiel, S., Peikert, C.: How to share a lattice trapdoor: threshold protocols for signatures and (H)IBE. In: Jacobson, M., Locasto, M., Mohassel, P., Safavi-Naini, R. (eds.) ACNS 2013. LNCS, vol. 7954, pp. 218–236. Springer, Heidelberg (2013). https://doi.org/10.1007/978-3-642-38980-1_14
11. Benhamouda, F., Camenisch, J., Krenn, S., Lyubashevsky, V., Neven, G.: Better zero-knowledge proofs for lattice encryption and their application to group signatures. In: Sarkar, P., Iwata, T. (eds.) ASIACRYPT 2014. LNCS, vol. 8873, pp. 551–572. Springer, Heidelberg (2014). https://doi.org/10.1007/978-3-662-45611-8_29
12. Benhamouda, F., Krenn, S., Lyubashevsky, V., Pietrzak, K.: Efficient zero-knowledge proofs for commitments from learning with errors over rings. In: ESORICS 2015, Part I. LNCS, vol. 9326, pp. 305–325. Springer, Heidelberg. https://doi.org/10.1007/978-3-319-24174-6_16
13. Bettaieb, S., Schrek, J.: Improved lattice-based threshold ring signature scheme. In: Gaborit, P. (ed.) PQCrypto 2013. LNCS, vol. 7932, pp. 34–51. Springer, Heidelberg (2013). https://doi.org/10.1007/978-3-642-38616-9_3
14. Bindel, N., et al.: qTESLA. Technical report, National Institute of Standards and Technology

15. Boneh, D., et al.: Threshold cryptosystems from threshold fully homomorphic encryption. In: Shacham, H., Boldyreva, A. (eds.) CRYPTO 2018. LNCS, vol. 10991, pp. 565–596. Springer, Cham (2018). https://doi.org/10.1007/978-3-319-96884-1_19
16. Bootle, J., Lyubashevsky, V., Seiler, G.: Algebraic techniques for short(er) exact lattice-based zero-knowledge proofs. In: Boldyreva, A., Micciancio, D. (eds.) CRYPTO 2019. LNCS, vol. 11692, pp. 176–202. Springer, Cham (2019). https://doi.org/10.1007/978-3-030-26948-7_7
17. Canetti, R., Makriyannis, N., Peled, U.: UC non-interactive, proactive, threshold ecdsa. Cryptology ePrint Archive, Report 2020/492
18. Cash, D., Hofheinz, D., Kiltz, E., Peikert, C.: Bonsai trees, or how to delegate a lattice basis. In: Gilbert, H. (ed.) EUROCRYPT 2010. LNCS, vol. 6110, pp. 523–552. Springer, Heidelberg (2010). https://doi.org/10.1007/978-3-642-13190-5_27
19. Castagnos, G., Catalano, D., Laguillaumie, F., Savasta, F., Tucker, I.: Two-party ECDSA from Hash proof systems and efficient instantiations. In: Boldyreva, A., Micciancio, D. (eds.) CRYPTO 2019. LNCS, vol. 11694, pp. 191–221. Springer, Cham (2019). https://doi.org/10.1007/978-3-030-26954-8_7
20. Castagnos, G., Catalano, D., Laguillaumie, F., Savasta, F., Tucker, I.: Bandwidth-efficient threshold EC-DSA. In: Kiayias, A., Kohlweiss, M., Wallden, P., Zikas, V. (eds.) PKC 2020. LNCS, vol. 12111, pp. 266–296. Springer, Cham (2020). https://doi.org/10.1007/978-3-030-45388-6_10
21. Cayrel, P.-L., Lindner, R., Rückert, M., Silva, R.: A Lattice-based threshold ring signature scheme. In: Abdalla, M., Barreto, P.S.L.M. (eds.) LATINCRYPT 2010. LNCS, vol. 6212, pp. 255–272. Springer, Heidelberg (2010). https://doi.org/10.1007/978-3-642-14712-8_16
22. Choi, R., Kim, K.: Lattice-based multi-signature with linear homomorphism. In: 2016 Symposium on Cryptography and Information Security (SCIS 2016)
23. Ciampi, M., Ostrovsky, R., Siniscalchi, L., Visconti, I.: Delayed-input non-malleable zero knowledge and multi-party coin tossing in four rounds. In: Kalai, Y., Reyzin, L. (eds.) TCC 2017. LNCS, vol. 10677, pp. 711–742. Springer, Cham (2017). https://doi.org/10.1007/978-3-319-70500-2_24
24. Ciampi, M., Ostrovsky, R., Siniscalchi, L., Visconti, I.: Four-round concurrent non-malleable commitments from one-way functions. In: Katz, J., Shacham, H. (eds.) CRYPTO 2017. LNCS, vol. 10402, pp. 127–157. Springer, Cham (2017). https://doi.org/10.1007/978-3-319-63715-0_5
25. Ciampi, M., Persiano, G., Scafuro, A., Siniscalchi, L., Visconti, I.: Improved OR-composition of Sigma-protocols. In: Kushilevitz, E., Malkin, T. (eds.) TCC 2016. LNCS, vol. 9563, pp. 112–141. Springer, Heidelberg (2016). https://doi.org/10.1007/978-3-662-49099-0_5
26. Cozzo, D., Smart, N.P.: Sharing the LUOV: threshold post-quantum signatures. In: Albrecht, M. (ed.) IMACC 2019. LNCS, vol. 11929, pp. 128–153. Springer, Cham (2019). https://doi.org/10.1007/978-3-030-35199-1_7
27. Dalskov, A., Keller, M., Orlandi, C., Shrishak, K., Shulman, H.: Securing DNSSEC keys via threshold ECDSA from generic MPC. Cryptology ePrint Archive, Report 2019/889
28. Damgård, I.: Efficient concurrent zero-knowledge in the auxiliary string model. In: Preneel, B. (ed.) EUROCRYPT 2000. LNCS, vol. 1807, pp. 418–430. Springer, Heidelberg (2000). https://doi.org/10.1007/3-540-45539-6_30
29. Damgård, I., Jakobsen, T.P., Nielsen, J.B., Pagter, J.I., Østergård, M.B.: Fast threshold ECDSA with honest majority. Cryptology ePrint Archive, Report 2020/501

30. Damgård, I., Orlandi, C., Takahashi, A., Tibouchi, M.: Two-round n-out-of-n and multi-signatures and trapdoor commitment from lattices. Cryptology ePrint Archive, Report 2020/1110
31. del Pino, R., Lyubashevsky, V., Seiler, G.: Lattice-based group signatures and zero-knowledge proofs of automorphism stability. In: ACM CCS 2018. pp. 574–591. ACM Press (2018)
32. Doerner, J., Kondi, Y., Lee, E., shelat, A.: Secure two-party threshold ECDSA from ECDSA assumptions. In: 2018 IEEE Symposium on Security and Privacy, pp. 980–997. IEEE Computer Society Press (2018)
33. Doerner, J., Kondi, Y., Lee, E., Shelat, A.: Threshold ECDSA from ECDSA assumptions: the multiparty case. In: 2019 IEEE Symposium on Security and Privacy, pp. 1051–1066. IEEE Computer Society Press (2019)
34. Doröz, Y., Hoffstein, J., Silverman, J.H., Sunar, B.: MMSAT: a scheme for multimessage multiuser signature aggregation. Cryptology ePrint Archive, Report 2020/520
35. Drijvers, M., et al.: On the security of two-round multi-signatures. In: 2019 IEEE Symposium on Security and Privacy, pp. 1084–1101. IEEE Computer Society Press (2019)
36. Ducas, L., Durmus, A., Lepoint, T., Lyubashevsky, V.: Lattice signatures and bimodal Gaussians. In: Canetti, R., Garay, J.A. (eds.) CRYPTO 2013. LNCS, vol. 8042, pp. 40–56. Springer, Heidelberg (2013). https://doi.org/10.1007/978-3-642-40041-4_3
37. Ducas, L., Lepoint, T., Lyubashevsky, V., Schwabe, P., Seiler, G., Stehlé, D.: Crystals-dilithium: digital signatures from module lattices
38. Ducas, L., Micciancio, D.: Improved short lattice signatures in the standard model. In: Garay, J.A., Gennaro, R. (eds.) CRYPTO 2014. LNCS, vol. 8616, pp. 335–352. Springer, Heidelberg (2014). https://doi.org/10.1007/978-3-662-44371-2_19
39. Esgin, M.F., Ersoy, O., Erkin, Z.: Post-quantum adaptor signatures and payment channel networks. Cryptology ePrint Archive, Report 2020/845
40. Esgin, M.F., Steinfeld, R., Liu, J.K., Liu, D.: Lattice-based zero-knowledge proofs: new techniques for shorter and faster constructions and applications. In: Boldyreva, A., Micciancio, D. (eds.) CRYPTO 2019. LNCS, vol. 11692, pp. 115–146. Springer, Cham (2019). https://doi.org/10.1007/978-3-030-26948-7_5
41. Esgin, M.F., Steinfeld, R., Sakzad, A., Liu, J.K., Liu, D.: Short lattice-based one-out-of-many proofs and applications to ring signatures. In: Deng, R.H., Gauthier-Umaña, V., Ochoa, M., Yung, M. (eds.) ACNS 2019. LNCS, vol. 11464, pp. 67–88. Springer, Cham (2019). https://doi.org/10.1007/978-3-030-21568-2_4
42. Fukumitsu, M., Hasegawa, S.: A tightly-secure lattice-based multisignature. In: APKC@AsiaCCS 2019, pp. 3–11. ACM (2019)
43. Fukumitsu, M., Hasegawa, S.: A lattice-based provably secure multisignature scheme in quantum random oracle model. In: Nguyen, K., Wu, W., Lam, K.Y., Wang, H. (eds.) ProvSec 2020. LNCS, vol. 12505, pp. 45–64. Springer, Cham (2020). https://doi.org/10.1007/978-3-030-62576-4_3
44. Gagol, A., Kula, J., Straszak, D., Swietek, M.: Threshold ECDSA for decentralized asset custody. Cryptology ePrint Archive, Report 2020/498
45. Genise, N., Micciancio, D.: Faster Gaussian sampling for trapdoor lattices with arbitrary modulus. In: Nielsen, J.B., Rijmen, V. (eds.) EUROCRYPT 2018. LNCS, vol. 10820, pp. 174–203. Springer, Cham (2018). https://doi.org/10.1007/978-3-319-78381-9_7
46. Gennaro, R., Goldfeder, S.: Fast multiparty threshold ECDSA with fast trustless setup. In: ACM CCS 2018, pp. 1179–1194. ACM Press (2018)

47. Gennaro, R., Goldfeder, S.: One round threshold ECDSA with identifiable abort. Cryptology ePrint Archive, Report 2020/540
48. Gennaro, R., Goldfeder, S., Narayanan, A.: Threshold-optimal DSA/ECDSA signatures and an application to bitcoin wallet security. In: Manulis, M., Sadeghi, A.-R., Schneider, S. (eds.) ACNS 2016. LNCS, vol. 9696, pp. 156–174. Springer, Cham (2016). https://doi.org/10.1007/978-3-319-39555-5_9
49. Gennaro, R., Jarecki, S., Krawczyk, H., Rabin, T.: Secure distributed key generation for discrete-log based cryptosystems. J. Cryptol. **20**(1), 51–83
50. Gentry, C., Peikert, C., Vaikuntanathan, V.: Trapdoors for hard lattices and new cryptographic constructions. In: 40th ACM STOC, pp. 197–206. ACM Press
51. Gentry, C., Sahai, A., Waters, B.: Homomorphic encryption from learning with errors: conceptually-simpler, asymptotically-faster, attribute-based. In: Canetti, R., Garay, J.A. (eds.) CRYPTO 2013. LNCS, vol. 8042, pp. 75–92. Springer, Heidelberg (2013). https://doi.org/10.1007/978-3-642-40041-4_5
52. Gorbunov, S., Vaikuntanathan, V., Wichs, D.: Leveled fully homomorphic signatures from standard lattices. In: 47th ACM STOC, pp. 469–477. ACM Press
53. Güneysu, T., Lyubashevsky, V., Pöppelmann, T.: Practical lattice-based cryptography: a signature scheme for embedded systems. In: Prouff, E., Schaumont, P. (eds.) CHES 2012. LNCS, vol. 7428, pp. 530–547. Springer, Heidelberg (2012). https://doi.org/10.1007/978-3-642-33027-8_31
54. Howgrave-Graham, N., Joux, A.: New generic algorithms for hard knapsacks. In: Gilbert, H. (ed.) EUROCRYPT 2010. LNCS, vol. 6110, pp. 235–256. Springer, Heidelberg (2010). https://doi.org/10.1007/978-3-642-13190-5_12
55. Kansal, M., Dutta, R.: Round optimal secure multisignature schemes from lattice with public key aggregation and signature compression. In: Nitaj, A., Youssef, A. (eds.) AFRICACRYPT 2020. LNCS, vol. 12174, pp. 281–300. Springer, Cham (2020). https://doi.org/10.1007/978-3-030-51938-4_14
56. Kiltz, E., Lyubashevsky, V., Schaffner, C.: A concrete treatment of Fiat-Shamir signatures in the quantum random-oracle model. In: Nielsen, J.B., Rijmen, V. (eds.) EUROCRYPT 2018. LNCS, vol. 10822, pp. 552–586. Springer, Cham (2018). https://doi.org/10.1007/978-3-319-78372-7_18
57. Komlo, C., Goldberg, I.: FROST: flexible round-optimized Schnorr threshold signatures. Cryptology ePrint Archive, Report 2020/852
58. Libert, B., Nguyen, K., Tan, B.H.M., Wang, H.: Zero-knowledge elementary databases with more expressive queries. In: Lin, D., Sako, K. (eds.) PKC 2019. LNCS, vol. 11442, pp. 255–285. Springer, Cham (2019). https://doi.org/10.1007/978-3-030-17253-4_9
59. Lindell, Y.: Fast secure two-party ECDSA signing. In: Katz, J., Shacham, H. (eds.) CRYPTO 2017. LNCS, vol. 10402, pp. 613–644. Springer, Cham (2017). https://doi.org/10.1007/978-3-319-63715-0_21
60. Lindell, Y., Nof, A.: Fast secure multiparty ECDSA with practical distributed key generation and applications to cryptocurrency custody. In: ACM CCS 2018, pp. 1837–1854. ACM Press (2018)
61. Liu, Z.Y., Tseng, Y.F., Tso, R.: Cryptanalysis of a round optimal lattice-based multisignature scheme. Cryptology ePrint Archive, Report 2020/1172
62. Lyubashevsky, V.: Fiat-Shamir with aborts: applications to lattice and factoring-based signatures. In: Matsui, M. (ed.) ASIACRYPT 2009. LNCS, vol. 5912, pp. 598–616. Springer, Heidelberg (2009). https://doi.org/10.1007/978-3-642-10366-7_35

63. Lyubashevsky, V.: Lattice signatures without trapdoors. In: Pointcheval, D., Johansson, T. (eds.) EUROCRYPT 2012. LNCS, vol. 7237, pp. 738–755. Springer, Heidelberg (2012). https://doi.org/10.1007/978-3-642-29011-4_43
64. Lyubashevsky, V.: Lattice-based zero-knowledge and applications. CIS 2019
65. Lyubashevsky, V., et al.: CRYSTALS-DILITHIUM. Technical report, National Institute of Standards and Technology
66. Lyubashevsky, V., Peikert, C., Regev, O.: A toolkit for ring-LWE cryptography. In: Johansson, T., Nguyen, P.Q. (eds.) EUROCRYPT 2013. LNCS, vol. 7881, pp. 35–54. Springer, Heidelberg (2013). https://doi.org/10.1007/978-3-642-38348-9_3
67. Ma, C., Jiang, M.: Practical lattice-based multisignature schemes for blockchains. IEEE Access **7**, 179765–179778
68. Ma, C., Weng, J., Li, Y., Deng, R.H.: Efficient discrete logarithm based multi-signature scheme in the plain public key model. Des. Codes Cryptogr. **54**(2), 121–133. https://doi.org/10.1007/s10623-009-9313-z
69. Maxwell, G., Poelstra, A., Seurin, Y., Wuille, P.: Simple Schnorr multi-signatures with applications to Bitcoin. Des. Codes Crypt. **87**(9), 2139–2164 (2019). https://doi.org/10.1007/s10623-019-00608-x
70. Micali, S., Ohta, K., Reyzin, L.: Accountable-subgroup multisignatures: extended abstract. In: ACM CCS 2001, pp. 245–254. ACM Press (2001)
71. Micciancio, D., Peikert, C.: Trapdoors for lattices: simpler, tighter, faster, smaller. In: Pointcheval, D., Johansson, T. (eds.) EUROCRYPT 2012. LNCS, vol. 7237, pp. 700–718. Springer, Heidelberg (2012). https://doi.org/10.1007/978-3-642-29011-4_41
72. Micciancio, D., Peikert, C.: Hardness of SIS and LWE with small parameters. In: Canetti, R., Garay, J.A. (eds.) CRYPTO 2013. LNCS, vol. 8042, pp. 21–39. Springer, Heidelberg (2013). https://doi.org/10.1007/978-3-642-40041-4_2
73. Nick, J., Ruffing, T., Seurin, Y.: MuSig2: simple two-round Schnorr multi-signatures. Cryptology ePrint Archive, Report 2020/1261
74. Nick, J., Ruffing, T., Seurin, Y., Wuille, P.: MuSig-DN: Schnorr multi-signatures with verifiably deterministic nonces. Cryptology ePrint Archive, Report 2020/1057
75. Nicolosi, A., Krohn, M.N., Dodis, Y., Mazières, D.: Proactive two-party signatures for user authentication. In: NDSS 2003. The Internet Society (2003)
76. Pass, R.: On deniability in the common reference string and random oracle model. In: Boneh, D. (ed.) CRYPTO 2003. LNCS, vol. 2729, pp. 316–337. Springer, Heidelberg (2003). https://doi.org/10.1007/978-3-540-45146-4_19
77. Pedersen, T.P.: Non-interactive and information-theoretic secure verifiable secret sharing. In: Feigenbaum, J. (ed.) CRYPTO 1991. LNCS, vol. 576, pp. 129–140. Springer, Heidelberg (1992). https://doi.org/10.1007/3-540-46766-1_9
78. Peikert, C.: An efficient and parallel Gaussian sampler for lattices. In: Rabin, T. (ed.) CRYPTO 2010. LNCS, vol. 6223, pp. 80–97. Springer, Heidelberg (2010). https://doi.org/10.1007/978-3-642-14623-7_5
79. Pointcheval, D., Stern, J.: Security arguments for digital signatures and blind signatures. J. Cryptol. **13**(3), 361–396
80. Schnorr, C.P.: Efficient identification and signatures for smart cards. In: Brassard, G. (ed.) CRYPTO 1989. LNCS, vol. 435, pp. 239–252. Springer, New York (1990). https://doi.org/10.1007/0-387-34805-0_22
81. Stinson, D.R., Strobl, R.: Provably secure distributed Schnorr signatures and a (t, n) threshold scheme for implicit certificates. In: Varadharajan, V., Mu, Y. (eds.) ACISP 2001. LNCS, vol. 2119, pp. 417–434. Springer, Heidelberg (2001). https://doi.org/10.1007/3-540-47719-5_33

82. Syta, E., et al.: Keeping authorities "honest or bust" with decentralized witness cosigning. In: 2016 IEEE Symposium on Security and Privacy, pp. 526–545. IEEE Computer Society Press (2016)
83. Toluee, R., Eghlidos, T.: An efficient and secure ID-based multi-proxy multi-signature scheme based on lattice. Cryptology ePrint Archive, Report 2019/1031
84. Torres, W.A., Steinfeld, R., Sakzad, A., Kuchta, V.: Post-quantum linkable ring signature enabling distributed authorised ring confidential transactions in blockchain. Cryptology ePrint Archive, Report 2020/1121
85. Tso, R., Liu, Z., Tseng, Y.: Identity-based blind multisignature from lattices. IEEE Access **7**, 182916–182923
86. Wagner, D.: A generalized birthday problem. In: Yung, M. (ed.) CRYPTO 2002. LNCS, vol. 2442, pp. 288–304. Springer, Heidelberg (2002). https://doi.org/10.1007/3-540-45708-9_19
87. Yang, R., Au, M.H., Zhang, Z., Xu, Q., Yu, Z., Whyte, W.: Efficient lattice-based zero-knowledge arguments with standard soundness: construction and applications. In: Boldyreva, A., Micciancio, D. (eds.) CRYPTO 2019. LNCS, vol. 11692, pp. 147–175. Springer, Cham (2019). https://doi.org/10.1007/978-3-030-26948-7_6

Isogeny-Based Key Compression Without Pairings

Geovandro C. C. F. Pereira[1,2(✉)] and Paulo S. L. M. Barreto[3]

[1] University of Waterloo, Waterloo, Canada
geovandro.pereira@uwaterloo.ca
[2] evolutionQ Inc., Kitchener, Canada
[3] University of Washington Tacoma, Tacoma, USA
pbarreto@uw.edu

Abstract. SIDH/SIKE-style protocols benefit from key compression to minimize their bandwidth requirements, but proposed key compression mechanisms rely on computing bilinear pairings. Pairing computation is a notoriously expensive operation, and, unsurprisingly, it is typically one of the main efficiency bottlenecks in SIDH key compression, incurring processing time penalties that are only mitigated at the cost of trade-offs with precomputed tables. We address this issue by describing how to compress isogeny-based keys without pairings. As a bonus, we also substantially reduce the storage requirements of other operations involved in key compression.

1 Introduction

Supersingular Isogeny Diffie-Hellman (SIDH) public keys are, in an abstract sense, triples $(A, x_P, x_Q) \in \mathbb{F}_{p^2}^3$ where A specifies an elliptic curve in Montgomery form $E : y^2 = x^3 + Ax^2 + x$, and x_P, x_Q are the x-coordinates of points P, Q on E (which in turn are the images of fixed points on a certain starting curve through a private prime-power-degree isogeny).

Although such triples naively take $6 \lg p$ bits of storage or bandwidth, better representations are known. Since P, Q are chosen to be in torsion subgroups of form $E[\ell^m]$ with $m \lg \ell \approx (1/2) \lg p$, they can be represented on some conventional public ℓ^m-torsion basis (R, S) in E by four coefficients from $\mathbb{Z}/\ell^m\mathbb{Z}$, namely $P = [a]R + [b]S$ and $Q = [c]R + [d]S$, so that the public key becomes $(A, a, b, c, d) \in \mathbb{F}_{p^2} \times (\mathbb{Z}/\ell^m\mathbb{Z})^4$ and the key bandwidth decreases to about $2 \lg p + 4 \cdot (1/2) \lg p = 4 \lg p$ bits [2]. Besides, for SIDH-style protocols only the subgroup $\langle P, Q \rangle$ is actually relevant, not the points P, Q themselves. This redundancy can be exploited for further compression, since only three out of those four point coefficients above are needed to specify that subgroup. Thus, each key is essentially represented by a tuple $(A, a, b, c) \in \mathbb{F}_{p^2} \times (\mathbb{Z}/\ell^m\mathbb{Z})^3$ (plus one bit to identify which coefficient is omitted). This finally brings the key size down to $3.5 \lg p$ bits, nearly halving the naive requirements above [5]. At the time of writing, this appears to be the minimum attainable (and hence optimal) bandwidth per key.

J. A. Garay (Ed.): PKC 2021, LNCS 12710, pp. 131–154, 2021.
https://doi.org/10.1007/978-3-030-75245-3_6

This size reduction, however, incurs a high computational overhead. Existing research works [2,5,11,17,18] have achieved substantial improvements, but they all rely on the computation of bilinear pairings to project (non-cyclic) elliptic discrete logarithm instances into the multiplicative group of units in $\mathbb{F}_{p^2}^*$, where variants of the Pohlig-Hellman algorithm [13] are effectively applied. Precomputed tables can substantially speed up pairing computations [11], but at the cost of increasing storage requirements, compounding with those incurred by the computation of discrete logarithms. More recently a work on reducing the storage component has been proposed [9].

Despite all improvements, pairing computation has consistently remained the efficiency bottleneck in all of those works (specially the case $\ell = 2$ per [11]).

Our Contribution: We describe how to compute discrete logarithms as required to obtain the four a, b, c, d coefficients (which can then be reduced down to three in the usual fashion) via tailored ECDLP instances without resorting to pairings. Our proposed method relies almost entirely on arithmetic for elliptic curve points defined over $\mathbb{F}_p$ for the discrete logarithm computation itself. Arithmetic over $\mathbb{F}_{p^2}$ is only ever needed in evaluating very simple and efficient maps between curves and groups, and to complete partially computed logarithms. Precomputation trade-offs are possible in the same way as they are for discrete logarithms on $\mathbb{F}_{p^2}^*$, and if adopted, only the tables for a single, fixed, public group generator are needed for each value of ℓ. Moreover, we show how to halve the storage requirements of windowed computation of discrete logarithm when the index of the prime-power group order is not a multiple of the window size.

The remainder of this paper is organized as follows. In Sect. 2 we define the fundamental notions and notations our proposal is based upon. We recap the basic Pohlig-Hellman algorithm in Sect. 3, and then we discuss the improvements made possible by the adoption of strategy graphs and propose several associated techniques in Sect. 4. We introduce our methods to compute elliptic curve discrete logarithms efficiently as required for SIDH key compression in Sect. 5, and assess its performance in Sect. 6. Finally, we discuss the results and conclude in Sect. 7.

2 Preliminaries

Consider a prime $p = 2^{e_2} \cdot q^{e_q} - 1$ for some $e_2 \geq 2$, some $e_q > 0$ and some small odd prime q (typically $q = 3$). We will represent the finite field $\mathbb{F}_{p^2} \simeq \mathbb{F}_p[i]/\langle i^2+1 \rangle$. Also, we will be mostly concerned with *supersingular* elliptic curves in Montgomery form $E : x^3 + Ax^2 + x$ with $A \in \mathbb{F}_{p^2}$ (or $A \in \mathbb{F}_p$ in a few cases). When required for clarity, the curve defined by a particular value of A will be denoted E_A.

Let $P, Q \in E[\ell^{e_\ell}]$ with $\ell \in \{2, q\}$. We say that P *is above* Q if $Q = [\ell^j]P$ for some $0 < j \leqslant e_\ell$.

The *trace map* on $E/\mathbb{F}_p$ is the linear map $\mathrm{tr} : E(\mathbb{F}_{p^2}) \to E(\mathbb{F}_p)$ defined as $\mathrm{tr}(P) := P + \Phi(P)$, where $\Phi : E(\mathbb{F}_{p^2}) \to E(\mathbb{F}_{p^2})$ is the Frobenius endomorphism,

$\Phi(x, y) := (x^p, y^p)$. If $P \in E(\mathbb{F}_p)$, then $\operatorname{tr}(P) = [2]P$. Conversely, if $\operatorname{tr}(P) = [2]P$, then $P \in E(\mathbb{F}_p)$.

A *distortion map* is an endomorphism $\psi : E \to E$ such that $\psi(P) \notin \langle P \rangle$. Efficiently computable distortion maps are hard to come by for most curves [8], but the special curve E_0 is equipped with a simple one, namely, $\psi : E_0 \to E_0$ defined as $\psi(x, y) := (-x, iy)$ in the Weierstrass and Montgomery models, or $\psi(x, y) := (ix, 1/y)$ in the Edwards model. Notice that $\psi^{-1} = -\psi$, since $\psi(\psi(x, y)) = (x, -y) = -(x, y)$. Besides, if $P \in E(\mathbb{F}_p)$ then $\operatorname{tr}(\psi(P)) = \mathcal{O}$, as one can see by directly computing $\operatorname{tr}(\psi(x, y)) = \operatorname{tr}(-x, iy) = (-x, iy) + ((-x)^p, (iy)^p) = (-x, iy) + (-x, -iy) = (-x, iy) - (-x, iy) = \mathcal{O}$. For convenience we also define the isomorphism $\tilde{\psi} : E_A \to E_{-A}$ that maps $\tilde{\psi}(x, y) := (-x, iy)$ in the Weierstrass and Montgomery models, and $\tilde{\psi}(x, y) := (ix, 1/y)$ in the Edwards model.

An *isogeny* between two elliptic curves E and E' over a field $\mathbb{K}$ is a morphism $\varphi : E(\overline{\mathbb{K}}) \to E'(\overline{\mathbb{K}})$ specified by rational functions, $\varphi(x, y) = (r(x), s(x)y)$ for some $r, s \in \mathbb{K}[x]$, satisfying $\varphi(\mathcal{O}_E) = \mathcal{O}_{E'}$. Writing $r(x) = n(x)/d(x)$ for $n, d \in \mathbb{K}[x]$ with $\gcd(n, d) = 1$, the *degree* of φ is $\deg \varphi := \max\{\deg n, \deg d\}$. For short, if $\deg \varphi = g$ we say that φ is a g-isogeny. If $r(x)$ is non-constant, φ is said to be *separable*, in which case $\deg \varphi = \# \ker \varphi = \#\{P \in E \mid \varphi(P) = \mathcal{O}\}$. An isogeny is said to be of *prime power* if $\deg \varphi = \ell^m$ for some small prime ℓ.

We will make extensive use of the 2-isogeny $\varphi_0 : E_0 \to E_6$ with kernel $\langle (i, 0) \rangle$ and its dual $\widehat{\varphi}_0 : E_6 \to E_0$ with kernel $\langle (0, 0) \rangle$.

Supersingular isogeny-based cryptosystems build prime-power isogenies starting from a fixed curve. The starting curve originally adopted for SIDH protocols is E_0, but since all power-of-2 isogenies leaving E_0 must necessarily pass through the 2-isogenous curve E_6, a recent trend pioneered by the SIKE scheme [1] is to adopt E_6 as the starting curve instead.

An SIDH-style private key will thus be an isogeny $\varphi : E_6 \to E$ of degree λ^{e_λ}, and the corresponding public key is, formally, a triple $(E, P := \varphi(P_6), Q := \varphi(Q_6))$ where (P_6, Q_6) is a basis of $E_6[\ell^{e_\ell}]$, where $\lambda \in \{2, q\}$ and $\ell \in \{2, q\} \setminus \{\lambda\}$.

The basic idea of compressing public keys is to unambiguously specify a public basis (R, S) for $E[\ell^{e_\ell}]$ and obtaining coefficients $a, b, c, d \in \mathbb{Z}/\ell^{e_\ell}\mathbb{Z}$ such that $P = [a]R + [b]S$ and $Q = [c]R + [d]S$. Since the dual isogeny $\widehat{\varphi} : E \to E_6$ is readily available and efficiently applicable during key pair generation [11], this process can be equivalently stated on curve E_6 itself. Namely, defining $R_6 := \widehat{\varphi}(R)$ and $S_6 := \widehat{\varphi}(S)$, that decomposition is equivalent to $\widehat{\varphi}(P) = [\lambda^{e_\lambda}]P_6 = [a]\widehat{\varphi}(R) + [b]\widehat{\varphi}(S) = [a]R_6 + [b]S_6$ and $\widehat{\varphi}(Q) = [\lambda^{e_\lambda}]Q_6 = [c]\widehat{\varphi}(R) + [d]\widehat{\varphi}(S) = [c]R_6 + [d]S_6$. Thus, if one can find $\hat{a}, \hat{b}, \hat{c}, \hat{d} \in \mathbb{Z}/\ell^{e_\ell}\mathbb{Z}$ such that

$$\begin{aligned} P_6 &= [\hat{a}]R_6 + [\hat{b}]S_6, \\ Q_6 &= [\hat{c}]R_6 + [\hat{d}]S_6, \end{aligned} \tag{1}$$

the desired coefficients for the compressed public key might be obtained from these after multiplying them by the scale factor λ^{e_λ}. Yet, this is actually unnecessary, since those four coefficients would be further compressed into a triple

$(b/a, c/a, d/a)$ or $(a/b, c/b, d/b)$ modulo ℓ^{e_ℓ} anyway, eliminating the need for any scale factor.

With this in mind, we henceforth assume that basis (R_6, S_6) has been prepared as outlined above, and we focus our attention to the specific task of finding $\hat{a}$, $\hat{b}$, $\hat{c}$, and $\hat{d}$ without any further reference to the private isogeny φ or its dual. Since we will also resort later to other curve models than Montgomery's in our algorithms, this assumption will also help keeping all computations contained in separate, well-delimited realms.

Being able to efficiently compute discrete logarithms is thus at the core of key compression methods. We next review the Pohlig-Hellman discrete logarithm algorithm and ways of making it as close to optimal as currently viable.

3 The Pohlig-Hellman Algorithm

The Pohlig-Hellman method (Algorithm 3.1) to compute the discrete logarithm of $P = [d]G \in \langle G \rangle$, where $\langle G \rangle$ is a cyclic Abelian group of smooth order ℓ^m, requires solving equations of form:

$$[\ell^{m-1-k}]P_k = [d_k]L$$

for $k = 0, \ldots, m-1$, where $L := [\ell^{m-1}]G$ has order ℓ, $d_k \in \{0, \ldots, \ell-1\}$ is the ℓ-ary digit of d, $P_0 := P$, and P_{k+1} depends on P_k and d_k.

Algorithm 3.1. Pohlig-Hellman discrete logarithm algorithm

INPUT: cyclic Abelian group $\langle G \rangle$, challenge $P \in \langle G \rangle$.
OUTPUT: d: base-ℓ digits of $\log_G P$, i.e. $[d]G = P$.

1: $L \leftarrow [\ell^{m-1}]G$ ▷ NB: $[\ell]L = \mathcal{O}$
2: $d \leftarrow 0$, $P_0 \leftarrow P$
3: **for** $k \leftarrow 0$ **to** $m-1$ **do**
4: $\quad V_k \leftarrow [\ell^{m-1-k}]P_k$
5: $\quad$ find $d_k \in \{0, \ldots, \ell-1\}$ such that $V_k = [d_k]L$
6: $\quad d \leftarrow d + d_k\ell^k$, $P_{k+1} \leftarrow P_k - [d_k\ell^k]G$
7: **end for** ▷ NB: $[d]G = P$
8: **return** d

A simple improvement for Algorithm 3.1 would be to precompute a table $\mathsf{T}[k][c] := [c]([\ell^k]G)$ for all $0 \le k < m$ and $0 \le c < \ell$. This way, the condition on line 5, which essentially solves a discrete logarithm instance in the subgroup $\langle L \rangle$ of small order ℓ, would read $V_k = \mathsf{T}[m-1][d_k]$, and the second assignment on line 6 would read $P_{k+1} \leftarrow P_k - \mathsf{T}[k][d_k]$ instead.

The running time of this algorithm is dominated by line 4 (and line 6 in the naive approach without tables), leading to an overall $O(m^2)$ complexity as measured in basic group operations. Shoup [14, Chapter 11] shows that this approach is far from optimal, but although his RDL algorithm [14, Section 11.2.3] provides a framework targeting optimality, it lacks an effective strategy to attain it. A practical technique for that purpose has been proposed by Zanon *et al.* [18, Section 6] that uses so-called *strategy graphs*. We next recap that technique in Sect. 4, which was originally proposed in the context of finite field discrete logarithms. We subsequently show (Sects. 4.1 to 4.5) how to adapt it for the ECDLP case.

4 Strategy Graphs

Let Δ be a graph with vertices $\{\Delta_{j,k} \mid j \geq 0,\ k \geq 0,\ j+k \leq m-1\}$ (that is, a triangular grid). Each vertex has either two downward outgoing edges, or no edges at all. Vertices $\Delta_{j,k}$ with $j+k < m-1$ are called internal vertices and have two weighted edges: a left-edge $\Delta_{j,k} \to \Delta_{j+1,k}$, and a right-edge $\Delta_{j,k} \to \Delta_{j,k+1}$. All left-edges are assigned weight $p > 0$ and all right-edges are assigned weight $q > 0$. Vertices $\Delta_{j,k}$ with $j+k = m-1$ are *leaves* since they have no outgoing edges. Vertex $\Delta_{0,0}$ is called the *root*.

A subgraph of Δ that contains a given vertex v, all leaves that can be reached from v and no vertex that cannot be reached from v is called a *strategy*. A *full* strategy is a strategy that contains the root.

Notice that a strategy is not required to contain all vertices reachable from v, and is thus not necessarily unique. This establishes the *optimal strategy problem*, that consists of finding a full strategy of minimum weight. This problem can be solved with the De Feo *et al.* $O(m^2)$ dynamic programming algorithm [7, Equation 5] or the Zanon *et al.* $O(m \lg m)$ method [18, Algorithm 6.2]. The latter is quoted in Appendix A.1 for reference.

Strategy graphs lend themselves to efficient prime-power-degree isogeny calculation [7], and can also model potential variants of the Pohlig-Hellman algorithm in a prime-power-order Abelian group [17,18]. Namely, an in-order traversal of a strategy spells out which operations are to be performed: left-edges correspond to multiplication by ℓ, and right-edges variously corresponds to applying ℓ-isogenies in the former case, or to erasing one base-ℓ digit from a discrete logarithm in the latter. Specifically in the solution of a discrete logarithm instance $P = [d]G$, these edge operations associate the value $[\ell^j](P - [d \bmod \ell^k]G)$ to vertex $\Delta_{j,k}$ for all j, k.

The reason this works is that, for those tasks, the overall calculation result (a prime-power-degree isogeny or a discrete logarithm) consists of a sequence of values computed at the leaves, and the value at each leaf depends only on the values computed at the leaves to its left. The original Pohlig-Hellman algorithm corresponds to a simple (non-optimal) traversal strategy whereby all $m(m+1)/2$ left-edges (i.e. multiplications by ℓ) are traversed top-down and left-to-right, while the only right-edges traversed (corresponding to the elimination of the least significant digits from the discrete logarithm being retrieved) are those on the rightmost diagonal of the strategy as a whole.

This idea is expressed in Algorithm 4.1, which is adapted from [17,18, Section 6]. Its complexity, measured by the number of edges traversed in a balanced strategy whereby the left-edge and right-edge costs are equal (and hence the number of leaves at each side of the strategy vertices is the same), is defined by the recurrence $T(m) = 2T(m/2) + m$ with $T(1) = 0$, yielding the overall cost $\Theta(m \lg m)$ which is very close to the minimal $\Theta(m \lg m / \lg \lg m)$ complexity [15]. The cost of an optimal albeit unbalanced strategy can be shown to lie asymptotically close to this [7, Equation 9].

Algorithm 4.1. Traverse($V, j, k, z, \mathsf{path}, \mathsf{T}$)

PURPOSE: retrieve d such that $[d]G = P$ for a cyclic Abelian group $\langle G \rangle$ of order ℓ^m.
INPUT: $V := [\ell^j](P - [d \bmod \ell^k]G)$: value associated to vertex $\Delta_{j,k}$;
j, k: coordinates of vertex $\Delta_{j,k}$;
z: number of leaves in the subtree rooted at $\Delta_{j,k}$;
path: traversal path (output of Algorithm A.1);
T: lookup table such that $\mathsf{T}[u][c] := [c]([\ell^u]G)$ for all $0 \leq u < m$ and $0 \leq c < \ell$.
OUTPUT: base-ℓ digits of d such that $[d]G = P$.
REMARK: the initial call is Traverse($P, 0, 0, m, \mathsf{path}, \mathsf{T}$).

1: **if** $z > 1$ **then**
2: $t \leftarrow \mathsf{path}[z]$ ▷ z leaves: t to the left exp, $z - t$ to the right
3: $V' \leftarrow [\ell^{z-t}]V$ ▷ go left $(z - t)$ times
4: Traverse($V', j + (z - t), k, t, \mathsf{path}, \mathsf{T}$)
5: $V' \leftarrow V - \sum_{h=k}^{k+t-1} \mathsf{T}[j + h][d_h]$ ▷ go right t times
6: Traverse($V', j, k + t, z - t, \mathsf{path}, \mathsf{T}$)
7: **else** ▷ leaf
8: find $d_k \in \{0, \ldots, \ell - 1\}$ such that $V = \mathsf{T}[m - 1][d_k]$ ▷ recover the k-th digit d_k of the discrete logarithm from $V = [d_k]([\ell^{m-1}]G)$
9: **end if**

4.1 Choosing the Curve Model

Algorithm 4.1 makes extensive use of point multiplications by (powers of) ℓ (line 3) and also point additions/subtractions (line 5). This makes the Montgomery model less suited for this task.

For the most important practical cases of $\ell = 2$ and $\ell = 3$, the (twisted) Edwards model [3] seems to be the most adequate, specifically *inverted twisted Edwards coordinates* for $\ell = 2$ and *projective twisted Edwards coordinates* for $\ell = 3$.

In the former case, with the adoption of inverted twisted Edwards coordinates point addition costs $9\mathbf{m}+1\mathbf{s}+6\mathbf{a}$ (or $8\mathbf{m}+1\mathbf{s}+6\mathbf{a}$ if one of the points is affine), and point doubling costs $3\mathbf{m} + 4\mathbf{s} + 6\mathbf{a}$. In the latter case, projective twisted Edwards coordinates enable point addition at the cost $10\mathbf{m} + 1\mathbf{s} + 6\mathbf{a}$ (or $9\mathbf{m} + 1\mathbf{s} + 6\mathbf{a}$ if one of the points is affine), and point tripling [4], which is here more relevant than point doubling, costs $9\mathbf{m} + 3\mathbf{s} + 9\mathbf{a}$.

4.2 Handling the Leaves

In a generalized, windowed implementation of Algorithm 4.1, that is, when expressing discrete logarithms in base ℓ^w for some $w \geqslant 1$ instead of simply sticking to base ℓ, finding digits $d_k \in \{0, \ldots, \ell^w - 1\}$ in line 8 depends on efficiently looking up the point V in a table containing the whole subgroup $\langle [\ell^{m-w}]G \rangle \subset E(\mathbb{F}_p)$, which consists of ℓ^w elements. Since point V is typically available in projective coordinates as discussed in Sect. 4.1, lookup operations are not straightforward in the sense that hash table or binary search techniques are not available. This will incur extra costs that must be carefully minimized.

First, we observe that, since the whole ℓ^w-torsion is searched, lookups can be initially restricted to one of the coordinates, namely, the y-coordinate in the Edwards models, since for each such value there are no more than two points of form (x, y) and $(-x, y)$ in the torsion. This reduces the table size in half.

Second, in either projective twisted or inverted twisted coordinates, the point comparisons are made between points of form $[X : Y : Z]$ against points of form $[x' : y' : 1]$, and in both cases equality holds iff $Y = y' \cdot Z$ and $X = x' \cdot Z$, where the second comparison is performed exactly once after identifying the correct y'. Since there are $\lceil \ell^w/2 \rceil$ distinct values of y' and they are expected to occur uniformly, the expected number of $\mathbb{F}_p$ multiplications is $\lceil \ell^w/4 \rceil + 1$.

This cost limits the values of w that can be chosen in practice, but these coincide with the values that make table T itself too large for practical deployment anyway [17,18].

4.3 Windowing and Signed Digits

In order to reduce processing time, Algorithm 4.1 can be optimized to use a more general base ℓ^w to express the digits. This reduces the number of leaves of Δ from m to m/w. In this case, although the total cost of left edge traversals is unchanged (since each left traversal now involves computing w multiplications by ℓ), the cost of right traversals is greatly reduced as we can now remove larger digits (i.e. digits modulo ℓ^w) at the same cost of removing a single digit modulo ℓ. This computation time reduction comes with an associated storage overhead because although the number of rows in table $\mathsf{T}[k][c]$ is divided by w, the number of columns grows exponentially in w, i.e., $\mathsf{T}[k][c] := [c]([\ell^k]G)$ for all $0 \leq k < \lceil m/w \rceil$ and $0 \leq c < \ell^w$.

A straightforward storage reduction by a factor of two can be achieved by using the technique of signed digits [10, Section 14.7.1], which requires storing only elements $0 \leq c \leq \lfloor \ell^w/2 \rfloor$ and then merely deciding whether to add or subtract the corresponding multiple of G. Note that storing the column corresponding to $c = 0$ is not needed in practice because 1) removing such digit is equivalent to subtracting the identity and no lookup is indeed required (remember that the discrete logarithm computation is not required to be constant time), and 2) testing if a leaf element corresponds to $c = 0$ reduces to a simple identity test. In this case, the number of columns is reduced by half since removing a negative digit is equivalent to subtracting the opposite of the table entry corresponding to the positive digit. Such storage reduction first appeared in the SIKE Round 3 submission [1] and was introduced by [9] in the context of key compression and was deployed in the official SIKE Round 3 implementation submitted to NIST. The above set of optimizations (adapted to elliptic curve discrete logarithms) is summarized by Algorithm 4.2.

Algorithm 4.2. TraverseWSign($V, j, k, z, \mathsf{path}, \mathsf{T}, w$)

PURPOSE: retrieve d such that $[d]G = P$ for a cyclic Abelian group $\langle G \rangle$ of order ℓ^m.
INPUT: $V := [L^j](P - [d \bmod L^k]G)$: value associated to vertex $\Delta_{j,k}$;
j, k: coordinates of vertex $\Delta_{j,k}$;
z: number of leaves in the subtree rooted at $\Delta_{j,k}$;
path: traversal path (output of Algorithm A.1);
T: lookup table such that $\mathsf{T}[u][c] := [c]([\ell^u]G)$ for all $0 \leq u < M := m/w$ and $1 \leq c \leq \lfloor L/2 \rfloor$.
w : window size such that $L := \ell^w$.
OUTPUT: base-L signed digits of d such that $[d]G = P$.
REMARK: the initial call is TraverseWSign($P, 0, 0, M, \mathsf{path}, \mathsf{T}, w$) and function $sign(\cdot) \in \{-, +\}$.

1: **if** $z > 1$ **then**
2: $t \leftarrow \mathsf{path}[z]$ ▷ z leaves: t to the left exp, $z - t$ to the right
3: $V' \leftarrow [L^{z-t}]V$ ▷ go left $(z - t)$ times
4: TraverseWSign($V', j + (z - t), k, t, \mathsf{path}, \mathsf{T}, w$)
5: $V' \leftarrow V - \sum_{h=k \ s.t. d_h \neq 0}^{k+t-1} sign(d_h)\mathsf{T}[j + h][|d_h|]$ ▷ go right t times
6: TraverseWSign($V', j, k + t, z - t, \mathsf{path}, \mathsf{T}, w$)
7: **else** ▷ leaf
8: find $d_k \in \{0, \pm 1, \ldots, \pm \lfloor L/2 \rfloor\}$ such that $V = \{\mathcal{O}, sign(d_k)\mathsf{T}[M - 1][|d_k|]\}$. ▷ recover the k-th digit d_k of the discrete logarithm from $V = [d_k]([\ell^{m-w}]G)$
9: **end if**

4.4 Halving Storage Requirements for Windowed Traversal

One can obtain the storage needed by Algorithm 4.2 by directly counting the number of $\mathbb{F}_p$ elements in table $T[u][c]$, i.e., $\#T = 2(m/w)\lfloor \ell^w/2 \rfloor$ elements.

Unfortunately, Algorithm 4.2 only works when w divides the exponent m, which is not the case in multiple SIKE parameters. For instance, in the ternary case ($\ell = 3$) of SIKEp434 and SIKEp751 we have $m = 137$ and $m = 239$, respectively, which are prime exponents and no w works. To circumvent this issue, authors in [18] suggested a modification to the traverse algorithm that requires using a second table of the same size of $T[u][c]$, imposing twice the storage.

We suggest a different approach that does not require an extra table and thus offers half of the storage of that proposed in [18] and adopted in subsequent works [11,12] including the official SIKE submission to NIST [1]. In order to achieve such reduction, assume that $m \equiv t \pmod{w}$ for any $t < w$, and write the discrete logarithm of P with respect to G as $d = q\ell^{m-t} + r$ with $0 \leq q < \ell^t$. Now, instead of invoking Algorithm 4.2 with the challenge P in the first argument we pass $[\ell^t]P$ which is a point whose order has index $m - t$ divisible by w. In this case, instead of recovering the full digit d, we get $r = d \pmod{\ell^{m-t}}$. Having r at hand, observe that the relation $P - [r]G = [q]([\ell^{m-t}]G)$ allows us to compare the point $P - [r]G$ (which can be efficiently computed using the technique described later in Sect. 4.5) against a very small precomputed table containing the points $[q]([\ell^{m-t}]G)$ for $0 \leq q < \ell^t$ in order to find the correct q. The original logarithm d can then be reconstructed with simple integer arithmetic. Also note that although this approach introduces an apparently extra small table, it also reduces the number of rows in table $T[u][d]$ due to the smaller order of the discrete logarithm instance, i.e. ℓ^{m-t} instead of ℓ^m. The storage of our method amounts to the following number of $\mathbb{F}_p$ elements:

$$\#T = \begin{cases} 2\left(\frac{m}{w}\right)\lfloor \ell^w/2 \rfloor, & \text{if } t = 0 \\ 2\left(\frac{(m-t)}{w}\lfloor \ell^w/2 \rfloor + \ell^t\right), & \text{otherwise} \end{cases} \tag{2}$$

4.5 Shifted Multiplications by Scalar

Besides retrieving d such that $[d]G = P$, Algorithm 4.1 can be slightly modified to yield more useful information. Specifically, we will need points of form $[\lfloor d/\ell^\sigma \rfloor]G$ for certain values of $\sigma > 0$, and although this could be carried out from the recovered value of d via multiplication by a scalar (d right-shifted by σ positions in base ℓ), it would incur additional cost that can be mostly averted.

However, when traversing the rightmost diagonal of the strategy graph (characterized by $j = 0$), chunks of ℓ-ary digits d_h from d are erased at line 5 (and implicitly at line 8 as well) by subtracting $[d_h]([\ell^h]G)$ from V. Since the subtracted points overall sum up to the original point $[d]G$ itself, for $h \geqslant \sigma$ one could add chunks of points of form $[d_h]([\ell^{h-\sigma}]G)$ at the same locations along the rightmost diagonal, preserve their sum H, and subtract $[\ell^\sigma]H$ at those locations instead. Since the erasure takes place at the branching points of the strategy graph and there are roughly $\lg m$ (or $\lg(m/w)$ in a windowed base-ℓ^w implementation) such locations along any path from the root to the leaves (including the rightmost diagonal), the additional cost incurred by this is roughly $\sigma \lg m$ multiplications by ℓ (in practice we will have $\ell = 2$, meaning plain doublings) and $\lg m$ additions, far less than the $O(m)$ extra doublings and additions that would be incurred by a plain scalar multiplication.

The result (adapted for base-ℓ^w) is summarized in Algorithm 4.3, which performs the strategy graph traversal, and Algorithm 4.4, which computes the actual discrete logarithms.

5 Projecting Elliptic Discrete Logarithms

As set forth in Eq. 1, we are given two bases of ℓ^m-torsion on E_6, (R_6, S_6) and (P_6, Q_6), the latter being fixed. Our task is to compute the coefficients

Algorithm 4.3. TraversePlus($V, m, j, k, z, \mathsf{path}, \mathsf{T}, \sigma, w$)

PURPOSE: retrieve d such that $[d]G = P$ for a cyclic Abelian group $\langle G \rangle$ of order ℓ^m.
INPUT: $V := [L^j](P - [d \bmod L^k]G)$: value associated to vertex $\Delta_{j,k}$;
m: exponent of group order ℓ^m;
j, k: coordinates of vertex $\Delta_{j,k}$;
z: number of leaves in the subtree rooted at $\Delta_{j,k}$;
path: traversal path (output of Algorithm A.1);
T: lookup table such that $\mathsf{T}[u][c] := [c]([L^u]G)$ for all $0 \leq u < m/w$ and $1 \leq c \leq \lfloor L/2 \rfloor$;
σ: shift in the computation of $[\lfloor d/L^\sigma \rfloor]G$.
w: window size such that $L := \ell^w$.
OUTPUT: base-L digits of d such that $[d]G = P$, and point $H := [\lfloor d/L^\sigma \rfloor]G$.

1: **if** $z > 1$ **then**
2: $t \leftarrow \mathsf{path}[z]$ ▷ z leaves: t to the left exp, $z - t$ to the right
3: $V' \leftarrow [L^{z-t}]V$ ▷ go left $(z - t)$ times
4: TraversePlus($V', m, j + (z - t), k, t, \mathsf{path}, \mathsf{T}, \sigma, w$)
5: $V' \leftarrow V$
6: **if** $j = 0$ **then** ▷ rightmost diagonal
7: $V' \leftarrow V' - \sum_{h=k \ s.t. d_h \neq 0}^{\min(\sigma-1, k+t-1)} sign(d_h)\mathsf{T}[h][|d_h|]$ ▷ σ least significant digits
8: $V_H \leftarrow \sum_{h=\max(k,\sigma) \ s.t. d_h \neq 0}^{k+t-1} sign(d_h)\mathsf{T}[h - \sigma][|d_h|]$ ▷ all remaining digits
9: **if** $V_H \neq \mathcal{O}$ **then**
10: $V' \leftarrow V' - [L^\sigma]V_H$
11: $H \leftarrow H + V_H$
12: **end if**
13: **else** ▷ internal diagonal
14: $V' \leftarrow V - \sum_{h=k \ s.t. d_h \neq 0}^{k+t-1} sign(d_h)\mathsf{T}[j + h][|d_h|]$ ▷ go right t times
15: **end if**
16: TraversePlus($V', m, j, k + t, z - t, \mathsf{path}, \mathsf{T}, \sigma, w$)
17: **else** ▷ leaf
18: find $d_k \in \{0, \pm 1, \ldots, \pm \lfloor L/2 \rfloor\}$ such that $V = \{\mathcal{O}, sign(d_k)\mathsf{T}[m/w - 1][|d_k|]\}$
19: **if** $j = 0$ and $k \geqslant \sigma$ and $d_k \neq 0$ **then**
20: $H \leftarrow H + sign(d_k)\mathsf{T}[k - \sigma][|d_k|]$
21: **end if**
22: **end if**

$\hat{a}, \hat{b}, \hat{c}, \hat{d} \in \mathbb{Z}/\ell^m\mathbb{Z}$ such that $P_6 = [\hat{a}]R_6 + [\hat{b}]S_6$ and $Q_6 = [\hat{c}]R_6 + [\hat{d}]S_6$. We will do this by projecting the elliptic curve discrete logarithms onto cyclic subgroups of points defined over $\mathbb{F}_p$, and to attain this goal, we will apply the trace map on carefully crafted torsion bases.

We will discuss the cases of odd ℓ and $\ell = 2$ separately, since the latter will require a somewhat different and more involved approach.

5.1 Handling Odd ℓ

Let $R_0 := \widehat{\varphi}_0(R_6)$, $S_0 := \widehat{\varphi}_0(S_6)$, $P_0 := \widehat{\varphi}_0(P_6)$, and $Q_0 := \widehat{\varphi}_0(Q_6)$.

Algorithm 4.4. Dlog$(P, m, \mathsf{path}, \mathsf{T}, \sigma, w)$

PURPOSE: retrieve d such that $[d]G = P$ for a cyclic Abelian group $\langle G \rangle$ of order ℓ^m, together with point $H := [\lfloor d/L^\sigma \rfloor]G$.

INPUT: P: point in $\langle G \rangle$;
m: exponent of group order ℓ^m;
path: traversal path (output of Algorithm A.1);
T: lookup table such that $\mathsf{T}[u][c] := [c]([L^u]G)$ for all $0 \leq u < m/w$ and $1 \leq c \leq \lfloor L/2 \rfloor$;
σ: shift in the computation of $[\lfloor d/L^\sigma \rfloor]G$.
w: window size such that $L := \ell^w$.

OUTPUT: base-L digits of d and point H.

REMARK: A call of form $d \leftarrow$ Dlog$(P, m, \mathsf{path}, \mathsf{T}, 0, w)$ is meant to disregard/discard H.

1: $d \leftarrow 0, \quad H \leftarrow \mathcal{O}$
2: TraversePlus$(P, m, 0, 0, m, \mathsf{path}, \mathsf{T}, \sigma, w)$ ▷ NB: this modifies both d and H
3: **return** d, H

Let $G \in E_0(\mathbb{F}_p)$ be a point of order ℓ^m. Then G generates the whole ℓ^m-torsion in $E_0(\mathbb{F}_p)$. Since the trace of a point on E_0 is always in $E_0(\mathbb{F}_p)$, we can write

$$\begin{aligned} \mathrm{tr}(R_0) &= [\zeta_R]G, \ \mathrm{tr}(\psi(R_0)) = [\xi_R]G, \\ \mathrm{tr}(S_0) &= [\zeta_S]G, \ \mathrm{tr}(\psi(S_0)) = [\xi_S]G, \end{aligned}$$

for some $\zeta_R, \zeta_S, \xi_R, \xi_S \in \mathbb{Z}/\ell^m\mathbb{Z}$. These four discrete logarithms can be retrieved by applying Algorithm 4.4 (with $\sigma = 0$, since we do not need the point H) to $\langle G \rangle$.

Analogously, we can write

$$\begin{aligned} \mathrm{tr}(P_0) &= [\mu_P]G, \ \mathrm{tr}(\psi(P_0)) = [\nu_P]G, \\ \mathrm{tr}(Q_0) &= [\mu_Q]G, \ \mathrm{tr}(\psi(Q_0)) = [\nu_Q]G, \end{aligned}$$

for some $\mu_P, \mu_Q, \nu_P, \nu_Q \in \mathbb{Z}/\ell^m\mathbb{Z}$. Since points P_0 and Q_0 are fixed, these discrete logarithms can be precomputed (in contrast with the previous four logarithms, which must be computed on demand).

With the above notation, applying the dual isogeny $\widehat{\varphi}_0$ to the decomposition of (P_6, Q_6) in base (R_6, S_6) yields:

$$\begin{cases} P_6 = [\hat{a}]R_6 + [\hat{b}]S_6 \\ Q_6 = [\hat{c}]R_6 + [\hat{d}]S_6 \end{cases} \overset{\widehat{\varphi}_0}{\Longrightarrow} \begin{cases} P_0 = [\hat{a}]R_0 + [\hat{b}]S_0 \\ Q_0 = [\hat{c}]R_0 + [\hat{d}]S_0 \end{cases}$$

Applying the trace map to the system on the right and grouping scalar coefficients together yields:

$$\begin{cases} P_0 = [\hat{a}]R_0 + [\hat{b}]S_0 \\ Q_0 = [\hat{c}]R_0 + [\hat{d}]S_0 \end{cases} \overset{\mathrm{tr}}{\Longrightarrow} \begin{cases} \mu_P = \hat{a}\zeta_R + \hat{b}\zeta_S \\ \mu_Q = \hat{c}\zeta_R + \hat{d}\zeta_S \end{cases} \pmod{\ell^m}$$

Correspondingly, applying the distortion map and then the trace map to that system yields:

$$\begin{cases} P_0 = [\hat{a}]R_0 + [\hat{b}]S_0 \\ Q_0 = [\hat{c}]R_0 + [\hat{d}]S_0 \end{cases} \xrightarrow{\operatorname{tr}\circ\psi} \begin{cases} \nu_P = \hat{a}\xi_R + \hat{b}\xi_S \\ \nu_Q = \hat{c}\xi_R + \hat{d}\xi_S \end{cases} \pmod{\ell^m}$$

Overall we are left with two similar linear systems, one for $\hat{a}$ and $\hat{b}$, the other for $\hat{c}$ and $\hat{d}$:

$$M \begin{bmatrix} \hat{a} \\ \hat{b} \end{bmatrix} = \begin{bmatrix} \mu_P \\ \nu_P \end{bmatrix}, \quad M \begin{bmatrix} \hat{c} \\ \hat{d} \end{bmatrix} = \begin{bmatrix} \mu_Q \\ \nu_Q \end{bmatrix} \pmod{\ell^m}$$

where

$$M := \begin{bmatrix} \zeta_R \ \zeta_S \\ \xi_R \ \xi_S \end{bmatrix} \pmod{\ell^m}$$

The formal solution of these systems is thus:

$$\begin{bmatrix} \hat{a} \\ \hat{b} \end{bmatrix} = M^{-1} \begin{bmatrix} \mu_P \\ \nu_P \end{bmatrix}, \quad \begin{bmatrix} \hat{c} \\ \hat{d} \end{bmatrix} = M^{-1} \begin{bmatrix} \mu_Q \\ \nu_Q \end{bmatrix} \pmod{\ell^m} \tag{3}$$

where

$$M^{-1} := \frac{1}{\zeta_R\xi_S - \zeta_S\xi_R} \begin{bmatrix} \xi_S & -\zeta_S \\ -\xi_R & \zeta_R \end{bmatrix} \pmod{\ell^m} \tag{4}$$

This solution, of course, requires $D := \zeta_R\xi_S - \zeta_S\xi_R$ to be invertible mod ℓ^m. This is the case for odd ℓ, for which Eqs. 3 and 4 completely solve the problem.

However, the same approach would not be complete for $\ell = 2$. For any $P_4 \in E_6[4]$, the composition of the 2-isogeny $\widehat{\varphi}_0$ followed by the trace maps pairs of points $(R_6, R_6 + P_4)$ on E_6 to the same point on E_0, and analogously for $(S_6, S_6 + P_4)$.

Efficiently solving this ambiguity requires a slightly different approach, which we will describe next. Indeed, we propose two solutions for this case: one that is slightly simpler conceptually, but requires tables twice as large for Algorithm 4.4, and another one that is considerably more involved in its one-time precomputation (in fact, it relies on the first method for that task), but minimizes the table space.

5.2 Handling $\ell = 2$, First Solution

The ideal feature needed to use the trace map as a projection onto a cyclic subgroup of 2^m-torsion would be a basis $(\tilde{P}_6, \tilde{Q}_6)$ where $\operatorname{tr}(\tilde{Q}_6) = \mathcal{O}$. However, this would require a point of form $\tilde{Q}_6 = (-x_Q, iy_Q)$ with $x_Q, y_Q \in \mathbb{F}_p$, or equivalently $(x_Q, y_Q) \in E_{-6}(\mathbb{F}_p)[2^m]$ of *full* order, and no such point exists (the maximum order one can get over $\mathbb{F}_p$ is 2^{m-1} [6, Lemma 1]).

Hence the best possible scenario is a basis $(\tilde{P}_6, \tilde{Q}_6)$ where $\operatorname{tr}([2]\tilde{Q}_6) = \mathcal{O}$, since this is compatible with the order restriction above. The fundamental constraint on $\tilde{Q}_6$ is thus $[2]\tilde{Q}_6 = (-x_H, iy_H) = \tilde{\psi}(H)$ where $H := (x_H, y_H) \in E_{-6}(\mathbb{F}_p)[2^m]$

is any point of order 2^{m-1}. In fact, the computation of discrete logarithms in $\langle[2]\tilde{Q}_6\rangle$ or a subgroup thereof can actually be carried out in $\langle H\rangle$ instead, with all arithmetic restricted to $\mathbb{F}_p$.

Besides, we want to keep the arithmetic carried out in the computation of discrete logarithms restricted as much as possible to $\mathbb{F}_p$. This constrains $\tilde{P}_6$ to being not only of full order and satisfying $\mathrm{tr}([2]\tilde{P}_6) \neq \mathcal{O}$, but also $[2]\tilde{P}_6 \in E_6(\mathbb{F}_p)$ even though $\tilde{P}_6 \in E_6(\mathbb{F}_{p^2}) \setminus E_6(\mathbb{F}_p)$. This is again compatible with the order restriction above.

With these constraints in mind, selecting a suitable basis $(\tilde{P}_6, \tilde{Q}_6)$ can be carried out as follows. Assume w.l.o.g. that basis (P_6, Q_6) is such that[1] Q_6 is above $(0, 0)$, while P_6 is above a different point of order 2. Since we seek any point $\tilde{Q}_6$ of full order with $\mathrm{tr}([2]\tilde{Q}_6) = \mathcal{O}$, we are free to look for a point of form

$$\tilde{Q}_6 = P_6 - [\alpha]Q_6$$

for some α, since more general linear combinations of basis (P_6, Q_6) would merely yield multiples of such a point or a similar one with the roles of P_6 and Q_6 reversed. This specific form also ensures that $\tilde{Q}_6$ is a point of full order. Doubling and then taking the trace from both sides of this equation yields the constraint $\mathcal{O} = \mathrm{tr}([2]\tilde{Q}_6) = \mathrm{tr}([2]P_6) - [\alpha]\mathrm{tr}([2]Q_6)$, that is:

$$\mathrm{tr}([2]P_6) = [\alpha]\mathrm{tr}([2]Q_6)$$

from which $\alpha \pmod{2^{m-2}}$ can be uniquely determined, once and for all, by applying Algorithm 4.4 (with $\sigma = 0$) to $\mathrm{tr}([2]P_6) \in \langle\mathrm{tr}([2]Q_6)\rangle \subset E_6(\mathbb{F}_p)$, and the same value of α can be lifted to a valid solution mod 2^m.

From the above discussion it must hold that $[2]\tilde{Q}_6 = \tilde{\psi}(H)$ for $H \in E_{-6}(\mathbb{F}_p)[2^m]$ of order 2^{m-1}. Because the points from E_{-6} of order 4 above $(0, 0)$ are $(1, \pm 2i)$ [7, Section 4.3.2], which are clearly not in $E_{-6}(\mathbb{F}_p)$, point H will necessarily be above one of the other points of order 2, and hence $\tilde{Q}_6$ will not be above $(0, 0)$ in $E_6(\mathbb{F}_p)$. Since Q_6 is chosen above $(0, 0)$, the pair $(Q_6, \tilde{Q}_6)$ constitutes a basis of 2^m-torsion.

We now seek $\tilde{P}_6$ satisfying $[2]\tilde{P}_6 \in E_6(\mathbb{F}_p)$ and $[2^{m-1}]\tilde{P}_6 = (0, 0)$. These two conditions imply $\mathrm{tr}([2]\tilde{P}_6) = [4]\tilde{P}_6 \neq \mathcal{O}$ (for $m > 2$) and the pair $(\tilde{P}_6, \tilde{Q}_6)$ constitutes a basis for $E_6[2^m]$. Yet, finding $\tilde{P}_6$ satisfying these constraints by trial and error is unlikely to be viable.

To overcome this obstacle, we express $\tilde{P}_6$ in basis $(Q_6, \tilde{Q}_6)$ as

$$\tilde{P}_6 = [\beta]Q_6 + [\gamma]\tilde{Q}_6$$

with the requirement that $\mathrm{tr}([2]\tilde{P}_6) = [4]\tilde{P}_6 = [\beta]\mathrm{tr}([2]Q_6)$ be a point of 2^{m-2}-torsion in $E_6(\mathbb{F}_p)$. In other words, pick any point $Q_6' \in E_6(\mathbb{F}_p)$ of order 2^{m-2} above $(0, 0)$ such that $Q_6' \in \langle\mathrm{tr}([2]Q_6)\rangle$, then simply choose $\tilde{P}_6$ so that $[4]\tilde{P}_6$ coincides with Q_6'. Now write

$$Q_6' = [\beta]\mathrm{tr}([2]Q_6)$$

[1] The actual SIKE setting matches this convention.

and retrieve the discrete logarithm $\beta \pmod{2^{m-2}}$ to the same base as for α, again once and for all. Now observe that $[4]\tilde{P}_6 - [4\beta]Q_6 = Q'_6 - [4\beta]Q_6 = [\gamma]([4]\tilde{Q}_6)$, and hence

$$\tilde{\psi}(Q'_6 - [4\beta]Q_6) = [\gamma]\tilde{\psi}([4]\tilde{Q}_6)$$

which constitutes a discrete logarithm instance in $\langle\tilde{\psi}([4]\tilde{Q}_6)\rangle \subset E_{-6}(\mathbb{F}_p)$. Solving it reveals $\gamma \pmod{2^{m-2}}$, once and for all as usual.

The last equation also shows that, although β is only determined mod 2^{m-2}, only the value 4β is required to satisfy the constraints above, so that same value can be lifted and taken as representative mod 2^m. The same observation holds for γ. This yields our choice $\tilde{P}_6$ and completes the basis $(\tilde{P}_6, \tilde{Q}_6)$ we seek for $E_6[2^m]$. This basis selection process is summarized in Algorithm 5.1.

Algorithm 5.1. Selecting a basis $(\tilde{P}_6, \tilde{Q}_6)$

INPUT: path: traversal path (output of Algorithm A.1);
(P_6, Q_6): arbitrary basis for $E_6[2^m]$.
OUTPUT: basis $(\tilde{P}_6, \tilde{Q}_6)$ for $E_6[2^m]$ such that $[2]\tilde{P}_6 \in E_6(\mathbb{F}_p)$, $[2^{m-1}]\tilde{P}_6 = (0,0)$, and $[2]\tilde{Q}_6 = \tilde{\psi}(H)$ for some $H \in E_{-6}(\mathbb{F}_p)$ of order 2^{m-1}.

1: prepare discrete logarithm table T for $\langle \mathrm{tr}([2]Q_6)\rangle$
2: $\alpha \leftarrow \mathrm{Dlog}(\mathrm{tr}([2]P_6), m-2, \mathsf{path}, \mathsf{T}, 0, w)$ ▷ via Algorithm 4.4
3: $\tilde{Q}_6 \leftarrow P_6 - [\alpha]Q_6$
4: prepare discrete logarithm table $\tilde{\mathsf{T}}$ for $\langle\tilde{\psi}([4]\tilde{Q}_6)\rangle$
5: pick $Q'_6 \in E_6(\mathbb{F}_p)$ of order 2^{m-2} above $(0,0)$ ▷ hence $Q'_6 \in \langle \mathrm{tr}([2]Q_6)\rangle$
6: $\beta \leftarrow \mathrm{Dlog}(\mathrm{tr}(Q'_6), m-2, \mathsf{path}, \mathsf{T}, 0, w)$ ▷ via Algorithm 4.4
7: $\gamma \leftarrow \mathrm{Dlog}(\tilde{\psi}([2]Q'_6 - [4\beta]Q_6), m-2, \mathsf{path}, \tilde{\mathsf{T}}, 0, w)$ ▷ via Algorithm 4.4
8: $\tilde{P}_6 \leftarrow [\beta]Q_6 + [\gamma]\tilde{Q}_6$
9: **return** $(\tilde{P}_6, \tilde{Q}_6)$

Computing Logarithms with Basis $(\tilde{P}_6, \tilde{Q}_6)$: Having found that special fixed basis, we reverse-decompose (R_6, S_6) as:

$$\begin{cases} R_6 = [a']\tilde{P}_6 + [b']\tilde{Q}_6 \\ S_6 = [c']\tilde{P}_6 + [d']\tilde{Q}_6 \end{cases}$$

Doubling and taking the trace from both sides yields:

$$\begin{cases} R_6 = [a']\tilde{P}_6 + [b']\tilde{Q}_6 \\ S_6 = [c']\tilde{P}_6 + [d']\tilde{Q}_6 \end{cases} \xrightarrow{\mathrm{tr}\circ[2]} \begin{cases} \mathrm{tr}([2]R_6) = [a']\mathrm{tr}([2]\tilde{P}_6) \\ \mathrm{tr}([2]S_6) = [c']\mathrm{tr}([2]\tilde{P}_6) \end{cases}$$

whereby $a', c' \pmod{2^{m-2}}$ are retrieved, and once they are known:

$$\begin{cases} R_6 = [a']\tilde{P}_6 + [b']\tilde{Q}_6 \\ S_6 = [c']\tilde{P}_6 + [d']\tilde{Q}_6 \end{cases} \xrightarrow{\tilde{\psi}\circ[4]} \begin{cases} \tilde{\psi}([4]R_6 - [4a']\tilde{P}_6) = [b']\tilde{\psi}([4]\tilde{Q}_6) \\ \tilde{\psi}([4]S_6 - [4c']\tilde{P}_6) = [d']\tilde{\psi}([4]\tilde{Q}_6) \end{cases}$$

whereby $b', d' \pmod{2^{m-2}}$ are similarly retrieved.

The computation of a' in $\langle \mathrm{tr}([2]\tilde{P}_6) \rangle$ by means of Algorithm 4.4 with $\sigma = 2$ yields, as a by-product, the point $P_a := [\lfloor a'/4 \rfloor]\mathrm{tr}([2]\tilde{P}_6) = [\lfloor a'/4 \rfloor]([4]\tilde{P}_6)$ which is almost the point $[4a']\tilde{P}_6$ needed for the computation of b', but not quite due to the loss of precision in $\lfloor a'/4 \rfloor$. To compensate for it, simply set $P_a \leftarrow P_a + [a' \bmod 4]\tilde{P}_6$, thereby ensuring that $[4]P_a = [4a']\tilde{P}_6$ at the cost of a single addition in $E_6(\mathbb{F}_{p^2})$ if the points $[u]\tilde{P}_6$ for $0 \leqslant u < 4$ are precomputed and stored in a small table. The same observations hold for the computation of d' from the by-product of c'.

So far we only recovered $a', b', c', d' \pmod{2^{m-2}}$, while we need these values mod 2^m instead. The complete values only differ by the retrieved ones by some amount in $D := \{k \cdot 2^{m-2} \mid 0 \leqslant k < 4\}$, that is, $R_6 - [a']\tilde{P}_6 - [b']\tilde{Q}_6 \in \{[u]\tilde{P}_6 + [v]\tilde{Q}_6 \mid u, v \in D\}$, and similarly for $S_6 - [c']\tilde{P}_6 - [d']\tilde{Q}_6$. Notice that the multiples of $\tilde{P}_6$ and $\tilde{Q}_6$ are essentially the by-products P_a, P_b, P_c, P_d of the computations of a', b', c', d' (points P_b and P_d must of course be mapped from E_{-6} back to E_6 via the $\tilde{\psi}^{-1} = -\tilde{\psi}$ map).

Thus, the missing terms u and v can be recovered from a lookup table L_6, incurring four point subtractions overall plus the search cost similar to that discussed in Sect. 4.2. Here, however, the set of points being searched always contains 16 points, so there are 9 distinct values of the y-coordinate in the twisted Edwards model, and the search for y incurs between 1 and 8 $\mathbb{F}_{p^2}$ multiplications, plus one more to determine the correct x for the retrieved y. In other words, the average search cost is 5.5 $\mathbb{F}_{p^2}$ multiplications, or about 16.5 $\mathbb{F}_p$ multiplications, and it never exceeds 27 $\mathbb{F}_p$ multiplications. Also, table L_6 only consists of 9 points, since the other ones are just the opposite of these.

This completely recovers the a', b', c', d' scalar factors, and a plain change of basis from $(\tilde{P}_6, \tilde{Q}_6)$ to (P_6, Q_6) yields $\hat{a}, \hat{b}, \hat{c}, \hat{d}$ as desired. This whole method is summarized in Algorithm 5.2.

Algorithm 5.2. $\mathrm{Dlog6}(R_6, \tilde{P}_6, \tilde{Q}_6, \mathsf{T}_P, \mathsf{T}_Q, \mathsf{path}, \mathsf{L}_6, w)$

PURPOSE: retrieve $a', b' \pmod{2^m}$ such that $R_6 = [a']\tilde{P}_6 + [b']\tilde{Q}_6$.
INPUT: $R_6 \in E_6(\mathbb{F}_{p^2})$: point to express in basis $(\tilde{P}_6, \tilde{Q}_6)$;
$(\tilde{P}_6, \tilde{Q}_6)$: special basis for $E_6(\mathbb{F}_{p^2})[2^m]$ (output of Algorithm 5.1);
T_P, T_Q: lookup tables for $\mathrm{tr}([2]\tilde{P}_6)$ and $\tilde{\psi}([4]\tilde{Q}_6)$, respectively;
path: traversal path (output of Algorithm A.1);
L_6: lookup table for pairs $(u := j \cdot 2^{m-2}, v := k \cdot 2^{m-2})$ for $j, k \in \{0 \dots 3\}$ with search key $[u]\tilde{P}_6 + [v]\tilde{Q}_6$ (see Section 4.2).
w : the window size.
OUTPUT: $a', b' \pmod{2^m}$ such that $R_6 = [a']\tilde{P}_6 + [b']\tilde{Q}_6$.

1: $a', P_a \leftarrow \mathrm{Dlog}(\mathrm{tr}([2]R_6), m-2, \mathsf{path}, \mathsf{T}_P, 2, w)$ ▷ via Algorithm 4.4
2: $P'_a \leftarrow P_a + [a' \bmod 4]\tilde{P}_6$
3: $b', P_b \leftarrow \mathrm{Dlog}(\tilde{\psi}([4](R_6 - P_a)), m-2, \mathsf{path}, \mathsf{T}_Q, 2, w)$ ▷ via Algorithm 4.4
4: $P'_b \leftarrow -\tilde{\psi}(P_b) + [b' \bmod 4]\tilde{Q}_6$
5: lookup $\delta_6 := R_6 - P'_a - P'_b$ in L_6 to retrieve (u, v) such that $[u]\tilde{P}_6 + [v]\tilde{Q}_6 = \delta_6$.
6: **return** $a' + u \pmod{2^m}$, $b' + v \pmod{2^m}$

This method requires computing logarithms in $\langle \mathrm{tr}([2]\tilde{P}_6) \rangle \subset E_6(\mathbb{F}_p)$ and $\tilde{\psi}([4]\tilde{Q}_6) \subset E_{-6}(\mathbb{F}_p)$. Therefore, two distinct tables would be required for Algorithm 4.4. We show next how to avoid this, thereby restricting all logarithm computations to a single subgroup over $\mathbb{F}_p$ with a somewhat more sophisticated method.

5.3 Handling $\ell = 2$, Second Solution

Our second solution involves mapping the discrete logarithm instances to curve E_0, where an efficient distortion map is available and enables using a single table for a subgroup of $E_0(\mathbb{F}_p)$ for all of those instances. However, a few obstacles must be overcome.

Namely, in this setting Algorithm 4.4 can only determine logarithms mod 2^{m-4} or mod 2^{m-3}, since the composition of the 2-isogeny between E_0 and E_6 with its dual introduces an extra factor 2 where one has already been placed by construction or indirectly by the trace map, thereby mapping to a point of incomplete order. This is slightly worse than our first solution, but more importantly, completing the values must still be done in E_6 where a', b', c', d' are properly defined, and the strategy graph traversal will no longer yield scalar multiples of points in E_6. Besides, if a change of basis is required to test the partial logarithms, it is likely to incur further point multiplications by scalars, introducing even more computational overhead.

We address these issues, coping with the incompleteness of computed discrete logarithms while avoiding multiplications by large scalars, by carefully picking a basis (P_0, Q_0) for $E_0[2^m]$ and a matching basis (P_6^*, Q_6^*) for $E_6[2^m]$ satisfying several constraints:

- P_0 must be a point of full order above $(i, 0)$, the generator of the kernel of the 2-isogeny φ_0, that is, $[2^{m-1}]P_0 = (i, 0)$, so that $\varphi_0(P_0)$ is a point of order exactly 2^{m-1} (NB: P_0 cannot be taken from $E_0(\mathbb{F}_p)$ since the only point of order 2 in $E_0(\mathbb{F}_p)$ is $(0, 0)$);
- $Q_0 := [2]P_0 - \mathrm{tr}(P_0)$, which is a point of trace zero, must satisfy $Q_0 = -\psi(\mathrm{tr}(P_0))$ which lies above $(0, 0)$ (NB: this specific choice is what enables using a single table to compute logarithms);
- P_6^* must be such that $[2]P_6^* = \varphi_0(P_0)$, so that $\varphi_0(\langle P_0 \rangle) \subset \langle P_6^* \rangle$ (NB: it is not possible for P_6^* to be defined as $\varphi_0(P_0)$ itself because P_0 is chosen above a point in the kernel of the isogeny, and hence its image will not be a point of full order);
- $Q_6^* := \varphi_0(Q_0)$ (NB: since Q_0 is not above the generator of the kernel of φ_0, Q_6^* is a point of full order 2^m).

While points Q_0 and Q_6^* are trivially determined, finding suitable points P_0 and P_6^* is not trivial. We now show how to find these. Notice that the following computations are only required once, that is, all of these points are fixed and can be precomputed.

Finding P_0: Pick any point $P_2 \in E_0[2^m]$ of full order above $(i, 0)$. Then $Q_2 := \psi(\mathrm{tr}(P_2)) \in E_0[2^m]$ is a linearly independent point of full order and trace zero. We can express $\mathrm{tr}(P_2)$ itself in basis (P_2, Q_2) as $\mathrm{tr}(P_2) = [u]P_2 + [v]Q_2$ for some $u, v \in \mathbb{Z}/2^m\mathbb{Z}$. Taking the trace from both sides of this equation yields $[2]\mathrm{tr}(P_2) = [u]\mathrm{tr}(P_2)$, from which we retrieve $u = 2 \pmod{2^m}$. Besides, applying the distortion map to that same equation and regrouping terms yields $\psi([2]P_2 - \mathrm{tr}(P_2)) = [v]\mathrm{tr}(P_2)$, from which we retrieve the discrete logarithm $v \pmod{2^m}$. Notice that v must be odd, since $\psi([2]P_2 - \mathrm{tr}(P_2))$ is a point of full order.

We now seek a point P_0 such that $[2]P_0 - \mathrm{tr}(P_0) = -\psi(\mathrm{tr}(P_0))$. Write $P_0 = [\alpha]P_2 + [\beta]Q_2$ for some α, β, and notice that $\mathrm{tr}(P_0) = [\alpha]\mathrm{tr}(P_2) = [2\alpha]P_2 + [v\alpha]Q_2$. Then $[2]P_0 - \mathrm{tr}(P_0) = [2\alpha]P_2 + [2\beta]Q_2 - [2\alpha]P_2 - [v\alpha]Q_2 = [2\beta - v\alpha]Q_2$, while $-\psi(\mathrm{tr}(P_0)) = -\psi([\alpha]\mathrm{tr}(P_2)) = -[\alpha]Q_2$, and hence $[2]P_0 - \mathrm{tr}(P_0) = -\psi(\mathrm{tr}(P_0)) \Rightarrow [2\beta - v\alpha]Q_2 = -[\alpha]Q_2 \Rightarrow [2\beta - v\alpha + \alpha]Q_2 = \mathcal{O}$, that is, $2\beta - v\alpha + \alpha = 0 \pmod{2^m}$ or simply $\beta = \alpha(v-1)/2 \pmod{2^m}$, where the division $(v-1)/2$ is exact because v is odd. Since any point P_0 satisfying this constraint is equally suitable, we simply take $\alpha = 1$ and $\beta = (v-1)/2$, that is, we choose $P_0 := P_2 + [(v-1)/2]Q_2$. This process is summarized in Algorithm 5.3.

Algorithm 5.3. Selecting a basis (P_0, Q_0)

INPUT: path: traversal path (output of Algorithm A.1).
OUTPUT: basis (P_0, Q_0) for $E_0[2^m]$ such that $P_0 \in E_0[2^m]$ is above $(i, 0)$ and $Q_0 := [2]P_0 - \mathrm{tr}(P_0) = -\psi(\mathrm{tr}(P_0))$.
REMARK: This algorithm is only used once, for precomputation.

1: pick $P_2 \in E_0(\mathbb{F}_{p^2})$ of order 2^m above $(i, 0)$
2: prepare discrete logarithm table T_2 for $\langle \mathrm{tr}(P_2) \rangle$
3: $v \leftarrow \mathrm{Dlog}(\psi([2]P_2 - \mathrm{tr}(P_2)), \mathsf{T}_2, m, \mathsf{path}, 0, w)$ ▷ via Algorithm 4.4
4: $P_0 \leftarrow P_2 + [\lfloor (v-1)/2 \rfloor]\psi(\mathrm{tr}(P_2))$
5: $Q_0 \leftarrow -\psi(\mathrm{tr}(P_0))$
6: **return** (P_0, Q_0)

Finding P_6^*: Find a basis $(\tilde{P}_6, \tilde{Q}_6)$ as prescribed in Sect. 5.2 (Algorithm 5.1). Since all that is required from P_6^* is that $[2]P_6^* = \varphi_0(P_0)$, we can write $\varphi_0(P_0) = [u']\tilde{P}_6 + [v']\tilde{Q}_6$, solve the discrete logarithms for u' and v' (which must be both even since $\varphi_0(P_0)$ is a point of order 2^{m-1}), and then choose $P_6^* := [u'/2]\tilde{P}_6 + [v'/2]\tilde{Q}_6$. This process is summarized in Algorithm 5.4.

Computing Logarithms with Bases (P_0, Q_0) and (P_6^*, Q_6^*): Algorithm 5.5 computes the decomposition of a point on $E_0[2^m]$ in the special basis (P_0, Q_0) precomputed by Algorithm 5.3, and also points $P_a^* = [\lfloor a^*/4 \rfloor]P_0$, $P_b^* = [\lfloor b^*/4 \rfloor]\mathrm{tr}(P_0)$.

Algorithm 5.4. Selecting a basis (P_6^*, Q_6^*)

INPUT: (P_0, Q_0): special basis for $E_0[2^m]$ (output of Algorithm 5.3);
$(\tilde{P}_6, \tilde{Q}_6)$: special basis for $E_6(\mathbb{F}_{p^2})[2^m]$ (output of Algorithm 5.1);
T_P, T_Q: lookup tables for $\mathrm{tr}([2]\tilde{P}_6)$ and $\tilde{\psi}([4]\tilde{Q}_6)$, respectively;
path: traversal path (output of Algorithm A.1);
L_6: lookup table for pairs $(u := j \cdot 2^{m-2}, v := k \cdot 2^{m-2})$ for $j, k \in \{0 \dots 3\}$ with search key $[u]\tilde{P}_6 + [v]\tilde{Q}_6$.
OUTPUT: basis (P_6^*, Q_6^*) for $E_6[2^m]$ such that $[2]P_6^* = \varphi_0(P_0)$ and $Q_6^* = \varphi(Q_0)$.
REMARK: This algorithm is only used once, for precomputation.

1: $T_6 \leftarrow \varphi_0(P_0)$
2: $u, v \leftarrow \mathrm{Dlog6}(T_6, \tilde{P}_6, \tilde{Q}_6, \mathsf{T}_P, \mathsf{T}_Q, \mathsf{path}, \mathsf{L}_6, w)$ ▷ via Algorithm 5.2
3: $P_6^* \leftarrow [\lfloor u/2 \rfloor]\tilde{P}_6 + [\lfloor v/2 \rfloor]\tilde{Q}_6$
4: $Q_6^* \leftarrow \varphi(Q_0)$
5: **return** (P_6^*, Q_6^*)

Algorithm 5.5. $\mathrm{Dlog0}(R_0, P_0, \mathsf{T}_0, \mathsf{path}, w)$

PURPOSE: retrieve $a^*, b^* \pmod{2^m}$ such that $R_0 = [a^*]P_0 + [b^*]Q_0$.
INPUT: $R_0 \in E_0(\mathbb{F}_{p^2})$: point to express in basis (P_0, Q_0);
$P_0 \in E_0[2^m]$: point of full order above $(i, 0)$ with $[2]P_0 - \mathrm{tr}(P_0) = -\psi(\mathrm{tr}(P_0))$ (output of Algorithm 5.3);
T_0: discrete logarithm lookup table for $\langle \mathrm{tr}(P_0) \rangle$;
path: traversal path (output of Algorithm A.1);
w : the window size.
OUTPUT: $a^*, b^* \pmod{2^m}$ such that $R_0 = [a^*]P_0 + [b^*]Q_0$ where $Q_0 = -\psi(\mathrm{tr}(P_0))$.

1: $a^*, P_a \leftarrow \mathrm{Dlog}(\mathrm{tr}(R_0), \mathsf{T}_0, m, \mathsf{path}, 3, w)$ ▷ via Algorithm 4.4
2: $P_a' \leftarrow [4]P_a + [(\lfloor a^*/2 \rfloor) \bmod 4]\mathsf{T}_0[0][1]$
3: $P_a' \leftarrow P_a' - \psi(P_a')$
4: $P_a^* \leftarrow P_a - \psi(P_a) + [(\lfloor a^*/4 \rfloor) \bmod 2]P_0$
5: $b^*, P_b^* \leftarrow \mathrm{Dlog}(\psi(R_0 - P_a'), \mathsf{T}_0, m, \mathsf{path}, 2, w)$ ▷ via Algorithm 4.4
6: **return** a^*, b^*, P_a^*, P_b^*

Analogously, algorithm 5.6 computes the decomposition of a point on $E_6[2^m]$ in the special basis (P_6^*, Q_6^*) precomputed by Algorithm 5.4. It does so by mapping the given discrete logarithm instance $R_6 \in E_6$ to a related instance $R_0 \in E_0$ via the dual isogeny $\widehat{\varphi}_0$, and then decomposing this instance in the special basis (P_0, Q_0), which is precomputed by Algorithm 5.3. The careful choice of this basis enables restricting the computations to a single subgroup of $E_0(\mathbb{F}_p)$ of full order. The obtained decomposition is finally mapped back from E_0 to E_6 via the isogeny φ_0. The isogeny evaluations only allow for a partial recovery of the desired logarithms, but the complete solution can now be retrieved at low cost by a lookup in a small table L_6^* of 9 entries, analogous to the L_6 table used in the first solution. The search overhead is the same as for the first solution for $\ell = 2$, namely, about $16.5\,\mathbb{F}_p$ multiplications on average, and no more than $27\,\mathbb{F}_p$ multiplications in any case.

Algorithm 5.6. Dlog2(R_6, P_0, T_0, path, L_6^*)

PURPOSE: retrieve a^*, b^* (mod 2^m) such that $R_6 = [a^*]P_6^* + [b^*]Q_6^*$.
INPUT: $R_6 \in E_6(\mathbb{F}_{p^2})$: point to express in basis (P_6^*, Q_6^*);
$P_0 \in E_0[2^m]$: point of full order above $(i, 0)$ with $[2]P_0 - \mathrm{tr}(P_0) = -\psi(\mathrm{tr}(P_0))$ (output of Algorithm 5.3);
T_0: discrete logarithm lookup table for $\langle \mathrm{tr}(P_0) \rangle$;
path: traversal path (output of Algorithm A.1);
L_6^*: lookup table for pairs $(u := h + j \cdot 2^{m-1}, v := k \cdot 2^{m-2})$ for $h, j \in \{0, 1\}$ and $k \in \{0 \ldots 3\}$ with search key $[u]P_6^* + [v]Q_6^*$.
OUTPUT: a^*, b^* (mod 2^m) such that $R_6 = [a^*]P_6^* + [b^*]Q_6^*$.

1: $R_0 \leftarrow [2]\widehat{\varphi}_0(R_6)$
2: $a^*, b^*, P_a^*, P_b^* \leftarrow$ Dlog0(R_0, P_0, T_0, path, w) ▷ via Algorithm 5.5
3: $a^* \leftarrow \lfloor a^*/4 \rfloor$, $b^* \leftarrow \lfloor b^*/4 \rfloor$
4: lookup $\delta_0 := R_6 - \widehat{\varphi}_0(P_a^*) + \widehat{\varphi}_0(\psi(P_b^*))$ in L_6^* to retrieve (u, v) such that $\delta_0 = [u]P_6^* + [v]Q_6^*$
5: **return** $2a^* + u$ (mod 2^m), $b^* + v$ (mod 2^m)

6 Experimental Results

Table 1 lists the average cost to decompose one point from $E_6(\mathbb{F}_{p^2})$ in basis $(\tilde{P}_6, \tilde{Q}_6)$, when Algorithm 5.2 is set to retrieve discrete logarithm digits in base 2, base 2^3, base 2^4 and base 2^6 (that is, with windows of size $w = 1$, $w = 3$, $w = 4$, and $w = 6$, respectively) for the official SIKE parameters. Fluctuations occur because, since a constant-time implementation is hardly needed for operations involving purely public information, one can omit dummy operations like point additions or multiplications by zero. Results are averaged over 1000 random discrete logarithm instances.

Table 1. Average cost of Algorithm 5.2 (in $\mathbb{F}_p$ multiplications) and (two) tables size (in $\#\mathbb{F}_{p^2}$ elements) to compute a', b' (mod 2^m) such that $R_6 = [a']\tilde{P}_6 + [b']\tilde{Q}_6$ for a random $R_6 \in E_6(\mathbb{F}_{p^2})[2^m]$.

Setting	$w = 1$		$w = 3$		$w = 4$		$w = 6$	
	Cost	Size	Cost	Size	Cost	Size	Cost	Size
SIKEp434	21148	428	13005	570	11420	852	10507	2256
SIKEp503	24901	496	15603	660	13792	992	12690	2628
SIKEp610	31464	606	19955	808	17530	1208	16003	3208
SIKEp751	39712	740	25051	986	21962	1476	20112	3920

Table 2 lists the corresponding costs for Algorithm 5.6. We see that the greater complexity of this method has a detectable effect on its cost, but it is quite modest compared to Algorithm 5.2: 0.8%–1.3% for $w = 1$, 2.3%–4.0% for $w = 3$, and 4.7%–8.4% for $w = 6$.

Table 2. Average cost of Algorithm 5.6 (in $\mathbb{F}_p$ multiplications) and table size (in $\#\mathbb{F}_{p^2}$ elements) to compute $a^*, b^* \pmod{2^m}$ such that $R_6 = [a^*]P_6^* + [b^*]Q^*$ for a random $R_6 \in E_6(\mathbb{F}_{p^2})[2^m]$.

Setting	$w = 1$		$w = 3$		$w = 4$		$w = 6$	
	Cost	Size	Cost	Size	Cost	Size	Cost	Size
SIKEp434	21420	216	13528	288	12027	432	11393	1152
SIKEp503	25194	250	16173	334	14435	500	13559	1328
SIKEp610	31781	305	20514	408	18187	610	16861	1632
SIKEp751	40035	372	25639	496	22632	744	21057	1984

Table 3 lists the costs for Algorithm 4.4 applied to $\ell = 3$ for its practical importance. Only values $w = 1$, $w = 3$, and $w = 4$ are listed; larger values would increase the table size without substantially improving processing efficiency (indeed, if w is too large we expect the overhead to exceed the gains anyway). However, in this case the costs are reported to decompose the whole basis (P_6, Q_6) in basis (R_6, Q_6), not just for one point, given the subtle difference between the methods for even and odd ℓ.

Table 3. Average cost of Algorithm 4.4 (in $\mathbb{F}_p$ multiplications) to compute $\hat{a}, \hat{b}, \hat{c}, \hat{d} \pmod{3^n}$ such that $P_6 = [\hat{a}]R_6 + [\hat{b}]S_6$ and $Q_6 = [\hat{c}]R_6 + [\hat{d}]S_6$ for $P_6, Q_6 \in E_6(\mathbb{F}_{p^2})[3^n]$.

Setting	$w = 1$		$w = 3$		$w = 4$	
	Cost	Size	Cost	Size	Cost	Size
SIKEp434	37073	137	21504	594	20702	1363
SIKEp503	43949	159	26333	689	24418	1587
SIKEp610	55003	192	33193	832	30489	1920
SIKEp751	71936	239	44191	1036	39888	2387

Direct comparisons with methods like [11] are hard, since we count basic operations in the underlying field $\mathbb{F}_p$ and developed our implementation in Magma, while that work only lists clock cycles for a C/assembly implementation.

Yet, one can make reasonably precise estimates of the joint cost of computing pairings and discrete logarithms with those techniques. When estimating the multiplications incurred *without* precomputed pairing tables, we assume the costs of the pairing algorithms from [18] which appear to be the most efficient currently available.

Results are summarized on Table 4. In all cases we list the results adopting $w = 3$ for the 2^m-torsion discrete logarithms, and $w = 4$ for the 3^n-torsion, to match the implementation in [11] and ensure the discrete logarithm tables take the same space[2].

Table 4. Average $\mathbb{F}_p$ multiplication counts of joint pairing and discrete logarithm computation from [11] and our pairingless method, for SIKEp751 ($m = 372$, $n = 239$).

Torsion	[11] w/precomp	[11] No precomp	Ours
2^m	33052	56253	45264
3^n	33144	65180	44191

Finally, we compare the storage requirements of our proposals, as measured equivalently either in $E(\mathbb{F}_p)$ points or in $\mathbb{F}_{p^2}$ elements, with prior techniques.

In general, Algorithm 4.1 and its variants (Algorithm 4.2 and 4.3) require tables of sizes given by Eq. 2. Thus, for instance, in the case of SIKEp751 this means $8 \cdot \lceil 372/4 \rceil = 744$ elements (points over $E(\mathbb{F}_p)$) for the 2^m-torsion and $w = 4$, and $13 \cdot (239 - 2)/3 + 3^2 = 1036$ elements for the 3^n-torsion with $w = 3$.

By contrast, both [11] and [18], which do not use the techniques we describe in Sects. 4.3 and 4.4, need up to *four* times as much space: $2^w \lceil m/w \rceil$ (resp. $3^w \lceil n/w \rceil$) elements if $w \mid m$ (resp. $w \mid n$), and twice as much for two separate sets of tables for each torsion if $w \nmid m$ (resp. $w \nmid n$). Thus, at the time of writing the official SIKEp751 implementation, which builds upon those two research works, takes $16 \cdot 372/4 = 1488$ elements for the 2^m-torsion and $w = 4$ (so $w \mid m$), and $2 \cdot 27 \cdot \lceil 239/3 \rceil = 4320$ elements for the 3^n-torsion with $w = 3$ (so $w \nmid m$).

Besides, in general the T_{P_2} and T_{Q_2} precomputed pairing tables as defined in [11, Section 5.3] require $6(m - 1)$ $\mathbb{F}_p$ elements altogether, while the T_P table as defined in [11, Section 5.4] requires space equivalent to that of $3(n - 1) + 2$ $\mathbb{F}_{p^2}$ elements (albeit in the form of individual $\mathbb{F}_p$ elements). For instance, for SIKEp751 this means $(372-1)\cdot 3 = 1113$ $\mathbb{F}_{p^2}$ elements for T_{P_2} and T_{Q_2} together, and $(239 - 1) \cdot 6 + 4 = 1432$ $\mathbb{F}_p$ elements for table T_P, equivalent to 716 $\mathbb{F}_{p^2}$ elements. Our techniques require none of that. This is summarized on Table 5. The storage requirements of our technique are less than 29% of the state of the art for the 2^m-torsion, and about 21% for the 3^n-torsion.

[2] For the binary torsion, our methods require an extra table, L_6 or L_6^*, containing just 9 points over $\mathbb{F}_{p^2}$, a small fraction of the space required for the other tables.

Table 5. Storage requirements, measured in $E(\mathbb{F}_p)$ points or equivalently in $\mathbb{F}_{p^2}$ elements for SIKEp751 ($m = 372$, $n = 239$).

Torsion	[11] and [18]	Ours	Ratio (%)
	dlogT ($\mathbb{F}_{p^2}$) + pairingT ($\mathbb{F}_{p^2}$)	dlogT ($E(\mathbb{F}_p)$)	
2^m	$1488 + 1113 = 2601$	744	28.6
3^n	$4320 + 716 = 5036$	1036	20.6

7 Discussion and Conclusion

Apart from initialization, both the method for odd ℓ in Sect. 5.1 and the second method for $\ell = 2$ in Sect. 5.3 require each a single table for all calls to Algorithm 4.4, that is, they are carried out in the same torsion group over $\mathbb{F}_p$.

As a consequence, those constructions require essentially the *same* table space as needed for discrete logarithms in $\mathbb{F}_{p^2}^*$, but *no* tables as required to speedup the computation of pairings as suggested in [11], since we avoid pairings altogether. Trade-offs between table size and processing speed are possible, particularly the windowed approach discussed in [18, Section 6.1].

We remark that solving two instances of the discrete logarithm in a subgroup of $E_0(\mathbb{F}_p)$ is computationally less expensive than solving a single instance in a subgroup of $E_0(\mathbb{F}_{p^2})$, given that the relative cost of the arithmetic over those fields is essentially the only difference between the two scenarios. This shows that adapting Teske's algorithm [16] to a strategy graph-based approach, thereby retrieving both u and v at once while keeping the number of group operations potentially the same as that of Algorithm 4.4, would incur not only an already larger computational cost due to the contrast between $\mathbb{F}_p$ and $\mathbb{F}_{p^2}$ arithmetic, but the precomputed tables themselves would have to be *quadratically* larger to cope with computing pairs of digits at once.

In this context, Sutherland's algorithm [15] extends Teske's approach and promises to be asymptotically faster, but it is far more involved in the way it retrieves the digits of a discrete logarithm. It is unclear how that method could avoid the larger cost of $\mathbb{F}_{p^2}$ arithmetic, nor how large the underlying group would have to be for the asymptotic speedup to overcome the corresponding overhead, nor even whether precomputed tables could be made any smaller than what Teske's method would require. For these reasons, neither of these two approaches seems practical for the task at hand.

We have thus described methods to compute discrete logarithms in the elliptic curve torsion groups of the starting curves in SIDH-style cryptosystems, as required to compress the corresponding public keys. Our methods do not rely on bilinear pairings, yet their efficiency is comparable to the best available pairing-based methods while vastly reducing the storage space needed for pairing computations. The table storage needed for discrete logarithm computation is essentially the same required for discrete logarithms in the $\mathbb{F}_{p^2}$ finite field over which the curves are defined, the excess space being constant and very small, limited to just a few extra points.

Acknowledgements. This work is supported in part by NSERC, CryptoWorks21, Canada First Research Excellence Fund, Public Works and Government Services Canada.

A The OptPath algorithm

Algorithm A.1. OptPath(p, q, e): optimal subtree traversal path

INPUT: p, q: left and right edge traversal cost; e: number of leaves of Δ.
OUTPUT: $\mathsf{path}[1 \ldots e]$: array of indices specifying an optimal traversal path.

▷ Define $C[1 \ldots e]$ as an array of costs.
$C[1] \leftarrow 0, \quad \mathsf{path}[1] \leftarrow 0$
for $k \leftarrow 2$ **to** e **do**
  $j \leftarrow 1, \quad z \leftarrow k - 1$
  while $j < z$ **do**
    $m \leftarrow j + \lfloor (z - j)/2 \rfloor, \quad w \leftarrow m + 1$
    $t_1 \leftarrow C[m] + C[k - m] + (k - m) \cdot p + m \cdot q$
    $t_2 \leftarrow C[w] + C[k - w] + (k - w) \cdot p + w \cdot q$
    if $t_1 \le t_2$ **then**
      $z \leftarrow m$
    else
      $j \leftarrow w$
    end if
  end while
  $C[k] \leftarrow C[j] + C[k - j] + (k - j) \cdot p + j \cdot q, \quad \mathsf{path}[k] \leftarrow j$
end for
return path

References

1. Azarderakhsh, R., et al.: Supersingular Isogeny Key Encapsulation. SIKE Team (2020). https://sike.org/
2. Azarderakhsh, R., Jao, D., Kalach, K., Koziel, B., Leonardi, C.: Key compression for isogeny-based cryptosystems. In: Proceedings of the 3rd ACM International Workshop on ASIA Public-Key Cryptography, pp. 1–10. ACM (2016)
3. Bernstein, D.J., Birkner, P., Joye, M., Lange, T., Peters, C.: Twisted Edwards Curves. In: Vaudenay, S. (ed.) AFRICACRYPT 2008. LNCS, vol. 5023, pp. 389–405. Springer, Heidelberg (2008). https://doi.org/10.1007/978-3-540-68164-9_26
4. Chuengsatiansup, C.: Optimizing curve-based cryptography. PhD thesis, Technische Universiteit Eindhoven (2017)

5. Costello, C., Jao, D., Longa, P., Naehrig, M., Renes, J., Urbanik, D.: Efficient Compression of SIDH Public Keys. In: Coron, J.-S., Nielsen, J.B. (eds.) EUROCRYPT 2017. LNCS, vol. 10210, pp. 679–706. Springer, Cham (2017). https://doi.org/10.1007/978-3-319-56620-7_24
6. Costello, C., Longa, P., Naehrig, M.: Efficient Algorithms for Supersingular Isogeny Diffie-Hellman. In: Robshaw, M., Katz, J. (eds.) CRYPTO 2016. LNCS, vol. 9814, pp. 572–601. Springer, Heidelberg (2016). https://doi.org/10.1007/978-3-662-53018-4_21
7. De Feo, L., Jao, D., Plût, J.: Towards quantum-resistant cryptosystems from supersingular elliptic curve isogenies. J. Math. Crypto. **8**(3), 209–247 (2014)
8. Galbraith, S.D., Rotger, V.: Easy decision-Diffie-Hellman groups. LMS J. Comput. Math. **7**, 201–218 (2004)
9. Hutchinson, A., Karabina, K., Pereira, G.: Memory Optimization Techniques for Computing Discrete Logarithms in Compressed SIKE. Cryptology ePrint Archive, Report 2021/368 (2020). http://eprint.iacr.org/2021/368
10. Menezes, A.J., van Oorschot, P.C., Vanstone, S.A.: Handbook of Applied Cryptography. CRC Press, Boca Raton, USA (1999)
11. Naehrig, M., Renes, J.: Dual Isogenies and Their Application to Public-Key Compression for Isogeny-Based Cryptography. In: Galbraith, S.D., Moriai, S. (eds.) ASIACRYPT 2019. LNCS, vol. 11922, pp. 243–272. Springer, Cham (2019). https://doi.org/10.1007/978-3-030-34621-8_9
12. Pereira, G., Doliskani, J., Jao, D.: x-only point addition formula and faster compressed SIKE. J. Cryptographic Eng. **11**(1), 1–13, (2020)
13. Pohlig, S.C., Hellman, M.E.: An improved algorithm for computing logarithms over $GF(p)$ and its cryptographic significance. IEEE Trans. Inf. Theory **24**(1), 106–110 (1978)
14. Shoup, V.: A Computational Introduction to Number Theory and Algebra. Cambridge University Press, Cambridge (2005)
15. Sutherland, A.V.: Structure computation and discrete logarithms in finite Abelian p-groups. Math. Comput. **80**, 477–500 (2011)
16. Teske, E.: The Pohlig-Hellman method generalized for group structure computation. J. Symbolic Comput. **27**(6), 521–534 (1999)
17. Zanon, G.H.M., Simplicio, M.A., Pereira, G.C.C.F., Doliskani, J., Barreto, P.S.L.M.: Faster Isogeny-Based Compressed Key Agreement. In: Lange, T., Steinwandt, R. (eds.) PQCrypto 2018. LNCS, vol. 10786, pp. 248–268. Springer, Cham (2018). https://doi.org/10.1007/978-3-319-79063-3_12
18. Zanon, G.H.M., Simplicio Jr., M.A., Pereira, G.C.C.F., Doliskani, J., Barreto, P.S.L.M.: Faster key compression for isogeny-based cryptosystems. IEEE Trans. Comput. **68**(5), 688–701 (2018)

Analysis of Multivariate Encryption Schemes: Application to Dob

Morten Øygarden[1(✉)], Patrick Felke[2], and Håvard Raddum[1]

[1] Simula UiB, Bergen, Norway
{morten.oygarden,haavardr}@simula.no
[2] University of Applied Sciences Emden/Leer, Emden, Germany
patrick.felke@hs-emden-leer.de

Abstract. In this paper, we study the effect of two modifications to multivariate public key encryption schemes: internal perturbation (*ip*), and Q_+. Focusing on the *Dob encryption scheme*, a construction utilising these modifications, we accurately predict the number of degree fall polynomials produced in a Gröbner basis attack, up to and including degree five. The predictions remain accurate even when fixing variables. Based on this new theory we design a novel attack on the Dob encryption scheme, which breaks Dob using the parameters suggested by its designers.

While our work primarily focuses on the Dob encryption scheme, we also believe that the presented techniques will be of particular interest to the analysis of other big–field schemes.

1 Introduction

Public key cryptography has played a vital role in securing services on the internet that we take for granted today. The security of schemes based on integer factorization and the discrete logarithm problem (DLP) is now well understood, and the related encryption algorithms have served us well over several decades.

In [25] it was shown that quantum computers can solve both integer factorization and DLP in polynomial time. While large scale quantum computers that break the actual implementations of secure internet communication have yet to be built, progress is being made in constructing them. This has led the community for cryptographic research to look for new public key primitives that are based on mathematical problems believed to be hard even for quantum computers, so called *post–quantum cryptography.*

In 2016 NIST launched a project aimed at standardizing post–quantum public key primitives. A call for proposals was made and many candidate schemes were proposed. The candidates are based on a variety of problems, including the shortest vector problem for lattices, the problem of decoding a random linear code, or the problem of solving a system of multivariate quadratic equations over a finite field (the MQ problem).

The first encryption scheme based on the MQ problem, named C^*, was proposed in [21] and was broken by Patarin in [23]. Since then, much work has

J. A. Garay (Ed.): PKC 2021, LNCS 12710, pp. 155–183, 2021.
https://doi.org/10.1007/978-3-030-75245-3_7

gone into designing new central maps, as well as modifications that can enhance the security of existing ones. Several multivariate schemes have been proposed following C^*, for instance [5,24,27,28]. While some of the schemes for digital signatures based on the MQ problem seem to be secure, it has been much harder to construct encryption schemes that are both efficient and secure. The papers [1,16,22,26,29], all present attacks on MQ-based public key encryption schemes, and as of now we are only aware of a few (e.g., [9,32]) that remain unbroken.

In [20] a new kind of central mapping is introduced, which can be used to construct both encryption and signature schemes. The novel feature of the central mapping is that it has a high degree over an extension field, while still being easy to invert. The encryption variant proposed in [20] is called Dob and uses two types of modifications to its basic construction.

Our Contribution

The initial part of our work provides a theoretical analysis of (combinations of) two modifications for multivariate cryptosystems. The Q_+–modification was (to the best of our knowledge) first proposed in [20], while the second, internal perturbation (*ip*), has been in use for earlier schemes [8,9,12]. More specifically, we develop the tools for computing the dimension of the ideal associated with these modifications, at different degrees. This in turn provides key insights into the complexity of algebraic attacks based on Gröbner basis techniques.

As an application, we focus on the Dob encryption scheme proposed in [20]. We are able to deduce formulas that predict the exact number of first fall polynomials for degrees 3,4 and 5. These formulas furthermore capture how the number of degree fall polynomials changes as an attacker fixes variables, which also allows for the analysis of hybrid methods (see e.g., [3]).

Finally, the newfound understanding allow us to develop a novel attack on the Dob encryption scheme. Through analyzing and manipulating smaller, projected polynomial systems, we are able to extract and isolate a basis of the secret modifiers, breaking the scheme. While the details of the attack have been worked out for the Dob encryption scheme, we believe the techniques themselves could be further generalised to include different central maps and modifications.

Organisation

The paper is organized as follows. In Sect. 2 we recall the relation between $\mathbb{F}_2^d$ and $\mathbb{F}_{2^d}$, as well as the necessary background for solving multivariate systems over $\mathbb{F}_2$. In Sect. 3 we develop the general theory that explores the effectiveness of the modifications Q_+ and *ip* . Section 4 introduces the Dob scheme, and we deduce formulas that predict the number of degree fall polynomials for this construction. Experimental data verifying the accuracy of these formulas is presented in Sect. 5. In Sect. 6 we develop the novel attack on the Dob encryption scheme, using the information learned from the previous sections. Finally, Sect. 7 concludes the work.

Table of definitions

Throughout the paper we will use the notation in Table 1. We list it here for easy reference.

Table 1. Notation used in the paper

Term	Meaning
$B(n)$	$B(n) = \mathbb{F}_2[x_1, \ldots, x_n]/\langle x_1^2 + x_1, \ldots, x_n^2 + x_n \rangle$
$\overline{B}(n)$	$\overline{B}(n) = \mathbb{F}_2[x_1, \ldots, x_n]/\langle x_1^2, \ldots, x_n^2 \rangle$
$\overline{B}(n)_\nu$	The set of homogeneous polynomials of degree ν in n variables
$\langle \mathcal{R} \rangle$	The ideal associated with the set of polynomials $\mathcal{R}$
$\langle \mathcal{R} \rangle_\nu$	The ν–th degree part of a graded ideal $\langle \mathcal{R} \rangle$
$\dim_\nu(\langle \mathcal{R} \rangle)$	The dimension of $\langle \mathcal{R} \rangle_\nu$ as an $\mathbb{F}_2$–vector space
$\mathcal{P}^h$	A set of homogeneous quadratic polynomials over $\overline{B}(n)_2$
$\mathrm{Syz}(\mathcal{P}^h)_\nu$	The grade ν part of the (first) syzygy module of $\mathcal{P}^h$. (See Sect. 2.1)
$\mathcal{T}(\mathcal{P}^h)_\nu$	The grade ν part of the trivial syzygy module of $\mathcal{P}^h$. (See Sect. 2.1)
$\mathcal{S}(\mathcal{P}^h)_\nu$	$\mathcal{S}(\mathcal{P})_\nu = \mathrm{Syz}(\mathcal{P})_\nu / \mathcal{T}(\mathcal{P}^h)_\nu$
Q_+, q_i, t	The Q_+ modifier, with $q_1, \ldots, q_t$ added quadratic polynomials
(ip), v_i, k	The *internal perturbation* modifier with $v_1, \ldots, v_k$ linear forms
$N_\nu^{(\alpha,\beta)}$	Estimate of the number of degree fall polynomials at degree ν

2 Preliminaries

Multivariate big–field encryption schemes are defined using the field $\mathbb{F}_{q^d}$ and the d-dimensional vector space over the base field, $\mathbb{F}_q^d$. In practical implementations, $q = 2$ is very often used, and we restrict ourselves to only consider this case in the paper.

2.1 Polynomial System Solving

A standard technique used in the cryptanalysis of multivariate schemes, is to compute a Gröbner basis associated with the ideal $\langle p_i + y_i \rangle_{1 \le i \le m}$, for a fixed ciphertext $y_1, \ldots, y_m$ (see for example [7] for more information on Gröbner bases). As we are interested in an encryption system, we can reasonably expect a unique solution in the boolean polynomial ring $B(n)$. In this setting the solution can be read directly from a Gröbner basis of any order.

One of the most efficient algorithms for computing Gröbner bases is F_4 [15]. In the usual setting, the algorithm proceeds in a step–wise manner; each step has an associated degree, D, where all the polynomial pairs of degree D are reduced simultaneously using linear algebra. The degree associated with the most time consuming step is known as the *solving degree*, D_{solv}, and time complexity of F_4 can be estimated to be:

$$\text{Complexity}_{\text{GB}} = \mathcal{O}\Big(\Big(\sum_{i=0}^{D_{solv}} \binom{d}{i} \Big)^{\omega} \Big), \tag{1}$$

where $2 \leq \omega \leq 3$ denotes the linear algebra constant. Determining D_{solv} is in general difficult, but there is an important class of polynomial systems that is well understood. Recall that a homogeneous polynomial system, $\mathcal{F}^h = (f_1^h, \dots, f_m^h) \in \overline{B}(n)^m$, is said to be *semi–regular* if the following holds; for all $1 \leq i \leq m$ and any $g \in \overline{B}(n)$ satisfying

$$g f_i^h \in \langle f_1^h, \dots, f_{i-1}^h \rangle \text{ and } \deg(g f_i) < D_{reg}, \tag{2}$$

then $g \in \langle f_1^h, \dots, f_i^h \rangle$ (note that f_i^h is included since we are over $\mathbb{F}_2$). Here D_{reg} is the *degree of regularity* as defined in [2], (for $i = 1$ the ideal generated by $\emptyset$ is the 0–ideal). We will also need a weaker version of this definition, where we say that $\mathcal{F}^h$ is D_0–semi–regular, if the same condition holds, but for $D_0 < D_{reg}$ in place of D_{reg} in Eq. (2). An inhomogeneous system $\mathcal{F}$ is said to be (D_0–)semi–regular if its upper homogeneous part is. For a quadratic, semi–regular system $\mathcal{F}$ over $\overline{B}(n)$, the Hilbert series of $\overline{B}(n)/\mathcal{F}$ is written as (Corollary 7 in [2]):

$$T_{m,n}(z) = \frac{(1+z)^n}{(1+z^2)^m}, \tag{3}$$

and the degree of regularity can be computed explicitly as the degree of the first non–positive term in this series. Determining whether a given polynomial system is semi–regular may, in general, be as hard as computing a Gröbner basis for it. Nevertheless, experiments seem to suggest that randomly generated polynomial systems behave as semi–regular sequences with a high probability [2], and the degree of regularity can in practice be used as the solving degree in Eq. (1). We will denote the degree of regularity for a semi–regular sequence of m polynomials in n variables as $D_{reg}(m, n)$. On the other hand, it is well known that many big–field multivariate schemes are not semi–regular (e.g., [5,16]). In these cases the *first fall degree* is often used to estimate the solving degree ([10,22]). The first fall degree, according to [10], will be defined in Definition 2, but before that we recall the definition of a *Macaulay matrix* associated to a polynomial system.

Definition 1. *Let $\mathcal{P}$ be an (inhomogeneous) polynomial system in $B(n)$, of degree two. An (inhomogeneous)* Macaulay matrix *of $\mathcal{P}$ at degree D, $M_D(\mathcal{P})$, is a matrix with entries in $\mathbb{F}_2$, such that:*

1. *The columns are indexed by the monomials of degree $\leq D$ in $B(n)$.*
2. *The rows are indexed by the possible combinations $x^\alpha p_i$, where $1 \leq i \leq n$ and $x^\alpha \in B(n)$ is a monomial of degree $\leq D - 2$. The entries in one row corresponds to the coefficients of the associated polynomial.*

Similarly, we define the homogeneous Macaulay matrix *of $\mathcal{P}$ at degree D, $\overline{M}_D(\mathcal{P})$, by considering $\mathcal{P}^h \in \overline{B}(n)$, only including monomials of degree D in the columns, and rows associated to combinations $x^\alpha p_i^h$, deg$(x^\alpha) = D - 2$.*

Syzygies and Degree Fall Polynomials. Let $\mathcal{P}^h = (p_1^h, \ldots, p_m^h) \in \overline{B}(n)_2^m$ denote a homogeneous quadratic polynomial system. The set $\mathcal{P}^h$ induces a map:

$$\begin{aligned} \psi^{\mathcal{P}^h} : \quad \overline{B}(n)^m &\longrightarrow \overline{B}(n) \\ (b_1, \ldots, b_m) &\longmapsto \textstyle\sum_{i=1}^m b_i p_i^h, \end{aligned} \tag{4}$$

which in turn splits into graded maps $\psi_{\nu-2}^{\mathcal{P}^h} : \overline{B}(n)_{\nu-2}^m \longrightarrow \overline{B}(n)_\nu$. The $\overline{B}(n)$–module $\text{Syz}(\mathcal{P}^h)_\nu = \text{Ker}(\psi_{\nu-2}^{\mathcal{P}^h})$ is known as the *ν–th grade of the (first) syzygy module of* $\mathcal{P}^h$. When $\nu = 4$, $\text{Syz}(\mathcal{P}^h)_4$ will contain the *Koszul Syzygies*[1], which are generated by $(0, ..., 0, p_j^h, 0, ..., 0, p_i^h, 0, ..., 0)$ (p_j^h is in position i and p_i^h is in position j), and the *field syzygies*, which are generated by $(0, ..., 0, p_i^h, 0, ..., 0)$ (p_i^h in position i). These syzygies correspond to the cancellations $p_j^h p_i^h + p_i^h p_j^h = 0$ and $(p_i^h)^2 = 0$. As they are always present, and not dependent of the structure of $\mathcal{P}^h$, they are sometimes referred to as the *trivial syzygies*. More generally, we will define the submodule $\mathcal{T}(\mathcal{P}^h)_\nu \subseteq \text{Syz}(\mathcal{P}^h)_\nu$ to be the ν–th graded component of the module generated by the Koszul and field syzygies, and denote $\mathcal{S}(\mathcal{P})_\nu = \text{Syz}(\mathcal{P}^h)_\nu / \mathcal{T}(\mathcal{P}^h)_\nu$.

Definition 2. *The* first fall degree *associated with the quadratic polynomial system $\mathcal{P}$ is the natural number*

$$D_{ff} = min\{\ D \geq 2 \mid \mathcal{S}(\mathcal{P})_D \neq 0\ \}.$$

Representations over Base and Extension Fields. For any fixed isomorphism $\mathbb{F}_2^d \simeq \mathbb{F}_{2^d}$, there is a one–to–one correspondence between d polynomials in $B(d)$ and a univariate polynomial in $\mathbb{F}_{2^d}[X]/\langle X^{2^d} + X\rangle$ (see 9.2.2.2 in [4] for more details). For an integer j, let $w_2(j)$ denote the number of nonzero coefficients in the binary expansion of j. For a univariate polynomial $H(X)$, we define $\max_{w_2}(H)$ as the maximal $w_2(j)$ where j is the degree of a term occurring in H. Let $P(X)$ be the univariate representation of the public key of a multivariate scheme, and suppose there exists a polynomial $H(X)$ such that

$$\max_{w_2}(H(X)P(X)) < \max_{w_2}(H(X)) + \max_{w_2}(P(X)). \tag{5}$$

Then the multivariate polynomials corresponding to the product $H(X)P(X)$ will yield degree fall polynomials from (multivariate) degree $\max_{w_2}(H) + \max_{w_2}(P)$ down to degree $\max_{w_2}(HP)$.

It was mentioned in [16] that the presence of polynomials satisfying Eq. (5) was the reason for Gröbner basis algorithms to perform exceptionally well on HFE–systems. Constructing particular polynomials that satisfy Eq. (5) has also been a central component in the security analyzes found in [10] and [22].

---

[1] Here we follow the nomenclature used, for instance, in [18].

3 Estimating the Number of Degree Fall Polynomials

We start by introducing a general setting, motivated by the Dob encryption scheme which we will focus on later. Let $\mathcal{F} : \mathbb{F}_2^n \rightarrow \mathbb{F}_2^m$ be a system of m quadratic polynomials over $B(n)$. Furthermore, consider the following two modifiers[2]:

1. The *internal perturbation* (*ip*) modification chooses k linear combinations $v_1, \ldots, v_k$, and adds a random quadratic polynomial in the v_i's to each polynomial in $\mathcal{F}$.
2. The Q_+ modifier selects t quadratic polynomials $q_1, \ldots, q_t$, and adds a random linear combination of them to each polynomial in $\mathcal{F}$.

Let H_{ip} be the random quadratic polynomials in $v_1, \ldots, v_k$ and H_{Q_+} the random linear combinations of $q_1, \ldots, q_t$. A modification of the system $\mathcal{F}$ can then be written as

$$\begin{aligned} \mathcal{P} : \mathbb{F}_2^n &\longrightarrow \mathbb{F}_2^m \\ x &\longmapsto \mathcal{F}(x) + H_{ip}(x) + H_{Q_+}(x). \end{aligned} \tag{6}$$

The problem we will be concerned with in this section is the following: given full knowledge of the degree fall polynomials of the system $\mathcal{F}$, what can we say about the degree fall polynomials of the system $\mathcal{P}$?

3.1 The Big Picture

Let $\mathcal{F}^h$ and $\mathcal{P}^h$ denote the homogeneous parts of the systems $\mathcal{F}$ and $\mathcal{P}$ respectively, and consider them over $\overline{B}(n)$. For a positive integer $\alpha \leq k$, we define V^α to be the homogeneous ideal in $\overline{B}(n)$ that is generated by all possible combinations of α linear forms from the *ip* modification, i.e.:

$$V^\alpha = \langle (v_{i_1} v_{i_2} \cdots v_{i_\alpha})^h \mid 1 \leq i_1 < i_2 < \ldots < i_\alpha \leq k \rangle. \tag{7}$$

In other words, V^α is the product ideal $\overbrace{V^1 \cdot V^1 \cdot \ldots \cdot V^1}^{\alpha}$. Similarly, for the quadratic polynomials associated with the Q_+ modifier we define Q^β for a positive integer $\beta \leq t$ to be the product ideal:

$$Q^\beta = \langle (q_{i_1} q_{i_2} \cdots q_{i_\beta})^h \mid 1 \leq i_1 < i_2 < \ldots < i_\beta \leq t \rangle. \tag{8}$$

Finally, for $0 \leq \alpha \leq k$ and $0 \leq \beta \leq t$, we define the ideal of different combinations of the modifiers, $M^{(\alpha,\beta)} = \langle V^\alpha, Q^\beta \rangle$, along with the boundary cases $M^{(\alpha,0)} = V^\alpha$, $M^{(0,\beta)} = Q^\beta$ and $M^{(0,0)} = \langle 1 \rangle$.

The following result is an important first step to understand how the degree fall polynomials in $\mathcal{F}$ behave when modifiers are introduced to the scheme.

[2] The authors of [20] named these two modifiers $\oplus$ and " + ". Note that in earlier literature (c.f. [31]), the " + " modification refers to a different modification than what is described in [20], and the $\oplus$ modification has been called *internal perturbation* (*ip*). (To the best of our knowledge, the " + " modification from [20] has not been used in earlier work). To avoid any confusion, we have chosen to stick with the name (*ip*) and use Q_+ for [20]'s "+".

Lemma 1. *Let $\mathcal{P}^h$, $\mathcal{F}^h$, $M^{(2,1)}$ be defined as above, and $\psi^{\mathcal{P}^h}$ be as defined in Eq. (4). Then $\langle \psi^{\mathcal{P}^h}(\mathcal{S}(\mathcal{F}))\rangle$ and $\langle \psi^{\mathcal{P}^h}(Syz(\mathcal{F}^h))\rangle$ are homogeneous subideals of $\langle \mathcal{P}^h \rangle \cap M^{(2,1)}$.*

Proof. We show the statement for $\langle \psi^{\mathcal{P}^h}(\mathrm{Syz}(\mathcal{F}^h))\rangle$; the case of $\langle \psi^{\mathcal{P}^h}(\mathcal{S}(\mathcal{F}))\rangle$ is similar. First note that $\psi^{\mathcal{P}^h}(\mathrm{Syz}(\mathcal{F}^h))$ is a group, as it is the image of a group under a group homomorphism. Secondly, for any element $\mathbf{a} = (a_1, \ldots, a_m) \in \mathrm{Syz}(\mathcal{F}^h)$, and any $r \in \overline{B}(n)$, we have $r\psi^{\mathcal{P}^h}(\mathbf{a}) = \psi^{\mathcal{P}^h}((ra_1, \ldots, ra_m))$, where also $(ra_1, \ldots, ra_m) \in \mathrm{Syz}(\mathcal{F}^h)$. It follows that $\psi^{\mathcal{P}^h}(\mathrm{Syz}(\mathcal{F}^h))$ is indeed an ideal.

The inclusion $\langle \psi^{\mathcal{P}^h}(\mathrm{Syz}(\mathcal{F}^h))\rangle \subseteq \langle \mathcal{P}^h\rangle$ follows directly from the definition of $\psi^{\mathcal{P}^h}$. For the other inclusion we note that, by construction, we can write $p_i^h = f_i^h + \sum_{j=1}^{t} b_{i,j} q_j^h + \sum_{j,l=0}^{k} c_{i,j,l}(v_j v_l)^h$, for all $1 \leq i \leq m$ and for suitable constants $b_{i,j}, c_{i,j,l} \in \mathbb{F}_2$, where f_i^h, p_i^h are the polynomials of $\mathcal{F}^h$ and $\mathcal{P}^h$ respectively. When $\mathbf{a} \in \mathrm{Syz}(\mathcal{F}^h)$, the f_i^h–parts in $\psi^{\mathcal{P}^h}(\mathbf{a})$ will vanish, and we are left with a polynomial that can be generated from the elements of V^2 and Q^1. Hence we also have $\langle \psi^{\mathcal{P}^h}(\mathrm{Syz}(\mathcal{F}^h))\rangle \subseteq M^{(2,1)}$.

In particular, there is the following chain of ideals

$$\langle \psi^{\mathcal{P}^h}(\mathcal{S}(\mathcal{F}))\rangle \subseteq \langle \psi^{\mathcal{P}^h}(\mathrm{Syz}(\mathcal{F}^h))\rangle \subseteq \langle \mathcal{P}^h\rangle \cap M^{(2,1)} \subseteq M^{(2,1)}. \tag{9}$$

We now allow ourselves to be slightly informal, in order to see how this all relates in practice to the cases we are interested in. At each degree ν, the dimension $\dim_\nu(M^{(2,1)})$ of $M_\nu^{(2,1)}$ as a vector space over $\mathbb{F}_2$ can be seen as a measure of how much information the modifiers can hide. An interesting case from an attacker's point of view is when $\langle \psi^{\mathcal{P}^h}(\mathcal{S}(\mathcal{F}))\rangle_{\nu_0}$ has the maximal dimension $\dim_{\nu_0}(\langle \psi^{\mathcal{P}^h}(\mathcal{S}(\mathcal{F}))\rangle) = \dim_{\nu_0}(M^{(2,1)})$, for a relatively small ν_0. While 'excess' polynomials in $\langle \psi^{\mathcal{P}^h}(\mathcal{S}(\mathcal{F}))\rangle_{\nu_0}$ will sum to 0 in $\overline{B}(n)$, there is a chance that the corresponding inhomogeneous polynomials will result in degree fall polynomials when treated over $B(n)$. In particular, this yields an upper bound $D_{ff} \leq \nu_0$ on the first fall degree. We can do even better in practice.

Note that $(M^{(2,1)}\langle \mathcal{P}^h\rangle)_\nu$ will be a subspace of (the row space of) the Macaulay matrix $\overline{M}_\nu(\mathcal{P})$. As this matrix can be constructed by an attacker, we should count the possible combinations of polynomials from both $(M^{(2,1)}\langle \mathcal{P}^h\rangle)$ and the image of $\psi^{\mathcal{P}^h}(\mathcal{S}(\mathcal{F}))$. Some caution is warranted when counting these combinations. For instance, $\psi^{\mathcal{P}^h}(ms) \in M^{(2,1)}\langle \mathcal{P}^h\rangle$ for any $m \in M^{(2,1)}$ and $s \in \mathcal{S}(\mathcal{F})$, so we need to be careful in order to not count the same elements twice. For now we will keep up with our informal theme and denote '$M^{(2,1)}\langle \mathcal{P}^h\rangle$ modulo these collisions' by $\mathcal{P}_{M^{(2,1)}}$. We will deal with it more properly when computing its dimension in Sect. 3.3. It is shown in Appendix A of [33] that $\langle \psi^{\mathcal{P}^h}(\mathcal{T}(\mathcal{F}^h))\rangle \subseteq M^{(2,1)}\langle \mathcal{P}^h\rangle$, which is why we will focus on $\langle \psi^{\mathcal{P}^h}(\mathcal{S}(\mathcal{F}))\rangle$ (as opposed to $\langle \psi^{\mathcal{P}^h}(\mathrm{Syz}(\mathcal{F}^h))\rangle$).

We now have everything needed to discuss estimates of the number of degree fall polynomials at different degrees. We start by assuming that none of the degree fall polynomials we get from $\mathcal{S}(\mathcal{F})$ (under $\psi^{\mathcal{P}^h}$) can be reduced by lower–degree Macaulay matrices of $\mathcal{P}$. This allows us to directly use $\dim_\nu(\mathcal{S}(\mathcal{F}))$. We furthermore add $\dim_\nu(\mathcal{P}_{M^{(2,1)}})$, and subtract by $\dim_\nu(M^{(2,1)})$. This yields the expression for our first estimate of degree fall polynomials, $N_\nu^{(0,0)}$, at degree ν:

$$N_\nu^{(0,0)} = \dim_\nu(\mathcal{S}(\mathcal{F})) + \dim_\nu(\mathcal{P}_{M^{(2,1)}}) - \dim_\nu(M^{(2,1)}). \tag{10}$$

In a sense, $N_\nu^{(0,0)}$ can be thought of as estimating the number of degree fall polynomials, as an effect of 'over saturating' $M_\nu^{(2,1)}$. When $N_\nu^{(0,0)}$ is a positive number, this is the number of degree fall polynomials we expect to find (based on this effect); if $N_\nu^{(0,0)}$ is negative, there is no such over saturation, and we do not expect any degree fall polynomials at degree ν. The benefits of having the expression in Eq. (10) is that the study of the relatively complex polynomial system $\mathcal{P}^h$ can be broken down to studying three simpler systems. The dimensions of $M^{(2,1)}$ and $\mathcal{P}_{M^{(2,1)}}$ can, in particular, be further studied under the assumptions that the modifiers form a semi–regular system. In addition to being a reasonable assumption as the modifiers are randomly chosen, this is also the ideal situation for the legitimate user, as this maximizes the dimension of $M^{(2,1)}$. Indeed, the study of $M^{(2,1)}$ and $\mathcal{P}_{M^{(2,1)}}$ will be continued in the following subsections. Before that, we will generalize the ideas presented so far, arriving at several expressions that can be used to estimate the number of degree fall polynomials.

Generalised Estimates of Degree Fall Polynomials. Let $M^{(\alpha,\beta)}\mathrm{Syz}(\mathcal{F})$ denote the module $\{ms \mid m \in M^{(\alpha,\beta)}, s \in \mathrm{Syz}(\mathcal{F})\}$ (which is well–defined since $\mathrm{Syz}(\mathcal{F})$ is a $\overline{B}(n)$–module), and define

$$\mathcal{S}(\mathcal{F})_{M^{(\alpha,\beta)}} := [M^{(\alpha,\beta)}\mathrm{Syz}(\mathcal{F})]/\mathcal{T}(\mathcal{F}).$$

Instead of considering *all* the syzygies $\mathcal{S}(\mathcal{F})$, we can start with submodules of the form $\mathcal{S}(\mathcal{F})_{M^{(\alpha,\beta)}}$. The benefit is that the ideal we need to 'over saturate' will now be $M^{(\alpha,\beta)}M^{(2,1)}$. In Sect. 5 we will see several examples where this yields a better estimate than $N_\nu^{(0,0)}$. Following through with this idea, along with the same considerations discussed prior to Eq. (10), we arrive at the following estimate for $\alpha, \beta \geq 0$:

$$\begin{aligned} N_\nu^{(\alpha,\beta)} &= \dim_\nu(\mathcal{S}(\mathcal{F})_{M^{(\alpha,\beta)}}) - \dim_\nu(M^{(\alpha,\beta)}M^{(2,1)}) \\ &\quad + \dim_\nu(\mathcal{P}^h_{M^{(\alpha,\beta)}M^{(2,1)}}). \end{aligned} \tag{11}$$

Recalling the convention that $M^{(0,0)} = \langle 1 \rangle$, this is indeed a generalisation of Eq. (10).

We now have several different estimates for degree fall polynomials, varying with the choice of α, β. Any of these may be dominating, depending on the parameters of the scheme. The general estimate at degree ν is then taken to be their maximum:

$$N_\nu = \max\{0, N_\nu^{(\alpha,\beta)} \mid 0 \leq \alpha \leq k \text{ and } 0 \leq \beta \leq t\}. \tag{12}$$

Note in particular that if $N_\nu = 0$, then all our estimates are non–positive, and we do not expect any degree fall polynomials at this degree.

Consider now the main assumptions underlying these estimates. Firstly, recall that we assumed that none of the degree fall polynomials that can be made from $\psi^{\mathcal{P}}(\mathcal{S}(\mathcal{F})_{M^{(\alpha,\beta)}})$ will be reduced to 0 when solving the system $\mathcal{P}$. Secondly, the formulas implicitly assume that all the polynomials in $M^{(\alpha,\beta)}M^{(2,1)}$ need to be reduced before we can observe degree fall polynomials. The third assumption, concerning $\mathcal{P}^h_{M^{(\alpha,\beta)}M^{(2,1)}}$, will be specified in Sect. 3.3.

Finally, we stress that the aim of this section has been to investigate one of the aspects that can lead to a system exhibiting degree fall polynomials. The estimates presented should not be used without care to derive arguments about lower bounds on the first fall degree. Nevertheless, we find that in practice these estimates and their assumptions seem to be reasonable. With the exception of a slight deviation in only two cases (see Sect. 4.3), the estimates lead to formulas that are able to describe all our experiments for the Dob encryption scheme that will be investigated in Sect. 4.

3.2 Dimension of the Modifiers

The estimate given in Eq. (11) requires knowledge of the dimension of (products of) the ideals $M^{(\alpha,\beta)}$. These will in turn depend on the chosen modifications V^α and Q^β. In this section we collect various results that will be needed to determine these dimensions. We start with the following elementary properties.

Lemma 2. *Consider $M^{(\alpha,\beta)} = (V^\alpha + Q^\beta)$, and positive integers $\alpha_0, \alpha, \beta_0, \beta, \nu$. Then the following holds:*

(i) $V^{\alpha_0}V^\alpha = V^{\alpha_0+\alpha}$ *and* $Q^{\beta_0}Q^\beta = Q^{\beta_0+\beta}$.

(ii) $V^{\alpha_0}Q^{\beta_0} \subseteq V^\alpha Q^\beta$ *if* $\alpha \leq \alpha_0$ *and* $\beta \leq \beta_0$.

(iii) $M^{(\alpha_0,\beta_0)}M^{(\alpha,\beta)} = M^{(\alpha_0+\alpha,\beta_0+\beta)} + V^{\alpha_0}Q^\beta + V^\alpha Q^{\beta_0}$.

(iv) $dim_\nu(M^{(\alpha,\beta)}) = dim_\nu(Q^\beta) + dim_\nu(V^\alpha) - dim_\nu(Q^\beta \cap V^\alpha)$.

(v)
$$\begin{aligned} dim_\nu(M^{(\alpha_0,\beta_0)}M^{(\alpha,\beta)}) &= dim_\nu(M^{(\alpha_0+\alpha,\beta_0+\beta)}) + dim_\nu(V^{\alpha_0}Q^\beta) \\ &+ dim_\nu(V^\alpha Q^{\beta_0}) - dim_\nu(M^{(\alpha_0+\alpha,\beta_0+\beta)} \cap V^{\alpha_0}Q^\beta) \\ &- dim_\nu(M^{(\alpha_0+\alpha,\beta_0+\beta)} \cap V^\alpha Q^{\beta_0}) - dim_\nu(V^{\alpha_0}Q^\beta \cap V^\alpha Q^{\beta_0}) \\ &+ dim_\nu(M^{(\alpha_0+\alpha,\beta_0+\beta)} \cap V^{\alpha_0}Q^\beta \cap V^\alpha Q^{\beta_0}). \end{aligned}$$

Proof. Properties (i) – (iv) follow from the appropriate definitions in a straightforward manner; we give a brief sketch of property (v) here. From property (iii) we know that $M^{(\alpha_0,\beta_0)}M^{(\alpha,\beta)}$ can be written as the sum of the three ideals $M^{(\alpha_0+\alpha,\beta_0+\beta)}$, $V^{\alpha_0}Q^\beta$ and $V^\alpha Q^{\beta_0}$. We start by summing the dimension of each of these three ideals individually. Any polynomial belonging to exactly two of these subideals is now counted twice, which is why we subtract by the combinations intersecting two of these ideals. Lastly, a polynomial belonging to all three of the subideals will, at this point, have been counted thrice, and then subtracted thrice. Hence, we add the dimension of intersecting all three subideals.

The dimension $\dim_\nu(V^\alpha)$ can be further inspected using the following result.

Lemma 3. *Suppose that $v_1, \ldots, v_k$ are k linearly independent linear forms in $\overline{B}(n)$. Then*

$$dim_\nu(V^\alpha) = \sum_{\substack{i \geq \alpha, j \geq 0 \\ i+j=\nu}} \binom{k}{i}\binom{n-k}{j} \tag{13}$$

holds under the conventions that $\binom{a}{b} = 0$ if $b > a$, and $\binom{a}{0} = 1$.

Proof. As $v_1, \ldots, v_k$ are linearly independent, we can choose $n-k$ linear forms of $\overline{B}(n)$, $w_{k+1}, \ldots, w_n$, that constitute a change of variables

$$\overline{B}(n) \simeq \overline{B}' = \mathbb{F}_2[v_1, \ldots, v_k, w_{k+1}, \ldots w_n]/\langle v_1^2, \ldots, w_n^2\rangle.$$

For any monomial $\gamma \in \overline{B}'$, we will define $\deg_v(\gamma)$ as its degree in the $v_1, \ldots, v_k$-variables, and $\deg_w(\gamma)$ as its degree in the variables $w_{k+1}, \ldots, w_n$. The elements of V^α of (total) degree ν, is now generated (in $\overline{B}'$ as an $\mathbb{F}_2$–vector space) by all monomials γ such that $\deg_v(\gamma) \geq \alpha$ and $\deg_v(\gamma) + \deg_w(\gamma) = \nu$. The number of all such monomials are counted in Eq. (13).

When $q_1^h, \ldots, q_t^h$ forms a D_0–Semi–regular system, we need only be concerned with the trivial syzygies when counting $\dim_\nu(Q^1)$, for $\nu < D_0$. For the particular cases we are interested in, this amounts to $\dim_3(Q^1) = tn$, $\dim_4(Q^1) = t\binom{n}{2} - [\binom{t}{2} + t]$ and $\dim_5(Q^1) = t\binom{n}{3} - n[\binom{t}{2} + t]$.

Lemma 4. *Suppose that $(v_1, \ldots, v_k, q_1, \ldots, q_t)$ is D_0–semi–regular, and consider $1 \leq \alpha \leq k$ and $1 \leq \beta \leq t$. Then*

$$(V^\alpha \cap Q^\beta)_\nu = (V^\alpha Q^\beta)_\nu,$$

holds for all $\nu < D_0$.

Proof. (Sketch) The product of any pair of ideals is contained in their intersection. For the other direction, consider a non–trivial element $e \in (V^\alpha \cap Q^\beta)_\nu$. Then, for some polynomials f_i, g_j, we can write $e = \sum f_i q_{i_1}^h \cdots q_{i_\beta}^h \in Q_\nu^\beta$, and $e = \sum g_j v_{j_1} \cdots v_{j_\alpha} \in V_\nu^\alpha$, which yields the syzygy

$$\sum f_i(q_{i_1}^h \cdots q_{i_\beta}^h) + \sum g_j(v_{j_1} \cdots v_{j_\alpha})^h = 0.$$

By assumption, all syzygies of degree $< D_0$ of $(v_1, \ldots, v_k, q_1^h, \ldots, q_t^h)$ will be generated by the field and Koszul syzygies of the v_i– and q_j^h–polynomials. It follows that (after possibly reducing by syzygies generated by only $q_1^h, \ldots, q_t^h$) we have $f_i \in V^\alpha$. Similarly, we have $g_j \in Q^\beta$. In particular, $e \in V^\alpha Q^\beta$.

A general characterisation of the ideal $V^\alpha Q^\beta$ is trickier. We are content with discussing some special cases of its dimension, which will be of interest to us.

Example 1. *Suppose that $(v_1, \ldots, v_k, q_1, \ldots, q_t)$ is D_0–semi–regular, and let $1 \le \alpha \le k$ and $1 \le \beta \le t$.*

(a) The generators of $V^\alpha Q^\beta$ are of degree $\alpha + 2\beta$, hence $dim_\nu(V^\alpha Q^\beta) = 0$ for all $\nu < \alpha + 2\beta$. (This also holds without the D_0-semi-regularity assumption).
(b) Suppose furthermore that $D_0 > \alpha + 2\beta + 1$. Then $dim_{(\alpha+2\beta+1)}(V^\alpha Q^\beta) = \binom{t}{\beta} dim_{\alpha+1}(V^\alpha)$. To see this, note that $\langle V^\alpha Q^\beta \rangle_{\alpha+2\beta+1}$ is generated by elements of the form $v_{l_1} \ldots v_{l_\alpha} q_{c_1} \ldots q_{c_\beta} x_r$, where $1 \le l_1 < \ldots < l_\alpha \le k$, $1 \le c_1 < \ldots < c_\beta \le t$ and $1 \le r \le n$. The semi-regularity assumption assures that there will be no cancellations (save for the ones already accounted for in $dim_{\alpha+1}(V^\alpha)$).
(c) Suppose furthermore that $D_0 > \alpha + 2\beta + 2$, then $dim_{(\alpha+2\beta+2)}(V^\alpha Q^\beta) = \binom{t}{\beta} dim_{\alpha+2}(V^\alpha) - \binom{k}{\alpha}\left[\binom{t}{\beta}t - \binom{t}{\beta+1}\right]$. The reasoning is similar to (b), with the difference that $dim_{\alpha+2}(V^\alpha)$ will now include the polynomials of the form $q_c^h(v_{l_1} \cdots v_{l_\alpha})^h$. There are $\binom{k}{\alpha}\left[\binom{t}{\beta}t - \binom{t}{\beta+1}\right]$ combinations of these that will reduce to 0 over $\overline{B}(n)$ (when multiplied with the combinations $q_{c_1}^h \ldots q_{c_\beta}^h$).

3.3 Dimension of $\mathcal{P}_{M^{(\alpha,\beta)}M^{(2,1)}}$

As noted in Sect. 3.1, we want $\mathcal{P}_{M^{(\alpha,\beta)}M^{(2,1)}}$ to be $M^{(\alpha,\beta)}M^{(2,1)}\langle \mathcal{P}^h \rangle$, modulo the polynomials of the form $\psi^{\mathcal{P}^h}(ms)$, for $ms \in \mathcal{S}(\mathcal{F})_{M^{(\alpha,\beta)}M^{(2,1)}}$. Computing the dimension of $(M^{(\alpha,\beta)}M^{(2,1)}\langle \mathcal{P}^h \rangle)_\nu$ directly might be difficult, seeing that $\mathcal{P}^h$ depends on $M^{(2,1)}$. To tackle this, we start with the assumption that the cancellations in $M^{(\alpha,\beta)}M^{(2,1)}\langle \mathcal{P}^h \rangle$ are only generated by the 'generic' cancellations, and cancellations coming from the underlying structure, depending on $\mathcal{F}$. By 'generic' cancellations we mean those generated by the Koszul– or field syzygies in either the p_i^h– or m_j–polynomials. The assumption furthermore implies that the second type of cancellations will lie in the image of $\psi^{\mathcal{P}^h}(\mathcal{S}(\mathcal{F})_{M^{(\alpha,\beta)}M^{(2,1)}})$. Let $\mathcal{G}_{SR}$ be a system of homogeneous quadratic polynomials, of the same size and number of variables as $\mathcal{P}^h$, such that $\{V^1, Q^1, \mathcal{G}_{SR}\}$ forms a semi–regular system. With the assumption outlined above, we have

$$\dim_\nu(\mathcal{P}_{M^{(\alpha,\beta)}M^{(2,1)}}) = \dim_\nu(M^{(\alpha,\beta)}M^{(2,1)}\mathcal{G}_{SR}) - \dim_\nu(\mathcal{S}(\mathcal{F})_{M^{(\alpha,\beta)}M^{(2,1)}}). \quad (14)$$

Indeed, any would–be cancellations that are over–counted in the term $\dim_\nu(M^{(\alpha,\beta)}M^{(2,1)}\mathcal{G}_{SR})$ would be subtracted in $-\dim_\nu(\mathcal{S}(\mathcal{F})_{M^{(\alpha,\beta)}M^{(2,1)}})$.

$\mathcal{S}(\mathcal{F})_{M^{(\alpha,\beta)}M^{(2,1)}}$ requires knowledge of the underlying central map, $\mathcal{F}$, and will be dealt with in the next section. Computing the dimensions of the product ideal $M^{(\alpha,\beta)}M^{(2,1)}\mathcal{G}_{SR}$ has many similarities with the work that was done in the previous subsection. In particular, the dimension at degree ν is zero if the degrees of all of its generators are $> \nu$. We conclude with the following short example, which covers the other cases that will be the most relevant to us.

Example 2. *Let $\mathcal{G}_{SR}$ be a system of d homogeneous quadratic polynomials over $\overline{B}(n)$, such that $\{V^1, Q^1, \mathcal{G}_{SR}\}$ forms a semi–regular system. Then*

$$dim_\nu(M^{(2,1)}\mathcal{G}_{SR}) = n\left[dim_{\nu-2}(Q^1) + dim_{\nu-2}(V^2)\right],$$

holds for $\nu = 4, 5$.

4 Number of Degree Fall Polynomials in the Dob Encryption Scheme

There are several ways to construct a central map $\mathcal{F} : \mathbb{F}_2^d \rightarrow \mathbb{F}_2^d$. For big–field schemes, the idea is to fix an isomorphism $\phi : \mathbb{F}_2^d \rightarrow \mathbb{F}_{2^d}$ between the vector space over the base field and the extension field, and choose two random invertible $d \times d$-matrices over $\mathbb{F}_2$, called S and T. $\mathcal{F}$ is then constructed as the composition $\mathcal{F} = S \circ \phi^{-1} \circ F \circ \phi \circ T$, where $F(X) \in \mathbb{F}_{2^d}[X]$, $\max_{w_2}(F) = 2$, and such that $F(X) = Y$ is easy to solve for any given Y. In particular, this ensures that $\mathcal{F}$ is a system of d quadratic polynomials, and ciphertexts can easily be decrypted with the knowledge of the secret S, T and F. There are two main ways in the literature to construct F with these properties:

1. $F(X) = X^e$, where $w_2(e) = 2$. This is the case for C^* [21].
2. $F(X) = \sum_{i=0}^{t} c_i X^{e_i}$, where we have $w_2(e_i) \leq 2$ for all i, and each e_i is bounded by a relatively small constant b. This is used in HFE [24].

Indeed, both C^* and HFE have been suggested with the *ip*–modification, known as PMI an ipHFE, respectively [8,12]. These schemes were broken in [14,17], by specialised attacks recovering the kernel of the linear forms of the *ip*–modification. Nevertheless, a later version of the C^* variant, PMI+ [9], also added the " + " modification in order to thwart this attack, and remains unbroken. We note that ipHFE, PMI and PMI+ all fits into the framework presented in Sect. 3, and the techniques presented here can be used to understand their resistance against algebraic attacks (recall that the " + " modification does not increase the security versus algebraic attacks). A comprehensive study of these schemes are beyond the scope of this work, as we focus on a newer construction that utilizes both the *ip*– and Q_+–modification.

4.1 The Dob Encryption Scheme

The *Two–Face* family, introduced in [20], presents a third way to construct a function $F(X)$. Writing $Y = F(X)$, we get the polynomial equation

$$E_1(X, Y) = Y + F(X) = 0.$$

When F has the Two–Face property, it can be transformed into a different polynomial $E_2(X, Y) = 0$, which has low degree in X and have 2–weight at most 2 for all exponents in X. The degree of E_2 in Y can be arbitrary. Given Y, it is then easy to compute an X that satisfies $E_2(X, Y) = 0$, or equivalently, $Y = F(X)$.

For a concrete instantiation, the authors of [20] suggest the polynomial

$$F(X) = X^{2^m+1} + X^3 + X, \tag{15}$$

where $d = 2m - 1$. Dobbertin showed in [13] that F is a permutation polynomial. In [20], based on the results of [13], it is further pointed out that

$$E_2(X, Y) = X^9 + X^6Y + X^5 + X^4Y + X^3(Y^{2^m} + Y^2) + XY^2 + Y^3 = 0$$

holds for any pair $Y = F(X)$. Note that F itself has high degree in X, but the highest exponent of X found in E_2 is 9 and all exponents have 2–weight at most 2.

The public key $\mathcal{F}$ associated with Eq. (15) under the composition described at the beginning of Sect. 4 is called *nude Dob*, and was observed in [20] to be weak. More precisely, experiments show that the associated multivariate system has solving degree three. Indeed, in Appendix D of [33] is is shown that this is the case for any d.

The (full) Dob encryption scheme is made by extending nude Dob with the two modifications, Q_+ and *ip*, as described at the beginning of Sect. 3. The public key is the d quadratic polynomials $\mathcal{P}$, constructed according to Eq. (6). The secret key consists of S, T, H_{ip} and H_{Q_+}. The plaintext space of the scheme is $\mathbb{F}_2^d$ and encryption is done by evaluating $y = \mathcal{P}(x)$, producing the ciphertext y.

To decrypt, the receiver of a ciphertext y guesses on the values of $v_i(x)$ and $q_j(x)$ for all $1 \leq i \leq k$ and $1 \leq j \leq t$, and computes the corresponding values of the polynomials in H_{ip} and H_{Q_+}. These values are added to y, removing the effect of the modifiers when the guess is correct. The resulting value y' is then the ciphertext of the nude Dob. This can be decrypted by first multiplying y' with S^{-1}, resulting in Y from the central mapping, which is then inverted using E_2 and multiplied with T^{-1} to recover the candidate plaintext x_0. The initial guess is then verified by checking if all $v_i(x_0)$ and $q_j(x_0)$ indeed evaluate to the guessed values.

In order for decryption to have an acceptable time complexity, the size of the modifications, k and t, can not be too large. To decrypt a ciphertext one must on the average do 2^{k+t-1} inversions of $\mathcal{P}$ before the correct plaintext is found. In [20] it is suggested to use $k = t = 6$ for 80–bit security.

For the remainder of this work, we let $\mathcal{F}$ and $\mathcal{P}$ denote the public keys of nude Dob and the (full) Dob encryption scheme, respectively.

4.2 Syzygies of the Unmodified Dob Scheme

The goal of this subsection is to estimate the dimension of $\mathcal{S}(\mathcal{F})_\nu$, for $\nu = 3, 4, 5$. We start by inspecting F (Eq. (15)) over the extension field $\mathbb{F}_{2^d}[X]/\langle X^{2^d} + X\rangle$. Note that $\max_{w_2}(F) = 2$, and consider the following polynomials:

$$G_1 = XF \qquad \text{and} \qquad G_2 = (X^{2^m} + X^2)F. \tag{16}$$

One finds that G_1 and G_2 are both products of F and a polynomial of 2–weight one, but the resulting polynomials still have $\max_{w_2}(G_i) = 2$. They are then examples of polynomials satisfying Eq. (5) from Sect. 2.1, and will correspond to $2d$ degree fall polynomials at degree three, down to quadratic polynomials. They form all the syzygies we expect at degree three, hence we set

$$\dim_3(\mathcal{S}(\mathcal{F})) = 2d. \tag{17}$$

Recall that it was noted in [20] that experiments of nude Dob had a solving degree of three, though the authors did not provide a proof that this is always the case. The presence of G_1 and G_2 ensures that the first fall degree of nude Dob is three. A complete proof that the solution of nude Dob can be found by only considering polynomials of degree three is a little more involved, and is provided in Appendix D of [33].

Things get more complicated for dimensions $\nu > 3$. While we expect the two polynomials G_1 and G_2 to generate a significant part of the syzygies, we also expect there to be other generators, as well as cancellations to keep track of. Due to the complexity of fully characterizing the higher degree parts of $\mathcal{S}(\mathcal{F})$, we instead found an expression for its dimension at degrees $\nu = 4, 5$ experimentally. The experimental setup is further described at the end of this subsection. Note that the formulas we present in this subsection will be a multiple of d. This strongly suggests that all the syzygies of the system come from its extension field structure. These relations could then, in principle, be written out analytically as was the case for $\nu = 3$. In particular, this makes it reasonable to expect the formulas to continue to hold for larger values of d (i.e., beyond our experimental capabilities).

In the subsequent formulas we introduce the following notation, which will be useful to us later. Whenever counting the syzygies that can be generated from syzygies of lower degree, we will multiply by n (the number of variables in an associated multivariate system), as opposed to d. For instance, let $(g_{i,1} \dots, g_{i,d})$, $1 \leq i \leq d$ denote the d multivariate syzygies associated with G_1. Then $x_j(g_{i,1} \dots, g_{i,d})$, $1 \leq j \leq n$ are syzygies at $\nu = 4$, and we will count all of these as[3] nd. For the Dob encryption scheme we of course have $n = d$, so this distinction may seem unnecessary at the moment, but later, in Sect. 5, we will also consider the case $n < d$ as an attacker may fix certain variables.

For $\nu = 4$, we find the following expression:

$$\dim_4(\mathcal{S}(\mathcal{F})) = (2n - 1)d, \tag{18}$$

where we note that the term $2nd$ has been generated by G_1 and G_2, as described above.

For $\nu = 5$, we have

$$\dim_5(\mathcal{S}(\mathcal{F})) = \left(2\binom{n}{2} - n - 2d - 20\right)d. \tag{19}$$

Once more, some of these terms can be understood from the syzygies of lower degrees. The contribution from the polynomials G_1 and G_2 from $\nu = 3$ will now be the $2\binom{n}{2}d$ term. The term '$-d$' from $\nu = 4$ will now cause the '$-nd$' term.

[3] Not all of these will be linearly independent in $\mathcal{S}(\mathcal{F})$. For example, the d syzygies associated with $(X^{2^m} + X^2)G_1$ will correspond to syzygies in $\mathcal{T}(\mathcal{F}^h)$. This does not really matter, as the expressions Eq. (18) and Eq. (19) corrects for this.

Experimental Setup. The experiments used to test Eq. (18) and Eq. (19) have been done as follows. The public polynomials of nude Dob are first generated, and we consider their upper homogeneous part, $\mathcal{F}^h$, over $\overline{B}(d)$. $\text{Dim}_\nu(\mathcal{S}(\mathcal{F}))$ is computed as the dimension of the kernel of the homogeneous Macaulay matrix $\overline{M}_\nu(\mathcal{F}^h)$, minus $\dim_\nu(\mathcal{T}(\mathcal{F}^h))$. For $\nu = 4, 5$ we tested all odd d, $25 \leq d \leq 41$, all matching the values predicted by Eq. (18) and Eq. (19).

4.3 Degree Fall Polynomials of the (modified) Dob Scheme

We now have all the tools needed to write out explicit formulas for (variants of) the estimates $N_\nu^{(\alpha,\beta)}$, $\nu \leq 5$, for the Dob scheme. The approach for the formulas is as follows. Equation (11) is used as a foundation, and $\dim_\nu(\mathcal{S}(\mathcal{F}))$ is given according to Sect. 4.2. For the dimension of the modifiers, and $\mathcal{P}_{M^{(\alpha,\beta)}M^{(2,1)}}$, we will combine the results discussed in Sect. 3.2 and Sect. 3.3. In particular, we will assume that the chosen modifying polynomials $\{v_1, \ldots, v_k, q_1, \ldots, q_t\}$ form a $(\nu+1)$–semi–regular system. The dimensions that are not covered by combining the results discussed so far, will be commented on separately. For the convenience of the reader, the non–trivial dimensions have been marked with an overbrace in the equations. The exceptions are Eq. (24) and Eq. (25), which are covered in greater depth in Appendix B of [33]. Recall also our convention that $\binom{a}{b} = 0$, if $b > a$, and $\binom{a}{0} = 1$.

$\boldsymbol{\nu = 3}$**.** At this degree we only consider $N^{(0,0)}$.

$$N_3^{(0,0)} = \overbrace{2d}^{\dim_3(\mathcal{S}(\mathcal{F}))} - \overbrace{\left((n-k)\binom{k}{2} + \binom{k}{3}\right)}^{\dim_3(V^2)} - \overbrace{nt}^{\dim_3(Q^1)} . \tag{20}$$

$\boldsymbol{\nu = 4}$**.**

$$\begin{aligned} N_4^{(0,0)} = {} & \overbrace{(2n-1)d}^{\dim_4(\mathcal{S}(\mathcal{F}))} + \overbrace{d\left(t + \binom{k}{2}\right)}^{\dim_4(\mathcal{P}_{M^{(2,1)}})} - \overbrace{\left(t\binom{n}{2} - \binom{t}{2} - t\right)}^{\dim_4(Q^1)} \\ & - \overbrace{\left(\binom{k}{2}\binom{n-k}{2} + \binom{k}{3}(n-k) + \binom{k}{4}\right)}^{\dim_4(V^2)} + \overbrace{t\binom{k}{2}}^{\dim_4(Q^1 \cap V^2)} . \end{aligned} \tag{21}$$

At $\nu = 4$, we also consider the estimate $N_4^{(1,0)}$, i.e., multiplying everything with the k linear forms from the *ip*–modifier. In particular, this means that $(\mathcal{S}(\mathcal{F})_{M^{(1,0)}})_4$ is spanned by the combinations $v_j^h(g_{i,1} \ldots, g_{i,d})$, $1 \leq j \leq k$ and $1 \leq i \leq 2d$, where we recall that $(g_{i,1} \ldots, g_{i,d})$ denote the $2d$ multivariate syzygies associated with G_1 and G_2 (Eq. (16))

$$
\begin{aligned}
N_4^{(1,0)} = \overbrace{2kd}^{\dim_4\left(\mathcal{S}(\mathcal{F})_{M^{(1,0)}}\right)} - \overbrace{\left(\binom{k}{3}(n-k)+\binom{k}{4}\right)}^{\dim_4(V^3)} \\
- t\overbrace{\left(k(n-k)+\binom{k}{2}\right)}^{\dim_4(Q^1V^1)}.
\end{aligned} \tag{22}
$$

$\boldsymbol{\nu = 5}$**.** At degree 5, $\mathcal{S}(\mathcal{F})_{M^{(2,1)}}$ (in Eq. (14)) is no longer trivial. Indeed, it will now consist of the possible combinations $v_{j_1}^h v_{j_2}^h(g_{i,1}\dots,g_{i,d})$ and $q_j^h(g_{i,1}\dots,g_{i,d})$.

$$
\begin{aligned}
N_5^{(0,0)} = \overbrace{\left(2\binom{n}{2} - n - 2d - 20\right)d}^{\dim_5(\mathcal{S}(\mathcal{F}))} - \overbrace{\left(t\binom{n}{3} - n\binom{t}{2} - tn\right)}^{\dim_5(Q^1)} \\
- \overbrace{\left(\binom{k}{2}\binom{n-k}{3} + \binom{k}{3}\binom{n-k}{2} + \binom{k}{4}(n-k) + \binom{k}{5}\right)}^{\dim_5(V^2)} \\
+ t\overbrace{\left(\binom{k}{2}(n-k) + \binom{k}{3}\right)}^{\dim_5(Q^1\cap V^2)} \\
\overbrace{+ ntd + d\left(\binom{k}{2}(n-k)+\binom{k}{3}\right) - 2dt - 2d\binom{k}{2}}^{\dim_5\left(\mathcal{P}_{M^{(2,1)}}\right)}.
\end{aligned} \tag{23}
$$

As mentioned above, it is a bit more involved to derive $N_5^{(1,1)}$ and $N_5^{(2,1)}$, and we will refer to Appendix B of [33] for more details. It would also appear that our assumptions are slightly off for these two estimates, as our experiments consistently yield $4d$ more degree fall polynomials than we are able to predict (see Remark 3, Appendix B of [33] for more details). We present the experimentally adjusted versions in Eqs. (24) and (25):

$$
\begin{aligned}
N_5^{(1,1)} = d\left(k(2n-k-2) + t(2+k) + \binom{k}{3} + 4\right) - \binom{t}{2}n - \binom{k}{3}\binom{n-k}{2} \\
- \binom{k}{5} - \binom{k}{4}(n-k) - t\left(k\binom{n-k}{2} + \binom{k}{2}(n-k) - kt\right).
\end{aligned} \tag{24}
$$

$$
\begin{aligned}
N_5^{(2,1)} = 2d\left(\binom{k}{2} + t + 2\right) - \left(\binom{k}{4}(n-k) + \binom{k}{5}\right) \\
- t\left(\binom{k}{2}(n-k) + \binom{k}{3}\right) - \binom{t}{2}n.
\end{aligned} \tag{25}
$$

5 Experimental Results on Degree Fall Polynomials

In the previous section we developed the theory on how to estimate the number of first fall polynomials, ending up with several formulas. This section is focused on the accuracy of these formulas, and how they can be used by an attacker. Note that since we are interested in the unique structure of the Dob encryption scheme, we will always assume that 'generic' degree fall polynomials do not interfere. More specifically, when inspecting a system of d polynomials in n variables at degree ν, we assume that d and n is chosen such that $D_{reg}(d, n) > \nu$.

5.1 Fixing Variables

The formulas separate d, the size of the field extension, and n, the number of variables. While the Dob encryption scheme uses $d = n$, an attacker can easily create an overdetermined system with $n < d$ by fixing some variables. This approach, known as the hybrid method, can be viewed as a trade–off between exhaustive search and Gröbner basis techniques, and its benefits are well–known for semi–regular sequences [3]. From Eqs. (20) to (25), we find that for the relevant choices of parameters (d, t, k), a greater difference between n and d can increase the number of degree fall polynomials. This means that a hybrid method will have a more intricate effect on a Dob system, than what we would expect from random systems. To a certain extent, an attacker can "tune" the number of degree fall polynomials, by choosing the amount of variables to fix. Of course, if the intent is to find a solution of the polynomial system through a Gröbner basis, this comes at the added cost of solving the system 2^r times, where r is the number of fixed variables, but in Sect. 6 we will present a different attack that circumvents this exponential factor.

Finally, one could ask whether it is reasonable to expect Eqs. (20) to (25) to be accurate after fixing a certain number of variables. It is, for instance, possible that different degree fall polynomials will cancel out, as certain variables are fixed. However, if past experience with the hybrid method is any indicator, such cancellations are very rare, and we see no reason that the extension field structure increases the probability for such cancellations to happen. As we will see in Sect. 5.3 this is supported by the experiments we have run; the formulas remain precise, even as n is varied.

5.2 Using the Degree Fall Formulas

We briefly recall how the formulas found in Sect. 4.3 relate to the public polynomials of a Dob encryption scheme. Let $\mathcal{P}$ be the polynomial system associated with a Dob scheme of fixed parameters (d, n, t, k) (where n is as described in Sect. 5.1). We expect the non–trivial dimension (i.e., the dimension of the part that is not generated by $\mathcal{T}(\mathcal{F})$) of the kernel of $\overline{M}_\nu(\mathcal{P})$ to be given by the maximal of the formulas $N_\nu^{(\alpha,\beta)}$, for $\nu = 3, 4, 5$.

If a step–wise algorithm such as F_4 is used, we expect the formulas to predict the number of degree falls polynomials, but *only* at the first fall degree. Suppose, for instance, that $N_3 = 0$, but $N_4 > 0$. Then this algorithm runs a second step at degree 4, using the newly found degree fall polynomials. This means that there are effectively more available polynomials in the system when (if) a step of degree 5 is performed, and in this case we do not expect the formulas we have for N_5 to be accurate.

Note in particular that if all the formulas we have are non–positive, an attacker is likely required to go up to step degree ≥ 6 in order to observe first fall polynomials.

5.3 Experimental Results

We have run a number of experiments with the Dob system of varying parameters (d, n, t, k). A subset of them is presented in Table 2, and the rest can be found in Appendix G of [33]. Gröbner bases of the systems were found using the F_4 algorithm implemented in the computational algebra system Magma. The script used for the experiments is available at [19].

In Table 2 we use the following notation. 'D_{ff}' is the experimentally found first fall degree. 'N (predicted)' is the number of first fall polynomials as predicted by the equations in Sect. 4.3. 'N (Magma)' is the number of first fall polynomials read from the verbose output of Magma, written as 'degree : {#degree fall polynomials at this degree}'. The solving degree D_{solv} was found experimentally by Magma. This has been measured as the degree where the most time consuming step of the algorithm took place. In the instances where the algorithm did not run to completion due to memory constraints, we give D_{solv} as $\geq X$, where X is the degree of the step where termination occurred. The degree of regularity for semi–regular systems of the same size, $D_{reg}(d, n)$, is also given. 'Step Degrees' lists the degrees of the steps that are being performed by F_4 up until linear relations are found. Once a sufficient number of linear relations are found, Magma restarts F_4 with the original system, as well as these linear relations. This restart typically needs a few rounds before the entire basis is found, but its impact on the running time of the algorithm is negligible, which is why we have chosen to exclude it when listing the step degrees. For convenience, the step where first fall polynomials are found is marked in blue and the solving step marked in red. Purple is used to mark the steps where these two coincide.

A first observation is that in all experiments we find that 'N (predicted)' matches 'N (Magma)'. We also find that fixing variables affects the cross–over point between the formulas $N_\nu^{(\alpha,\beta)}$, as for instance seen in the rows 6 and 7. We note that $N_\nu^{(0,0)}$ tend to be dominant when $n << d$, and that $N_5^{(2,1)}$ only seems to have an impact when k is large and t is small.

For the majority of cases we observe that $D_{ff} = D_{solv}$ or $D_{solv} + 1$, but one should be careful in drawing any conclusions from this, seeing that our experiments are in practice limited to computations of $D < 6$. The relation between n and D_{solv} is also noteworthy. For instance, in row 9 we have $d = 57$ and $n = 38$; D_{ff} is 5, but $D_{solv} \geq 6$. In row 10 we fix one more variable, $n = 37$ (while keeping everything else as before), and find $D_{solv} = 5$.

Table 2. Degree fall polynomials for Dob encryption schemes of various parameters.

d	n	t (+)	k (ip)	D_{ff}	N (predicted)	N (Magma)	D_{solv} $(D_{reg}(d,n))$	Step Degrees
53	53	0	0	3	$N_3^{(0,0)}$: 106	2:106	3 (9)	2,3,3
53	53	0	3	4	$N_4^{(0,0)}$: 1999	3:1999	4 (9)	2,3,4,4
53	53	3	0	4	$N_4^{(0,0)}$: 1596	3:1596	4 (9)	2,3,4,4
59	29	0	7	4	$N_4^{(1,0)}$: 21	3:21	5 (5)	2,3,4,4,5
37	25	2	3	4	$N_4^{(0,0)}$: 692	3:692	4 (5)	2,3,4,4
31	29	0	8	5	$N_5^{(1,1)}$: 478	4:478	5 (6)	2,3,4,5,5,5
31	30	0	8	5	$N_5^{(2,1)}$: 264	4:264	5 (6)	2,3,4,5,5,5,4
39	37	1	7	5	$N_5^{(2,1)}$: 136	4:136	≥ 6 (7)	2,3,4,5,5,5,6...
57	38	4	6	5	$N_5^{(1,1)}$: 2086	4:2086	≥ 6 (6)	2,3,4,5,5,6...
57	37	4	6	5	$N_5^{(1,1)}$: 2847	4:2847	5 (6)	2,3,4,5,5
129	50	6	6	5	$N_5^{(0,0)}$: 64024	4:64024	≥ 5 (6)	2,3,4,5,5

Impact on Known Attacks. The solving degree of big field schemes are often estimated using the first fall degree. In cases where $D_{solv} > D_{ff}$, we observed instances where it is beneficial for an attacker to fix (a few) variables in order to lower the D_{solv} for each guess. Without a better understanding of D_{solv} and how it is affected by fixing variables, it seems that the approximation $D_{ff} \approx D_{solv}$ is conservative, yet reasonable, when estimating the complexity of direct/hybrid attacks against Dob system.

Another attack that may greatly benefit from the detailed formulas for degree fall polynomials obtained in Sect. 3, is an adapted version of the distinguishing attack that was proposed for HFEv- (Section 5 in [11]). An attacker fixes random linear forms, and distinguishes between the cases where (some of) the fixed linear forms are in the span of $\langle v_1, \ldots, v_k \rangle$, and when none of them are, by the use of Gröbner basis techniques. Indeed, if *one* of the fixed linear forms are in this span, the number of degree fall polynomials will be the same as for a system with $k-1$ ip linear forms. Hence, a distinguisher based on the formulas presented here will work even without a drop in first fall degree, making the attack more versatile.

The deeper understanding for how the modifiers work allows for an even more efficient attack on the Dob scheme, which we now present.

6 A New Attack on the Dob Encryption Scheme

In the previous two sections we have studied how degree fall polynomials can occur in the Dob scheme, and have verified the accuracy of our resulting formulas through experiments. In this section we will show how all these insights can be combined to a novel attack. In Sect. 6.1, we shall see that adding an extra polynomial to the system can leak information about the modification polynomials. We will see how this information can be used to retrieve (linear combinations of) the secret *ip* linear forms, and the homogeneous quadratic part of the Q_+ modification, in Sects. 6.2 and 6.3. We investigate how Gröbner basis algorithms perform with this extra information in Sect. 6.4, and finally discuss the complexity of the entire attack in Sect. 6.5.

6.1 Adding an Extra Polynomial

In Sect. 3.1 we discussed how products of the modifiers and public polynomials affect the number of degree fall polynomials, through $\mathcal{P}_{M^{(2,1)}}$. One would also expect a similar effect to take place when adding a random polynomial to the system.

Consider a set of parameters for the Dob scheme, where the number of first fall polynomials is determined by $N_\nu^{(0,0)}$, for some $\nu > 3$. Let $\mathcal{P}$ be the public key of this scheme, and consider a randomly chosen homogeneous polynomial p_R of degree $\nu - 2$. As it is unlikely that the randomly chosen p_R has any distinct interference with $\mathcal{P}$, we expect $(\langle p_R \rangle \cap M^{(2,1)})_\nu$ to be generated by the possible combinations $p_R q_i^h$, and $p_R(v_j v_l)^h$. Furthermore, since the generators of $\mathcal{S}(\mathcal{F})$ have degree at least 3, we do not expect any collision between $\psi^{\mathcal{P}^h}(\mathcal{S}(\mathcal{F}))$ and $\langle p_R \rangle$ at degree ν (cf. Sect. 3.3). From these considerations, we estimate the number of degree fall polynomials for the system $\{\mathcal{P}, p_R\}$ at degree ν to be:

$$N_\nu(\{\mathcal{P}, p_R\}) = N_\nu^{(0,0)}(\mathcal{P}) + t + \binom{k}{2}. \tag{26}$$

We ran a few experiments that confirm this intuition, the details are given in Table 3. First, we confirmed that the degree fall polynomials of $\mathcal{P}$ were indeed given by $N_\nu^{(0,0)}(\mathcal{P})$, before applying Magma's implementation of the F_4 algorithm on the system $\{\mathcal{P}, p_R\}$. Recall also our convention that $\binom{0}{2} = 0$ when applying Eq. (26).

With all this in mind, assume for the moment that $d = n$, and consider a homogeneous Macaulay matrix of $\{\mathcal{P}^h, p_R\}$ at degree ν, $\overline{M}_\nu(\{\mathcal{P}^h, p_R\})$. Any element in the (left) kernel of this matrix can in general be written as:

$$h_R p_R + \sum_{i=1}^{d} h_i p_i^h = 0, \tag{27}$$

Table 3. First fall polynomials of Dob encryption schemes with an added, randomly chosen polynomial p_R.

d	n	$\deg(p_R)$	t (Q_+)	k (ip)	D_{ff}	N (predicted)	N (Magma)
31	29	2	2	2	4	$N_4 : 705$	3:705
45	30	2	6	0	4	$N_4 : 342$	3:342
75	39	3	6	6	5	$N_5 : 4695$	4:4695
39	37	3	6	0	5	$N_5 : 9036$	4:9036

for some homogeneous quadratic polynomials $h_i \in \overline{B}(d)_{\nu-2}$, $1 \le i \le d$, and $h_R \in \overline{B}(d)_2$. From the discussion above, we expect that the only way p_R contributes to these kernel elements is through the trivial syzygies, multiplications with p_i^h or p_R, and through multiplying with the generators of $M^{(2,1)}$. It follows that any polynomial h_R, from Eq. (27), will be in the span of[4]

$$\mathcal{H} := \{p_1^h, \ldots, p_d^h, p_R, q_1^h, \ldots, q_t^h, (v_1v_2)^h, \ldots, (v_{k-1}v_k)^h\}. \tag{28}$$

Hence, given enough kernel elements of $\overline{M}_\nu(\{\mathcal{P}^h, p_R\})$, a set of generators of $\mathrm{Span}(\mathcal{H})$ can be found. In the next subsection we will generalise this observation to the case where a number of variables are fixed, i.e. $n < d$.

6.2 Gluing Polynomials

Let W_η denote a non-empty subset of r variables, i.e. $W_\eta = \{x_{\eta_1}, \ldots, x_{\eta_r}\}$ for integers $1 \le \eta_1 < \ldots < \eta_r \le d$. For $n = d - r$, there is a natural projection map associated to W_η, $\pi_{W_\eta} : B(d) \to B(d)/W_\eta \simeq B(n)$, that fixes the variables in W_η to 0. For any polynomial system $\mathcal{R}$ over $B(d)$, we will also write $\pi_{W_\eta}(\mathcal{R})$ to mean the system consisting of all polynomials in $\mathcal{R}$ under π_{W_η}. Suppose now that the number of first fall polynomials of a Dob system $\mathcal{P}$ is given by $N_\nu^{(0,0)}$, after fixing r variables to 0, i.e., $n = d - r$. Let W_η be the set of variables we fix. Following a similar line of reasoning as in Sect. 6.1, we find that $\pi_{W_\eta}(h_R)$ from a kernel element of the Macaulay matrix associated with $\pi_{W_\eta}(\{P^h, p_R\})$ will no longer be in the span of $\mathcal{H}$, but rather lie in the span of $\pi_{W_\eta}(\mathcal{H})$. To ease notation, we will write $\mathcal{H}_\eta = \pi_{W_\eta}(\mathcal{H})$. A natural question is whether we can recover $\mathcal{H}$, by using different variable sets $W_1, \ldots, W_\rho$, and finding generators for the associated polynomial sets $\mathcal{H}_1, \ldots, \mathcal{H}_\rho$. We answer this question positively in this subsection.

Let $\widetilde{W}_\eta := \{x_1, \ldots, x_d\} \setminus W_\eta$ denote the complement of W_η, and note that $\mathcal{H}_\eta$ only contains information about the set of monomials $A(W_\eta) := \{x_ix_j \mid x_i, x_j \in \widetilde{W}_\eta\}$. In order to guarantee that the family $\mathcal{H}_1, \ldots, \mathcal{H}_\rho$ can give complete information about $\mathcal{H}$ we need to ensure that for any choice of $1 \le i < j \le d$, we have $x_i, x_j \in \widetilde{W}_\eta$ for at least one $1 \le \eta \le \rho$. In other words, the sets $\widetilde{W}_1, \ldots, \widetilde{W}_\rho$ must cover all possible quadratic monomials.

In practice, both d and the size r of the variable sets will be determined by the chosen Dob parameters[5]. This naturally leads to the following problem:

[4] If p_R has degree ≥ 3, then the syzygy $p_R^2 + p_R = 0$ will be of degree $> \nu$. In this case p_R will not be among the generators of $\mathcal{H}$. We shall see later, in Remark (1), that the effect of p_R can also be removed in the degree 2 case, but at an added cost to the run time.

[5] We will see later that the gluing also requires some overlap between the variable sets, but this is not a problem for the parameters we are interested in.

Definition 3 (The (Quadratic) (r,d)–Covering Problem). *For integers $1 < r < d - 1$, find the smallest number ρ of variable sets, each of size r, such that*

$$A(W_1) \cup \ldots \cup A(W_\rho) = \{x_i x_j \mid 1 \leq i < j \leq d\}.$$

Appendix E of [33] presents a constructive solution to this problem, which provides a good upper bound for ρ that is sufficient for our use case. The upper bound is given by the following lemma

Lemma 5. *The (Quadratic) (r,d)–Covering Problem is upper bounded by*

$$\rho \leq \binom{\left\lceil \frac{d}{\lfloor (d-r)/2 \rfloor} \right\rceil}{2}.$$

We illustrate the strategy for recovering $\mathcal{H}$ in the simple case when $d = 3r$. In this particular case, the method above yields $\rho = 3$, where W_1, W_2 and W_3 are pairwise, disjoint variable sets. We may write the following matrix:

$$\begin{array}{c} \\ H_1 \\ H_2 \\ H_3 \end{array} \begin{array}{cccccc} W_1 * W_1 & W_1 * W_2 & W_1 * W_3 & W_2 * W_2 & W_2 * W_3 & W_3 * W_3 \\ \end{array}$$
$$\begin{bmatrix} 0 & 0 & 0 & * & * & * \\ * & 0 & * & 0 & 0 & * \\ * & * & 0 & * & 0 & 0 \end{bmatrix}$$

Here $W_i * W_j$, $i, j \in \{1, 2, 3\}$, is understood as a list of the monomials $x_a x_b$ where $x_a \in W_i$ and $x_b \in W_j$ (under any fixed ordering and $a \neq b$), and we write H_l to mean the rows associated with a fixed set of generators for $\mathcal{H}_l$. A 0 in the matrix means that the respective submatrix is the zero matrix, whereas $*$ denotes that the submatrix may take non-zero values. By construction, if the submatrix whose rows are H_l, and columns are $W_i * W_j$, is denoted by $*$, then it forms a set of generators for $\mathcal{H}$ restricted to the monomials in $W_i * W_j$. In particular, the submatrix with columns $W_3 * W_3$ and rows H_1 spans the same row-space as the submatrix with columns $W_3 * W_3$ and rows H_2. We will use this observation to construct a new matrix, denoted $H_1 \cap_{W_3} H_2$, that combine the useful information from H_1 and H_2 in the following procedure.

1. Since $\{p_1^h, \ldots, p_d^h, p_R\}$ are known, we start by finding $t + \binom{k}{2}$ vectors in the row space of H_2 that are linearly independent of $\pi_{W_2}(\{p_1^h, \ldots, p_d^h, p_R\})$. Denote the set of these vectors Y_2.
2. If $|W_3 * W_3| >> d + t + \binom{k}{2} + 1$, then for each vector $y_i \in Y_2$, we can expect a unique vector z_i in the row space of H_1, such that $y_i + z_i$ is 0 along the columns associated with $W_3 * W_3$. Find such an z_i for each $y_i \in Y_2$ through Gaussian elimination.
3. We now have $t + \binom{k}{2}$ pairs (y_i, z_i) that are used to define the $(t + \binom{k}{2}) \times \binom{d}{2}$ matrix $(H_1 \cap_{W_3} H_2)$ over $\mathbb{F}_2$ in the following manner. For each row index i_0 and column index j_0, we define the entry at $[i_0, j_0]$ to be

$$(H_1 \cap_{W_3} H_2)[i_0, j_0] = \begin{cases} y_{i_0}[j_0], & \text{if } j_0 \text{ is associated with a monomial in } W_3 * W_3 \\ y_{i_0}[j_0] + z_{i_0}[j_0], & \text{otherwise.} \end{cases}$$

The above procedure uses the common information found in the columns of $W_3 * W_3$ to combine vectors from H_1 and H_2. We may think of this as "gluing" polynomials along $W_3 * W_3$, hence the name of the technique. Now consider the following matrix.

$$\begin{array}{c} \\ (H_1 \cap_{W_3} H_2) \\ H_3 \end{array} \begin{array}{c} \begin{array}{cccccc} W_1 * W_1 & W_1 * W_2 & W_1 * W_3 & W_2 * W_2 & W_2 * W_3 & W_3 * W_3 \end{array} \\ \left[\begin{array}{cccccc} * & 0 & * & * & * & * \\ * & * & 0 & * & 0 & 0 \end{array} \right] \end{array}$$

Note in particular that the polynomials associated with $(H_1 \cap_{W_3} H_2)$ forms a set of generators for $\pi_{W_1 * W_2}(\mathcal{H})$. In order to recover the information of the monomials in $W_1 * W_2$, we need only glue the vectors of $(H_1 \cap_{W_3} H_2)$, with combinations from the row space of H_3, using the same procedure as described above. Since both $(H_1 \cap_{W_3} H_2)$ and H_3 may take non–zero values at $W_1 * W_1$ and $W_2 * W_2$, we expect the gluing to result in $t + \binom{k}{2}$ unique polynomials if $|(W_1 * W_1) \cup (W_2 * W_2)| >> d + t + \binom{k}{2} + 1$. By construction, all of the resulting $t + \binom{k}{2}$ polynomials associated with $(H_1 \cap_{W_3} H_2) \cap_{W_1} H_3$ will be in the span of $\langle p_1^h, \dots, p_d^h, p_R, q_1^h, \dots, q_t^h, \dots (v_i v_j)^h \dots \rangle$, but none of them in the span of $\langle p_1^h, \dots, p_d^h, p_R \rangle$. Hence we define $\mathcal{G}$ to be the set consisting of the polynomials $\{p_1^h, \dots, p_d^h, p_R\}$, as well as the polynomials associated with $(H_1 \cap_{W_3} H_2) \cap_{W_1} H_3$, and note that $\mathcal{G}$ is, by construction, a system of polynomials that are linearly equivalent to $\mathcal{H}$.

As a proof of concept, we implemented retrieving $\mathcal{G}$ from a toy example of the Dob scheme, with $d = 45$, $t = 6$ and $k = 0$, using the method described above. The interested reader can find more details by consulting Example 3, Appendix C in [33].

The General Case. In the case of a general family of variable sets $W_1, \dots, W_\rho$, we will not be able to set up the straightforward matrices that was shown above. The gluing process can still be done in a similar, iterative manner. For instance, the submatrix associated with $\mathcal{H}_\eta$ will have 0 for each monomial $x_i x_j$ where x_i or $x_j \in W_\eta$, and $*$ otherwise. As above, we expect to be able to glue $\mathcal{H}_\eta$ with $\mathcal{H}_\psi$ if the number of their common $*$–monomials exceeds $d + t + \binom{k}{2} + 1$.

6.3 Retrieving the Linear Forms from *ip*

Suppose now that a set of generators $\mathcal{G}$ for Span($\mathcal{H}$) has been found, as described in Sect. 6.2. The goal is to recover k linear forms that are generators for $\langle v_1, \dots, v_k \rangle$. In order to simplify our arguments we will assume $k \geq 5$. The special cases $2 \leq k \leq 4$ does not provide more security, and are dealt with in Remark 1, [33].

Consider the kernel of the homogeneous Macaulay matrix $\overline{M}_3(\mathcal{G})$. From the definition of $\mathcal{H}$ (Eq. (28)), we find that Span($\mathcal{H}$) contains all the homogeneous nude Dob–polynomials $f_1^h, \ldots, f_d^h$, as well as all the combinations $(v_i v_j)^h$, $1 \le i < j \le k$. Each polynomial $(v_i v_j)^h$ generates the two kernel elements $v_i(v_i v_j)^h$ and $v_j(v_i v_j)^h$ (which are trivial when working over $\overline{B}(d)$). The nude Dob–polynomials will generate the $2d$ kernel elements associated with the degree fall polynomials discussed in Sect. 4.2. We would like to separate these two types of kernel elements. To this end, we suggest constructing a smaller system, $\mathcal{G}'$, by removing three polynomials from $\mathcal{G}$, that are in the span of $\{p_1^h, \ldots, p_d^h\}$. Indeed, the idea is that this will work as a self–imposed minus modifier, which will remove the effect of the Dob–polynomials of $\mathcal{G}$ at degree 3.

On the other hand, some kernel elements generated by combinations of the $(v_i v_j)^h$–elements can still be observed for $\mathcal{G}'$ at degree 3. More specifically, suppose $\mathcal{G}'$ was created from $\mathcal{G}$ by removing p_1^h, p_2^h and p_3^h. Then Span($\mathcal{G}'$) may not necessarily contain $(v_1 v_j)^h$ itself, for any $2 \le j \le k$, but it will contain the combination $(v_1 v_j)^h + b_{1,j} p_1^h + b_{2,j} p_2^h + b_{3,j} p_3^h$, for some $b_{1,j}, b_{2,j}, b_{3,j} \in \mathbb{F}_2$. By considering these equations for all j, and eliminating p_1^h, p_2^h and p_3^h, we find that Span($\mathcal{G}'$) will contain a polynomial $z_1 = \sum_{j=2}^{k} a_j (v_1 v_j)^h$, where $a_2, \ldots, a_k \in \mathbb{F}_2$ are not all 0, using the assumption that $k \ge 5$. The polynomial $v_1 z_1$ will subsequently be reduced to 0 over $\overline{B}(d)$. Similarly, we are guaranteed to find polynomials $z_2, \ldots, z_k$. We assume that these are the only contributors to the kernel. In particular, this means that each kernel element of $\overline{M}_3(\mathcal{G}')$ can be written as $\sum l_i g_i = 0$, with $g_i \in \mathcal{G}'$, and each l_i a linear form in Span($\{v_1, \ldots, v_k\}$). It follows that an attacker can retrieve a basis $v_1^*, \ldots, v_k^*$ of $\langle v_1, \ldots, v_k \rangle$, by determining k linearly independent l_i's from these kernel elements.

The retrieval of $\mathcal{G}$ and $v_1^*, \ldots, v_k^*$, as described in this subsection, has been implemented and verified on the toy example with parameters $d = 63$, $t = 1$ and $k = 4$. This is further described in Example 4, Appendix C of [33].

6.4 Solving the Extended Dob System

Assume now that an attacker has followed the steps described in the previous subsections, and has recovered a system $\mathcal{G}$ (Sect. 6.2), as well as a basis $\{v_1^*, \ldots, v_k^*\}$ that generates $\langle v_1, \ldots, v_k \rangle$ (Sect. 6.3). Now fix a set of generators $q_1^*, \ldots, q_k^*$ for the polynomials that are in Span($\mathcal{G}$), but not in

$$\mathrm{Span}(\{p_1^h, \ldots, p_d^h, p_R, (v_i^* v_j^*)^h \mid 1 \le i < j \le k\}).$$

With all this information, we consider the associated *extended Dob system*, $\mathcal{P}_E$, defined by:

$$\mathcal{P}_E := \{p_1, \ldots, p_d, p_R, q_1^*, \ldots, q_t^*, v_1^*, \ldots, v_k^*\}. \tag{29}$$

For any given ciphertext, an attacker with access to an extended Dob system can guess constant values for the polynomials $p_R, q_1^*, \ldots, q_t^*, v_1^*, \ldots, v_k^*$, and check the guess by finding a Gröbner basis for $\mathcal{P}_E$.

Remark 1. A system $\mathcal{P}_E$ that is independent of the randomly chosen polynomial p_R can be obtained by running the steps described in Sects. 6.2 and 6.3 for two different elements p_R, and combine the results. More information can be found by consulting Remark 2 in [33].

In order to get a better understanding of solving extended Dob systems, we introduce the following modification for multivariate schemes.

Definition 4. *For a polynomial system $\mathcal{P}'$, we define the modification $\mathcal{L}_+$ by choosing l_0 linear forms, and appending linear combinations of them to each polynomial in $\mathcal{P}'$.*

Consider an extended Dob system, $\mathcal{P}_E$, where all coefficients have been guessed correctly. Since q_i^* does not contain any information about the linear part of the q_i–polynomials, it follows that $\text{Span}(\mathcal{P}_E)$ will contain a Dob system that is only modified with the $\mathcal{L}_+$–modification, where $l_0 = t$. Moreover, this Dob system has d equations and $d-k$ variables[6]. The problem of estimating the complexity of finding a solution to $\mathcal{P}_E$, can then be reduced to that of estimating the complexity of finding a Gröbner basis for Dob with the $\mathcal{L}_+$–modification. While a thorough analysis of this $\mathcal{L}_+$–modification is beyond the scope of this work, we point out a couple of immediate properties.

Firstly, seeing that the first fall degree only depends on the upper homogeneous part of a polynomial system, it is unaffected by the $\mathcal{L}_+$–modification. In particular, we expect $2d$ degree fall polynomials at degree 3, as in the case for nude Dob (Sect. 4.2). Secondly, if running an algorithm such as F_4, a second batch of degree fall polynomials will emerge at the first step of degree 4. To see this, note that Dob with the $\mathcal{L}_+$–modification can be written over the quotient ring $\mathbb{F}_{2^d}[X]/\langle X^{2^d} + X \rangle$ as

$$F_{\mathcal{L}_+}(X) = X(X^{2^m} + X^2) + L(X) + C_E, \tag{30}$$

where C_E is a constant in $\mathbb{F}_{2^d}$, and $L(X) = \sum_{i=1}^{m} c_i X^{2^i}$, with $c_i \in \mathbb{F}_{2^d}$, is a polynomial of binary weight one. $XF_{\mathcal{L}_+}$ is one of the combinations that induce degree fall polynomials at degree 3, and $X^4XF_{\mathcal{L}_+}$ will correspond to cubic[7] (multivariate) polynomials found at the second step of degree 3. Upon running a subsequent step at degree 4, the polynomial $L(X)X^4XF_{\mathcal{L}_+}$ will correspond to d multivariate cubic polynomials, and would hence be counted as degree fall polynomials.

We ran a few experiments for extended Dob systems, $\mathcal{P}_E$, the results of which can be found in Appendix F of [33].

---

[6] Here we implicitly assume that k variables have been eliminated by the linear forms v_i^*.

[7] For nude Dob, the polynomial X^5F can be used to create linear polynomials (see Equation (35), Appendix D in [33]). The crucial difference is that in this case, the linear term X can be cancelled out at degree 3, whereas this is not possible for a general $L(X)$.

6.5 Complexity of the Attack

The attack proposed in this section has two main parts. The first step is to construct an extended Dob system, $\mathcal{P}_E$. In the second step, an attacker solves this system for a particular ciphertext. Suppose an attacker fixes $d-n$ variables in order to find ρ polynomial systems $\mathcal{H}_1, \dots, \mathcal{H}_\rho$ from the kernel elements of Macaulay matrices of degree $D_0 \geq 3$. The gluing operations, determining the linear forms $v_1^*, \dots, v_k^*$, and the quadratic forms $q_1^*, \dots, q_t^*$ only involve Macaulay matrices of degree at most three. Hence, we expect the first step to be dominated by recovering generators for the polynomial systems $\mathcal{H}_i$. While the optimal choice of attack parameters may depend on the parameters of the Dob encryption scheme, as a rule of thumb it seems best to first minimize D_0, then n, and lastly ρ. In practice, minimizing n involves choosing the smallest n such that $D_{reg}(d,n) > D_0$, for a fixed d. Kernel elements of the resulting sparse, homogeneous Macaulay matrix can be found using a variant of the Wiedemann algorithm [30] (see also [6] for an implementation of a version adapted to the XL algorithm). Section VI of [30] shows that one kernel vector can be retrieved after three iterations with probability > 0.7, and as a simplification we estimate the complexity of finding a sufficient number of kernel elements in each of the ρ Macaulay matrices as $\frac{3}{0.7}\left(t + \binom{k}{2}\right)\binom{n}{D_0}^2\binom{n}{2}$. Recall from Remark 1 that the first step is performed twice if the attacker wishes to remove the effect of p_R from $\mathcal{P}_E$; let $\delta = 1$ denote if this is the case, and $\delta = 0$ otherwise. It follows that the total attack complexity can be estimated as

$$\mathcal{C}_{\text{Attack}} = \max\left\{ 2^\delta \rho \frac{3}{0.7}\left(t + \binom{k}{2}\right)\binom{n}{D_0}^2\binom{n}{2}, \mathcal{C}_{\mathcal{P}_E,\delta} \;\middle|\; \delta \in \{0,1\} \right\}, \tag{31}$$

where $\mathcal{C}_{\mathcal{P}_E,\delta}$ denotes the complexity of finding a solution for $\mathcal{P}_E$ (with or without p_R, depending on δ). While we do not have a general estimate for the complexity this second step, we discuss how to estimate it in the case of the 80–bit secure parameter set proposed in Sect. 2.4 of [20], in the following.

Security of the Suggested Parameters. Let $d = 129$, and $t = k = 6$ for the Dob encryption scheme. Using Eqs. (3) and (21) we find that it is not possible to choose an n such that $N_4^{(0,0)}$ is positive, and $D_{reg}(129, n) > 4$. For degree 5, we find that $n = 50$ is the smallest number such that $N_5^{(0,0)}$ is positive, and $D_{reg}(129, 50) > 5$. Indeed, for this choice of parameters, we get:

$$N_5^{(0,0)}(129, 50, 6, 6) = 64024,$$

which is exactly the number of degree fall polynomials observed in the last row of Table 2. For this choice of parameters, ρ is upper bounded by 15, due to Lemma 5. In this case we can do even better, and use $\rho = 11$, as described in Appendix E of [33]. Choosing $\delta = 1$, we find that the first step requires about 2^{63} operations. For step two, we note from the experiments we ran, provided in Table 4 Appendix F of [33], that the extended Dob system with modifications $t = k = 6$ has a solving degree of 4 in all the experiments we can run. Conjecturing that this behaviour extends to $d = 129$, we estimate the complexity of step two to be $\mathcal{C}_{\mathcal{P}_E,1} = 2^{12}\binom{123}{4}^{\omega}$, where the factor 2^{12} is the cost of finding the correct constants for $q_1^*, \ldots, q_6^*$ and $v_1^*, \ldots, v_6^*$. We have also used $123 = 129 - 6$ as the number of variables in this system, seeing that 6 variables are eliminated by the linear forms v_i^*.

Using $\omega = 2.4$, step two is estimated at 2^{67}. Using Strassen's algorithm with $\omega = 2.8$ (a rather pessimistic choice for an attacker as it assumes that it is not possible to take advantage of the sparse matrix structure of the systems), the estimate is 2^{77} for step two. Either option leads to a time complexity below the proposed 80–bit security.

7 Conclusions

We have presented an analysis on the security provided by the Q_+ and *ip* modifications against algebraic attacks. The theory was then applied to the Dob encryption scheme, along with a novel attack on this construction. Not only does the attack break the suggested parameter set, but the effectiveness of how crucial information regarding the modifications can be retrieved allows us to conclude that the Dobbertin permutation seems unsuited for use in encryption schemes. The reader may consult Section 7 in [33] for a more in–depth discussion on this. We emphasize that this work has not covered the Dob *signature* scheme, nor the generalized central maps introduced in [20]; their security remains an open question.

There are several directions where the ideas presented here may inspire future work. Firstly, the modifications are treated as ideals, whose dimensions can be examined. If different types of modifications, such as minus and vinegar, can be included in this framework, it could lead to a deeper understanding of the security of an even larger subclass of big–field schemes. Secondly, the attack introduces new tools for the cryptanalysis of multivariate schemes. The gluing technique allows an attacker to collect useful information after fixing a number of variables. As there is no need for correct guesses, the exponential factor usually associated with hybrid methods is avoided. Furthermore, the technique does not rely on heuristic assumptions on the relation between the first fall and solving degrees.

In light of this, we believe that security analyses of big–field multivariate schemes ought not only focus on the first fall degree directly, but also how this degree changes when fixing variables. Cryptographers wishing to design encryption schemes by adding limited modification to an otherwise weak polynomial system should be particularly aware of the effect presented in this work.

Acknowledgements. Morten Øygarden has been funded by The Research Council of Norway through the project "qsIoT: Quantum safe cryptography for the Internet of Things". The authors would like to thank Carlos Cid for useful discussions on this work.

References

1. Apon, D., Moody, D., Perlner, R., Smith-Tone, D., Verbel, J.: Combinatorial rank attacks against the rectangular simple matrix encryption scheme. In: Ding, J., Tillich, J.-P. (eds.) PQCrypto 2020. LNCS, vol. 12100, pp. 307–322. Springer, Cham (2020). https://doi.org/10.1007/978-3-030-44223-1_17
2. Bardet, M., Faugère, J.-C., Salvy, B.: Complexity of Gröbner basis computation for Semi-regular Overdetermined sequences over $\mathbb{F}_2$ with solutions in $\mathbb{F}_2$. (2003). [Research Report] RR-5049, INRIA, inria-00071534
3. Bettale, L., Faugère, J.-C., Perret, L.: Hybrid approach for solving multivariate systems over finite fields. J. Math. Cryptology **3**(3), 177–197 (2009)
4. Carlet. S.: Vectorial boolean functions for cryptography. In: Crama, Y., Hammer, P.L., (eds.), Boolean Models and Methods in Mathematics, Computer Science, and Engineering, pp. 398–469. Cambridge University Press (2010)
5. Cartor, R., Smith-Tone, D.: EFLASH: a new multivariate encryption scheme. In: Cid Jr., C., Jacobson, M. (eds.) Selected Areas in Cryptography - SAC 2018, vol. 11349, pp. 281–299. Springer, Heidelberg (2019). https://doi.org/10.1007/978-3-030-10970-7_13
6. Cheng, Chen-Mou, Chou, Tung, Niederhagen, Ruben, Yang, Bo-Yin: Solving quadratic equations with XL on parallel architectures. In: Prouff, Emmanuel, Schaumont, Patrick (eds.) CHES 2012. LNCS, vol. 7428, pp. 356–373. Springer, Heidelberg (2012). https://doi.org/10.1007/978-3-642-33027-8_21
7. Cox, D.A., Little, J., O'shea, D.: Using Algebraic Geometry. Springer, Heidelberg (2006). https://doi.org/10.1007/b138611
8. Ding, J.: A new variant of the matsumoto-imai cryptosystem through perturbation. In: Bao, F., Deng, R., Zhou, J. (eds.) PKC 2004. LNCS, vol. 2947, pp. 305–318. Springer, Heidelberg (2004). https://doi.org/10.1007/978-3-540-24632-9_22
9. Ding, J., Gower, J.E.: Inoculating multivariate schemes against differential attacks. In: Yung, M., Dodis, Y., Kiayias, A., Malkin, T. (eds.) PKC 2006. LNCS, vol. 3958, pp. 290–301. Springer, Heidelberg (2006). https://doi.org/10.1007/11745853_19
10. Ding, J., Hodges, T.J.: Inverting HFE systems is quasi-polynomial for all fields. In: Rogaway, P. (ed.) CRYPTO 2011. LNCS, vol. 6841, pp. 724–742. Springer, Heidelberg (2011). https://doi.org/10.1007/978-3-642-22792-9_41
11. Ding, J., Perlner, R., Petzoldt, A., Smith-Tone, D.: Improved cryptanalysis of HFEv- via projection. In: Lange, T., Steinwandt, R. (eds.) PQCrypto 2018. LNCS, vol. 10786, pp. 375–395. Springer, Cham (2018). https://doi.org/10.1007/978-3-319-79063-3_18
12. Ding, J., Schmidt, D.: Cryptanalysis of HFEv and internal perturbation of HFE. In: Vaudenay, S. (ed.) PKC 2005. LNCS, vol. 3386, pp. 288–301. Springer, Heidelberg (2005). https://doi.org/10.1007/978-3-540-30580-4_20
13. Dobbertin, H.: Almost perfect nonlinear power functions on GF (2/sup n/): the welch case. IEEE Trans. Inf. Theory **45**(4), 1271–1275 (1999)
14. Dubois, V., Granboulan, L., Stern, J.: Cryptanalysis of HFE with internal perturbation. In: Okamoto, T., Wang, X. (eds.) PKC 2007. LNCS, vol. 4450, pp. 249–265. Springer, Heidelberg (2007). https://doi.org/10.1007/978-3-540-71677-8_17
15. Faugère, J.-C.: A new efficient algorithm for computing Gröbner bases (F4). J. Pure Appl. algebra **139**(1–3), 61–88 (1999)
16. Faugère, J.-C., Joux, A.: Algebraic cryptanalysis of hidden field equation (HFE) cryptosystems using Gröbner bases. In: Boneh, D. (ed.) CRYPTO 2003. LNCS, vol. 2729, pp. 44–60. Springer, Heidelberg (2003). https://doi.org/10.1007/978-3-540-45146-4_3

17. Fouque, P.-A., Granboulan, L., Stern, J.: Differential cryptanalysis for multivariate schemes. In: Cramer, R. (ed.) EUROCRYPT 2005. LNCS, vol. 3494, pp. 341–353. Springer, Heidelberg (2005). https://doi.org/10.1007/11426639_20
18. Hoffman, J.W., Jia, X., Wang, H.: Commutative Algebra: An Introduction. Stylus Publishing, LLC (2016)
19. https://github.com/Simula-UiB/Attack-On-The-Dob-Encryption-Scheme
20. Macario-Rat, G., Patarin, J.: Two-face: new public key multivariate schemes. In: Joux, A., Nitaj, A., Rachidi, T. (eds.) AFRICACRYPT 2018. LNCS, vol. 10831, pp. 252–265. Springer, Cham (2018). https://doi.org/10.1007/978-3-319-89339-6_14
21. Matsumoto, T., Imai, H.: Public quadratic polynomial-tuples for efficient signature-verification and message-encryption. In: Barstow, D., et al. (eds.) EUROCRYPT 1988. LNCS, vol. 330, pp. 419–453. Springer, Heidelberg (1988). https://doi.org/10.1007/3-540-45961-8_39
22. Øygarden, M., Felke, P., Raddum, H., Cid, C.: Cryptanalysis of the multivariate encryption scheme EFLASH. In: Jarecki, S. (ed.) CT-RSA 2020. LNCS, vol. 12006, pp. 85–105. Springer, Cham (2020). https://doi.org/10.1007/978-3-030-40186-3_5
23. Patarin, J.: Cryptanalysis of the matsumoto and imai public key scheme of eurocrypt 1988. In: Coppersmith, D. (ed.) CRYPTO 1995. LNCS, vol. 963, pp. 248–261. Springer, Heidelberg (1995). https://doi.org/10.1007/3-540-44750-4_20
24. Patarin, J.: Hidden fields equations (HFE) and isomorphisms of polynomials (IP): Two new families of asymmetric algorithms. In: Maurer, U. (ed.) EUROCRYPT 1996. LNCS, vol. 1070, pp. 33–48. Springer, Heidelberg (1996). https://doi.org/10.1007/3-540-68339-9_4
25. Shor, P.W.: Algorithms for quantum computation: discrete logarithms and factoring. In: Proceedings 35th Annual Symposium on Foundations of Computer Science, pp. 124–134. IEEE (1994)
26. Smith-Tone, D., Verbel, J.: A rank attack against extension field cancellation. In: Ding, J., Tillich, J.-P. (eds.) PQCrypto 2020. LNCS, vol. 12100, pp. 381–401. Springer, Cham (2020). https://doi.org/10.1007/978-3-030-44223-1_21
27. Szepieniec, A., Ding, J., Preneel, B.: Extension field cancellation: a new central trapdoor for multivariate quadratic systems. In: Takagi, T. (ed.) PQCrypto 2016. LNCS, vol. 9606, pp. 182–196. Springer, Cham (2016). https://doi.org/10.1007/978-3-319-29360-8_12
28. Tao, C., Xiang, H., Petzoldt, A., Ding, J.: Simple matrix-a multivariate public key cryptosystem (MPKC) for encryption. Finite Fields Appl. **35**, 352–368 (2015)
29. Wang, Y., Ikematsu, Y., Duong, D.H., Takagi, T.: The secure parameters and efficient decryption algorithm for multivariate public key cryptosystem EFC. IEICE Trans. Fundam. Electron. Commun. Comput. Sci. **102**(9), 1028–1036 (2019)
30. Wiedemann, D.: Solving sparse linear equations over finite fields. IEEE Trans. Inf. Theory **32**(1), 54–62 (1986)
31. Wolf, C., Preneel, B.: Taxonomy of public key schemes based on the problem of multivariate quadratic equations. Cryptology ePrint Archive, Report 2005/077 (2005). https://eprint.iacr.org/2005/077
32. Yasuda, T., Wang, Y., Takagi, T.: Multivariate encryption schemes based on polynomial equations over real numbers. In: Ding, J., Tillich, J.-P. (eds.) PQCrypto 2020. LNCS, vol. 12100, pp. 402–421. Springer, Cham (2020). https://doi.org/10.1007/978-3-030-44223-1_22
33. Øygarden, M., Felke, P., Raddum, H.: Analysis of Multivariate Encryption Schemes: Application to Dob. Cryptology ePrint Archive, Report 2020/1442 (2020). https://eprint.iacr.org/2020/1442 (Extended Version)

On the Integer Polynomial Learning with Errors Problem

Julien Devevey[1(✉)], Amin Sakzad[2], Damien Stehlé[1,3], and Ron Steinfeld[2]

[1] ENS de Lyon, Laboratoire LIP (University of Lyon, CNRS, ENSL, INRIA, UCBL), Lyon, France
julien.devevey@ens-lyon.fr

[2] Faculty of Information Technology, Monash University, Clayton, Australia

[3] Institut Universitaire de France, Paris, France

Abstract. Several recent proposals of efficient public-key encryption are based on variants of the polynomial learning with errors problem (PLWE^f) in which the underlying *polynomial* ring $\mathbb{Z}_q[x]/f$ is replaced with the (related) modular *integer* ring $\mathbb{Z}_{f(q)}$; the corresponding problem is known as *Integer Polynomial Learning with Errors* ($\mathsf{I\text{-}PLWE}^f$). Cryptosystems based on $\mathsf{I\text{-}PLWE}^f$ and its variants can exploit optimised big-integer arithmetic to achieve good practical performance, as exhibited by the ThreeBears cryptosystem. Unfortunately, the average-case hardness of $\mathsf{I\text{-}PLWE}^f$ and its relation to more established lattice problems have to date remained unclear.

We describe the first polynomial-time average-case reductions for the search variant of $\mathsf{I\text{-}PLWE}^f$, proving its computational equivalence with the search variant of its counterpart problem PLWE^f. Our reductions apply to a large class of defining polynomials f. To obtain our results, we employ a careful adaptation of Rényi divergence analysis techniques to bound the impact of the integer ring arithmetic carries on the error distributions. As an application, we present a deterministic public-key cryptosystem over integer rings. Our cryptosystem, which resembles ThreeBears, enjoys one-way (OW-CPA) security provably based on the search variant of $\mathsf{I\text{-}PLWE}^f$.

1 Introduction

The Learning with Errors (LWE) problem was first introduced by Regev in [Reg09]. This problem, in its search form, consists in finding $\mathbf{s} \in \mathbb{Z}_q^m$ for some parameters $q > 2$ and $m \geq 1$, given arbitrarily many samples of the form $(\mathbf{a}_i, \langle \mathbf{a}_i, \mathbf{s} \rangle + e_i)$ over $\mathbb{Z}_q^m \times \mathbb{Z}_q$. Here, the so-called error e_i is a random small-magnitude integer and $\mathbf{a}_i$ is uniform in $\mathbb{Z}_q^m$. A variant of this problem can be defined by replacing $\mathbb{Z}$ by a polynomial ring $\mathbb{Z}[x]/f$, where $f \in \mathbb{Z}[x]$ is monic and irreducible. In that case, the problem is called Polynomial-LWE (PLWE) if $m = 1$ [SSTX09], and Module-LWE (MLWE) if $m \geq 1$ [BGV12]. As illustrated by their prominence in the NIST post-quantum cryptography project [NIS], in practice, these problems over polynomial rings are typically preferred to LWE, as

J. A. Garay (Ed.): PKC 2021, LNCS 12710, pp. 184–214, 2021.
https://doi.org/10.1007/978-3-030-75245-3_8

they lead to more efficient cryptographic constructions. Their intractability has been (quantumly) linked to some worst-case problems for some restricted classes of Euclidean lattices (see, e.g., [SSTX09, LPR10, LS15, AD17, PRS17, RSW18]).

More recently, Gu [Gu17, Gu19] introduced another variant of LWE which we will refer to as the Integer Polynomial Learning With Errors problem (I-PLWE), by consistency with PLWE (in [Gu17, Gu19], it is called integer ring learning with errors). It is related to PLWE, as follows. For an integer q, evaluation in q is a homomorphism from $\mathbb{Z}[x]/f$ to $\mathbb{Z}_{f(q)}$. Note that it does not naturally extend to a homomorphism from $\mathbb{Z}_q[x]/f$ to $\mathbb{Z}_{f(q)}$ (this will actually be the main source of technical difficulty throughout this article). Nevertheless, for a polynomial $a(x) = \sum_{i<\deg f} a_i x^i \in \mathbb{Z}_q[x]/f$, we can assume that $a_i \in (-q/2, q/2]$ for all i and consider the integer $a(q) := \sum_{i<\deg f} a_i q^i \in \mathbb{Z}_{f(q)}$. This allows to relate an element of $\mathbb{Z}_q[x]/f$ to an integer $\mathbb{Z}_{f(q)}$. In this spirit, I-PLWE asks to find $s \in \mathbb{Z}_{f(q)}$ given arbitrarily many samples of the form $(a_i, a_i s + e_i)$ over $\mathbb{Z}_{f(q)} \times \mathbb{Z}_{f(q)}$, where the a_i's are uniform in $\mathbb{Z}_{f(q)}$ and the e_i's have a centered q-ary decomposition with small-magnitude coefficients (we refer the reader to Sect. 2 for a formal definition). This problem was investigated for $f = x^m + 1$ in [Gu17, Gu19], which also contain an asymptotically efficient public-key encryption scheme with IND-CPA security inherited from I-PLWE's presumed hardness. This encryption scheme was generalized in [BCSV20]. A module extension of I-PLWE was considered for $f = x^m - x^{m/2} - 1$ in the ThreeBears candidate [Ham17] to the NIST PQC project [NIS]. Taking I-PLWE (or its module extension) allows to replace a polynomial ring by large integers, and to take advantage of efficient large-integer arithmetic algorithms and libraries. A somewhat similar intractability assumption was considered in [AJPS18, Sze17], with error terms of small Hamming weight in their binary decomposition.

The presence of *carries* in the integer operations underlying those integer-ring problems distinguishes them from their carry-free polynomial analogues, and creates technical annoyances when analyzing their intractability and building cryptosystems. In particular, the only reduction from PLWE to I-PLWE known so far, due to [Gu17], holds only for a worst-case variant of I-PLWE, in which the error terms are arbitrary (among small-magnitude errors). The reduction proceeds by converting PLWE samples (i.e., polynomials) to I-PLWE samples (i.e., integers). The reduction analysis only shows that the error terms resulting from the conversion have q-ary decompositions with small-magnitude coefficients (see [Gu17, Lemma 3.7]). As noted in [Gu19], which mentions proving hardness of I-PLWE as an open problem, this is insufficient to support the intractability of the average-case variant I-PLWE, with random error terms. The situation is identical for the converse direction, from I-PLWE to PLWE. Unfortunately, it seems very difficult to design a public-key encryption scheme with security inherited from the intractability of this worst-case variant of I-PLWE. For example, Gu's encryption scheme [Gu17, Gu19] is proved secure under the presumed intractability of a *decision* and *average-case* variant of I-PLWE, in which the error terms are randomly distributed, and one only asks to distinguish I-PLWE samples from uniform samples rather than finding the secret s from I-PLWE samples.

A concrete security analysis of I-PLWE is given in [BCF20] against certain attacks, such as classical meet-in-the-middle and lattice-based attacks. When $f = x^m + 1$ with m composite with an odd divisor, they give an improved attack that can be viewed as the I-PLWE analogue of Gentry's attack on NTRU with a composite defining polynomial [Gen01]. This improved attack does not apply when f is irreducible. In particular, classical meet-in-the-middle and lattice-based techniques are combined in order to build an improved lattice-based attack for $f = x^m + 1$ with m composite with an odd divisor.

Contributions. We exhibit polynomial-time reductions between the *search* and *average-case* variant of $\mathsf{I\text{-}PLWE}^{(f)}$ and the *search* and *average-case* variant of $\mathsf{PLWE}^{(f)}$, for a large class of defining polynomials f: the reductions only require that f is monic.[1] Compared to [Gu17], the reduction analyses do consider the error term distributions. Our results show the hardness equivalence of search I-PLWE and search PLWE. The reduction loss in success probability depends on the degree of f, its expansion factor (the definition of the expansion factor is recalled in Sect. 2), the relative magnitude of the error terms and secret, and the number of samples. In particular, we can set q polynomial in the degree of f such that the loss is polynomial for a constant number of samples.

These reductions handle random error terms, but are limited to the *search* variants, as opposed to the *decision* variants. This makes it complicated to devise a public-key encryption scheme with security based on the presumed intractability of PLWE. In particular, we do not know how to prove the security of Gu's encryption scheme under well-established assumptions: indeed, this scheme was designed to provide IND-CPA security based on the presumed intractability of the decision version of I-PLWE. As our second main contribution, we exhibit a *deterministic* public-key encryption scheme, which can be viewed as a mild variant of Gu's. It is designed to provide one-way security under chosen plaintext attacks (OW-CPA), under the *search* I-PLWE and the *decision* PLWE intractability assumptions. By adapting the techniques developed in [RSW18], one can devise reductions between appropriately defined search and decision versions of PLWE for large families of defining polynomials f and with limited parameter losses. Thanks to our first contribution, this means that our scheme can be adapted to enjoy security based on any single intractability assumption among search I-PLWE, search PLWE and decision PLWE. Finally, we note that a deterministic public-key encryption scheme enjoying OW-CPA security can be converted in an IND-CCA key-exchange mechanism in the random oracle model [HHK17].

Our techniques and results readily extend to the module case: one can define I-MLWE analogously to I-PLWE, and reduce the search variants of I-MLWE and MLWE to one another. Our deterministic encryption scheme can also be adapted to the module case, and it then somewhat resembles the ThreeBears candidate to the NIST PQC project [Ham17].

[1] As commonly done, we also impose irreducibility of f in the problem definitions, to avoid weaknesses such as those pointed out in [BCF20].

Techniques. In the reductions to/from I-PLWE from/to PLWE, the main idea is to convert integers into polynomials and vice-versa via the 'approximate' (due to the 'small' carries) relations between the integer and polynomial ring operations studied in Sect. 3. We then use the Rényi divergence analysis approach [LSS14, BLRL+18] to show that, for suitably chosen parameters, the small carry errors incurred by the format conversions do not shift the error distribution "too far" from the desired distribution. This allows to reduce these average-case problems to one another. The restriction to search problems (as opposed to decision problems) in our hardness results is inherited from the use of the Rényi divergence.

Beyond the distributional analysis of the error terms, our reductions are also more general than those of [Gu17] as they apply for any monic defining polynomial f. The main difficulty here is to handle the homomorphism defect of the map from $\mathbb{Z}_q[x]$ to $\mathbb{Z}_{f(q)}$ by taking a polynomial a with coefficients a_i viewed as integers in $(-q/2, q/2]$ and computing $a(q) := \sum_{i<\deg f} a_i q^i \in \mathbb{Z}_{f(q)}$. In particular, we distinguish two cases, depending whether $f(q) > q^{\deg f}$, for which this map is injective, or $f(q) < q^{\deg f}$, for which it is surjective. When the map is injective, we randomize it so that it reaches the whole range, and when it is surjective, we consider a randomized inverse mapping. Overall, this leads to four reductions, corresponding to converting integers to polynomials or polynomials to integers, depending on whether $f(q) > q^{\deg f}$ or $f(q) < q^{\deg f}$. Importantly, for our reductions to go through, we need the I-PLWE secret s to have a q-ary decomposition with small coefficients, which corresponds to taking a small-coefficient secret in PLWE: in our analysis, this is needed to ensure that carries due the multiplication $a_i \cdot s$ remain small.

The design of the encryption scheme is relatively standard. We use an I-PLWE sample $\mathsf{pk} := (a, b) = (a, as + e)$ as a public key. We encrypt a triple (t, e', e'') of integers with q-ary decompositions with small coefficients, by generating two I-PLWE samples $(c_1, c_2) := (at + Ke', bt + Ke'')$. Here K is a small integer that enables decryption: given $c_2 - c_1 s$, one recovers t by reducing the q-ary decomposition coefficients modulo K and dividing the resulting integer by e modulo $f(q)$. Once t is known, one may recover e' and e''. Overall, this provides a deterministic public-key encryption scheme. The proof of OW-CPA security exploits the intractability of decision PLWE to argue that pk is somewhat close to uniform: this is achieved by game hops with distributional updates on pk whose effects on the OW-CPA winning probability are controlled by Rényi divergence arguments. The compatibility of OW-CPA security with the Rényi divergence was similarly exploited in the security proof of the Frodo candidate to the NIST PQC project [ABD+17]. Finally, once pk is replaced by a uniform pair $(a, b) \in \mathbb{Z}_{f(q)}^2$, OW-CPA security follows from the presumed intractability of I-PLWE.

Open Problems. Similarly to I-PLWE, the one-dimensional LWE problem also involves samples of the form $(a_i, a_i s + e_i)$ over $\mathbb{Z}_p \times \mathbb{Z}_p$ for some integer p. Reductions between one-dimensional LWE and standard multi-dimensional LWE have been given in [BLP+13], hence supporting the hardness of one-dimensional LWE (for a large modulus p). Unfortunately, one-dimensional LWE is different from I-PLWE in that the error term e_i is small compared to p in one-dimensional LWE, and has a q-ary decomposition with small coefficients in I-PLWE. Obtaining a reduction from one-dimensional LWE to I-PLWE would be an interesting avenue to prove hardness of PLWE (with polynomially-bounded modulus) under LWE.

Interestingly, converting an error-free I-PLWE sample (a, as) into a PLWE sample $(A, AS + E)$ creates a non-zero error E, due to the carries in the multiplication of a by s modulo $f(q)$. This PLWE variant is insecure as one can recover s by dividing as by a modulo $f(q)$. Error-free I-PLWE resembles the polynomial-ring variant of Learning With Rounding [BPR12]: in the first, the error term is a deterministic function of (A, S), whereas in the second it is a deterministic function of AS. This raises the question of studying which functions of (A, S) lead to secure or insecure deterministic-error variants of PLWE.

One limitation of our techniques is due to the fact that the Rényi divergence is convenient to study search problems but not so for decision problems, notably because of the probability preservation property (see Definition 1) which is not meaningful in the case where the probabilities are close to $\frac{1}{2}$ instead of 0. For this reason, it is unclear how to extend our analysis to obtain reductions between decision I-PLWE and decision PLWE. Finding a reduction between decision I-PLWE and decision PLWE would require different techniques from ours. To prove hardness of decision I-PLWE, an alternative path would be to obtain a search to decision reduction. Unfortunately, it is also unclear whether existing search to decision reductions for PLWE (see [LPR10, PRS17, RSW18]) could be adapted to I-PLWE, mainly because of the highly structured noise distribution.

2 Preliminaries

We let $x \hookleftarrow D$ denote the action of sampling x from distribution D. We let $\mathcal{U}(S)$ denote the uniform distribution over any finite set S and we write $x \hookleftarrow S$ instead of $x \hookleftarrow \mathcal{U}(S)$. For any $P = \sum_i P_i x^i \in \mathbb{Z}[x]$, $P \bmod q$ denotes $\sum_i (P_i \bmod q) x^i$.

2.1 Integer Gaussian Distributions

For $\sigma > 0$, we define the centered Gaussian function of standard deviation parameter σ as $\rho_\sigma(\mathbf{x}) = \exp(-\pi \|\mathbf{x}\|^2/\sigma^2)$, for any $\mathbf{x} \in \mathbb{R}^m$. We define the centered integer Gaussian distribution $D_{\mathbb{Z}^m,\sigma}$ of standard deviation parameter σ by

$$\forall \mathbf{x} \in \mathbb{Z}^m : \; D_{\mathbb{Z}^m,\sigma}(\mathbf{x}) = \rho_\sigma(\mathbf{x})/\rho_\sigma(\mathbb{Z}^m).$$

For $B > 0$, we use $D_{\mathbb{Z}^m,\sigma,B}$ to denote the distribution obtained from $D_{\mathbb{Z}^m,\sigma}$ by cutting its tail (by rejection sampling) to take values in $(-B/2, B/2]^m$. Since we are going to reduce polynomials sampled from this distribution to $\mathbb{Z}_q[x]$, by reducing each of their coefficients modulo q, and then look at the representatives of said coefficients in $(-q/2, q/2]$, we will use $D_{\mathbb{Z}^{<m}[x],\sigma,q}$ to sample such polynomials. Doing so gives us polynomials whose coefficients are not affected by reductions modulo q.

We will let $D_{\mathbb{Z}^{<m}[x],\sigma,B}$ denote the distribution over integer polynomials of degree $< m$ obtained by sampling the coefficient vector according to $D_{\mathbb{Z}^m,\sigma,B}$. We also write $D_{\mathbb{Z}[x]/f,\sigma,B}$ for $f \in \mathbb{Z}[x]$ monic of degree m to denote the distribution $D_{\mathbb{Z}^{<m}[x],\sigma,B}$ while insisting that we view the sample as an element of $\mathbb{Z}[x]/f$.

2.2 The Rényi Divergence

The Rényi divergence is a prominent tool that we use throughout this work. Its relevance to security proofs in lattice-based cryptography was stressed in [BLRL+18].

Definition 1 (Rényi Divergence). *Let P and Q be two discrete probability distributions, such that we have $\mathrm{Supp}(P) \subseteq \mathrm{Supp}(Q)$. The Rényi divergences of orders 2 and ∞ are respectively defined as follows:*

$$R(P||Q) := \sum_{x \in \mathrm{Supp}(P)} \frac{P(x)^2}{Q(x)} \quad \text{and} \quad R_\infty(P||Q) := \max_{x \in \mathrm{Supp}(P)} \frac{P(x)}{Q(x)}.$$

The following lemma, listing classical properties of the Rényi divergence, is borrowed from [BLRL+18].

Lemma 1. *Let P and Q be two discrete probability distributions such that we have $\mathrm{Supp}(P) \subseteq \mathrm{Supp}(Q)$. The following properties hold.*

- ***Log. Positivity:*** $R(P||Q) \geq R(P||P) = 1$.
- ***Data Processing Inequality:*** $R(P^f||Q^f) \leq R(P||Q)$ *for any function f, where X^f denotes the distribution of $f(x)$ when sampling $x \hookleftarrow X$.*
- ***Multiplicativity:*** *Let P and Q be two distributions of a pair of random variables X_1 and X_2 and P_i and Q_i denote the marginal distribution of X_i under P and Q, respectively. If X_1 and X_2 are independent, then $R(P||Q) = R(P_1||Q_1)R(P_2||Q_2)$. Otherwise, we have $R(P||Q) \leq R_\infty(P_1||Q_1) \cdot \max_{x_1 \in \mathrm{Supp}(P_1)} R((P_2|x_1)||(Q_2|x_1))$.*
- ***Probability Preservation:*** *Let $E \subseteq \mathrm{Supp}(Q)$ be an arbitrary event. Then, we have $Q(E) \geq P(E)^2/R(P||Q)$.*

2.3 The Polynomial Learning with Errors Problem

We recall here the PLWE problem studied, e.g., in [SSTX09, LPR10, RSW18]. Here we choose to tail-cut the Gaussian distribution such that each coefficient of the error already belongs to $(-q/2, q/2]$.

Definition 2 (P distribution). *Let $q \geq 2$, $f \in \mathbb{Z}[x]$ monic and $\sigma > 0$. Given $s \in \mathbb{Z}_q[x]/f$, we define the distribution $\mathsf{P}_{q,\sigma}^{(f)}(s)$ over $\mathbb{Z}_q[x]/f \times \mathbb{Z}[x]/f$ obtained by sampling $a \hookleftarrow \mathbb{Z}_q[x]/f$, $e \hookleftarrow D_{\mathbb{Z}[x]/f,\sigma,q}$ and returning $(a, b = a \cdot s + e) \in \mathbb{Z}_q[x]/f \times \mathbb{Z}_q[x]/f$.*

The distribution above is sometimes generalized to arbitrary covariance matrices. Our results carry over to this setting, as their proofs do not involve arguments specific to spherical Gaussians. For the sake of simplicity, we describe them using spherical Gaussian distributions.

Definition 3 (Search PLWE). *Let $q \geq 2$, $f \in \mathbb{Z}[x]$ irreducible and monic, and $\sigma > \sigma' > 0$. The problem $\mathsf{sPLWE}^{(f)}_{q,\sigma,\sigma'}$ consists in finding $s \hookleftarrow D_{\mathbb{Z}[x]/f,\sigma',q}$, given arbitrarily many samples from $\mathsf{P}^{(f)}_{q,\sigma}(s)$. For an algorithm $\mathcal{A}$, we define $\mathsf{Adv}^{\mathsf{sPLWE}}_{f,q,\sigma,\sigma'}(\mathcal{A})$ as the probability that $\mathcal{A}$ returns s (over the randomness of s, the samples and $\mathcal{A}$'s internal randomness). For $t \geq 1$, we write $\mathsf{sPLWE}^{(f)}_{q,\sigma,\sigma',t}$ to restrict the number of samples to at most t.*

For technical convenience, we use an average-case variant of search PLWE. It is computationally equivalent (by random self-reducibility) to the more standard worst-case variant in which s is arbitrary. We also assume that s is sampled from a Gaussian distribution, rather than the more common choice of uniform distribution. By adapting the technique from [ACPS09], sPLWE with uniform secret and error distribution $D_{\mathbb{Z}[x]/f,\sigma',q}$ reduces to $\mathsf{sPLWE}^{(f)}_{q,\sigma',\sigma',t}$ with identical secret and error distribution equal to $D_{\mathbb{Z}[x]/f,\sigma',q}$. By adding independent Gaussian samples to the second components of the sPLWE samples, one can reduce $\mathsf{sPLWE}^{(f)}_{q,\sigma',\sigma',t}$ to $\mathsf{sPLWE}^{(f)}_{q,\sigma',\sigma,t}$. The Gaussian sum may be analyzed using [BF11, Lemma 4.12]. Letting $m = \deg f$, one may set $\sigma' = \Omega(\sqrt{m})$ (to obtain a Gaussian error term) and $q = \Omega(\sigma\sqrt{m})$ (to handle the Gaussian tail-cutting), to limit the advantage loss to an additive $2^{-\Omega(m)}$ term.

Definition 4 (Decision PLWE). *Let $q \geq 2$, $f \in \mathbb{Z}[x]$ irreducible and monic, and $\sigma > \sigma' > 0$. The problem $\mathsf{dPLWE}^{(f)}_{q,\sigma,\sigma'}$ consists in distinguishing between oracle accesses to $D_0 = \mathcal{U}(\mathbb{Z}_q[x]/f \times \mathbb{Z}[x]/f)$ and $D_1 = \mathsf{P}^{(f)}_{q,\sigma}(s)$ where $s \hookleftarrow D_{\mathbb{Z}[x]/f,\sigma',q}$ is sampled once and for all. For an algorithm $\mathcal{A}$, we define*

$$\mathsf{Adv}^{\mathsf{dPLWE}}_{f,q,\sigma,\sigma'}(\mathcal{A}) = \left|\Pr[\mathcal{A}^{D_0} \to 1] - \Pr[\mathcal{A}^{D_1} \to 1]\right|.$$

For $t \geq 1$, we write $\mathsf{dPLWE}^{(f)}_{q,\sigma,\sigma',t}$ to restrict the number of samples to at most t.

The techniques from [RSW18] can be adapted to reduce sPLWE to dPLWE for exponentially many defining polynomials f as a function of the degree m. Note that for this reduction to go through, one needs to use non-spherical Gaussian distributions and to sample the covariance matrix from a specific distribution. The reduction incurs an increase of the maximum singular value of that covariance matrix, which is polynomial in m and the expansion factor of f.

Definition 5 (Expansion Factor). *Let $q \geq 2$. Let $f \in \mathbb{Z}[x]$ of degree m. The expansion factor of f, denoted $\mathsf{EF}(f)$ is defined as:*

$$\mathsf{EF}(f) := \max_{g \in \mathbb{Z}^{<2m-1}[x] \setminus \{0\}} (\|g \bmod f\|_\infty / \|g\|_\infty).$$

As an example of polynomial f with $\mathsf{EF}(f) \leq \mathrm{poly}(m)$, we can mention gap polynomials $f = x^m + g$ with $\deg(g) \leq m/2$ and $\|g\|_\infty \leq \mathrm{poly}(m)$ (see [LM06]).

2.4 The Integer Polynomial Learning with Errors Problem

The integer variant I-PLWE of PLWE is parameterized by a monic polynomial f and an integer $q > 2$ (and a noise parameters, as we will see below). It is defined using the set $\mathbb{Z}_{f(q)}$ of integers modulo $f(q)$. This set can be viewed as polynomials in $\mathbb{Z}_q[x]/f$, via the map consisting in taking the representative in $(-q/2, q/2]$ of every coefficient and evaluating the resulting polynomial in q. This format conversion is at the core of the reductions between I-PLWE and PLWE that we will describe. Unfortunately, this conversion is imperfect, most visibly because the two sets do not have the same sizes (unless $f = x^m$ for some integer m, but this case is excluded as PLWE is defined for f irreducible).

Before introducing I-PLWE, we define the integer range $I_{f,q}$ from where we choose the representatives of $\mathbb{Z}_{f(q)}$. It is not always $(-f(q)/2, f(q)/2]$. This oddity stems from the fact that when q is even, the set of evaluations in q of polynomials in $\mathbb{Z}_q[x]/f$ with their coefficients seen as integers in $(-q/2, q/2]$, is not zero-centered. The specific definition of $I_{f,q}$ is justified by Lemma 4.

Definition 6 (Representatives range for $\mathbb{Z}_{f(q)}$). *Let $q > 2$ and $f \in \mathbb{Z}[x]$ monic of degree $m > 0$. We define:*

$$I_{f,q} = \begin{cases} \left(\frac{q}{2}\frac{q^m-1}{q-1} - f(q), \frac{q}{2}\frac{q^m-1}{q-1}\right] & \text{if } q \text{ even and } q\frac{q^m-1}{q-1} \geq f(q) \geq q^m, \\ \left(-\frac{q-2}{2}\frac{q^m-1}{q-1}, f(q) - \frac{q-2}{2}\frac{q^m-1}{q-1}\right] & \text{if } q \text{ even and } q^m > f(q) > (q-2)\frac{q^m-1}{q-1}, \\ (-f(q)/2, f(q)/2] & \text{otherwise.} \end{cases}$$

Whenever we consider an element $\bar{a}$ of $\mathbb{Z}_{f(q)}$ and want to choose a representative a in $\mathbb{Z}$ for it, we will choose it such that $a \in I_{f,q}$.

We now recall (and generalize) the I-PLWE problem introduced by Gu [Gu19].

Definition 7 (IP distribution). *Let $q > 2$, $f \in \mathbb{Z}[x]$ monic of degree $m > 0$, and $\sigma > 0$. We first define the distribution $D_{\mathbb{Z}_{f(q)},\sigma,q}$ as the distribution obtained by sampling $E \hookleftarrow D_{\mathbb{Z}^{<m+1}[x],\sigma,q}$, setting $e = E(q)$ and rejecting if it does not belong to $I_{f,q}$. Given $s \in \mathbb{Z}_{f(q)}$, we define the distribution $\mathsf{IP}^{(f)}_{q,\sigma}(s)$ over $\mathbb{Z}_{f(q)} \times \mathbb{Z}_{f(q)}$ obtained by sampling $a \hookleftarrow \mathbb{Z}_{f(q)}$, $e \hookleftarrow D_{\mathbb{Z}_{f(q)},\sigma,q}$ and returning $(a, b = a \cdot s + e) \in \mathbb{Z}_{f(q)} \times \mathbb{Z}_{f(q)}$.*

Note that this definition slightly diverges from Gu's, as we choose a different noise distribution. Previously, the noise was sampled from $D_{\mathbb{Z}^{<m}[x],\sigma}$, evaluated on q and reduced modulo $f(q)$. To sample from the distribution $D_{\mathbb{Z}_{f(q)},\sigma,q}$ from Definition 7, one can do the following:

- If $f(q) < q^m$, sample $E \hookleftarrow D_{\mathbb{Z}^{<m}[x],\sigma,q}$ and reject it if $E(q) \notin I_{f,q}$. This greatly reduces the rejection probability while still defining a probability distribution over the whole set $I_{f,q}$.
- If $f(q) \geq q^m$, sample $E \hookleftarrow D_{\mathbb{Z}^{<m}[x],\sigma,q}$. Compute $e' := E(q)$. Next let $C := 1 + 2\exp(-\pi/\sigma^2)$ and $p := \exp(-\pi/\sigma^2)/C$. Then set $e'' = q^m$ with probability p, $e'' = -q^m$ with probability p and $e'' := 0$ else. Finally set $e := e' + e''$ and reject it if it does not belong to $I_{f,q}$. In that case, the rejection probability is at most $2p = 2\exp(-\pi/\sigma^2)/C$.

The different claims made here can be proven using the results from Lemma 4.

Our reductions will only concern the search version of I-PLWE, so we only define this one. The definition can be adapted to a decision version.

Definition 8 (Search I-PLWE). *Let $q > 2$, $f \in \mathbb{Z}[x]$ irreducible and monic, and $\sigma > \sigma' > 0$. The problem $\mathsf{sI\text{-}PLWE}^{(f)}_{q,\sigma,\sigma'}$ consists in finding $s \hookleftarrow D_{\mathbb{Z}_{f(q)},\sigma',q}$, given arbitrarily many samples from $\mathsf{IP}^{(f)}_{q,\sigma}(s)$. For an algorithm $\mathcal{A}$, we define $\mathsf{Adv}^{\mathsf{sI\text{-}PLWE}}_{f,q,\sigma,\sigma'}(\mathcal{A})$ as the probability that $\mathcal{A}$ returns s (over the randomness of s, the samples and $\mathcal{A}$'s internal randomness). For $t \geq 1$, we write $\mathsf{sI\text{-}PLWE}^{(f)}_{q,\sigma,t}$ to restrict the number of samples to at most t.*

2.5 Public-Key Encryption

We recall the definition of deterministic encryption with perfect correctness.

Definition 9 (Deterministic public-key encryption). *A deterministic public-key encryption scheme is a triple of polynomial-time algorithms $(\mathsf{KeyGen}, \mathsf{Enc}, \mathsf{Dec})$ with the following specifications.*

- $\mathsf{KeyGen}(1^\lambda)$. *Algorithm* KeyGen *is probabilistic. It takes as input the security parameter λ (in unary) and outputs a public key* pk *and a secret key* sk. *We assume that the keys contain descriptions of a plaintext set $\mathcal{M}_\lambda$ and a ciphertext set $\mathcal{C}_\lambda$ that depend only on λ.*
- $\mathsf{Enc}(\mathsf{pk}, M)$. *Algorithm* Enc *is deterministic. It takes as input a public key* pk *and a plaintext $M \in \mathcal{M}$, and outputs a ciphertext $C \in \mathcal{C}_\lambda$.*
- $\mathsf{Dec}(\mathsf{sk}, C)$. *Algorithm* Dec *is deterministic. It takes as input a secret key* sk *and a ciphertext $C \in \mathcal{C}$, and outputs a plaintext $M \in \mathcal{M}_\lambda$.*

The correctness requirement states that for all $(\mathsf{pk}, \mathsf{sk})$ output by KeyGen *and all $M \in \mathcal{M}$, we have $\mathsf{Dec}(\mathsf{sk}, \mathsf{Enc}(\mathsf{pk}, M)) = M$.*

For such a deterministic encryption scheme, we consider the security notion of One-Wayness under Chosen Plaintext Attacks (OW-CPA). Note that the security game is of a search type (the adversary should recover a plaintext), which will be convenient for two reasons. First, OW-CPA security of our encryption scheme will be proven under the presumed hardness of the search version of I-PLWE rather than its decision counterpart (recall that we obtain reductions between I-PLWE and PLWE only for the search variant of I-PLWE). Second, in the security proof of our scheme, we will rely on arguments based on the Rényi divergence, which is more amenable to search problems than decision problems.

Note that OW-CPA security is typically defined with respect to the uniform distribution on plaintexts. We consider a variant that handles more general plaintext distributions.

Definition 10 (OW-CPA security). OW-CPA *security of a deterministic public-key encryption scheme $\mathsf{PKE} = (\mathsf{KeyGen}, \mathsf{Enc}, \mathsf{Dec})$ with respect to a family of distributions $\{D_{\mathcal{M}_\lambda}\}_\lambda$ over the plaintext spaces $\{\mathcal{M}_\lambda\}_\lambda$ is defined using the following game between a challenger and a adversary $\mathcal{A}$.*

- *The challenger runs* $\mathsf{KeyGen}(1^\lambda)$ *to obtain a public key* pk *and a secret key* sk. *It sends* pk *to* $\mathcal{A}$.
- *The challenger samples* M *from* $D_{\mathcal{M}_\lambda}$ *and sends* $C = \mathsf{Enc}(\mathsf{pk}, M)$ *to* $\mathcal{A}$.
- *Given* pk *and* C, *the adversary* $\mathcal{A}$ *replies with a plaintext* M'. *It wins the game if* $M' = M$.

The advantage $\mathsf{Adv}^{\mathsf{OW\text{-}CPA}}_{\mathsf{PKE},D_{\mathcal{M}_\lambda}}(\mathcal{A})$ *of the adversary* $\mathcal{A}$ *is defined as the probability that* $\mathcal{A}$ *wins the game.*

As seen in [HHK17] (see also [BP18]), a OW-CPA-secure deterministic encryption scheme can be tightly converted into a Key Encapsulation Mechanism that is secure under Chosen Ciphertext Attacks (CCA-secure KEM), in the Random Oracle Model (ROM). The advantage loss in this conversion is an additive term $q_D \cdot 2^{-H_\infty(D_{\mathcal{M}_\lambda})}$, where q_D is the number of decryption queries made to the KEM, and $H_\infty(D_{\mathcal{M}_\lambda}) = -\log \max_M D_{\mathcal{M}_\lambda}[M]$ is the min-entropy of $D_{\mathcal{M}_\lambda}$. Note that [HHK17, Theorem 3.6] involves a term $q_D/|\mathcal{M}_\lambda|$, as it considers the uniform distribution on plaintexts, but the proof can be readily adapted to non-uniform plaintext distributions, leading to the adapted advantage loss.

In the Quantum Random Oracle Model (QROM), in which the adversary has a quantum access to the random oracle, a deterministic OW-CPA secure encryption scheme can also be converted into a CCA-secure KEM, but the currently known proofs are not tight (see, e.g., [HHK17,BHH+19,KSS+20]), unless one requires additional properties on the deterministic encryption scheme [SXY18]. For our scheme, we do not know how to ensure the disjoint simulatability property required of [SXY18] under standard assumptions.

3 Relations Between Computations over the Polynomial and Integer Rings

In order to relate the PLWE and I-PLWE problems, we first compare the rings over which they are defined: PLWE takes place over some polynomial ring $\mathbb{Z}_q[x]/(f)$ whereas I-PLWE takes place over some integer ring $\mathbb{Z}_{f(q)}$. We first show how operations over $\mathbb{Z}$ can be converted to operations in $\mathbb{Z}_q[x]$, and then how to adapt this conversion to the rings $\mathbb{Z}_q[x]/f$ and $\mathbb{Z}_{f(q)}$.

3.1 Computations over $\mathbb{Z}_q[x]$

A natural way to convert an integer to an element of $\mathbb{Z}_q[x]$ would be to write the q-ary decomposition of an element of $\mathbb{Z}$ to get a polynomial. We rather use a centered q-ary decomposition, which is better suited to capture the smallness of the I-PLWE error terms. In this centered q-ary decomposition, the coefficients are taken in $(-q/2, q/2]$ rather than $[0, q)$. In the following, we exclude the case of $q = 2$, as we cannot represent a negative integer as a combination of powers of 2 with coefficients in $(-q/2, q/2] = \{0, 1\}$.

Definition 11 (Centered q-ary decomposition of an integer). *Let $q > 2$ and $a \in \mathbb{Z}$. For all $0 \leq i \leq \lceil \log_q a \rceil$ we recursively define the i-th coefficient of a in the q-ary decomposition as:*

$$a_i := \frac{a - \sum_{j<i} a_j q^j}{q^i} \bmod q,$$

where the mod *operation outputs the representative that belongs to $(-q/2, q/2]$.*

We now define the map Φ_q that converts an integer a into the polynomial whose coefficients are the coefficients of the centered q-ary decomposition of a.

Definition 12 (Conversion from $\mathbb{Z}$ to $\mathbb{Z}_q[x]$). *Let $q > 2$. The map $\Phi_q : \mathbb{Z} \longrightarrow \mathbb{Z}_q[x]$ is defined as follows*

$$\Phi_q : a \longmapsto \sum_{i=0}^{\lceil \log_q a \rceil} a_i x^i.$$

The map $\Phi_q^{-1} : \mathbb{Z}_q[x] \longrightarrow \mathbb{Z}$ is defined as follows

$$\Phi_q^{-1} : P = \sum_i P_i x^i \longmapsto \sum_i \overline{P}_i q^i,$$

where $\overline{P}_i \in \mathbb{Z}$ is the representative of $P_i \in \mathbb{Z}_q$ belonging to $(-q/2, q/2]$.

Note that indeed Φ_q^{-1} is the inverse of Φ_q, and hence both of them are bijections. Moreover, the equality $f(q) = \Phi_q^{-1}(f \bmod q)$ holds for any $f \in \mathbb{Z}[x]$ whose coefficients belong to $(-q/2, q/2)$. This drives us to always require that $q > 2\|f\|_\infty$ in the following. If $\Phi_q(a)$ has every coefficient with representative in $(-q/2, q/2)$ then $\Phi_q(-a) = -\Phi_q(a)$. Importantly, note that even though Φ_q maps a ring to another ring, it is *not* a ring homomorphism: it is not compatible with addition and multiplication. For instance, for $q = 3$, we have $\Phi_q(1+1) = x - 1 \neq -1 = \Phi_q(1) + \Phi_q(1)$ and $\Phi_q(2 \cdot 2) = x + 1 \neq (x-1)^2 = \Phi_q(2) \cdot \Phi_q(2)$.

Below, our goal is to evaluate how far Φ_q is from being a ring homomorphism, by bounding the quantities $\Phi_q(a+b) - (\Phi_q(a) + \Phi_q(b))$ and/or $\Phi_q(a \cdot b) - \Phi_q(a) \cdot \Phi_q(b)$ for $a, b \in \mathbb{Z}$. When adding (resp. multiplying) two integers in $\mathbb{Z}$ via schoolbook addition (resp. multiplication) in base q, the computation of a given digit may interfere with the computation of the next digit, because of carries. Oppositely, when adding (resp. multiplying) two polynomials in $\mathbb{Z}_q[x]$, there are no carries: computations can be done in parallel. Moreover, if we choose an even basis q, computing $-a$ may not be as simple as taking the opposite of each one of its coefficients.

For the next lemma it will be useful to recall how to compute the Euclidean division with 0-centered remainder: let $a \in \mathbb{Z}$ and $q \geq 2$. The "standard" Euclidean division of $a + \lfloor (q-1)/2 \rfloor$ by q can be written as:

$$a + \left\lfloor \frac{q-1}{2} \right\rfloor = r + \left\lfloor \frac{a + \lfloor (q-1)/2 \rfloor}{q} \right\rfloor \cdot q,$$

with $r \in [0, q)$. We thus have:

$$a = r - \left\lfloor \frac{q-1}{2} \right\rfloor + \left\lfloor \frac{a + \lfloor (q-1)/2 \rfloor}{q} \right\rfloor \cdot q,$$

and since $r - \lfloor (q-1)/2 \rfloor \in (-q/2, q/2]$ we have $a \bmod q = r - \lfloor (q-1)/2 \rfloor$.

Definition 13 (Carries). *Let $q > 2$. Define $q' = \lfloor (q-1)/2 \rfloor$. For all $a, b \in \mathbb{Z}$ and $a_i = \frac{a - \sum_{j=0}^{i-1} a_j q^j}{q^i} \bmod q \in (-q/2, q/2]$ defined for $i \leq \lceil \log_q a \rceil$ and $b_i = \frac{b - \sum_{j=0}^{i-1} b_j q^j}{q^i} \bmod q \in (-q/2, q/2]$ defined for $i \leq \lceil \log_q b \rceil$, we recursively define the additive, multiplicative and opposite carries as follows.*

- *Addition carries $\mathbf{c}^{(a)}(a, b) \in \mathbb{Z}^{\lceil \max(\log_q |a|, \log_q |b|) \rceil + 1}$:*

$$\mathbf{c}^{(a)}(a, b) := \left(0 \ \left\lfloor \frac{a_0 + b_0 + q'}{q} \right\rfloor \ \ldots \ \left\lfloor \frac{c^{(a)}(a,b)_{i-1} + a_{i-1} + b_{i-1} + q'}{q} \right\rfloor \ \ldots \right)^\top.$$

- *Multiplication carries $\mathbf{c}^{(m)}(a, b) \in \mathbb{Z}^{\lceil \log_q |a| \rceil + \lceil \log_q |b| \rceil + 1}$:*

$$\mathbf{c}^{(m)}(a, b) := \left(0 \ \left\lfloor \frac{a_0 \cdot b_0 + q'}{q} \right\rfloor \ \ldots \ \left\lfloor \frac{c^{(m)}(a,b)_{i-1} + \sum_{j+k=i-1} a_j \cdot b_k + q'}{q} \right\rfloor \ldots \right)^\top.$$

- *Opposite carries: If q is odd, then $\mathbf{c}^{(o)}(a) := \mathbf{0}$. Else, define $h : a \mapsto \{1 \text{ if } a = q/2,\ 0 \text{ else}\}$ and*

$$\mathbf{c}^{(o)}(a) := \left(0 \ -h(a_0) \ \ldots \ -h(\mathbf{c}^{(o)}(a)_{i-1} + a_{i-1}) \ \ldots \right)^\top \in \mathbb{Z}^{\lceil \log_q |a| \rceil}.$$

Finally, define the associated carry polynomials $c^{(o)}(a) := \sum_{j=0} c^{(o)}(a)_j x^j$ and $c^{(i)}(a, b) := \sum_{j=0} (c^{(i)}(a, b)_j \bmod q) x^j$ for $i \in \{a, m\}$.

After having defined these carries, we move on to prove that the difference between operations in $\mathbb{Z}$ and $\mathbb{Z}_q[x]$ is the carry polynomial that stems from computations in $\mathbb{Z}$.

Lemma 2. *Let $q > 2$ and $a, b \in \mathbb{Z}$. Then the decomposition of their sum is $\Phi_q(a + b) = \Phi_q(a) + \Phi_q(b) + c^{(a)}(a, b)$. The decomposition of their product is $\Phi_q(a \cdot b) = \Phi_q(a) \cdot \Phi_q(b) + c^{(m)}(a, b)$. Finally the decomposition of the opposite of a is $\Phi_q(-a) = -\Phi_q(a) + c^{(o)}(a)$.*

The proof proceeds by induction. It is postponed to the appendix of the full version, where we only prove it for the addition, as the other two cases are similar. We now bound the magnitudes of the carries. Note that multiplication carries can be much larger than addition carries.

Lemma 3 (Bounds on carries). *Let $q > 2$ and $a, b \in \mathbb{Z}$. Define $q' = \lfloor (q-1)/2 \rfloor$. We have:*

$$\|c^{(a)}(a,b)\|_\infty \leq 1 \quad \textit{and} \quad \|c^{(o)}(a)\|_\infty \leq 1,$$
$$\|c^{(m)}(a,b)\|_\infty \leq \frac{q + q' + \min(\|a\|_\infty \cdot \|b\|_1, \|b\|_\infty \cdot \|a\|_1)}{q-1}.$$

The proof of this lemma is also postponed to the appendix of the full version, and also proceeds by induction.

3.2 Carries of $\mathbb{Z}_{f(q)}$ Operations in $\mathbb{Z}_q[x]/f$

Remember that the problems defined in Sect. 2 take place in a ring, either polynomial $\mathbb{Z}_q[x]/f$ or integer $\mathbb{Z}_{f(q)}$. Our understanding of the carries from $\mathbb{Z}$ in $\mathbb{Z}_q[x]$ from the previous subsection needs to be refined to understand what happens when we convert elements of $\mathbb{Z}_{f(q)}$ into elements of $\mathbb{Z}_q[x]/f$. We move on to study carries of $\mathbb{Z}_{f(q)}$ operations in $\mathbb{Z}_q[x]/f$.

So far, we introduced a conversion Φ_q from $\mathbb{Z}$ to $\mathbb{Z}_q[x]$ (for an arbitrary $q > 2$), and studied its homomorphism defect (concretely, carries of the basic operations over $\mathbb{Z}$). We progressively refine it so that it maps $\mathbb{Z}_{f(q)}$ to $\mathbb{Z}_q[x]/f$.

Definition 14. *Let $q > 2$ and $f \in \mathbb{Z}[x]$ a monic polynomial. The map $\Phi_q^{(f)} : \mathbb{Z} \to \mathbb{Z}_q[x]/f$ is defined as follows:*

$$\Phi_q^{(f)} : a \mapsto \Phi_q(a) \bmod f.$$

If $\bar{a}$ is an element of $\mathbb{Z}_{f(q)}$, then $\Phi_q^{(f)}(\bar{a})$ is defined as $\Phi_q^{(f)}(a)$ where a is the representative of $\bar{a}$ in $I_{f,q}$, as defined in Definition 6.

Since its input and output sets are not the same size, the map $\Phi_q^{(f)} : \mathbb{Z}_{f(q)} \to \mathbb{Z}_q[x]/f$ cannot be a bijection. The following lemma shows that depending on the value of $f(q)$ compared to q^m, the map $\Phi_q^{(f)}$ or the evaluation map in q is surjective. Note that the choice of $I_{f,q}$, which may look somewhat arbitrary for q even and $f(q) \approx q^m$, is justified to guarantee this lemma.

Lemma 4. *Let $q > 2$ and $f \in \mathbb{Z}[x]$ be a monic polynomial whose coefficients belong to $(-q/2, q/2)$. Then:*

- *If $f(q) \geq q^m$, for all $P \in \mathbb{Z}_q[x]/f$, we have $\Phi_q^{(f)}(P(q) \bmod f(q)) = P$, i.e., the map $\Phi_q^{(f)}$ is surjective from $\mathbb{Z}_{f(q)}$ to $\mathbb{Z}_q[x]/f$ and the map $P \mapsto P(q) \bmod f(q)$ is injective from $\mathbb{Z}_q[x]/f$ to $\mathbb{Z}_{f(q)}$.*
- *If $f(q) < q^m$, for all $a \in I_{f,q}$, we have $(\Phi_q^{(f)}(a))(q) = a \bmod f(q)$, i.e., the map $\Phi_q^{(f)}$ is injective from $\mathbb{Z}_{f(q)}$ to $\mathbb{Z}_q[x]/f$ and the map $P \mapsto P(q) \bmod f(q)$ is surjective from $\mathbb{Z}_q[x]/f$ to $\mathbb{Z}_{f(q)}$.*

We exclude $q/2$ from the set of possible values of the coefficients of f, as it creates technical complications (with potential carries) and in our reductions we will impose that q is significantly larger than $2\|f\|_\infty$.

Proof. The first property is satisfied if $P(q) \bmod f(q) = P(q)$ for any polynomial $P \in \mathbb{Z}_q[x]/f$. This is equivalent to $\Phi_q^{-1}(\mathbb{Z}_q[x]/f) \subseteq I_{f,q}$. The second property is satisfied if $\Phi_q^{(f)}(a) = \Phi_q(a)$ for any $a \in \mathbb{Z}_{f(q)}$. This one is equivalent to $I_{f,q} \subseteq \Phi_q^{-1}(\mathbb{Z}_q[x]/f)$.

In the case where q is odd, we have $\Phi_q^{-1}(\mathbb{Z}_q[x]/f) = [-\frac{q^m-1}{2}, \frac{q^m-1}{2}]$ and $I_{f,q} = (-\frac{f(q)}{2}, \frac{f(q)}{2}]$. The claimed inclusions can be checked by direct computations.

Assume now that q is even. Then:

$$\Phi_q^{-1}(\mathbb{Z}_q[x]/f) = \mathbb{Z} \cap \frac{q^m-1}{q-1} \cdot \left(-\frac{q}{2}, \frac{q}{2}\right] = \left[-\frac{q-2}{2} \cdot \frac{q^m-1}{q-1}, \frac{q}{2} \cdot \frac{q^m-1}{q-1}\right]$$

is not zero-centered.

In the case $f(q) \geq q^m$, it is possible that $\frac{q}{2} \cdot \frac{q^m-1}{q-1} > \frac{f(q)}{2}$: if that is true, we choose $\frac{q}{2} \cdot \frac{q^m-1}{q-1}$ as the right side of the representative interval $I_{f,q}$. In that case, the left side of $I_{f,q}$ is (using $f(q) \geq q^m - 1$):

$$\frac{q}{2} \cdot \frac{q^m-1}{q-1} - f(q) \leq \frac{q}{2} \cdot \frac{q^m-1}{q-1} - (q^m - 1) = -\frac{q-2}{2}\frac{q^m-1}{q-1}.$$

We see here that our choice of $I_{f,q}$ leads to $\Phi_q^{-1}(\mathbb{Z}_q[x]/f) \subseteq I_{f,q}$.

In the case $f(q) < q^m$, it is possible that $-\frac{q-2}{2} \cdot \frac{q^m-1}{q-1} > -\frac{f(q)}{2}$: if that is true, we choose $-\frac{q-2}{2} \cdot \frac{q^m-1}{q-1}$ as the left side of the representative interval $I_{f,q}$. In that case, the right side of $I_{f,q}$ is (using $f(q) \leq q^m - 1$):

$$f(q) - \frac{q-2}{2} \cdot \frac{q^m-1}{q-1} \leq (q^m - 1) - \frac{q-2}{2} \cdot \frac{q^m-1}{q-1} = \frac{q}{2}\frac{q^m-1}{q-1}.$$

We see here that our choice of $I_{f,q}$ leads to $I_{f,q} \subseteq \Phi_q^{-1}(\mathbb{Z}_q[x]/f)$. □

Our understanding of the effect of $\Phi_q^{(f)}$ can be even more refined. In the case where $f(q) < q^m$, the next lemma states that each element of $\mathbb{Z}_{f(q)}$ has at most two predecessors by the map $P \mapsto P(q) \bmod f(q)$ from $\mathbb{Z}_q[x]/f$.

Lemma 5 (Surjectivity of the evaluation, when $f(q) < q^m$). *Let $q > 2$ and $f \in \mathbb{Z}[x]$ be a monic polynomial of degree m such that $f(q) < q^m$ and whose coefficients belong to $(-q/2, q/2)$. Then for any $a \in \mathbb{Z}_{f(q)}$, there exist at most 2 polynomials $P, Q \in \mathbb{Z}_q[x]/f$ such that $P(q) \bmod f(q) = Q(q) \bmod f(q) = a$. When evaluating P in q, the coefficients of P are taken in $(-q/2, q/2]$.*

Proof. We first note the following about f:

$$f(q) \geq q^m - \left\lfloor \frac{q-1}{2} \right\rfloor \frac{q^m-1}{q-1} \geq q^m - \frac{q-1}{2} \cdot \frac{q^m-1}{q-1} > \frac{q^m}{2}.$$

The equality $P(q) \bmod f(q) = Q(q) \bmod f(q)$ holds if and only if there exists some $k \in \mathbb{Z}$ such that $P(q) = Q(q) + kf(q)$. Since $|P(q) - Q(q)| \leq q^m$, we obtain:

$$|k| \leq \frac{q^m}{f(q)}.$$

Using the previous lower bound on $f(q)$, this is < 2. We must hence have $k \in \{-1, 0, 1\}$. Assume that an element $a \in \mathbb{Z}_{f(q)}$ has three predecessors $P, Q, R \in \mathbb{Z}_q[x]/f$ such that $P(q) = Q(q) + \delta_0 f(q)$ and $P(q) = R(q) + \delta_1 f(q)$ with δ_0, δ_1 both nonzero. This implies that $Q(q) - R(q) = (\delta_1 - \delta_0) f(q)$. By the above, we must have $|\delta_0 - \delta_1| \leq 1$, which implies that $Q(q) = R(q)$. Therefore, the element a has at most 2 predecessors. □

In the next lemma, we explore the case $f(q) \geq q^m$ and show that each polynomial has at most three predecessors in $\mathbb{Z}_{f(q)}$ by the map $\Phi_q^{(f)}$.

Lemma 6 (Surjectivity of the map $\Phi_q^{(f)}$, when $f(q) \geq q^m$). *Let $q > 2$ and $f \in \mathbb{Z}[x]$ be a monic polynomial of degree m such that $f(q) \geq q^m$ and whose coefficients belong to $(-q/2, q/2)$. For any $P \in \mathbb{Z}_q[x]/f$, there exist at most 3 integers $a, b, c \in \mathbb{Z}_{f(q)}$ such that $P = \Phi_q^{(f)}(a) = \Phi_q^{(f)}(b) = \Phi_q^{(f)}(c)$. Remember that when applying $\Phi_q^{(f)}$ on a, the representative of a is taken in $I_{f,q}$.*

Proof. We note that $\Phi_q^{(f)}(a) = \Phi_q^{(f)}(b)$ holds if and only if there exists some $\delta \in \mathbb{Z}$ such that $\Phi_q(a) = \Phi_q(b) + \delta f$. We have $\delta = a_m - b_m$, where $a = \sum_{i \leq m} a_i q^i, b = \sum_{i \leq m} b_i q^i$ with $a_i, b_i \in (-q/2, q/2]$ for all $i < m$ and $a_m, b_m \in \{-1, 0, 1\}$, by our choice of f and $I_{f,q}$. This implies that any $P \in \mathbb{Z}_q[x]/f$ has at most 3 predecessors. □

To study the carries from operations over $\mathbb{Z}$ in the ring of polynomials modulo f, it suffices to see that these carries are the same as in the previous section, but reduced modulo f. This observation helps bounding them, by using the expansion factor and Lemma 3. We now study the carries of operations done modulo $f(q)$ as seen in the ring of polynomials modulo f. To interpret operations from $\mathbb{Z}_{f(q)}$ in $\mathbb{Z}_q[x]/f$, one can first compute in $\mathbb{Z}$, reduce modulo $f(q)$, apply Φ_q and finally reduce modulo f. We define, for $a, b \in I_{f,q}$:

$$c_f^{(a)}(a, b) := \Phi_q^{(f)}(a + b \bmod f(q)) - \Phi_q^{(f)}(a) - \Phi_q^{(f)}(b),$$
$$c_f^{(m)}(a, b) := \left(\Phi_q^{(f)}(a \cdot b \bmod f(q)) - \Phi_q^{(f)}(a) \cdot \Phi_q^{(f)}(b)\right) \bmod f,$$

where assume that the output of the "mod $f(q)$" operation is an integer in $I_{f,q}$.

Lemma 7 (Carries of $\mathbb{Z}_{f(q)}$ in $\mathbb{Z}_q[x]/f$). *Let $q > 2$ and $f \in \mathbb{Z}[x]$ be a monic polynomial of degree m whose coefficients belong to $(-q/2, q/2)$. Let $a, b \in I_{f,q}$. We assume that the output of the "mod $f(q)$" operation is an integer in $I_{f,q}$.*

- *Addition carries. We have, for some* $\delta_0, \delta_1 \in \{-1, 0, 1\}$*:*

  $$\Phi_q^{(f)}(a+b \bmod f(q)) = \Phi_q(a)+\Phi_q(b)+c^{(a)}(a,b)+c^{(a)}(a+b, \delta_0 f(q))+(\delta_0+\delta_1)f.$$

  In particular:

  $$c_f^{(a)}(a,b) = c^{(a)}(a,b) + c^{(a)}(a+b, \delta_0 f(q)) + (\delta_0 + \delta_1 + a_m + b_m) \cdot f,$$

  where $a = \sum_{i \le m} a_i q^i, b = \sum_{i \le m} b_i q^i$ *with* $a_i, b_i \in (-q/2, q/2]$ *for all* $i < m$ *and* $a_m, b_m \in \{-1, 0, 1\}$*.*
- *Multiplication carries. We have:*

  $$c_f^{(m)}(a,b) = \Big(c^{(m)}(a,b) + c^{(m)}\left(-\delta, f(q)\right) + c^{(a)}\left(a \cdot b, -\delta f(q)\right)\Big) \bmod f,$$

  where $\delta = \lfloor (a \cdot b - (a \cdot b \bmod f(q)))/f(q) \rfloor$*.*

Note that the lemma statement on addition carries is more detailed than for multiplication carries. We use this extra information on addition carries to prove Lemma 8 below. Apart from this, it will be sufficient to note that $c_f^{(a)}(a,b) = (c^{(a)}(a,b) + c^{(a)}(a+b, \delta_0 f(q))) \bmod f$.

Proof. We study addition carries first. As $a, b \in I_{f,q}$ and the "mod $f(q)$" map takes values in $I_{f,q}$, there exists $\delta_0 \in \{-1, 0, 1\}$ such that $a + b \bmod f(q) = a + b + \delta_0 f(q)$. Using Lemma 2, we obtain:

$$\Phi_q(a + b \bmod f(q)) = \Phi_q(a) + \Phi_q(b) + c^{(a)}(a,b) + \delta_0 f + c^{(a)}(a + b, \delta_0 f(q)).$$

Here we used the fact that $\Phi_q(\delta_0 f(q)) = \delta_0 f$, which holds because $\delta_0 \in \{-1, 0, 1\}$ and the coefficients of f belong to $(-q/2, q/2)$, so there are no opposition carries. We now reduce the latter polynomial modulo f:

$$\begin{aligned}\Phi_q^{(f)}(a + b \bmod f(q)) &= \Phi_q(a) + \Phi_q(b) + c^{(a)}(a,b) + c^{(a)}(a + b, \delta_0 f(q)) \\ &\quad + \delta_0 f - \left\lfloor \frac{\Phi_q(a + b \bmod f(q))}{f} \right\rfloor f \\ &= \Phi_q(a) + \Phi_q(b) + c^{(a)}(a,b) + c^{(a)}(a + b, +\delta_0 f(q)) \\ &\quad + (\delta_0 + \delta_1) f.\end{aligned}$$

Note that for any $a \in I_{f,q}$, we have $|a| < 3q^m/2$, which implies that $\delta_1 \in \{-1, 0, 1\}$. The second statement on addition carries follows from the same fact that for any $a \in I_{f,q}$, we have $|a| < 3q^m/2$. This implies that $a_m, b_m \in \{-1, 0, 1\}$.

We now consider multiplication carries. By definition of δ, we have $a \cdot b \bmod f(q) = a \cdot b - \delta f(q)$. Using Lemma 2, we obtain:

$$\begin{aligned}\Phi_q(a \cdot b \bmod f(q)) &= \Phi_q(a \cdot b) + \Phi_q\left(-\delta \cdot f(q)\right) + c^{(a)}(a \cdot b, -\delta f(q)) \\ &= \Phi_q(a) \cdot \Phi_q(b) + c^{(m)}(a,b) + \Phi_q\left(-\delta\right) \cdot f \\ &\quad + c^{(m)}\left(-\delta, f(q)\right) + c^{(a)}\left(a \cdot b, -\delta f(q)\right).\end{aligned}$$

Finally, by reducing both sides modulo f, we obtain the lemma statement. □

In the following section, we will be confronted to expressions of the form $b + E(q) \bmod f(q)$, where $b \in \mathbb{Z}_{f(q)}$ and $E \in \mathbb{Z}_q[x]/f$, and we will turn them into polynomials by applying $\Phi_q^{(f)}$. From what precedes, we already know that:

$$\begin{aligned}
&\Phi_q^{(f)}(b + E(q) \bmod f(q)) \\
&\quad = \Phi_q^{(f)}(b) + \Phi_q^{(f)}(E(q) \bmod f(q)) + c_f^{(a)}(b, E(q) \bmod f(q)) \\
&\quad = \Phi_q^{(f)}(b) + E + c_f^{(a)}(b, E(q) \bmod f(q)) + c^{(a)}(E(q), \delta f(q)),
\end{aligned}$$

where $\delta = \lfloor [E(q) - \overline{E(q)}]/f(q) \rfloor$ and $\overline{E(q)} = E(q) \bmod f(q)$. During the computations, we will remove the constant term $\Phi_q^{(f)}(b)$, and do separate computations on the carries and on E. We will end up with expressions:

$$E + \ell \cdot c_f^{(a)}(b, E(q) \bmod f(q)) + \ell \cdot c^{(a)}(E(q), \delta f(q)),$$

where $\ell = -1$ or $\ell = 2$ depending on which reduction between PLWE and I − PLWE we are currently working on. To analyze the reductions, we use the fact that this expression, when seen as a map with input E, is injective.

Lemma 8 (Injectivity of the carries). *Let $q > 2$ and $f \in \mathbb{Z}[x]$ be a monic polynomial of degree m whose coefficients belong to $(-q/2, q/2)$. Let $b \in I_{f,q}$. We assume that the output of the "mod $f(q)$" operation is an integer in $I_{f,q}$. We define, for $\delta_1, \delta_2, \delta_3 \in \{-1, 0, 1\}$:*

$$\begin{aligned}
I_{\delta_1,\delta_2,\delta_3}^{(b)} := \Bigg\{ P \in \mathbb{Z}_q[x]/f : &\left\lfloor \frac{P(q) - \overline{P(q)}}{f(q)} \right\rfloor = \delta_1 \\
&\wedge \left\lfloor \frac{(b + \overline{P(q)}) - (b + \overline{P(q)} \bmod f(q))}{f(q)} \right\rfloor = \delta_2 \\
&\wedge \left\lfloor \frac{\Phi_q(b + P(q) \bmod f(q))}{f} \right\rfloor = \delta_3 \Bigg\},
\end{aligned}$$

where $\overline{P(q)} = (P(q) \bmod f(q)) \in I_{f,q}$. Then the following two statements hold.

1. *We have that:*
$$\mathbb{Z}_q[x]/f = \bigsqcup_{\delta_1,\delta_2,\delta_3 \in \{-1,0,1\}} I_{\delta_1,\delta_2,\delta_3}^{(b)}.$$

2. *For any non-zero $\ell \in \mathbb{Z}$, define $g_\ell : P \mapsto P + \ell \cdot c^{(a)}(\overline{P(q)}, \delta_1(P) \cdot f(q)) + \ell \cdot c_f^{(a)}(b, P(q))$, where the map δ_1 from $\mathbb{Z}_q[x]/f$ to itself is defined as $\delta_1 : P \mapsto \lfloor (P(q) - \overline{P(q)})/f(q) \rfloor$. For any $\delta_1, \delta_2, \delta_3 \in \{-1, 0, 1\}$, the restriction of g_ℓ to $I_{\delta_1,\delta_2,\delta_3}^{(b)}$ is injective over $\mathbb{Z}_q[x]/f$.*

Proof. We have the following partition of $\mathbb{Z}_q[x]/f$:

$$\mathbb{Z}_q[x]/f = \bigsqcup_{\delta_1,\delta_2,\delta_3 \in \mathbb{Z}} I_{\delta_1,\delta_2,\delta_3}^{(b)},$$

and hence it suffices to prove that $I^{(b)}_{\delta_1,\delta_2,\delta_3} = \emptyset$ for $(\delta_1,\delta_2,\delta_3) \notin \{-1,0,1\}^3$. We distinguish two cases. In the case where $f(q) < q^m$, since $q^m/2 < f(q) < q^m$, the integer $P(q)$ is reduced at most once modulo $f(q)$, thus $\delta_1 \in \{-1,0,1\}$ captures all possibilities for δ_1. In the case where $f(q) \geq q^m$, the integer $P(q)$ cannot be non-trivially reduced modulo $f(q)$, thanks to our choice of $I_{f,q}$. In this case, the set $\{0\}$ captures all possibilities for δ_1. For δ_2 and δ_3, note that they correspond to the δ's defined in the addition carries of Lemma 7.

To prove the second item, let $\delta_1,\delta_2,\delta_3 \in \{-1,0,1\}$ and $P,Q \in I^{(b)}_{\delta_1,\delta_2,\delta_3}$ such that $g_\ell(P) = g_\ell(Q)$. Since they are in the same $I^{(b)}_{\delta_1,\delta_2,\delta_3}$, it means that the δ's corresponding to the addition carries between b and $\overline{P(q)}$, and to those between b and $\overline{Q(q)}$, are identical (these are δ_2 and δ_3). Moreover, it holds by definition that $\delta_1(P) = \delta_1(Q) = \delta_1$. As $g_\ell(P) = g_\ell(Q)$, we have, using Lemma 7:

$$\begin{aligned}\frac{P-Q}{\ell} &= (c_f^{(a)}(b,\overline{Q(q)}) - c_f^{(a)}(b,\overline{P(q)})) + (c^{(a)}(Q(q),\delta_1 f(q)) - c^{(a)}(P(q),\delta_1 f(q)))\\ &= (c^{(a)}(b,\overline{Q(q)}) - c^{(a)}(b,\overline{P(q)}) + c^{(a)}(b+\overline{Q(q)},\delta_2 f(q))\\ &\quad - c^{(a)}(b+\overline{P(q)},\delta_2 f(q))) + (c^{(a)}(Q(q),\delta_1 f(q)) - c^{(a)}(P(q),\delta_1 f(q))).\end{aligned}$$

We will show by induction that the above implies that $P = Q$. Define (H_k) as "$P_n = Q_n$ for all $n \leq k$". Note that (H_0) follows from the definition of $c^{(a)}$. Assume now that (H_k) holds for some $0 \leq k < m$. Recall the definitions of $\overline{P(q)} = P(q) - \delta_1(P)f(q)$ and $\overline{Q(q)} = Q(q) - \delta_1(Q)f(q)$, so $\overline{P(q)}_n = \overline{Q(q)}_n$ holds for all $n \leq k$.

1. As the addition carry at rank $k+1$ only depends on $\overline{P(q)}_n = \overline{Q(q)}_n$ and b_n for $n \leq k$, we have $c^{(a)}(b,\overline{P(q)})_{k+1} = c^{(a)}(b,\overline{Q(q)})_{k+1}$. Similarly, we have $c^{(a)}(P(q),\delta_1 f(q))_{k+1} = c^{(a)}(Q(q),\delta_1 f(q))_{k+1}$.
2. Similarly, we also have $(b+\overline{P(q)})_n = (b+\overline{Q(q)})_n$ for all $n \leq k+1$.
3. For the same reason, we obtain $c^{(a)}(b+\overline{P(q)},\delta_2 f(q))_{k+1} = c^{(a)}(b+\overline{Q(q)},\delta_2 f(q))_{k+1}$.

By the above equality on $\frac{P-Q}{\ell}$, we obtain that $P_{k+1} = Q_{k+1}$. This completes the induction, and the proof that $P = Q$. Therefore, the restriction of g_ℓ to $I^{(b)}_{\delta_1,\delta_2,\delta_3}$ is indeed injective. □

4 Reductions Between sPLWE and sI-PLWE

We exhibit reductions between the search variants of the PLWE and I-PLWE problems, as defined in Sect. 2, for a large class of defining polynomials f. As discussed in Sect. 1, our reductions fill some missing gaps in the prior work of Gu [Gu19] for $f = x^m + 1$, and generalize the results to many different defining polynomials f. For each reduction, the study depends on whether the integer set has more elements than the polynomial set or not. The four reductions and their analyses are very similar, yet each of them has its own subtleties. Nonetheless, the following lemma will be used in every case.

Lemma 9 (Carries of an IP sample). *Let $q > 2$ and $f \in \mathbb{Z}[x]$ monic and irreducible of degree m, whose coefficients belong to $(-q/2, q/2)$. Define $C(P,Q) := \Phi_q^{(f)}(Q(q) - P(q)s \bmod f(q)) - (Q - PS \bmod q)$ and $b := -P(q)s \bmod f(q)$, for any $P, Q, S \in \mathbb{Z}_q[x]/f$ and $s := S(q) \bmod f(q)$. Then:*

- $\|C(P,Q)\|_\infty \leq \mathsf{EF}(f) \cdot (6 + \|f\|_1 + 2m\|S\|_\infty)$
- *For fixed $P \in \mathbb{Z}_{f(q)}$ and any $\delta_1, \delta_2, \delta_3 \in \{-1, 0, 1\}$ and $\ell \in \mathbb{Z}_q \backslash 0$, the map $Q \mapsto Q + \ell C(P,Q) - PS$ is injective from $I^{(b)}_{\delta_1,\delta_2,\delta_3}$ to $\mathbb{Z}_q[x]/f$, where $I^{(b)}_{\delta_1,\delta_2,\delta_3}$ is as defined in Lemma 8.*

Note that we will use this lemma only for $\ell = -1$ and $\ell = 2$. Due to space constraints, the proof of this lemma and several results from this section are postponed to the appendix of the full version.

4.1 Reducing sPLWE to sI-PLWE when $f(q) < q^m$

In this subsection, we are given samples from the P distribution and we try to obtain samples from the IP distribution. Since the polynomial set is bigger than the integer one, we can evaluate it for q and get a distribution whose support is $(\mathbb{Z}_{f(q)})^2$. Moreover the next lemma will prove that it is indeed close enough to IP to use an adversary against sI-PLWE to solve sPLWE.

Lemma 10. *Let $q \geq 3$, $m > 0$, $f \in \mathbb{Z}_q[x]$ be a monic polynomial of degree m such that $f(q) < q^m$ and whose coefficients belong to $(-q/2, q/2)$. Let $\sigma > 0$. Let $S \in \mathbb{Z}_q[x]/f$ and $s \in \mathbb{Z}_{f(q)}$ such that $S(q) = s \bmod f(q)$. Given a sample $(A, B) \hookleftarrow \mathsf{P}^{(f)}_{q,\sigma}(S)$, set $(a, b) := (A(q) \bmod f(q), B(q) \bmod f(q))$. Then:*

$$R_{\mathsf{IP\ to\ P}} := R(\mathsf{IP}^{(f)}_{q,\sigma}(s) \| (a,b)) \leq 216 \exp\left(38\, m^3 \frac{\mathsf{EF}(f)^2(\|f\|_\infty + \|S\|_\infty)^2}{\sigma^2}\right).$$

Proof. We start by proving that the divergence is well defined. Recall that the support of $\mathsf{IP}^{(f)}_{q,\sigma}(s)$ is $\mathbb{Z}_{f(q)} \times \mathbb{Z}_{f(q)}$. Since $\Phi_q^{-1}(I_{f,q}) \subseteq \mathbb{Z}_q[x]/f$, the divergence is well-defined as the support of (a, b) is exactly $(\mathbb{Z}_{f(q)})^2$.

We move on to bounding the divergence:

$$R_{\mathsf{IP\ to\ P}} = \sum_{(i,j) \in (\mathbb{Z}_{f(q)})^2} \frac{\Pr_{a' \hookleftarrow \mathbb{Z}_{f(q)}, e' \hookleftarrow D_{\mathbb{Z}_{f(q)},\sigma,q}}(a' = i \wedge a's + e' \bmod f(q) = j)^2}{\Pr_{a,b}(a = i \wedge b = j)}$$

$$\leq \sum_{(i,j) \in (\mathbb{Z}_{f(q)})^2} \frac{q^m}{f(q)^2} \cdot \frac{D_{\mathbb{Z}_{f(q)},\sigma,q}(\Phi_q(j - is \bmod f(q)))^2}{\sum\limits_{\substack{A \in \mathbb{Z}_q[x]/f \\ A(q) = i \bmod f(q)}} \Pr\limits_{e \hookleftarrow D_{\mathbb{Z}[x]/f,\sigma,q}}((AS + e \bmod f)(q) = j \bmod f(q))},$$

where we condition on the values of a' and A. Since $\Phi_q^{(f)}(i)(q) = i \bmod f(q)$, we bound from below the sum at the denominator by keeping only the term $A = \Phi_q^{(f)}(i)$. Moreover, we notice that $j = \Phi_q^{(f)}(j)(q) = [\Phi_q^{(f)}(i)S + \Phi_q^{(f)}(j) -$

$\Phi_q^{(f)}(i)S](q)$, which implies that the denominator is at least $D_{\mathbb{Z}[x]/f,\sigma,q}(\Phi_q^{(f)}(j) - \Phi_q^{(f)}(i)S)$. We therefore obtain the bound:

$$R_{\mathsf{IP\ to\ P}} \leq \sum_{(i,j)\in(\mathbb{Z}_{f(q)})^2} \frac{q^m}{f(q)^2} \frac{D_{\mathbb{Z}_{f(q)},\sigma,q}(j - is \bmod f(q))^2}{D_{\mathbb{Z}[x]/f,\sigma,q}(\Phi_q^{(f)}(j) - \Phi_q^{(f)}(j)S)}.$$

To bound the Gaussian ratio, we can split the work into bounding two ratios:

- The first one is a ratio of Gaussian functions and can be thus expressed as a difference $\exp(-\pi(2\|\Phi_q^{(f)}(j - is \bmod f(q))\|^2 - \|(\Phi_q^{(f)}(j) - \Phi_q^{(f)}(i)S)\|^2)/\sigma^2)$.
- The second one is the ratio of normalization constants of the Gaussian distributions $\rho_\sigma(\mathbb{Z}_q[x]/f)/\rho_\sigma(\mathbb{Z}_{f(q)})$.

First, let $C(i,j) := \Phi_q^{(f)}(j - is \bmod f(q)) - \Phi_q^{(f)}(j) - \Phi_q^{(f)}(i)S \in \mathbb{Z}_q[x]/f$. Recall the identity $2\|\mathbf{x}+\mathbf{y}\|^2 - \|\mathbf{x}\|^2 = \|\mathbf{x}+2\mathbf{y}\|^2 - 2\|\mathbf{y}\|^2$. In our case, we instantiate this with $\mathbf{x} = \Phi_q^{(f)}(j) - \Phi_q^{(f)}(i)S$ and $\mathbf{y} = C(i,j)$. We now have to study $\|C(i,j)\|_\infty$ and the map $j \mapsto \Phi_q^{(f)}(j) - \Phi_q^{(f)}(i)S + 2C(i,j)$.

If we let $P = \Phi_q^{(f)}(i)$ and $Q = \Phi_q^{(f)}(j)$, we notice that $C(i,j)$ corresponds to the $C(P,Q)$ defined in the Lemma 9. Recalling here the results from its analysis, we know that $\|C(i,j)\|_\infty \leq \mathsf{EF}(f)(6 + \|f\|_1 + 2m\|S\|_\infty)$ and that the map $j \mapsto \Phi_q^{(f)}(j) - \Phi_q^{(f)}(i)S + 2C(i,j)$ is injective from each of the 27 intervals defined in Lemma 8 to $\mathbb{Z}_q[x]/f$, where we moreover recall that $\Phi_q^{(f)}$ is injective from $\mathbb{Z}_{f(q)}$ to $\mathbb{Z}_q[x]/f$ in the case $f(q) < q^m$. It is then possible to reindex each of the 27 summation terms, to get:

$$\sum_{(i,j)\in(\mathbb{Z}_{f(q)})^2} \exp(-\pi\|\Phi_q^{(f)}(j) - \Phi_q^{(f)}(i)S + 2C(i,j)\|^2/\sigma^2) \leq 27 \cdot \sum_{i\in\mathbb{Z}_{f(q)}} \rho_\sigma(\mathbb{Z}_q[x]/f)$$
$$\leq 27 \cdot f(q) \cdot \rho_\sigma(\mathbb{Z}_q[x]/f).$$

Recalling that $q^m < 2f(q)$, we then get the bound:

$$R_{\mathsf{IP\ to\ P}} \leq 54 \cdot \frac{\rho_\sigma(\mathbb{Z}_q[x]/f)^2}{\rho_\sigma(\mathbb{Z}_{f(q)})^2} \cdot \exp\left(2\pi m \frac{\mathsf{EF}(f)^2(6 + \|f\|_1 + 2m\|S\|_\infty)^2}{\sigma^2}\right).$$

We now move on to bounding the ratio $\rho_\sigma(\mathbb{Z}_q[x]/f)/\rho_\sigma(\mathbb{Z}_{f(q)})$. We write:

$$\frac{\rho_\sigma(\mathbb{Z}_q[x]/f)}{\rho_\sigma(\mathbb{Z}_{f(q)})} = \frac{\sum_{Q\in\mathbb{Z}_q[x]/f} \exp(-\pi\|Q\|^2/\sigma^2)}{\sum_{P\in\Phi_q^{(f)}(\mathbb{Z}_{f(q)})} \exp(-\pi\|P\|^2/\sigma^2)}$$
$$= 1 + \frac{\sum_{Q\in\mathbb{Z}_q[x]/f\setminus\Phi_q^{(f)}(\mathbb{Z}_{f(q)})} \exp(-\pi\|Q\|^2/\sigma^2)}{\sum_{P\in\Phi_q^{(f)}(\mathbb{Z}_{f(q)})} \exp(-\pi\|P\|^2/\sigma^2)}.$$

First, notice that the Φ_q map preserves ordering, if the ordering considered for polynomials is the lexicographical ordering: $m < n$ if and only if $\Phi_q(m) < \Phi_q(n)$.

Let $P \in \mathbb{Z}_q[x]/f \setminus \Phi_q^{(f)}(\mathbb{Z}_{f(q)})$. Assume that its leading coefficient is positive, up to replacing P with $-P$. Then, since it holds that $f(q) > \sum_{i=0}^{m-1} \lfloor q/2 \rfloor q^i$ and $P(q) \geq f(q)/2$, the leading coefficient of P is at least $q' := \lceil \lfloor q/2 \rfloor /2 \rceil$. This proves that $P - q'x^{m-1} \in \Phi_q^{(f)}(\mathbb{Z}_{f(q)})$ as either its degree is now strictly smaller than $m-1$ or its leading coefficient is strictly smaller than q', since $2q' > q/2$. Moreover, $P - q'x^{m-1} > 0$. The same kind of reasoning can be held for P with negative leading coefficient, to map it to an element of $\Phi_q^{(f)}(\mathbb{Z}_{f(q)})$ with negative leading coefficient. Both maps are injective as they are translations. Their image sets do not overlap and the image of any element has smaller norm than said element. By combining these two maps, this proves that there exists an injective map $g : \mathbb{Z}_q[x]/f \setminus \Phi_q^{(f)}(\mathbb{Z}_{f(q)}) \to \Phi_q^{(f)}(\mathbb{Z}_{f(q)})$ such that $\|g(P)\| \leq \|P\|$ holds for any $P \in \mathbb{Z}_q[x]/f \setminus \Phi_q^{(f)}(\mathbb{Z}_{f(q)})$. This proves that

$$\sum_{Q \in \mathbb{Z}_q[x]/f \setminus \Phi_q^{(f)}(\mathbb{Z}_{f(q)})} \exp\Big(-\pi \frac{\|Q\|^2}{\sigma^2}\Big) \leq \sum_{P \in \Phi_q^{(f)}(\mathbb{Z}_{f(q)})} \exp\Big(-\pi \frac{\|P\|^2}{\sigma^2}\Big),$$

and hence that the ratio is ≤ 2. The total multiplicative constant is then 216. □

The result below follows from the Rényi divergence probability preservation.

Theorem 1. *Let $q > 2$ and $f \in \mathbb{Z}[x]$ irreducible and monic of degree $m > 0$ such that $f(q) < q^m$ and whose coefficients belong to $(-q/2, q/2)$. Let $\sigma > \sigma' > 0$ such that $q > \sqrt{m}\sigma$. Let t be a number of samples, such that:*

$$\exp\Big(6t + 38tm^3 \frac{\mathsf{EF}(f)^2(\|f\|_\infty + m^{1/2}\sigma')^2}{\sigma^2}\Big) = \mathsf{poly}(m).$$

Then $\mathsf{sPLWE}^{(f)}_{q,\sigma,\sigma',t}$ reduces to $\mathsf{sl\text{-}PLWE}^{(f)}_{q,\sigma,\sigma',t}$.

We refer to the discussion just after Theorem 2 for how to set parameters so that the theorem conditions are fulfilled.

Proof. Assume that there exists an adversary $\mathcal{A}$ with success probability ε_0 against the $\mathsf{sl\text{-}PLWE}^{(f)}_{q,\sigma,\sigma',t}$ game. We introduce a sequence of games to prove the theorem:

Game 0: This is the genuine $\mathsf{sl\text{-}PLWE}^{(f)}_{q,\sigma,\sigma',t}$ game.

Game 1: In this game, we change the distribution of the secret. We now sample $s \hookleftarrow D_{\mathbb{Z}_{f(q)},\sigma',\sigma'\sqrt{m}}$. Recall that the statistical distance between $D_{\mathbb{Z}_{f(q)},\sigma',q}$ and $D_{\mathbb{Z}_{f(q)},\sigma',\sigma'\sqrt{m}}$ is $2^{-\Omega(m)}$, since $q > \sqrt{m}\sigma'$.

Game 2: In this game we change the distribution of samples. They are now sampled according to the process introduced in Lemma 10, where the polynomial secret S is sampled according to $D_{\mathbb{Z}[x]/f,\sigma',\sqrt{m}\sigma'}$ and $s := S(q) \bmod f(q)$.

Game 3: In this game, we change the distribution of the secret S: it is now sampled according to $D_{\mathbb{Z}[x]/f,\sigma',q}$. The statistical distance between the distribution of the polynomial secret in this game and the previous one is $2^{-\Omega(m)}$.

Call ε_i the success probability of $\mathcal{A}$ in Game i. From the remarks on statistical distance, it already holds that $|\varepsilon_0 - \varepsilon_1| < 2^{-\Omega(m)}$ and $|\varepsilon_2 - \varepsilon_3| < 2^{-\Omega(m)}$. In the context of Game 1 versus Game 2, by using the probability preservation and multiplicativity of the Rényi divergence, it holds that

$$\varepsilon_2 \geq \frac{\varepsilon_1^2}{R_\infty(D_1||D_2) \cdot \max_{S:\|S\|_\infty \leq \sqrt{m}\sigma'} R^t_{\mathsf{P} \text{ to } \mathsf{IP}}},$$

where D_1 and D_2 denote the distributions of the secret s in Games 1 and 2, respectively. Note that in D_2, for a given integer secret s, there are at most two polynomial secrets S_i such that $s = S_i(q) \bmod f(q)$. We can bound from below the probability by keeping only $S := \Phi_q^{(f)}(s) \in \mathbb{Z}_q[x]/f$. We compute the divergence.

$$\begin{aligned} R_\infty(D_1||D_2) &\leq \max_{s \in \mathrm{Supp}(D_1)} \frac{D_{\mathbb{Z}_{f(q)},\sigma',\sigma'\sqrt{m}}(s)}{D_{\mathbb{Z}[x]/f,\sigma',\sigma'\sqrt{m}}(\Phi_q^{(f)}(s))} \\ &\leq \frac{\rho_{\sigma'}(\mathbb{Z}^{<m}_{\sigma'\sqrt{m}}[x])}{\rho_{\sigma'}(\Phi_q(\mathrm{Supp}(D_1)))} \max_{s \in \mathrm{Supp}(D_1)} \frac{\exp(-\pi\|\Phi_q(s)\|^2)/\sigma'^2}{\exp(-\pi\|\Phi_q^{(f)}(s)\|^2)/\sigma'^2}. \end{aligned}$$

Since s is in $I_{f,q}$, we have $\Phi_q^{(f)}(s) = \Phi_q(s)$ and the rightmost ratio is always 1. Recall the existence of the g injective map from Lemma 10. This maps every element of $\mathbb{Z}^{<m}_{\sigma'\sqrt{m}}[x]$ that is not in $\Phi_q(\mathrm{Supp}(D_1))$ to an element in $\Phi_q(\mathrm{Supp}(D_1))$, which has smaller norm. This implies that $R_\infty(D_1||D_2) \leq 2$, by partitioning. This shows with our choice of parameters that the success probability loss is at most polynomial in m when switching from Game 1 to Game 2.

Finally we build an adversary $\mathcal{B}$ against the $\mathsf{sPLWE}^{(f)}_{q,\sigma,\sigma',t}$ game. It suffices to notice that $\mathcal{B}$ can exactly simulate $\mathcal{A}$'s view in Game 3. Moreover, if $\mathcal{A}$ wins, then its output s is such that $s = S(q) \bmod f(q)$, where S is the secret that $\mathcal{B}$ has to guess. Then $\mathcal{B}$ outputs S uniformly among the predecessors of s by the evaluation map $P \mapsto P(q) \bmod f(q)$. Since this set is comprised of at most two integers, the probability that $\mathcal{B}$ wins is $\geq \varepsilon_3/2$. □

4.2 Reducing sPLWE to sI-PLWE when $f(q) \geq q^m$

In this subsection we are given polynomial samples from a ring that is smaller than the target integer ring. To compensate, we will not simply evaluate our samples for q but instead choose uniformly an integer pair among the predecessors of the sample by the map $\Phi_q(f)$. The following lemma proves that the resulting distribution is close to IP.

Lemma 11. *Let $q > 2$, $f \in \mathbb{Z}[x]$ monic and irreducible of degree m such that $f(q) \geq q^m$ and whose coefficients belong to $(-q/2, q/2)$. Let $\sigma > 0$, $S \in \mathbb{Z}_q[x]/f$*

and $s \in \mathbb{Z}_{f(q)}$ *such that* $S = \Phi_q^{(f)}(s)$. *Let* $(A, B) \hookleftarrow \mathsf{P}_{q,\sigma}^{(f)}(S)$. *Choose* (a, b) *uniformly randomly in* $\{(i,j) \in \mathbb{Z}_{f(q)} | \Phi_q^{(f)}(i,j) = (A,B)\}$. *Then:*

$$R_{\mathsf{IP\ to\ P}} := R(\mathsf{IP}_{q,\sigma}^{(f(q))}(s) || (a,b)) \leq 243 \exp\left(114 \frac{m^3 \mathsf{EF}(f)^2 (\|f\|_\infty + \|S\|_\infty)^2}{\sigma^2}\right).$$

Proof. We start by proving that the divergence is well-defined. We already know that $\Phi_q^{(f)}$ is surjective from $\mathbb{Z}_{f(q)}$ to $\mathbb{Z}_q[x]/f$ in the case where $f(q) \geq q^m$. Since the support of (A, B) is $(\mathbb{Z}_q[x]/f)^2$, this implies that the support of (a, b) is $(\mathbb{Z}_{f(q)})^2$. We can now start bounding it:

$$R_{\mathsf{IP\ to\ P}} = \sum_{(i,j) \in (\mathbb{Z}_{f(q)})^2} \frac{\Pr_{a' \hookleftarrow \mathbb{Z}_{f(q)}, e \hookleftarrow D_{\mathbb{Z}_{f(q)},\sigma,q}}(a' = i \wedge a's + e = j)^2}{\Pr_{(a,b)}(a = i \wedge b = j)}$$

$$\leq \sum_{(i,j) \in (\mathbb{Z}_{f(q)})^2} \frac{\left(\frac{1}{f(q)} D_{\mathbb{Z}_{f(q)},\sigma,q}(j - is \bmod f(q))\right)^2}{\frac{1}{q^m} \cdot \Pr_{(A,B)}(\Phi_q^{(f)}(j) = B | \Phi_q^{(f)}(i) = A) \cdot \Pr_b(b = j | B = \Phi_q^{(f)}(j))},$$

using the chain rule. We moreover know the following facts for the denominator:

- we already used that $\Pr_{A \hookleftarrow \mathbb{Z}_q[x]/f}(\Phi_q^{(f)}(i) = A) = 1/q^m$.
- For $E = \Phi_q^{(f)}(j) - \Phi_q^{(f)}(i) S \bmod f$, it holds that $\Phi_q^{(f)}(j) = AS + E$, under the hypothesis that $\Phi_q^{(f)}(i) = A$. Thus it holds that:

$$\Pr_{(A,B)}(\Phi_q^{(f)}(j) = B | \Phi_q^{(f)}(i) = A) \geq \Pr_{E \hookleftarrow D_{\mathbb{Z}[x]/f,\sigma,q}}(\Phi_q^{(f)}(i) S + E = \Phi_q^{(f)}(j)).$$

- Since any polynomial in $\mathbb{Z}_q[x]/f$ has at most 3 predecessors in $\mathbb{Z}_{f(q)}$ by $\Phi_q^{(f)}$, it holds that the probability $\Pr_{(a,b)}(b = j | \Phi_q^{(f)}(b) = \Phi_q^{(f)}(j))$ is at least 1/3.

The above three statements give:

$$R_{\mathsf{IP\ to\ P}} \leq \sum_{(i,j) \in (\mathbb{Z}_{f(q)})^2} \frac{3q^m}{f(q)^2} \cdot \frac{D_{\mathbb{Z}_{f(q)},\sigma,q}(j - is \bmod f(q))^2}{D_{\mathbb{Z}[x]/f,\sigma,q}(\Phi_q^{(f)}(j) - \Phi_q^{(f)}(i) S)}.$$

Recall that in the case $f(q) \geq q^m$, $\mathbb{Z}_q[x]/f \subseteq \Phi_q(I_{f,q})$. This immediately shows $\rho_\sigma(\mathbb{Z}_q[x]/f) \leq \rho_\sigma(\Phi_q(I_{f,q}))$. We then have:

$$R_{\mathsf{IP\ to\ P}} \leq \frac{3q^m}{\rho_\sigma(\Phi_q(\mathbb{Z}_{f(q)})) f(q)^2} \cdot \sum_{(i,j) \in (\mathbb{Z}_{f(q)})^2} \frac{\exp(-2\pi \|\Phi_q(j - is \bmod f(q))\|^2 / \sigma^2)}{\exp(-\pi \|\Phi_q^{(f)}(j) - \Phi_q^{(f)}(i) S\|^2 / \sigma^2)}.$$

Define $C(i,j) := \Phi_q^{(f)}(j - is \bmod f(q)) - \Phi_q^{(f)}(j) - \Phi_q^{(f)}(i) S \bmod f$, as we previously did. The mod$f$ may not be trivial and we know that there exists some $\delta \in \{-1, 0, 1\}$ such that $\Phi_q(j - is \bmod f(q)) = \Phi_q^{(f)}(j - is \bmod f(q)) + \delta f$.

Instead of guessing for each pair (i, j) which δ is the right one, we simply bound the divergence by a sum over each of the three possible values for δ:

$$R_{\mathsf{IP\ to\ P}} \leq \frac{3q^m}{f(q)^2} \cdot \sum_{\substack{\delta\in\{-1,0,1\} \\ (i,j)\in(\mathbb{Z}_{f(q)})^2}} \frac{\exp(-2\pi\|(\Phi_q^{(f)}(j) - \Phi_q^{(f)}(i)S \bmod f) + C(i,j) + \delta f\|^2/\sigma^2)}{\rho_\sigma(\Phi_q(\mathbb{Z}_{f(q)}))\exp(-\pi\|\Phi_q^{(f)}(j) - \Phi_q^{(f)}(i)S \bmod f\|^2/\sigma^2)}.$$

We know that $P(i,j) := \Phi_q^{(f)}(j) - \Phi_q^{(f)}(i)S \bmod f$ and $C(i,j)$ have degree $\leq m$. Recall the identity $2\|\mathbf{x}+\mathbf{y}\|^2 - \|\mathbf{x}\|^2 = \|\mathbf{x}+2\mathbf{y}\|^2 - 2\|\mathbf{y}\|^2$. In our case, we instantiate this with $\mathbf{x} = \Phi_q^{(f)}(j) - \Phi_q^{(f)}(i)S$ and $\mathbf{y} = C(i,j)$. To bound the last norm, we recall that the analysis of $C(P,Q)$ done in Lemma 9, applies here by setting $P = \Phi_q^{(f)}(i)$ and $Q = \Phi_q^{(f)}(j)$. Then we have:

$$\|C(i,j) + \delta f\|^2 \leq 1 + m\mathsf{EF}(f)^2(6 + \|f\|_1 + 2m\|S\|_\infty)^2 + m\|f\|_\infty^2.$$

Let us fix $i \in \mathbb{Z}_{f(q)}$. We study $j \mapsto P(i,j) + 2C(i,j)$. As proved in Lemma 9, this is injective over each of $(\Phi_q^{(f)})^{-1}(I_{\delta_1,\delta_2,\delta_3}^{(-is)})$ where $I_{\delta_1,\delta_2,\delta_3}^{(-is)}$ are the intervals introduced in Lemma 8. Since $f(q) \geq q^m$, $I_{\delta_1,\delta_2,\delta_3}^{(-is)}$ is empty if $i \neq 0$. We have:

$$\|P(i,j) + 2C(i,j) + \delta f\|^2 = \delta^2 + \|P(i,j) + 2C(i,j) + 2\delta(f - x^m)\|^2,$$

and note how $\exp(-\pi\delta^2/\sigma^2) \leq 1$ and $f(q) \geq q^m$. Our global bound becomes:

$$R_{\mathsf{IP\ to\ P}} \leq 27\exp\left(2\pi\frac{3m\mathsf{EF}(f)^2(6 + m\|f\|_\infty + 2m\|S\|_\infty)^2}{\sigma^2}\right) \cdot \sum_{\substack{\delta\in\{-1,0,1\} \\ j\in\mathbb{Z}_{f(q)}}} \frac{\exp(-\pi\|\Phi_q^{(f)}(j) + \delta(f - x^m)\|^2/\sigma^2)}{\rho_\sigma(\mathbb{Z}_{f(q)})}.$$

Moreover, we know that every $P \in \mathbb{Z}_q[x]/f$ has at most 3 predecessors by $\Phi_q^{(f)}$ from $\mathbb{Z}_{f(q)}$. We can thus replace the sum over $j \in \mathbb{Z}_{f(q)}$ by 3 times a sum over $P \in \mathbb{Z}_q[x]/f$. Since $P \mapsto P + \delta(f - x^m)$ is a bijection of $\mathbb{Z}_q[x]/f$, we get:

$$R_{\mathsf{IP\ to\ P}} \leq 243\exp\left(6\pi\frac{m\mathsf{EF}(f)^2(6 + m\|f\|_\infty + 2m\|S\|_\infty)^2}{\sigma^2}\right)\frac{\rho_\sigma(\mathbb{Z}_q[x]/f)}{\rho_\sigma(\mathbb{Z}_{f(q)})}.$$

To conclude, we recall $\rho_\sigma(\mathbb{Z}_q[x]/f) \leq \rho_\sigma(\mathbb{Z}_{f(q)})$ since $\mathbb{Z}_q[x]/f \subseteq \Phi_q(\mathbb{Z}_{f(q)})$. □

The below result follows from the Rényi divergence probability preservation.

Theorem 2. *Let $q > 2$ and $f \in \mathbb{Z}[x]$ irreducible and monic of degree $m > 0$ such that $f(q) \geq q^m$ and whose coefficients belong to $(-q/2, q/2)$. Let $\sigma > \sigma' > 0$ such that $q > \sqrt{m}\sigma$. Let t be a number of samples, such that:*

$$\exp\left(\frac{7\,m\|f\|_\infty^2}{\sigma'^2} + 114t\left(1 + \frac{m^3\mathsf{EF}(f)^2(\|f\|_\infty + m^{1/2}\sigma')^2}{\sigma^2}\right)\right) = \mathsf{poly}(m).$$

Then $\mathsf{sPLWE}_{q,\sigma,\sigma',t}^{(f)}$ reduces to $\mathsf{sI\text{-}PLWE}_{q,\sigma,\sigma',t}^{(f)}$.

Along with Theorem 1, this provides a concrete way to find a range of parameters for which sPLWE reduces to sl-PLWE. One should start by choosing an irreducible monic polynomial f of degree $m > 0$. Note that f already determines which theorem will be used: if the second highest nonzero coefficient of f is negative (resp. positive), it holds that $f(q) < q^m$ (resp. $f(q) \geq q^m$) for any integer $q \geq 2\|f\|_\infty$. The value of $t = O(\log m)$ can then be fixed depending on the needs. In Sect. 5, we will have $t = 2$.

The next step is to choose the noise parameter $\sigma' > 0$. When $f(q) \leq q^m$, it can be chosen freely, whereas in the case where $f(q) \geq q^m$, it must satisfy $\sigma' = \Omega(\|f\|_\infty \sqrt{m/\log(m)})$. Then the other noise parameter $\sigma > 0$ should be chosen such that $\sigma^2 \geq \Omega(tm^3 \mathsf{EF}(f)^2 (\|f\|_\infty + m^{1/2}\sigma')^2/\log(m))$. Last is to choose an integer $q > \max(2\|f\|_\infty, \sqrt{m}\sigma)$. In Sect. 5, further conditions are discussed as they are needed for the encryption application.

4.3 Reducing sl-PLWE to sPLWE when $f(q) < q^m$

When reducing sl-PLWE to sPLWE, we are given samples from the IP distribution, and we want to obtain samples from the P distribution. Here, the integer set is smaller than the polynomial one, so the mapping cannot be deterministic if we want to cover the whole range. For this purpose, we uniformly choose polynomials that are predecessors of our samples by the evaluation $P \mapsto P(q) \bmod f(q)$.

Lemma 12 (Divergence between P and IP, when $f(q) < q^m$). *Let $q > 2$ and $f \in \mathbb{Z}[x]$ monic and irreducible of degree $m > 0$ such that $f(q) < q^m$ and whose coefficients belong to $(-q/2, q/2)$. Let $\sigma > 0$. Let $S \in \mathbb{Z}[x]/f$ and $s = S(q) \bmod f(q) \in I_{f,q}$. Sample $(a, b) \hookleftarrow \mathsf{IP}_{q,\sigma}^{(f)}(s)$ and choose A (resp. B) uniformly in the set of predecessors of a $\{P \in \mathbb{Z}_q[x]/f : P(q) \bmod f(q) = a\}$ (resp. the set of predecessors of b $\{P \in \mathbb{Z}_q[x]/f : P(q) \bmod f(q) = b\}$) via the evaluation map. Then:*

$$R_{\mathsf{P}\text{ to }\mathsf{IP}} := R(\mathsf{P}_{q,\sigma}^{(f)}(S)\|(A,B)) \leq 108 \exp\left(38 \cdot m^3 \mathsf{EF}(f)^2 \frac{(\|f\|_\infty + \|S\|_\infty)^2}{\sigma^2}\right).$$

The below result follows from the Rényi divergence probability preservation.

Theorem 3. *Let $q > 2$ and $f \in \mathbb{Z}[x]$ irreducible and monic of degree $m > 0$ such that $f(q) < q^m$ and whose coefficients belong to $(-q/2, q/2)$. Let $\sigma > \sigma' > 0$ such that $q > \sqrt{m}\sigma$. Let t be a number of samples, such that:*

$$\exp\left(\frac{7m\|f\|_\infty^2}{\sigma'^2} + 76t\left(1 + m^3 \mathsf{EF}(f)^2 \frac{(\|f\|_\infty + m^{1/2}\sigma')^2}{\sigma^2}\right)\right) \leq \mathsf{poly}(m).$$

Then $\mathsf{sl\text{-}PLWE}_{q,\sigma,\sigma',t}^{(f)}$ *reduces to* $\mathsf{PLWE}_{q,\sigma,\sigma',t}^{(f)}$.

4.4 Reducing sl-PLWE to sPLWE Reduction when $f(q) \geq q^m$

In this subsection, the integer set is bigger than the polynomial set. Simply applying $\Phi_q^{(f)}$ on the samples that we get is thus enough to get a distribution that covers the entirety of $(\mathbb{Z}_q[x]/f)^2$. Moreover, the next lemma proves that this distribution is close to P.

Lemma 13. *Let $q > 2$, $f \in \mathbb{Z}[x]$ monic and irreducible of degree m such that $f(q) \geq q^m$ and whose coefficients belong to $(-q/2, q/2)$. Let $\sigma > 0$, $S \in \mathbb{Z}_q[x]/f$ and $s \in \mathbb{Z}_{f(q)}$ such that $\Phi_q^{(f)}(s) = S$. Then we have:*

$$R_{\mathsf{P} \text{ to } \mathsf{IP}} := R(\mathsf{P}_{q,\sigma}^{(f)}(S) || \Phi_q^{(f)}(\mathsf{IP}_{q,\sigma}^{(f)}(s))) \leq 162 \exp\Big(114 \frac{m^3 \mathsf{EF}(f)^2 (\|f\|_\infty + \|S\|_\infty)^2}{\sigma^2}\Big).$$

The below result follows from the Rényi divergence probability preservation.

Theorem 4. *Let $q > 2$ and $f \in \mathbb{Z}[x]$ irreducible and monic of degree $m > 0$ such that $f(q) < q^m$ and whose coefficients belong to $(-q/2, q/2)$. Let $\sigma > \sigma' > 0$ such that $q > \sqrt{m}\sigma$. Let t be a number of samples, such that:*

$$\exp\Big(114 t \Big(1 + 114 m^3 \mathsf{EF}(f)^2 \frac{(\|f\|_\infty + m^{1/2}\sigma')^2}{\sigma^2}\Big)\Big) = \mathsf{poly}(m).$$

Then $\mathsf{sl\text{-}PLWE}_{q,\sigma,\sigma',t}^{(f)}$ *reduces to* $\mathsf{sPLWE}_{q,\sigma,\sigma',t}^{(f)}$.

5 A Public-Key Encryption Scheme Based on sl-PLWE

We now describe a deterministic public-key encryption scheme, whose OW-CPA security will be proved based on the presumed hardness of sl-PLWE and dPLWE.

KeyGen(1^λ)**.** On input the security parameter, the key generation algorithm first chooses parameters $\mathsf{pp} := (f, q, \sigma, \sigma', K)$ as explained below. First, let $m := \deg f$. Define $\mathcal{C} = \mathbb{Z}_{f(q)} \times \mathbb{Z}_{f(q)}$ and

$$\mathcal{M} = \Big\{ \Big(\sum_i t_i q^i, \sum_i e'_i q^i, \sum_i e''_i q^i\Big) \in \mathbb{Z}_{f(q)}^3 \mid \forall i : |t_i| \leq \sigma'\sqrt{m} \ \wedge \ |e'_i|, |e''_i| \leq \sigma\sqrt{m} \Big\}.$$

Sample $a \hookleftarrow \mathcal{U}(\mathbb{Z}_{f(q)})$, $s \hookleftarrow D_{\mathbb{Z}_{f(q)},\sigma',\sigma'\sqrt{m}}$ and $e \hookleftarrow D_{\mathbb{Z}_{f(q)},\sigma,\sigma\sqrt{m}}$. If $e = 0$, then restart. Compute $b = as + e \in \mathbb{Z}_{f(q)}$ and output:

$$\mathsf{pk} := (\mathsf{pp}, a, b) \text{ and } \mathsf{sk} := (\mathsf{pp}, s, e).$$

Enc(pk, M)**.** On input the public key $\mathsf{pk} = (\mathsf{pp}, a, b)$ and any valid plaintext message $M = (t, e', e'') \in \mathcal{M}$, compute and output:

$$(c_1, c_2) := (a \cdot t + K \cdot e',\ b \cdot t + K \cdot e'') \in \mathbb{Z}_{f(q)} \times \mathbb{Z}_{f(q)}.$$

Dec$(\mathsf{sk}, (c_1, c_2))$**.** On input the secret key $\mathsf{sk} = (\mathsf{pp}, s, e)$ comprised of the public parameters and two short vectors, and a ciphertext (c_1, c_2), the decryption algorithm first computes:

$$d := c_2 - c_1 \cdot s.$$

Writing $d = \sum_i d_i q^i$, it computes $d' = \sum_i (d_i \bmod K) \cdot q^i \bmod f(q)$. It then recovers the message $t = d'/e \bmod f(q)$, $e' = (c_1 - at)/K \bmod f(q)$ and $e'' = (c_2 - bt)/K \bmod f(q)$. Finally, it outputs (t, e', e'').

We make a few comments on the scheme. By a standard tail bound, the distributions $D_{\mathbb{Z}_{f(q)},\sigma,\sigma\sqrt{m}}$ and $D_{\mathbb{Z}_{f(q)},\sigma',\sigma'\sqrt{m}}$ can be efficiently sampled by rejection sampling from $D_{\mathbb{Z}_{f(q)},\sigma}$ and $D_{\mathbb{Z}_{f(q)},\sigma'}$, respectively. Also, the probability that $e = 0$ is $2^{-\Omega(m)}$. We explicitly exclude this possibility to prove perfect correctness. We will prove OW-CPA security with respect to the distribution

$$D_{\mathcal{M}} = D_{\mathbb{Z}_{f(q)},\sigma',\sigma'\sqrt{m}} \times D_{\mathbb{Z}_{f(q)},\sigma,\sigma\sqrt{m}} \times D_{\mathbb{Z}_{f(q)},\sigma,\sigma\sqrt{m}}$$

over the plaintext space $\mathcal{M}$. For the same reasons as above, it can be sampled efficiently, and its min-entropy is $H_\infty(D_{\mathcal{M}}) = \Omega(m \log \sigma)$. Finally, in the decryption algorithm, we make several divisions modulo $f(q)$. To guarantee its possibility, we impose that $f(q)$ is prime and make sure that e and K are non-zero.

We choose $f \in \mathbb{Z}[x]$ monic and irreducible of degree $m > 0$. We choose $q > 2$ such that $f(q)$ is prime. Note that $f(q)$ has bit-length $\approx m \log q$, so if q is $\Omega(m^{1+\varepsilon})$ for any $\varepsilon > 0$, we heuristically expect that $f(q)$ is prime after a polynomial number of trials for q will make $f(q)$ prime. Note that in full generality, it may not be possible to find any q that makes $f(q)$ prime (for example, consider $f = x^2 + x + 4$).

The other parameters are set as follows. For correctness (Theorem 5), we impose that $K > 14\sigma\sigma' m^2 \|f\|_\infty \mathsf{EF}(f)$ and $q > 84Km^2\|f\|_\infty \mathsf{EF}(f)\sigma\sigma'$. For OW-CPA security (Theorem 6), we impose that $\sigma > \sqrt{m}\mathsf{EF}(f)(\|f\|_1 + m^{3/2}\sigma')$ and $\sigma' \geq \sqrt{m}$. These inequalities can be handled by first setting σ', then σ, K and q. For security against known PLWE attacks, one may choose $m = \Omega(\lambda)$ and $q, \sigma, \sigma' \in \mathrm{poly}(m)$.

Theorem 5 (Correctness). *Assume that $K > 14\sigma\sigma' m^2 \|f\|_\infty \mathsf{EF}(f)$ and also $q > 84K\sigma\sigma' m^2\|f\|_\infty \mathsf{EF}(f)$. Then the above encryption scheme is correct.*

Proof. Let (c_1, c_2) be an encryption of $M = (t, e', e'') \in \mathcal{M}$ under pk. We want to show that given sk and (c_1, c_2), the decryption algorithm indeed recovers M. Note first that $d = c_2 - c_1 \cdot s = K \cdot (e'' - e' \cdot s) + e \cdot t \bmod f(q)$. By carries analysis from Lemma 14 found in appendix of the full version, we have

$$\forall i < m : d_i = d_i' + K \cdot d_i'' \text{ with } |d_i'| < K/2 \text{ and } d' = \sum_i d_i' q^i = e \cdot t \bmod f(q).$$

This exploits the parameter conditions on K and q. Once the decryption algorithm has recovered $d' = e \cdot t \bmod f(q)$, it can recover t, e' and e'' using division in the field $\mathbb{Z}_{f(q)}$. □

Lemma 14. *Let* $K > 14\sigma\sigma' m^2 \|f\|_\infty \mathsf{EF}(f)$ *and* $q > 84K\sigma\sigma' m^2 \|f\|_\infty \mathsf{EF}(f)$. *Let* (c_1, c_2) *be an encryption of* $M = (t, e', e'') \in \mathcal{M}$ *under* $\mathsf{pk} = (a, as + e)$. *Then let* $d = \sum_i d_i q^i := c_2 - c_1 \cdot s$ *and write* $d_i = d_i' + K \cdot d_i''$ *with* $|d_i'| < K/2$, *for any* $i < m$. *Then* $d' := \sum_i d_i' q^i = e \cdot t \bmod f(q)$.

We now study the OW-CPA security of the above deterministic cryptosystem.

Theorem 6 (Security). *Assuming that* $\sigma \geq \sqrt{m}\mathsf{EF}(f) \cdot (\|f\|_1 + m^{3/2}\sigma')$ *and* $\sigma' \geq \sqrt{m}$, *the above* PKE *scheme is* OW-CPA *secure for distribution* $D_{\mathcal{M}}$, *under the* $\mathsf{sI\text{-}PLWE}^{(f)}_{q,\sigma,\sigma',2}$ *and* $\mathsf{dPLWE}^{(f)}_{q,\sigma,\sigma',1}$ *assumptions. More concretely, if there exists a* OW-CPA *adversary* $\mathcal{A}$, *then there exist algorithms* $\mathcal{B}$ *and* $\mathcal{C}$ *for* dPLWE *and* sI-PLWE, *respectively, with run-times similar to the run-time of* $\mathcal{A}$ *and such that:*

$$\mathsf{Adv}^{\mathsf{OW\text{-}CPA}}_{\mathsf{PKE},D_{\mathcal{M}}}(\mathcal{A}) \leq O\left(\mathsf{Adv}^{\mathsf{sI\text{-}PLWE}}_{f,q,\sigma,\sigma'}(\mathcal{C})^{1/4} + \mathsf{Adv}^{\mathsf{dPLWE}}_{f,q,\sigma,\sigma'}(\mathcal{B})^{1/2}\right) + 2^{-\Omega(m)}.$$

Our security proof relies on two security assumptions: the search problem sI-PLWE and the decision problem dPLWE. As recalled in Sect. 2, dPLWE and sPLWE can be set so that they reduce to one another (up to some limited parameter losses). From Sect. 4, we know that sPLWE and sI-PLWE reduce to one another. Therefore, Theorem 6 could be adapted to make security rely on a single hardness assumption, e.g., sI-PLWE.

Proof. Assume that there exists an adversary $\mathcal{A}$ against the OW-CPA game of the PKE with non-negligible success probability ε_0. We define the following games:

Game 0**:** This is the OW-CPA game.
Game 1**:** In this game, we sample $s \hookleftarrow D_{\mathbb{Z}_{f(q)},\sigma'}$ and $e \hookleftarrow D_{\mathbb{Z}_{f(q)},\sigma}$ instead of $s \hookleftarrow D_{\mathbb{Z}_{f(q)},\sigma',\sigma'\sqrt{m}}$ and $e \hookleftarrow D_{\mathbb{Z}_{f(q)},\sigma,\sigma\sqrt{m}}$, respectively. Also, we do not reject when $e = 0$.
Game 2**:** In this game, we change the distribution of the public key pk. First we start by sampling $A \hookleftarrow \mathcal{U}(\mathbb{Z}_q[x]/f)$, $S \hookleftarrow D_{\mathbb{Z}[x]/f,\sigma',q}$ and $E \hookleftarrow D_{\mathbb{Z}[x]/f,\sigma,q}$ and then set $B = AS + E \bmod f$. Then

- If $f(q) \geq q^m$, choose a and b uniformly among the predecessors of A and B by the map $\Phi_q^{(f)}$, respectively.
- If $f(q) < q^m$, compute $(a, b) = (A(q) \bmod f(q), B(q) \bmod f(q))$.

Game 3**:** In this game, we change the generation of B. Instead of sampling (A, B) as above, we sample $(A, B) \hookleftarrow \mathcal{U}((\mathbb{Z}_q[x]/f)^2)$.
Game 4**:** In this game, we change the generation of (a, b) once more. Instead of sampling $(A, B) \hookleftarrow \mathcal{U}((\mathbb{Z}_q[x]/f)^2)$ and computing predecessors (a, b), we directly sample $a, b \hookleftarrow \mathcal{U}(\mathbb{Z}_{f(q)})$.

Let ε_i denote the success probability of $\mathcal{A}$ in Game i. By definition, we have $\varepsilon_0 = \mathsf{Adv}^{\mathsf{OW\text{-}CPA}}_{\mathsf{PKE},D_{\mathcal{M}}}(\mathcal{A})$. For any random variables (a, b, t, e, e', a', b'), the following inequality holds by using the data processing inequality and the multiplicativity of the Rényi divergence:

$$R((a, b, at + Ke, bt + Ke')\|(a', b', a't + Ke, b't + Ke')) \leq R((a, b)\|(a', b')). \quad (1)$$

In the context of $\mathsf{Game}\ 0$ versus $\mathsf{Game}\ 1$, note that the statistical distance between $D_{\mathbb{Z}_{f(q)},\sigma}$ and $D_{\mathbb{Z}_{f(q)},\sigma,\sigma\sqrt{m}}$ is $2^{-\Omega(m)}$. The same holds for $D_{\mathbb{Z}_{f(q)},\sigma'}$ and $D_{\mathbb{Z}_{f(q)},\sigma',\sigma'\sqrt{m}}$. Further, the probability that $e = 0$ is also $2^{-\Omega(m)}$. Therefore, we have $|\varepsilon_0 - \varepsilon_1| \leq 2^{-\Omega(m)}$.

In the context of $\mathsf{Game}\ 1$ versus $\mathsf{Game}\ 2$, we can instantiate (1) with (a, b) as in $\mathsf{Game}\ 1$ and (a', b') as in $\mathsf{Game}\ 2$. By Lemmas 10 and 11 and thanks to our choice of parameters, this divergence is $\leq O(1)$. Then, by the probability preservation property, we have: $\varepsilon_2 \geq \Omega(\varepsilon_1^2)$.

For $\mathsf{Game}\ 2$ versus $\mathsf{Game}\ 3$, we use the hardness of dPLWE. Indeed, one can build an algorithm $\mathcal{B}$ against dPLWE that would exploit a behavioural difference of $\mathcal{A}$ between $\mathsf{Game}\ 2$ and $\mathsf{Game}\ 3$. We have:

$$\mathsf{Adv}^{\mathsf{dPLWE}}_{f,q,\sigma,\sigma'}(\mathcal{B}) \geq |\varepsilon_3 - \varepsilon_2| - 2^{-\Omega(m)}.$$

In the context of $\mathsf{Game}\ 3$ versus $\mathsf{Game}\ 4$, we instantiate (1) with (a, b) as in $\mathsf{Game}\ 3$ and (a', b') as in $\mathsf{Game}\ 4$. In $\mathsf{Game}\ 3$, the probability of $a = k$ for a given $k \in \mathbb{Z}_{f(q)}$ is $\leq 3/q^m$, and the same holds for b. Therefore:

$$R((a,b)||(a',b')) \leq f(q)^2 \cdot \frac{(3/q^m)^4}{1/f(q)^2} = 81 \cdot \frac{f(q)^4}{q^{4m}}.$$

Since $f(q) < 2q^m$, the divergence is ≤ 1296. By using the probability preservation probability, we have that $\varepsilon_4 \geq \Omega(\varepsilon_3^2)$. Finally, we handle $\mathsf{Game}\ 4$ using hardness of $\mathsf{sl\text{-}PLWE}$. We build an $\mathsf{sl\text{-}PLWE}$ algorithm $\mathcal{C}$ as follows. Upon receiving two $\mathsf{sl\text{-}PLWE}$ samples $(a, a \cdot t + e')$ and $(b, b \cdot t + e'')$, it sets

$$\begin{aligned} \mathsf{pk} &:= (K \cdot a, K \cdot b), \\ c_1 &:= K \cdot (a \cdot t + e') = (K \cdot a) \cdot t + K \cdot e', \\ c_2 &:= K \cdot (b \cdot t + e') = (K \cdot b) \cdot t + K \cdot e''. \end{aligned}$$

It then calls the OW-CPA adversary $\mathcal{A}$ on the challenge $\mathsf{pk}, (c_1, c_2)$ and waits for its answer (t, e, e'). Then $\mathcal{C}$ outputs t. As K is coprime to $f(q)$, multiplication by K modulo $f(q)$ is a bijection, and the view of $\mathcal{A}$ is as in $\mathsf{Game}\ 4$. As a result, we have that $\mathsf{Adv}^{\mathsf{sl\text{-}PLWE}}_{f,q,\sigma,\sigma'}(\mathcal{C}) \geq \varepsilon_3$. The result follows by collecting terms. □

Acknowledgments. This work was supported in part by European Union Horizon 2020 Research and Innovation Program Grant 780701, Australian Research Council Discovery Project Grant DP180102199, and by BPI-France in the context of the national project RISQ (P141580).

References

[ABD+17] Alkim, E., et al.: Frodo: Candidate to NIS (2017)

[ACPS09] Applebaum, B., Cash, D., Peikert, C., Sahai, A.: Fast cryptographic primitives and circular-secure encryption based on hard learning problems. In: Halevi, S. (ed.) CRYPTO 2009. LNCS, vol. 5677, pp. 595–618. Springer, Heidelberg (2009). https://doi.org/10.1007/978-3-642-03356-8_35

[AD17] Albrecht, M.R., Deo, A.: Large modulus ring-LWE $\geq$ module-LWE. In: Takagi, T., Peyrin, T. (eds.) ASIACRYPT 2017. LNCS, vol. 10624. Springer, Cham (2017). https://doi.org/10.1007/978-3-319-70694-8

[AJPS18] Aggarwal, D., Joux, A., Prakash, A., Santha, M.: A new public-key cryptosystem via Mersenne numbers. In: Shacham, H., Boldyreva, A. (eds.) CRYPTO 2018. LNCS, vol. 10993, pp. 459–482. Springer, Cham (2018). https://doi.org/10.1007/978-3-319-96878-0_16

[BCF20] Budroni, A., Chetioui, B., Franch, E.: Attacks on integer-RLWE. IACR Cryptol. ePrint Arch. **2020**, 1007 (2020)

[BCSV20] Bootland, C., Castryck, W., Szepieniec, A., Vercauteren, F.: A framework for cryptographic problems from linear algebra. J. Math. Cryptol. **14**(1), 202–217 (2020)

[BF11] Boneh, D., Freeman, D.M.: Linearly homomorphic signatures over binary fields and new tools for lattice-based signatures. In: Catalano, D., Fazio, N., Gennaro, R., Nicolosi, A. (eds.) PKC 2011. LNCS, vol. 6571, pp. 1–16. Springer, Heidelberg (2011). https://doi.org/10.1007/978-3-642-19379-8_1

[BGV12] Brakerski, Z., Gentry, C., Vaikuntanathan, V.: (Leveled) fully homomorphic encryption without bootstrapping. In: ITCS 2012 (2012)

[BHH+19] Bindel, N., Hamburg, M., Hövelmanns, K., Hülsing, A., Persichetti, E.: Tighter proofs of CCA security in the quantum random oracle model. In: Hofheinz, D., Rosen, A. (eds.) TCC 2019. LNCS, vol. 11892, pp. 61–90. Springer, Cham (2019). https://doi.org/10.1007/978-3-030-36033-7_3

[BLP+13] Brakerski, Z., Langlois, A., Peikert, C., Regev, O., Stehlé, D.: Classical hardness of learning with errors. In: STOC 2013 (2013)

[BLRL+18] Bai, S., Lepoint, T., Roux-Langlois, A., Sakzad, A., Stehlé, D., Steinfeld, R.: Improved security proofs in lattice-based cryptography: using the Rényi divergence rather than the statistical distance. J. Cryptol. **31**(2), 610–640 (2018)

[BP18] Bernstein, D.J., Persichetti, E.: Towards KEM unification. IACR Cryptol. ePrint Arch. **2018**, 526 (2018)

[BPR12] Banerjee, A., Peikert, C., Rosen, A.: Pseudorandom functions and lattices. In: Pointcheval, D., Johansson, T. (eds.) EUROCRYPT 2012. LNCS, vol. 7237, pp. 719–737. Springer, Heidelberg (2012). https://doi.org/10.1007/978-3-642-29011-4_42

[Gen01] Gentry, C.: Key recovery and message attacks on NTRU-composite. In: Pfitzmann, B. (ed.) EUROCRYPT 2001. LNCS, vol. 2045, pp. 182–194. Springer, Heidelberg (2001). https://doi.org/10.1007/3-540-44987-6_12

[Gu17] Gu, C.: Integer version of ring-LWE and its applications. IACR Cryptol. ePrint Arch. **2017**, 641 (2017)

[Gu19] Gu, C.: Integer version of ring-LWE and its applications. In: Meng, W., Furnell, S. (eds.) SocialSec 2019. CCIS, vol. 1095, pp. 110–122. Springer, Singapore (2019). https://doi.org/10.1007/978-981-15-0758-8_9

[Ham17] Hamburg, M.: Three bears: Candidate to NIS (2017)

[HHK17] Hofheinz, D., Hövelmanns, K., Kiltz, E.: A modular analysis of the Fujisaki-Okamoto transformation. In: Kalai, Y., Reyzin, L. (eds.) TCC 2017. LNCS, vol. 10677, pp. 341–371. Springer, Cham (2017). https://doi.org/10.1007/978-3-319-70500-2_12

[KSS+20] Kuchta, V., Sakzad, A., Stehlé, D., Steinfeld, R., Sun, S.-F.: Measure-rewind-measure: tighter quantum random oracle model proofs for one-way to hiding and CCA security. In: Canteaut, A., Ishai, Y. (eds.) EUROCRYPT 2020. LNCS, vol. 12107, pp. 703–728. Springer, Cham (2020). https://doi.org/10.1007/978-3-030-45727-3_24

[LM06] Lyubashevsky, V., Micciancio, D.: Generalized compact knapsacks are collision resistant. In: Bugliesi, M., Preneel, B., Sassone, V., Wegener, I. (eds.) ICALP 2006. LNCS, vol. 4052, pp. 144–155. Springer, Heidelberg (2006). https://doi.org/10.1007/11787006_13

[LPR10] Lyubashevsky, V., Peikert, C., Regev, O.: On ideal lattices and learning with errors over rings. In: Gilbert, H. (ed.) EUROCRYPT 2010. LNCS, vol. 6110, pp. 1–23. Springer, Heidelberg (2010). https://doi.org/10.1007/978-3-642-13190-5_1

[LS15] Langlois, A., Stehlé, D.: Worst-case to average-case reductions for module lattices. Des. Codes Crypt. **75**(3), 565–599 (2014). https://doi.org/10.1007/s10623-014-9938-4

[LSS14] Langlois, A., Stehlé, D., Steinfeld, R.: GGHLite: more efficient multilinear maps from ideal lattices. In: Nguyen, P.Q., Oswald, E. (eds.) EUROCRYPT 2014. LNCS, vol. 8441, pp. 239–256. Springer, Heidelberg (2014). https://doi.org/10.1007/978-3-642-55220-5_14

[NIS] NIST: Post-Quantum Cryptography Project. https://csrc.nist.gov/Projects/Post-Quantum-Cryptography/

[PRS17] Peikert, C., Regev, O., Stephens-Davidowitz, N.: Pseudorandomness of ring-LWE for any ring and modulus. In: STOC 2017 (2017)

[Reg09] Regev, O.: On lattices, learning with errors, random linear codes, and cryptography. J. ACM **56**(6), 34 (2009)

[RSW18] Rosca, M., Stehlé, D., Wallet, A.: On the ring-LWE and polynomial-LWE problems. In: Nielsen, J.B., Rijmen, V. (eds.) EUROCRYPT 2018. LNCS, vol. 10820, pp. 146–173. Springer, Cham (2018). https://doi.org/10.1007/978-3-319-78381-9_6

[SSTX09] Stehlé, D., Steinfeld, R., Tanaka, K., Xagawa, K.: Efficient public key encryption based on ideal lattices. In: Matsui, M. (ed.) ASIACRYPT 2009. LNCS, vol. 5912, pp. 617–635. Springer, Heidelberg (2009). https://doi.org/10.1007/978-3-642-10366-7_36

[SXY18] Saito, T., Xagawa, K., Yamakawa, T.: Tightly-secure key-encapsulation mechanism in the quantum random oracle model. In: Nielsen, J.B., Rijmen, V. (eds.) EUROCRYPT 2018. LNCS, vol. 10822, pp. 520–551. Springer, Cham (2018). https://doi.org/10.1007/978-3-319-78372-7_17

[Sze17] Szepieniec, A.: Ramstake: Candidate to NIS (2017)

Shorter Lattice-Based Zero-Knowledge Proofs via One-Time Commitments

Vadim Lyubashevsky[1(✉)], Ngoc Khanh Nguyen[1,2], and Gregor Seiler[1,2]

[1] IBM Research - Zurich, Ruschlikon, Switzerland
{vad,nkn}@zurich.ibm.com
[2] ETH Zurich, Zurich, Switzerland
gseiler@inf.ethz.ch

Abstract. There has been a lot of recent progress in constructing efficient zero-knowledge proofs for showing knowledge of an $\vec{s}$ with small coefficients satisfying $\boldsymbol{A}\vec{s} = \vec{t}$. For typical parameters, the proof sizes have gone down from several megabytes to a bit under 50KB (Esgin et al., Asiacrypt 2020). These are now within an order of magnitude of the sizes of lattice-based signatures, which themselves constitute proof systems which demonstrate knowledge of something weaker than the aforementioned equation. One can therefore see that this line of research is approaching optimality. In this paper, we modify a key component of these proofs, as well as apply several other tweaks, to achieve a further reduction of around 30% in the proof output size. We also show that this savings propagates itself when these proofs are used in a general framework to construct more complex protocols.

1 Introduction

Zero-knowledge proofs and commit-and-prove protocols form the foundations of virtually all privacy-based protocols. In preparing for the (eventual) coming of quantum computing, there has been a lot of focus in recent years on building such protocols based on quantum-safe assumptions. Quantum-safe PCP/IOP schemes whose security is just based on the collision-resistance of cryptographic hash functions have existed for decades, and there has been a lot of recent work around them. The main feature of these constructions is that their outputs are sublinear in the statement size. The main downside is that they can be very slow and memory intensive. Furthermore, there is a lower bound of around 100KB for proofs of statements that have small size. So it's quite likely that they are not the best solution for all scenarios.

In the last few years, new techniques emerged in lattice cryptography that made it a promising foundation for quantum-safe privacy-based protocols. These techniques have been used for blockchain applications [EZS+19], verifiable random functions [EKS+20], and for proofs of arithmetic statements [LNS20a]. In all of these scenarios, lattice schemes appear to be the best solutions available. For example, a commit-and-prove protocol for integer products is significantly smaller and several orders of magnitude faster than other quantum-safe solutions.

J. A. Garay (Ed.): PKC 2021, LNCS 12710, pp. 215–241, 2021.
https://doi.org/10.1007/978-3-030-75245-3_9

These results show that lattices might eventually be very reasonable substitutes for the classical cryptography that is currently embedded in those protocols.

At the core of many of the recent privacy-based protocols is the BDLOP commitment scheme [BDL+18] which is able to commit to an arbitrary message vector $\vec{m}$ modulo q. In [BDL+18], it was also shown how one can prove knowledge of $\vec{m}$ by only proving knowledge of the commitment randomness $\vec{r}$. The proof technique was essentially using the "Fiat-Shamir with Aborts" [Lyu09] framework to keep the proofs small and avoid leaking any information about $\vec{r}$. If one uses the Gaussian rejection sampling procedure [Lyu12], then the magnitude of each coefficient of the $\vec{r}'$ output in the proof is around $12 \cdot \kappa\|\vec{r}\|$; where the κ is some constant that comes from the challenge and the 12 comes from a Gaussian tail bound needed for (statistical) zero-knowledge.

The increased coefficient size means that the proof is noticeably larger than the randomness itself (and gives rise to a vicious cycle of having to increase the modulus and dimension of the underlying lattice). It nevertheless seems necessary because leaking some information about the randomness can be dangerous. For example, if one were to repeatedly perform proofs of knowledge for the same commitment and leaking something about the same randomness each time, eventually the entire randomness could be recovered by even a passive observer.

1.1 One-Time Commitments

If one looks closer at how the BDLOP commitment is being used in many of the privacy-based protocols, one would notice that the scheme is used to commit to some intermediate value, give a proof-of-knowledge of the value (i.e. proof of knowledge of the commitment randomness), and then discards the commitment. So only *one* proof of knowledge is performed. In this case, it's not immediately clear whether some leakage of the randomness vector is problematic. Still, it seems somewhat risky to only perform a minimal perturbation on the randomness and hope that this is good enough for LWE to remain secure. Instead of relying completely on heuristic security, it would be good to have a technique which lowers the proof size, and at the same time concretely allows one to understand exactly how the LWE problem is affected by the leakage.

For efficiency purposes, the BDLOP commitment instantiation is only computationally hiding (i.e. based on LWE), so one cannot use prior techniques to prove that enough entropy remains in the randomness after the leakage. While there are techniques that show that LWE-based encryption schemes can tolerate some leakage, the results are asymptotic and it's unclear what the actual practical implication of the leakage is [DGK+10, GKPV10, BD20]. There has also been some work examining the practical aspects of leakage in the Ring-LWE setting [DDGR20], and the security of the scheme is barely affected when the leakage is small.

We show that a particular rejection sampling strategy information-theoretically leaks just one bit of randomness, and allows us to exactly quantify what this leakage is. More specifically, in addition to the public LWE samples, there is also a short public vector $\vec{z}$, and we require that the whoe LWE secret (i.e. the secret concatenated with the error vector) has a non-negative inner product with it. Because the LWE secret is uniformly distributed around 0, the probability that the inner product will be non-negative is greater than 1/2, and so this extra restriction loses (less than) one bit of entropy.

We observe that the leakage essentially transforms the LWE problem instance into (a much less leaky version of) an extended-LWE one, which was shown to be equivalent to LWE in [AP12]. The decisional extended-LWE problem asks to distinguish between the distributions $(\boldsymbol{B}, \boldsymbol{B}\vec{\boldsymbol{r}}, \vec{z}, \langle\vec{\boldsymbol{r}}, \vec{\boldsymbol{z}}\rangle)$ and $(\boldsymbol{B}, \vec{\boldsymbol{u}}, \vec{z}, \langle\vec{\boldsymbol{r}}, \vec{\boldsymbol{z}}\rangle)$, where $\vec{\boldsymbol{r}}$ is sampled from the secret/noise domain of the LWE problem, $\vec{\boldsymbol{u}}$ is uniformly random, and $\vec{z}$ is sampled from some efficiently sampleable distribution. One caveat is that for efficiency, we use a structured matrix $\boldsymbol{B}$, and the proof in [AP12] does not carry over to our setting.[1]

Furthermore, it's clear that there is an equivalence between the *search* versions of extended Ring-LWE and Ring-LWE – and so a separation between the decisional versions would be quite interesting because all the best current lattice algorithms work by trying to solve the search problem. In short, we do not believe that this one bit of leakage has any practical consequences on the hardness of the Ring-LWE problem. It would actually be interesting if this assumption found even more applications, beside the original ones (e.g. [OPW11]) that inspired the Extended-LWE assumption, for improving the efficiency of lattice schemes.[2]

1.2 Technical Overview

The last prover move of a Schnorr-type Σ-protocol is a value $\vec{\boldsymbol{z}} = \vec{\boldsymbol{y}} + \vec{\boldsymbol{v}}$, where $\vec{\boldsymbol{y}}$ is a "masking" vector that the prover created during the first move and $\vec{\boldsymbol{v}}$ is the combination of the secret and the challenge (usually their product, but this is unimportant for our purposes and we can consider the whole $\vec{\boldsymbol{v}}$ to be secret). If we would like $\vec{\boldsymbol{z}}$ to have small norm, then we cannot choose the coefficients of $\vec{\boldsymbol{y}}$ to be so large that the sum $\vec{\boldsymbol{y}} + \vec{\boldsymbol{v}}$ statistically hides $\vec{\boldsymbol{v}}$. Instead we use rejection sampling to force the distribution of $\vec{\boldsymbol{z}}$ to be independent of $\vec{\boldsymbol{v}}$. In particular, if we would like the distribution of the output to be f, while the distribution of $\vec{\boldsymbol{z}}$ is g, then one should output $\vec{\boldsymbol{z}}$ with probability $f(\vec{\boldsymbol{z}})/(M \cdot g(\vec{\boldsymbol{z}}))$, where M is some positive integer set so that this ratio is never larger than 1. Since $1/M$ is the probability that something will be output, we also want to have M as small as possible. Combining these two requirements, it's easy to see that M should be set to $\max_{\vec{\boldsymbol{z}}}(g(\vec{\boldsymbol{z}})/f(\vec{\boldsymbol{z}}))$.

If we follow [Lyu12] where the target distribution f is a discrete Gaussian with standard deviation $\mathfrak{s}$ and the distribution g is a shifted Gaussian (by $\vec{\boldsymbol{v}}$) with the same standard deviation, then via [Lyu12, Lemma 4.5], the value for M is derived as

[1] For the readers familiar with the *sample-preserving* reduction between search and decisional LWE problems [MM11], the underlying obstacles for that reduction and the extended-LWE reduction not carrying over to the Ring-LWE setting are similar.

[2] Indeed, much of the progress in constructions of practical classical cryptography has come from making stronger, but still plausible, assumptions that stem from discrete log or factoring.

$$\exp\left(\frac{-2\langle\vec{z},\vec{v}\rangle+\|\vec{v}\|^2}{2\mathfrak{s}^2}\right)\le\exp\left(\frac{24\mathfrak{s}\|\vec{v}\|+\|\vec{v}\|^2}{2\mathfrak{s}^2}\right)=M.$$

To obtain the inequality, one uses a standard 1-dimensional tail bound for the inner product of a discrete Gaussian with arbitrary vector (c.f. [Lyu12, Lemma 4.3]). And in fact, it is this tail bound that contributes the most to M. For example, if we would like to have $M = \exp(1)$, then we would need to set $\mathfrak{s} \approx 12\|\vec{v}\|$. On the other hand, if we knew that $\langle\vec{z},\vec{v}\rangle \ge 0$, then we could set $\mathfrak{s} \approx \|\vec{v}\|/\sqrt{2}$, a decrease of around a factor of 17. So the intuition is for the prover to throw away the potential outputs $\vec{z}$ that have the aforementioned inner product be negative-valued. The effect of this is that it leaks information about $\vec{z}$ – in particular, the fact that its inner product with the secret is positive.

Interestingly, the new value of $\mathfrak{s}$ is identical to what one would get by using bimodal rejection sampling, as in the BLISS signature scheme [DDLL13]. We cannot directly apply the technique from that paper because it required that the public value $\boldsymbol{B}_0$ be set up such that $\boldsymbol{B}_0\vec{r} = q \pmod{2q}$. Intuitively, with this setup, leaking the sign of the secret $\vec{r}$ doesn't matter because both $\vec{r}$ and $-\vec{r}$ satisfy the equality. Since we do not have this setup, the bimodal technique from BLISS would leak some information. At this point, we do not see a way to quantify the leakage stemming from the bimodal distribution, unlike the fairly simple leakage that we proposed instead. We should also mention that a recent work [TWZ20] showed how to apply the bimodal technique to the BDLOP commitment scheme without any leakage. Their transformation is not for free, though – it increases the length of the output, and also has a technical subtlety that makes it difficult to apply to our current result. The issue is that a part of our security proof requires that the challenge space has a particular distribution over $\{-1, 0, 1\}$ (it's necessary for Lemma 2.1, which is crucial for the product proof over fully-splitting rings). In the proof in [TWZ20], on the other hand, the challenges are masked by the prover and so their distribution is possibly determined in an adversarial fashion.

1.3 Applications and Paper Overview

A good benchmark for the progress of the development of lattice-based proof techniques is the simple proof of knowledge of a trinary secret vector $\vec{s}$ satisfying $\boldsymbol{B}\vec{s} = \vec{t}$. Up until a few years ago, for a particular real-world parametrization of the problem ($\boldsymbol{B}$ being a 1024×2048 dimensional matrix over $\mathbb{Z}_q$ for $q \approx 2^{32}$), the smallest proof used "Stern proofs" [Ste93] ported to lattices [LNSW13], and had proof sizes of several megabytes. Switching the proof strategy to showing that a coefficient s_i is trinary by using a commit-and-prove strategy by proving the algebraic equation $(s_i - 1) \cdot s_i \cdot (s_i + 1) = 0$ lowered the proof sizes to around 300KB [YAZ+19, BLS19]. Then even more recently, by utilizing more efficient product proofs [EZS+19, ALS20], it was shown in [ENS20] how to obtain proofs of size under 50KB.

In Sect. 3, we apply our new technique to the aforementioned benchmark, as well as to the recent framework in [LNS20a] for proving integer relations.

Proving	[ENS20]	[LNS20a]	**this work**	heuristic masking with no rejection sampling
Knowledge of an LWE Sample	47KB	47KB	**33.3** KB	27 KB
Integer Addition	–	24.8KB	**16.9** KB	13.8 KB
Integer Multiplication	–	40.2KB	**28.2** KB	23 KB

Fig. 1. Proof size comparisons for secure commit-and prove protocols for proving knowledge of a (Module)-LWE sample of total dimension (secret and error vector) 2048, and 128-bit integer addition and multiplication. In the last column we list the proof sizes when only masking the secret vector $c\vec{r}$ with a uniformly random masking vector that has the same infinity norm bound than the secret vector and not performing any rejection sampling. This is possibly still secure, but lacks a security proof at this point.

[LNS20b, Appendix B] shows how this framework can be further optimised using commitment compression from [DKL+18]. In total, we obtain a size reduction of around 30% for these proofs (see Fig. 1). As a side note, the proofs in [ENS20, LNS20a] used the uniform distribution instead of discrete Gaussians. The reason was that Gaussians did not provide much of a size reduction (a few kilobytes) and are a bit more cumbersome to work with. But in light of our modified rejection sampling, which only appears to apply to the Gaussian technique, we believe that it is now worthwhile to switch in order to take advantage of the additional size reduction.

To see how far our new rejection sampling procedure is from the (almost) best possible, we also compute the proof size for the case in which we don't do *any* rejection sampling when giving a proof of knowledge of the commitment randomness. In particular, we heuristically mask the secret by adding a random masking vector whose coefficients are as big as those of the vector. This undoubtedly leaks something about the randomness, but it may still be reasonable to hope that the message in the commitment remains hidden because there is still enough entropy in the LWE secret (i.e. the randomness of the commitment).[3] This strategy leads to proof sizes that are around 20% smaller. We do not see how one can get any sort of security reduction for this approach, but we don't see an attack either. It is therefore an interesting open problem whether this approach can lead to something with a security proof. This would lead to essentially optimal parameters for this approach of creating zero-knowledge proofs.

Since our basic proofs are fairly close to optimal (as far as this line of research goes), we find it worthwhile to give further applications of them. Combined with a few extra tricks we develop along the way, we believe this leads to the shortest current constructions for certain primitives. Section 4 describes how one constructs a verifiable decryption scheme for Kyber [BDK+18], which is a finalist of the NIST PQC competition. This approach can be easily extended to other lattice-based KEM finalists, such as Saber [DKRV18] or NTRU [HPS98].

[3] Even smaller sizes would be of course obtained if one does no masking at all, but then the scheme would be clearly insecure.

Complementing the previous section, which requires range proofs in the infinity norm, in [LNS20b, Appendix E] we further consider range proofs with respect to the Euclidean norm. Concretely, we show how to prove that a vector $\vec{v}$ has $\|\vec{v}\| < a$ for some integer a. In [LNS20b, Appendix F], we describe an alternative approach for creating an important ingredient in some proofs – namely, *approximate* range proofs [BL17,BN20,LNS20a] – by using bimodal Gaussians [DDLL13] which further increases the efficiency of the aforementioned protocol. We also remark that the latter two sections make use of the improved framework from [LNS20a] defined in Sect. 3.

2 Preliminaries

2.1 Notation

Denote $\mathbb{Z}_p$ to be the ring of integers modulo p. Let q be an odd prime. We write $\vec{v} \in R^m$ to denote vectors over a ring R and matrices over R will be written as regular capital letters M. Define I_n to be the $n \times n$ identity matrix over $\mathbb{Z}_q$. For an integer a, we define a vector $\vec{a} = (a, \ldots, a)$ unless stated otherwise. By default, all vectors are column vectors. We write $\vec{v} \| \vec{w}$ for a usual concatenation of $\vec{v}$ and $\vec{w}$ (which is still a column vector). For $\vec{v}, \vec{w} \in \mathbb{Z}_q^k$, $\vec{v} \circ \vec{w}$ is the usual component-wise multiplication. For simplicity, we denote $\vec{u}^2 = \vec{u} \circ \vec{u}$. We write $x \leftarrow S$ when $x \in S$ is sampled uniformly at random from the finite set S and similarly $x \leftarrow D$ when x is sampled according to the distribution D. We write $[n]$ to denote the set $\{1, \ldots, n\}$. Given two functions $f, g : \mathbb{N} \rightarrow [0, 1]$, we write $f(\mu) \approx g(\mu)$ if $|f(\mu) - g(\mu)| < \mu^{-\omega(1)}$. A function f is negligible if $f \approx 0$. We write $\mathsf{negl}(n)$ to denote an unspecified negligible function in n.

For a power of two d, denote $\mathcal{R}$ and $\mathcal{R}_q$ respectively to be the rings $\mathbb{Z}[X]/(X^d + 1)$ and $\mathbb{Z}_q[X]/(X^d + 1)$. Bold lower-case letters denote elements in $\mathcal{R}$ or $\mathcal{R}_q$ and bold lower-case letters with arrows represent column vectors with coefficients in $\mathcal{R}$ or $\mathcal{R}_q$. We also write bold upper-case letters for matrices in $\mathcal{R}$ or $\mathcal{R}_q$. By default, for a polynomial denoted as a bold letter, we write its i-th coefficient as its corresponding regular font letter subscript i, e.g. $f_0 \in \mathbb{Z}_q$ is a constant coefficient of $\boldsymbol{f} \in \mathcal{R}_q$.

Modular Reductions. We define $r' = r \bmod^{\pm} q$ to be the unique element r' in the range $-\frac{q-1}{2} \leq r' \leq \frac{q-1}{2}$ such that $r' \equiv r \pmod q$. We also denote $r' = r \bmod^{+} q$ to be the unique element r' in the range $0 \leq r' < q$ such that $r' \equiv r \pmod q$. When the exact representation is not important, we simply write $r \bmod q$.

Sizes of Elements. For an element $w \in \mathbb{Z}_q$, we write $\|w\|_\infty$ to mean $|w \bmod^{\pm} q|$. Define the ℓ_∞ and ℓ_p norms for $\boldsymbol{w} = w_0 + w_1 X + \ldots + w_{d-1} X^{d-1} \in \mathcal{R}$ as follows:

$$\|\boldsymbol{w}\|_\infty = \max_j \|w_j\|_\infty, \quad \|\boldsymbol{w}\|_p = \sqrt[p]{\|w_0\|_\infty^p + \ldots + \|w_{d-1}\|_\infty^p}.$$

If $\vec{\boldsymbol{w}} = (\boldsymbol{w}_1, \ldots, \boldsymbol{w}_m) \in \mathcal{R}^m$, then

$$\|\vec{\boldsymbol{w}}\|_\infty = \max_j \|\boldsymbol{w}_j\|_\infty, \quad \|\vec{\boldsymbol{w}}\|_p = \sqrt[p]{\|\boldsymbol{w}_1\|^p + \ldots + \|\boldsymbol{w}_k\|^p}.$$

By default, we denote $\|\vec{\boldsymbol{w}}\| := \|\vec{\boldsymbol{w}}\|_2$.

2.2 Cyclotomic Rings

Suppose (q) splits into l prime ideals of degree d/l in $\mathcal{R}$. This means $X^d + 1 \equiv \varphi_1 \ldots \varphi_l \pmod{q}$ with irreducible polynomials φ_j of degree d/l modulo q. We assume that $\mathbb{Z}_q$ contains a primitive $2l$-th root of unity $\zeta \in \mathbb{Z}_q$ but no elements whose order is a higher power of two, i.e. $q - 1 \equiv 2l \pmod{4l}$. Therefore, we have

$$X^d + 1 \equiv \prod_{j \in \mathbb{Z}_{2l}^\times} \left(X^{\frac{d}{l}} - \zeta^j \right) \pmod{q} \tag{1}$$

where ζ^j $(j \in \mathbb{Z}_{2l}^\times)$ ranges over all the l primitive $2l$-th roots of unity.

Let $\mathcal{M}_q := \{\boldsymbol{p} \in \mathbb{Z}_q[X] : \deg(\boldsymbol{p}) < d/l\}$. We define the Number Theoretic Transform (NTT) of a polynomial $\boldsymbol{p} \in \mathcal{R}_q$ as follows:

$$\mathsf{NTT}(\boldsymbol{p}) := \begin{bmatrix} \hat{\boldsymbol{p}}_0 \\ \vdots \\ \hat{\boldsymbol{p}}_{l-1} \end{bmatrix} \in \mathcal{M}_q^l \text{ where } \hat{\boldsymbol{p}}_j = \boldsymbol{p} \bmod (X^{\frac{d}{l}} - \zeta^{2j+1}).$$

We also define the inverse NTT operation. Namely, for a vector $\vec{v} \in \mathcal{M}_q^l$, $\mathsf{NTT}^{-1}(\vec{v})$ is the polynomial $\boldsymbol{p} \in \mathcal{R}_q$ such that $\mathsf{NTT}(\boldsymbol{p}) = \vec{v}$.

2.3 Automorphisms

The ring $\mathcal{R}_q$ has a group of automorphisms $\mathrm{Aut}(\mathcal{R}_q)$ that is isomorphic to $\mathbb{Z}_{2d}^\times \cong \mathbb{Z}_2 \times \mathbb{Z}_{d/2}$,

$$i \mapsto \sigma_i \colon \mathbb{Z}_{2d}^\times \to \mathrm{Aut}(\mathcal{R}_q),$$

where σ_i is defined by $\sigma_i(X) = X^i$. Note that for $i \in \mathbb{Z}_{2d}^\times$ and odd j it holds that $(\sigma_i(X - \zeta^j)) = (X - \zeta^{ji^{-1}})$ in $\mathcal{R}_q$ (as ideals), and for $\boldsymbol{f} \in \mathcal{R}_q$,

$$\sigma_i \left(\boldsymbol{f} \bmod (X - \zeta^j) \right) = \sigma_i(\boldsymbol{f}) \bmod \left(X - \zeta^{ji^{-1}} \right).$$

Let k be a divisor of l and $\sigma := \sigma_{2l/k+1} \in \mathsf{Aut}(\mathcal{R}_q)$. Then, we can write

$$(X^d + 1) = \prod_{j \in \mathbb{Z}_{2l/k}^\times} \prod_{i=0}^{k-1} \sigma^i \left(X^{\frac{d}{l}} - \zeta^j \right).$$

2.4 Challenge Space

Let $\mathcal{C} := \{-1,0,1\}^d \subset \mathcal{R}_q$ be the challenge set of ternary polynomials with coefficients $-1,0,1$. We define the following probability distribution $C : \mathcal{C} \rightarrow [0,1]$. The coefficients of a challenge $\boldsymbol{c} \leftarrow C$ are independently identically distributed with $P(0) = 1/2$ and $\Pr(1) = \Pr(-1) = 1/4$.

Consider the coefficients of the polynomial $\boldsymbol{c} \bmod (X^{d/l} - \zeta^j)$ for $\boldsymbol{c} \leftarrow C$. Then, all coefficients follow the same distribution over $\mathbb{Z}_q$. Let us write Y for the random variable over $\mathbb{Z}_q$ that follows this distribution. Attema et al. [ALS20] give an upper bound on the maximum probability of Y.

Lemma 2.1. *Let the random variable Y over $\mathbb{Z}_q$ be defined as above. Then for all $x \in \mathbb{Z}_q$,*

$$\Pr(Y = x) \leq \frac{1}{q} + \frac{2l}{q} \sum_{j \in \mathbb{Z}_q^\times / \langle \zeta \rangle} \prod_{i=0}^{l-1} \left| \frac{1}{2} + \frac{1}{2} \cos(2\pi j y \zeta^i / q) \right|. \tag{2}$$

In particular, [ALS20,ENS20] computed that for $q \approx 2^{32}$, the maximum probability for each coefficient of $c \bmod X^{d/l} - \zeta^j$ is around $2^{-31.4}$. In general, we will call this probability p.

An immediate consequence of Lemma 2.1 is that polynomial $\boldsymbol{c} \leftarrow C$ is invertible in $\mathcal{R}_q$ with overwhelming probability as long as parameters q, d, l are selected so that $q^{-d/l}$ is negligible.

Let k be a divisor of d such that $q^{-kd/l}$ is negligible and set $\sigma = \sigma_{2l/k+1}$. Let us define a probability distribution $\tilde{C}$ over $\mathcal{R}^k$ which first samples $\boldsymbol{c} = \boldsymbol{c}_0 + \boldsymbol{c}_1 X + \ldots + \boldsymbol{c}_{k-1} X^{k-1} \leftarrow C$ and outputs $(\boldsymbol{c}_0, \ldots, \boldsymbol{c}_{k-1})$ where each $\boldsymbol{c}_i$ is defined as $\boldsymbol{c}_i = \sum_{j=0}^{d/k-1} c_{jk+i} X^{jk}$. Clearly, we have

$$\boldsymbol{c} = \sum_{i=0}^{k-1} \boldsymbol{c}_i X^i.$$

2.5 Module-SIS and Module-LWE Problems

Security of the [BDL+18] commitment scheme used in our protocols relies on the well-known computational lattice problems, namely Module-LWE (M-LWE) and Module-SIS (M-SIS) [LS15]. Both problems are defined over $\mathcal{R}_q$.

Definition 2.2 (M-SIS$_{\kappa,m,B}$). *Given $\boldsymbol{A} \leftarrow \mathcal{R}_q^{\kappa \times m}$, the* Module-SIS *problem with parameters $\kappa, m > 0$ and $0 < B < q$ asks to find $\vec{\boldsymbol{z}} \in \mathcal{R}_q^m$ such that $\boldsymbol{A}\vec{\boldsymbol{z}} = \vec{\boldsymbol{0}}$ over $\mathcal{R}_q$ and $0 < \|\vec{\boldsymbol{z}}\| \leq B$. An algorithm $\mathcal{A}$ is said to have advantage ϵ in solving M-SIS$_{\kappa,m,B}$ if*

$$\Pr\left[0 < \|\vec{\boldsymbol{z}}\| \leq B \wedge \boldsymbol{A}\vec{\boldsymbol{z}} = \vec{\boldsymbol{0}} \,\middle|\, \boldsymbol{A} \leftarrow \mathcal{R}_q^{\kappa \times m};\ \vec{\boldsymbol{z}} \leftarrow \mathcal{A}(\boldsymbol{A})\right] \geq \epsilon.$$

Definition 2.3 (M-LWE$_{m,\lambda,\chi}$). *The* Module-LWE *problem with parameters $m, \lambda > 0$ and an error distribution χ over $\mathcal{R}$ asks the adversary $\mathcal{A}$ to distinguish between the following two cases: 1) $(\boldsymbol{A}, \boldsymbol{A}\vec{s} + \vec{e})$ for $\boldsymbol{A} \leftarrow \mathcal{R}_q^{m\times\lambda}$, a secret vector $\vec{s} \leftarrow \chi^\lambda$ and error vector $\vec{e} \leftarrow \chi^m$, and 2) $(\boldsymbol{A}, \vec{b}) \leftarrow \mathcal{R}_q^{m\times\lambda} \times \mathcal{R}_q^m$. Then, $\mathcal{A}$ is said to have advantage ϵ in solving M-LWE$_{m,\lambda,\chi}$ if*

$$\Big|\Pr\big[b = 1 \,\big|\, \boldsymbol{A} \leftarrow \mathcal{R}_q^{m\times\lambda};\ \vec{s} \leftarrow \chi^\lambda;\ \vec{e} \leftarrow \chi^m;\ b \leftarrow \mathcal{A}(\boldsymbol{A}, \boldsymbol{A}\vec{s} + \vec{e})\big] \qquad (3)$$
$$- \Pr\Big[b = 1 \,\Big|\, \boldsymbol{A} \leftarrow \mathcal{R}_q^{m\times\lambda};\ \vec{b} \leftarrow \mathcal{R}_q^m;\ b \leftarrow \mathcal{A}(\boldsymbol{A}, \vec{b})\Big]\Big| \geq \epsilon.$$

For our constructions in this work, the practical hardness of either of the problems against known attacks is not affected by the parameter m. Therefore, we sometimes simply write M-SIS$_{\kappa,B}$ or M-LWE$_{\lambda,\chi}$. The parameters κ and λ denote the *module ranks* for M-SIS and M-LWE, respectively.

2.6 Probability Distributions

For sampling randomness in the commitment scheme that we use, and to define a variant of the Ring Learning with Errors problem, we need to define an error distribution χ^d on $\mathcal{R}$. In this paper we sample the coefficients of the random polynomials in the commitment scheme using the distribution χ on $\{-1, 0, 1\}$ where ± 1 both have probability $5/16$ and 0 has probability $6/16$. This distribution is chosen (rather than the more "natural" uniform one) because it is easy to sample given a random bitstring by computing $a_1 + a_2 - b_1 - b_2 \bmod 3$ with uniformly random bits a_i, b_i.

Discrete Gaussian Distribution. We now define the discrete Gaussian distribution used for the rejection sampling.

Definition 2.4. *The* discrete Gaussian distribution *on $\mathcal{R}^\ell$ centered around $\vec{v} \in \mathcal{R}^\ell$ with standard deviation $\mathfrak{s} > 0$ is given by*

$$D_{\vec{v},\mathfrak{s}}^{\ell d}(\vec{z}) = \frac{e^{-\|\vec{z}-\vec{v}\|^2/2\mathfrak{s}^2}}{\sum_{\vec{z}'\in\mathcal{R}^\ell} e^{-\|\vec{z}'\|^2/2\mathfrak{s}^2}}.$$

When it is centered around $\vec{0} \in \mathcal{R}^\ell$ we write $D_{\mathfrak{s}}^{\ell d} = D_{\vec{0},\mathfrak{s}}^{\ell d}$.

2.7 Approximate Range Proofs

Baum and Lyubashevsky [BL17] showed that if $B\vec{s}$ has small coefficients, for a vector $\vec{s}$ over $\mathbb{Z}_q$ and uniformly random binary matrix B, then with high probability $\vec{s}$ must have small coefficients as well. More recently, Lyubashevsky et al. [LNS20a] generalise their result for $B\vec{s} + \vec{e}$ where $\vec{e}$ is an arbitrary vector over $\mathbb{Z}_q$. We extend the lemma for the case when B is sampled from a distribution centered at 0. The main advantage of this approach is that the infinity norm of $B\vec{s}$ decreases significantly, which is essential for the rejection sampling.

Concretely, we define the probability distribution $\mathsf{C} : \{-1, 0, 1\} \to [0, 1]$ such that $\Pr_{c \leftarrow \mathsf{C}}[c = 0] = p$ and $\Pr_{c \leftarrow \mathsf{C}}[c = 1] = \Pr_{c \leftarrow \mathsf{C}}[c = -1] = (1 - p)/2$ for some $p \in [0, 1]$. Then, we have the following lemma.

Lemma 2.5. *Let $\vec{s} \in \mathbb{Z}_q^m$ and $\vec{y} \in \mathbb{Z}_q^n$. Then*

$$\Pr\left[\|B\vec{s} + \vec{y}\|_\infty < \frac{1}{2}\|\vec{s}\|_\infty : B \leftarrow \mathsf{C}^{n \times m}\right] \le \max\{p, 1 - p\}^n.$$

We provide the proof of Lemma 2.5 in [LNS20b, Appendix A].

2.8 Commit-and-Prove

Let R_L be a polynomial-time verifiable relation containing (ck, x, w). We will call ck the commitment key, x the statement and w the witness. Also, we define a language L_{ck} as the set of statements x for which there exists a witness w such that $(ck, x, w) \in R_L$.

We define the commit-and-prove functionality similarly as in [EG14, CLOS02] for a relation R_L. Roughly speaking, we want to commit to messages $m_1, \ldots, m_n$ and prove certain statements about them. Therefore, $w = (m_1, \ldots, m_n)$ constitutes a witness for $x \in L_{ck}$.

Formally, a commit-and-prove functionality (CP) consists of four algorithms $CP = (\mathsf{Gen}, \mathsf{Com}, \mathsf{Prove}, \mathsf{Verify})$. We require $\mathsf{Com}, \mathsf{Verify}$ to be deterministic whereas $\mathsf{Gen}, \mathsf{Prove}$ are probabilistic.

- $\mathsf{Gen}(1^\mu)$: Given a security parameter μ, generates a commitment key ck. The commitment key specifies a message space $\mathcal{M}_{ck}$ a randomness space $\mathcal{R}_{ck}$ and commitment space $\mathcal{C}_{ck}$.
- $\mathsf{Com}_{ck}(m; r)$: Given a commitment key ck, a message $m \in \mathcal{M}_{ck}$ and randomness $r \in \mathcal{R}_{ck}$ returns a commitment $c \in \mathcal{C}_{ck}$.
- $\mathsf{Prove}_{ck}(x, ((m_1, r_1), \ldots, (m_n, r_n)))$: Given a commitment key ck, statement x and commitment openings $m_i \in \mathcal{M}_{ck}, r_i \in \mathcal{R}_{ck}$ and $(ck, x, (m_1, \ldots, m_n)) \in R_L$ returns a proof π.
- $\mathsf{Verify}_{ck}(x, c_1, \ldots, c_n, \pi)$: Given a commitment key ck, a statement x, a proof π and commitments $c_i \in \mathcal{C}_{ck}$, outputs 1 (accept) or 0 (reject).

Definition 2.6 (Correctness). *The commit-and-prove functionality CP has statistical correctness with correctness error $\rho : \mathbb{N} \to [0, 1]$ if for all adversaries $\mathcal{A}$:*

$$\Pr\left[\begin{array}{l} ck \leftarrow \mathsf{Gen}(1^\mu); (x, m_1, r_1 \ldots, m_n, r_n) \leftarrow \mathcal{A}(ck); c_i = \mathsf{Com}_{ck}(m_i; r_i); \\ \pi \leftarrow \mathsf{Prove}_{ck}(x, ((m_1, r_1), \ldots, (m_n, r_n))) : \mathsf{Verify}_{ck}(x, c_1, \ldots, c_n, \pi) = 0 \end{array}\right] \le \rho(\mu) \quad (4)$$

where $\mathcal{A}$ outputs $m_i \in \mathcal{M}_{ck}, r_i \in \mathcal{R}_{ck}$ so that $(ck, x, (m_1, \ldots, m_n)) \in R_L$.

Definition 2.7 (Knowledge Soundness). *The commit-and-prove functionality CP is knowledge sound with knowledge error $\epsilon : \mathbb{N} \to [0, 1]$ if for all PPT $\mathcal{A}$ there exists an expected polynomial time extractor $\mathcal{E}$ so that :*

$$\Pr\left[\begin{array}{l} ck \leftarrow \mathsf{Gen}(1^\mu); (x, c_1, \ldots, c_n, \pi) \leftarrow \mathcal{A}(ck); ((m_1^*, r_1^*) \ldots, (m_n^*, r_n^*)) \leftarrow \mathcal{E}(c_1, \ldots, c_n) : \\ \mathsf{Verify}_{ck}(x, c_1, \ldots, c_n, \pi) = 1 \wedge ((ck, x, (m_1^*, \ldots, m_n^*)) \notin R_L \vee \exists i, \mathsf{Com}(m_i^*; r_i^*) \neq c_i) \end{array}\right] \quad (5)$$

is less or equal to $\epsilon(\mu)$*, where* $\mathcal{E}$ *outputs* $m_i^* \in \mathcal{M}_{ck}$ *and* $r_i^* \in \mathcal{R}_{ck}$*.*

In lattice-based zero-knowledge proofs, it is sometimes useful to relax the definition of knowledge soundness by only requiring $r_1^*, \ldots, r_n^* \in \bar{\mathcal{R}}_{ck}$ where $\mathcal{R}_{ck} \subseteq \bar{\mathcal{R}}_{ck}$. However, the definition still makes sense if one can argue that the extracted commitments are still binding. This is what we do by additionally defining notions of *weak opening* (Definition 2.9).

The next property is a new notion called *simulatability*. Informally, it means that there exists an efficient simulator $\mathcal{S}$ which can simulate both the commitment generation and the proof at the same time.

Definition 2.8 (Simulatability). *The commit-and-prove functionality* CP *is simulatable if there exist PPT simulators* SimCom *and* SimProve *such that for all PPT adversaries* $\mathcal{A}$*:*

$$\begin{aligned}
&\Pr\left[\begin{array}{l} ck \leftarrow \mathsf{Gen}(1^\mu); (x, m_1, \ldots, m_n) \leftarrow \mathcal{A}(ck); r_1, \ldots, r_n \leftarrow \xi; \forall i, c_i = \mathsf{Com}_{ck}(m_i, r_i); \\ \pi \leftarrow \mathsf{Prove}_{ck}(x, (m_1, r_1), \ldots, (m_n, r_n)) : (ck, x, (m_1, \ldots, m_n)) \in R_L \wedge \mathcal{A}(c_1, \ldots, c_n, \pi) = 1 \end{array}\right] \\
&\approx \Pr\left[\begin{array}{l} ck \leftarrow \mathsf{Gen}(1^\mu); (x, m_1, \ldots, m_n) \leftarrow \mathcal{A}(ck); , c_1, \ldots, c_n \leftarrow \mathsf{SimCom}_{ck}(x); \\ \pi \leftarrow \mathsf{SimProve}_{ck}(x, c_1, \ldots, c_n) : (ck, x, (m_1, \ldots, m_n)) \in R_L \wedge \mathcal{A}(c_1, \ldots, c_n, \pi) = 1 \end{array}\right]
\end{aligned} \tag{6}$$

where ξ *is a probability distribution on* $\mathcal{R}_{ck}$*.*

The difference between simulatability and zero-knowledge is that randomness $r_1, \ldots, r_n$ is directly generated from ξ as it would in the real-world protocol rather than chosen from adversary. This property becomes crucial when using the BDLOP commitments [BDL+18].

2.9 Commitment Scheme

We recall the BDLOP commitment scheme from [BDL+18] used in our constructions as well as previous works [ALS20, ENS20, LNS20a]. Suppose that we want to commit to a message vector $\vec{\boldsymbol{m}} = (\boldsymbol{m}_1, \ldots, \boldsymbol{m}_n) \in \mathcal{R}_q^n$ for $n \geq 1$ and that module ranks of κ and λ are required for M-SIS and M-LWE security, respectively. Then, in the key generation, a matrix $\boldsymbol{B}_0 \leftarrow \mathcal{R}_q^{\kappa \times (\kappa+\lambda+n)}$ and vectors $\vec{\boldsymbol{b}}_1, \ldots, \vec{\boldsymbol{b}}_n \leftarrow \mathcal{R}_q^{\kappa+\lambda+n}$ are generated and output as public parameters. Note that one could choose to generate $\boldsymbol{B}_0, \vec{\boldsymbol{b}}_1, \ldots, \vec{\boldsymbol{b}}_n$ in a more structured way as in [BDL+18] since it saves some computation. However, for readability, we write the commitment matrices in the "Knapsack" form as above. In our case, the hiding property of the commitment scheme is established via the duality between the Knapsack and MLWE problems. We refer to [EZS+19, Appendix C] for a more detailed discussion.

To commit to the message $\vec{\boldsymbol{m}}$, we first sample $\vec{\boldsymbol{r}} \leftarrow \chi^{d \cdot (\kappa+\lambda+n)}$. Now, there are two parts of the commitment scheme: the binding part and the message encoding part. In particular, we compute

$$\begin{aligned}
\vec{\boldsymbol{t}}_0 &= \boldsymbol{B}_0 \vec{\boldsymbol{r}} \bmod q, \\
\boldsymbol{t}_i &= \langle \vec{\boldsymbol{b}}_i, \vec{\boldsymbol{r}} \rangle + \boldsymbol{m}_i \bmod q,
\end{aligned}$$

for $i \in [n]$, where $\vec{t}_0$ forms the binding part and each $\boldsymbol{t}_i$ encodes a message polynomial $\boldsymbol{m}_i$.

We recall the notion of a weak opening [ALS20].

Definition 2.9. *A* weak opening *for the commitment* $\vec{t} = \vec{t}_0 \parallel \boldsymbol{t}_1 \parallel \cdots \parallel \boldsymbol{t}_n$ *consists of* d *polynomials* $\bar{\boldsymbol{c}}_i \in \mathcal{R}_q$*, a randomness vector* $\vec{\boldsymbol{r}}^*$ *over* $\mathcal{R}_q$ *and messages* $\boldsymbol{m}_1^*, \ldots, \boldsymbol{m}_n^* \in \mathcal{R}_q$ *such that*

$$\begin{aligned}
&\left\|\bar{\boldsymbol{c}}_i\right\|_1 \leq 2\mathsf{k} \text{ and } \bar{\boldsymbol{c}}_i \bmod X - \zeta^{2i+1} \neq 0 \text{ for all } 0 \leq i < d, \\
&\left\|\bar{\boldsymbol{c}}_i \vec{\boldsymbol{r}}^*\right\|_2 \leq 2\beta \text{ for all } 0 \leq i < d, \\
&\boldsymbol{B}_0 \vec{\boldsymbol{r}}^* = \vec{\boldsymbol{t}}_0, \\
&\langle \vec{\boldsymbol{b}}_i, \vec{\boldsymbol{r}}^* \rangle + \boldsymbol{m}_i^* = \boldsymbol{t}_i \text{ for } i \in [n]
\end{aligned}$$

Attema et al. show that the commitment scheme is still binding with respect to weak openings.

2.10 Framework by Lyubashevsky et al. [LNS20a]

Recently, Lyubashevsky et al. [LNS20a] proposed a general framework for proving linear and multiplicative relations between committed messages. Concretely, suppose that the prover $\mathcal{P}$ has a vector of n messages $\vec{m} = (\vec{m}_1, \ldots, \vec{m}_n) \in \mathbb{Z}_q^{nl}$. Let pp be a public set of polynomials $P : \left(\mathbb{Z}_q^l\right)^n \rightarrow \mathbb{Z}_q^l$ of n variables over $\mathbb{Z}_q^l$ with standard component-wise addition and multiplication and define $\alpha = \max_{P \in \mathsf{pp}} \deg(P)$[4]. For readability, we will often "concatenate" polynomials in pp, i.e. we will write $\mathsf{pp} = \{P_1, \ldots, P_t\}$ where each $P_i : \left(\mathbb{Z}_q^l\right)^n \rightarrow \mathbb{Z}_q^{u_i l}$ and $u_1, \ldots, u_t > 0$.

For the linear relations, let us set $\mathsf{ulp} = (A, \vec{u}) \in \mathbb{Z}_q^{vl \times nl} \times \mathbb{Z}_q^{vl}$. In practice, A can have arbitrary number of rows but then we would have to pad rows with zeroes in order to get a multiple of l.

Overall, [LNS20a] provides a protocol $\boldsymbol{\pi} = (\mathsf{Com}_{n,\alpha}, \Pi_n^\alpha(\mathsf{pp}, \mathsf{ulp}))$ where the prover $\mathcal{P}$ first generates the BDLOP commitments to $\vec{m}$ (sub-protocol $\mathsf{Com}_{n,\alpha}$) and then wants to prove that $\vec{m} \in \mathcal{L}_n(\mathsf{pp}, \mathsf{ulp})$ (sub-protocol $\Pi_n^\alpha(\mathsf{pp}, \mathsf{ulp})$) where

$$\mathcal{L}_n(\mathsf{pp}, \mathsf{ulp}) := \{\vec{m} \in \mathbb{Z}_q^{nl} : \forall P \in \mathsf{pp}, P(\vec{m}) = \vec{0} \text{ and } A\vec{m} = \vec{u}\}. \quad (7)$$

In this paper we are only interested in applying the LNS framework only for the case $l = d$, i.e. $X^d + 1$ splits completely into linear factors modulo q, unless stated otherwise.

Let us formulate the protocol π in terms of the commit-and-prove functionality from Sect. 2.8. First, the relation R_{LNS} we are interested in here is

$$(ck, (\mathsf{pp}, \mathsf{ulp}), \vec{m}) \in R_{LNS} \iff \vec{m} \in \mathcal{L}_n(\mathsf{pp}, \mathsf{ulp}).$$

We define a CP functionality $LNS = (\mathsf{LNSGen}, \mathsf{LNSCom}, \mathsf{LNSProve}^U, \mathsf{LNSVerify}^U)$ for the relation R_{LNS} as follows:

[4] Although Lyubashevsky et al. only consider the case $\alpha \leq 3$, it can be easily generalised by sending more garbage commitments.

- $\mathsf{LNSGen}(1^\mu)$: It outputs a commitment key ck specifies the message space $\mathcal{M}_{ck} = \mathbb{Z}_q^{nd}$, randomness space $\mathcal{R}_{ck} = \{-1,0,1\}^{d\cdot(\kappa+\lambda+n+\alpha)}$[5] and the commitment space $\mathcal{C}_{ck} = \mathcal{R}_q^{\kappa+n}$. It also generates the matrix $\boldsymbol{B}_0 \leftarrow \mathcal{R}_q^{\kappa\times(\kappa+\lambda+n+\alpha)}$ and vectors $\vec{\boldsymbol{b}}_1,\ldots,\vec{\boldsymbol{b}}_{n+\alpha} \leftarrow \mathcal{R}_q^{\kappa+\lambda+n+\alpha}$.
- $\mathsf{LNSCom}_{ck}((\vec{m}_1,\ldots,\vec{m}_n);\vec{\boldsymbol{r}})$ outputs $(\vec{\boldsymbol{t}}_0,\boldsymbol{t}_1,\ldots,\boldsymbol{t}_n)$ where

$$\vec{\boldsymbol{t}}_0 = \boldsymbol{B}_0\vec{\boldsymbol{r}} \bmod q,$$
$$\boldsymbol{t}_i = \langle\vec{\boldsymbol{b}}_i,\vec{\boldsymbol{r}}\rangle + \mathsf{NTT}^{-1}(\vec{m}_i) \bmod q \text{ for } i\in[n].$$

- $\mathsf{LNSProve}^U_{ck}((\mathsf{pp},\mathsf{ulp}),\vec{m}_1,\ldots,\vec{m}_n,\vec{\boldsymbol{r}})$: It runs the non-interactive version of the protocol $\Pi_n^\alpha(\mathsf{pp},\mathsf{ulp})$ (e.g. [LNS20a, Fig. 8]), using the Fiat-Shamir transform, and outputs the proof π. Letter U denotes that the algorithm uses uniform rejection sampling.
- $\mathsf{LNSVerify}^U_{ck}\left((\mathsf{pp},\mathsf{ulp}),\vec{\boldsymbol{t}}_0,\boldsymbol{t}_1,\ldots,\boldsymbol{t}_n,\pi\right)$: Check the verification equations of $\Pi_n^\alpha(\mathsf{pp},\mathsf{ulp})$ (e.g. [LNS20a, Fig. 9]).

Eventually, Lyubashevsky et al. show that the commit-and-prove functionality LNS defined above for the relation R_{LNS} is both knowledge sound with negligible knowledge error under the Module-SIS assumption and simulatable under the Module-LWE assumption where the randomness $\vec{\boldsymbol{r}}$ distribution is defined over $\xi = \chi^{d\cdot(\kappa+\lambda+n+\alpha)}$.

3 Opening Proof with Improved Rejection Sampling

In lattice-based zero-knowledge proofs, e.g.[BLS19, ALS20], the prover will want to output a vector $\vec{\boldsymbol{z}}$ whose distribution should be independent of a secret randomness vector $\vec{\boldsymbol{r}}$, so that $\vec{\boldsymbol{z}}$ cannot be used to gain any information on the prover's secret. During the protocol, the prover computes $\vec{\boldsymbol{z}} = \vec{\boldsymbol{y}} + \boldsymbol{c}\vec{\boldsymbol{r}}$ where $\vec{\boldsymbol{r}}$ is the randomness used to commit to the prover's secret, $\boldsymbol{c} \leftarrow C$ is a challenge polynomial, and $\vec{\boldsymbol{y}}$ is a "masking" vector. In order to remove the dependency of $\vec{\boldsymbol{z}}$ on $\vec{\boldsymbol{r}}$, one applies the *rejection sampling* technique.

Lemma 3.1 ([BLS19]). *Let $V \subseteq \mathcal{R}^\ell$ be a set of polynomials with norm at most T and $\rho\colon V \to [0,1]$ be a probability distribution. Also, write $\mathfrak{s} = 11T$ and $M = 3$. Now, sample $\vec{\boldsymbol{v}} \leftarrow \rho$ and $\vec{\boldsymbol{y}} \leftarrow D_{\mathfrak{s}}^{\ell d}$, set $\vec{\boldsymbol{z}} = \vec{\boldsymbol{y}} + \vec{\boldsymbol{v}}$, and run $b \leftarrow \mathsf{Rej}_0(\vec{\boldsymbol{z}},\vec{\boldsymbol{v}},\mathfrak{s})$ as defined in Fig. 2. Then, the probability that $b = 0$ is at least $(1-2^{-100})/M$ and the distribution of $(\vec{\boldsymbol{v}},\vec{\boldsymbol{z}})$, conditioned on $b = 0$, is within statistical distance of $2^{-100}/M$ of the product distribution $\rho \times D_{\mathfrak{s}}^{\ell d}$.*

Let us recall how parameters $\mathfrak{s}$ and M are usually selected. Namely, the repetition rate M is chosen to be an upper-bound on:

$$\frac{D_{\mathfrak{s}}^{\ell d}(\vec{\boldsymbol{z}})}{D_{\vec{\boldsymbol{v}},\mathfrak{s}}^{\ell d}(\vec{\boldsymbol{z}})} = \exp\left(\frac{-2\langle\vec{\boldsymbol{z}},\vec{\boldsymbol{v}}\rangle + \|\vec{\boldsymbol{v}}\|^2}{2\mathfrak{s}^2}\right) \le \exp\left(\frac{24\mathfrak{s}\|\vec{\boldsymbol{v}}\| + \|\vec{\boldsymbol{v}}\|^2}{2\mathfrak{s}^2}\right) = M. \quad (8)$$

[5] Note that the length of $\vec{\boldsymbol{r}}$ is not $\kappa+\lambda+n$ as in Sect. 2.9 since the prover will later in the protocol commit to α garbage polynomials using the same $\vec{\boldsymbol{r}}$.

$\mathrm{Rej}_0(\vec{z}, \vec{v}, \mathfrak{s})$	$\mathrm{Rej}_1(\vec{z}, \vec{v}, \mathfrak{s})$
01 $u \leftarrow [0,1)$	01 If $\langle \vec{z}, \vec{v} \rangle < 0$
02 If $u > \frac{1}{M} \cdot \exp\left(\frac{-2\langle \vec{z}, \vec{v}\rangle + \|\vec{v}\|^2}{2\mathfrak{s}^2}\right)$	02 return 1
03 return 1	03 $u \leftarrow [0,1)$
04 Else	04 If $u > \frac{1}{M} \cdot \exp\left(\frac{-2\langle \vec{z}, \vec{v}\rangle + \|\vec{v}\|^2}{2\mathfrak{s}^2}\right)$
05 return 0	05 return 1
	06 Else
	07 return 0

Fig. 2. Two rejection sampling algorithms: the one used in previous works (left) and the one proposed in this section (right).

For the inequality we used the tail bound which says that with probability at least $1 - 2^{100}$ we have $|\langle \vec{z}, \vec{v}\rangle| < 12\mathfrak{s}\|\vec{v}\|$ for $\vec{z} \leftarrow D_{\mathfrak{s}}^{\ell d}$ [Ban93, Lyu12]. Hence, by setting $\mathfrak{s} = 11\|\vec{v}\|$ we obtain $M \approx 3$.

In this section we propose a new way to apply rejection sampling. Namely, we force $\vec{z}$ to satisfy $\langle \vec{z}, \vec{v}\rangle \geq 0$, otherwise we abort. With this additional assumption, we can set M in the following way:

$$\exp\left(\frac{-2\langle \vec{z}, \vec{v}\rangle + \|\vec{v}\|^2}{2\mathfrak{s}^2}\right) \leq \exp\left(\frac{\|\vec{v}\|^2}{2\mathfrak{s}^2}\right) = M. \tag{9}$$

Hence, for $M \approx 3$ one would select $\mathfrak{s} = 0.675 \cdot \|\vec{v}\|$. Note that the probability for $\vec{z} \leftarrow D_{\sigma}^{\ell d}$ that $\langle \vec{z}, \vec{v}\rangle \geq 0$ is at least $1/2$. Hence, the expected number of rejections would be at most $2M = 6$. On the other hand, if one aims for $M = 6$ repetitions using (8), then $\mathfrak{s} = 6.74 \cdot \|\vec{v}\|$. Thus, we manage to reduce the standard deviation by around a factor of 10.

Subset Rejection Sampling. In order to prove security of our new rejection sampling algorithm, we need the following modification of the rejection sampling lemma by Lyubashevsky [Lyu12].

Lemma 3.2 (Subset Rejection Sampling). *Let V be an arbitrary set and $h : V \to \mathbb{R}, f : \mathbb{Z}^m \to \mathbb{R}$ be probability distributions. Also define a family of set $S_v \subseteq \mathbb{Z}^m$ for $v \in V$ and $S = \{(z, v) \subseteq V \times \mathbb{Z}^m : z \in S_v\}$. Suppose $g_v : \mathbb{Z}^m \to \mathbb{R}$ is a family distributions indexed by all $v \in V$ and there exist $M, \gamma \geq 0$ which satisfy:*

$$\begin{aligned} &\forall v \in V, z \in S_v : M g_v(z) \geq f(z) \\ &\forall v \in V : \sum_{z \in S_v} f(z) \geq \gamma. \end{aligned} \tag{10}$$

Then the distributions of the output of $\mathcal{A}$ and $\mathcal{F}$, defined in Fig. 3, are identical. Moreover, the probability that $\mathcal{A}$ and $\mathcal{F}$ output something is at least $\frac{\gamma}{M}$.

$\mathcal{A}$	$\mathcal{F}$
01 $v \leftarrow h$	01 $v \leftarrow h$
02 $z \leftarrow g_v$	02 $z \leftarrow f$
03 if $z \notin S_v$ then abort	03 if $z \notin S_v$ then abort
04 output (z, v) with probability $\frac{f(z)}{Mg_v(z)}$	04 output (z, v) with probability $\frac{1}{M}$.

Fig. 3. Algorithms $\mathcal{A}$ and $\mathcal{F}$ for Lemma 3.2.

Proof. Let $v \in V$. If $z \in S_v$, the probability that $\mathcal{A}$ outputs z is equal to $g_v(z) \cdot \frac{f(z)}{Mg_v(z)} = \frac{f(z)}{M}$. Otherwise, the probability that $\mathcal{A}$ outputs $z \notin S_v$ is exactly 0. Hence

$$\Pr[\mathcal{A} \text{ outputs something}] = \sum_{v \in V} h(v) \sum_{z \in S_v} \frac{f(z)}{M} \geq \frac{\gamma}{M}.$$

Moreover, the probability that $\mathcal{F}$ outputs something is also $\frac{\sum_{(z,v)\in S} h(v)f(z)}{M}$. Hence:

$$\begin{aligned}
\Delta(\mathcal{A}, \mathcal{F}) &= \frac{1}{2}\left(\sum_{(z,v)\in S} |\mathcal{A}(z,v) - \mathcal{F}(z,v)|\right) \\
&= \frac{1}{2}\sum_{v\in V} h(v)\left(\sum_{z\in S_v}\left|g_v(z)\cdot\frac{f(z)}{Mg_v(z)} - \frac{f(z)}{M}\right|\right) \\
&= \frac{1}{2}\sum_{v\in V} h(v)\left(\sum_{z\in S_v}\left|\frac{f(z)}{M} - \frac{f(z)}{M}\right|\right) = 0.
\end{aligned}$$

□

Later on, we will consider the special case when $f := D^m_{\mathfrak{s}}, g_{\vec{v}} := D^m_{\vec{v},\mathfrak{s}}$ for $\vec{v} \in V \subseteq \mathbb{Z}^m$ and

$$S_v := \{\vec{z} \in \mathbb{Z}^m : \langle \vec{v}, \vec{z} \rangle \geq 0\}.$$

Then, the probability that $\mathcal{A}$ outputs something is at least:

$$\frac{1}{M}\sum_{\vec{v}\in V} h(\vec{v}) \Pr_{\vec{z}\leftarrow D^m_{\mathfrak{s}}}[\langle \vec{v}, \vec{z}\rangle \geq 0] \geq \frac{1}{2M}.$$

Therefore, we can set $\gamma = 1/2$. Here, we used the fact that $\Pr_{\vec{z}\leftarrow D^m_{\mathfrak{s}}}[\langle \vec{v}, \vec{z}\rangle > 0] = \Pr_{\vec{z}\leftarrow D^m_{\mathfrak{s}}}[\langle \vec{v}, \vec{z}\rangle < 0]$. We also highlight that the value M we chose in (9) indeed satisfies Eq. 10.

Extended M-LWE. One observes that with the new approach, the verifier learns some new information about the secret. Indeed, if a prover $\mathcal{P}$ returns $\vec{z}$ then the verifier $\mathcal{V}$ knows that $\langle \vec{z}, \vec{v}\rangle \geq 0$. However, later on we will show that the opening proof from [ALS20] using the new rejection sampling is still simulatable assuming that a new problem, which we call *Extended M-LWE*, is computationally hard. For readability, we will describe it in a "knapsack" form.

Definition 3.3 (Extended M-LWE$_{m,k,\lambda,\chi,\xi_1,\xi_2}$). *The* Extended Module-LWE *problem with parameters $m, \lambda > 0$ and error distributions χ, ξ_1 and ξ_2 over $\mathcal{R}$ and $\mathcal{R}^k$ respectively, asks the adversary $\mathcal{A}$ to distinguish between the following two cases:*

1. $\left(\boldsymbol{B}, \boldsymbol{B}\vec{\boldsymbol{r}}, \boldsymbol{c}_1, \ldots, \boldsymbol{c}_k, \vec{\boldsymbol{z}}, \mathsf{sign}\left(\left\langle \vec{\boldsymbol{z}}, \begin{pmatrix} \boldsymbol{c}_1\vec{\boldsymbol{r}} \\ \vdots \\ \boldsymbol{c}_k\vec{\boldsymbol{r}} \end{pmatrix} \right\rangle\right)\right)$ *for $\boldsymbol{B} \leftarrow \mathcal{R}_q^{m\times(m+\lambda)}$, a secret vector $\vec{\boldsymbol{r}} \leftarrow \chi^{m+\lambda}$ and $(\vec{\boldsymbol{z}}, \boldsymbol{c}_1, \ldots, \boldsymbol{c}_k) \leftarrow \xi_1^{k(m+\lambda)} \times \xi_2$*
2. $\left(\boldsymbol{B}, \vec{\boldsymbol{u}}, \boldsymbol{c}_1, \ldots, \boldsymbol{c}_k, \vec{\boldsymbol{z}}, \mathsf{sign}\left(\left\langle \vec{\boldsymbol{z}}, \begin{pmatrix} \boldsymbol{c}_1\vec{\boldsymbol{r}} \\ \vdots \\ \boldsymbol{c}_k\vec{\boldsymbol{r}} \end{pmatrix} \right\rangle\right)\right)$ *for $\boldsymbol{B} \leftarrow \mathcal{R}_q^{m\times(m+\lambda)}, \vec{\boldsymbol{u}} \leftarrow \mathcal{R}_q^m$ and $(\vec{\boldsymbol{z}}, \boldsymbol{c}_1, \ldots, \boldsymbol{c}_k) \leftarrow \xi_1^{k(m+\lambda)} \times \xi_2$*

where $\mathsf{sign}(a) = 1$ *if $a \geq 0$ and 0 otherwise. Then, $\mathcal{A}$ is said to have advantage ϵ in solving Extended M-LWE$_{m,k,\lambda,\chi,\xi_1,\xi_2}$ if*

$$\Big|\Pr\Big[b = 1 \Big| \boldsymbol{B} \leftarrow \mathcal{R}_q^{m\times(m+\lambda)};\ \vec{\boldsymbol{r}} \leftarrow \chi^{m+\lambda};\ \vec{\boldsymbol{z}} \leftarrow \xi_1^{k(m+\lambda)};\ \vec{\boldsymbol{c}} \leftarrow \xi_2;\ b \leftarrow \mathcal{A}(\boldsymbol{B}, \boldsymbol{B}\vec{\boldsymbol{r}}, \vec{\boldsymbol{z}}, \vec{\boldsymbol{c}}, s)\Big]$$
$$- \Pr\Big[b = 1 \Big| \boldsymbol{B} \leftarrow \mathcal{R}_q^{m\times\lambda};\ \vec{\boldsymbol{u}} \leftarrow \mathcal{R}_q^m;\ \vec{\boldsymbol{z}} \leftarrow \xi_1^{k(m+\lambda)};\vec{\boldsymbol{c}} \leftarrow \xi_2\,;\ b \leftarrow \mathcal{A}(\boldsymbol{B}, \vec{\boldsymbol{u}}, \vec{\boldsymbol{z}}, \vec{\boldsymbol{c}}, s)\Big]\Big| \geq \epsilon.$$

where

$$s = \mathsf{sign}\left(\left\langle \vec{\boldsymbol{z}}, \begin{pmatrix} \boldsymbol{c}_1\vec{\boldsymbol{r}} \\ \vdots \\ \boldsymbol{c}_k\vec{\boldsymbol{r}} \end{pmatrix} \right\rangle\right) \quad \text{and } \vec{\boldsymbol{c}} = (\boldsymbol{c}_1, \ldots, \boldsymbol{c}_k).$$

To simplify notation, we will write Extended M-LWE$_{m,\lambda}$ to denote Extended M-LWE$_{m,1,\lambda,\chi^d,D_{\mathfrak{s}}^d,C}$ where χ is defined in Sect. 2.6.

We note that the LWE problem with various side information has already been discussed in e.g. [DGK+10, AP12, DDGR20]. As far as we are aware, our new variant of M-LWE is the closest to the Extended LWE problem defined by Alperin-Sheriff and Peikert [AP12][6]. Indeed, in [LNS20b, Appendix D] we show that hardness of the non-algebraic version of our Extended M-LWE (i.e. without any polynomial ring structure) can be reduced to plain LWE using similar techniques as in [AP12].

Hardness of Ring/Module-LWE is often analysed as an LWE problem since, so far, the best known attacks do not make use of the algebraic structure of the polynomial ring [ADPS15]. Then, the only two attacks which would be relevant to our Module-LWE problem are be the primal and dual attacks

[6] In [AP12] the hint is the inner product $\langle\vec{r}, \vec{z}\rangle$ of the secret vector $\vec{r}$ and some $\vec{z}$ sampled from a given distribution D.

[Alb17, AGVW17, APS15]. Interestingly, the concrete analysis suggests that solving search-LWE (using the primal attack) is more efficient than solving the decisional version of LWE (using the dual attack). Thus, we believe that the search Extended-MLWE problem should still be hard with one bit, i.e. s, leaked since the vector $\vec{r}$ has high enough entropy.

3.1 Concrete Instantiation

We describe how to apply our rejection sampling in the opening proof by Attema et al. [ALS20]. For readability, we consider the simple version of the protocol without any commitment compression [DKL+18] or Galois automorphisms [LNS20a, Appendix A.3] for boosting soundness. We discuss how to apply all those improvements in Sect. 3.2 and [LNS20b, Appendix B].

One observes that the protocol presented in Fig. 4 is not very meaningful since it only shows that prover $\mathcal{P}$ has a polynomial $\boldsymbol{m} \in \mathcal{R}_q$. However, it is a key ingredient to prove linear [ENS20] and multiplicative [ALS20] relations between committed messages.

Formally, let us define the following the commit-and-prove functionality $CP = (\mathsf{Gen}, \mathsf{Com}, \mathsf{Prove}, \mathsf{Verify})$:

- $\mathsf{Gen}(1^\mu)$: Given a security parameter μ, generates a commitment key ck which specifies a message space $\mathcal{M}_{ck} = R_q$, a randomness space $\mathcal{R}_{ck} = \{-1, 0, 1\}^{(\lambda+\kappa+1)d}$ and commitment space $\mathcal{C}_{ck} = \mathcal{R}_q^{\kappa+1}$. It also generates the matrix $\boldsymbol{B}_0 \leftarrow \mathcal{R}_q^{\kappa \times (\kappa+\lambda+1)}$ and the vector $\vec{\boldsymbol{b}}_1 \leftarrow \mathcal{R}_q^{\kappa+\lambda+1}$.
- $\mathsf{Com}_{ck}(\boldsymbol{m}; \vec{\boldsymbol{r}})$: Given a commitment key ck, a message $\boldsymbol{m} \in \mathcal{M}_{ck}$ and randomness $\vec{\boldsymbol{r}} \in \mathcal{R}_{ck}$ returns a commitment $(\vec{\boldsymbol{t}}_0, \boldsymbol{t}_1) = (\boldsymbol{B}_0\vec{\boldsymbol{r}}, \langle \vec{\boldsymbol{b}}_1, \vec{\boldsymbol{r}} \rangle + \boldsymbol{m}) \in \mathcal{C}_{ck}$.
- $\mathsf{Prove}_{ck}(x, \boldsymbol{m}, \vec{\boldsymbol{r}})$: It first generates $\vec{\boldsymbol{y}} \leftarrow D_{\mathfrak{s}}^{\kappa+\lambda+1}$ and computes $\boldsymbol{c} = H(\boldsymbol{B}_0\vec{\boldsymbol{y}})$. Then, it computes $\vec{\boldsymbol{z}} = \vec{\boldsymbol{y}} + \boldsymbol{c}\vec{\boldsymbol{r}}$ and gets $b \leftarrow \mathsf{Rej}_1(\vec{\boldsymbol{z}}, \boldsymbol{c}\vec{\boldsymbol{r}}, \mathfrak{s})$. If $b = 0$, it outputs $\pi = (\boldsymbol{c}, \vec{\boldsymbol{z}})$.
- $\mathsf{Verify}_{ck}\left(x, \vec{\boldsymbol{t}}_0, \boldsymbol{t}_1, \pi\right)$: Parse $\pi = (\boldsymbol{c}, \vec{\boldsymbol{z}})$. If $\|\vec{\boldsymbol{z}}\| \leq \mathfrak{s}\sqrt{2(\lambda + \kappa + 1)d}$ and $\boldsymbol{c} = H(\vec{\boldsymbol{B}}_0\vec{\boldsymbol{z}} - \boldsymbol{c}\vec{\boldsymbol{t}}_0)$, return 1. Otherwise, return 0.

Here, $H : \{0, 1\}^* \to \{-1, 0, 1\}^d \subset \mathcal{R}_q$ is a random oracle which generates output from the distribution C (see Sect. 2.4). The language R_L, for which CP is defined, is trivial: $(ck, x, \boldsymbol{m}) \in R_L \iff \boldsymbol{m} \in \mathcal{R}_q$.

Correctness and knowledge soundness of CP can be proven almost identically as in [ALS20, Theorem 4.4]. Hence, we will only focus on simulatability.

Theorem 3.4. *Suppose Extended M-LWE*$_{\kappa+1,\lambda}$ *is computationally hard. Then, the commit-and-prove functionality* $CP = (\mathsf{Gen}, \mathsf{Com}, \mathsf{Prove}, \mathsf{Verify})$ *defined above for the language* R_L *is simulatable in the random oracle model* H.

Proof. Let us consider the following hybrid algorithms.

- $\mathsf{Prove}^1_{ck}(x, \boldsymbol{m}, \vec{\boldsymbol{r}})$: It first generates $\vec{\boldsymbol{y}} \leftarrow D_{\mathfrak{s}}^{\kappa+\lambda+1}, \boldsymbol{c} \leftarrow C$. Then, it computes $\vec{\boldsymbol{z}} = \vec{\boldsymbol{y}} + \boldsymbol{c}\vec{\boldsymbol{r}}$ and gets $b \leftarrow \mathsf{Rej}_1(\vec{\boldsymbol{z}}, \boldsymbol{c}\vec{\boldsymbol{r}}, \mathfrak{s})$. If $b = 1$, it outputs $\pi = (\boldsymbol{c}, \vec{\boldsymbol{z}})$ and programs $\boldsymbol{c} = H(\boldsymbol{B}_0\vec{\boldsymbol{z}} - \boldsymbol{c}\vec{\boldsymbol{t}}_0)$.

Prover $\mathcal{P}$		Verifier $\mathcal{V}$
Inputs:		
$\boldsymbol{B}_0 \in \mathcal{R}_q^{\kappa\times(\lambda+\kappa+1)}, \vec{\boldsymbol{b}}_1 \in \mathcal{R}_q^{\lambda+\kappa+1}$		$\boldsymbol{B}_0, \vec{\boldsymbol{b}}_1$
$\boldsymbol{m} \in \mathcal{R}_q$		
$\vec{\boldsymbol{r}} \leftarrow \chi^{(\lambda+\kappa+1)d}$		
$\vec{\boldsymbol{t}}_0 = \boldsymbol{B}_0\vec{\boldsymbol{r}}$		
$\boldsymbol{t}_1 = \langle \vec{\boldsymbol{b}}_1, \vec{\boldsymbol{r}}\rangle + \boldsymbol{m}$		
$\vec{\boldsymbol{y}} \leftarrow D_{\mathfrak{s}}^{(\lambda+\kappa+1)d}$		
$\vec{\boldsymbol{w}} = \boldsymbol{B}_0\vec{\boldsymbol{y}}$		
	$\xrightarrow{\vec{\boldsymbol{t}}_0, \boldsymbol{t}_1, \vec{\boldsymbol{w}}}$	
	$\xleftarrow{\boldsymbol{c}}$	$\boldsymbol{c} \leftarrow C$
$\vec{\boldsymbol{z}} = \vec{\boldsymbol{y}} + \boldsymbol{c}\vec{\boldsymbol{r}}$		
If $\mathsf{Rej}_b(\vec{\boldsymbol{z}}, \boldsymbol{c}\vec{\boldsymbol{r}}, \mathfrak{s}) = 1$, abort	$\xrightarrow{\vec{\boldsymbol{z}}}$	
		For $i = 0, \ldots, k-1$:
		$\|\vec{\boldsymbol{z}}\|_2 \overset{?}{\leq} \beta = \mathfrak{s}\sqrt{2(\lambda+\kappa+1)d}$
		$\boldsymbol{B}_0\vec{\boldsymbol{z}} \overset{?}{=} \vec{\boldsymbol{w}} + \boldsymbol{c}\vec{\boldsymbol{t}}_0$

Fig. 4. Opening proof for the commitment scheme. If $b = 0$ then the protocol is identical to the one described in [ALS20] and uses Rej_0 defined in Fig. 2. On the other hand, if $b = 1$ then we apply the new rejection sampling algorithm Rej_1 in Fig. 2.

– $\mathsf{Prove}^2_{ck}(x, \boldsymbol{m}, \vec{\boldsymbol{r}})$: It first generates $\vec{\boldsymbol{z}} \leftarrow D_{\mathfrak{s}}^{\kappa+\lambda+1}, \boldsymbol{c} \leftarrow C$. If $\langle \vec{\boldsymbol{z}}, \boldsymbol{c}\vec{\boldsymbol{r}}\rangle \geq 0$ then with probability $1/M$ it outputs $\pi = (\boldsymbol{c}, \vec{\boldsymbol{z}})$ and programs $\boldsymbol{c} = H(\boldsymbol{B}_0\vec{\boldsymbol{z}} - \boldsymbol{c}\vec{\boldsymbol{t}}_0)$.

It is easy to see that the difference between Prove and Prove^1 is that the algorithm programs the random oracle at one particular value $\boldsymbol{B}\vec{\boldsymbol{y}}$ (without checking whether it was already set). Hence, by arguing similarly as for zero-knowledge in [KLS18, DKL+18] we have that for all PPT adversaries $\mathcal{A}$:

$$\begin{aligned}\Pr&\begin{bmatrix} ck \leftarrow \mathsf{Gen}(1^\mu); (x, \boldsymbol{m}) \leftarrow \mathcal{A}(ck); \vec{\boldsymbol{r}} \leftarrow \chi^{(\lambda+\kappa+1)d}; (\vec{\boldsymbol{t}}_0, \boldsymbol{t}_1) = \mathsf{Com}_{ck}(\boldsymbol{m}; \vec{\boldsymbol{r}}); \\ \pi \leftarrow \mathsf{Prove}_{ck}(x, \boldsymbol{m}, \vec{\boldsymbol{r}}) : (ck, x, \boldsymbol{m}) \in R_L \wedge \mathcal{A}(\vec{\boldsymbol{t}}_0, \boldsymbol{t}_1, \pi) = 1 \end{bmatrix} \\ \approx \Pr&\begin{bmatrix} ck \leftarrow \mathsf{Gen}(1^\mu); (x, \boldsymbol{m}) \leftarrow \mathcal{A}(ck); \vec{\boldsymbol{r}} \leftarrow \chi^{(\lambda+\kappa+1)d}; (\vec{\boldsymbol{t}}_0, \boldsymbol{t}_1) = \mathsf{Com}_{ck}(\boldsymbol{m}; \vec{\boldsymbol{r}}); \\ \pi \leftarrow \mathsf{Prove}^1_{ck}(x, \boldsymbol{m}, \vec{\boldsymbol{r}}) : (ck, x, \boldsymbol{m}) \in R_L \wedge \mathcal{A}(\vec{\boldsymbol{t}}_0, \boldsymbol{t}_1, \pi) = 1 \end{bmatrix}.\end{aligned} \tag{11}$$

For the next hybrid, we apply Lemma 3.2. Namely, let $m = (\lambda + \kappa + 1)d$ and $V = \{\boldsymbol{c}\vec{\boldsymbol{r}} : \boldsymbol{c} \in \{-1, 0, 1\}^d, \vec{\boldsymbol{r}} \in \{-1, 0, 1\}^m\}$. Set the probability distribution $h : V \rightarrow \mathbb{R}$ as

$$h(\vec{\boldsymbol{v}}) = \Pr[\boldsymbol{c}\vec{\boldsymbol{r}} = \vec{\boldsymbol{v}} : \boldsymbol{c} \leftarrow C, \vec{\boldsymbol{r}} \leftarrow \chi^m].$$

Next, we set $f := D_{\mathfrak{s}}^m, g_{\vec{v}} := D_{\vec{v},\mathfrak{s}}^m$ for $\vec{v} \in V$ and

$$S_{\vec{v}} := \{\vec{z} \in \mathcal{R}_q^{\lambda+\kappa+1} : \langle \vec{v}, \vec{z} \rangle \geq 0\}.$$

Then, by Lemma 3.2 we have:

$$\Pr\left[\begin{matrix} ck \leftarrow \mathsf{Gen}(1^\mu); (x, \boldsymbol{m}) \leftarrow \mathcal{A}(ck); \vec{r} \leftarrow \chi^{(\lambda+\kappa+1)d}; (\vec{t}_0, \boldsymbol{t}_1) = \mathsf{Com}_{ck}(\boldsymbol{m}; \vec{r}); \\ \pi \leftarrow \mathsf{Prove}_{ck}^1(x, \boldsymbol{m}, \vec{r}) : (ck, x, \boldsymbol{m}) \in R_L \wedge \mathcal{A}(\vec{t}_0, \boldsymbol{t}_1, \pi) = 1 \end{matrix}\right]$$
$$= \Pr\left[\begin{matrix} ck \leftarrow \mathsf{Gen}(1^\mu); (x, \boldsymbol{m}) \leftarrow \mathcal{A}(ck); \vec{r} \leftarrow \chi^{(\lambda+\kappa+1)d}; (\vec{t}_0, \boldsymbol{t}_1) = \mathsf{Com}_{ck}(\boldsymbol{m}; \vec{r}); \\ \pi \leftarrow \mathsf{Prove}_{ck}^2(x, \boldsymbol{m}, \vec{r}) : (ck, x, \boldsymbol{m}) \in R_L \wedge \mathcal{A}(\vec{t}_0, \boldsymbol{t}_1, \pi) = 1 \end{matrix}\right] \quad (12)$$

for all adversaries $\mathcal{A}$. Now we define two algorithms SimCom and SimProve responsible for the simulation.

- $\mathsf{SimCom}_{ck}(x)$: It samples $\vec{t}_0$ and $\boldsymbol{t}_1$ uniformly at random from $\mathcal{R}_q^\kappa$ and $\mathcal{R}_q$ respectively and returns $(\vec{t}_0, \boldsymbol{t}_1)$.
- $\mathsf{SimProve}_{ck}\left(x, \vec{t}_0, \boldsymbol{t}_1\right)$: It first generates $\vec{z} \leftarrow D_{\mathfrak{s}}^{\kappa+\lambda+1}, \vec{r}^* \leftarrow \chi^{\lambda+\kappa+1}$ and $\boldsymbol{c} \leftarrow C$. Then, if $\langle \vec{z}, \boldsymbol{c}\vec{r}^* \rangle \geq 0$ then with probability $1/M$ it outputs $\pi = (\boldsymbol{c}, \vec{z})$ and programs $\boldsymbol{c} = H(\boldsymbol{B}_0\vec{z} - \boldsymbol{c}\vec{t}_0)$.

For the sake of contradiction suppose there exists a PPT adversary $\mathcal{A}$ such that

$$\left|\Pr\left[\begin{matrix} ck \leftarrow \mathsf{Gen}(1^\mu); (x, \boldsymbol{m}) \leftarrow \mathcal{A}(ck); \vec{r} \leftarrow \chi^{(\lambda+\kappa+1)d}; (\vec{t}_0, \boldsymbol{t}_1) = \mathsf{Com}_{ck}(\boldsymbol{m}; \vec{r}); \\ \pi \leftarrow \mathsf{Prove}_{ck}^2(x, \boldsymbol{m}, \vec{r}) : (ck, x, \boldsymbol{m}) \in R_L \wedge \mathcal{A}(\vec{t}_0, \boldsymbol{t}_1, \pi) = 1 \end{matrix}\right]\right.$$
$$\left. - \Pr\left[\begin{matrix} ck \leftarrow \mathsf{Gen}(1^\mu); (x, \boldsymbol{m}) \leftarrow \mathcal{A}(ck); (\vec{t}_0, \boldsymbol{t}_1) \leftarrow \mathsf{SimCom}_{ck}(x); \\ \pi \leftarrow \mathsf{SimProve}_{ck}(x, \vec{t}_0, \boldsymbol{t}_1); (ck, x, \boldsymbol{m}) \in R_L \wedge \mathcal{A}(\vec{t}_0, \boldsymbol{t}_1, \pi) = 1 \end{matrix}\right]\right| = \epsilon. \quad (13)$$

Let us construct an adversary $\mathcal{B}$ which solves the Extended M-LWE$_{\kappa+1,\lambda}$ also with probability ϵ using the algorithm $\mathcal{A}$. Concretely, suppose that $\mathcal{B}$ is given a tuple $\left((\boldsymbol{B}_0 \| \vec{b}_1), (\vec{t}_0 \| \boldsymbol{u}_1), \vec{z}, \boldsymbol{c}, \mathsf{sign}(\langle \vec{z}, \boldsymbol{c}\vec{r} \rangle)\right)$ for $\vec{z} \leftarrow D_{\mathfrak{s}}^{(\lambda+\kappa+1)d}, \boldsymbol{c} \leftarrow C$ and $\vec{r} \leftarrow \chi^{(\lambda+\kappa+1)d}$. Firstly, $\mathcal{A}$ outputs a pair $(x, \boldsymbol{m})$. Then, $\mathcal{B}$ sets $\boldsymbol{t}_1 = \boldsymbol{u}_1 + \boldsymbol{m}$. Finally, if $\mathsf{sign}(\langle \vec{z}, \boldsymbol{c}\vec{r} \rangle) \geq 0$ then $\mathcal{B}$ sets $\pi = (\boldsymbol{c}, \vec{z})$ and with probability $1/M$ sends $(\vec{t}_0, \boldsymbol{t}_1, \pi)$. Otherwise, it aborts. At the end, $\mathcal{B}$ outputs the bit sent from $\mathcal{A}$.

First, suppose that $\vec{t}_0 = \boldsymbol{B}\vec{r}$ and $\boldsymbol{u}_1 = \langle \vec{b}_1, \vec{r} \rangle$. Then, $(\boldsymbol{t}_0, \boldsymbol{t}_1)$ constructed by $\mathcal{B}$ is indeed equal to $\mathsf{Com}_{ck}(\boldsymbol{m}; \vec{r})$. Then, the way π is built is identical as in Prove^2. In this case, the probability that $\mathcal{B}$ outputs bit 1 is equal to

$$\Pr\left[\begin{matrix} ck \leftarrow \mathsf{Gen}(1^\mu); (x, \boldsymbol{m}) \leftarrow \mathcal{A}(ck); \vec{r} \leftarrow \chi^{(\lambda+\kappa+1)d}; (\vec{t}_0, \boldsymbol{t}_1) = \mathsf{Com}_{ck}(\boldsymbol{m}; \vec{r}); \\ \pi \leftarrow \mathsf{Prove}_{ck}^2(x, \boldsymbol{m}, \vec{r}) : (ck, x, \boldsymbol{m}) \in R_L \wedge \mathcal{A}(\vec{t}_0, \boldsymbol{t}_1, \pi) = 1 \end{matrix}\right].$$

On the other hand, assume that $\vec{t}_0$ and $\boldsymbol{u}_1$ are chosen uniformly at random and also independently of $\vec{r}$. Then, $\boldsymbol{t}_1$ is random as well. Hence, the probability that $\mathcal{B}$ outputs 1 is indeed equal to

$$\Pr\left[\begin{matrix} ck \leftarrow \mathsf{Gen}(1^\mu); (x, \boldsymbol{m}) \leftarrow \mathcal{A}(ck); (\vec{t}_0, \boldsymbol{t}_1) \leftarrow \mathsf{SimCom}_{ck}(x); \\ \pi \leftarrow \mathsf{SimProve}_{ck}(x, \vec{t}_0, \boldsymbol{t}_1); (ck, x, \boldsymbol{m}) \in R_L \wedge \mathcal{A}(\vec{t}_0, \boldsymbol{t}_1, \pi) = 1 \end{matrix}\right].$$

Thus, $\mathcal{B}$ can efficiently distinguish between the two Extended M-LWE cases with probability ϵ. Since, we assumed that the problem is computationally hard, this implies that ϵ is negligible. Then, the statement holds by the hybrid argument. □

3.2 Boosting Soundness and Decreasing Standard Deviation

The protocol in Fig. 4 has soundness error around $q^{-d/l}$ which is not necessarily negligible. In order to boost soundness, Attema et al. [ALS20] apply Galois automorphisms. We recall the extended opening proof protocol below.

Prover $\mathcal{P}$ first generates $\vec{\boldsymbol{y}}_0, \ldots, \vec{\boldsymbol{y}}_{k-1} \leftarrow D_{\mathfrak{s}}^{(\lambda+\kappa+1)d}$ and $\vec{\boldsymbol{r}}, \vec{\boldsymbol{t}}_0, \boldsymbol{t}_1$ as before. Next, it outputs $(\vec{\boldsymbol{t}}_0, \boldsymbol{t}_1, \vec{\boldsymbol{w}}_0, \ldots, \vec{\boldsymbol{w}}_{k-1})$ where $\vec{\boldsymbol{w}}_i = \boldsymbol{B}_0\vec{\boldsymbol{y}}_i$. After receiving a challenge $\boldsymbol{c} \leftarrow C$ from the verifier, $\mathcal{P}$ computes

$$\vec{\boldsymbol{z}}_i = \vec{\boldsymbol{y}}_i + \sigma^i(\boldsymbol{c})\vec{\boldsymbol{r}} \text{ for } i = 0, \ldots, k-1$$

where $\sigma := \sigma_{2d/k+1}$ where k is a divisor of d. Then, the prover applies rejection sampling $\mathsf{Rej}_1(\vec{\boldsymbol{z}}, \vec{\boldsymbol{v}}, \mathfrak{s})$ where $\vec{\boldsymbol{z}} = \vec{\boldsymbol{z}}_0 \parallel \cdots \parallel \vec{\boldsymbol{z}}_{k-1}$ and $\vec{\boldsymbol{v}} = \sigma^0(\boldsymbol{c})\vec{\boldsymbol{r}} \parallel \cdots \parallel \sigma^{k-1}(\boldsymbol{c})\vec{\boldsymbol{r}}$. If it does not abort, then $\mathcal{P}$ outputs $\vec{\boldsymbol{z}}$. Finally, the verifier checks that $\vec{\boldsymbol{z}}$ is small and

$$\boldsymbol{B}_0\vec{\boldsymbol{z}}_i = \vec{\boldsymbol{w}}_i + \sigma^i(\boldsymbol{c})\vec{\boldsymbol{t}}_0$$

for $i = 0, \ldots, k-1$. As argued by Attema et al., this protocol has soundness around $q^{-dk/l}$.

More recently, Lyubashevsky et al. [LNS20a, Appendix A.6] (also mentioned in [ENS20]) improved this opening proof by applying a simple modification. Suppose $X^n + 1$ splits completely modulo q, i.e. $l = d$. Let us write the challenge $\boldsymbol{c} = \boldsymbol{c}_0 + \boldsymbol{c}_1 X + \ldots + \boldsymbol{c}_{k-1}X^{k-1} \leftarrow C$ where

$$\boldsymbol{c}_i = \sum_{j=0}^{d/k-1} c_{jk+i}X^{jk}.$$

By definition of $\sigma = \sigma_{2d/k+1}$, we have that $\sigma(\boldsymbol{c}_i) = \boldsymbol{c}_i$ for each i. Therefore, we have:

$$\sigma^i(\boldsymbol{c}) = \sum_{j=0}^{k-1} \sigma^i(X^j)\boldsymbol{c}_j.$$

The modified opening proof protocol is presented as follows. Prover $\mathcal{P}$ samples $\vec{\boldsymbol{y}}'_0, \ldots, \vec{\boldsymbol{y}}'_{k-1}$ from $D_{\mathfrak{s}}^{(\lambda+\kappa+1)d}$ as before. Then, the prover sends $\vec{\boldsymbol{w}}'_i = \boldsymbol{B}_0\vec{\boldsymbol{y}}'_i$. After getting a challenge $\boldsymbol{c} \leftarrow C$, it computes $\boldsymbol{c}_0, \ldots, \boldsymbol{c}_{k-1}$ as above and calculates $\vec{\boldsymbol{z}}'_i$ as:

$$\begin{pmatrix} \vec{\boldsymbol{z}}'_0 \\ \vec{\boldsymbol{z}}'_1 \\ \vdots \\ \vec{\boldsymbol{z}}'_{k-1} \end{pmatrix} = \begin{pmatrix} \vec{\boldsymbol{y}}'_0 \\ \vec{\boldsymbol{y}}'_1 \\ \vdots \\ \vec{\boldsymbol{y}}'_{k-1} \end{pmatrix} + \begin{pmatrix} \boldsymbol{c}_0\vec{\boldsymbol{r}} \\ \boldsymbol{c}_1\vec{\boldsymbol{r}} \\ \vdots \\ \boldsymbol{c}_{k-1}\vec{\boldsymbol{r}} \end{pmatrix}.$$

Since each $\boldsymbol{c}_i$ has only at most d/k non-zero coefficients, we manage to decrease the standard deviation possibly by a factor of k (in practice the improvement is smaller if one upper-bounds $\|\sigma^i(\boldsymbol{c})\vec{\boldsymbol{r}}\|$ more cleverly).

Eventually, the prover applies rejection sampling $\mathsf{Rej}_1(\vec{\boldsymbol{z}}, \vec{\boldsymbol{v}}, \mathfrak{s})$ where $\vec{\boldsymbol{z}} = \vec{\boldsymbol{z}}'_0 \parallel \cdots \parallel \vec{\boldsymbol{z}}'_{k-1}$ and $\vec{\boldsymbol{v}} = \boldsymbol{c}_0\vec{\boldsymbol{r}} \parallel \cdots \parallel \boldsymbol{c}_{k-1}\vec{\boldsymbol{r}}$. After receiving vectors $\vec{\boldsymbol{z}}'_j$, $\mathcal{V}$ first checks whether

$$\boldsymbol{B}_0\vec{\boldsymbol{z}}'_i \stackrel{?}{=} \vec{\boldsymbol{w}}'_i + \boldsymbol{c}_i\vec{\boldsymbol{t}}_0.$$

for $i = 0, \ldots, k-1$ and that each $\vec{\boldsymbol{z}}_i$ is small.

Note that by computing

$$\vec{\boldsymbol{y}}_i = \sum_{j=0}^{k-1} \sigma^i(X^j)\vec{\boldsymbol{y}}'_j,\ \vec{\boldsymbol{z}}_i = \sum_{j=0}^{k-1} \sigma^i(X^j)\vec{\boldsymbol{z}}'_j$$

and $\vec{\boldsymbol{w}}_i = \boldsymbol{B}_0\vec{\boldsymbol{y}}_i$ for $i = 0, \ldots, k-1$, we have:

$$\boldsymbol{B}_0\vec{\boldsymbol{z}}_i = \vec{\boldsymbol{w}}_i + \sigma^i(\boldsymbol{c})\vec{\boldsymbol{t}}_0$$

which is the exact verification equation as in [ALS20]. This observation is crucial in [LNS20a] in order to still be able to prove linear and multiplicative relations using techniques from [ALS20, ENS20].

Lyubashevsky et al. bound $\|\vec{\boldsymbol{v}}\|$ by first finding α so that

$$\Pr\left[\exists i, \|\boldsymbol{c}_i\vec{\boldsymbol{r}}\|_\infty > \alpha : \boldsymbol{c} \leftarrow C, \vec{\boldsymbol{r}} \leftarrow \chi^{(\lambda+\kappa+1)d}\right] < 2^{-128}$$

and then setting the bound $\|\vec{\boldsymbol{v}}\| \leq \alpha\sqrt{\lambda+\kappa+1}$. In [LNS20b, Appendix C] we describe a more optimal way to compute an upper-bound on $\|\vec{\boldsymbol{v}}\|$ using almost identical methods as in [DDLL13].

3.3 Applications

We apply the new rejection sampling technique in the protocol by Esgin et al. [ENS20, Appendix B] to prove knowledge of secrets in LWE samples. Concretely, for $n = 2048$, we want to prove knowledge of a ternary vector $\vec{s} \in \{-1, 0, 1\}^n$ such that

$$\vec{u} = (A' \parallel I_m) \cdot \vec{s} \pmod{q},$$

where I_m is the m-dimensional identity matrix, $A' \in \mathbb{Z}_q^{m\times(n-m)}$ is a public matrix chosen uniformly at random and q is a modulus of about 32 bits (i.e., $\log q \approx 32$). Note that $\vec{s}$ here corresponds to the concatenation of a secret vector and an error vector of 1024 dimension each in the usual LWE setting. For fair comparison, we will use the protocol described in [ENS20, Fig. 3] with the following two modifications (i) we do the Gaussian rejection sampling according to Rej_1 instead of the uniform one and (ii) we apply the commitment compression techniques as in [LNS20b, Appendix B].

We set parameters $(q, d, l, k) = (\approx 2^{32}, 128, 128, 4)$ similarly as in [ENS20]. Esgin et al. choose the expected number of repetitions to be 18.87. Since sampling from a discrete Gaussians is much less efficient than from a uniform distribution, for fairness we set $\mathfrak{s} = T$ and $M \approx 3.3$ where T is the upper-bound on $\|\vec{v}\|$ where $\vec{v} = c_0\vec{r} \| \cdots \| c_{k-1}\vec{r}$. Esgin et al. use the fact that $\|\vec{v}\|_\infty \leq d/k = 32$ and thus they set $T = 32\sqrt{(\lambda + \kappa + 3 + 16)d}$. We, however, apply the bound described in [LNS20b, Appendix C] and observe that for (κ, λ) selected in the next paragraph, our bound on $\|\vec{v}\|$ is around five times smaller than in [ENS20].

Now we set λ and κ such that M-LWE and M-SIS are hard against known attacks. We measure the hardness with the root Hermite factor δ and aim for $\delta \approx 1.0043$ [ENS20, EZS+19, BLS19]. By assuming that the Extended M-LWE is almost equally hard as M-LWE, we set $\lambda = 10$ as in [ENS20]. On the other hand, for the M-SIS hardness we manage to set $\kappa = 8$ due to having smaller standard deviation $\mathfrak{s}$. Hence, without using the compression techniques, we obtain the proof of size 41.35KB compared to 47KB by [ENS20]. After applying the additional improvements described in [LNS20b, Appendix B] we reduce the proof size to 33.6KB.

Similarly, we can consider the LNS functionality defined in Sect. 2.10 where $\mathsf{LNSProve}^U$ use our new Gaussian rejection sampling in Fig. 2 instead of a uniform one. We will denote this variant of the protocol as $\mathsf{LNSProve}^D$ and the corresponding CP functionality for the language R_L as

$$LNS^D = (\mathsf{LNSGen}, \mathsf{LNSCom}, \mathsf{LNSProve}^D, \mathsf{LNSVerify}^D).$$

The total proof size (when using Discrete Gaussians and without any Dilithium compression techniques) is about

$$(n + \kappa + \alpha + 1)d \log q \; + \; k(\lambda + \kappa + n + \alpha)d \cdot \log(12\mathfrak{s}) \quad \text{bits.} \tag{14}$$

Here, n, α are defined in Sect. 2.10, k is a divisor of d such that q^{-k} is negligible and $\mathfrak{s}$ is the standard deviation used for the rejection sampling. For efficiency, we also apply Dilithium compression methods described in [LNS20b, Appendix B].

We present the proof sizes for proving n-bit integer addition and multiplication using LNS^D in Fig. 1.

4 Verifiable Decryption

In this section we apply the improved LNS framework with the rejection sampling from Sect. 3 to the problem of constructing a verifiable decryption scheme. We restrict our attention the Kyber key encapsulation scheme [BDK+18] and its NIST level 1 parameter set Kyber512. Kyber is a finalist in the NIST PQC standardization effort. Our techniques work equally well for any of the other lattice-based KEMs in round 3 of the NIST process, i.e. Saber [DKRV18] and NTRU [HPS98]. Kyber512 uses module rank 2 over the ring $\mathcal{R}_q = \mathbb{Z}_q[X]/(X^{256} + 1)$ with modulus $q = 3329$. The public key is given by an MLWE vector $\vec{t} = \boldsymbol{A}\vec{s} + \vec{e}$ where $\boldsymbol{A} \in \mathcal{R}_q^{2\times 2}$ is a uniform public matrix and $\vec{s}$ and $\vec{e}$ are short secret vectors with coefficients in the interval $[-2, 2]$. The encryption of a binary polynomial $\boldsymbol{m} \in \{0,1\}^{256}$ encoding a 256-bit key consists of the rounded vector and polynomial

$$\vec{\boldsymbol{u}} = \mathsf{Compress}_{10}\left(\boldsymbol{A}^T\vec{\boldsymbol{s}}' + \vec{\boldsymbol{e}}_u\right) = \boldsymbol{A}^T\vec{\boldsymbol{s}}' + \vec{\boldsymbol{e}}'_u$$
$$\boldsymbol{v} = \mathsf{Compress}_4\left(\langle \vec{\boldsymbol{t}}, \vec{\boldsymbol{s}}'\rangle + \boldsymbol{e}_v + \left\lceil \frac{q}{2} \right\rfloor \boldsymbol{m}\right) = \langle \vec{\boldsymbol{t}}, \vec{\boldsymbol{s}}'\rangle + \boldsymbol{e}'_v + \left\lceil \frac{q}{2} \right\rfloor \boldsymbol{m}$$

where $\vec{\boldsymbol{s}}'$, $\vec{\boldsymbol{e}}_u$ and $\boldsymbol{e}_v$ are again short, the functions $\mathsf{Compress}_{10}$ and $\mathsf{Compress}_4$ compress to 10 and 4 bits per coefficient, and $\vec{\boldsymbol{e}}'_u$, $\boldsymbol{e}'_v$ include the errors coming from the compression. Finally, decryption uses the observation

$$\boldsymbol{v} - \langle \vec{\boldsymbol{s}}, \vec{\boldsymbol{u}}\rangle = \langle \vec{\boldsymbol{e}}, \vec{\boldsymbol{s}}'\rangle - \langle \vec{\boldsymbol{s}}, \vec{\boldsymbol{e}}'_u\rangle + \boldsymbol{e}'_v + \left\lceil \frac{q}{2} \right\rfloor \boldsymbol{m},$$

which implies

$$\left\| \boldsymbol{v} - \langle \vec{\boldsymbol{s}}, \vec{\boldsymbol{u}}\rangle - \left\lceil \frac{q}{2} \right\rfloor \boldsymbol{m} \right\|_\infty < \frac{q}{4}$$

with overwhelming probability. In fact, the decryption algorithm will recover $\boldsymbol{m}$ precisely if this norm bound is true. In the scheme there is no guarantee for this bound and encrypted keys can fail to be decryptable with probability around 2^{-139}.

Now, for a verifiable decryption scheme we need to be able to prove knowledge of a vector $\vec{\boldsymbol{s}}$ and polynomials $\boldsymbol{m}$, $\boldsymbol{x}$ such that

$$\boldsymbol{v} - \langle \vec{\boldsymbol{s}}, \vec{\boldsymbol{u}}\rangle - \left\lceil \frac{q}{2} \right\rfloor \boldsymbol{m} = \boldsymbol{x} \tag{15}$$
$$\vec{\boldsymbol{s}} \in \{-2,-1,0,1,2\}^{512} \tag{16}$$
$$\boldsymbol{m} \in \{0,1\}^{256} \tag{17}$$
$$\|\boldsymbol{x}\|_\infty < \frac{q}{4} \tag{18}$$

The first three properties (15), (16), (17) can in principle directly be proven with the LNS framework. For the fourth one we can use a small-base decomposition approach for doing range proofs. A small problem is posed by the magnitude of the Kyber modulus $q = 3329$. While it is possible to instantiate the LNS framework in a way that allows to directly prove linear equations modulo such small primes, this results in quite large soundness error and many repetitions in the opening proof. To circumvent this problem and arrive at a more efficient protocol, we use the framework with a much larger modulus q' and lift Eq. (15) to the integers. This means that we instead prove

$$\boldsymbol{v} - \langle \vec{\boldsymbol{s}}, \vec{\boldsymbol{u}}\rangle - \left\lceil \frac{q}{2} \right\rfloor \boldsymbol{m} + \boldsymbol{d}q \equiv \boldsymbol{x} \pmod{q'} \tag{19}$$

for another secret polynomial $\boldsymbol{d} \in \mathbb{Z}[X]/(X^{256}+1)$ whose range $\|\boldsymbol{d}\|_\infty \leq 2^{10}$ we also need to prove. Note that Eq. (19) for $q' > 2^{23}$ together with the range proofs implies Eq. (15) since from the ranges of the individual terms we know that the equation must hold over the integers, which in turn implies (15) since the additional term, which is a multiple of q, vanishes modulo q.

4.1 Range Proofs

In the protocol sketched above there are the two range proofs $\|\boldsymbol{d}\|_\infty \leq 2^{10}$ and $\|\boldsymbol{x}\|_\infty < q/4$. For the first range proof it is actually enough to prove that $q\,\|\boldsymbol{d}\|_\infty < q'/4$. We use a 64-bit prime q' for the LNS framework protocol. Then, there is enough head-room between the actual range 2^{10} of $\boldsymbol{d}$ and $q'/(4q) > 2^{50}$ so that we can use the approximate shortness proof. On the other hand, for proving the range of $\boldsymbol{x}$ it is important to not have any slack in the proof. So here we decompose $\boldsymbol{x}$ in base 5. We choose base 5, since for proving the coefficients of $\vec{s}$ to lie in the interval $[-2, 2]$ we already have degree-5 product relations and hence can prove the base-5 decomposition without any additional garbage commitments. The interval of the coefficients of $\boldsymbol{x}$ has length $q/2 = 1664$ and hence we need 5 base-5 digits for each coefficient. Now, since 1664 is not a power of 5 we write each coefficient of $\boldsymbol{x}$ in the form

$$a_0 + a_1 5 + a_2 5^2 + a_3 5^3 + a_4 260$$

with $a_4 \in 0, \dots, 4$. This decomposition is not unique but precisely maps to the integers in the interval $[0, 1664]$.

4.2 Proof Size

We compute the size of the verifiable decryption scheme for Kyber512 from above. As commitment messages we have the vector $\boldsymbol{s}$ of $\mathbb{Z}$-dimension 512, the polynomial $\boldsymbol{m}$ of dimension 256, the masking polynomial for the approximate range proof for $\boldsymbol{d}$, and the expansion of $\boldsymbol{x}$ in base-5, which has $\mathbb{Z}$-dimension $5 \cdot 256 = 1280$. This amounts to a total message dimension of $n = 2176$. We then computed that the full LNS protocol with 64-bit modulus, MLWE rank 20 and MSIS rank 5 has a proof size of 43.6KB.

Acknowledgement. We would like to thank the anonymous reviewers for useful comments. This work was supported by the SNSF ERC Transfer Grant CRETP2-166734 FELICITY.

References

ADPS15. Alkim, E., Ducas, L., Pöppelmann, T., Schwabe, P.: Post-quantum key exchange - a new hope. IACR Cryptol. ePrint Arch. **2015**, 1092 (2015)

AGVW17. Albrecht, M.R., Göpfert, F., Virdia, F., Wunderer, T.: Revisiting the expected cost of solving uSVP and applications to LWE. In: Takagi, T., Peyrin, T. (eds.) ASIACRYPT 2017. LNCS, vol. 10624, pp. 297–322. Springer, Cham (2017). https://doi.org/10.1007/978-3-319-70694-8_11

Alb17. Albrecht, M.R.: On dual lattice attacks against small-secret LWE and parameter choices in HElib and SEAL. In: Coron, J.-S., Nielsen, J.B. (eds.) EUROCRYPT 2017. LNCS, vol. 10211, pp. 103–129. Springer, Cham (2017). https://doi.org/10.1007/978-3-319-56614-6_4

ALS20. Attema, T., Lyubashevsky, V., Seiler, G.: Practical product proofs for lattice commitments. In: Micciancio, D., Ristenpart, T. (eds.) CRYPTO 2020. LNCS, vol. 12171, pp. 470–499. Springer, Cham (2020). https://doi.org/10.1007/978-3-030-56880-1_17

AP12. Alperin-Sheriff, J., Peikert, C.: Circular and KDM security for identity-based encryption. In: Fischlin, M., Buchmann, J., Manulis, M. (eds.) PKC 2012. LNCS, vol. 7293, pp. 334–352. Springer, Heidelberg (2012). https://doi.org/10.1007/978-3-642-30057-8_20

APS15. Albrecht, M.R., Player, R., Scott, S.: On the concrete hardness of learning with errors. Cryptology ePrint Archive, Report 2015/046 (2015). https://eprint.iacr.org/2015/046

Ban93. Banaszczyk, W.: New bounds in some transference theorems in the geometry of numbers. Math. Ann. **296**(1), 625–635 (1993)

BD20. Brakerski, Z., Döttling, N.: Hardness of LWE on general entropic distributions. In: Canteaut, A., Ishai, Y. (eds.) EUROCRYPT 2020. LNCS, vol. 12106, pp. 551–575. Springer, Cham (2020). https://doi.org/10.1007/978-3-030-45724-2_19

BDK+18. Bos, J.W. et al.: CRYSTALS - kyber: A cca-secure module-lattice-based KEM. In: 2018 IEEE European Symposium on Security and Privacy, EuroS&P, pp. 353–367 (2018)

BDL+18. Baum, C., Damgård, I., Lyubashevsky, V., Oechsner, S., Peikert, C.: More efficient commitments from structured lattice assumptions. In: Catalano, D., De Prisco, R. (eds.) SCN 2018. LNCS, vol. 11035, pp. 368–385. Springer, Cham (2018). https://doi.org/10.1007/978-3-319-98113-0_20

BL17. Baum, C., Lyubashevsky, V.: Simple amortized proofs of shortness for linear relations over polynomial rings. IACR Cryptology ePrint Archive **2017**, 759 (2017)

BLS19. Bootle, J., Lyubashevsky, V., Seiler, G.: Algebraic techniques for Short(er) exact lattice-based zero-knowledge proofs. In: Boldyreva, A., Micciancio, D. (eds.) CRYPTO 2019. LNCS, vol. 11692, pp. 176–202. Springer, Cham (2019). https://doi.org/10.1007/978-3-030-26948-7_7

BN20. Baum, C., Nof, A.: Concretely-efficient zero-knowledge arguments for arithmetic circuits and their application to lattice-based cryptography. In: Kiayias, A., Kohlweiss, M., Wallden, P., Zikas, V. (eds.) PKC 2020. LNCS, vol. 12110, pp. 495–526. Springer, Cham (2020). https://doi.org/10.1007/978-3-030-45374-9_17

CLOS02. Canetti, R., Lindell, Y., Ostrovsky, R., Sahai, A.: Universally composable two-party and multi-party secure computation. In: STOC, pp. 494–503. ACM (2002)

DDGR20. Dachman-Soled, D., Ducas, L., Gong, H., Rossi, M.: LWE with side information: attacks and concrete security estimation. In: Micciancio, D., Ristenpart, T. (eds.) CRYPTO 2020. LNCS, vol. 12171, pp. 329–358. Springer, Cham (2020). https://doi.org/10.1007/978-3-030-56880-1_12

DDLL13. Ducas, L., Durmus, A., Lepoint, T., Lyubashevsky, V.: Lattice signatures and bimodal gaussians. In: Canetti, R., Garay, J.A. (eds.) CRYPTO 2013. LNCS, vol. 8042, pp. 40–56. Springer, Heidelberg (2013). https://doi.org/10.1007/978-3-642-40041-4_3

DGK+10. Dodis, Y., Goldwasser, S., Tauman Kalai, Y., Peikert, C., Vaikuntanathan, V.: Public-key encryption schemes with auxiliary inputs. In: Micciancio, D. (ed.) TCC 2010. LNCS, vol. 5978, pp. 361–381. Springer, Heidelberg (2010). https://doi.org/10.1007/978-3-642-11799-2_22

DKL+18. Ducas, L., et al.: Crystals-dilithium: a lattice-based digital signature scheme. IACR Trans. Cryptogr. Hardw. Embed. Syst. **2018**(1), 238–268 (2018)

DKRV18. D'Anvers, J.-P., Karmakar, A., Sinha Roy, S., Vercauteren, F.: Saber: module-LWR based key exchange, CPA-secure encryption and CCA-secure KEM. In: Joux, A., Nitaj, A., Rachidi, T. (eds.) AFRICACRYPT 2018. LNCS, vol. 10831, pp. 282–305. Springer, Cham (2018). https://doi.org/10.1007/978-3-319-89339-6_16

EG14. Escala, A., Groth, J.: Fine-tuning groth-sahai proofs. In: Krawczyk, H. (ed.) PKC 2014. LNCS, vol. 8383, pp. 630–649. Springer, Heidelberg (2014). https://doi.org/10.1007/978-3-642-54631-0_36

EKS+20. Esgin, M.F., et al.: Practical post-quantum few-time verifiable random function with applications to algorand. Cryptology ePrint Archive, Report 2020/1222 (2020). https://eprint.iacr.org/2020/1222

ENS20. Esgin, M.F., Nguyen, N.K., Seiler, G.: Practical exact proofs from lattices: new techniques to exploit fully-splitting rings. In: Moriai, S., Wang, H. (eds.) ASIACRYPT 2020. LNCS, vol. 12492, pp. 259–288. Springer, Cham (2020). https://doi.org/10.1007/978-3-030-64834-3_9

EZS+19. Esgin, M.F., Zhao, R.K., Steinfeld, R., Liu, J.K., Liu, D.: Matrict: Efficient, scalable and post-quantum blockchain confidential transactions protocol. In: CCS, pp. 567–584. ACM (2019)

GKPV10. Goldwasser, S., Kalai, Y.T., Peikert, C., Vaikuntanathan, V.: Robustness of the learning with errors assumption. In: ICS, pp. 230–240. Tsinghua University Press (2010)

HPS98. Hoffstein, J., Pipher, J., Silverman, J.H.: NTRU: a ring-based public key cryptosystem. In: ANTS, pp. 267–288 (1998)

KLS18. Kiltz, E., Lyubashevsky, V., Schaffner, C.: A concrete treatment of fiat-Shamir signatures in the quantum random-oracle model. In: Nielsen, J.B., Rijmen, V. (eds.) EUROCRYPT 2018. LNCS, vol. 10822, pp. 552–586. Springer, Cham (2018). https://doi.org/10.1007/978-3-319-78372-7_18

LNS20a. Lyubashevsky, V., Nguyen, N.K., Seiler, G.: Practical lattice-based zero-knowledge proofs for integer relations. In: IACR Cryptology ePrint Archive, 2020. ACM CCS (2020). http://eprint.iacr.org/2020/1183

LNS20b. Lyubashevsky, V., Nguyen, N.K., Seiler, G.: Shorter lattice-based zero-knowledge proofs via one-time commitments. Cryptology ePrint Archive, Report 2020/1448 (2020). https://eprint.iacr.org/2020/1448

LNSW13. Ling, S., Nguyen, K., Stehlé, D., Wang, H.: Improved zero-knowledge proofs of knowledge for the ISIS problem, and applications. In: PKC, pp. 107–124 (2013)

LS15. Langlois, A., Stehlé, D.: Worst-case to average-case reductions for module lattices. Des. Codes Crypt. **75**(3), 565–599 (2014). https://doi.org/10.1007/s10623-014-9938-4

Lyu09. Lyubashevsky, V.: Fiat-Shamir with aborts: Applications to lattice and factoring-based signatures. In: ASIACRYPT, pp. 598–616 (2009)

Lyu12. Lyubashevsky, V.: Lattice signatures without trapdoors. In: EUROCRYPT, pp. 738–755 (2012)

MM11. Micciancio, D., Mol, P.: Pseudorandom knapsacks and the sample complexity of LWE search-to-decision reductions. In: Rogaway, P. (ed.) CRYPTO 2011. LNCS, vol. 6841, pp. 465–484. Springer, Heidelberg (2011). https://doi.org/10.1007/978-3-642-22792-9_26

OPW11. O'Neill, A., Peikert, C., Waters, B.: Bi-deniable public-key encryption. In: Rogaway, P. (ed.) CRYPTO 2011. LNCS, vol. 6841, pp. 525–542. Springer, Heidelberg (2011). https://doi.org/10.1007/978-3-642-22792-9_30

Ste93. Stern, J.: A new identification scheme based on syndrome decoding. In: CRYPTO, pp. 13–21 (1993)

TWZ20. Tao, Y., Wang, X., Zhang, R.: Short zero-knowledge proof of knowledge for lattice-based commitment. In: Ding, J., Tillich, J.-P. (eds.) PQCrypto 2020. LNCS, vol. 12100, pp. 268–283. Springer, Cham (2020). https://doi.org/10.1007/978-3-030-44223-1_15

YAZ+19. Yang, R., Au, M.H., Zhang, Z., Xu, Q., Yu, Z., Whyte, W.: Efficient lattice-based zero-knowledge arguments with standard soundness: construction and applications. In: Boldyreva, A., Micciancio, D. (eds.) CRYPTO 2019. LNCS, vol. 11692, pp. 147–175. Springer, Cham (2019). https://doi.org/10.1007/978-3-030-26948-7_6

Multivariate Public Key Cryptosystem from Sidon Spaces

Netanel Raviv[1(✉)], Ben Langton[2], and Itzhak Tamo[3]

[1] Department of Computer Science and Engineering, Washington University in St. Louis, St. Louis, MO 63103, USA
netanel.raviv@wustl.edu

[2] Department of Mathematics, Harvey Mudd College, Claremont, CA 91711, USA
blangton@g.hmc.edu

[3] Department of Electrical Engineering–Systems, Tel-Aviv University, Tel-Aviv, Israel
tamo@tauex.tau.ac.il

Abstract. A Sidon space is a subspace of an extension field over a base field in which the product of any two elements can be factored uniquely, up to constants. This paper proposes a new a public-key cryptosystem of the multivariate type which is based on Sidon spaces, and has the potential to remain secure even if quantum supremacy is attained. This system, whose security relies on the hardness of the well-known MinRank problem, is shown to be resilient to several straightforward algebraic attacks. In particular, it is proved that the two popular attacks on the MinRank problem, the kernel attack and the minor attack, succeed only with exponentially small probability. The system is implemented in software, and its hardness is demonstrated experimentally.

Keywords: Multivariate public key cryptosystem · MinRank problem · Sidon spaces

1 Introduction

Public key cryptosystems (PKCs), such as RSA, are essential in many communication scenarios. However, most number-theoretic PKCs are prone to quantum attacks, and will become obsolete once quantum supremacy is attained. Hence, it is important to devise PKCs whose hardness relies on problems that are hard to solve even with quantum computers at hand. One such problem that has gained increasing attention lately is solving a system of multivariate polynomial (usually quadratic) equations [22,28], which is NP-hard in general [10]. PKCs whose hardness relies on solving multivariate polynomial equations are called *Multivariate Public Key Cryptosystems* (MPKCs).

Nearly all MPKCs in the literature were either cryptanalyzed or their efficiency was proved to be limited. Recently, the so-called ABC cryptosystem [28], that relies on simple matrix multiplication as the encryption scheme, seems to

J. A. Garay (Ed.): PKC 2021, LNCS 12710, pp. 242–265, 2021.
https://doi.org/10.1007/978-3-030-75245-3_10

have been broken by [13]. Earlier works include the Hidden Field Equations (HFE) cryptosystem [22] that has been broken by a MinRank attack [15], and the TTM scheme [19] that experienced a similar fate [14]. In addition, some variants of the HFE scheme, such as ZHFE [25] and HFE- [7] were also successfully attacked by [23] and [30]. The MPKC of [27] was also broken by a MinRank attack. Additional candidates include the oil-and-vinegar scheme [16], Rainbow [8], and Gui [24]. In light of these recent advances, in this paper we propose a new MPKC which seems to be inherently robust against several natural attacks. This MPKC is based on a newly defined algebraic concept called *Sidon spaces*.

Let $\mathbb{F}_q$ denote a finite field with q elements, and let $\mathbb{F}_q^* \triangleq \mathbb{F}_q \setminus \{0\}$. For an integer n let $\mathbb{F}_{q^n}$ be the algebraic extension of degree n of $\mathbb{F}_q$, and let $[n] \triangleq \{1, 2, \ldots, n\}$. Simply put, a Sidon space V is a subspace of $\mathbb{F}_{q^n}$ over $\mathbb{F}_q$ such that the product of any two nonzero elements of V has a unique factorization over V, up to a constant multiplier from $\mathbb{F}_q$. Sidon spaces were recently defined in [2] as a tool for studying certain multiplicative properties of subspaces, and their application to error correction in network coding, alongside several explicit constructions that are employed herein, were studied in [26].

In this paper we suggest the *Sidon Cryptosystem*, an MPKC based on Sidon spaces. In a nutshell, this cryptosystem enables the sender to transmit the product of two elements in a secret Sidon space V, without knowing its structure. The receiver uses the structure of V in order to factor the given product and obtain the plaintext efficiently. A malicious attacker, however, cannot extract the plaintext from the product due to insufficient knowledge about V. The suggested Sidon cryptosystem is based on a specific optimal construction of a Sidon space from [26], and yet, other Sidon spaces with comparable parameters can be used similarly. The security of the suggested system relies on the hardness of solving multivariate polynomial equations, and the hardness of the MinRank problem.

In the MinRank problem, which is believed to be hard even for quantum computers, one must find a low-rank target matrix in the linear span of matrices that are given as input; it arises in settings where one solves a quadratic system of equations via linearization. Cryptographic systems that are based on the MinRank attack are often broken by either of two attacks, the minor attack and the kernel attack (also known as the Kipnis-Shamir attack) [12]. In the minor attack, one formulates an equation system by setting all small minors of the target matrix to zero, and solves the resulting system (usually) by linearization. The kernel attack exploits the fact that vectors in the kernel of the target matrix give rise to linear equations in the coefficients of its combination; successfully guessing sufficiently many of those will break the system.

In the sequel we analyze the Sidon cryptosystem in the face of these two attacks, and both are proved to succeed only with exponentially small probability. We additionally analyze attacks that are specific to the Sidon cryptosystem and are not in either of those forms, and show that these require solving polynomial equations outside the range of feasibility. We emphasize that unfortunately, a rigorous proof of hardness that does not rely on a particular attack structure is yet to be found.

This paper is organized as follows. The definition of a Sidon space, alongside relevant constructions and their efficient factorization algorithm, are given in Sect. 2. The details of the Sidon cryptosystem are given in Sect. 3, and its efficiency is discussed. MinRank attacks, namely, the kernel attack and the minor attack, are discussed in Sect. 4. Attacks which are specifically designed for the Sidon cryptosystem are discussed in Sect. 5. Finally, experimental results are reported in Sect. 6, and concluding remarks are given in Sect. 7.

We adopt the following notational conventions. Scalars are denoted by $a, b, \ldots$ or $\alpha, \beta, \ldots$; matrices by $\mathbf{A}, \mathbf{B} \ldots$; sets by $\mathcal{U}, \mathcal{W}, \ldots$; linear subspaces and polynomials by $V, U, \ldots$; and vectors, all of which are row vectors, by $\mathbf{v}, \boldsymbol{\nu}, \ldots$.

2 Preliminaries

For integers k and n let $\mathcal{G}_q(n,k)$ be the set of all k-dimensional subspaces of $\mathbb{F}_{q^n}$ over $\mathbb{F}_q$. *Sidon spaces* were recently defined in [2] as a tool for studying certain multiplicative properties of subspaces. As noted in [2], the term "Sidon space" draws its inspiration from a *Sidon set.* A set of integers is called a Sidon set if the sums of any two (possibly identical) elements in it are distinct; thus, Sidon spaces may be seen as a multiplicative and linear variant of Sidon sets. In the following definition, for $a \in \mathbb{F}_{q^n}$, let $a\mathbb{F}_q \triangleq \{\lambda a | \lambda \in \mathbb{F}_q\}$, which is the subspace over $\mathbb{F}_q$ spanned by a.

Definition 1 ([2, **Sect. 1**]). *A subspace $V \in \mathcal{G}_q(n,k)$ is called a Sidon space if for all nonzero $a,b,c,d \in V$, if $ab = cd$ then $\{a\mathbb{F}_q, b\mathbb{F}_q\} = \{c\mathbb{F}_q, d\mathbb{F}_q\}$.*

It is shown in [2, Thm. 18] and in [26, Prop. 3] that if $V \in \mathcal{G}_q(n,k)$ is a Sidon space, then

$$2k \leq \dim(V^2) \leq \binom{k+1}{2}, \tag{1}$$

where $V^2 \triangleq \operatorname{span}_{\mathbb{F}_q}\{u \cdot v | u, v \in V\}$, and consequently it follows that $k \leq n/2$. Sidon spaces which attain the upper bound are called *max-span* Sidon spaces, and are rather easy to construct; it is an easy exercise to verify that $\operatorname{span}_{\mathbb{F}_q}\{\delta^{n_i}\}_{i=1}^k$ is a max-span Sidon space in $\mathbb{F}_{q^n}$ for $n > 2k^2(1 + o_k(1))$, where δ is a primitive element of $\mathbb{F}_{q^n}$, and $\{n_1, \ldots, n_k\} \subseteq [\lfloor n/2 \rfloor]$ is an optimal (i.e., largest) Sidon set [21]. Sidon spaces which attain the lower bound in (1) are called *min-span* Sidon spaces, and are paramount to our work; it will be shown in the sequel that having $k = \Theta(n)$ is essential to the security of the system. The cryptosystem which is given in this paper employs a min-span Sidon space whose construction is given in the remainder of this section.

Motivated by applications in network coding, constructions of Sidon spaces in several parameter regimes were suggested in [26]. In particular, the following construction provides a Sidon space $V \in \mathcal{G}_q(rk, k)$ for any k and any $r \geq 3$. A slightly more involved variant of this construction is shown in the sequel to provide a Sidon space in $\mathcal{G}_q(2k, k)$, which will be used in our cryptosystem.

Construction 1 *[26, Const. 11]. For integers $r \geq 3$, k, and q a prime power, let $\gamma \in \mathbb{F}_{q^{rk}}^*$ be a root of an irreducible polynomial of degree r over $\mathbb{F}_{q^k}$. Then, $V \triangleq \{u + u^q\gamma | u \in \mathbb{F}_{q^k}\}$ is a Sidon space in $\mathcal{G}_q(rk, k)$.*

By choosing the element γ judiciously, a similar construction provides a Sidon space in $\mathcal{G}_q(2k, k)$ for any $q \geq 3$ as follows. For any given nonnegative integer k, let $\mathcal{W}_{q-1} \triangleq \{u^{q-1} | u \in \mathbb{F}_{q^k}\}$ and $\overline{\mathcal{W}}_{q-1} \triangleq \mathbb{F}_{q^k} \setminus \mathcal{W}_{q-1}$. The next construction requires an element $\gamma \in \mathbb{F}_{q^{2k}}$ that is a root of an irreducible quadratic polynomial $x^2 + bx + c$ over $\mathbb{F}_{q^k}$, where $c \in \overline{\mathcal{W}}_{q-1}$. According to [26, Lemma 13], for any $c \in \overline{\mathcal{W}}_{q-1}$ there exist many b's in $\mathbb{F}_{q^k}$ such that $x^2 + bx + c$ is irreducible over $\mathbb{F}_{q^k}$, and hence such γ elements abound[1].

Construction 2 *[26, Const. 15]. For a prime power $q \geq 3$ and a positive integer k, let $n = 2k$, and let $\gamma \in \mathbb{F}_{q^n}^*$ be a root of an irreducible polynomial x^2+bx+c over $\mathbb{F}_{q^k}$ with $c \in \overline{\mathcal{W}}_{q-1}$. The subspace $V \triangleq \{u + u^q\gamma | u \in \mathbb{F}_{q^k}\}$ is a Sidon space in $\mathcal{G}_q(2k, k)$.*

The Sidon space V of Construction 2 will be used in the sequel to devise an MPKC. This subspace admits the following efficient algorithm [26, Thm. 16] that for every nonzero a and b in V, factors ab to a and b up to constant factors from $\mathbb{F}_q$; note that since $ab = (\frac{1}{\lambda}a)(\lambda b)$ for any $a, b \in V$ and any $\lambda \in \mathbb{F}_q^*$, this algorithm is capable of identifying a and b only up to a multiplicative factor in $\mathbb{F}_q$.

Given ab, denote $a = u + u^q\gamma$ for some nonzero $u \in \mathbb{F}_{q^k}$ and $b = v + v^q\gamma$ for some nonzero $v \in \mathbb{F}_{q^k}$. Notice that since γ is a root of $x^2 + bx + c$ it follows that

$$\begin{aligned} ab &= (u + u^q\gamma)(v + v^q\gamma) \\ &= (uv - (uv)^q c) + (uv^q + u^q v - b(uv)^q)\gamma , \end{aligned}$$

and since $\{1, \gamma\}$ is a basis of $\mathbb{F}_{q^n}$ over $\mathbb{F}_{q^k}$, it follows that one can obtain the values of $q_0 \triangleq uv - (uv)^q c$ and $q_1 \triangleq uv^q + u^q v - b(uv)^q$ by representing ab over this basis.

Since $c \in \overline{\mathcal{W}}_{q-1}$, it follows that the linearized polynomial $T(x) = x - cx^q$ is invertible on $\mathbb{F}_{q^k}$. Hence, it is possible to extract uv from $q_0 = T(uv)$ by applying T^{-1}.

Knowing uv, extracting $uv^q + vu^q$ from q_1 is possible by adding $b(uv)^q$. Therefore, the polynomial $uv + (uv^q + u^q v)x + (uv)^q x^2$ can be assembled, and its respective roots $-1/u^{q-1}$ and $-1/v^{q-1}$ can be found. Since these roots determine $u\mathbb{F}_q$ and $v\mathbb{F}_q$ uniquely, it follows that a and b are identified up to order and up to a multiplicative factor in $\mathbb{F}_q$.

---

[1] Since $|\overline{\mathcal{W}}_{q-1}| = q^k - \frac{q^k-1}{q-1} - 1$, a crude lower bound for the number of such elements γ is $\approx \frac{q-2}{q-1} \cdot q^k$.

3 The Sidon Cryptosystem

In general, for a Sidon space $V \in \mathcal{G}_q(n,k)$ and $a, b \in V$, factoring ab to a and b requires knowledge about the structure of V, as can be seen from the factoring algorithm suggested above. This intuition leads to the following MPKC, called the *Sidon Cryptosystem*. The crux of devising this system is enabling Bob to encrypt his message into a product ab, without the need to know the precise construction of V by Alice. This is done by exploiting the bilinear nature of multiplication in finite field extensions.

To this end, we introduce the notion of a *multiplication table* of a subspace. For a given vector $\mathbf{v} = (v_1, \ldots, v_k) \in \mathbb{F}_{q^n}^k$ let $\mathbf{M}(\mathbf{v}) \triangleq \mathbf{v}^\intercal \mathbf{v}$. For an ordered basis $\mathbf{b} = (b_1, b_2, \ldots, b_n)$ of $\mathbb{F}_{q^n}$ over $\mathbb{F}_q$, express $\mathbf{M}(\mathbf{v})$ as a linear combination of matrices over $\mathbb{F}_q$, i.e.,

$$\begin{aligned}\mathbf{M}(\mathbf{v}) &= b_1\mathbf{M}^{(1)} + b_2\mathbf{M}^{(2)} + \ldots + b_n\mathbf{M}^{(n)}, \text{ and let}\\ \mathbf{M}(\mathbf{v},\mathbf{b}) &\triangleq (\mathbf{M}^{(1)}, \mathbf{M}^{(2)}, \ldots, \mathbf{M}^{(n)}).\end{aligned}$$

The matrix $\mathbf{M}(\mathbf{v})$ is called *the multiplication table* of $\mathbf{v}$, and the entries of $\mathbf{M}(\mathbf{v},\mathbf{b})$ are called the *coefficient matrices* of $\mathbf{v}$ with respect to $\mathbf{b}$. This notion will be of interest when $\{v_1, \ldots, v_k\}$ is a basis of a Sidon space.

The following cryptosystem relies on choosing a random Sidon space by Construction 2 (which amounts to randomly choosing a proper γ), fixing an arbitrary ordered basis $\boldsymbol{\nu} = (\nu_1, \ldots, \nu_k)$ of V, and interpreting the product of two elements $a \triangleq \sum_{i=1}^k a_i\nu_i$ and $b \triangleq \sum_{i=1}^k b_i\nu_i$ in V as the bilinear form $\mathbf{a}\mathbf{M}(\boldsymbol{\nu})\mathbf{b}^\intercal$, where $\mathbf{a} = (a_1, \ldots, a_k) \in \mathbb{F}_q^k$ and $\mathbf{b} = (b_1, \ldots, b_k) \in \mathbb{F}_q^k$. Even though the suggested cryptosystem relies on Construction 2, any Sidon space for which an efficient factorization algorithm exists may be used similarly. A remark about the required ratio k/n is given shortly.

To describe the message set in the following cryptosystem, let $\sim$ be an equivalence relation on $\mathbb{F}_q^{k\times k}$ such that $\mathbf{A} \sim \mathbf{B}$ if $\mathbf{A} = \mathbf{B}^\intercal$, for any $\mathbf{A}, \mathbf{B} \in \mathbb{F}_q^{k\times k}$. Further, let $\mathcal{Q}_k$ be the set of $k \times k$ rank one matrices over $\mathbb{F}_q$, modulo the equivalence relation $\sim$. That is, $\mathcal{Q}_k$ is a set of equivalence classes, each of which contains either one symmetric matrix of rank one, or two non-symmetric matrices of rank one, where one is the transpose of the other. It is shown in Lemma 3 in Appendix A that $|\mathcal{Q}_k| = \frac{(q^k-1)(q^k-q)}{2(q-1)} + q^k - 1$. In what follows, Alice chooses a random Sidon space V by Construction 2, and publishes its coefficient matrices according to a random basis of V and a random basis of $\mathbb{F}_{q^n}$. Bob then sends Alice an encrypted message by exploiting the bilinear nature of multiplication in field extensions.

Parameters: An integer k and a field size $q \geq 3$.
Private key: Alice chooses

1. **A random representation of $\mathbb{F}_{q^n}$ over $\mathbb{F}_q$:** i.e., a polynomial $P_A(x) \in \mathbb{F}_q[x]$ of degree $n = 2k$ which is irreducible over $\mathbb{F}_q$.
2. **A random Sidon space by Construction** 2**:** i.e., a random element $c \in \overline{W}_{q-1}$ and an element $b \in \mathbb{F}_{q^k}$ such that $P_{b,c}(x) \triangleq x^2 + bx + c$ is irreducible

over $\mathbb{F}_{q^k}$, a $\gamma \in \mathbb{F}_{q^n}^*$ such that $P_{b,c}(\gamma) = 0$; this γ defines the Sidon space $V \triangleq \{u + u^q\gamma | u \in \mathbb{F}_{q^k}\}$.

3. **A random *ordered* basis $\boldsymbol{\nu} = (\nu_1, \ldots, \nu_k)$ of V:** which is equivalent to choosing a random invertible $k \times k$ matrix over $\mathbb{F}_q$.
4. **A random *ordered* basis $\boldsymbol{\beta} = (\beta_1, \ldots, \beta_n)$ of $\mathbb{F}_{q^n}$ over $\mathbb{F}_q$:** which is equivalent to choosing a random invertible $n \times n$ matrix over $\mathbb{F}_q$.

Public key: Alice publishes $\mathbf{M}(\boldsymbol{\nu}, \boldsymbol{\beta}) = (\mathbf{M}^{(1)}, \ldots, \mathbf{M}^{(n)})$.

Encryption: The message to be encrypted is seen as an equivalence class in $\mathcal{Q}_k$. Bob chooses arbitrary $\mathbf{a} = (a_1, \ldots, a_k)$ and $\mathbf{b} = (b_1, \ldots, b_k)$ that correspond to his message (i.e., such that $\mathbf{a}^\intercal\mathbf{b}$ is in the corresponding equivalence class in $\mathcal{Q}_k$), and sends $E(\mathbf{a}, \mathbf{b}) \triangleq \left(\mathbf{a}\mathbf{M}^{(i)}\mathbf{b}^\intercal\right)_{i=1}^n$ to Alice.

Decryption: Alice assembles

$$\sum_{i=1}^{n} \mathbf{a}\mathbf{M}^{(i)}\mathbf{b}^\intercal \cdot \beta_i = \mathbf{a}\mathbf{M}(\boldsymbol{\nu})\mathbf{b}^\intercal = \mathbf{a}\boldsymbol{\nu}^\intercal\boldsymbol{\nu}\mathbf{b}^\intercal = \left(\sum_{i=1}^{k} a_i\nu_i\right)\left(\sum_{i=1}^{k} b_i\nu_i\right) \triangleq ab\,.$$

Since a and b are in the Sidon space V, they can be retrieved from ab up to order and up to a multiplicative factor from $\mathbb{F}_q$ (see Sect. 2). The respective $\mathbf{a}$ and $\mathbf{b}$ are then retrieved by representing a and b over $\boldsymbol{\nu}$. Since $\mathbf{a}$ and $\mathbf{b}$ correspond to a unique equivalence class in $\mathcal{Q}_k$, it follows that they determine the message sent by Bob uniquely.

An alternative scheme which employs randomization is given in Appendix B. One clear advantage of the above system is that its *information rate* approaches 1 as k grows. The information rate is defined as the ratio between the number of bits in Bob's message and the number of bits that are required to transmit the corresponding cyphertext. Due to the size of $\mathcal{Q}_k$, given earlier, it follows that the number of information bits in Bob's message approaches $2k\log_2 q$ as k grows; this is identical to the number of information bits in the cyphertext $E(\mathbf{a}, \mathbf{b})$.

On the other hand, a clear disadvantage is that the public key is relatively large in comparison with the size of the plaintext; due to the symmetry of the coefficient matrices, the public key contains $k^2(k+1)$ elements[2] in $\mathbb{F}_q$, whereas the plaintext contains approximately $2k$ elements in $\mathbb{F}_q$. This disadvantage is apparent in some other MPKCs as well. For instance, in the ABC cryptosystem [28, Sect. 3], to transmit a message of k field elements, $2k$ quadratic polynomials in k variables are evaluated. Hence, the information rate is $\frac{1}{2}$, and in order to transmit k field elements, a public key of $k^2(k+1)$ field elements is required. Our system suffers from a large public key as many other MPKCs, albeit at information rate which approaches 1.

Remark 1 (A note about performance). Both encoding and decoding require only elementary operations over finite fields. Given $\mathbf{a}$ and $\mathbf{b}$, Bob encrypts by computing n bi-linear transforms in $O(k^3)$. Given the cypertext, Alice obtains ab using $O(k^2)$ operations, and follows the factorization algorithm from Sect. 2. This algorithm includes change-of-basis to $\{1, \gamma\}$, which is equivalent to solving

[2] That is, $n = 2k$ matrices, each containing $\binom{k+1}{2}$ elements.

a linear equation, followed by applying a pre-determined linear transform T^{-1}, solving a univariate quadratic polynomial over $\mathbb{F}_{q^n}$, and finally two computation of inverse (e.g., by the extended Euclidean algorithm) and two extractions of $(q-1)$'th root (e.g., by the $O(k^3)$ algorithm of [4]). Overall, assuimg q is constant, both encoding and decoding require $O(k^3)$ operations. Key generation can be done via a simple randomized process, and experimental results are given in Sect. 6.

Remark 2 (A note about parameters). The fact that $n = 2k$ (or more generally, that $k = \Theta(n)$) in the Sidon cryptosystem above seems to be essential to the security of the system. For example, using a max-span Sidon space [26, Sect. IV], in which the set $\{\nu_i\nu_j\}_{i,j\in[k]}$ is linearly independent over $\mathbb{F}_q$ and thus $n \geq \binom{k+1}{2}$, is detrimental to the security of the system—it is easy to verify that if V is a max-span Sidon space, then $\text{span}_{\mathbb{F}_q}(\{\mathbf{M}^{(i)}\}_{i=1}^n)$ is the set of all $k \times k$ symmetric matrices over $\mathbb{F}_q$. Hence, given $E(\mathbf{a}, \mathbf{b}) = (\mathbf{a}\mathbf{M}^{(i)}\mathbf{b}^\intercal)_{i=1}^n$, by using linear operations one can have $(\mathbf{a}\mathbf{C}_{i,j}\mathbf{b}^\intercal)_{i,j\in[k]}$, where $\mathbf{C}_{i,j}$ is a matrix which contains 1 in its (i,j)-th entry, 1 in its (j,i)-th entry, and zero elsewhere, and as a result the expressions $\{a_ib_i\}_{i=1}^k$ and $\{a_ib_j + a_jb_i\}_{i>j}$ are obtained. Clearly, these values are the coefficients of $p_a \cdot p_b$, where

$$p_a(x_1, \ldots, x_k) \triangleq \sum_{i\in[k]} a_ix_i, \qquad \text{and} \qquad p_b(x_1, \ldots, x_k) \triangleq \sum_{i\in[k]} b_ix_i \ ,$$

and thus $\mathbf{a}$ and $\mathbf{b}$ could be identified by factoring $p_a \cdot p_b$.

4 MinRank Attacks

In what follows, we consider several attacks that are based on the well-known NP-complete problem[3] MinRank [10]. In all of these attacks, it is shown that breaking the system requires solving some special case of MinRank, and the feasibility of success is discussed.

The MinRank problem.
Input: Integers k, n, r and linearly independent matrices $\mathbf{N}^{(0)}, \mathbf{N}^{(1)}, \ldots, \mathbf{N}^{(n)}$ in $\mathbb{F}^{k\times k}$ for some field $\mathbb{F}$.
Output: A tuple $(\lambda_1, \ldots, \lambda_n) \in \mathbb{F}^n$, not all zero, such that

$$\text{rank}_{\mathbb{F}}\left(\sum_{i=1}^n \lambda_i\mathbf{N}^{(i)} - \mathbf{N}^{(0)}\right) \leq r.$$

In this section, the purpose of the attacker Eve is to find an equivalent secret key V'. That is, Eve begins by guessing an irreducible polynomial $P_E(x)$ of degree $n = 2k$ to define $F_E = \mathbb{F}_q[x] \bmod (P_E(x)) = \mathbb{F}_{q^n}$, where $(P_E(x))$ is the ideal generated by $P_E(x)$ in $\mathbb{F}_q[x]$. Then, since there exists a field isomorphism f :

[3] Or more precisely, the *square* MinRank *search* problem.

$F_A \to F_E$, and since $\nu_s\nu_t = \sum_{i=1}^{n}(\mathbf{M}^{(i)})_{s,t}\beta_i$ by the definition of the system, it follows that

$$f(\nu_s\nu_t) = f(\nu_s)f(\nu_t) = f\left(\sum_{i=1}^{n}\mathbf{M}_{s,t}^{(i)}\beta_i\right) = \sum_{i=1}^{n}\mathbf{M}_{s,t}^{(i)}f(\beta_i). \tag{2}$$

Namely, the tuple $(f(\beta_i))_{i=1}^{n}$ is a solution to the MinRank problem whose parameters are $r = 1$, $\mathbf{N}^{(0)} = 0$, $n = 2k$, $\mathbb{F} = F_E$, and $\mathbf{N}^{(i)} = \mathbf{M}^{(i)}$ for $i \in [n]$. Then, factoring the resulting rank one matrix $\sum_{i=1}^{n}\mathbf{M}^{(i)}f(\beta_i)$ to $f(\boldsymbol{\nu})^\intercal f(\boldsymbol{\nu})$ enables Eve to find $V' = f(V)$, i.e., the subspace in F_E which is isomorphic to V in F_A. With $f(V)$ at her disposal, Eve may break the cryptosystem.

To the best of the authors' knowledge, this solution is not necessarily unique; furthermore, it is unclear if breaking the system is possible if a solution is found which is not a basis of F_E over $\mathbb{F}_q$, or if the resulting V' is not a Sidon space. Nevertheless, we focus on the hardness of finding *any* solution. Moreover, due to (2), for convenience of notation we omit the isomorphism f from the discussion.

4.1 The Kernel Attack

The kernel formulation of MinRank relies on the fact that any nonzero vector $\mathbf{v} \in \mathbb{F}_{q^n}^k$ in $K \triangleq \ker_{\mathbb{F}_{q^n}}(\sum_{i\in[n]}\beta_i\mathbf{M}^{(i)})$ gives rise to k $\mathbb{F}_{q^n}$-linear equations in $y_1, \ldots, y_n$, namely, the k equations given by $(\sum_{i=1}^{n} y_i\mathbf{M}^{(i)})\mathbf{v}^\intercal = 0$. To find the correct $y_1, \ldots, y_n \in \mathbb{F}_{q^n}$, sufficiently many $\mathbf{v}$'s in K must be found. For example, finding $\mathbf{v}_1 \in K$ yields k equations in $n = 2k$ variables, and hence there are at least $(q^n)^k$ possible solutions, depending on the linear dependence of these equations. Finding an additional $\mathbf{v}_2 \in K$ adds another k equations, which are likely to reduce the number of possible values for $y_1, \ldots, y_n$ further. By repeating this process, the attacker wishes to reduce the dimension of the solution space sufficiently so that the solution $y_1, \ldots, y_n$ could be found.

Since K is unknown, the attacker resorts to uniformly random guesses of $\mathbf{v}_1, \mathbf{v}_2 \in \mathbb{F}_{q^n}^k$, hoping to get them both in K. However, since $\dim K = k - 1$, it follows that

$$\Pr_{\mathbf{v}\in\mathbb{F}_{q^n}^k}(\mathbf{v} \in K) = \frac{|K|}{|\mathbb{F}_{q^n}^k|} = \frac{(q^n)^{k-1}}{(q^n)^k} = \frac{1}{q^n}, \tag{3}$$

and hence the probability of finding even *a single* $\mathbf{v} \in K$ is exponentially small in the message length.

Remark 3 (Kernel attack over the base field). Recall that $\mathbf{M}(\boldsymbol{\nu}) = \sum_{i\in[n]}\beta_i\mathbf{M}^{(i)}$. In order to make the above attack feasible, one may suggest to guess nonzero vectors $\mathbf{v} \in \mathbb{F}_q^k$ rather than $\mathbf{v} \in \mathbb{F}_{q^n}^k$. However, it is easy to see that for any nonzero vector $\mathbf{v} \in \mathbb{F}_q^k$ we have $\mathbf{M}(\boldsymbol{\nu})\mathbf{v} \neq 0$, and in fact it is a vector with no nonzero entries. Indeed, $\mathbf{M}(\boldsymbol{\nu})$ is the multiplication table of $\boldsymbol{\nu} = (\nu_1, \ldots, \nu_k)$, which is a basis of the Sidon space V. Hence, $\mathbf{M}(\boldsymbol{\nu})\mathbf{v}$ is a vector whose i'th coordinate equals $\nu_i(\sum_{j\in[k]} v_j\nu_j)$. Since the ν_j's are linearly independent over $\mathbb{F}_q$ and $\mathbf{v}$ is nonzero, the second term in the product is nonzero, and hence so is the product.

Remark 4 (Kipnis-Shamir formulation). In a variant of this attack, one guesses kernel vectors in a systematic form, rather than in a general form. That is, the system

$$\left(\sum_{i=1}^{n} y_i \mathbf{M}^{(i)}\right) \begin{pmatrix} 1 & 0 & \dots & 0 \\ 0 & 1 & \dots & 0 \\ \vdots & \vdots & \ddots & \vdots \\ 0 & 0 & \dots & 1 \\ z_1 & z_2 & \dots & z_{k-1} \end{pmatrix} = 0.$$

has a solution with $y_1, \dots, y_n, z_1, \dots, z_{k-1} \in \mathbb{F}_{q^n}$ (technically, the position of the non-unit row in the r.h.s matrix can be arbitrary; however, this can be amended by repeating the algorithm k times with different positions, or by random guessing). Similar to the attack above, one can guess two column vectors from the r.h.s matrix, and solve the resulting system, which is linear in the y_i's. However, it is readily verified that the probability to guess each z_i correctly is q^{-n}, and hence analysis similar to (3) applies. Alternatively, one can treat both the y_i's and the z_i's as variables over $\mathbb{F}_{q^n}$, and solve the resulting quadratic system using Gröbner basis algorithms. Very recently [3,31], it was shown that in some parameter regimes, such Gröbner basis algorithms admit an inherent structure that can be utilized to reduce the computation time, often significantly (e.g., for the HFE cryptosystem). Whether the Sidon cryptosystem admits a similar structure remains to be studied.

4.2 The Minor Attack

In the minor attack of MinRank, one considers the system of homogeneous quadratic equations given by setting all 2×2 minors of $\sum_{i \in [n]} y_i \mathbf{M}^{(i)}$ to zero, and (usually) solves by linearization. That is, the system is considered as a linear one in the $\binom{n+1}{2}$ variables $\{z_{i,j}\}_{i \leq j, i,j \in [n]}$, where $z_{i,j}$ represents $y_i y_j$ for every i and j. The resulting homogeneous linear system has a right kernel of dimension at least one; if it happens to be at most one, the attacker finds a nonzero solution $\mathbf{w} = (w_{i,j})_{i \leq j}$ and arranges it in a symmetric matrix

$$\text{mat}(\mathbf{w}) = \begin{pmatrix} w_{1,1} & w_{1,2} & \cdots & w_{1,n} \\ w_{1,2} & w_{2,2} & \cdots & w_{2,n} \\ \vdots & \dots & \ddots & \vdots \\ w_{1,n} & w_{2,n} & \cdots & w_{n,n} \end{pmatrix}. \quad (4)$$

Then, the attacker finds a rank one decomposition $(w_1, \dots, w_n)^\intercal (w_1, \dots, w_n)$ of (4) (which is guaranteed to exist, since the solution $z_{i,j} = y_i y_j$ has a rank one decomposition, and the dimension of the kernel is one), which provides a solution.

In most systems the dimension of the kernel will indeed be at most one. Otherwise the attacker is left with yet another MinRank problem, that we call *secondary*, in which a "rank-one vector" (that is, a vector $\mathbf{w}$ such that $\text{mat}(\mathbf{w})$ is of rank one) must be found in the kernel. In what follows it is shown that this attack on the Sidon cryptosystem results in the latter scenario. That is, attempting to solve the minor attack via linearization results in a linear system with a large kernel. Moreover, it is shown that the secondary (and tertiary, etc.) attack suffers from the same effect.

Let $\boldsymbol{\Omega}$ be the quadratic system which results from setting all 2×2 minors of $\sum_{i\in[n]} y_i \mathbf{M}^{(i)}$ to zero. This system contains $\binom{k}{2}^2$ equations, each is a linear combination over $\mathbb{F}_q$ of the $\binom{n+1}{2}$ monomials $y_1^2, \ldots, y_n^2, y_1y_2, \ldots, y_{n-1}y_n$. To break the cryptosystem, the values of $y_1, \ldots, y_n$ in a solution to $\boldsymbol{\Omega}$ should form a basis to $\mathbb{F}_{q^n}$ over $\mathbb{F}_q$, and as discussed earlier, it is unclear if the system can be broken otherwise. Yet, for generality we focus on the hardness of finding *any* solution.

Let $\boldsymbol{\Omega}_{\text{lin}}$ be the matrix which results from linearizing $\boldsymbol{\Omega}$. That is, each of the $\binom{n+1}{2}$ columns of $\boldsymbol{\Omega}_{\text{lin}}$ is indexed by a monomial y_sy_t, and each row is indexed by a minor $((i,j),(\ell,d))$ (i.e., the minor that is computed from the i'th and j'th rows and the ℓ's and d'th columns). The value of an entry in column y_sy_t and row $((i,j),(\ell,d))$ is the coefficient of y_sy_t in the equation for the 2×2 minor of $(\sum_{i\in[n]} y_i\mathbf{M}^{(i)})$ in rows i and j, and columns ℓ and d. Note that a solution to $\boldsymbol{\Omega}$ corresponds to a vector in the right kernel of $\boldsymbol{\Omega}_{\text{lin}}$, but the inverse is not necessarily true.

We begin by discussing several aspects of $\boldsymbol{\Omega}_{\text{lin}}$. First, since the matrices $\mathbf{M}^{(i)}$ are symmetric, many rows in $\boldsymbol{\Omega}_{\text{lin}}$ are identical; minor $((i,j),(\ell,d))$ identical to minor $((\ell,d),(i,j))$. Hence, the effective number of rows is at most

$$\binom{\binom{k}{2}+1}{2}. \tag{5}$$

Second, $\boldsymbol{\Omega}_{\text{lin}}$ is over $\mathbb{F}_q$, while the required solution is in $\mathbb{F}_{q^n}$. One way to circumvent this is by representing every y_i using n variables over $\mathbb{F}_q$. The resulting linearized system can be described using Kronecker products. By using the fact that the rank of a Kronecker product is the product of the individual ranks, it can be easily shown that this system has a large kernel, and thus solving by linearization is not feasible. The full details of this approach are given in Appendix C.

More importantly, in contrast to Remark 3, one can simply find $\ker_{\mathbb{F}_q}(\boldsymbol{\Omega}_{\text{lin}})$; since $\text{rank}_{\mathbb{F}_q}(\boldsymbol{\Omega}_{\text{lin}}) = \text{rank}_{\mathbb{F}_{q^n}}(\boldsymbol{\Omega}_{\text{lin}})$, it follows that the true solution $(z_{i,j})_{i\le j} = (\beta_i\beta_j)_{i\le j}$ lies in $\text{span}_{\mathbb{F}_{q^n}}(\ker_{\mathbb{F}_q}(\boldsymbol{\Omega}_{\text{lin}}))$. Put differently, one can solve $\boldsymbol{\Omega}$ via linearization over $\mathbb{F}_q$ (i.e., obtain an $\mathbb{F}_q$-basis to $\boldsymbol{\Omega}_{\text{lin}}$'s right kernel), span it over $\mathbb{F}_{q^n}$, and search for a rank one vector. However, in what follows it is shown that the rank of $\boldsymbol{\Omega}_{\text{lin}}$ is low (specifically, $\text{rank}(\boldsymbol{\Omega}_{\text{lin}}) \le \binom{n+1}{2} - n$), and hence this approach is not feasible either. One might wonder if the secondary MinRank problem that emerges is itself solvable by linearization, for which we show that the answer is negative, and the proof is similar.

Bounding the Rank of $\boldsymbol{\Omega}_{\text{lin}}$. Let $\boldsymbol{\nu} = (\nu_1, \ldots, \nu_k)$ be the secret basis of V and let $\mathbf{u} = (\nu_1, \ldots, \nu_n)$ be an extension of $\boldsymbol{\nu}$ to a complete basis of $\mathbb{F}_{q^n}$

over $\mathbb{F}_q$. Let $\boldsymbol{\beta} = (\beta_1, \ldots, \beta_n)$ be the secret basis of $\mathbb{F}_{q^n}$. Therefore, we have that $\mathbf{u}^\intercal \mathbf{u} = \sum_{i\in[n]} \beta_i \mathbf{N}^{(i)}$ for some matrices $\mathbf{N}^{(i)} \in \mathbb{F}_q^{n\times n}$. It is readily verified that for every $i \in [n]$, the upper left $k \times k$ submatrix of $\mathbf{N}^{(i)}$ is the public key coefficient matrix $\mathbf{M}^{(i)}$. In addition, let $\mathbf{E} \in \mathbb{F}_q^{n\times n}$ be the change-of-basis matrix such that $\boldsymbol{\beta} = \mathbf{uE}$, and then

$$\boldsymbol{\beta}^\intercal \boldsymbol{\beta} = \mathbf{E}^\intercal \mathbf{u}^\intercal \mathbf{u} \mathbf{E} = \sum_{i\in[n]} \beta_i \mathbf{E}^\intercal \mathbf{N}^{(i)} \mathbf{E}. \tag{6}$$

Construct a system $\boldsymbol{\Gamma}$ of quadratic equations in the variables $y_1, \ldots, y_n$ by setting all the 2×2 minors of $\sum_{i\in[n]} y_i \mathbf{N}^{(i)}$ to zero, and let $\boldsymbol{\Gamma}_{\text{lin}}$ be the linearization of the set of equations in $\boldsymbol{\Gamma}$, obtained by replacing each monomial $y_i y_j$ by the variable $z_{i,j}$. Notice that one obtains $\boldsymbol{\Omega}_{\text{lin}}$ from $\boldsymbol{\Gamma}_{\text{lin}}$ by omitting every row $((i,j),(\ell,d))$ of $\boldsymbol{\Gamma}_{\text{lin}}$ with either one of i, j, ℓ, d larger than k. Therefore, it follows that $\ker(\boldsymbol{\Gamma}_{\text{lin}}) \subseteq \ker(\boldsymbol{\Omega}_{\text{lin}})$.

We claim that each matrix $\mathbf{E}^\intercal \mathbf{N}^{(l)} \mathbf{E}, l \in [n]$ defines a valid solution to $\boldsymbol{\Gamma}_{\text{lin}}$ simply by setting $z_{i,j} = (\mathbf{E}^\intercal \mathbf{N}^{(l)} \mathbf{E})_{i,j} = (\mathbf{E}^\intercal \mathbf{N}^{(l)} \mathbf{E})_{j,i}$. Then, it will be shown that $\{\mathbf{E}^\intercal \mathbf{N}^{(l)} \mathbf{E}\}_{l\in[n]}$ are linearly independent, and thus so are the solutions they define. This would imply that the dimension of the solution space of $\boldsymbol{\Gamma}_{\text{lin}}$ is at least n, and since $\ker(\boldsymbol{\Gamma}_{\text{lin}}) \subseteq \ker(\boldsymbol{\Omega}_{\text{lin}})$, it would also imply that the dimension of the solution space of $\boldsymbol{\Omega}_{\text{lin}}$ is at least n.

For an element $\alpha \in \mathbb{F}_{q^n}$ and $i \in [n]$ let $(\alpha)_i \in \mathbb{F}_q$ be the coefficient of β_i in the expansion of α as a linear combination of the β_j's over $\mathbb{F}_q$, i.e., $\alpha = \sum_{i\in[n]} (\alpha)_i \beta_i$. Then, it follows from the definition of the $\mathbf{N}^{(l)}$'s that $\mathbf{N}^{(l)}_{i,j} = (\nu_i \nu_j)_l$. Similarly, it follows from (6) that $(\mathbf{E}^\intercal \mathbf{N}^{(l)} \mathbf{E})_{i,j} = (\beta_i \beta_j)_l$.

Lemma 1. *For every $l \in [n]$ the assignment $z_{i,j} = (\mathbf{E}^\intercal \mathbf{N}^{(l)} \mathbf{E})_{i,j}$ is a solution for $\boldsymbol{\Gamma}_{lin}$.*

Proof. Let $\begin{pmatrix} a & b \\ c & d \end{pmatrix} \in \mathbb{F}_{q^n}^{2\times 2}$ be an arbitrary 2×2 submatrix of $\mathbf{u}^\intercal \mathbf{u} = \sum_{i\in[n]} \beta_i \mathbf{N}^{(i)}$. First, notice that the respective equation in $\boldsymbol{\Gamma}$ is

$$\left(\sum_{i\in[n]} (a)_i y_i\right) \left(\sum_{i\in[n]} (d)_i y_i\right) - \left(\sum_{i\in[n]} (b)_i y_i\right) \left(\sum_{i\in[n]} (c)_i y_i\right) = 0,$$

which after linearization becomes

$$\sum_{i,j\in[n]} (a)_i (d)_j z_{i,j} - \sum_{i,j\in[n]} (b)_i (c)_j z_{i,j} = 0. \tag{7}$$

Second, since $\mathbf{u}^\intercal \mathbf{u}$ is a rank one matrix, so is any of its 2×2 submatrices, and therefore $ad - bc = 0$. Since this implies that $(ad - bc)_l = 0$ for every $l \in [n]$, it follows that

$$\begin{aligned}
0 &= (ad - bc)_l = (ad)_l - (bc)_l \\
&= \left(\textstyle\sum_{i,j\in[n]}(a)_i(d)_j\beta_i\beta_j\right)_l - \left(\textstyle\sum_{i,j\in[n]}(b)_i(c)_j\beta_i\beta_j\right)_l \\
&= \textstyle\sum_{i,j\in[n]}(a)_i(d)_j(\beta_i\beta_j)_l - \sum_{i,j\in[n]}(b)_i(c)_j(\beta_i\beta_j)_l \\
&= \textstyle\sum_{i,j\in[n]}(a)_i(d)_j(\mathbf{E}^\intercal\mathbf{N}^{(l)}\mathbf{E})_{i,j} - \sum_{i,j\in[n]}(b)_i(c)_j(\mathbf{E}^\intercal\mathbf{N}^{(l)}\mathbf{E})_{i,j}.
\end{aligned}$$

Therefore, it follows from (7) that for every $l \in [n]$, the assignments $z_{i,j} = (\mathbf{E}^\intercal\mathbf{N}^{(l)}\mathbf{E})_{i,j}$ is a zero of $\mathbf{\Gamma}_{\text{lin}}$, as needed.

Lemma 2. *The n matrices $\mathbf{E}^\intercal\mathbf{N}^{(l)}\mathbf{E}, l \in [n]$ are linearly independent over $\mathbb{F}_q$.*

Proof. Since $\mathbf{E}$ is invertible, the claim follows by showing that the matrices $\{\mathbf{N}^{(l)}\}_{l\in[n]}$ are linearly independent over $\mathbb{F}_q$. For $l \in [n]$ let $\mathbf{a} = (a_i)_{i\in[n]}$ and $\mathbf{b} = (b_i)_{i\in[n]}$ be nonzero vectors in $\mathbb{F}_q^n$ such that $(\sum_{i\in[n]} a_i\nu_i)(\sum_{j\in[n]} b_j\nu_j) = \beta_l$. Then, it follows that

$$\beta_l = \left(\textstyle\sum_{i\in[n]}a_i\nu\right)\left(\textstyle\sum_{j\in[n]}b_j\nu_j\right) = \mathbf{a}\mathbf{u}^\intercal\mathbf{u}\mathbf{b}^\intercal = \sum_{i\in[n]}\beta_i\mathbf{a}\mathbf{N}^{(i)}\mathbf{b}^\intercal,$$

and hence

$$\mathbf{a}\mathbf{N}^{(i)}\mathbf{b}^\intercal = \begin{cases} 1 & i = l \\ 0 & i \neq l \end{cases}.$$

This readily implies that every $\mathbf{N}^{(l)}$ is linearly independent of the remaining matrices $\{\mathbf{N}^{(j)}\}_{j\neq l}$; otherwise, a nontrivial linear combination $\mathbf{N}^{(l)} = \sum_{j\neq l}\alpha_i\mathbf{N}^{(j)}$ would imply that $1 = 0$ by multiplying from the left by $\mathbf{a}$ and from the right by $\mathbf{b}^\intercal$. Since this holds for every $l \in [n]$, the claim follows.

Remark 5. We have experimentally verified for a wide range of q and n values that $\text{rank}(\mathbf{\Omega}_{\text{lin}}) = \binom{n+1}{2} - 2n$, namely, that $\dim\ker(\mathbf{\Omega}_{\text{lin}}) = 2n$. In the above it is proved that $\dim\ker(\mathbf{\Omega}_{\text{lin}}) \geq n$, and the remaining n dimensions remain unexplained. One might conjecture that different extensions of $\nu_1, \ldots, \nu_k$ to $\mathbf{u}$ might result in different kernels of $\mathbf{\Gamma}_{\text{lin}}$, which might explain the missing n dimensions in $\ker(\mathbf{\Omega}_{\text{lin}})$. However, it is shown in Appendix D that this is not the case, and all possible extensions of $\nu_1, \ldots, \nu_k$ to $\boldsymbol{\nu}$ result in identical $\ker(\mathbf{\Gamma}_{\text{lin}})$.

Secondary Minor Attack. In the above it is shown that by attempting to solve the minor attack via linearization, one is left with yet another MinRank problem, which we call *secondary*. That is, in the secondary problem one must find a rank one vector in the $\mathbb{F}_{q^n}$-span of $\ker(\mathbf{\Omega}_{\text{lin}})$ (i.e., a rank one matrix in $\{\text{mat}(\mathbf{y})|\mathbf{y} \in \text{span}_{\mathbb{F}_{q^n}}(\ker_{\mathbb{F}_q}(\mathbf{\Omega}_{\text{lin}}))\}$, where $\text{mat}(\cdot)$ is defined in (4)). To show the hardness of the *primary* minrank attack, it was shown earlier that it is not feasible to find a rank one matrix in the $\mathbb{F}_{q^n}$-span of $\{\mathbf{N}^{(i)}\}_{i\in[n]}$ via linearization. According to Lemma 1, to show that hardness of the *secondary* attack it suffices to show that that it is not feasible to find a rank one matrix in the $\mathbb{F}_{q^n}$-span of $\{\mathbf{E}^\intercal\mathbf{N}^{(i)}\mathbf{E}\}_{i\in[n]}$. Since $\mathbf{E}$ is invertible, it readily follows that a solution to the primary attack is also a solution to the secondary, and vice versa. Therefore, solving the secondary minor attack via linearization is not feasible either.

Moreover, in the secondary attack and in the subsequent ones (tertiary, quaternary, etc.), we observe the following intriguing circular phenomenon. Let $\{\mathbf{B}^{(i)}\}_{i\in[n]} \subseteq \mathbb{F}_q^{n\times n}$ such that $\boldsymbol{\beta}^\intercal\boldsymbol{\beta} = \sum_{i\in[n]}\beta_i\mathbf{B}^{(i)}$. Since $\boldsymbol{\beta} = \mathbf{uE}$ and $\mathbf{u}^\intercal\mathbf{u} = \sum_{i\in[n]}\beta_i\mathbf{N}^{(i)}$, it follows that

$$\mathbf{u}^\intercal\mathbf{u} = (\mathbf{E}^{-1})^\intercal\boldsymbol{\beta}^\intercal\boldsymbol{\beta}\mathbf{E}^{-1} = \sum_{i\in[n]}\beta_i(\mathbf{E}^{-1})^\intercal\mathbf{B}^{(i)}\mathbf{E}^{-1} = \sum_{i\in[n]}\beta_i\mathbf{N}^{(i)},$$

and hence $\mathbf{E}^\intercal\mathbf{N}^{(i)}\mathbf{E} = \mathbf{B}^{(i)}$. That is, in the secondary attack one should find an $\mathbb{F}_{q^n}$-assignment to $y_1,\ldots,y_n$ so that $\sum_{i\in[n]}y_i\mathbf{B}^{(i)}$ is of rank one. Then, one repeats the proof of hardness for $\sum_{i\in[n]}y_i\mathbf{N}^{(i)}$ for the special case where $\mathbf{u} = \boldsymbol{\beta}$, i.e., where $\mathbf{N}^{(i)} = \mathbf{B}^{(i)}$ and $\mathbf{E} = \mathbf{I}$. Lemma 1 then implies that $z_{i,j} = (\mathbf{B}^{(l)})_{i,j}$ is in the kernel of the linearized system, for every $\ell \in [n]$. Consequently, while attempting to solve the secondary attack by linearization, one encounters a *tertiary* attack, where one should find an $\mathbb{F}_{q^n}$ assignment to $y_1,\ldots,y_n$ so that $\sum_{i\in[n]}y_i\mathbf{B}^{(i)}$ is of rank one. Clearly, this tertiary attack is *identical* to the secondary one. Moreover, by following the same arguments we have that all subsequent attacks (quaternary, quinary, etc.) are identical to the secondary one.

Remark 6. As mentioned earlier, we have verified experimentally for a wide range of q and k values over many randomized constructions, that $\dim\ker(\boldsymbol{\Omega}_{\text{lin}}) = 2n$, but as of yet have not been able to explain that mathematically. In the context of the secondary attack, one might suggest to take a basis $\mathbf{v}_1,\ldots,\mathbf{v}_{2n}$ of $\ker(\boldsymbol{\Omega}_{\text{lin}})$, and search for a rank one matrix in the $\mathbb{F}_{q^n}$-span of $\{\text{mat}(\mathbf{v}_i)\}_{i\in[2n]}$, again using linearization. We have verified experimentally that the resulting system is of the same rank as $\boldsymbol{\Omega}_{\text{lin}}$, hence not feasibly solvable via linearization, albeit having $\binom{2n+1}{2}$ columns rather than $\binom{n+1}{2}$.

5 Other Attacks

5.1 Finding a Structured Sidon Space

In this section we present an attack which is specific to the structure of the Sidon space V from Construction 2. By guessing an alternative construction of $\mathbb{F}_{q^n}$, Eve may assemble a certain set of polynomial equations, which is guaranteed to have a solution. Each such solution defines a subspace V', most likely a Sidon space, whose coefficient matrices are identical to those of the secret Sidon space V, and hence, it can be used to break the system. However, the resulting equation set is only slightly underdetermined, and hence it is unlikely that a suitable polynomial algorithm exists.

In this attack, Eve guesses an irreducible polynomial $P_E(x) \in \mathbb{F}_q[x]$ of degree n, and constructs $\mathbb{F}_{q^n}$ as $F_E \triangleq \mathbb{F}_q[x] \bmod (P_E(x))$, where $(P_E(x))$

denotes the ideal in $\mathbb{F}_q[x]$ which is generated by $P_E(x)$. Further, she guesses a basis $\omega_1, \ldots, \omega_n$ of F_E over $\mathbb{F}_q$ such that $\omega_1, \ldots, \omega_k$ is a basis for G_E, the unique subfield of size q^k of F_E.

To find $\boldsymbol{\nu}' \triangleq (\nu'_1, \ldots, \nu'_k) \in \mathbb{F}_{q^n}^k$ and $\boldsymbol{\beta}' \triangleq (\beta'_1, \ldots, \beta'_n) \in \mathbb{F}_{q^n}^n$ such that $\mathbf{M}(\boldsymbol{\nu}, \boldsymbol{\beta}) = \mathbf{M}(\boldsymbol{\nu}', \boldsymbol{\beta}')$, Eve defines variables $\{u_{i,j}\}_{i,j\in[k]}$, $\{b_{i,j}\}_{i,j\in[n]}$, and $\{g_i\}_{i=1}^n$, all of which represent elements in $\mathbb{F}_q$, and

$$\gamma' \triangleq \sum_{j=1}^{n} g_j\omega_j \ ,$$

$$\begin{aligned}\nu'_i &\triangleq \left(\sum_{j=1}^{k} u_{i,j}\omega_j\right) + \left(\sum_{j=1}^{n} g_j\omega_j\right)\left(\sum_{j=1}^{k} u_{i,j}\omega_j\right)^q \\ &= \left(\sum_{j=1}^{k} u_{i,j}\omega_j\right) + \left(\sum_{j=1}^{n} g_j\omega_j\right)\left(\sum_{j=1}^{k} u_{i,j}\omega_j^q\right) \text{ for all } i \in [k], \text{ and}\end{aligned}$$

$$\beta'_i \triangleq \sum_{j=1}^{n} b_{i,j}\omega_j \text{ for all } i \in [n] \ .$$

Eve then defines the following $\binom{k+1}{2}$ equations over $\mathbb{F}_{q^n}$,

$$\nu'_s\nu'_t = \sum_{i=1}^{n} M_{s,t}^{(i)}\beta'_i \text{ for all } s,t \in [k],\ s \geq t \ . \tag{8}$$

Finally, by expressing each side of every equation as a linear combination of $\{\omega_i\}_{i\in[n]}$ and comparing coefficients, Eve obtains $n \cdot \binom{k+1}{2} = k^2(k+1)$ equations over $\mathbb{F}_q$ in $n^2+k^2+n = 5k^2+2k$ variables. The left hand sides of these equations are polynomials in $k^2+n = k^2+2k$ variables and degree four, and the right hand sides are linear polynomials in $n^2 = 4k^2$ variables.

Since the isomorphism f exists (2), the system is guaranteed to have a solution. The resulting subspace $V' \triangleq \text{span}\{\nu'_i\}_{i\in[n]}$ is a Sidon space if the corresponding γ' satisfies the conditions of Construction 2. However, it seems that the straightforward algorithms for obtaining a solution are infeasible.

Notice that the terms on the left hand side of (8) are of either of the forms

$$u_{s,t}u_{\ell,r},\ g_ju_{s,t}u_{\ell,r},\ \text{or}\ g_ig_ju_{s,t}u_{\ell,r},$$

for $s,t,\ell,r \in [k]$ and $i,j \in [n]$. Hence, a straightforward reduction to the quadratic case includes replacing those terms by $u_{s,t,\ell,r}$, $g_j \cdot u_{s,t,\ell,r}$, and $g_{i,j}u_{s,t,\ell,r}$, respectively. In the resulting quadratic equation set, the number of equations remains $e \triangleq k^2(k+1)$. The number of variables however, comprises of k^4 variables of the form $u_{s,t,\ell,r}$, $4k^2$ of the form $g_{i,j}$, $4k^2$ of the form $b_{i,j}$, and $2k$ of the form g_j. Thus, the overall number of variables is $v \triangleq k^4+8k^2+2k$ and the equation set is *underdetermined* ($e < v$), with $v = \Theta(e^{4/3})$.

Algorithms for solving underdetermined systems of quadratic equations were studied in [6,18,29]. It is known that highly underdetermined systems ($v = \Omega(e^2)$) and highly overdetermined systems ($e = \Omega(v^2)$) are solvable in randomized polynomial time. On the other hand, if $e = v \pm O(1)$ then the current state-of-the-art algorithms are exponential. The results in our case ($v = \Theta(e^{4/3})$) seem inconclusive. In our experimental section it is shown that standard Gröbner basis algorithms are far from feasible for solving this system for $k < 10$.

5.2 Extracting the Message from the Cyphertext

It is readily verified that extracting $\mathbf{a}$ and $\mathbf{b}$ from $E(\mathbf{a}, \mathbf{b}) = (\mathbf{a}\mathbf{M}^{(i)}\mathbf{b}^\intercal)_{i=1}^n$ and $\mathbf{M}(\boldsymbol{\nu}, \boldsymbol{\beta}) = (\mathbf{M}^{(i)})_{i=1}^n$ is equivalent to solving the corresponding non-homogeneous bilinear system of $2k$ equations and $2k$ variables. It seems that the state-of-the-art algorithm for solving a bilinear system is given by [11, Cor. 3], whose complexity is

$$O\left(\binom{n_a + n_b + \min(n_a + 1, n_b + 1)}{\min(n_a + 1, n_b + 1)}^\omega\right),$$

where n_a and n_b are the number of entries in $\mathbf{a}$ and $\mathbf{b}$, and ω is the exponent of matrix multiplication. However, this specialized algorithm requires homogeneity, and in any case applying it to our problem requires $O(\binom{3k+1}{k+1}^\omega)$, which is infeasible even for small values of k.

We also note that it is possible to apply algorithms that do not exploit the *bilinear* nature of the system, but rather only its quadratic one. However, evidence show that standard Gröbner basis algorithms for solving quadratic equations perform very poorly on quadratic equation sets in which the number of equations and the number of variables is equal. Following Remark 2, it should be noted that if one would employ a max-span Sidon space as the private key, the resulting bilinear system has $\Theta(k^2)$ equations and $2k$ variables, and hence it is easy to solve by [5, Sect. 6.5] and references therein.

6 Experiments

Experiments were run using a computer with an Intel i7-9750H CPU with 16 GB of RAM. Computations were done on an engineering cluster node with 2 Intel x86 E5 2650 processors with 64 gigabytes of RAM. For reproducibility, the code for all experiments is given [1]. Throughout this section we denote the number of equations by e and number of variables by v.

Before discussing attacks, we discuss the performance of the system itself. Encoding and decoding use simple finite field operations, and had marginal affect on run-times (see Remark 1). The significant part of the key generation algorithm is the choice of γ, which defines the secret Sidon space; this amounts to choosing the quadratic polynomial $P_{a,b}$ so that it is irreducible over $\mathbb{F}_{q^k}$ with $c \in \overline{\mathcal{W}_{q-1}}$. This was done at random, and mean success times for different k and q values over 10 trials are given in Fig. 1.

The easiest attack to implement seems to be the bilinear one (Sect. 5.2), due to the small size of the associated inhomogeneous bilinear system ($v = e = 2k$). Specialized algorithms for improved performance on bilinear systems [11] are inapplicable, since they require homogeneity and have exponential complexity. We used the `F4` algorithm from the `FGb` library [9] in combination with `FGb_sage` [32]. The system was homogenized before the Gröbner basis was computed. Attacks were efficiently carried out for $k \leq 10$ (i.e., $v = 21$ and $e = 20$). The field size q was varied between $q = 3$ and $q = 65521$, but had marginal effect on running times. Past $k = 10$, the `F4` algorithm exceeded the $50 \cdot 10^6$ bound on the dimension of the matrix. Average running times, that are given below in Fig. 2, are consistent with the exponential growth one would expect.

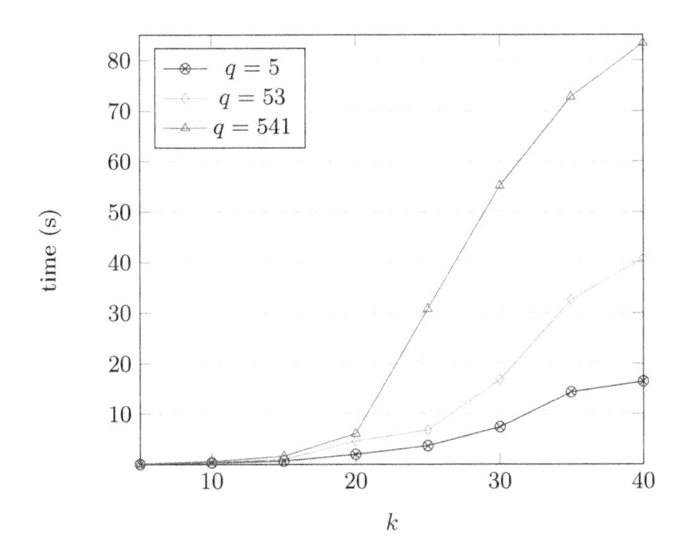

Fig. 1. Average running times of randomized key generation for various q values.

Next, executing the minor attack (Sect. 4.2) past $k = 2$ proved difficult. The first class of algorithms considered for this attack were of the eXtended Linearization (XL) family [5], but were not promising for a number of reasons. First, XL algorithms require a unique solution, which is not the case in our systems. Second, complexity analysis shows poor asymptotic performance; XL algorithms are polynomial if $\varepsilon \triangleq \frac{e}{v^2}$ is fixed, but are in general exponential otherwise. In our case ε approaches 0 as k increases, and thus we resorted to Gröbner basis algorithms.

Experimental evidence shows that while the attack generates $\Theta(k^5)$ Eq. (10), only $2k^2(2k-3)$ of them are independent (an upper bound of $2k^2(2k+1)$ is given in (11)). Benchmarks for fast Gröbner basis algorithms [17] show that the $k = 3$ system exists on the borderline of what has been computed, and that is supported by experimental evidence. Both implementations of `F5` as well as

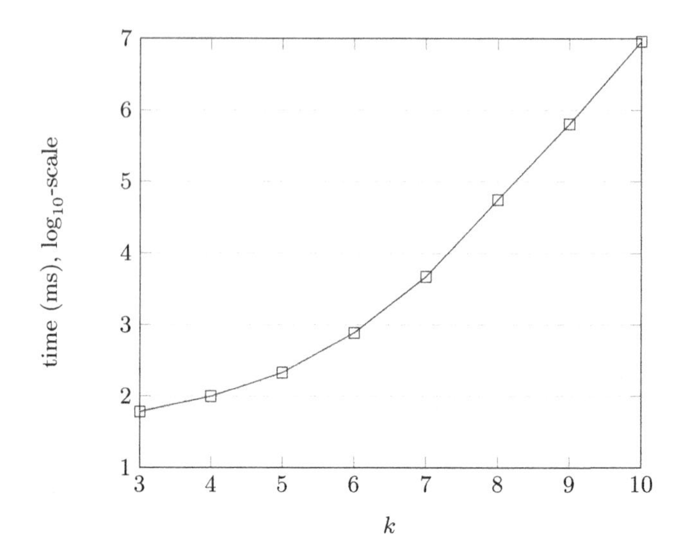

Fig. 2. Average running times for the bilinear attack (Sect. 5.2) on randomly chosen Sidon cryptosystems. Standard deviations are given in light shaded area, which is barely visible.

the FGb library were used to try and compute Gröbner bases for this system, but neither performed well, with the FGb library quickly surpassing the $50 \cdot 10^6$ matrix bound and the F5 algorithm not terminating after several days of running. For $k = 4$ and $k = 5$ we were able to compute the degree of regularity, which was 8.

The structured attack in Sect. 5.1, which has $v = \Theta(k^2)$ and $e = \Theta(k^3)$ proved to be the least feasible, where $k = 3$ ($v = 36$ and $e = 54$) and up were completely unsolvable. The system can be reduced to a quadratic one with $v = \Theta(k^4)$ variables, which did not seem to accelerate the computation.

7 Discussion

In this paper the Sidon cryptosystem was introduced, and several straightforward attacks were given. These attacks were shown to induce instances of several problems for which it is unlikely that a polynomial algorithm exists. Nevertheless, a finer analysis of the algebraic nature of Sidon spaces might shed some light on the structure of these instances, and consequently, might prove the system insecure. On the other hand, a rigorous proof for the hardness of the Sidon cryptosystem, which has yet to be found, will be a significant achievement in post-quantum cryptography.

The first order of business in extending this work is finding the remaining n dimensions in the kernel of $\mathbf{\Omega}_{\text{lin}}$, and we have verified experimentally that these additional n dimensions do not exist in $\mathbf{\Gamma}_{\text{lin}}$. More broadly, we suggest that applications of Sidon spaces to cryptography extend beyond what is discussed in the paper. Other than using different constructions of Sidon spaces (e.g., [20]) in the framework described above, we suggest to study the following concepts in order to strengthen the resulting systems.

r-Sidon spaces. The Sidon spaces in this paper enable the product of every two elements to be factored uniquely (up to constants). This is a special case of r-Sidon spaces, in which the product of any r elements can be factored uniquely (see [26, Sect. VI]). This would extend the hardness of the system from solving bilinear systems to r-linear ones.

High rank multiplication table. Most of the susceptibility of the Sidon cryptosystem lies in the matrix $\mathbf{M}(\boldsymbol{\nu})$ (see Sect. 3) being of rank one. To remedy that, let $U, V \in \mathcal{G}_q(4k, k)$ be min-span Sidon spaces such that V is spanned by $\boldsymbol{\nu} = (\nu_i)_{i=1}^k$, U is spanned by $\boldsymbol{\upsilon} = (\upsilon_i)_{i=1}^k$ and $U^2 \cap V^2 = \{0\}$. It is readily verified that Bob in able to decrypt the ciphertext even if the matrix $\mathbf{M}(\boldsymbol{\nu}) = \boldsymbol{\nu}^\intercal \boldsymbol{\nu}$ is replaced by $\boldsymbol{\nu}^\intercal \boldsymbol{\nu} + \boldsymbol{\upsilon}^\intercal \boldsymbol{\upsilon}$: Bob will begin by extracting $\mathbf{a}\boldsymbol{\nu}^\intercal \boldsymbol{\nu}\mathbf{b}$ from the ciphertext, which is possible since $U^2 \cap V^2 = \{0\}$, and continue similarly. If the vectors $\boldsymbol{\nu}$ and $\boldsymbol{\upsilon}$ are independent over $\mathbb{F}_{q^n}$, the resulting matrix is of rank two, and hence the system's resilience against MinRank attacks is increased.

Funding. This work was partially supported by the European Research Council (ERC grant number 852953) and by the Israel Science Foundation (ISF grant number 1030/15).

Appendix A

An Omitted Proof.

Lemma 3. *For any prime power q and an integer k, the size of $\mathcal{Q}_k$ (see Sect. 3) is* $\frac{(q^k-1)(q^k-q)}{2(q-1)} + q^k - 1$.

Proof. The following statements, which are easy to prove, are left as an exercise to the reader.

1. For every $\mathbf{a}$ and $\mathbf{b}$ in $\mathbb{F}_q^k \setminus \{0\}$, the matrix $\mathbf{a}^\intercal \mathbf{b}$ is symmetric if and only if $\mathbf{a} \in \operatorname{span}_{\mathbb{F}_q}(\mathbf{b})$.
2. Every $\mathbf{a}, \mathbf{b}$ in $\mathbb{F}_q^k \setminus \{0\}$ and every $\lambda, \mu \in \mathbb{F}_q^*$ satisfy that $\mathbf{a}^\intercal \cdot (\lambda \mathbf{a}) = \mathbf{b}^\intercal \cdot (\mu \mathbf{b})$ if and only if $\mu\lambda^{-1}$ is a quadratic residue, and $\mathbf{a} = \sqrt{\mu\lambda^{-1}} \cdot \mathbf{b}$.
3. Every $\mathbf{a}, \mathbf{b}, \mathbf{c}$, and $\mathbf{d}$ in $\mathbb{F}_q^k$ such that $\mathbf{a} \notin \operatorname{span}_{\mathbb{F}_q}(\mathbf{b})$ and $\mathbf{c} \notin \operatorname{span}_{\mathbb{F}_q}(\mathbf{d})$ satisfy that $\mathbf{a}^\intercal \mathbf{b} = \mathbf{c}^\intercal \mathbf{d}$ if and only if $\mathbf{a} = \lambda \mathbf{c}$ and $\mathbf{b} = \lambda^{-1} \mathbf{d}$ for some $\lambda \in \mathbb{F}_q^*$.

Therefore, 1 and 2 imply that $\mathcal{Q}_k$ contains $q^k - 1$ equivalence classes of size one. In addition, 1 and 3 imply that $\mathcal{Q}_k$ contains $\frac{(q^k-1)(q^k-q)}{2(q-1)}$ equivalence classes of size two.

Appendix B

Randomized Encryption. In certain cryptographic scenarios it is imperative that repeated messages will not induce repeated cyphertexts. That is, Eve must not know that Bob wishes to send Alice a message which has already been sent before. A common solution to this constraint is to use randomness, as suggested below.

In this section it is shown that this can be attained at the price of a slightly larger public key and half of the information rate. Roughly speaking, the idea behind the suggested scheme is to modify the Sidon cryptosystem so that one of the elements $\mathbf{a}$ and $\mathbf{b}$ (see Sect. 3) is random.

To achieve the above goal, Alice randomly chooses an additional irreducible polynomial $P_R(x) \in \mathbb{F}_q[x]$ of degree $k = n/2$, which is appended to the public key, and fixes a canonical basis $z_1, \ldots, z_k$ of $F_R \triangleq \mathbb{F}_q[x] \bmod (P_R(x))$ over $\mathbb{F}_q$. Rather than encoding into the set $\mathcal{Q}_k$, Bob encodes his message as $\mathbf{a} = (a_i)_{i=1}^k \in \mathbb{F}_q^k \setminus \{0\}$. By randomly picking $\mathbf{b} = (b_i)_{i=1}^k \in \mathbb{F}_q^k \setminus \{0\}$ and using the canonical basis $z_1, \ldots, z_k$, Bob defines

$$\hat{a} \triangleq \sum_{i=1}^{k} a_i z_i , \qquad \hat{b} \triangleq \sum_{i=1}^{k} b_i z_i ,$$

$$\hat{a}/\hat{b} \triangleq \hat{c} = \sum_{i=1}^{k} c_i z_i , \text{ and} \qquad \mathbf{c} \triangleq (c_1, \ldots, c_k) ,$$

and sends $E(\mathbf{c}, \mathbf{b})$ to Alice. Upon receiving $E(\mathbf{c}, \mathbf{b})$, Alice decrypts $E(\mathbf{c}, \mathbf{b})$ as in Sect. 3, obtains $\{\mathbf{c}', \mathbf{b}'\} \triangleq \{\lambda \cdot (c_1, \ldots, c_k), \frac{1}{\lambda} \cdot (b_1, \ldots, b_k)\}$, for some unknown $\lambda \in \mathbb{F}_q$, and computes

$$\left(\lambda \sum_{i=1}^{k} c_i z_i\right) \left(\frac{1}{\lambda} \sum_{i=1}^{k} b_i z_i\right) = \lambda \hat{c} \cdot \tfrac{1}{\lambda} \hat{b} = \hat{a}.$$

By representing $\hat{a}$ over $z_1, \ldots, z_k$, Alice obtains $\mathbf{a}$, the plaintext by Bob. It is evident from this scheme that repeatedly transmitting a message $\mathbf{a}$ is highly unlikely to produce identical cyphertexts.

Appendix C

Linearization Attack Over $\mathbb{F}_q$. To obtain an $\mathbb{F}_{q^n}$-solution to $\mathbf{\Omega}_{\text{lin}}$, set $y_s = \sum_{j \in [n]} y_{s,j} \delta_j$ for every $s \in [n]$, where $\{\delta_i\}_{i \in [n]}$ is any basis of $\mathbb{F}_{q^n}$ that the attacker chooses, and the $y_{i,j}$'s are variables that represent $\mathbb{F}_q$ elements. This transition to $\mathbb{F}_q$ can be described using Kronecker products as follows. Let $\{c_d^{(i,j)}\}_{i,j,d \in [n]}$ so that $\delta_i \delta_j = \sum_{d \in [n]} c_d^{(i,j)} \delta_d$ for every i and j. Then, an equation of the form $\sum_{s,t} \alpha_{s,t} y_s y_t = 0$, where $\alpha_{s,t} \in \mathbb{F}_q$, is written as

$$0 = \sum_{s,t} \alpha_{s,t} \left(\sum_{j \in [n]} y_{s,j} \delta_j \right) \left(\sum_{i \in [n]} y_{t,i} \delta_i \right) = \sum_{s,t} \alpha_{s,t} \sum_{i,j} \left(\sum_{d \in [n]} c_d^{(i,j)} \delta_d \right) y_{s,j} y_{t,i}$$

$$= \sum_{d\in[n]} \delta_d \sum_{s,t,i,j} \alpha_{s,t} c_d^{(i,j)} y_{s,j} y_{t,i}.$$

Hence, since $\{\delta_d\}_{d\in[n]}$ is a basis, and since the remaining scalars are in $\mathbb{F}_q$, this equation induces the n equations

$$\sum_{s,t,i,j} \alpha_{s,t} c_a^{(i,j)} y_{s,j} y_{t,i} = 0 \text{ for every } a \in [n]. \tag{9}$$

To describe the resulting $\mathbb{F}_q$-system, recall that the $\binom{n+1}{2}$ columns of $\mathbf{\Omega}_{\text{lin}}$ are indexed by the monomials $y_s y_t$, and the rows are indexed by minors $((i,j),(\ell,d))$. The value of an entry in column $y_s y_t$ and row $((i,j),(\ell,d))$ is the coefficient of $y_s y_t$ in the equation for the 2×2 zero minor of $(\sum_{i\in[n]} y_i \mathbf{M}^{(i)})$ in rows i and j, and columns ℓ and d. It follows from (9) that by performing the transition to $\mathbb{F}_q$ we obtain the coefficient matrix $\mathbf{\Omega}_q \triangleq \mathbf{\Omega}_{\text{lin}} \otimes \mathbf{C}$, where $\mathbf{C} \in \mathbb{F}_q^{n\times n^2}$ is a matrix which contains the $c_d^{(i,j)}$'s[4], and $\otimes$ denotes the Kronecker product.

In the resulting system $\mathbf{\Omega}_q$ the columns are indexed by $y_{s,j} y_{t,i}$ with $s \le t$, and the rows are indexed by $(((i,j),(\ell,d)),a)$ (i.e., a pair which represents a minor, up to the symmetry in (5), and an index a from (9)). This matrix contains

$$\begin{aligned} &\binom{n+1}{2} \cdot n^2 = 8k^4 + 4k^3 \triangleq k' \text{ columns, and} \\ &\binom{\binom{k}{2}+1}{2} \cdot n = \frac{2k^5 - 4k^4 + 6k^3 - 4k^2}{8} \text{ rows,} \end{aligned} \tag{10}$$

and a satisfying assignment for the $y_{i,j}$'s corresponds to a vector over $\mathbb{F}_q$ in its right kernel. As explained earlier, since there exists a solution (the secret key in the Sidon cryptosystem), the dimension of the right kernel of $\mathbf{\Omega}_q$ is at least one. Since the system has more rows than columns, one would expect the dimension of the kernel to be at most one, and the solution should be found by standard linearization techniques (see below). However, we have that

$$\begin{aligned} \text{rank}(\mathbf{\Omega}_q) &= \text{rank}(\mathbf{\Omega} \otimes \mathbf{C}) = \text{rank}(\mathbf{\Omega}) \cdot \text{rank}(\mathbf{C}) \\ &\le \binom{n+1}{2} \cdot n = 4k^3 + 2k^2 \ll k', \end{aligned} \tag{11}$$

and therefore, the attacker is left with yet another MinRank problem, where a rank-one solution (in a sense that will be made clear shortly) should be found in the linear span of at least $4k^4 - 2k^2$ matrices $\{\text{mat}(\mathbf{v}_i)\}$, where $\{\mathbf{v}_i\} \subseteq \mathbb{F}_q^{k'}$ span $\ker(\mathbf{\Omega}_q)$.

To describe in what sense a solution of $\mathbf{\Omega}_q$ is of "rank one," index the columns of $\mathbf{\Omega}_q$ by tuples $\mathcal{R} \triangleq \{(s,j,t,i) | s,j,t,i \in [n], s \le t\}$, where each

[4] More precisely, $\mathbf{C}$ contains $c_d^{(i,j)}$ in entry $(d,(i,j))$, where the n^2 columns are indexed by all pairs (i,j), $i,j \in [n]$.

column corresponds to the monomial $y_{s,j}y_{t,i}$. Then, one must finds a vector $\mathbf{z} = (z_{s,j,t,i})_{(s,j,t,i)\in\mathcal{R}} \in \mathbb{F}_q^{\binom{n+1}{2}n^2}$ in the right kernel of $\mathbf{\Omega}_q$, and wishes to decompose it to find the respective values for $\{y_{s,j}\}_{s,j\in[n]}$.

To find that a solution $\mathbf{z}$ is not parasitic, i.e., that it corresponds to some solution $\hat{\mathbf{y}} = (\hat{y}_{s,j})_{s,j\in[n]}$ to the original quadratic system, one must verify that all the following matrices are of rank one, and moreover, that there exist $\hat{\mathbf{y}}$ which satisfies the following rank one decompositions.

$$\begin{pmatrix} z_{1,1,1,1} & \cdots & z_{1,1,1,n} & z_{1,1,2,1} & \cdots & z_{1,1,2,n} & \cdots & z_{1,1,n,1} & \cdots & z_{1,1,n,n} \\ z_{1,2,1,1} & \cdots & z_{1,2,1,n} & z_{1,2,2,1} & \cdots & z_{1,2,2,n} & \cdots & z_{1,2,n,1} & \cdots & z_{1,2,n,n} \\ \vdots & \ddots & \vdots & \vdots & \ddots & \vdots & \ddots & \vdots & \ddots & \vdots \\ z_{1,n,1,1} & \cdots & z_{1,n,1,n} & z_{1,n,2,1} & \cdots & z_{1,n,2,n} & \cdots & z_{1,n,n,1} & \cdots & z_{1,n,n,n} \end{pmatrix} = (\hat{y}_{1,1},\ldots,\hat{y}_{1,n})^\intercal \hat{\mathbf{y}}$$

$$\begin{pmatrix} z_{2,1,2,1} & \cdots & z_{2,1,2,n} & \cdots & z_{2,1,n,1} & \cdots & z_{2,1,n,n} \\ z_{2,2,2,1} & \cdots & z_{2,2,2,n} & \cdots & z_{2,2,n,1} & \cdots & z_{2,2,n,n} \\ \vdots & \ddots & \vdots & \ddots & \vdots & \ddots & \vdots \\ z_{2,n,2,1} & \cdots & z_{2,n,2,n} & \cdots & z_{2,n,n,1} & \cdots & z_{2,n,n,n} \end{pmatrix} = (\hat{y}_{2,1},\ldots,\hat{y}_{2,n})^\intercal (\hat{y}_{2,1}\ldots,\hat{y}_{n,n})$$

$$\vdots$$

$$\begin{pmatrix} z_{n,1,n,1} & \cdots & z_{n,1,n,n} \\ z_{n,2,n,1} & \cdots & z_{n,2,n,n} \\ \vdots & \ddots & \vdots \\ z_{n,n,n,1} & \cdots & z_{n,n,n,n} \end{pmatrix} = (\hat{y}_{n,1},\ldots,\hat{y}_{n,n})^\intercal (\hat{y}_{n,1}\ldots,\hat{y}_{n,n})$$

It is readily verified that $\mathbf{z}$ is non-parasitic if and only if all the above are met. However, it is difficult to find such a solution, since the dimension of the right kernel of $\mathbf{\Omega}_q$ is at least

$$\begin{aligned} \text{num. of columns} - \operatorname{rank}(\mathbf{\Omega}_q) &= k' - \operatorname{rank}(\mathbf{\Omega}_q) \\ &\geq 8k^4 + 4k^3 - \left(\binom{n+1}{2} - n\right) n = 8k^4 + 2k^2. \end{aligned}$$

Appendix D

Different Basis Extension. In the spirit of Remark 5, when trying to find different extensions of $\nu_1,\ldots,\nu_k$ to a basis of $\mathbb{F}_{q^n}$ such that the resulting $\mathbf{\Gamma}$ and $\mathbf{\Gamma}'$ have disjoint kernels, we discover the following. For $\boldsymbol{\nu} = (\nu_1,\ldots,\nu_k)$, let $\mathbf{u}_1 = (\boldsymbol{\nu},\boldsymbol{\mu}_1)$, $\mathbf{u}_2 = (\boldsymbol{\nu},\boldsymbol{\mu}_2)$ be two possible extensions, with respective matrices $\mathbf{E}_1,\mathbf{E}_2$ (i.e., such that $\boldsymbol{\beta} = \mathbf{u}_1\mathbf{E}_1 = \mathbf{u}_2\mathbf{E}_2$), respective $\{\mathbf{N}^{(i)}\}_{i\in[n]}$, $\{\tilde{\mathbf{N}}^{(i)}\}_{i\in[n]}$, and respective kernel vectors $\{\mathbf{n}_i\}_{i\in[n]}$ and $\{\tilde{\mathbf{n}}_i\}_{i\in[n]}$. Let $\boldsymbol{\beta}^\intercal\boldsymbol{\beta} = \sum_{i\in[n]}\beta_i\mathbf{B}^{(i)}$, and observe that

$$\mathbf{u}_1^\intercal\mathbf{u}_1 = (\mathbf{E}_1^{-1})^\intercal\boldsymbol{\beta}^\intercal\boldsymbol{\beta}\mathbf{E}_1^{-1} = \sum_{i\in[n]}\beta_i(\mathbf{E}_1^{-1})^\intercal\mathbf{B}^{(i)}\mathbf{E}_1^{-1}$$

$$= \sum_{i\in[n]} \beta_i \mathbf{N}^{(i)}, \text{ and therefore } \mathbf{E}_1^\intercal \mathbf{N}^{(i)} \mathbf{E}_1 = \mathbf{B}^{(i)}. \text{ Similarly,}$$

$$\mathbf{u}_2^\intercal \mathbf{u}_2 = (\mathbf{E}_2^{-1})^\intercal \beta^\intercal \beta \mathbf{E}_2^{-1} = \sum_{i\in[n]} \beta_i (\mathbf{E}_2^{-1})^\intercal \mathbf{B}^{(i)} \mathbf{E}_2^{-1}$$

$$= \sum_{i\in[n]} \beta_i \tilde{\mathbf{N}}^{(i)} \text{ and therefore } \mathbf{E}_2^\intercal \tilde{\mathbf{N}}^{(i)} \mathbf{E}_2 = \mathbf{B}^{(i)}.$$

Hence, the respective kernel vectors $\{\mathbf{n}_i\}_{i\in[n]}$ and $\{\tilde{\mathbf{n}}_i\}_{i\in[n]}$ are *identical.*

References

1. Raviv, N., Langton B., Tamo I.,: The Sidon Cryptosystem (2021). https://github.com/b-langton/Sidon-Cryptosystem
2. Bachoc, C., Serra, O., Zémor, G.: An analogue of Vosper's theorem for extension fields. In: arXiv:1501.00602 [math.NT] (2015)
3. Bardet, M., et al.: Improvements of algebraic attacks for solving the rank decoding and MinRank problems. In: Moriai, S., Wang, H. (eds.) ASIACRYPT 2020. LNCS, vol. 12491, pp. 507–536. Springer, Cham (2020). https://doi.org/10.1007/978-3-030-64837-4_17
4. Barreto, P., Voloch, J.F.: Efficient computation of roots in finite fields. Des. Codes Crypt. **39**(2), 275–280 (2006)
5. Courtois, N., Klimov, A., Patarin, J., Shamir, A.: Efficient algorithms for solving overdefined systems of multivariate polynomial equations. In: Preneel, B. (ed.) EUROCRYPT 2000. LNCS, vol. 1807, pp. 392–407. Springer, Heidelberg (2000). https://doi.org/10.1007/3-540-45539-6_27
6. Cheng, C.-M., Hashimoto, Y., Miura, H., Takagi, T.: A polynomial-time algorithm for solving a class of underdetermined multivariate quadratic equations over fields of odd characteristics. In: Mosca, M. (ed.) PQCrypto 2014. LNCS, vol. 8772, pp. 40–58. Springer, Cham (2014). https://doi.org/10.1007/978-3-319-11659-4_3
7. Ding, J., Kleinjung, T.: Degree of regularity for HFE-. IACR Cryptology ePrint Archive, p. 570 (2011)
8. Ding, J., Schmidt, D.: Rainbow, a new multivariable polynomial signature scheme. In: Ioannidis, J., Keromytis, A., Yung, M. (eds.) ACNS 2005. LNCS, vol. 3531, pp. 164–175. Springer, Heidelberg (2005). https://doi.org/10.1007/11496137_12
9. Faugère, J.-C.: FGb: a library for computing gröbner bases. In: Fukuda, K., Hoeven, J., Joswig, M., Takayama, N. (eds.) ICMS 2010. LNCS, vol. 6327, pp. 84–87. Springer, Heidelberg (2010). https://doi.org/10.1007/978-3-642-15582-6_17
10. Faugère, J.-C., Levy-dit-Vehel, F., Perret, L.: Cryptanalysis of MinRank. In: Wagner, D. (ed.) CRYPTO 2008. LNCS, vol. 5157, pp. 280–296. Springer, Heidelberg (2008). https://doi.org/10.1007/978-3-540-85174-5_16
11. Faugère, J.C., El-Din, M.S., Spaenlehauer, P.J.: Gröbner bases of bihomogeneous ideals generated by polynomials of bidegree (1, 1): algorithms and complexity. J. Symbolic Comput. **46**(4), 406–437 (2011)
12. Faugère, J.C., El-Din, M.S., Spaenlehauer, P.J.: Computing loci of rank defects of linear matrices using Gröbner bases and applications to cryptology. In: Proceedings of the International Symposium on Symbolic and Algebraic Computation, pp. 257–264 (2010)

13. Gu, C.: Cryptanalysis of Simple Matrix Scheme for Encryption. IACR Cryptology ePrint Archive, p. 1075 (2016)
14. Goubin, L., Courtois, N.T.: Cryptanalysis of the TTM cryptosystem. In: Okamoto, T. (ed.) ASIACRYPT 2000. LNCS, vol. 1976, pp. 44–57. Springer, Heidelberg (2000). https://doi.org/10.1007/3-540-44448-3_4
15. Kipnis, A., Shamir, A.: Cryptanalysis of the HFE public key cryptosystem by relinearization. In: Wiener, M. (ed.) CRYPTO 1999. LNCS, vol. 1666, pp. 19–30. Springer, Heidelberg (1999). https://doi.org/10.1007/3-540-48405-1_2
16. Kipnis, A., Patarin, J., Goubin, L.: Unbalanced oil and vinegar signature schemes. In: Stern, J. (ed.) EUROCRYPT 1999. LNCS, vol. 1592, pp. 206–222. Springer, Heidelberg (1999). https://doi.org/10.1007/3-540-48910-X_15
17. Makarim, R.H., tevens M.: M4GB: an efficient Gröbner-basis algorithm. In: Proceedings of the 2017 ACM on International Symposium on Symbolic and Algebraic Computation, pp. 293–300 (2017)
18. Miura, H., Hashimoto, Y., Takagi, T.: Extended algorithm for solving underdefined multivariate quadratic equations. In: Gaborit, P. (ed.) PQCrypto 2013. LNCS, vol. 7932, pp. 118–135. Springer, Heidelberg (2013). https://doi.org/10.1007/978-3-642-38616-9_8
19. Moh, T.T.: A fast public key system with signature and master key functions. In: Proceedings of CrypTEC 1999, International Workshop on Cryptographic Techniques and E-Commerce, pp. 63–69. Hong-Kong City University Press (1999)
20. Niu, Y., Qin, Y., Yansheng, W.: Several kinds of large cyclic subspace codes via Sidon spaces. Discrete Math. **343**(5), 111788 (2020)
21. O'Bryant, K.: A complete annotated bibliography of work related to Sidon sequences. In: arXiv preprint math/0407117 (2004)
22. Patarin, J.: Hidden fields equations (HFE) and isomorphisms of polynomials (IP): two new families of asymmetric algorithms. In: Maurer, U. (ed.) EUROCRYPT 1996. LNCS, vol. 1070, pp. 33–48. Springer, Heidelberg (1996). https://doi.org/10.1007/3-540-68339-9_4
23. Perlner, R., Smith-Tone, D.: Security analysis and key modification for ZHFE. In: Takagi, T. (ed.) PQCrypto 2016. LNCS, vol. 9606, pp. 197–212. Springer, Cham (2016). https://doi.org/10.1007/978-3-319-29360-8_13
24. Petzoldt, A., Chen, M.-S., Yang, B.-Y., Tao, C., Ding, J.: Design principles for HFEv- based multivariate signature schemes. In: Iwata, T., Cheon, J.H. (eds.) ASIACRYPT 2015. LNCS, vol. 9452, pp. 311–334. Springer, Heidelberg (2015). https://doi.org/10.1007/978-3-662-48797-6_14
25. Porras, J., Baena, J., Ding, J.: ZHFE, a new multivariate public key encryption scheme. In: Mosca, M. (ed.) PQCrypto 2014. LNCS, vol. 8772, pp. 229–245. Springer, Cham (2014). https://doi.org/10.1007/978-3-319-11659-4_14
26. Roth, R.M., Raviv, N., Tamo, I.: Construction of Sidon spaces with applications to coding. IEEE Trans. Inf. Th. **64**(6), 4412–4422 (2017)
27. Schulman, L.J.: Cryptography from tensor problems. In: IACR Cryptol. ePrint Arch. (2012)
28. Tao, C., Diene, A., Tang, S., Ding, J.: Simple matrix scheme for encryption. In: Gaborit, P. (ed.) PQCrypto 2013. LNCS, vol. 7932, pp. 231–242. Springer, Heidelberg (2013). https://doi.org/10.1007/978-3-642-38616-9_16
29. Thomae, E., Wolf, C.: Solving underdetermined systems of multivariate quadratic equations revisited. In: Fischlin, M., Buchmann, J., Manulis, M. (eds.) PKC 2012. LNCS, vol. 7293, pp. 156–171. Springer, Heidelberg (2012). https://doi.org/10.1007/978-3-642-30057-8_10

30. Vates, J., Smith-Tone, D.: Key recovery attack for all parameters of HFE. In: Lange, T., Takagi, T. (eds.) PQCrypto 2017. LNCS, vol. 10346, pp. 272–288. Springer, Cham (2017). https://doi.org/10.1007/978-3-319-59879-6_16
31. Verbel, J., Baena, J., Cabarcas, D., Perlner, R., Smith-Tone, D.: On the complexity of "Superdetermined" minrank instances. In: Ding, J., Steinwandt, R. (eds.) PQCrypto 2019. LNCS, vol. 11505, pp. 167–186. Springer, Cham (2019). https://doi.org/10.1007/978-3-030-25510-7_10
32. Wageringel M.: A Sage interface for FGb (2020). https://github.com/mwageringel/fgb_sage

Banquet: Short and Fast Signatures from AES

Carsten Baum[1(✉)], Cyprien Delpech de Saint Guilhem[2], Daniel Kales[3], Emmanuela Orsini[2], Peter Scholl[1], and Greg Zaverucha[4]

[1] Department of Computer Science, Aarhus University, Aarhus, Denmark
cbaum@cs.au.dk
[2] imec-COSIC, KU Leuven, Leuven, Belgium
[3] Graz University of Technology, Graz, Austria
[4] Microsoft Research, Redmond, USA

Abstract. This work introduces Banquet, a digital signature scheme with post-quantum security, constructed using only symmetric-key primitives. The design is based on the MPC-in-head paradigm also used by Picnic (CCS 2017) and BBQ (SAC 2019). Like BBQ, Banquet uses only standardized primitives, namely AES and SHA-3, but signatures are more than 50% shorter, making them competitive with Picnic (which uses a non-standard block cipher to improve performance). The MPC protocol in Banquet uses a new technique to verify correctness of the AES S-box computations, which is efficient because the cost is amortized with a batch verification strategy. Our implementation and benchmarks also show that both signing and verification can be done in under 10ms on a current x64 CPU. We also explore the parameter space to show the range of trade-offs that are possible with the Banquet design, and show that Banquet can nearly match the signature sizes possible with Picnic (albeit with slower, but still practical run times) or have speed within a factor of two of Picnic (at the cost of larger signatures).

1 Introduction

Digital signatures such as RSA and ECDSA form the backbone of authentication mechanisms on the Internet, and are central to many uses of cryptography. While being highly efficient, it is also known that in the presence of quantum computers, nearly all such currently deployed constructions will be rendered insecure.

This has led to a search for efficient, plausibly post-quantum-secure constructions of digital signatures that do not rely on assumptions such as factoring or the hardness of the discrete logarithm problem. There are a multitude of candidates with different design ideas: some rely on plausibly hard problems over (structured) lattices [21,24,33], others rely on the hardness of certain problems from multivariate cryptography [13] or isogenies [15].

The full version of this paper is available as IACR ePrint Report 2021/068 [4].

J. A. Garay (Ed.): PKC 2021, LNCS 12710, pp. 266–297, 2021.
https://doi.org/10.1007/978-3-030-75245-3_11

While these signature schemes all rely on number-theoretic, or structured hardness assumptions, digital signatures can be built from symmetric-key primitives alone, offering the possibility of relying on "less structured" and better-studied assumptions compared with public-key encryption, where this is not known to be possible. The Picnic signature scheme [14, 36] is one example which uses the following paradigm: the public key is a plaintext-ciphertext pair (x, y) while the secret key k defines a one-way function F_k, instantiated with a block cipher. A signature is then a non-interactive zero-knowledge proof showing that the prover (the signer) knows a key k such that $y = F_k(x)$.

As the proof size depends on proving statements about the chosen block cipher in zero knowledge, the authors of Picnic chose a special block cipher called LowMC [1] that is optimized for a low number of AND gates in its Boolean circuit representation. While LowMC has so far withstood cryptanalytic efforts in the context of Picnic, its security is still less established than standards like AES, and there have been attacks on older versions of LowMC [18, 35] or in applications where more than one plaintext-ciphertext pair is available [32].

MPC (in the Head). The zero-knowledge proof of the Picnic scheme is based on the so-called MPC-in-the-Head (MPCitH) paradigm [27]. We will now explain this paradigm in more detail before we continue to describe our contributions.

We consider interactive multi-party computation (MPC) protocols, where a set of N parties $\mathcal{P}_1, \ldots, \mathcal{P}_N$ securely and correctly evaluate a function f on a secret input x. In order to do so, each $\mathcal{P}_i$ obtains as input a secret share of the input x. Then, all parties together run an interactive computation where they exchange messages with the goal of ending up with a secret-sharing of the output, $f(x)$. These shares are then sent to whomever should learn the output. Assuming an adversary controls at most t of the N parties (i.e., a corruption threshold t), the MPC protocol guarantees that no information beyond $f(x)$ is leaked. For the types of MPCitH protocols related to this work, we only consider the case of passive security, where all parties are assumed to follow the protocol. Typically, the function f is described as a Boolean circuit or an arithmetic circuit over a finite field $\mathbb{F}$. We say that the MPC protocol uses preprocessing if, before the input x is specified, $\mathcal{P}_1, \ldots, \mathcal{P}_N$ are given secret-shares of correlated, random values that are sampled according to some known distribution.

The idea of MPCitH is that such an MPC scheme can be turned into a zero-knowledge proof, in the following way: the witness of a statement is secret-shared as the input x, while f will be a verification function that outputs 0 iff x is a valid witness. The prover *simulates* all N parties locally (hence the name *in the head*) and sends the verifier commitments to each parties' input shares, secret random tapes, and all communicated messages. Additionally, it sends the output shares of the parties (that should reconstruct to 0) to the verifier. Then, the verifier randomly chooses t of the parties' commitments to be opened, and verifies that the committed messages are consistent with an honest execution of the MPC protocol according to the opened input shares and random tapes, and the previously received output shares. Since only t parties are opened, the verifier learns nothing about the secret input x, while the random choice of the opened parties ensures that enough simulations of the other parties must also be correct (with some probability), ensuring soundness of the proof. Typically, to make the soundness error small enough, several parallel repetitions of the basic protocol are carried out.

Digital Signatures from MPCitH. To obtain a signature scheme, Picnic uses an MPCitH protocol to prove knowledge of a secret key k such that $y = F_k(x)$, for a one-way function F_k. This gives a zero-knowledge identification protocol, which can be turned into a signature scheme with the Fiat–Shamir transform. Making this approach practical requires an MPC protocol that efficiently evaluates the one-way function since the communication complexity of most MPC protocols scales with the number of AND (or multiplication) gates in the circuit, and multiple parallel repetitions are required.

As mentioned earlier, Picnic uses a one-way function based on the LowMC cipher, which has a relatively low AND gate count (around 600, at the 128-bit security level). However, this means that Picnic relies inherently on a non-standard assumption. A direct instantiation using, say, AES instead of LowMC would remove this assumption, but increase the signature size by around 4–5x due to the much larger AND gate count in the AES circuit. Since AES has a relatively compact description using operations over $\mathbb{F}_{2^8}$, it is natural to also consider using MPC protocols tailored for this field instead of $\mathbb{F}_2$. This was the approach recently taken in the BBQ scheme [16], which reduced AES-based signature sizes by 40% compared to the binary circuit approach. However, AES-based signatures are still about 2–3x larger than LowMC-based signatures.

1.1 Our Contributions

In this work, we present Banquet, a novel approach to constructing AES-based identification and signature schemes. Compared with the previous AES-based approach in BBQ [16], Banquet reduces signature size, and our implementation results show that Banquet can be made almost as efficient as Picnic.

First, we leverage the prover's full knowledge of the secret MPC input in an MPCitH protocol to design a protocol that does not "recompute" the AES function, but "verifies" it instead. As it turns out, verifying that $y = \mathsf{AES}_k(x)$ for public x, y is cheaper than encrypting x under k, as the prover knows all AES evaluation intermediate states, which must then be shown to be consistent.

To achieve this, we construct a new test for batch verification of multiple intermediate states in the AES encryption circuit at once, instead of verifying them individually. This batch test also allows us to avoid a preprocessing step, unlike previous work (BBQ and Picnic), reducing costs of the entire protocol. Our amortization technique does come with higher computational costs due to polynomial operations, and an increase in the number of rounds from 3 or 5 in previous MPCitH constructions up to 7, which affects concrete security bounds when using Fiat–Shamir.

We show that our approach reduces signatures sizes when compared with BBQ by around 50%, for the same security level. Interestingly, these signatures are now very close in size to Picnic[1], meaning that Banquet is comparable in signature size to the state of the art of MPCitH-based signatures while using a standard block cipher.

See Table 1 for a high-level comparison of the signature size and run times.

Table 1. Signature size (in bytes) and run times (if available) for Picnic2, Picnic3, AES Binary, BBQ and Banquet for comparable MPCitH parameters and 128 bit security, where N denotes the number of MPCitH parties.

Protocol	N	Sign (ms)	Verify (ms)	Size (bytes)
Picnic2	64	41.16	18.21	12 347
	16	10.42	5.00	13 831
Picnic3	16	5.33	4.03	12 466
AES Bin	64	-	-	51 876
BBQ	64	-	-	31 876
Banquet	16	6.36	4.86	19 776
	107	21.13	18.96	14 784

Moreover, we provide a full prototype implementation of Banquet that works for a wide variety of parameter sets, and give a detailed analysis of how to securely choose parameters. At the 128-bit classical security level (corresponding to NIST's L1 category), our optimized implementation can sign messages in 6.4ms, about 1.2x slower than the 5.3 ms required for Picnic3 (the latest version of Picnic), while our signature size is 19.8kB, around 50% larger than Picnic3's 12.5kB. At higher security levels (NIST's L3 and L5), Banquet's signing speed ranges from 1.5–10x slower than Picnic, and signatures are 1.2–2x larger, depending on the choices of parameters.

At all security levels, our signature size is around 40–50% smaller than the AES-based scheme BBQ, which is itself much smaller than a naive AES-based scheme instantiated with a binary circuit and MPCitH [31] (denoted AES Bin in Table 1). Note that there is no reported implementation of BBQ, so we cannot compare runtimes here.

SPHINCS+ [6] is a hash-based signature scheme based on standard, symmetric-key primitives, like Banquet. At NIST's L1 security level, we show that Banquet can outperform the SPHINCS+ -fast parameters in both signature size and signing time, but with slower verification. At higher security levels SPHINCS+ obtains smaller signatures, but sometimes with slower signing time.

1.2 Our Techniques

Our main building block to achieve smaller signatures in Banquet is a new amortized inverse verification check, which replaces the solution from BBQ. Recall

[1] Using the Picnic3 parameter sets, see [30].

that in AES, the only non-linear operations are the S-box evaluations, which can be seen as inversions in $\mathbb{F}_{2^8}$, with the difference that 0 maps to 0. In BBQ, these were evaluated with preprocessed multiplication triples based on techniques from MPC, with a modification to the AES key generation phase to ensure that 0 is never inverted (which reduces the key space by 1 bit).

At a high level, our approach for verifying inverses works in four steps.

Inject Inverses. We provide the outputs of all m S-box evaluations already as part of the witness, and only verify that the product of the input and output for each of the m S-box instances is 1. Already, this optimization simplifies the original BBQ construction and reduces its main communication cost down from 4 to 3 field elements per S-box (per MPC execution).

Amortize the Verification of Multiplicative Relations. Then, we observe that it is not necessary to multiply all m S-box inputs with all outputs that are claimed to be correct independently. Instead, one multiplication of secret shared values is sufficient. This is done by arranging all inputs and outputs of the S-boxes into polynomials $S(\cdot)$ and $T(\cdot)$ (which can be done using free linear operations), providing a product polynomial P (that guarantees the required relation) as part of the witness and checking that $P(\cdot)$ is indeed the product of $S(\cdot)$ and $T(\cdot)$ by performing only one multiplication by evaluating at a random point. The prover additionally needs to send m field elements to specify the polynomial $P(\cdot)$.

Boost the Soundness. The product test, which relies on the Schwartz–Zippel Lemma, has soundness that depends on the gap between the degree of $P(\cdot)$ and the size of the underlying field. In $\mathbb{F}_{2^8}$ this gives quite poor soundness in practice, so we boost soundness by lifting all polynomials to an extension field and performing the test there.

Reduce Communication with Linear Combinations. Finally, we split our test from one polynomial triple $S(\cdot), T(\cdot), P(\cdot)$ with S, T of degree m into $\approx \sqrt{m}$ polynomial triples with factors of degree $\approx \sqrt{m}$ each. This stage is inspired by a recent zero-knowledge proof technique which was used to verify a batch of low-degree relations [10]. To verify these polynomial products, we then take a random linear combination of the polynomials to reduce the verification of all S-box evaluations down to a single check on polynomials of degree $\approx \sqrt{m}$, which reduces communication further.

1.3 Related Work

MPCitH was introduced in [27] and first shown to be feasible in practice with the ZKBoo protocol [25] and its follow-up work ZKB++ [14]. Later, Katz et al. introduced preprocessing to MPCitH-type protocols [31], which was further developed by Baum and Nof [3]. This paradigm of constructing signatures from MPCitH was first used in Picnic [14] and further developed in several later works [7,8,28,30,31].

Other paradigms for generic zero-knowledge proofs from symmetric-key primitives could also be used to instantiate our approach, such as Ligero [2] or Aurora [5]. These systems are not particularly well-suited to signatures, however, since despite good asymptotic performance, their proof sizes are quite large for small circuits like AES. For instance, a recent variant of Ligero was suggested for constructing post-quantum signatures [9], but when using AES as the one-way function, it achieves a signature size of 224KB and signing time of 256 ms, which (although on different hardware) are both significantly worse than Banquet.

A recent, alternative suggestion for MPCitH is to use the Legendre symbol as a one-way function [8]. This improves upon Picnic in terms of both speed and signature size, but also relies on a somewhat esoteric assumption, which has not seen much quantum cryptanalysis.

In addition to Picnic, there are several other signature schemes in the 3rd round of the NIST Post Quantum Cryptography Standardization Process[2]. The current finalists are the two lattice-based proposals Dilithium [21] and Falcon [23], as well as Rainbow [17], based on multivariate polynomials. "Alternate Candidates" are, in addition to Picnic, the SPHINCS+ [6] framework which is hash-based and GeMSS [13] which also uses multivariate polynomials. We will compare Banquet to Picnic, BBQ and SPHINCS+ since they are all based on symmetric key primitives.

2 Preliminaries

We let κ denote the computational security parameter. We denote by $[n]$ the set of integers $\{1, \dots, n\}$ and by $[0, n]$ the set $\{0, \dots, n\}$ with 0 included. We use L1, L3 and L5 to refer to the three security levels defined by NIST [34] in the call for post-quantum proposals, which match or exceed the brute-force security of AES-128, AES-192 and AES-256, respectively.

2.1 Definitions

We use the standard security notion for digital signature schemes, namely, existential unforgeability under adaptive chosen-message attacks (EUF-CMA) [26]. As a stepping stone to EUF-CMA security, we will first prove security of our scheme against key-only attacks (EUF-KO) where the adversary is given the public key but no access to a signing oracle. See the full version [4] for formal definitions.

2.2 MPC in the Head

We now recall the MPC-in-the-Head (MPCitH) scheme used in Picnic and other previous works. In zero-knowledge proofs based on the MPCitH paradigm, the prover simulates N parties $\mathcal{P}_1, \dots, \mathcal{P}_N$ for a computation over a field $\mathbb{F}$. As a

[2] https://csrc.nist.gov/projects/post-quantum-cryptography/round-3-submissions.

single computation usually does not achieve a negligible soundness error, the prover evaluates τ independent instances of the MPC scheme we describe below.

For simplicity, we focus on one MPC instance only. We describe the protocol from the view of the individual parties, although it is actually the prover simulating each such party who performs these actions.

First, each $\mathcal{P}_i$ obtains a tape of private randomness derived from a seed $\mathsf{sd}^{(i)}$. These seeds are used whenever a party needs to generate pseudorandom values or randomness for commitments. In order to secret-share a value $x \in \mathbb{F}$, the parties $\mathcal{P}_1, \ldots, \mathcal{P}_N$ first locally generate a pseudo-random share $x^{(i)} \in \mathbb{F}$, which $\mathcal{P}_1$ adjusts to $x^{(1)} \leftarrow x - \sum_{i=1}^{N} x^{(i)}$, so that $x^{(1)}, \ldots, x^{(N)}$ form the secret-sharing $\langle x \rangle$ of x. Observe that all parties can easily, without communication, generate a secret-sharing $\langle r \rangle$ of a pseudorandom value r by each deterministically deriving shares from $\mathsf{sd}^{(i)}$. In order to open a secret-shared value $\langle x \rangle$, each $\mathcal{P}_i$ simply broadcasts its share $x^{(i)}$ of x to all other parties.

Initially, before the parties obtain the secret-shares of the secret input, they may first obtain shares of random triples a, b, c, such that $c = a \cdot b$. The process of establishing shares of such random triples is usually part of a preprocessing step. Each party commits to all shares from the preprocessing.

If all parties have enough shares of random triples and also obtained shares of the input (to which they also commit) then they can perform the computation. Let C be a circuit over $\mathbb{F}$ the parties evaluate as follows:

- For the secret-shared values $\langle x \rangle, \langle y \rangle$ the parties can compute a secret sharing $\langle x + y \rangle$ or $\langle \alpha \cdot x + \beta \rangle$ for publicly known $\alpha, \beta \in \mathbb{F}$ by using the linearly homomorphic property of the secret-sharing scheme. The parties can therefore compute shares of the outcome of the operation *without interaction.*
- To compute a secret-sharing $\langle x \cdot y \rangle$, from secret-shared values $\langle x \rangle, \langle y \rangle$, the parties take an unused sharing of a random triple $\langle a \rangle, \langle b \rangle, \langle c \rangle$, open the two values $\langle \delta \rangle = \langle a - x \rangle, \langle \epsilon \rangle = \langle b - y \rangle$, locally reconstruct δ and ϵ and then use the communication-free linear operations to compute a sharing of $\langle z \rangle = \delta \cdot \langle y \rangle + \epsilon \cdot \langle x \rangle - \delta \cdot \epsilon - \langle c \rangle$, which is correct if all shares were opened correctly and a, b, c indeed form a correct multiplicative triple.

When broadcasting values, each party locally commits to the values that it sends to and receives from other parties. Finally, each party locally sends its share of the output of the computation to the verifier, together with all the aforementioned commitments.

The verifier chooses a party $\mathcal{P}_i$ which should not be opened, whereupon the prover will send the verifier the openings for all commitments and seeds of the remaining $N-1$ parties, as well as all values that the un-opened party broadcast in the process. The verifier then re-computes all messages that are sent by each opened party and checks if these are consistent with the commitments as well as the pseudorandom seeds. It accepts if all these checks go through. In order to also verify the preprocessing, one would have also have to verify the preprocessing independently [3,31]. We do not describe such checks here since our signature scheme, in comparison to BBQ [16], does not require preprocessed data.

One can see that the output, which the verifier obtains as shares from all N parties, must be correct with probability at least $1/N$, as the prover could have cheated in at most one party (the one which is not opened to the verifier). But in order to do so it would have had to anticipate the verifier's choice before making the commitments as it cannot undo cheating later. As mentioned before, the soundness error can be reduced by running the aforementioned scheme τ times in parallel. Note that by only revealing the secret states of $N-1$ parties, the protocol we described above does not leak any information about the secret input to the verifier, as every $N-1$ out of N shares appear pseudorandom and the remaining shares are hidden inside commitments.

2.3 AES

AES is a 128-bit block-cipher based on a substitution-permutation network (SPN). It allows key lengths of 128, 192 or 256 bits, where the SPN uses 10, 12 or 14 rounds respectively. The state of AES always consists of 128 bits and can be considered as a 4×4 matrix of elements in $\mathbb{F}_{2^8}$. The round function is composed of four operations on the state, of which only one called *SubBytes* is non-linear. SubBytes transforms each of the 16 bytes of the state by applying an S-box to each byte. The AES S-box computes a multiplicative inverse in the field $\mathbb{F}_{2^8}$, followed by an invertible affine transformation, and can be seen as

$$S : s \mapsto \phi^{-1}\left(\mathbf{A} \cdot \phi\left(s^{-1}\right) + \mathbf{b}\right), \tag{1}$$

where $\phi : \mathbb{F}_{2^8} \rightarrow (\mathbb{F}_2)^8$ is an isomorphism of vector spaces and $\mathbf{A} \in (\mathbb{F}_2)^{8\times 8}$ and $\mathbf{b} \in (\mathbb{F}_2)^8$ are the public parameters of the affine transformation. For completeness, $s^{-1} = 0$ if $s = 0$. The key schedule function is mostly linear, except for the application of the same S-box to up to four bytes of the round key.

2.4 The BBQ Signature Scheme

The BBQ signature scheme [16] follows the blueprint of Picnic [14], except for two main differences: 1) While Picnic uses LowMC as a one-way function (OWF), BBQ relies on the well-studied AES; 2) BBQ does not consider AES as a binary circuit with AND and XOR gates, but rather as an arithmetic circuit over $\mathbb{F}_{2^8}$ where the only non-linear operation is the S-box inversion.

The reason why AES naturally fits to be evaluated inside MPCitH, is that all its operations can either be expressed as linear transformations or field operations over $\mathbb{F}_{2^8}$ (as mentioned in Sect. 2.3). If one uses the MPCitH scheme that was outlined in Sect. 2.2 over the field $\mathbb{F}_{2^8}$, then only evaluating the S-boxes requires communication between the parties (beyond obtaining shares of the input). The S-box evaluation is therefore the only additional contribution to the size of the signature.

The approach of BBQ for evaluating the S-box inside MPCitH is as follows:

1: A random multiplication triple $(\langle a \rangle, \langle b \rangle, \langle c \rangle)$ comes from preprocessing.

2: $\langle s \rangle$ is held by the parties.
3: $\langle r \rangle$ is sampled at random from $\mathbb{F}_{2^8}$.
4: $\langle t \rangle \leftarrow \langle s \rangle \cdot \langle r \rangle$ which is computed using $(\langle a \rangle, \langle b \rangle, \langle c \rangle)$.
5: $t \leftarrow \mathsf{Open}(\langle t \rangle)$.
6: $\langle s^{-1} \rangle \leftarrow t^{-1} \cdot \langle r \rangle = \langle s^{-1} \cdot r^{-1} \cdot r \rangle$.

This approach, in the ideal case, only communicates 4 field elements per S-box: one field element for the preprocessed multiplication triple where only $\langle c \rangle$ is non-random, two for the multiplication $\langle s \rangle \cdot \langle r \rangle$ and one for the opening of $\langle t \rangle$. Two crucial properties of this protocol are:

1. It requires that s is invertible for every S-box as a computation that branches based on s being 0 or not would be much more costly.
2. It is necessary that $r \neq 0$, as the inversion does not work if $r = 0$.

The first drawback can be easily worked around, as shown in [16], by restricting key generation to choose an AES key and input such that S-box inputs are always non-zero. The authors show that this only reduces the key-space by 1.1 to 2.9 bits for AES-128 and AES-256 (respectively).

3 Identification Scheme with Amortized Verification of Inverses

In this section we present our novel technique for efficient amortized verification of inverses in MPC in more detail. This technique builds upon the sacrificing-based multiplication verification of [3], but improves upon their work in a novel and interesting way, by adapting a recent polynomial-based technique for verifying multiplications in distributed zero-knowledge proofs [10].

Our first observation is that we can replace the MPC-oriented inversion algorithm by an MPCitH-friendly version instead. In BBQ, the parties in the MPCitH first compute a masked version $\langle t \rangle$ of the input $\langle s \rangle$ to the S-box (i.e. $\langle t \rangle \leftarrow \langle s \rangle \cdot \langle r \rangle$, then invert t in the clear and finally remove the mask. This computes an inversion of $\langle s \rangle$ as one would do in regular MPC protocols, but it does not take the additional knowledge of the prover into account. Namely, the prover can directly inject a sharing of the inverse $\langle t \rangle = \langle s^{-1} \rangle$ into the protocol execution. This is possible because in an MPCitH protocol, the prover knows the evaluated circuit as well as all secret-shared values in advance. This also removes the random value $\langle r \rangle$ that was used in the inversion algorithm before, which is an advantage as BBQ required extra costs to ensure that this random $\langle r \rangle$ was non-zero in order for the inversion to be correct. However, the prover could still share a wrong value for $\langle t \rangle$, so the MPCitH parties must now run a checking procedure to ensure that the inverse values are correct.

After completing the circuit for evaluating AES, the parties now hold shares for $2m$ values, where m denotes the number of S-boxes: the inputs $\langle s_1 \rangle, \ldots, \langle s_m \rangle$ and their corresponding alleged inverses $\langle t_1 \rangle, \ldots, \langle t_m \rangle$. These $2m$ values should all pairwise multiply to 1, which can be verified using the standard multiplication verification procedure that uses a random multiplication triple for each pair

$\langle s_\ell \rangle, \langle t_\ell \rangle, \ell \in [m]$. In the following we will show an alternative method to check inverses that requires less communication, contributing to shorter signatures. Here we will again exploit that the prover knows the entire secret inputs of the MPCitH protocol and can provide additional, although possibly faulty, secret inputs to the computation.

3.1 Polynomial-Based Checking of Inverses

Consider a random polynomial $S(x) \in \mathbb{F}_{2^8}[x]$ of degree m that has $S(\ell - 1) = s_\ell$, for all $\ell \in [m]$. Similarly, consider such a polynomial $T(x) \in \mathbb{F}_{2^8}[x]$ with $T(\ell - 1) = t_\ell$, also of degree m. We can construct these polynomials by interpolating the m points (ℓ, s_ℓ), and one extra, random point.

By defining the polynomial $P = S \cdot T$ of degree $2m$, it holds that $P(\ell - 1) = 1$ for $\ell \in [m]$ if all the $\langle t_i \rangle$ were correctly provided. All $S(\cdot), T(\cdot), P(\cdot)$ are known to the prover at proof time. To perform the amortized test, observe that the MPCitH parties (1) can compute shares of the polynomials $S(\cdot)$, $T(\cdot)$ and $P(\cdot)$, which the prover will have committed to, without communication using Lagrange interpolation, and (2) can check that $P = S \cdot T$ by receiving a random value R from the verifier, locally evaluating the three polynomials at R, jointly reconstructing $P(R)$, $S(R)$, $T(R)$ and allowing the verifier to check that $P(R) = S(R) \cdot T(R)$.

Both $S(\cdot), T(\cdot)$ are already provided in the form of the shares $\langle s_\ell \rangle, \langle t_\ell \rangle$ and no extra communication is necessary[3] to interpolate these. For $P(\cdot)$, observe that m of its evaluations can be hard-coded as equal to 1, as we want to achieve that $P(0) = \cdots = P(m-1) = 1$. The proof therefore only has to communicate $m+1$ further evaluation points of $P(\cdot)$ in secret-shared form. The prover may cheat doing so, but the multiplication test on a random R chosen by the verifier detects such cheating behavior. The probability that this check fails to reveal cheating when verifying $P(\cdot)$ can be bounded using the Schwartz–Zippel Lemma, which we can use to bound the number of zeroes of the polynomial $Q = P - S \cdot T$, which is non-zero only when $P \neq S \cdot T$.

Lemma 1 (Schwartz–Zippel Lemma). *Let $Q(x) \in \mathbb{F}[x]$ be a non-zero polynomial of degree $d \geq 0$. For any finite subset S of $\mathbb{F}$,* $\Pr_{r \xleftarrow{\$} S}[Q(r) = 0] \leq \frac{d}{|S|}$.

In summary, in addition to the m injected inverses, the prover will additionally have to provide the remaining $m+1$ points that define $P(\cdot)$ fully as part of the proof, and will have to open $S(R), T(R), P(R)$ to the verifier.

3.2 Generalized Polynomial-Based Checking

We now generalize the protocol from the previous subsection to reduce the number of field elements that need to be opened by the MPCitH parties. This gen-

[3] Both $S(\cdot), T(\cdot)$ are actually defined by m shares and one share of a random value only known to the prover, which will later simplify the simulation of the protocol for its zero-knowledge property. This sharing of a random value can be obtained for free in MPCitH.

eralization reduces the transcript size from around $2m$ elements to $m + O(\sqrt{m})$ by instead checking $O(\sqrt{m})$ inner products of size $\sqrt{m}$. It is based on a zero-knowledge proof from [10, Section 4.2] (also described in [12, Section 4.1]).

The idea of the improved check is to first compute $O(\sqrt{m})$ random inner products and use these to define $O(\sqrt{m})$ pairs of polynomials $S_j(\cdot)$ and $T_j(\cdot)$. These are then used to define a single random polynomial $P(\cdot)$, still subjected to a constraint based on the inverse relation, which is then checked against its constituent polynomials as before. We also modify this test by lifting the random polynomial evaluations to an extension field, which improves the soundness bound from the Schwartz-Zippel lemma.

Let λ be a lifting parameter and let $m = m_1 \cdot m_2$ where $m_2 < 8\lambda$. Fix an injective homomorphism to lift shares from $\mathbb{F}_{2^8}$ to $\mathbb{F}_{2^{8\lambda}}$, which can be computed locally by each of the parties of the MPCitH protocol. We also write $f(k)$ for a polynomial $f(\cdot)$ and an integer k, to mean f evaluated at the k-th element of $\mathbb{F}_{2^{8\lambda}}$ (according to a fixed ordering). The following procedure describes the non-secret-shared verification protocol.

Given inputs $s_1, \ldots, s_m$ and $t_1, \ldots, t_m \in \mathbb{F}_{2^8}$:

1: Lift $s_1, \ldots, s_m$ and $t_1, \ldots, t_m$ to $\mathbb{F}_{2^{8\lambda}}$.

2: For $j \in [m_1]$, sample additional random points $\bar{s}_j, \bar{t}_j \leftarrow \mathbb{F}_{2^{8\lambda}}$.

3: Sample $r_j \leftarrow \mathbb{F}_{2^{8\lambda}}$, for $j \in [m_1]$. ▷ Randomizing the inner products.

4: Compute $s'_{j,k} = r_j \cdot s_{j+m_1 k}$ and write $t'_{j,k} = t_{j+m_1 k}$, for $j \in [m_1], k \in [0, m_2 - 1]$. Observe that when all $s_i t_i = 1$,

$$\begin{pmatrix} s'_{1,k} & \cdots & s'_{m_1,k} \end{pmatrix} \begin{pmatrix} t'_{1,k} \\ \vdots \\ t'_{m_1,k} \end{pmatrix} = \sum_{j \in [m_1]} r_j \qquad \text{for } k \in [0, m_2 - 1].$$

5: Define polynomials $S_j(\cdot), T_j(\cdot)$ such that

$$\begin{aligned} S_j(k) &= s'_{j,k}, & T_j(k) &= t'_{j,k} \qquad \text{for } k \in [0, m_2 - 1], \\ S_j(m_2) &= \bar{s}_j, & T_j(m_2) &= \bar{t}_j. \end{aligned}$$

By definition each such polynomial has degree m_2.

6: Let $P = \sum_j S_j \cdot T_j$ be of degree $2m_2$, where it is guaranteed that $P(k) = \sum_j r_j$, for $k \in [0, m_2 - 1]$ and $j \in [m_1]$.

7: Sample $R \leftarrow \mathbb{F}_{2^{8\lambda}} \setminus [0, m_2 - 1]$. ▷ Schwartz–Zippel challenge.

8: Compute $P(R)$ as well as $S_j(R)$ and $T_j(R)$, for $j \in [m_1]$, and verify whether $P(R) = \sum_j S_j(R) \cdot T_j(R)$.

Secret-Shared Checking. Since polynomial interpolation is linear, the parties in the MPCitH protocol can interpolate the shares of the coefficients of polynomials $S_j(\cdot)$ and $T_j(\cdot)$ from shares of $s'_{j,k}$ and $t'_{j,k}$ as well as $\bar{s}_j, \bar{t}_j$. This does not require any communication as the challenges r_j are public and $\bar{s}_j, \bar{t}_j$ can be freely generated by the MPCitH scheme. From this, each party can compute their share of $S_j(R)$ and $T_j(R)$ for each j and then reveal it in order to perform the check.

As mentioned above, the only non-linear part is the computation of the polynomial $P(\cdot)$. Here the prover adjusts the shares for m_2+1 values of P, as another m_2 values are already specified by the publicly known $P(k) = \sum_j r_j$ for each $k \in [0, m_2-1]$, in the same way that it injects a correction value for the inverses. With those $2m_2+1$ shares, the parties locally interpolate shares of the coefficients of P and then compute and reveal their shares of $P(R)$.

In summary, each party $\mathcal{P}_i$ performs the following operations.

1: Lift $s_1^{(i)}, \dots, s_m^{(i)}$ and $t_1^{(i)}, \dots, t_m^{(i)}$ to $\mathbb{F}_{2^{8\lambda}}$.
2: For $j \in [m_1]$, sample $\bar{s}_j^{(i)}, \bar{t}_j^{(i)} \leftarrow \mathbb{F}_{2^{8\lambda}}$.
3: Receive challenges $r_j \in \mathbb{F}_{2^{8\lambda}}$ for $j \in [m_1]$.
4: Compute $s'^{(i)}_{j,k} = r_j \cdot s^{(i)}_{j+m_1k}$ and write $t'^{(i)}_{j,k} = t^{(i)}_{j+m_1k}$ for $j \in [m_1], k \in [0, m_2-1]$.
5: Interpolate polynomials $S_j^{(i)}(\cdot)$ and $T_j^{(i)}(\cdot)$ such that:

$$S_j^{(i)}(m_2) = \bar{s}_j^{(i)}, \quad T_j^{(i)}(m_2) = \bar{t}_j^{(i)}$$

and

$$S_j^{(i)}(k) = \bar{s}'^{(i)}_{j,k}, \quad T_j^{(i)}(k) = \bar{t}'^{(i)}_{j,k} \text{ for } k \in [0, m_2-1].$$

6: Receive m_2+1 shares $P^{(i)}(k)$, for $k \in \{m_2, \dots, 2m_2\}$ ($k = m_2$ is included as parties cannot compute $\sum_j \bar{s}_j \cdot \bar{t}_j$ locally) from the prover. For $k \in [0, m_2-1]$, if $i = 1$, set $P^{(i)}(k) = \sum_j r_j$; if $i \neq 1$, set $P^{(i)}(k) = 0$. Interpolate $P^{(i)}$ from those $2m_2+1$ points.
7: Receive the challenge $R \in \mathbb{F}_{2^{8\lambda}} \setminus [0, m_2-1]$ from the verifier.
8: Compute $P^{(i)}(R), S_j^{(i)}(R)$ and $T_j^{(i)}(R)$ and open all these $2m_1+1$ values.
9: Check that $P^{(i)}(R) = \sum_{j \in [m_1]} S_j^{(i)}(R) \cdot T_j^{(i)}(R)$.

Soundness Error of the Generalized Check. Assume that each party honestly follows the protocol but there exists $\ell \in [m]$ such that $s_\ell \cdot t_\ell \neq 1$. Since the embedding into $\mathbb{F}_{2^{8\lambda}}$ is an injective homomorphism, it must then also hold that $s_\ell \cdot t_\ell \neq 1$ over $\mathbb{F}_{2^{8\lambda}}$. Assuming that the above protocol succeeds, then one of the following conditions must hold:

1. In Step 2, the values $r_1, \dots, r_{m_1}$ were sampled such that $\sum_{j \in [m_1]} S_j(k) \cdot T_j(k) = 1$ for $k \in [0, m_2-1]$.
2. In Step 6 a value R was chosen such that $P(R) = \sum_j S_j(R) \cdot T_j(R)$ while $P \neq \sum_j S_j \cdot T_j$.

For the first condition, by assumption we have that $\exists j, k$ such that $\sum_j r_j = \sum_j s'_{j,k} \cdot t'_{j,k}$ while $r_j \neq s'_{j,k} \cdot t'_{j,k}$. By the choice of r_j this will happen with probability at most $2^{-8\lambda}$. In the second case, the polynomials on both sides are of degree $2m_2$ and can have at most $2m_2$ points in common. By Lemma 1, the probability of choosing such a value of R is at most $2m_2/(2^{8\lambda} - m_2)$.

The overall soundness error is therefore at most $2^{-8\lambda} + 2m_2/(2^{8\lambda} - m_2)$.

Simulatability of the Generalized Check. We now construct a simulator for the aforementioned protocol to argue that it does not leak any information. The simulator obtains $N-1$ shares of $\{s_\ell, t_\ell\}_{\ell \in [m]}$ as inputs, w.l.o.g. it misses the N-th share. It first chooses $r_1, \ldots, r_{m_1}$ uniformly at random from $\mathbb{F}_{2^{8\lambda}}$ and R uniformly from the appropriate set.

For $i \in [N-1]$, it samples $\bar{s}_j^{(i)}$ and $\bar{t}_j^{(i)}$ as in the protocol and interpolates $S_j^{(i)}$ and $T_j^{(i)}$ for $j \in [m_1]$. It then samples $S_j(R)$ and $T_j(R)$ at random. It fixes m pairs of shares $\{s_\ell^{(N)}, t_\ell^{(N)}\}$ arbitrarily, sets $S_j^{(N)}(R) = S_j(R) - \sum_{i=1}^{N-1} S_j^{(i)}(R)$ and similarly for $T_j^{(N)}(R)$, and interpolates $S_j^{(N)}$ and $T_j^{(N)}$ using these values (instead of sampling $\bar{s}_j^{(N)}$ and $\bar{t}_j^{(N)}$ at random). Because the uniform sampling of $\bar{s}_j$ and $\bar{t}_j$ in the protocol imply a uniform distribution for $S_j(R)$ and $T_j(R)$, the values produced by the simulator (including the opened shares $S_j^{(N)}(R)$ and $T_j^{(N)}(R)$), are identically distributed.

The simulator then computes the product polynomial P defined by the shared S_j and T_j polynomials it interpolated before and honestly samples the m_2+1 shares for each party. Instead of opening $P^{(N)}(R)$ honestly, the simulator computes $P^{(N)}(R) = P(R) - \sum_{i=1} N - 1 P^{(i)}(R)$ and opens that instead. Because $P(R)$ is computed honestly from $S_j(R)$ and $T_j(R)$, the computed $P^{(N)}(R)$ is distributed identically to an honest run of the protocol.

By construction, all opened values are consistent with the protocol definition and are perfectly indistinguishable from a real run. Furthermore, all secret-shared values by linearity generate a correct transcript.

Communication Cost. Steps 1–4 and 6 are local given public knowledge of r_j and R. The only parts which add communication are Step 5, which introduces $8\lambda(m_2+1)$ bits into the transcript unless $\mathcal{P}_1$ is opened (as injecting shares can be done with $\mathcal{P}_2, \ldots, \mathcal{P}_N$ sampling random shares and $\mathcal{P}_1$ receiving a correction share), and Step 7, which always adds $8\lambda(2m_1+1)$ bits. This gives a total average overhead per S-box of $8\lambda\left(\frac{N-1}{N}(m_2+1) + 2m_1 + 1\right)/m$ bits.

For instance, in our concrete instantiation at the L1 security level (see Sect. 6.1), we use $m = 200$, with $N = 16$ parties, $\lambda = 4$, $m_1 = 10$ and $m_2 = 20$ to obtain an overhead of 6.51 bits per S-box. This is significantly less than the direct approach of checking with m MPC multiplications, which would require around 16 bits per multiply (8 for the last party's share of the multiplication triple, and 8 for the unopened party's broadcast value).

4 The Banquet Signature Scheme

In this section we present the Banquet signature scheme obtained by using the zero-knowledge identification scheme from the previous section with the Fiat–Shamir transform [22]. We state and prove its security theorem in Sect. 5.

At a high level, Banquet works exactly as previous MPCitH-based signatures, like Picnic and BBQ. Given a key pair consisting of a random secret key $\mathsf{sk} = k$

and a public key $\mathsf{pk} = (x, y)$ such that $\mathsf{AES}_k(x) = y$, and to sign a message μ one generates a non-interactive zero-knowledge proof of knowledge of k in a way that binds μ to the proof. More concretely, we start with a 7-round, interactive identification scheme for proving knowledge of k, and compile this to a non-interactive proof using the Fiat–Shamir transform. The verifier's three random challenges are generated using random oracles, with the message and public key used as initial inputs to bind these to the signature.

Additionally, to sample the MPC parties' randomness we use a deterministic seed expansion function, Expand, which we instantiate using SHAKE. Each seed s used as input to Expand defines a distinct random tape t, such that every call to $\mathsf{Sample}(t)$ reads the next bits of the tape defined by t, keeping track of the current position on the tape. As introduced in [31], to reduce communication when opening seeds that were randomly challenged, we generate all seeds as the leaves of a binary tree derived from a master seed at the root. This allows $N-1$ of N seeds to be communicated by revealing only $\log N$ seeds.

Parameters. The scheme depends on the following values: the security parameter κ, the total number of parties N in the underlying MPC protocol, the total number of S-boxes m, the number of parallel repetitions τ, and m_1, m_2, and λ be as described in the previous section.

Key Generation. $\mathsf{Gen}(1^\kappa)$ samples $k, x \leftarrow \{0,1\}^\kappa$, computes $\mathsf{AES}_k(x) = y$, and repeats this until there are no S-boxes in the computation of y with input 0. It then sets $\mathsf{sk} = k$ and $\mathsf{pk} = (x, y)$, and returns $(\mathsf{pk}, \mathsf{sk})$.

The security of the key generation directly follows from the security analysis in [16], which we review in Sect. 5.

We recall that for security reasons the key generation algorithm requires the block-size and the key-size to be equal [14]. While this is true for AES-128, this is not the case for AES-192 and AES-256. Two solutions to this problem were proposed in [16]: the first one relies on the use of the Rijndael cipher with 192-bit (resp. 256-bit) blocks and keys; the second on the combination of two copies of AES-192 (resp. AES-256) in ECB mode.

Signature Generation and Verification Algorithm. The $\mathsf{Sign}(\mathsf{sk}, \mathsf{pk}, \mu)$ algorithm is formally described in Figs. 1, 2 and 3. We describe the protocol in phases and give the rationale behind each one. The challenges h_1, h_2 and h_3 are generated using three random oracles H_1, H_2 and H_3, respectively. The MPC-in-the-Head computation is divided into two steps: the AES *execution* and then the *verification* of the inverse injections.

In Phase 1 (Fig. 1) the prover commits to τ executions of AES, generating the first signature component σ_1, which consists of a 2κ-bit salt st, commitments to the seeds $\{\mathsf{C}_e^{(i)}\}_{i \in [N]}$, the injection of the secret key sk, the injection of the m inverse values $t_{e,\ell}$ and the broadcast of the output ct_e, for each execution $e \in [\tau]$ and S-box $\ell \in [m]$. These values suffice to uniquely determine the output values of the distributed AES circuit. The first challenge, h_1, is generated in Phase 2 (Fig. 2) by hashing together σ_1, the message μ and the public key pk. The next

We use e to index executions, i to index parties, and ℓ to index S-boxes.
$\mathsf{Sign}(\mathsf{sk}, \mu)$:
Phase 1: Committing to the seeds and the execution views of the parties.

1: Sample a random salt $\mathsf{st} \xleftarrow{\$} \{0,1\}^{2\kappa}$.
2: **for** each parallel execution e **do**
3: Sample a root seed: $\mathsf{sd}_e \xleftarrow{\$} \{0,1\}^{\kappa}$.
4: Compute parties' seeds $\mathsf{sd}_e^{(1)}, \ldots, \mathsf{sd}_e^{(N)}$ as leaves of binary tree from sd_e.
5: **for** each party i **do**
6: Commit to seed: $\mathsf{C}_e^{(i)} \leftarrow \mathsf{Commit}(\mathsf{st}, e, i, \mathsf{sd}_e^{(i)})$.
7: Expand random tape: $\mathsf{tape}_e^{(i)} \leftarrow \mathsf{Expand}(\mathsf{st}, e, i, \mathsf{sd}_e^{(i)})$
8: Sample witness share: $\mathsf{sk}_e^{(i)} \leftarrow \mathsf{Sample}(\mathsf{tape}_e^{(i)})$.
9: Compute witness offset: $\Delta\mathsf{sk}_e \leftarrow \mathsf{sk} - \sum_i \mathsf{sk}_e^{(i)}$.
10: Adjust first share: $\mathsf{sk}_e^{(1)} \leftarrow \mathsf{sk}_e^{(1)} + \Delta\mathsf{sk}_e$.
11: **for** each S-box ℓ **do**
12: For each party i, compute the local linear operations to obtain the share $s_{e,\ell}^{(i)}$ of the S-box input $s_{e,\ell}$.
13: Compute the S-box output: $t_{e,\ell} = \left(\sum_i s_{e,\ell}^{(i)}\right)^{-1}$.
14: For each party i, sample the share of the output: $t_{e,\ell}^{(i)} \leftarrow \mathsf{Sample}(\mathsf{tape}_e^{(i)})$.
15: Compute output offset: $\Delta t_{e,\ell} = t_{e,\ell} - \sum_i t_{e,\ell}^{(i)}$.
16: Adjust first share: $t_{e,\ell}^{(1)} \leftarrow t_{e,\ell}^{(1)} + \Delta t_{e,\ell}$.
17: Broadcast each party's share $\mathsf{ct}_e^{(i)}$ of the output.
18: Set $\sigma_1 \leftarrow (\mathsf{st}, (\mathsf{C}_e^{(i)})_{i\in[N]}, (\mathsf{ct}_e^{(i)})_{i\in[N]}, \Delta\mathsf{sk}_e, (\Delta t_{e,\ell})_{\ell\in[m]})_{e\in[\tau]}$.

Fig. 1. Signature scheme - Phase 1. Commitment to executions of AES.

phases are devoted to the verification of the AES executions. In particular, in Phase 3 (Fig. 2) the prover generates the commitments to the checking polynomial $P_e(\cdot)$, for each execution $e \in [\tau]$, as described in Sect. 3.2, and computes a challenge for them in Phase 4. Phases 5 and 6 (Fig. 3) describe the computation of the challenge for the committed checking polynomial and the commitments to the views of the check openings for each execution, respectively. Finally, Phase 7 outputs the signature σ.

The verification algorithm $\mathsf{Verify}(\mathsf{pk}, \mu, \sigma)$ is described in Fig. 4. It performs similar computations to those made during generation of the signature, thereby checking the consistency of $N-1$ of the N parties in each of the τ instances.

5 Security Proof

We prove Banquet is EUF-CMA-secure (unforgeability against chosen-message attacks, Theorem 1) by first proving that Banquet is EUF-KO-secure (unforgeability against key-only attacks) in Lemma 2.

Phase 2: Challenging the multiplications.

1: Compute challenge hash: $h_1 \leftarrow H_1(\mu, \mathsf{pk}, \sigma_1)$.
2: Expand hash: $(r_{e,j})_{e\in[\tau],j\in[m_1]} \leftarrow \mathsf{Expand}(h_1)$ where $r_{e,j} \in \mathbb{F}_{2^{8\lambda}}$.

Phase 3: Committing to the checking polynomials.

1: **for** each execution e **do**
2: **for** each party i **do**
3: Lift $s^{(i)}_{e,\ell}, t^{(i)}_{e,\ell} \hookrightarrow \mathbb{F}_{2^{8\lambda}}$, for $\ell \in [m]$.
4: **for** $j \in [m_1]$ **do**
5: Set $s'^{(i)}_{e,j,k} \leftarrow r_{e,j} \cdot s^{(i)}_{e,j+m_1 k}$ and $t'^{(i)}_{e,j,k} \leftarrow t^{(i)}_{e,j+m_1 k}$, for $k \in [0, m_2]$.
6: Sample additional random points: $\bar{s}^{(i)}_{e,j}, \bar{t}^{(i)}_{e,j} \leftarrow \mathsf{Sample}(\mathsf{tape}^{(i)}_e)$.
7: Define $S^{(i)}_{e,j}(k) = s'^{(i)}_{e,j,k}$ and $T^{(i)}_{e,j}(k) = t'^{(i)}_{e,j,k}$ for $k \in [0, m_2 - 1]$ as well as $S^{(i)}_{e,j}(m_2) = \bar{s}^{(i)}_{e,j}$ and $T^{(i)}_{e,j}(m_2) = \bar{t}^{(i)}_{e,j}$.
8: Interpolate polynomials $S^{(i)}_{e,j}(\cdot)$ and $T^{(i)}_{e,j}(\cdot)$ of degree m_2 using defined $m_2 + 1$ points.
9: Compute product polynomial: $P_e \leftarrow \sum_{j\in[m_1]} \left(\sum_i S^{(i)}_{e,j}\right) \cdot \left(\sum_i T^{(i)}_{e,j}\right)$.
10: **for** each party i **do**
11: For $k \in [0, m_2 - 1]$: $P^{(i)}_e(k) = \begin{cases} \sum_j r_{e,j} & \text{if } i = 1 \\ 0 & \text{if } i \neq 1 \end{cases}$
12: For $k \in \{m_2, \ldots, 2m_2\}$, sample $P^{(i)}_e(k) \leftarrow \mathsf{Sample}(\mathsf{tape}^{(i)}_e)$.
13: **for** $k \in \{m_2, \ldots, 2m_2\}$ **do**
14: Compute offset: $\Delta P_e(k) = P_e(k) - \sum_i P^{(i)}_e(k)$.
15: Adjust first share: $P^{(1)}_e(k) \leftarrow P^{(1)}_e(k) + \Delta P_e(k)$.
16: For each party i, interpolate $P^{(i)}_e$ using defined $2m_2 + 1$ points.
17: Set $\sigma_2 \leftarrow \left((\Delta P_e(k))_{k\in\{m_2,\ldots,2m_2\}}\right)_{e\in[\tau]}$.

Fig. 2. Signature scheme - Phases 2 and 3. Computation of randomized inner product checking polynomials.

Lemma 2. *Let* Commit, H_1, H_2 *and* H_3 *be modeled as random oracles,* Expand *be modeled as a random function, and let* (N, τ, m_2, λ) *be parameters for the Banquet scheme. Let* $\mathcal{A}$ *be a probabilistic* $\mathsf{poly}(\kappa)$*-time adversary against the* EUF-KO *security of the signature scheme that makes* Q_c, Q_1, Q_2 *and* Q_3 *queries to the respective oracles. Then there exists a probabilistic* $\mathsf{poly}(\kappa)$*-time adversary* $\mathcal{B}$ *against the* OWF *security of* $f_{\mathbf{x}}$ *such that*

$$\mathbf{Adv}^{\mathsf{OWF}}_{\mathcal{B}}(1^\kappa) \geq \mathbf{Adv}^{\mathsf{EUF\text{-}KO}}_{\mathcal{A}}(1^\kappa) - \varepsilon(Q_c, Q_1, Q_2, Q_3),$$

with

$$\varepsilon(Q_c, Q_1, Q_2, Q_3) = \frac{(\tau N + 1)(Q_c + Q_1 + Q_2 + Q_3)^2}{2^{2\kappa}} + \Pr[X + Y + Z = \tau]$$

where $X = \max_{q_1\in\mathcal{Q}_1}\{X_{q_1}\}$ *with* $X_{q_1} \sim \mathfrak{B}(\tau, 1/2^{8\lambda})$, $Y = \max_{q_2\in\mathcal{Q}_2}\{Y_{q_2}\}$ *with* $Y_{q_2} \sim \mathfrak{B}(\tau - X, 2m_2/(2^{8\lambda} - m_2))\forall q_2$ *and* $Z = \max_{q_3\in\mathcal{Q}_3}\{Z_{q_3}\}$ *with* $Z_{q_3} \sim \mathfrak{B}(\tau -$

Phase 4: Challenging the checking polynomials.

1: Compute challenge hash: $h_2 \leftarrow H_2(h_1, \sigma_2)$.

2: Expand hash: $(R_e)_{e\in[\tau]} \leftarrow \mathsf{Expand}(h_2)$ where $R_e \in \mathbb{F}_{2^{8\lambda}} \setminus [0, m_2 - 1]$.

Phase 5: Committing to the views of the checking protocol.

1: **for** each execution e **do**

2: **for** each party i **do**

3: For $j \in [m_1]$, compute: $a_{e,j}^{(i)} \leftarrow S_{e,j}^{(i)}(R_e)$ and $b_{e,j}^{(i)} \leftarrow T_{e,j}^{(i)}(R_e)$.

4: Compute: $c_e^{(i)} \leftarrow P_e^{(i)}(R_e)$.

5: Open c_e, and $a_{e,j}$, $b_{e,j}$ for $j \in [m_1]$.

6: Set $\sigma_3 \leftarrow (((a_{e,j}^{(i)}, b_{e,j}^{(i)})_{j\in[m_1]}, c_e^{(i)})_{i\in[N]})_{e\in[\tau]}$.

Phase 6: Challenging the views of the checking protocol.

1: Compute challenge hash: $h_3 \leftarrow H_3(h_2, \sigma_3)$.

2: Expand hash: $(\bar{i}_e)_{e\in[\tau]} \leftarrow \mathsf{Expand}(h_3)$ where $\bar{i}_e \in [N]$.

Phase 7: Opening the views of the checking protocol.

1: **for** each execution e **do**

2: $\mathsf{seeds}_e \leftarrow \{\log_2(N)$ nodes needed to compute $\mathsf{sd}_{e,i}$ for $i \in [N] \setminus \{\bar{i}_e\}\}$.

3: Output $\sigma \leftarrow (\mathsf{st}, h_1, h_3, (\mathsf{seeds}_e, \mathsf{C}_e^{(\bar{i}_e)}, \Delta\mathsf{sk}_e, (\Delta t_{e,\ell})_{\ell\in[m]},$
$(\Delta P_e(k))_{k\in\{m_2,\ldots,2m_2\}}, P_e(R_e), (S_{e,j}(R_e), T_{e,j}(R_e))_{j\in[m_1]})_{e\in[\tau]})$.

Fig. 3. Signature scheme - Phases 4–7. Computation of the views of the randomized check openings, challenging and opening of the views of the checking protocol.

$X - Y, 1/N)\forall q_3$, where $\mathfrak{B}(n,p)$ denotes the binomial probability distribution with n samples each with probability p of success.

Remark 1. Due to the mix of different distributions, we do not express the second term of $\varepsilon(Q_,, Q_1, Q_2, Q_3)$ as a closed function; we will later compute parameters τ, m_2, κ and N such that ε is negligible in λ. This will then imply that if $\mathcal{A}$ has a non-negligible advantage in the EUF-KO game with these parameters, then $\mathcal{B}$ also has non-negligible advantage in the corresponding OWF game.

Proof. The proof follows a similar strategy to that of [8, Lemma 2, Appendix B] and is included in the full version [4].

Theorem 1. *The Banquet signature scheme is EUF-CMA-secure, assuming that* Commit*, H_1, H_2 and H_3 are modelled as random oracles,* Expand *is a PRG with output computationally ϵ_{PRG}-close to uniform, the seed tree construction is computationally hiding, the (N, τ, m_2, λ) parameters are appropriately chosen, and the key generation function $f_{\mathbf{x}}$: $\mathsf{sk} \mapsto \mathsf{pk}$ is a one-way function.*

Proof. Fix an attacker $\mathcal{A}$. We define a sequence of games where the first corresponds to $\mathcal{A}$ interacting with the real signature scheme in the EUF-CMA game. Through a series of hybrid arguments we show that this is indistinguishable from a simulated game, under the assumptions above. Let G_0 be the unmodified EUF-CMA game and let $\mathcal{B}$ denote an adversary against the EUF-KO game that acts

```
Verify(pk, μ, σ) :
1: Parse σ ← (st, h_1, h_3, (seeds_e, C_e^(ī_e), Δsk_e, (Δt_{e,ℓ})_{ℓ∈[m]},
   (ΔP_e(k))_{k∈{m_2,...,2m_2}}, P_e(R_e), (S_{e,j}(R_e), T_{e,j}(R_e))_{j∈[m_1]})_{e∈[τ]}).
2: Compute h'_2 ← H_2(h_1, ((ΔP_e(k))_{k∈{m_2,...,2m_2}})_{e∈[τ]}).
3: Expand hashes as (r_{e,j})_{e∈[M],j∈[m_1]} ← Expand(h_1), (R_e)_{e∈[M]} ← Expand(h'_2)
   and (ī_e)_{e∈[M]} ← Expand(h_3).
4: for each execution e do
5:   Use seeds_e to compute sd_e^(i) for i ∈ [N] \ ī_e.
6:   for each party i ∈ [N] \ ī_e do
7:     Recompute C_e^(i) ← Commit(st, e, i, sd_e^(i)), tape_e^(i) ← Expand(st, e, i, sd_e^(i))
       and sk_e^(i) ← Sample(tape_e^(i)).
8:     if i =? 1 then
9:       Adjust first share: sk_e^(i) ← sk_e^(i) + Δsk_e.
10:    for each S-box ℓ do
11:      Compute local linear operations to obtain s_{e,ℓ}^(i).
12:      Sample output share: t_{e,ℓ}^(i) ← Sample(tape_e^(i)).
13:      if i =? 1 then
14:        Adjust first share: t_{e,ℓ}^(i) ← t_{e,ℓ}^(i) + Δt_{e,ℓ}.
15:    Recompute output broadcast ct_e^(i) and missing ct_e^(ī_e) = ct − Σ_{i≠ī_e} ct_e^(i).
16:    Do as in Phase 3, lines 3–8 to interpolate S_{e,j}^(i), T_{e,j}^(i) for j ∈ [m_1].
17:    for k from 0 to m_2 − 1 do
18:      If i =? 1, set P_e^(i)(k) = Σ_j r_{e,j}; otherwise set P_e^(i)(k) = 0.
19:    for k from m_2 to 2m_2 do
20:      Sample share: P_e^(i)(k) ← Sample(tape_e^(i)).
21:      if i =? 1 then
22:        Adjust first share: P_e^(i)(k) ← P_e^(i)(k) + ΔP_e(k).
23:    Interpolate P_e^(i) and compute c_e^(i) ← P_e^(i)(R_e).
24:    For j ∈ [m_1], compute a_{e,j}^(i) ← S_{e,j}^(i)(R_e) and b_{e,j}^(i) ← T_{e,j}^(i)(R_e).
25:  Compute missing shares c_e^(ī_e) ← P_e(R_e) − Σ_{i≠ī_e} c_e^(i) and for j ∈ [m_1]:
       a_{e,j}^(ī_e) ← S_{e,j}(R_e) − Σ_{i≠ī_e} a_{e,j}^(i) and b_{e,j}^(ī_e) ← T_{e,j}(R_e) − Σ_{i≠ī_e} b_{e,j}^(i)
26: Set h'_1 ← H_1(st, ((C_e^(i))_{i∈[N]}, (ct_e^(i))_{i∈[N]}, Δsk_e, (Δt_{e,ℓ})_{ℓ∈[m]})_{e∈[τ]}).
27: Set h'_3 ← H_3( h'_2, (P_e(R_e), (c_e^(i))_{i∈[N]},
       (S_{e,j}(R_e), T_{e,j}(R_e), (a_{e,j}^(i), b_{e,j}^(i))_{i∈[N]})_{j∈[m_1]})_{e∈[τ]} ).
28: Output accept iff h'_1 =? h_1, h'_3 =? h_3 and for all executions e it holds that
    P_e(R_e) =? Σ_j S_{e,j}(R_e) · T_{e,j}(R_e).
```

Fig. 4. Verification algorithm.

as a simulator of EUF-CMA game to $\mathcal{A}$. (In the random oracle model: when $\mathcal{A}$ queries one of its random oracles, $\mathcal{B}$ first checks if that query has been recorded before; if so, then it responds with the recorded answer; if not, $\mathcal{B}$ forwards the query to its corresponding random oracle, records the query and the answer it receives and forwards the answer to $\mathcal{A}$.). Let G_i denote the probability that $\mathcal{A}$ succeeds in game G_i. At a high level, the sequence of games is as follows:

G_0: $\mathcal{B}$ knows a real witness and can compute signatures honestly;
G_1: $\mathcal{B}$ replaces real signatures with simulated ones which no longer use sk;
G_2: $\mathcal{B}$ then uses the EUF-KO challenge pk^* in its simulation to $\mathcal{A}$.

We note that $\mathbf{Adv}_{\mathcal{A}}^{\mathsf{EUF\text{-}CMA}} = \mathsf{G}_0 = (\mathsf{G}_0 - \mathsf{G}_1) + \mathsf{G}_1$ and we obtain a bound on G_0 by bounding first $\mathsf{G}_0 - \mathsf{G}_1$ and then G_1.

Hopping to Game G_1. When $\mathcal{A}$ queries the signing oracle, $\mathcal{B}$ simulates a signature σ by sampling a random witness, picking a party P_{i^*} and cheating in the verification phase and in the broadcast of the output shares $\mathsf{ct_e}^{(i)}$ such that the circuit still outputs the correct AES ciphertext, and finally ensuring that the values observed by $\mathcal{A}$ are sampled independently of the incorrect witness and with the same distribution as in a real signature. It programs both the second random oracle to return the R_e values that it sampled, and also the third random oracle to hide the party for which it has cheated in the verification and opening phases.

We now argue that simulating the signatures as in G_1 is indistinguishable from signatures in G_0. We list a series of (sub) game hops which begins with G_0, where the witness is known and signatures are created honestly, and ends with G_1, where signatures are simulated without using the witness. With each change to $\mathcal{B}$'s behavior, we give an argument as to why the simulation remains indistinguishable, and quantify these below.

1. The initial $\mathcal{B}$ knows the real witness and can compute honest signatures as in the protocol. It only aborts if the salt that it samples in Phase 1 has already been queried. As its simulation is perfect, $\mathcal{B}$ is indistinguishable from the real EUF-CMA game as long as it does not abort.
2. Before beginning, the next $\mathcal{B}$ samples h_3 at random and expands it to obtain $(i_e^*)_{e\in[\tau]}$; these are the unopened parties, which $\mathcal{B}$ will use for cheating. It proceeds as before and programs the random oracle H_3 so that it outputs h_3 when queried in Phase 6. If that query has already been made, $\mathcal{B}$ aborts the simulation.
3. In Phase 1, the next $\mathcal{B}$ replaces $\mathsf{sd}_e^{(i^*)}$ in the binary tree, for each $e \in [\tau]$, by a randomly sampled one. This is indistinguishable from the previous hybrid assuming that the tree structure is hiding.
4. The next $\mathcal{B}$ replaces all outputs of $\mathsf{Expand}(\mathsf{st}, e, i^*, \mathsf{sd}_e^{(i^*)})$ by random outputs (independent of the seed). This is indistinguishable from the previous reduction assuming that Expand is indistinguishable from a random function.
5. The next $\mathcal{B}$ replaces the commitments of the unopened parties $C_e^{(i^*)}$ with random values (i.e., without querying Commit).
6. Before starting Phase 3, the next $\mathcal{B}$ samples h_2 at random and expands it to obtain $(R_e)_{e\in[\tau]}$; this will enable it to sample the checking values at random. It then proceeds as before and programs the random oracle H_2 to output h_2 in Phase 4. If that query has already been made, $\mathcal{B}$ aborts the simulation.

7. In Phase 3, the next $\mathcal{B}$ interpolates $S_{e,j}^{(i)}$ for $i \in [N] \setminus \{i^*\}$, samples the values $S_{e,j}(R_e)$ at random, computes $S_{e,j}^{(i^*)}(R_e) = S_{e,j}(R_e) - \sum_{i \neq i^*} S_{e,j}^{(i)}$ and interpolates $S_{e,j}^{(i^*)}$ using $k \in \{0, \ldots, m2-1\} \cup \{R_e\}$. It does the same for the T polynomials and computes P_e and the offsets according to the protocol. As the uniform distribution of honestly generated $S_{e,j}(R_e)$ and $T_{e,j}(R_e)$ (opened in Phase 5) comes from the uniform distribution of $\bar{s}_{e,j}$ and $\bar{t}_{e,j}$ given by the random function (and which are hidden from $\mathcal{A}$ as $\mathsf{sd}_e^{(i^*)}$ is no longer used), this is indistinguishable from the previous hybrid. The same holds for the shares of party $\mathcal{P}_{i^*}$ that are opened in Phase 5. The distribution of the ΔP_e offsets is therefore also indistinguishable from a real signature as they are computed honestly from indistinguishable elements. (At this stage the P_e polynomials always satisfy the check since $\mathcal{B}$ is still using a correct witness.)
8. In Phase 5, the next $\mathcal{B}$ replaces $c_e^{(i^*)} \leftarrow P_e^{(i^*)}(R_e)$ with $c_e^{(i)} \leftarrow P_e(R_e) - \sum_{i \neq i^*} P_e^{(i)}(R_e)$. This is indistinguishable because the $P_e^{(i)}(R_e)$ values, for $i \neq i^*$, are computed honestly, and the $P_e(R_e)$ value is distributed identically to an honest signature (because $S_{e,j}$ and $T_{e,j}$ are). From now on, the Schwartz–Zippel check always passes, even if the product relation doesn't hold, and the distribution of everything that $\mathcal{A}$ can observe is indistinguishable from an honest signature and independent of hidden values.
9. The final $\mathcal{B}$ replaces the real sk by a fake witness sk^* and cheats on the broadcast of party P_{i^*}'s output share $\mathsf{ct}_e^{(i^*)}$ such that it matches what is expected, given the $N-1$ other shares. As $\mathsf{sk}_e^{(i^*)}$ is independent from the seeds $\mathcal{A}$ observes, the distribution of $\Delta\mathsf{sk}_e^*$ is identical and $\mathcal{A}$ has no information about sk^*. As $\mathcal{P}_{i^*}$ is never opened, $\mathcal{B}$'s cheating on $\mathsf{ct}_e^{(i^*)}$ can't be detected.

We can conclude that $\mathcal{B}$'s simulation of the signing oracle is indistinguishable and that $\mathcal{A}$ behaves exactly as in the real EUF-CMA game unless an abort happens.

There are four points at which $\mathcal{B}$ could abort: if the salt it sampled has been used before, if the commitment it replaces is queried, or if its queries to H_2 and H_3 have been made previously. Let Q_{st} denote the number of different salts queried during the game (by both $\mathcal{A}$ and $\mathcal{B}$); each time $\mathcal{B}$ simulates a signature, it has a maximum probability of $Q_{\mathsf{st}}/2^{2\kappa}$ of selecting an existing salt and aborting. Let Q_c denote the number of queries made to Commit by $\mathcal{A}$, including those made during signature queries. Since Commit is a random oracle, and $\mathsf{sd}_e^{(i^*)}$ is a uniformly random κ-bit value not used by $\mathcal{B}$ elsewhere, each time $\mathcal{B}$ attempts a new signature, it has a maximum probability of $Q_c/2^{\kappa}$ of replacing an existing commitment and aborting.

Similarly for H_2, resp. H_3, $\mathcal{B}$ has a maximum probability of $Q_2/2^{2\kappa}$, resp. $Q_3/2^{2\kappa}$ of aborting, where Q_2 and Q_3 denote the number of queries made to each random oracle during the game. Note that $\mathcal{B}$ samples one salt, replaces τ commitments and makes one query to both H_2 and H_3 for each signature query.

Therefore

$$\mathsf{G}_0 - \mathsf{G}_1 \leq Q_s \cdot \left(\tau \cdot \epsilon_{\mathrm{PRG}} + \mathbf{Adv}_{\mathsf{Tree}}^{\mathsf{Hiding}} + \Pr[\mathcal{B} \text{ aborts}]\right)$$

where

$$\Pr[\mathcal{B} \text{ aborts}] \leq Q_{\mathsf{st}}/2^{2\kappa} + Q_c/2^{\kappa} + Q_2/2^{2\kappa} + Q_3/2^{2\kappa}$$
$$= (Q_{\mathsf{st}} + Q_2 + Q_3)/2^{2\kappa} + Q_c/2^{\kappa} .$$

Bounding G_1. In G_1, $\mathcal{B}$ is no longer using the witness and is instead simulating signatures only by programming the random oracles; it therefore replaces the honestly computed pk with and instance pk^* of the EUF-KO game. We see that if $\mathcal{A}$ wins G_1, i.e. outputs a valid signature, then $\mathcal{B}$ outputs a valid signature in the EUF-KO game, and so we have

$$\mathsf{G}_1 \leq \epsilon_{\mathrm{KO}} \leq \epsilon_{\mathrm{OWF}} + \varepsilon(Q_,, Q_1, Q_2, Q_3)$$

where the bound on advantage ϵ_{KO} of a EUF-KO attacker follows from Lemma 2. By a union bound, we have that

$$\mathbf{Adv}_{\mathcal{A}}^{\mathsf{EUF\text{-}CMA}} \leq \epsilon_{\mathrm{OWF}} + \varepsilon(Q_,, Q_1, Q_2, Q_3)$$
$$+ Q_s \cdot \left(\tau \cdot \epsilon_{\mathrm{PRG}} + \mathbf{Adv}_{\mathsf{Tree}}^{\mathsf{Hiding}} + \frac{Q_{\mathsf{st}} + Q_2 + Q_3}{2^{2\kappa}} + \frac{Q_c}{2^{\kappa}} \right) .$$

Assuming that Expand is a PRG, that the seed tree construction is hiding, that $f_{\mathbf{x}}$ is a one-way function and that parameters (N, τ, m_2, λ) are appropriately chosen implies that $\mathbf{Adv}_{\mathcal{A}}^{\mathsf{EUF\text{-}CMA}}$ is negligible in κ.

Strong Unforgeability. Our analysis uses the EUF-CMA definition and therefore does not rule out the case that an attacker can find a new signature for a previously signed message (for instance, by mauling a signature output by the signer in such a way that it remains valid on the same message). Intuitively, since the intermediate seeds from the tree are the only part of the signature that the verifier does not hash directly during verification (the verifier only hashes the leaf seeds of the tree), as a minimum we require that (i) it is difficult to find a set of intermediate seeds in the tree that derive the same leaf seeds used in a signature, and (ii) it is difficult to find a different seed that produces the same outputs when input to Expand as a seed used in the signature. Since we use cryptographic hash functions to derive seeds and to instantiate Expand, these requirements should be met under the assumption that the hash function is 2nd-preimage resistant (or is a random oracle). A formal proof of strong unforgeability is nevertheless an interesting open question.

QROM Security. The quantum ROM is a stronger version of the ROM that allows attackers to make superposition queries to the RO; this models attacks on PQ primitives which make use of a quantum computer. As Banquet aims to provide post-quantum security, whether our analysis holds in the QROM is a natural question. The most promising approach seems to be the general results for multi-round Fiat–Shamir type signatures [19,20], since our current reduction makes essential use of the RO query history, ruling out the "history-free" approach of [11]. However, in order to apply the QROM EUF-CMA result [19, Theorem 23] would require that we formulate Banquet as Σ-protocol, and prove multiple properties about it, which is beyond the scope of the current paper. Finally we note that the amount of assurance provided by QROM for signature schemes is debatable, as there are no known non-contrived schemes that are secure in the ROM, but insecure in the QROM.

6 Parameters, Implementation and Performance

We first describe how we chose parameters for Banquet, and give some options. We then describe our implementation[4] and the optimizations we use to improve performance of Sign and Verify, which can be improved significantly over a direct implementation of the scheme from Sect. 4. We then compare Banquet to some other post-quantum signature schemes, and finally discuss some other features of the design. In this section all times are given in milliseconds, by averaging over 100 runs, on an Intel Xeon W-2133 CPU @ 3.60GHz, unless noted otherwise.

6.1 Parameter Selection

The soundness error of the signature scheme from Sect. 4 depends on the parameters $(\kappa, N, \lambda, m_1, m_2, \tau)$. Our analysis of Banquet is similar to the analysis of the 7-round ID schemes in [8] and the five-round schemes in [29]. We can bound the probability of cheating by assuming that the attacker can cheat by guessing any one of the challenges in a given parallel repetition. Let τ_1 be the number of repetitions for which the attacker will guess the first challenge, and τ_2 be the number for which she will guess the second challenge. Since the attacker is successful in a repetition by being successful in any of the challenges, the number of repetitions where the challenge must be guessed in the third round is $\tau_3 = \tau - \tau_1 - \tau_2$. The cost of the attack is given by

$$C = 1/P_1 + 1/P_2 + 1/P_3$$

where P_i is the probability of correctly guessing τ_i sub-challenges in challenge step i. We call a triple (τ_1, τ_2, τ_3) an attack *strategy*. Our goal is to choose parameters such that $C > 2^{\kappa}$ for all strategies.

The first challenge space (Phase 2) has size $2^{8\lambda m_1}$, and the probability that a given challenge allows cheating is $2^{-8\lambda}$ (as shown in Sect. 3.2). Therefore, the probability of guessing τ_1 of τ challenges is

$$P_1 = \sum_{k=\tau_1}^{\tau} \mathsf{PMF}(k, \tau, 2^{-8\lambda}) \ ,$$

where PMF is the probability mass function:

$$\mathsf{PMF}(k, \tau, p) = \binom{\tau}{k} p^k (1-p)^{\tau - k}$$

[4] The implementation is publicly available at https://github.com/dkales/banquet.

which gives the probability of getting exactly k successes in τ independent trials each having probability p of success.

The second challenge space (Phase 4) has size $2^{8\lambda} - m_2$, and the probability that a given challenge allows cheating is $2m_2/(2^{8\lambda} - m_2)$. The probability of guessing τ_2 of $\tau - \tau_1$ challenges correctly is therefore

$$P_2(\tau_2) = \sum_{k=\tau_2}^{\tau-\tau_1} \mathsf{PMF}(k, \tau - \tau_1, 2m_2/(2^{8\lambda} - m_2)).$$

The third challenge space (Phase 6) has size N, and the attacker must guess the challenge in the remaining repetitions correctly, therefore

$$P_3(\tau_3) = N^{-\tau_3}.$$

To choose parameters, we fix $(\kappa, N, \lambda, m_1, m_2)$, then start with $\tau = 1$, and increase it, at each step checking the attack costs for all possible strategies (τ_1, τ_2, τ_3). When we reach τ where the attack cost exceeds 2^κ for all strategies, we output τ as the number of repetitions required for κ-bit security. Since τ is always less than 100, and τ_3 is fixed once τ_1 and τ_2 are chosen, using a script to perform this exhaustive search is practical.

Choice of m_1, m_2. We found that choosing $m_1 \approx \sqrt{m}$ gave good performance in practice. For example at L1, when $m = 200$, we chose $m_1 = 10$, and $m_2 = 20$. The signature size and runtime does not change significantly for small changes in m_i (e.g., $m_1 = 8$, $m_2 = 25$ is about the same), but signature sizes increase as we move m_1 further away from $\sqrt{m}$.

Number of Parties. Increasing N allows us to decrease signature size, but increases the cost of signing and verification. The choices of N we found interesting are powers of two from 16 to 256, with 64 being a sweet spot on the curve. Our search started at these powers of two, but often we were able to decrease N slightly without increasing τ, which improves sign and verify times.

Choice of λ. We generated parameters for $\lambda = 2, 3, 4, 5, 6$ so that field arithmetic happens in fields of size 16 to 48 bits, which are convenient for processor word sizes, and these values provide sufficient soundness. We benchmarked multiple parameter sets with $\lambda = 4$ and $\lambda = 6$, and in general $\lambda = 6$ is slightly faster, but has slightly larger signatures (about 0.5-1KB larger). Table 2 shows the differences.

L3 and L5 Parameters. As in the BBQ scheme, scaling the Banquet design to the 192 and 256-bit security levels presents a challenge because the block size of AES is limited to 128 bits. Simply using AES-256 with 128-bit outputs does not provide 256-bit security; intuitively, in this case there are a large number of 256-bit keys that produce the same ciphertext for any fixed plaintext, and finding any one of them allows an attacker to create a forgery.

BBQ explores two options for higher security parameters. The first is to use the Rijndael cipher, which has parameter sets with 192 and 256-bit block sizes, and the second is to make two calls to AES-192 or AES-256 in ECB mode (using two different plaintext blocks), which we refer to as AES-192x2 and AES-256x2 respectively.

The Rijndael option has 80 fewer S-boxes at the 192-bit level, and we estimate that Banquet signatures with Rijndael would be $\approx$ 2KB shorter. At L5 however, two calls to AES-256 has 60 fewer S-boxes, as the Rijndael key schedule is more expensive. Since the difference is small, we use only AES at all three levels.

Public-Key Uniqueness. As noted in [16], the ECB construction trivially has two public keys for each secret key, where the plaintext and ciphertext blocks in the public key are swapped. Since the Banquet design includes the public key as an input to the challenge computation (prepending the public key to the signed message), this ensures that the verifier is using the same public key as the signer.

6.2 Implementation and Optimizations

We have implemented Banquet in C++ in order to determine the running time of sign and verify operations. We began with a direct implementation of the scheme, as presented in Sect. 4, where all field and polynomial operations were done with the NTL library[5]. However, sign and verify times were on the order of multiple seconds, due to the cost of the polynomial operations in Phase 3.

As a first optimization, note that when interpolating a set of points (x_i, y_i), the x_i values are fixed, therefore, we can precompute the Lagrange coefficients, and save computation later. However, we can avoid most interpolation altogether. Rather than computing the per-party shares of the polynomials $S^{(i)}$, $T^{(i)}$, by interpolating shares of points, the prover can first reconstruct the points from the shares and interpolate them to get S, T and P (in unshared form). Then in Phase 4, the shares of points previously used to interpolate $S^{(i)}, T^{(i)}$ are used to compute $(a^{(i)}, b^{(i)})$. Applying this technique to polynomials S and T (and P in a similar fashion) reduces the number of interpolations from $Nm_1\tau$ to $m_1\tau$ (of polynomials of degree m_2), while for P, the number drops from $N\tau$ to τ interpolations (of degree $2m_2+1$). We can reduce this further, observing that in each of the τ instances, the polynomials S, T are defined using the same set of points, except for the additional randomizing points $\bar{s}, \bar{t}$ (and a constant random multiplier for S). We therefore interpolate each of these only once for all instances, and then adjust to the correct polynomial in each instance by adding a multiple of the Lagrange polynomial corresponding to the last point. Incorporating this into the computation of P, we do $2m_1$ interpolations in total to compute P, however, some of the steps in the protocol still require the evaluation of the polynomials $S^{(i)}$, $T^{(i)}$ at the point R_e. For this calculation, we also do not need to interpolate the polynomials, but instead evaluate the Lagrange coefficients at the common evaluation point R_e beforehand, reducing the needed work from a full interpolation to a single inner product.

[5] https://shoup.net/ntl/.

Table 2. Performance metrics of different parameter sets for Banquet. All instances for AES-128 have $(m, m_1, m_2) = (200, 10, 20)$ for AES-192x2 we have $(416, 16, 26)$ and for AES-256x2 we have $(500, 20, 25)$.

Scheme	N	λ	τ	Sign (ms)	Verify (ms)	Size (bytes)
AES-128	16	4	41	6.36	4.86	19776
	16	6	37	5.91	4.51	20964
	31	4	35	8.95	7.46	17456
	31	6	31	8.19	6.76	18076
	57	4	31	14.22	12.30	15968
	57	6	27	12.45	10.75	16188
	107	4	28	24.15	21.71	14880
	107	6	24	21.13	18.96	14784
	255	4	25	51.10	46.88	13696
	255	6	21	43.81	40.11	13284
AES-192x2	16	4	62	17.25	13.15	51216
	16	6	57	16.52	12.50	53936
	31	4	53	25.82	21.66	45072
	31	6	47	24.00	19.89	45624
	64	4	46	43.03	38.00	40240
	64	6	40	39.07	34.15	39808
	116	4	42	69.37	62.68	37760
	116	6	36	61.95	55.55	36704
	256	4	38	135.29	124.50	35088
	256	6	32	119.01	108.53	33408
AES-256x2	16	4	84	27.78	21.67	83488
	16	6	75	25.71	19.88	84610
	31	4	72	41.40	35.20	73888
	31	6	63	37.67	31.76	73114
	62	4	63	67.99	60.33	66688
	62	6	54	60.79	53.39	64420
	119	4	56	112.62	102.52	61088
	119	6	48	100.66	90.76	58816
	256	4	50	213.58	196.27	56160
	256	6	43	190.58	174.70	54082

Taken together, these optimizations reduced the time of sign and verify by more than 30x, to be on the order of 100 ms. Finally, we replaced NTL with a dedicated field arithmetic implementation optimized for our application (avoiding dynamic memory allocation, and other options NTL has to be flexible) and the small binary fields that we are working with. This reduced the runtime by a further factor of 4x. However, we have not invested the resources to ensure that our implementation runs in constant time, some parts of the implementation may be susceptible to timing and/or memory access leaks. In our final implementation, we make use of hardware instructions for binary field multiplication (`PCLMUL`) and the AES hardware instructions (`AES-NI`) whenever possible, although the structure of the MPC execution does not allow a straightforward application of the AES instructions due to the injection of the inverse values in the protocol. However, we can still use small tricks like implementing the MixColumns layer by a trifold application of the inverse MixColumns instruction (for the AES MixColumns matrix it holds that $M = (M^{-1})^3$), giving us a speedup of about 10% compared to a naive implementation.

At L1, the final implementation (for $N = 57, \tau = 31, \lambda = 4$) spends about 3% of the time on computing the MPC evaluation of the AES circuit(s), 38% on finite field arithmetic, 31% on hashing, and about 25% on allocating/copying memory. Our implementation uses the SHAKE extensible output function both as a hash function and PRG (details are given in [4]).

6.3 Performance

In Table 3, we compare the proof size of Banquet with BBQ [16], and a Picnic-like signature scheme with a binary circuit for AES based on the KKW protocol [31]. Our Banquet instances provide much smaller signatures than all previous MPCitH-based signatures using AES. We cannot compare the performance here since no implementation is available for BBQ or AES Bin. However, we can estimate the performance of BBQ and AES Bin based on the implementation of Picnic, where a large part of the signing and verification cost is comprised of similar operations such as the seed tree generation, hashing of messages and computation of the pre-processing phase. The only difference is that the LowMC circuit is replaced by the AES circuit, but again, the structure of the MPC operations does not allow straightforward use of AES hardware instructions. In addition, since the internal states of the parties are larger due to the larger circuit of AES, we expect most of the hashing and seed expansion to take slightly longer. Overall, we would estimate the performance of a highly optimized implementation of BBQ or AES Bin to match the performance of Picnic2 instances, however with significantly larger signatures.

In Table 4 we compare the signature size and signing/verification times for Banquet to other post-quantum signature schemes: Picnic2 and Picnic3 [30], the previous and latest version of Picnic (based on KKW and LowMC), respectively, and SPHINCS$^+$ [6]. At the L1 security level, our Banquet implementation can sign a message in 6.36 ms and verify it in 4.86 ms. Compared to Picnic3 this corresponds to a slowdown of factor of only 1.2x, while the signature size is about 50% larger than that of Picnic3. However, different parameter sets for Banquet can reduce its signature size at the cost of slower signing and verification speeds. When comparing to SPHINCS$^+$, Banquet can offer faster signing speeds and smaller signatures, however SPHINCS$^+$ verification is faster. At the L3 and L5 security levels, the relative performance of Picnic3 and Banquet remains

Table 3. Comparison of signature sizes. N is the number of parties used in the MPC, M is the total number of MPC instances (when preprocessing is used), and τ is the number of online executions (equal to the number of parallel repetitions in Banquet). The rows are grouped by security level in order L1, L3, L5.

Protocol	N	M	τ	Size (bytes)
AES Bin	64	343	27	51 876
BBQ	64	343	27	31 568
Banquet	16	-	41	19 776
	107	-	24	14 784
	255	-	21	13 284
AES Bin	64	570	39	149 134
BBQ	64	570	39	86 888
Banquet	16	-	62	51 216
	116	-	36	36 704
	256	-	32	33 408
AES Bin	64	803	50	233 696
BBQ	64	803	50	137 670
Banquet	16	-	84	83 488
	119	-	48	58 816
	256	-	43	54 082

similar: our 16-party Banquet instances are about 1.6x slower than Picnic3 with signatures that are about 50% larger. Banquet signing speeds are still comparable to SPHINCS$^+$, however SPHINCS$^+$ signatures are smaller.

Interactive Identification. The signature scheme of Sect. 4 may be used as an interactive protocol between a prover and verifier, where the prover runs phases 1, 3 and 5, while the verifier runs phases 2, 4 and 6. For phase 2, the prover sends a commitment to σ_1, and the verifier responds with a random bitstring h_1. Similarly, in phase 4, and 6 the prover sends commitments to σ_2, σ_3 (respectively) and the verifier responds with random bitstrings h_2, h_3.

Let p_1, p_2 and p_3 denote the probability of guessing the first, second or third challenge (respectively). Recall that $p_1 = 2^{-8\lambda}$, $p_2 = m_2/(2^{8\lambda} - m_2)$ and $p_3 = 1/N$. The soundness error of the interactive protocol is

$$\epsilon = p_1 + (1 - p_1)p_2 + (1 - p_1)(1 - p_2)p_3$$

since a dishonest prover wins if: either she gets the first challenge right, or not the first but the second or neither the first nor the second but the third. We can reduce the soundness error to ϵ^τ by running τ parallel repetitions.

To target t bits of interactive security we choose τ so that $\epsilon^\tau < 2^{-t}$. Table 5 gives some of the costs when $t = 40$. We see that Banquet needs very few parallel repetitions, and can use a very small field size $\lambda = 2$. When compared to the

Table 4. Comparison of signature sizes and run times for various MPCitH-based signature schemes and SPHINCS$^+$ (using "`sha256simple`" parameter sets). N is the number of parties, M is the total number of MPC instances (when preprocessing is used), and τ is the number of online executions (equal to the number of parallel repetitions in Banquet). The rows are grouped by security level in order L1, L3, L5.

Protocol	N	M	τ	Sign (ms)	Ver (ms)	Size (bytes)
Picnic2	64	343	27	41.16	18.21	12 347
	16	252	36	10.42	5.00	13 831
Picnic3	16	252	36	5.33	4.03	12 466
SPHINCS$^+$-fast	-	-	-	14.42	1.74	16 976
SPHINCS$^+$-small	-	-	-	239.34	0.73	8 080
Banquet	16	-	41	6.36	4.86	19 776
	107	-	24	21.13	18.96	14 784
	255	-	21	43.81	40.11	13 284
Picnic2	64	570	39	123.21	41.25	27 173
	16	420	52	29.85	11.77	30 542
Picnic3	16	419	52	11.01	8.49	27 405
SPHINCS$^+$-fast	-	-	-	19.05	2.82	35 664
SPHINCS$^+$-small	-	-	-	493.17	1.12	17 064
Banquet	16	-	62	17.25	13.15	51 216
	116	-	36	61.95	55.55	36 704
	256	-	32	119.01	108.53	33 408
Picnic2	64	803	50	253	71.32	46 162
	16	604	68	61.09	21.19	52 860
Picnic3	16	601	68	18.82	13.56	48 437
SPHINCS$^+$-fast	-	-	-	38.71	2.89	49 216
SPHINCS$^+$-small	-	-	-	310.37	1.46	29 792
Banquet	16	-	84	27.78	21.67	83 488
	119	-	48	100.66	90.76	58 816
	256	-	43	190.85	174.70	54 082

Picnic3 ID scheme (details in [30, §7]), the communication costs with 16 parties are about the same, and then are less with Banquet as N increases. A similar tradeoff could be made with Picnic3, which also requires less time. Finally, the reduced number of roundtrips make Picnic easier to fit into existing flows of network protocols. That said, the performance of Banquet remains competitive in this setting, and it has a more conservative security assumption.

Table 5. Benchmarks of interactive identification schemes at security level L1. All Banquet parameters have $m_1 = 10$, $m_2 = 20$ and $\lambda = 2$. The column "Rep" gives the number of parallel repetitions τ used in Banquet, and (M, τ) the number of MPC instances and online executions in Picnic3.

Scheme	N	Rep.	Prover (ms)	Verifier (ms)	Communication (bytes)
Banquet	16	11	1.94	1.44	4 452
	23	9	2.06	1.60	3 804
	55	7	3.15	2.66	3 092
	109	6	4.70	4.16	2 760
Picnic3	16	$(72, 12)$	1.73	1.33	4 070
	16	$(48, 16)$	1.16	0.92	4 750

Acknowledgements. Cyprien Delpech de Saint Guilhem and Emmanuela Orsini have been supported in part by the Defense Advanced Research Projects Agency (DARPA) under Contract No. HR001120C0085, by CyberSecurity Research Flanders under reference number No. VR20192203, and by ERC Advanced Grant ERC-2015-AdG-IMPaCT. Carsten Baum and Peter Scholl have been supported by the Defense Advanced Research Projects Agency (DARPA) under Contract No. HR001120C0085. Baum has been additionally supported in part by the European Research Council (ERC) under the European Unions's Horizon 2020 research and innovation programme under grant agreement No. 669255 (MPCPRO), and Scholl by a starting grant from Aarhus University Research Foundation.
Daniel Kales has been supported in part by the European Unions's Horizon 2020 research and innovation programme under grant agreement No. 871473 (KRAKEN).

Any opinions, findings and conclusions or recommendations expressed in this material are those of the author(s) and do not necessarily reflect the views of any of the funders. The U.S. Government is authorized to reproduce and distribute reprints for governmental purposes notwithstanding any copyright annotation therein.

References

1. Albrecht, M.R., Rechberger, C., Schneider, T., Tiessen, T., Zohner, M.: Ciphers for MPC and FHE. In: Oswald, E., Fischlin, M. (eds.) EUROCRYPT 2015. LNCS, vol. 9056, pp. 430–454. Springer, Heidelberg (2015). https://doi.org/10.1007/978-3-662-46800-5_17
2. Ames, S., Hazay, C., Ishai, Y., Venkitasubramaniam, M.: Ligero: lightweight sublinear arguments without a trusted setup. In: ACM CCS 2017, pp. 2087–2104. ACM Press, November 2017
3. Baum, C., Nof, A.: Concretely-efficient zero-knowledge arguments for arithmetic circuits and their application to lattice-based cryptography. In: Kiayias, A., Kohlweiss, M., Wallden, P., Zikas, V. (eds.) PKC 2020. LNCS, vol. 12110, pp. 495–526. Springer, Cham (2020). https://doi.org/10.1007/978-3-030-45374-9_17
4. Baum, C., de Saint Guilhem, C.D., Kales, D., Orsini, E., Scholl, P., Zaverucha, G.: Banquet: short and fast signatures from AES. Cryptology ePrint Archive, Report 2021/068 (2021). Full version of this paper: https://eprint.iacr.org/2021/068

5. Ben-Sasson, E., Chiesa, A., Riabzev, M., Spooner, N., Virza, M., Ward, N.P.: Aurora: transparent succinct arguments for R1CS. In: Ishai, Y., Rijmen, V. (eds.) EUROCRYPT 2019. LNCS, vol. 11476, pp. 103–128. Springer, Cham (2019). https://doi.org/10.1007/978-3-030-17653-2_4
6. Bernstein, D.J., Hülsing, A., Kölbl, S., Niederhagen, R., Rijneveld, J., Schwabe, P.: The SPHINCS$^+$ signature framework. In: Cavallaro, L., Kinder, J., Wang, X., Katz, J. (eds.) ACM CCS 2019, pp. 2129–2146. ACM Press, November 2019
7. Beullens, W.: Sigma protocols for MQ, PKP and SIS, and fishy signature schemes. In: Canteaut, A., Ishai, Y. (eds.) EUROCRYPT 2020, Part III. LNCS, vol. 12107, pp. 183–211. Springer, Cham (2020). https://doi.org/10.1007/978-3-030-45727-3_7
8. Beullens, W., Delpech de Saint Guilhem, C.: LegRoast: efficient post-quantum signatures from the Legendre PRF. In: Ding, J., Tillich, J.-P. (eds.) PQCrypto 2020. LNCS, vol. 12100, pp. 130–150. Springer, Cham (2020). https://doi.org/10.1007/978-3-030-44223-1_8
9. Bhadauria, R., Fang, Z., Hazay, C., Venkitasubramaniam, M., Xie, T., Zhang, Y.: Ligero++: a new optimized sublinear IOP. In: CCS, pp. 2025–2038. ACM (2020)
10. Boneh, D., Boyle, E., Corrigan-Gibbs, H., Gilboa, N., Ishai, Y.: Zero-knowledge proofs on secret-shared data via fully linear PCPs. In: Boldyreva, A., Micciancio, D. (eds.) CRYPTO 2019, Part III. LNCS, vol. 11694, pp. 67–97. Springer, Cham (2019). https://doi.org/10.1007/978-3-030-26954-8_3
11. Boneh, D., Dagdelen, Ö., Fischlin, M., Lehmann, A., Schaffner, C., Zhandry, M.: Random oracles in a quantum world. In: Lee, D.H., Wang, X. (eds.) ASIACRYPT 2011. LNCS, vol. 7073, pp. 41–69. Springer, Heidelberg (2011). https://doi.org/10.1007/978-3-642-25385-0_3
12. Boyle, E., Gilboa, N., Ishai, Y., Nof, A.: Practical fully secure three-party computation via sublinear distributed zero-knowledge proofs. In: Cavallaro, L., Kinder, J., Wang, X., Katz, J. (eds.) ACM CCS 2019, pp. 869–886. ACM Press, November 2019
13. Casanova, A., Faugere, J.C., Macario-Rat, G., Patarin, J., Perret, L., Ryckeghem, J.: GeMSS: a great multivariate short signature. Submission to the NIST's post-quantum cryptography standardization process (2017)
14. Chase, M., et al.: Post-quantum zero-knowledge and signatures from symmetric-key primitives. In: Thuraisingham, B.M., Evans, D., Malkin, T., Xu, D. (eds.) ACM CCS 2017, pp. 1825–1842. ACM Press, October–November 2017
15. De Feo, L., Galbraith, S.D.: SeaSign: compact isogeny signatures from class group actions. In: Ishai, Y., Rijmen, V. (eds.) EUROCRYPT 2019, Part III. LNCS, vol. 11478, pp. 759–789. Springer, Cham (2019). https://doi.org/10.1007/978-3-030-17659-4_26
16. de Saint Guilhem, C.D., De Meyer, L., Orsini, E., Smart, N.P.: BBQ: using AES in Picnic signatures. In: Paterson, K.G., Stebila, D. (eds.) SAC 2019. LNCS, vol. 11959, pp. 669–692. Springer, Cham (2020). https://doi.org/10.1007/978-3-030-38471-5_27
17. Ding, J., Schmidt, D.: Rainbow, a new multivariable polynomial signature scheme. In: Ioannidis, J., Keromytis, A., Yung, M. (eds.) ACNS 2005. LNCS, vol. 3531, pp. 164–175. Springer, Heidelberg (2005). https://doi.org/10.1007/11496137_12
18. Dinur, I., Liu, Y., Meier, W., Wang, Q.: Optimized interpolation attacks on LowMC. In: Iwata, T., Cheon, J.H. (eds.) ASIACRYPT 2015. LNCS, vol. 9453, pp. 535–560. Springer, Heidelberg (2015). https://doi.org/10.1007/978-3-662-48800-3_22

19. Don, J., Fehr, S., Majenz, C.: The measure-and-reprogram technique 2.0: multi-round Fiat-Shamir and more. In: Micciancio, D., Ristenpart, T. (eds.) CRYPTO 2020. LNCS, vol. 12172, pp. 602–631. Springer, Cham (2020). https://doi.org/10.1007/978-3-030-56877-1_21
20. Don, J., Fehr, S., Majenz, C., Schaffner, C.: Security of the Fiat-Shamir transformation in the quantum random-oracle model. In: Boldyreva, A., Micciancio, D. (eds.) CRYPTO 2019, Part II. LNCS, vol. 11693, pp. 356–383. Springer, Cham (2019). https://doi.org/10.1007/978-3-030-26951-7_13
21. Ducas, L., Kiltz, E., Lepoint, T., Lyubashevsky, V., Schwabe, P., Seiler, G., Stehlé, D.: CRYSTALS-Dilithium: a lattice-based digital signature scheme. IACR TCHES **2018**(1), 238–268 (2018)
22. Fiat, A., Shamir, A.: How to prove yourself: practical solutions to identification and signature problems. In: Odlyzko, A.M. (ed.) CRYPTO 1986. LNCS, vol. 263, pp. 186–194. Springer, Heidelberg (1987). https://doi.org/10.1007/3-540-47721-7_12
23. Fouque, P.A., et al.: Falcon: fast-Fourier lattice-based compact signatures over NTRU. Submission to the NIST's post-quantum cryptography standardization process (2018)
24. Gentry, C., Peikert, C., Vaikuntanathan, V.: Trapdoors for hard lattices and new cryptographic constructions. In: Ladner, R.E., Dwork, C. (eds.) 40th ACM STOC, pp. 197–206. ACM Press, May 2008
25. Giacomelli, I., Madsen, J., Orlandi, C.: ZKBoo: faster zero-knowledge for Boolean circuits. In: Holz, T., Savage, S. (eds.) USENIX Security 2016, pp. 1069–1083. USENIX Association, August 2016
26. Goldwasser, S., Micali, S., Rivest, R.L.: A digital signature scheme secure against adaptive chosen-message attacks. SIAM J. Comput. **17**(2), 281–308 (1988)
27. Ishai, Y., Kushilevitz, E., Ostrovsky, R., Sahai, A.: Zero-knowledge from secure multiparty computation. In: Johnson, D.S., Feige, U. (eds.) 39th ACM STOC, pp. 21–30. ACM Press, June 2007
28. Kales, D., Ramacher, S., Rechberger, C., Walch, R., Werner, M.: Efficient FPGA implementations of LowMC and Picnic. In: Jarecki, S. (ed.) CT-RSA 2020. LNCS, vol. 12006, pp. 417–441. Springer, Cham (2020). https://doi.org/10.1007/978-3-030-40186-3_18
29. Kales, D., Zaverucha, G.: An attack on some signature schemes constructed from five-pass identification schemes. In: Krenn, S., Shulman, H., Vaudenay, S. (eds.) CANS 2020. LNCS, vol. 12579, pp. 3–22. Springer, Cham (2020). https://doi.org/10.1007/978-3-030-65411-5_1
30. Kales, D., Zaverucha, G.: Improving the performance of the Picnic signature scheme. IACR TCHES **2020**(4), 154–188 (2020)
31. Katz, J., Kolesnikov, V., Wang, X.: Improved non-interactive zero knowledge with applications to post-quantum signatures. In: Lie, D., Mannan, M., Backes, M., Wang, X. (eds.) ACM CCS 2018, pp. 525–537. ACM Press, October 2018
32. Liu, F., Isobe, T., Meier, W.: Cryptanalysis of full LowMC and LowMC-M with algebraic techniques. Cryptology ePrint Archive, Report 2020/1034 (2020)
33. Lyubashevsky, V.: Lattice signatures without trapdoors. In: Pointcheval, D., Johansson, T. (eds.) EUROCRYPT 2012. LNCS, vol. 7237, pp. 738–755. Springer, Heidelberg (2012). https://doi.org/10.1007/978-3-642-29011-4_43
34. National Institute of Standards and Technology: Round 3 Submissions for the NIST Post-Quantum Cryptography Project (2020). https://csrc.nist.gov/Projects/post-quantum-cryptography/round-3-submissions. Accessed 11 Nov 2020

35. Rechberger, C., Soleimany, H., Tiessen, T.: Cryptanalysis of low-data instances of full LowMCv2. IACR Trans. Symm. Cryptol. **2018**(3), 163–181 (2018)
36. Zaverucha, G., et al.: Picnic. Technical report, National Institute of Standards and Technology (2019). https://csrc.nist.gov/projects/post-quantum-cryptography/round-2-submissions

Cryptographic Primitives and Schemes

Improving Revocation for Group Signature with Redactable Signature

Olivier Sanders(✉)

Applied Crypto Group, Orange Labs, Cesson-Sévigné, France
olivier.sanders@orange.com

Abstract. Group signature is a major cryptographic tool allowing anonymous access to a service. However, in practice, access to a service is usually granted for some periods of time, which implies that the signing rights must be deactivated the rest of the time. This requirement thus calls for complex forms of revocation, reminiscent of the concept of time-bound keys. However, schemes implementing this concept are rare and only allow revocation with limited granularity. That is, signing keys are associated with an expiry time and become definitively useless once the latter has passed.

In this paper, we revisit the notion of group signatures with time-bound keys with several contributions. Firstly, we extend this notion to allow high granularity revocation: a member's signing key can in particular be deactivated at some moments and then be automatically reinstated. Secondly, we show that this complex property is actually simple to achieve using redactable signature. In particular, we consider in this context a recent redactable signature scheme from PKC 20 that we improve by dramatically reducing the size of the public key. The resulting construction is of independent interest.

1 Introduction

Group signature, introduced by Chaum and van Heyst [10], enables anonymous, yet accountable, authentication to a service. In such a system, a so-called group manager has the responsibility of a group of users who can issue anonymous signatures on behalf of the group. More specifically, anyone can check that the resulting signatures were issued by a group member but it is impossible, except for the group manager, to identify the actual signer. This means for example that a service provider can check that the user has the right to access the service whereas the user has the assurance that this authentication leaks as little information as possible.

This ability to reconcile the interests of all parties makes it an ideal solution in many scenarios, which explains the countless papers on this topic. We in particular note that some simple variants such as DAA or EPID are today massively deployed [1,25]. Group signature has also been proposed in the context of public transport (*e.g.* [12,15]) to implement an anonymous version of a transport subscription pass such as, for example, the Navigo pass [19] in Paris,

J. A. Garay (Ed.): PKC 2021, LNCS 12710, pp. 301–330, 2021.
https://doi.org/10.1007/978-3-030-75245-3_12

that allows a passenger to take unlimited trips within some fixed periods of time. With group signature, this passenger could prove that he has the right to access the transport service without being identified by the transport operator.

This use-case thus highlights the benefits of group signatures at first glance but also reveals their limitations when we consider more thoroughly a real-world application. Indeed, access to a service is usually not granted for ever but only for some periods of time. For example, the user of a public transport system typically pays for a 1 month or year subscription starting from a date of his choice. We can also envision alternative cases where one would subscribe to a pass providing unlimited access but only during weekends.

Providing signing rights without the ability to limit them to some time periods is therefore extremely problematic in practice. We in particular note that this cannot be fixed by revealing these time periods in the signature as it would break anonymity. We here touch a weak point of group signatures. Although most schemes come with efficient enrolment procedures, the problem of limiting the signing rights is rarely considered in papers, and usually only through the concept of revocation that can be implemented in three different ways.

The first kind of revocation approach is the one where the group manager regularly changes the group public key, thus resetting the group. This is compatible with any scheme but is highly impractical in practice as it is becomes necessary to issue a new group signing key for each user at the beginning of each time period.

The second kind of revocation is the one where the group manager provides at each time period an updated information on the current set of non-revoked members. This information is then used by the group members during the generation of the signature to prove that they are still part of the group. In other words, a group member can no longer issue a valid group signature once he is revoked. This approach may offer nice asymptotic complexity (e.g. [16,17]) but increases both the computational cost and the size of a group signature while forcing the user to regularly update their group signing key.

The last kind of revocation is based on the notion of revocation lists formalized by Boneh and Shacham under the name of Verifier-Local Revocation (VLR) [6]. Here, a member is revoked by adding a specific information in a revocation list allowing the verifiers to trace all signatures issued by this member, at least for a certain time. This revocation technique is interesting because it does not require to update group members' signing keys and has no impact on the complexity of the group signature itself. Unfortunately, it makes the verification process linear in the number of revoked users and so can only be used in situations where this revocation list remains relatively short. In particular, we cannot use it directly in the context of public transport to deactivate users' signing keys when their subscription is over as it would quickly lead to revocation lists containing millions of elements. It can only be used for exceptional situations such as the theft or loss of some user's smartphone.

To address this problem, Chu *et al.* [11] proposed to improve VLR group signatures by associating signing keys with an expiry time beyond which the group member loses his ability to sign, hence the name of group signature with time-bound keys. Such systems thus deal with two kinds of revocation, a *natural* revocation that automatically excludes users once their expiry time has passed and a *premature* revocation that works exactly as in a standard VLR scheme. This way, such systems dramatically limit the size of the revocation list and so the computational cost of the verification process.

Following [11], Emura *et al.* [13] recently proposed an improved security model for this primitive along with an efficient construction that blends the last two kinds of revocation we mentioned above. Concretely, the natural revocation is based on [17] by providing at each time period an information that enables non-revoked users to issue group signatures while premature revocation is still based on VLR. The resulting construction has nice asymptotic complexity but suffers from the limitations listed above, namely the need to prove in each signature that the signing key is still active and the need to update the latter at each time period.

Our Contribution. We propose in this paper to improve group signature with time-bound keys in several ways.

Firstly, we allow the group manager to associate a group signing key with any set of time periods and not just an expiry time as in previous works. Concretely, this means that a user may be able to sign at some time period t_1 and then be considered as revoked during the subsequent time periods before being automatically reinstated at a later time period t_2. This can for example be useful in the case mentioned above where a user would have access to a service only during weekends. The signing key will then be active only during the weekends and not during the other days of the week. This thus improves the granularity of the revocation but raises some privacy issues as it now means that revocation is not necessarily permanent: we must therefore ensure both backward and forward unlinkability for revoked users. We also allow opening queries in our anonymity experiment, contrarily to [13], and thus achieve a stronger notion of privacy.

Our second contribution is a construction of a very efficient scheme satisfying our new definition based on unlinkable redactable signatures (URS) [9,22]. An URS scheme enables to issue a signature σ on a set of messages $\{m_i\}_{i=1}^n$ and then to publicly derive from σ an unlinkable signature σ' that only proves authenticity of a subset of messages $\{m_i\}_{i\in\mathcal{I}}$, for some $\mathcal{I} \subset [1, n]$. Here, unlinkability means that σ' does not leak information on the set of *redacted* messages $\{m_i\}_{i\notin\mathcal{I}}$ and cannot be linked to σ beyond the fact that both signatures coincide on $\mathcal{I}$.

We use URS to construct group signature with time-bound keys as follows. During the enrolment process a group manager will issue a redacted signature σ on a set of messages $\{m_i\}_{i=1}^n$ where $m_i \neq 0$ if and only if the new member has the right to issue group signatures at the time period i. To generate a group signature at a time period t this member then only has to redact all the messages $\{m_i\}_{i=1}^n$ but m_t and then send the resulting derived signature σ' attesting that $m_t \neq 0$. Intuitively, thanks to unlinkability of URS schemes, we do not have to hide σ' or the redacted messages, which leads to a very efficient and simple protocol. Similarly, signatures from an unregistered member or an illicit extension of signing rights (*i.e.* a member that manages to sign outside his periods of activity) imply a forgery against the URS scheme. It then essentially remains to add a premature revocation mechanism that still retains backward and forward unlinkability but this can be done using rather standard techniques. An interesting outcome of our approach based on URS is that our group members no longer need to update their signing keys at each time period. They only need to know their original signing key and the current time period to generate a group signature.

So far we have shown that URS schemes lead to simple constructions of group signature with time-bound keys. However, this result is of practical significance only if we can propose an efficient candidate for the URS scheme. An interesting candidate was proposed very recently at PKC 20 [22], with extremely short signatures containing only four elements and which can be verified with essentially one exponentiation by non-redacted message. This might seem perfect in our context (as each group signature only involves one non-redacted element) but unfortunately the construction in [22] suffers from a large public key, quadratic in n. In the context of public transport, where it seems reasonable to consider one-day time period and a public key valid for the next 3 years, this means that the public parameters would contain millions of elements, which can be cumbersome. We therefore propose an improved version of the construction of [22], which retains all the nice features of the latter but with a public key only *linear* in n. We believe that this contribution is of independent interest, although its security analysis is done in the generic group model and the random oracle model.

Organisation. We recall in Sect. 2 the notion of bilinear groups and present the computational assumptions that underlay the security of our protocols. Section 3 is dedicated to URS and contains in particular a new construction with shorter public keys. Section 4 presents an improved model for group signature with time-bound keys whereas Sect. 5 shows how to instantiate this primitive with URS. Finally, the last section compares the efficiency of our contributions with the most relevant schemes from the state-of-the-art.

2 Preliminaries

Bilinear Groups. Our construction requires bilinear groups whose definition is recalled below.

Definition 1. *Bilinear groups are a set of three groups $\mathbb{G}_1$, $\mathbb{G}_2$, and $\mathbb{G}_T$ of order p along with a map, called pairing, $e : \mathbb{G}_1 \times \mathbb{G}_2 \rightarrow \mathbb{G}_T$ that is*

1. *bilinear: for any $g \in \mathbb{G}_1, \widetilde{g} \in \mathbb{G}_2$, and $a, b \in \mathbb{Z}_p$, $e(g^a, \widetilde{g}^b) = e(g, \widetilde{g})^{ab}$;*
2. *non-degenerate: for any $g \in \mathbb{G}_1^*$ and $\widetilde{g} \in \mathbb{G}_2^*$, $e(g, \widetilde{g}) \neq 1_{\mathbb{G}_T}$;*
3. *efficient: for any $g \in \mathbb{G}_1$ and $\widetilde{g} \in \mathbb{G}_2$, $e(g, \widetilde{g})$ can be efficiently computed.*

As most recent cryptographic papers, we only consider bilinear groups of prime order with *type 3* pairings [14], meaning that no efficiently computable homomorphism is known between $\mathbb{G}_1$ and $\mathbb{G}_2$.

Computational Assumptions. The security analysis of our protocols will make use of the following two assumptions.

- SDL assumption: Given $(g, g^a) \in \mathbb{G}_1^2$ and $(\widetilde{g}, \widetilde{g}^a) \in \mathbb{G}_2^2$, this assumption states that it is hard to recover a. It thus essentially extends the standard discrete logarithm assumption to the case of bilinear groups.
- EDDH assumption: Given $(\{g^{a \cdot c^i}\}_{i=0}^{2n^2}, \{g^{b \cdot c^i}\}_{i=0}^{n-1}, \{g^{c^i}\}_{i=1}^{3n^2}, \{g^{d \cdot c^i}\}_{i=1}^{2n^2}, g^z) \in \mathbb{G}_1^{7n^2+n+2}$ and $(\{\widetilde{g}^{c^i}\}_{i=1}^{2n^2}, \widetilde{g}^d, \{\widetilde{g}^{a \cdot c^i}\}_{i \in [1,2n^2] \setminus]n^2-n, n^2+n[}) \in \mathbb{G}_2^{4n^2-2n+1}$, the EDDH assumption states that it is hard to decide whether $z = a \cdot b \cdot c^{n^2} + b \cdot d$ or z is random.

We note that our EDDH assumption is an instance of the generic BBG assumption [8]. The hardness of the underlying problem is studied in the generic group model in the full version [23] but it is intuitively based on the following rationale. A non-random z is the sum of two monomials, $a \cdot b \cdot c^{n^2}$ and $b \cdot d$, that are both multiple of b. As b is only provided in $\mathbb{G}_1$ with $\{g^{b \cdot c^i}\}_{i=0}^{n-1}$, any attempt to distinguish z from randomness will intuitively require to pair an element of this set with an element of $\mathbb{G}_2$. If the latter belongs to $\{\widetilde{g}^{a \cdot c^i}\}_{i \in [1,2n^2] \setminus]n^2-n, n^2+n[}$, then we get an element of $\mathbb{G}_T$ whose exponent is of the form $a \cdot b \cdot c^i$ for some $i \in [1, n^2-1] \cup [n^2+n, 2n^2]$. This is not sufficient to distinguish the first monomial in z so we must pair g^z with some g^{c^i} for $i \geq n$, resulting (once we remove the first monomial) in an element $e(g, \widetilde{g})^{b \cdot d \cdot c^i}$ with $i \geq n$. The latter element cannot be computed from the EDDH instance as we only have $g^{b \cdot c^i}$, for $i < n$, in $\mathbb{G}_1$ and $\widetilde{g}^d$ in $\mathbb{G}_2$. The same reasoning applies if we start by trying to remove the second monomial.

3 Redactable Signatures with Linear Size Public Key

3.1 Unlinkable Redactable Signature

Before presenting our construction, we recall the notion of unlinkable redactable signature (URS) from [9], using the notations from [22]. The core idea of this primitive is that a signature σ issued on a set[1] of messages $\{m_i\}_{i=1}^n$ can be publicly redacted so as to be valid only on a subset $\{m_i\}_{i \in \mathcal{I}}$, for some $\mathcal{I} \subset [1, n]$. This feature is important both for efficiency and privacy reasons. The set of redacted messages is then $\{m_i\}_{i \in \overline{\mathcal{I}}}$, where $\overline{\mathcal{I}} = [1, n] \setminus \mathcal{I}$.

[1] We stress that the index of each message is important as the term "set" might lead to a confusion. Here, m_i means that this message has been signed under the i-th element of the public key and is only valid for this position. In particular, deriving from σ a signature on $\{m_{\pi(i)}\}_{i=1}^n$ for some permutation π would constitute a forgery.

Syntax. An URS scheme consists of the 4 following algorithms.

- $\texttt{Keygen}(1^\lambda, n)$: On input a security parameter 1^λ and an integer n, this algorithm returns a key pair $(\mathsf{sk}, \mathsf{pk})$ supporting signatures on sets of n messages $\{m_i\}_{i=1}^n$.
- $\texttt{Sign}(\mathsf{sk}, \{m_i\}_{i=1}^n)$: On input n messages $\{m_i\}_{i=1}^n$ and the signing key sk, this algorithm outputs a signature σ.
- $\texttt{Derive}(\mathsf{pk}, \sigma, \{m_i\}_{i=1}^n, \mathcal{I})$: On input a signature σ on $\{m_i\}_{i=1}^n$, the public key pk and a subset $\mathcal{I} \subseteq [1, n]$, this algorithm returns a redacted (or derived) signature $\sigma_{\mathcal{I}}$ on the subset of messages $\{m_i\}_{i \in \mathcal{I}}$.
- $\texttt{Verify}(\mathsf{pk}, \sigma, \{m_i\}_{i \in \mathcal{I}})$: On input the public key pk, a set of messages $\{m_i\}_{i \in \mathcal{I}}$ and a signature σ (generated by $\texttt{Sign}$ or $\texttt{Derive}$), this algorithm outputs 1 (valid) or 0 (invalid).

Security Model. As any signature, a redactable signature must be unforgeable, meaning that it is impossible to output a valid signature on an unsigned set (or subset) of messages. However, a subtlety arises if we consider the generation of a new derived signature as an attack, even if the latter is only valid on an already signed subset of messages. Following the terminology of standard signature schemes, a construction preventing generation of new signatures is said to be strongly unforgeable. As its name suggests, strong unforgeability implies unforgeability. In [22], these two notions were defined as in Fig. 1. These experiments make use of the following oracles that define a counter c and three tables, Q_1, Q_2 and Q_3:

- $\mathcal{O}\texttt{Sign}^*(\{m_i\}_{i=1}^n)$: on input a set of n messages, this oracle returns $\texttt{Sign}(\mathsf{sk}, \{m_i\}_{i=1}^n)$, stores $Q_1[c] = (\sigma, \{m_i^{(c)}\}_{i=1}^n)$ and increments $c \leftarrow c + 1$.
- $\mathcal{O}\texttt{Sign}(\{m_i\}_{i=1}^n)$: on input a set of n messages, this oracle computes $\sigma \leftarrow \texttt{Sign}(\mathsf{sk}, \{m_i\}_{i=1}^n)$, stores $Q_1[c] = (\sigma, \{m_i^{(c)}\}_{i=1}^n)$ and increments $c \leftarrow c + 1$.
- $\mathcal{O}\texttt{Derive}(k, \mathcal{I})$: on input an index k and a set $\mathcal{I}$, this algorithm returns $\perp$ if $Q_1[k] = \emptyset$ or if $\mathcal{I} \nsubseteq [1, n]$. Else, it uses σ and $\{m_i\}_{i=1}^n$ stored in $Q_1[k]$ to return $\texttt{Derive}(\mathsf{pk}, \sigma, \{m_i\}_{i=1}^n, \mathcal{I})$. The set $\{m_i\}_{i \in \mathcal{I}}$ is then added to Q_2.
- $\mathcal{O}\texttt{Reveal}(k)$: on input an index k, this algorithm returns $\perp$ if $Q_1[k] = \emptyset$ and $Q_1[k] = (\sigma, \{m_i^{(k)}\}_{i=1}^n)$ otherwise. The set $\{m_i^{(k)}\}_{i=1}^n$ is then added to Q_3.

The difference between $\mathcal{O}\texttt{Sign}^*$ and $\mathcal{O}\texttt{Sign}$ is that the latter does not return anything. $\mathcal{O}\texttt{Sign}$ indeed simply generates a signature that can be used as input of subsequent $\mathcal{O}\texttt{Derive}$ queries. Finally, we also recall in the same figure the notion of unlinkability that provides strong privacy guarantees as it ensures that no information leak on redacted messages and that it is impossible to link the input (σ) and the output (σ') of the $\texttt{Derive}$ algorithm beyond the fact that they both coincide on the set $\{m_i\}_{i \in \mathcal{I}}$ of revealed messages.

Let $\mathcal{A}$ be a probabilistic polynomial adversary. An URS scheme is

- unforgeable if $\texttt{Adv}^{uf}(\mathcal{A}) = |\Pr[\texttt{Exp}_{\mathcal{A}}^{uf}(1^\lambda, n) = 1]|$ is negligible for any $\mathcal{A}$.

Unforgeability

$\mathtt{Exp}_{\mathcal{A}}^{uf}(1^\lambda, n)$

1. $c \leftarrow 0$; $Q_1 \leftarrow \emptyset$;
2. $(\mathsf{sk}, \mathsf{pk}) \leftarrow \mathtt{Keygen}(1^k, n)$
3. $(\sigma^*, \{m_i\}_{i \in \mathcal{I}}) \leftarrow \mathcal{A}^{\mathcal{O}\mathtt{Sign}^*}(\mathsf{pk})$
4. Return 1 if $\mathcal{I} \neq \emptyset$ and $\mathtt{Verify}(\mathsf{pk}, \sigma^*, \{m_i\}_{i \in \mathcal{I}}) = 1$ and $\forall j < c, \exists k_j \in \mathcal{I} : m_{k_j} \neq m_{k_j}^{(j)}$
5. Else, return 0

Strong Unforgeability

$\mathtt{Exp}_{\mathcal{A}}^{suf}(1^\lambda, n)$

1. $Q_1, Q_2, Q_3 \leftarrow \emptyset$;
2. $(\mathsf{sk}, \mathsf{pk}) \leftarrow \mathtt{Keygen}(1^k, n)$
3. $(\sigma^*, \{m_i\}_{i \in \mathcal{I}}) \leftarrow \mathcal{A}^{\mathcal{O}\mathtt{Sign}, \mathcal{O}\mathtt{Derive}, \mathcal{O}\mathtt{Reveal}}(\mathsf{pk})$
4. Return 1 if $\mathcal{I} \neq \emptyset$ and $\mathtt{Verify}(\mathsf{pk}, \sigma^*, \{m_i\}_{i \in \mathcal{I}}) = 1$ and $\{m_i\}_{i \in \mathcal{I}} \notin Q_2$ and $\forall \{m_i^\ell\}_{i=1}^n \in Q_3$: $\exists k_j \in \mathcal{I} : m_{k_j} \neq m_{k_j}^\ell$
5. Else, return 0

Unlinkability

$\mathtt{Exp}_{\mathcal{A}}^{unl-b}(1^\lambda, n)$

1. $(\mathsf{pk}, \mathcal{I}, \{m_i^{(0)}\}_{i=1}^n, \{m_i^{(1)}\}_{i=1}^n, \sigma^{(0)}, \sigma^{(1)}) \leftarrow \mathcal{A}()$
2. If $\exists b' \in \{0, 1\}$: $\mathtt{Verify}(\mathsf{pk}, \sigma^{(b')}, \{m_i^{(b')}\}_{i=1}^n) = 0$, return 0
3. If $\exists j \in \mathcal{I} : m_j^{(0)} \neq m_j^{(1)}$, return 0
4. $\sigma_{\mathcal{I}}^{(b)} \leftarrow \mathtt{Derive}(\mathsf{pk}, \sigma^{(b)}, \{m_i^{(b)}\}_{i=1}^n, \mathcal{I})$
5. $b^* \leftarrow \mathcal{A}(\sigma_{\mathcal{I}}^{(b)})$
6. Return $(b^* = b)$.

Fig. 1. Security notions for redactable signatures

- strongly unforgeable if $\mathtt{Adv}^{suf}(\mathcal{A}) = |\Pr[\mathtt{Exp}_{\mathcal{A}}^{suf}(1^\lambda, n) = 1]|$ is negligible for any $\mathcal{A}$.
- unlinkable $\mathtt{Adv}^{unl} = |\Pr[\mathtt{Exp}_{\mathcal{A}}^{unl-1}(1^\lambda, n) = 1] - \Pr[\mathtt{Exp}_{\mathcal{A}}^{unl-0}(1^\lambda, n) = 1]|$ is negligible for any $\mathcal{A}$.

3.2 Our Construction

Intuition. The system of [22] is constructed upon the Pointcheval-Sanders (PS) signature scheme [20] for blocks of n messages, by aggregating the redacted messages in one element and then proving, thanks to an additional element, that the latter was honestly generated. Unfortunately, in [22], this is done by adding a quadratic number (in n) of elements in the public key, which quickly becomes inefficient.

Our approach shares some similarities with [22] but differs in several important ways. Our first difference is that we do not start from the original PS signature scheme but rather from a specific instantiation where the secret key only contains two scalars x and y and where a signature $(\sigma_1, \sigma_2) \in \mathbb{G}_1^2$ on a set of messages $\{m_i\}_{i=1}^n$ is $(h, h^{x+\sum_{i=1}^n y^i \cdot m_i})$, for some random element $h \in \mathbb{G}_1$. Concretely, this implicitly sets $y_i = y_1^i$, for $i \geq 2$, in the original PS signature scheme. The original proof of PS signatures in the generic group model readily adapts to this particular settings. Actually, this instantiation has been recently studied by McDonald [18]. In any case, the validity of σ can be checked by simply testing whether the following equation holds:

$$e(\sigma_1, \widetilde{g}^x \cdot \prod_{i=1}^{n} \widetilde{g}^{y^i \cdot m_i}) = e(\sigma_2, \widetilde{g}),$$

where $\widetilde{g}^x$ and $\{\widetilde{g}^{y^i}\}_{i=1}^n$ are parts of the public key. As in [22], we can compute an element $\widetilde{\sigma} \leftarrow \prod_{i \in \overline{\mathcal{I}}} \widetilde{g}^{y^i \cdot m_i}$ that aggregates all the redacted messages but we must then ensure that $\widetilde{\sigma}$ will not be used by an adversary to cheat the verification procedure. Concretely, since the `Verify` algorithm now checks the following equation:

$$e(\sigma_1, \widetilde{g}^x \cdot \widetilde{\sigma} \cdot \prod_{i \in \mathcal{I}} \widetilde{g}^{y^i \cdot m_i}) = e(\sigma_2, \widetilde{g}),$$

one must intuitively ensure that $\widetilde{\sigma}$ has not been used to aggregate illicit elements of the form $\widetilde{g}^{-x}$ or $\widetilde{g}^{y^i \cdot m_i'}$, for some $i \in \mathcal{I}$, which would lead to trivial forgeries. Here, we can't use the solution from [22] anymore because our secret key is different, but primarily because it would entail a public key containing $O(n^2)$ elements.

The first step of our new strategy is to notice that the following pairing

$$G = e(\prod_{i \in \mathcal{I}} g^{y^{n+1-i}}, \widetilde{\sigma})$$

is of the form $e(g^{\sum_{i \in \mathcal{I}, j \in \overline{\mathcal{I}}} y^{n+1-i+j} \cdot m_j}, \widetilde{g})$ for an honestly generated $\widetilde{\sigma}$. Since $\mathcal{I} \cap \overline{\mathcal{I}} = \emptyset$, we note that the first input of the resulting pairing can be computed without the knowledge of $g^{y^{n+1}}$. In particular, it can be computed only from the $2n-1$ elements g^{y^i}, for $i \in [1, n] \cup [n+2, 2n]$, that we add to the public key.

Now, following [22], it might be tempting to conclude that there is an equivalence here, namely that an ill-formed $\widetilde{\sigma}$ will necessarily lead to a pairing G involving $g^{y^{n+1}}$ or an element of the form $g^{x \cdot y^u}$, for some $u > 0$, that are not provided in the public key.

Unfortunately, this is not true because, in the case where G is computed from an ill-formed $\widetilde{\sigma} \leftarrow \prod_{i=1}^{n} \widetilde{g}^{y^i \cdot m_i'}$ (for example, one such that $\exists i \in \mathcal{I}$ with $m_i' \neq 0$), we have:

$$G = e(g^{\sum_{u=1}^{2n} y^u \cdot a_u}, \widetilde{g})$$

with $a_{n+1} = \sum_{i \in \mathcal{I}} m_i'$. It is thus trivial for the adversary to select values m_i', for $i \in \mathcal{I}$, that will cancel the coefficient a_{n+1} of y^{n+1}. In such a case, it can create a forgery using only the elements g^{y^i}, for $i \in [1, n] \cup [n+2, 2n]$, which are provided in the public key.

This solution therefore does not work as it is, but this does not mean that we should completely discard it either. Instead, we will keep the same approach but add some unpredictability in the coefficient a_{n+1} to thwart the previous attack.

To this end, we will generate the hash outputs $c_i \leftarrow \mathtt{H}(\sigma_1||\sigma_2||\widetilde{\sigma}||\mathcal{I}||i)$, for $i \in \mathcal{I}$, and use them to compute a different pairing

$$e(\prod_{i\in\mathcal{I}} g^{y^{n+1-i}\cdot c_i}, \widetilde{\sigma}) = e(g^{\sum\limits_{i\in\mathcal{I},j\in\overline{\mathcal{I}}} y^{n+1-i+j}\cdot c_i \cdot m_j}, \widetilde{g}).$$

Here, our previous remark is still valid: for a honestly generated $\widetilde{\sigma}$, there is no monomial in y^{n+1}. But now, in the case of an ill-formed $\widetilde{\sigma}$ as above, the coefficient a_{n+1} of y^{n+1} is $\sum_{i\in\mathcal{I}} c_i \cdot m_i'$. Since c_i depends on $\widetilde{\sigma}$ and so on m_i', we see that any strategy to choose the scalars m_i' in such a way that $a_{n+1} = 0$ is unlikely to succeed as any change in a value of m_i' will lead to a completely new set of values $\{c_i\}_{i\in\mathcal{I}}$. This solution is reminiscent of the approach to prevent rogue key attacks in aggregate signature or multi-signature schemes (see *e.g.* [5]) but we use it here for another purpose and with a significant difference. We can't indeed derive c_i directly from the messages m_i as it would prevent efficient proofs of knowledge of m_i but rather from the first elements $(\sigma_1, \sigma_2, \widetilde{\sigma})$ of the signature. One of the difficulties of the security proof is to show that the adversary can't leverage this fact to create forgeries.

At this stage, we have an unforgeable redactable signature scheme. To achieve unlinkability, we use exactly the same trick as in [22], namely we aggregate a signature on a random message t under a dummy public key and then redact t to perfectly hide the set $\{m_i\}_{i\in\overline{\mathcal{I}}}$. Together with the re-randomizability of the PS signatures (that our variant inherits) this leads to an unlinkable redactable signature scheme, as defined in Sect. 3.1.

The Scheme

- $\mathtt{Keygen}(1^\lambda, n)$: this algorithm generates $(g, \widetilde{g}) \xleftarrow{\$} \mathbb{G}_1^* \times \mathbb{G}_2^*$ along with two random scalars $(x, y) \xleftarrow{\$} \mathbb{Z}_p^2$ and computes the following elements:
  - $\widetilde{X} \leftarrow \widetilde{g}^x$;
  - $\widetilde{Y}_i \leftarrow \widetilde{g}^{y^i}, \forall 1 \leq i \leq n$;
  - $Y_i \leftarrow g^{y^i}, \forall i \in [1, n] \cup [n+2, 2n]$.

  The secret key sk is then (x, y) whereas the public key pk is $(\mathtt{H}, g, \widetilde{g}, \{Y_i\}_{i=1}^n, \{Y_i\}_{i=n+2}^{2n}, \widetilde{X}, \{\widetilde{Y}_i\}_{i=1}^n)$, where $\mathtt{H} : \{0,1\}^* \to \mathbb{Z}_p^*$ is the description of a hash function.
- $\mathtt{Sign}(\mathsf{sk}, \{m_i\}_{i=1}^n)$: to sign n messages $m_1, \ldots, m_n$, the signer selects a random element $\sigma_1 \xleftarrow{\$} \mathbb{G}_1$, computes $\sigma_2 \leftarrow \sigma_1^{x+\sum_{i=1}^n y^i\cdot m_i}$ and then outputs the signature $\sigma = (\sigma_1, \sigma_2)$.
- $\mathtt{Derive}(\mathsf{pk}, \sigma, \{m_i\}_{i=1}^n, \mathcal{I})$: on input a signature $\sigma = (\sigma_1, \sigma_2)$ on $\{m_i\}_{i=1}^n$, the public key pk and a subset $\mathcal{I} \subset [1, n]$, this algorithm generates two random scalars $(r, t) \xleftarrow{\$} \mathbb{Z}_p^2$ and computes:
  - $\sigma_1' \leftarrow \sigma_1^r$;
  - $\sigma_2' \leftarrow \sigma_2^r \cdot (\sigma_1')^t$;
  - $\widetilde{\sigma}' \leftarrow \widetilde{g}^t \cdot \prod_{j\in\overline{\mathcal{I}}} \widetilde{Y}_j^{m_j}$.

Then, for all $i \in \mathcal{I}$, it computes the scalar $c_i \leftarrow \mathtt{H}(\sigma_1'||\sigma_2'||\widetilde{\sigma}'||\mathcal{I}||i)$ that is used to generate:

$$\sigma_3' \leftarrow \prod_{i\in\mathcal{I}}[Y_{n+1-i}^t \cdot \prod_{j\in\overline{\mathcal{I}}} Y_{n+1-i+j}^{m_j}]^{c_i}.$$

where $\overline{\mathcal{I}} = [1,n] \setminus \mathcal{I}$. Finally, the signer returns the derived signature $\sigma_{\mathcal{I}} = (\sigma_1', \sigma_2', \sigma_3', \widetilde{\sigma}')$ on $\{m_i\}_{i\in\mathcal{I}}$.

- `Verify`($\mathsf{pk}, \sigma, \{m_i\}_{i\in\mathcal{I}}$): this algorithm parses σ as $(\sigma_1, \sigma_2, \sigma_3, \widetilde{\sigma}) \in \mathbb{G}_1^3 \times \mathbb{G}_2$, setting $\sigma_3 = 1_{\mathbb{G}_1}$ and $\widetilde{\sigma} = 1_{\mathbb{G}_2}$ if $\sigma \in \mathbb{G}_1^2$ (*i.e.* if σ has not been derived). If $\sigma_1 = 1_{\mathbb{G}_1}$, then it returns $\perp$. Else, the algorithm tests if the following equations hold, in which case it returns 1.
  1. $e(\sigma_1, \widetilde{X} \cdot \widetilde{\sigma} \cdot \prod_{i\in\mathcal{I}} \widetilde{Y}_i^{m_i}) = e(\sigma_2, \widetilde{g})$;
  2. $e(\sigma_3, \widetilde{g}) = e(\prod_{i\in\mathcal{I}} Y_{n+1-i}^{c_i}, \widetilde{\sigma})$;

  where $c_i \leftarrow \mathtt{H}(\sigma_1||\sigma_2||\widetilde{\sigma}||\mathcal{I}||i)$. If (at least) one of these equations is not satisfied, then the algorithm returns 0.

Remark 2. 1) We note that the elements provided in the public key are sufficient to compute derived signatures, and in particular the element σ_3' since, for all $i \in \mathcal{I}$ and $j \in \overline{\mathcal{I}}$, we have $n+1-i \in [1,n]$ and $n+1-i+j \in [1,n] \cup [n+2, 2n]$.

2) We have defined σ_3' as $\prod_{i\in\mathcal{I}}[Y_{n+1-i}^t \cdot \prod_{j\in\overline{\mathcal{I}}} Y_{n+1-i+j}^{m_j}]^{c_i}$ for ease of exposition but we note that applying directly this formula to compute this element would be rather inefficient in most cases as it would entail $|\mathcal{I}|(n-|\mathcal{I}|+1)$ exponentiations. For all $u \in [1,n] \cup [n+2, 2n]$, let us define $t_u = t$ if $u = n+1-i$ for some $i \in \mathcal{I}$ and $t_u = 0$ otherwise. Then, σ_3' can also be written as follows:

$$\sigma_3' = \prod_{u\in[1,n]\cup[n+2,2n]} Y_u^{t_u+s_u}$$

where $s_u = \sum_{\substack{i\in\mathcal{I}, j\in\overline{\mathcal{I}}:\\ j-i=u-n-1}} c_i \cdot m_j$, for all $u \in [1,n] \cup [n+2, 2n]$. Computing σ_3' this way requires at most 2n-1 exponentiations.

Correctness. We prove here that the `Verify` algorithm returns 1 for any signature σ returned by the `Sign` or the `Derive` algorithm.

First, in the case where σ has not been derived, we note that the second verification equation is trivially satisfied as σ_3 and $\widetilde{\sigma}$ are the neutral elements of respectively $\mathbb{G}_1$ and $\mathbb{G}_2$. Moreover, in this case, we have $e(\sigma_2, \widetilde{g}) = e(\sigma_1^{x+\sum_{i=1}^n y^i \cdot m_i}, \widetilde{g}) = e(\sigma_1, \widetilde{g}^{x+\sum_{i=1}^n y^i \cdot m_i}) = e(\sigma_1, \widetilde{X} \cdot \prod_{i=1}^n \widetilde{Y}_i^{m_i})$, which concludes the proof.

Let us now assume that σ is an output of the `Derive` algorithm for some subset $\mathcal{I}$. We have

$$\begin{aligned}
e(\sigma_1', \widetilde{X} \cdot \widetilde{\sigma}' \cdot \prod_{i \in \mathcal{I}} \widetilde{Y}_i^{m_i}) &= e(\sigma_1', \widetilde{g}^{x + \sum_{i \in \mathcal{I}} y^i \cdot m_i} \cdot \widetilde{g}^t \cdot \prod_{j \in \overline{\mathcal{I}}} \widetilde{Y}_j^{m_j}) \\
&= e(\sigma_1', \widetilde{g}^{t + x + \sum_{i=1}^n y^i \cdot m_i}) \\
&= e((\sigma_1')^{x + \sum_{i=1}^n y^i \cdot m_i} \cdot (\sigma_1')^t, \widetilde{g}) \\
&= e(\sigma_2', \widetilde{g})
\end{aligned}$$

and

$$\begin{aligned}
e(\prod_{i \in \mathcal{I}} Y_{n+1-i}^{c_i}, \widetilde{\sigma}') &= e(\prod_{i \in \mathcal{I}} Y_{n+1-i}^{c_i}, \widetilde{g}^{t + \sum_{j \in \overline{\mathcal{I}}} y^j \cdot m_j}) \\
&= e([\prod_{i \in \mathcal{I}} Y_{n+1-i}^{c_i}]^{t + \sum_{j \in \overline{\mathcal{I}}} y^j \cdot m_j}, \widetilde{g}) \\
&= e(\prod_{i \in \mathcal{I}} [Y_{n+1-i}^{t + \sum_{j \in \overline{\mathcal{I}}} y^j \cdot m_j}]^{c_i}, \widetilde{g}) \\
&= e(\prod_{i \in \mathcal{I}} [Y_{n+1-i}^t \cdot \prod_{j \in \overline{\mathcal{I}}} Y_{n+1-i+j}^{m_j}]^{c_i}, \widetilde{g}),
\end{aligned}$$

which means that both equations are satisfied.

3.3 Security Analysis

By modelling `H` as a random oracle, we can prove the strong unforgeability (and hence the basic unforgeability) of our construction in the generic group model. We note that relying on a q-type assumption, as it was done in [21] for PS signatures, seems extremely difficult here as the use of several powers of the secret value y prevents to use the strategy from [21]. Fortunately, proving the unlinkability of our scheme does not require such kinds of assumption as we show that this property holds unconditionally. This is formally stated by the following theorem, proven below.

Theorem 3.
- *In the random oracle and generic group models, our construction is strongly unforgeable.*
- *Our construction is unconditionally unlinkable.*

Proof of Strong Unforgeability

Lemma 4. *In the generic group model, no adversary can break the strong unforgeability of our scheme with probability greater than* $\frac{q_H + 2 + 2n \cdot (3n + 2 + 2q_R + 4q_D + q_G)^2}{2p}$, *where* q_H *is a bound on the number of random oracle queries,* q_G *is a bound on the number of group oracle queries,* q_D *is a bound on the number of* $\mathcal{O}$`Derive` *queries and* q_R *is a bound on the number of* $\mathcal{O}$`Reveal` *queries.*

Proof. In the generic group model, the adversary $\mathcal{A}$ has only access to the elements from the public key and the ones resulting from queries to the different oracles. Each of these elements is associated with a polynomial whose formal variables are the scalars unknown to the adversary (either the values from the secret key or the random scalars r and t used to derive signatures). Concretely, the adversary has access to

- $\mathsf{pk} = (\{g^{y^i}\}_{i=0}^{n}, \{g^{y^i}\}_{i=n+2}^{2n}, \widetilde{g}^x, \{\widetilde{g}^{y^i}\}_{i=0}^{n})$;
- $(g^{r_k}, g^{r_k(x+\sum_{i=1}^{n} y^i\cdot m_{k,i})})$ obtained, for $k \in [1, q_R]$, via the $\mathcal{O}\mathtt{Reveal}$ oracle on a set of messages $\{m_{k,i}\}_{i=1}^{n}$ adaptively chosen by the adversary;
- $(g^{r'_\ell}, g^{r'_\ell(x+t_\ell+\sum_{i=1}^{n} y^i\cdot m_{\ell,i})}, \widetilde{g}^{t_\ell} \cdot \prod_{j\in\overline{\mathcal{I}}_\ell} \widetilde{g}^{y^j\cdot m_{\ell,j}}, \prod_{i\in\mathcal{I}_\ell}[\prod_{j\in\overline{\mathcal{I}}_\ell}(g^{y^{n+1-i+j}\cdot m_j}) \cdot g^{y^{n+1-i}\cdot t_\ell}]^{c_{\ell,i}})$ obtained through $\mathcal{O}\mathtt{Derive}$ queries, for $\ell \in [1, q_D]$, where $c_{\ell,i}$ is computed as described in Sect. 3.2, namely by hashing the first three elements of the signature concatenated with $\mathcal{I}_\ell$ and i.

From these elements, $\mathcal{A}$ must create a signature $\sigma = (\sigma_1, \sigma_2, \sigma_3, \widetilde{\sigma})$ on a set of messages $\{m_i\}_{i\in\mathcal{I}}$ (we may have $\mathcal{I} = [1, n]$) that would be considered as a valid forgery by the strong unforgeability experiment. We note that we may have $(\sigma_3, \widetilde{\sigma}) = (1_{\mathbb{G}_1}, 1_{\mathbb{G}_2})$ so we can consider a four-elements forgery without loss of generality.

In this proof, we will use a register $\mathtt{L}$ to handle random oracle queries. For each query x, we first check whether $\mathtt{L}[x]$ already contains a scalar $y \in \mathbb{Z}_p^*$, in which case we return the latter. Else, we generate a random $y \xleftarrow{\$} \mathbb{Z}_p^*$ that is returned to $\mathcal{A}$ and then stored in $\mathtt{L}[x]$.

In the generic group model, σ must have been created as a combination of the elements above. This means that there are known scalars $\{(\alpha_{1,i}, \beta_{1,i}, \gamma_{1,i}\}_{i\in[0,n]\cup[n+2,2n]}$, δ_2, $\{\delta_{3,i}\}_{i\in[0,n]}$, $\{(\alpha_{4,k,b}, \beta_{4,k,b}, \gamma_{4,k,b})\}_{k\in[1,q_R],b\in[1,2]}$, $\{(\alpha_{5,\ell,b}, \beta_{5,\ell,b}, \gamma_{5,\ell,b})\}_{\ell\in[1,q_R],b\in[1,3]}$ and $\{\delta_{5,\ell}\}_{\ell\in[1,q_R]}$ such that:

- $[\sigma_1] = \sum_{i\in[0,n]\cup[n+2,2n]} \alpha_{1,i}\cdot y^i + \sum_{k=1}^{q_R} \alpha_{4,k,1}\cdot r_k + \alpha_{4,k,2}\cdot r_k(x + \sum_{i=1}^{n} y^i \cdot m_{k,i}) + \sum_{\ell=1}^{q_D} (\alpha_{5,\ell,1}\cdot r'_\ell + \alpha_{5,\ell,2}\cdot r'_\ell(x + t_\ell + \sum_{i=1}^{n} y^i\cdot m_{\ell,i}) + \alpha_{5,\ell,3} \cdot \sum_{i\in\mathcal{I}_\ell} c_{\ell,i}[y^{n+1-i}\cdot t_\ell + \sum_{j\in\overline{\mathcal{I}}_\ell} y^{n+1-i+j}\cdot m_j]$
- $[\sigma_2] = \sum_{i\in[0,n]\cup[n+2,2n]} \beta_{1,i}\cdot y^i + \sum_{k=1}^{q_R} \beta_{4,k,1}\cdot r_k + \beta_{4,k,2}\cdot r_k(x + \sum_{i=1}^{n} y^i \cdot m_{k,i}) + \sum_{\ell=1}^{q_D} (\beta_{5,\ell,1}\cdot r'_\ell + \beta_{5,\ell,2}\cdot r'_\ell(x + t_\ell + \sum_{i=1}^{n} y^i\cdot m_{\ell,i}) + \beta_{5,\ell,3} \cdot \sum_{i\in\mathcal{I}_\ell} c_{\ell,i}[y^{n+1-i}\cdot t_\ell + \sum_{j\in\overline{\mathcal{I}}_\ell} y^{n+1-i+j}\cdot m_j]$

- $[\sigma_3] = \sum_{i\in[0,n]\cup[n+2,2n]} \gamma_{1,i} \cdot y^i + \sum_{k=1}^{q_R} \gamma_{4,k,1} \cdot r_k + \gamma_{4,k,2} \cdot r_k(x + \sum_{i=1}^{n} y^i \cdot m_{k,i}) + \sum_{\ell=1}^{q_D}(\gamma_{5,\ell,1} \cdot r'_\ell + \gamma_{5,\ell,2} \cdot r'_\ell(x + t_\ell + \sum_{i=1}^{n} y^i \cdot m_{\ell,i}) + \gamma_{5,\ell,3} \cdot \sum_{i\in\mathcal{I}_\ell} c_{\ell,i}[y^{n+1-i} \cdot t_\ell + \sum_{j\in\overline{\mathcal{I}}_\ell} y^{n+1-i+j} \cdot m_j]$
- $[\widetilde{\sigma}] = \delta_2 \cdot x + \sum_{i=0}^{n} \delta_{3,i} \cdot y^i + \sum_{\ell=0}^{q_D} \delta_{5,\ell}(t_\ell + \sum_{j\in\overline{\mathcal{I}}_\ell} y^j \cdot m_{\ell,j})$

where $\sigma_i \leftarrow g^{[\sigma_i]}$ and $\widetilde{\sigma} \leftarrow \widetilde{g}^{[\widetilde{\sigma}]}$. As σ is expected to be a valid signature, the following two conditions must be satisfied:

1. $e(\sigma_1, \widetilde{X} \cdot \widetilde{\sigma} \cdot \prod_{i\in\mathcal{I}} \widetilde{Y}_i^{m_i}) = e(\sigma_2, \widetilde{g})$;
2. $e(\sigma_3, \widetilde{g}) = e(\prod_{i\in\mathcal{I}} Y_{n+1-i}^{c_i}, \widetilde{\sigma})$;

but these are just necessary conditions. The set $\{m_i\}$ returned by the adversary must indeed also satisfy the following two conditions:

1. $\forall k \in [1, q_R]$, $\{m_i\}_{i\in\mathcal{I}} \not\subseteq \{m_{k,i}\}_{i=1}^{n}$;
2. $\forall \ell \in [1, q_D]$ either $\mathcal{I} \neq \mathcal{I}_\ell$ or $\{m_i\}_{i\in\mathcal{I}} \neq \{m_{\ell,i}\}_{i\in\mathcal{I}_\ell}$.

We here need to distinguish two cases:

- Case 1: $[\widetilde{\sigma}] = 0$;
- Case 2: $[\widetilde{\sigma}] \neq 0$.

Case 1. Here, we can only consider the first equation of the verification process and get the following relation:

$$[\sigma_1](x + \sum_{i\in\mathcal{I}} y^i \cdot m_i) = [\sigma_2]$$

As there is no monomial of degree 2 in x in $[\sigma_2]$, we can conclude that $\alpha_{4,k,2} = \alpha_{5,\ell,2} = 0\ \forall\ k \in [1, q_R]$ and $\ell \in [1, q_D]$. Similarly, there are no elements of the form $x \cdot y^u$ for $u > 0$, which implies that $\alpha_{1,i} = 0$, $\forall i > 0$, and that $\alpha_{5,\ell,3} = 0\ \forall \ell \in [1, q_D]$. We can then significantly simplify $[\sigma_1]$:

$$[\sigma_1] = \alpha_{1,0} + \sum_{k=1}^{q_R} \alpha_{4,k,1} \cdot r_k + \sum_{\ell=1}^{q_D} \alpha_{5,\ell,1} \cdot r'_\ell$$

Now, we note that any monomial of degree 1 in x in $[\sigma_2]$ also involves some r_k or r'_ℓ. We must then have $\alpha_{1,0} = 0$, meaning that any monomial on the left hand side also involves some r_k or r'_ℓ. This allows us to conclude that $\beta_{1,i} = 0$ $\forall i$ and that $\beta_{5,\ell,3} = 0\ \forall \ell \in [1, q_D]$. Finally, the factor $(x + \sum_{i\in\mathcal{I}} y^i \cdot m_i)$ in the previous relation means that any monomial in $[\sigma_2]$ is at least of degree 1 in x or y. This means that $\beta_{4,k,1} = \beta_{5,\ell,1} = 0$, $\forall\ k \in [1, q_R]$ and $\ell \in [1, q_D]$. We can then also simplify $[\sigma_2]$:

$$[\sigma_2] = \sum_{k=1}^{q_R} \beta_{4,k,2} \cdot r_k(x + \sum_{i=1}^{n} y^i \cdot m_{k,i}) + \sum_{\ell=1}^{q_D} \beta_{5,\ell,2} \cdot r'_\ell(x + t_\ell + \sum_{i=1}^{n} y^i \cdot m_{\ell,i})$$

In our case, there are no terms in t_ℓ in the left member of the equation, which means that $\beta_{5,\ell,2} = 0 \ \forall \ell \in [1, q_D]$. We can therefore also remove the monomials involving r'_ℓ in $[\sigma'_1]$.

At this stage, we have:

- $[\sigma_1] = \sum_{k=1}^{q_R} \alpha_{4,k,1} \cdot r_k$;
- $[\sigma_2] = \sum_{k=1}^{q_R} \beta_{4,k,2} \cdot r_k(x + \sum_{i=1}^{n} y^i \cdot m_{k,i})$.

This implies that $\alpha_{4,k,1} = \beta_{4,k,2}$, $\forall k \in [1, q_R]$. Moreover, for any k such that $\alpha_{4,k,1} \neq 0$, we must have $m_i = m_{k,i}$ $\forall i \in \mathcal{I}$, in which case σ would not be a valid forgery. The only other possibility is $\alpha_{4,k,1} = 0$ $\forall k \in [1, q_R]$ but, here again, this would mean that σ is not a valid forgery. Hence, no adversary can output a valid forgery in Case 1.

Case 2. Let us now consider the second case, and more specifically the second equation of the verification process (which is not trivial in this case):

$$[\sigma_3] = [\widetilde{\sigma}](\sum_{i \in \mathcal{I}} c_i \cdot y^{n+1-i})$$

where $c_i = \mathtt{H}(\sigma_1||\sigma_2||\widetilde{\sigma}||\mathcal{I}||i)$. As there are no terms in $x \cdot y^u$, for $u > 0$, in $[\sigma_3]$, we can conclude that $\delta_2 = 0$. This means that the coefficients of all monomials involving x in $[\sigma_3]$ are zero: $\gamma_{4,k,2} = \gamma_{5,\ell,2} = 0$, $\forall\ k \in [1, q_R]$ and $\ell \in [1, q_D]$. Similarly, we note that we can remove the monomials involving r_k or r'_ℓ as there are not present in the right member. We thus get:

- $[\sigma_3] = \sum_{i \in [0,n] \cup [n+2,2n]} \gamma_{1,i} \cdot y^i + \sum_{\ell=1}^{q_D} \gamma_{5,\ell,3} \cdot \sum_{i \in \mathcal{I}_\ell} c_{\ell,i}[y^{n+1-i} \cdot t_\ell + \sum_{j \in \overline{\mathcal{I}}_\ell} y^{n+1-i+j} \cdot m_j]$;
- $[\widetilde{\sigma}] = \sum_{i=0}^{n} \delta_{3,i} \cdot y^i + \sum_{\ell=0}^{q_D} \delta_{5,\ell}(t_\ell + \sum_{j \in \overline{\mathcal{I}}_\ell} y^j \cdot m_{\ell,j})$.

Let us define, for all $i \in [0, n]$, $\delta'_{3,i} = \delta_{3,i} + \sum_{\ell \in [1,q_D] : i \in \overline{\mathcal{I}}_\ell} \delta_{5,\ell} \cdot m_{\ell,i}$. Then, $[\widetilde{\sigma}]$ can be written as follows:

$$[\widetilde{\sigma}] = \sum_{i=0}^{n} \delta'_{3,i} \cdot y^i + \sum_{\ell=0}^{q_D} \delta_{5,\ell} \cdot t_\ell.$$

We note that the coefficient of the monomial y^{n+1} of $[\widetilde{\sigma}](\sum_{i \in \mathcal{I}} c_i \cdot y^{n+1-i})$ is exactly $\sum_{i \in \mathcal{I}} c_i \cdot \delta'_{3,i}$. As there is no monomial of degree $n+1$ in $[\sigma_3]$, we know that this sum is necessarily 0 but we need to show that this can be true only if $\delta'_{3,i} = 0$ $\forall i \in \mathcal{I}$. This will be done at the end of this proof where we will show that the event $\sum_{i \in \mathcal{I}} c_i \cdot \delta'_{3,i} = 0$ and $\exists j \in \mathcal{I}$ such that $\delta'_{3,j} \neq 0$ is very unlikely.

Right now, we assume this result and so consider that $\delta'_{3,i} = 0$, $\forall i \in \mathcal{I}$:

$$[\widetilde{\sigma}] = \sum_{i \in [0,n] \setminus \mathcal{I}} \delta'_{3,i} \cdot y^i + \sum_{\ell=0}^{q_D} \delta_{5,\ell} \cdot t_\ell$$

We can now focus on the first equation of verification:

$$[\sigma_1](x + [\widetilde{\sigma}] + \sum_{i \in \mathcal{I}} y^i \cdot m_i) = [\sigma_2]$$

Although the relation is not the same as in Case 1 because $[\widetilde{\sigma}]$ is not necessarily 0, some parts of the previous analysis are still relevant. In particular, for the same reasons as above, we have:

- $\alpha_{4,k,2} = \alpha_{5,\ell,2} = \alpha_{5,\ell,3} = 0$, $\forall\ k \in [1, q_R]$ and $\ell \in [1, q_D]$;
- $\alpha_{1,i} = 0$, $\forall i \geq 0$;
- $\beta_{1,i} = 0\ \forall i$ and $\beta_{5,\ell,3} = 0\ \forall \ell \in [1, q_D]$.

We can then simplify both σ_1 and σ_2 as follows:

- $[\sigma_1] = \sum_{k=1}^{q_R} \alpha_{4,k,1} \cdot r_k + \sum_{\ell=1}^{q_D} \alpha_{5,\ell,1} \cdot r'_\ell$
- $[\sigma_2] = \sum_{k=1}^{q_R} (\beta_{4,k,1} \cdot r_k + \beta_{4,k,2} \cdot r_k(x + \sum_{i=1}^{n} y^i \cdot m_{k,i})) + \sum_{\ell=1}^{q_D} (\beta_{5,\ell,1} \cdot r'_\ell + \beta_{5,\ell,2} \cdot r'_\ell(x + t_\ell + \sum_{i=1}^{n} y^i \cdot m_{\ell,i}))$

We must now distinguish two subcases:

- Case 2.1: $\exists \ell \in [1, q_D]$ such that $\delta_{5,\ell} \neq 0$.
- Case 2.2: $\forall \ell \in [1, q_D], \delta_{5,\ell} = 0$.

In the first case, we have $\alpha_{4,k,1} = 0$ for all $k \in [1, q_R]$ as there are no terms in $r_k \cdot t_\ell$ in $[\sigma_2]$. We must therefore also have $\beta_{4,k,1} = \beta_{4,k,2} = 0$, $\forall k \in [1, q_R]$. This means that, $\forall \ell \in [1, q_D]$,

$$\alpha_{5,\ell,1} \cdot r'_\ell(x + \sum_{i \in [0,n] \setminus \mathcal{I}} \delta'_{3,i} \cdot y^i + \delta_{5,\ell} \cdot t_\ell + \sum_{i \in \mathcal{I}} y^i \cdot m_i)$$
$$= \beta_{5,\ell,1} \cdot r'_\ell + \beta_{5,\ell,2} \cdot r'_\ell(x + t_\ell + \sum_{i=1}^{n} y^i \cdot m_{\ell,i})$$

which implies that $\alpha_{5,\ell,1} = \beta_{5,\ell,2}$. Hence, $m_{\ell,i} = m_i$, $\forall i \in \mathcal{I}$, and $\delta_{5,\ell} = 1$ (assuming that $\alpha_{5,\ell,1} \neq 0$ as this is trivial otherwise). σ can then be a valid forgery only if $\mathcal{I} \neq \mathcal{I}_\ell$, for such a ℓ. However, we recall that $[\sigma_3]$ and $[\widetilde{\sigma}]$ must satisfy:

$$[\sigma_3] = [\widetilde{\sigma}](\sum_{i \in \mathcal{I}} c_i \cdot y^{n+1-i})$$

On the right hand side, the monomials involving t_ℓ are exactly $c_i \cdot y^{n+1-i} \cdot t_\ell$, for $i \in \mathcal{I}$. On the left hand side, they are $\gamma_{5,\ell,3} \cdot c_{\ell,i} \cdot y^{n+1-i} \cdot t_\ell$ for $i \in \mathcal{I}_\ell$. Since $\mathtt{H}$ returns non-zero scalars, this equation can be satisfied only if $\mathcal{I} \subset \mathcal{I}_\ell$. However, since $\mathcal{I} \neq \mathcal{I}_\ell$, we know that there is at least one index i^* such that $i^* \in \mathcal{I}_\ell$ and $i^* \notin \mathcal{I}$. For this index, the monomial $\gamma_{5,\ell,3} \cdot c_{\ell,i^*} \cdot y^{n+1-i^*} \cdot t_\ell$ has no counterpart in the right member of the equation, which means that $\gamma_{5,\ell,3} = 0$

and therefore that $\beta_{5,\ell,2} = 0$. In case 2.1, the adversary can then succeed only by using $[\sigma_1] = 0$, which makes the forgery σ invalid.

Let us now consider the case 2.2. Here, the situation is simpler as we have:

- $[\sigma_1] = \sum_{k=1}^{q_R} \alpha_{4,k,1} \cdot r_k + \sum_{\ell=1}^{q_D} \alpha_{5,\ell,1} \cdot r'_\ell$;
- $[\sigma_2] = \sum_{k=1}^{q_R} (\beta_{4,k,1} \cdot r_k + \beta_{4,k,2} \cdot r_k(x + \sum_{i=1}^{n} y^i \cdot m_{k,i})) + \sum_{\ell=1}^{q_D} \beta_{5,\ell,1} \cdot r'_\ell$;
- $[\widetilde{\sigma}] = \sum_{i \in [0,n] \setminus \mathcal{I}} \delta'_{3,i} \cdot y^i$.

From $[\sigma_1](x + [\widetilde{\sigma}] + \sum_{i \in \mathcal{I}} y^i \cdot m_i) = [\sigma_2]$, we can deduce that $\alpha_{4,k,1} = \beta_{4,k,2}$, $\forall k \in [1, q_R]$. Therefore, either $m_{k,i} = m_i$ for all $i \in \mathcal{I}$ or $\alpha_{4,k,1} = 0$. The former case means that the forgery is invalid so we can assume that $\alpha_{4,k,1} = \beta_{4,k,2} = 0$, $\forall k \in [1, q_R]$. There are then no longer terms involving x in $[\sigma_2]$, which implies that $[\sigma_1]$ must be zero and so that σ is also invalid.

We now need to bound the probability of some bad events that would make our simulation in the generic group model incorrect. The first one is the event where the adversary returns a forgery $(\sigma_1, \sigma_2, \sigma_3, \widetilde{\sigma})$ for a set $\mathcal{I}$, where $\widetilde{\sigma}$ was generated using some scalars $\delta'_{3,i}$, as described above, such that

1. $\exists j \in \mathcal{I}$ such that $\delta'_{3,j} \neq 0$;
2. $\sum_{i \in \mathcal{I}} c_i \cdot \delta'_{3,i} = 0$, with $c_i \leftarrow \mathtt{H}(\sigma_1 || \sigma_2 || \widetilde{\sigma} || \mathcal{I} || i) \in \mathbb{Z}_p^*$.

We distinguish two cases. Either $\mathcal{A}$ has queried $\sigma_1 || \sigma_2 || \widetilde{\sigma} || \mathcal{I} || i$, $\forall i$ such that $\delta'_{3,i} \neq 0$, or there is at least one such index for which the corresponding string has not been queried to the random oracle before $\mathcal{A}$ outputs its forgery. In the second case, at least one random $c_i \in \mathbb{Z}_p^*$ is generated after the adversary has returned the forgery σ, which means that the second condition can only be satisfied with probability at most $\frac{1}{p}$.

So let us focus on the first case. In the generic group model, each set of values $\{\delta'_{3,i}\}_{i \in \mathcal{I}}$ generates a different element $\widetilde{\sigma}$. As $\widetilde{\sigma}$ is taken as input by the random oracle $\mathtt{H}$ to generate the random, non-zero scalars c_i, this means that $\{\delta'_{3,i}\}_{i \in \mathcal{I}}$ is distributed independently of $\{c_i\}_{i \in \mathcal{I}}$. The probability that $\sum_{i \in \mathcal{I}} c_i \cdot \delta'_{3,i} = 0$ with some non-zero $\delta'_{3,i}$ is then at best $\frac{1}{p}$ for a given set of values $\{\delta'_{3,i}\}_{i \in \mathcal{I}}$. Now, we note that the sum $\sum_{i \in \mathcal{I}} c_i \cdot \delta'_{3,i}$ needs at least two non-zero terms to be equal to zero because $c_i \neq 0$. This means that any tentative by the adversary to satisfy both conditions consume at least two queries to the random oracle. We can therefore bound the probability of $\mathcal{A}$ succeeding in this second case by $\frac{q_H}{2p}$, which is negligible as long as $\mathcal{A}$ makes only a polynomial number of queries to the random oracle. In the end, the probability that this bad event occurs is at most $\frac{q_H+2}{2p}$.

The second event we need to bound is the one where two of the formal polynomials used above evaluate to the same value. Indeed, the two elements associated with these polynomials would be equal in practice but would be considered as different by our simulation. The number of polynomials involved in our proof is $3n + 2 + 2q_R + 4q_D + q_G$, each of them being of degree at most $2n$. Using the Schwartz-Zippel lemma, we can bound the probability of such an event by $\frac{2n\cdot(3n+2+2q_R+4q_D+q_G)^2}{2p}$, which is negligible.

Proof of Unlinkability. We here prove that a derived signature $\sigma_{\mathcal{I}}$ on $\{m_i\}_{i\in\mathcal{I}}$ is distributed independently of the original signature $\sigma = (\sigma_1, \sigma_2, \sigma_3, \widetilde{\sigma})$ and of the set of redacted messages $\{m_i\}_{i\in\overline{\mathcal{I}}}$.

Let $h = g^v$ be some random element of $\mathbb{G}_1$, t be a random scalar and s be such that $\sigma_1 = g^s$. We can then define $u = t + \sum_{j\in\overline{\mathcal{I}}} y^j \cdot m_j$ along with:

- $\sigma'_1 \leftarrow h$;
- $\sigma'_2 \leftarrow h^{x+\sum_{i\in\mathcal{I}} y^i\cdot m_i} \cdot h^u$;
- $\sigma'_3 \leftarrow [\prod_{i\in\mathcal{I}} Y_{n+1-i}^{c_i}]^u$;
- $\widetilde{\sigma}' \leftarrow \widetilde{g}^u$.

We note that:

$$(\prod_{i\in\mathcal{I}} Y_{n+1-i}^{c_i})^u = \prod_{i\in\mathcal{I}} (Y_{n+1-i}^u)^{c_i} = \prod_{i\in\mathcal{I}} [Y_{n+1-i}^t \cdot \prod_{j\in\overline{\mathcal{I}}} Y_{n+1-i+j}^{m_j}]^{c_i}.$$

Therefore $\sigma' = (\sigma'_1, \sigma'_2, \sigma'_3, \widetilde{\sigma}')$ is exactly the derived signature that one would get by running the `Derive` algorithm with scalars t and $r = \frac{v}{s}$. Moreover, σ' is distributed as a valid output of this algorithm since both t and r are random.

Now, we note that the scalar u is random because t is random, so the four elements of $\sigma'_{\mathcal{I}}$ are distributed independently of σ and $\{m_i\}_{i\in\overline{\mathcal{I}}}$, which concludes the proof.

4 Group Signature with Time-Bound Keys

In this section, we recall and extend the definition of a group signature scheme with time-bound keys from [13]. There are three main differences with the latter paper. Firstly, as we explain in the introduction, we associate each signing key usk_k with a set of *active* time periods $\mathcal{T}_k$ and not just an expiry time. This means that the user k can issue valid group signatures for all time periods $t \in \mathcal{T}_k$, which are not necessarily contiguous. Concretely, the user can be considered as revoked at some time period $t \notin \mathcal{T}_k$ and then be automatically reinstated at a later period $t' \in \mathcal{T}_k$. This definition clearly generalizes the previous ones [11,13] that only consider expiry time. Our second difference is that we allow $\mathcal{O}$`Open` queries for the adversary during the anonymity game. Such queries were indeed forbidden in [13], resulting in a weaker notion of anonymity. Finally, our group manager does not need to provide the so-called "expiration information" for each period, which simplifies both the management process and the signature algorithm. Our group members indeed only need to know the current time period (and their original signing key) to issue a signature and in particular do not need to update their signing key with such information at each time period.

4.1 Syntax

As in [13], our group signature is composed of the following algorithms, involving three types of entities: the group manager, the users and the verifiers.

- $\texttt{GKeygen}$: on input a security parameter 1^λ and a bound n on the number of time periods, this algorithms generates the group key pair $(\mathsf{gsk}, \mathsf{gpk})$ and initializes a register $\texttt{Reg}$. The group public key gpk is then considered as known by all the other parties.
- $\texttt{Join}$: this is a two-party interactive protocol between the group manager and a new group member k. Both of them take as input gpk along with the set of active time periods $\mathcal{T}_k$[2] for this user. The group manager additionally takes as input gsk along with the current version of $\texttt{Reg}$. After successful completion of this protocol, the user obtains his group signing key usk_k that contains in particular his secret key sk_k and $\mathcal{T}_k$ whereas the group manager stores a revocation token rt_k and $\mathcal{T}_k$ in $\texttt{Reg}[k]$.
- $\texttt{Sign}$: on input a group signing key usk_k, the group public key gpk, the current time period t and a message m, this algorithm returns a group signature σ.
- $\texttt{Revoke}$: on input $(\mathsf{gsk}, \mathsf{gpk})$, $\texttt{Reg}$, a time period t and a set $\mathcal{R}$ of users to revoke, this algorithm returns a revocation list $\texttt{RL}_t$ specific to this period.
- $\texttt{Verify}$: on input gpk, a time period t, a revocation list $\texttt{RL}_t$, a group signature σ and a message m, this algorithms returns either 1 (valid) or 0 (invalid).
- $\texttt{Open}$: on input gsk, $\texttt{Reg}$, a group signature σ, a message m and a period t, this algorithm returns either a user identifier k or a failure message $\perp$.

Remark 5. Previous works [11,13] distinguish two kinds of revocation, the natural revocation that automatically excludes the users from the group once their expiry time has passed and the premature revocation that is called to exclude users before their expiry time. This terminology is coherent with their setting but not with ours where each user may alternate between periods of activity and inactivity. We then rather consider, for each time period t, a set of *active* users (*i.e.* those such that $t \in \mathcal{T}_k$) and a set of inactive ones. A user k is then said to be *revoked* at period t only if the $\texttt{Revoke}$ algorithm has been run on a set $\mathcal{R} \ni k$ and t, which corresponds to the premature revocation in [11,13]. In particular, the revocation list $\texttt{RL}_t$ is independent of the set of inactive users.

4.2 Security Model

A group signature should achieve correctness, anonymity, traceability and non-frameability as defined below. Our definitions are adapted from [13] and include the differences discussed at the beginning of this section. We refer to [13] for a formal definition of correctness but it intuitively requires that an honestly generated signature, issued by an active and non-revoked group member, is considered as valid by the verification algorithm and can be opened by the group manager.

[2] We associate each time period with an integer t in $[1, n]$. We can then talk of "time period t" without loss of generality.

As in [13], we ensure anonymity of users as long as their secret key do not leak. This is quite standard for group signature with revocation lists as the revocation tokens for a user can usually be generated from his secret key. This therefore corresponds to the notion of selfless-anonymity [6]. We nevertheless consider an anonymity definition that extends the notion of backward unlinkability to our setting. That is, we even allow revocation of challenge users (those targeted by the adversary) at any time period t different from the one of issuance of the challenge group signature. We thus ensure both backward and forward unlinkability.

Our traceability and non-frameability notions are standard. Intuitively, the former ensures that any group signature valid for a period t can be linked back to a group member k *active* at this time period whereas the latter ensures that k has indeed taken part in the generation of this signature.

All these security definitions make use of the following oracles that define $\mathcal{H}$ (resp. $\mathcal{C}$) as the set of honest (resp. corrupt) users. As the corrupt entities differ according to the experiments, we consider several oracles to add new members to the groups. All of them associate a group member to a unique index k and then return $\perp$ if they are run on an existing k.

- $\mathcal{O}\texttt{Add}(k, \mathcal{T}_k)$ is an oracle that can be used to add a new honest user k for the set of time periods $\mathcal{T}_k$. It runs Join with the corresponding inputs, thus generating a group signing key along with the associated revocation tokens. It does not return any data but adds k to $\mathcal{H}$.
- $\mathcal{O}\texttt{J}_U(k, \mathcal{T}_k)$ is an oracle that plays the user's side of the Join protocol. It can be used by an adversary $\mathcal{A}$ playing the role of a corrupt group manager to add a new user k for the time periods $\mathcal{T}_k$.
- $\mathcal{O}\texttt{J}_{GM}(k, \mathcal{T}_k)$ is the counterpart of the $\mathcal{O}\texttt{J}_U$ oracle that can be used by a corrupt user to join the group. k is then added to $\mathcal{C}$.
- $\mathcal{O}\texttt{Cor}(k)$ is an oracle that returns the group signing key of an honest user k. k is then removed from $\mathcal{H}$ and added to $\mathcal{C}$.
- $\mathcal{O}\texttt{Sign}(i, m, t)$ is an oracle that returns $\texttt{Sign}(\mathsf{gpk}, \mathsf{usk}_i, m, t)$, provided that k is an honest user that has already joined the group.
- $\mathcal{O}\texttt{Open}(\sigma, m, t)$ is an oracle that returns $\texttt{Open}(\mathsf{gsk}, \mathsf{gpk}, \texttt{Reg}, \sigma, m, t)$.
- $\mathcal{O}\texttt{Revoke}(\mathcal{R}, t)$ is an oracle that returns $\texttt{Revoke}(\mathsf{gsk}, \mathsf{gpk}, \texttt{Reg}, \mathcal{R}, t)$. The adversary may adaptively run several times this algorithm for the same time period t.
- $\mathcal{O}\texttt{Ch}_b(i_0, i_1, m, t)$ is an oracle that takes as inputs the index of two honest users active at the time period t and returns $\texttt{Sign}(\mathsf{gpk}, \mathsf{usk}_{i_b}, m, t)$.

In both the traceability and the non-frameability experiments, by including Reg in the adversary input we mean that it has read access to this register. We could also provide write access but this would require a more intricate Join protocol where the new user would sign the entry of the register with a specific key, as in [3] for example. We believe this would unnecessarily complicate our security model and so only consider this simpler scenario in our paper. Should the need arise, it would be straightforward to upgrade our model and our construction to handle write access.

$\mathtt{Exp}^{an}_{\mathcal{A}}(1^\lambda)$ – Anonymity Security Game
1. $b \xleftarrow{\$} \{0,1\}$
2. $(\mathsf{gsk}, \mathsf{gpk}, \mathtt{Reg}) \leftarrow \mathtt{GKeygen}()$
3. $b^* \leftarrow \mathcal{A}^{\mathcal{O}\mathtt{Add},\mathcal{O}\mathtt{Cor},\mathcal{O}\mathtt{Sign},\mathcal{O}\mathtt{Open},\mathcal{O}\mathtt{Revoke},\mathcal{O}\mathtt{Ch}_b}(\mathsf{gpk})$
4. If $\mathcal{O}\mathtt{Open}$ is queried on the output of $\mathcal{O}\mathtt{Ch}_b$, then return 0
5. If $\mathcal{O}\mathtt{Cor}$ has been run on an input of $\mathcal{O}\mathtt{Ch}_b$, then return 0
6. If both $\mathcal{O}\mathtt{Ch}_b(k_0, k_1, m, t)$ and $\mathcal{O}\mathtt{Revoke}(\mathcal{R}, t)$ are queried, with $\{k_0, k_1\} \cap \mathcal{R} \neq \emptyset$, then return 0
7. Return $(b = b^*)$

$\mathtt{Exp}^{tra}_{\mathcal{A}}(1^\lambda)$ – Traceability Security Game
1. $(\mathsf{gsk}, \mathsf{gpk}) \leftarrow \mathtt{GKeygen}()$
2. $(\sigma, m, t) \leftarrow \mathcal{A}^{\mathcal{O}\mathtt{Add},\mathcal{O}\mathtt{J}_{GM},\mathcal{O}\mathtt{Cor},\mathcal{O}\mathtt{Open},\mathcal{O}\mathtt{Revoke},\mathcal{O}\mathtt{Sign}}(\mathsf{gpk}, \mathtt{Reg})$
3. If $0 \leftarrow \mathtt{Verify}(\mathsf{gpk}, \mathtt{RL}_t, \sigma, m, t)$, then return 0
4. If $\perp \leftarrow \mathtt{Open}(\mathsf{gsk}, \mathsf{gpk}, \mathbf{Reg}, \sigma, m, t)$, then return 1
5. If $k \leftarrow \mathtt{Open}(\mathsf{gsk}, \mathsf{gpk}, \mathbf{Reg}, \sigma, m, t)$ and $t \notin \mathcal{T}_k$, then return 1
6. Return 0

$\mathtt{Exp}^{nf}_{\mathcal{A}}(1^\lambda)$ – Non-Frameability Security Game
1. $(\mathsf{gsk}, \mathsf{gpk}) \leftarrow \mathtt{GKeygen}(pp)$
2. $(\sigma, m, t) \leftarrow \mathcal{A}^{\mathcal{O}\mathtt{Add},\mathcal{O}\mathtt{J}_{U},\mathcal{O}\mathtt{Cor},\mathcal{O}\mathtt{Open},\mathcal{O}\mathtt{Revoke},\mathcal{O}\mathtt{Sign}}(\mathsf{gsk}, \mathtt{Reg})$
3. $k \leftarrow \mathtt{Open}(\mathsf{gsk}, \mathsf{gpk}, \mathbf{Reg}, \sigma, m, t)$
4. If $0 \leftarrow \mathtt{Verify}(\mathsf{gpk}, \mathtt{RL}_t, \sigma, m, t)$, then return 0
5. If $\mathcal{O}\mathtt{Sign}$ returned σ, then return 0
6. If $k \notin \mathcal{H}$, then return 0
7. Return 1

Fig. 2. Security games for group signature

Let $\mathcal{A}$ be a probabilistic polynomial adversary. A group signature scheme with time-bound keys is (Fig. 2)

- anonymous if $\mathtt{Adv}^{an}(\mathcal{A}) = |\Pr[\mathtt{Exp}^{an}_{\mathcal{A}}(1^\lambda) = 1] - 1/2|$ is negligible for any $\mathcal{A}$;
- traceable if $\mathtt{Adv}^{tra}(\mathcal{A}) = \Pr[\mathtt{Exp}^{tra}_{\mathcal{A}}(1^\lambda) = 1]$ is negligible for any $\mathcal{A}$;
- non-frameable if $\mathtt{Adv}^{nf}(\mathcal{A}) = \Pr[\mathtt{Exp}^{nf}_{\mathcal{A}}(1^\lambda) = 1]$ is negligible for any $\mathcal{A}$.

5 Instantiation from Redactable Signature

5.1 Our Construction

Intuition. The core idea behind our construction is rather simple once we have identified redactable signature as a suitable building block for group signature with time-bound keys. However, there are still some issues to address to get a scheme achieving the strong security properties of Sect. 4.

Indeed, the core idea is that any user k joining the group for a set of time periods $\mathcal{T}_k$ receives a redactable signature on a set of n messages $\{m_i\}_{i=1}^n$ where $m_i = 0$ if $i \notin \mathcal{T}_k$. This leads to a very compact group signing key that essentially consists of this signature. To issue a group signature at a time period i, a member only has to run the Derive algorithm on the subset $\mathcal{I} = \{i\}$ to get a redacted signature σ'. The latter can be straightforwardly used by the verifier to check if this member is active at this time period, as this signature would be valid on "0" otherwise. To achieve non-frameability while allowing revocation, it might be tempting to follow [22] and simply add a signature on a secret value sk_k. As in [20] the knowledge of $\widetilde{g}^{\mathsf{sk}_k}$ would then be enough to revoke (or, alternatively, open) signatures issued by k. Unfortunately, this would prevent revocation for specific time periods and in particular backward and forward unlinkability. We therefore proceed differently and define $m_i = \mathsf{sk}_k$ for any $i \in \mathcal{T}_k$. This way we can revoke a user for any time period i (and only for this time period) by simply providing a way to test whether the redacted signature σ' (derived on $\{i\}$) is valid on sk_k.

The Scheme. Our construction heavily relies on the redactable signature scheme described in Sect. 3.2 that we refer to as Σ.

- GKeygen($1^\lambda, n$): This algorithms runs Σ.Keygen($1^\lambda, n$) to get a pair (x, y) along with $\mathsf{pk} = (\mathtt{H}, g, \widetilde{g}, \{Y_i\}_{i=1}^n, \{Y_i\}_{i=n+2}^{2n}, \widetilde{X}, \{\widetilde{Y}_i\}_{i=1}^n)$. It then sets $\mathsf{gsk} = (x, y)$ and $\mathsf{gpk} = \mathsf{pk}$, and initializes a register Reg.
- Join: To join the group for the set of time periods $\mathcal{T}_k$, a new user k first selects a random secret key $\mathsf{sk}_k \xleftarrow{\$} \mathbb{Z}_p$ and sends $(g^{\mathsf{sk}_k}, \widetilde{g}^{\mathsf{sk}_k})$ to the group manager. He then proves knowledge of sk_k using for example the Schnorr's algorithm [24]. If the proof is valid and if $e(g^{\mathsf{sk}_k}, \widetilde{g}) = e(g, \widetilde{g}^{\mathsf{sk}_k})$, it selects a random scalar r and returns $(\sigma_1, \sigma_2) \leftarrow (g^r, [g^x \cdot (g^{\mathsf{sk}_k})^{\sum_{j\in\mathcal{T}_k} y^j}]^r)$. Note that this is a valid redactable signature on a set $\{m_i\}_{i=1}^n$, with $m_i = \mathsf{sk}_k$ if $i \in \mathcal{T}_k$ and 0 otherwise. The user is then able to check the validity of (σ_1, σ_2) by running the Σ.Verify algorithm. It then sets usk_k as $\{\mathsf{sk}_k, (\sigma_1, \sigma_2), \mathcal{T}_k\}$. In the meantime, the group manager stores $\widetilde{g}^{\mathsf{sk}_k}$ and $\mathcal{T}_k$ in Reg[k].
- Sign: to sign a message m for the current time period t, the user runs Σ.Derive(pk, $(\sigma_1, \sigma_2), \{m_i\}_{i=1}^n, \{t\}$) with $\{m_i\}_{i=1}^n$ defined as above. It then gets a derived $\sigma_\mathcal{I} = (\sigma_1', \sigma_2', \sigma_3', \widetilde{\sigma}')$ for $\mathcal{I} = \{t\}$ and must now prove that it is valid on a message $m_t = \mathsf{sk}_k \neq 0$. As the second equation defined in Σ.Verify can be tested with the sole knowledge of $\sigma_\mathcal{I}$, this means that he must simply prove knowledge of sk_k such that:

$$e(\sigma_1, \widetilde{X} \cdot \widetilde{\sigma} \cdot \widetilde{Y}_t^{\mathsf{sk}_k}) = e(\sigma_2, \widetilde{g})$$

  Concretely, it generates $a \xleftarrow{\$} Z_p$ and computes $K = e(\sigma_1, \widetilde{Y}_t)^a$ along with $c \leftarrow \mathtt{H}(K, \sigma_\mathcal{I}, m)$ and $s = a + c \cdot \mathsf{sk}_k$. It then outputs the group signature $\sigma \leftarrow (\sigma_\mathcal{I}, c, s)$.
- Revoke: For each user k to revoke for the time period t, the group manager recovers $\widetilde{g}^{\mathsf{sk}_k}$ from Reg[k] and adds $(\widetilde{g}^{\mathsf{sk}_k})^{y^t}$ to $\mathtt{RL}_t$.
- Verify: To verify a group signature $\sigma = (\sigma_1, \sigma_2, \sigma_3, \widetilde{\sigma}, c, s)$ on a message m for a time period t, the verifier first checks whether the second equation of Σ.Verify is satisfied. That is, $(\sigma_1, \sigma_2, \sigma_3, \widetilde{\sigma})$ must verify

$$e(\sigma_3, \widetilde{g}) = e(Y_{n+1-t}^{c_t}, \widetilde{\sigma})$$

where $c_t \leftarrow \mathtt{H}(\sigma_1||\sigma_2||\widetilde{\sigma}||\{t\}||t)$. It then checks whether $m_t = 0$ by testing if the following equation holds:

$$e(\sigma_1, \widetilde{X} \cdot \widetilde{\sigma}) = e(\sigma_2, \widetilde{g})$$

in which case it returns 0. Else, it verifies the proof of knowledge by computing $K' \leftarrow e(\sigma_1, \widetilde{Y}_t)^s \cdot [e(\sigma_2, \widetilde{g}) \cdot e(\sigma_1^{-1}, \widetilde{X} \cdot \widetilde{\sigma})]^{-c}$ and checking if $c = \mathtt{H}(K', \sigma_{\mathcal{I}}, m)$. If the proof is correct, then the signature is valid but it could have been generated with a revoked key.
For each element $\widetilde{h}_k$ in $\mathtt{RL}_t$, this algorithm then tests whether $e(\sigma_1, \widetilde{h}_k) = e(\sigma_2, \widetilde{g}) \cdot e(\sigma_1^{-1}, \widetilde{X} \cdot \widetilde{\sigma})$. If one of these conditions is satisfied, the algorithm returns 0. Else it returns 1.
- `Open`: For each active user k at time period t, this algorithm recovers $\widetilde{g}^{\mathsf{sk}_k}$ from $\mathtt{Reg}[k]$ and tests whether $e(\sigma_1, \widetilde{g}^{\mathsf{sk}_k}) = [e(\sigma_2, \widetilde{g}) \cdot e(\sigma_1^{-1}, \widetilde{X} \cdot \widetilde{\sigma})]^{y^{-t}}$ until it gets a match, in which case it returns the corresponding identifier k.

Remark 6. As the size of the group signature is the usual benchmark in the literature, we chose to present the version of our construction that optimizes it. However, this version requires to perform operations in $\mathbb{G}_T$ to generate the NIZK in the group signature. This may be a problem if one favours computational complexity as operations in $\mathbb{G}_T$ are notoriously less efficient than their counterparts in $\mathbb{G}_1$. In such a case, one can use a standard trick (*e.g.* [2,4]) which consists in adding the element $\sigma_1^{\mathsf{sk}_k} \in \mathbb{G}_1$ to the group signature and then proving knowledge of sk_k directly in $\mathbb{G}_1$. This shifts all computations from $\mathbb{G}_T$ to $\mathbb{G}_1$, improving efficiency at the cost of a small increase of the group signature size. The security proofs can be straightforwardly adapted to this new version.

Remark 7. We note that we are in a very favourable case when evaluating the Σ.`Derive` algorithm in the `Sign` protocol. Indeed, we have $|\mathcal{I}| = |\{t\}| = 1$ and all the involved messages are either 0 or sk_k. Computing $\widetilde{\sigma}$ thus only requires two exponentiations in $\mathbb{G}_2$ as we have $\widetilde{\sigma} = \widetilde{g}^u \cdot (\prod_{j \in \mathcal{T}_k \setminus \{t\}} \widetilde{Y}_j)^{\mathsf{sk}_k}$. Moreover, the latter product $P_t = \prod_{j \in \mathcal{T}_k \setminus \{t\}} \widetilde{Y}_j$ can be efficiently updated from one active time period i to the next one i' as $P_{i'} = P_i \cdot \widetilde{Y}_i \cdot \widetilde{Y}_{i'}^{-1}$. For the same reasons, σ_3 can be computed with essentially 2 exponentiations in $\mathbb{G}_1$. This complexity is therefore much lower than the generic one of our `Derive` algorithm. We provide more details in the next section.

5.2 Security Analysis

The security of our group signature scheme is stated by the next theorem, proved below.

Theorem 8. *In the random oracle model, our group signature is*

- *non-frameable under the* SDL *assumption;*
- *anonymous under the* EDDH *assumption and the non-frameability of our construction;*
- *traceable under the unforgeability of the redactable signature scheme* Σ.

Proof of Anonymity. The unlinkability property of a redactable signature scheme Σ implies that the set of redacted messages ($\{m_i\}_{i \in \overline{\mathcal{I}}}$) is perfectly hidden but does not provide any guarantee for the messages in $\{m_i\}_{i \in \mathcal{I}}$. In each of our group signatures, the latter set is exactly $\{\mathsf{sk}_k\}$, where sk_k is the group member's secret key. We can't therefore only rely on the unlinkability of Σ to prove anonymity and will then build a more intricate proof.

Game 1. Our first game is exactly the anonymity experiment where the adversary $\mathcal{A}$ is expected to win with probability ϵ.

Game 2. In our second game, we proceed as usual except that our reduction $\mathcal{R}$ makes a guess on the time period t^* targeted by the adversary. If $\mathcal{O}\mathtt{Ch}_b$ is run on a different time period, then $\mathcal{R}$ aborts. The new success probability is then at least $\frac{\epsilon}{n}$.

Game 3. In this game, the reduction $\mathcal{R}$ now makes a guess on the user k^* targeted by the adversary. If $\mathcal{O}\mathtt{Ch}_b$ is run with $k_b \neq k^*$, then $\mathcal{R}$ aborts. The new success probability is then at least $\frac{\epsilon}{n \cdot q}$, where q is a bound on the number of group members.

Game 4. In this game, $\mathcal{R}$ proceeds as in the previous game except that it stores all the signatures issued on behalf of k^* by $\mathcal{O}\mathtt{Sign}$ in a specific list $\mathtt{L}$ and deletes the information contained in $\mathtt{Reg}[k^*]$. Upon receiving an $\mathcal{O}\mathtt{Open}$ query, it first proceeds as usual but then tests whether the signature to open belongs to $\mathtt{L}$. In such a case, it returns k^*. Else, it returns $\perp$.

Game 5. In this last game, $\mathcal{R}$ generates two random elements σ_1 and σ_2 and defines $\widetilde{\sigma} \leftarrow \widetilde{g}^s$ and $\sigma_3 \leftarrow Y_{n+1-t^*}^{s \cdot c_i}$, where $c_i \leftarrow \mathtt{H}(\sigma_1' || \sigma_2' || \widetilde{\sigma}' || \mathcal{I} || t^*)$ and s is random. It then returns $(\sigma_1, \sigma_2, \sigma_3, \widetilde{\sigma})$ along with a simulated proof (c, s') of validity when $\mathcal{A}$ queries the oracle $\mathcal{O}\mathtt{Ch}_b$ for the time period t^*. As this group signature is perfectly independent of the users targeted by $\mathcal{A}$, the latter can only succeed with probability negligibly close to $\frac{1}{2}$.

Game 3 $\rightarrow$ *Game 4.* The only difference between Game 3 and Game 4 is the opening of signatures issued on behalf of k^*. As we keep track of all signatures returned by $\mathcal{O}\mathtt{Sign}$, there can be a problem only if the adversary manages to forge a valid group signature which can be traced back to k^*. In such a case our reduction will fail to correctly simulate the opening process as it will return $\perp$ instead of k^*.

However, such an adversary can be trivially converted into an adversary against non-frameability. Indeed, the latter property provides at least the same oracle queries and inputs than in the anonymity experiment. If we denote by ϵ_4 the advantage of the adversary in Game 4, we then get $\frac{\epsilon}{n \cdot q} \leq \mathtt{Adv}^{nf}(\mathcal{A}) + \epsilon_4$.

Game 4 $\rightarrow$ *Game 5*. Let us consider a EDDH instance $(\{g^{a\cdot c^i}\}_{i=0}^{2n^2}, \{g^{b\cdot c^i}\}_{i=0}^{n-1}, \{g^{c^i}\}_{i=1}^{3n^2}, \{g^{d\cdot c^i}\}_{i=1}^{2n^2}) \in \mathbb{G}_1^{7n^2+n+1}$ and $(\{\widetilde{g}^{a\cdot c^i}\}_{i\in[1,2n^2]\setminus]n^2-n,n^2+n[}, \{\widetilde{g}^{c^i}\}_{i=1}^{2n^2}, \widetilde{g}^d) \in \mathbb{G}_2^{4n^2-2n+1}$ along with g^z. We show that any adversary able to distinguish Game 4 from Game 5 can be used to solve the associated problem. In our proof, we will implicitly define $\mathsf{sk}_{k^*} = a$ and proceed as usual for all the other users. We therefore only need to explain how to generate the group public key and to deal with oracle queries involving this user.

To avoid confusion with the elements provided in the EDDH instance, we will denote the generators of $\mathbb{G}_1$ and $\mathbb{G}_2$ in our group public key by respectively Y_0 and $\widetilde{Y}_0$. Let $k = \lfloor \frac{n^2}{t^*} \rfloor$. We note that we have $k \geq n$ and $0 < n^2 - kt^* < n$ as $t^* \in [1, n]$. This in particular implies that $n^2 + k(t - t^*) \notin]n^2 - n, n^2 + n[\ \forall t \neq t^*$.

First, the reduction $\mathcal{R}$ generates a random $x \in \mathbb{Z}_p$ and define the elements of the public key as follows:

- $(Y_0, \widetilde{Y}_0) \leftarrow (g^{c^{n^2-kt^*}}, \widetilde{g}^{c^{n^2-kt^*}})$
- $\widetilde{X} \leftarrow (\widetilde{g}^{c^{n^2-kt^*}})^x$;
- $\widetilde{Y}_i \leftarrow \widetilde{g}^{c^{n^2+k(i-t^*)}}, \forall 1 \leq i \leq n$;
- $Y_i \leftarrow g^{c^{n^2+k(i-t^*)}}, \forall i \in [1, n] \cup [n + 2, 2n]$.

We note that all the necessary elements are provided in the EDDH instance, no matter the value of t^*, thanks to the definition of k. $\mathcal{R}$ can now answer all the oracle queries involving k^*:

- $\mathcal{O}\mathtt{Add}$: As explained above, $\mathcal{R}$ implicitly defines $\mathsf{sk}_{k^*} = a$ and then issues a signature $(\sigma_1, \sigma_2) \leftarrow ((Y_0)^r, [(Y_0)^x \cdot (\prod_{i\in\mathcal{T}_k} Y_i)^a]^r)$ for some random r. All the involved elements are provided in the EDDH instance.
- $\mathcal{O}\mathtt{Cor}$: Since Game 3, we know that this oracle is not used on k^*, so $\mathcal{R}$ can answer any such queries.
- $\mathcal{O}\mathtt{Sign}$: A group signature issued at time period i on behalf of k^* is a derived signature for $\mathcal{I} = \{i\}$ along with a non-interactive proof of knowledge of $\mathsf{sk}_{k^*} = a$. As the latter can be simulated, it only remains to explain how to generate the derived signature $\sigma_\mathcal{I} = (\sigma'_1, \sigma'_2, \sigma'_3, \widetilde{\sigma}')$.
  The reduction generates a random r and s and acts as if the scalar $t = s - \sum_{j\in\mathcal{T}_k\setminus\{i\}} a \cdot c^{k\cdot j}$, leading to:
  - $\sigma'_1 \leftarrow (Y_0)^r$;
  - $\sigma'_2 \leftarrow (Y_0^{(s+(x+a\cdot c^{k\cdot i})})^r$;
  - $\widetilde{\sigma}' \leftarrow (\widetilde{Y}_0)^t \cdot \prod_{j\in\mathcal{T}_k\setminus\{i\}} \widetilde{Y}_j^a = (\widetilde{Y}_0)^s$
  - $\sigma'_3 \leftarrow [Y_{n+1-i}^t \cdot \prod_{j\in\mathcal{T}_k\setminus\{i\}} Y_{n+1-i+j}^a]^{c_i} = Y_{n+1-i}^{s\cdot c_i}$

  where $c_i \leftarrow \mathtt{H}(\sigma'_1||\sigma'_2||\widetilde{\sigma}'||\mathcal{I}||i)$. All these values can be generated from our EDDH instance. We note that both r and t are correctly distributed as s is random. Our reduction then returns the resulting signature $\sigma_\mathcal{I}$ along with a simulated proof of knowledge (c, s').

- $\mathcal{O}$Revoke: Since Game 3, we know that this oracle is not queried on a list of users containing k^* for the time period t^*. If $\mathtt{RL}_t$ does not contain k^*, then $\mathcal{R}$ proceeds as usual. Else, this means that k^* is revoked for a time period $t \neq t^*$ and $\mathcal{R}$ then returns $\widetilde{Y}_t^a = \widetilde{g}^{a \cdot c^{n^2+k(t-t^*)}}$.
- $\mathcal{O}$Open : we proceed as explained in Game 4.
- $\mathcal{O}\mathtt{Ch}_b$: Since Game 3, we know that $\mathcal{R}$ must return a group signature on behalf of k^* for the time period t^*. We set $\sigma_1' = (Y_0)^b$ (which implicitly defines $r = b$) and acts as if $t = \frac{d}{c^{n^2-kt^*}} - \sum_{j \in \mathcal{T}_k \setminus \{t^*\}} a \cdot c^{k \cdot j}$. This gives us:
  - $\widetilde{\sigma}' \leftarrow (\widetilde{Y}_0)^t \cdot \prod_{j \in \mathcal{T}_k \setminus \{t^*\}} \widetilde{Y}_j^a = \widetilde{g}^d$;
  - $\sigma_3' \leftarrow [Y_{n+1-t^*}^t \cdot \prod_{j \in \mathcal{T}_k \setminus \{t^*\}} Y_{n+1-t^*+j}^a]^{c_{t^*}} = (g^{c^{k(n+1-t^*)}})^{d \cdot c_{t^*}}$.

  Moreover we set $\sigma_2' = (Y_0^b)^x \cdot g^z$.
  First, note that σ_1' is perfectly distributed. All the required elements are provided in the EDDH instance, in particular because $n^2 - k \cdot t^* < n$. There are then only two cases. If $z = a \cdot b \cdot c^{n^2} + b \cdot d$, then we have $\sigma_2' = (\sigma_1')^{t + (x + a \cdot c^{k \cdot t^*} + \sum_{j \in \mathcal{T}_k \setminus \{t^*\}} a \cdot c^{k \cdot j})}$ and we are playing Game 4. If z is random then σ_1' and σ_2' are random and independent elements and we are playing Game 5. We then have $\epsilon_4 \leq \mathtt{Adv}^{\mathsf{EDDH}}(\mathcal{A}) + \epsilon_5$.

In the end, we have $\frac{\epsilon}{n \cdot q} \leq \mathtt{Adv}^{nf}(\mathcal{A}) + \mathtt{Adv}^{\mathsf{EDDH}}(\mathcal{A}) + \epsilon_5$ with a negligible ϵ_5, which concludes our proof.

Proof of Non-frameability. Intuitively, as our group signatures contain a proof of knowledge of the user's secret key, any adversary framing an honest user must have first recovered his secret key. We will use this fact to solve the SDL problem.

Indeed, let $(g, g^a) \in \mathbb{G}_1$ and $(\widetilde{g}, \widetilde{g}^a) \in \mathbb{G}_2$ be a SDL instance. We make a guess on k^*, the honest user that $\mathcal{A}$ aims to frame and implicitly sets his secret key $\mathsf{sk}_{k^*} = a$. We abort if this guess is wrong.

By using g^a and $\widetilde{g}^a$, and by simulating the proof of knowledge of a, we can perfectly simulate the Join protocol. We then explain how we can deal with $\mathcal{O}$Sign queries for a time period i. Our reduction $\mathcal{R}$ generates random $u, v \xleftarrow{\$} \mathbb{Z}_p$ and computes $\sigma_1' \leftarrow g^u$ and $\sigma_2' \leftarrow g^{u(v+x)} \cdot (g^a)^{u \cdot y^i}$, which sets $t = v - \sum_{j \in \mathcal{T}_k \setminus \{i\}} a \cdot y^j$ in the Derive process. It then remains to send $\widetilde{\sigma}' = \widetilde{g}^v$ and $\sigma_3' = Y_{n+1-i}^{v \cdot c_i}$, where $c_i \leftarrow \mathtt{H}(\sigma_1' || \sigma_2' || \widetilde{\sigma}' || \mathcal{I} || i)$ along with a simulated proof of knowledge.

Eventually, the adversary returns a group signature $\sigma = (\sigma_1, \sigma_2, \sigma_3, \widetilde{\sigma}, c, s)$ for a time period i that can be traced back to k^* which means that $e(\sigma_1, \widetilde{g}^a) = [e(\sigma_2, \widetilde{g}) \cdot e(\sigma_1^{-1}, \widetilde{X} \cdot \widetilde{\sigma})]^{y^{-i}}$. Therefore, we have $e(\sigma_1, \widetilde{Y}_i^a) = e(\sigma_2, \widetilde{g}) \cdot e(\sigma_1^{-1}, \widetilde{X} \cdot \widetilde{\sigma})$ and thus $e(\sigma_1, \widetilde{X} \cdot \widetilde{\sigma} \cdot \widetilde{Y}_i^a) = e(\sigma_2, \widetilde{g})$. The proof of knowledge contained in σ is then a proof of knowledge of a that $\mathcal{R}$ can extract to solve the SDL problem.

Any adversary $\mathcal{A}$ succeeding against the non-frameability of our scheme with probability ϵ can then be used to solve the SDL problem with probability $\frac{\epsilon}{q}$, where q is a bound on the number of group members.

Proof of Traceability. A successful adversary $\mathcal{A}$ against traceability returns a valid group signature for a time period t that either foils the opening process (*i.e.* Open returns $\perp$) or that is traced back to a user k that is inactive at this time period (*i.e.* $t \notin \mathcal{T}_k$). We show in this proof that both cases lead to a forgery against the underlying redactable signature scheme Σ.

We construct a reduction $\mathcal{R}$ that acts as an adversary in the unforgeability experiment for Σ, with the goal to output a valid forgery by using $\mathcal{A}$. $\mathcal{R}$ then gets a public key pk that it sets as the group public key. To answer $\mathcal{O}\mathtt{J}_{GM}$ query, $\mathcal{R}$ simply extracts the user's secret signing key from the proof of knowledge and then queries the signing oracle for Σ. All the other queries are trivial to address as $\mathcal{R}$ does not need to know the secret key (x, y). In the end, $\mathcal{A}$ returns a valid group signature $\sigma = (\sigma_{\{t\}}, c, s)$ that corresponds to one of the two cases mentioned above. In all cases, the fact that σ is valid implies that $\sigma_{\{t\}}$ is a valid derived signature for the subset $\{t\}$ and on some message m_t whose knowledge is proven by (c, s). We can then extract m_t from this proof and distinguish two cases. In all cases $m_t \neq 0$, otherwise the group signature would be rejected by the verification algorithm.

- Case 1: Open returns $\perp$ on σ. As this algorithm tests whether $m_t = \mathsf{sk}_k$ for every registered member k, this means that $m_t \notin \mathsf{L}_t = \{0, \{\mathsf{sk}_k\}_k\}$. However, every query to the signing oracle of Σ was on sets of messages $\{m'_i\}_{i=1}^n$ with $m'_i \in \mathsf{L}_t$. This means that $\sigma_{\{t\}}$ and m_t constitute a valid forgery against Σ.
- Case 2: Open returns k with $t \notin \mathcal{T}_k$. This case means that $m_t = \mathsf{sk}_k$. However, as $t \notin \mathcal{T}_k$, $\mathcal{R}$ has queried for this user a signature on a set $\{m'_i\}_{i=1}^n$ with $m'_t = 0$. Therefore, here again, $\sigma_{\{t\}}$ and m_t necessarily constitute a forgery against Σ.

Both cases then lead to a forgery against Σ. An adversary against the traceability of our construction can then be used to attack the unforgeability of Σ with the same success probability, which concludes our proof.

6 Efficiency

6.1 Redactable Signature

We compare in Table 1 the efficiency of our unlinkable redactable signature with the recent one from [22]. Regarding the public key and the signature sizes, the comparison is provided both in terms of group elements and in bits, by implementing our bilinear groups using the BLS12 curve from ZCash [7]. The latter corresponds to a 128-bits security level, yielding elements of 256 bits ($\mathbb{Z}_p$), 382 bits ($\mathbb{G}_1$), 763 bits ($\mathbb{G}_2$) and 4572 bits ($\mathbb{G}_1$).

Table 1 shows that the main features of these two schemes are essentially the same (constant size derived signature, $O(k)$ verification complexity, etc.) except in the case of the public key. In [22], pk contains $O(n^2)$ elements whereas it only contains $O(n)$ elements in our scheme. The concrete improvement is thus extremely significant, except for very small values of n.

Table 1. Complexity of our redactable rignature scheme and the one from [22]. The costs of `Derive` and `Verify` are provided for a set $\{m_i\}_{i \in \mathcal{I}}$ of k elements. Here, H denotes the evaluation of a hash function, r_i denotes the generation of a random element in $\mathbb{G}_i$, e_i denotes an exponentiation in $\mathbb{G}_i$, for $i \in \{1, 2\}$, and p_k denotes an equation involving k pairings.

	pk	σ	Sign	Derive	Verify
[22]	$\frac{n^2+n+2}{2}\mathbb{G}_1 + n\mathbb{G}_2$ $= 191(n^2+n+2)$ bits	$2\mathbb{G}_1 + 2\mathbb{G}_2 = 2290$ bits	$1\mathsf{r}_2 + 1\mathsf{e}_2$	$2(n-k+1)\mathsf{e}_1$ $+3\mathsf{e}_2$	$k\mathsf{e}_1 + 2\mathsf{p}_2$
Ours	$(1+2n)\mathbb{G}_1 + (n+1)\mathbb{G}_2$ $= 382(4n+3)$ bits	$3\mathbb{G}_1 + 1\mathbb{G}_2$ $= 1909$ bits	$1\mathsf{r}_1 + 1\mathsf{e}_1$	$2(n+1)\mathsf{e}_1 + k\mathsf{H}$ $+(n-k+1)\mathsf{e}_2$	$k(\mathsf{e}_1 + \mathsf{e}_2 + \mathsf{H})$ $+2\mathsf{p}_2$

Table 2. Size complexities of our group signature scheme and [13]. `Update` here refers to the information (called expiration information in [13]) required to update the group signing key at each time period whereas `RL` is the size of the revocation list (only required by the verifiers) to revoke R users. We use the same notations as in the previous table and define $m = \mathtt{log}\ n$.

	pk	usk	Update	RL	σ
[13]	$8\mathbb{G}_1 + 3\mathbb{G}_2 = 5345$ bits	$1\mathbb{Z}_p +$ $(1\mathbb{G}_1 + 2\mathbb{Z}_p)m$ $= 256 + 894m$ bits	$1\mathbb{G}_1 +$ $(1\mathbb{G}_1 + 2\mathbb{Z}_p)m$ $= 382 + 894m$ bits	$R(2\mathbb{G}_1 + 1\mathbb{G}_2)$ $= 1527R$ bits	$6\mathbb{G}_1 + 1\mathbb{G}_2 + 11\mathbb{Z}_p$ $= 5871$ bits
Ours	$(1+2n)\mathbb{G}_1$ $+(n+1)\mathbb{G}_2$ $= 382(4n+3)$ bits	$2\mathbb{G}_1 + \mathbb{Z}_p = 1020$ bits	-	$R\mathbb{G}_2 1.9\,cm$ $= 763R$ bits	$3\mathbb{G}_1 + 1\mathbb{G}_2 + 2\mathbb{Z}_p$ $= 2421$ bits

6.2 Group Signature with Time-Bound Keys

We compare in Tables 2 and 3 the efficiency of our construction with the one of the most efficient scheme [13] from the state-of-the-art, using the same bilinear groups as above. We nevertheless note that this comparison has some limitations as our schemes do not have exactly the same features. For example, we allow $\mathcal{O}$`Open` queries in our anonymity experiment (hence achieving so-called CCA anonymity) contrarily to [13], but have a less efficient opening process. Similarly, our signing key can be associated with any set of time periods (thus offering a better granularity) and do not need to be updated, contrarily to [13], but we need a larger group public key. We also rely on different computational assumptions. In all cases, these tables show that our whole authentication process (issuance of group signature and verification) is more efficient regarding both computational complexity and the size of the elements. We believe this is a very interesting feature of our scheme as this authentication process is the usual bottleneck of use-cases involving group signatures.

As several parameters depend on n, it might be interesting to evaluate the concrete complexity in real-world scenarios. For example, in the case of a transit pass, it seems reasonable to consider time periods of one day for efficient revocation. A value $n \sim 1000$ allows then to issue group signing keys for the next three years. Such a value of n only impacts our public key, that would represent 191 KB, which is within the reach of any smartphone. If this is a problem in more constrained environments, we note that this large public key is only necessary

Table 3. Computational complexities of our group signature scheme and [13].

	`Sign`	`Verify`
[13]	$23\mathsf{e}_1 + 1\mathsf{e}_2 + 1\mathsf{p}_6 + 1\mathsf{p}_5 + \mathsf{H}$	$24\mathsf{e}_1 + 1\mathsf{p}_2 + 2\mathsf{p}_8 + \mathsf{H}$
Ours	$6\mathsf{e}_1 + 2\mathsf{e}_2 + 2\mathsf{H} + 1\mathsf{p}_1$	$3\mathsf{e}_1 + 1\mathsf{p}_3 + 2\mathsf{H} + 2\mathsf{p}_2$

to run `Derive`. In an alternative solution, the group manager could simply send, for each time period, the elements $\prod_{j\in\overline{\mathcal{I}}} \widetilde{Y}_j$, $\prod_{j\in\overline{\mathcal{I}}} Y_{n+1-i+j}$ and Y_{n+1-i} that are sufficient, for all group members, to run this algorithm. This would dramatically reduce the size of the public key for the group members and for the verifiers. This would not be a disadvantage compared to [13] as the latter already requires to send (larger) update information at each time period.

Conclusion

In this paper, we have proposed an extension of group signature with time-bound keys that allows for a better revocation granularity while removing the need to update member's secret keys at each time period. This has two important practical consequences. Firstly, by providing a way to precisely limit the signing rights of a group member we make group signature even more suitable for real-world applications, as most of the latter are unlikely to grant unlimited access to users. This in particular limits the need for premature revocation whose complexity increases with the number of revoked members. Secondly, this simplifies key management for both the group manager (that no longer needs to publish expiration information at the beginning of each period) and the group members (that no longer need to recover this information).

We have also shown in this paper that we can implement such a complex primitive with remarkable efficiency. Our group signatures are indeed only 300 Bytes long, which is rather surprising as (efficient) revocation for group signature is usually quite hard to achieve. This was made possible by a variant of a recent redactable signature scheme that we have introduced and that we believe to be of independent interest.

Acknowledgement. The author thanks R. Kabaleeshwaran for pointing out that a previous version of the EDDH assumption did not hold. The author is grateful for the support of the ANR through project ANR-16-CE39-0014 PERSOCLOUD and project ANR-18-CE-39-0019-02 MobiS5.

References

1. AlLee, G.: EPID for IoT Identity (2016). https://img.en25.com/Web/McAfeeE10BuildProduction/a6dd7393-63f8-4c08-b3aa-89923182a7e5_EPID_Overview_Public_2016-02-08.pdf

2. Barki, A., Desmoulins, N., Gharout, S., Traoré, J.: Anonymous attestations made practical. In: Noubir, G., Conti, M., Kasera, S.K. (eds.) WiSec 2017 (2017)
3. Bellare, M., Shi, H., Zhang, C.: Foundations of group signatures: the case of dynamic groups. In: Menezes, A. (ed.) CT-RSA 2005. LNCS, vol. 3376, pp. 136–153. Springer, Heidelberg (2005). https://doi.org/10.1007/978-3-540-30574-3_11
4. Bernhard, D., Fuchsbauer, G., Ghadafi, E., Smart, N.P., Warinschi, B.: Anonymous attestation with user-controlled linkability. Int. J. Inf. Secur. **12**, 219–249 (2013)
5. Boneh, D., Drijvers, M., Neven, G.: Compact multi-signatures for smaller blockchains. In: Peyrin, T., Galbraith, S. (eds.) ASIACRYPT 2018. LNCS, vol. 11273, pp. 435–464. Springer, Cham (2018). https://doi.org/10.1007/978-3-030-03329-3_15
6. Boneh, D., Shacham, H.: Group signatures with verifier-local revocation. In: Atluri, V., Pfitzmann, B., McDaniel, P. (eds.) ACM CCS 2004, pp. 168–177. ACM Press, October 2004
7. Bowe, S.: BLS12-381: New zk-SNARK Elliptic Curve Construction (2017). https://electriccoin.co/blog/new-snark-curve/
8. Boyen, X.: The uber-assumption family. In: Galbraith, S.D., Paterson, K.G. (eds.) Pairing 2008. LNCS, vol. 5209, pp. 39–56. Springer, Heidelberg (2008). https://doi.org/10.1007/978-3-540-85538-5_3
9. Camenisch, J., Dubovitskaya, M., Haralambiev, K., Kohlweiss, M.: Composable and modular anonymous credentials: definitions and practical constructions. In: Iwata, T., Cheon, J.H. (eds.) ASIACRYPT 2015, Part II. LNCS, vol. 9453, pp. 262–288. Springer, Heidelberg (2015). https://doi.org/10.1007/978-3-662-48800-3_11
10. Chaum, D., van Heyst, E.: Group signatures. In: Davies, D.W. (ed.) EUROCRYPT 1991. LNCS, vol. 547, pp. 257–265. Springer, Heidelberg (1991). https://doi.org/10.1007/3-540-46416-6_22
11. Chu, C.-K., Liu, J.K., Huang, X., Zhou, J.: Verifier-local revocation group signatures with time-bound keys. In: Youm, H.Y., Won, Y. (eds.) ASIACCS 2012, pp. 26–27. ACM Press, May 2012
12. Desmoulins, N., Lescuyer, R., Sanders, O., Traoré, J.: Direct anonymous attestations with dependent basename opening. In: Gritzalis, D., Kiayias, A., Askoxylakis, I. (eds.) CANS 2014. LNCS, vol. 8813, pp. 206–221. Springer, Cham (2014). https://doi.org/10.1007/978-3-319-12280-9_14
13. Emura, K., Hayashi, T., Ishida, A.: Group signatures with time-bound keys revisited: a new model and an efficient construction. In: Karri, R., Sinanoglu, O., Sadeghi, A.-R., Yi, X. (eds.) ASIACCS 2017, pp. 777–788. ACM Press, April 2017
14. Galbraith, S.D., Paterson, K.G., Smart, N.P.: Pairings for cryptographers. Discret. Appl. Math. **156**(16), 3113–3121 (2008)
15. Libert, B., Mouhartem, F., Nguyen, K.: A lattice-based group signature scheme with message-dependent opening. In: Manulis, M., Sadeghi, A.-R., Schneider, S. (eds.) ACNS 2016. LNCS, vol. 9696, pp. 137–155. Springer, Cham (2016). https://doi.org/10.1007/978-3-319-39555-5_8
16. Libert, B., Peters, T., Yung, M.: Group signatures with almost-for-free revocation. In: Safavi-Naini, R., Canetti, R. (eds.) CRYPTO 2012. LNCS, vol. 7417, pp. 571–589. Springer, Heidelberg (2012). https://doi.org/10.1007/978-3-642-32009-5_34
17. Libert, B., Peters, T., Yung, M.: Scalable group signatures with revocation. In: Pointcheval, D., Johansson, T. (eds.) EUROCRYPT 2012. LNCS, vol. 7237, pp. 609–627. Springer, Heidelberg (2012). https://doi.org/10.1007/978-3-642-29011-4_36

18. McDonald, K.L.: The landscape of pointcheval-sanders signatures: Mapping to polynomial-based signatures and beyond. IACR Cryptology ePrint Archive 2020:450 (2020)
19. Navigo (2020). https://www.iledefrance-mobilites.fr/titres-et-tarifs/liste?d=forfaits
20. Pointcheval, D., Sanders, O.: Short randomizable signatures. In: Sako, K. (ed.) CT-RSA 2016. LNCS, vol. 9610, pp. 111–126. Springer, Cham (2016). https://doi.org/10.1007/978-3-319-29485-8_7
21. Pointcheval, D., Sanders, O.: Reassessing security of randomizable signatures. In: Smart, N.P. (ed.) CT-RSA 2018. LNCS, vol. 10808, pp. 319–338. Springer, Cham (2018). https://doi.org/10.1007/978-3-319-76953-0_17
22. Sanders, O.: Efficient redactable signature and application to anonymous credentials. In: Kiayias, A., Kohlweiss, M., Wallden, P., Zikas, V. (eds.) PKC 2020. LNCS, vol. 12111, pp. 628–656. Springer, Cham (2020). https://doi.org/10.1007/978-3-030-45388-6_22
23. Sanders, O.: Improving revocation for group signature with redactable group signature (full version of this work). IACR Cryptology ePrint Archive 2020:856 (2020)
24. Schnorr, C.P.: Efficient identification and signatures for smart cards. In: Quisquater, J.-J., Vandewalle, J. (eds.) EUROCRYPT 1989. LNCS, vol. 434, pp. 688–689. Springer, Heidelberg (1990). https://doi.org/10.1007/3-540-46885-4_68
25. TCG (2015). https://trustedcomputinggroup.org/authentication/

Bootstrapping Fully Homomorphic Encryption over the Integers in Less than One Second

Hilder Vitor Lima Pereira(✉)

COSIC, KU Leuven, Leuven, Belgium

Abstract. One can bootstrap LWE-based fully homomorphic encryption (FHE) schemes in less than one second, but bootstrapping AGCD-based FHE schemes, also known as FHE over the integers, is still very slow. In this work we propose a fast bootstrapping method for FHE over the integers, closing thus this gap between these two types of schemes. We use a variant of the AGCD problem to construct a new GSW-like scheme that can natively encrypt polynomials, then, we show how the single-gate bootstrapping method proposed by Ducas and Micciancio (EUROCRYPT 2015) can be adapted to FHE over the integers using our scheme, and we implement a bootstrapping that, using around 400 MB of key material, runs in less than one second in a common personal computer.

Keywords: Fully homomorphic encryption · AGCD · Bootstrapping

1 Introduction

The two main families of fully homomorphic encryption (FHE) schemes are the ones based on lattices, mainly on the Learning with Errors (LWE) problem, and the schemes over the integers, based on the Approximate Greatest Common Divisor (AGCD) problem. Immediately after the first FHE scheme was proposed by Gentry [Gen09], a scheme over the integers was put forth as a simpler alternative [DGHV10]. Thereafter, several techniques were proposed to improve the efficiency of FHE, and one always found ways to apply those techniques to both families of homomorphic schemes. For example, a method to reduce the noise by scaling a ciphertext and switching the modulus of the ciphertext space, known as modulus switching, was proposed in [BV11] and was soon adapted for schemes over the integers [CNT12]. A technique known as batching, which consists in encrypting several messages into a single ciphertext so that each homomorphic operation acts in parallel on all the encrypted messages, has also been applied to RLWE schemes [BGV12, GHS12] and to schemes over the integers [CCK+13]. Finally, in 2013, Gentry, Sahai, and Waters introduced a FHE scheme that uses a decomposition technique to turn the noise growth of homomorphic products

This paper was written while the author was working at the University of Luxembourg.

J. A. Garay (Ed.): PKC 2021, LNCS 12710, pp. 331–359, 2021.
https://doi.org/10.1007/978-3-030-75245-3_13

roughly additive [GSW13], i.e., the homomorphic product of two ciphertexts c and c' yields a ciphertext c_{mult} whose noise is approximately the noise of c plus the noise of c'. Even this technique was adapted to the schemes over the integers [BBL17].

However, new fast bootstrapping techniques, one of the last great achievements of FHE, has only been availed for (R)LWE schemes: In [ASP14], it was proposed to bootstrap a base scheme whose ciphertext space is $\mathbb{Z}_q$ by using a GSW-like scheme whose plaintext space contains $\mathbb{Z}_q$. Because of the slow noise growth of GSW-like schemes, the final noise accumulated in the refreshed ciphertext is only polynomial in the security parameter λ, therefore, it is not necessary to set large parameters for the base scheme as it was done in previous bootstrapping methods, where the parameters have to allow a scheme to evaluate its own decryption function. Then, in [DM15], the authors found an efficient way to represent $\mathbb{Z}_q$, removed the expensive final step of the method proposed in [ASP14], and implemented a boostrapping that runs in less than one second in a common laptop using a GSW-like scheme based on the RLWE problem. The running times of [DM15] were further improved in [CGGI16] and a base scheme based on LWE was bootstrapped in less than 0.1 s also using a RLWE-based GSW-like scheme. Nevertheless, none of those techniques has been adapted to FHE over the integers.

The main difficulties one has to deal with when trying to create similar bootstrapping methods for FHE over the integers are:

1. One needs an efficient GSW-like scheme based on the AGCD problem. For instance, the GSW-like scheme proposed in [BBL17] is far from practical. The scheme of [Per20] has better running times and, at first glance, seems to be a good choice, however, the size of the bootstrapping keys that it produces is huge.
2. The modulus p is secret: the decryption function of (R)LWE-based schemes is defined modulo a *public* integer q, thus, all the homomorphic operations performed during the bootstrapping can safely disclose q, but for AGCD-based schemes, we have an integer p which is at the same time the modulus and the secret key, hence, the bootstrapping must hide p.
3. The modulus p is exponentially large in λ: in (R)LWE-based schemes, one can set the modulus q to be just polynomially large in the security parameter, while in FHE over the integers we have $p \in \Omega(2^\lambda)$, and the fast bootstrapping of [DM15] would require the message space of the GSW-like scheme to contain polynomials of degree bigger than p. But then, all the homomorphic operations would take exponential time, since they would be performed by adding and multiplying polynomials of degree $\Omega(2^\lambda)$.

Thus, in this work we address these three issues and propose fast bootstrapping methods for FHE over the integers, aiming then to close the gap between LWE- and AGCD-based schemes. Namely, we introduce a new hardness problem that cannot be easier than the AGCD problem, then we use it to construct an efficient GSW-like scheme that works homomorphically on polynomial rings of the form $\mathbb{Z}_t[x]/\langle f \rangle$. Therewith we show how to perform gate bootstrapping, as in [DM15,CGGI16]. We implemented a proof-of-concept in C++ and refreshed ciphertexts of FHE schemes over the integers in less than one second.

1.1 Overview of Our Techniques and Results

New Underlying Problem and GSW-like Scheme: Our first contribution is to use the AGCD problem to construct a GSW-like homomorphic encryption scheme that operates efficiently and natively on polynomial rings. We remark that given N AGCD instances $c_i := pq_i + r_i$, one can represent them as a polynomial $c(x) := \sum_{i=0}^{N-1} c_i x^i$, which can then be written as $c(x) = pq(x) + r(x)$. Thus, if we extend the AGCD problem to sample polynomials $q(x)$ and $r(x)$ and return $pq(x) + r(x)$, we obtain an equivalent problem. But now, by fixing a polynomial ring R, for example, $R = \mathbb{Z}[x]/\langle x^N + 1\rangle$, and a secret polynomial $k(x) \in R$, we can obtain randomized samples of the form $(pq(x) + r(x))k(x)$. Because we are randomizing a problem that is equivalent to the AGCD, we obtain a problem that cannot be easier than the AGCD problem. We call it Randomized (Polynomial) AGCD (RAGCD) problem. Moreover, as it was noticed in [CP19], solving randomized versions of the AGCD problem seems to be harder than solving the original AGCD problem, therefore, we can select smaller parameters. In particular, each AGCD sample is a γ-bit integer, but in our case each coefficient of the polynomials will be an integer with bit length around γ/N, where N is the degree of $k(x)$. Hence, we can use the RAGCD problem to encrypt a degree-N polynomial m into a degree-N polynomial c whose total bit-length is then $N \cdot \gamma/N = \gamma$, while using the AGCD problem would require one γ-bit ciphertext for each coefficient, resulting in a total of $N\gamma$ bits.

Thus, using the RAGCD problem, we propose a GSW-like scheme that can encrypt a polynomial $m \in R$ in two formats:

- Scalar format: $(pq + r + \alpha m) \cdot k \in R$, for some integer α.
- Vector format: $(p\mathbf{q} + \mathbf{r}) \cdot k + \mathbf{g}m \in R^\ell$, where $\mathbf{g} = (b^0, ..., b^{\ell-1})$ for some $b \in \mathbb{Z}$.

Therewith we can define an efficient mixed homomorphic multiplication from $R \times R^\ell$ to R that is akin to the external product used in [CGGI16]. We notice that the main source of efficiency of the bootstrapping method proposed in [CGGI16] is the use of this external product, hence, we have the first piece of a fast bootstrapping for FHE over the integers.

Fast Bootstrapping for FHE over the Integers: Firstly, notice that simply trying to implement the bootstrapping procedures of [DM15] or [CGGI16] with our scheme would not work, since it would require us to use $N > p \in \Omega(2^\lambda)$, which is not efficient, and it would also leak p. Therefore, to solve these issues related to the size and the privacy of the modulus used in the decryption of AGCD-based schemes, we propose to perform a "hidden approximate modulus switching". Namely, consider a message $m \in \mathbb{Z}_t$ and a ciphertext $c = pq + r + mp/t$ to be bootstrapped. Multiplying c by N/p would switch the modulus, resulting in $c' = Nq + r' + mN/t$, for a potentially small N that could be managed by our scheme. Of course, we cannot do it before refreshing because having access to N/p would leak p. Even if we could perform the modulus switching in a secure way, without revealing p, as in [CNT12], the resulting ciphertext c' would leak the message m, because N is known. Thus, we propose that the product $c \cdot N/p$ be performed as part of the refreshing procedure, so that the secret key p is encrypted in the bootstrapping keys and the resulting ciphertext c' is only produced in an encrypted form.

Essentially, since $y := x^2$ has order N in $R := \mathbb{Z}[x]/\langle x^N + 1\rangle$, we have $y^a \cdot y^b = y^{a+b \bmod N}$, so we can use our GSW-like scheme, which we name GAHE, to work homomorphically over $\mathbb{Z}_N$. Thus, we would like to define the bootstrapping keys as encryptions of $y^{2^i N/p}$ for $0 \leq i < \gamma$, and then, to refresh a γ-bit ciphertext $c = pq + r + mp/t$ of the base scheme, we would decompose c in base two obtaining the bits $(c_0, ..., c_{\gamma-1})$ and use the homomorphic mixed product to multiply the bootstrapping keys and obtain a GAHE ciphertext $\tilde{c}$ encrypting

$$\prod_{i=0}^{\gamma-1} y^{c_i 2^i N/p \bmod N} = y^{\sum_{i=0}^{\gamma-1} c_i 2^i N/p \bmod N} = y^{cN/p \bmod N} = y^{r'+mN/t}.$$

After this, we could apply techniques similar to those of [DM15] to transform $\tilde{c}$ into a base scheme ciphertext encrypting m. The problem now is that $2^i N/p$ is not integer. Hence, we encrypt $y^{\lfloor 2^i N/p \rceil}$ instead of $y^{2^i N/p}$. By noticing that $\lfloor 2^i N/p \rceil = 2^i N/p + \epsilon_i$ for some $\epsilon_i \in [-1/2, 1/2]$, we see that computing the same sequence of homomorphic products yields a GAHE encryption of $y^{r'+mN/t+\epsilon}$ for some term ϵ that is not too big. Finally, we propose a functional key-switching to transform this GAHE ciphertext into a base scheme (AGCD-based) encryption of m. By choosing the parameters carefully, the noise term of the final ciphertext is smaller than the initial noise.

Functional Key Switching: We propose a procedure to transform ciphertexts by switching the secret key under which they are encrypted and also applying some function to the message that is encrypted. Namely, given a ciphertext c encrypting a message m under key sk, our functional key-switching procedure produces a new ciphertext $\bar{c}$ that encrypts $\phi(m) \cdot \mathbf{u}$, where $\phi(m)$ is the vector of coefficients of m and $\mathbf{u}$ is an arbitrary vector. Depending on how the parameters are chosen, this procedure can be used to switch the underlying problem from the RAGCD to the original AGCD problem and vice versa; or to reduce the noise of a ciphertext; or to change the message that is encrypted. In our bootstrapping method, the functional key switching is used as follows: for a value $e \in \mathbb{Z}$ depending on the message m, we transform a GAHE encryption of y^e into a ciphertext of the base scheme (the scheme that is being bootstrapped) encrypting m. An overview of our bootstrapping procedure is illustrated in Fig. 1. Furthermore, when compared to other key- or modulus-switching procedures for AGCD-based schemes, as the one proposed in [CNT12], our procedure is more general and seems more straightforward.

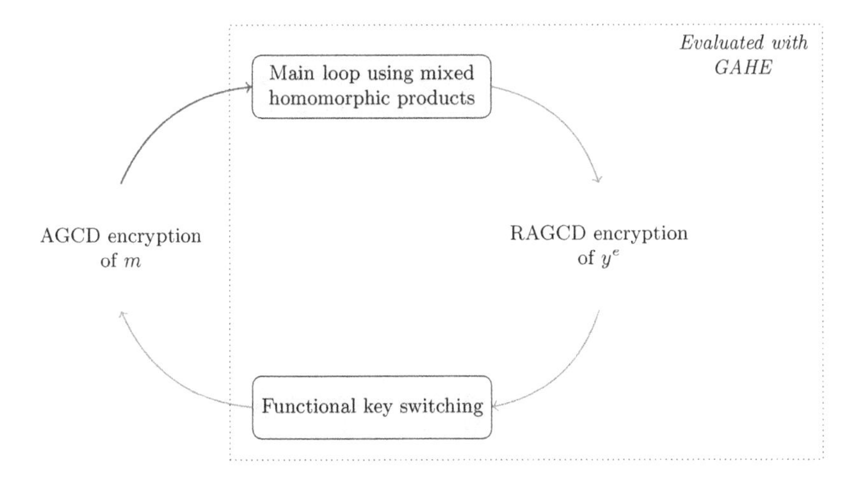

Fig. 1. Two steps of our single-bit bootstrapping. Its input is an encryption of m under the AGCD problem with large noise and the output is an encryption of the same message with less noise.

Implementation and Practical Results: We implemented our bootstrapping procedures in C++ and executed experiments similar to [DM15] and [CGGI16]. Although our implementation is not optimized, we obtained running times and memory consumption similar to [DM15], i.e., we could bootstrap the base scheme in less than one second. For the best of our knowledge, all the previous bootstrapping methods for FHE over the integers took several seconds (or even minutes). Our implementation is publicly available. All the details are shown in Sect. 6.

2 Theoretical Background and Related Works

2.1 Notation and Basic Facts

We use R to denote the cyclotomic ring $\mathbb{Z}[x]/\langle x^N+1\rangle$, where N is a power of two. When we refer to an element f of R, we always mean the unique representative of degree smaller than N, thus, writing $f = \sum_{i=0}^{N-1} f_i x^i$ is unambiguous and we can define the coefficient vector of f as $\phi(f) := (f_0, ..., f_{N-1})$. The anti-circulant matrix of f is the matrix $\boldsymbol{\Phi}(f) \in \mathbb{Z}^{N\times N}$ such that the i-th row is equal to $\phi(x^{i-1}\cdot f)$ for $1 \le i \le N$. It is worth noticing that for $a, b \in \mathbb{Z}$ and $f, g \in R$, we have $\phi(af + bg) = a\phi(f) + b\phi(g)$ and $\phi(f)\boldsymbol{\Phi}(g) = \phi(f \cdot g)$.

We denote vectors by bold lowercase letters and use the infinity-norm $\|\mathbf{v}\| := \|\mathbf{v}\|_\infty$. For any $f \in R$, we define $\|f\| = \|\phi(f)\|$. Notice that $\|fg\| \le N\|f\|\|g\|$. We denote matrices by bold capital letters and use the max-norm $\|\mathbf{A}\| := \|\mathbf{A}\|_{\max} = \max\{|a_{i,j}| : a_{i,j}$ is an entry of $\mathbf{A}\}$. If the entries of both $\mathbf{A}$ and $\mathbf{B}$ belong to R, then, $\|\mathbf{A}\cdot\mathbf{B}\| \le mN\|\mathbf{A}\|\cdot\|\mathbf{B}\|$, where m is the number of rows of $\mathbf{B}$. If at least one of the matrices is integral, then $\|\mathbf{A}\cdot\mathbf{B}\| \le m\|\mathbf{A}\|\cdot\|\mathbf{B}\|$.

Integer intervals are denoted with double brackets, e.g., an integer interval open on a and closed on b is $]\!]a, b]\!] = \mathbb{Z} \cap]a, b]$. The notation $[x]_m$ means the only integer y in $[-m/2, m/2[$ such that $x = y \bmod m$. When applied to vectors or matrices, $[\cdot]_m$ is applied entry-wise, when applied to polynomials, it is applied to each coefficient. We define the column vector $\mathbf{g} := (1, b, b^2, ..., b^{\ell-1})^T$. For any $a \in]\!] - b^\ell, b^\ell [\![$, let $g^{-1}(a)$ be the signed base-b decomposition of a such that the inner product $g^{-1}(a)\mathbf{g}$ is equal to a. For a polynomial f with coefficients in $]\!] - b^\ell, b^\ell [\![$, we define $g^{-1}(f) := \sum_{i=0}^{\deg(f)} g^{-1}(f_i)x^i$. Thus, $g^{-1}(f)\mathbf{g} = f$. At some points, instead of writing $r + \lfloor p/t \rceil m$ with $r \in \mathbb{Z}$, we can simply write $r' + mp/t$. In such cases, we are supposing that $r' = r - \epsilon m \in \mathbb{Q}$, where $\lfloor p/t \rceil = p/t - \epsilon$.

2.2 Approximate-GCD Problem

The Approximate Greatest Common Divisor problem (also known as Approximate Common Divisor problem, ACD) was introduced in [HG01] and since then it has been used to construct several homomorphic encryption schemes [DGHV10,CCK+13,CS15]. The best known attacks against it run in exponential time [GGM16] and it is believed to be quantumly hard [BBL17]. Moreover, a variant of the problem in which the noise is sampled from a different distribution is equivalent to the LWE problem [CS15]. Now, we define this problem formally:

Definition 1. *Let ρ, η, γ, and p be integers such that $\gamma > \eta > \rho > 0$ and $2^{\eta-1} \leq p \leq 2^\eta$. The distribution $\mathcal{D}_{\gamma,\rho}(p)$, whose support is $[\![0, 2^\gamma[\![$ is defined as*

$$\mathcal{D}_{\gamma,\rho}(p) := \{\text{Sample } q \leftarrow [\![0, 2^\gamma/p\ [\![\text{ and } r \leftarrow]\!] - 2^\rho, 2^\rho[\![\ :\ \text{Output } x := pq + r\}.$$

Definition 2 (AGCD problem). *The (ρ, η, γ)-approximate-GCD problem is the problem of finding p, given arbitrarily many samples from $\mathcal{D}_{\gamma,\rho}(p)$.*

The (ρ, η, γ)-decisional-approximate-GCD problem is the problem of distinguishing between $\mathcal{D}_{\gamma,\rho}(p)$ and $\mathcal{U}([\![0, 2^\gamma[\![)$.

2.3 Related Work

Fast Bootstrapping Using Polynomial Rings. In [DM15], the authors observed that in the polynomial ring $\mathbb{Z}[x]/\langle x^N + 1\rangle$, the element $y := x^{2N/q}$ has order q. Thus, the multiplicative group $\mathcal{G} := \langle y \rangle$ is isomorphic to $\mathbb{Z}_q$, in other words, we can map $a_i \in \mathbb{Z}_q$ to $y^{a_i} \in \mathcal{G}$ and $a_i + a_j \bmod q$ corresponds to $y^{a_i} \cdot y^{a_j} \bmod x^N + 1 = y^{a_i + a_j \bmod q}$. Additionally, representing $\mathbb{Z}_q$ with $\mathcal{G}$ is more efficient than using symmetric groups, as it was proposed in [ASP14], since it allows us to instantiate a GSW-like scheme with the RLWE instead of the LWE problem and to evaluate the decryption function of the base scheme by multiplying low-dimensional polynomial matrices instead of high-dimensional integral matrices.

Then, [DM15] proposes a gate bootstrapping, i.e., they propose a simple base scheme that encrypts one bit and can evaluate one binary gate homomorphically, then it has to be bootstrapped. Thus, evaluating a binary circuit with this scheme requires that we perform the refreshing function after each gate. The binary gates are very efficient as they require only $\Theta(n)$ simple additions modulo q, hence, refreshing the resulting ciphertext is the expensive part. The base scheme uses the LWE problem to encrypt a message m as $\mathbf{c} := (\mathbf{a}, b := \mathbf{as}+e+mq/t \bmod q) \in \mathbb{Z}_q^{n+1}$. The bootstrapping keys are GSW encryptions of the secret key $\mathbf{s}$ essentially as follows: $\mathfrak{K}_{i,j} = \mathsf{GSW.Enc}(y^{-2^i \cdot s_j})$ for $0 \leq i \leq \ell := \lceil \log(q) \rceil$ and $1 \leq j \leq n$. Then, given a ciphertext $\mathbf{c} = (\mathbf{a}, b)$ to be refreshed, we write $\mathbf{a} = (a_1, ..., a_n)$, decompose each a_j in base 2, obtaining $(a_{0,j}, ..., a_{\ell-1,j})$, and the first step consists in using GSW's homomorphic product to compute $b - \mathbf{as} = e + mq/t \bmod q$, i.e.:

$$\mathsf{GSW.Enc}(y^b) \prod_{j=1}^{n} \prod_{0 \leq i < \ell} \mathfrak{K}_{i,j} = \mathsf{GSW.Enc}(y^{b - \sum_{j=1}^{n} a_j s_j \bmod q}).$$

The second step consists in transforming a GSW encryption of $y^{e+mq/t}$ in a base scheme ciphertext encrypting m. Roughly speaking, this is done by taking the coefficient vector of one specific row of the GSW ciphertext and multiplying it by a fixed vector, then, applying a modulus- and a key-switching.

In [CGGI16], the authors noticed that instead of simply using the GSW homomorphic product, which consists in multiplying matrices of polynomials, we can perform the bootstrapping using a mixed product in which one operand is an RLWE ciphertext (thus, a vector) and the other one is a GSW ciphertext (thus, a matrix), resulting then in an RLWE ciphertext (again a vector). The authors called it an external product. This speeds up the bootstrapping since it replaces matrix-matrix products by vector-matrix multiplications.

Notice that in the context of AGCD-based schemes, q would be replaced by a secret $p \in \Omega(2^\lambda)$ and we would need $N \approx p$, thus, the degree of the polynomials encrypted by the GSW-like scheme would be exponentially large. Moreover, since N would be public and $2N \in p\mathbb{Z}$, it would be possible to recover p.

GSW-Like Schemes over the Integers. In [BBL17], the authors use the AGCD problem to construct a GSW-like leveled homomorphic encryption scheme that encrypts a single bit m into a vector $\mathbf{c} := p\mathbf{q} + \mathbf{r} + m\mathbf{g} \in \mathbb{Z}^\gamma$ where $p\mathbf{q}+\mathbf{r} \leftarrow (\mathcal{D}_{\gamma,\rho}(p))^\gamma$ and $\mathbf{g} = (2^0, 2^1, \ldots, 2^{\gamma-1})$. To perform homomorphic products, they define the operator $\mathbf{G}^{-1}(\mathbf{c}) \in \{0,1\}^{\gamma \times \gamma}$ as a matrix such that each column j is $g^{-1}(c_j)$, that is, the binary decomposition of the j-th entry of $\mathbf{c}$. Notice that $\mathbf{g}\mathbf{G}^{-1}(\mathbf{c}) = \mathbf{c}$, thus, two ciphertexts $\mathbf{c}_i := p\mathbf{q}_i + \mathbf{r}_i + m_i\mathbf{g}$ (for $i = 1, 2$) are multiplied homomorphically as

$$\begin{aligned} \mathbf{c}_{mult} &:= \mathbf{c}_1 \mathbf{G}^{-1}(\mathbf{c}_2) \\ &= p\mathbf{q}_1 \mathbf{G}^{-1}(\mathbf{c}_2) + \mathbf{r}_1 \mathbf{G}^{-1}(\mathbf{c}_2) + m_1 \mathbf{g}\mathbf{G}^{-1}(\mathbf{c}_2) \\ &= p\underbrace{(\mathbf{q}_1 \mathbf{G}^{-1}(\mathbf{c}_2) + m_1 \mathbf{q}_2)}_{\mathbf{q}_{mult}} + \underbrace{(\mathbf{r}_1 \mathbf{G}^{-1}(\mathbf{c}_2) + m_1 \mathbf{r}_2)}_{\mathbf{r}_{mult}} + m_1 m_2 \mathbf{g}. \end{aligned}$$

We see that the noise growth due to the homomorphic product is approximately additive, i.e., $\|\mathbf{r}_{mult}\| \leq \left\|\mathbf{r}_1 \mathbf{G}^{-1}(\mathbf{c}_2)\right\| + m_1 \|\mathbf{r}_2\| \leq \gamma \|\mathbf{r}_1\| + \|\mathbf{r}_2\|$. However, this scheme is not practical. Their authors report that performing one single multiplication takes several seconds in a modern CPU. The main reason for this inefficiency is the huge ciphertext expansion, as it encrypts one bit into γ^2 bits and, typically, γ is much bigger than λ.

Trying to amend this issue, in [Per20] it is proposed to expand the message space of [BBL17] so that instead of encrypting only bits, it is possible to encrypt vectors and matrices with non-binary entries. Furthermore, the ciphertexts are randomized with a hidden matrix $\mathbf{K}$, since, as it was observed in [CP19], all the attacks against the AGCD problem become much more expensive when the AGCD samples are multiplied by a random matrix and, thus, one can choose smaller parameters, in particular, one can decrease the size of γ and have better ciphertext expansion. The resulting scheme is a GSW-like leveled homomorphic scheme that can perform operations with matrices and vectors, in particular, it is possible to do homomorphic vector-matrix products. Notice that by using coefficient vectors and circulant matrices to represent elements of R, we can use this scheme to operate homomorphically over R. In particular, we could, in principle, use it in a bootstrapping procedure *à la* [DM15]. However, by doing so, we would encrypt a degree-N polynomial into a matrix ciphertext of dimension $N\ell \times N$, with $\ell = \Theta(\gamma)$, which would yield very large bootstrapping keys.

Hence, we go one step further and propose to randomize the AGCD problem with a random polynomial $k(x)$ instead of a random matrix. Thereby we can encrypt a polynomial of degree N into an ℓ-dimensional vector whose each entry is a degree-N polynomial, gaining thus a factor N. We also define two types of ciphertexts and we provide an efficient homomorphic product between them. This corresponds to the vector-matrix product of [Per20] and to the external product of [CGGI16].

3 Randomized (Polynomial) AGCD Problem

We start by extending the AGCD problem to a problem that is strictly equivalent, but that works on polynomials. Then, we propose to randomize this problem with a hidden polynomial $k(x)$, obtaining thus the underlying problem that will be used in our scheme.

Definition 3 (Underlying distribution of PAGCD). *Let N, ρ, η, γ, and p be integers such that $\gamma > \eta > \rho > 0$ and p is an η-bit integer. The distribution $\mathcal{P}_{N,\gamma,\rho}(p)$, whose support is $[\![0, 2^\gamma - 1]\!]^N$, is defined as*

$$\mathcal{P}_{N,\gamma,\rho}(p) := \left\{ \textit{Sample } c_0, ..., c_{N-1} \leftarrow \mathcal{D}_{\gamma,\rho}(p) : \textit{ Output } c := \sum_{i=0}^{N-1} c_i x^i \right\}.$$

Definition 4 (PAGCD). *The (N, ρ, η, γ)-polynomial-approximate-GCD problem is the problem of finding p, given many samples from $\mathcal{P}_{N,\gamma,\rho}(p)$.*

The (N, ρ, η, γ)-decisional-PAGCD problem is the problem of distinguishing between $\mathcal{P}_{N,\gamma,\rho}(p)$ and $\mathcal{U}([\![0, 2^\gamma[\![^N)$.

Because each coefficient of each polynomial output by $\mathcal{P}_{N,\gamma,\rho}(p)$ is an independent sample of $\mathcal{D}_{\gamma,\rho}(p)$, having N samples of the AGCD problem is the same as having one sample of the PAGCD problem, hence, it is clear that the PAGCD and the original AGCD problem are equivalent.

Now, aiming to choose smaller parameters and following the ideas of [CP19] and [Per20], we propose a randomized version of this problem, but instead of randomizing a vector of AGCD samples with a hidden matrix $\mathbf{K}$, we randomize a sample of $\mathcal{P}_{N,\gamma,\rho}(p)$ with a hidden polynomial k, performing the operations in the ring $R := \mathbb{Z}[x]/\langle f \rangle$, for some f of degree N.

Definition 5 (Underlying distribution of RAGCD). *Let N, ρ, η, γ, and p be integers such that $\gamma > \eta > \rho > 0$ and p has η bits. Let f be a degree-N integral polynomial, $R := \mathbb{Z}[x]/\langle f \rangle$, x_0 be a sample from $\mathcal{D}_{\gamma,\rho}(p)$, and k be an random invertible polynomial of R/x_0R. The distribution $\mathcal{R}_{N,\gamma,\rho,x_0}(p,k)$, whose support is R/x_0R is defined as*

$$\mathcal{R}_{N,\gamma,\rho,x_0}(p,k) := \{\mathit{Sample}\ c \leftarrow \mathcal{P}_{N,\gamma,\rho}(p) :\ \mathit{Output}\ \tilde{c} := c \cdot k \in R/x_0R\}.$$

Definition 6 (RAGCD). *The $(x_0, N, \rho, \eta, \gamma)$-RAGCD problem is the problem of finding p and k, given arbitrarily many samples from $\mathcal{R}_{N,\gamma,\rho,x_0}(p,k)$.*

The $(x_0, N, \rho, \eta, \gamma)$-decisional-RAGCD problem is the problem of distinguishing between $\mathcal{R}_{N,\gamma,\rho,x_0}(p,k)$ and $\mathcal{U}(R/x_0R)$.

We can instantiate this problem using any polynomial ring $\mathbb{Z}[x]/\langle f \rangle$, however, one has to carefully choose the polynomial used as the modulus, in particular, if f is not irreducible in $\mathbb{Z}[x]$, then its factors can lead to attacks on easier instances of the RAGCD problem. In Sect. 6.1, a detailed discussion about the choice of f is presented. For our bootstrapping procedure, we use $f = x^N + 1$ with N being a power of two.

Notice that given many instances of PAGCD problem, we can select one coefficient of any polynomial to be the scalar x_0, then sample a random invertible k, and multiply each PAGCD instance by k in R/x_0R, obtaining thus valid instances of the RAGCD problem. Thus, this problem cannot be easier than the PAGCD problem. Therefore, because the PAGCD and the original AGCD problem are equivalent, the RAGCD problem is not easier than the AGCD problem.

However, for the decisional version of the problems, this argument is not valid, since we would still have to prove that the distribution $\mathcal{U}([\![0, 2^\gamma[\![^N)$ from the decisional-PAGCD problem is mapped to the corresponding distribution $\mathcal{U}(R/x_0R)$ of the decisional-RAGCD. So, in the next lemma, we prove that if we fix $x_0 \geq 2^{\gamma-1}$ and restrict the distribution $\mathcal{R}_{N,\gamma,\rho,x_0}(p,k)$ so that it only randomizes polynomials with coefficients smaller than x_0, then we obtain a distribution that is indistinguishable from $\mathcal{U}(R/x_0R)$ under the hardness of the decisional AGCD problem. In other words, under the decisional-AGCD assumption, this "restricted version" of the decisional-RAGCD assumption holds.

Lemma 1. *Let x_0 be a sample of $\mathcal{D}_{\gamma,\rho}(p)$ such that $x_0 \geq 2^{\gamma-1}$. Let $\mathcal{D}_{<x_0}$ be the distribution obtained by rejecting samples of $\mathcal{D}_{\gamma,\rho}(p)$ that are bigger than or*

equal to x_0. *Let* $\mathcal{R}_{<x_0}$ *be defined as* $\mathcal{R}_{N,\gamma,\rho,x_0}(p,k)$, *but randomizing polynomials with coefficients smaller than* x_0, *that is:*

$$\mathcal{R}_{<x_0} := \left\{ \textit{Sample } c \leftarrow \sum_{i=0}^{N-1} x^i \cdot \mathcal{D}_{<x_0} : \ \textit{Output } \tilde{c} := c \cdot k \in R/x_0R \right\}.$$

Then, distinguishing between $\mathcal{R}_{<x_0}$ *and* $\mathcal{U}(R/x_0R)$ *is computationally hard under the decisional-AGCD assumption.*

Proof. Let $x_0 \geq 2^{\gamma-1}$ be an AGCD sample and $\mathcal{A}$ be a PPT adversary with non-negligible advantage $\mathsf{Adv}(\mathcal{A})$ in distinguishing $\mathcal{R}_{<x_0}$ and $\mathcal{U}(R/x_0R)$. We will show that $\mathcal{A}$ can be used to distinguish between $\mathcal{U}(\mathbb{Z}_{x_0})$ and $\mathcal{D}_{<x_0}$.

Given samples $x_1, ..., x_M$ from $\mathcal{U}(\mathbb{Z}_{x_0})$ or $\mathcal{D}_{<x_0}$, we can sample a polynomial k invertible on R/x_0R, group the samples N by N, represent them as polynomials $c_1, ..., c_{\lfloor M/N \rfloor} \in R$ and multiply by k on R/x_0R, obtaining $\tilde{c}_i := c_i \cdot k \in R/x_0R$. At last, we output $\mathcal{A}(\tilde{c}_1, ..., \tilde{c}_{\lfloor M/N \rfloor})$.

It is clear that if the samples x_i's follow $\mathcal{U}(\mathbb{Z}_{x_0})$, then, each c_i is uniform distributed on R/x_0R. Moreover, because k is invertible modulo x_0, multiplying by it does not change the uniform distribution, thus, $\tilde{c}_i$ follows $\mathcal{U}(R/x_0R)$ as well. On the other hand, if the x_i's are sampled from $\mathcal{D}_{<x_0}$, then $\tilde{c}_i$'s follow $\mathcal{R}_{<x_0}$ by the definition of $\mathcal{R}_{<x_0}$.

Therefore, $\mathcal{A}$ receives inputs following valid distributions and the advantage we have in distinguishing $\mathcal{U}(\mathbb{Z}_{x_0})$ from $\mathcal{D}_{<x_0}$ is also $\mathsf{Adv}(\mathcal{A})$.

However, because $x_0 \geq 2^{\gamma-1}$, from Lemma 3 of (the full version of) [Per20], we know that the distributions $\mathcal{D}_{<x_0}$ and $\mathcal{U}(\mathbb{Z}_{x_0})$ are indistinguishable under the decisional-AGCD assumption, hence, such $\mathcal{A}$ cannot exist. □

4 GSW-Like AGCD-Based Homomorphic Encryption

In this section, we present the GSW-like AGCD-based Homomorphic Encryption (GAHE) scheme that will be used to perform the bootstrapping. First of all, let N be a power of two and $R := \mathbb{Z}[x]/\langle x^N + 1 \rangle$. We start with a basic scheme that can encrypt a polynomial $m \in R$ into a vector $\mathbf{c} \in R^\ell$. Then, by assuming circular security, we extend the definition of the scheme so that we also have scalar ciphertexts. Finally, we define a functional key-switching. For brevity and because in our main applications, the fast bootstrapping procedure, we only use the mixed homomorphic product, we omit the other homomorphic operations, like additions and "vector-vector" product, presenting them only in Appendix A. Furthermore, to ease the presentation, specially the noise-growth analysis, we keep the modulus x_0 private. Hence, the homomorphic operations are performed on R instead of R/x_0R, which means that the bit length of the ciphertext grows. However, in our bootstrapping procedure, this growth is small and independent of the multiplicative depth of the homomorphic evaluation.

- $\mathsf{GAHE.KeyGen}(1^\lambda, N, t, b)$: Choose the parameters η, ρ, and γ. Sample an η-bit random prime p. Sample x_0 from $p \cdot \mathcal{U}([\![1, 2^\gamma/p]\!])$, until $x_0 \geq 2^{\gamma-1}$.

Then, sample k uniformly from R/x_0R until k^{-1} exists over R/x_0R. Define $\ell_0 := \lceil \log_b(2^\gamma) \rceil$ and $\ell := \lceil \ell_0 + \log_b(N) + 1 + \log_b(\ell_0 + \log_b(N) + 1) \rceil$[1]. The public parameters are $\mathsf{params} := \{N, t, \ell, b, \eta, \gamma, \rho\}$ and secret key is $\mathsf{sk} := (p, k, x_0)$.

- $\mathsf{GAHE.EncVec}(\mathsf{sk}, m)$: Given a polynomial $m \in R/tR$, construct a vector $\mathbf{x} := (p\mathbf{q} + \mathbf{r})k \in R^\ell$ by sampling each entry x_i independently from $\mathcal{R}_{N,\gamma,\rho,x_0}(p, k)$, then output the following vector $\mathbf{c}$:

$$\mathbf{c} := [\mathbf{x} + \mathbf{g} \cdot m]_{x_0} \in R^\ell.$$

- $\mathsf{GAHE.DecVec}(\mathsf{sk}, \mathbf{c})$: Let $\alpha := \lfloor p/t \rceil$. Compute $c := \langle g^{-1}([\alpha k]_{x_0}), \mathbf{c} \rangle$ over R/x_0R. Then do $c' := c \cdot k^{-1} \in R/x_0R$ and output

$$\left\lfloor \frac{t \cdot [c']_p}{p} \right\rceil \bmod t.$$

4.1 Assuming Circular Security to Extend the Scheme

In this section we show that, by assuming circular security, we can encrypt an element of R/tR into a single element of R instead of into a vector. We call a ciphertext produced by this new encryption method a scalar ciphertext and the ones produced by the encryption function defined before are vector ciphertexts. Moreover, we define the mixed homomorphic product between a vector and a scalar ciphertext. It is worth noticing that circular security is regarded as a weak assumption and has been used extensively in all types of homomorphic encryption schemes.

Thus, notice that by assuming circular security, we can use $\mathsf{GAHE.EncVec}$ to encrypt $m \cdot k \cdot \lfloor p/t \rceil$, obtaining $\mathbf{c} = (p\mathbf{q} + \mathbf{r})k + (m \cdot k \cdot \lfloor p/t \rceil)\mathbf{g} = (p\mathbf{q} + \mathbf{r} + m \cdot \lfloor p/t \rceil \cdot \mathbf{g})k$. But then, because the first entry of $\mathbf{g}$ is 1, we see that the first entry of $\mathbf{c}$ has the following format: $c_1 = (pq_1 + r_1 + m \cdot \lfloor p/t \rceil)k \in R$. Thus, we can extend our scheme with the following procedures:

- $\mathsf{GAHE.EncScalar}(\mathsf{sk}, m)$: Given a polynomial $m \in R/tR$, let $\alpha := \lfloor p/t \rceil$, sample $x := (pq + r)k \leftarrow \mathcal{R}_{N,\gamma,\rho,x_0}(p, k)$ and output

$$c := [x + m \cdot \alpha \cdot k]_{x_0} \in R.$$

- $\mathsf{GAHE.DecScalar}(\mathsf{sk}, c)$: Output $\left\lfloor \frac{t \cdot [c']_p}{p} \right\rceil \bmod t$ where $c' := c \cdot k^{-1} \in R/x_0R$.
- $\mathsf{GAHE.MultMix}(c, \mathbf{c})$: to perform a homomorphic mixed product, we decompose and multiply the scalar ciphertext c by the vector ciphertext $\mathbf{c}$, outputting the following inner product over R: $c_{mult} := g^{-1}(c) \cdot \mathbf{c} \in R$.

[1] If we were publishing x_0, then the homomorphic operations could be done modulo x_0 and we could set $\ell = \ell_0$, without adding these extra logarithmic terms.

4.2 Correctness of Decryption

In this section we define the noise of a ciphertext and show the necessary conditions for the decryption functions to work.

Definition 7 (Noise of scalar ciphertext). *Let* $c = (pq + r + \lfloor p/t \rceil m)k$ *be a scalar ciphertext encrypting a message* $m \in R/tR$. *We define the noise of* c *as* $\mathsf{err}(c) := [(c \cdot k^{-1} - \lfloor p/t \rceil m) \bmod x_0]_p$. *Notice that* $\mathsf{err}(c)$ *is exactly* r *if* $\|r\| < p/2$.

Definition 8 (Noise of vector ciphertext). *Let* $\mathbf{c} = (p\mathbf{q} + \mathbf{r})k + \mathbf{g}m$ *be a vector encryption of* $m \in R/tR$. *We define the noise of* $\mathbf{c}$ *as* $\mathsf{err}(\mathbf{c}) := [(\mathbf{c} - \mathbf{g}m) \cdot k^{-1} \bmod x_0)]_p$. *Notice that* $\mathsf{err}(\mathbf{c})$ *is* $\mathbf{r}$ *if* $\|\mathbf{r}\| < p/2$.

Lemma 2 (Upper bound on the noises). *Let* $c = (pq + r + \alpha m_1)k \in R$ *be a scalar ciphertext and* $\mathbf{c} = (p\mathbf{q} + \mathbf{r})k + \mathbf{g}m_2 \in R^\ell$ *be a vector ciphertext. Assuming that* $\|\mathsf{err}(c)\|$ *and* $\|\mathsf{err}(\mathbf{c})\|$ *are both smaller than* $p/2$, *it holds that* $\|\mathsf{err}(c)\| = \|r\|$ *and* $\|\mathsf{err}(\mathbf{c})\| = \|\mathbf{r}\|$. *In particular, if* c *and* $\mathbf{c}$ *are fresh ciphertexts, then* $\|\mathsf{err}(c)\| < 2^\rho$ *and* $\|\mathsf{err}(\mathbf{c})\| < 2^\rho$.

Let's first analyze GAHE.DecScalar. Then, the correctness of GAHE.DecVec follows basically by the same argument.

Lemma 3 (Correctness of scalar decryption). *Let* c *be a scalar encryption of* $m \in R/tR$. *If* $\|\mathsf{err}(c)\| < \frac{p}{3t}$, *then* $\mathsf{GAHE.DecScalar}(\mathsf{sk}, c)$ *outputs* m.

Proof. Let $c = (pq+r+\lfloor p/t \rceil m)k$. Consider the polynomial $c' = c \cdot k^{-1} \in R/x_0R$ defined in GAHE.DecScalar. We can write it as $c' = pq' + r + \lfloor p/t \rceil m \in R$. Then, when we perform the reduction modulo p, we obtain $\bar{c} = [r + \lfloor p/t \rceil m]_p = [\mathsf{err}(c) + \lfloor p/t \rceil m]_p = \mathsf{err}(c) + \epsilon + mp/t - pu$ for some $\epsilon, u \in R$ with $\|\epsilon\| \leq 1/2$.

Thus, in the next step of the decryption function, we have

$$\frac{t\bar{c}}{p} = \frac{t(\mathsf{err}(c) + \epsilon)}{p} + m - ut.$$

But because $\|\mathsf{err}(c)\| < \frac{p}{3t}$, we have $\|t(\mathsf{err}(c) + \epsilon)/p\| < 1/3 + \|t\epsilon/p\| < 1/2$. Hence, since $m - ut$ has integer coefficients, the rounding function outputs

$$\left\lfloor \frac{t\bar{c}}{p} \right\rceil = \left\lfloor \frac{t(\mathsf{err}(c) + \epsilon)}{p} \right\rceil + m - ut = m - ut.$$

Therefore, the reduction modulo t indeed gives us m. □

Lemma 4 (Sufficient conditions for correctness of vector decryption). *Let* $\mathbf{c}$ *be a vector encryption of* $m \in R/tR$. *If* $\|\mathsf{err}(\mathbf{c})\| < \frac{p}{3N\ell bt}$, *then* $\mathsf{GAHE.DecVec}(\mathsf{sk}, \mathbf{c})$ *outputs* m.

Proof. Let $\alpha := \lfloor p/t \rceil$. Notice that $\mathsf{GAHE.DecVec}(\mathsf{sk}, \mathbf{c})$ can be rewritten as

1. Compute a scalar encryption of the same message m, i.e., $c := g^{-1}([\alpha k]_{x_0}) \cdot \mathbf{c}$.
2. Output $\mathsf{GAHE.DecScalar}(\mathsf{sk}, c)$.

But by Definitions 7 and 8, we have

$$\mathsf{err}(c) = [(c \cdot k^{-1} - \alpha m \bmod x_0)]_p = [g^{-1}([\alpha k]_{x_0}) \cdot \mathsf{err}(\mathbf{c})]_p.$$

But $\left\|g^{-1}([\alpha k]_{x_0}) \cdot \mathsf{err}(\mathbf{c})\right\| \leq N\ell b \left\|\mathsf{err}(\mathbf{c})\right\| < p/(3t)$. Therefore, the output of $\mathsf{GAHE.DecScalar}(\mathsf{sk}, c)$ is m by Lemma 3. □

4.3 Analysis of Mixed Homomorphic Product

L $\mathbf{c}$ be a vector encryption of v and c be a scalar encryption of s. Also, let $\mathbf{y} := g^{-1}(c) \in R^\ell$. In the definition of $\mathsf{GAHE.MultMix}(c, \mathbf{c})$ we have $c_{mult} := \mathbf{y} \cdot \mathbf{c}$, thus, the following holds:

$$\begin{aligned} c_{mult} &= (p\mathbf{y}\mathbf{q} + \mathbf{y}\mathbf{r})k + \mathbf{y}\mathbf{g}v && \text{(By definition of } \mathbf{c}\text{)} \\ &= (p\mathbf{y}\mathbf{q} + \mathbf{y}\mathbf{r})k + cv && \text{(Because } \mathbf{y}\mathbf{g} = c\text{)} \\ &= (p\underbrace{(\mathbf{y}\mathbf{q} + qv)}_{q_{mult}} + \underbrace{(\mathbf{y}\mathbf{r} + rv)}_{r_{mult}} + \lfloor p/t \rceil sv)k && \text{(By definition of } c\text{)} \end{aligned}$$

Therefore, the mixed homomorphic product takes encryptions of s and v and produces $c_{mult} = (pq_{mult} + r_{mult} + \lfloor p/t \rceil sv)k \in R$, which is a valid scalar encryption of the product of the messages, as expected.

As for the noise growth, we now show that a sequence of n mixed homomorphic products increases the noise just linearly in n.

Lemma 5 (Noise growth of mixed products). *Let $n \in \mathbb{N}^*$. For all $i \in [\![1, n]\!]$, let $\mathbf{c}_i$ be a vector encryption of m_i. Let also c_0 be a scalar encryption of m_0. Assume that B is an upper bound to the norm of the products of plaintexts, i.e., $\left\|\prod_{i=j}^{n} m_i\right\| \leq B$ for $0 \leq j \leq n$. Finally, for $1 \leq i \leq n$, define $c_i :=$ $\mathsf{GAHE.MultMix}(c_{i-1}, \mathbf{c}_i) \in R$ (notice that c_i is a scalar encryption of $\prod_{j=0}^{i} m_j$). Then,*

$$\|\mathsf{err}(c_n)\| < NB \|\mathsf{err}(c_0)\| + \sum_{i=1}^{n} N^2 B\ell b \|\mathsf{err}(\mathbf{c}_i)\|. \quad (1)$$

In particular, if c_0 and all the $\mathbf{c}_i$'s are fresh ciphertexts, then

$$\|\mathsf{err}(c_n)\| < 2N^2 B\ell b n 2^\rho. \quad (2)$$

Proof. By the analysis done above, we know that the term r_i of c_i is $g^{-1}(c_{i-1})\mathbf{r}_i + r_{i-1}m_i$. Hence, the term r_n after n homomorphic products is

$$r_n = r_0 \prod_{i=1}^{n} m_i + \sum_{i=1}^{n} g^{-1}(\mathbf{c}_{i-1})\mathbf{r}_i \left(\prod_{j=i+1}^{n} m_j\right) \in R.$$

Thus,

$$\|r_n\| \leq N \|r_0\| \left\| \prod_{i=1}^{n} m_i \right\| + \sum_{i=1}^{n} N\ell \left\| g^{-1}(\mathbf{c}_i) \right\| \left\| \mathbf{r}_i \left(\prod_{j=i+1}^{n} m_j \right) \right\|$$
$$\leq NB \|r_0\| + \sum_{i=1}^{n} N^2 \ell b B \|\mathbf{r}_i\| .$$

Therefore, Inequality 1 holds. By Lemma 2, if all the operands are fresh ciphertexts, then, $\|r_0\| < 2^\rho$ and $\|\mathbf{r}_i\| < 2^\rho$, and the particular case also holds. □

4.4 Functional Key-Switching

In this section we define a procedure that will play a main role in our bootstrapping, namely, a *functional* key-switching. Therewith we can change the keys and the dimension of the polynomial ring of a ciphertext and at the same time apply some function to the plaintext. That is to say, given two integers N_1 and N_2, we define two polynomial rings $R_i := \mathbb{Z}[x]/\langle x^{N_i} + 1\rangle$. Then, we can transform a scalar ciphertext $c_1 \in R_1$ that encrypts a message $m \in R_1/tR_1$ under key (p_1, k_1) into a ciphertext c_2 encrypting $\phi(m) \cdot \mathbf{u}$ under another key (p_2, k_2) for any $\mathbf{u} \in R_2^{N_1}$, where $\phi(m) \in \mathbb{Z}^{N_1}$ is the coefficient vector of m.

Like the key-switching procedures of LWE-based schemes, our functional key-switching consists in two parts: firstly, we need both private keys to generate a functional key-switching key; then, using this key, we can publicly perform the transformation.

- $\mathsf{FuncKeySwtGen}(\mathsf{sk}_1, \mathsf{sk}_2, \mathsf{params}, \mathbf{u})$: given $\mathsf{params} = (N_1, N_2, \tilde{b}, \tilde{\ell}, \tilde{\gamma}, \tilde{\rho})$, secret keys $\mathsf{sk}_i = (p_i, k_i) \in \mathbb{Z} \times R_i$, and a vector $\mathbf{u} \in R_2^{N_1}$, proceed as follows:
  1. Define $\mathbf{g}_{\tilde{b}} := (\tilde{b}^0, ..., \tilde{b}^{\tilde{\ell}-1}) \in \mathbb{Z}^{\tilde{\ell}\times 1}$ and $\mathbf{G} = \mathbf{I}_{N_1} \otimes \mathbf{g}_{\tilde{b}} \in \mathbb{Z}^{N_1\tilde{\ell}\times N_1}$.
  2. Let $\mathbf{v} := \left\lfloor \frac{p_2}{p_1} \mathbf{G}\boldsymbol{\Phi}(k_1^{-1})\mathbf{u} \right\rceil \in R_2^{N_1\tilde{\ell}}$, where p_2/p_1 must be interpreted as a fraction in $\mathbb{Q}$ and the inverse of k_1 is computed on R_1/p_1R_1.
  3. Sample M from $p_2 \cdot \mathcal{U}([0, 2^{\tilde{\gamma}}/p_2])$.
  4. Sample $\mathbf{y}$ from $(\mathcal{P}_{N_2,\tilde{\gamma},\tilde{\rho}}(p_2))^{N_1\tilde{\ell}}$.
  5. Output $\mathsf{swk} := [(\mathbf{y} + \mathbf{v}) \cdot k_2]_M$. Notice that the output is of the form

$$\left(p_2\mathbf{q} + \mathbf{r} + \left\lfloor \frac{p_2}{p_1} \mathbf{G}\boldsymbol{\Phi}(k_1^{-1})\mathbf{u} \right\rceil\right) \cdot k_2 \in R_2^{N_1\tilde{\ell}}.$$

- $\mathsf{FuncKeySwt}(c_1, \mathsf{swk})$: Given a scalar ciphertext $c_1 \in R_1$ and a functional key-switching key $\mathsf{swk} \in R_2^{N_1\tilde{\ell}}$, define $\mathbf{z} := \phi(c_1) \in \mathbb{Z}^{N_1}$, decompose each entry of $\mathbf{z}$ in base $\tilde{b}$ as $\mathbf{w} := (g^{-1}(z_1), ..., g^{-1}(z_{N_1})) \in \mathbb{Z}^{N_1\tilde{\ell}}$, and output $c_2 := \mathbf{w} \cdot \mathsf{swk} \in R_2$.

Lemma 6 (Correctness of functional key switching). *Let* $\mathbf{u} \in R_2^{N_1}$, $\mathsf{sk}_i := (p_i, k_i) \in \mathbb{Z} \times R_i$, *and* $\mathsf{params} := (N_1, N_2, \tilde{b}, \tilde{\ell}, \tilde{\gamma}, \tilde{\rho})$. *Let also*

$\mathsf{swk} := \mathsf{FuncKeySwtGen}(\mathsf{sk}_1, \mathsf{sk}_2, \mathsf{params}, \mathbf{u})$. *Then, for any* $c_1 \in R_1$ *encrypting* $m \in R_1/tR_1$ *under key* sk_1, *it holds that* $c_2 := \mathsf{FuncKeySwt}(c_1, \mathsf{swk})$ *is a valid encryption of* $\phi(m) \cdot \mathbf{u} \in R_2$ *under key* sk_2, *if* $\|c_1\| < \tilde{b}^{\tilde{\ell}}$. *Moreover, the noise term of* c_2 *is bounded as follows:*

$$\|\mathsf{err}(c_2)\| \leq \tilde{\ell} N_1 \tilde{b} 2^{\tilde{\rho}} + 2^{\eta_2 - \eta_1 + 2} N_1 \|\mathbf{u}\| \|\mathsf{err}(c_1)\|$$

where η_i *is the bit length of* p_i.

Proof. Let $c_1 = (p_1 q_1 + r_1 + \alpha_1 m) k_1 \in R_1$, where $\alpha_1 := \lfloor p_1/t \rceil$. Notice that $\mathbf{w}$ defined in FuncKeySwt satisfies $\mathbf{wG} = \phi(c_1)$ because $\|c_1\| < \tilde{b}^{\tilde{\ell}}$. Moreover, $\phi(c_1)\boldsymbol{\Phi}(k_1^{-1}) = p_1 \mathbf{q}_1 + \phi(r_1) + \alpha_1 \phi(m)$. Therefore, the output of FuncKeySwt is

$$\begin{aligned} c_2 &= (p_2 \mathbf{wq} + \mathbf{wr} + \mathbf{w}\epsilon + \frac{p_2}{p_1} \mathbf{wG}\boldsymbol{\Phi}(k_1^{-1})\mathbf{u}) \cdot k_2 && \text{(For some } \|\epsilon\| \leq 1/2) \\ &= (p_2 \mathbf{wq} + \mathbf{w}(\mathbf{r} + \epsilon) + \frac{p_2}{p_1}(p_1 \mathbf{q}_1 + \phi(r_1) + \alpha_1 \phi(m))\mathbf{u}) k_2 \\ &= (p_2 q_2 + \mathbf{w}(\mathbf{r} + \epsilon) + \frac{p_2}{p_1}(\phi(r_1) + \alpha_1 \phi(m))\mathbf{u}) \cdot k_2 && \text{(For } q_2 := \mathbf{wq} + \mathbf{q}_1 \mathbf{u}) \\ &= (p_2 q_2 + \mathbf{w}(\mathbf{r} + \epsilon) + \frac{p_2}{p_1}(\phi(r_1) + \epsilon \phi(m))\mathbf{u} + \frac{p_2}{t}\phi(m)\mathbf{u}) \cdot k_2 && \text{(For some } \epsilon \in R_2) \end{aligned}$$

Therefore, c_2 is indeed an encryption of $\phi(m)\mathbf{u}$ with respect to the key sk_2, that is, $c_2 = (pq_2 + r_2 + p_2 \phi(m)\mathbf{u}/t) k_2 \in R_2$ with $\mathsf{err}(c_2) = r_2 = \mathbf{w}(\mathbf{r} + \epsilon) + \frac{p_2}{p_1}(\phi(r_1) + \epsilon \phi(m))\mathbf{u}$. Furthermore,

$$\begin{aligned} \|\mathsf{err}(c_2)\| &\leq \|\mathbf{wr}\| + \|\mathbf{w}\epsilon\| + \left\| \frac{p_2}{p_1}(\phi(r_1) + \epsilon \phi(m))\mathbf{u} \right\| \\ &\leq \tilde{\ell} N_1 \tilde{b} \|\mathbf{r}\| + \tilde{\ell} N_1 \tilde{b}/2 + 2^{\eta_2 - \eta_1 + 1} N_1 \|\mathbf{u}\| (\|\mathsf{err}(c_1)\| + t/2) \\ &\leq \tilde{\ell} N_1 \tilde{b} 2^{\tilde{\rho}} + 2^{\eta_2 - \eta_1 + 2} N_1 \|\mathbf{u}\| \|\mathsf{err}(c_1)\|. \end{aligned}$$

□

It turns out that this procedure is very general. For example, if we set $\mathbf{u} = (1, x, ..., x^{N_1})$, then, $\phi(m)\mathbf{u} = \sum_{i=0}^{N_1} m_i x^i = m$, therefore, by using such $\mathbf{u}$, our functional key-switching works as an ordinary key-switching, outputting an encryption of the same message m but in the ring R_2 and under the key sk_2. By setting $\mathbf{u} = (1, z, ..., z^{N_1})$ for any $z \in \mathbb{Z}$, we obtain an encryption of $\phi(m)\mathbf{u} = m(z)$, i.e., the evaluation of m at the point z. Also notice that when $N_i = 1$, we have $R_i \simeq \mathbb{Z}$, thus, not only our procedure is well defined for $N_i = 1$, but it also switches the underlying problem from the AGCD to the RAGCD problem or vice versa. In Table 1, all the possible ways of using our functional key switching are shown. The third column shows the underlying problems used to encrypt the input and the output message depending on whether each N_i is bigger than one or not. For instance, if $N_1 = 1$ and $N_2 > 1$, then the vector $\mathbf{u} \in R_2^{N_1}$ collapses to a scalar, that is, a polynomial of R_2, thus we are taking a message $m \in \mathbb{Z}$ encrypted using the AGCD problem and we are producing a ciphertext that encrypts the polynomial $m \cdot u$ using the RAGCD problem.

Table 1. Possible usages of the functional key-switching procedure.

N_1	N_2	Underlying problems	Encrypted message
>1	>1	RAGCD $\longrightarrow$ RAGCD	$\sum_{i=0}^{N_1-1} m_i x^i \mapsto \sum_{i=0}^{N_1-1} m_i \cdot u_i$ with $u_i \in R_2$
>1	$=1$	RAGCD $\longrightarrow$ AGCD	$\sum_{i=0}^{N_1-1} m_i x^i \mapsto \sum_{i=0}^{N_1-1} m_i \cdot u_i$ with $u_i \in \mathbb{Z}$
$=1$	>1	AGCD $\longrightarrow$ RAGCD	$m \in \mathbb{Z} \mapsto m \cdot u$ with $u \in R_2$
$=1$	$=1$	AGCD $\longrightarrow$ AGCD	$m \in \mathbb{Z} \mapsto m \cdot u$ with $u \in \mathbb{Z}$

4.5 Semantic Security

The function $\mathsf{GAHE.EncVec}$ encrypts a message $m \in R$ into a vector whose each entry is of the form $x_i + b^i \cdot m \bmod x_0$ for a value x_i sampled from $\mathcal{R}_{N,\gamma,\rho,x_0}(p,k)$ and a fixed $b \in \mathbb{N}$. Thus, if we assume that it is hard to distinguish between $\mathcal{U}(R/x_0R)$ and $\mathcal{R}_{N,\gamma,\rho,x_0}(p,k)$, we can use a hybrid argument to firstly replace x_i by $u_i \leftarrow \mathcal{U}(R/x_0R)$, then argue that $u_i + b^i \cdot m \bmod x_0$ also follows a uniform distribution, thus, can be replaced in another hybrid by $u_i' \leftarrow \mathcal{U}(R/x_0R)$. Because the final hybrid does not depend on m the advantage of an attacker in distinguishing vector encryptions of a pair of messages m_0 and m_1 is negligible. Moreover, our scalar encryption can be viewed as a particular case of vector encryption if we assume circular security. Therefore, we have the following result.

Lemma 7. *Under the decisional-RAGCD assumption and the circular-security assumption, encryptions of any pair of polynomials are computationally indistinguishable.*

Alternatively, it is possible to prove the security relying solely on the decisional-AGCD problem. For this, we have to replace the distribution $\mathcal{R}_{N,\gamma,\rho,x_0}(p,k)$ by $\mathcal{R}_{<x_0}$ in $\mathsf{GAHE.EncVec}$ and $\mathsf{GAHE.EncScalar}$, then use Lemma 1 to argue that $\mathcal{R}_{<x_0}$ is computationally indistinguishable from $\mathcal{U}(R/x_0R)$, and finally use the same hybrid argument as in Lemma 7.

Lemma 8. *Replace the distribution $\mathcal{R}_{N,\gamma,\rho,x_0}(p,k)$ by $\mathcal{R}_{<x_0}$ in the encryption functions. Then, under the decisional-AGCD assumption and the circular-security assumption, encryptions of any pair of polynomials are computationally indistinguishable.*

5 Single-Gate Bootstrapping

In this section, we show how to use our scheme to bootstrap a simple AGCD-based "single-gate" homomorphic encryption scheme as it was done in the RLWE-based fast bootstrapping methods of [DM15, CGGI16].

5.1 Base Scheme

Consider the following simple AGCD-based scheme that will be used as the base scheme, that is, as the scheme that will be bootstrapped. As it is done in [DM15, CGGI16], this base scheme is a leveled scheme with two levels only, thus, fresh ciphertexts are at level-1, we can evaluate one homomorphic binary gate by performing some simple additions, obtaining a ciphertext at level-2, and then we have to refresh the ciphertext to reduce the noise and to go back to level 1. Since all the binary gates can be written as compositions of logical NAND gates, to keep the presentation simple, we just present this binary gate. Furthermore, to avoid confusion, we represent the parameters of the base scheme with an overscore. For instance, the secret key of the base scheme is a prime $\bar{p}$ of bit length $\bar{\eta}$, while GAHE's secret key has an η-bit prime p.

- $\mathsf{HE.ParamGen}(\lambda)$: Choose $\bar{\rho} = \lambda$, $\bar{\eta} = \bar{\rho} + \beta$ for some small constant β, and $\bar{\gamma} = \Omega(\beta^2\lambda/\log(\lambda))$. Output $\mathsf{params} := (\bar{\gamma}, \bar{\eta}, \bar{\rho}, \lambda)$.
- $\mathsf{HE.KeyGen}(\mathsf{params})$: Sample a random prime $\bar{p}$ from $[\![2^{\bar{\eta}-1}, 2^{\bar{\eta}}]\!]$ and $\bar{p}q_{\mathsf{ek}} + r_{\mathsf{ek}} \leftarrow \mathcal{D}_{\bar{\gamma},\bar{\rho}}(\bar{p})$. Define the evaluation key as $\bar{\mathsf{ek}} := \bar{p}q_{\mathsf{ek}} + r_{\mathsf{ek}} + \lfloor 5\bar{p}/8 \rceil$ and the secret key as $\bar{\mathsf{sk}} := \bar{p}$.
- $\mathsf{HE.Enc}(\bar{\mathsf{sk}}, m, L)$: To encrypt a bit m, sample $\bar{p}q + r \leftarrow \mathcal{D}_{\bar{\gamma},\bar{\rho}}(\bar{p})$ and output the level-L ciphertext $c = \bar{p}q + r + \lfloor L\bar{p}/4 \rceil m$.
- $\mathsf{HE.Dec}(\bar{\mathsf{sk}}, c)$: To decrypt a level-1 c, compute $c' := [c]_{\bar{p}}$, then output $\left[\left\lfloor \frac{4c'}{\bar{p}} \right\rceil\right]_2$.
- $\mathsf{HE.Nand}(c_1, c_2, \bar{\mathsf{ek}})$: Let c_0 and c_1 be level-1 ciphertexts encrypting m_1 and m_2, respectively. Output $c := \bar{\mathsf{ek}} - c_1 - c_2$.

The function $\mathsf{HE.ParamGen}$ chooses the parameters in a way that guarantees the correctness of $\mathsf{HE.Dec}$. Namely, because $|r| < 2^{\bar{\rho}}$, we have $|r + \lfloor \bar{p}/4 \rceil m| < \bar{p}/2$, therefore, $c' = [c]_{\bar{p}} = r + \lfloor \bar{p}/4 \rceil m$ in $\mathbb{Z}$. And since $\lfloor \bar{p}/4 \rceil > 2^{\bar{\rho}+1} > 2|r|$, we have $\lfloor 4r/\bar{p} \rceil = 0$, then, the output is $\lfloor 4c'/\bar{p} \rceil = \lfloor 4r/\bar{p} \rceil + m = m$.

Our NAND gate is the same of [DM15, CGGI16], thus it outputs

$$c = \bar{p}\underbrace{(q_{\mathsf{ek}} - q_1 - q_2)}_{q_{nand}} + \underbrace{r_{\mathsf{ek}} - r_1 - r_2 \pm \frac{\bar{p}}{8}}_{r_{nand}} + \lfloor \bar{p}/2 \rceil (1 - m_1 m_2)$$

which is a level-2 encryption of $NAND(m_1, m_2)$ with noise $|r_{nand}| < 3 \cdot 2^{\bar{\rho}} + \bar{p}/8$.

By standard techniques [DGHV10, CS15, BBL17] one can prove that this base scheme is CPA-secure if the AGCD problem is computationally hard. Moreover, the parameters chosen in $\mathsf{HE.ParamGen}$ provide security of λ bits.

5.2 Generating the Bootstrapping Keys

To generate the key material used to bootstrap, we need to fix a base $B \geq 2$ in which we decompose the ciphertexts of the base scheme when they are refreshed. Then, we define $L := \lceil \log_B(2^{\bar{\gamma}}) \rceil$, which is the number of words needed to decompose the given ciphertexts. Moreover, the number of homomorphic mixed products that we perform during the refresh procedure is $\Theta(L)$, thus, there is a

Algorithm 1: GenBootstrapKeys

Input: Decomposition base B, secret key $\bar{p}$ of the base scheme
Output: Bootstrapping key bk

1 $y \leftarrow x^2$
2 $L \leftarrow \lceil \bar{\gamma} \cdot \log_B(2) \rceil$
3 **for** $s = 1$ until $B - 1$ **do**
4   **for** $i = 0$ until $L - 1$ **do**
5         $\mathfrak{K}_{s,i} \leftarrow \mathsf{GAHE.EncVec}\left(y^{\lfloor sB^i N/\bar{p} \rceil}\right)$
6         $\epsilon_{s,i} \leftarrow sB^i N/\bar{p} - \lfloor sB^i N/\bar{p} \rceil$
7 Choose $\Delta \in \mathbb{N}$ such that $|\sum_{i=0}^{L-1} \epsilon_{s_i,i}| < \Delta$ for any $(s_0, ..., s_{L-1})$, e.g., $\Delta = L/2$
8 $\delta \leftarrow \lceil \Delta + (3 \cdot 2^{\bar{\rho}} + \bar{p}/8) N/\bar{p} \rceil$
9 $\mathfrak{K}_\delta \leftarrow \mathsf{GAHE.EncScalar}(y^\delta)$ using $\alpha := \lfloor p/8 \rceil$
10 $\gamma_{\mathsf{ek}} \leftarrow \lfloor \bar{\gamma} - \log(\ell N b) \rfloor$ and $\rho_{\mathsf{ek}} \leftarrow \lfloor \bar{\rho} - \log(\ell N b) - 2 \rfloor$
11 $\mathsf{params} \leftarrow (N, 1, b, \ell, \gamma_{\mathsf{ek}}, \rho_{\mathsf{ek}})$
12 $\mathbf{u} \leftarrow (1, 1, ..., 1) \in \mathbb{Z}^N$
13 $\mathsf{ek} \leftarrow \mathsf{FuncKeySwtGen}(\mathsf{sk} := (p, k), \bar{\mathsf{sk}} := (\bar{p}, 1), \mathsf{params}, \mathbf{u}) \in \mathbb{Z}^{N\ell}$
14 $\mathfrak{K}_8 \leftarrow \mathcal{D}_{\bar{\gamma}, \bar{\rho}-1}(\bar{p}) + \lfloor \bar{p}/8 \rceil$
15 **return** $\mathsf{bk} := \left(\mathsf{ek}, \mathfrak{K}_\delta, \mathfrak{K}_8, \{\mathfrak{K}_{s,i}\}_{\substack{1 \le s < B \\ 0 \le i < L}}\right)$

time-memory tradeoff, as the amount of memory increases in general when we increase B, but at the same time, L decreases.

The bootstrapping procedure consists in two main steps: in the first one, we use the GAHE scheme to homomorphically multiply a given ciphertext $\bar{c}$ by $N/\bar{p}$, obtaining a GAHE's scalar ciphertext c; in the second step, we transform c in a valid base scheme ciphertext c'. To perform the first step, we would like to encrypt values of the form $y^{sB^i N/\bar{p}}$, where $y := x^2$, but the exponent would not be integer, thus, we encrypt $y^{\lfloor sB^i N/\bar{p} \rceil}$, that is, we define $\mathfrak{K}_{s,i} := \mathsf{GAHE.EncVec}\left(y^{\lfloor sB^i N/\bar{p} \rceil}\right)$ for $1 \le s < B$ and $0 \le i < L$. In addition, we also encrypt an integer δ that is added to the result obtained in the first step, so that the final result is contained in the interval $[\![0, N-1]\!]$. Thus, we define $\mathfrak{K}_\delta := \mathsf{GAHE.EncScalar}(y^\delta) \in R$.

Notice that $\mathfrak{K}_\delta$ is a scalar ciphertext, while $\mathfrak{K}_{s,i}$'s are vector ciphertexts. During the refresh procedure, we use the mixed homomorphic product to multiply them. Hence, at the end of the first step, we have a scalar ciphertext $c = (pq + r + \alpha y^e)k$ for some $e \in [\![0, N-1]\!]$ whose value depends on the message m. Then, to extract m, we define a test vector $\mathbf{u} \in \{0,1\}^N$, such that $\phi(y^e) \cdot \mathbf{u} = 1 - 2m$ and use our functional key-switching to transform c into a ciphertext that encrypts $\phi(y^e) \cdot \mathbf{u}$ under the base scheme key $\bar{\mathsf{sk}}$. Thus, we also append the following key to the bootstrapping keys:

$$\mathsf{ek} := \mathsf{FuncKeySwtGen}(\mathsf{sk} := (p, k), \bar{\mathsf{sk}} := (\bar{p}, 1), \mathbf{u}).$$

In Algorithm 1 we present in detail the procedure to generate the bootstrapping key bk.

5.3 Refreshing a Ciphertext

The goal of the bootstrapping is to take a level-2 ciphertext $c = \bar{p}q + r + \lfloor \bar{p}/2 \rceil m \in \mathbb{Z}$ whose noise term satisfies $|r| < 3 \cdot 2^{\bar{\rho}} + \bar{p}/8$ and to output a level-1 ciphertext $c' = \bar{p}q' + r' + \lfloor \bar{p}/4 \rceil m$ with $|r'| < 2^{\bar{\rho}}$. The refreshing procedure is shown thoroughly in Algorithm 2 and it consists in two main steps: in the first one, we decompose c in the base B obtaining $(c_0, c_1, ..., c_{L-1})$, then we use the bootstrapping key and GAHE's mixed homomorphic multiplication to obtain a scalar encryption of y^e, where $y := x^2$ and

$$y^e = y^\delta \cdot \prod_{i=0}^{\ell-1} y^{\lfloor c_i b^i N/\bar{p} \rceil} = y^{\delta + cN/\bar{p} + \epsilon \bmod N} = y^{\delta + rN/\bar{p} + mN/2 + \epsilon}$$

for some small value ϵ.

Algorithm 2: REFRESH

Input: Level-2 ciphertext c of the base scheme, bootstrapping key bk
Output: Level-1 ciphertext c of the base scheme
1 Let $(c_0, c_1, ..., c_{L-1})$ be a decomposition of c in base B.
2 $z \leftarrow \mathfrak{K}_\delta$
3 **for** $i = 0$ until $L - 1$ **do**
4   **if** $c_i > 0$ **then**
5         $z \leftarrow$ GAHE.MultMix$(z, \mathfrak{K}_{c_i,i})$

▷ `Second step: extract the message.`
6 $\tilde{c} \leftarrow$ FuncKeySwt(z, ek)
7 $c' \leftarrow \mathfrak{K}_8 - \tilde{c}$
8 **return** c'

Then, notice that $\phi(y^e) = \phi(x^{2e})$, thus, if $0 \leq e < N/2$, then, the only non-zero entry of $\phi(y^e)$ is 1, otherwise, it is -1. But as we show in Lemma 9, we have $0 \leq e < N/2$ if $m = 0$ and $N/2 \leq e \leq N - 1$ if $m = 1$, therefore, the vector $\mathbf{u} := (1, ..., 1) \in \mathbb{Z}^N$ satisfies $\phi(y^e) \cdot \mathbf{u} = 1 - 2m$. Thus, because we used $\mathbf{u}$ to generate ek, when we apply the functional key-switching in the second step of Algorithm 2, we switch from GAHE to the base scheme and we obtain an encryption of $\phi(x^e) \cdot \mathbf{u} = 1 - 2m$, that is, we obtain $\tilde{c} = \bar{p}\tilde{q} + \tilde{r} + (1 - 2m) \cdot \lfloor p/8 \rceil$. Therefore, subtracting $\tilde{c}$ from $\mathfrak{K}_8$ yields a valid level-one base scheme encryption of m, that is, $c' := \mathfrak{K}_8 - \tilde{c} = \bar{p}q' + r' + m \lfloor p/4 \rceil$.

In which follows, we prove the correctness of the refreshing procedure.

Lemma 9. *Let c be a level-2 encryption of $m \in \{0, 1\}$ with noise bounded by $3 \cdot 2^{\bar{\rho}} + \bar{p}/8$. Let $N \geq 4\delta$ where δ is the integer defined in Algorithm 1. Then,* *the ciphertext $z \in R$ obtained at the end of the main loop of Algorithm 2 is an encryption of x^{2e} where $e \in [\![0, N-1]\!]$. Moreover, $m = 0 \iff 0 \leq e < N/2$ and $m = 1 \iff N/2 \leq e < N$.*

Proof. Let $y := x^2$. We initialize z with a scalar encryption of y^δ and at each iteration i, we add $\lfloor c_i b^i N/\bar{p} \rceil$ to the exponent, thus, because y has order N in R, it is clear that at the end of the loop z encrypts y^e where $e = \delta + \sum_{i=0}^{L-1} \lfloor c_i B^i N/\bar{p} \rceil \bmod N$.

Now, let $\epsilon_i := \lfloor c_i B^i N/\bar{p} \rceil - c_i B^i N/\bar{p}$ and $\epsilon := \sum_{i=0}^{L-1} \epsilon_i$. Then,

$$e = \delta + \epsilon + (N/\bar{p}) \cdot \sum_{i=0}^{L-1} c_i B^i = \delta + \epsilon + cN/\bar{p} = \delta + \epsilon + rN/\bar{p} + mN/2 \bmod N$$

Notice that $|\epsilon + rN/\bar{p}| < \Delta + (3 \cdot 2^{\bar{\rho}} + \bar{p}/8)N/\bar{p} \leq \delta$. Also, because $N \geq 4\delta$ by hypothesis, we have $2\delta \leq N/2$. Thus, we can see that

$$\delta + \epsilon + rN/\bar{p} + mN/2 < 2\delta + \frac{N}{2} \leq N.$$

Similarly, $\delta + \epsilon + rN/\bar{p} + mN/2 \geq \delta - \Delta - \frac{(3 \cdot 2^{\bar{\rho}} + \bar{p}/8)N}{\bar{p}} \geq \delta - \delta = 0$. Therefore, we conclude that $0 \leq e < N$. But because e is integer, we have $0 \leq e \leq N-1$, as expected.

Thereby, $e = \delta + \epsilon + rN/\bar{p} + mN/2$ over $\mathbb{Z}$, without the reduction modulo N. Thus,

$$\begin{cases} m = 0 \implies e = \delta + \epsilon + rN/\bar{p} < 2\delta \leq N/2 \\ m = 1 \implies e = \delta + \epsilon + rN/\bar{p} + N/2 \geq N/2 \end{cases}$$ □

Lemma 10. *Let $m \in \{0, 1\}$ and $\delta \in \mathbb{N}^*$ as defined in Algorithm 1. Let $e \in [\![0, N-1]\!]$ such that $m = 0 \iff 0 \leq e < N/2$. Let z be a scalar encryption of x^{2e} with $\alpha = \lfloor p/8 \rceil$ and noise bounded by some value B_z. Then, when given z as input, the second step of Algorithm 2 outputs a base scheme level-1 encryption of m with noise bounded by $2^{\bar{\rho}-1} + NB_z 2^{\bar{\eta}-\eta+2}$.*

Proof. We know that $z = (pq_z + r_z + \lfloor p/8 \rceil x^{2e})k$ and that ek is a functional switching key from $\mathsf{sk} = (p, k)$ to $\bar{\mathsf{sk}} = (\bar{p}, 1)$ with respect to $\mathbf{u} = (1, ..., 1)$. Then, by Lemma 6, the output of $\mathsf{FuncKeySwt}(z, \mathsf{ek})$ is

$$\tilde{c} = \bar{p}\tilde{q} + \tilde{r} + \left\lfloor \frac{\bar{p}}{8} \right\rceil \phi(x^{2e})\mathbf{u} \in \mathbb{Z},$$

where $|\mathsf{err}(\tilde{c})| \leq 2^{\bar{\rho}-2} + NB_z 2^{\bar{\eta}-\eta+2}$ and $\phi(x^{2e})\mathbf{u} = 1 - 2m$.

Notice that $\lfloor p/8 \rceil - (1-2m)\lfloor p/8 \rceil = 2m \lfloor p/8 \rceil = m \lfloor p/4 \rceil + \epsilon$, therefore, the output $c' := \mathfrak{K}_8 - \tilde{c}$ is indeed of the form $\bar{p}q' + r' + m\lfloor p/4 \rceil$, which a valid base scheme level-1 encryption of m. Moreover, $\mathsf{err}(c') \leq \mathsf{err}(\mathfrak{K}_8) + \mathsf{err}(\tilde{c}) \leq 2^{\bar{\rho}-1} + NB_z 2^{\bar{\eta}-\eta+2}$ □

Theorem 1 (Correctness of bootstrapping). *Let c be a level-2 encryption of $m \in \{0,1\}$ with noise bounded by $3 \cdot 2^{\bar{\rho}} + \bar{p}/8$. Let $N \geq 4\delta$ where δ is the integer defined in Algorithm 1. Let $\bar{\rho} \geq \rho + \bar{\eta} - \eta + \log(N^3 \ell b L) + 4$. Then, the refresh procedure, Algorithm 2, outputs a valid base scheme level-1 encryption of m with noise smaller than $2^{\bar{\rho}}$.*

Proof. By Lemma 9, we know that the ciphertext z produced at the end of the first step of Refresh is of the form $(pq_z + r_z + \lfloor p/8 \rceil x^{2e})k$ for some $e \in [\![0, N-1]\!]$ such that $m = 0 \iff 0 \leq e < N/2$. Therefore, by Lemma 10, the output of Refresh is a base scheme level-1 ciphertext $c' = \bar{p}q' + r' + \lfloor \bar{p}/4 \rceil m$ with $|r'| < 2^{\bar{\rho}-1} + N \cdot \|\mathsf{err}(z)\| \cdot 2^{\bar{\eta}-\eta+2}$. But because z is computed with a sequence of L mixed homomorphic products, by Lemma 5, we have $\|\mathsf{err}(z)\| < 2N^2 \ell b L 2^{\rho}$, therefore, $|r'| < 2^{\bar{\rho}-1} + 2^{\rho+\bar{\eta}-\eta+\log(N^3\ell b L)+3} \leq 2^{\bar{\rho}-1} + 2^{\bar{\rho}-1} = 2^{\bar{\rho}}$. □

5.4 Truncating Ciphertexts to Speed up Refreshing

When we encrypt a message m with the base scheme, we multiply it by a constant α that is bigger than the noise. This has the effect of shifting the message so that it is encrypted "between" the noise and the key. It has already been noticed [Bra12, CS15] that when we use noisy encryption schemes that encrypt messages in this way, we can discard the least significant bits of the ciphertexts, at the expend of increasing the noise, to use less memory to represent encrypted messages. But in our case, because the main loop of Algorithm 2 ignores bits equal to zero, we can also save some homomorphic multiplications and speed up the bootstrapping. Moreover, we do not need to generate bootstrapping keys $\mathfrak{K}_{s,i}$'s for these truncated bits.

In detail, given a base scheme ciphertext $c = \bar{p}q + r + \bar{\alpha}m$, we can set the first μ bits to zero, for example, by subtracting $s := c \bmod 2^{\mu}$ from c. Notice that we obtain then $c' := c - s = \bar{p}q + (r - s) + \bar{\alpha}m$, that is a valid encryption m, but with a new noise term potentially bigger, satisfying $\mathsf{err}(c') \leq \mathsf{err}(c) + 2^{\mu}$. Then, when we decompose c' in base B in the refreshing procedure, the first $\mu_B := \lfloor \mu \cdot \log_B(2) \rfloor$ words are ignored and the keys $\mathfrak{K}_{s,i}$ for $0 \leq i < \mu_B$ are never used. Thus, we reduce the number of mixed homomorphic products from L to $L - \mu_B$ and the number of keys from $(B-1)L$ to $(B-1)(L-\mu_B)$.

6 Practical Results

In this section we show how to choose the parameters for our scheme, we present the running times and memory usage of our bootstrapping procedure, and we compare our results with previous works. Our proof-of-concept was implemented in C++ using the Number Theory Library[2] (NTL) and the source code is publicly available[3]. We ran the experiments on a single core of a processor Intel Core i5-8600K 3.60 GHz, of a machine with 32 GB of RAM memory. We stress

[2] https://www.shoup.net/ntl/.
[3] https://github.com/hilder-vitor/FHEZ/.

that our implementation is not optimized and the running times that we present below, although being enough to show that our techniques are practical, can certainly be improved.

6.1 Cryptanalysis and Parameter Selection

Firstly we recall the definitions of the parameters used in our GAHE scheme:

- N: we work over the cyclotomic ring $R := \mathbb{Z}[x]/\langle x^N + 1\rangle$;
- η: we sample the secret prime p uniformly from $[\![2^{\eta-1}, 2^{\eta}]\!]$;
- ρ: during encryption, we sample the noise terms uniformly from $]\!] - 2^{\rho}, 2^{\rho}[\![$;
- γ: the private modulus x_0 satisfies $2^{\gamma-1} \leq x_0 < 2^{\gamma}$
- t: the message space is $R/tR = \mathbb{Z}_t[x]/\langle x^N + 1\rangle$;
- b: base in which we perform the decomposition g^{-1};
- ℓ: number of words used in g^{-1}. Vector ciphertexts belong to R^{ℓ}.

In [CP19] and [Per20], the authors analyzed a randomized version of the AGCD problem in which the AGCD samples are arranged as vectors and multiplied by a hidden random matrix $\mathbf{K} \in \mathbb{Z}^{N\times N}$. Namely, for fixed p and $\mathbf{K}$, an attacker has access to many vectors $\tilde{\mathbf{v}}_i = \mathbf{v}_i\mathbf{K} \in \mathbb{Z}^N$, where $\mathbf{v}_i = p\mathbf{q}_i + \mathbf{r}_i \in \mathbb{Z}^N$. In our case, an attacker has access to polynomials $\tilde{c}_i := c_i \cdot k = (pq_i + r_i)k \in R$ output from $\mathcal{R}_{N,\gamma,\rho,x_0}(p, k)$. But, denoting by $\mathbf{K} \in \mathbb{Z}^{N\times N}$ the anti-circulant matrix of k, we can write $\phi(\tilde{c}_i) = \phi(c_i)\mathbf{K} = (p\phi(q_i) + \phi(r_i))\mathbf{K} \in \mathbb{Z}^N$ which can be viewed as the randomized AGCD problem of [CP19,Per20], but with a structured matrix $\mathbf{K}$ instead of a completely random. Hence, we use the cryptanalysis done in [CP19,Per20] without taking advantage of the structure of the circulant matrix of k. The parallel with the RLWE problem is worthy of note: the attacks against the RLWE problem are adapted from the cryptanalysis of the LWE problem, since the RLWE can be seen as a structured version of the LWE. Also, in practice, such structure is ignored because there is no known way of exploiting it.

Thus, to guarantee the security, we must set $\gamma \in \Omega\left(\frac{\lambda(\eta-\rho)^2}{N\log\lambda}\right)$ to rule out orthogonal lattice attacks and $\rho \in \Omega(\lambda/N)$ to avoid GCD attacks [CP19,Per20]. A simple choice for the modulus polynomial f when instantiating the RAGCD problem is $f = x^N + 1$ with N being a power of two, because in this case, f is a cyclotomic polynomial, therefore, irreducible on $\mathbb{Z}[x]$. However, other choices of f are possible, but we suggest that f must be irreducible, since using a reducible polynomial f makes other attacks possible, as we discuss now.

Polynomial Evaluation: Consider that we define the ring R as $\mathbb{Z}[x]/\langle f\rangle$ for some degree-N polynomial f. Given an instance RAGCD $c := (pq + r)k \in R$, there is a polynomial u such that the following holds over $\mathbb{Z}[x]$: $c = (pq+r)k - uf$. Therefore, when we evaluate c at some integer z, we obtain $c(z) = (pq(z) + r(z))k(z) - u(z)f(z) \in \mathbb{Z}$. Now, if z is a root of f, we have $c(z) = (pq(z) + r(z))k(z)$, which can be viewed as an instance of the original AGCD problem, but masked by an integer $k(z)$. Even for small values of N, we expect $r(z)$ to be bigger than p in general. For instance, setting $\lambda = \eta = 100$ and $N = 32$, the power z^{N-1} alone would already be bigger than p for any z such that $|z| > 10$, thus, it is very likely that $|r(z)| = |\sum_{i=0}^{N-1} r_i \cdot z^i|$ is also bigger than p. In this case, $c(z)$ is an ill formed AGCD sample and we can not recover p from it.

However, if $r(z)$ happens to be small, then $c(z)$ is an AGCD sample with noise term $r(z)$ and we could use the attacks against the original AGCD problem instead of the attacks against the vector AGCD problem. This could be problematic because we would be attacking an AGCD instance with parameters much smaller than what it is needed to guarantee the security, since parameters of the vector AGCD problem (and thus, the ones of the RAGCD problem) are usually equal to the parameters of the AGCD problem divided by the dimension of the vectors, in this case, the value N.

As a concrete example, consider that one tries to instantiate the RAGCD problem using the ring $R = \mathbb{Z}[x]/\langle x^N - 1\rangle$. To achieve security of λ bits, one could set, say, $\rho = \lambda/N$. But then, the noise term $r = \sum_{i=0}^{N-1} r_i \cdot x^i \in \mathbb{Z}[x]$ satisfies $|r_i| < 2^{\lambda/N}$. Now, the problem is that $x^N - 1$ has a very small root, namely, the value 1, thus, it holds that $c(1) = (pq(1) + r(1))k(1)$, and $|r(1)| \leq \sum_{i=0}^{N-1} |r_i| \leq N \cdot 2^{\lambda/N}$. In other words, evaluating any RAGCD instance c at 1 produces a "masked" AGCD instance with small noise term, around $N \cdot 2^{\lambda/N}$. One could, for instance, run Lee-Seo's GCD attack [LS14], which would recover the secret p in time and memory $\tilde{O}(2^{\lambda/N})$, that is, in much less time than the $\Omega(2^{\lambda})$ that the chosen security level is supposed to guarantee.

Dimension Reduction: Actually, evaluating a polynomial c at a point z is equivalent to reducing c modulo $(x - z)$. And assuming that z is an integer and a root of f is the same as assuming that $x - z$ is a factor of f. Thus, we can generalize the previous attack as follows: Consider that one instantiates the RAGCD problem using the ring $\mathbb{Z}[x]/\langle f\rangle$ for a polynomial f that has a non-trivial factor g, that is, the degree of g is at least one and g divides f on $\mathbb{Z}[x]$.

Then, because an RAGCD instance c can be written as $c = (pq+r)k - uf$, for some $u \in \mathbb{Z}[x]$, we can reduce c modulo g obtaining $c' = (p[q]_g + [r]_g) \cdot [k]_g - vg$, for some $v \in \mathbb{Z}[x]$. But this c' is a new RAGCD instance over the "smaller" ring $\mathbb{Z}[x]/\langle g\rangle$, because the degree of g is less than the degree of f. For some polynomials g, the norm of $[r]_g$ will be bigger than p and c' will be an ill defined RAGCD instance from which we cannot recover p. However, depending on the degree and on the coefficients of g, the infinity norm of $[r]_g$ can be just slightly larger than the norm of r, which means that c' can be effectively used in an attack in lower dimension (thus, in an easier RAGCD instance).

For example, let N be even and consider that the $g(x) = x^{N/2}+1$ is a factor of f. Then, reducing c modulo g yields $c' = (p[q]_g+[r]_g)\cdot[k]_g - vg$, for some $v \in \mathbb{Z}[x]$, where c' is a polynomial with half the degree of the original c. Moreover, by defining $r := \sum_{i=0}^{N-1} r_i \cdot x^i$, we have $[r]_g = \sum_{i=0}^{N/2-1} (r_i + r_{i+N/2}) \cdot x^i$, hence, $\|[r]_g\| \leq 2\|r\|$. The same holds for q, i.e., $\|[q]_g\| \leq 2\|q\|$. Thus, we essentially reduce an RAGCD instance with parameters N, γ, η, and ρ, to a much easier RAGCD instance with parameters $N/2$, $\gamma + 1$, η, and $\rho + 1$. To illustrate that: the time complexity of the GCD attacks would decrease from $\tilde{O}(2^{N\rho})$ to $\tilde{O}(2^{N(\rho+1)/2})$ and orthogonal lattice attacks would have their costs reduced from $2^{\Omega(\gamma N/(\eta-\rho)^2)}$ to $2^{\Omega(\frac{N}{2}\cdot(\gamma+1)/(\eta-\rho-1)^2)}$, thus, attacking this new RAGCD instance would take roughly the square root of the time needed to attack the original instance.

Parameters for Security: To guarantee the security level of λ bits, we must set $\gamma \in \Omega\left(\frac{\lambda(\eta-\rho)^2}{N\log\lambda}\right)$ to rule out orthogonal lattice attacks and $\rho \in \Omega(\lambda/N)$ to avoid GCD attacks (where $N = 1$ for the AGCD problem and $N > 1$ for the RAGCD problem). More concretely, the number of integer operations of the GCD attacks is bigger than $(N\rho)^2 \cdot 2^{N\rho}$ [Per20], thus, we set $\rho \geq \lambda/N$, to guarantee that this type of attack takes more than 2^λ CPU clock cycles.

Considering several different cryptanalysis [DGHV10,CS15,GGM16,CP19], we see that lattice attacks on the AGCD problem and its variants boil down to running a lattice-basis reduction algorithm on a lattice of dimension d and rank $d - N$, where d that can be chosen by the attacker, $N = 1$ for the original AGCD problem and $N > 1$ for the randomized versions. The goal is then to find short enough d-dimensional vectors $\mathbf{v}_i$'s that are orthogonal to vectors $\mathbf{r}_i$'s whose components are ρ-bit noise terms. We basically need $\|\mathbf{v}_i\|_2 \cdot \|\mathbf{r}_i\|_2 < p$. Considering that $\|\mathbf{r}_i\|_2 \approx 2^\rho$, we obtain then $\|\mathbf{v}_i\|_2 < 2^{\eta-\rho}$. Taking into account the root-Hermite factor ζ of the lattice-basis reduction algorithm and the determinant of the lattice, we can estimate $\|\mathbf{v}_i\|_2$ as $\zeta^d \cdot (2^{\gamma N})^{1/d}$, thus, we end up with the necessary condition

$$d\log(\zeta) + \gamma N/d < \eta - \rho.$$

This inequality is equivalent to $\log(\zeta)d^2 - (\eta-\rho)d + \gamma N < 0$ and it has no solution if its discriminant is negative, i.e., if $(\eta-\rho)^2 - 4\log(\zeta)\gamma N < 0$. Hence, we obtain the following concrete restriction on γ:

$$\gamma > \frac{(\eta-\rho)^2}{4N\log(\zeta)}. \tag{3}$$

Therefore, to guarantee a security level of λ bits, we just have to choose a small enough ζ such that any lattice-basis reduction achieving such root-Hermite factor costs more than 2^λ operations, then fix $\gamma = \left\lceil \frac{(\eta-\rho)^2}{4N\log(\zeta)} \right\rceil$, where $N = 1$ for the AGCD problem.

Parameters for Correctness: If we let L be the maximum multiplicative depth to be evaluated, then, the correctness of the decryption functions imposes the following constraint: By Lemmas 3 and 4, decryption works if the final noise is smaller than $p/(3t)$. Thus, we can use $2^\eta/(6t) < p/(3t)$ as an acceptable bound to the noise. By Lemma 5, the final noise is upper bounded by $2N^2BL\ell b2^\rho$, thus, we need $2N^2BL\ell b2^\rho \leq 2^\eta/(6t)$, or, equivalently,

$$\eta \geq \rho + \log(tN^2BL\ell b) + \log(12).$$

In Sect. 6.2 we propose concrete parameters sufficient to evaluate our bootstrapping method.

6.2 Running Times and Memory Requirements of Our Bootstrapping

In this section we present our practical results for the bootstrapping procedure described in Sect. 5. Our experiment consisted in encrypting two random bits m_1 and m_2 into c_1 and c_2, computing $c := \mathsf{HE.Nand}(c_1, c_2)$, then refreshing c. Because the homomorphic nand gate is performed with three simple integer additions, its running time is negligible and we only measured the refreshing step. To show the time-memory trade-off explicitly, we used several values for the base B. All the parameters were chosen to guarantee a security level of more than 100 bits. For this, we used the root-Hermite factor $\zeta = 1.0064$ in Inequality 3, which is the same value used in [DM15]. Notice that the BKZ algorithm requires a block size greater than 190 and much more than 2^{100} CPU clock cycles to achieve such root-Hermite factor [CN11,DM15].

Thus, for the base scheme, we proceed as described in Sect. 5.1 by fixing $\beta = 5$, $\bar{\eta} = 105$, $\bar{\rho} = 100$, and $\bar{\gamma} = \left\lceil \frac{(\bar{\eta}-\bar{\rho})^2}{4\log(\zeta)} \right\rceil = \left\lceil \frac{25}{4\log(1.0064)} \right\rceil = 680$. We also truncated $\mu = \bar{\rho} - 5$ bits of the ciphertexts, as explained in Sect. 5.4. We recall that when we generate bk, we must choose an upper-bound Δ for the sum of the rounding errors $\epsilon_{s,i}$'s. Because $|\epsilon_{s,i}| \leq 1/2$, it is clear that we can choose $\Delta = L/2$, however, this bound is not realistic and we can use much smaller values of Δ in practice, thus, we used $\Delta \approx (L - \lambda \log_B(2))/6$. Hence, for each B, we defined L and Δ, then N was set as the smallest power of two larger than $16 \cdot \Delta$. GAHE's parameters are presented in Table 2.

Table 2. We show the practical results of our bootstrapping for three sets of parameters. The two last rows show [DM15] and [CGGI16], which used only one fixed set of parameters. We show the running times they reported on a 3.0 GHz processor and also these timings multiplied by $\frac{3}{3.6}$ to make the comparison with our results more senseful. The security level is $\lambda = 100$ for the three schemes and we always used $\eta = 100$ and $\gamma \geq \lceil (\eta - \rho)^2/(4N\log(1.0064)) \rceil$ for our GAHE scheme.

	B	Δ	L	N	γ	ρ	$\log b$	ℓ	Size bk	Refreshing
Ours	2^6	16	114	256	206	56	24	10	412 MB	0.94 s
	2^7	14	98	256	206	56	24	10	712 MB	0.81 s
	2^8	8	86	128	204	69	11	21	1.3 GB	0.48 s
[DM15]	-								1.3 GB	0.69 s ($\times \frac{3}{3.6} = 0.57$ s)
[CGGI16]	-								52 MB	0.05 s ($\times \frac{3}{3.6} = 0.04$ s)

Our running times are comparable with those of [DM15] and around 10 times larger than those of [CGGI16]. A full comparison is presented in Table 2. We stress that this comparison is to be taken with care, because we used a 3.6 GHz processor while they used a 3.0 GHz one. On the other hand, while we used our own (very simple) implementation of the Fast Fourier Transform (FFT) to perform polynomial multiplication, they used very optimized FFT libraries (they work with polynomials whose coefficients are small, thus, they can use well-known FFT libraries implemented with floating-point numbers). Therefore, our running times can surely be improved.

Appendix

A Other Homomorphic Operations

- GAHE.AddVec($\mathbf{c}_1, \mathbf{c}_2$): to homomorphically add two ciphertexts, just add them entry-wise: $\mathbf{c}_{add} := \mathbf{c}_1 + \mathbf{c}_2 \in R^\ell$.
- GAHE.MultVec($\mathbf{c}_1, \mathbf{c}_2$): to perform a homomorphic product, apply g^{-1} to each entry of $\mathbf{c}_1$ obtaining a $\ell \times \ell$ matrix of polynomials, i.e., $\mathbf{A} := (g^{-1}(c_{1,1}) \dots g^{-1}(c_{1,\ell}))$, then perform a vector-matrix product over R: $\mathbf{c}_{mult} := \mathbf{c}_2 \cdot \mathbf{A} \in R^\ell$.
- GAHE.AddScalar(c_1, c_2): to perform a homomorphic addition, just add the ciphertexts: $c_{add} := c_1 + c_2 \in R$.
- GAHE.AddPlaintext($\mathbf{c}_1, h$) and GAHE.MultPlaintext($\mathbf{c}_1, h$): to add a plaintext h, output $\mathbf{c}_1 + \mathbf{g} \cdot h$. To multiply, simply multiply each entry of $\mathbf{c}_1$ by h in R, i.e., output $h \cdot \mathbf{c}_1 \in R^\ell$.

A.1 Correctness of Homomorphic Operations

The mixed homomorphic product was analyzed in Sect. 4.3. We now show that the other homomorphic operations are also correct. For $i \in \{1, 2\}$, let $\mathbf{c}_i$ a be vector encryption of v_i and c_i be a scalar encryption of s_i. Thus, we have $\mathbf{c}_i = (p\mathbf{q}_i + \mathbf{r}_i)k + \mathbf{g}v_i$ and $c_i = (pq_i + r_i + \alpha s_i)k$.

Hence, it is easy to see that the homomorphic additions produce valid ciphertexts, i.e.,

- $c_1 + c_2 = (p(q_1 + q_2) + (r_1 + r_2) + \alpha(s_1 + s_2))k \in R$.
- $\mathbf{c}_1 + \mathbf{c}_2 = (p(\mathbf{q}_1 + \mathbf{q}_2) + (\mathbf{r}_1 + \mathbf{r}_2))k + \mathbf{g}(v_1 + v_2) \in R^\ell$.

To see that the homomorphic product of two vector ciphertexts is correct, notice that we decompose one of the operands, say, $\mathbf{c}_1$, as $\mathbf{A} = (g^{-1}(c_{1,1}) \dots g^{-1}(c_{1,\ell})) \in R^{\ell \times \ell}$, and when we multiply $\mathbf{A}$ by $\mathbf{g}$, we obtain again $\mathbf{c}_1$, i.e., $\mathbf{g} \cdot \mathbf{A} = \mathbf{c}_1$. Hence, we have the following:

$$\begin{aligned}
\mathbf{c}_{mult} &= \mathbf{c}_2 \cdot \mathbf{A} \\
&= (p\mathbf{q}_2\mathbf{A} + \mathbf{r}_2\mathbf{A})k + \mathbf{g}\mathbf{A}v_2 \\
&= (p\mathbf{q}_2\mathbf{A} + \mathbf{r}_2\mathbf{A})k + ((p\mathbf{q}_1 + \mathbf{r}_1)k + \mathbf{g}v_1)v_2 \\
&= (p\underbrace{(\mathbf{q}_2\mathbf{A} + \mathbf{q}_1 v_2)}_{\mathbf{q}_{mult}} + \underbrace{(\mathbf{r}_2\mathbf{A} + \mathbf{r}_1 v_2)}_{\mathbf{r}_{mult}})k + \mathbf{g}v_1 v_2
\end{aligned}$$

Therefore, the homomorphic multiplication yields a valid encryption of the product of the messages.

A.2 Noise Growth of Homomorphic Operations

In this section we show that the noise in the ciphertexts grows basically additively when we perform any homomorphic operation, including products. Using the analysis done in Sect. 4.3, it is easy to derive upper bounds to the noise accumulated by the homomorphic operations.

Lemma 11 (Noise of homomorphic additions). *Let n be an integer bigger than or equal to 2. For $i \in [\![1, n]\!]$, let c_i be a scalar encryption of s_i and $\mathbf{c}_i$ be a vector encryption of v_i. Compute the homomorphic sum of these ciphertexts as follows: $c := \sum_{i=1}^{n} c_i \in R$ and $\mathbf{c} := \sum_{i=1}^{n} \mathbf{c}_i \in R^{\ell}$. Then, $\mathsf{err}(c) = \sum_{i=1}^{n} \mathsf{err}(c_i)$ and $\mathsf{err}(\mathbf{c}) = \sum_{i=1}^{n} \mathsf{err}(\mathbf{c}_i)$. In particular, if all c_i's and $\mathbf{c}_i$'s are fresh ciphertexts, we have*

$$\|\mathsf{err}(c)\| < n2^{\rho} \text{ and } \|\mathsf{err}(\mathbf{c})\| < n2^{\rho}.$$

Proof. Because each c_i is of the form $(pq_i + r_i + \lfloor p/t \rceil s_i)k$, it is clear that $\mathsf{err}(c) = \sum_{i=1}^{n} r_i = \sum_{i=1}^{n} \mathsf{err}(c_i)$. By Lemma 2, if all c_i's are fresh ciphertexts, we have $\|\mathsf{err}(c)\| \leq \sum_{i=1}^{n} \|\mathsf{err}(c_i)\| < n2^{\rho}$ and the particular case holds.

Basically the same argument holds for vector ciphertexts. □

The noise growth of a sequence of homomorphic products involving only vector ciphertexts is essentially equal to the one of mixed products.

Lemma 12 (Noise growth of products of vector ciphertexts). *Let n be an integer bigger than or equal to 1. For $i \in [\![0, n]\!]$, let $\mathbf{c}_i$ be an encryption of m_i. Let also $\mathbf{c}'_0 := \mathbf{c}_0$ and $\mathbf{c}'_i := \mathsf{GAHE.MultVec}(\mathbf{c}'_{i-1}, \mathbf{c}_i)$ for $i > 0$. (Notice that $\mathbf{c}'_i$ is an encryption of $\prod_{j=0}^{i} m_j$). Assume that B is an upper bound to the product of the plaintexts, i.e., $\left\|\prod_{i=j}^{n} m_i\right\| \leq B$ for $0 \leq j \leq n$. Then,*

$$\|\mathsf{err}(\mathbf{c}'_n)\| < NB\,\|\mathsf{err}(\mathbf{c}_0)\| + \sum_{i=1}^{n} N^2 B\ell b\,\|\mathsf{err}(\mathbf{c}_i)\|\,.$$

In particular, if all the products only involve fresh ciphertexts, then

$$\|\mathsf{err}(\mathbf{c}'_n)\| < 2N^2 B\ell b n 2^{\rho}.$$

Proof. This proof is basically equal to the one of Lemma 5, hence, we omit it. □

References

[ASP14] Alperin-Sheriff, J., Peikert, C.: Faster bootstrapping with polynomial error. In: Garay, J.A., Gennaro, R. (eds.) CRYPTO 2014. LNCS, vol. 8616, pp. 297–314. Springer, Heidelberg (2014). https://doi.org/10.1007/978-3-662-44371-2_17

[BBL17] Benarroch, D., Brakerski, Z., Lepoint, T.: FHE over the Integers: decomposed and Batched in the Post-Quantum Regime. In: Fehr, S. (ed.) PKC 2017. LNCS, vol. 10175, pp. 271–301. Springer, Heidelberg (2017). https://doi.org/10.1007/978-3-662-54388-7_10

[BGV12] Brakerski, Z., Gentry, C., Vaikuntanathan, V.: (Leveled) fully homomorphic encryption without bootstrapping. In: Proceedings of the 3rd Innovations in Theoretical Computer Science Conference, ITCS 2012, pp. 309–325. ACM, New York (2012)

[Bra12] Brakerski, Z.: Fully homomorphic encryption without modulus switching from classical GapSVP. In: Safavi-Naini, R., Canetti, R. (eds.) CRYPTO 2012. LNCS, vol. 7417, pp. 868–886. Springer, Heidelberg (2012). https://doi.org/10.1007/978-3-642-32009-5_50

[BV11] Brakerski, Z., Vaikuntanathan, V.: Efficient fully homomorphic encryption from (standard) LWE. In: 2011 IEEE 52nd Annual Symposium on Foundations of Computer Science, pp. 97–106, October 2011

[CCK+13] Cheon, J.H., et al.: Batch fully homomorphic encryption over the integers. In: Johansson, T., Nguyen, P.Q. (eds.) EUROCRYPT 2013. LNCS, vol. 7881, pp. 315–335. Springer, Heidelberg (2013). https://doi.org/10.1007/978-3-642-38348-9_20

[CGGI16] Chillotti, I., Gama, N., Georgieva, M., Izabachène, M.: Faster fully homomorphic encryption: bootstrapping in less than 0.1 seconds. In: Cheon, J.H., Takagi, T. (eds.) ASIACRYPT 2016. LNCS, vol. 10031, pp. 3–33. Springer, Heidelberg (2016). https://doi.org/10.1007/978-3-662-53887-6_1

[CN11] Chen, Y., Nguyen, P.Q.: BKZ 2.0: better lattice security estimates. In: Lee, D.H., Wang, X. (eds.) ASIACRYPT 2011. LNCS, vol. 7073, pp. 1–20. Springer, Heidelberg (2011). https://doi.org/10.1007/978-3-642-25385-0_1

[CNT12] Coron, J.-S., Naccache, D., Tibouchi, M.: Public key compression and modulus switching for fully homomorphic encryption over the integers. In: Pointcheval, D., Johansson, T. (eds.) EUROCRYPT 2012. LNCS, vol. 7237, pp. 446–464. Springer, Heidelberg (2012). https://doi.org/10.1007/978-3-642-29011-4_27

[CP19] Coron, J.-S., Pereira, H.V.L.: On Kilian's randomization of multilinear map encodings. In: Galbraith, S.D., Moriai, S. (eds.) ASIACRYPT 2019. LNCS, vol. 11922, pp. 325–355. Springer, Cham (2019). https://doi.org/10.1007/978-3-030-34621-8_12, https://eprint.iacr.org/2018/1129

[CS15] Cheon, J.H., Stehlé, D.: Fully homomophic encryption over the integers revisited. In: Oswald, E., Fischlin, M. (eds.) EUROCRYPT 2015. LNCS, vol. 9056, pp. 513–536. Springer, Heidelberg (2015). https://doi.org/10.1007/978-3-662-46800-5_20

[DGHV10] van Dijk, M., Gentry, C., Halevi, S., Vaikuntanathan, V.: Fully homomorphic encryption over the integers. In: Gilbert, H. (ed.) EUROCRYPT 2010. LNCS, vol. 6110, pp. 24–43. Springer, Heidelberg (2010). https://doi.org/10.1007/978-3-642-13190-5_2

[DM15] Ducas, L., Micciancio, D.: FHEW: bootstrapping homomorphic encryption in less than a second. In: Oswald, E., Fischlin, M. (eds.) EUROCRYPT 2015. LNCS, vol. 9056, pp. 617–640. Springer, Heidelberg (2015). https://doi.org/10.1007/978-3-662-46800-5_24

[Gen09] Gentry, C.: A fully homomorphic encryption scheme. Ph.D. thesis, Stanford University (2009). https://crypto.stanford.edu/craig/

[GGM16] Galbraith, S.D., Gebregiyorgis, S.W., Murphy, S.: Algorithms for the approximate common divisor problem. LMS J. Comput. Math. **19**(A), 58–72 (2016)

[GHS12] Gentry, C., Halevi, S., Smart, N.P.: Fully homomorphic encryption with polylog overhead. In: Pointcheval, D., Johansson, T. (eds.) EUROCRYPT

2012. LNCS, vol. 7237, pp. 465–482. Springer, Heidelberg (2012). https://doi.org/10.1007/978-3-642-29011-4_28
[GSW13] Gentry, C., Sahai, A., Waters, B.: Homomorphic encryption from learning with errors: conceptually-simpler, asymptotically-faster, attribute-based. In: Canetti, R., Garay, J.A. (eds.) CRYPTO 2013. LNCS, vol. 8042, pp. 75–92. Springer, Heidelberg (2013). https://doi.org/10.1007/978-3-642-40041-4_5
[HG01] Howgrave-Graham, N.: Approximate integer common divisors. In: Silverman, J.H. (ed.) CaLC 2001. LNCS, vol. 2146, pp. 51–66. Springer, Heidelberg (2001). https://doi.org/10.1007/3-540-44670-2_6
[LS14] Lee, H.T., Seo, J.H.: Security analysis of multilinear maps over the integers. In: Garay, J.A., Gennaro, R. (eds.) CRYPTO 2014. LNCS, vol. 8616, pp. 224–240. Springer, Heidelberg (2014). https://doi.org/10.1007/978-3-662-44371-2_13
[Per20] Pereira, H.V.L.: Efficient AGCD-based homomorphic encryption for matrix and vector arithmetic. Cryptology ePrint Archive, Report 2020/491 (2020). https://eprint.iacr.org/2020/491

Group Signatures with User-Controlled and Sequential Linkability

Jesus Diaz[1(✉)] and Anja Lehmann[2]

[1] IBM Research – Zurich, Rüschlikon, Switzerland
jdv@zurich.ibm.com
[2] Hasso-Plattner-Institute, University of Potsdam, Potsdam, Germany
anja.lehmann@hpi.de

Abstract. Group signatures allow users to create signatures on behalf of a group while remaining anonymous. Such signatures are a powerful tool to realize privacy-preserving data collections, where e.g., sensors, wearables or vehicles can upload authenticated measurements into a data lake. The anonymity protects the user's privacy yet enables basic data processing of the uploaded unlinkable information. For many applications, full anonymity is often neither desired nor useful though, and selected parts of the data must eventually be correlated after being uploaded. Current solutions of group signatures do not provide such functionality in a satisfactory way: they either rely on a trusted party to perform opening or linking of signatures, which clearly conflicts with the core privacy goal of group signatures; or require the user to decide upon the linkability of signatures *before* they are generated.

In this paper we propose a new variant of group signatures that provides linkability in a flexible and user-centric manner. Users – and only they – can decide before and after signature creation whether they should remain linkable or be correlated. To prevent attacks where a user omits certain signatures when a *sequence* of events in a certain section (e.g., time frame), should be linked, we further extend this new primitive to allow for sequential link proofs. Such proofs guarantee that the provided sequence of data is not only originating from the same signer, but also occurred in that exact order and contains *all* of the user's signatures within the time frame. We formally define the desired security and privacy properties, propose a provably secure construction based on DL-related assumptions and report on a prototypical implementation of our scheme.

1 Introduction

Group signatures [5,17] extend conventional signatures to protect the signers' identity. Signers remain anonymous within the anonymity set defined by the members of a group formed by users who request to join and are accepted by the manager. Anyone with the group public key can verify signatures. To avoid abusing anonymity, an *opener* can usually re-identify the signer of any signature. This enables accountability and further processing if data needs to be more identifiable or linked, but requires full trust on the opener to ensure privacy.

J. A. Garay (Ed.): PKC 2021, LNCS 12710, pp. 360–388, 2021.
https://doi.org/10.1007/978-3-030-75245-3_14

Schemes with Trusted Openers. To reduce this dependency, alternatives quickly sprouted. In group signatures with Verifier Local Revocation, verifiers can keep local lists of *revoked* signers, not requiring them to open incoming signatures [10]. Traceable signatures [18,24] add an extra trusted entity who, after opening a signature by any given member, can produce member-specific trapdoors that can be used to link signatures originating by them. Convertably linkable signatures remove the opener, but incorporate a party who can (non-transitively) blindly link signatures within sets of queried signatures [23]. Recently, also blind variants for central opening have been proposed [26]. Still, all these alternatives use some sort of central entity for opening or linking, which needs to be fully trusted to ensure privacy. While this trust can be distributed [13], this still gives control to a set of central entities rather than users.

Schemes with User-Controlled Linkability. Instead of relying on trusted parties, it may suffice to let signers control which signatures will be linkable, and when. This is also ideal from a privacy perspective, as users retain full control. In this vein, Direct Anonymous Attestation (DAA) [6,12] and anonymous credential systems [15], also aimed at preserving signer/holder privacy, follow this approach. They enable user-controlled linkability through deterministically computed pseudonyms (from a scope and the user's key) within each signature. This makes all signatures for the same scope automatically linkable. Otherwise, they remain unlinkable. Such *implicit linking* has the drawback of being static: a signature that was decided to be unlinkable to some or all other signatures, will remain unlinkable forever. Thus, use cases with even a remote probability of needing to link signatures a posteriori would require to make them all linkable by default, eliminating all privacy.

Further, relying on the more privacy-friendly option of user-controlled and implicit linkability instead of having an almighty opener, makes formally defining the desired security and privacy properties of such group signatures much more challenging. In fact, to date no satisfactory security model for DAA in the form of accessible game-based security notions is known; we refer to [6,12] for a summary of the long line of failed security notions in that respect.

Alternatively, some existing group signatures offer user-controlled a posteriori linking or opening of previously anonymous signatures: In [29] users can claim signatures by outputting their secret key which allows to test whether a signature stemmed from that user. But this is an all-or-nothing approach, immediately destroying privacy of all the user's signatures and thus is unsuitable for most realistic scenarios. The recent work by Krenn et al. [26] implement a more flexible *explicit linking* by enabling users to issue link proofs for two (or, in theory, more) signatures. However, their model still crucially relies on the presence of a trusted opener to model and prove the desired security properties. Thus, even if only explicit linking would be needed, the scheme must allow full opening through a central entity in order to fit their model and hope for any provable security guarantees.

Ideally, one would hope for group signatures supporting both implicit and explicit linking to increase utility and, for scenarios handling sensitive data, without trusted parties that can unilaterally remove privacy.

1.1 Our Contributions

In this paper we provide the first provably secure group signatures that are purely user-centric, i.e., where only the user can control the linkage of her signatures. To allow for the necessary flexibility, our solution supports both implicit and explicit linkability. That is, the user can make signatures linkable with respect to pseudonyms when she generates them, and also link signatures with different pseudonyms afterwards through explicit link proofs.

Security Model Without Opener, and for Implicit and Explicit Linking. Our first challenge was to provide meaningful security notions when no opener is available that can be leveraged, e.g., to express who is a valid member of the group. Instead, we take inspiration from security models for DAA [6,12] to express membership of groups through linking. We define *anonymity* by requiring that it must not be possible to link signatures by the same user, except when she decides to make them linkable by default, or when she explicitly links them. For *traceability*, (1) it must not be possible to create signatures that are not traceable to any valid member of the group, and (2) it must not be possible to explicitly link signatures originating from different (possibly corrupt) users. Finally, for *non-frameability* we require that (1) no signature can be implicitly linkable to another honest signature unless it was honestly generated by the same user – who also made both signatures linkable by default, and (2) no adversary can explicitly link honest and dishonest signatures, or honest signatures that have not been explicitly linked by their signer. Note that we give two variants for both traceability and non-frameability. This is needed due to the possibility to implicitly and explicitly link signatures, and is a direct consequence of leveraging linkability to replace the opener. We emphasize that, to the best of our knowledge, implicit linking has not been modelled previously for group signatures – let alone in combination with explicit linking.

Sequential Link Proofs. When the pseudonymous signatures are over data with inherent order properties – e.g., time series – just re-establishing linkage is not enough. Therein, it may be needed to attest that the linked messages are given in the same order in which they were produced, and without omitting (possibly relevant) ones. For instance, smart vehicles in Intelligent Transportation Systems (ITSs) are required to send measurements to a data lake. There, the order of a sequence of events may be useful to detect anomalies: e.g., a vehicle reporting 35-45-30-40 l of fuel in a short timespan is probably an anomaly, while one reporting 45-40-35-30 is probably not. Or, again, in contact tracing systems, where pseudonyms are reused during a limited time, after which new ones are derived. Users may eventually be required to reveal their pseudonymous data spanning several of those pseudonyms, and omitting specific chunks of this data (or altering the order) may preclude effective contact tracing. In these use cases, the number of pseudonymously signed messages that may be required to be linked can be expected to be of at least many tens (and possibly a few hundreds) of signatures, in short time spans. Additionally, order may be relevant in less throughput-demanding scenarios. For instance, it may have very different implications when a person fails to pay X mortgage fees in a row, than the case when the X defaults correspond to months very distant in time.

This motivates our next contribution. We extend our previous model and construction to enable sequential link proofs: signers can prove that a sequence of signatures was produced in the specified order, and no signature is being omitted. To model this, we introduce a new unforgeability property, *sequentiality*, ensuring that honest-then-corrupt users cannot create sequential proofs for wrongly ordered sequences, nor omitting signatures. Our extended construction builds on efficient hash-chain ideas from anonymous payment systems [27].

Efficient Construction with Batch Proofs for Linking. We give an efficient construction realizing our model. Pseudonymous signatures are computed using the scope-exclusive nym approach from DAA and anonymous credentials, where the pseudonym is deterministically derived from a scope and the same secret key in the user's credential. This gives implicit linkage. For explicitly linking signatures, we propose a new way to batch the signatures being linked, leveraging the fact that pseudonyms are group elements that can be "aggregated". This leads to an efficient mechanism for linking large sets of signatures.

Implementation and Comparison. To further assess efficiency of our constructions, we implement them and report on the obtained experimental results (check Appendix A for notes on the implementation and a demo). Both the basic scheme and sequential extension outperform the most related previous work [26]: we link sets of ~100 signatures in ~40 ms, while [26] requires ~300 ms for linking only 2 signatures (besides requiring a trusted opener.)

2 Preliminaries

Notation. $\mathbb{G} = \langle g \rangle$ denotes a cyclic group $\mathbb{G}$ generated by g, $a \leftarrow A(\cdot)$ denotes a obtained by applying algorithm A, $a \leftarrow_\$ S$ means a is picked uniformly from set S, and $[n]$ denotes the closed interval $[1, n]$. H and H' are cryptographic hash functions. Signed messages are represented as a tuple of elements. When arguing about sets of such tuples, $\boldsymbol{\Sigma}$ denotes a set, and Σ_i the i-th element in $\boldsymbol{\Sigma}$. $\boldsymbol{\Sigma}_o$ is an ordered set, and $A_o \in_o S_o$ denotes that A_o appears in S_o, respecting order.

Bilinear Maps. Let $\mathbb{G}_1 = \langle g_1 \rangle, \mathbb{G}_2 = \langle g_2 \rangle, \mathbb{G}_T$ be three cyclic groups of prime order p, where an efficient mapping $e : \mathbb{G}_1 \times \mathbb{G}_2 \rightarrow \mathbb{G}_T$ exists. e satisfies bilinearity, i.e., $e(g_1^x, g_2^y) = e(g_1, g_2)^{xy}$; non-degeneracy, i.e., $e(g_1, g_2)$ generates $\mathbb{G}_T$; and efficiency, i.e., there exists $\mathsf{PG}(1^\tau)$ efficiently generating bilinear groups $(p, \mathbb{G}_1, \mathbb{G}_2, \mathbb{G}_T, g_1, g_2, e)$ as above, and computing $e(a, b)$ is efficient for any $a \in \mathbb{G}_1, b \in \mathbb{G}_2$. Moreover, we use Type-III bilinear maps [22], i.e., $\mathbb{G}_1 \neq \mathbb{G}_2$ and there are no efficiently computable homomorphisms between them.

Hardness Assumptions. We base the security of our scheme in the well known Discrete Logarithm and DDH assumptions [16] and in the q-SDH assumption for Type-III pairings [9], which we informally recall next.

q-SDH assumption (for Type-III pairings [9]*.)* Given $g_1 \in \mathbb{G}_1$, $g_2 \in \mathbb{G}_2$, $\chi \in \mathbb{Z}_p$, and a $(\mathbb{G}_1^{q+1}, \mathbb{G}_2^2)$ tuple $(g_1, g_1^{\chi}, g_1^{(\chi^2)}, ..., g_1^{(\chi^q)}, g_2, g_2^{\chi})$, it is computationally unfeasible for any polynomial-time machine to output a tuple $(g_1^{\frac{1}{x+\chi}}, x) \in \mathbb{G}_1 \times \mathbb{Z}_p \setminus \{-\chi\}$.

BBS+ Signatures and Pseudonyms. We rely on the BBS+ signature scheme proposed in [1] for Type-II pairings, and Type-III pairings in [11].

We use the following convention for BBS+ operations, for some previously generated Type-III pairing group $(p, \mathbb{G}_1, \mathbb{G}_2, \mathbb{G}_T, g_1, g_2, e)$:

- **Key Generation.** Compute $(h_1, h_2) \leftarrow_{\$} \mathbb{G}_1^2$, $y \leftarrow_{\$} \mathbb{Z}_p^*$, $W \leftarrow_{\$} g_2^y$. Set $sk \leftarrow y$ and $pk \leftarrow (W, h_1, h_2)$.
- **Signing.** Given a message m (assumed to be in $\mathbb{Z}_p$, pick $x, s \leftarrow_{\$} \mathbb{Z}_p^*$ and compute $A \leftarrow (g_1 h_1^s h_2^m)^{\frac{1}{x+y}}$. The signature is the tuple (A, x, s).
- **Verification.** Given a signature (A, x, s) over a message m, supposedly from $pk = (W, h_1, h_2)$, check that $e(A, W g_2^x) = e(g_1 h_1^s h_2^m, g_2)$.

We extend the proof of knowledge in BBS+ signatures to prove correctness of the pseudonyms that signers generate.

For pseudonyms, we follow [14]. Roughly, with the help of a hash function, pseudonyms are deterministically generated from a scope *scp* and a private key *sk* as $\mathsf{H}(scp)^{sk}$.

Proof Protocols. We use non-interactive proofs of knowledge obtained through the Fiat-Shamir transform [21]. $\mathsf{SPK}\{(x, r) : h = h_1^x h_2^r\}(ctx, m)$, denotes a signature of knowledge of (x, r) meeting the condition to the right of the colon, for public message m, and parameters ctx to prevent malleability attacks [7]. For verification, we write $\mathsf{SPKVerify}(\pi, ctx, m)$, returning 1 (correct) or 0 (incorrect).

Additional Building Blocks. We rely on an append-only bulletin board BB and pseudo random functions (PRFs). PRFs generate pseudorandom output from a secret key and arbitrary inputs. $\mathsf{PRF.KeyGen}(1^{\tau}) \rightarrow k$ generates the keys, and $\mathsf{PRF.Eval}(k, m) \rightarrow r$ pseudorandomness r from key k and message m. The BB is assumed to verify the data before writing, and written data cannot be erased.

3 Scheme with User-Controlled Linkability (UCL)

In this section we present our basic group signature scheme with user-controlled and selective linkability. We start by presenting the general syntax, then describe how the desired security properties can be formulated without the presence of an opening entity, and finally present our secure instantiation.

The core contribution of this section is the new security model that captures the desired security and privacy properties without a central (trusted) entity and allows for selective, user-centric linkability. The proposed scheme follows in most parts the standard approach of group signatures, integrates the pseudonym idea from DAA, and provides a new way to prove linkage of a *batch* of signatures.

3.1 Syntax

In group signatures, an *issuer* interacts with *users* who want to join the group and become group members. Members create anonymous signatures on behalf of the group, which verifiers can check without learning the signers' identity. In our setting, the anonymity of the signer is steered via *pseudonyms*, generated with every signature, as well as explicit *link proofs*. More precisely, a UCL scheme supports two types of linkability (see Fig. 1 for a pictorial representation):

Implicit Linkability: Every signature is accompanied with a pseudonym, generated by the user for a particular scope. Re-using the same scope leads to the same pseudonym, making all signatures generated for the same *scope* immediately linkable for the verifier. Pseudonymous signatures for different scopes cannot be linked, except via explicit link proofs generated by the user.

Explicit Linkability: After the signatures have been generated, they can be claimed and linked by the user: given a set of signatures, the user proves that she created all of them, i.e., links the signatures in the set.

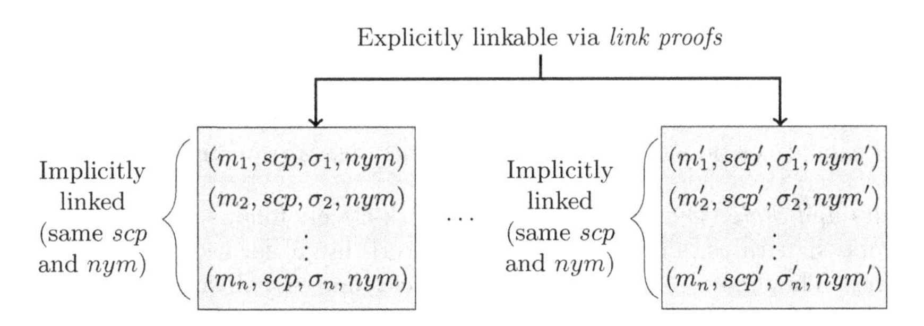

Fig. 1. Implicit vs explicit linkability on signatures by a same user, controlled by the user via scopes, pseudonyms and link proofs.

We emphasize that users have full control on the scopes, which can be any arbitrary (bit)string. For instance, in the contact tracing example given in Sect. 1, where identifiers are reused during 15 min, the scope could be derived from publicly available information, such as the current epoch. Alternatively, using randomly chosen scopes would lead to unlinkable signatures.

A UCL group signature scheme consists of the following algorithms:

$\mathsf{Setup}(1^\tau) \rightarrow param$: Generates the public parameters for the scheme.

$\mathsf{IKGen}(param) \rightarrow (isk, ipk)$: Generates the issuer's keypair (isk, ipk).

$\langle \mathsf{Join}(ipk), \mathsf{Issue}(ipk, isk) \rangle \rightarrow (usk, \perp)$: To become a member of the group, the user runs the interactive join protocol with the issuer. If successful, the user obtains a user secret key usk.

$\mathsf{Sign}(ipk, usk, m, scp) \rightarrow (\sigma, nym)$: Signs a message m w.r.t. scope scp via user secret key usk. The output is a pseudonym nym and group signature σ.

$\mathsf{Verify}(ipk, \Sigma) \rightarrow 0/1$: On input a group public key ipk and tuple $\Sigma = (m, scp, \sigma, nym)$, containing a group signature σ and a pseudonym nym, purportedly corresponding to m and scp, returns 1 when the tuple is valid and 0 otherwise.

$\mathsf{Link}(ipk, usk, lm, \boldsymbol{\Sigma}) \rightarrow \pi_l/\perp$: On input a set of signature tuples $\boldsymbol{\Sigma} = \{\Sigma_i\}_{i \in [n]}$ and user secret key usk, produces a proof π_l of these signatures being linked or $\perp$ indicating failure. The link proof is also done for a specific message lm, which can be used e.g., to ensure freshness of the proof.

$\mathsf{VerifyLink}(ipk, lm, \boldsymbol{\Sigma}, \pi_l) \rightarrow 0/1$: Returns 1 if π_l is a valid proof for the statement that $\boldsymbol{\Sigma} = \{\Sigma_i\}_{i \in [n]}$ were produced by the same signer and for link message lm, or 0 otherwise.

We delay the definition of the correctness properties for a UCL scheme after introducing some extra notation in the next section.

3.2 Security Model

A UCL group signature scheme should provide the following privacy and security properties: For privacy, signatures should not leak anything about the signer's identity beyond what is exposed by the user through implicit and explicit linkability (**anonymity**). Security is expressed through a number of properties covering the desired unforgeability guarantees: signatures should only be created by users that have correctly joined the group (**traceability**), and even a corrupt issuer should not be able to impersonate honest users (**non-frameability**).

Oracles and State. Our definitional framework closely follows the existing work of group signatures, and in particular the work by [5] for security of dynamic schemes. They make use of a number of oracles and global variables that allow the adversary to engage with honest parties, and which we adjust to our setting.

ADDU: Runs ⟨Join, Issue⟩ between an honest user and an honest issuer, allowing the adversary to enroll honest users. The new user key is stored as USK[uid].

SNDU: (The SeND to User oracle.) Runs the Join process on behalf of an honest user, against an adversarially controlled issuer. The new user key is stored as USK[uid].

SNDI: (The SeND to Issuer oracle.) Runs the Issue process on behalf of an honest issuer, allowing the adversary to join in the role of corrupt users in games with an honest issuer. Updates transcript[uid] with a transcript of the exchanged messages.

SIGN/LINK: Allow the adversary to obtain honest users' signatures/link proofs for messages/signatures of his choice (with restrictions in anonymity game).

$\mathsf{CH\text{-}SIGN}_b/\mathsf{CH\text{-}LINK}_b$: Challenge oracles in the anonymity game that allow the adversary to get signatures and link proofs for a challenge user uid_b.

Figure 2 presents the details of the oracles used in our games: the standard ADDU, SNDU, and SNDI oracles as defined in [5], and SIGN and $\mathsf{CH\text{-}SIGN}_b$, which we modify from [5], and LINK and $\mathsf{CH\text{-}LINK}_b$, which are specific to our model.

Table 1. Information stored by the global state variables.

Variable	Content
uid_b^*	Challenge user in anon-b. Ignored in the other games
HUL	uids of honest users that have joined
CUL	uids of corrupt users that have joined (needed when issuer is honest)
SIG[uid]	Signature tuples (m, scp, σ, nym) produced by SIGN for user uid
CSIG	Signatures tuples (m, scp, σ, nym) by uid_b^* produced via $\mathsf{CH\text{-}SIGN}_b$
LNK[uid]	Link queries $(lm, \boldsymbol{\Sigma})$ sent to LINK for uid
CLNK	Link queries $(lm, \boldsymbol{\Sigma})$ made to $\mathsf{CH\text{-}LINK}_b$
USK[uid]	Signing key of honest user uid
transcript[uid]	Messages from join protocol between user uid & Honest issuer

Helper Function Identify. In some security games we need to determine if a certain user secret key was used to create a given signature. For this we follow DAA work [6,12] and assume the availability of a function $\mathsf{Identify}(ipk, usk, \Sigma) \to 0/1$, returning 1 when $\Sigma = (m, scp, \sigma, nym)$ was produced by usk, or 0 otherwise.

We assume the following behaviour of Identify: for all $(isk, ipk) \leftarrow \mathsf{IKGen}(param)$, and all $\Sigma = (m, scp, \sigma, nym)$ where $\mathsf{Verify}(ipk, \Sigma) = 1$ there must exist *exactly one* usk (from the user secret key space induced by $\langle \mathsf{Join}(ipk), \mathsf{Issue}(ipk, isk) \rangle$) such that $\mathsf{Identify}(ipk, usk, \Sigma) = 1$.

We use the function for keys of both honest and corrupt users. Abusing notation, we write $\mathsf{Identify}(\mathsf{uid}, \Sigma)$ to indicate that Identify is run for the secret key usk of user uid (where ipk is clear from the context). For honest users, Identify simply uses USK[uid]; while keys of corrupt users can be extracted from the join transcript. For the latter, note that Identify is only used in games where the issuer is honest, i.e., such a transcript is available. In our concrete scheme we exploit the random oracle to extract a user's keys via rewinding. If online-extractable proofs are used, then Identify will also receive the trapdoor information as input.

We now formally capture the expected security properties.

ADDU (uid) // From [5]

if uid $\in$ HUL $\cup$ CUL : **return** $\perp$
HUL $\leftarrow$ HUL $\cup$ {uid}
$\mathsf{dec}^{\mathsf{uid}} \leftarrow \mathsf{cont}, st^{\mathsf{uid}}_{\mathsf{Join}} \leftarrow ipk, st^{\mathsf{uid}}_{\mathsf{Issue}} \leftarrow (isk, ipk)$
$(st^{\mathsf{uid}}_{\mathsf{Join}}, \mathsf{M}_{\mathsf{Issue}}, \mathsf{dec}^{\mathsf{uid}}) \leftarrow \mathsf{Join}(st^{\mathsf{uid}}_{\mathsf{Join}}, \perp)$
while $\mathsf{dec}^{\mathsf{uid}} = \mathsf{cont}$:
  $(st^{\mathsf{uid}}_{\mathsf{Issue}}, \mathsf{M}_{\mathsf{Join}}, \mathsf{dec}^{\mathsf{uid}}) \leftarrow \mathsf{Issue}(st^{\mathsf{uid}}_{\mathsf{Issue}}, \mathsf{M}_{\mathsf{Issue}})$
  if $\mathsf{dec}^{\mathsf{uid}} = \mathsf{accept}$: transcript[uid] $\leftarrow st^{\mathsf{uid}}_{\mathsf{Issue}}$
  $(st^{\mathsf{uid}}_{\mathsf{Join}}, \mathsf{M}_{\mathsf{Issue}}, \mathsf{dec}^{\mathsf{uid}}) \leftarrow \mathsf{Join}(st^{\mathsf{uid}}_{\mathsf{Join}}, \mathsf{M}_{\mathsf{Join}})$
if $\mathsf{dec}^{\mathsf{uid}} = \mathsf{accept}$: USK[uid] $\leftarrow st^{\mathsf{uid}}_{\mathsf{Join}}$
return accept

SIGN(uid, m, scp) // Modified from [5]

if uid $\notin$ HUL $\vee$ USK[uid] $= \perp$: **return** $\perp$
$(\sigma, nym) \leftarrow \mathsf{Sign}(ipk, \mathsf{USK}[\mathsf{uid}], m, scp)$
$\Sigma \leftarrow (m, scp, \sigma, nym), \mathsf{SIG}[\mathsf{uid}] \leftarrow \mathsf{SIG}[\mathsf{uid}] \cup \{\Sigma\}$
return (σ, nym)

CH-SIGN$_b$(m, scp) // Modified from [5]

// Initialized with $\mathsf{uid}^*_b, \mathsf{uid}^*_{1-b}$ by the experiment
$(\sigma, nym) \leftarrow \mathsf{Sign}(ipk, \mathsf{USK}[\mathsf{uid}^*_b], m, scp)$
$\Sigma \leftarrow (m, scp, \sigma, nym), \mathsf{CSIG} \leftarrow \mathsf{CSIG} \cup \{\Sigma\}$
return (σ, nym)

CH-LINK$_b$(lm, $\boldsymbol{\Sigma}$) // New w.r.t. [5]

// Initialized with uid^*_b by the experiment
$\mathsf{CLNK} \leftarrow \mathsf{CLNK} \cup (lm, \boldsymbol{\Sigma})$
$\pi_l \leftarrow \mathsf{Link}(ipk, \mathsf{USK}[\mathsf{uid}^*_b], lm, \boldsymbol{\Sigma})$
return π_l

SNDU(uid, M_{in}) // From [5]

if uid $\notin$ HUL :
  HUL $\leftarrow$ HUL $\cup$ {uid}
  $\mathsf{M}_{in} \leftarrow \perp, \mathsf{dec}^{\mathsf{uid}} \leftarrow \mathsf{cont}$
if $\mathsf{dec}^{\mathsf{uid}} \neq \mathsf{cont}$: **return** $\perp$
if $st^{\mathsf{uid}}_{\mathsf{Join}} = \perp : st^{\mathsf{uid}}_{\mathsf{Join}} \leftarrow ipk$
$(st^{\mathsf{uid}}_{\mathsf{Join}}, \mathsf{M}_{out}, \mathsf{dec}^{\mathsf{uid}}) \leftarrow \mathsf{Join}(st^{\mathsf{uid}}_{\mathsf{Join}}, \mathsf{M}_{in})$
if $\mathsf{dec}^{\mathsf{uid}} = \mathsf{accept}$: USK[uid] $\leftarrow st^{\mathsf{uid}}_{\mathsf{Join}}$
return $(\mathsf{M}_{out}, \mathsf{dec}^{\mathsf{uid}})$

SNDI (uid, M_{in}) // From [5]

if uid $\in$ HUL : **return** $\perp$
if uid $\notin$ CUL :
  CUL $\leftarrow$ CUL $\cup$ {uid}, $\mathsf{dec}^{\mathsf{uid}} \leftarrow \mathsf{cont}$
if $\mathsf{dec}^{\mathsf{uid}} \neq \mathsf{cont}$: **return** $\perp$
if $st^{\mathsf{uid}}_{\mathsf{Issue}} = \perp : st^{\mathsf{uid}}_{\mathsf{Issue}} \leftarrow (isk, ipk)$
$(st^{\mathsf{uid}}_{\mathsf{Issue}}, \mathsf{M}_{out}, \mathsf{dec}^{\mathsf{uid}}) \leftarrow \mathsf{Issue}(st^{\mathsf{uid}}_{\mathsf{Issue}}, \mathsf{M}_{in})$
if $\mathsf{dec}^{\mathsf{uid}} = \mathsf{accept}$:
  transcript[uid] $\leftarrow st^{\mathsf{uid}}_{\mathsf{Issue}}$
return $(\mathsf{M}_{out}, \mathsf{dec}^{\mathsf{uid}})$

LINK(uid, lm, $\boldsymbol{\Sigma}$) // New w.r.t. [5]

if uid $\notin$ HUL $\vee$ USK[uid] $= \perp$: **return** $\perp$
$\mathsf{LNK}[\mathsf{uid}] \leftarrow \mathsf{LNK}[\mathsf{uid}] \cup (lm, \boldsymbol{\Sigma})$
$\pi_l \leftarrow \mathsf{Link}(ipk, \mathsf{USK}[\mathsf{uid}], lm, \boldsymbol{\Sigma})$
return π_l

Fig. 2. Detailed oracles available in our model.

Correctness. We formalize the correctness of Sign and correctness of Link properties in the full version [19].

Anonymity. We adapt the classic privacy notion to our setting. It expresses that signatures must not reveal anything about the signer's identity beyond what was intended by her, even when the issuer is corrupt. The adversary plays the role of the issuer and can trigger honest users to join, sign and link. Eventually, he chooses two honest users uid^*_0 and uid^*_1, and one becomes the challenge user uid^*_b. The adversary can receive signatures and link proofs of uid^*_b (via CH-SIGN$_b$ and CH-LINK$_b$) and must determine b better than by random guessing.

As our signatures support user-controlled linkability, we must be careful to exclude trivial wins leveraging it. There are two ways in which the adversary can trivially win. First, by leveraging implicit linkability: signatures by the same user and with the same scope are directly linkable. The adversary could exploit this by calling $\mathsf{CH\text{-}SIGN}_b$ and SIGN (the latter, for uid_0^* or uid_1^*) with the same scope. Second, the adversary can leverage explicit linkability by obtaining link proofs via LINK or $\mathsf{CH\text{-}LINK}_b$ for a set of signatures that contains challenge signatures, obtained though $\mathsf{CH\text{-}SIGN}_b$, and non-challenge signatures (for a challenge user), obtained from SIGN.

Definition 1. *(Anonymity). A group signature scheme* UCL *with user-controlled linkability is anonymous if for all ppt adversaries* $\mathcal{A}$*, the following is negligible in* τ*:* $|\Pr[\mathbf{Exp}_{\mathcal{A},\mathsf{UCL}}^{\mathsf{anon\text{-}1}}(\tau) = 1] - \Pr[\mathbf{Exp}_{\mathcal{A},\mathsf{UCL}}^{\mathsf{anon\text{-}0}}(\tau) = 1]|$.

Experiment: $\mathbf{Exp}_{\mathcal{A},\mathsf{UCL}}^{\mathsf{anon\text{-}}b}(\tau)$

$param \leftarrow \mathsf{Setup}(1^\tau), (ipk, isk) \leftarrow \mathsf{IKGen}(param)$
$(\mathsf{uid}_0^*, \mathsf{uid}_1^*, \mathsf{state}) \leftarrow \mathcal{A}^{\mathsf{SNDU,SIGN,LINK}}(\text{choose}, ipk, isk)$
if $\mathsf{USK}[\mathsf{uid}_d^*] \neq \bot$ for $d = 0, 1$:
  Initialize $\mathsf{CH\text{-}SIGN}_b$ and $\mathsf{CH\text{-}LINK}_b$ with uid_b^*
else :
  return $\bot$
$b' \leftarrow \mathcal{A}^{\mathsf{SNDU,SIGN,LINK,CH\text{-}SIGN}_b\mathsf{,CH\text{-}LINK}_b}(\text{guess}, \mathsf{state})$
// Trivial wins via implicit linking:
// $\mathcal{A}$ used the same scope in $\mathsf{CH\text{-}SIGN}_b$ and SIGN for one of the challenge user
if $\exists(*, scp, *) \in \mathsf{CSIG} \wedge \exists(*, scp, *) \in \mathsf{SIG}[\mathsf{uid}_d^*]$ for $d \in \{0, 1\}$:
  return $\bot$
// Trivial wins via explicit linking:
// $\mathcal{A}$ queried LINK or $\mathsf{CH\text{-}LINK}_b$ with both challenge and non-challenge sigs.
if $\exists \boldsymbol{\Sigma}$ s.t. $(\boldsymbol{\Sigma} \cap \mathsf{CSIG} \neq \emptyset \wedge (*, \boldsymbol{\Sigma}) \in \mathsf{LNK}[*]) \vee$
  $(\boldsymbol{\Sigma} \cap \mathsf{SIG}[\mathsf{uid}_d^*] \neq \emptyset \wedge (*, \boldsymbol{\Sigma}) \in \mathsf{CLNK}$ for $d \in \{0, 1\})$:
  return $\bot$
return b'

Traceability. This property covers the desired unforgeability guarantees for corrupt users of groups with an honest issuer. Intuitively, it guarantees that only legitimate members of the group are able to generate valid signatures on behalf of that group. The traditional approach in group signature models [5,26] is to ask the adversary for a forgery and leverage the trusted opener to check whether the forged signature opens to any user that has joined the group.

As our setting does not have such an opening entity, we cannot follow this approach and instead take inspiration from the DAA security models [6,12]. Therein, one uses the implicit availability of an $\mathsf{Identify}$ function (introduced above) which allows to check whether a given signature belongs to a certain user secret key (which we know from honest users, and can extract from corrupt ones). The adversary wins if he can produce valid signatures (or link proofs) that cannot be traced back via Identify to any member of the group. This alone would not be sufficient though, as our signatures also carry some information in their implicit and explicit linkability, which an adversary should not be able to manipulate either. That is, the adversary also wins if he can produce more standalone signatures that are unlinkable (for the same scope) than he controls corrupt users, or if he manages to produce a valid link proof for signatures of different corrupt users.

We have grouped these properties along the statement that the adversary has to forge, i.e., we have signature traceability for forgeries of standalone signatures, and link traceability that works analogously for the link proofs.

Definition 2. *(Signature Traceability). A group signature scheme* UCL *with user-controlled linkability provides signature traceability if for all ppt adversaries* $\mathcal{A}$, $|\Pr[\mathbf{Exp}^{\mathsf{sign\text{-}trace}}_{\mathcal{A},\mathsf{UCL}}(\tau) = 1]|$ *is negligible in* τ.

Definition 3. *(Link Traceability). A group signature scheme* UCL *with user-controlled linkability provides link traceability if for all ppt adversaries* $\mathcal{A}$*, the following is negligible in* τ*:* $|\Pr[\mathbf{Exp}^{\mathsf{link\text{-}trace}}_{\mathcal{A},\mathsf{UCL}}(\tau) = 1]|$.

Experiment: $\mathbf{Exp}^{\mathsf{sign\text{-}trace}}_{\mathcal{A},\mathsf{UCL}}(\tau)$

$param \leftarrow \mathsf{Setup}(1^\tau), (ipk, isk) \leftarrow \mathsf{IKGen}(param)$

$(\Sigma_1, \ldots, \Sigma_n) \leftarrow \mathcal{A}^{\mathsf{ADDU,SNDI,SIGN,LINK}}(ipk)$

return 1 **if** :

$\forall i : \mathsf{Verify}(ipk, \Sigma_i) = 1 \ \wedge \ \Sigma_i = (m_i, scp, \sigma_i, nym_i)$ // the scope is the same in all sigs

and one of the following conditions holds:

// Signature of non-member

1) $\exists \Sigma_i$ s.t. $\forall \mathsf{uid} \in \mathsf{HUL} \cup \mathsf{CUL} : \mathsf{Identify}(\mathsf{uid}, \Sigma_i) = 0$

// More unlinkable sigs than corrupt users

2) $\forall i, j : nym_i \neq nym_j \ \wedge \ \Sigma_i \notin \mathsf{SIG}[*] \ \wedge \ |\mathsf{CUL}| < n$

Experiment: $\mathbf{Exp}^{\mathsf{link\text{-}trace}}_{\mathcal{A},\mathsf{UCL}}(\tau)$

$param \leftarrow \mathsf{Setup}(1^\tau), (ipk, isk) \leftarrow \mathsf{IKGen}(param)$

$(lm, \boldsymbol{\Sigma}, \pi_l) \leftarrow \mathcal{A}^{\mathsf{ADDU,SNDI,SIGN,LINK}}(ipk)$

return 1 **if** :

$\mathsf{VerifyLink}(ipk, lm, \boldsymbol{\Sigma}, \pi_l) = 1$

and one of the two conditions holds:

// Contains signature of non-member

1) $\exists \Sigma \in \boldsymbol{\Sigma}$ s.t. $\forall \mathsf{uid} \in \mathsf{HUL} \cup \mathsf{CUL} : \mathsf{Identify}(\mathsf{uid}, \Sigma) = 0$

// sigs by different users

2) $\exists \mathsf{uid} \neq \mathsf{uid}', \Sigma \neq \Sigma' \in \boldsymbol{\Sigma}$ s.t. $\mathsf{Identify}(\mathsf{uid}, \Sigma) = 1 \wedge \mathsf{Identify}(\mathsf{uid}', \Sigma') = 1$

Non-frameability. This property guarantees that an honest user cannot be framed by the adversary, even when the issuer is corrupt. In our setting such framing can be done when signatures of an honest user are linkable to signatures that she has not generated. As we support two different types of linkability, we again need a dedicated variant of that property for each of them. The first captures non-frameability from standalone signatures, i.e., via implicit linking. In this case, the adversary can only frame an honest user by producing a signature that holds for the same pseudonym that an honest signature generated for that scope. Linkability (and thus framing attacks) across scopes is not possible and thus does not have to be considered here. Such linkage for different scopes is only possible via explicit link proofs. The second property we define captures non-frameability for these proofs, which the adversary can leverage to frame an honest user in two ways: producing a proof that (1) links honestly generated signatures with adversarial ones; or (2) producing a proof that links honestly generated signatures by the same user, but the honest user did not create that proof – i.e., it is the proof itself that is forged and aims to impersonate the honest user.

Definition 4. *(Signature Non-frameability). A group signature scheme* UCL *with user-controlled linkability is secure against signature framing if for all ppt adversaries* $\mathcal{A}$*, the following is negligible in* τ*:* $|\Pr[\mathbf{Exp}_{\mathcal{A},\mathsf{UCL}}^{\mathsf{sign\text{-}frame}}(\tau) = 1]|$.

Definition 5. *(Link Non-frameability). A group signature scheme* UCL *with user-controlled linkability is secure against link framing if for all ppt adversaries* $\mathcal{A}$*, the following is negligible in* τ*:* $|\Pr[\mathbf{Exp}_{\mathcal{A},\mathsf{UCL}}^{\mathsf{link\text{-}frame}}(\tau) = 1]|$.

Experiment: $\mathbf{Exp}_{\mathcal{A},\mathsf{UCL}}^{\mathsf{sign\text{-}frame}}(\tau)$

$param \leftarrow \mathsf{Setup}(1^\tau), (ipk, isk) \leftarrow \mathsf{IKGen}(param)$

$(\Sigma = (m, scp, \sigma, nym)) \leftarrow \mathcal{A}^{\mathsf{SNDU,SIGN,LINK}}(ipk, isk)$

return 1 **if** :

$\mathsf{Verify}(ipk, \Sigma) = 1$ and :

$\exists \mathsf{uid}$ s.t. $\Sigma \notin \mathsf{SIG}[\mathsf{uid}] \;\wedge\; (*, scp, *, nym) \in \mathsf{SIG}[\mathsf{uid}]$

Experiment: $\mathbf{Exp}_{\mathcal{A},\mathsf{UCL}}^{\mathsf{link\text{-}frame}}(\tau)$

$param \leftarrow \mathsf{Setup}(1^\tau), (ipk, isk) \leftarrow \mathsf{IKGen}(param)$

$(lm, \boldsymbol{\Sigma}, \pi_l) \leftarrow \mathcal{A}^{\mathsf{SNDU,SIGN,LINK}}(ipk, isk)$

return 1 **if** :

$\mathsf{VerifyLink}(ipk, lm, \boldsymbol{\Sigma}, \pi_l) = 1$

and one of the following conditions hold:

// Contains honest and adversarial sigs.

1) $\exists \mathsf{uid}$ s.t. $\exists \Sigma, \Sigma' \in \boldsymbol{\Sigma} : \Sigma \in \mathsf{SIG}[\mathsf{uid}] \wedge \Sigma' \notin \mathsf{SIG}[\mathsf{uid}]$

// Honestly created sigs., but π_l was forged

2) $\exists \mathsf{uid}$ s.t. $\forall \Sigma \in \boldsymbol{\Sigma}, \Sigma \in \mathsf{SIG}[\mathsf{uid}] \;\wedge (lm, \boldsymbol{\Sigma}) \notin \mathsf{LNK}[\mathsf{uid}]$

Definition 6. *(Security of* UCL*). A group signature scheme* UCL *with user-controlled linkability is secure if it ensures the previous anonymity, traceability and non-frameability properties.*

3.3 Construction

We now present our scheme satisfying the desired security and privacy properties. The core of our constructions follows the standard approach of group signatures (see, e.g., [8]): during join, users receive from the issuer a membership credential, and signing essentially is a proof of knowledge of such a credential. We use BBS+ signatures for such blindly issued membership credentials.

Adding **implicit linkability:** Whereas standard group signatures usually include an encryption of the user's identity (for opening) in her signature, we use the pseudonym idea of DAA and anonymous credentials instead [6,12,14] and, specifically, of [11]. That is, when creating a signature, the user also reveals a pseudonym $nym \leftarrow \mathsf{H}(scp)^y$ for her key y and a particular scope scp. Clearly, these pseudonyms are scope-exclusive, i.e., there is only one valid pseudonym per scope and user key [14]. The user also proves that she has computed the pseudonym from her key.

Adding **explicit linkability:** The existing solution for link proofs [14,26] of signatures with different pseudonyms is to let the user provide a fresh proof that all pseudonyms are all based on the same user key. So far, this approach has been proposed for linking only two signatures, and will grow linearly when being used for many signatures. For our proofs, we instead use the observation that all individual pseudonyms the signatures are associated to can form a "meta-nym" $\overline{nym} = \prod_{i \in [n]} nym_i = \prod_{i \in [n]} \mathsf{H}(scp_i)^y$. That is, the user can simply prove that she knows the secret key y such that $\overline{nym} \leftarrow \overline{hscp}^y$, where $\overline{nym}$ and $\overline{hscp} = \prod_{i \in [n]} \mathsf{H}(scp_i)$ are uniquely determined by the signatures.

We stress that we do not claim novelty of the main parts of the group signatures. The core contribution here is (1) the simple trick for making efficient batched link proofs, and (2) making the pseudonym idea of credentials and DAA also formally available for group signatures.

Our Construction Π_{UCL}. Our concrete construction works as follows:

$\mathsf{Setup}(1^\tau) \rightarrow param$. Generates a bilinear group $(p, \mathbb{G}_1, \mathbb{G}_2, \mathbb{G}_T, g_1, g_2, e) \leftarrow \mathsf{PG}(1^\tau)$ and two further generators $h_1, h_2 \in \mathbb{G}_1$ (for the BBS+ credentials).

$\mathsf{IKGen}(param) \rightarrow (isk, ipk)$. Outputs $isk \leftarrow_\$ \mathbb{Z}_p^*$ and $ipk \leftarrow g_2^{isk}$.

$\langle \mathsf{Join}(ipk), \mathsf{Issue}(ipk, isk) \rangle \rightarrow (usk, \bot)$. This interactive protocol lets the user blindly obtain a BBS+ signature by the issuer on her secret key y:

- Issuer: sends a random nonce $n \leftarrow \mathbb{Z}_p^*$ to the user.
- User: $y \leftarrow_\$ \mathbb{Z}_p^*, Y \leftarrow h_1^y$, $\pi_Y \leftarrow \mathsf{SPK}\{(y) : Y \leftarrow h_1^y\}((param, h_1, Y), n)$. Sends (Y, π_Y) back to the issuer.
- Issuer: Only proceeds if π_Y is valid. Computes BBS+ signature on y as $x, s \leftarrow_\$ \mathbb{Z}_p^*$, $A \leftarrow (Y h_2^s g_1)^{1/(isk+x)}$. Sends (A, x, s) to user.

- User: If $A \neq 1_{\mathbb{G}_1}, e(A, g_2)^x e(A, ipk) = e(g_1 Y h_2^s, g_2)$ outputs $usk \leftarrow (A, x, y, s)$.

$\mathsf{Sign}(ipk, usk, m, scp) \rightarrow (\sigma, nym)$. To sign a message m for scope scp, the user generates the pseudonym $nym \leftarrow \mathsf{H}(scp)^y$ and computes a proof that the pseudonym was computed for a key that she has a BBS+ credential on, including the message m in the Fiat-Shamir hash of the proof.

- Parse usk as (A, x, y, s).
- Compute the pseudonym as: $nym \leftarrow \mathsf{H}(scp)^y$.
- Re-randomize the BBS+ credential as $r_1, r_2 \leftarrow_\$ \mathbb{Z}_p^*$, $r_3 \leftarrow r_1^{-1}$ and $s' \leftarrow s - r_2 r_3$, $A' \leftarrow A^{r_1}$, $\hat{A} \leftarrow (A')^{-x}(g_1 h_1^y h_2^s)^{r_1}$, $d \leftarrow (g_1 h_1^y h_2^s)^{r_1} h_2^{-r_2}$.
- Compute $\pi_\sigma \leftarrow \mathsf{SPK}\{(x, y, r_2, r_3, s') : nym = \mathsf{H}(scp)^y \wedge$
$$\hat{A}/d = (A')^{-x} h_2^{r_2} g_1 h_1^y = d^{r_3} h_2^{-s'}\}(ctx, m)$$
for $ctx \leftarrow (param, A', \hat{A}, d, nym)$.
- $\sigma \leftarrow (A', \hat{A}, d, \pi_\sigma)$. Return (σ, nym).

$\mathsf{Verify}(ipk, \Sigma)$. Parses σ in Σ as $(A', \hat{A}, d, \pi_\sigma)$, checks that $A' \neq 1_{\mathbb{G}_1}$, $e(A', ipk) = e(\hat{A}, g_2)$,and outputs 1 if the SPK in Σ is valid for message m and scope scp.

$\mathsf{Link}(ipk, lm, \boldsymbol{\Sigma}) \rightarrow \pi_l/\perp$. Linking signatures is done by batching all nyms and scopes into $\overline{nym}$ and $\overline{hscp}$, and proving knowledge of the discrete logarithm of $\overline{nym}$ w.r.t. $\overline{hscp}$. The link message lm is included in the hash of the proof.

- Parse usk as (A, x, y, s), and $\boldsymbol{\Sigma}$ as $\{\Sigma_i = (m_i, scp_i, \sigma_i, nym_i)\}_{i \in [n]}$.
- If $\exists i \in [n]$ s.t. $\mathsf{H}(scp_i)^y \neq nym_i$, or $\mathsf{Verify}(ipk, \Sigma_i) = 0$, return $\perp$.
- Set $ctx \leftarrow (param, \{scp_i\}_{i \in [n]}, \{nym_i\}_{i \in [n]})$.
- Compute $\overline{hscp} \leftarrow \prod_{i \in [n]} \mathsf{H}(scp_i)$ and $\overline{nym} \leftarrow \overline{hscp}^y$.
- Output $\pi_l \leftarrow \mathsf{SPK}\{(y) : \overline{nym} = \overline{hscp}^y\}(ctx, lm)$.

$\mathsf{VerifyLink}(ipk, lm, \boldsymbol{\Sigma}, \pi_l) \rightarrow 0/1$. The verifier recomputes the meta-scope $\overline{hscp}$ and meta-nym $\overline{nym}$ from the individual signatures, verifies all signatures and π_l:

- Parse $\boldsymbol{\Sigma}$ as $\{\Sigma_i = (m_i, scp_i, \sigma_i, nym_i)\}_{i \in [n]}$.
- If $\exists i \in [n]$ s.t. $\mathsf{Verify}(ipk, \Sigma_i) = 0$, return 0.
- If $\exists i \neq j \in [n]$ s.t. $scp_i = scp_j \wedge nym_i \neq nym_j$, return 0.
- $\overline{hscp} = \prod_{i \in [n]} \mathsf{H}(scp_i)$, $\overline{nym} = \prod_{i \in [n]} nym_i$.
- Output result of verifying π_l for $\overline{hscp}$ and $\overline{nym}$.

3.3.1 Security of Our Construction

Theorem 1. *Assuming* SPK *is zero-knowledge and simulation-sound, our construction is secure under the discrete logarithm, DDH, and q-SDH assumptions, in the random oracle model for* H *and* SPK.

Proof Sketch. Under the DDH assumption [28], *anonymity* follows from zero-knowledgeness and simulation-soundness of the SPKs, and the fact that pseudonyms are indistinguishable from random when different scopes are used.

We realize Identify with the help of the pseudonyms. Given a signature (m, scp, σ, nym), Identify fetches y from the usk of the specified uid and, if $\mathsf{H}(scp)^y = nym$, returns 1; else, returns 0. Scope-exclusiveness of pseudonyms ensures the required uniqueness [14]. Then, *signature traceability* follows from unforgeability of the BBS+ credentials, and zero-knowledgeness and soundness of SPK: if the adversary produces, for the same scope, more unlinkable signatures than corrupt users, or a signature from a non-member, we extract a forged BBS+ credential and can break the q-SDH assumption [11]. Winning condition 1 of *link traceability* is shown similarly. For condition 2, soundness of SPK ensures the individual signatures and the link proof are valid discrete logarithm proofs. Also, after the uniqueness property of pseudonyms, no two nyms in the same link proof can have different values if derived from the same *scp*. This prevents malleability attacks: e.g., corrupt users joining with $y = a$ and $y = b - a$ and using nyms derived from those keys and the same *scp* in the same link proof. Thus, an adversary can only try to subvert the proof with nyms derived from different scopes. But this requires to find non-trivial roots in an equation of the form $g^{\alpha_1 y_1} ... g^{\alpha_n y_n} = 1$, where the y_i's are controlled by the adversary, but the α_i's are not, as the g^{α_i}'s are produced by H (a random oracle). We show that a successful adversary can be used to break the discrete logarithm assumption.

For *signature non-frameability*, we rely on the uniqueness property of the pseudonyms and zero-knowledgeness and soundness of SPK. We break the discrete logarithm assumption from an adversary forging a signature with the same scope and nym that a signature of an honest user. For *link non-frameability*, we rely on the zero-knowledgeness and soundness of SPK. First, a similar argument as in traceability ensures that the link proof must be over the same exponents. We leverage this to embed a DL challenge into the nyms and link proofs of an honest user. If the adversary forges a signature (for winning condition 1) or a link proof (winning condition 2) for this user, we can extract a solution to the challenge.

The full proofs are given in the full version of this work [19].

3.3.2 Leveraging a Trusted Bulletin Board

Our UCL group signatures target a setting where signatures are generated and collected in a pseudonymous manner, and where linkability can still be refined later on by the users. Such a setting implicitly assumes the storage and availability of the originally exposed group signatures, e.g., in form of a central data lake that collects all individual signatures. In applications where the data lake is trusted by the verifiers (or even maintained by them), we can leverage this to improve the efficiency of our scheme. For clarity, we refer to such a trusted data lake and the additional functionality it must provide as *bulletin board* (BB), which can be used as follows:

- All signatures Σ_i are sent to the BB, who verifies and appends them, if valid.
- Link and VerifyLink no longer check the validity of all Σ_i in $\boldsymbol{\Sigma}$, but simply check whether all signatures are in the BB.

By using such a trusted BB we can improve the efficiency of Link and VerifyLink significantly – of course for the price of trusting a central entity again. This trust assumption would be necessary for the anonymity, link traceability and link non-frameability properties. However, the functionality of the BB can easily be distributed, e.g., using a blockchain; or the trust enforced and verified via regular audits where verifiers randomly pick signatures in the BB and check their validity. Thus, we believe that such a trust assumption is much more relaxed than trusting an entity that can single-handedly revoke the anonymity of all users.

Requirements on long-term storage capacity of the bulletin board depend on the use case. However, it seems reasonable to assume that, for most real world settings, a maximum timespan for storing past signatures can be established.

4 Scheme with Sequential Linkability (sUCL)

We extend our basic UCL scheme to allow for sequential link proofs. These sequential proofs target a setting where the originally signed (and unlinkable) data has an inherent order, e.g., time series data when sensors or vehicles continuously upload their measurements into a data lake. While the data is collected in unlinkable form, the eventual subsequent link proof must re-establish not only the correlation but also the order of a selected subset in an immutable manner.

We start by describing the minor syntax changes needed for our sequential group signatures (sUCL), and then discuss the additional security property we want such a sUCL scheme to achieve. Roughly, when making a sequential link proof, a corrupt user should not be able to swap, omit or insert signatures within the selected interval – and yet, this proves, nor reveals, nothing about signatures *outside* the proven interval. For this *sequentiality* property, we consider security against honest-then-corrupt users. While this may seem too lenient, note that it fits many real world applications where signing is an automatic process performed in the background by some device or application. In those cases, the need to alter sequences will only arise *after* the signatures have been created and sent. But, as described, the produced signatures – which contain extra information to enable proving order – are assumed to be stored in a data lake. Then, eventually, users have to make some claim that involves proving order with respect to those previously stored signatures. But this limits the options of malicious users. E.g., assume signatures Σ_1, Σ_2 and Σ_3 are produced in that order (i.e., first Σ_1, then Σ_2 and finally Σ_3), but a malicious user $\mathcal{A}$ wants to prove the reverse order. Then, $\mathcal{A}$ needs to commit to that strategy *before* sending the signatures by consequently altering the order information embedded in the signatures. Our argument is that, in many real world cases, $\mathcal{A}$ will not know which order he will be interested to prove in the future. For instance, in a contact tracing scenario (for a pandemic), malicious users will not know what order they are interested to prove until *after* learning which has been the risky contact.

Moreover, which specific alteration might be needed would also depend on the originally produced (and signed) data, and uninformed/random alterations may very well be useless or even counterproductive for the purposes of a malicious user. Nevertheless, even modeling this weak property requires a non-trivial approach. In Sect. 6, we give some insight about what seems to be possible beyond the honest-then-corrupt approach.

Finally, we present a simple extension to our Π_{UCL} scheme that uses the trusted bulletin board sketched in Sect. 3.3.2 and includes a hidden hash-chain into the group signatures, which allows to re-establish the order of signatures.

Syntax of sUCL. The signatures—despite being unlinkable per se—must now have an implicit order that can be recovered and verified through SLink and VerifySLink respectively. Abusing notation, we consider the set of signatures $\boldsymbol{\Sigma}_o$ to be given as an *ordered* set, and the proof and verification is done with respect to. this order. Further, to allow signatures to have an implicit order, we need to turn SSign into a stateful algorithm. That is, in addition to the standard input, it also receives a state st and outputs an updated state st'. We model that the state is initially set together with usk during the Join protocol. In summary, a sUCL scheme follows the UCL syntax from Sect. 3.1 with the following modifications:

$\langle \mathsf{Join}(ipk), \mathsf{Issue}(ipk, isk)\rangle \rightarrow ((usk, st), \perp)$: Initializes user state st.
$\mathsf{SSign}(ipk, usk, st, m, scp) \rightarrow ((\tilde{\sigma}, nym), st')$: Stateful sign algorithm.
$\mathsf{SLink}(ipk, usk, lm, \boldsymbol{\Sigma}_o) \rightarrow \pi_{seq}/\perp$: Sequential link proof for the ordered set $\boldsymbol{\Sigma}_o$.
$\mathsf{VerifySLink}(ipk, lm, \boldsymbol{\Sigma}_o, \pi_{seq}) \rightarrow 0/1$: Verifies π_{seq} w.r.t. the order in $\boldsymbol{\Sigma}_o$.

4.1 Security Model for sUCL

We want the sUCL scheme to have (essentially) the same traceability, non-frameability and anonymity properties as in Sect. 3.2—and additionally guarantee the correctness and security of the re-established sequential order.

Traceability and Non-frameability. These properties cover the security expected through the controlled linkage (not order) and only need minor adjustments to cater for the changed syntax: In the games, we use SSIGN/SLINK instead of SIGN/LINK.

4.1.1 Sequentiality

This property captures the security we can expect from proofs that reveal the sequential order of several signatures issued by a same user. Namely, when a user makes a sequential link proof for an ordered set $\boldsymbol{\Sigma}_o = \Sigma_1, \ldots, \Sigma_n$, we want to ensure that $\Sigma_1, \ldots, \Sigma_n$ have occurred indeed in that order and that no signature is omitted or inserted. The latter prevents attacks where a corrupt user tries to "hide" or add certain signatures, e.g., when a driver is asked to reveal the speed measurements from a certain time interval and wants to omit the moment she was speeding.

We follow the classic unforgeability style of definition and ask the adversary to output a forged link proof with an incorrect sequence. Clearly, such a definition needs to be able to capture what the "right order" of signatures is, in order to quantify whether a forgery violates that order or not. To do so, we opted for a two-stage game where the adversary can engage with honest users and make them sign (and link) messages of his choice. This ensures that we know the correct order in which the signatures are generated. Eventually, the adversary picks one of the honest users uid^*, upon which uid^* becomes corrupted and the adversary receives her secret key and current state. The adversary wins if he outputs a valid sequential link proof that violates the sequence produced by the originally honest user, e.g., re-orders, omits or inserts signatures.

Clearly we must allow the adversary to possibly include maliciously generated signatures in his forgery, but must be careful to avoid trivial wins: as soon as we give the adversary the secret key of uid^* he can trivially (re-)generate signatures on behalf of the honest user. Thus, we ask the adversary to commit to a set of maliciously generated signatures $\boldsymbol{\Sigma}'$ *before* corrupting uid^* and request that his link forgery for alleged ordered signatures $\boldsymbol{\Sigma}^*$ must be a subset of $\boldsymbol{\Sigma}' \cup \mathsf{SIG}[\mathsf{uid}^*]$.

Definition 7. *(Sequentiality). A group signature scheme* sUCL *with user-controlled sequential linkability ensures sequentiality if for all ppt adversaries* $\mathcal{A}$*, the following is negligible in* τ*:* $|\Pr[\mathbf{Exp}^{\mathsf{sequential}}_{\mathcal{A},\mathsf{sUCL}}(\tau) = 1]|$.

Experiment: $\mathbf{Exp}^{\mathsf{sequential}}_{\mathcal{A},\mathsf{sUCL}}(\tau)$

$param \leftarrow \mathsf{Setup}(1^\tau), (ipk, isk) \leftarrow \mathsf{IKGen}(param)$
$(\mathsf{uid}^*, \boldsymbol{\Sigma}', \mathsf{state}) \leftarrow \mathcal{A}^{\mathsf{ADDU},\mathsf{SNDI},\mathsf{SSIGN},\mathsf{SLINK}}(\text{choose}, ipk)$
if $\mathsf{USK}[\mathsf{uid}^*] = \bot$: **return** 0
else : $\mathsf{HUL} \leftarrow \mathsf{HUL} \setminus \{\mathsf{uid}^*\}, \mathsf{CUL} \leftarrow \mathsf{CUL} \cup \{\mathsf{uid}^*\}$
// $\mathsf{USK}[\mathsf{uid}^*]$ contains (usk, st) of uid^*
$(lm^*, \boldsymbol{\Sigma}^*, \pi^*_{seq}) \leftarrow \mathcal{A}^{\mathsf{ADDU},\mathsf{SNDI},\mathsf{SSIGN},\mathsf{SLINK}}(\text{forge}, \mathsf{state}, \mathsf{USK}[\mathsf{uid}^*])$
return 1 **if** :
$\mathsf{VerifySLink}(ipk, lm^*, \boldsymbol{\Sigma}^*, \pi^*_{seq}) = 1 \ \wedge$
$\boldsymbol{\Sigma}^* \cap \mathsf{SIG}[\mathsf{uid}^*] \neq \emptyset \ \wedge$
$\boldsymbol{\Sigma}^* \subseteq \boldsymbol{\Sigma}' \cup \mathsf{SIG}[\mathsf{uid}^*] \ \wedge$
$\boldsymbol{\Sigma}^* \notin_o \mathsf{SIG}[\mathsf{uid}^*]$ // $\in_o$ means ordered check

4.1.2 Anonymity

In the basic scheme (UCL), we defined anonymity with the typical approach: the adversary first picks two honest users and must then guess which one is used to produce challenge signatures and link proofs. In UCL, we just needed to prevent the adversary from leveraging implicit linkability and explicit linkability. This boils down to not allowing the reuse of scopes between calls to $\mathsf{CH\text{-}SIGN}_b$ and SIGN (for challenge users), and not allowing to link signatures produced by $\mathsf{CH\text{-}SIGN}_b$ and SIGN (again, for challenge users).

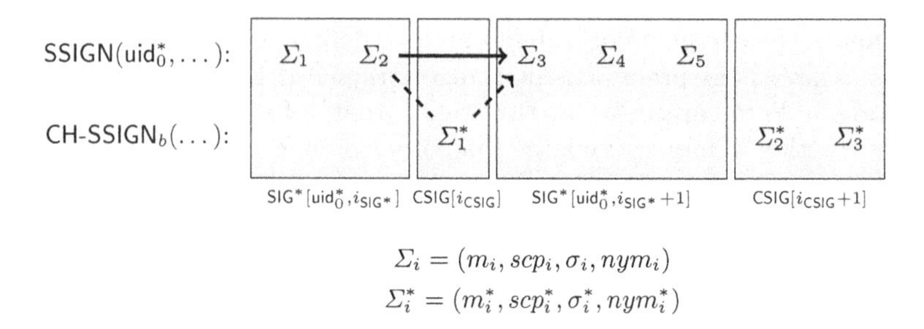

Fig. 3. Sketch of a strategy leading to a trivial win by $\mathcal{A}$ leveraging order information in sUCL, and the model to detect it.

In the sequential extension (sUCL), the idea is still the same, i.e., the adversary has to guess which is the chosen challenge user out of the two he picked up. However, the adversary has more ways to trivially learn the challenge user by leveraging the order information unavoidably revealed by the sequential link queries. Take, for instance, the scenario sketched in Fig. 3. There, the adversary interleaves a call to CH-SSIGN$_b$ (the one producing Σ_1^*) between calls to SSIGN for the same challenge user (the call that produces Σ_2 and the calls producing Σ_3–Σ_5). If the adversary makes a call to SLINK with the signatures produced before and after the call to CH-SSIGN$_b$ (e.g., including Σ_2, Σ_3 in Fig. 3) and the call fails, then the challenge user is the same as the one used in the calls to SSIGN. Indeed, the link call fails because one signature is missing in the sequence (and, in Fig. 3 the correct sequence would be the dashed one). Similarly, if the call succeeds, then the challenge user is not the one used in the calls to SSIGN (and the correct sequence in Fig. 3 is the solid one). Note that this works even when the scopes in all signatures are different: hence, it would not constitute a disallowed action in the UCL model. A similar strategy interleaving a call to SSIGN between calls to CH-SSIGN$_b$ also applies.

Oracles and State. In the previous example, we saw that calls to CH-SSIGN$_b$ and SSIGN (the latter for uid$_0^*$ or uid$_1^*$) can later be used to (trivially) expose the challenge user – by linking signatures produced before those calls, with signatures produced after. However, linking signatures produced within the same interval of such calls should not leak any information about the challenge user. To capture those intervals, we assign every honestly generated signature to a cluster (set of signatures). Since the calls to CH-SSIGN$_b$ and SSIGN are the events defining the linkage of which signatures would lead to trivial wins, we use those calls to mark when we need to start assigning signatures to a new cluster.

More specifically, to keep track of the cluster to which we need to assign signatures by challenge users, we resort to two counters: i_{SIG^*} and i_{CSIG}. Every time the adversary makes a call to CH-SSIGN$_b$, we dump all signatures produced by SSIGN(uid$_b^*$, . . .) since the last call to CH-SSIGN$_b$ to a new cluster SIG*[uid$_b^*$, i_{SIG^*}], and increment i_{SIG^*}. Similarly, when a call to SSIGN(uid$_b^*$, . . .)

Table 2. New/modified global state variables in the sequential UCL scheme.

Variable	Content
$\mathsf{SIG}[\mathsf{uid}]$	Signature tuples $(m, scp, \tilde{\sigma}, nym)$ Produced by SSIGN for user uid
$\mathsf{SIG}^*[\mathsf{uid}_b^*, i]$	i-th cluster of signature tuples for uid_b^* produced by SSIGN
$\mathsf{CSIG}[i]$	i-th cluster of challenge signature tuples $(m, scp, \tilde{\sigma}, nym)$
i_{SIG^*}	Counter for SIG^* clusters. Incremented when $\mathsf{CH\text{-}SSIGN}_b$ is called
i_{CSIG}	Counter for CSIG clusters. Incremented when SSIGN is called

$\mathsf{SSIGN}(\mathsf{uid}, m, scp)$

$\textbf{if } \mathsf{uid} \notin \mathsf{HUL} \vee \mathsf{USK}[\mathsf{uid}] = \perp : \textbf{return } \perp$
$((\tilde{\sigma}, nym), st'_{\mathsf{uid}}) \leftarrow \mathsf{SSign}(ipk, \mathsf{USK}[\mathsf{uid}], st_{\mathsf{uid}}, m, scp)$
$\Sigma \leftarrow (m, scp, \tilde{\sigma}, nym)$
$\mathsf{SIG}[\mathsf{uid}] \leftarrow \mathsf{SIG}[\mathsf{uid}] \cup \{\Sigma\},\ st_{\mathsf{uid}} \leftarrow st'_{\mathsf{uid}}$
// If anon game and challenge user,
// counter for challenge cluster gets incremented
$\textbf{if } \mathsf{uid} = \mathsf{uid}_d^* \text{ for } d \in \{0,1\} : i_{\mathsf{CSIG}} \leftarrow i_{\mathsf{CSIG}} + 1$
$\textbf{return } (\tilde{\sigma}, nym)$

$\mathsf{CH\text{-}SSIGN}_b(m, scp)$

// Initialized with uid_b^* by the experiment
$((\tilde{\sigma}, nym), st'_{\mathsf{uid}_b^*}) \leftarrow \mathsf{SSign}(ipk, \mathsf{USK}[\mathsf{uid}_b^*], st_{\mathsf{uid}_b^*}, m, scp)$
$\Sigma \leftarrow (m, scp, \tilde{\sigma}, nym)$
$\mathsf{CSIG}[i_{\mathsf{CSIG}}] \leftarrow \mathsf{CSIG}[i_{\mathsf{CSIG}}] \cup \{\Sigma\},\ st_{\mathsf{uid}_b^*} \leftarrow st'_{\mathsf{uid}_b^*}$
// Create new sigs. cluster for challenge users
$\textbf{for } d = 0,1 :$
$\quad \mathsf{SIG}^*[\mathsf{uid}_d^*, i_{\mathsf{SIG}^*}] \leftarrow \mathsf{SIG}[\mathsf{uid}_d^*],\ \mathsf{SIG}[\mathsf{uid}_d^*] \leftarrow \emptyset$
$i_{\mathsf{SIG}^*} \leftarrow i_{\mathsf{SIG}^*} + 1$
$\textbf{return } (\tilde{\sigma}, nym)$

$\mathsf{SLINK}(\mathsf{uid}, lm, \boldsymbol{\Sigma}_o)$

$\textbf{if } \mathsf{uid} \notin \mathsf{HUL} \vee \mathsf{USK}[\mathsf{uid}] = \perp : \textbf{return } \perp$
$\mathsf{LNK}[\mathsf{uid}] \leftarrow \mathsf{LNK}[\mathsf{uid}] \cup (lm, \boldsymbol{\Sigma}_o)$
$\pi_{seq} \leftarrow \mathsf{SLink}(ipk, \mathsf{USK}[\mathsf{uid}], lm, \boldsymbol{\Sigma}_o)$
$\textbf{return } \pi_{seq}$

$\mathsf{CH\text{-}SLINK}_b(lm, \boldsymbol{\Sigma}_o)$

// Initialized with uid_b^* by the experiment
$\mathsf{CLNK} \leftarrow \mathsf{CLNK} \cup (lm, \boldsymbol{\Sigma}_o)$
$\pi_{seq} \leftarrow \mathsf{SLink}(ipk, \mathsf{USK}[\mathsf{uid}_b^*], lm, \boldsymbol{\Sigma}_o)$
$\textbf{return } \pi_{seq}$

Fig. 4. Modified versions of the SIGN, SLINK, $\mathsf{CH\text{-}SIGN}_b$ and $\mathsf{CH\text{-}LINK}_b$ oracles.

is made, we increment i_{CSIG} so that all signatures produced by $\mathsf{CH\text{-}SSIGN}_b$ from that point onwards start being assigned to a new cluster $\mathsf{CSIG}[i_{\mathsf{CSIG}}]$.

In the example in Fig. 3, this restricts the adversary to making SLINK queries containing signatures in either $\mathsf{SIG}^*[\mathsf{uid}_0^*, i_{\mathsf{SIG}^*}]$, $\mathsf{CSIG}[i_{\mathsf{CSIG}}]$, $\mathsf{SIG}^*[\mathsf{uid}_0^*, i_{\mathsf{SIG}^*} + 1]$, or $\mathsf{CSIG}[i_{\mathsf{CSIG}} + 1]$, but not of any combination of (subsets of) those clusters.

The oracles used to model sUCL are summarized next and fully defined in Fig. 4. The state variables are summarized in Table 2. We emphasize that the new modifications only affect the anonymity property, while the other properties just need to adjust for the updated syntax.

$\mathsf{Adjacent}(\mathsf{LNK}[\mathsf{uid}], \mathsf{CLNK})$

if $\mathsf{uid} \notin \{\mathsf{uid}_0^*, \mathsf{uid}_1^*\}$: **return** 0
return 1 **if** $\exists(lm, \boldsymbol{\Sigma} = \{\Sigma_i\}_{i\in[n]}) \in \mathsf{LNK}[\mathsf{uid}], (lm', \boldsymbol{\Sigma}' = \{\Sigma_i'\}_{i\in[n']}) \in \mathsf{CLNK}$
and one of the following conditions holds:
1) Σ_0 was produced by SSIGN immediately after $\Sigma_{n'}'$ being produced by $\mathsf{CH\text{-}SSIGN}_b$
2) Σ_0' was produced by $\mathsf{CH\text{-}SSIGN}_b$ inmmediately after Σ_n being produced by SSIGN

Fig. 5. Definition of the helper function Adjacent.

- SSIGN/SLINK extend SIGN/LINK. SSIGN uses st_{uid}, the state of user uid, to call SSign, and updates it with the returned st'_{uid}. SLINK gets an ordered set.
- $\mathsf{CH\text{-}SSIGN}_b/\mathsf{CH\text{-}SLINK}_b$. Challenge oracles for the anonymity game, allowing the adversary to get signatures and link proofs for the challenge user.

Helper Function Adjacent. We rely on a helper function, $\mathsf{Adjacent}(\mathsf{LNK}[\mathsf{uid}], \mathsf{CLNK}) \to 0/1$. It explores LNK to check link queries for honest signatures and CLNK to check link queries for challenge signatures. It returns 1 if SLINK and $\mathsf{CH\text{-}SLINK}_b$ have been respectively queried with two sets of signatures that were sequentially generated, or 0 otherwise. This is an artifact of our specific construction rather than a general requirement, though. In Π_{sUCL}, given two adjacent signatures Σ_n, Σ_{n+1}, if Σ_n is included in a link proof and Σ_{n+1} in *another* link proof, it is possible to determine that they were sequentially issued. Consequently, if one is a challenge signature and the other is not, it would be possible to trivially guess the bit b in the anonymity game. The Adjacent function is defined in Fig. 5.

Anonymity Definition. Beyond the cumbersome changes required to prevent the new trivial wins, and the extra Adjacent check required by our specific construction, we capture anonymity in sUCL as in UCL. Specifically, the adversary controls the issuer and allows users to join, sign and link signatures. He chooses a pair of honest users, one of which is randomly picked to initialize the challenge oracles. Eventually, the adversary needs to guess which one of the users was chosen, task for which he can query again the oracles, subject to the restrictions described above. The formal definition is given next.

Definition 8. *(Anonymity). A group signature scheme* sUCL *with user-controlled sequential linkability ensures anonymity if for all ppt adversaries $\mathcal{A}$, the following is negligible in τ:* $|\Pr[\mathbf{Exp}^{\mathsf{sanon\text{-}1}}_{\mathcal{A},\mathsf{sUCL}}(\tau) = 1] - \Pr[\mathbf{Exp}^{\mathsf{sanon\text{-}0}}_{\mathcal{A},\mathsf{sUCL}}(\tau) = 1]|$.

Experiment: $\mathbf{Exp}^{\mathsf{sanon}\text{-}b}_{\mathcal{A},\mathsf{sUCL}}(\tau)$

$param \leftarrow \mathsf{Setup}(1^\tau), (ipk, isk) \leftarrow \mathsf{IKGen}(param)$

$(\mathsf{uid}_0^*, \mathsf{uid}_1^*, \mathsf{state}) \leftarrow \mathcal{A}^{\mathsf{SNDU,SSIGN,SLINK}}(\text{choose}, ipk, isk)$

if $\mathsf{USK}[\mathsf{uid}_d^*] \neq \bot$ for $d = 0, 1$: Initialize $\mathsf{CH\text{-}SSIGN}_b$ and $\mathsf{CH\text{-}SLINK}_b$ with uid_b^*

else : **return** $\bot$

$b' \leftarrow \mathcal{A}^{\mathsf{SNDU,SSIGN,SLINK,CH\text{-}SSIGN}_b\mathsf{,CH\text{-}SLINK}_b}(\text{guess}, \mathsf{state})$

if $\mathsf{Adjacent}(\mathsf{LNK}[\mathsf{uid}_d^*], \mathsf{CLNK}) = 1$ for $d \in \{0,1\}$: **return** $\bot$

// Trivial wins via implicit linking: $\mathcal{A}$ used same scp in calls to SIGN and CH-SSIGN$_b$

if $\exists(*, scp, *) \in \bigcup_{\forall i_{\mathsf{CSIG}}} \mathsf{CSIG}[i_{\mathsf{CSIG}}] \wedge \exists(*, scp, *) \in \mathsf{SIG}[\mathsf{uid}_d^*] \bigcup_{\forall i_{\mathsf{SIG}^*}} \mathsf{SIG}^*[\mathsf{uid}_d^*, i_{\mathsf{SIG}^*}]$ **for** $d \in \{0,1\}$:

  return $\bot$

// Trivial win via explicit linking (1): $\mathcal{A}$ queried SLINK with challenge sigs, or sigs in different clusters

if $\exists \boldsymbol{\Sigma}_o$ s.t. $(*, \boldsymbol{\Sigma}_o) \in \mathsf{LNK}[\mathsf{uid}_d^*] \wedge$

  $(\boldsymbol{\Sigma}_o \cap \mathsf{CSIG} \neq \emptyset \vee \boldsymbol{\Sigma}_o \notin \mathsf{SIG}[\mathsf{uid}_d^*] \vee \nexists i_{\mathsf{SIG}^*}$ s.t. $\boldsymbol{\Sigma}_o \in \mathsf{SIG}^*[\mathsf{uid}_d^*, i_{\mathsf{SIG}^*}])$ for $d \in \{0,1\}$:

  return $\bot$

// Trivial win via explicit linking (2): $\mathcal{A}$ queried CH-SSIGN$_b$ with challenge sigs in different clusters

if $\exists \boldsymbol{\Sigma}_o$ s.t. $(*, \boldsymbol{\Sigma}_o) \in \mathsf{CLNK} \wedge \nexists i_{\mathsf{CSIG}}$ s.t. $\boldsymbol{\Sigma}_o \in \mathsf{CSIG}[i_{\mathsf{CSIG}}]$:

  return $\bot$

return b'

4.2 Sequential Construction

We describe how we add such sequential behaviour to Π_{UCL} while preserving the desired anonymity. Recall that signatures must remain unlinkable and *not* reveal user-specific order (such as being the 5-th signature of some user). The order is only guaranteed and re-established for the subset of signatures linked via SLink.

Adding Order Information. Our construction leverages well known hash-chain structures [27]. Roughly, every i-th signature is extended with information linking it to the $(i-1)$-th signature by the same user. For this, we use pseudorandom numbers. First, x_i is generated for the i-th signature, and combined with x_{i-1}, from the previous signature, by computing $\mathsf{H}(x_i \oplus x_{i-1})$. The result of this hash and $\mathsf{H}(x_i)$ are added to the signature. In sequential link proofs, besides the basic link proof, the signer reveals the x_i's of all the signatures in the sequence.

Trusting an Append-only Bulletin Board BB. In our sequential scheme construction, the BB is *required.* It now also checks that the commitments to the pseudorandom numbers specified above are unique across all the uploaded signatures: this is critical to prevent malleable sequences. Also, being *append-only* prevents removing signatures once added, avoiding tampering with order.

Our Construction Π_{sUCL}. For brevity, we only describe the modified functions.

$\langle \mathsf{Join}(ipk), \mathsf{Issue}(ipk, isk)\rangle \rightarrow ((usk, st), \bot)$. Operates as in Π_{UCL}, but the user adds $k \leftarrow \mathsf{PRF.KeyGen}(\tau)$ to her usk and sets $st \leftarrow 1$.

$\mathsf{SSign}(ipk, usk, st, m, scp) \rightarrow ((\tilde{\sigma}, nym), st')$. Computes (σ, nym) as in $\Pi_{\mathsf{UCL}}.\mathsf{Sign}$ and extends σ with the anonymous sequence seq using the key k and state st:

- Parse usk as (A, x, y, s, k) and compute (σ, nym) as in Sign.
- Compute $n_{st} \leftarrow \mathsf{PRF.Eval}(k, 0||st)$, $n_{st-1} \leftarrow \mathsf{PRF.Eval}(k, 0||st-1)$.
- Compute $x_{st} \leftarrow \mathsf{PRF.Eval}(k, 1||n_{st})$, $x_{st-1} \leftarrow \mathsf{PRF.Eval}(k, 1||n_{st-1})$.
- Compute $seq_1 \leftarrow \mathsf{H}'(x_{st}), seq_2 \leftarrow \mathsf{H}'(x_{st} \oplus x_{st-1}), seq_3 \leftarrow n_{st}$.
- Set $seq \leftarrow (seq_1, seq_2, seq_3)$, $st \leftarrow st + 1$.
- Return $(((\sigma, seq), nym), st)$.

The signatures in our construction are required to be uploaded to the bulletin board BB. The entity responsible to do so may depend on the use case. BB verifies $(m, scp, (\sigma, (seq_1, seq_2, seq_3)), nym)$ and checks uniqueness of seq, rejecting the signature if either check fails. Uniqueness of seq ensures that no $\Sigma' = (\cdot, \cdot, (\cdot, (seq'_1, seq'_2, \cdot)), \cdot)$ exists in BB, such that $seq_1 = seq'_1$ or $seq_2 = seq'_2$.

$\mathsf{SLink}(ipk, usk, lm, \boldsymbol{\Sigma}_o) \rightarrow \pi_{seq}/\bot$. Sequential link proofs are computed as previous link proofs, but adding to the proof the commitment openings. Namely:

- Parse usk as (A, x, y, s, k) and $\boldsymbol{\Sigma}_o$ as $\{\Sigma_i = (\cdot, \cdot, (\cdot, (\cdot, \cdot, seq_{i,3})), \cdot)\}_{i \in [n]}$
- If any Σ_i does not exist in BB, abort. Else, compute π_l as in Link.
- For all Σ_i in $\boldsymbol{\Sigma}_o$, compute $x_i \leftarrow \mathsf{PRF.Eval}(k, 1||seq_{i,3})$.
- Return $\pi_{seq} \leftarrow (\pi_l, \{x_i\}_{i \in [n]})$.

$\mathsf{VerifySLink}(ipk, lm, \boldsymbol{\Sigma}_o, \pi_{seq}) \rightarrow 0/1$. Verifiers check the link proof as in the basic scheme, and recompute and compare the hash-chain:

- Parse π_{seq} as $(\pi_l, \{x_i\}_{i \in [n]})$, and $\boldsymbol{\Sigma}_o$ as $\{\Sigma_i = (\cdot, \cdot, (\cdot, (seq_{i,1}, seq_{i,2}, \cdot)), \cdot)\}_{i \in [n]}$.
- If any Σ_i does not exist in BB, return 0. Else, verify π_l as in VerifyLink.
- Check $seq_{1,1} = \mathsf{H}'(x_1)$. If not, reject.
- For $i \in [2, n]$, check $seq_{i,1} = \mathsf{H}'(x_i)$ and $seq_{i,2} = \mathsf{H}'(x_i \oplus x_{i-1})$. If not, reject.

Efficiently Fetching Previously Created Signatures. Finally, note that users can leverage the n_{st} values to easily fetch signatures from the bulletin board BB. If a user has a rough idea of the value of st when the signature was created, she can use PRF to recompute n_{st} for near st values. Otherwise, it is always possible to iterate from the initial value until finding the desired signature (as opposed to locally storing all signatures, or iterating through all signatures in BB).

4.2.1 Security of Our Construction

Theorem 2. *Assuming zero-knowledgeness and simulation-soundness of* SPK*, collision resistance of* H′*, pseudorandomness of* PRF*, and a trusted* BB *verifying signatures and checking uniqueness of seq (across all signatures in* BB*), our construction is secure under the discrete logarithm, DDH, and q-SDH assumptions, in the random oracle model for* H*,* H′ *and* SPK*.*

Proof Sketch. Proving *anonymity* essentially requires showing that the newly added *seq* components can be simulated, which follows from pseudorandomness of PRF and the modelling of H and H′ as random oracles.

For *sequentiality*, we show how to find collisions in H′, assuming a trusted BB verifying signatures and checking uniqueness of their *seq* components, and pseudorandomness of PRF. Since honest signatures must exist in $\boldsymbol{\Sigma}^*$, all the attacker can do is to remove or swap honest signatures, or insert dishonest signatures before or after honest ones. However, the adversary commits to the set $\boldsymbol{\Sigma}'$ of dishonest signatures in the first stage of the game, and he can only use signatures in this set and SIG[uid*] to produce $\boldsymbol{\Sigma}^*$. First, the uniqueness checks by BB prevent the adversary from creating multiple signatures with the same *seq* values and re-order them as desired. Then, we show that to remove or swap honest signatures, or insert malicious ones, the adversary must find different openings to the seq_1 or seq_2 values in the committed signatures that are consistent with their hash chain, implying a collision in H′. This ensures that, before corrupting the user, the probability of the adversary producing a dishonest signature that can be "chained" with an honest one, is negligible.

Full proofs for the new and modified properties are given the full version of this work [19]. The rest of the properties are proven as in the basic scheme.

5 Evaluation and Measurements

Table 3 summarises the functionality provided by the UCL and sUCL variants proposed in the present work, as well as that of the most related works [23,26]. The table focuses on the linkability aspects, and on which are the entities that can perform such linking.

Table 3. Functionality comparison between the schemes presented here and [23,26].

	User-controlled Linking	Authority-controlled linking	Sequential proofs
UCL (Sect. 3)	Yes	No	No
sUCL (Sect. 4)	Yes	No	Yes
GL19 [23]	No	Yes	No
KSS19 [26]	Yes	Yes	No

We now analyse the computational and space costs of our constructions, comparing with related work. In Table 4, we denote with $\mathsf{e}_{\mathbb{G}_X}$, p and h, respectively, an exponentiation (in $\mathbb{G}_X$), a pairing and a computation of a hash function; and with $n\mathbb{G}_1$, $n\mathbb{Z}_p$, $n\mathsf{h}$, n elements in $\mathbb{G}_1$, $\mathbb{Z}_p$ and hashes, respectively (also, elements associated to the Paillier encryption used in [23] are denoted with $\mathbb{Z}_{n^2}$). For the SPKs, we use the Fiat-Shamir transform, and for the PRF an HMAC construction [4]. The used curve is BLS12-381 [2,3]. The costs derived from verifying and storing the individual signatures involved in Link and VerifyLink are omitted, i.e., we only account for the costs derived from storing/computing or verifying the linkability proof itself. Note also that [23] does not include a linking functionality per se. The (mostly) equivalent functionality is a combination of their `Blind`, `Convert` and `Unblind` operations. Thus, in the table we show the aggregate of their costs. In addition, other operations supported by [26], but not compatible with our model, are also omitted. These include their `Opn`, `Lnk` and `LnkJdg` functions (in Table 4, `Link` and `VerifyLink` refers to `SLnk` and `SLnkJdg` in [26]).

Table 4. Computational (top) and space (bottom) costs. In the "Our scheme" column, we show in black font the costs of the UCL scheme (Sect. 3), and the text in red corresponds to the added costs of the sUCL scheme (Sect. 4). Since [23,26] only support explicit linkability, we only compare the linking costs in those schemes against the explicit linking of our schemes. Link costs for [23] aggregate their blinding, converting and unblinding costs. Operations from [26] that are not compatible with our model are omitted.

Algorithm	Our scheme	KSS19 [26]	GL19 [23]
Join	$3\mathsf{p} + 1\mathsf{e}_{\mathbb{G}_T} + 3\mathsf{e}_{\mathbb{G}_1} + 1\mathsf{h}$	$8\mathsf{p}$	$3\mathsf{p} + 1\mathsf{e}_{\mathbb{G}_T} + 3\mathsf{e}_{\mathbb{G}_1} + 1\mathsf{h}$
Issue	$4\mathsf{e}_{\mathbb{G}_1} + 1\mathsf{h}$	$6\mathsf{e}_{\mathbb{G}_1} + 1\mathsf{e}_{\mathbb{G}_2}$	$4\mathsf{e}_{\mathbb{G}_1} + 1\mathsf{h}$
$\underline{\mathsf{S}}$Sign	$14\mathsf{e}_{\mathbb{G}_1} + 2\mathsf{h} + 10\mathsf{h}$	$9\mathsf{p} + 13\mathsf{e}_{\mathbb{G}_1} + 6\mathsf{e}_{\mathbb{G}_T} + 2\mathsf{h}$	$16\mathsf{e}_{\mathbb{G}_1} + 15\mathsf{e}_{\mathbb{Z}_{n^2}} + 1\mathsf{h}$
Verify	$2\mathsf{p} + 9\mathsf{e}_{\mathbb{G}_1} + 2\mathsf{h}$	$9\mathsf{p} + 12\mathsf{e}_{\mathbb{G}_1} + 7\mathsf{e}_{\mathbb{G}_T} + 2\mathsf{h}$	$2\mathsf{p} + 12\mathsf{e}_{\mathbb{G}_1} + 11\mathsf{e}_{\mathbb{Z}_{n^2}} + 1\mathsf{h}$
$\underline{\mathsf{S}}$Link (s sigs.)	$(s+1)\mathsf{h} + (s+2)\mathsf{e}_{\mathbb{G}_1} + 2s\mathsf{h}$	$2s\mathsf{e}_{\mathbb{G}_1} + (s+1)\mathsf{h}$	$(7s+8)\mathsf{e}_{\mathbb{G}_1}$
Verify$\underline{\mathsf{S}}$Link (s sigs.)	$(s+1)\mathsf{h} + 2\mathsf{e}_{\mathbb{G}_1} + (2s-1)\mathsf{h}$	$2s\mathsf{e}_{\mathbb{G}_1} + 1\mathsf{h}$	N/A
	Our scheme	KSS19 [26]	GL19 [23]
Signature	$4\mathbb{G}_1 + 1\mathsf{H} + 5\mathbb{Z}_p + 3\mathsf{H}$	$6\mathbb{G}_1 + 1H + 5\mathbb{Z}_p$	$3\mathbb{G}_1 + 6\mathbb{Z}_p + 1\mathsf{H} + 6\mathbb{Z}^*_{n^2}$
Linkability proof (s sigs.)	$1\mathsf{H} + 1\mathbb{Z}_p + s\mathbb{Z}_p$	$1H + s\mathbb{Z}_p$	N/A

Figure 6 shows the results of experiments obtained with a C implementation of both variants of our scheme (run on a MacBook Pro 2.5 GHz Quad-Core Intel i7, 16 GB 2133 MHz LPDDR3 RAM), and iterating every trial 1000 times. Setup, Join and Issue are omitted, as they will typically take place either rarely or in non time-critical contexts. Sign and Verify run in well below 5 ms. For Link and VerifyLink (and the sequential variants), we experiment with sets of 10, 50 and 100 signatures. As in Table 4, this does not include verification of individual signatures. Note that even in the case of 100 signatures, we are still in the order of 40 ms for linking and 20 ms for verifying the proofs. For comparison, [26] reports signing and signature verification times around 100–150 ms, and linking and link verification times (for only two signatures) in the order of 330 ms.

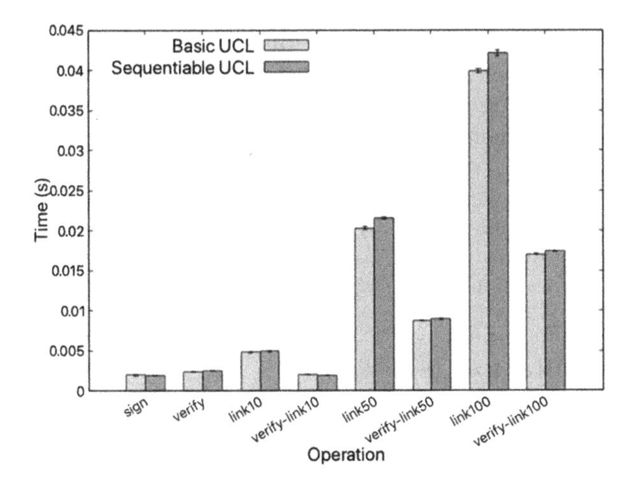

Fig. 6. Costs for Sign, Verify and Link (with 10, 50 and 100 signatures).

6 Conclusion

We have presented a new variant of group signatures that allows users to explicitly link large sets of signatures, supports implicit signature linking, and does not rely on a trusted opener. We have then extended this to allow proving order within a sequence of linked signatures, including that no signature has been omitted which was originally produced between the first and last signatures of the sequence. We have also given a formal model capturing the extended unforgeability and privacy properties in this setting, and efficient constructions realizing our model, which we have proved secure under discrete logarithm related assumptions. We have also reported on experimental evaluation obtained from an implementation of our schemes.

Several lines of further work are possible. First, we give an unforgeability property ensuring that order is maintained against honest-then-corrupt users, but we do not consider the equivalent for initially corrupt ones. While we argue that modelling honest-then-corrupt users is applicable to many real-world use cases, it is interesting to consider the stronger variant. In that case, initially, it seems that we can only hope to detect inconsistent proofs. Otherwise, if we only consider independent sequence proofs, a malicious signer may just "pre-compute" the sequence in the order he intends to prove afterwards, even if he publishes the signatures in a different order. Also, being able to prove non-linkage of signatures may be an interesting functionality – which would also impact the model. In practice, there may be use cases where proving not having issued a (set of) signature(s) can be useful. For instance, as a basic mechanism for (privacy respectful) blacklisting. Efficiency-wise, taking inspiration on [20,25], a great improvement would be to study the incorporation of batch verification of signatures (in addition to batch linking). On a more specific note, our construction for proving linked sequences introduces an artifact that affects the anonymity property. Namely, separately linking two adjacent sequences (i.e., where the last signature of one sequence was created immediately before the first signature of the other) makes both sequences linkable. Hence, removing this constraint would be an obvious improvement.

Acknowledgements. This work has been supported by the European Union's Horizon 2020 research and innovation program under Grant Agreement Number 768953 (ICT4CART). Jesus thanks Patrick Towa for very insightful and helpful discussions. Part of Anja's work was done while she was at IBM Research – Zurich.

A Implementation Notes

We have implemented the basic and sequential instantiations of our scheme. The efficiency analysis presented in Sect. 5 is based on that implementation, which is available at https://github.com/IBM/libgroupsig. Additionally, we have prepared a demo web application that leverages our implementation. It can be accessed from any PC with access to the Internet and a local installation of Docker[1] via the following commands:

```
$ docker pull jdiazvico/sucl:latest
$ docker run -p 5000:5000 jdiazvico/sucl
```

Where the first command downloads a Docker image that has a local installation of the compiled code, and the second command runs the demo. After successfully running both commands, the demo – which contains explanatory instructions on how to use it – can be accessed by going to http://127.0.0.1:5000 on any web browser.

References

1. Au, M.H., Susilo, W., Mu, Y.: Constant-size dynamic k-TAA. In: De Prisco, R., Yung, M. (eds.) SCN 2006. LNCS, vol. 4116, pp. 111–125. Springer, Heidelberg (2006). https://doi.org/10.1007/11832072_8
2. Barbulescu, R., Duquesne, S.: Updating key size estimations for pairings. J. Cryptol. **32**(4), 1298–1336 (2019)
3. Barreto, P.S.L.M., Lynn, B., Scott, M.: Constructing elliptic curves with prescribed embedding degrees. In: Cimato, S., Persiano, G., Galdi, C. (eds.) SCN 2002. LNCS, vol. 2576, pp. 257–267. Springer, Heidelberg (2003). https://doi.org/10.1007/3-540-36413-7_19
4. Bellare, M., Canetti, R., Krawczyk, H.: Keying hash functions for message authentication. In: Koblitz, N. (ed.) CRYPTO 1996. LNCS, vol. 1109, pp. 1–15. Springer, Heidelberg (1996). https://doi.org/10.1007/3-540-68697-5_1
5. Bellare, M., Shi, H., Zhang, C.: Foundations of group signatures: the case of dynamic groups. In: Menezes, A. (ed.) CT-RSA 2005. LNCS, vol. 3376, pp. 136–153. Springer, Heidelberg (2005). https://doi.org/10.1007/978-3-540-30574-3_11

[1] https://www.docker.com/. Last access on October 10th, 2020.

6. Bernhard, D., Fuchsbauer, G., Ghadafi, E., Smart, N.P., Warinschi, B.: Anonymous attestation with user-controlled linkability. Int. J. Inf. Sec. **12**(3), 219–249 (2013). https://doi.org/10.1007/s10207-013-0191-z
7. Bernhard, D., Pereira, O., Warinschi, B.: How not to prove yourself: Pitfalls of the Fiat-Shamir heuristic and applications to Helios. In: Wang, X., Sako, K. (eds.) ASIACRYPT 2012. LNCS, vol. 7658, pp. 626–643. Springer, Heidelberg (2012). https://doi.org/10.1007/978-3-642-34961-4_38
8. Bichsel, P., Camenisch, J., Neven, G., Smart, N.P., Warinschi, B.: Get shorty via group signatures without encryption. In: Garay, J.A., De Prisco, R. (eds.) SCN 2010. LNCS, vol. 6280, pp. 381–398. Springer, Heidelberg (2010). https://doi.org/10.1007/978-3-642-15317-4_24
9. Boneh, D., Boyen, X.: Short signatures without random Oracles and the SDH assumption in bilinear groups. J. Cryptol. **21**(2), 149–177 (2008)
10. Boneh, D., Shacham, H.: Group signatures with verifier-local revocation. In: ACM CCS 2004, pp. 168–177 (2004)
11. Camenisch, J., Drijvers, M., Lehmann, A.: Anonymous attestation using the strong Diffie Hellman assumption revisited. In: Franz, M., Papadimitratos, P. (eds.) Trust 2016. LNCS, vol. 9824, pp. 1–20. Springer, Cham (2016). https://doi.org/10.1007/978-3-319-45572-3_1
12. Camenisch, J., Drijvers, M., Lehmann, A.: Universally composable direct anonymous attestation. In: Cheng, C.-M., Chung, K.-M., Persiano, G., Yang, B.-Y. (eds.) PKC 2016. LNCS, vol. 9615, pp. 234–264. Springer, Heidelberg (2016). https://doi.org/10.1007/978-3-662-49387-8_10
13. Camenisch, J., Drijvers, M., Lehmann, A., Neven, G., Towa, P.: Short threshold dynamic group signatures. IACR Cryptology ePrint Archive 2020/16 (2020)
14. Camenisch, J., Krenn, S., Lehmann, A., Mikkelsen, G.L., Neven, G., Pedersen, M.Ø.: Formal treatment of privacy-enhancing credential systems. In: Dunkelman, O., Keliher, L. (eds.) SAC 2015, Revised Selected Papers. LNCS, vol. 9566, pp. 3–24. Springer, Cham (2016). https://doi.org/10.1007/978-3-319-31301-6_1
15. Camenisch, J., Lysyanskaya, A.: An efficient system for non-transferable anonymous credentials with optional anonymity revocation. In: Pfitzmann, B. (ed.) EUROCRYPT 2001. LNCS, vol. 2045, pp. 93–118. Springer, Heidelberg (2001). https://doi.org/10.1007/3-540-44987-6_7
16. Cash, D., Kiltz, E., Shoup, V.: The twin Die-Hellman problem and applications. In: Advances in Cryptology-EUROCRYPT 2008, 27th Annual International Conference on the Theory and Applications of Cryptographic Techniques, Istanbul, Turkey, 13–17 April 2008, Proceedings, pp. 127–145 (2008)
17. Chaum, D., van Heyst, E.: Group signatures. In: Davies, D.W. (ed.) EUROCRYPT 1991. LNCS, vol. 547, pp. 257–265. Springer, Heidelberg (1991). https://doi.org/10.1007/3-540-46416-6_22
18. Choi, S.G., Park, K., Yung, M.: Short traceable signatures based on bilinear pairings. In: Yoshiura, H., Sakurai, K., Rannenberg, K., Murayama, Y., Kawamura, S. (eds.) IWSEC 2006. LNCS, vol. 4266, pp. 88–103. Springer, Heidelberg (2006). https://doi.org/10.1007/11908739_7
19. Diaz, J., Lehmann, A.: Group signatures with user-controlled and sequential linkability. Cryptology ePrint Archive, Report 2021/181 (2021). https://eprint.iacr.org/2021/181
20. Ferrara, A.L., Green, M., Hohenberger, S., Pedersen, M.Ø.: Practical short signature batch verification. In: Fischlin, M. (ed.) CT-RSA 2009. LNCS, vol. 5473, pp. 309–324. Springer, Heidelberg (2009). https://doi.org/10.1007/978-3-642-00862-7_21

21. Fiat, A., Shamir, A.: How to prove yourself: practical solutions to identification and signature problems. In: Odlyzko, A.M. (ed.) CRYPTO 1986. LNCS, vol. 263, pp. 186–194. Springer, Heidelberg (1987). https://doi.org/10.1007/3-540-47721-7_12
22. Galbraith, S.D., Paterson, K.G., Smart, N.P.: Pairings for cryptographers. Discrete Appl. Math. **156**(16), 3113–3121 (2008)
23. Garms, L., Lehmann, A.: Group signatures with selective linkability. In: Lin, D., Sako, K. (eds.) PKC 2019. LNCS, vol. 11442, pp. 190–220. Springer, Cham (2019). https://doi.org/10.1007/978-3-030-17253-4_7
24. Kiayias, A., Tsiounis, Y., Yung, M.: Traceable signatures. In: Cachin, C., Camenisch, J.L. (eds.) EUROCRYPT 2004. LNCS, vol. 3027, pp. 571–589. Springer, Heidelberg (2004). https://doi.org/10.1007/978-3-540-24676-3_34
25. Kim, H., Lee, Y., Abdalla, M., Park, J.H.: Practical dynamic group signature with efficient concurrent joins and batch verifications. Cryptology ePrint Archive, Report 2020/921 (2020). https://eprint.iacr.org/2020/921
26. Krenn, S., Samelin, K., Striecks, C.: Practical group-signatures with privacy-friendly openings. In: ARES 2019, pp. 10:1–10:10 (2019)
27. Malavolta, G., Moreno-Sanchez, P., Kate, A., Maffei, M., Ravi, S.: Concurrency and privacy with payment-channel networks. In: CCS 2017, pp. 455–471 (2017)
28. Naor, M., Reingold, O.: Number-theoretic constructions of efficient pseudo-random functions. J. ACM **51**(2), 231–262 (2004)
29. Song, D.X.: Practical forward secure group signature schemes. In: CCS 2001, Proceedings, pp. 225–234 (2001)

Impossibility on Tamper-Resilient Cryptography with Uniqueness Properties

Yuyu Wang[1(✉)], Takahiro Matsuda[2], Goichiro Hanaoka[2], and Keisuke Tanaka[3]

[1] University of Electronic Science and Technology of China, Chengdu, China
wangyuyu@uestc.edu.cn
[2] National Institute of Advanced Industrial Science and Technology (AIST), Tokyo, Japan
{t-matsuda,hanaoka-goichiro}@aist.go.jp
[3] Tokyo Institute of Technology, Tokyo, Japan
keisuke@is.titech.ac.jp

Abstract. In this work, we show negative results on the tamper-resilience of a wide class of cryptographic primitives with uniqueness properties, such as unique signatures, verifiable random functions, signatures with unique keys, injective one-way functions, and encryption schemes with a property we call unique-message property. Concretely, we prove that for these primitives, it is impossible to derive their (even extremely weak) tamper-resilience from any common assumption, via black-box reductions. Our proofs exploit the simulatable attack paradigm proposed by Wichs (ITCS '13), and the tampering model we treat is the plain model, where there is no trusted setup.

Keywords: Black-box separation · Simulatable attack · Tamper-resilience · Uniqueness

1 Introduction

1.1 Background

Motivated by the fact that an adversary may maliciously modify the secret information of a cryptographic scheme by executing tampering attacks (e.g., heating up devices or injecting faults [12,13]) and observe the effect of the changes, Bellare and Kohno [10] and Gennaro et al. [37] independently initiated the study on tamper-resilient primitives. Bellare and Kohno proposed block-cipher against restricted tampering attacks (i.e., the class of tampering functions used by the

[1] Here, tampering functions mean functions used by adversaries that take as input original keys and output tampered keys.

Y. Wang—Research was conducted at Tokyo Institute of Technology.

J. A. Garay (Ed.): PKC 2021, LNCS 12710, pp. 389–420, 2021.
https://doi.org/10.1007/978-3-030-75245-3_15

adversary is restricted[1]), and gave a negative result showing that there exists no tamper-resilient block-cipher against arbitrary tampering functions. In their model (called the plain model in our paper), secret keys are potentially tampered with and there is no trusted setup. Gennaro et al. treated primitives against arbitrary tampering functions, whereas secret keys implicitly contain trusted public keys in their model (called the on-line model in [35]). Although most following works [7,8,11,17,23,24,28,34,35,49,53,62,67] did not adopt the on-line model, they assumed the existence of trusted common reference strings (CRSs), due to the difficulty of achieving tamper-resilience in the plain model. Amongst them, several works [17,23,24,28,35] are secure even when tampering functions could be arbitrary. Such strong security notions are worth considering since it is hard to restrict the range of attacks in practice. However, it is not desirable to put a strong trust on the entity that sets up public parameters in practice, and the assumption that tamper-proof public parameters are available is very strong. Especially, an adversary, who can execute fault attacks on secret keys, should also be able to alter CRSs stored together with the keys in the device. Therefore, it is desirable to understand what kind of primitives can be tamper-resilient in the plain model. The research by Dziembowski et al. [27] showed us a promising way to achieve tamper-resilience in the plain model, which utilizes non-malleable codes. Indeed, combining non-malleable codes with standard primitives can straightforwardly derive primitives (even with uniqueness properties) secure against (at least one-time) tampering attacks in the plain model. However, this work requires restrictions on tampering functions (and so do the following works (e.g., [6,18,22,29,30,46])). Another work by Ateniese et al. [4] proved that unique signatures are secure against subversion attacks, which allow an adversary to maliciously modify signing algorithms and hence capture tampering attacks. However, their results assume that the attacks meet an undetectability property or cryptographic reverse firewalls are available.

Up until now, all the (positive or negative) results on tamper-resilient primitives against arbitrary tampering functions either assumed tamper-proof public parameters (e.g., [23,24,28,35,49]), or focused on symmetric cryptography [10]. Hence, it remains unclear whether public key primitives can achieve (full) tamper-resilience in the plain model. In this paper, we study public key cryptography in this model and show broad negative results.

1.2 Our Results

We focus on the impossibility of proving the tamper-resilience of a wide class of cryptographic primitives via black-box reductions, and show several negative results. The type of black-box reduction we consider is the so-called fully black-box reduction, which does not use the code of adversaries. Moreover, a reduction algorithm should break the underlying assumption as long as the utilized adversary successfully breaks the tamper-resilience, no matter how much computing power the adversary has. We remark that most cryptographic primitives are proved to be secure via such type of reductions. We detail our results below.

Impossibility on Provable Deterministic Primitives (PDPs) and Signatures. At first, we consider a negative result on a class of primitives called

PDPs, which were firstly defined by Abe et al. [2]. A PDP evaluates a function by using a secret key and generates a proof for the input/output pair, and it is required that there exist only one valid output for each input. The definition of PDPs captures various primitives such as verifiable random functions (VRFs) [44,54,55], verifiable unpredictable functions (VUFs) [54,55], and unique signatures [39,54,55]. The (perfect) uniqueness property of these primitives prevents malicious signers from easily outputting many signatures on the same input, and thus prevents a simple denial-of service attack on a verifier forced to verify many outputs on the same input, even when the key pairs are selected by the signer in a subtle way. Also, due to this property, PDPs can be viewed as perfectly binding commitments to an exponential number of (perhaps random-looking) outputs [54], and thus can play important roles in micropayments [57], resettable zero-knowledge proofs [56], updatable zero-knowledge databases [52], verifiable transaction escrow schemes [47], etc. On account of the wide usage of PDPs, their security under tampering attacks is important and worth studying.

For these primitives, we show that it is impossible to achieve their tamper-resilience via black-box reductions. More specifically, we show that if a PDP is weakly unpredictable,[2] then there exists no black-box reduction deriving its tamper-resilience from any assumption captured by the notion of a cryptographic game [38,40,68], where a (possibly inefficient) challenger interacts with a monolithic adversary.[3] Here, weak unpredictability only requires that any probabilistic polynomial-time (PPT) adversary, neither allowed to make a query nor given a public key, cannot come up with a valid input/output pair. It is clear that any non-trivial PDP should satisfy such weak security. Furthermore, differently from negative results in [35,37], we treat very weak tamper-resilience, where an adversary only makes one tampering query and one computing query.[4] Hence, our result also captures tamper-resilient PDPs with self-destructive or key-updating mechanism.[5] We prove our result by using the simulatable attack paradigm proposed by Wichs [68], which is discussed in more details in the next subsection. By slightly modifying this proof, we can extend our negative result for a more general notion called re-randomizable signatures [43,66].

As by-product results, we prove the same negative result on weakly unforgeable unique-key signatures, in which there exists only one valid secret key for each public key, and injective one-way functions (OWFs). Here, weak unforgeability is defined in the same way as weak unpredictability, and up until now, a broad

[2] Unless explicitly stated otherwise, when referring to weak unpredictability, we mean computational weak unpredictability, not statistical weak unpredictability. The same argument is made for other security notions.

[3] By a monolithic adversary, we mean an adversary that is a single entity. Its antonym is a "multi-stage" adversary that consists of two or more components among which the state information cannot be passed freely [63].

[4] When focusing on negative results, the defined tamper-resilience is desirable to be as weak as possible.

[5] Self-destructive mechanism prevents an adversary from learning information by making further queries when tampering is detected, and key-updating mechanism allows a device to update its secret information.

class of existing signature schemes, e.g., ones where secret keys are discrete logarithms or factoring of public keys, or key pairs are in the Diffie-Hellman form, is captured by the notion of unique-key signatures (e.g., [21,36,45,51,66]). These results not only show the reason why many existing schemes cannot be proven tamper-resilient, but also indicate that when constructing signatures and OWFs in the presence of tampering attacks, one should circumvent the unique-key property and injectiveness. Note that there is no contradiction between our work and tamper-resilient unique signatures (implicitly) implied by previous results on non-malleable codes or subversion-resilient signatures [4,6,18,27,29,30,46], since those results require either restrictions on tampering functions or reverse firewalls as mentioned before.

Impossibility on Encryption Schemes. Next, we give a negative result on a class of public key encryption (PKE) schemes that we call *unique-message* PKE schemes, where for a ciphertext (possibly outside the support of the encryption algorithm), all the valid secret keys with respect to a public key (possibly outside the support of the key generation algorithm) lead to the same decryption result. More specifically, for a unique-message PKE scheme, in addition to ordinary algorithms as a PKE scheme, we require that there be an algorithm that we call the "plaintext-recovering" algorithm. Its syntax is exactly the same as the ordinary decryption algorithm. We require that it satisfy the usual correctness as the decryption algorithm. What makes it different from the ordinary decryption algorithm is that for each public key and each ciphertext, it holds that the decryption results are the same for all valid secret keys with respect to the public key (see Definition 15 for the formal definition). We note that the plaintext-recovering algorithm may be the original decryption algorithm, but in general it need not be so.

Our negative result shows that if a unique-message PKE scheme is weakly one-way, then there exists no black-box reduction deriving its tamper-resilience from any assumption captured by the notion of a *restricted* cryptographic game (i.e., any common falsifiable assumption [38,59]), where the challenger is restricted to be PPT. Here, weak one-wayness is defined in the same way as standard one-wayness, except that we only treat adversaries that are not allowed to see the public key. In other words, it only requires that any PPT adversary, neither allowed to make decryption queries nor given a public key, cannot recover the message from a randomly generated ciphertext. This is clearly a very weak security notion, and should be satisfied by any non-trivial PKE scheme. Furthermore, similarly to the cases of PDPs and signatures, we consider very weak tamper-resilience, where an adversary only makes one tampering query and one decryption query. Unlike our result for PDPs, this result does not capture black-box reductions to non-falsifiable assumptions where challengers are computationally unbounded, unless we assume that the PKE scheme is statistically weakly one-way. However, statistical weak one-wayness is not necessarily implied by (computational) one-wayness. We will give more details in Sect. 4.2. Here, notice that [23] also shows a negative result with respect to adversaries making a single tampering and decryption query. However, it only treats a strong type of tampering queries called "post-challenge" tampering queries, which can be dependent on the challenge ciphertext. Their negative result can be circumvented when considering challenge-independent tampering queries which capture a-prior tampering attacks in practice. Moreover, their negative result holds only for indistinguishability against chosen ciphertext attacks. It was unclear whether tamper resilient one-wayness against (even weak) chosen ciphertext attacks is achievable, while we give a partial but strong negative answer.

Although the definition of a unique-message PKE scheme has never been formalized before, it captures many naturally constructed PKE schemes (e.g., [15, 20, 36, 41, 64]). More specifically, since a PKE scheme is required to satisfy correctness, all the valid ciphertexts (i.e., ones in the support of the encryption algorithm) should be decrypted to a unique message, while invalid ciphertexts usually lead the decryption algorithm to abort, in order to prevent adversaries from learning useful information from the answers of decryption queries. Hence, a ciphertext is typically decrypted to a unique message if the used secret key is correct. However, due to possible difficulties of directly proving some implementations to be a unique-message PKE scheme, instead of insisting that the original decryption algorithm decrypt any ciphertext to a unique message, we give a relaxation by introducing the notion of the plaintext-recovering algorithm mentioned in the above paragraph. For ease of understanding the rationale behind our definition, as an instance, we show how it captures the Cramer-Shoup scheme [20] in the full paper. Furthermore, one can also see that unique-key PKE schemes, where there exists only one valid secret key for each public key, can be cast as unique-message PKE schemes (see the full paper for details). Similar to our negative results for signatures, our results for PKE schemes clearly show the exact barrier when proving tamper-resilience for existing schemes, and also give a guideline for future works on tamper-resilient PKE schemes.

Remark on the Plain Model. Our research focuses on tamper-resilient primitives in the plain model. This model might seem strong and assuming the existence of tamper-proof public parameters may be reasonable to some extent. However, such an assumption is not always realistic since fault attacks allow adversaries to maliciously modify CRSs stored in the devices. Besides, another line of works on subversion-resilient non-interactive proof systems (e.g., [1, 9, 33]) also alerted the danger of trusting CRSs. Therefore, in addition to previous positive results mentioned before [4, 6, 18, 27, 29, 30, 46], it is desirable to deepen the understanding of tamper-resilient primitives in the plain model. Moreover, we believe that trying to circumvent our negative results is a good starting point for future positive works, as we will mention in the open problems in Sect. 5.

1.3 High-Level Idea and Technique

Tamper-resilient primitives are secure against adversaries that try to tamper with the secret key, make (computing, signing, or decryption) queries, and output a forgery or recover a message. To prove the tamper-resilience of a primitive under some cryptographic assumption via a (fully) black-box reduction, one needs to construct a reduction algorithm that has access to any successful adversary against the tamper-resilience and breaks the assumption. Therefore, to show the impossibility on black-box reductions from tamper-resilience to common assumptions, what we need to do is to rule out the existence of reduction algorithms which can obtain useful information from any successful adversary, in any cryptographic game. Our basic idea for proving this is to show that any reduction algorithm cannot answer the queries made by some successful adversary, or it cannot benefit from the outputs of the adversary.

Tamper-Resilience Model. Before describing how we achieve our goal, we describe how we model a valid adversary against tamper-resilience in more details. Such an adversary consists of three independent components $(\mathbf{Tamper}, \mathbf{Break1}, \mathbf{Break2})$, which are allowed to share states before the security game but do not have communicating tapes once the game begins.[6] **Tamper** models a tampering function that on input the original secret key tries to output some tampered key helpful to $(\mathbf{Break1}, \mathbf{Break2})$. **Break1** makes a (computing, signing, or decryption) query. On input the answer generated via the tampered key, **Break2** tries to output some forgery (or recover a message from the challenge ciphertext). The model we consider captures the very weak type of tampering attacks where the adversary can only make one selectively determined tampering query, which in turn makes our negative results very strong. Notice that $(\mathbf{Break1}, \mathbf{Break2})$ learns no information on the secret key other than the information leaked from the answer of the, say, computing query, since $(\mathbf{Break1}, \mathbf{Break2})$ and **Tamper** (which sees the secret key) do not share any state generated during the security game. It is the same as the case that an adversary $(\mathbf{Break1}, \mathbf{Break2})$ determines the way to tamper with the secret key at the beginning of the game and tries to benefit from the answer of the computing query. We justify our model as follows.

Remark on Our Model. In our model, we define the tampering function as part of the adversary and the reduction can only have black-box access to it, while in previous works [23,24,28,35] considering arbitrary tamper attacks, the tampering functions are defined as tampering queries made by the adversary. Therefore, one may wonder whether the reductions considered by us are more restricted. We stress that in the security proofs of all these works, the reductions also access the functions in a black-box manner. Indeed, those reductions sometimes change the functions by hard-wiring other functions or values in the tampering functions, which make the functions seem "non-black-box". However, such procedures can be treated as changing the input of the functions rather than exploiting the structure of the functions themselves. Therefore, such modification for tampering functions is also allowed in our model. For instance, the reduction can query the hard-wired function to its challenger and give the answer back to **Tamper** as its input. As a result, our model does not make any additional restrictions on the reduction.

[6] We forbid the communication between **Break1** and **Break2** for simplicity, and such restriction makes our results stronger since we focus on negative results.

We also stress that we can model an adversary in the way that (**Break**1, **Break**2) sends a (selectively determined) tampering function **Tamper** to modify a secret key sk to a tampered key $\mathbf{Tamper}(sk)$ as in previous works (e.g., [23,24,28,35]), while for a fully black-box reduction, which only has black-box access to **Tamper**, this does not make any difference. We define **Tamper** as part of the adversary only for simplicity. Our model does not rule out reductions exploiting the structures of arbitrary tampering functions (rather than restricted ones), while it would be surprising if there would be any.

Our Intuition. We now describe an intuition behind our proofs. For ease of understanding, we talk about the case of unique signatures. Let $\mathcal{R}$ be a reduction algorithm trying to attack some underlying assumption captured by a typical cryptographic game with access to a successful adversary $\mathcal{A} = (\mathbf{Tamper}, \mathbf{Break}1, \mathbf{Break}2)$. To benefit from $\mathcal{A}$, $\mathcal{R}$ has to answer the signing query made by **Break**1. However, we observe that if $\mathcal{R}$ has not given **Tamper** a valid secret key previously,[7] it may have no idea what the tampered key is, in which case *answering the signing query is as difficult as breaking the underlying security of the unique signature scheme for* $\mathcal{R}$. On the other hand, if $\mathcal{R}$ has given a valid key to **Tamper**, then it is able to forge a signature by itself. In this case, since *a signature forged by* **Break**2 *must be the same as the one forged by* $\mathcal{R}$ *due to uniqueness, it does little help to* $\mathcal{R}$. As a result, the access to $\mathcal{A}$ may not benefit $\mathcal{R}$ in the cryptographic game, which gives us the conflict. Note that when formally showing the existence of such a successful but "useless" adversary $\mathcal{A}$, we need to take care of more details (e.g., the way for $\mathcal{A}$ to check the validity of a secret key without having a key checking algorithm), which we do not mention here for simplicity.

The above intuition is also adopted to show negative results on VRFs, VUFs, unique-key signatures, injective OWFs, and unique-message PKE schemes, while in the case of unique-message PKE schemes, our proof exploits the difficulty of answering decryption queries (instead of signing queries). Like the case of unique signatures, the uniqueness properties of these primitives ensure that the outputs of $\mathcal{A}$ and $\mathcal{R}$ are identical.

We formalize our intuition by using meta-reductions, which have appeared in a great deal of previous works (e.g., [3,5,14,19,22,31,32,38,42,50,58,60,61, 68,69]). Roughly speaking, we firstly give an inefficient (but valid) adversary $\mathcal{A}$ breaking the tamper-resilience of a class of schemes, and then a PPT algorithm **Sim** (which does not necessarily have the structure of a valid adversary) simulating the action of $\mathcal{A}$. For any black-box reduction $\mathcal{R}$ deriving the tamper-resilience of these schemes from some cryptographic game $\mathcal{G}$, we could obtain a PPT adversary $\mathcal{R}^{\mathbf{Sim}}$ breaking $\mathcal{G}$ with the same advantage as $\mathcal{R}^{\mathcal{A}}$, which is infeasible if $\mathcal{G}$ is hard to break. Hence, we can derive the non-existence of $\mathcal{R}$. More specifically, we give our proof under the simulatable attack paradigm, a meta-reduction method proposed by Wichs [68]. Most negative results proved using meta-reductions implicitly fall under this paradigm, and recent works [16,26]

[7] Here, a valid secret key means a secret key passing the key checking procedure executed by **Tamper**.

explicitly used this paradigm to show negative results on entropic search learning with errors and extractors for entropy extractor-dependent sources. What we have to do is to show that any (possibly inefficient) oracle-access machine cannot distinguish $\mathcal{A}$ and **Sim**. By doing this we can separate the tamper-resilience of our target schemes from any cryptographic game $\mathcal{G}$ rather than some particular one. We remark that when proving the impossibility result on unique-message PKE schemes, the oracle-access machine is required to be efficient, in which case we separate the tamper-resilience from any *restricted* cryptographic game. We refer the reader to Sects. 3.3 and 4.3 for the details of our adversaries and simulators and the ideas behind their constructions.

Comparison with Previous Works. Finally, let us highlight the differences between the work by Wichs and ours. In [68], Wichs showed that there is no black box reduction for proving the security of leakage-resilient unique witness one-way relations, leaky pseudo-entropy generators, entropy condensers, and correlation-resilient OWFs from the assumptions captured by cryptographic games.[8] His negative results for the latter two primitives are vastly different stories, since the adversaries are modeled in different ways, while those for the former two are more related to our results, in the sense that both leakage-resilient and tamper-resilient primitives prevent attacks on memory. However, it should be noticed that leakage-resilience treats adversaries directly obtaining leaked information, while tamper-resilience treats ones observing the effect of malicious modifications. Since the restrictions on adversaries are completely different, our results and those by Wichs do not imply each other, and designing inefficient adversaries and PPT simulators in our case is never easy. Furthermore, our proofs utilize a new methodology that proves the indistinguishability between adversaries and simulators based on computational security assumptions. This is quite different from Wichs' results since the proofs in his work do not use them.

Other Related Negative Results on Unique Primitives. Coron [19] showed impossibility on simple reductions deriving the tight security of unique sigantures from non-interactive assumptions. Later Kakvi and Kiltz [48] fixed Coron's result by giving a stricter definition of unique signatures. Hofheinz et al. [43] extended the negative results in [19,48] for the notion of re-randomizable signatures, which is more general and hence captures more instantiations, such as the Waters signature scheme [66] and its variant [43]. Recently, Morgan and Pass [58] proposed an impossibility result by ruling out any linear-preserving black-box reduction deriving the security of unique signatures from bounded-round assumptions. In another line, Wang et al. [65] ruled out memory-tight black-box reductions deriving the multi-challenge security of signatures from any computational assumption.

[8] Interestingly, in [68], Wichs also mentioned a negative result on leakage-resilient unique signatures.

1.4 Outline of This Paper

In Sect. 2, we recall the definitions of cryptographic games (and properties) and simulatable attacks. In Sect. 3, we give our negative results on PDPs, unique-key signatures, and injective OWFs. In Sect. 4, we give our negative results on unique-message PKE schemes. In Sect. 5, we discuss open problems.

2 Preliminaries

In this section, we review several definitions and terminologies that are necessary to describe our results.

Notation. *negl* denotes an unspecified negligible function. If $\mathcal{X}$ is a finite set, then $x \leftarrow \mathcal{X}$ denotes the process of uniformly sampling x at random from the set $\mathcal{X}$. If $\mathcal{A}$ is a deterministic (respectively, probabilistic) algorithm, then $y = \mathcal{A}(x)$ (respectively, $y \leftarrow \mathcal{A}(x)$) means that $\mathcal{A}$ on input x outputs y. Letting the internal randomness space of a probabilistic algorithm $\mathcal{A}$ be $\mathcal{R}_a$, computing $y \leftarrow \mathcal{A}(x)$ is equivalent to sampling $r \leftarrow \mathcal{R}_a$ and then computing $y = \mathcal{A}(x; r)$.

2.1 Cryptographic Game (Property)

In this subsection, we recall the definitions of a cryptographic game and a cryptographic property.

Definition 1 (Cryptographic game [40]**).** *A cryptographic game $\mathcal{G}$ consists of a (possibly inefficient) random system (called the challenger) $\mathcal{CH}$ and a constant $c \in [0, 1)$. For some security parameter 1^λ, $\mathcal{CH}(1^\lambda)$ interacts with some adversary $\mathcal{A}(1^\lambda)$, and outputs a bit b. This interaction is denoted by $b \leftarrow (\mathcal{A}(1^\lambda) \leftrightharpoons \mathcal{CH}(1^\lambda))$, and the advantage of $\mathcal{A}$ in $\mathcal{G}$ is $\mathbf{Adv}_{\mathcal{G}}^{\mathcal{A}}(\lambda) = \Pr[1 \leftarrow (\mathcal{A}(1^\lambda) \leftrightharpoons \mathcal{CH}(1^\lambda))] - c$.*

A cryptographic game $\mathcal{G}$ is secure if for any PPT adversary $\mathcal{A}$, $\mathbf{Adv}_{\mathcal{G}}^{\mathcal{A}}(\lambda) \leq negl(\lambda)$.

As noted in [38,68], all commonly used assumptions in cryptography fall under the framework of cryptographic games.

A restricted version of the above definition, which only considers PPT challengers and captures most *falsifiable* assumptions [38,59], is given as follows.

Definition 2 (Restricted cryptographic game [38]**).** *A* restricted cryptographic game *is defined in exactly the same way as a cryptographic game, except that we replace "(possibly inefficient) random system" with* "PPT random system".

Cryptographic Property. As noted by Wichs [68], although the definition of a cryptographic game captures all common assumptions, it does not capture some cryptographic properties against stateless adversaries consisting of multiple independent components (e.g., leakage-resilience of one-way relations defined in [68] and tamper-resilience of PDPs, signatures, and PKE schemes defined later in our paper). Following [68], we give a very general definition of an arbitrary cryptographic property $\mathcal{P}$ and use $\mathbf{Adv}_{\mathcal{P}}^{\mathcal{A}_\lambda}(\lambda)$ to denote the advantage of $\mathcal{A}_\lambda$ in breaking a cryptographic property $\mathcal{P}$, where λ is the security parameter. $\mathcal{P}$ is said to be secure if for any PPT adversary $\mathcal{A}$, $\mathbf{Adv}_{\mathcal{P}}^{\mathcal{A}_\lambda}(\lambda)$ is negligible in λ.

2.2 Simulatable Attack

The simulatable attack paradigm is a meta-reduction method formalized by Wichs [68]. Showing the existence of simulatable attacks on cryptographic properties is a general way to show the impossibility of deriving these properties from common assumptions via black-box reductions. We now recall the definitions of a black-box reduction and simulatable attack as follows. Our definition here is based on [68].

Definition 3 (Black-box reduction). *Let $\mathcal{P}$ be some cryptographic property and $\mathcal{G}$ be some cryptographic game. An oracle-access PPT machine $\mathcal{R}^{(\cdot)}$ is said to be a* black-box reduction *deriving the security of $\mathcal{P}$ from $\mathcal{G}$, if for any (possibly inefficient, non-uniform) adversary $\mathcal{A}_\lambda$ such that $\mathbf{Adv}_{\mathcal{P}}^{\mathcal{A}_\lambda}(\lambda) = 1$, there exists a non-negligible function ϵ such that we have $\mathbf{Adv}_{\mathcal{G}}^{\mathcal{R}^{\mathcal{A}_\lambda}}(\lambda) \geq \epsilon(\lambda)$.*

In the above definition, we require $\mathbf{Adv}_{\mathcal{P}}^{\mathcal{A}_\lambda}(\lambda)$ to be 1 (rather than non-negligible), which makes the defined reduction very restrictive. Since our focus is on a black-box separation, the more restricted the type of black-box reductions is, the stronger our negative results become. Furthermore, the definition in [68] is strengthened by requiring that a black-box reduction $\mathcal{R}$ have noticeable advantage in breaking $\mathcal{G}$, while we only require $\mathcal{R}$ to have a non-negligible advantage, which is more common.[9]

A simulatable attack on a cryptographic property $\mathcal{P}$ consists of a valid but possibly inefficient adversary $\mathcal{A}$ and a possibly invalid but efficient simulator $\mathbf{Sim}$.[10] If $\mathcal{A}$ breaks $\mathcal{P}$ and is indistinguishable from $\mathbf{Sim}$ for any oracle-access machine, then the existence of a black-box reduction $\mathcal{R}$ deriving the security of $\mathcal{P}$ from some cryptographic game $\mathcal{G}$ implies that breaking the assumption captured by $\mathcal{G}$ is not hard. This follows from the fact that the success of $\mathcal{R}^{\mathcal{A}}$ implies the success of $\mathcal{R}^{\mathbf{Sim}}$ in $\mathcal{G}$.

Definition 4 (Simulatable attack [68]). *A* simulatable attack *on a cryptographic property $\mathcal{P}$ consists of: (a) an ensemble of (possibly inefficient) stateless non-uniform adversaries $\{\mathcal{A}_{\lambda,f}\}_{\lambda\in\mathbb{N},f\in\mathbb{F}_\lambda}$ where $\{\mathbb{F}_\lambda\}_\lambda$ are some finite sets, and (b) a PPT stateful simulator $\mathbf{Sim}$. Furthermore, the following two properties are required to hold.*

- *For all $\lambda \in \mathbb{N}$ and $f \in \mathbb{F}_\lambda$, $\mathbf{Adv}_{\mathcal{P}}^{\mathcal{A}_{\lambda,f}}(\lambda) = 1$.*

[9] We note that as discussed in [68], all the proofs given by Wichs can be extended to the case that the advantage of $\mathcal{R}$ is only required to be non-negligible.

[10] In our case, a valid (respectively, invalid) adversary means a stateless (respectively, stateful) adversary.

– *For all (possibly inefficient) oracle-access probabilistic machines $\mathcal{B}^{(\cdot)}$ making at most polynomially many queries to its oracle, we have*

$$|\Pr_{f \leftarrow \mathbb{F}_\lambda}[1 \leftarrow \mathcal{B}^{\mathcal{A}_{\lambda,f}}(1^\lambda)] - \Pr[1 \leftarrow \mathcal{B}^{\mathbf{Sim}(1^\lambda)}(1^\lambda)]| \leq negl(\lambda).$$

Definition 5 (Weak simulatable attack). *A* weak simulatable attack *is defined in exactly the same way as a simulatable attack, except that we replace "(possibly inefficient) oracle-access probabilistic machines $\mathcal{B}^{(\cdot)}$" with "oracle-access PPT machines $\mathcal{B}^{(\cdot)}$".*

Note that in the above definitions, $\mathbb{F}_\lambda$ is a set, and an adversary is modeled as an ensemble of algorithms $\mathcal{A}_{\lambda,f}$ where each instance hardwires an element $f \in \mathbb{F}_\lambda$. Note also that the simulator **Sim** is only required to simulate the behavior of adversaries $\mathcal{A}_{\lambda,f}$ in the situation where f is chosen uniformly at random from $\mathbb{F}_\lambda$. Like in [68], we set $\mathbb{F}_\lambda$ as a set of all functions with some specific domain and range when showing our negative results. This ensures that the outputs of f look like real randomness in the view of $\mathcal{B}$, and they can be simulated by $\mathbf{Sim}(1^\lambda)$ by executing lazy sampling. We refer the reader to Sects. 3.3 and 4.3 for the details.

The following theorem by Wichs [68] shows that the existence of a (weak) simulatable attack on some cryptographic property $\mathcal{P}$ implies the impossibility of deriving the security of $\mathcal{P}$ from any (restricted) cryptographic game $\mathcal{G}$ via black-box reductions.

Theorem 1 ([68]). *If there exists a simulatable attack (respectively, weak simulatable attack) on some cryptographic property $\mathcal{P}$ and a black-box reduction deriving the security of $\mathcal{P}$ from the security of some cryptographic game (respectively, restricted cryptographic game) $\mathcal{G}$, then there exists some PPT adversary $\mathcal{A}$ that has non-negligible advantage in $\mathcal{G}$.*

We refer the reader to [68] for the proof of Theorem 1. Notice that the original proof in [68] did not show that a weak simulatable attack implies the black-box separation with respect to restricted cryptographic games, and it asks the reduction algorithm to have a noticeable advantage. However, extending it to show the above theorem is straightforward.

3 Impossibility on Provable Deterministic Primitives and Unique-Key Signatures

In this section, we give negative results on tamper-resilient PDPs (including tamper-resilient VUFs, VRFs, and unique signatures as special cases) and tamper-resilient unique-key signatures. Our results show that if a PDP or unique-key signature scheme satisfies some "extremely" weak unpredictability or unforgeability, then there exists no black-box reduction deriving its tamper-resilience in the plain model from any commonly used assumption.

The rest of this section is organized as follows. In Sect. 3.1, we recall the definitions of PDPs and signatures. In Sect. 3.2, we define several security notions. In Sect. 3.3, we show the existence of simulatable attacks on the tamper-resilience of PDPs and signatures. In Sect. 3.4, we summarize our negative results.

3.1 Definitions of PDPs and Signatures

At first, we recall the definition of a PDP, which is formalized in [2] and captures VUFs, VRFs, and unique signatures as special cases.

Definition 6 (Provable deterministic primitive (PDP) [2]). *A PDP consists of the polynomial-time (PT) algorithms* $(\mathsf{Gen}, \mathsf{Comp}, \mathsf{Prove}, \mathsf{Verify})$. *(a)* Gen *is a probabilistic algorithm that takes as input* 1^λ, *and returns a public/secret key pair* $(pk, sk) \in \{0,1\}^p \times \{0,1\}^s$ *for some polynomials* $p = p(\lambda)$ *and* $s = s(\lambda)$. *The set of all secret keys (output by* $\mathsf{Gen}(1^\lambda)$*) and the (internal) randomness space of* Gen *are respectively denoted by* $\mathcal{SK}$ *and* $\mathcal{R}_g$. *(b)* Comp *is a deterministic algorithm that takes as input a secret key* sk *and* $x \in \mathcal{X}$, *where* $\mathcal{X}$ *denotes the domain, and returns some value* y. *(c)* Prove *is a probabilistic algorithm that takes as input a secret key* sk *and* x, *and returns a proof* π. *The (internal) randomness space of* Prove *is denoted by* $\mathcal{R}_p$. *(d)* Verify *is a deterministic algorithm that takes as input a public key* pk, x, y, *and a proof* π, *and returns* 1 *(accept) or* 0 *(reject).*

A PDP is required to satisfy uniqueness *and* correctness. *Uniqueness is said to be satisfied if for all* $\lambda \in \mathbb{N}$, *all* $pk \in \{0,1\}^p$ *(possibly outside the support of* Gen*) and all* $x \in \mathcal{X}$, *there exists no tuple* (y, π, y', π') *that simultaneously satisfies* $y \neq y'$ *and* $\mathsf{Verify}_{pk}(x, y, \pi) = \mathsf{Verify}_{pk}(x, y', \pi') = 1$. *Correctness is said to be satisfied if* $\mathsf{Verify}_{pk}(x, \mathsf{Comp}_{sk}(x), \mathsf{Prove}_{sk}(x)) = 1$ *holds for all* $\lambda \in \mathbb{N}$, *all* $(pk, sk) \leftarrow \mathsf{Gen}(1^\lambda)$, *and all* $x \in \mathcal{X}$.

The syntax of a PDP is exactly the same as that of a VRF and a VUF, and it also captures unique signature schemes, which we discuss later in this subsection. Notice that the definition of uniqueness is different from that in [2], which additionally requires the public parameter (including the bilinear group) to be correctly generated since it treats structure-preserving constructions. Other than that we do not consider public parameters separately or some other relaxed uniqueness notions (e.g., uniqueness holding for most public keys), one can see that our definition is equivalent to the original definitions of uniqueness in [54,55]. Such original definitions prevent denial-of service attacks and provide perfect binding properties when PDPs are used as a special type of commitments in their applications (e.g., micropayments [57], resettable zero-knowledge proofs [56], updatable zero-knowledge databases [52], verifiable transaction escrow schemes [47]), even in the presence of maliciously chosen CRSs and public keys.

We now recall the definition of a (digital) signature scheme.

Definition 7 (Digital signature). *A signature scheme consists of the PT algorithms* $(\mathsf{Gen}, \mathsf{Sign}, \mathsf{Verify})$. *(a)* Gen *is a probabilistic algorithm that takes as* *input* 1^λ, *and returns a public/secret key pair* $(pk, sk) \in \{0,1\}^p \times \{0,1\}^s$ *for some polynomials* $p = p(\lambda)$ *and* $s = s(\lambda)$. *The set of all secret keys (output by* $\mathsf{Gen}(1^\lambda)$*) and the (internal) randomness space of* Gen *are respectively denoted by* $\mathcal{SK}$ *and* $\mathcal{R}_g$. *(b)* Sign *is a probabilistic algorithm that takes as input a secret key* sk *and a message* $m \in \mathcal{M}$, *where* $\mathcal{M}$ *is the message space, and returns a signature* σ. *The (internal) randomness space of* Sign *is denoted by* $\mathcal{R}_s$. *(c)* Verify *is a deterministic algorithm that takes as input a public key* pk, *a message* m, *and a signature* σ, *and returns* 1 *(accept) or* 0 *(reject).*

A signature scheme is required to satisfy correctness, which means that $\mathsf{Verify}_{pk}(m, \sigma) = 1$ *holds for all* $\lambda \in \mathbb{N}$, *all* $(pk, sk) \leftarrow \mathsf{Gen}(1^\lambda)$, *all* $m \in \mathcal{M}$, *and all* $\sigma \leftarrow \mathsf{Sign}_{sk}(m)$.

We now recall the definition of a unique signature scheme, in which the signing algorithm is deterministic and there exists only one valid signature for each pair of public key (not necessarily output by $\mathsf{Gen}(1^\lambda)$) and message.

Definition 8 (Unique signature [54]). *A signature scheme* (Gen, Sign, Verify) *is said to be a* unique signature scheme *if (a)* Sign *is deterministic, and (b) for all* $\lambda \in \mathbb{N}$, *all* $pk \in \{0,1\}^p$ *(possibly outside the support of* Gen*), and all* $m \in \mathcal{M}$, *there exists no pair* (σ, σ') *that simultaneously satisfies* $\sigma \neq \sigma'$ *and* $\mathsf{Verify}_{pk}(m, \sigma) = \mathsf{Verify}_{pk}(m, \sigma') = 1$.

One can easily see that a unique signature scheme can be cast as a PDP where Comp is the signing algorithm and Prove always returns the empty string.

We now define unique-key signatures, where there exists only one valid secret key for each public key (not necessarily output by $\mathsf{Gen}(1^\lambda)$).

Definition 9 (Unique-key signature). *A signature scheme* (Gen, Sign, Verify) *is said to be a* unique-key signature scheme *if there exists a deterministic PT algorithm* UKCheck *such that (a)* $\mathsf{UKCheck}(pk, sk) = 1$ *holds for all* $\lambda \in \mathbb{N}$ *and all* $(pk, sk) \leftarrow \mathsf{Gen}(1^\lambda)$, *and (b) for all* $\lambda \in \mathbb{N}$ *and all* $pk \in \{0,1\}^p$ *(possibly outside the support of* Gen*), there exists no pair* $(sk, sk') \in \{0,1\}^s \times \{0,1\}^s$ *that simultaneously satisfies* $sk \neq sk'$ *and* $\mathsf{UKCheck}(pk, sk) = \mathsf{UKCheck}(pk, sk') = 1$.

3.2 Security Notions for PDPs and Signatures

In this subsection, we define several security notions, called weak unpredictability, weak unforgeability, and weak tamper-resilience, for PDPs and signatures.

In [2], two security notions were defined for PDPs: unpredictability and pseudorandomness. A PDP satisfying the former (respectively, latter) security notion is a VUF (respectively, VRF). Moreover, unpredictability is weaker than pseudorandomness (see [2, Lemma 5]). In this paper, we define weak unpredictability, which is weaker than standard unpredictability. This security notion only guarantees that a PPT adversary, which is allowed to neither learn *pk* nor make any query, cannot output a valid input/output pair.[11] We also define a similar security notion, called weak unforgeability, for signatures. Furthermore, we define

[11] Since we aim at proving the impossibility on tamper-resilience of primitives, we would like to define their underlying security in a way as weak as possible.

two additional security notions, called statistical weak unpredictability and statistical weak unforgeability, which treat possibly inefficient adversaries. We also refer the reader to the full paper for the standard security of unpredictability and unforgeability.

Definition 10 ((Statistical) weak unpredictability). *A PDP* $(\mathsf{Gen}, \mathsf{Comp}, \mathsf{Prove}, \mathsf{Verify})$ *is said to be* weakly unpredictable *(respectively,* statistically weakly unpredictable*), if for any PPT adversary (respectively, possibly inefficient adversary)* $\mathcal{A}$*, we have*

$$\Pr[(pk, sk) \leftarrow \mathsf{Gen}(1^\lambda), (x^*, y^*) \leftarrow \mathcal{A}(1^\lambda) : \mathsf{Comp}_{sk}(x^*) = y^*] \leq negl(\lambda).$$

Definition 11 ((Statistical) weak unforgeability). *A signature scheme* $(\mathsf{Gen}, \mathsf{Sign}, \mathsf{Verify})$ *is said to be* weakly unforgeable *(respectively,* statistically weakly unforgeable*), if for any PPT adversary (respectively, possibly inefficient adversary)* $\mathcal{A}$*, we have*

$$\Pr[(pk, sk) \leftarrow \mathsf{Gen}(1^\lambda), (m^*, \sigma^*) \leftarrow \mathcal{A}(1^\lambda) : \mathsf{Verify}_{pk}(m^*, \sigma^*) = 1] \leq negl(\lambda).$$

One can easily see that weak unpredictability and weak unforgeability are much weaker than standard unpredictability and unforgeability notions, respectively. However, this does not straightforwardly mean that statistical weak unpredictability and statistical weak unforgeability are also weak since they treat possibly inefficient adversaries. Now we give two lemmas showing the equivalence between weak unpredictability and statistical weak unpredictability, and that between weak unforgeability and statistical weak unforgeability.

Lemma 1. *A PDP satisfies weak unpredictability (against non-uniform adversaries) if and only if it satisfies statistical weak unpredictability.*

Proof (of Lemma 1). Since it is straightforward that statistical weak unpredictability implies weak unpredictability, we focus on the opposite direction.

If a PDP $\Phi = (\mathsf{Gen}, \mathsf{Comp}, \mathsf{Prove}, \mathsf{Verify})$ is not statistically weakly unpredictable, then there exists a (possibly inefficient) adversary $\mathcal{A}$ that, on input a security parameter 1^λ, can output x^* and y^* such that $\Pr[(pk, sk) \leftarrow \mathsf{Gen}(1^\lambda) : y^* = \mathsf{Comp}_{sk}(x^*)]$ is non-negligible. Therefore, we can hard-wire such (x^*, y^*) in a (non-uniform) PPT adversary $\mathcal{B}$, which can easily break the weak unpredictability of Φ by outputting (x^*, y^*), on input 1^λ. Hence, weak unpredictability implies statistical weak unpredictability. □

Lemma 2. *A signature scheme satisfies weak unforgeability (against non-uniform adversaries) if and only if it satisfies statistical weak unforgeability.*

We omit the proof of Lemma 2 since it is exactly the same except that we replace the winning condition $y^* = \mathsf{Comp}_{sk}(x^*)$ with $\mathsf{Verify}_{pk}(x^*, y^*) = 1$.

We now define weak tamper-resilience (WTR) for PDPs and signatures. An adversary against such security notions consists of three independent components $(\mathbf{Tamper}, \mathbf{Break1}, \mathbf{Break2})$. **Tamper** models a tampering function which determines a tampered secret key, on input a public/secret key pair. **Break1** takes as input a public key and makes a computing or signing query. On receiving the answer generated by using the tampered secret key, **Break2** tries to output a valid forgery. For simplicity, we allow the adversary to make only one tampering query and one signing query, and forbid the communication between **Break1** and **Break2**. These security notions are (strictly) extremely weak versions of the unforgeability under chosen message and tampering attacks defined in [28,35] and there have already been several positive results satisfying them [23,24,28,35], except that we treat the plain model. As explained before, the more restrictive the adversary is, the stronger our negative results are. Here, notice that although we treat **Tamper** as a component of the adversary, it is essentially a tampering query made by the adversary since ($\mathbf{Break}_1, \mathbf{Break}_2$) can neither learn its inputs nor communicate with it. The formal definitions are as follows.

Definition 12 (Weak tamper-resilient (WTR) PDP). *A PDP* (Gen, $\mathsf{Comp}, \mathsf{Prove}, \mathsf{Verify}$) *is said to satisfy* WTR security, *if for any PPT adversary* $\mathcal{A} = (\mathbf{Tamper}, \mathbf{Break1}, \mathbf{Break2})$, *we have*

$$\Pr[(pk, sk) \leftarrow \mathsf{Gen}(1^\lambda), sk' \leftarrow \mathbf{Tamper}(1^\lambda, pk, sk), x \leftarrow \mathbf{Break1}(1^\lambda, pk), \\ y = \mathsf{Comp}_{sk'}(x), (x^*, y^*) \leftarrow \mathbf{Break2}(1^\lambda, pk, y) : \\ x^* \neq x \wedge sk' \in \mathcal{SK} \wedge y^* = \mathsf{Comp}_{sk}(x^*)] \leq negl(\lambda).$$

The winning condition that $sk' \in \mathcal{SK}$ follows [28]. It makes our results stronger since the adversary is more restricted.

Definition 13 (Weak tamper-resilient (WTR) signature). *A signature scheme* ($\mathsf{Gen}, \mathsf{Sign}, \mathsf{Verify}$) *is said to satisfy* WTR security, *if for any PPT adversary* $\mathcal{A} = (\mathbf{Tamper}, \mathbf{Break1}, \mathbf{Break2})$, *we have*

$$\Pr[(pk, sk) \leftarrow \mathsf{Gen}(1^\lambda), sk' \leftarrow \mathbf{Tamper}(1^\lambda, pk, sk), m \leftarrow \mathbf{Break1}(1^\lambda, pk), \\ \sigma \leftarrow \mathsf{Sign}_{sk'}(m), (m^*, \sigma^*) \leftarrow \mathbf{Break2}(1^\lambda, pk, \sigma) : \\ m^* \neq m \wedge sk' \in \mathcal{SK} \wedge \mathsf{Verify}_{pk}(m^*, \sigma^*) = 1] \leq negl(\lambda).$$

Notice that when showing impossibility of black-box reductions for proving WTR security, we need to consider reduction algorithms that can exploit an adversary $\mathcal{A} = (\mathbf{Tamper}, \mathbf{Break1}, \mathbf{Break2})$ in any way they want, i.e., adaptively make queries to **Tamper**, **Break1**, and **Break2** in any order and for any times (on condition that the total number of queries is polynomial in λ). This is an obstacle we need to overcome in our formal proofs. Also, note that unlike previous works treating arbitrary tampering attacks [23,24,28,35], we define **Tamper** as part of the adversary. However, we do this only for simplicity and this does not make any additional restriction on the reductions we consider. We refer the reader to Sect. 1.3 for the remark on our model for a further discussion.

3.3 Simulatable Attacks for WTR Secure PDPs and Signatures

In this subsection, we focus on showing the existence of simulatable attacks on the WTR security of PDPs and unique signatures, which implies the impossibility of deriving their WTR security from any commonly used assumption via black-box reductions, due to Theorem 1.

Simulatable Attack for WTR Secure PDPs. We start with giving a theorem showing that if a PDP satisfies weak unpredictability, then there exists a simulatable attack on its WTR security.

Theorem 2. *For any weakly unpredictable PDP* $\Phi = (\mathsf{Gen}, \mathsf{Comp}, \mathsf{Prove}, \mathsf{Verify})$, *there exists a simulatable attack on the WTR security of* Φ.

Overview and Idea of the Proof. Let $\mathbb{F}_\lambda$ be the set of all functions $f : \{0,1\}^p \rightarrow \mathcal{R}_g \times \mathcal{R}_p$, and (x, x^*) be elements in $\mathcal{X}$ such that $x \neq x^*$. We firstly construct an inefficient adversary $\mathcal{A}$, which is an ensemble of stateless algorithms $\{\mathcal{A}_{\lambda,f} = (\mathbf{Tamper}_{\lambda,f}, \mathbf{Break1}_{\lambda,f}, \mathbf{Break2}_{\lambda,f})\}_{\lambda\in\mathbb{N}, f\in\mathbb{F}_\lambda}$. Each $\mathcal{A}_{\lambda,f}$ hard-wires (x, x^*) and an element f in $\mathbb{F}_\lambda$. We show that each $\mathcal{A}_{\lambda,f}$ breaks the WTR security of Φ. Then we show the existence of a PPT stateful simulator **Sim** that can simulate the behavior of $\mathcal{A}_{\lambda,f}$, in the case that f is randomly chosen from $\mathbb{F}_\lambda$ (and hence is a random function with domain $\{0,1\}^p$ and range $\mathcal{R}_g \times \mathcal{R}_p$). We design $\mathcal{A}_{\lambda,f}$ as follows.

$\mathbf{Tamper}_{\lambda,f}(1^\lambda, pk, sk)$ runs $(r_g, r_p) = f(pk)$ and $(pk', sk') = \mathsf{Gen}(1^\lambda; r_g)$ (where r_p is an internal random coin of Prove that is used when checking the validity of (pk, sk) which we will explain later). If (pk, sk) is valid, it outputs sk' as the tampered key. $\mathbf{Break1}_{\lambda,f}(pk)$ outputs x as the computing query. $\mathbf{Break2}_{\lambda,f}(pk, y)$ runs $(r_g, r_p) = f(pk)$ and $(pk', sk') = \mathsf{Gen}(1^\lambda; r_g)$, and checks whether y is a correct answer for x (i.e., whether $y = \mathsf{Comp}_{sk'}(x)$). If the check works, it does an exhaustive search to find (y^*, π^*) such that $\mathsf{Verify}_{pk}(x^*, y^*, \pi^*) = 1$, and outputs (x^*, y^*) as a forgery. Otherwise, it aborts. One can see that $\mathcal{A}_{\lambda,f}$ breaks the WTR security of Φ due to correctness and uniqueness.

Next we explain why we can have a PPT stateful simulator **Sim** which is indistinguishable from $\mathcal{A}_{\lambda,f}$ (where $f \leftarrow \mathbb{F}_\lambda$) in the view of any (possibly inefficient) oracle-access machine $\mathcal{B}$. To make $\mathbf{Break2}_{\lambda,f}$ output a forgery (rather than abort), $\mathcal{B}$ has to answer the query x made by $\mathbf{Break1}_{\lambda,f}$. However, without having given $\mathbf{Tamper}_{\lambda,f}$ a valid key pair (pk, sk) previously, $\mathcal{B}$ would learn no information on (pk', sk'). The reason is that $\mathcal{B}$ only has black-box access to $\mathbf{Tamper}_{\lambda,f}$ and cannot see the structure of f. When $\mathbf{Tamper}_{\lambda,f}(pk, sk)$ aborts, no information on $f(pk)$ is revealed. In this case, $\mathcal{B}$ cannot answer x due to the weak unpredictability of Φ. Therefore, we can construct **Sim**, who simulates the outputs of f by executing lazy sampling (i.e., by randomly choosing (r_g, r_p) and keeping them in its internal list), and outputs a forgery by using a valid key sk having appeared in a **Tamper** query made by $\mathcal{B}$ previously.[12] If such sk does

[12] This is possible since **Sim** is stateful and can record the previously queried keys in its internal list.

not exist, **Sim** aborts. Due to uniqueness, the final outputs of $\mathbf{Break2}_{\lambda,f}$ and **Sim** must be identical, which guarantees that the interactions with $\mathcal{A}_{\lambda,f}$ and with **Sim** are indistinguishable in the view of $\mathcal{B}$.

More specifically, we show the indistinguishability by giving hybrid machines $\mathcal{A}_0$ and $\mathcal{A}_1$. $\mathcal{A}_0$ interacts with $\mathcal{B}$ in the same way as $\mathcal{A}_{\lambda,f}$ (where $f \leftarrow \mathbb{F}_\lambda$) does, except that it simulates the outputs of f by executing lazy sampling. $\mathcal{A}_1$ runs in the same way as $\mathcal{A}_0$ does except that it aborts if $\mathcal{B}$ makes a **Break**2 query (pk, y), where a valid secret key sk for pk has not appeared in a **Tamper** query previously. The indistinguishability between $\mathcal{A}_{\lambda,f}$ and $\mathcal{A}_0$ follows from the fact that the outputs of f look perfectly random in the view of $\mathcal{B}$. Furthermore, $\mathcal{A}_0$ is indistinguishable from $\mathcal{A}_1$, since without having given $\mathcal{A}_0$ a valid key pair (pk, sk) previously, all the **Break**2 queries including pk that $\mathcal{B}$ makes will lead $\mathcal{A}_0$ to abort. Otherwise, we can construct an adversary breaking the statistical weak unpredictability of Φ. However, since statistical weak unpredictability is equivalent to (computational) weak unpredictability (see Lemma 1), such an adversary cannot exist due to the weak unpredictability of Φ. At last, we need to show that $\mathcal{A}_1$ is indistinguishable from **Sim**. The only difference between them is that to output a forgery, $\mathcal{A}_1$ does an exhaustive search, while **Sim** exploits a valid secret key having appeared in a **Tamper** query previously. Due to the uniqueness of Φ, their forgeries (with respect to the same pk) must be identical, and hence $\mathcal{B}$ cannot distinguish the interactions with $\mathcal{A}_{\lambda,f}$ and with **Sim**.

Notice that we need to ensure that $\mathbf{Tamper}_{\lambda,f}$ and **Sim** output a tampered key only if they receive a valid key pair (pk, sk). Otherwise, **Sim** cannot simulate the behavior of $\mathcal{A}_{\lambda,f}$. Nevertheless, one may wonder how they check the validity, since there seems to be no checking algorithm for key pairs. To deal with this issue, we make them verify whether $\mathsf{Verify}_{pk}(x^*, \mathsf{Comp}_{sk}(x^*), \mathsf{Prove}_{sk}(x^*; r_p)) = 1$ instead. Although such a procedure does not check the validity of (pk, sk) directly, it guarantees that if (pk, sk) passes the verification, then $\mathbf{Break2}_{\lambda,f}$ can absolutely find a forgery for x^* with respect to pk by using its brute force, and **Sim** can output the same forgery by using sk.

Proof (of Theorem 2). For each $\lambda \in \mathbb{N}$, let $\mathbb{F}_\lambda$ be the set of all functions $f : \{0,1\}^p \rightarrow \mathcal{R}_g \times \mathcal{R}_p$, and x and x^* be arbitrary elements in $\mathcal{X}$ such that $x \neq x^*$. We define an inefficient class of stateless adversaries $\{\mathcal{A}_{\lambda,f} = (\mathbf{Tamper}_{\lambda,f}, \mathbf{Break1}_{\lambda,f}, \mathbf{Break2}_{\lambda,f})\}_{\lambda\in\mathbb{N}, f\in\mathbb{F}_\lambda}$, where x and x^* are hard-wired, as follows.

$\mathbf{Tamper}_{\lambda,f}(pk, sk)$:[13]

1. Compute $(r_g, r_p) = f(pk)$.
2. Compute $(pk', sk') = \mathsf{Gen}(1^\lambda; r_g)$.
3. If $\mathsf{Verify}_{pk}(x^*, \mathsf{Comp}_{sk}(x^*), \mathsf{Prove}_{sk}(x^*; r_p)) = 1$, return sk'. Otherwise, return $\perp$.

[13] For simplicity, we omit the procedure of length-checking since the security parameter is implicitly taken as input. The same argument is made for other algorithms.

Break1$_{\lambda,f}(pk)$:

1. Return x.

Break2$_{\lambda,f}(pk, y)$:

1. Compute $(r_g, r_p) = f(pk)$.
2. Compute $(pk', sk') = \mathsf{Gen}(1^\lambda; r_g)$.
3. If $y = \mathsf{Comp}_{sk'}(x)$, then do an exhaustive search to find the lexicographically first pair (y^*, π^*) such that $\mathsf{Verify}_{pk}(x^*, y^*, \pi^*) = 1$, and return (x^*, y^*). If $y \neq \mathsf{Comp}_{sk'}(x)$ or such (y^*, π^*) does not exist, return $\perp$.

It is clear that $\mathsf{Verify}_{pk}(x^*, y^*, \pi^*) = 1$ implies $y^* = \mathsf{Comp}_{sk}(x^*)$ if (pk, sk) is an honestly sampled key pair, due to the correctness and uniqueness of Φ. Furthermore, the checks done by **Tamper**$_{\lambda,f}$ and **Break2**$_{\lambda,f}$ must work in a WTR security game due to correctness, and we have $x \neq x^*$. Hence, for each $f \in \mathbb{F}_\lambda$, $\mathcal{A}_{\lambda,f}$ breaks the WTR security of Φ with advantage 1.

We now define the PPT stateful simulator **Sim**(1^λ). It internally keeps a list Ł (which is initially empty) as a state, and answers queries as follows.

- On receiving a **Tamper** query (pk, sk):
  1. Search $(pk, \overline{sk}, r_g, r_p) \in$ Ł.[14] If the searching process failed (i.e., pk is not currently in Ł), randomly choose $(r_g, r_p) \leftarrow \mathcal{R}_g \times \mathcal{R}_p$, and add $(pk, \overline{sk}, r_g, r_p)$ (where $\overline{sk} = \perp$) to Ł.
  2. Compute $(pk', sk') = \mathsf{Gen}(1^\lambda; r_g)$.
  3. If $\mathsf{Verify}_{pk}(x^*, \mathsf{Comp}_{sk}(x^*), \mathsf{Prove}_{sk}(x^*; r_p)) = 1$, replace $\overline{sk}$ with sk in Ł (if $\overline{sk} = \perp$), and return sk'. Otherwise, return $\perp$.
- On receiving a **Break1** query pk:
  1. Return x.
- On receiving a **Break2** query (pk, y):
  1. Search $(pk, \overline{sk}, r_g, r_p) \in$ Ł. If the searching process failed or $\overline{sk} = \perp$, return $\perp$.
  2. Compute $(pk', sk') = \mathsf{Gen}(1^\lambda; r_g)$.
  3. If $y = \mathsf{Comp}_{sk'}(x)$, compute $y^* = \mathsf{Comp}_{\overline{sk}}(x^*)$ and return (x^*, y^*). Otherwise, return $\perp$.

Let $\mathcal{B}^{(\cdot)}$ be any (possibly inefficient) oracle-access probabilistic machine that makes at most polynomially many queries. We show that $|\Pr_{f \leftarrow \mathbb{F}_\lambda}[1 \leftarrow \mathcal{B}^{\mathcal{A}_{\lambda,f}}(1^\lambda)] - \Pr[1 \leftarrow \mathcal{B}^{\mathbf{Sim}(1^\lambda)}(1^\lambda)]| \leq negl(\lambda)$ by giving hybrid machines.[15]

Hybrid Machine $\mathcal{A}_0$: We define an inefficient *stateful* machine $\mathcal{A}_0$ as follows.

- On receiving a **Tamper** query (pk, sk):

[14] Searching processes succeed even if $\overline{sk}$ is $\perp$.

[15] Recall that during the execution of $\mathcal{B}^{\mathcal{A}_{\lambda,f}}(1^\lambda)$ or $\mathcal{B}^{\mathbf{Sim}(1^\lambda)}(1^\lambda)$, $\mathcal{B}$ can adaptively make **Tamper**, **Break1**, and **Break2** queries in any order and for any times (on condition that the total number of queries is polynomial in λ).

1. Search $(pk, \overline{sk}, r_g, r_p) \in \text{Ł}$ (where Ł is initialized with $\emptyset$). If the searching process failed, randomly choose $(r_g, r_p) \leftarrow \mathcal{R}_g \times \mathcal{R}_p$, and add $(pk, \overline{sk}, r_g, r_p)$ (where $\overline{sk} = \perp$) to Ł.
2. Compute $(pk', sk') = \mathsf{Gen}(1^\lambda; r_g)$.
3. If $\mathsf{Verify}_{pk}(x^*, \mathsf{Comp}_{sk}(x^*), \mathsf{Prove}_{sk}(x^*; r_p)) = 1$, replace $\overline{sk}$ with sk in Ł (if $\overline{sk} = \perp$), and return sk'. Otherwise, return $\perp$.

- On receiving a **Break**1 query pk:
  1. Return x.
- On receiving a **Break**2 query (pk, y):
  1. Search $(pk, \overline{sk}, r_g, r_p) \in \text{Ł}$. If the searching process failed, then randomly choose $(r_g, r_p) \leftarrow \mathcal{R}_g \times \mathcal{R}_p$, and add $(pk, \perp, r_g, r_p)$ to Ł.
  2. Compute $(pk', sk') = \mathsf{Gen}(1^\lambda; r_g)$.
  3. If $y = \mathsf{Comp}_{sk'}(x)$, then do an exhaustive search to find the lexicographically first pair (y^*, π^*) such that $\mathsf{Verify}_{pk}(x^*, y^*, \pi^*) = 1$, and return (x^*, y^*). If $y \neq \mathsf{Comp}_{sk'}(x)$ or such (y^*, π^*) does not exist, return $\perp$.

Lemma 3. $\Pr_{f \leftarrow \mathbb{F}_\lambda}[1 \leftarrow \mathcal{B}^{\mathcal{A}_{\lambda,f}}(1^\lambda)] = \Pr[1 \leftarrow \mathcal{B}^{\mathcal{A}_0(1^\lambda)}(1^\lambda)]$.

Proof (of Lemma 3). Since f (used by $\mathcal{A}_{\lambda,f}$) is randomly sampled from $\mathbb{F}_\lambda$, the outputs of f are perfect randomness in the view of $\mathcal{B}$. Moreover, what $\mathcal{A}_0$ does is just simulating f by executing lazy sampling. Then this lemma follows from the fact that the views of $\mathcal{B}$ in the interactions with $\mathcal{A}_{\lambda,f}$ (where $f \leftarrow \mathbb{F}_\lambda$) and with $\mathcal{A}_0$ are identical. □

Hybrid Machine $\mathcal{A}_1$: We now define an inefficient stateful machine $\mathcal{A}_1$ which is the same as $\mathcal{A}_0$, except that on receiving a **Break**2 query (pk, y), $\mathcal{A}_1$ aborts if there is no valid secret key $\overline{sk}$ for pk stored in Ł. In other words, $\mathcal{A}_1$ aborts if pk has not appeared in a **Tamper** query previously, the answer of which is not $\perp$. Formally, on receiving a **Break**2 query (pk, y), $\mathcal{A}_1$ runs as follows. (Bellow, the difference from $\mathcal{A}_0$ is only in Step 1, and is *emphasized.*)

1. Search $(pk, \overline{sk}, r_g, r_p) \in \text{Ł}$. *If the searching process failed or* $\overline{sk} = \perp$, *return* $\perp$.
2. Compute $(pk', sk') = \mathsf{Gen}(1^\lambda; r_g)$.
3. If $y = \mathsf{Comp}_{sk'}(x)$, do an exhaustive search to find the lexicographically first pair (y^*, π^*) such that $\mathsf{Verify}_{pk}(x^*, y^*, \pi^*) = 1$, and return (x^*, y^*). If $y \neq \mathsf{Comp}_{sk'}(x)$ or such (y^*, π^*) does not exist, return $\perp$.

Lemma 4. $|\Pr[1 \leftarrow \mathcal{B}^{\mathcal{A}_1(1^\lambda)}(1^\lambda)] - \Pr[1 \leftarrow \mathcal{B}^{\mathcal{A}_0(1^\lambda)}(1^\lambda)]| \leq negl(\lambda)$.

Proof (of Lemma 4). Let E be the event that during the execution of $\mathcal{B}^{\mathcal{A}_0(1^\lambda)}(1^\lambda)$, $\mathcal{B}$ makes a **Break**2 query (pk, y) such that

- pk has not appeared in a valid **Tamper** query (the answer of which is not $\perp$) previously, and
- the answer to this **Break**2 query is *not* $\perp$.

If E does not occur during the execution of $\mathcal{B}^{\mathcal{A}_0(1^\lambda)}(1^\lambda)$, then the view of $\mathcal{B}$ is identical to its view in the interaction with $\mathcal{A}_1$. Therefore, we have $|\Pr[1 \leftarrow \mathcal{B}^{\mathcal{A}_1(1^\lambda)}(1^\lambda)] - \Pr[1 \leftarrow \mathcal{B}^{\mathcal{A}_0(1^\lambda)}(1^\lambda)]| \leq \Pr[E]$. It remains to show that $\Pr[E]$ is negligible.

Claim 1. *Let the total number of (all kinds of) queries made by $\mathcal{B}$ be q. Then there exists an inefficient adversary $\mathcal{E}$ that breaks the statistical weak unpredictability of Φ with probability at least* $\Pr[E]/q^2$.

Proof Idea of Claim 1. A tampered key is generated as $(pk', sk') \leftarrow \mathsf{Gen}(1^\lambda; r_g)$ where r_g is a randomness linked with a public key pk. If $\mathcal{B}$ does not make a valid **Tamper** query (which does not lead $\mathcal{A}_0$ to output $\perp$) including pk, it would learn no information on (pk', sk').[16] In this case, making a **Break**2 query, such that pk is included in this query but $\mathcal{A}_0$ does not return $\perp$, means forging a valid input/output pair under pk', due to the check done at the third step in the response to a **Break**2 query. Therefore, $\mathcal{B}$ can be used to break the statistical weak unpredictability of Φ. The formal proof is as follows.

Proof. (of Claim 1*).* The description of $\mathcal{E}$ is as follows.

The challenger samples $(pk', sk') \leftarrow \mathsf{Gen}(1^\lambda)$ and gives 1^λ to $\mathcal{E}$. Then $\mathcal{E}$ randomly chooses $\hat{i}, \hat{j} \leftarrow \{1, \cdots, q\}$, and interacts with $\mathcal{B}$ in the same way as $\mathcal{A}_0$ does (during the execution of $\mathcal{B}^{\mathcal{A}_0(1^\lambda)}(1^\lambda)$), except that

1. From the $\hat{i}$th query, every time when receiving a **Tamper** or **Break**2 query including pk used in the $\hat{i}$th query, $\mathcal{E}$ returns $\perp$ to $\mathcal{B}$ (except for the $\hat{j}$th query).[17]
2. On receiving the $\hat{j}$th query, if it is a **Break**2 query denoted by (pk, y), $\mathcal{E}$ returns (x, y) to the challenger and terminates. Otherwise $\mathcal{E}$ aborts.

Now we argue that $\mathcal{E}$ returns (x, y) such that $y = \mathsf{Comp}_{sk'}(x)$ with probability at least $\Pr[E]/q^2$.

During the execution of $\mathcal{B}^{\mathcal{A}_0(1^\lambda)}(1^\lambda)$, when E occurs, $\mathcal{B}$ must have made a **Break**2 query (pk, y), such that (a) there exists no entry $(pk, \overline{sk}, r_g, r_p) \in \mathrm{L}$ such that $\overline{sk} \neq \perp$, but (b) $\mathcal{A}_0$ does not return $\perp$ as its answer. Therefore, for randomly sampled $\hat{i}, \hat{j} \leftarrow \{1, \cdots, q\}$ (not learnt by $\mathcal{B}$), when E occurs, the probability that

- the $\hat{j}$th query is the first **Break**2 query satisfying the above two conditions (a) and (b), and
- the $\hat{j}$th query includes pk, which is firstly used in the $\hat{i}$th query,

is at least $1/q^2$. Since $\mathcal{E}$ perfectly simulates $\mathcal{A}_0$ in the interaction with $\mathcal{B}$ in this case (till the termination), it returns (x, y) such that $y = \mathsf{Comp}_{sk'}(x)$ with probability at least $\Pr[E]/q^2$. Notice that in this case, r_g linked with pk (used

[16] As explained in the idea of the proof, since $\mathcal{B}$ only has black-box access to $\mathbf{Tamper}_{\lambda,f}$ and cannot see the structure of f, when $\mathbf{Tamper}_{\lambda,f}(pk, sk)$ aborts, no information on $f(pk)$ is revealed.

[17] $\mathcal{E}$ may terminate before receiving the $\hat{i}$th query.

in the $\hat{j}$th query) is not used by $\mathcal{E}$, and we view (pk', sk') (generated by the challenger and not learnt by $\mathcal{E}$) as the key pair generated by using r_g. This completes the proof of Claim 1. □

Due to the equivalence between weak unpredictability and statistical weak unpredictability (see Lemma 1) and the assumption that Φ is weakly unpredictable, $\Pr[E]/q^2$ is negligible. Therefore, $\Pr[E]$ is negligible, completing the proof of Lemma 4. □

Lemma 5. $\Pr[1 \leftarrow \mathcal{B}^{\mathbf{Sim}(1^\lambda)}(1^\lambda)] = \Pr[1 \leftarrow \mathcal{B}^{\mathcal{A}_1(1^\lambda)}(1^\lambda)]$.

Proof (of Lemma 5). The difference between **Sim** and $\mathcal{A}_1$ is that to return a correct input/output pair, **Sim** computes $y^* = \mathsf{Comp}_{\overline{sk}}(x^*)$ while $\mathcal{A}_1$ does an exhaustive search to find the lexicographically first pair (y^*, π^*) such that $\mathsf{Verify}_{pk}(x^*, y^*, \pi^*) = 1$. One can see that during the execution of $\mathcal{B}^{\mathcal{A}_1(1^\lambda)}(1^\lambda)$ and $\mathcal{B}^{\mathbf{Sim}(1^\lambda)}(1^\lambda)$, $\mathsf{Verify}_{pk}(x^*, \mathsf{Comp}_{\overline{sk}}(x^*), \mathsf{Prove}_{\overline{sk}}(x^*; r_p)) = 1$ holds for all $(pk, \overline{sk}, r_g, r_p) \in \mathrm{L}$ where $\overline{sk} \neq \bot$, due to the check done in the third step in the response to a **Tamper** query. Furthermore, there exists only one y^* such that $\mathsf{Verify}_{pk}(x^*, y^*, \pi^*) = 1$ for some π^*, due to the uniqueness of Φ. Therefore, the forgeries output by **Sim** and $\mathcal{A}$ with respect to the same *pk* are the same, i.e., the views of $\mathcal{B}$ in the interactions with **Sim** and with $\mathcal{A}_1$ are identical. □

Due to Lemmas 3 to 5, we have $|\Pr_{f \leftarrow \mathbb{F}_\lambda}[1 \leftarrow \mathcal{B}^{\mathcal{A}_{\lambda,f}}(1^\lambda)] - \Pr[1 \leftarrow \mathcal{B}^{\mathbf{Sim}(1^\lambda)}(1^\lambda)]| \leq negl(\lambda)$, completing the proof of Theorem 2. □

Simulatable Attack for WTR Secure Unique-Key Signatures. Next we give our negative result on tamper-resilient unique-key signatures.

Theorem 3. *For any weakly unforgeable unique-key signature scheme* $\Sigma = (\mathsf{Gen}, \mathsf{Sign}, \mathsf{Verify})$, *there exists a simulatable attack on the WTR security of* Σ.

We refer the reader to the full paper for the adversaries and simulator in this simulatable attack. Unlike those in the proof of Theorem 2, the adversaries and simulator in this simulatable attack check the validity of a key pair in a direct way by using the key checking algorithm UKCheck, and the adversaries exhaustively search a secret key and forge a signature by using it. We omit the proof of the indistinguishability between the adversaries and simulator since it can be done by slightly modifying the proof of Theorem 2.

3.4 Summary of Negative Results on PDPs and Signatures

Since we have shown the existence of simulatable attacks on the WTR security of any weakly unpredictable PDP and any weakly unforgeable unique-key signature scheme, we obtain the following corollary, which is the first main result in our paper. It directly follows from Theorems 1, 2, and 3.

Corollary 1. *Let Φ (respectively, Σ) be a PDP (respectively, a unique-key signature scheme). If Φ (respectively, Σ) is weakly unpredictable (respectively, weakly unforgeable), then there exists no black-box reduction deriving the WTR security of Φ (respectively, Σ) from the security of any cryptographic game.*

This corollary implies the impossibility of deriving the (even extremely weak) tamper-resilience of PDPs and unique-key signatures from any common assumption, via black-box reductions.

As explained before, VRFs, VUFs, and unique signatures can be cast as PDPs. Furthermore, the security notions for VRFs and VUFs, called pseudorandomness and unpredictability respectively (see [2] for the formal definitions), are stronger than weak unpredictability, and a weakly unforgeable unique signature scheme can be viewed as a weakly unpredictable PDP. Hence, we obtain the following corollary derived from Corollary 1.

Corollary 2. *Let Φ be a VRF, a VUF, or a weakly unforgeable unique signature scheme. There exists no black-box reduction deriving the WTR security of Φ from the security of any cryptographic game.*

Negative Result on Injective OWFs. In [68], Wichs gave a negative result on leakage-resilient unique-key one-way relations. One may also wonder whether tamper-resilient injective OWFs are achievable. Indeed, Faonio and Venturi [28] implicitly used a tamper-resilient OWF, and we can follow them to combine a tamper-resilient injective OWF with the framework in [25] to obtain tamper-resilient unique-key signatures in the CRS model, where it is assumed that tamper-proof public parameters are available. However, a simplified version of the proof of Theorem 2 can be adopted to show the non-existence of black-box reductions deriving the tamper-resilience of OWFs from the security of any cryptographic game. We refer the reader to the full paper for the definition, security notion, and simulatable attack for tamper-resilient injective OWFs. Notice that this negative result does not imply those on unique-key signatures and encryption schemes, since a public/secret key pair is not necessarily an output/input pair of an OWF, and a signature or a ciphertext does not necessarily include public keys.

Negative Result on Re-randomizable Signatures. In [43], Hofheinz et al. extended the negative results on tight security of unique signatures, which was firstly proved by Coron [19] and then fixed by Kakvi and Kiltz [48], for the notion of re-randomizable signatures. This notion is more general and hence captures more instantiations, such as the Waters signature scheme [66] and its variant [43]. We argue that such an extension can also be adopted in our case. Namely, by slightly changing the proof of Theorem 2, we can prove the impossibility on re-randomizable signatures with tamper-resilience. Intuitively, like the uniqueness of a PDP, which guarantees that the outputs of the adversary and the simulator are the same, the re-randomizability guarantees that their (re-randomized) outputs are indistinguishable in the view of any (possibly inefficient) distinguisher.

We refer the reader to the full paper for the definition of re-randomizable signatures and the simulatable attack on their WTR security. We omit the formal proof since it can be done by slightly modifying the proof of Theorem 2.

We can also extend the negative result on unique-key signatures for signatures with key re-randomization [5], and the same extension can be adopted for the above mentioned result on injective OWFs and our result on PKE schemes introduced in the next section. These extensions are similar to the above one and hence we omit the details.

Remark on Self-destructive and Key-Updating Mechanisms. The tamper-resilience notions of many constructions are guaranteed by self-destructive or key-updating mechanism (e.g., [23,27,35,37,49]). The former allows a device to erase all internal data when tampering is detected, so that an adversary cannot obtain any information from further queries. The latter allows a device to update its secret information. Since we treat adversaries that only make one tampering query and one computing query, our results (in both this section and the next section) capture tamper-resilient primitives with these two mechanisms as well.

4 Impossibility on Unique-Message PKE Schemes

In this section, we give a negative result on unique-message PKE schemes. Our result shows that if a unique-message PKE scheme satisfies some "extremely" weak security, then there exists no black-box reduction deriving its tamper-resilience in the plain model from any commonly used falsifiable assumption.

The rest of this section is organized as follows. In Sect. 4.1, we give the definition of a unique-message PKE scheme. In Sect. 4.2, we define several security notions. In Sect. 4.3, we show the existence of a weak simulatable attack on the tamper-resilience of unique-message PKE schemes. In Sect. 4.4, we summarize our negative result.

4.1 Definition of PKE Schemes

We now give the definition of a PKE scheme.

Definition 14 (Public key encryption (PKE)). *A PKE scheme consists of the PT algorithms* $(\mathsf{Gen}, \mathsf{Enc}, \mathsf{Dec})$. *(a)* Gen *is a probabilistic algorithm that takes as input* 1^λ*, and returns a public/secret key pair* $(pk, sk) \in \{0,1\}^p \times \{0,1\}^s$ *for some polynomials* $p = p(\lambda)$ *and* $s = s(\lambda)$*. The set of all secret keys (output by* $\mathsf{Gen}(1^\lambda)$*) and the (internal) randomness space of* Gen *are denoted by* $\mathcal{SK}$ *and* $\mathcal{R}_g$*, respectively. (b)* Enc *is a probabilistic algorithm that takes as input a public key* pk *and a message* $m \in \mathcal{M}$*, where* $\mathcal{M}$ *is the message space, and returns a ciphertext* $ct \in \{0,1\}^c$ *for some polynomial* $c = c(\lambda)$*. The (internal) randomness space of* Enc *is denoted by* $\mathcal{R}_e$*. (c)* Dec *is a deterministic algorithm that takes as input a secret key* sk *and a ciphertext* ct*, and returns a message* $m \in \mathcal{M}$ *or* $\perp$*.*

A PKE scheme is required to satisfy correctness, *which means that* $\mathsf{Dec}_{sk}(ct) = m$ *holds for all* $\lambda \in \mathbb{N}$, *all* $(pk, sk) \leftarrow \mathsf{Gen}(1^\lambda)$, *all* $m \in \mathcal{M}$, *and all* $ct \leftarrow \mathsf{Enc}_{pk}(m)$.

We now define unique-message PKE schemes. For a unique-message PKE scheme, there exists a plaintext-recovering algorithm which can correctly decrypt a ciphertext, and it is required that when using it to decrypt a ciphertext (possibly outside the support of Enc), all valid secret keys with respect to a public key (possibly outside the support of Gen) should lead to the same decryption result.

Definition 15 (Unique-message PKE). *A PKE scheme* (Gen, Enc, Dec) *is said to be a* unique-message PKE scheme *if there exist two deterministic PT algorithm* (UMCheck, Rec) *such that (a)* $\mathsf{UMCheck}(pk, sk) = 1$ *holds for all* $\lambda \in \mathbb{N}$ *and all* $(pk, sk) \leftarrow \mathsf{Gen}(1^\lambda)$, *(b)* (Gen, Enc, Rec) *satisfies correctness, and (c) for all* $\lambda \in \mathbb{N}$, *all* $pk \in \{0,1\}^p$, *and all* $ct \in \{0,1\}^c$ *(possibly outside the support of* Gen *and* Enc *respectively), there exists no pair* $(sk, sk') \in \{0,1\}^s \times \{0,1\}^s$ *that simultaneously satisfies* $\mathsf{UMCheck}(pk, sk) = \mathsf{UMCheck}(pk, sk') = 1$ *and* $\mathsf{Rec}_{sk}(ct) \neq \mathsf{Rec}_{sk'}(ct)$.

For ease of understanding the rationale behind the above definition, as an instance, we show how it captures the Cramer-Shoup scheme [20] in the full paper. Furthermore, we argue that this definition captures all the unique-key PKE schemes, which are defined in the same way as unique-key signatures, namely, there exists only one valid secret key for each public key (not necessarily output by $\mathsf{Gen}(1^\lambda)$). We refer the reader to the full paper for the formal definition and the proof that all unique-key PKE schemes fall under the definition of unique-message PKE schemes.

4.2 Security Notions for PKE Schemes

In this subsection, we define weak one-wayness and WTR security for PKE schemes.

At first, we give the definition of weak one-wayness. Such security only guarantees that an adversary, which is allow to neither learn *pk* nor make any decryption query, cannot recover a message from a randomly generated ciphertext.

Definition 16 (Weak one-wayness). *A PKE scheme* (Gen, Enc, Dec) *is said to be* weakly one-way, *if for any PPT adversary* $\mathcal{A}$, *we have*

$$\Pr[(pk, sk) \leftarrow \mathsf{Gen}(1^\lambda), m \leftarrow \mathcal{M}, ct \leftarrow \mathsf{Enc}_{pk}(m), \\ m' \leftarrow \mathcal{A}(1^\lambda, ct) : m = m'] \leq negl(\lambda).$$

Remark. We can also define statistical weak one-wayness by replacing "PPT adversary" with "(possibly inefficient) adversary". However, unlike the cases of unpredictability and unforgeability notions defined for PDPs and signatures, statistical weak one-wayness is *not necessarily* implied by weak one-wayness. Specifically, for a one-way PKE scheme, one can see that its security does not change if we put the public key into the ciphertext. The one-way security of the original PKE scheme implies the weak one-wayness of this modified scheme. However, if the public key is part of the ciphertext, the scheme cannot be statistically weakly one-way because an inefficient adversary can find a secret key corresponding to the public key and decrypt the challenge ciphertext.

We now define WTR security for PKE schemes. Like WTR security for signatures, an adversary in the security game consists of three independent components (**Tamper**, **Break**1, **Break**2). **Tamper** determines a tampered secret key, on input a public/secret key pair. **Break**1 takes as input a public key and makes a decryption query. On receiving the answer generated by using the tampered secret key and a challenge ciphertext, **Break**2 tries to decrypt the challenge ciphertext. Similarly to WTR security for signatures, we allow the adversary to make only one tampering query and one decryption query, and forbid the communication between **Break**1 and **Break**2. If the message space is super-polynomially large, one may consider this security notion as an extremely weak version of the indistinguishability under chosen ciphertext attacks and tampering attacks defined in [28,35], except that we treat the plain model. As noted before, the more restrictive the adversary is, the stronger our negative result is. The formal definition is as follows.

Definition 17 (Weak tamper-resilient (WTR) PKE). *A PKE scheme* $(\mathsf{Gen}, \mathsf{Enc}, \mathsf{Dec})$ *is said to satisfy* WTR security, *if for any PPT adversary* $\mathcal{A} = (\mathbf{Tamper}, \mathbf{Break}1, \mathbf{Break}2)$, *we have*

$$\Pr[(pk, sk) \leftarrow \mathsf{Gen}(1^\lambda), sk' \leftarrow \mathbf{Tamper}(1^\lambda, pk, sk), ct \leftarrow \mathbf{Break}1(1^\lambda, pk), m = \mathsf{Dec}_{sk'}(ct), m^* \leftarrow \mathcal{M}, ct^* \leftarrow \mathsf{Enc}_{pk}(m^*), m' \leftarrow \mathbf{Break}2(1^\lambda, pk, m, ct^*) : sk' \in \mathcal{SK} \wedge m' = m^*] \leq negl(\lambda).$$

4.3 Weak Simulatable Attack for WTR Secure Unique-Message PKE Schemes

Next we give a theorem showing the existence of a weak simulatable attack on the WTR security of unique-message PKE schemes satisfying weak one-wayness. The basic idea of the proof is similar to that of Theorem 2. The main difference is that in this case, the indistinguishability between the inefficient adversary $\mathcal{A}$ and the PPT simulator **Sim** follows from the fact that without making a valid **Tamper** query (which does not lead $\mathcal{A}$ to output $\perp$), the distinguisher cannot answer a decryption query (rather than a signing query). Similarly to the simulatable attack for Theorem 3 (see the full paper for details), $\mathcal{A}$ and **Sim** check the validity of a key pair in a direct way, by using the key checking algorithm $\mathsf{UMCheck}$.

Theorem 4. *For any weakly one-way unique-message PKE scheme* $\Pi = (\mathsf{Gen}, \mathsf{Enc}, \mathsf{Dec})$, *there exists a weak simulatable attack on its WTR security.*

We give the overview and idea of the proof of Theorem 4 as below, and refer the reader to the full paper for details.

Overview and Idea of the Proof of Theorem 4. Let $\mathsf{UMCheck}$ and Rec be the key checking algorithm and plaintext-recovering algorithm of Π, respectively, and $\mathbb{F}_\lambda$ be the set of all functions $f : \{0,1\}^p \to \mathcal{R}_g \times \mathcal{R}_e \times \mathcal{M}$. We firstly construct an inefficient adversary $\mathcal{A}$, which is an ensemble of stateless algorithms $\{\mathcal{A}_{\lambda,f} = (\mathbf{Tamper}_{\lambda,f}, \mathbf{Break1}_{\lambda,f}, \mathbf{Break2}_{\lambda,f})\}_{\lambda\in\mathbb{N}, f\in\mathbb{F}_\lambda}$. Each $\mathcal{A}_{\lambda,f}$ hard-wires an element f in $\mathbb{F}_\lambda$. We show that each $\mathcal{A}_{\lambda,f}$ breaks the WTR security of Π, and there exists a PPT stateful simulator **Sim** that can simulate the behavior of $\mathcal{A}_{\lambda,f}$, in the case that f is chosen uniformly at random from $\mathbb{F}_\lambda$ (and hence is a random function with domain $\{0,1\}^p$ and range $\mathcal{R}_g \times \mathcal{R}_e \times \mathcal{M}$). We design $\mathcal{A}_{\lambda,f}$ as follows.

$\mathbf{Tamper}_{\lambda,f}(1^\lambda, pk, sk)$ runs $(r_g, r_e, m) = f(pk)$ and $(pk', sk') = \mathsf{Gen}(1^\lambda; r_g)$. If (pk, sk) is valid (i.e., $\mathsf{UMCheck}(pk, sk) = 1$), it outputs sk' as the tampered key. $\mathbf{Break1}_{\lambda,f}(pk)$ runs $(r_g, r_e, m) = f(pk)$ and outputs $ct = \mathsf{Enc}_{pk'}(m; r_e)$ as the decryption query. $\mathbf{Break2}_{\lambda,f}(pk, m', ct^*)$ runs $(r_g, r_e, m) = f(pk)$ and $(pk', sk') = \mathsf{Gen}(1^\lambda; r_g)$, and checks whether the answer of the decryption query is correct (i.e., whether $m' = m$). If the check works, it does an exhaustive search to find a secret key sk such that $\mathsf{UMCheck}(pk, sk) = 1$, and outputs $m^* = \mathsf{Rec}_{sk}(ct^*)$. Otherwise, it aborts. One can see that $\mathcal{A}_{\lambda,f}$ breaks the WTR security of Π due to the correctness of Π and $(\mathsf{Gen}, \mathsf{Enc}, \mathsf{Rec})$, and the unique-message property of Π.

Next we explain why we can have a PPT stateful simulator **Sim** which is indistinguishable from $\mathcal{A}_{\lambda,f}$ (where $f \leftarrow \mathbb{F}_\lambda$) in the view of any oracle-access PPT machine $\mathcal{B}$. To make $\mathbf{Break2}_{\lambda,f}$ recover ct^* (rather than abort), $\mathcal{B}$ has to answer the query ct made by $\mathbf{Break1}_{\lambda,f}$. However, without having given $\mathbf{Tamper}_{\lambda,f}$ a valid key pair (pk, sk) previously, ct is just a randomly generated ciphertext in the view of $\mathcal{B}$, and $\mathcal{B}$ learns no information on (pk', sk'). The reason is that $\mathcal{B}$ only has black-box access to $\mathbf{Tamper}_{\lambda,f}$ and cannot see the structure of f. When $\mathbf{Tamper}_{\lambda,f}(pk, sk)$ aborts, no information on $f(pk)$ is revealed. In this case, $\mathcal{B}$ cannot answer ct due to the weak one-wayness of Π. Therefore, we can construct **Sim**, who simulates the outputs of f by executing lazy sampling, and decrypts ct^* by using a valid key having appeared in a **Tamper** query made by $\mathcal{B}$ previouly. If such a key does not exist, **Sim** aborts. Due to the unique-message property, the final outputs of $\mathbf{Break2}_{\lambda,f}$ and **Sim** must be identical, which guarantees that the interactions with $\mathcal{A}_{\lambda,f}$ and with **Sim** are indistinguishable in the view of $\mathcal{B}$.

More specifically, we show the indistinguishability by giving hybrid machines $\mathcal{A}_0$ and $\mathcal{A}_1$. $\mathcal{A}_0$ interacts with $\mathcal{B}$ in the same way as $\mathcal{A}_{\lambda,f}$ (where $f \leftarrow \mathbb{F}_\lambda$) does, except that it simulates the outputs of f by executing lazy sampling. $\mathcal{A}_1$ runs in the same way as $\mathcal{A}_0$ does except that on receiving a **Break**2 query (pk, m', ct^*) where m' is a correct answer for the decryption query, if a valid secret key sk for pk has appeared in a **Tamper** query previously, $\mathcal{A}_1$ directly computes $\mathsf{Rec}_{sk}(ct^*)$. Otherwise, it exhaustively searches sk and then computes $\mathsf{Rec}_{sk}(ct^*)$. The indistinguishability between $\mathcal{A}_{\lambda,f}$ and $\mathcal{A}_0$ follows from the fact that the outputs of f look perfectly random in the view of $\mathcal{B}$. Furthermore, due to the unique-message property of Π, the decryption results output by $\mathcal{A}_0$ and $\mathcal{A}_1$ (with respect to the same pk and ct^*) must be identical. Hence, $\mathcal{A}_0$ is indistinguishable from $\mathcal{A}_1$ in the view of $\mathcal{B}$. At last, we need to show that $\mathcal{A}_1$ is indistinguishable from **Sim**. The only difference between them is that when $\mathcal{B}$ makes a **Break**2 query (pk, m', ct^*), where a valid secret key sk for pk has not appeared in a **Tamper** query previously, $\mathcal{A}_1$ checks whether m' is a correct answer of the decryption query and exhaustively searches a secret key to decrypt ct^* (if the check works), while **Sim** just aborts. Then the indistinguishability between $\mathcal{A}_1$ and **Sim** follows from the fact that without having given $\mathcal{A}_1$ a valid key pair (pk, sk) previously, all the **Break**2 queries including pk that $\mathcal{B}$ makes will lead $\mathcal{A}_1$ to abort. Otherwise, we can construct an adversary breaking the weak one-wayness of Π.

Remark. By slightly modifying the above proof, we can also prove that if a unique-message PKE scheme satisfies statistical weak one-wayness, then there exists a simulatable attack on its WTR security.

Furthermore, it is clear that for any honestly generated ciphertext, any honestly generated secret key should lead to the same decryption result, due to correctness. Therefore, we can slightly modify the proof of Theorem 4 to show that for a weakly one-way (respectively, statistically weakly one-way) PKE scheme $(\mathsf{Gen}, \mathsf{Enc}, \mathsf{Dec})$, if there exists an algorithm that can efficiently check whether a secret key and a ciphertext are in the support of Gen and Enc (with respect to a public key) respectively, then there exists a weak simulatable attack (respectively, (standard) simuatable attack) on its WTR security.

4.4 Summary of a Negative Result on Unique-Message PKE

Since we have shown the existence of a weak simulatable attack on the WTR security of any weakly one-way unique-message PKE schemes in the last subsection, we obtain the following corollary, which is the second main result in our paper. It follows directly from Theorems 1 and 4.

Corollary 3. *Let Π be a unique-message PKE scheme. If Π is weakly one-way, then there exists no black-box reduction deriving the WTR security of Π from the security of any restricted cryptographic game.*

This result implies the impossibility of deriving the (even extremely weak) tamper-resilience of a large class of PKE schemes from any common falsifiable assumption, via black-box reductions.

5 Open Problems

Primitives Circumventing Our Results. Our impossibility results capture a wide class of tamper-resilient cryptographic primitives in the plain model, while it remains open whether achieving ones (against arbitrary tampering attacks) outside of the class is possible. One may try to circumvent our results by giving a tamper-resilient PKE scheme, which is weakly one-way but not statistically weakly one-way, under non-falsifiable assumptions. Furthermore, it might be promising to combine such a PKE scheme with an NIZK proof system against untrusted CRSs [9] to construct a tamper-resilient signature scheme, under the framework proposed by Dodis et al. [25].

Impossibility on Primitives in the CRS Model. One may also wonder whether it is possible to construct primitives captured by our negative results in the CRS model (where the existence of tamper-proof public parameters is assumed). If we strengthen the notions of statistical weak unpredictability and unforgeability, and weak one-wayness by allowing the public parameter to be a maliciously generated one (rather than an honestly sampled one), then our impossibility results also hold in this model. However, it is apparent that such security notions are not implied by standard ones. Studying PKE schemes satisfying standard security but not satisfying ones against maliciously generated public parameters might serve as a starting point.

Acknowledgement. A part of this work was supported by the National Natural Science Foundation for Young Scientists of China under Grant Number 62002049, the Fundamental Research Funds for the Central Universities under Grant Numbers ZYGX2020J017, ZYGX2020ZB020, ZYGX2020ZB019, the Sichuan Science and Technology Program under Grant Numbers 2019YFG0506, 2020YFG0292, 2019YFG0505, 2020YFG0460, 2020YFG0462, Input Output Cryptocurrency Collaborative Research Chair funded by IOHK, JST OPERA JPMJOP1612, JST CREST JPMJCR14D6, JSPS KAKENHI JP16H01705, JP17H01695.

References

1. Abdolmaleki, B., Baghery, K., Lipmaa, H., Zając, M.: A subversion-resistant SNARK. In: Takagi, T., Peyrin, T. (eds.) ASIACRYPT 2017. LNCS, vol. 10626, pp. 3–33. Springer, Cham (2017). https://doi.org/10.1007/978-3-319-70700-6_1
2. Abe, M., Camenisch, J., Dowsley, R., Dubovitskaya, M.: On the impossibility of structure-preserving deterministic primitives. In: Lindell, Y. (ed.) TCC 2014. LNCS, vol. 8349, pp. 713–738. Springer, Heidelberg (2014). https://doi.org/10.1007/978-3-642-54242-8_30
3. Abe, M., Groth, J., Ohkubo, M.: Separating short structure-preserving signatures from non-interactive assumptions. In: Lee, D.H., Wang, X. (eds.) ASIACRYPT 2011. LNCS, vol. 7073, pp. 628–646. Springer, Heidelberg (2011). https://doi.org/10.1007/978-3-642-25385-0_34
4. Ateniese, G., Magri, B., Venturi, D.: Subversion-resilient signature schemes. In: ACM CCS 2015 (2015)
5. Bader, C., Jager, T., Li, Y., Schäge, S.: On the impossibility of tight cryptographic reductions. In: Fischlin, M., Coron, J.-S. (eds.) On the impossibility of tight cryptographic reductions. LNCS, vol. 9666, pp. 273–304. Springer, Heidelberg (2016). https://doi.org/10.1007/978-3-662-49896-5_10
6. Ball, M., Dachman-Soled, D., Kulkarni, M., Malkin, T.: Non-malleable codes for bounded depth, bounded fan-in circuits. In: Fischlin, M., Coron, J.-S. (eds.) EUROCRYPT 2016. LNCS, vol. 9666, pp. 881–908. Springer, Heidelberg (2016). https://doi.org/10.1007/978-3-662-49896-5_31

7. Bellare, M., Cash, D.: Pseudorandom functions and permutations provably secure against related-key attacks. In: Rabin, T. (ed.) CRYPTO 2010. LNCS, vol. 6223, pp. 666–684. Springer, Heidelberg (2010). https://doi.org/10.1007/978-3-642-14623-7_36
8. Bellare, M., Cash, D., Miller, R.: Cryptography secure against related-key attacks and tampering. In: Lee, D.H., Wang, X. (eds.) ASIACRYPT 2011. LNCS, vol. 7073, pp. 486–503. Springer, Heidelberg (2011). https://doi.org/10.1007/978-3-642-25385-0_26
9. Bellare, M., Fuchsbauer, G., Scafuro, A.: NIZKs with an untrusted CRS: security in the face of parameter subversion. In: Cheon, J.H., Takagi, T. (eds.) ASIACRYPT 2016. LNCS, vol. 10032, pp. 777–804. Springer, Heidelberg (2016). https://doi.org/10.1007/978-3-662-53890-6_26
10. Bellare, M., Kohno, T.: A theoretical treatment of related-key attacks: RKA-PRPs, RKA-PRFs, and applications. In: Biham, E. (ed.) EUROCRYPT 2003. LNCS, vol. 2656, pp. 491–506. Springer, Heidelberg (2003). https://doi.org/10.1007/3-540-39200-9_31
11. Bellare, M., Paterson, K.G., Thomson, S.: rka security beyond the linear barrier: IBE, encryption and signatures. In: Wang, X., Sako, K. (eds.) ASIACRYPT 2012. LNCS, vol. 7658, pp. 331–348. Springer, Heidelberg (2012). https://doi.org/10.1007/978-3-642-34961-4_21
12. Biham, E., Shamir, A.: Differential fault analysis of secret key cryptosystems. In: Kaliski, B.S. (ed.) CRYPTO 1997. LNCS, vol. 1294, pp. 513–525. Springer, Heidelberg (1997). https://doi.org/10.1007/BFb0052259
13. Boneh, D., DeMillo, R.A., Lipton, R.J.: On the importance of eliminating errors in cryptographic computations. J. Cryptol. **14**(2), 101–119 (2001)
14. Boneh, D., Venkatesan, R.: Breaking RSA may not be equivalent to factoring. In: Nyberg, K. (ed.) EUROCRYPT 1998. LNCS, vol. 1403, pp. 59–71. Springer, Heidelberg (1998). https://doi.org/10.1007/BFb0054117
15. Boyen, X., Mei, Q., Waters, B.: Direct chosen ciphertext security from identity-based techniques. In: ACM CCS (2005)
16. Brakerski, Z., Döttling, N.: Hardness of LWE on general entropic distributions. In: Canteaut, A., Ishai, Y. (eds.) EUROCRYPT 2020. LNCS, vol. 12106, pp. 551–575. Springer, Cham (2020). https://doi.org/10.1007/978-3-030-45724-2_19
17. Chakraborty, S., Prabhakaran, M., Wichs, D.: Witness maps and applications. In: Kiayias, A., Kohlweiss, M., Wallden, P., Zikas, V. (eds.) PKC 2020. LNCS, vol. 12110, pp. 220–246. Springer, Cham (2020). https://doi.org/10.1007/978-3-030-45374-9_8
18. Chen, Yu., Qin, B., Zhang, J., Deng, Y., Chow, S.S.M.: Non-malleable functions and their applications. In: Cheng, C.-M., Chung, K.-M., Persiano, G., Yang, B.-Y. (eds.) PKC 2016. LNCS, vol. 9615, pp. 386–416. Springer, Heidelberg (2016). https://doi.org/10.1007/978-3-662-49387-8_15
19. Coron, J.-S.: Optimal security proofs for PSS and other signature schemes. In: Knudsen, L.R. (ed.) EUROCRYPT 2002. LNCS, vol. 2332, pp. 272–287. Springer, Heidelberg (2002). https://doi.org/10.1007/3-540-46035-7_18
20. Cramer, R., Shoup, V.: Design and analysis of practical public-key encryption schemes secure against adaptive chosen ciphertext attack. SIAM J. Comput. **33**(1), 167–226 (2003)
21. Cramer, R., Shoup, V.: Signature schemes based on the strong RSA assumption. ACM Trans. Inf. Syst. Secur. **3**(3), 161–185 (2000)

22. Dachman-Soled, D., Kulkarni, M.: Upper and lower bounds for continuous non-malleable codes. In: Lin, D., Sako, K. (eds.) PKC 2019. LNCS, vol. 11442, pp. 519–548. Springer, Cham (2019). https://doi.org/10.1007/978-3-030-17253-4_18
23. Damgård, I., Faust, S., Mukherjee, P., Venturi, D.: Bounded tamper resilience: how to go beyond the algebraic barrier. J. Cryptol. **30**(1), 152–190 (2017)
24. Damgård, I., Faust, S., Mukherjee, P., Venturi, D.: The chaining Lemma and its application. In: Lehmann, A., Wolf, S. (eds.) ICITS 2015. LNCS, vol. 9063, pp. 181–196. Springer, Cham (2015). https://doi.org/10.1007/978-3-319-17470-9_11
25. Dodis, Y., Haralambiev, K., López-Alt, A., Wichs, D.: Efficient public-key cryptography in the presence of key leakage. In: Abe, M. (ed.) ASIACRYPT 2010. LNCS, vol. 6477, pp. 613–631. Springer, Heidelberg (2010). https://doi.org/10.1007/978-3-642-17373-8_35
26. Dodis, Y., Vaikuntanathan, V., Wichs, D.: Extracting randomness from extractor-dependent sources. In: Canteaut, A., Ishai, Y. (eds.) EUROCRYPT 2020. LNCS, vol. 12105, pp. 313–342. Springer, Cham (2020). https://doi.org/10.1007/978-3-030-45721-1_12
27. Dziembowski, S., Pietrzak, K., Wichs, D.: Non-malleable codes. In: ICS (2010)
28. Faonio, A., Venturi, D.: Efficient public-key cryptography with bounded leakage and tamper resilience. In: Cheon, J.H., Takagi, T. (eds.) ASIACRYPT 2016. LNCS, vol. 10031, pp. 877–907. Springer, Heidelberg (2016). https://doi.org/10.1007/978-3-662-53887-6_32
29. Faust, S., Mukherjee, P., Nielsen, J.B., Venturi, D.: Continuous non-malleable codes. In: Lindell, Y. (ed.) TCC 2014. LNCS, vol. 8349, pp. 465–488. Springer, Heidelberg (2014). https://doi.org/10.1007/978-3-642-54242-8_20
30. Faust, S., Mukherjee, P., Venturi, D., Wichs, D.: Efficient non-malleable codes and key derivation for poly-size tampering circuits. IEEE Trans. Inf. Theory **62**(12), 7179–7194 (2016)
31. Fischlin, M., Harasser, P., Janson, C.: Signatures from sequential-OR proofs. In: Canteaut, A., Ishai, Y. (eds.) EUROCRYPT 2020. LNCS, vol. 12107, pp. 212–244. Springer, Cham (2020). https://doi.org/10.1007/978-3-030-45727-3_8
32. Fischlin, M., Schröder, D.: On the impossibility of three-move blind signature schemes. In: Gilbert, H. (ed.) EUROCRYPT 2010. LNCS, vol. 6110, pp. 197–215. Springer, Heidelberg (2010). https://doi.org/10.1007/978-3-642-13190-5_10
33. Fuchsbauer, G.: Subversion-zero-knowledge SNARKs. In: Abdalla, M., Dahab, R. (eds.) PKC 2018. LNCS, vol. 10769, pp. 315–347. Springer, Cham (2018). https://doi.org/10.1007/978-3-319-76578-5_11
34. Fujisaki, E., Xagawa, K.: Efficient RKA-Secure KEM and IBE Schemes Against Invertible Functions. In: Lauter, K., Rodríguez-Henríquez, F. (eds.) LATINCRYPT 2015. LNCS, vol. 9230, pp. 3–20. Springer, Cham (2015). https://doi.org/10.1007/978-3-319-22174-8_1
35. Fujisaki, E., Xagawa, K.: Public-key cryptosystems resilient to continuous tampering and leakage of arbitrary functions. In: Cheon, J.H., Takagi, T. (eds.) ASIACRYPT 2016. LNCS, vol. 10031, pp. 908–938. Springer, Heidelberg (2016). https://doi.org/10.1007/978-3-662-53887-6_33
36. Gamal, T.E.: A public key cryptosystem and a signature scheme based on discrete logarithms. IEEE Trans. Inf. Theory **31**(4), 469–472 (1985)
37. Gennaro, R., Lysyanskaya, A., Malkin, T., Micali, S., Rabin, T.: Algorithmic Tamper-Proof (ATP) security: theoretical foundations for security against hardware tampering. In: Naor, M. (ed.) TCC 2004. LNCS, vol. 2951, pp. 258–277. Springer, Heidelberg (2004). https://doi.org/10.1007/978-3-540-24638-1_15

38. Gentry, C., Wichs, D.: Separating succinct non-interactive arguments from all falsifiable assumptions. In: STOC (2011)
39. Goldwasser, S., Ostrovsky, R.: *Invariant* signatures and non-interactive zero-knowledge proofs are equivalent. In: Brickell, E.F. (ed.) CRYPTO 1992. LNCS, vol. 740, pp. 228–245. Springer, Heidelberg (1993). https://doi.org/10.1007/3-540-48071-4_16
40. Haitner, I., Holenstein, T.: On the (im)possibility of key dependent encryption. In: Reingold, O. (ed.) TCC 2009. LNCS, vol. 5444, pp. 202–219. Springer, Heidelberg (2009). https://doi.org/10.1007/978-3-642-00457-5_13
41. Haralambiev, K., Jager, T., Kiltz, E., Shoup, V.: Simple and efficient public-key encryption from computational Diffie-Hellman in the standard model. In: Nguyen, P.Q., Pointcheval, D. (eds.) PKC 2010. LNCS, vol. 6056, pp. 1–18. Springer, Heidelberg (2010). https://doi.org/10.1007/978-3-642-13013-7_1
42. Hesse, J., Hofheinz, D., Kohl, L.: On tightly secure non-interactive key exchange. In: Shacham, H., Boldyreva, A. (eds.) CRYPTO 2018. LNCS, vol. 10992, pp. 65–94. Springer, Cham (2018). https://doi.org/10.1007/978-3-319-96881-0_3
43. Hofheinz, D., Jager, T., Knapp, E.: Waters signatures with optimal security reduction. In: Fischlin, M., Buchmann, J., Manulis, M. (eds.) PKC 2012. LNCS, vol. 7293, pp. 66–83. Springer, Heidelberg (2012). https://doi.org/10.1007/978-3-642-30057-8_5
44. Hohenberger, S., Waters, B.: Constructing verifiable random functions with large input spaces. In: Gilbert, H. (ed.) EUROCRYPT 2010. LNCS, vol. 6110, pp. 656–672. Springer, Heidelberg (2010). https://doi.org/10.1007/978-3-642-13190-5_33
45. Hohenberger, S., Waters, B.: Short and stateless signatures from the RSA assumption. In: Halevi, S. (ed.) CRYPTO 2009. LNCS, vol. 5677, pp. 654–670. Springer, Heidelberg (2009). https://doi.org/10.1007/978-3-642-03356-8_38
46. Jafargholi, Z., Wichs, D.: Tamper detection and continuous non-malleable codes. In: Dodis, Y., Nielsen, J.B. (eds.) TCC 2015. LNCS, vol. 9014, pp. 451–480. Springer, Heidelberg (2015). https://doi.org/10.1007/978-3-662-46494-6_19
47. Jarecki, S., Shmatikov, V.: Handcuffing big brother: an abuse-resilient transaction Escrow scheme. In: Cachin, C., Camenisch, J.L. (eds.) EUROCRYPT 2004. LNCS, vol. 3027, pp. 590–608. Springer, Heidelberg (2004). https://doi.org/10.1007/978-3-540-24676-3_35
48. Kakvi, S.A., Kiltz, E.: Optimal security proofs for full domain hash, revisited. In: Pointcheval, D., Johansson, T. (eds.) EUROCRYPT 2012. LNCS, vol. 7237, pp. 537–553. Springer, Heidelberg (2012). https://doi.org/10.1007/978-3-642-29011-4_32
49. Kalai, Y.T., Kanukurthi, B., Sahai, A.: Cryptography with tamperable and leaky memory. In: Rogaway, P. (ed.) CRYPTO 2011. LNCS, vol. 6841, pp. 373–390. Springer, Heidelberg (2011). https://doi.org/10.1007/978-3-642-22792-9_21
50. Kiltz, E., Masny, D., Pan, J.: Optimal security proofs for signatures from identification schemes. In: Robshaw, M., Katz, J. (eds.) CRYPTO 2016. LNCS, vol. 9815, pp. 33–61. Springer, Heidelberg (2016). https://doi.org/10.1007/978-3-662-53008-5_2
51. Kravitz, D.W.: Digital signature algorithm. US Patent 5,231,668
52. Liskov, M.: Updatable zero-knowledge databases. In: Roy, B. (ed.) ASIACRYPT 2005. LNCS, vol. 3788, pp. 174–198. Springer, Heidelberg (2005). https://doi.org/10.1007/11593447_10
53. Liu, F.-H., Lysyanskaya, A.: Tamper and leakage resilience in the split-state model. In: Safavi-Naini, R., Canetti, R. (eds.) CRYPTO 2012. LNCS, vol. 7417, pp. 517–532. Springer, Heidelberg (2012). https://doi.org/10.1007/978-3-642-32009-5_30

54. Lysyanskaya, A.: Unique signatures and verifiable random functions from the DH-DDH separation. In: Yung, M. (ed.) CRYPTO 2002. LNCS, vol. 2442, pp. 597–612. Springer, Heidelberg (2002). https://doi.org/10.1007/3-540-45708-9_38
55. Micali, S., Rabin, M.O., Vadhan, S.P.: Verifiable random functions. In: FOCS (1999)
56. Micali, S., Reyzin, L.: Soundness in the public-key model. In: Kilian, J. (ed.) CRYPTO 2001. LNCS, vol. 2139, pp. 542–565. Springer, Heidelberg (2001). https://doi.org/10.1007/3-540-44647-8_32
57. Micali, S., Rivest, R.L.: Micropayments revisited. In: Preneel, B. (ed.) CT-RSA 2002. LNCS, vol. 2271, pp. 149–163. Springer, Heidelberg (2002). https://doi.org/10.1007/3-540-45760-7_11
58. Morgan, A., Pass, R.: On the security loss of unique signatures. In: Beimel, A., Dziembowski, S. (eds.) TCC 2018. LNCS, vol. 11239, pp. 507–536. Springer, Cham (2018). https://doi.org/10.1007/978-3-030-03807-6_19
59. Naor, M.: On cryptographic assumptions and challenges. In: Boneh, D. (ed.) CRYPTO 2003. LNCS, vol. 2729, pp. 96–109. Springer, Heidelberg (2003). https://doi.org/10.1007/978-3-540-45146-4_6
60. Paillier, P., Vergnaud, D.: Discrete-log-based signatures may not be equivalent to discrete log. In: Roy, B. (ed.) ASIACRYPT 2005. LNCS, vol. 3788, pp. 1–20. Springer, Heidelberg (2005). https://doi.org/10.1007/11593447_1
61. Pass, R.: Limits of provable security from standard assumptions. In: STOC (2011)
62. Qin, B., Liu, S., Yuen, T.H., Deng, R.H., Chen, K.: Continuous non-malleable key derivation and its application to related-key security. In: Katz, J. (ed.) PKC 2015. LNCS, vol. 9020, pp. 557–578. Springer, Heidelberg (2015). https://doi.org/10.1007/978-3-662-46447-2_25
63. Ristenpart, T., Shacham, H., Shrimpton, T.: Careful with composition: limitations of the indifferentiability framework. In: Paterson, K.G. (ed.) EUROCRYPT 2011. LNCS, vol. 6632, pp. 487–506. Springer, Heidelberg (2011). https://doi.org/10.1007/978-3-642-20465-4_27
64. Rivest, R.L., Shamir, A., Adleman, L.M.: A method for obtaining digital signatures and public-key cryptosystems (reprint). Commun. ACM **26**(1), 96–99 (1983)
65. Wang, Y., Matsuda, T., Hanaoka, G., Tanaka, K.: Memory lower bounds of reductions revisited. In: Nielsen, J.B., Rijmen, V. (eds.) EUROCRYPT 2018. LNCS, vol. 10820, pp. 61–90. Springer, Cham (2018). https://doi.org/10.1007/978-3-319-78381-9_3
66. Waters, B.: Efficient identity-based encryption without random Oracles. In: Cramer, R. (ed.) EUROCRYPT 2005. LNCS, vol. 3494, pp. 114–127. Springer, Heidelberg (2005). https://doi.org/10.1007/11426639_7
67. Wee, H.: Public key encryption against related key attacks. In: Fischlin, M., Buchmann, J., Manulis, M. (eds.) PKC 2012. LNCS, vol. 7293, pp. 262–279. Springer, Heidelberg (2012). https://doi.org/10.1007/978-3-642-30057-8_16
68. Wichs, D.: Barriers in cryptography with weak, correlated and leaky sources. In: ITCS (2013)
69. Zhang, J., Zhang, Z., Chen, Yu., Guo, Y., Zhang, Z.: Black-box separations for one-more (static) CDH and its generalization. In: Sarkar, P., Iwata, T. (eds.) ASIACRYPT 2014. LNCS, vol. 8874, pp. 366–385. Springer, Heidelberg (2014). https://doi.org/10.1007/978-3-662-45608-8_20

Rate-1 Key-Dependent Message Security via Reusable Homomorphic Extractor Against Correlated-Source Attacks

Qiqi Lai[1,2(✉)], Feng-Hao Liu[3], and Zhedong Wang[3]

[1] School of Computer Science, Shaanxi Normal University, Xi'an, China
laiqq@snnu.edu.cn

[2] State Key Laboratory of Integrated Service Networks, Xidian University, Xi'an, China

[3] Florida Atlantic University, Boca Raton, FL, USA
{fenghao.liu,wangz}@fau.edu

Abstract. In this work, we first present general methods to construct information rate-1 PKE that is $\mathsf{KDM}^{(n)}$-secure with respect to *block-affine* functions for any unbounded polynomial n. To achieve this, we propose a new notion of extractor that satisfies *reusability*, *homomorphic*, and *security against correlated-source attacks*, and show how to use this extractor to improve the information rate of the KDM-secure PKE of Brakerski et al. (Eurocrypt 18). Then, we show how to amplify KDM security from block-affine function class into general bounded size circuits via a variant of the technique of Applebaum (Eurocrypt 11), achieving better efficiency. Furthermore, we show how to generalize these approaches to the IBE setting.

Additionally, our PKE and IBE schemes are also leakage resilient, with leakage rates $1 - o(1)$ against a slightly smaller yet still general class – block leakage functions. We can instantiate the required building blocks from LWE or DDH.

1 Introduction

The classic notion of *semantic security* by Goldwasser and Micali [18] guarantees security when the secret key is generated randomly and independently of the message being encrypted. This notion however, is not sufficient in various scenarios, e.g., [1,10,13,24]. To tackle this issue, [8,9] formally defined *Key Dependent Message* (KDM) security, which requires $\mathsf{Enc}(\mathsf{pk}, \mathfrak{f}(\mathsf{sk}))$ to be indistinguishable from $\mathsf{Enc}(\mathsf{pk}, 0)$ for all $\mathfrak{f}$ in a certain class. The setting can be generalized to n-users, i.e., $\mathsf{KDM}^{(n)}$-security, where security holds even when the attacker obtains the encryption of $\mathfrak{f}(\mathsf{sk}_1, \ldots, \mathsf{sk}_n)$ under some user's (public) key. The community has established various theoretical feasibility results – we know how to construct $\mathsf{KDM}^{(n)}$-secure PKE for unbounded polynomial n from the LWE [5], DDH [9], or LPN [5,16,23] assumption, for bounded polynomial n from QR/DCR assumption [10], and for $n = 1$ from CDH [12].

J. A. Garay (Ed.): PKC 2021, LNCS 12710, pp. 421–450, 2021.
https://doi.org/10.1007/978-3-030-75245-3_16

On the other hand however, all the prior constructions have relatively small information rate[1] even for the class of linear functions, resulting in very large overhead in scenarios that require encrypting large data, e.g., storing large encrypted files in the cloud, or streaming encrypted high-resolution movies over the internet. To remove this limitation and enhance usability, it is necessary to determine whether a low information rate is inherent for KDM security.

As folklore, this issue (low information rate) can be solved easily for regular PKE, as one can always achieve rate $1 - o(1)$ by using the technique of hybrid encryption (the KEM-DEM paradigm). It is however, not clear whether KDM security can be preserved under a general hybrid encryption [22]. This direction has remained an important open problem (ref. [9,10]). Therefore, we ask:

Main Question: Can we construct a $\mathsf{KDM}^{(n)}$-secure PKE with better information rate, e.g. $1 - o(1)$, even for $n = 1$ and linear functions?

1.1 Our Contributions

This work answers the main question and makes the following contributions:

Contribution 1. We show how to construct a $\mathsf{KDM}^{(1)}$-secure PKE with information rate $1 - o(1)$ with respect to *block-affine* functions, a slightly more restricted class than that of bit-affine functions. To achieve this, we first propose a new primitive – *reusable homomorphic extractor against correlated-source attacks*, and instantiate it based on DDH or LWE. Next, we show how to use this primitive to improve the approach of Batch Encryption (BE) [12], which was used to derive $\mathsf{KDM}^{(1)}$-secure PKE (albeit low information rates.)

Particularly, we identify that BE implies a weak hash proof system (wHPS) with important additional properties. Then we show that our new extractor can be integrated with such a wHPS to achieve $\mathsf{KDM}^{(1)}$-security with information rate $1 - o(1)$. Our proof technique connects wHPS and the new reusable homomorphic extractor in a novel way, which deviates from the prior simulation approach [5,7,9–12]. The new extractor and proof technique can be of independent interest.

Contribution 2. We show how to upgrade the above approach to achieve $\mathsf{KDM}^{(n)}$-secure PKE for unbounded polynomial n. Particularly, we identify the technical barrier of the current BE-based approach [12], which inherently can only achieve a bounded polynomial n. To tackle this, we construct an enhanced variant of the current BE by adding a new *reusable* property. By using this stronger BE as the underlying building block of wHPS, the scheme in Contribution 1 can be proved $\mathsf{KDM}^{(n)}$-secure for any unbounded polynomial n. For instantiations, we construct the required extractor and BE from DDH or LWE. Thus, either of these assumptions implies $\mathsf{KDM}^{(n)}$-secure PKE with the optimal information rate, i.e., $1 - o(1)$.

[1] Information rate is defined as the message-to-ciphertext ratio when one encrypts sufficiently long plaintexts.

Our design of KDM-PKE is quite modular, which might open a path for further constructions from other assumptions, as long as we can construct the required building blocks.

Contribution 3. We generalize the above approach in two directions. First, we show that the class of block-affine function is still sufficient for KDM amplification to the class of general bounded-sized circuits via a variant of the technique in [4], even the class of block-affine functions is more restricted, i.e., it does not contain all projection functions, so that the generic KDM amplification of Applebaum [4] does not work. Thus, the affine function class is still sufficiently general, and can yield more efficient constructions.

Second, we construct $\mathsf{KDM}^{(n)}$-secure IBE for unbounded n with the $1 - o(1)$ information rate. The corresponding KDM function class here is slightly smaller than the allowable KDM class for our PKE. We discuss this allowable class next. Moreover, the required building blocks can be instantiated based on DDH in the bilinear group or LWE.

In addition to KDM security, our PKE schemes (both DDH and LWE-based) are leakage resilient. The leakage rate is optimal, i.e., $1 - o(1)$, against block leakage, which is slightly smaller than the general leakage class[2]. The IBE schemes are as well leakage resilient. For the same class of leakage functions, the IBE leakage rate can achieve $1 - o(1)$ under LWE or DDH with respect to some bilinear maps.

1.2 Technical Overview

In this section, we present a technical overview of our contributions. We start with the construction of $\mathsf{KDM}^{(1)}$-secure PKE with information rate $1 - o(1)$. To achieve this target, we first identify several new properties from (Identity-based) weak Hash Proof Systems (wHPS) [2,21], Batch Encryption (BE) [12], and randomness extractors [3], and then describe our new idea to integrate these properties. Before describing our new insights, we first review the following two important tools – wHPS and BE.

(Weak) Hash Proof System. A hash proof system can be described as a key encapsulation mechanism that consists of four algorithms $(\mathsf{Setup}, \mathsf{Encap}, \mathsf{Encap}^*, \mathsf{Decap})$: (1) Setup generates a key pair $(\mathsf{pk}, \mathsf{sk})$, (2) $\mathsf{Encap}(\mathsf{pk})$ outputs a pair $(\mathsf{CT}, \mathsf{k})$ where k is a key encapsulated in a "valid" ciphertext CT, (3) $\mathsf{Encap}^*(\mathsf{pk})$ outputs an "invalid" ciphertext CT^*, and (4) $\mathsf{Decap}(\mathsf{sk}, \mathsf{CT})$ outputs a key k'. A (weak) hash proof system needs to satisfy the following three properties:

- **Correctness.** For a valid ciphertext CT, the Decap algorithm always outputs the encapsulated key k' such that $\mathsf{k}' = \mathsf{k}$, where $(\mathsf{CT}, \mathsf{k}) \xleftarrow{\$} \mathsf{Encap}(\mathsf{pk})$.

[2] When the secret key is stored in blocks, a block leakage function can leak individual blocks one after another, as long as the blocks still remain a block source.

- **Ciphertext Indistinguishability.** Valid ciphertexts and invalid ciphertexts are computationally indistinguishable, *even given the secret key* sk. This property is essential for achieving leakage resilience and KDM security.
- **Universal.** The wHPS is (ℓ, w)-universal if given the public key pk and an invalid ciphertext CT^*, the decapsulated key length is ℓ and the conditional min-entropy of the decapsulation of CT^* is greater or equal to w, i.e., $H_\infty(\mathsf{Decap}(\mathsf{sk}, \mathsf{CT}^*) \mid \mathsf{pk}, \mathsf{CT}^*) \geq w$. A wHPS only requires this property to hold for a random invalid ciphertext, i.e. $\mathsf{CT}^* \overset{\$}{\leftarrow} \mathsf{Encap}^*(\mathsf{pk})$, while a full-fledged HPS requires it to hold for any invalid ciphertext.

We note that wHPS has been used to achieve leakage resilience (LR) in prior work [2,25]. Homomorphic wHPS has been used to achieve $\mathsf{KDM}^{(1)}$-security [27]. It was not clear whether wHPS can be used to achieve $\mathsf{KDM}^{(1)}$-security with the optimal information rate.

Batch Encryption [12]**.** A Batch Encryption (BE) consists of four algorithms: $(\mathsf{Setup}, \mathsf{KeyGen}, \mathsf{Enc}, \mathsf{Dec})$. The secret key is a vector $\boldsymbol{x} \in \mathbb{Z}_B^n$ for $B, n \in \mathbb{N}$. The Setup algorithm simply outputs a random common reference string CRS, and $\mathsf{KeyGen}(\mathsf{CRS}, \boldsymbol{x})$ is a projection function that outputs (a short) hash value h of $\boldsymbol{x}$ and CRS. The encryption algorithm takes an $n \times B$ matrix $\mathbf{M}$ and (CRS, h) as input, and outputs a ciphertext $\mathsf{CT} \leftarrow \mathsf{Enc}((\mathsf{CRS}, h), \mathbf{M})$. The decryption algorithm taking as input a ciphertext CT and a secret key $\boldsymbol{x}$, can only recover M_{i,x_i}, i.e., the x_i-th entry in the i-th row, for $1 \leq i \leq n$, while the other entries remain hidden *even given* the secret key $\boldsymbol{x}$. The work [12] showed that BE can be instantiated from LWE, CDH, and LPN with the *succinctness* property, i.e. the size of $|h|$ depends only on the security parameter and can be set as $o(n)$. Using a succinct BE as a central building block, the work [12] constructed a PKE that simultaneously achieves $\mathsf{KDM}^{(1)}$-security for affine functions and leakage resilience with the optimal leakage rate, i.e., $1 - o(1)$.

Even though the above tools have been demonstrated powerful, there are two common limitations for the current techniques – (1) KDM-security can be achieved only for bounded users, and (2) the information rate is quite low, e.g., $\frac{1}{O(\lambda)}$. Next, we present our new insights to break these technical barriers.

Our New Insights

We start with a simple observation that BE can be used to construct wHPS with additional structures, which are critical in achieving KDM-security. Then we introduce our new variant of random extractor, and sketch its instantiations from DDH and LWE. With all these preparations, we show our new ideas to achieve KDM security.

wHPS from BE. We can construct a wHPS from BE in the following simple way. $\mathsf{wHPS.sk}$ is a random $\boldsymbol{x} \in \mathbb{Z}_B^n$, and $\mathsf{wHPS.pk} = (\mathsf{CRS}, h)$ where CRS, h are generated according to the underlying BE. The valid encapsulation algorithm $\mathsf{wHPS.Encap}$ just samples a random vector $\boldsymbol{k} = (k_1, \ldots, k_n)^\top \in \mathbb{Z}_B^n$ as the encapsulated key and generates the ciphertext by $\mathsf{BE.Enc}(\mathbf{M})$, where the i-th row of $\mathbf{M}$

is set as $(k_i, k_i, \dots, k_i)$ for $i \in [n]$. On the other hand, the invalid encapsulation algorithm wHPS.Encap* generates an invalid ciphertext $\mathsf{CT}^* \leftarrow \mathsf{BE.Enc}(\mathbf{M})$ by first sampling a random vector $\boldsymbol{k}' = (k'_1, \dots, k'_n)^\top$ and then setting the i-th row of $\mathbf{M}$ as $(k'_i + 0, k'_i + 1, \dots, k'_i + B - 1)$ for $i \in [n]$. Moreover, the decapsulation algorithm wHPS.Decap simply outputs the decryption result of $\mathsf{BE.Dec}(\boldsymbol{x}, \mathsf{CT})$.

It is not hard to show that this construction is an $(n \log B, n \log B - |h|)$-universal wHPS, which can be used to achieve a LR-PKE that tolerates $(n \log B - |h| - k)$-bit leakage by using a (k, ε)-extractor (ref. [2,25]).[3] Particularly, the corresponding leakage resilient public-key encryption scheme PKE_1 can be constructed as follows: $\mathsf{PKE}_1.\mathsf{pk} = \mathsf{wHPS.pk}$ and $\mathsf{PKE}_1.\mathsf{sk} = \mathsf{wHPS.sk}$. To encrypt a message m, the encryption algorithm first generates $(\mathsf{CT}, \boldsymbol{k}) \leftarrow \mathsf{wHPS.Encap}$ and samples $\boldsymbol{r}$ as the randomness of a strong randomness extractor $\mathsf{Ext}(\cdot, \cdot)$, and then outputs $(\mathsf{CT}, \boldsymbol{r}, \mathsf{Ext}(\boldsymbol{r}, \boldsymbol{k}) + m)$ as the ciphertext.

Generally, a plain extractor is not sufficient to derive KDM security for PKE_1 in the above paradigm. Interestingly, this task is possible if we use our reusable homomorphic extractor against correlated-source attacks, and the wHPS has appropriate additional structures. Next, we describe the required extractor.

Our New Notion of Extractor and Constructions. We identify three properties of an extractor: (1) reusable, (2) homomorphic, and (3) secure against correlated-source attacks.

Let $\mathsf{Ext}(\boldsymbol{r}, \boldsymbol{s})$ be an extractor, where $\boldsymbol{s}$ is the source and $\boldsymbol{r}$ is the seed. A reusable extractor requires that the same source $\boldsymbol{s}$ can be repeatedly extracted by different seeds for any polynomially many times while maintaining pseudorandomness. That is, for any $m = \mathsf{poly}(\lambda)$ and source $\boldsymbol{s}$ with sufficient entropy, we have $(\boldsymbol{r}_1, \dots, \boldsymbol{r}_m, \mathsf{Ext}(\boldsymbol{r}_1, \boldsymbol{s}), \dots, \mathsf{Ext}(\boldsymbol{r}_m, \boldsymbol{s})) \approx (\boldsymbol{r}_1, \dots, \boldsymbol{r}_m, u_1, \dots, u_m)$, where each u_i is uniformly random.[4] Previously, the work [3,14,25] showed that under computational assumptions, e.g., DDH or LWE, the reusability can be achieved.

The extractor $\mathsf{Ext}(\boldsymbol{r}, \boldsymbol{s})$ is (output) homomorphic with respect to a function $\mathfrak{h}$ if there exists a related function $\mathfrak{h}'$ such that $\mathsf{Ext}(\boldsymbol{r}, \boldsymbol{s}) + \mathfrak{h}(\boldsymbol{s}) = \mathsf{Ext}(\mathfrak{h}'(\boldsymbol{r}), \boldsymbol{s})$. Similar to the work of [27], we will use this homomorphic property in a critical way to achieve KDM security.

We say the (reusable) extractor $\mathsf{Ext}(\boldsymbol{r}, \boldsymbol{s})$ is secure against correlated-source attacks if for functions (perhaps chosen adaptively by the attacker) in some class $\mathcal{F}$, such that for $m = \mathsf{poly}(\lambda)$ and $\mathfrak{g}_1, \dots, \mathfrak{g}_m \in \mathcal{F}$, the extractor remains pseudorandom as follows:[5]

$$(\boldsymbol{r}_1, \dots, \boldsymbol{r}_m, \mathsf{Ext}(\boldsymbol{r}_1, \mathfrak{g}_1(\boldsymbol{s})), \dots, \mathsf{Ext}(\boldsymbol{r}_m, \mathfrak{g}_m(\boldsymbol{s}))) \approx (\boldsymbol{r}_1, \dots, \boldsymbol{r}_m, u_1, \dots, u_m).$$

[3] The extractor can extract uniform string (up to statistical distance ε) for any source with min-entropy k.

[4] Clearly, this notion cannot be achieved unconditionally, as an information-theoretic extractor requires (conditional) min-entropy from the source, which would be exhausted after a bounded number of extractions.

[5] Clearly, this notion is stronger than the reusable extractor, which can be viewed as a special case where $\mathfrak{g}_i$'s are all the identity function. Thus, this notion is only possible under computational assumptions.

Our notion of correlated-source attacks is similar to that of a recent work by Goyal and Song [19], yet with the following major differences. First, the security requirements are different. The work [19] considers information-theoretic indistinguishability of *one* instance of extraction from the *original source*, even given multiple extractions from the modified source, i.e.,

$$(\boldsymbol{r}, \mathsf{Ext}(\boldsymbol{r}, \boldsymbol{s}), \{\boldsymbol{r}_i, \mathsf{Ext}(\boldsymbol{r}_i, \mathfrak{g}_i(\boldsymbol{s}))\}_{i\in m}) \approx (\boldsymbol{r}, u, \{\boldsymbol{r}_i, \mathsf{Ext}(\boldsymbol{r}_i, \mathfrak{g}_i(\boldsymbol{s}))\}_{i\in m}).$$

In contrast, our notion requires that all instances of $\mathsf{Ext}(\boldsymbol{r}_i, \mathfrak{g}_i(\boldsymbol{s}))$ remain pseudorandom, which is a stronger requirement (in this aspect).

Second, the ranges of feasible function classes are different. Specifically, our notion is too strong to achieve for the class of all functions. For example, if $\mathfrak{g}_i$ is a constant function, then $\mathsf{Ext}(\boldsymbol{r}_i, \mathfrak{g}_i(\boldsymbol{s}))$ becomes a fixed value given $\boldsymbol{r}_i$, and thus cannot be pseudorandom. This indicates a necessary condition for feasibility that the function must be entropy preserving. However, the notion in [19] is possible to achieve even unconditionally for the class of all functions, as their challenge instance is extracted from an unmodified source.

Third, to achieve information-theoretic extraction for all arbitrary input correlated functions, the number m of extraction samples given extra in the distribution in [19] must be bounded inherently, and thus cannot be fully reusable.

Summing up the above analyses, we conclude that our security requirement is stronger, resulting in a relatively smaller feasible function class. Moreover, our notion requires reusability for an unbounded polynomial samples, and thus a computational assumption is necessary.

Next, we discuss how to construct such an extractor that simultaneously achieves all the three properties.

Construction Based on DDH. We start with a review of the existing DDH-based reusable extractor. Let $\mathbb{G}$ be the DDH group of order q, $\boldsymbol{r} \in \mathbb{G}^n$ be seed, and $\boldsymbol{s} \in \mathbb{Z}_q^n$ be source. The following function has been proved to be a reusable extractor in [3,25]: $\mathsf{Ext}(\boldsymbol{r}, \boldsymbol{s}) = \prod_{i=1}^n r_i^{s_i}$. Moreover, we notice the following two properties about this extractor: (1) it is output homomorphic with respect to functions of the form $\mathfrak{h}_{\boldsymbol{b}}(\boldsymbol{s}) = \prod_{i=1}^n b_i^{s_i}$, as $\mathsf{Ext}(\boldsymbol{r}, \boldsymbol{s}) \cdot \mathfrak{h}_{\boldsymbol{b}}(\boldsymbol{s}) = \prod_{i=1}^n (r_i \cdot b_i)^{s_i} = \mathsf{Ext}(\boldsymbol{r} \circ \boldsymbol{b}, \boldsymbol{s})$, where $\circ$ is the component-wise group multiplication; (2) the extractor remains pseudorandom against the correlated source attacks with respect to linear shift functions of the form $\mathfrak{g}_{\boldsymbol{v}}(\boldsymbol{s}) = \boldsymbol{s}+\boldsymbol{v}$. Due to the fact $\mathsf{Ext}(\boldsymbol{r}, \boldsymbol{s}+\boldsymbol{v}) = \prod_{i=1}^n r_i^{s_i+v_i} = \mathsf{Ext}(\boldsymbol{r}, \boldsymbol{s}) \cdot \mathsf{Ext}(\boldsymbol{r}, \boldsymbol{v})$, we can simulate $\mathsf{Ext}(\boldsymbol{r}, \mathfrak{g}_{\boldsymbol{v}}(\boldsymbol{s}))$ given $(\boldsymbol{r}, \mathsf{Ext}(\boldsymbol{r}, \boldsymbol{s}))$ and $\mathfrak{g}_{\boldsymbol{v}}$. Via this simple reduction, the security of the reusable extractor directly translates to the security against correlated-source attacks with respect to linear shifts.

At first, it seems that the existing construction already fulfills the three required properties. However, when considering the application to KDM-secure PKE, we notice an obstacle that this extractor is still not compatible with the above mentioned framework of the weak hash proof system based on batch encryption (BE). Below, we sketch the major reason for this incompatibility, and discuss our solution in the following.

Particularly, the BE-based system requires that each component of the secret vector comes from a polynomial-sized domain, i.e., $\boldsymbol{s} \in S^n$ for $|S| = \mathsf{poly}(\lambda)$.

However, the above construction has the domain $\mathbb{G}^n$, which is clearly too large, as DDH assumption holds only when the order q is super-polynomial. To tackle this issue, one might set $S = \mathbb{Z}_p$ for some small p. However, for a subtle reason this approach faces an additional technical difficulty. More specifically, due to the BE feature, the linear shift should work in $\mathbb{Z}_p$, i.e., $\mathfrak{g}_v(s) = s + v \mod p$. However, this equation might not hold for the above mentioned reduction on correlated-source security, i.e., $\mathsf{Ext}(r, (s + v \mod q)) = \mathsf{Ext}(r, s) \cdot \mathsf{Ext}(r, v) \neq \mathsf{Ext}(r, (s + v \mod p))$. Thus, it is unclear whether we can achieve correlated-source security against linear shifts (modulo p) by using the linearity of the extractor, which essentially works only in modulo q.

To solve this issue, we set $S = \mathbb{Z}_2$, and use another route of reduction that avoids using the above linearity equation. Particularly, we show a way to transform an instance of the form $(r, z = \mathsf{Ext}(r, s))$ into $(r', \mathsf{Ext}(r', (s + b \mod 2)))$ given b, without using the linearity of the extractor. Furthermore, via a reduction from the reusability of the extractor, we can establish security against correlated-source attacks for linear shifts in modulo 2. This would suffice to achieve KDM security as we discuss later. More formally, the transformation works as follow:

- For $i \in [n]$, if $b_i = 0$, set $r'_i = r_i$ and $z'_i = 1$; otherwise for $b_i = 1$, set $r'_i = r_i^{-1}$ and $z'_i = r_i^{-1}$.
- Output $(r', z \cdot \prod_{i=1}^{n} z'_i)$.

We note that if $b_i = 0$, then the term $r_i^{s_i}$ would appear in z, or otherwise $r_i^{1-s_i}$. With a simple check, our transformation is consistent with this fact. It is not hard to formalize the security proof using this idea.

Construction Based on LWE. Next we look at the LWE-based reusable extractor [3]. Let $q > p > 1$ be parameters, S be some small set over $\mathbb{Z}_q$, $r \in \mathbb{Z}_q^n$ be seed, and $s \in S^n$ be source. The work [3,6] showed that $\mathsf{Ext}(r, s) = \lceil \langle r, s \rangle \rfloor_p$ is a reusable extractor where $\lceil \cdot \rfloor$ is some rounding function, and the number of reusable samples can be any arbitrary polynomial if $q/p = \lambda^{\omega(1)}$. For general settings of parameters however, this extractor might not be output homomorphic, as linearity might not hold for rounding of inner products. Nevertheless, we identify that if $p|q$, then the extractor is output homomorphic with respect to linear functions (i.e. $\mathfrak{h}_b(s) = \langle b, s \rangle \mod p$) by using the following equation:

$$\lceil \langle r, s \rangle \rfloor_p + \langle b, s \rangle = \lceil \langle r, s \rangle + (q/p) \langle b, s \rangle \rfloor_p = \lceil \langle r + (q/p) b, s \rangle \rfloor_p.$$

Thus, we can set $\mathfrak{h}'_b(r) = r + (q/p)b$, achieving the desired property.

Next, we would like to show that the construction is secure against correlated-source attacks for linear shifts. Similar to the DDH construction, we need to tackle the issue that $\mathfrak{g}_b(s)$ and $\mathsf{Ext}(r, s)$ are working on different moduli. To solve this issue, we first apply the same idea by setting $S = \mathbb{Z}_2^n$, and then hopefully a similar reduction would work. However, this method does not work in a straight-forward way as rounding breaks linearity. Let us consider a simple case where $b = (1, 0, 0, \dots, 0)^T$, i.e., only $b_1 = 1$ and others 0. Then the reduction would need to simulate $\lceil r_1(1-s_1)+\sum_{i=2}^{n} r_i s_i \rfloor_p = \lceil -r_1' + r_1' s_1 + \sum_{i=2}^{n} r_i' s_i \rfloor_p$, where $r_1' = -r_1$ and $r_i' = r_i$ for $i = 2 \sim n$. However, $\lceil -r_1' + r_1' s_1 + \sum_{i=2}^{n} r_i' s_i \rfloor_p \neq \lceil -r_1' \rfloor_p + \lceil r_1' s_1 + \sum_{i=2}^{n} r_i' s_i \rfloor_p$ in general, and thus the previous transformation would break down.

To solve this, we use the proof technique of [6], who first switches the rounded inner products into rounded LWE samples. Then we show that LWE is resilient to correlated-source attacks for linear shifts, translating to security of the whole construction. More specifically, we first switch $\lceil \langle \boldsymbol{r}, \boldsymbol{s} \rangle \rfloor_p$ to $\lceil \langle \boldsymbol{r}, \boldsymbol{s} \rangle + e \rfloor_p$. The switch incurs a negligible statistical distance if $q/p = \lambda^{\omega(1)}$, which is required for the reusability for an arbitrary polynomial samples anyway (under current proof techniques). Then by using the above idea, we can easily show that samples of the form $\langle \boldsymbol{r}, (\boldsymbol{s} + \boldsymbol{b} \mod 2) \rangle + e$ are computationally indistinguishable from random samples, and therefore so are their rounded versions. This describes the proof ideas.

$\mathsf{KDM}^{(1)}$-PKE with $1 - o(1)$ Rate via the Extractor

Achieving $\mathsf{KDM}^{(1)}$-Security. To illustrate our idea, we consider the case where Ext is homomorphic with respect to linear functions and secure against correlated-attacks with respect to linear shifts. Next, we identify three important *additional structures* of wHPS from the above construction:

1. The secret key of wHPS (and PKE_1) is just a vector $\boldsymbol{x} \in \mathbb{Z}_B^n$ as the BE.
2. The decapsulation of an invalid ciphertext CT^* has the following form: $\mathsf{Decap}(\boldsymbol{x}, \mathsf{CT}^*) = \boldsymbol{x} + \boldsymbol{k}'$, where $\boldsymbol{k}' \in \mathbb{Z}_B^n$ is certain vector related to CT^*.
3. Given $\boldsymbol{k}'$, the above CT^* can be simulated faithfully.

Let $\mathfrak{h}$ be some linear functions, and let us take a look at the equation of upon a KDM query of an encryption of $\mathfrak{h}(\mathsf{sk})$.

$$
\begin{aligned}
&\mathsf{PKE}_1.\mathsf{Enc}(\mathfrak{h}(\mathsf{sk})) && \\
=&(\mathsf{CT}, \boldsymbol{r}, \mathsf{Ext}(\boldsymbol{r}, \boldsymbol{k}) + \mathfrak{h}(\boldsymbol{x})) && \text{By Structure 1}\\
=&(\mathsf{CT}, \boldsymbol{r}, \mathsf{Ext}(\boldsymbol{r}, \mathsf{Decap}(\boldsymbol{x}, \mathsf{CT})) + \mathfrak{h}(\boldsymbol{x})) && \text{Correctness of wHPS}\\
\approx&(\mathsf{CT}^*, \boldsymbol{r}, \mathsf{Ext}(\boldsymbol{r}, \mathsf{Decap}(\boldsymbol{x}, \mathsf{CT}^*)) + \mathfrak{h}(\boldsymbol{x})) && \text{Ciphertext indistinguishability}\\
=&(\mathsf{CT}^*, \boldsymbol{r}, \mathsf{Ext}(\boldsymbol{r}, \boldsymbol{x} + \boldsymbol{k}') + \mathfrak{h}(\boldsymbol{x})) && \text{By Structure 2}\\
=&(\mathsf{CT}^*, \boldsymbol{r}, \mathsf{Ext}(\boldsymbol{r}, \boldsymbol{x}') + \mathfrak{h}(\boldsymbol{x}' - \boldsymbol{k}')) && \text{Change of variable}\\
=&(\mathsf{CT}^*, \boldsymbol{r}, \mathsf{Ext}(\boldsymbol{r}, \boldsymbol{x}') + \mathfrak{h}(\boldsymbol{x}') - \mathfrak{h}(\boldsymbol{k}')) && \text{Linearity of } \mathfrak{h}\\
=&(\mathsf{CT}^*, \boldsymbol{r}, \mathsf{Ext}(\mathfrak{h}'(\boldsymbol{r}), \boldsymbol{x}') - \mathfrak{h}(\boldsymbol{k}')) && \text{Homomorphism of Ext}\\
=&(\mathsf{CT}^*, \mathfrak{h}'^{-1}(\boldsymbol{r}), \mathsf{Ext}(\boldsymbol{r}, \boldsymbol{x}') - \mathfrak{h}(\boldsymbol{k}')) && \text{Change of variable}\\
=&(\mathsf{CT}^*, \mathfrak{h}'^{-1}(\boldsymbol{r}), \mathsf{Ext}(\boldsymbol{r}, \boldsymbol{x} + \boldsymbol{k}') - \mathfrak{h}(\boldsymbol{k}')) && \text{Change of variable}
\end{aligned}
$$

Via a hybrid argument, we can switch all the adversary's KDM queries to the form in the last equation. However, as $\mathsf{Ext}(\boldsymbol{r}, \boldsymbol{x} + \boldsymbol{k}') - \mathfrak{h}(\boldsymbol{k}')$ still depends on the secret key $\boldsymbol{x}$, we cannot follow the prior proof technique in [5,7,9–12], which requires to simulate the KDM queries without using the secret key. To handle this, we observe that now the adversary's view of his Q queries is of the form $\{(\mathsf{CT}_i^*, \mathfrak{h}_i'^{-1}(\boldsymbol{r}_i), \mathsf{Ext}(\boldsymbol{r}_i, \boldsymbol{x}+\boldsymbol{k}_i') - \mathfrak{h}(\boldsymbol{k}_i'))\}_{i\in[Q]}$. We can then leverage the security of the extractor to switch these outputs of the extractor to uniformly random strings at one shot. Since CT_i^* can be generated given $\boldsymbol{k}_i'$ (the third additional property of wHPS), and Ext is secure against correlated-source attacks (even given $\boldsymbol{k}_i'$'s), we can prove that $\{\mathsf{PKE}_1.\mathsf{Enc}(\mathfrak{h}_i(\mathsf{sk}))\}_{i\in[Q]}$ is indistinguishable from random via a simple reduction from the required extractor. We refer the details to Sect. 5.1.

Improving Information Rate. The information rate of the above scheme is $\frac{w}{|\mathsf{CT}|+|\boldsymbol{r}|+w}$, where w denotes the length of the output of extractor. In our instantiations of the extractor, we have $|\mathsf{CT}| > |\boldsymbol{k}|\lambda$ and $|\boldsymbol{k}| \geq w$, and thus $|\mathsf{CT}|$ dominates the denominator, resulting in the ratio at most $O(1/\lambda)$. To improve the rate, we use the same CT (encapsulation) and repeatedly extract from the same source with different seeds when encrypting many different messages. That is, we consider the following scheme PKE_2, where $\mathsf{PKE}_2.\mathsf{pk}$ and $\mathsf{PKE}_2.\mathsf{sk}$ are the same as the above PKE_1. The encryption algorithm is modified as below:

$$\begin{aligned}&\mathsf{PKE}_2.\mathsf{Enc}((m_1, m_2, \ldots, m_t))\\&\quad= (\mathsf{CT}, \boldsymbol{r}_1, \mathsf{Ext}(\boldsymbol{r}_1, \boldsymbol{k}) + m_1, \boldsymbol{r}_2, \mathsf{Ext}(\boldsymbol{r}_2, \boldsymbol{k}) + m_2, \ldots, \boldsymbol{r}_t, \mathsf{Ext}(\boldsymbol{r}_t, \boldsymbol{k}) + m_t).\end{aligned}$$

By using the same proof idea of PKE_1, we can show that suppose the reusable extractor is homomorphic with respect to linear functions and secure against correlated-source attacks, then the scheme PKE_2 is $\mathsf{KDM}^{(1)}$-secure with respect to affine functions. In this case, the information rate would be $\frac{wt}{|\mathsf{CT}|+|\boldsymbol{r}|t+wt}$, approaching $\frac{w}{|\boldsymbol{r}|+w}$ for sufficiently large t.

However, in our both LWE and DDH instantiations, $w \ll |\boldsymbol{r}|$, and thus the rate is still far from the optimal. To tackle this issue, we use a parallel repetition of the source, i.e., let $\boldsymbol{k} = (\boldsymbol{k}_1, \boldsymbol{k}_2, \ldots, \boldsymbol{k}_d)$, and define

$$\mathsf{Ext}_{||}(\boldsymbol{r}, \boldsymbol{k}) = (\mathsf{Ext}(\boldsymbol{r}, \boldsymbol{k}_1), \mathsf{Ext}(\boldsymbol{r}, \boldsymbol{k}_2), \ldots, \mathsf{Ext}(\boldsymbol{r}, \boldsymbol{k}_d)).$$

We can show that suppose $\boldsymbol{k}$ forms a block source, then the output of $\mathsf{Ext}_{||}$ will be computationally indistinguishable from random. Moreover, $\mathsf{Ext}_{||}$ is as well homomorphic and secure against correlated-source attacks for appropriate classes. By using $\mathsf{Ext}_{||}$, we can still derive $\mathsf{KDM}^{(1)}$ security, for a slightly weaker class of *block*-affine functions. Now, the information rate would be $\frac{wd}{|\boldsymbol{r}|+wd}$, approaching $1-o(1)$ by setting d such that $|\boldsymbol{r}| = o(wd)$.

Achieving Arbitrary Polynomial $\bar{n}$
Next, we discuss how to upgrade the above framework to achieve $\mathsf{KDM}^{(\bar{n})}$-security for an unbounded polynomial $\bar{n}$. Before presenting our approach, we first abstract some important features from the above schemes PKE_1 and PKE_2 – (1) the schemes are based on BE as the most underlying tool, and (2) they have the following features: (a) the secret key is just a vector $\boldsymbol{x}$, and (b) the public key has the form $(\mathsf{CRS}, \mathsf{H}(\mathsf{CRS}, \boldsymbol{x}))$, where H denotes the projection function $\mathsf{KeyGen}(\cdot,\cdot)$ of BE in [12]. We call this type of schemes as BE-based public key encryption scheme.

Next we generalize the idea of [9], showing that if a BE-based scheme satisfies certain key and ciphertext homomorphic properties, then one can prove $\mathsf{KDM}^{(\bar{n})}$-security from $\mathsf{KDM}^{(1)}$ by the following two steps: Let Π be a BE-based PKE.

1. First we define an intermediate scheme $\Pi^{\bar{n}}$ that runs $\bar{n}$ times the encryption algorithm of Π to encrypt the same message, with $\bar{n}$ distinct public parameters but corresponding to the same secret key. Particularly, $\Pi^{\bar{n}}.\mathsf{sk} = \Pi.\mathsf{sk} = \boldsymbol{x}$, and $\Pi^{\bar{n}}.\mathsf{pk} = (\Pi.\mathsf{pk}_1, \dots, \Pi.\mathsf{pk}_{\bar{n}})$, where $\Pi.\mathsf{pk}_i = (\mathsf{CRS}_i, h_i = \mathsf{H}(\mathsf{CRS}_i, \boldsymbol{x}))$ for all $i \in [\bar{n}]$. The encryption algorithm works as follows:
$$\Pi^{\bar{n}}.\mathsf{Enc}(m) = (\Pi.\mathsf{Enc}(\mathsf{pk}_1, m), \Pi.\mathsf{Enc}(\mathsf{pk}_2, m), \dots, \Pi.\mathsf{Enc}(\mathsf{pk}_{\bar{n}}, m)).$$
2. Then we show, if $\Pi^{\bar{n}}$ is $\mathsf{KDM}^{(1)}$-secure with respect to affine functions, then Π is $\mathsf{KDM}^{(\bar{n})}$-secure with respect to affine functions.

Thus, to show that PKE_2 is $\mathsf{KDM}^{(\bar{n})}$ secure, it suffices to show that its intermediate scheme, i.e., $\mathsf{PKE}_2^{\bar{n}}$, is $\mathsf{KDM}^{(1)}$ secure.

However, the current instantiation of the underlying BE [12] can only derive $\mathsf{KDM}^{(1)}$ security of $\mathsf{PKE}_2^{\bar{n}}$ for a bounded polynomial $\bar{n}$. When $\bar{n}$ becomes too large, $\mathsf{PKE}_2^{\bar{n}}$ may completely loses security. As each $h_i = \mathsf{H}(\mathsf{CRS}_i, \boldsymbol{x})$ leaks some small information of the secret $\boldsymbol{x}$, thus the secret might have no entropy given too many hashes in the pk_i's. Even worse, in the LWE-based instantiation of [12], one can obtain $\boldsymbol{x}$ given only n (the dimension of $\boldsymbol{x}$) hashes of h_i's by simply solving linear equations. This approach seems to hit an entropy barrier, inherently.

To tackle this challenge, we propose a new pseudorandom property of BE (and BE-based PKE) by adding *reusability* to the projection function H. Particularly, the reusable property requires that the following two distributions are indistinguishable, even in conjunction with the reusable extractor against correlated-source attacks for any $\bar{n}, m = \mathsf{poly}(\lambda)$:

$$\left(\{\mathsf{CRS}_i, \mathsf{H}(\mathsf{CRS}_i, \boldsymbol{x})\}_{i\in[\bar{n}]}, \{\boldsymbol{r}_j, \mathsf{Ext}(\boldsymbol{r}, \mathfrak{h}_j(\boldsymbol{x}))\}_{j\in[m]}\right) \approx_c \left(\{\mathsf{CRS}_i, u_i\}_{i\in[\bar{n}]}, \{\boldsymbol{r}_j, u'_j\}_{j\in[m]}\right)$$

Conceptually, this would guarantee secrecy of $\boldsymbol{x}$ even if the adversary can obtain many hashes on the same $\boldsymbol{x}$ and samples from the reusable extractor (under correlated-source attacks).

As a result, by using a BE with this reusable property as the underlying building block of wHPS, we are able to show that $\mathsf{PKE}_2^{\bar{n}}$ is $\mathsf{KDM}^{(1)}$-secure for any $\bar{n} = \mathsf{poly}(\lambda)$, implying that PKE_2 is $\mathsf{KDM}^{(\bar{n})}$-secure for any $\bar{n} = \mathsf{poly}(\lambda)$.

New BE Constructions. To instantiate the required BE, we observe that the CDH-based scheme in [12] as is, can achieve the reusability property if DDH is further assumed. However, the LWE-based scheme becomes insecure if n hashes are given to the adversaries as we stated before, where n is the dimension of $\boldsymbol{x}$. To solve this, we design a new projection function H' that makes a simple yet essential modification of the original H of [12]. Particularly, $\mathsf{H}'(\mathsf{CRS}, \boldsymbol{x}) = \mathsf{H}(\mathsf{CRS}, \boldsymbol{x}) + \boldsymbol{e}$, for some appropriate noise $\boldsymbol{e}$. In this way, the distribution $(\mathsf{CRS}, \mathsf{H}'(\mathsf{CRS}, \boldsymbol{x}))$ in this modified BE would be a sample of LWE, which is pseudorandom even when polynomially many samples are given, and can be used in conjunction with the LWE-based reusable extractor. This enables us to achieve $\mathsf{KDM}^{(\bar{n})}$-PKE for any unbounded polynomial $\bar{n}$ with optimal information rate with respect to affine functions.

Amplification. We first notice that the class of block-affine functions does not contain all projection functions, so the generic technique of Applebaum [4] does not apply to amplify the class. Nevertheless, we show that this class can still be used to encode the labels of Garbled Circuits (a common realization of randomized encoding), and thus we can amplify the class to be any bounded-sized boolean circuits.

As our scheme can encrypt messages of an indefinite length, we are able to further achieve KDM function class for $(\mathcal{F}_s||\mathcal{Q}^\tau)$, where $\mathcal{F}_s$ is the class of circuits up to sized s, $\mathcal{Q}^\tau$ is the class of affine functions with τ-element outputs, and $(\mathcal{F}_s||\mathcal{Q}^\tau)$ denotes the concatenation of two classes, i.e., every function $\mathfrak{f}$ in the class can be represented by $\mathfrak{f} = (\mathfrak{h}, \mathfrak{q})$ for some $\mathfrak{h} \in \mathcal{F}_s$ and $\mathfrak{q} \in \mathcal{Q}^\tau$ such that $\mathfrak{f}(\mathsf{sk}) = (\mathfrak{h}(\mathsf{sk})||\mathfrak{q}(\mathsf{sk}))$. For the parameter range $\tau \gg s$, our scheme achieves the optimal information rate, i.e., $1 - o(1)$.

Upgrade to KDM-IBE

The above framework can be further generalized to construct IBE with KDM-security and leakage resilience. Particularly, we design a new compiler that uses an IB-wHPS to amply the on-the-fly KDM-security (a new notion) of PKE into KDM-security of IBE, and simultaneously the resulting IBE achieves leakage resilience. This improves the compiler of [23], which might not be leakage resilient.

Our compiler is straight-forward. Let Π be a BE-based PKE and IB-wHPS be an identity-based wHPS that has additional structures: (1) the secret key has the structure $\mathsf{sk}_{\mathsf{id}} = (\boldsymbol{x}, \mathsf{sk}_{\mathsf{id},\boldsymbol{x}})$, (2) $\mathsf{IB\text{-}wHPS.Decap}(\mathsf{sk}_{\mathsf{id}}, \mathsf{CT}^*) = \boldsymbol{x} + \boldsymbol{k}$, and (3) given $\boldsymbol{k}$, the above CT^* can be simulated faithfully. (This is similar to the additional structures of our required wHPS above). Then we can design an $\mathsf{IBE}.\{\mathsf{Setup}, \mathsf{KeyGen}, \mathsf{Enc}, \mathsf{Dec}\}$ as follows. $\mathsf{IBE}.\{\mathsf{Setup}, \mathsf{KeyGen}\}$ and $\mathsf{IBE}.\{\mathsf{mpk}, \mathsf{msk}, \mathsf{sk}_{\mathsf{id}}\}$ are the same as those of IB-wHPS. To encrypt a message m with an id, IBE.Enc first generates an encapsulation $(\mathsf{CT}_1, \boldsymbol{k}) \leftarrow \mathsf{IB\text{-}wHPS.Encap}(\mathsf{mpk}, \mathsf{id})$, then generates $\mathsf{pk} = (\mathsf{CRS}, \mathfrak{h}(\mathsf{CRS}, \boldsymbol{k}))$ from the BE, and then computes $\mathsf{CT}_2 \leftarrow \Pi.\mathsf{Enc}(\mathsf{pk}, m)$. The resulting ciphertext would be $(\mathsf{CT}_1, \mathsf{pk}, \mathsf{CT}_2)$.

Next we present a simple case that demonstrates the key idea of our KDM-security proof. Consider the simple case of only one KDM query, i.e., an encryption for some message $\mathfrak{f}(\mathsf{sk}_{\mathsf{id}}) = \mathfrak{f}(\boldsymbol{x}, \mathsf{sk}_{\mathsf{id},\boldsymbol{x}})$ (by Structure 2 of IB-wHPS) with respect to some id. We can derive the following:

$$
\begin{aligned}
&\mathsf{IBE.Enc}(\mathfrak{f}(\boldsymbol{x}, \mathsf{sk}_{\mathsf{id},\boldsymbol{x}})) \\
=&(\mathsf{CT}_1, \mathsf{CRS}, \mathsf{H}(\mathsf{CRS}, \boldsymbol{k}), \mathsf{CT}_2) \\
\approx_c&(\mathsf{CT}_1^*, \mathsf{CRS}, \mathsf{H}(\mathsf{CRS}, \mathsf{IB\text{-}wHPS.Decap}(\mathsf{CT}_1^*)), \mathsf{CT}_2) && \text{Valid/Invalid Ciphertext Indistinguishability} \\
=&(\mathsf{CT}_1^*, \mathsf{CRS}, \mathsf{H}(\mathsf{CRS}, \boldsymbol{x} + \boldsymbol{k}'), \mathsf{CT}_2) && \text{By Structure 1} \\
=&\Big(\mathsf{CT}_1^*, \mathsf{CRS}, \mathsf{H}(\mathsf{CRS}, \boldsymbol{x}'), \Pi.\mathsf{Enc}\big(\mathsf{CRS}, \mathsf{H}(\mathsf{CRS}, \boldsymbol{x}'), \\
&\qquad \mathfrak{f}((\boldsymbol{x}' - \boldsymbol{k}'), \mathsf{sk}_{\mathsf{id},(\boldsymbol{x}'-\boldsymbol{k}')})\big)\Big) && \text{Change of Variable} \\
=&\Big(\mathsf{CT}_1^*, \mathsf{CRS}, \mathsf{H}(\mathsf{CRS}, \boldsymbol{x}'), \Pi.\mathsf{Enc}\big(\mathsf{CRS}, \mathsf{H}(\mathsf{CRS}, \boldsymbol{x}'), \mathfrak{g}(\boldsymbol{x}')\big)\Big) && \text{(*) Explain Below} \\
\approx_c&\Big(\mathsf{CT}_1^*, \mathsf{CRS}, \mathsf{H}(\mathsf{CRS}, \boldsymbol{x}'), \Pi.\mathsf{Enc}\big(\mathsf{CRS}, \mathsf{H}(\mathsf{CRS}, \boldsymbol{x}'), u\big)\Big) && \mathsf{KDM}\ \text{of}\ \Pi
\end{aligned}
$$

We observe that if $\mathfrak{f}((\boldsymbol{x}' - \boldsymbol{k}'), \mathsf{sk}_{(\boldsymbol{x}'-\boldsymbol{k}')})$ can be expressed as $\mathfrak{g}(\boldsymbol{x}')$ and the underlying Π is KDM-secure with respect to the function $\mathfrak{g}$, then the resulting IBE is KDM-secure with respect to $\mathfrak{f}$. We further identify that the equation (*) holds even if the master secret key msk of IB-wHPS is given. Thus, we can hardcode msk and $\boldsymbol{k}'$ and randomness r into $\mathfrak{g}$ and set the function as follow: $\mathfrak{g}_{\mathsf{msk},\boldsymbol{k}',r}(\boldsymbol{x}')$ first computes $\mathsf{sk}_{\mathsf{id},\boldsymbol{x}'-\boldsymbol{k}'} = \mathsf{IB\text{-}wHPS.KeyGen}(\mathsf{msk}, \mathsf{id}, \boldsymbol{x}' - \boldsymbol{k}'; r)$ and then outputs $\mathfrak{f}((\boldsymbol{x}' - \boldsymbol{k}'), \mathsf{sk}_{\mathsf{id},(\boldsymbol{x}'-\boldsymbol{k}')})$. We can instantiate Π by using the above mentioned schemes PKE_1 or PKE_2 and the bootstrapping technique of Applebaum [4]. In this way, we can obtain a KDM-secure PKE with respect to the class of bounded polynomial circuits, which includes the required $\mathfrak{g}$.

The above idea cannot be trivially extended to the general case where there are many KDM queries. A simple reason is that pk needs to be generated on-the-fly for each ciphertext. This does not match the traditional notion of KDM-security for PKE. To handle this technical issue, we propose a new notion called *on-the-fly* KDM-security, where there is no pk upfront, and the adversary receives an on-the-fly $\mathsf{pk} = (\mathsf{CRS}, \mathsf{H}(\mathsf{CRS}, \boldsymbol{x}'))$ with respect to the same secret key $\boldsymbol{x}'$ upon each KDM query. By using this on-the-fly KDM-PKE with the IB-wHPS, we are able to achieve KDM-IBE. Moreover, we can prove that the above PKE_2 satisfies the on-the-fly notion. We refer details to full version.

2 Preliminaries

We use several standard mathematical notations, whose detailed descriptions are deferred to the full version. In the full version we present the formal definitions of KDM-security and leakage resilience. Below, we present the syntax of two important tools – *batch encryption* and *weak hash proof systems*. Due to space limit, we defer their detailed security properties to the full version.

Definition 2.1 (Batch Encryption in [12]). *A batch encryption (*BE*) scheme consists of the following four algorithms* {Setup, KeyGen, Enc, Dec}*:*

- $\mathsf{Setup}(1^\lambda, 1^n)$*: The algorithm takes as input the security parameter λ and key length n, and outputs a common reference string* CRS *which includes a parameter $B = B(\lambda, n)$.*

- $\mathsf{KeyGen}(\mathsf{CRS}, \boldsymbol{x})$: *Given a common reference string* CRS *and the secret key* $\boldsymbol{x} \in \mathbb{Z}_B^n$ *as input, the algorithm projects the secret key* $\boldsymbol{x}$ *to a public key* h.
- $\mathsf{Enc}(\mathsf{CRS}, h, \mathbf{M})$: *Given a common reference string* CRS, *a public key* h, *and a message matrix* $\mathbf{M} = (M_{i,j})_{i \in [n], j \in \mathbb{Z}_B} \in \mathbb{Z}_B^{n \times B}$ *as input, the algorithm outputs a ciphertext* CT.
- $\mathsf{Dec}(\mathsf{CRS}, \boldsymbol{x}, \mathsf{CT})$: *Given a common reference string* CRS, *a secret key* $\boldsymbol{x}$, *and a ciphertext* CT *as input, the algorithm outputs a message vector* $\boldsymbol{m}' = (M_{i,x_i})_{i \in [n]}$.

Remark 2.2. *Let* $\hat{\ell}$ *denote the bit-length of the public key* h. *Then we notice that given the public key* pk, *the conditional min-entropy of* sk *is* $H_\infty(\mathsf{sk}|\mathsf{pk}) = H_\infty(\boldsymbol{x}|h) \geq n \log B - \hat{\ell}$.

Definition 2.3 (Weak Hash Proof System in [21]). *A weak hash proof system (*wHPS*) with the encapsulated-key-space* $\mathcal{K}$ *consists of four algorithms* $\mathsf{wHPS}.\{\mathsf{Setup}, \mathsf{Encap}, \mathsf{Encap}^*, \mathsf{Decap}\}$ *as follows. (We will omit* wHPS *when the context is clear).*

- **Key generation.** $\mathsf{Setup}(1^\lambda)$ *takes a security parameter* λ *as input, and generates a pair of public key and secret key* $(\mathsf{pk}, \mathsf{sk})$.
- **Valid encapsulation.** $\mathsf{Encap}(\mathsf{pk})$ *takes a public key* pk *as input, and outputs a valid ciphertext* CT *and its corresponding encapsulated key* $\mathsf{k} \in \mathcal{K}$.
- **Invalid encapsulation.** $\mathsf{Encap}^*(\mathsf{pk})$ *takes a public key* pk *as input, and outputs an invalid ciphertext* CT^*.
- **Decapsulation.** $\mathsf{Decap}(\mathsf{sk}, \mathsf{CT})$ *takes as input a secret key* sk *and ciphertext* CT, *and deterministically outputs* $\mathsf{k} \in \mathcal{K}$.

Additionally, we define the following function families that are useful for our results on KDM security.

Definition 2.4 (Linear, Affine and Shift Functions). *Let* $\mathcal{X}, \mathcal{Y}$ *be some additive groups. A function* $\mathfrak{g} : \mathcal{X} \to \mathcal{Y}$ *is linear if for every* $x, x' \in \mathcal{X}$, *we have* $\mathfrak{g}(x + x') = \mathfrak{g}(x) + \mathfrak{g}(x')$; *a function* $\mathfrak{h} : \mathcal{X} \to \mathcal{Y}$ *is affine if there exist a linear function* $\mathfrak{g} : \mathcal{X} \to \mathcal{Y}$ *and a constant* $a \in \mathcal{Y}$ *such that* $\mathfrak{h}(x) = \mathfrak{g}(x) + a$ *for every* $x \in \mathcal{X}$. *Moreover, a function* $\mathfrak{s} : \mathcal{X} \to \mathcal{X}$ *indexed by certain element* $x \in \mathcal{X}$ *is shift, if for every* $x, x' \in \mathcal{X}$, *we have* $\mathfrak{s}_x(x') = x + x'$.

Definition 2.5. *Let* $\mathcal{X}, \mathcal{Y}$ *be some additive groups. Given a class of linear functions* $\mathcal{G} = \{\mathfrak{g} : \mathcal{X} \to \mathcal{Y}\}$, *we define a related class of affine functions* $\mathcal{G}^t = \{\mathfrak{g}' : \mathcal{X} \to \mathcal{Y}^t\}$ *where each* $\mathfrak{g}' \in \mathcal{G}^t$ *can be indexed by a constant vector* $\boldsymbol{a} = (a_1, \ldots, a_t)^\top \in \mathcal{Y}^t$ *and* t *functions in* $\mathcal{G}$, *i.e.,* $\mathfrak{g}_1, \mathfrak{g}_2, \ldots, \mathfrak{g}_t \in \mathcal{G}$, *such that for every* $x \in \mathcal{X}$, $\mathfrak{g}'(x) = (\mathfrak{g}_1(x), \mathfrak{g}_2(x), \ldots, \mathfrak{g}_t(x))^\top + \boldsymbol{a} = (\mathfrak{g}_1(x) + a_1, \mathfrak{g}_2(x) + a_2, \ldots, \mathfrak{g}_t(x) + a_t)^\top$.

Besides, if the underlying linear functions $\mathfrak{g} \in \mathcal{G}$ *is a block function, i.e., each output component of* $\mathfrak{g}$ *depends only on one block of its input, then the resulting functions* $\mathfrak{g}' \in \mathcal{G}^t$ *are called block-affine function.*

3 Randomness Extractor and Its Variants

In this section, we first define a new variant of (computational) randomness extractors, which serve as the most important tools of this paper. Then, we instantiate the required extractors based on LWE or DDH, respectively.

3.1 Our New Variant of Randomness Extractors

We require an extractor that is (1) reusable, (2) secure against correlated-source attacks, and (3) homomorphic. We present their definitions below.

Definition 3.1 (Reusable Extractor in [3]). *Let $\mathcal{X}, \mathcal{S}, \mathcal{Y}$ be efficient ensembles parameterized by the security parameter λ. An efficient function $\mathsf{Ext} : \mathcal{X} \times \mathcal{S} \to \mathcal{Y}$ is an (e, t)-reusable-extractor*[6]*, if for any correlated random variables (s, aux) where s is over $\mathcal{S}$ and $H_\infty(s|\mathsf{aux}) \geq e$, the following two distributions are computationally (statistically) indistinguishable:*

$$(\mathsf{aux}, r_1, \ldots, r_t, \mathsf{Ext}(r_1, s), \ldots, \mathsf{Ext}(r_t, s)) \approx (\mathsf{aux}, r_1, \ldots, r_t, u_1, \ldots, u_t),$$

where the strings $\{r_i \xleftarrow{\$} \mathcal{X}\}$, $\{u_i \xleftarrow{\$} \mathcal{Y}\}$ are sampled independently.

If $e > t \log |\mathcal{Y}| + O(\log(1/\varepsilon))$ for some $\varepsilon = \mathsf{negl}(\lambda)$, we can construct an (e, t)-reusable extractor information theoretically, e.g.,. Leftover hash lemma [15]. On the other hand for $e < t \log |\mathcal{Y}| + O(\log(1/\varepsilon))$, it is still possible to construct (e, t)-reusable extractor under appropriate computational assumptions, such as DDH or LWE [3,25], for t being a bounded or even any arbitrary polynomial depending on the parameter settings.

Definition 3.2 (Reusable Extractor against Correlated-Source Attacks). *Let $\mathsf{Ext} : \mathcal{X} \times \mathcal{S} \to \mathcal{Y}$ be some function, and $\mathcal{F} = \{\mathfrak{f} : \mathcal{S} \to \mathcal{Y}\}$ be some function class. We say Ext is an (e, t)-reusable extractor against correlated-source attacks with respect to $\mathcal{F}$, if for every random variables s, aux where s is over $\mathcal{S}$ and $\mathsf{H}_\infty(s|\mathsf{aux}) \geq e$, the following oracles, $O_s(\cdot)$ and $U(\cdot)$, are computationally indistinguishable given up to t queries:*

- *$O_s(\cdot)$: Take a function $\mathfrak{f} \in \mathcal{F}$ as input, sample a fresh random $r \leftarrow \mathcal{X}$, and return $(r, \mathsf{Ext}(r, \mathfrak{f}(s)))$ upon each query.*
- *$U(\cdot)$: Take a function $\mathfrak{f} \in \mathcal{F}$ as input, return a uniform sample $(r, u) \leftarrow (\mathcal{X}, \mathcal{Y})$ upon each query.*

Remark 3.3. *The above Definition 3.2 can also be described in the indistinguishability form – for any correlated random variables (s, aux) such that s is over $\mathcal{S}$ and $H_\infty(s|\mathsf{aux}) \geq e$, the following two distributions are computationally (statistically) indistinguishable: $\left(\mathsf{aux}, \{r_i, \mathsf{Ext}(r_i, \mathfrak{f}_i(s))\}_{i\in[t]}\right) \approx \left(\mathsf{aux}, \{r_i, u_i\}_{i\in[t]}\right)$, where the strings $\{r_i \xleftarrow{\$} \mathcal{X}\}_{i\in[t]}$, $\{u_i \xleftarrow{\$} \mathcal{Y}\}_{i\in[t]}$ are sampled independently, and $\{\mathfrak{f}_i \in \mathcal{F}\}_{i\in[t]}$ are chosen (adaptively) by any PPT adversary $\mathcal{A}$.*

[6] Here, t denotes the number of times the weak source being reused.

Clearly, an (e, t)-reusable extractor is also one against correlated-source attacks with respect to the identity function.

Definition 3.4 (Homomorphic Extractor). *Let $\mathcal{Y}$ be a group associated with operation '$\circ$', $\mathsf{Ext} : \mathcal{X} \times \mathcal{S} \to \mathcal{Y}$ be an extractor following the syntax as in Definition 3.1, and $\mathcal{H} = \{\mathfrak{h} : \mathcal{S} \to \mathcal{Y}\}$ be some function class. We say that Ext is homomorphic with respect to $\mathcal{H}$, if for any function $\mathfrak{h} \in \mathcal{H}$, there exists an invertible function $\mathfrak{h}' : \mathcal{X} \to \mathcal{X}$ (efficiently computable given $\mathfrak{h}$) such that for any $x \in \mathcal{X}$ and $s \in \mathcal{S}$, we have $\mathsf{Ext}(x, s) \circ \mathfrak{h}(s) = \mathsf{Ext}(\mathfrak{h}'(x), s)$.*

3.2 Instantiations from LWE and DDH

Definition 3.5. *For integers n and δ, we define the linear function class.*

- *$\mathcal{SF}_{\delta,n} = \{\mathfrak{s}_{\boldsymbol{a}} : \mathbb{Z}_\delta^n \to \mathbb{Z}_\delta^n\}$ where each function $\mathfrak{s}_{\boldsymbol{a}}$ is indexed by a vector $\boldsymbol{a} \in \mathbb{Z}_\delta^n$ such that $\mathfrak{s}_{\boldsymbol{a}}(\boldsymbol{x}) = \boldsymbol{x} + \boldsymbol{a} \bmod \delta$, for every $\boldsymbol{x} \in \mathbb{Z}_\delta^n$.*

Construction 3.6 (LWE-Based Extractor). *Let $\mathcal{X} = \mathbb{Z}_q^n$, $\mathcal{S} = \mathbb{Z}_2^n$ and $\mathcal{Y} = \mathbb{Z}_p$, where p is a prime and $p|q$. We define $\mathsf{Ext} : \mathcal{X} \times \mathcal{S} \to \mathcal{Y}$ as:*

$$\mathsf{Ext}(\boldsymbol{a}, \boldsymbol{s}) = \lfloor \langle \boldsymbol{a}, \boldsymbol{s} \rangle \mod q \rceil_{q,p},$$

where $\boldsymbol{a} \in \mathcal{X}, \boldsymbol{s} \in \mathcal{S}$ and $\lfloor \cdot \rceil_{q,p}$ is defined as the definition of LWR in [6]. The construction has ratio $\frac{|\mathcal{Y}|}{|\mathcal{X}|} = \frac{\log p}{n \log q}$.

Theorem 3.7. *Let λ be the security parameter, q, p, d, β, σ be parameters such that $q \geq p\beta\lambda^{\omega(1)}$, $\beta = \sigma\lambda^{\omega(1)}$, and $p|q$. Let χ be some σ-bounded distribution over $\mathbb{Z}_q^n$, $e \geq (d + \Omega(\lambda)) \log q$. Assuming the hardness of $\mathsf{LWE}_{d,q,\chi}$, then Ext in Construction 3.6 is an $(e, \ell = \mathsf{poly}(\lambda))$-reusable extractor against correlated-source attacks with respect to the function class $\mathcal{SF}_{2,n}$. Furthermore, this Ext is homomorphic with respect to the function class $\mathcal{G}_{p,n} = \{\mathfrak{g}_{\boldsymbol{b}} : \mathbb{Z}_2^n \to \mathbb{Z}_p\}$, where each function $\mathfrak{g}_{\boldsymbol{b}}$ is indexed by a vector $\boldsymbol{b} \in \mathbb{Z}_q^n$ such that $\mathfrak{g}_{\boldsymbol{b}}(\boldsymbol{x}) = \langle \boldsymbol{b}, \boldsymbol{x} \rangle \bmod p$, for every $\boldsymbol{x} \in \mathbb{Z}_2^n$.*

Due to space limit, we defer the detailed proof to the full version.

Construction 3.8 (DDH-Based Extractor). *Let $\mathbb{G}$ be a group of prime order q, $\mathcal{X} = \mathbb{G}^n$, $\mathcal{S} = \mathbb{Z}_2^n$, and $\mathcal{Y} = \mathbb{G}$. We define $\mathsf{Ext} : \mathcal{X} \times \mathcal{S} \to \mathcal{Y}$ as:*

$$\mathsf{Ext}(\boldsymbol{a}, \boldsymbol{s}) = \prod_{i=1}^{n} a_i^{s_i},$$

where $\boldsymbol{a} \in \mathcal{X}$, $\boldsymbol{s} \in \mathbb{Z}_2^n$. The construction has ratio $\frac{|\mathcal{Y}|}{|\mathcal{X}|} = \frac{1}{n}$.

Theorem 3.9. *Let λ be the security parameter, $\mathbb{G}$ be a group of prime order q. Assuming that DDH is hard with respect to the group $\mathbb{G}$ and $e \geq \log q + 2\log(1/\varepsilon)$ where $\varepsilon \in (0, 1)$ is negligible, then Ext defined as Definition 3.8 is an $(e, t = \mathsf{poly}(\lambda))$-reusable extractor against correlated-source attacks with respect to the function class $\mathcal{SF}_{2,n}$. Furthermore, Ext is homomorphic with respect to the function class $\mathcal{G}'_{q,n}$, where each $\mathfrak{g} \in \mathcal{G}'_{q,n}$ is indexed by certain vector $\boldsymbol{b} \in \mathbb{G}^n$, i.e., $\mathfrak{g}_{\boldsymbol{b}}(\boldsymbol{s}) = \prod_{i=1}^{n} b_i^{s_i}$ for input $\boldsymbol{s} \in \mathbb{Z}_2^n$.*

Due to space limit, we defer the detailed proof to the full version.

4 wHPS and Its Instantiation from Batch Encryption

In this section, we first identify several new important structures of wHPS, and then show an instantiation of the required wHPS from BE.

4.1 Additional Structure of wHPS

Definition 4.1 (wHPS with Additional Structures). *We say that Π is a* wHPS *with additional structures, if the following conditions hold:*

1. *Π satisfies all conditions for a* wHPS *defined in Definition 2.3;*
2. *The secret key,* sk, *of Π can be written as* $\mathsf{sk} := (\boldsymbol{a}, \mathsf{sk}_{\boldsymbol{a}}) \in \mathbb{Z}_m^n \times \{0,1\}^*$, *for certain positive integers $m, n \in \mathbb{Z}$. In particular, $\mathsf{sk}_{\boldsymbol{a}} \in \{0,1\}^*$ can be viewed as an arbitrary bit string, but is related to the prefix vector $\boldsymbol{a} \in \mathbb{Z}_m^n$.*
3. *The decapsulation of an invalid ciphertext,* $\mathsf{Decap}(\mathsf{sk}, \mathsf{CT}^*)$, *can be written as $\mathfrak{s}_{\boldsymbol{k}'}(\boldsymbol{a}) = \boldsymbol{a} + \boldsymbol{k}' \mod m$, where the $\boldsymbol{a}$ is the first part of the secrete key* sk, *and $\boldsymbol{k}' \in \mathbb{Z}_m^n$ is the index vector related to the invalid ciphertext* CT^*.
4. *Given some $\boldsymbol{k}' \in \mathbb{Z}_m^n$, one can generate* CT^* *such that* $\mathsf{Decap}(\mathsf{sk}, \mathsf{CT}^*) = \mathfrak{s}_{\boldsymbol{k}'}(\boldsymbol{a})$ *and the distribution of* CT^* *is identical to that of* $\mathsf{Encap}^*(\mathsf{pk})$.

Remark 4.2. *This additional structure can also be generalized to the notion of* IB-wHPS *described in full version. In particular, for the case of* $\mathsf{sk}_{\mathsf{id}} := (\boldsymbol{a}, \mathsf{sk}_{\boldsymbol{a},\mathsf{id}})$ *in the* IB-wHPS, $\mathsf{sk}_{\boldsymbol{a},\mathsf{id}}$ *is the output of an integrated algorithm* $\mathsf{IB\text{-}wHPS.KeyGen}(\mathsf{msk}, \mathsf{id}, \boldsymbol{a})$, *where* msk *denotes the master secret key.*

4.2 wHPS from BE

Construction 4.3 (Construction of wHPS from BE). *Let $\Pi = \Pi.\{\mathsf{Setup}, \mathsf{KeyGen}, \mathsf{Enc}, \mathsf{Dec}\}$ be a batch encryption scheme with the message space $\mathbb{Z}_B^{n\times B}$, the secret-key space $\mathbb{Z}_B^n$ and the projected public key size $\hat{\ell}$. Then, we construct a weak hash proof system* HPS *scheme $\Pi_{\mathsf{wHPS}} = \Pi_{\mathsf{wHPS}}.\{\mathsf{Setup}, \mathsf{Encap}, \mathsf{Encap}^*, \mathsf{Decap}\}$ with the same ciphertext space as Π and the encapsulated key space $\mathcal{K} = \mathbb{Z}_B^n$ as follows:*

- $\Pi_{\mathsf{wHPS}}.\mathsf{Setup}(1^\lambda)$: *The algorithm runs $\mathsf{CRS} \xleftarrow{\$} \Pi.\mathsf{Setup}(1^\lambda, 1^n)$ for an integer $n \in \mathbb{N}$, and then runs $\Pi.\mathsf{KeyGen}(\mathsf{CRS}, \boldsymbol{x})$ to generate h for a randomly chosen vector $\boldsymbol{x} \in \mathbb{Z}_B^n$. Finally, the algorithm outputs $\mathsf{pk} := (\mathsf{CRS}, h)$ and $\mathsf{sk} := \boldsymbol{x}$.*
- $\Pi_{\mathsf{wHPS}}.\mathsf{Encap}(\mathsf{pk})$: *Given a public-key* pk *as input, the algorithm first chooses a random vector $\boldsymbol{k} = (k_1, \dots, k_n)^\top \in \mathbb{Z}_B^n$, and set matrix $\mathbf{M} = (M_{i,j})_{i\in[n], j\in\mathbb{Z}_B}$ such that $M_{i,j} = k_i$ for every $i \in [n], j \in \mathbb{Z}_B$, i.e., all components in each row of $\mathbf{M}$ are the same. Then the algorithm runs $\mathsf{CT} \xleftarrow{\$} \Pi.\mathsf{Enc}(\mathsf{CRS}, h, \mathbf{M})$, and outputs* CT *and $\boldsymbol{k}$ as a valid ciphertext and its encapsulated key, respectively.*
- $\Pi_{\mathsf{wHPS}}.\mathsf{Encap}^*(\mathsf{pk})$: *Given a public-key* pk *as input, the algorithm chooses a random vector $\boldsymbol{k} = (k_1, \dots, k_n)^\top \in \mathbb{Z}_B^n$, and set matrix $\mathbf{M} = (M_{i,j})_{i\in[n], j\in\mathbb{Z}_B}$ such that $M_{i,j} = k_i + j \mod B$ for every $i \in [n], j \in \mathbb{Z}_B$. (In this way, every element in a row is different from the others in the same row.) Then the algorithm runs $\mathsf{CT}^* \xleftarrow{\$} \Pi.\mathsf{Enc}(\mathsf{CRS}, h, \mathbf{M})$, and outputs CT^* as an invalid ciphertext.*

– $\Pi_{\mathsf{wHPS}}.\mathsf{Decap}(\mathsf{sk},\mathsf{CT})$: *Given a ciphertext* CT *and a secret key* $\mathsf{sk} := \boldsymbol{x}$ *as input, the algorithm runs* $\boldsymbol{m}' = \Pi.\mathsf{Dec}(\mathsf{CRS},\boldsymbol{x},\mathsf{CT})$, *and outputs* $\boldsymbol{m}'$ *as the encapsulated key.*

It is clear that this construction of wHPS satisfies the additional structures in Definition 4.1. Moreover, the secret key of wHPS does not have the second part $\mathsf{sk}_{\boldsymbol{a}}$, which is one of our key points to prove the KDM security. Below we present the formal theorem and its proof.

Theorem 4.4 (wHPS from BE). *Suppose* Π *is a semantically secure batch encryption scheme with the message space* $\mathbb{Z}_B^{n\times B}$, *the secret-key space* $\mathbb{Z}_B^n$ *and the projected public key size* $\hat{\ell}$. *Then Construction 4.3 is an* $(n\log B, w)$-*universal weak hash proof system with the encapsulated key space* $\mathcal{K} = \mathbb{Z}_B^n$ *and* $w = n\log B - \hat{\ell}$, *and has the additional structure as Definition 4.1.*

Proof. According to the definition of a wHPS, we need to prove the following three properties: correctness, universality and ciphertext indistinguishability.

Correctness. Correctness of this wHPS follows directly from the correctness of the underlying BE.

Universality and the Additional Structure as Definition 4.1. Given the public key pk and a random invalid ciphertext $\mathsf{CT}^* \xleftarrow{\$} \Pi.\mathsf{Enc}(\mathsf{CRS},h,\mathbf{M})$, we have

$$\Pi_{\mathsf{wHPS}}.\mathsf{Decap}(\mathsf{sk},\mathsf{CT}^*) = \Pi_{\mathsf{wHPS}}.\mathsf{Decap}(\boldsymbol{x},\mathsf{CT}^*) = \boldsymbol{x}+\boldsymbol{k}',$$

where $\boldsymbol{k}'$ is the vector used to generate the invalid ciphertext. Clearly, this function is an efficiently computable and invertible permutation, i.e., the decryption function can be written as the permutation $\mathfrak{s}_{\boldsymbol{k}'}(\boldsymbol{x}) = \boldsymbol{x}+\boldsymbol{k}'$.

As this is an injective function of $\boldsymbol{x}$ (for any fixed $\boldsymbol{k}'$), the min-entropy of $\boldsymbol{x}$ remains the same after applying this function, i.e., $H_\infty(\mathsf{Decap}(\mathsf{sk},\mathsf{CT}^*)|(h,\mathsf{CT}^*)) = H_\infty(\boldsymbol{x}+\boldsymbol{k}'|(h,\mathsf{CT}^*)) = H_\infty(\boldsymbol{x}|(h,\mathsf{CT}^*))$. Moreover, we note that given h, CT^* is independent of $\boldsymbol{x}$, so $H_\infty(\boldsymbol{x}|(h,\mathsf{CT}^*)) = H_\infty(\boldsymbol{x}|h)$. Therefore, we have

$$H_\infty(\boldsymbol{x}+\boldsymbol{k}|(h,\mathsf{CT}^*)) = H_\infty(\boldsymbol{x}|(h,\mathsf{CT}^*)) = H_\infty(\boldsymbol{x}|h) \geq H_\infty(\boldsymbol{x}) - |h| = n\log B - \hat{\ell}.$$

It is also clear from the argument that the scheme Π_{wHPS} satisfies the additional structure as Definition 4.1, i.e. the secret key sk has the structure $\boldsymbol{x}\in\mathbb{Z}_B^n$, and $\Pi_{\mathsf{wHPS}}.\mathsf{Decap}(\mathsf{sk},\mathsf{CT}^*) = \boldsymbol{x}+\boldsymbol{k}'$, where $\boldsymbol{k}'$ is a vector related to the invalid ciphertext CT^*.

Ciphertext Indistinguishability. Directly from the security of BE, we can prove that the ciphertexts output by $\Pi_{\mathsf{wHPS}}.\mathsf{Encap}(\mathsf{pk})$ and $\Pi_{\mathsf{wHPS}}.\mathsf{Encap}^*(\mathsf{pk})$ are computationally indistinguishable, even given the secret key $\boldsymbol{x}$. □

5 Generic Construction PKE from wHPS

In this section, we show that a weak hash proof system with the additional structure as Definition 4.1 can be used to obtain a public-key encryption scheme that is simultaneously leakage resilient and KDM secure.

Before presenting our generic construction, we introduce a useful definition of block source, and a parallel repetition description of randomness extractor.

Definition 5.1 (Block Source [26]). *A random variable* $S = (S_1, \ldots, S_m)$ *is a* $(e_1, \ldots, e_m)$ *block source if for every* $s_1, \ldots, s_{i-1}$, $S_i|_{S_1=s_1, S_2=s_2, \ldots, S_{i-1}=s_{i-1}}$ *is a* e_i*-source. If* $e_1 = e_2 = \cdots = e_m = e$*, then we call* S *an* $m \times e$ *block source.*

Definition 5.2 (Parallel Repetition of Extractor). *For any input* $\boldsymbol{s} = (s_1, \ldots, s_m) \in \mathcal{S}^m$ *and an underlying extractor* $\mathsf{Ext} : \mathcal{R} \times \mathcal{S} \rightarrow \mathcal{Y}$*, we use* $\mathsf{Ext}_{||}(r, \boldsymbol{s}) = (r, \mathsf{Ext}(r, s_1), \ldots, \mathsf{Ext}(r, s_m))$ *to denote a parallel repetition of extractor.*

Next, our generic construction of PKE can be derived from wHPS and Ext in the following way.

Construction 5.3 (PKE from wHPS and Ext). *Suppose that* $\Pi_{\mathsf{wHPS}} = \Pi_{\mathsf{wHPS}}.\{\mathsf{Setup}, \mathsf{Encap}, \mathsf{Encap}^*, \mathsf{Decap}\}$ *is a* wHPS *with the secret key space and the encapsulated key space being* $\mathcal{S} = \mathcal{K} = \mathbb{Z}_B^n$ *with* $n = n' \cdot m$*, and* $\mathsf{Ext} : \mathcal{R} \times \mathbb{Z}_B^{n'} \rightarrow \mathcal{M}$ *is an* (e, poly)*-reusable extractor. Then, for any polynomial integer* t*, we define a public-key encryption scheme* $\Pi_{\mathsf{PKE}} = \Pi_{\mathsf{PKE}}.\{\mathsf{KeyGen}, \mathsf{Enc}, \mathsf{Dec}\}$ *with message space* $\mathcal{M}^{t \times m}$ *as follows:*

- $\Pi_{\mathsf{PKE}}.\mathsf{KeyGen}(1^\lambda)$*: The algorithm runs* $(\mathsf{pk}^{\Pi_{\mathsf{wHPS}}}, \mathsf{sk}^{\Pi_{\mathsf{wHPS}}}) \xleftarrow{\$} \Pi_{\mathsf{wHPS}}.\mathsf{Setup}(1^\lambda)$*, and then outputs* $\mathsf{pk} := \mathsf{pk}^{\Pi_{\mathsf{wHPS}}}$ *and* $\mathsf{sk} := \mathsf{sk}^{\Pi_{\mathsf{wHPS}}}$.
- $\Pi_{\mathsf{PKE}}.\mathsf{Enc}(\mathsf{pk}, \boldsymbol{\mu})$*: Given a public-key* pk *and a message* $\boldsymbol{\mu} = (\boldsymbol{\mu}_1, \ldots, \boldsymbol{\mu}_t) \in \mathcal{M}^{t \times m}$ *as input with each* $\boldsymbol{\mu}_j \in \mathcal{M}^m$*, the algorithm runs* wHPS.Encap *to generate* $(\mathsf{CT}_0, \boldsymbol{k}) \xleftarrow{\$} \Pi_{\mathsf{wHPS}}.\mathsf{Encap}(\mathsf{pk})$ *for* $\boldsymbol{k} \in \mathbb{Z}_B^n$*. The algorithm interprets* $\boldsymbol{k} \in (\mathbb{Z}_B^{n'})^m$*, and then samples* $r_j \xleftarrow{\$} \mathcal{R}$ *for* $j \in [t]$*. Furthermore, the algorithm computes and outputs* $\mathsf{CT} = (\mathsf{CT}_0, \mathsf{CT}_1, \ldots, \mathsf{CT}_t)$*, where*

$$\mathsf{CT}_j = (\mathsf{CT}_j^{(1)}, \mathsf{CT}_j^{(2)}) = (r_j, \mathsf{Ext}_{||}(r_j, \boldsymbol{k}) + \boldsymbol{\mu}_j), \text{ for } j \in [t].$$

- $\Pi_{\mathsf{PKE}}.\mathsf{Dec}(\mathsf{sk}, \mathsf{CT})$*: Given a ciphertext* $\mathsf{CT} = (\mathsf{CT}_0, \mathsf{CT}_1, \ldots, \mathsf{CT}_t)$ *and a secret key* sk *as input, the algorithm first computes* $\boldsymbol{k}' = \mathsf{wHPS.Decap}(\mathsf{sk}, \mathsf{CT}_0)$*, and then outputs* $\boldsymbol{\mu} = (\boldsymbol{\mu}_1', \ldots, \boldsymbol{\mu}_t')$*, where*

$$\boldsymbol{\mu}_j' = \mathsf{CT}_j^{(2)} - \mathsf{Ext}_{||}(\mathsf{CT}_j^{(1)}, \boldsymbol{k}').$$

Our construction achieves KDM security and leakage-resilience simultaneously. We summarize the results in the following theorem.

Theorem 5.4. *Assume that (1) Π_{wHPS} is a $(n \log B, w)$-universal* wHPS *with the secret key space and the encapsulated key space being $\mathcal{S} = \mathcal{K} = \mathbb{Z}_B^n$, $n = mn'$, $w = n \log B - \hat{\ell}$, where $\hat{\ell}$ denotes the bit length of* pk*, and $n' \log B \geq \hat{\ell} + \lambda + e$, (2) Π_{wHPS} has the additional structures as Definition 4.1 and the secret key does not have the additional string sk_x, (3) the extractor $\mathsf{Ext} : \mathcal{R} \times \mathbb{Z}_B^{n'} \to \mathcal{M}$ is an (e, poly)-reusable extractor, which is also homomorphic with respect to the class of linear functions $\mathcal{G} : \{\mathfrak{g} : \mathbb{Z}_B^{n'} \to \mathcal{M}\}$ and robust against correlated-source attacks with respect to the class of the shift functions $\mathcal{SF}_{B,n'} : \{\mathfrak{s} : \mathbb{Z}_B^{n'} \to \mathbb{Z}_B^{n'}\}$. Then the above scheme Π_{PKE} is*

1. *leakage-resilient against block leakage*[7]*, with block leakage rate $(1 - \frac{e+\hat{\ell}+\lambda}{n' \log B})$ per block.*
2. $\mathsf{KDM}^{(1)}$*-secure with respect to the block-affine function class $\mathcal{G}^t = \{\mathfrak{g}' : \mathbb{Z}_B^n \to \mathcal{M}^{m \times t}\}$ as defined in Definition 2.5.*
3. *The information rate is $\frac{|\mathcal{M}|mt}{|\mathsf{CT}_0| + |\mathcal{R}|t + |\mathcal{M}|mt}$, where $|\cdot|$ denotes the bit description length of its elements. As a result, for large enough t and m, we obtain rate-1* KDM*-secure* PKE *scheme.*

Remark 5.5. *We note that any* wHPS *(without the additional structures) and reusable extractor (without the homomorphic and robust property) already suffice to prove leakage resilience, which detailed proof is deferred to full version due to space limit. The extra properties will be used for deriving* KDM *security, which will be formally presented in Sects. 5.1 and 6. In Sect. 3.2, we have presented homomorphic extractors from* DDH *and* LWE.

5.1 Proof of $\mathsf{KDM}^{(1)}$-security

In this section, we present the proof of the second part of Theorem 5.4. Our proof takes the following high-level steps:

- We first define a modified encryption algorithm Enc', and then switch the responses of the KDM queries by using Enc' instead of the real Enc. By a hybrid argument, we argue that the adversary cannot distinguish whether he is answered by Enc or Enc'.
- We next modify the KDM responses by using Enc'', which essentially generates random strings as the ciphertexts. We argue that this is indistinguishable from the above case by the security of the reusable extractor robust against correlated-source attacks with respect to the class of shift functions (ref. Definition 2.4);
- Finally, we show that even given multiple KDM encryption queries, Enc'' is indistinguishable from $\mathsf{Enc}(0)$, implying KDM-security.

[7] Just as described in full version, block leakage means that each block of source is leaked by an independent function and remain enough entropy conditioned on leakage against other blocks.

Below, we first define the modified encryption algorithm Enc'. On input a public-key pk, a secret-key $\mathsf{sk} := \boldsymbol{x} \in \mathbb{Z}_B^n = (\mathbb{Z}_B^{n'})^m$ and a function $\mathfrak{g}' \in \mathcal{G}^t$, where $\mathfrak{g}'$ can be indexed by a vector $\boldsymbol{a} = (\boldsymbol{a}_1^\top, \ldots, \boldsymbol{a}_t^\top)^\top \in \mathcal{M}^{m \times t}$ and t functions $\mathfrak{g}_1, \ldots, \mathfrak{g}_t \in \mathcal{G}$ (ref. Definition 2.5), where for each $j \in [t]$, $\boldsymbol{a}_j = (a_{j,1}, \ldots, a_{j,m})^\top \in \mathcal{M}^m$, $\mathfrak{g}_j = (\mathfrak{g}_{j,1}, \ldots, \mathfrak{g}_{j,m})$ with $\mathfrak{g}_{j,l} : \mathbb{Z}_B^{n'} \to \mathcal{M}$ and $l \in [m]$, the algorithm does the following:

1. Generate an invalid ciphertext CT_0^*. By Property 4 in Definition 4.1, set $\boldsymbol{x}' := \mathsf{Decap}(\mathsf{sk}, \mathsf{CT}_0^*) = \boldsymbol{x} + \boldsymbol{k}'$ for some $\boldsymbol{k}'$.
2. Compute $t \cdot m$ invertible functions $\{\mathfrak{h}_{1,l}\}_{l \in [m]}, \ldots, \{\mathfrak{h}_{t,l}\}_{l \in [m]}$ such that $\mathsf{Ext}_{||}(r, \boldsymbol{s}) + \mathfrak{g}_j(\boldsymbol{s}) = (\mathsf{Ext}(r, \boldsymbol{s}_1), \ldots, \mathsf{Ext}(r, \boldsymbol{s}_m)) + (\mathfrak{g}_{j,1}(\boldsymbol{s}_1), \ldots, \mathfrak{g}_{j,m}(\boldsymbol{s}_m)) = (\mathsf{Ext}(\mathfrak{h}_{j,1}(r), \boldsymbol{s}_1), \ldots, \mathsf{Ext}(\mathfrak{h}_{j,m}(r), \boldsymbol{s}_m))$ for any $j \in [t]$, by the property of homomorphic extractor (ref. Definition 3.4). Here, $\boldsymbol{s}$ is a block source, i.e., $\boldsymbol{s} = (\boldsymbol{s}_1, \ldots, \boldsymbol{s}_m)$.
3. Then sample t random seeds $r_1, \ldots, r_t \in \mathcal{R}$ for the extractor, and compute $z_j = \{\mathsf{Ext}(\mathfrak{h}_{j,l}(r_j), \boldsymbol{x}_l') - \mathfrak{g}_{j,l}(\boldsymbol{k}_l') + a_{j,l}\}_{l \in [m]}$ for $j \in [t]$, where $\boldsymbol{x}' = (\boldsymbol{x}_l')_{l \in [m]}$ and $\boldsymbol{k}' = (\boldsymbol{k}_l')_{l \in [m]}$.
4. Output the ciphertext CT': $\big(\mathsf{CT}_0^*, r_1, z_1, \ldots, r_t, z_t\big)$.

Then, we define the other modified encryption algorithm Enc'':

1. Generate an invalid ciphertext CT_0^*.
2. Then for each $j \in [t]$, sample $r_j \xleftarrow{\$} \mathcal{R}$ and $z_j \xleftarrow{\$} \mathcal{M}^m$;
3. Output the ciphertext CT'': $\big(\mathsf{CT}_0^*, r_1, z_1, \ldots, r_t, z_t\big)$.

Furthermore, we define a series of hybrids as follows:

- **Hybrid H_0**: This hybrid is identical to the original KDM queries case, i.e. the responses of all the Q KDM queries are generated as the real encryptions of the $\mathfrak{g}'^{(i)}(\mathsf{sk})$ for $i \in [Q]$.
- **Hybrid $\mathsf{H}_{0.i}$** for each $i \in [Q]$: Upon receiving the first i KDM queries, this hybrid uses Enc' to reply and then generates the remaining KDM responses according to the original encryption algorithm as H_0.
- **Hybrid H_1**: This hybrid replies all KDM queries with Enc''.
- **Hybrid H_2**: This hybrid replies all KDM queries with $\mathsf{Enc}(0)$.

Let events $\mathcal{E}_0$, $\mathcal{E}_1$, $\mathcal{E}_2$ denote that the KDM adversary $\mathcal{A}$ outputs 1 in H_0, H_1, and H_2, respectively. Similarly, we define events $\mathcal{E}_{0.i}$. To show that $\mathsf{Pr}[\mathcal{E}_0] \approx \mathsf{Pr}[\mathcal{E}_2]$, we will take the following path:

$$\mathsf{Pr}[\mathcal{E}_0] \approx \mathsf{Pr}[\mathcal{E}_{0.1}] \approx \cdots \approx \mathsf{Pr}[\mathcal{E}_{0.Q}] \approx \mathsf{Pr}[\mathcal{E}_1] \approx \mathsf{Pr}[\mathcal{E}_2].$$

We note that proving indistinguishability of H_1 and H_2 follows essentially the same idea from proving its semantic security. This can be captured in the proof of leakage resilience in the full version, so we just omit the proof to avoid repetition. For notational convenience, we define $\mathsf{H}_{0.0} := \mathsf{H}_0$.

Finally, we use the following three lemmas to accomplish the above mentioned proof idea. Due to space limit, we defer the detailed proof to the full version.

Lemma 5.6. *For $i \in [Q]$, $\left|\Pr[\mathcal{E}_{0.i-1}] - \Pr[\mathcal{E}_{0.i}]\right| \leq \mathsf{negl}(\lambda)$, assuming the ciphertext indistinguishability of the underlying* wHPS.

Lemma 5.7. $\left|\Pr[\mathcal{E}_{0.Q}] - \Pr[\mathcal{E}_1]\right| \leq \mathsf{negl}(\lambda)$, *assuming that (e, poly)-reusable extractor is homomorphic with respect to the class of linear functions $\mathcal{G} : \{\mathfrak{g} : \mathbb{Z}_B^{n'} \to \mathcal{M}\}$ and robust against correlated-source attacks with respect to the class of the shift functions $\mathcal{SF}_{B,n'} : \{\mathfrak{s} : \mathbb{Z}_B^{n'} \to \mathbb{Z}_B^{n'}\}$.*

Lemma 5.8. *For $i \in [Q]$, $\left|\Pr[\mathcal{E}_1] - \Pr[\mathcal{E}_2]\right| \leq \mathsf{negl}(\lambda)$, assuming the ciphertext indistinguishability of the underlying* wHPS.

Combining Lemma 5.6, 5.7 and 5.8, we can conclude that the advantage $\mathbf{Adv}^{\mathcal{F}\text{-}\mathsf{KDM}}_{\mathsf{PKE},\mathcal{A}}(\lambda)$ of $\mathcal{A}$ in the KDM security game satisfies that:

$$\mathbf{Adv}^{\mathcal{F}\text{-}\mathsf{KDM}}_{\mathsf{PKE},\mathcal{A}}(\lambda) \leq (Q+2) \cdot \mathsf{negl}(\lambda) \leq \mathsf{negl}(\lambda).$$

This completes the proof that Π_{PKE} in Construction 5.3 is $\mathsf{KDM}^{(1)}$-secure with respect to $\mathcal{G}^t$.

6 Achieving $\mathsf{KDM}^{(\bar{n})}$-security from $\mathsf{KDM}^{(1)}$-security

In this section, we show how to upgrade our Construction 5.3 to achieve $\mathsf{KDM}^{(\bar{n})}$-security for an unbounded polynomial $\bar{n}$. To achieve this, we first define a more general design paradigm called BE-*based scheme*, capturing several important features of Construction 5.3. Then we identify two homomorphic properties of BE-based scheme, which only implies the $\mathsf{KDM}^{(\bar{n})}$-security for bounded polynomial $\bar{n}$. Finally, we define an additional pseudorandom property for BE-based scheme, and prove $\mathsf{KDM}^{(\bar{n})}$-security for unbounded polynomial $\bar{n}$ with all these properties.

6.1 BE-Based PKEand Its Two Key-Homomorphic Properties

Definition 6.1 (BE-based PKE). *Let* BE *be a batch encryption as Definition 2.1. A* BE*-based* PKE *Π is a public-key encryption scheme with the following properties: (1) the secret key of Π is a vector $\boldsymbol{x} \in \mathbb{Z}_B^n$ for some $B, n \in \mathbb{Z}$, as in the scheme* BE, *(2) the public key is* $(\mathsf{CRS}, \mathsf{H}(\mathsf{CRS}, \boldsymbol{x}))$, *where* CRS *is generated by* BE.Setup, *and* $\mathsf{H}(\cdot,\cdot) = \mathsf{BE.KeyGen}(\cdot,\cdot)$ *is the projection function of* BE. *In this way,* CRS *is independent of the secret key.*

Clearly, Construction 5.3 is BE-based PKE. Next, we identify two crucial key-homomorphic properties on BE-based PKE schemes, which can be used to achieve the $\mathsf{KDM}^{(\bar{n})}$-security.

Property 1: There is a deterministic algorithm $\mathcal{T}_1$ that takes as input a pair $(\mathsf{CRS}, \mathsf{H}(\mathsf{CRS}, \boldsymbol{x}))$ and a vector $\boldsymbol{k} \in \mathbb{Z}_B^n$, and outputs $(\mathsf{CRS}', \mathsf{H}(\mathsf{CRS}', \boldsymbol{x}+\boldsymbol{k}))$, i.e., $\mathcal{T}_1(\mathsf{CRS}, \mathsf{H}(\mathsf{CRS}, \boldsymbol{x}), \boldsymbol{k}) = (\mathsf{CRS}', \mathsf{H}(\mathsf{CRS}', \boldsymbol{x}+\boldsymbol{k}))$.

Moreover, for any vectors $\boldsymbol{x}, \boldsymbol{k} \in \mathbb{Z}_B^n$ and $\mathsf{CRS} \xleftarrow{\$} \Pi.\mathsf{Setup}(1^\lambda, 1^n)$, the following two distributions are identical (or statistically close):

$$(\mathsf{CRS}, \mathsf{H}(\mathsf{CRS}, \boldsymbol{x} + \boldsymbol{k}), \boldsymbol{x}, \boldsymbol{k}) \equiv (\mathcal{T}_1(\mathsf{CRS}, \mathsf{H}(\mathsf{CRS}, \boldsymbol{x}), \boldsymbol{k}), \boldsymbol{x}, \boldsymbol{k}).$$

Property 2: There exists a deterministic algorithm $\mathcal{T}_2$ that takes a pair $(\mathsf{CT}, \boldsymbol{k})$ as input and outputs a ciphertext CT', i.e., $\mathcal{T}_2(\mathsf{CT}, \boldsymbol{k}) = \mathsf{CT}'$. Moreover, for any message $\mu \in \mathcal{M}$, vectors $\boldsymbol{x}, \boldsymbol{k} \in \mathbb{Z}_B^n$, and CRS, the following distributions are identical (or statistically close):

$$(\mathsf{CT}_1, \mathcal{T}_1(\mathsf{CRS}, \mathsf{H}(\mathsf{CRS}, \boldsymbol{x}), \boldsymbol{k}), \boldsymbol{x}, \boldsymbol{k}) \equiv (\mathcal{T}_2(\mathsf{CT}, \boldsymbol{k}), \mathcal{T}_1(\mathsf{CRS}, \mathsf{H}(\mathsf{CRS}, \boldsymbol{x}), \boldsymbol{k}), \boldsymbol{x}, \boldsymbol{k}),$$

where $\mathsf{CT} \leftarrow \Pi.\mathsf{Enc}(\mathsf{CRS}, \mathsf{H}(\mathsf{CRS}, \boldsymbol{x}), \mu)$, and $\mathsf{CT}_1 \leftarrow \Pi.\mathsf{Enc}(\mathsf{CRS}, \mathsf{H}(\mathsf{CRS}, \boldsymbol{x} + \boldsymbol{k}), \mu)$.

Remark 6.2. *These two properties can also be defined for* BE *schemes. Furthermore, if the underlying* BE *scheme has these two properties, Construction 5.3 would inherit these two properties, due to its designs of public key and ciphertext.*

6.2 Intermediate Scheme $\Pi^{\bar{n}}$

Following the above mentioned BE-based PKE scheme $\Pi = \Pi.\{\mathsf{KeyGen}, \mathsf{Enc}, \mathsf{Dec}\}$, we define the following intermediate scheme $\Pi^{\bar{n}}$.

Construction 6.3 (Intermediate BE-based PKE $\Pi^{\bar{n}}$). *Given a* BE*-based* PKE $\Pi = \Pi.\{\mathsf{KeyGen}, \mathsf{Enc}, \mathsf{Dec}\}$ *with the message space* $\mathcal{M}$*, we construct a new scheme* $\Pi^{\bar{n}} = \Pi^{\bar{n}}.\{\mathsf{KeyGen}, \mathsf{Enc}, \mathsf{Dec}\}$ *with the same message space* $\mathcal{M}$ *as follows:*

- $\Pi^{\bar{n}}.\mathsf{KeyGen}(1^\lambda, 1^{\bar{n}})$*: The algorithm does the following steps:*
  1. *Take the security parameter* λ *and an integer* $\bar{n} \in \mathbb{N}$ *as input, run* $\Pi.\mathsf{KeyGen}$ *for* $\bar{n}$ *times to obtain* $\mathsf{CRS}_i \xleftarrow{\$} \Pi.\mathsf{KeyGen}(1^\lambda, 1^{\bar{n}})$ *for* $1 \leq i \leq \bar{n}$*, where all these* CRS_i *contain the same size parameter* $B \in \mathbb{Z}$.
  2. *Choose a random vector* $\boldsymbol{x} \xleftarrow{\$} \mathbb{Z}_B^n$ *to generates* $h_i = \mathsf{H}(\mathsf{CRS}_i, \boldsymbol{x})$ *for* $1 \leq i \leq \bar{n}$;
  3. *Output* $\mathsf{pk} := (\mathsf{pk}_i)_{1 \leq i \leq \bar{n}}$ *and* $\mathsf{sk} := \boldsymbol{x}$*, where* $\mathsf{pk}_i = (\mathsf{CRS}_i, h_i)$.
- $\Pi^{\bar{n}}.\mathsf{Enc}(\mathsf{pk}, \mu)$*: Given a public-key* pk *and a message* $\mu \in \mathcal{M}$ *as input, the algorithm runs* $\Pi.\mathsf{Enc}$ *for* $\bar{n}$ *times to generate* $\mathsf{CT}_i \xleftarrow{\$} \Pi.\mathsf{Enc}(\mathsf{pk}_i, \mu)$ *for* $1 \leq i \leq \bar{n}$*, and then outputs* $\mathsf{CT} = (\mathsf{CT}_1, \ldots, \mathsf{CT}_{\bar{n}})$ *as the ciphertext of* $\mu \in \mathcal{M}$.
- $\Pi^{\bar{n}}.\mathsf{Dec}(\mathsf{sk}, \mathsf{CT})$*: Given a ciphertext* $\mathsf{CT} = (\mathsf{CT}_1, \ldots, \mathsf{CT}_{\bar{n}})$ *and a secret key* sk *as input, the algorithm runs* $\Pi.\mathsf{Dec}$ *to generate* $\mu' = \Pi.\mathsf{Dec}(\mathsf{sk}, \mathsf{CT}_i)$ *for some* $i \in [\bar{n}]$*, and then output* μ' *as a plaintext for* CT.

We note that the correctness of the scheme $\Pi^{\bar{n}}$ follows clearly from that of Π. Next we present a KDM-security reduction between Π and $\Pi^{\bar{n}}$.

Theorem 6.4 ($\mathsf{KDM}^{(\bar{n})}$-security of Π). *Suppose that (1) a* BE*-based* PKE *scheme Π satisfies Properties 1 and 2 in Sect. 6.1, and (2) the intermediate scheme $\Pi^{\bar{n}}$ in Definition 6.3 is $\mathsf{KDM}^{(1)}$-security with respect to the class $\mathcal{G} = \{\mathfrak{g} : \mathcal{SK} \to \mathcal{M}\}$ of all affine (resp., block-affine) functions from $\mathcal{SK}$ to $\mathcal{M}$. Then Π is $\mathsf{KDM}^{(\bar{n})}$-secure with respect to the class $\mathcal{F} = \{\mathfrak{f} : \mathcal{SK}^{\bar{n}} \to \mathcal{M}\}$ of all affine (resp., block-affine) functions from $\mathcal{SK}^{\bar{n}}$ to $\mathcal{M}$.*

Due to the limitation of space, the detailed proof is deferred to the full version.

Remark 6.5. *Our construction can support more general relationship between $\mathcal{F}$ and $\mathcal{G}$. Particularly, the theorem also holds for the following relation. For every $\boldsymbol{k}_1, \ldots, \boldsymbol{k}_{\bar{n}}$ and $\mathfrak{h} \in \mathcal{F}$, we have $\mathfrak{g}_{\boldsymbol{k}_1,\ldots,\boldsymbol{k}_{\bar{n}}}(\boldsymbol{x}) := \mathfrak{h}(\boldsymbol{x} + \boldsymbol{k}_1, \ldots, \boldsymbol{x} + \boldsymbol{k}_{\bar{n}}) \in \mathcal{G}$.*

6.3 Proving $\mathsf{KDM}^{(1)}$-Security of $\Pi^{\bar{n}}$

In this section, we first define the required new pseudorandom property, and then show how it derives $\mathsf{KDM}^{(1)}$-security of $\Pi^{\bar{n}}_{\mathsf{PKE}}$ for unbounded polynomial $\bar{n}$. In the next section, we show how to construct such an underlying BE.

Definition 6.6. *Let $\mathsf{Ext} : \mathcal{R} \times \mathbb{Z}_B^n \to \mathcal{M}$ be some (reusable) extractor. A* BE*-based* PKE *satisfies an additional pseudorandom property if the following holds. For any polynomial $\bar{n} = \mathsf{poly}(\lambda)$, the following two distributions are computationally indistinguishable:*

$$\left(\begin{pmatrix} \mathsf{CRS}_1, \cdots, \mathsf{CRS}_{\bar{n}} \\ h_1, \quad \cdots, \quad h_{\bar{n}} \end{pmatrix}, \{r_i, \mathsf{Ext}(r_i, \boldsymbol{x} + \boldsymbol{k}_i)\}_{i \in [t]} \right)$$
$$\approx_c \left(\begin{pmatrix} \mathsf{CRS}_1, \cdots, \mathsf{CRS}_{\bar{n}} \\ u_1, \quad \cdots, \quad u_{\bar{n}} \end{pmatrix}, \{r_i, u'_i\}_{i \in [t]} \right)$$

where $\{\mathsf{CRS}_i\}_{i \in [\bar{n}]}$, $\{u_i\}_{i \in [\bar{n}]}$ and $\{u'_i\}_{i \in [\bar{t}]}$ are uniformly random, $\boldsymbol{x} \xleftarrow{\$} \mathbb{Z}_B^n$, and $h_i = \mathsf{H}(\mathsf{CRS}_i, \boldsymbol{x})$ for all $i \in [\bar{n}]$.

Theorem 6.7. *Let Π_{PKE} be the* BE*-based scheme as Construction 5.3. Suppose the underlying* BE *satisfies the pseudorandom property as Definition 6.6. Then for any polynomial $\bar{n}$, the intermediate scheme $\Pi^{\bar{n}}_{\mathsf{PKE}}$ is $\mathsf{KDM}^{(1)}$-secure with respect to all block-affine functions.*

The proof of this theorem is similar to that of Theorem 5.4. Particularly, we would switch all the real KDM responses to Enc' as in the **Hybrid** $\mathsf{H}_{0,Q}$, and then use the reusable extractor (against shift functions) to further switch the responses to Enc'' as in the **Hybrid** H_1. The key observation is the following: $\mathsf{H}(\mathsf{CRS}, \boldsymbol{x})$ does not leak $\boldsymbol{x}$ in the computational sense and can be used in connection with the extractor. Thus, the same argument of Theorem 5.4 goes through in this case.

Due to the limitation of space, we defer the detailed proof and the constructions of the required BE to the full version.

Summing up Theorems 6.4, 6.7 and the instantiations of the required BE in full version, we conclude that for any polynomial $\bar{n}$, Construction 5.3 is $\mathsf{KDM}^{(\bar{n})}$-secure with respect to block-affine functions.

7 Putting Things Together

By instantiating Construction 5.3 with (1) the specific reusable extractor from LWE in Construction 3.6 and (2) the LWE-based BE in full version. we are able to achieve the following corollary via Theorems 6.4, 6.7.

Corollary 7.1. *Assuming that* LWE *is hard, there exists a rate-1 (both information and leakage rates)* PKE *that is leakage resilient against block leakage and* $\mathsf{KDM}^{(\bar{n})}$*-secure w.r.t.* block-*affine functions for any unbounded polynomial* $\bar{n}$.

Similarly, by instantiating Construction 5.3 with (1) the specific reusable extractor from DDH in Construction 3.8 and (2) the DDH-based BE in full version, we are able to achieve the following corollary via Theorems 6.4, 6.7:

Corollary 7.2. *Assuming that* DDH *is hard, there exists a rate-1 (both information and leakage rates)* PKE *that is leakage resilient against block leakage and* $\mathsf{KDM}^{(\bar{n})}$*-secure w.r.t.* block-*affine functions for any unbounded polynomial* $\bar{n}$.

We notice that the overall construction of the DDH-based scheme resembles a modification of the scheme of [9]. We do not present this variant. Instead, we take a more modular approach by identifying a framework that suffices for KDM security and can be instantiated from various assumptions.

Remark 7.3. *The class of block affine functions is more restricted than the regular (bit) affine class. In particular, each output component of a block affine function can depend only on one block of the input, whereas the output of a bit affine function can depend on every bit of the input. Nevertheless, this restricted class already suffices for* KDM *amplification to any bounded-size functions, and moreover allows constructions with better information rate. We discuss how to amplify the function class in the following section.*

8 Extensions

In this section, we further extend our above results in Sect. 7 in two directions: the first one is to enlarge the class of KDM functions via Garbled Circuits; the second one is to generalize our results to the setting of IBE.

8.1 Garbled Circuits

In this section, we recall the key ingredient for the KDM amplification of Applebaum [4]: Garbled Circuits.

Definition 8.1 (Garbled Circuits [12]). *A garbling scheme consists of three algorithms* (Garble, Eval, Sim) *as follows:*

- $\mathsf{Garble}(1^\lambda, 1^n, 1^m, C)$ *is a* PPT *algorithm that first takes as input* λ, *a circuit* $C : \{0,1\}^n \rightarrow \{0,1\}^m$ *together with its input length* n *and output length* m, *and then outputs a garbled circuit* $\widehat{C}$ *along with labels* $\{\mathsf{lab}_{i,b}\}_{i\in[n],b\in\{0,1\}}$, *where each label* $\mathsf{lab}_{i,b} \in \{0,1\}^\lambda$.

- $\mathsf{Eval}(1^\lambda, \widehat{C}, \widehat{L})$ *is a deterministic algorithm that first takes as input a garbled circuit* $\widehat{C}$ *along with a set of* n *labels* $\widehat{L} = \{\mathsf{lab}_i\}_{i\in[n]}$, *and then outputs a string* $y \in \{0,1\}^m$.
- $\mathsf{Sim}(1^\lambda, 1^{|C|}, 1^n, y)$ *is a* PPT *algorithm that first takes as input* λ *and a bit description length of circuit* C, *an input length* n *and a string* $y \in \{0,1\}^m$, *then outputs a simulated garbled circuit* $\widetilde{C}$ *and labels* $\widetilde{L} = \{\widetilde{\mathsf{lab}_i}\}_{i\in[n]}$.

Moreover, the garbling scheme needs to satisfy the following two properties.

1. ***Correctness.*** *For any circuit* $C : \{0,1\}^n \to \{0,1\}^m$, *any input* $x = (x_i)_{i\in[n]} \in \{0,1\}^n$, *and any* $(\widehat{C}, \{\mathsf{lab}_{i,b}\}) \leftarrow \mathsf{Garble}(C)$, *it holds* $\mathsf{Eval}(\widehat{C}, \widehat{L}) = C(x)$ *where* $\widehat{L} = \{\mathsf{lab}_{i,x_i}\}_{i\in n}$.
2. ***Simulation Security.*** *For any circuit* $C : \{0,1\}^n \to \{0,1\}^m$, *any input* $x = (x_i)_{i\in[n]} \in \{0,1\}^n$, *the following two distributions are computational indistinguishability:*

$$\begin{aligned}&\{(\widehat{C}, \widehat{L}) : (\widehat{C}, \{\mathsf{lab}_{i,b}\}) \leftarrow \mathsf{Garble}(C), \widehat{L} = \{\mathsf{lab}_{i,x_i}\}_{i\in n}\}\\ \approx&\{(\widetilde{C}, \widetilde{L}) : (\widetilde{C}, \widetilde{L}) \leftarrow \mathsf{Sim}(1^\lambda, 1^{|C|}, 1^n, C(x))\}.\end{aligned}$$

8.2 Bootstrapping to Larger Classes of KDM Functions

We first present a bootstrapped variant of Construction 5.3 by using the technique of garbled circuits.[8] Then, we analyze the KDM-security and information rate of this improved scheme.

Construction 8.2 (Amplification of Our KDM Security). *Let* $\Pi = \Pi.\{\mathsf{KeyGen}, \mathsf{Enc}, \mathsf{Dec}\}$ *be the* PKE *of Construction 5.3 instantiated with parameter* $B = 2$ *such that its secret key size* $|\mathsf{sk}| = n = n' \cdot m$. *And let* $\mathsf{GC} = \mathsf{GC}.(\mathsf{Garble}, \mathsf{Eval}, \mathsf{Sim})$ *be a garbled scheme, whose label size* $|\mathsf{lab}_{i,j}|$ *is equivalent to the bit length of element in* $\mathcal{M}$. *Then, we construct a new scheme* $\widehat{\Pi} = \widehat{\Pi}.\{\mathsf{KeyGen}, \mathsf{Enc}, \mathsf{Dec}\}$ *with the message space* $\widehat{\mathcal{M}} = \mathcal{M}^{(t-n'+1)\times m}$ *as follows:*

- $\widehat{\Pi}.\mathsf{KeyGen}(1^\lambda)$: *The algorithm gets* $(\mathsf{pk}, \mathsf{sk})$ *just as* $\Pi.\mathsf{KeyGen}(1^\lambda)$.
- $\widehat{\Pi}.\mathsf{Enc}(\mathsf{pk}, \mu)$: *Given a public-key* pk *and a message* $\mu = \{\mu_{i,j}\}_{i\in[t-n'+1],j\in[m]} \in \mathcal{M}^{(t-n'+1)\times m}$ *as input, the algorithm first invokes* $(\widetilde{C}, \widetilde{L}) \leftarrow \mathsf{GC}.\mathsf{Sim}(\mu_{1,1}, \ldots, \mu_{1,m})$ *with* $\widetilde{L} = \{\mathsf{lab}_{i,j}\}_{i\in[n'],j\in[m]}$, *and then runs* $\Pi.\mathsf{Enc}$ *to output the ciphertext*

$$\begin{aligned}\mathsf{CT} :=&\Big(\widetilde{C}, \Pi.\mathsf{Enc}(\mathsf{pk}, \widetilde{L}, \{\mu_{i,j}\}_{i\in[2,t-n'+1],j\in[1,m]})\Big)\\ =&\Big(\widetilde{C}, \mathsf{CT}_0, r_1, \{\mathsf{Ext}(r_1, \boldsymbol{k}_1) + \mathsf{lab}_{1,1}, \ldots, \mathsf{Ext}(r_1, \boldsymbol{k}_m) + \mathsf{lab}_{1,m}\},\\ &\ldots, r_{n'}, \{\mathsf{Ext}(r_{n'}, \boldsymbol{k}_1) + \mathsf{lab}_{n',1}, \ldots, \mathsf{Ext}(r_{n'}, \boldsymbol{k}_m) + \mathsf{lab}_{n',m}\},\\ &r_{n'+1}, \{\mathsf{Ext}(r_{n'+1}, \boldsymbol{k}_1) + \mu_{2,1}, \ldots, \mathsf{Ext}(r_{n'+1}, \boldsymbol{k}_m) + \mu_{2,m}\},\\ &\ldots, r_t, \{\mathsf{Ext}(r_t, \boldsymbol{k}_1) + \mu_{(t-n'+1),1}, \ldots, \mathsf{Ext}(r_t, \boldsymbol{k}_m) + \mu_{(t-n'+1),m}\}\Big).\end{aligned}$$

[8] In [4], Applebaum leverages the abstract notion of randomized encoding to achieve KDM amplification. Here, we directly amplify our scheme through using Garbled Circuits, which is a well-known instantiation of randomized encoding.

Here, we use $\{\mathsf{lab}_{i,j}\}_{i\in[n']}$ *to denote the garbled results of the j-th block of* sk *for any* $j \in [m]$.

- $\widehat{\Pi}.\mathsf{Dec}(\mathsf{sk}, \mathsf{CT})$: *Given a ciphertext* CT *and a secret key* sk *as input, the algorithm first runs* $\Pi.\mathsf{Dec}$ *to recover all* $\{\mathsf{lab}_{i,j}\}_{i\in[n'],j\in[m]}$ *and* $\{\mu'_{i,j}\}_{i\in[2,t-n'+1],j\in[m]}$, *and then runs* $\mathsf{GC.Dec}(\widetilde{C}, \{\mathsf{lab}_{i,j}\})$ *to get* $\{\mu'_{1,j}\}_{j\in[m]}$. *Finally, the algorithm outputs*

$$\mu' = \{\mu'_{i,j}\}_{i\in[t-n'+1],j\in[m]} \in \mathcal{M}^{(t-n'+1)\times m}.$$

Remark 8.3. *For simplicity of presentation, we have implicitly assumed that* $|\mathsf{lab}_{i,j}| = |\mathcal{M}|$. *For the more general case such that* $|\mathsf{lab}_{i,j}| > |\mathcal{M}|$, *we can easily handle through using many more elements in* $\mathcal{M}$ *to cover each* $\mathsf{lab}_{i,j}$.

It is not hard to verify that the correctness of $\widehat{\Pi}$ follows from that of the underlying scheme Π and garble scheme GC. Below, we first argue the KDM-security of the scheme $\widehat{\Pi}$, and then analyze its information rate.

Before presenting the formal theorem about the KDM security of $\widehat{\Pi}$, we define a particular KDM function class $\hat{\mathcal{F}} = (\mathcal{F}_s||\mathcal{Q}^\tau)$ as follows.

Definition 8.4. *Let* $\mathcal{F}_s$ *be the class of functions of the secret key* $\mathsf{sk} := \boldsymbol{x} \in \mathbb{Z}_B^n$, *where the circuit size of each function in* $\mathcal{F}_s$ *is up to* s. *Let* $\mathcal{Q}^\tau$ *denote the block-affine function class* $\{\mathfrak{g}' : \mathbb{Z}_B^n \to \mathcal{M}^{\tau\times m}\}$, *which is defined similarly as in Definition 2.5. Moreover,* $(\mathcal{F}_s||\mathcal{Q}^\tau)$ *denotes the concatenation of two classes, i.e., every function* $\mathfrak{f}$ *in the class can be represented by* $\mathfrak{f} = (\mathfrak{h}, \mathfrak{q})$ *for some* $\mathfrak{h} \in \mathcal{F}_s$ *and* $\mathfrak{q} \in \mathcal{Q}^\tau$ *such that* $\mathfrak{f}(\mathsf{sk}) = (\mathfrak{h}(\mathsf{sk})||\mathfrak{q}(\mathsf{sk}))$.

Theorem 8.5. *For the parameter setting in Construction 8.2, if* Π *is* $\mathsf{KDM}^{(1)}$-*secure with respect to* $\mathcal{G}^t = \{\mathfrak{g}' : \mathbb{Z}_B^n \to \mathcal{M}^{t\times m}\}$ *as defined in Definition 2.5, and* GC *is a secure garbling scheme, then* $\widehat{\Pi}$ *is* $\mathsf{KDM}^{(1)}$-*secure with respect to* $\widehat{\mathcal{F}} = (\mathcal{F}_s||\mathcal{Q}^\tau)$ *as defined in Definition 8.4.*

Proof (Sketch). As pointed out by [4], we just need to focus on KDM reduction from $\mathcal{F}_s$ to the corresponding part of block-affine function class $\mathcal{G}^t$, denoted by $\mathcal{G}^{n'}$, i.e., $\mathcal{F}_s \leq_{\mathsf{KDM}} \mathcal{G}^{n'}$. Particularly, it suffices to show that block-affine functions in $\mathcal{G}^{n'}$ can encode any bounded size circuits of $\boldsymbol{x} \in \mathbb{Z}_2^n$, according to Applebaum's concepts on the KDM reduction in [4].

More specifically, suppose that $\mathcal{A}$ is the adversary against the KDM-security of $\widehat{\Pi}$ with respect to $\mathfrak{h} \in \mathcal{F}_s$, and $\mathcal{C}$ is the challenger for the KDM-security of Π with respect to $\mathcal{G}^{n'}$. Then, through using $\mathcal{A}$ as a building block, we can establish a reduction algorithm $\mathcal{B}$ to break the KDM-security of Π with the same advantage as that of $\mathcal{A}$.

In particular, after receiving a function $\mathfrak{h}(\cdot) \in \mathcal{F}_s$ of sk from $\mathcal{A}$, $\mathcal{B}$ conducts the followings

1. Choose $2n$ labels $\{\mathsf{lab}_{i,j,0}, \mathsf{lab}_{i,j,1}\}_{i\in[n'],j\in[m]}$, with $|\mathsf{sk}| = n = n' \cdot m$.
2. For each $j \in [m]$,

- Set a matrix $\mathbf{A}^{(j)} = (\boldsymbol{a}_1^{(j)}, \ldots, \boldsymbol{a}_{n'}^{(j)})$ of dimension $(n' \times n')$, where for $l \in [n']$, the l-th component of $\boldsymbol{a}_l^{(j)}$ is $(\mathsf{lab}_{l,j,1} - \mathsf{lab}_{l,j,0})$ and all others are 0.
- Set a vector $\boldsymbol{b}^{(j)} = (\mathsf{lab}_{1,j,0}, \ldots, \mathsf{lab}_{n',j,0})^\top$ of n' dimension.
- Take $(\mathbf{A}^{(j)})^\top$ and $\boldsymbol{b}^{(j)}$ as the index of the j-th block-affine function $\mathfrak{g}_j(\mathsf{sk}_j) = (\mathbf{A}^{(j)})^\top \cdot \mathsf{sk}_j + \boldsymbol{b}^{(j)}$, where $\mathsf{sk}_j \in \{0,1\}^{n'}$ is the j-th block of sk.

3. Send the indexes of all m block-affine functions to $\mathcal{C}$ to conduct KDM query.
4. Receive the KDM ciphertexts $\{\mathsf{ct}_{i,j}\}_{i \in [n'], j \in [m]}$ from $\mathcal{C}$.
5. Run the algorithm GC.Garble to obtain the garbled circuit $\widehat{C}$ with respect to the KDM query function $\mathfrak{h}(\cdot)$ from $\mathcal{A}$.
6. Send $\mathsf{CT} := (\widehat{C}, \{\mathsf{ct}_{i,j}\}_{i \in [n'], j \in [m]})$ to $\mathcal{A}$.
7. Finally, $\mathcal{B}$ outputs whatever $\mathcal{A}$ outputs.

It is not hard to verify that $\mathsf{ct}_{i,j}$ will be a encryption of $\mathsf{lab}_{i,j,b}$ for $b := \mathsf{sk}_{i,j}$. Thus, the above reduction process is clearly set up. Finally, this theorem holds. □

Remark 8.6. *Although Theorem 8.5 just focuses on the case of* $\mathsf{KDM}^{(1)}$, *the above construction and analysis can be easily (though somewhat tedious) extended to* $\mathsf{KDM}^{(\bar{n})}$ *for any polynomially unbounded* $\bar{n}$.

Finally, we focus on the information rate of the above construction. We remark that for this amplified KDM function class $\hat{\mathcal{F}} = (\mathcal{F}_s || \mathcal{Q}^\tau)$, the parameters t, s and τ should satisfy: $\tau < t$ and s is the size of circuits amplified from block-affine function with outputs $(t - \tau)$ vectors over $\mathcal{M}^m$.

By setting $\tau \gg s$, our scheme achieves the optimal information rate, i.e., $1 - o(1)$. This is because although the additional garble circuit in the ciphertext and the encryption of labels will increase the ciphertext length to certain bounded size, we can use large enough $\tau \gg s$ such that the last τ part of ciphertext dominates the whole information rate.

8.3 Upgrade to KDM-Secure and Leakage Resilient IBE

In this section, we present our general compiler to construct an IBE that is both KDM-secure and leakage resilient. The compiler uses as key ingredients an IB-wHPS (described in full version) with additional structure (ref. Remark 4.2) and an on-the-fly KDM-secure PKE (described in full version). Conceptually, this general IBE scheme can be view as the hybrid encryption of the IB-wHPS and PKE: to encrypt a message m, the IBE encryption algorithm first generates (1) a pair of encapsulated key and ciphertext $(\mathsf{CT}, \boldsymbol{k})$ according to the IB-wHPS, and then generates (2) a pair of session public-key and ciphertext according to the PKE, i.e., $\mathsf{pk} = (\mathsf{CRS}, \mathsf{H}(\mathsf{CRS}, \boldsymbol{k}))$ and $\mathsf{Enc}(\mathsf{pk}, m)$, respectively, under the same encapsulated key $\boldsymbol{k}$. By connecting the two security properties in a novel way, we are able to derive the desired IBE.

Construction 8.7 (KDM-secure IBE). *Let* $\Pi_{\mathsf{IB\text{-}wHPS}} = \Pi_{\mathsf{IB\text{-}wHPS}}.\{\mathsf{Setup}, \mathsf{KeyGen}, \mathsf{Encap}, \mathsf{Encap}^*, \mathsf{Decap}\}$ *be an* IB-wHPS *with the encapsulated key space* $\mathcal{K}$ *and the identity space* $\mathcal{ID}$. *Let* $\Pi_{\mathsf{PKE}} = \Pi_{\mathsf{PKE}}.\{\mathsf{KeyGen}, \mathsf{Enc}, \mathsf{Dec}\}$ *be a* BE*-based* PKE. *Then, we construct an* IBE *scheme* $\Pi_{\mathsf{IBE}} = \Pi_{\mathsf{IBE}}.\{\mathsf{Setup}, \mathsf{KeyGen}, \mathsf{Enc}, \mathsf{Dec}\}$ *for message space* $\mathcal{M}$ *as follows.*

- $\Pi_{\mathsf{IBE}}.\mathsf{Setup}(1^\lambda)$: *The algorithm runs* $(\mathsf{mpk}^{\Pi_{\mathsf{IB\text{-}wHPS}}}, \mathsf{msk}^{\Pi_{\mathsf{IB\text{-}wHPS}}}) \xleftarrow{\$} \Pi_{\mathsf{IB\text{-}wHPS}}.\mathsf{Setup}(1^\lambda)$, *and then outputs* $\mathsf{mpk} := \mathsf{mpk}^{\Pi_{\mathsf{IB\text{-}wHPS}}}$ *and* $\mathsf{msk} := \mathsf{msk}^{\Pi_{\mathsf{IB\text{-}wHPS}}}$.
- $\Pi_{\mathsf{IBE}}.\mathsf{KeyGen}(\mathsf{msk}, \mathsf{id})$: *Given a master secret-key* msk *and an identity* $\mathsf{id} \in \mathcal{ID}$ *as input, the algorithm runs* IB-wHPS.KeyGen *to generate and output* $\mathsf{sk}_{\mathsf{id}} := \mathsf{sk}_{\mathsf{id}}^{\Pi_{\mathsf{IB\text{-}wHPS}}} \xleftarrow{\$} \Pi_{\mathsf{IB\text{-}wHPS}}.\mathsf{KeyGen}(\mathsf{msk}, \mathsf{id})$.
- $\Pi_{\mathsf{IBE}}.\mathsf{Enc}(\mathsf{mpk}, \mathsf{id}, \mu)$: *Given a master public-key* mpk, *an identity* $\mathsf{id} \in \mathcal{ID}$ *and a message* $m \in \mathcal{M}$ *as input, the algorithm does the following steps:*
  1. *Generates* $(\mathsf{CT}_1, \boldsymbol{k}) \leftarrow \Pi_{\mathsf{IB\text{-}wHPS}}.\mathsf{Encap}(\mathsf{mpk}, \mathsf{id})$;
  2. *Chooses an on-the-fly common reference string* CRS *for* Π_{PKE};
  3. *Computes* $\mathsf{CT}_2 = \Pi_{\mathsf{PKE}}.\mathsf{Enc}(\mathsf{CRS}, h, \mu)$ *where* $h = \mathsf{H}(\mathsf{CRS}, \boldsymbol{k})$;
  4. *Outputs* $\mathsf{CT} = (\mathsf{CT}_1, \mathsf{CRS}, h, \mathsf{CT}_2)$ *as the ciphertext of* m *under the identity* id.
- $\Pi_{\mathsf{IBE}}.\mathsf{Dec}(\mathsf{sk}_{\mathsf{id}}, \mathsf{CT})$: *Given a ciphertext* $\mathsf{CT} = (\mathsf{CT}_1, \mathsf{CRS}, h, \mathsf{CT}_2)$ *and a secret key* $\mathsf{sk}_{\mathsf{id}}$ *as input, the algorithm does the following steps:*
  1. *Run* $\Pi_{\mathsf{IB\text{-}wHPS}}.\mathsf{Decap}$ *to generate* $\boldsymbol{k}' = \Pi_{\mathsf{IB\text{-}wHPS}}.\mathsf{Decap}(\mathsf{sk}_{\mathsf{id}}, \mathsf{CT}_1)$;
  2. *Output* $m' = \Pi_{\mathsf{PKE}}.\mathsf{Dec}(\mathsf{CRS}, \boldsymbol{k}', \mathsf{CT}_2)$.

We sketch that the above construction can be proven to be a rate-1 (both information and leakage rates) IBE that is leakage resilient against block leakage and $\mathsf{KDM}^{(\bar{n})}$-secure w.r.t. a restricted block-function class for any polynomial unbounded $\bar{n}$. Due to space limit, the corresponding formal theorem statement and its detailed proof are deferred to the full version.

Acknowledgements. We would like to thank the anonymous reviewers of PKC 2021 for their insightful advices. Qiqi Lai is supported by the National Key R&D Program of China (2017YFB0802000), the National Natural Science Foundation of China (61802241, U2001205, 61772326, 61802242), the Natural Science Basic Research Plan in Shaanxi Province of China (2019JQ-360), the National Cryptography Development Foundation during the 13th Five-year Plan Period (MMJJ20180217), and the Fundamental Research Funds for the Central Universities (GK202103093). Feng-Hao Liu and Zhedong Wang are supported by an NSF Award CNS-1657040 and an NSF Career Award CNS-1942400. Any opinions, findings, and conclusions or recommendations expressed in this material are those of the author(s) and do not necessarily reflect the views of the sponsors.

References

1. Adão, P., Bana, G., Herzog, J., Scedrov, A.: Soundness of formal encryption in the presence of key-cycles. In: di Vimercati, S.C., Syverson, P., Gollmann, D. (eds.) ESORICS 2005. LNCS, vol. 3679, pp. 374–396. Springer, Heidelberg (2005). https://doi.org/10.1007/11555827_22

2. Alwen, J., Dodis, Y., Naor, M., Segev, S. Walfish, G., Wichs, D.: Public-key encryption in the bounded-retrieval model. In: Gilbert [17], pp. 113–134
3. Alwen, J., Krenn, S., Pietrzak, K., Wichs, D.: Learning with rounding, revisited. In: Canetti, R., Garay, J.A. (eds.) CRYPTO 2013. LNCS, vol. 8042, pp. 57–74. Springer, Heidelberg (2013). https://doi.org/10.1007/978-3-642-40041-4_4
4. Applebaum, B.: Key-dependent message security: generic amplification and completeness. In: Paterson, K.G. (ed.) EUROCRYPT 2011. LNCS, vol. 6632, pp. 527–546. Springer, Heidelberg (2011). https://doi.org/10.1007/978-3-642-20465-4_29
5. Applebaum, B., Cash, D., Peikert, C., Sahai, A.: Fast cryptographic primitives and circular-secure encryption based on hard learning problems. In: Halevi [20], pp. 595–618
6. Banerjee, A., Peikert, C., Rosen, A.: Pseudorandom functions and lattices. In: Pointcheval, D., Johansson, T. (eds.) EUROCRYPT 2012. LNCS, vol. 7237, pp. 719–737. Springer, Heidelberg (2012). https://doi.org/10.1007/978-3-642-29011-4_42
7. Barak, B., Haitner, I., Hofheinz, D., Ishai, Y. Bounded key-dependent message security. In: Gilbert [17], pp. 423–444
8. Black, J., Rogaway, P., Shrimpton, T.: Encryption-scheme security in the presence of key-dependent messages. In: Nyberg, K., Heys, H. (eds.) SAC 2002. LNCS, vol. 2595, pp. 62–75. Springer, Heidelberg (2003). https://doi.org/10.1007/3-540-36492-7_6
9. Boneh, D., Halevi, S., Hamburg, M., Ostrovsky, R.: Circular-secure encryption from decision Diffie-Hellman. In: Wagner, D. (ed.) CRYPTO 2008. LNCS, vol. 5157, pp. 108–125. Springer, Heidelberg (2008). https://doi.org/10.1007/978-3-540-85174-5_7
10. Brakerski, Z., Goldwasser, S.: Circular and leakage resilient public-key encryption under subgroup indistinguishability. In: Rabin, T. (ed.) CRYPTO 2010. LNCS, vol. 6223, pp. 1–20. Springer, Heidelberg (2010). https://doi.org/10.1007/978-3-642-14623-7_1
11. Brakerski, Z., Goldwasser, S., Kalai, Y.T.: Black-box circular-secure encryption beyond affine functions. In: Ishai, Y. (ed.) TCC 2011. LNCS, vol. 6597, pp. 201–218. Springer, Heidelberg (2011). https://doi.org/10.1007/978-3-642-19571-6_13
12. Brakerski, Z., Lombardi, A., Segev, G., Vaikuntanathan, V.: Anonymous IBE, leakage resilience and circular security from new assumptions. In: Nielsen, J.B., Rijmen, V. (eds.) EUROCRYPT 2018. LNCS, vol. 10820, pp. 535–564. Springer, Cham (2018). https://doi.org/10.1007/978-3-319-78381-9_20
13. Camenisch, J., Lysyanskaya, A.: An efficient system for non-transferable anonymous credentials with optional anonymity revocation. In: Pfitzmann, B. (ed.) EUROCRYPT 2001. LNCS, vol. 2045, pp. 93–118. Springer, Heidelberg (2001). https://doi.org/10.1007/3-540-44987-6_7
14. Dodis, Y., Kalai, Y.T., Lovett, S.: On cryptography with auxiliary input. In: Mitzenmacher, M. (ed.) 41st ACM STOC, pp. 621–630. ACM Press, May/June (2009)
15. Dodis, Y., Ostrovsky, R., Reyzin, L., Smith, A.D.: Fuzzy extractors: how to generate strong keys from biometrics and other noisy data. SIAM J. Comput. **38**(1), 97–139 (2008)
16. Döttling, N.: Low noise LPN: KDM secure public key encryption and sample amplification. In: Katz, J. (ed.) PKC 2015. LNCS, vol. 9020, pp. 604–626. Springer, Heidelberg (2015). https://doi.org/10.1007/978-3-662-46447-2_27
17. Gilbert, H. (ed.): EUROCRYPT 2010, volume 6110 of LNCS. Springer, Heidelberg, May/June 2010

18. Goldwasser, S., Micali, S.: Probabilistic encryption. J. Comput. Syst. Sci. **28**(2), 270–299 (1984)
19. Goyal, V., Song, Y.: Correlated-source extractors and cryptography with correlated-random tapes. In: Ishai, Y., Rijmen, V. (eds.) EUROCRYPT 2019. LNCS, vol. 11476, pp. 562–592. Springer, Cham (2019). https://doi.org/10.1007/978-3-030-17653-2_19
20. Halevi, S. (ed.): CRYPTO 2009. LNCS, vol. 5677. Springer, Heidelberg (2009). https://doi.org/10.1007/978-3-642-03356-8
21. Hazay, C., López-Alt, A., Wee, H., Wichs, D.: Leakage-resilient cryptography from minimal assumptions. In: Johansson, T., Nguyen, P.Q. (eds.) EUROCRYPT 2013. LNCS, vol. 7881, pp. 160–176. Springer, Heidelberg (2013). https://doi.org/10.1007/978-3-642-38348-9_10
22. Hofheinz, D., Unruh, D.: Towards key-dependent message security in the standard model. In: Smart, N. (ed.) EUROCRYPT 2008. LNCS, vol. 4965, pp. 108–126. Springer, Heidelberg (2008). https://doi.org/10.1007/978-3-540-78967-3_7
23. Kitagawa, F., Tanaka, K.: Key dependent message security and receiver selective opening security for identity-based encryption. In: Abdalla, M., Dahab, R. (eds.) PKC 2018, Part I. LNCS, vol. 10769, pp. 32–61. Springer, Cham (2018). https://doi.org/10.1007/978-3-319-76578-5_2
24. Laud, P., Corin, R.: Sound computational interpretation of formal encryption with composed keys. In: Lim, J.-I., Lee, D.-H. (eds.) ICISC 2003. LNCS, vol. 2971, pp. 55–66. Springer, Heidelberg (2004). https://doi.org/10.1007/978-3-540-24691-6_5
25. Naor, M., Segev, G.: Public-key cryptosystems resilient to key leakage. In: Halevi [20], pp. 18–35
26. Vadhan, S.P.: Pseudorandomness. Found. Trends® Theor. Comput. Sci. **7**(1–3), 1–336 (2012)
27. Wee, H.: KDM-security via homomorphic smooth projective hashing. In: Cheng, C.-M., Chung, K.-M., Persiano, G., Yang, B.-Y. (eds.) PKC 2016, Part II. LNCS, vol. 9615, pp. 159–179. Springer, Heidelberg (2016). https://doi.org/10.1007/978-3-662-49387-8_7

Two-Party Adaptor Signatures from Identification Schemes

Andreas Erwig[1(✉)], Sebastian Faust[1], Kristina Hostáková[2], Monosij Maitra[1], and Siavash Riahi[1]

[1] Technische Universität Darmstadt, Darmstadt, Germany
{andreas.erwig,sebastian.faust,monosij.maitra, siavash.riahi}@tu-darmstadt.de
[2] ETH Zürich, Zürich, Switzerland
kristina.hostakova@inf.ethz.ch

Abstract. Adaptor signatures are a novel cryptographic primitive with important applications for cryptocurrencies. They have been used to construct second layer solutions such as payment channels or cross-currency swaps. The basic idea of an adaptor signature scheme is to tie the signing process to the revelation of a secret value in the sense that, much like a regular signature scheme, an adaptor signature scheme can authenticate messages, but simultaneously leaks a secret to certain parties. Recently, Aumayr et al. provide the first formalization of adaptor signature schemes, and present provably secure constructions from ECDSA and Schnorr signatures. Unfortunately, the formalization and constructions given in this work have two limitations: (1) current schemes are limited to ECDSA and Schnorr signatures, and no generic transformation for constructing adaptor signatures is known; (2) they do not offer support for aggregated two-party signing, which can significantly reduce the blockchain footprint in applications of adaptor signatures.

In this work, we address these two shortcomings. First, we show that signature schemes that are constructed from identification (ID) schemes, which additionally satisfy certain homomorphic properties, can generically be transformed into adaptor signature schemes. We further provide an impossibility result which proves that unique signature schemes (e.g., the BLS scheme) cannot be transformed into an adaptor signature scheme. In addition, we define two-party adaptor signature schemes with aggregatable public keys and show how to instantiate them via a generic transformation from ID-based signature schemes. Finally, we give instantiations of our generic transformations for the Schnorr, Katz-Wang and Guillou-Quisquater signature schemes.

K. Hostáková—Research partially conducted at Technische Universität Darmstadt, Germany.

M. Maitra—Research partially conducted at Indian Institute of Technology Madras, India.

J. A. Garay (Ed.): PKC 2021, LNCS 12710, pp. 451–480, 2021.
https://doi.org/10.1007/978-3-030-75245-3_17

1 Introduction

Blockchain technologies, envisioned first in 2009 [34], have spurred enormous interest by academia and industry. This technology puts forth a decentralized payment paradigm, where financial transactions are stored in a decentralized data structure – often referred to as the blockchain. The main cryptographic primitive used by blockchain systems is the one of digital signature schemes, which allow users to authenticate payment transactions. Various different flavors of digital signature schemes are used by blockchain systems, e.g., ring signatures [39] add privacy-preserving features to cryptocurrencies [40], while threshold signatures and multi-signatures are used for multi-factor authorization of transactions [18].

Adaptor signatures (sometimes also referred to as scriptless scripts) are another important type of digital signature scheme introduced by the cryptocurrency community [37] and recently formalized by Aumayr et al. [2]. In a nutshell, adaptor signatures tie together authorization of a message and the leakage of a secret value. Namely, they allow a *signer* to produce a *pre-signature* under her secret key such that this pre-signature can be *adapted* into a valid signature by a *publisher* knowing a certain secret value. If the completed signature gets published, the signer is able to extract the embedded secret used by the publisher.

To demonstrate the concept of adaptor signatures, let us discuss the simple example of a preimage sale which serves as an important building block in many blockchain applications such as payment channels [2,6,10,38], payment routing in payment channel networks (PCNs) [13,30,33] or atomic swaps [11,21]. Assume that a seller offers to reveal a preimage of a hash value h in exchange for c coins from a concrete buyer. This is a classical instance of a fair exchange problem, which can be solved using the blockchain as follows. The buyer locks c coins in a transaction which can be spent by another transaction if it is authorized by the seller and contains a preimage of the hash value h.

While this solution implements the preimage sale, it has various drawbacks: (i) The only hash functions that can be used are the ones supported by the underlying blockchain. For example, the most popular blockchain-based cryptocurrency, Bitcoin, supports only SHA-1, SHA-256 and RIPEMD-160 [5]. This makes the above solution unsuitable for applications like privacy-preserving payment routing in PCNs [13,30] that crucially rely on the preimage sale instantiated with a *homomorphic* hash function. (ii) The hash value has to be fixed at the beginning of the sale and cannot be changed later without a new transaction being posted on the blockchain. This is problematic in, e.g., generalized payment channels [2], where users utilize the ideas from the preimage sale to repeatedly update channel balances without any blockchain interaction. (iii) Finally, the blockchain script is non-standard as, in addition to a signature verification, it contains a hash preimage verification. This does not only make the transaction more expensive but also allows parties who are maintaining the blockchain (also known as *miners*) to censor transactions belonging to a preimage sale.

The concept of adaptor signatures allows us to implement a preimage sale in a way that overcomes most of the aforementioned drawbacks. The protocol works at a high level as follows. The buyer locks c coins in a transaction which can be spent by a transaction authorized by *both* the seller and the buyer. Thereafter, the buyer pre-signs a transaction spending the c coins with respect to the hash value h. If the seller knows a preimage of h, she can adapt the pre-signature of the buyer, attach her own signature and claim the c coins. The buyer can then extract a preimage from the adapted signature. Hence, parties are not restricted to the hash functions supported by the blockchain, i.e., drawback (i) is addressed. Moreover, the buyer can pre-sign the spending transaction with respect to multiple hash values which overcomes drawback (ii). However, the third drawback remains. While the usage of adaptor signatures avoids the hash preimage verification in the script, it adds a signature verification (i.e., there are now 2 signature verifications in total) which makes this type of exchange easily distinguishable from a normal payment transaction. Hence, the sale remains rather expensive and censorship is not prevented.

The idea of *two-party* adaptor signatures is to replace the two signature verifications by one. The transaction implementing a preimage sale then has exactly the same format as a transaction simply transferring coins. As a result the price (in terms of fees paid to the miners) of the preimage sale transaction is the same as the price for a normal payment. Moreover, censorship is prevented as miners cannot distinguish the transactions belonging to the preimage sale from a standard payment transaction. Hence, point (iii) is fully addressed.

The idea of replacing two signatures by one has already appeared in the literature in the context of payment channels. Namely, Malavolta et al. [30] presented protocols for two-party threshold adaptor signatures based on Schnorr and ECDSA digital signatures. However, they did not present a standalone definition for the threshold primitive and hence security for these schemes has not been analyzed. Furthermore, the key generation of the existing threshold adaptor signature schemes is interactive which is undesirable. Last but not least, their constructions are tailored to Schnorr and ECDSA signature schemes and hence is not generic. From the above points, the following natural question arises:

Is it possible to define and instantiate two-party adaptor signature schemes with non-interactive key generation in a generic way?

1.1 Our Contribution

Our main goal is to define two-party adaptor signatures and explore from which digital signature we can instantiate this new primitive. We proceed in three steps which we summarize below and depict in Fig. 1.

Step 1: From ID Schemes to Adaptor Signatures. Our first goal is to determine if there exists a specific class of signature schemes which can be generically transformed into adaptor signatures. Given the existing Schnorr-based construction [2,37], a natural choice is to explore signature schemes constructed in a similar fashion. To this end, we focus on signature schemes built from identification (ID) schemes using the Fiat-Shamir transform [25]. We show that ID-based signature schemes satisfying certain additional properties can be transformed to adaptor signature schemes generically. In addition to Schnorr signatures [41], this class includes Katz-Wang and Guillou-Quisquater signatures [22,24]. As an additional result, we show that adaptor signatures *cannot* be built from unique signatures, ruling out constructions from, e.g., BLS signatures [9].

Our generic transformation of adaptor signatures from ID schemes has multiple benefits. Firstly, by instantiating it with the Guillou-Quisquater signature scheme, we obtain the first RSA-based adaptor signature scheme. Secondly, since Katz-Wang signatures offers tight security (under the decisional Diffie-Hellman (DDH) assumption), and our generic transformation also achieves tight security, our result shows how to construct adaptor signatures with a tight reduction to the underlying DDH assumption.

Step 2: From ID Schemes to Two-Party Signatures. Our second goal is to generically transform signature schemes built from ID schemes into two-party signature schemes with aggregatable public keys. Unlike threshold signatures, these signatures have non-interactive key generation. This means that parties can independently generate their key pairs and later collaboratively generate signatures that are valid under their *combined* public key. For our transformation, we require the signature scheme to satisfy certain aggregation properties which, as we show, are present in the three aforementioned signature schemes. While this transformation serves as a middle step towards our main goal of constructing two-party adaptor signatures, we believe it is of independent interest.

Step 3: From ID Schemes to Two-Party Adaptor Signatures. Finally, we define two-party adaptor signature schemes with aggregatable public keys. In order to instantiate this novel cryptographic primitive, we use similar techniques as in step 1 where we "lifted" standard signature schemes to adaptor signature schemes. More precisely, we present a transformation turning a two-party signature scheme based on an ID scheme into a two-party adaptor signature scheme.

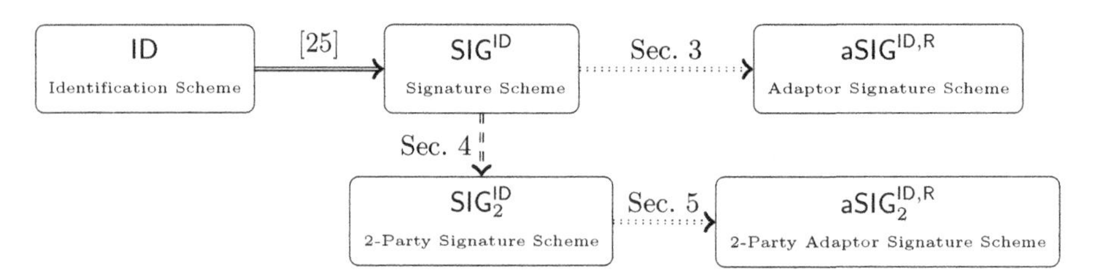

Fig. 1. Overview of our results. Full arrow represents a generic transformation, dotted and dashed arrows represent a generic transformation which requires additional homomorphic or aggregation properties respectively.

Remark 1. Let us point out that Fig. 1 presents our transformation steps from signature schemes based on ID schemes to two-party adaptor signatures.

Despite the fact that we generically construct our two-party adaptor signature scheme from two-party signature schemes based on ID schemes, we reduce its security to the strong unforgeability of the underlying single party signature scheme. Therefore, we do not need the two-party signature scheme from ID schemes to be strongly unforgeable. This gives us a more general result than proving security based on strong unforgeability of the two-party signature scheme from ID schemes. We note that any ID scheme can be transformed to a signature scheme with strong unforgeability by Bellare and Shoup [4].

Let us further mention that our security proofs are in the random oracle model. Proving the security of our constructions and the original constructions from [2] in the standard model remains an interesting open problem.

1.2 Related Work

Adaptor Signatures. The notion of adaptor signatures was first introduced by Poelstra [37] and has since been used in many blockchain related applications, such as PCNs [30], payment channel hubs [43] or atomic swaps [11]. However, the adaptor signatures as a standalone primitive were only formalized later by Aumayr et al. [2], where they were used to generalize the concept of payment channels. Concurrently, Fournier [17] attempted to formalize adaptor signatures, however, as pointed out in [2], his definition is weaker than the one given in [2] and not sufficient for certain applications. All the previously mentioned works constructed adaptor signatures only from Schnorr and ECDSA signatures, i.e., they did not show generic transformations for building adaptor signature schemes. As previously mentioned, a two-party threshold variant of adaptor signatures was presented by Malavolta et al. [30]. Their construction requires interactive key generation, thereby differing from our two-party adaptor signature notion. Moreover, no standalone definition of the threshold primitive was provided.

Two works [15,44] have recently introduced post-quantum secure adaptor signature schemes, i.e., schemes that remain secure even in presence of an adversary having access to a quantum computer. In order to achieve post-quantum security, [15] based its scheme on standard and well-studied lattice assumptions, namely Module-SIS and Module-LWE, while the scheme in [44] is based on lesser known assumptions for isogenies. Both works additionally show how to construct post-quantum secure PCNs from their respective adaptor signature schemes.

Multi-Signatures and ID Schemes. Multi-Signatures have been subject to extensive research in the past (e.g., [23,35,36]). In a nutshell, multi-signatures allow a set of signers to collaboratively generate a signature for a common message such that the signature can be verified given the public key of each signer. More recently, the notion of multi-signatures with aggregatable public keys has been introduced [31] and worked on [8,26], which allows to aggregate the public keys of all signers into one single public key. We use some results from the work of

Kiltz et al. [25], which provides a concrete and modular security analysis of signatures schemes from ID schemes obtained via the Fiat-Shamir transformation. Our paper builds up on their work and uses some of their notation.

2 Preliminaries

In this section, we introduce notation that we use throughout this work and preliminaries on adaptor signatures and identification schemes. Due to space limitations, we provide formal definitions of digital signature schemes, non-interactive zero-knowledge proofs and extractable commitments in the full version of this paper [14].

Notation. We denote by $x \leftarrow_{\$} \mathcal{X}$ the uniform sampling of x from the set $\mathcal{X}$. Throughout this paper, n denotes the security parameter. By $x \leftarrow \mathsf{A}(y)$ we denote a *probabilistic polynomial time* (PPT) algorithm A that on input y, outputs x. When A is a *deterministic polynomial time* (DPT) algorithm, we use the notation $x := \mathsf{A}(y)$. A function $\nu\colon \mathbb{N} \to \mathbb{R}$ is *negligible in* n if for every $k \in \mathbb{N}$, there exists $n_0 \in \mathbb{N}$ s.t. for every $n \geq n_0$ it holds that $|\nu(n)| \leq 1/n^k$.

Hard Relation. Let $\mathsf{R} \subseteq \mathcal{D}_S \times \mathcal{D}_{\mathsf{w}}$ be a relation with statement/witness pairs $(Y, y) \in \mathcal{D}_S \times \mathcal{D}_{\mathsf{w}}$ and let the language $L_{\mathsf{R}} \subseteq \mathcal{D}_S$ associated to R be defined as $L_{\mathsf{R}} := \{Y \in \mathcal{D}_S \mid \exists y \in \mathcal{D}_{\mathsf{w}} \text{ s.t. } (Y, y) \in \mathsf{R}\}$. We say that R is a *hard relation* if: (i) There exists a PPT sampling algorithm $\mathsf{GenR}(1^n)$ that on input the security parameter outputs a pair $(Y, y) \in \mathsf{R}$; (ii) The relation R is poly-time decidable; (iii) For all PPT adversaries $\mathcal{A}$, the probability that $\mathcal{A}$ outputs a valid witness $y \in \mathcal{D}_{\mathsf{w}}$ for $Y \in L_{\mathsf{R}}$ is negligible.

2.1 Adaptor Signatures

We now recall the definition of adaptor signatures, recently put forward in [2].

Definition 1 (Adaptor Signature). *An adaptor signature scheme w.r.t. a hard relation* R *and a signature scheme* $\mathsf{SIG} = (\mathsf{Gen}, \mathsf{Sign}, \mathsf{Vrfy})$ *consists of a tuple of four algorithms* $\mathsf{aSIG}_{\mathsf{R},\mathsf{SIG}} = (\mathsf{pSign}, \mathsf{Adapt}, \mathsf{pVrfy}, \mathsf{Ext})$ *defined as:*

$\mathsf{pSign}_{sk}(m, Y)$*: is a PPT algorithm that on input a secret key sk, message* $m \in \{0,1\}^*$ *and statement* $Y \in L_{\mathsf{R}}$*, outputs a pre-signature* $\widetilde{\sigma}$*.*

$\mathsf{pVrfy}_{pk}(m, Y; \widetilde{\sigma})$*: is a DPT algorithm that on input a public key pk, message* $m \in \{0,1\}^*$*, statement* $Y \in L_{\mathsf{R}}$ *and pre-signature* $\widetilde{\sigma}$*, outputs a bit b.*

$\mathsf{Adapt}_{pk}(\widetilde{\sigma}, y)$*: is a DPT algorithm that on input a pre-signature* $\widetilde{\sigma}$ *and witness* y*, outputs a signature* σ*.*

$\mathsf{Ext}_{pk}(\sigma, \widetilde{\sigma}, Y)$*: is a DPT algorithm that on input a signature* σ*, pre-signature* $\widetilde{\sigma}$ *and statement* $Y \in L_{\mathsf{R}}$*, outputs a witness y such that* $(Y, y) \in \mathsf{R}$*, or* $\perp$*.*

An adaptor signature scheme, besides satisfying plain digital signature correctness, should also satisfy pre-signature correctness that we formalize next.

Definition 2 (Pre-Signature Correctness). *An adaptor signature* $\mathsf{aSIG}_{\mathsf{R,SIG}}$ *satisfies* pre-signature correctness, *if for all* $n \in \mathbb{N}$ *and* $m \in \{0,1\}^*$*:*

$$\Pr\left[\begin{array}{c|l} \mathsf{pVrfy}_{pk}(m, Y; \widetilde{\sigma}) = 1 \wedge & (sk, pk) \leftarrow \mathsf{Gen}(1^n), (Y, y) \leftarrow \mathsf{GenR}(1^n) \\ \mathsf{Vrfy}_{pk}(m; \sigma) = 1 \wedge & \widetilde{\sigma} \leftarrow \mathsf{pSign}_{sk}(m, Y), \sigma := \mathsf{Adapt}_{pk}(\widetilde{\sigma}, y) \\ (Y, y') \in \mathsf{R} & y' := \mathsf{Ext}_{pk}(\sigma, \widetilde{\sigma}, Y) \end{array}\right] = 1.$$

An adaptor signature scheme $\mathsf{aSIG}_{\mathsf{R,SIG}}$ is called *secure* if it satisfies three security properties: *existential unforgeablity under chosen message attack for adaptor signatures, pre-signature adaptability* and *witness extractability.* Let us recall the formal definition of these properties next.

The notion of unforgeability for adaptor signatures is similar to existential unforgeability under chosen message attacks for standard digital signatures but additionally requires that producing a forgery σ for some message m^* is hard even given a pre-signature on m^* w.r.t. a random statement $Y \in L_{\mathsf{R}}$.

Definition 3 (aEUF−CMA Security). *An adaptor signature scheme* $\mathsf{aSIG}_{\mathsf{R,SIG}}$ *is unforgeable if for every PPT adversary* $\mathcal{A}$ *there exists a negligible function* ν *such that:* $\Pr[\mathsf{aSigForge}_{\mathcal{A},\mathsf{aSIG}_{\mathsf{R,SIG}}}(n) = 1] \le \nu(n)$*, where the definition of the experiment* $\mathsf{aSigForge}_{\mathcal{A},\mathsf{aSIG}_{\mathsf{R,SIG}}}$ *is as follows:*

$\mathsf{aSigForge}_{\mathcal{A},\mathsf{aSIG}_{\mathsf{R,SIG}}}(n)$	$\mathcal{O}_{\mathrm{S}}(m)$	$\mathcal{O}_{\mathrm{pS}}(m, Y)$
$1: \mathcal{Q} := \emptyset, (sk, pk) \leftarrow \mathsf{Gen}(1^n)$	$1: \sigma \leftarrow \mathsf{Sign}_{sk}(m)$	$1: \widetilde{\sigma} \leftarrow \mathsf{pSign}_{sk}(m, Y)$
$2: m^* \leftarrow \mathcal{A}^{\mathcal{O}_{\mathrm{S}}, \mathcal{O}_{\mathrm{pS}}}(pk)$	$2: \mathcal{Q} := \mathcal{Q} \cup \{m\}$	$2: \mathcal{Q} := \mathcal{Q} \cup \{m\}$
$3: (Y, y) \leftarrow \mathsf{GenR}(1^n), \widetilde{\sigma} \leftarrow \mathsf{pSign}_{sk}(m^*, Y)$	$3:$ **return** σ	$3:$ **return** $\widetilde{\sigma}$
$4: \sigma^* \leftarrow \mathcal{A}^{\mathcal{O}_{\mathrm{S}}, \mathcal{O}_{\mathrm{pS}}}(\widetilde{\sigma}, Y)$		
$5:$ **return** $(m^* \notin \mathcal{Q} \wedge \mathsf{Vrfy}_{pk}(m^*; \sigma^*))$		

A natural requirement for an adaptor signature scheme is that any valid pre-signature w.r.t. Y (possibly produced by a malicious signer) can be completed into a valid signature using a witness y with $(Y, y) \in \mathsf{R}$.

Definition 4 (Pre-Signature Adaptability). *An adaptor signature scheme* $\mathsf{aSIG}_{\mathsf{SIG,R}}$ *satisfies pre-signature adaptability, if for all* $n \in \mathbb{N}$*, messages* $m \in \{0,1\}^*$*, statement/witness pairs* $(Y, y) \in \mathsf{R}$*, public keys pk and pre-signatures* $\widetilde{\sigma} \leftarrow \{0,1\}^*$ *we have* $\mathsf{pVrfy}_{pk}(m, Y; \widetilde{\sigma}) = 1$*, then* $\mathsf{Vrfy}_{pk}(m; \mathsf{Adapt}_{pk}(\widetilde{\sigma}, y)) = 1$.

The last property that we are interested in is *witness extractability.* Informally, it guarantees that a valid signature/pre-signatue pair $(\sigma, \widetilde{\sigma})$ for message/statement (m, Y) can be used to extract a corresponding witness y.

Definition 5 (Witness Extractability). *An adaptor signature scheme* $\mathsf{aSIG}_{\mathsf{R}}$ *is* witness extractable *if for every PPT adversary* $\mathcal{A}$*, there exists a negligible function* ν *such that the following holds:* $\Pr[\mathsf{aWitExt}_{\mathcal{A},\mathsf{aSIG}_{\mathsf{R,SIG}}}(n) = 1] \le \nu(n)$*, where the experiment* $\mathsf{aWitExt}_{\mathcal{A},\mathsf{aSIG}_{\mathsf{R,SIG}}}$ *is defined as follows:*

$\mathsf{aWitExt}_{\mathcal{A},\mathsf{aSIG}_{\mathsf{R},\mathsf{SIG}}}(n)$	$\mathcal{O}_{\mathrm{S}}(m)$	$\mathcal{O}_{\mathrm{pS}}(m, Y)$
$1: \mathcal{Q} := \emptyset, (sk, pk) \leftarrow \mathsf{Gen}(1^n)$	$1: \sigma \leftarrow \mathsf{Sign}_{sk}(m)$	$1: \widetilde{\sigma} \leftarrow \mathsf{pSign}_{sk}(m, Y)$
$2: (m^*, Y^*) \leftarrow \mathcal{A}^{\mathcal{O}_{\mathrm{S}}, \mathcal{O}_{\mathrm{pS}}}(pk)$	$2: \mathcal{Q} := \mathcal{Q} \cup \{m\}$	$2: \mathcal{Q} := \mathcal{Q} \cup \{m\}$
$3: \widetilde{\sigma} \leftarrow \mathsf{pSign}_{sk}(m^*, Y^*)$	$3:$ **return** σ	$3:$ **return** $\widetilde{\sigma}$
$4: \sigma^* \leftarrow \mathcal{A}^{\mathcal{O}_{\mathrm{S}}, \mathcal{O}_{\mathrm{pS}}}(\widetilde{\sigma})$		
$5: y := \mathsf{Ext}_{pk}(\sigma^*, \widetilde{\sigma}, Y^*)$		
$6:$ **return** $(m^* \notin \mathcal{Q} \wedge (Y^*, y) \notin \mathsf{R} \wedge \mathsf{Vrfy}_{pk}(m^*; \sigma^*))$		

Let us stress that while the witness extractability experiment aWitExt looks fairly similar to the experiment aSigForge, there is one crucial difference; namely, the adversary is allowed to choose the forgery statement Y^*. Hence, we can assume that it knows a witness for Y^* and can thus generate a valid signature on the forgery message m^*. However, this is not sufficient to win the experiment. The adversary wins *only* if the valid signature does not reveal a witness for Y^*.

2.2 Identification and Signature Schemes

In this section we recall the definition of identification schemes and how they are transformed to signature schemes as described in [25].

Definition 6 (Canonical Identification Scheme [25]**).** *A canonical identification scheme* ID *is defined as a tuple of four algorithms* ID := (IGen, P, ChSet, V).

- *The key generation algorithm* IGen *takes the system parameters* par *as input and returns secret and public key* (sk, pk)*. We assume that pk defines the set of challenges, namely* ChSet.
- *The prover algorithm* P *consists of two algorithms namely* P_1 *and* P_2*:*
  - P_1 *takes as input the secret key sk and returns a commitment* $R \in \mathcal{D}_{\mathsf{rand}}$ *and a state St.*
  - P_2 *takes as input the secret key sk, a commitment* $R \in \mathcal{D}_{\mathsf{rand}}$*, a challenge* $h \in \mathsf{ChSet}$*, and a state St and returns a response* $s \in \mathcal{D}_{\mathsf{resp}}$*.*
- *The verifier algorithm* V *is a deterministic algorithm that takes the public key pk and the conversation transcript as input and outputs* 1 *(acceptance) or* 0 *(rejection).*

We require that for all $(sk, pk) \in \mathsf{IGen}(\mathsf{par})$*, all* $(R, St) \in \mathsf{P}_1(sk)$*, all* $h \in \mathsf{ChSet}$ *and all* $s \in \mathsf{P}_2(sk, R, h, St)$*, we have* $\mathsf{V}(pk, R, h, s) = 1$.

We recall that an identification scheme ID is called *commitment-recoverable*, if V first internally calls a function V_0 which recomputes $R_0 = \mathsf{V}_0(pk, h, s)$ and then outputs 1, iff $R_0 = R$. Using Fiat-Shamir heuristic one can transform any identification scheme ID of the above form into a digital signature scheme $\mathsf{SIG}^{\mathsf{ID}}$. We recall this transformation in Fig. 2 when ID is commitment-recoverable.

$\mathsf{Gen}(1^n)$	$\mathsf{Sign}_{sk}(m)$	$\mathsf{Vrfy}_{pk}(m;(h,s))$
$1: (sk, pk) \leftarrow \mathsf{IGen}(n)$	$1: (R, St) \leftarrow \mathsf{P}_1(sk)$	$1: R := \mathsf{V}_0(pk, h, s)$
$2:$ **return** (sk, pk)	$2: h := \mathcal{H}(R, m)$	$2:$ **return** $h = \mathcal{H}(R, m)$
	$3: s \leftarrow \mathsf{P}_2(sk, R, h, St)$	
	$4:$ **return** (h, s)	

Fig. 2. $\mathsf{SIG}^{\mathsf{ID}}$: Digital signature schemes from identification schemes [25]

3 Adaptor Signatures from $\mathsf{SIG}^{\mathsf{ID}}$

Our first goal is to explore and find digital signature schemes which can generically be transformed to adaptor signatures. Interestingly, we observe that both existing adaptor signature schemes, namely the Schnorr-based and the ECDSA-based schemes, utilize the randomness used during signature generation to transform digital signatures to adaptor signatures [2]. We first prove a negative result, namely that it is impossible to construct an adaptor signature scheme from a unique signature scheme [19,29,42]. Thereafter, we focus on signature schemes constructed from identification schemes (cf. Fig. 2) and show that if the underlying ID-based signature scheme $\mathsf{SIG}^{\mathsf{ID}}$ satisfies certain additional properties, then we can generically transform it into an adaptor signature scheme. To demonstrate the applicability of our generic transformation, we show in the full version of this paper [14] that many existing $\mathsf{SIG}^{\mathsf{ID}}$ instantiations satisfy the required properties.

3.1 Impossibility Result for Unique Signatures

An important class of digital signatures are those where the signing algorithm is deterministic and the generated signatures are unique. Given the efficiency of deterministic signature schemes along with numerous other advantages that come from signatures being unique [19,29,42], it would be tempting to design adaptor signatures based on unique signatures. However, we show in Theorem 1 that if the signature scheme has unique signatures, then it is impossible to construct a secure adaptor signature scheme from it.

Theorem 1. *Let* R *be a hard relation and* $\mathsf{SIG} = (\mathsf{Gen}, \mathsf{Sign}, \mathsf{Vrfy})$ *be a signature scheme with unique signatures. Then there does not exist an adaptor signature scheme* $\mathsf{aSIG}_{\mathsf{R},\mathsf{SIG}}$.

Proof. We prove this theorem by contradiction. Assume there exists an adaptor signature scheme where the underlying signature scheme, SIG, has unique signatures. We construct a PPT algorithm $\mathcal{A}$ which internally uses the adaptor signature and breaks the hardness of R. In other words, $\mathcal{A}$ receives $(1^n, Y)$ as input and outputs y, such that $(Y, y) \in \mathsf{R}$. Below, we describe $\mathcal{A}$ formally.

On input $(1^n, Y)$, $\mathcal{A}$ proceeds as follows:

1 : Sample a new key pair $(sk, pk) \leftarrow \mathsf{Gen}(1^n)$.
2 : Choose an arbitrary message m from the signing message space.
3 : Generate a pre-signature, $\widetilde{\sigma} \leftarrow \mathsf{preSign}_{sk}(m, Y)$.
4 : Generate a signature, $\sigma := \mathsf{Sign}_{sk}(m)$.
5 : Compute and output $y := \mathsf{Ext}_{pk}(\sigma, \widetilde{\sigma}, Y)$.

We now show that y returned by $\mathcal{A}$ is indeed a witness of Y, i.e., $(Y, y) \in \mathsf{R}$. From the correctness of the adaptor signature scheme, we know that for any y' s.t. $(Y, y') \in \mathsf{R}$ the signature $\sigma' := \mathsf{Adapt}(\widetilde{\sigma}, y')$ is a valid signature, i.e., $\mathsf{Vrfy}_{pk}(m, \sigma') = 1$. Moreover, we know that $y'' := \mathsf{Ext}_{pk}(\sigma', \widetilde{\sigma}, Y)$ is such that $(Y, y'') \in \mathsf{R}$. As SIG is a unique signature scheme, this implies that $\sigma' = \sigma$ which in turn implies that the witness y returned by $\mathcal{A}$ is y''. Hence, $\mathcal{A}$ breaks the hardness of R with probability 1.

Let us briefly discuss which signature schemes are affected by our impossibility result. Unique signature schemes (also known as verifiable unpredictable functions (VUF)) have been first introduced in [19]. Furthermore, many follow-up works such as [29,32] and most recently [42], have shown how to instantiate this primitive in the standard model. Another famous example of a unique signature scheme is BLS [9]. Naturally, due to our impossibility result, an adaptor signature scheme cannot be instantiated from these signature schemes.

3.2 Generic Transformation to Adaptor Signatures

We now describe how to generically transform a randomized digital signature scheme $\mathsf{SIG}^{\mathsf{ID}}$ from Fig. 2 into an adaptor signature scheme w.r.t. a hard relation R. For brevity, we denote the resulting adaptor signature scheme as $\mathsf{aSIG}^{\mathsf{ID},\mathsf{R}}$ instead of $\mathsf{aSIG}_{\mathsf{R},\mathsf{SIG}^{\mathsf{ID}}}$. The main idea behind our transformation is to *shift* the public randomness of the Sign procedure by a statement Y for the relation R in order to generate a modified signature called a *pre-signature*. Using a corresponding witness y (i.e., $(Y, y) \in \mathsf{R}$), the shift of the public randomness in the pre-signature can be reversed (or adapted), in order to obtain a regular (or full) signature. Moreover, it should be possible to extract a witness given both the pre-signature and the full-signature. To this end, let us formalize three new *deterministic* functions which we will use later in our transformation.

1. For the randomness shift, we define a function $f_{\mathsf{shift}} \colon \mathcal{D}_{\mathsf{rand}} \times L_{\mathsf{R}} \rightarrow \mathcal{D}_{\mathsf{rand}}$ that takes as input a commitment value $R \in \mathcal{D}_{\mathsf{rand}}$ of the identification scheme and a statement $Y \in L_{\mathsf{R}}$ of the hard relation, and outputs a new commitment value $R' \in \mathcal{D}_{\mathsf{rand}}$.
2. For the adapt operation, we define $f_{\mathsf{adapt}} \colon \mathcal{D}_{\mathsf{resp}} \times \mathcal{D}_{\mathsf{w}} \rightarrow \mathcal{D}_{\mathsf{resp}}$ that takes as input a response value $\tilde{s} \in \mathcal{D}_{\mathsf{resp}}$ of the identification scheme and a witness $y \in \mathcal{D}_{\mathsf{w}}$ of the hard relation, and outputs a new response value $s \in \mathcal{D}_{\mathsf{resp}}$.

3. Finally, for witness extraction, we define $f_{\mathsf{ext}}\colon \mathcal{D}_{\mathsf{resp}} \times \mathcal{D}_{\mathsf{resp}} \to \mathcal{D}_{\mathsf{w}}$ that takes as input two response values $\tilde{s}, s \in \mathcal{D}_{\mathsf{resp}}$ and outputs a witness $y \in \mathcal{D}_{\mathsf{w}}$.

Our transformation from $\mathsf{SIG}^{\mathsf{ID}}$ to $\mathsf{aSIG}^{\mathsf{ID,R}}$ is shown in Fig. 3.

$\mathsf{pSign}_{sk}(m, Y)$	$\mathsf{pVrfy}_{pk}(m, Y; (h, \tilde{s}))$	$\mathsf{Adapt}_{pk}((h, \tilde{s}), y)$
$1: (R_{\mathsf{pre}}, St) \leftarrow \mathsf{P}_1(sk)$	$1: \widehat{R}_{\mathsf{pre}} := \mathsf{V}_0(pk, h, \tilde{s})$	$1: s = f_{\mathsf{adapt}}(\tilde{s}, y)$
$2: R_{\mathsf{sign}} := f_{\mathsf{shift}}(R_{\mathsf{pre}}, Y)$	$2: \widehat{R}_{\mathsf{sign}} := f_{\mathsf{shift}}(\widehat{R}_{\mathsf{pre}}, Y)$	$2: \mathbf{return}\ (h, s)$
$3: h := \mathcal{H}(R_{\mathsf{sign}}, m)$	$3: b := (h = \mathcal{H}(\widehat{R}_{\mathsf{sign}}, m))$	$\mathsf{Ext}_{pk}((h, s), (h, \tilde{s}), Y)$
$4: \tilde{s} \leftarrow \mathsf{P}_2(sk, R_{\mathsf{pre}}, h, St)$	$4: \mathbf{return}\ b$	$1: \mathbf{return}\ f_{\mathsf{ext}}(s, \tilde{s})$
$5: \mathbf{return}\ (h, \tilde{s})$		

Fig. 3. Generic transformation from $\mathsf{SIG}^{\mathsf{ID}}$ to a $\mathsf{aSIG}^{\mathsf{ID,R}}$ scheme

$\mathsf{IGen}(n)$	$\mathsf{P}_1(sk)$	$\mathsf{P}_2(sk, R, h, r)$	$\mathsf{V}_0(pk, h, s)$
$1: sk \leftarrow_{\$} \mathbb{Z}_q, pk = g^{sk}$	$1: r \leftarrow_{\$} \mathbb{Z}_q, R = g^r$	$1: s = r + h \cdot sk$	$1: R = g^s \cdot pk^{-h}$
$2: \mathbf{return}\ (sk, pk)$	$2: \mathbf{return}\ (R, r)$	$2: \mathbf{return}\ s$	$2: \mathbf{return}\ (R)$

Fig. 4. Schnorr signature scheme

In order for $\mathsf{aSIG}^{\mathsf{ID,R}}$ to be an adaptor signature scheme, we need the functions f_{shift}, f_{adapt} and f_{ext} to satisfy two properties. The first property is a homomorphic one and relates the functions f_{shift} and f_{adapt} to the commitment-recoverable component V_0 and the hard relation R. Informally, for all $(Y, y) \in \mathsf{R}$, we need the following to be equivalent: (i) Extract the public randomness from a response $\tilde{s}$ using V_0 and then apply f_{shift} to shift the public randomness by Y, and (ii) apply f_{adapt} to shift the *secret* randomness in $\tilde{s}$ by y and then extract the public randomness using V_0. Formally, for any public key pk, any challenge $h \in \mathsf{ChSet}$, any response value $\tilde{s} \in \mathcal{D}_{\mathsf{resp}}$ and any statement/witness pair $(Y, y) \in \mathsf{R}$, it must hold that:

$$f_{\mathsf{shift}}(\mathsf{V}_0(pk, h, \tilde{s}), Y) = \mathsf{V}_0(pk, h, f_{\mathsf{adapt}}(\tilde{s}, y)). \tag{1}$$

The second property requires that the function $f_{\mathsf{ext}}(\tilde{s}, \cdot)$ is the inverse function of $f_{\mathsf{adapt}}(\tilde{s}, \cdot)$ for any $\tilde{s} \in \mathcal{D}_{\mathsf{resp}}$. Formally, for any $y \in \mathcal{D}_{\mathsf{w}}$ and $\tilde{s} \in \mathcal{D}_{\mathsf{resp}}$, we have

$$y = f_{\mathsf{ext}}(f_{\mathsf{adapt}}(\tilde{s}, y), \tilde{s}). \tag{2}$$

To give an intuition about the functions f_{shift}, f_{adapt} and f_{ext} and their purpose, let us discuss their concrete instantiations for Schnorr signatures and show that they satisfy Equations (1) and (2). The instantiations for Katz-Wang signatures and Guillou-Quisquater signatures can be found in the full version of this paper [14].

Example 1 (Schnorr signatures). Let $\mathbb{G} = \langle g \rangle$ be a cyclic group of prime order p where the discrete logarithm problem in $\mathbb{G}$ is hard. The functions IGen, P_1, P_2 and V_0 for Schnorr's signature scheme are defined in Fig. 4.

Let us consider the hard relation $\mathsf{R} = \{(Y, y) \mid Y = g^y\}$, i.e., group elements and their discrete logarithms, and let us define the functions $f_{\mathsf{shift}}, f_{\mathsf{adapt}}, f_{\mathsf{ext}}$ as:

$$f_{\mathsf{shift}}(Y, R) := Y \cdot R, \quad f_{\mathsf{adapt}}(\tilde{s}, y) := \tilde{s} + y, \quad f_{\mathsf{ext}}(s, \tilde{s}) := s - \tilde{s}.$$

Intuitively, the function f_{shift} is *shifting* randomness in the group while the function f_{adapt} *shifts* randomness in the exponent. To prove that Eq. (1) holds, let us fix an arbitrary public key $pk \in \mathbb{G}$, a challenge $h \in \mathbb{Z}_q$, a response value $s \in \mathbb{Z}_q$ and a statement witness pair $(Y, y) \in \mathsf{R}$, i.e., $Y = g^y$. We have

$$\begin{aligned} f_{\mathsf{shift}}(\mathsf{V}_0(pk, h, s), Y) &= f_{\mathsf{shift}}(g^s \cdot pk^{-h}, Y) = g^s \cdot pk^{-h} \cdot Y \\ &= g^{s+y} \cdot pk^{-h} = \mathsf{V}_0(pk, h, s+y) = \mathsf{V}_0(pk, h, f_{\mathsf{adapt}}(s, y)) \end{aligned}$$

which is what we wanted to prove. In order to show that Eq. (2) holds, let us fix an arbitrary witness $y \in \mathbb{Z}_q$ and a response value $s \in \mathbb{Z}_q$. Then we have

$$f_{\mathsf{ext}}(f_{\mathsf{adapt}}(s, y), s) = f_{\mathsf{ext}}(s + y, s) = s + y - s = y$$

and hence Eq. (2) is satisfied as well.

We now show that the transformation from Fig. 3 is a secure adaptor signature scheme if functions $f_{\mathsf{shift}}, f_{\mathsf{adapt}}, f_{\mathsf{ext}}$ satisfying Equations (1) and (2) exist.

Theorem 2. *Assume that* $\mathsf{SIG}^{\mathsf{ID}}$ *is a* $\mathsf{SUF\text{-}CMA}$*-secure signature scheme transformed using Fig. 2, let* $f_{\mathsf{shift}}, f_{\mathsf{adapt}}$ *and* f_{ext} *be functions satisfying the relations from Equations* (1) *and* (2)*, and* R *be a hard relation. Then the resulting* $\mathsf{aSIG}^{\mathsf{ID},\mathsf{R}}$ *scheme from the transformation in Fig. 3 is a secure adaptor signature scheme in the random oracle model.*

In order to prove Theorem 2, we must show that $\mathsf{aSIG}^{\mathsf{ID},\mathsf{R}}$ satisfies *pre-signature correctness*, $\mathsf{aEUF\text{-}CMA}$*security*, *pre-signature adaptability* and *witness extractability* properties described in Definitions 2 to 5 respectively.

Lemma 1. (Pre-Signature Correctness). *Under the assumptions of Theorem 2,* $\mathsf{aSIG}^{\mathsf{ID},\mathsf{R}}$ *satisfies pre-signature correctness as for Definition 2.*

Proof. Let us fix an arbitrary message m and a statement witness pair $(Y, y) \in \mathsf{R}$. Let $(sk, pk) \leftarrow \mathsf{Gen}(1^n)$, $\widetilde{\sigma} \leftarrow \mathsf{pSign}_{sk}(m, Y)$, $\sigma := \mathsf{Adapt}_{pk}(\widetilde{\sigma}, y)$ and $y' := \mathsf{Ext}_{pk}(\sigma, \widetilde{\sigma}, Y)$. From Fig. 3 we know that $\widetilde{\sigma} = (h, \tilde{s})$, $\sigma = (h, s)$ and $y' = f_{\mathsf{ext}}(s, \tilde{s})$, where we have $s := f_{\mathsf{adapt}}(\tilde{s}, y)$, $\tilde{s} \leftarrow \mathsf{P}_2(sk, R_{\mathsf{pre}}, h, St)$, $h := \mathcal{H}(R_{\mathsf{sign}}, m)$, $R_{\mathsf{sign}} := f_{\mathsf{shift}}(R_{\mathsf{pre}}, Y)$ and $(R_{\mathsf{pre}}, St) \leftarrow \mathsf{P}_1(sk)$. We first show $\mathsf{pVrfy}_{pk}(m, Y; \widetilde{\sigma}) = 1$. From completeness of the ID scheme, we know that $\mathsf{V}_0(pk, h, \tilde{s}) = R_{\mathsf{pre}}$. Hence:

$$\mathcal{H}(f_{\mathsf{shift}}(\mathsf{V}_0(pk, h, \tilde{s}), Y), m) = \mathcal{H}(f_{\mathsf{shift}}(R_{\mathsf{pre}}, Y), m) = \mathcal{H}(R_{\mathsf{sign}}, m) = h \quad (3)$$

which is what we needed to prove. We now show that $\mathsf{Vrfy}_{pk}(m;\sigma) = 1$. By Fig. 2, we need to show that $h = \mathcal{H}(\mathsf{V}_0(pk, h, s), m)$. This follows from the property of f_{shift}, f_{adapt} (cf. Eq. (1)) and Eq. (3) as follows:

$$\begin{aligned}\mathcal{H}(\mathsf{V}_0(pk, h, s), m) =& \mathcal{H}(\mathsf{V}_0(pk, h, f_{\mathsf{adapt}}(\tilde{s}, y)), m) \\ \overset{(1)}{=}& \mathcal{H}(f_{\mathsf{shift}}(\mathsf{V}_0(pk, h, \tilde{s}), Y), m) \overset{(3)}{=} h.\end{aligned}$$

Finally, we need to show that $(Y, y') \in \mathsf{R}$. This follows from (2) since:

$$y' = f_{\mathsf{ext}}(s, \tilde{s}) = f_{\mathsf{ext}}(f_{\mathsf{adapt}}(\tilde{s}, y), \tilde{s}) \overset{(2)}{=} y.$$

Lemma 2 (**$\mathsf{aEUF-CMA}$-Security**). *Under the assumptions of Theorem 2, $\mathsf{aSIG}^{\mathsf{ID,R}}$ satisfies the $\mathsf{aEUF-CMA}$ security as for Definition 3.*

Let us give first a high level overview of the proof. Our goal is to provide a reduction such that, given an adversary $\mathcal{A}$ who can win the experiment $\mathsf{aSigForge}_{\mathcal{A},\mathsf{aSIG}^{\mathsf{ID,R}}}$, we can build a simulator who can win the $\mathsf{strongSigForge}$ experiment of the underlying signature or can break the hardness of the relation R. In the first case, we check if $\mathcal{A}$'s forgery σ^* is equal to $\mathsf{Adapt}_{pk}(\widetilde{\sigma}, y)$. If so, we use $\mathcal{A}$ to break the hardness of the relation R by extracting the witness $y = \mathsf{Ext}(\sigma^*, \widetilde{\sigma}, Y)$. Otherwise, $\mathcal{A}$ was able to forge a signature "unrelated" to the pre-signature provided to it. In this case, it is used to win the $\mathsf{strongSigForge}$ experiment. All that remains is to answer $\mathcal{A}$'s signing and pre-signing queries using $\mathsf{strongSigForge}$'s signing queries. This is done by programming the random oracle such that the full-signatures generated by the challenger in the $\mathsf{strongSigForge}$ game look like pre-signatures for $\mathcal{A}$.

Proof. We prove the lemma by defining a series of game hops. The modifications for each game hop is presented in code form in the full version of this paper [14].

Game G_0: This game is the original $\mathsf{aSigForge}$ experiment, where the adversary $\mathcal{A}$ outputs a valid forgery σ^* for a message m of its choice, while having access to pre-signing and signing oracles $\mathcal{O}_{\mathrm{pS}}$ and $\mathcal{O}_{\mathrm{S}}$ respectively. Being in the random oracle model, all the algorithms of the scheme and the adversary have access to the random oracle $\mathcal{H}$. Since G_0 corresponds to $\mathsf{aSigForge}$, it follows that $\Pr[\mathsf{aSigForge}_{\mathcal{A},\mathsf{aSIG}^{\mathsf{ID,R}}}(n) = 1] = \Pr[G_0 = 1]$.

Game G_1: This game works as G_0 except when the adversary outputs a forgery σ^*, the game checks if adapting the pre-signature $\widetilde{\sigma}$ using the secret witness y results in σ^*. If so, the game aborts.

Claim. Let Bad_1 be the event where G_1 aborts. Then $\Pr[\mathsf{Bad}_1] \leq \nu_1(n)$, where ν_1 is a negligible function in n.

Proof: This claim is proven by a reduction to the relation R. We construct a simulator $\mathcal{S}$ which breaks the hardness of R using $\mathcal{A}$ that causes G_1 to abort with non-negligible probability. The simulator receives a challenge Y^*, and generates a key pair $(sk, pk) \leftarrow \mathsf{Gen}(1^n)$ in order to simulate $\mathcal{A}$'s queries to the oracles $\mathcal{H}$, $\mathcal{O}_{\mathrm{pS}}$ and $\mathcal{O}_{\mathrm{S}}$. This simulation of the oracles work as described in $\boldsymbol{G_1}$.

Upon receiving the challenge message m^* from $\mathcal{A}$, $\mathcal{S}$ computes a pre-signature $\widetilde{\sigma} \leftarrow \mathsf{pSign}_{sk}(m^*, Y^*)$ and returns the pair $(\widetilde{\sigma}, Y)$ to the adversary. Upon $\mathcal{A}$ outputting a forgery σ^* and assuming that Bad_1 happened (i.e., $\mathsf{Adapt}(\widetilde{\sigma}, y) = \sigma$), pre-signature correctness (Definition 2) implies that the simulator can extract y^* by executing $\mathsf{Ext}(\sigma^*, \widetilde{\sigma}, Y^*)$ in order to obtain $(Y^*, y^*) \in \mathsf{R}$.

We note that the view of $\mathcal{A}$ in this simulation and in $\boldsymbol{G_1}$ are indistinguishable, since the challenge Y^* is an instance of the hard relation R and has the same distribution to the public output of GenR. Therefore, the probability that $\mathcal{S}$ breaks the hardness of R is equal to the probability that the event Bad_1 happens. Hence, we conclude that Bad_1 only happens with negligible probability. ■

Since games $\boldsymbol{G_1}$ and $\boldsymbol{G_0}$ are equivalent except if event Bad_1 occurs, it holds that $\Pr[\boldsymbol{G_0} = 1] \leq \Pr[\boldsymbol{G_1} = 1] + \nu_1(n)$.

Game $\boldsymbol{G_2}$: This game is similar to the previous game except for a modification in the $\mathcal{O}_{\mathrm{pS}}$ oracle. After the execution of $\mathsf{preSign}_{sk}$, the oracle obtains a pre-signature $\widetilde{\sigma}$ from which it extracts the randomness $R_{\mathsf{pre}} \leftarrow \mathsf{V}_0(pk, \widetilde{\sigma})$. The oracle computes $R_{\mathsf{sign}} = f_{\mathsf{shift}}(R_{\mathsf{pre}}, Y)$ and checks if $\mathcal{H}$ was already queried on the inputs $R_{\mathsf{pre}} \| m$ or $R_{\mathsf{sign}} \| m$ *before* the execution of pSign_{sk}. In this case the game aborts.

Claim. Let Bad_2 be the event that $\boldsymbol{G_2}$ aborts in $\mathcal{O}_{\mathrm{pS}}$. Then $\Pr[\mathsf{Bad}_2] \leq \nu_2(n)$, where ν_2 is a negligible function in n.

Proof: We first recall that the output of P_1 (i.e., R_{pre}) is uniformly random from a super-polynomial set of size q in the security parameter. From this it follows that R_{sign} is distributed uniformly at random in the same set. Furthermore, $\mathcal{A}$ being a PPT algorithm, it can only make polynomially many queries to $\mathcal{H}$, $\mathcal{O}_{\mathrm{S}}$ and $\mathcal{O}_{\mathrm{pS}}$ oracles. Denoting ℓ as the total number of queries to $\mathcal{H}$, $\mathcal{O}_{\mathrm{S}}$ and $\mathcal{O}_{\mathrm{pS}}$, we have: $\Pr[\mathsf{Bad}_2] = \Pr[H'[R_{\mathsf{pre}} \| m] \neq \bot \vee H'[R_{\mathsf{sign}} \| m] \neq \bot] \leq 2\frac{\ell}{q} \leq \nu_2(n)$. This follows from the fact that ℓ is polynomial in the security parameter. ■

Since games $\boldsymbol{G_2}$ and $\boldsymbol{G_1}$ are identical except in the case where Bad_2 occurs, it holds that $\Pr[\boldsymbol{G_1} = 1] \leq \Pr[\boldsymbol{G_2} = 1] + \nu_2(n)$.

Game $\boldsymbol{G_3}$: In this game, upon a query to the $\mathcal{O}_{\mathrm{pS}}$, the game produces a full-signature instead of a pre-signature by executing Sign_{sk} instead of $\mathsf{preSign}_{sk}$. Accordingly, it programs the random oracle $\mathcal{H}$ to make the full-signature "look like" a pre-signature from the point of view of the adversary $\mathcal{A}$. This is done by:

1. It sets $\mathcal{H}(R_{\mathsf{pre}} \| m)$ to the value stored at position $\mathcal{H}(R_{\mathsf{sign}} \| m)$.
2. It sets $\mathcal{H}(R_{\mathsf{sign}} \| m)$ to a fresh value chosen uniformly at random.

The above programming makes sense as our definition of f_{shift} requires it to be deterministic and to possess the same domain and codomain with respect to the commitment set $\mathcal{D}_{\mathsf{rand}}$. Note further that $\mathcal{A}$ can only notice that $\mathcal{H}$ was programmed if it was previously queried on either $R_{\mathsf{pre}} \| m$ or $R_{\mathsf{sign}} \| m$. But as described in the previous game, we abort if such an event happens. Hence, we have that $\Pr[\boldsymbol{G_2} = 1] = \Pr[\boldsymbol{G_3} = 1]$.

Game G_4: In this game, we impose new checks during the challenge phase that are same as the ones imposed in G_2 during the execution of $\mathcal{O}_{\mathrm{pS}}$.

Claim. Let Bad_3 be the event that G_4 aborts in the challenge phase. Then $\Pr[\mathsf{Bad}_3] \leq \nu_3(n)$, where ν_3 is a negligible function in n.

Proof: The proof is identical to the proof in G_2. ■

It follows that $\Pr[G_4 = 1] \leq \Pr[G_3 = 1] + \nu_3(n)$.

Game G_5: Similar to game G_3, we generate a signature instead of a pre-signature in the challenge phase and program $\mathcal{H}$ such that the full-signature looks like a correct pre-signature from $\mathcal{A}$'s point of view. We get $\Pr[G_5 = 1] = \Pr[G_4 = 1]$.

Now that the transition from the original aSigForge experiment (game G_0) to game G_5 is indistinguishable, it only remains to show the existence of a simulator $\mathcal{S}$ that can perfectly simulate G_5 and uses $\mathcal{A}$ to win the strongSigForge game. The modifications from games G_1 - G_5 and the simulation in code form can be found in the full version of this paper [14].

We emphasize that the main differences between the simulation and Game G_5 are syntactical. Namely, instead of generating the public and secret keys and computing the algorithm Sign_{sk} and the random oracle $\mathcal{H}$, $\mathcal{S}$ uses its oracles $\mathsf{SIG}^{\mathsf{ID}}$ and $\mathcal{H}^{\mathsf{ID}}$. Therefore, $\mathcal{S}$ perfectly simulates G_5. It remains to show that $\mathcal{S}$ can use the forgery output by $\mathcal{A}$ to win the strongSigForge game.

Claim. (m^*, σ^*) constitutes a valid forgery in game strongSigForge.

Proof: To prove this claim, we show that the tuple (m^*, σ^*) has not been returned by the oracle $\mathsf{SIG}^{\mathsf{ID}}$ before. First note that $\mathcal{A}$ wins the experiment if it has not queried on the challenge message m^* to $\mathcal{O}_{\mathrm{pS}}$ or $\mathcal{O}_{\mathrm{S}}$. Therefore, $\mathsf{SIG}^{\mathsf{ID}}$ is queried on m^* only during the challenge phase. If $\mathcal{A}$ outputs a forgery σ^* that is equal to the signature σ as output by $\mathsf{SIG}^{\mathsf{ID}}$, it would lose the game since this signature is not valid given the fact that $\mathcal{H}$ is programmed.

Hence, $\mathsf{SIG}^{\mathsf{ID}}$ has never output σ^* when queried on m^* before, thus making (m^*, σ^*) a valid forgery for game strongSigForge. ■

From games $G_0 - G_5$, we have that $\Pr[G_0 = 1] \leq \Pr[G_5 = 1] + \nu(n)$, where $\nu(n) = \nu_1(n) + \nu_2(n) + \nu_3(n)$ is a negligible function in n. Since $\mathcal{S}$ simulates game G_5 perfectly, we also have that $\Pr[G_5 = 1] = \Pr[\mathsf{strongSigForge}_{\mathcal{S}^{\mathcal{A}},\mathsf{SIG}}(n) = 1]$. Combining this with the probability statement in G_0, we obtain the following:

$\Pr[\mathsf{aSigForge}_{\mathcal{A},\mathsf{aSIG}^{\mathsf{ID},\mathsf{R}}}(n) = 1] \leq \Pr[\mathsf{strongSigForge}_{\mathcal{S}^{\mathcal{A}},\mathsf{SIG}^{\mathsf{ID}}}(n) = 1] + \nu(n)$.

Recall that the negligible function $\nu_1(n)$, contained in the sum $\nu(n)$ above, precisely quantifies the adversary's advantage in breaking the hard relation R. Thus, the probability of breaking the unforgeability of the $\mathsf{aSIG}^{\mathsf{ID},\mathsf{R}}$ is clearly bounded above by that of breaking either R or the strong unforgeability of $\mathsf{SIG}^{\mathsf{ID}}$.

Lemma 3 (Pre-Signature Adaptability). *Under the assumptions of Theorem 2,* $\mathsf{aSIG}^{\mathsf{ID},\mathsf{R}}$ *satisfies the pre-signature adaptability as for Definition 4.*

Proof. Assume $\mathsf{pVrfy}_{pk}(m, Y; \tilde{\sigma}) = 1$, with the notations having their usual meanings from Fig. 3, which means $h = \mathcal{H}(f_{\mathsf{shift}}(\mathsf{V}_0(pk, h, \tilde{s}), Y), m)$. For any valid pair $(Y, y) \in R$, we can use the homomorphic property from Eq. (1). Then, for such a pair $(Y, y) \in R$, plugging $f_{\mathsf{shift}}(\mathsf{V}_0(pk, h, \tilde{s}), Y) = \mathsf{V}_0(pk, h, f_{\mathsf{adapt}}(\tilde{s}, y))$ in the above equation implies $h = \mathcal{H}(\mathsf{V}_0(pk, h, f_{\mathsf{adapt}}(\tilde{s}, y)), m)$. This directly implies $\mathsf{Vrfy}_{pk}(m; \sigma) = 1$, where $s = f_{\mathsf{adapt}}(\tilde{s}, y)$ and $\sigma = (h, s)$. Therefore, adapting the valid pre-signature would also result in a valid full-signature.

Lemma 4 (Witness Extractability). *Under the assumptions of Theorem 2,* $\mathsf{aSIG}^{\mathsf{ID},\mathsf{R}}$ *satisfies the witness extractability as for Definition 5.*

This proof is very similar to the proof of Lemma 2 with the mere difference that we only need to provide a reduction to the $\mathsf{strongSigForge}$ experiment. This is because in the $\mathsf{aWitExt}_{\mathcal{A},\mathsf{aSIG}_{R_g,\mathsf{SIG}^{\mathsf{ID}}}}$ experiment, $\mathcal{A}$ provides the public value Y^* and must forge a valid full-signature σ^* such that $(Y^*, \mathsf{Ext}_{pk}(\sigma^*, \widetilde{\sigma}, Y^*)) \notin \mathsf{R}$. The full proof can be found in the full version of this paper [14].

Remark 2. We note that our proofs for the $\mathsf{aEUF{-}CMA}$ security and witness extractability are in its essence reductions to the strong unforgeability of the underlying signature schemes. Yet the Fiat-Shamir transformation does not immediately guarantee the resulting signature scheme to be strongly unforgeable. However, we first note that many such signature schemes are indeed strongly unforgeable, for instance Schnorr [25], Katz-Wang (from Chaum-Pedersen identification scheme) [24] and Guillou-Quisquater [1] signature schemes all satisfy strong unforgeability. Moreover, one can transform any Fiat-Shamir based existentially unforgeable signature scheme into a strongly unforgeable one via the generic transformation using the results of Bellare et.al. [4].

4 Two-Party Signatures with Aggregatable Public Keys from Identification Schemes

Before providing our definition and generic transformation for two-party adaptor signatures, we show how to generically transform signature schemes based on identification schemes into two-party signature schemes with aggregatable public keys denoted by SIG_2. In Sect. 5, we then combine the techniques used in this section with the ones from Sect. 3 in order to generically transform identification schemes into two-party adaptor signature schemes.

Informally, a SIG_2 scheme allows two parties to jointly generate a signature which can be verified under their combined public keys. An application of such signature schemes can be found in cryptocurrencies where two parties wish to only allow conditional payments such that both users have to sign a transaction in order to spend some funds. Using SIG_2, instead of submitting two separate signatures, the parties can submit a single signature while enforcing the same condition (i.e., a transaction must have a valid signature under the combined key) and hence reduce the communication necessary with the blockchain. Importantly and unlike threshold signature schemes, the key generation here is non-interactive. In other words, parties generate their public and secret keys independently and anyone who knows both public keys can compute the joint public key of the two parties.

We use the notation $\Pi_{\mathsf{Func}\langle x_i, x_{1-i}\rangle}$ to represent a two-party interactive protocol Func between P_i and P_{1-i} with respective secret inputs x_i, x_{1-i} for $i \in \{0,1\}$. Furthermore, if there are common public inputs e.g., $y_1, \cdots, y_n$ we use the notation $\Pi_{\mathsf{Func}\langle x_i, x_{1-i}\rangle}(y_1, \cdots, y_n)$. We note that the execution of a protocol might not be symmetric, i.e., party $\mathcal{P}_i$ executes the procedures $\Pi_{\mathsf{Func}\langle x_i, x_{1-i}\rangle}$ while party $\mathcal{P}_{1-i}$ executes the procedures $\Pi_{\mathsf{Func}\langle x_{1-i}, x_i\rangle}$.

4.1 Two-Party Signatures with Aggregatable Public Keys

We start with defining a two-party signature scheme with aggregatable public keys. Our definition is inspired by the definitions from prior works [7,8,26].

Definition 7 (Two-Party Signature with Aggregatable Public Keys). *A two-party signature scheme with aggregatable public keys is a tuple of PPT protocols and algorithms* $\mathsf{SIG}_2 = (\mathsf{Setup}, \mathsf{Gen}, \Pi_{\mathsf{Sign}}, \mathsf{KAg}, \mathsf{Vrfy})$, *formally defined as:*

$\mathsf{Setup}(1^n)$: *is a PPT algorithm that on input a security parameter n, outputs public parameters pp.*

$\mathsf{Gen}(pp)$: *is a PPT algorithm that on input public parameter pp, outputs a key pair (sk, pk).*

$\Pi_{\mathsf{Sign}\langle sk_i, sk_{1-i}\rangle}(pk_0, pk_1, m)$: *is an interactive, PPT protocol that on input secret keys sk_i from party $\mathcal{P}_i$ with $i \in \{0,1\}$ and common values $m \in \{0,1\}^*$ and pk_0, pk_1, outputs a signature σ.*

$\mathsf{KAg}(pk_0, pk_1)$: *is a DPT algorithm that on input two public keys pk_0, pk_1, outputs an aggregated public key apk.*

$\mathsf{Vrfy}_{apk}(m; \sigma)$: *is a DPT algorithm that on input public parameters pp, a public key apk, a message $m \in \{0,1\}^*$ and a signature σ, outputs a bit b.*

The *completeness* property of SIG_2 guarantees that if the protocol Π_{Sign} is executed correctly between the two parties, the resulting signature is a valid signature under the aggregated public key.

Definition 8 (Completeness). *A two-party signature with aggregatable public keys SIG_2 satisfies completeness, if for all key pairs $(sk, pk) \leftarrow \mathsf{Gen}(1^n)$ and messages $m \in \{0,1\}^*$, the protocol $\Pi_{\mathsf{Sign}\langle sk_i, sk_{1-i}\rangle}(pk_0, pk_1, m)$ outputs a signature σ to both parties $\mathcal{P}_0, \mathcal{P}_1$ such that $\mathsf{Vrfy}_{apk}(m; \sigma) = 1$ where $apk := \mathsf{KAg}(pk_0, pk_1)$.*

A two-party signature scheme with aggregatable public keys should satisfy *unforgeability*. At a high level, this property guarantees that if one of the two parties is malicious, this party is not able to produce a valid signature under the aggregated public key without cooperation of the other party. We formalize the property through an experiment $\mathsf{SigForge}^b_{\mathcal{A},\mathsf{SIG}_2}$, where $b \in \{0,1\}$ defines which of the two parties is corrupt. This experiment is initialized by a security parameter n and run between a challenger $\mathcal{C}$ and an adversary $\mathcal{A}$, which proceeds as follows. The challenger first generates the public parameters pp by running the setup procedure $\mathsf{Setup}(1^n)$ as well as a signing key pair (sk_{1-b}, pk_{1-b}) by executing

$\mathsf{Gen}(1^n)$, thereby simulating the honest party $\mathcal{P}_{1-b}$. Thereafter, $\mathcal{C}$ forwards pp_{C} and pk_{1-b} to the adversary $\mathcal{A}$ who generates its own key pair (sk_b, pk_b), thereby emulating the malicious party P_b, and submits (sk_b, pk_b) to $\mathcal{C}$. The adversary $\mathcal{A}$ additionally obtains access to an *interactive* and stateful signing oracle $\mathcal{O}^b_{\Pi_{\mathsf{S}}}$, which simulates the honest party $\mathcal{P}_{1-b}$ during the execution of $\Pi^{\mathcal{A}}_{\mathsf{Sign}\langle sk_{1-b},\cdot\rangle}$. Furthermore, every queried message m is stored in a query list $\mathcal{Q}$.

Eventually, $\mathcal{A}$ outputs a forgery in form of a $\mathsf{SIG}_2^{\mathsf{ID}}$ signature σ^* and a message m^*. $\mathcal{A}$ wins the experiment if σ^* is a valid signature for m^* under the aggregated public key $apk := \mathsf{KAg}(pk_0, pk_1)$ and m^* was never queried before, i.e., $m^* \notin \mathcal{Q}$. Below, we give a formal definition of the unforgeability game.

Definition 9 (2-EUF−CMASecurity). *A two-party, public key aggregatable signature scheme* SIG_2 *is unforgeable if for every PPT adversary* $\mathcal{A}$*, there exists a negligible function* ν *such that: for* $b \in \{0,1\}$*,* $\Pr[\mathsf{SigForge}^b_{\mathcal{A},\mathsf{SIG}_2}(n) = 1] \leq \nu(n)$*, where the experiment* $\mathsf{SigForge}^b_{\mathcal{A},\mathsf{SIG}_2}(n)$ *is defined as follows:*

$\mathsf{SigForge}^b_{\mathcal{A},\mathsf{SIG}_2}(n)$	$\mathcal{O}^b_{\Pi_{\mathsf{S}}}(m)$
$1: \mathcal{Q} := \emptyset, pp \leftarrow \mathsf{Setup}(1^n)$	$1: \mathcal{Q} := \mathcal{Q} \cup \{m\}$
$2: (sk_{1-b}, pk_{1-b}) \leftarrow \mathsf{Gen}(pp)$	$2: \sigma \leftarrow \Pi^{\mathcal{A}}_{\mathsf{Sign}\langle sk_{1-b},\cdot\rangle}(pk_0, pk_1, m)$
$3: (sk_b, pk_b) \leftarrow \mathcal{A}(pp, pk_{1-b})$	
$4: (\sigma^*, m^*) \leftarrow \mathcal{A}^{\mathcal{O}^b_{\Pi_{\mathsf{S}}}(\cdot)}(pk_{1-b}, sk_b, pk_b)$	
$5:$ **return** $\left(m^* \notin \mathcal{Q} \wedge \mathsf{Vrfy}_{\mathsf{KAg}(pk_0,pk_1)}(m^*; \sigma^*)\right)$	

Remark 3 (On Security Definition). There are two different approaches for modeling signatures with aggregatable public keys in the literature, namely the plain public-key model [3] (also known as key-verification model [12]) and the knowledge-of-secret-key (KOSK) model [7]. In the plain public-key setting the adversary chooses a key pair (sk_b, pk_b) and only declares the public key pk_b to the challenger in the security game. However, security proofs in this setting typically require rewinding techniques with the forking lemma. This is undesirable for the purpose of this paper, as we aim to construct adaptor signatures and its two-party variant generically as building blocks for further applications such as payment channels [2]. Payment channels are proven secure in the UC framework that does not allow the use of rewinding techniques in order to ensure concurrency. Thus, the plain public-key model does not seem suitable for our purpose. In the KOSK setting, however, the adversary outputs its (possibly maliciously chosen) key pair (sk_b, pk_b) to the challenger. In practice this means that the parties need to exchange zero-knowledge proofs of knowledge of their secret key[1]. Similar to previous works [7,28], we do not require the forking lemma or rewinding in the KOSK setting and hence follow this approach.

[1] Using techniques from [16,20] it is possible to obtain NIZKs which allow for witness extraction without rewinding.

4.2 Generic Transformation from $\mathsf{SIG}^{\mathsf{ID}}$ to $\mathsf{SIG}_2^{\mathsf{ID}}$

We now give a generic transformation from $\mathsf{SIG}^{\mathsf{ID}}$ schemes to two-party signature schemes with aggregatable public keys.

At a high level, our transformation turns the signing procedure into an interactive protocol which is executed between the two parties $\mathcal{P}_0, \mathcal{P}_1$. The main idea is to let both parties engage in a randomness exchange protocol in order to generate a joint public randomness which can then be used for the signing procedure. In a bit more detail, to create a joint signature, each party $\mathcal{P}_i$ for $i \in \{0, 1\}$ can individually create a partial signature with respect to the *joint randomness* by using the secret key sk_i and exchange her partial signature with $\mathcal{P}_{1-i}$. The joint randomness ensures that both partial signatures can be combined to one jointly computed signature.

In the following, we describe the randomness exchange protocol that is executed during the signing procedure in more detail, as our transformation heavily relies on it. The protocol, denoted by $\Pi_{\mathsf{Rand\text{-}Exc}}$, makes use of two cryptographic building blocks, namely an extractable commitment scheme $\mathsf{C} = (\mathsf{Gen}, \mathsf{Com}, \mathsf{Dec}, \mathsf{Extract})$ and a NIZK proof system $\mathsf{NIZK} = (\mathsf{Setup_R}, \mathsf{Prove}, \mathsf{Verify})$. Consequently, the common input to both parties $\mathcal{P}_0$ and $\mathcal{P}_1$ are the public parameters pp_{C} of the commitment scheme, while each party P_i takes as secret input her secret key sk_i. In the following, we give description of the $\Pi_{\mathsf{Rand\text{-}Exc}\langle sk_0, sk_1\rangle}(pp_{\mathsf{C}}, \mathsf{crs})$ protocol and present it in a concise way in Fig. 5.

$\mathcal{P}_0(pp_{\mathsf{C}}, \mathsf{crs}, sk_0)$		$\mathcal{P}_1(pp_{\mathsf{C}}, \mathsf{crs}, sk_1)$
$(R_0, St_0) \leftarrow \mathsf{P}_1(sk_0)$		
$\pi_0 \leftarrow \mathsf{NIZK.Prove}(\mathsf{crs}, R_0, sk_0)$		
$(c, d) \leftarrow \mathsf{C.Com}(pp_{\mathsf{C}}, (R_0, \pi_0))$	$\xrightarrow{c}$	$(R_1, St_1) \leftarrow \mathsf{P}_1(sk_1)$
	$\xleftarrow{R_1, \pi_1}$	$\pi_1 \leftarrow \mathsf{NIZK.Prove}(\mathsf{crs}, R_1, sk_1)$
	$\xrightarrow{d}$	$R_0' \leftarrow \mathsf{C.Dec}(pp_{\mathsf{C}}, c, d)$
If $\mathsf{NIZK.Verify}(\mathsf{crs}, R_1, \pi_1) = 0$, then abort		If $\mathsf{NIZK.Verify}(\mathsf{crs}, R_0', \pi_0) = 0$, then abort
R_0, St_0, R_1		R_1, St_1, R_0

Fig. 5. $\Pi_{\mathsf{Rand\text{-}Exc}}$ Protocol

1. Party $\mathcal{P}_0$ generates her public randomness R_0 using algorithm P_1 from the underlying ID scheme alongside a NIZK proof $\pi_0 \leftarrow \mathsf{NIZK.Prove}(\mathsf{crs}, R_0, sk_0)$ that this computation was executed correctly with the corresponding secret value sk_0. $\mathcal{P}_0$ executes $(c, d) \leftarrow \mathsf{C.Com}(pp, (R_0, \pi_0))$ to commit to R_0 and π_0 and sends the commitment c to $\mathcal{P}_1$.
2. Upon receiving the commitment c from $\mathcal{P}_0$, party $\mathcal{P}_1$ generates her public randomness R_1 using algorithm P_1. She also computes a NIZK proof as $\pi_1 \leftarrow \mathsf{NIZK.Prove}(\mathsf{crs}, R_1, sk_1)$, which proves correct computation of R_1, and sends R_1 and π_1 to $\mathcal{P}_0$.
3. Upon receiving R_1 and π_1 from $\mathcal{P}_1$, $\mathcal{P}_0$ sends the opening d to her commitment c to $\mathcal{P}_1$.

4. $\mathcal{P}_1$ opens the commitment in this round. At this stage, both parties check that the received zero-knowledge proofs are valid. If the proofs are valid, each party $\mathcal{P}_i$ for $i \in \{0,1\}$ outputs R_i, St_i, R_{1-i}.

Our transformation can be found in Fig. 6. Note that we use a deterministic function $f_{\mathsf{com\text{-}rand}}(\cdot,\cdot)$ in step 3 in the signing protocol which combines the two public random values R_0 and R_1. In step 6 of the same protocol, we assume that the partial signatures are exchanged between the parties via the protocol Π_{Exchange} upon which the parties can combine them using a deterministic function $f_{\mathsf{com\text{-}sig}}(\cdot,\cdot)$ in step 7. Further, a combined signature can be verified under a combined public key of the two parties. In more detail, to verify a combined signature $(h,s) := f_{\mathsf{com\text{-}sig}}(h,(s_0,s_1))$, in step 7, there must exist an additional deterministic function $f_{\mathsf{com\text{-}pk}}(\cdot,\cdot)$ (in step 1 of the KAg algorithm) such that:

$\mathsf{Setup}(1^n)$	$\Pi_{\mathsf{Sign}\langle sk_i, sk_{1-i}\rangle}(pk_i, pk_{1-i}, m)$
$1: pp_{\mathsf{C}} \leftarrow \mathsf{C.Gen}(1^n)$	$1:$ Parse $pk_i = ((1^n, pp_{\mathsf{C}}, \mathsf{crs}), pk_i')$
$2: \mathsf{crs} \leftarrow \mathsf{NIZK.Setup_R}(1^n)$	$2: (R_i, St_i, R_{1-i}) \leftarrow \Pi_{\mathsf{Rand\text{-}Exc}\langle sk_i, sk_{1-i}\rangle}(pp_{\mathsf{C}}, \mathsf{crs})$
$3:$ **return** $pp := (1^n, pp_{\mathsf{C}}, \mathsf{crs})$	$3: R_{\mathsf{sign}} := f_{\mathsf{com\text{-}rand}}(R_0, R_1)$
$\mathsf{Gen}(pp)$	$4: h := \mathcal{H}(R_{\mathsf{sign}}, m)$
$1:$ Parse $pp = (1^n, pp_{\mathsf{C}}, \mathsf{crs})$	$5: s_i \leftarrow \mathsf{P}_2(sk_i, R_i, h, St_i)$
$2: (sk, pk') \leftarrow \mathsf{IGen}(n)$	$6: s_{1-i} \leftarrow \Pi_{\mathsf{Exchange}}\langle s_i, s_{1-i}\rangle$
$3: pk := (pp, pk')$	$7: (h, s) := f_{\mathsf{com\text{-}sig}}(h, (s_0, s_1))$
$4:$ **return** (sk, pk)	$8:$ **return** (h, s)
$\mathsf{KAg}(pk_0, pk_1)$	$\mathsf{Vrfy}_{apk}(m; (h, s))$
$1: apk := f_{\mathsf{com\text{-}pk}}(pk_0, pk_1)$	$1: R_{\mathsf{sign}} := \mathsf{V}_0(apk, h, s)$
$2:$ **return** apk	$2:$ **return** $h := \mathcal{H}(R_{\mathsf{sign}}, m)$

Fig. 6. $\mathsf{SIG}_2^{\mathsf{ID}}$: SIG_2 scheme from identification scheme.

$$\Pr\left[\mathsf{Vrfy}_{apk}(m;(h,s)) = 1 \;\middle|\; \begin{array}{l} (pk_0, sk_0) \leftarrow \mathsf{IGen}(n), (pk_1, sk_1) \leftarrow \mathsf{IGen}(n) \\ (h,s) \leftarrow \Pi_{\mathsf{Sign}\langle sk_0, sk_1\rangle}(pk_0, pk_1, m) \\ apk := f_{\mathsf{com\text{-}pk}}(pk_0, pk_1) \end{array}\right] = 1. \tag{4}$$

We also require that given a full signature and a secret key sk_i with $i \in \{0,1\}$, it is possible to extract a valid partial signature under the the public key pk_{1-i} of the other party. In particular, there exists a function $f_{\mathsf{dec\text{-}sig}}(\cdot,\cdot,\cdot)$ such that:

$$\Pr\left[\mathsf{Vrfy}_{pk_{1-i}}(m;(h,s_{1-i})) = 1 \;\middle|\; \begin{array}{l} (pk_0, sk_0) \leftarrow \mathsf{IGen}(n), (pk_1, sk_1) \leftarrow \mathsf{IGen}(n) \\ (h,s) \leftarrow \Pi_{\mathsf{Sign}\langle sk_0, sk_1\rangle}(pk_0, pk_1, m) \\ (h, s_{1-i}) := f_{\mathsf{dec\text{-}sig}}(sk_i, pk_i, (h,s)) \end{array}\right] = 1. \tag{5}$$

Note that Eqs. 4 and 5 implicitly define $f_{\mathsf{com\text{-}sig}}$ through the execution of Π_{Sign} in the conditional probabilities.

The instantiations of these functions for Schnorr, Katz-Wang signatures and Guillou-Quisquater signatures can be found in the full version of this paper [14].

We note the similarity between this transformation with that in Fig. 3. In particular, both of them compute the public randomness R_{sign} by shifting the original random values. Note also that running the algorithm V_0 on the inputs (pk_i, h, s_i) would return $R_i, \forall i \in \{0, 1\}$.

Below, we show that the transformation in Fig. 6 provides a secure two-party signature with aggregatable public keys. To this end, we show that $\mathsf{SIG}_2^{\mathsf{ID}}$ satisfies SIG_2 *completeness* and *unforgeability* from Definitions 8 and 9, respectively.

Theorem 3. *Assume that* $\mathsf{SIG}^{\mathsf{ID}}$ *is a signature scheme based on the transformation from an identification scheme as per Fig. 2. Further, assume that the functions* $f_{\mathsf{com\text{-}sig}}$, $f_{\mathsf{com\text{-}pk}}$ *and* $f_{\mathsf{dec\text{-}sig}}$ *satisfy the relations, Equations* (4) *and* (5) *respectively. Then the resulting* $\mathsf{SIG}_2^{\mathsf{ID}}$ *scheme from the transformation in Fig. 6 is a secure two-party signature scheme with aggregatable public keys in the random oracle model.*

Lemma 5. *Under the assumptions of Theorem 3,* $\mathsf{SIG}_2^{\mathsf{ID}}$ *satisfies Definition 8.*

Proof. The proof follows directly from Eq. 4 and the construction of KAg algorithm in Fig. 6.

Lemma 6. *Under the assumptions of Theorem 3,* $\mathsf{SIG}_2^{\mathsf{ID}}$ *satisfies Definition 9.*

Proof. We prove this lemma by exhibiting a simulator $\mathcal{S}$ that breaks the unforgeability of the $\mathsf{SIG}^{\mathsf{ID}}$ scheme if it has access to an adversary that can break the unforgeability of the $\mathsf{SIG}_2^{\mathsf{ID}}$ scheme. More precisely, we show a series of games, starting with the $\mathsf{SigForge}^b_{\mathcal{A},\mathsf{SIG}_2}$ experiment, such that each game is computationally indistinguishable from the previous one. The last game is modified in such a way that the simulator can use the adversary's forgery to create its own forgery for the unforgeability game against the $\mathsf{SIG}^{\mathsf{ID}}$ scheme.

To construct this simulator, we note that the $\Pi_{\mathsf{Rand\text{-}Exc}}$ protocol in Fig. 6 must satisfy two properties (similar to [27]). First, the commitment scheme must be extractable for the simulator, and second, the NIZK proof used must be simulatable. The reasons for these two properties become evident in the proof.

We prove Lemma 6 by separately considering the cases of the adversary corrupting party $\mathcal{P}_0$ or party $\mathcal{P}_1$, respectively.

Adversary Corrupts $\mathcal{P}_0$. In the following we give the security proof in case the adversary corrupts party $\mathcal{P}_0$.

Game G_0: This is the regular $\mathsf{SigForge}^0_{\mathcal{A},\mathsf{SIG}_2}(n)$ experiment, in which the adversary plays the role of party $\mathcal{P}_0$. In the beginning of the game, the simulator generates the public parameters as $pp \leftarrow \mathsf{Setup}(1^n)$. Note that the Setup procedure, apart from computing $\mathsf{crs} \leftarrow \mathsf{NIZK.Setup_R}(1^n)$, includes the execution of $\mathsf{C.Gen}$ through which the simulator learns the trapdoor tr for the commitment scheme C. Further, $\mathcal{S}$ generates a fresh signing key pair $(sk_1, pk_1) \leftarrow \mathsf{Gen}(1^n)$, sends pp and pk_1 to $\mathcal{A}$ and receives the adversary's key pair (pk_0, sk_0). The simulator simulates the experiment honestly. In particular, it simulates the interactive signing oracle $\mathcal{O}^0_{\Pi_S}$ honestly by playing the role of party $\mathcal{P}_1$.

Game G_1: This game proceeds exactly like the previous game, with a modification in the simulation of the signing oracle. Upon $\mathcal{A}$ initiating the signing protocol by calling the interactive signing oracle, $\mathcal{S}$ receives the commitment c to its public randomness R_0 from $\mathcal{A}$. The simulator, using the trapdoor tr, then extracts a randomness $R'_0 \leftarrow \mathsf{C.Extract}(pp, tr, c)$ and computes the joint randomness as $R_{\mathsf{sign}} \leftarrow f_{\mathsf{com\text{-}rand}}(R'_0, R_1)$. $\mathcal{S}$ honestly computes the zero-knowledge proof to its own randomness R_1 and sends it to $\mathcal{A}$. Upon receiving the opening d to c from the adversary, $\mathcal{S}$ checks if $R'_0 = \mathsf{C.Dec}(pp, c, d)$. If this does not hold, $\mathcal{S}$ aborts, otherwise $\mathcal{S}$ continues to simulate the rest of the experiment honestly.

Claim. Let Bad_1 be the event that G_1 aborts in the signing oracle. Then, we have $\Pr[\mathsf{Bad}_1] \leq \nu_1(n)$, where ν_1 is a negligible function in n.

Proof: Note that game G_1 aborts only if the extracted value R'_0 from commitment c is not equal to the actual committed value R_0 in c, i.e., if $\mathsf{C.Extract}(pp, tr, c) \neq \mathsf{C.Dec}(pp, c, d)$. By the extractability property of C this happens only with negligible probability. In other words, it holds that $\Pr[\mathsf{Bad}_1] \leq \nu_1(n)$, where ν_1 is a negligible function in n. ■

Game G_2: This game proceeds as game G_1, with a modification to the signing oracle. Upon input message m, instead of generating its signature (h, s_0) with respect to the joint public randomness R_{sign}, the simulator generates it only with respect to its own randomness R_0. Further, the simulator programs the random oracle in the following way: as in the previous game, it computes the joint randomness R_{sign} and then programs the random oracle in a way such that on input (R_{sign}, m) the random oracle returns h.

It is easy to see that this game is indistinguishable from G_1 if the adversary has not queried the random oracle on input (R_{sign}, m) before the signing query. If, however, the adversary has issued this random oracle query before the signing query (i.e., $\mathcal{H}(R_{\mathsf{sign}}, m) \neq \perp$)), then the simulation aborts.

Claim. Let Bad_2 be the event that G_2 aborts in the signing oracle. Then, we have $\Pr[\mathsf{Bad}_2] \leq \nu_2(n)$, where ν_2 is a negligible function in n.

Proof: We first recall that the output of P_1 (i.e., R_{pre}) is uniformly random from a super-polynomial set of size q in the security parameter. From this it follows that R_{sign} is distributed uniformly at random in the same set. Furthermore, $\mathcal{A}$ being a PPT algorithm, can only make polynomially many queries to $\mathcal{H}$ and $\mathcal{O}_{\mathrm{pS}}$ oracles. Denoting ℓ as the total number of queries to $\mathcal{H}$ and $\mathcal{O}_{\mathrm{S}}$, we have: $\Pr[\mathsf{Bad}_2] = \Pr[\mathcal{H}(R_{\mathsf{sign}}, m) \neq \perp] \leq \frac{\ell}{q} \leq \nu_2(n)$. This follows from the fact that ℓ is polynomial in the security parameter. ■

Game G_3: In this game, the only modification as compared to the previous game is that during the Setup procedure, the simulator executes the algorithm

$(\widetilde{\mathsf{crs}}, \tau) \leftarrow \mathsf{NIZK.Setup}'_{\mathsf{R}}(1^n)$ instead of $\mathsf{crs} \leftarrow \mathsf{Setup}_{\mathsf{R}}(1^n)$, which allows the simulator to learn the trapdoor τ. Since the two distributions $\{\mathsf{crs} : \mathsf{crs} \leftarrow \mathsf{Setup}_{\mathsf{R}}(1^n)\}$ and $\{\widetilde{\mathsf{crs}} : (\widetilde{\mathsf{crs}}, \tau) \leftarrow \mathsf{Setup}'_{\mathsf{R}}(1^n)\}$ are indistinguishable to $\mathcal{A}$ except with negligible probability, we have that $\Pr[\boldsymbol{G_2} = 1] \leq \Pr[\boldsymbol{G_3} = 1] + \nu_3(n)$ where ν_3 is a negligible function in n.

Game $\boldsymbol{G_4}$: This game proceeds exactly like the previous game except that the simulator does not choose its own key pair, but rather uses its signing oracle from the EUF−CMA game to simulate the adversary's interactive signing oracle $\mathcal{O}^0_{\Pi_{\mathsf{S}}}$. More concretely, upon the adversary calling $\mathcal{O}^0_{\Pi_{\mathsf{S}}}$ on message m, the simulator calls its own signing oracle which provides a signature (h, s_1) for m under secret key sk_1. Note that the simulator does not know sk_1 or the secret randomness r_1 used in s_1. Therefore, the simulator has to additionally simulate the NIZK proof that proves knowledge of r_1 in s_1. More concretely, the simulator executes $\pi_{\mathsf{S}} \leftarrow \mathsf{S}(\widetilde{\mathsf{crs}}, \tau, R_1)$, where R_1 is the public randomness used in s_1. Due to the fact that the distributions $\{\pi : \pi \leftarrow \mathsf{Prove}(\widetilde{\mathsf{crs}}, R_1, r_1)\}$ and $\{\pi_{\mathsf{S}} : \pi_{\mathsf{S}} \leftarrow \mathsf{S}(\widetilde{\mathsf{crs}}, \tau, R_1)\}$ are indistinguishable to $\mathcal{A}$ except with negligible probability, it holds that $\Pr[\boldsymbol{G_3} = 1] \leq \Pr[\boldsymbol{G_4} = 1] + \nu_4(n)$ where ν_4 is a negligible function in n.

It remains to show that the simulator can use a valid forgery output by $\mathcal{A}$ to break unforgeability of the $\mathsf{SIG}^{\mathsf{ID}}$ scheme.

Claim. A valid forgery $(m^*, (h^*, s^*))$ output by $\mathcal{A}$ in game $\mathsf{SigForge}_{\mathcal{A},\mathsf{SIG}_2^{\mathsf{ID}}}$ can be transformed into a valid forgery $(m^*, (h^*, s_1^*))$ in game $\mathsf{SigForge}_{\mathcal{S},\mathsf{SIG}^{\mathsf{ID}}}$.

Proof: When $\mathcal{A}$ outputs a valid forgery $(m^*, (h^*, s^*))$, $\mathcal{S}$ extracts the partial signature (h^*, s_1^*) by executing $f_{\mathsf{dec\text{-}sig}}(sk_0, pk_0, (h^*, s^*))$ (from Eq. (5)). Note that the simulator knows the adversary's key pair (sk_0, pk_0). The simulator then submits $(m^*, (h^*, s_1^*))$ as its own forgery to the EUF−CMA challenger. By definition, $\mathcal{A}$ wins this game if it has not queried a signature on m^* before. Thus, $\mathcal{S}$ has also not queried the EUF−CMA signing oracle on m^* before. Further, Eq. (5) implies that $(m^*, (h^*, s_1^*))$ is a valid forgery under the public key pk_1. ■

From games $\boldsymbol{G_0} - \boldsymbol{G_4}$, we have that $\Pr[\boldsymbol{G_0} = 1] \leq \Pr[\boldsymbol{G_4} = 1] + \nu(n)$, where $\nu(n) = \nu_1(n) + \nu_2(n) + \nu_3(n) + \nu_4(n)$ is a negligible function in n. Thus, we have $\Pr[\mathsf{SigForge}_{\mathcal{A},\mathsf{SIG}_2^{\mathsf{ID}}}(n) = 1] \leq \Pr[\mathsf{SigForge}_{\mathcal{S},\mathsf{SIG}^{\mathsf{ID}}}(n) = 1] + \nu(n)$.

Adversary Corrupts $\mathcal{P}_1$. In case the adversary corrupts $\mathcal{P}_1$, the simulator has to simulate $\mathcal{P}_0$. The proof for this case follows exactly the same steps as above with the exception that game $\boldsymbol{G_1}$ is not required. This is due to the reason that the simulator now plays the role of the committing party in the randomness exchange and hence does not have to extract $\mathcal{A}$'s randomness from the commitment c.

5 Two-Party Aggregatable Adaptor Signatures

We are now ready to formally introduce the notion of two-party adaptor signatures with aggregatable public keys which we denote by aSIG_2. Our definition can be seen as a combination of the definition of adaptor signatures from Sect. 3

and the definition of two-party signatures with aggregatable public keys from Sect. 4. Unlike the single party adaptor signatures, in aSIG_2 both parties have the role of the signer and generate pre-signatures cooperatively. Furthermore, both parties can adapt the pre-signature given a witness value y. We note that both the pre-signature and the full-signature are valid under the aggregated public keys of the two parties. We formally define an aSIG_2 scheme w.r.t. a SIG_2 scheme (which is in turn defined w.r.t. a SIG scheme) and a hard relation R.

Afterwards, we show how to instantiate our new definition. Concretely, we present a generic transformation that turns a $\mathsf{SIG}_2^{\mathsf{ID}}$ scheme with certain homomorphic properties into a two-party adaptor signatures scheme. As a $\mathsf{SIG}_2^{\mathsf{ID}}$ scheme is constructed w.r.t. a $\mathsf{SIG}^{\mathsf{ID}}$ scheme (cf. Sect. 4), the construction presented in this section can implicitly transform digital signatures based on ID schemes to two-party adaptor signatures.

The definition of a two-party adaptor signature scheme aSIG_2 is similar to the definition of a standard adaptor signature scheme as for Definition 1. The main difference lies in the pre-signature generation. Namely, the algorithm pSign is replaced by a *protocol* Π_{pSign} which is executed between two parties.

Definition 10 (Two-Party Adaptor Signature Scheme with Aggregatable Public Keys). *A two-party adaptor signature scheme with aggregatable public keys is defined w.r.t. a hard relation* R *and a two-party signature scheme with aggregatable public keys* $\mathsf{SIG}_2 = (\mathsf{Setup}, \mathsf{Gen}, \Pi_{\mathsf{Sign}}, \mathsf{KAg}, \mathsf{Vrfy})$. *It is run between parties* $\mathcal{P}_0, \mathcal{P}_1$ *and consists of a tuple* $\mathsf{aSIG}_2 = (\Pi_{\mathsf{pSign}}, \mathsf{Adapt}, \mathsf{pVrfy}, \mathsf{Ext})$ *of efficient protocols and algorithms which are defined as follows:*

$\Pi_{\mathsf{pSign}\langle sk_i, sk_{1-i}\rangle}(pk_0, pk_1, m, Y)$: *is an interactive protocol that on input secret keys* sk_i *from party* $\mathcal{P}_i$ *with* $i \in \{0,1\}$ *and common values public keys* pk_i, *message* $m \in \{0,1\}^*$ *and statement* $Y \in L_{\mathsf{R}}$, *outputs a pre-signature* $\widetilde{\sigma}$.

$\mathsf{pVrfy}_{apk}(m, Y; \widetilde{\sigma})$: *is a DPT algorithm that on input an aggregated public key* apk, *a message* $m \in \{0,1\}^*$, *a statement* $Y \in L_{\mathsf{R}}$ *and a pre-signature* $\widetilde{\sigma}$, *outputs a bit* b.

$\mathsf{Adapt}_{apk}(\widetilde{\sigma}, y)$: *is a DPT algorithm that on input an aggregated public key* apk, *a pre-signature* $\widetilde{\sigma}$ *and witness* y, *outputs a signature* σ.

$\mathsf{Ext}_{apk}(\sigma, \widetilde{\sigma}, Y)$: *is a DPT algorithm that on input an aggregated public key* apk, *a signature* σ, *pre-signature* $\widetilde{\sigma}$ *and statement* $Y \in L_{\mathsf{R}}$, *outputs a witness* y *such that* $(Y, y) \in \mathsf{R}$, *or* $\perp$.

We note that in aSIG_2, the pVrfy algorithm enables public verifiability of the pre-signatures, e.g., aSIG_2 can be used in a three-party protocol where the third party needs to verify the validity of the generated pre-signatrue.

In the following, we formally define properties that a two-party adaptor signature scheme with aggregatable public keys aSIG_2 has to satisfy. These properties are similar to the ones for single party adaptor signature schemes. We start by defining two-party pre-signature correctness which, similarly to Definition 2 states that an honestly generated pre-signature and signature are valid, and it is possible to extract a valid witness from them.

Definition 11 (Two-Party Pre-Signature Correctness). *A two-party adaptor signature with aggregatable public keys* aSIG_2 *satisfies two-party pre-signature correctness, if for all* $n \in \mathbb{N}$*, messages* $m \in \{0,1\}^*$*, it holds that:*

$$\Pr\left[\begin{array}{c|l} \mathsf{pVrfy}_{apk}(m, Y; \widetilde{\sigma}) = 1 & pp \leftarrow \mathsf{Setup}(1^n), (sk_0, pk_0) \leftarrow \mathsf{Gen}(pp) \\ \wedge & (sk_1, pk_1) \leftarrow \mathsf{Gen}(pp), (Y, y) \leftarrow \mathsf{GenR}(1^n) \\ \mathsf{Vrfy}_{apk}(m; \sigma) = 1 & \widetilde{\sigma} \leftarrow \Pi_{\mathsf{pSign}\langle sk_0, sk_1 \rangle}(pk_0, pk_1, m, Y) \\ \wedge & apk := \mathsf{KAg}(pk_0, pk_1) \\ (Y, y') \in \mathsf{R} & \sigma := \mathsf{Adapt}_{apk}(\widetilde{\sigma}, y), y' := \mathsf{Ext}_{apk}(\sigma, \widetilde{\sigma}, Y) \end{array}\right] = 1.$$

The unforgeability security definition is similar to Definition 9, except the adversary interacts with two oracles $\mathcal{O}^b_{\Pi_{\mathrm{S}}}, \mathcal{O}^b_{\Pi_{\mathrm{pS}}}$ in order to generate signatures and pre-signatures, as in Definition 3. More precisely, in the $\mathsf{aSigForge}^b_{\mathcal{A},\mathsf{aSIG}_2}(n)$ experiment defined below, $\mathcal{A}$ obtains access to *interactive*, stateful signing and pre-signing oracles $\mathcal{O}^b_{\Pi_{\mathrm{S}}}$ and $\mathcal{O}^b_{\Pi_{\mathrm{pS}}}$ respectively. Oracles $\mathcal{O}^b_{\Pi_{\mathrm{S}}}$ and $\mathcal{O}^b_{\Pi_{\mathrm{pS}}}$ simulate the honest party $\mathcal{P}_{1-b}$ during an execution of the protocols $\Pi^{\mathcal{A}}_{\mathsf{Sign}\langle sk_{1-b}, \cdot \rangle}$ and $\Pi^{\mathcal{A}}_{\mathsf{pSign}\langle sk_{1-b}, \cdot \rangle}$ respectively. Similar to Definition 9, both the protocols $\Pi^{\mathcal{A}}_{\mathsf{Sign}\langle sk_{1-b}, \cdot \rangle}, \Pi^{\mathcal{A}}_{\mathsf{pSign}\langle sk_{1-b}, \cdot \rangle}$ employed by the respective oracles $\mathcal{O}^b_{\Pi_{\mathrm{S}}}, \mathcal{O}^b_{\Pi_{\mathrm{pS}}}$ gets an oracle access to $\mathcal{A}$ as well.

Definition 12 (2-aEUF−CMA Security). *A two-party adaptor signature with aggregatable public keys* aSIG_2 *is unforgeable if for every PPT adversary* $\mathcal{A}$ *there exists a negligible function* ν *such that:* $\Pr[\mathsf{aSigForge}_{\mathcal{A},\mathsf{aSIG}_2}(n) = 1] \leq \nu(n)$*, where the experiment* $\mathsf{aSigForge}_{\mathcal{A},\mathsf{aSIG}_2}(n)$ *is defined as follows:*

$\mathsf{aSigForge}^b_{\mathcal{A},\mathsf{aSIG}_2}(n)$

1 : $\mathcal{Q} := \emptyset, pp \leftarrow \mathsf{Setup}(1^n)$
2 : $(sk_{1-b}, pk_{1-b}) \leftarrow \mathsf{Gen}(pp)$
3 : $(sk_b, pk_b) \leftarrow \mathcal{A}(pp, pk_{1-b})$
4 : $m^* \leftarrow \mathcal{A}^{\mathcal{O}^b_{\Pi_{\mathrm{S}}}, \mathcal{O}^b_{\Pi_{\mathrm{pS}}}}(pk_{1-b}, sk_b, pk_b)$
5 : $(Y, y) \leftarrow \mathsf{GenR}(1^n)$
6 : $\widetilde{\sigma} \leftarrow \Pi^{\mathcal{A}}_{\mathsf{pSign}\langle sk_{1-b}, \cdot \rangle}(m^*, Y)$
7 : $\sigma^* \leftarrow \mathcal{A}^{\mathcal{O}^b_{\Pi_{\mathrm{S}}}, \mathcal{O}^b_{\Pi_{\mathrm{pS}}}}(\widetilde{\sigma}, Y)$
8 : **return** $\left(m^* \notin \mathcal{Q} \wedge \mathsf{Vrfy}_{\mathsf{KAg}(pk_0, pk_1)}(m^*; \sigma^*)\right)$

$\mathcal{O}^b_{\Pi_{\mathrm{S}}}(m)$

1 : $\mathcal{Q} := \mathcal{Q} \cup \{m\}$
2 : $\sigma \leftarrow \Pi^{\mathcal{A}}_{\mathsf{Sign}\langle sk_{1-b}, \cdot \rangle}(pk_0, pk_1, m)$

$\mathcal{O}^b_{\Pi_{\mathrm{pS}}}(m, Y)$

1 : $\mathcal{Q} := \mathcal{Q} \cup \{m\}$
2 : $\widetilde{\sigma} \leftarrow \Pi^{\mathcal{A}}_{\mathsf{pSign}\langle sk_{1-b}, \cdot \rangle}(pk_0, pk_1, m, Y)$

The definition of two-party pre-signature adaptability follows Definition 4 closely. The only difference is that in this setting the pre-signature must be valid under the aggregated public keys.

Definition 13 (Two-Party Pre-Signature Adaptability). *A two-party adaptor signature scheme with aggregatable public keys* aSIG_2 *satisfies two-party pre-signature adaptability, if for all* $n \in \mathbb{N}$*, messages* $m \in \{0,1\}^*$*, statement and witness pairs* $(Y, y) \in \mathsf{R}$*, public keys* pk_0 *and* pk_1*, and pre-signatures* $\widetilde{\sigma} \in \{0,1\}^*$ *satisfying* $\mathsf{pVrfy}_{apk}(m, Y; \widetilde{\sigma}) = 1$ *where* $apk := \mathsf{KAg}(pk_0, pk_1)$*, we have* $\Pr[\mathsf{Vrfy}_{apk}(m; \mathsf{Adapt}_{apk}(\widetilde{\sigma}, y)) = 1] = 1$.

Finally, we define two-party witness extractability.

Definition 14 (Two-Party Witness Extractability). *A two-party public key aggregatable adaptor signature scheme* aSIG_2 *is* witness extractable *if for every PPT adversary* $\mathcal{A}$*, there exists a negligible function* ν *such that the following holds:* $\Pr[\mathsf{aWitExt}_{\mathcal{A},\mathsf{aSIG}_2}(n) = 1] \leq \nu(n)$*, where the experiment* $\mathsf{aWitExt}_{\mathcal{A},\mathsf{aSIG}_2}$ *is defined as follows:*

$\mathsf{aWitExt}^b_{\mathcal{A},\mathsf{aSIG}_2}(n)$	$\mathcal{O}^b_{\Pi_\mathsf{S}}(m)$
$1: \mathcal{Q} := \emptyset, pp \leftarrow \mathsf{Setup}(1^n)$	$1: \mathcal{Q} := \mathcal{Q} \cup \{m\}$
$2: (sk_{1-b}, pk_{1-b}) \leftarrow \mathsf{Gen}(pp)$	$2: \sigma \leftarrow \Pi^{\mathcal{A}}_{\mathsf{Sign}\langle sk_{1-b}, \cdot \rangle}(pk_0, pk_1, m)$
$3: (sk_b, pk_b) \leftarrow \mathcal{A}(pp, pk_{1-b})$	
$4: (m^*, Y^*) \leftarrow \mathcal{A}^{\mathcal{O}^b_{\Pi_\mathsf{S}}, \mathcal{O}^b_{\Pi_\mathsf{pS}}}(pk_{1-b}, sk_b, pk_b)$	$\mathcal{O}^b_{\Pi_\mathsf{pS}}(m, Y)$
$5: \widetilde{\sigma} \leftarrow \Pi^{\mathcal{A}}_{\mathsf{pSign}\langle sk_{1-b}, \cdot \rangle}(m^*, Y^*)$	$1: \mathcal{Q} := \mathcal{Q} \cup \{m\}$
$6: \sigma^* \leftarrow \mathcal{A}^{\mathcal{O}^b_{\Pi_\mathsf{S}}, \mathcal{O}^b_{\Pi_\mathsf{pS}}}(\widetilde{\sigma})$	$2: \widetilde{\sigma} \leftarrow \Pi^{\mathcal{A}}_{\mathsf{pSign}\langle sk_{1-b}, \cdot \rangle}(pk_0, pk_1, m, Y)$
$7: apk := \mathsf{KAg}(pk_0, pk_1), y' := \mathsf{Ext}_{apk}(\sigma^*, \widetilde{\sigma}, Y^*)$	
$8:$ **return** $(m^* \notin \mathcal{Q} \wedge (Y^*, y') \notin \mathsf{R} \wedge \mathsf{Vrfy}_{apk}(m^*; \sigma^*))$	

Note that the only difference between this experiment and the $\mathsf{aSigForge}_{\mathcal{A},\mathsf{aSIG}_2}$ experiment is that here the adversary is allowed to choose the statement/witness pair (Y^*, y^*) and that the winning condition additionally requires that for the extracted witness $y' \leftarrow \mathsf{Ext}_{apk}(\sigma^*, \widetilde{\sigma}, Y^*)$ it holds that $(Y^*, y') \notin \mathsf{R}$.

A two-party adaptor signature scheme with aggregatable public keys aSIG_2 is called *secure* if it satisfies the properties 2aEUF−CMA security, *two-party pre-signature adaptability* and *two-party witness extractability.*

5.1 Generic Transformation from $\mathsf{SIG}_2^{\mathsf{ID}}$ to $\mathsf{aSIG}_2^{\mathsf{ID,R}}$

We now present our generic transformation to achieve two-party adaptor signature schemes with aggregatable public keys from identification schemes. In its essence, this transformation is a combination of the transformations presented in Figs. 3 and 6. More precisely, similar to the transformation from $\mathsf{SIG}^{\mathsf{ID}}$ to $\mathsf{aSIG}^{\mathsf{ID,R}}$ presented in Fig. 3, we assume the existence of functions f_{shift}, f_{adapt} and f_{ext} with respect to the relation R. We then make use of the $\Pi_{\mathsf{Rand\text{-}Exc}}$ protocol from the transformation in Fig. 6 to let parties agree on the randomness that is going to be used during the pre-signing process. However, unlike the transformation in Fig. 6, the resulting randomness is shifted by a statement Y for relation R using the function f_{shift}. The transformation can be found in Fig. 7.

Theorem 4. *Assume that* $\mathsf{SIG}^{\mathsf{ID}}$ *is an* $\mathsf{SUF-CMA}$*-secure signature scheme transformed using Fig. 2. Let* $f_{\mathsf{shift}}, f_{\mathsf{adapt}}$ *and* f_{ext} *be functions satisfying the relations from Equations* (1) *and 2, and* R *be a hard relation. Further, assume that* $f_{\mathsf{com\text{-}sig}}, f_{\mathsf{com\text{-}pk}}$ *and* $f_{\mathsf{dec\text{-}sig}}$ *satisfy the relation from Equations* (4) *and* (5). *Then the resulting* $\mathsf{aSIG}_2^{\mathsf{ID,R}}$ *scheme from the transformation in Fig. 7 is a secure two-party adaptor signature scheme with aggregatable public keys in the random oracle model.*

$\Pi_{\mathsf{pSign}\langle sk_0, sk_1\rangle}(pk_0, pk_1, m, Y)$	$\mathsf{pVrfy}_{apk}(m, Y; (h, \tilde{s}))$
$1:$ Parse $pk_i = ((1^n, pp_{\mathsf{C}}, \mathsf{crs}), pk_i'), i \in \{0,1\}$	$1: \widehat{R}_{\mathsf{pre}} := \mathsf{V}_0(apk, h, \tilde{s})$
$2: (R_i, St_i, R_{1-i}) \leftarrow \Pi_{\mathsf{Rand\text{-}Exc}\langle sk_i, sk_{1-i}\rangle}(pp_{\mathsf{C}}, \mathsf{crs})$	$2:$ **return** $h = \mathcal{H}(f_{\mathsf{shift}}(\widehat{R}_{\mathsf{pre}}, Y), m)$
$3: R_{\mathsf{pre}} := f_{\mathsf{com\text{-}rand}}(R_0, R_1)$	$\mathsf{Adapt}_{pk}((h, \tilde{s}), y)$
$4: R_{\mathsf{sign}} := f_{\mathsf{shift}}(R_{\mathsf{pre}}, Y), h := \mathcal{H}(R_{\mathsf{sign}}, m)$	$1:$ **return** $(h, f_{\mathsf{adapt}}(\tilde{s}, y))$
$5: \tilde{s}_i \leftarrow \mathsf{P}_2(sk_i, R_i, h, St_i)$	$\mathsf{Ext}_{pk}((h, s), (h, \tilde{s}), Y)$
$6: \tilde{s}_{1-i} \leftarrow \Pi_{\mathsf{Exchange}}\langle \tilde{s}_i, \tilde{s}_{1-i}\rangle$	$1:$ **return** $f_{\mathsf{ext}}(s, \tilde{s})$
$7: (h, \tilde{s}) := f_{\mathsf{com\text{-}sig}}(h, (\tilde{s}_i, \tilde{s}_{1-i}))$	
$8:$ **return** $(h, \tilde{s})$	

Fig. 7. A two-party adaptor signature scheme with aggregatable public keys $\mathsf{aSIG}_2^{\mathsf{ID,R}}$ defined with respect to a $\mathsf{SIG}_2^{\mathsf{ID}}$ scheme and a hard relation R.

In order to prove Theorem 4, we must show that $\mathsf{aSIG}_2^{\mathsf{ID,R}}$ satisfies the *pre-signature correctness*, 2-$\mathsf{aEUF-CMA}$ *security*, *pre-signature adaptability* and *witness extractability* properties as described in Definitions 11 to 14 respectively. We provide the full proofs of the following lemmas in the full version of this paper [14] and only mention the intuition behind the proofs here. As mentioned in the introduction of this work, despite the fact that $\mathsf{aSIG}_2^{\mathsf{ID,R}}$ is constructed from $\mathsf{SIG}_2^{\mathsf{ID}}$, we require only $\mathsf{SIG}^{\mathsf{ID}}$ to be $\mathsf{SUF-CMA}$-secure in order to prove 2-$\mathsf{aEUF-CMA}$ security for $\mathsf{aSIG}_2^{\mathsf{ID,R}}$.

Lemma 7 (Two-Party Pre-Signature Correctness). *Under the assumptions of Theorem 4,* $\mathsf{aSIG}_2^{\mathsf{ID,R}}$ *satisfies Definition 11.*

The proof of Lemma 7 follows directly from Equations (1) to (2) and the correctness of SIG_2 from Lemma 5.

Lemma 8 (2-$\mathsf{aEUF-CMA}$-Security). *Under the assumptions of Theorem 4,* $\mathsf{aSIG}_2^{\mathsf{ID,R}}$ *satisfies Definition 12.*

Proof Sketch: In a nutshell the proof of this lemma is a combination of the proofs of Lemmas 2 and 6, i.e., the proof is done by a reduction to the hardness of the relation R and the $\mathsf{SUF-CMA}$ of the underlying signature scheme. During the signing process, the challenger queries its $\mathsf{SUF-CMA}$ signing oracle and receives a signature σ. As in the proof of Lemma 6, the challenger

programs the random oracle such that σ appears like a signature generated with the combined randomness of the challenger and the adversary. Simulating the pre-signing process is similar with the exception that before programming the random oracle, the randomness must be shifted using the function f_{shift}. Finally, the challenger and the adversary generate a pre-signature $\widetilde{\sigma}^* = (h, \tilde{s})$ on the challenge message m^* and the adversary outputs the forgery $\sigma^* = (h, s)$. If $f_{\mathsf{ext}}(s, \tilde{s})$ returns the y generated by the challenger, as in the proof of Lemma 2, the hardness of the relation R can be broken. Otherwise, using $f_{\mathsf{dec\text{-}sig}}$, it is possible to use the forgery provided by the adversary to extract a forgery for the $\mathsf{SUF-CMA}$ game.

Lemma 9 (Two-Party Pre-Signature Adaptability). *Under the assumptions of Theorem 4,* $\mathsf{aSIG}_2^{\mathsf{ID},\mathsf{R}}$ *satisfies Definition 13.*

Proof Sketch: The proof of Lemma 9 is analogous to the proof of Lemma 3.

Lemma 10 (Two-Party Witness Extractability). *Under the assumptions of Theorem 4,* $\mathsf{aSIG}_2^{\mathsf{ID},\mathsf{R}}$ *satisfies Definition 14.*

Proof Sketch: The proof of Lemma 10 is very similar to the proof of Lemma 8 except that the adversary chooses Y now and thus, no reduction to the hardness of the relation R is needed.

Acknowledgments. This work was partly supported by the German Research Foundation (DFG) Emmy Noether Program *FA 1320/1-1*, by the *DFG CRC 1119 CROSSING* (project S7), by the German Federal Ministry of Education and Research (BMBF) *iBlockchain project* (grant nr. 16KIS0902) and by *NSCX project* (project number CS1920241NSCX008801) on *Design and Development of Blockchain based Technologies* in the *Department of Computer Science and Engineering, IIT Madras.*

References

1. Abdalla, M., et al.: Tighter reductions for forward-secure signature schemes. In: PKC 2013 (2013)
2. Aumayr, L., et al.: Generalized bitcoin-compatible channels. Cryptology ePrint Archive, Report 2020/476. https://eprint.iacr.org/2020/476.pdf (2020)
3. Bellare, M., Neven, G.: Multi-signatures in the plain public-Key model and a general forking lemma. In: ACM CCS 2006 (2006)
4. Bellare, M., Shoup, S.: Two-tier signatures, strongly unforgeable signatures, and Fiat-Shamir without random oracles. In: PKC 2007 (2007)
5. Bitcoin Scripts. https://en.bitcoin.it/wiki/Script#Crypto
6. Bitcoin Wiki: Payment Channels. https://en.bitcoin.it/wiki/Payment_channels

7. Boldyreva, A.: Threshold signatures, multisignatures and blind signatures based on the Gap-Diffie-Hellman-group signature scheme. In: P-KC 2003 (2003)
8. Boneh, D., et al.: Compact multi-signatures for smaller blockchains. In: ASIACRYPT 2018, Part II (2018)
9. Boneh, D., et al.: Short signatures from the weil pairing. In: ASIACRYP- T 2001 (2001)
10. Decker, C., Wattenhofer, R.: A fast and scalable payment network with bitcoin duplex micropayment channels. In: Stabilization, Safety, and Security of Distributed Systems 2015 (2015)
11. Deshpande, A., Herlihy, M.: Privacy-preserving cross-chain atomic swaps. In: FC 2020 (2020)
12. Drijvers, M., et al.: On the security of two-round multi-signatures. In: 2019 IEEE Symposium on Security and Privacy (2019)
13. Eckey, L., et al.: Splitting payments locally while routing interdimensionally. Cryptology ePrint Archive, Report 2020/555. https://eprint.iacr.org/2020/555 (2020)
14. Erwig, A., et al.: Two-party adaptor signatures from identification schemes. Cryptology ePrint Archive, Report 2021/150. https://eprint.iacr.org/2021/150 (2021)
15. Esgin, M.F., et al.: Post-quantum adaptor signatures and payment channel networks. In: ESORICS 2020 (2020)
16. Fischlin, M.: Communication-efficient non-interactive proofs of knowledge with online extractors. In: CRYPTO 2005 (2005)
17. Fournier, L.: One-time verifiably encrypted signatures A.K.A. Adaptor Signatures. https://github.com/LLFourn/one-time-VES/blob/master/main.pdf (2019)
18. Gennaro, R., et al.: Threshold-optimal DSA/ECDSA signatures and an application to bitcoin wallet security. In: ACNS 16 (2016)
19. Goldwasser, S., Ostrovsky, R.: Invariant signatures and non-interactive zero-knowledge proofs are equivalent. In: Annual International Cryptology Conference. Springer (1992)
20. Groth, J., et al.: Perfect non-interactive zero knowledge for NP In: EU- ROCRYPT 2006 (2006)
21. Gugger, J.: Bitcoin-monero cross-chain atomic swap. Cryptology ePrint Archive, Report 2020/1126. https://eprint.iacr.org/2020/1126 (2020)
22. Guillou, L.C., Quisquater, J.-J.: A "Paradoxical" indentity-based signature scheme resulting from zero-knowledge. In: CRYPTO'88 (1990)
23. Hardjono, T., Zheng, Y.: A practical digital multisignature scheme based on discrete logarithms (extended abstract). In: Advances in Cryp- tology – AUSCRYPT'92 (1993)
24. Katz, J., Wang, N.: Efficiency improvements for signature schemes with tight security reductions. In: ACM CCS 2003 (2003)
25. Kiltz, E., et al.: Optimal security proofs for signatures from identification schemes. In: CRYPTO 2016, Part II (2016)
26. Le, D.-P., et al.: DDH-based multisignatures with public key aggregation. Cryptology ePrint Archive, Report 2019/771. https://eprint.iacr.org/2019/771 (2019)
27. Lindell, Y.: Fast secure two-party ECDSA signing. In: CRYPTO 2017, Part II (2017)
28. Lu, S., et al.: Sequential aggregate signatures and multisignatures without random oracles. In: EUROCRYPT 2006 (2006)
29. Lysyanskaya, A.: Unique signatures and verifiable random functions from the DH-DDH separation. In: Annual International Cryptology Conference. Springer (2002)
30. Malavolta, G., et al.: Anonymous multi-hop locks for blockchain scalability and interoperability. In: NDSS 2019 (2019)

31. Maxwell, G., et al.: Simple Schnorr multi-signatures with applications to Bitcoin. In: Designs, Codes and Cryptography 2019 (2019)
32. Micali, S., et al.: Verifiable random functions. In: 40th FOCS (1999)
33. Miller, A., et al.: Sprites and state channels: payment networks that go faster than lightning. In: FC 2019 (2019)
34. Nakamoto, S.: Bitcoin: a peer-to-peer electronic cash system. http://bitcoin.org/bitcoin.pdf (2009)
35. Ohta, K., Okamoto, T.: A digital multisignature scheme based on the Fiat-Shamir scheme. In: Advances in Cryptology – ASIACRYPT'91 (1993)
36. Okamoto, T.: A digital multisignature scheme using bijective public-key cryptosystems. ACM Trans. Comput. Syst. **4** (1988)
37. Poelstra, A.: Scriptless scripts. https://download.wpsoftware.net/bitcoin/wizardry/mw-slides/2017-03-mit-bitcoin-expo/slides.pdf (2017)
38. Poon, J., Dryja, T.: The bitcoin lightning network: scalable O-chain instant payments. https://lightning.network/lightning-network-paper.pdf (2016)
39. Rivest, R.L., et al.: How to leak a secret. In: ASIACRYPT 2001 (2001)
40. van Saberhagen, N.: CryptoNote v 2.0. https://bytecoin.org/old/whitepaper.pdf
41. Schnorr, C.-P.: Efficient signature generation by smart cards. J. Cryptol. **3** (1991)
42. Shen, S.-T., et al.: Unique signature with short output from CDH assumption. In: International Conference on Provable Security. Springer (2015)
43. Tairi, E., et al.: A^2L: anonymous atomic locks for scalability in payment channel hubs. Cryptology ePrint Archive, Report 2019/589. https://eprint.iacr.org/2019/589 (2019)
44. Tairi, E., et al.: Post-quantum adaptor signature for privacy-preserving O-chain payments. FC (to appear, 2021). https://eprint.iacr.org/2020/1345

Compact Zero-Knowledge Proofs for Threshold ECDSA with Trustless Setup

Tsz Hon Yuen[1(✉)], Handong Cui[1], and Xiang Xie[2]

[1] The University of Hong Kong, Pok Fu Lam, Hong Kong
{thyuen,hdcui}@cs.hku.hk
[2] Shanghai Key Laboratory of Privacy-Preserving Computation, MatrixElements Technologies, Shanghai, China
xiexiang@matrixelements.com

Abstract. Threshold ECDSA signatures provide a higher level of security to a crypto wallet since it requires more than t parties out of n parties to sign a transaction. The state-of-the-art bandwidth efficient threshold ECDSA used the additive homomorphic Castagnos and Laguillaumie (CL) encryption based on an unknown order group G, together with a number of zero-knowledge proofs in G. In this paper, we propose compact zero-knowledge proofs for threshold ECDSA to lower the communication bandwidth, as well as the computation cost. The proposed zero-knowledge proofs include the discrete-logarithm relation in G and the well-formedness of a CL ciphertext.

When applied to two-party ECDSA, we can lower the bandwidth of the key generation algorithm by 47%, and the running time for the key generation and signing algorithms are boosted by about 35% and 104% respectively. When applied to threshold ECDSA, our first scheme is more optimized for the key generation algorithm (about 70% lower bandwidth and 85% faster computation in key generation, at a cost of 20% larger bandwidth in signing), while our second scheme has an all-rounded performance improvement (about 60% lower bandwidth, 46% faster computation in key generation without additional cost in signing).

Keywords: Threshold signature · ECDSA · Zero-knowledge proof

1 Introduction

Threshold signature allows n parties to share the message signing ability without trusting each other, such that no coalition of $t < n$ or fewer users can generate a valid signature. Threshold ECDSA signatures become a popular research topic recently since ECDSA is adopted in Bitcoin and other cryptocurrencies. Threshold ECDSA signatures are useful for managing keys in crypto wallet. For example, two-party ECDSA [4,13] (with $t = 1, n = 2$) is useful for smart contract building blocks such as Coinswap and Lightning Network. A threshold signature with $t = 1, n = 3$ is useful for a hot wallet of a crypto exchange: the exchange

J. A. Garay (Ed.): PKC 2021, LNCS 12710, pp. 481–511, 2021.
https://doi.org/10.1007/978-3-030-75245-3_18

holds a private key for online transaction and a private key for paper backup, and a separate security firm holds the third key to validate transactions. In this case, losing one key from the exchange or the security firm does not compromise the hot wallet. General threshold ECDSA signatures were proposed in [5,11,14].

1.1 Additive Homomorphic CL Encryption in Threshold ECDSA

Using additive homomorphic encryption is one of the most popular techniques for generating efficient two-party or threshold ECDSA. Some earlier papers [11,13,14] used Paillier encryption. Recently, Castagnos *et al.* [4] used the additive homomorphic Castagnos and Laguillaumie (CL) encryption [7] based on an unknown order group G, which contains a subgroup F in which the discrete logarithm (DL) problem is tractable. We call the group G as the HSM group since we require that the *hard subgroup membership* assumption holds in G. It was shown in [1] that the HSM group G can be constructed from class groups of quadratic fields. The advantage of using CL encryption over Paillier encryption is that the generation of the class group is trustless, and the size of a class group element is smaller than that of a Paillier group element (for the same security level).

Zero-Knowledge Proofs for CL Encryption. One of the technical difficulties for using the CL encryption for threshold ECDSA is the design of zero-knowledge (ZK) proofs in the HSM group. In particular, we need the ZK proofs related to (1) the discrete-logarithm (DL) of an unknown order group element, and (2) the well-formedness of a CL ciphertext. In [4], the authors used a ZK proof with a single bit challenge. In order to achieve soundness error of $2^{-\epsilon_s}$, the protocol has to be repeated for ϵ_s-times and hence the resulting algorithm is inefficient. In [5], the authors tackled the first DL problem by using a *lowest common multiple* (*lcm*) tricks, which reduces the repetition of the ZK proof to about $\epsilon_s/10$-times. The authors tackled the second CL ciphertext well-formedness problem based on a strong root assumption in the HSM group.

Although the ZK proof for a CL ciphertext in [5] is highly efficient, it does not allow a fast, trustless setup. The strong root assumption used in [5] assumes that when given a random group element $w \in G\backslash F$, it is difficult to output a group element u and a positive integer $e \neq 2^k$ such that $u^e = w$.[1] In their security proof, it requires that w is a random group generator, which can be obtained from a standardized group, or jointly generated by all participating parties during the interactive key generation algorithm. In the former case, all users have to trust the standardizing authority and it is not desirable for decentralized applications such as public blockchain. In the latter case, it greatly increases the round complexity and the bandwidth used for the interactive key generation algorithm.

[1] This special requirement on e is needed since computing square roots in class groups of quadratic fields is easy [4]. The assumptions used in this paper do not require such a special arrangement.

Algorithm 1: Insecure ZK Proof for the relation $\mathcal{R}$

1 Verifier sends a random λ-bit prime ℓ.
2 Prover finds $q' \in \mathbb{Z}$ and $r \in [0, \ell - 1]$ s.t. $x = q'\ell + r$. Prover sends $Q = g^{q'}$ and r to the verifier.
3 Verifier accepts if $r \in [0, \ell - 1]$ and $Q^{\ell} g^{r} = w$.

1.2 Compact Zero-Knowledge Proof with Fast Trustless Setup

In this paper, we propose compact ZK proofs for the DL relation of HSM group element, and the well-formedness of CL ciphertext with a fast trustless setup. We first consider a ZK proof for a simple DL relation $\mathcal{R}$ in an unknown order group G for some group elements $g, w \in G \setminus F$:[2]

$$\mathcal{R} = \{x \in \mathbb{Z} : w = g^{x}\}.$$

The subgroup F makes the ZK proof on the relation $\mathcal{R}$ much more complicated.

First Attempt. We start by adopting the adaptive root assumption [1] in the group G with order q subgroup F. In short, the adversary first outputs a group element $w \in G \setminus F$ (which can be verified by $w^{q} \neq 1$). When given a random prime ℓ, we assume that no polynomial time adversary can output a group element u such that $u^{\ell} = w$ with non-negligible probability. Given such an assumption, we can construct a simple ZK proof for $\mathcal{R}$ based on [1] in Algorithm 1.

However, this trivial construction is not secure since there exists a known order subgroup $F \subset G$. Suppose that the prover knows x and y such that $w = g^{x} f^{y}$ for some $f \in F$. The prover can compute $Q' = g^{q'} f^{\frac{y}{\ell}}$ since the order of f is known. It can pass the verification since:

$$Q'^{\ell} g^{r} = (g^{q'} f^{\frac{y}{\ell}})^{\ell} g^{r} = g^{x} f^{y} = w.$$

Our Solution. We propose the use of an extra round of challenge to eliminate the elements of order q in w. This extra round simply uses q instead of using the prime number ℓ. We give a simplified ZK proof for the relation $\mathcal{R}$ in Algorithm 2. (It is the simplified version of Algorithm 4 by setting $n = 1$).

Note that our protocol only runs for one time only for a soundness error of $2^{-\epsilon_s} \approx 2^{\log \lambda - \lambda}$, as compared to ϵ_s-times for [4] and $\epsilon_s/10$-times for [5] for a soundness error of $2^{-\epsilon_s}$. Based on our efficient ZK proof for DL relation of a class group element, we can later formulate an efficient ZK proof for the well-formedness of a CL ciphertext. The major technical difficulty of this paper lies in the security proof and the security model.

[2] Since it is easy to compute $\log_g w$ if $g \in F$, it is impossible to construct a ZK proof for $\mathcal{R}$ if $g \in F$. Hence, we restrict that $g \in G \setminus F$.

Algorithm 2: Simplified ZK Proof for the relation $\mathcal{R}$

Param: A security parameter B.

1 Prover chooses $k \xleftarrow{\$} [-B, B]$ and sends $R = g^k$ to the verifier.
2 Verifier sends $c \xleftarrow{\$} [0, q-1]$ to the prover.
3 Prover computes $s = k + cx$. Prover finds $d \in \mathbb{Z}$, $e \in [0, q-1]$ s.t. $s = dq + e$ and sends $D = g^d$ and e to the verifier.
4 If $e \in [0, q-1]$ and $D^q g^e = Rw^c$, verifier sends a random λ-bit prime ℓ.
5 Prover finds $q' \in \mathbb{Z}$ and $r \in [0, \ell-1]$ s.t. $s = q'\ell + r$. Prover sends $Q = g^{q'}$ and r to the verifier.
6 Verifier accepts if $r \in [0, \ell-1]$ and $Q^\ell g^r = Rw^c$.

1.3 Our Contribution

Our contribution is twofold: (1) In theoretical aspect, we give compact ZK proofs for the well-formedness of a CL ciphertext and for the DL relation in the HSM group with a fast and trustless setup. (2) In practical aspect, we improve the performance of two-party ECDSA and threshold ECDSA with trustless setup by using our ZK proofs.

We observe that by using the generic group model, we can build a more compact ZK proof for two-party/threshold ECDSA. Since ECDSA is known to be secure in the generic group model [2], the security of two-party/threshold ECDSA also indirectly relies on the generic group model. Using our compact ZK proof for two-party/threshold ECDSA still relies on the generic group model.

ZK Proofs and the Generic Group Model. We propose the *first* generic group model for the HSM group (including the class group of imaginary quadratic group order), by defining group operations with the main group G, as well as the subgroup F. Equipped with the new generic group model, we are able to analyse the security of the hard subgroup membership assumption and the adaptive root subgroup assumption in the generic group model. The technical difficulty for the generic group mode is how to maintain the correctness of group operations among elements in G and F, where the discrete logarithm of elements in F is known. Denote $G = G^q \times F$ where G^q is a subgroup of G. For all $g \in G$, we represent g by an element in G^q and an element in F. We handle the group operations in G^q and F separately in order to ensure the correctness of DL computation in F.

Afterwards, we propose some building blocks, such as the proof of knowledge of an exponent for a group element in G, and a zero-knowledge proof of knowledge for a group element representation in G (a generalization of the DL relation), and then a zero-knowledge proof of knowledge for the well-formedness of a CL ciphertext. As shown in Fig. 1, our ZK proof for DL in the HSM group is around 97% shorter than CCL + 19 [4] and around 74% shorter than CCL + 20 ([5], Sect. 5.1) with the same level of soundness error and statistical distance of 2^{-80}.

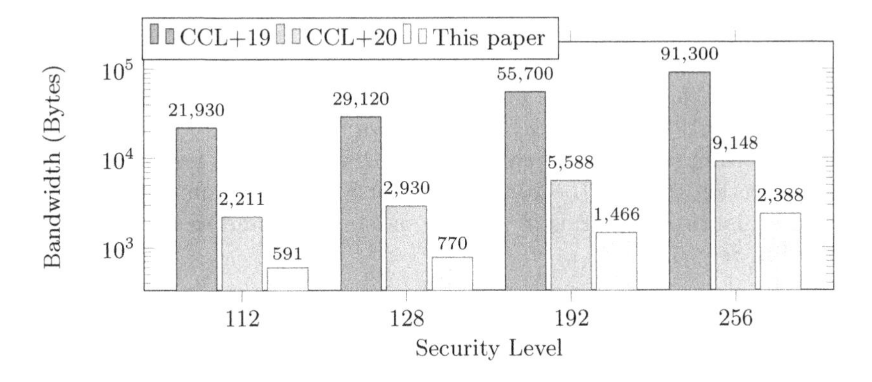

Fig. 1. Comparison of ZK Proof of DL relation in HSM group.

As compared with ZK proofs in [5], their strong root assumption is similar to the strong RSA assumption, while our adaptive root assumption is more similar to the RSA assumption. On the other hand, the security of our ZK proofs requires the use of generic group model while the security of the ZK proofs in [5] does not.

Two-party ECDSA. The two-party ECDSA scheme CCL + 19 [4] has an efficient ISign algorithm, with the drawback of running the IKeyGen algorithm with a communication size of >50 kB and a running time of >60 s for 128-bit security level. Recently, [5] improved the IKeyGen algorithm in [4] by adding an *lcm* trick upon it (we denote it as CCL + 19-*lcm*). In this paper, we implement these schemes and find out that CCL + 19-*lcm* has a non-obvious cost of doubling the running of ISign as compared with CCL + 19.

We propose a new two-party ECDSA (Sect. 5.1) by modifying the ZK proof of the well-formedness of CL ciphertext, such that the plaintext encrypted is related to an ECC group element. As compared with CCL + 19 [4] or CCL + 19-*lcm* ([5] Sect. 5.1), we use a single round ZK proof to replace the multiple rounds of ZK proofs. Our new two-party ECDSA outperforms the state-of-the-art CCL + 19-*lcm* in most aspects. Our scheme uses 47% less bandwidth in IKeyGen than the CCL + 19-*lcm* for 128-bit security. The running time of our IKeyGen is 35% faster, and the running time of our ISign is 104% faster. Detailed comparison in terms of security assumptions and security models are discussed in Sect. 5.1.

Threshold ECDSA. For threshold ECDSA, the major bottleneck for the IKeyGen algorithm for the threshold ECDSA in CCL + 20 [5] is that the ZK proof for the well-formedness of a CL ciphertext requires a random group generator g_q as discussed above (from the strong root assumption). As a result, their IKeyGen algorithm requires an additional interactive ISetup algorithm to generate such g_q. This ISetup algorithm requires a ZK proof of DL relation in the class group for n parties.

By using our bandwidth efficient ZK proof of DL relation, we can remove this complicated IKeyGen algorithm. It is because our underlying adaptive root assumption does not require a random group generator g_q. We can build a bandwidth efficient threshold ECDSA (Scheme 2 in Sect. 5.2) with about 60% smaller bandwidth than [5] for (t, n) = (1,3), (2,4) and (2,5)[3]. The running time of our $\mathsf{IKeyGen}$ is 46–65% faster. Our scheme 1 is even more optimized for the key generation algorithm (about 70% lower bandwidth and 85–90% faster computation in key generation than CCL + 20), at a cost of 20% larger bandwidth in signing. Detailed comparison in terms of security assumptions and security models are discussed in Sect. 5.2.

2 Backgrounds

We review some definitions of groups and introduce some intractability assumptions in these groups. In particular, we will use a group where the *hard subgroup membership* assumption [4] holds.

For a distribution $\mathcal{D}$, we write $d \hookleftarrow \mathcal{D}$ to refer to d being sampled from $\mathcal{D}$ and $b \overset{\$}{\leftarrow} B$ if b is sampled uniformly in the set B. We use $\mathsf{negl}(\lambda)$ (resp. $\mathsf{exp}(\lambda)$) to represent a negligible (resp. exponential) function in λ. We denote $\mathrm{ord}_{\mathbb{G}}(g)$ as the order of $g \in \mathbb{G}$. We denote ϵ_s and ϵ_d as the parameter for soundness error and statistical distance respectively.

2.1 Groups

We define some group generation algorithms as in [4]:

- On input a security parameter 1^λ, the $\mathsf{GGen}_{\mathrm{ECC}}$ algorithm generates a cyclic group $\hat{G}$ with prime order q and $\hat{P}$ is a generator of $\hat{G}$. It outputs $\mathcal{G}_{\mathrm{ECC}} = (\hat{G}, q, \hat{P})$.
- On input a security parameter 1^λ and a prime number q, the $\mathsf{GGen}_{\mathrm{HSM}}$ algorithm outputs $\mathcal{G}_{\mathrm{HSM}} = (\tilde{s}, g, f, g_q, \tilde{G}, G, F, G^q)$.

  The set $(\tilde{G}, \cdot)$ is a finite abelian group of order $q \cdot \hat{s}$, where the length of $\hat{s}$ is a function of λ and $\gcd(q, \hat{s}) = 1$. The value $\tilde{s}$ is the upper bound of $\hat{s}$. One can decide if an element is in $\tilde{G}$ in polynomial time. The set $(F, \cdot)$ is the unique cyclic subgroup of $\tilde{G}$ of order q, generated by f. The group $G^q := \{x^q, x \in G\}$ is the subgroup of order s of G, generated by g_q. The set $(G, \cdot)$ is a cyclic subgroup of $\tilde{G}$ of order $q \cdot s$, where s divides $\hat{s}$. By construction $F \subset G$, it holds that $G = G^q \times F$ and $g := f \cdot g_q$ is the generator of G. The discrete logarithm problem in F can be solved by a polynomial time algorithm Solve:

$$x \leftarrow \mathsf{Solve}_{\mathcal{G}_{\mathrm{HSM}}, q}(f^x), \quad \forall x \overset{\$}{\leftarrow} \mathbb{Z}_q.$$

  We drop the subscript for Solve when the context is clear. For simplicity, we will call this group the *HSM group*.

[3] These are the most popular types of threshold signatures in Bitcoin's P2SH transactions as shown in https://txstats.com/dashboard/db/p2sh-repartition-by-type?orgId=1. Hence we use these 3 settings for comparison in this paper.

Class Groups of Imaginary Quadratic Order. The HSM group can be instantiated by class groups of imaginary quadratic order.

The $\mathsf{GGen}_{\mathrm{HSM}}$ algorithm picks a random prime $\tilde{q}$ such that $q\tilde{q} \equiv 1 \pmod 4$ and $(q/\tilde{q}) = -1$. It computes $\Delta_K = -q\tilde{q}, \Delta_q = q^2\Delta_K$. Denote $\widehat{G}$ as the class group $Cl(\Delta_q)$, whose order is $h(\Delta_q) = q \cdot h(\Delta_K)$. It computes $\tilde{s} := \left\lceil \frac{1}{\pi} \log|\Delta_K|\sqrt{|\Delta_K|} \right\rceil$ such that $h(\Delta_K) < \tilde{s}$.

It sets $f = [(q^2, q)] \in Cl(\Delta_q)$ and $F = \langle f \rangle$. Let r be a small prime, with $r \neq q$ and $(\frac{\Delta_K}{r}) = 1$. It sets I as an ideal lying above r. Denote φ_q^{-1} as the surjection defined in the Algorithm 1 of [6]. It computes $g_q = [\varphi_q^{-1}(I^2)]^q \in Cl(\Delta_q)$ and sets $G^q = \langle g_q \rangle$. It computes $g = f \cdot g_q$ and sets $G = \langle g \rangle$. It outputs $\mathcal{G}_{\mathrm{HSM}} = (\tilde{s}, g, f, g_q, \widehat{G}, G, F, G^q)$.

2.2 ECDSA

We review the ECDSA below.

Setup. On input a security parameter 1^λ, it runs $\mathcal{G}_{\mathrm{ECC}} \leftarrow \mathsf{GGen}_{\mathrm{ECC}}(1^\lambda)$. It outputs $\mathsf{param} = \mathcal{G}_{\mathrm{ECC}}$. The input param is omitted for other algorithms for simplicity.

KeyGen. It picks a random secret key $x \xleftarrow{\$} \mathbb{Z}_q$ and computes a public key $\hat{Q} = \hat{P}^x$. It returns $(\hat{Q}, x)$.

Sign. On input a message m, it picks $k \xleftarrow{\$} \mathbb{Z}_q$. It computes $\hat{R} = (r_x, r_y) = \hat{P}^k$, $r = r_x \bmod q$ and $s = k^{-1}(xr + H(m)) \bmod q$. It outputs the signature (r, s).

Verify. On input a public key $\hat{Q}$, a message m and a signature (r, s), it computes $\hat{R} = (r_x, r_y) = (\hat{Q}^r \hat{P}^{H(m)})^{1/s}$. It outputs 1 if $r = r_x \bmod q$. Otherwise, it outputs 0.

2.3 CL Encryption from HSM Group

Castagnos and Laguillaumie [7] introduced a framework of a group with an easy DL subgroup. We review the additive homomorphic CL encryption algorithm instantiated from class groups of quadratic fields [4].

Setup. On input a security parameter 1^λ and a prime q, it runs $\mathcal{G}_{\mathrm{HSM}} \leftarrow \mathsf{GGen}_{\mathrm{HSM},q}(1^\lambda)$. It parses $\mathcal{G}_{\mathrm{HSM}} = (\tilde{s}, g, f, g_q, \widehat{G}, G, F, G^q)$. Define $S = \tilde{s} \cdot 2^{\epsilon_d}$ for some statistical distance ϵ_d. It outputs $\mathsf{param} = \mathcal{G}_{\mathrm{HSM}}$. The input param is omitted for other algorithms for simplicity.

KeyGen. It picks a random $\mathsf{sk} \xleftarrow{\$} [0, S]$ and computes $\mathsf{pk} = g_q^{\mathsf{sk}}$. It returns $(\mathsf{sk}, \mathsf{pk})$.

$\mathsf{Encrypt}$. On input a public key pk and a message m, it picks a random $\rho \xleftarrow{\$} [0, S]$ and outputs the ciphertext $C = (C_1, C_2)$, where:

$$C_1 = f^m \mathsf{pk}^\rho, \quad C_2 = g_q^\rho.$$

$\mathsf{Decrypt}$. On input a secret key sk and a ciphertext $C = (C_1, C_2)$, it computes $M = C_1 / C_2^{\mathsf{sk}}$ and returns $m \leftarrow \mathsf{Solve}(M)$.

EvalScal. On input a public key pk, a ciphertext $C = (C_1, C_2)$ and a scalar s, it outputs $C' = (C'_1 = C_1^s, C'_2 = C_2^s)$.

EvalSum. On input a public key pk, two ciphertexts $C = (C_1, C_2)$ and $C' = (C'_1, C'_2)$, it outputs $\hat{C} = (\hat{C}_1 = C_1 C'_1, \hat{C}_2 = C_2 C'_2)$.

3 Generic Group Model for HSM Group

We use the generic group model for groups of unknown order [8] together with groups of known order to model the HSM group.

A group $\mathbb{G} = \mathbb{G}_1 \times \mathbb{G}_2$ is parameterized by three integer public parameters q, A, B such that the order of $\mathbb{G}_1$ is sampled uniformly from $[A, B]$ and the order of $\mathbb{G}_2$ is q. The group $\mathbb{G}$ is defined by a random injective function $\sigma : \mathbb{Z}_{|\mathbb{G}_1| \times q} \rightarrow \{0,1\}^{\ell}$. for some ℓ where $2^{\ell} \gg |\mathbb{G}_1| \times q$. The group elements are $\sigma(0), \sigma(1), \ldots, \sigma(|\mathbb{G}_1| \times q - 1)$. We further define a function $\pi(a, b) = qa + b$ for $a \in \mathbb{Z}_{|\mathbb{G}_1|}$ and $b \in \mathbb{Z}_q$.

A generic group algorithm $\mathcal{A}$ is a probabilistic algorithm. Let $\mathcal{L} = \mathcal{L}_0 \cup \mathcal{L}_1$ be a list that is initialized with the encodings. $\mathcal{A}$ is given $(q, \mathcal{L})$ as input. The algorithm can query two generic group oracles:

- $\mathcal{O}_1$ takes a bit b'. If $b' = 0$, it samples a random $a \in \mathbb{Z}_{|\mathbb{G}_1|}$, $b \in \mathbb{Z}_q$ and returns $\sigma(\pi(a, b))$. It is appended to the list of encodings $\mathcal{L}_0$. If $b' = 1$, it samples a random $b \in \mathbb{Z}_q$ and returns $\sigma(\pi(0, b))$[4]. It is appended to the list of encodings $\mathcal{L}_1$.
- When $\mathcal{L}$ has size $\tilde{q}$, the second oracle $\mathcal{O}_2(i, j, \pm)$ takes two indices $i, j \in [1, \tilde{q}]$ and a sign bit, and returns $\sigma(\pi(a_i \pm a_j \mod |\mathbb{G}_1|, b_i \pm b_j \mod q)$, which is appended to $\mathcal{L}_1$ if $a_i \pm a_j \neq 0 \mod |\mathbb{G}_1|$. Otherwise, it is appended to $\mathcal{L}_0$.

For the group $\mathcal{G}_{\mathrm{HSM}}$, this model treats the output of $\mathcal{O}_1(1)$ as the elements in F and the output of $\mathcal{O}_1(0)$ as the elements in G. The generator g_q in G^q is initialized as $\sigma(\pi(a, 0))$ for some random a. Given the output of $\mathcal{O}_1(0)$, it is difficult to distinguish if it is in G^q or not. Suppose that f is initialized as $\sigma(\pi(0, b^*))$ for some $b^* \in \mathbb{Z}_q$. The Solve algorithm for input $\tilde{f} \in F$ can be modelled by finding the encoding of $\tilde{f}$ in $\mathcal{L}_1$ as $\sigma(\pi(0, \tilde{b}))$ for some $\tilde{b} \in \mathbb{Z}_q$ and returning $\tilde{b}/b^* \mod q$.

Lemma 1 (Element Representation [15]). *Let $\mathbb{G}$ be a generic group and $\mathcal{A}$ be a generic algorithm making q_1 queries to $\mathcal{O}_1$ and q_2 queries to $\mathcal{O}_2$. Let $\{g_1, \ldots, g_m\}$ be the outputs of $\mathcal{O}_1$. There is an efficient algorithm* Ext *that given as input the transcript of $\mathcal{A}$s interaction with the generic group oracles, produces for every element $u \in \mathbb{G}$ that $\mathcal{A}$ outputs, a tuple $(\alpha_1, \ldots, \alpha_m) \in \mathbb{Z}^m$ such that $u = \prod_{i=1}^{m} g_i^{\alpha_i}$ and $\alpha_i \leq 2^{q_2}$.*

[4] The random encoding for DL-easy subgroup is necessary, since the adversary may obtain some $g' = \sigma(\pi(a_1, b_1))$ and $f' = \sigma(\pi(0, b_2))$ from $\mathcal{O}_1$. The adversary can obtain $g' \cdot f'$ or $(g')^2/f'$ from $\mathcal{O}_2$. The encodings b_1 and b_2 ensure that the value in the DL-easy subgroup is always correct even when the computation involves elements in $\mathbb{G}_1$.

Lemma 2 (Subgroup Element Representation). *Let $\mathbb{G}$ be a generic group and $\mathcal{A}$ be a generic algorithm making q_1 queries to $\mathcal{O}_1$ and q_2 queries to $\mathcal{O}_2$. Let $\{g_1, \ldots, g_{m_0}\}$ be the outputs of $\mathcal{O}_1(0)$. There is an efficient algorithm* Ext *that given as input the transcript of $\mathcal{A}$s interaction with the generic group oracles, produces for every element $u \in \mathbb{G}$ that $\mathcal{A}$ outputs, a tuple $(\alpha_1, \ldots, \alpha_{m_0}) \in \mathbb{Z}^m$ and $\gamma \in \mathbb{Z}_q$ such that $u = f^\gamma \cdot \prod_{i=1}^{m_0} g_i^{\alpha_i}$ and $\alpha_i \leq 2^{q_2}$.*

Proof. Suppose that there is an algorithm $\mathcal{A}$ of this lemma and we will show how to build the extractor Ext. Ext first runs as an algorithm $\mathcal{A}'$ in the Lemma 1. $\mathcal{A}'$ is given initial encodings from its challenger and forwards them to $\mathcal{A}$. When $\mathcal{A}$ makes an oracle query, $\mathcal{A}'$ forwards them to its challenger to get the answer. Finally, $\mathcal{A}$ outputs an element $u \in \mathbb{G}$. $\mathcal{A}'$ forwards u to its challenger. By Lemma 1, there exists an extractor Ext' that outputs, a tuple $(\alpha_1, \ldots, \alpha_m) \in \mathbb{Z}^m$ such that $u = \prod_{i=1}^{m} g_i^{\alpha_i}$ and $\{g_1, \ldots, g_m\}$ are the outputs of $\mathcal{O}_1$. W.l.o.g., assume that $(g_1, \ldots, g_{m_0})$ are the outputs of $\mathcal{O}_1(0)$ and $(g_{m_0+1}, \ldots, g_m)$ are the outputs of $\mathcal{O}_1(1)$. Ext can compute $\beta_i = \log_f g_i \in \mathbb{Z}_q$ for $i \in [m_0 + 1, m]$ by running the Solve algorithm. Hence, Ext can compute $\gamma = \sum_{i=m_0+1}^{m} \beta_i \alpha_i \bmod q$ and can output $(\alpha_1, \ldots, \alpha_{m_0}, \gamma)$ such that $u = f^\gamma \cdot \prod_{i=1}^{m_0} g_i^{\alpha_i}$ and $\alpha_i \leq 2^{q_2}$. □

Lemma 3 (Subgroup Hidden Order). *Let $\mathbb{G} = \mathbb{G}_1 \times \mathbb{G}_2$ be a generic group where $|\mathbb{G}_1|$ is a uniformly chosen integer in $[A, B]$. Let $\mathcal{A}$ be a generic algorithm making q_1 queries to $\mathcal{O}_1(0)$ and q_2 queries to $\mathcal{O}_2$. The probability that $\mathcal{A}$ succeeds in computing $0 \neq k \in \mathbb{N}$ such that for a g which is a response to an $\mathcal{O}_1(0)$ query $g^k = 1$ is at most $\frac{(q_1+q_2)^3}{M}$, where $1/M$ is negligible whenever $|B - A| = \mathsf{exp}(\lambda)$.*

It follows from the Lemma 3 of [1]. If there is an $\mathcal{A}$ succeeds in this lemma, it is easy to build an algorithm $\mathcal{A}'$ which succeeds in the Lemma 3 of [1].

Lemma 4 (Subgroup Discrete Logarithm). *Let $\mathbb{G} = \mathbb{G}_1 \times \mathbb{G}_2$ be a generic group where $|\mathbb{G}_1|$ is a uniformly chosen integer in $[A, B]$ and $1/A$ and $1/|B - A|$ are negligible in λ. Let $\mathcal{A}$ be a polynomial time generic algorithm and let $\{g_1, \ldots, g_{m_0}\}$ be the outputs of $\mathcal{O}_1(0)$. The probability that $\mathcal{A}$ succeeds in outputting $\alpha_1, \ldots, \alpha_{m_0}, \beta_1, \ldots, \beta_{m_0} \in \mathbb{Z}$ and $\gamma, \delta \in \mathbb{Z}_q$, such that $f^\gamma \prod_{i=1}^{m_0} g_i^{\alpha_i} = f^\delta \prod_{i=1}^{m_0} g_i^{\beta_i} \in \mathbb{G}$, $\alpha_i \neq \beta_i$ and $\gamma \neq \delta \bmod q$, is negligible.*

Proof. By Lemma 2, every group element u in $\mathbb{G}$ that the adversary obtains from the $\mathcal{O}_2$ query can be written as $u = f^\gamma \prod_{i=1}^{m_0} g_i^{\alpha_i}$ for some known $\alpha_i \in \mathbb{Z}$, $\gamma \in \mathbb{Z}_q$. Let $h = f^\delta \prod_{i=1}^{m_0} g_i^{\beta_i}$ be another such a group element.

If there is some $i \in [1, m_0]$ for which $\alpha_i \not\equiv \beta_i \bmod \mathrm{ord}_{\mathbb{G}}(g_i)$ or $\gamma \not\equiv \delta \bmod q$, then the probability that $u = h$ is at most $\frac{(q_1+q_2)^2}{A}$ as shown in [8]. Therefore when $f^\gamma \prod_{i=1}^{m_0} g_i^{\alpha_i} = f^\delta \prod_{i=1}^{m_0} g_i^{\beta_i}$, then $\alpha_i \equiv \beta_i \bmod \mathrm{ord}_{\mathbb{G}}(g_i)$ and $\gamma \equiv \delta \bmod q$ with non-negligible probability if $1/A$ is negligible.

If $\alpha_i \equiv \beta_i \bmod \mathrm{ord}_{\mathbb{G}}(g_i)$, we have either $\alpha_i = \beta_i$ or $\alpha_i = \beta_i + K \cdot \mathrm{ord}_{\mathbb{G}}(g_i)$ for some integer K. By Lemma 3, $\alpha_i = \beta_i$ with overwhelming probability $(1 - \frac{(q_1+q_2)^3}{M}$, where $1/M$ is negligible whenever $|B - A| = \mathsf{exp}(\lambda))$. □

3.1 Assumptions

Let $\mathcal{D}$ (resp. $\mathcal{D}_q$) be a distribution over the integers such that the distribution $\{g^x, x \xleftarrow{\$} \mathcal{D}\}$ (resp. $\{g_q^x, x \xleftarrow{\$} \mathcal{D}_q\}$) is at a distance less than 2^λ from the uniform distribution in G (resp. G^q).

Hard Subgroup Membership Assumption. The hard subgroup membership assumption for the group $\mathcal{G}_{\text{HSM}}$ means that it is hard to distinguish the elements of G^q in G. It means that for every polynomial time algorithm $\mathcal{A}$:

$$\left| \Pr\left[b = b^* \middle| \begin{array}{l} \mathcal{G}_{\text{HSM}} \leftarrow \mathsf{GGen}_{\text{HSM},q}(1^\lambda), x \hookleftarrow \mathcal{D}, x' \hookleftarrow \mathcal{D}_q, \\ b \xleftarrow{\$} \{0,1\}, Z_0 = g^x, Z_1 = g_q^{x'}, \\ b^* \leftarrow \mathcal{A}(\mathcal{G}_{\text{HSM}}, Z_b, \mathsf{Solve}(\cdot)) \end{array} \right] - \frac{1}{2} \right| \leq \mathsf{negl}(\lambda).$$

Adaptive Root Subgroup Assumption. We define the adaptive root subgroup assumption, which is the modification of the adaptive root assumption [1] in the group $\mathcal{G}_{\text{HSM}}$. We denote $\mathsf{Primes}(\lambda)$ as the set of odd primes less than 2^λ.

The adaptive root subgroup assumption holds for the group $\mathcal{G}_{\text{HSM}}$ if for all polynomial time algorithms $(\mathcal{A}_0, \mathcal{A}_1)$:

$$\Pr\left[\begin{array}{l} u^\ell = w, \\ w^q \neq 1 \end{array} \middle| \begin{array}{l} q > 2^\lambda, \mathcal{G}_{\mathsf{HSM}} \leftarrow \mathsf{GGen}_{\mathsf{HSM},q}(1^\lambda), (w, \mathsf{state}) \leftarrow \mathcal{A}_0(\mathcal{G}_{\mathsf{HSM}}), \\ \ell \xleftarrow{\$} \mathsf{Primes}(\lambda), u \leftarrow \mathcal{A}_1(\ell, \mathsf{state}) \end{array} \right] \leq \mathsf{negl}(\lambda).$$

The next two corollaries show that the adaptive root subgroup problem and the non-trivial order element problem are intractable in a generic group model.

Corollary 1. *(Adaptive Root Subgroup Hardness). Let $G \in \mathcal{G}_{\mathsf{HSM}}$ be a generic group where $|G^q|$ is a uniformly chosen integer in $[A, B]$ such that $1/A$ and $1/|B-A|$ are negligible in λ. Any generic adversary $\mathcal{A}$ that performs a polynomial number of queries to oracle $\mathcal{O}_2$ succeeds in breaking the adaptive root subgroup assumption on $\mathcal{G}_{\mathsf{HSM}}$ with at most negligible probability in λ.*

Proof. Recall that the adversary outputs $u, w \in G$ for a challenge ℓ such that $u^\ell = w$ and $w^q \neq 1$. According to Lemma 2, we can write $u = f^\gamma \prod_{i=1}^m g_i^{\alpha_i}$ and $w = f^\delta \prod_{i=1}^m g_i^{\beta_i}$, where $\{g_1, \dots, g_m\}$ is the outputs of $\mathcal{O}_1(0)$. Since $w^q \neq 1$, there exists some $i^* \in [1, m]$ such that $\beta_{i^*} \neq 0$.

According to Lemma 4, we know that $\alpha_{i^*}\ell = \beta_{i^*} \bmod \mathrm{ord}_{\mathbb{G}}(g_{i^*})$ with overwhelming probability $1 - \epsilon$. Hence, $\alpha_{i^*}\ell = \beta_{i^*} + k{\cdot}\mathrm{ord}_{\mathbb{G}}(g_{i^*})$ for some $k \in \mathbb{Z}$. According to Lemma 3, an efficient adversary can compute a multiple of the order of the group G^q with at most negligible probability ϵ'. It follows that $k = 0$ and $\alpha_{i^*}\ell = \beta_{i^*}$ with probability greater than $1 - \epsilon - \epsilon'$ Hence, ℓ must divides β_{i^*}. However, β_{i^*} is chosen before ℓ and if $\mathcal{A}$ makes q_2 generic group queries then $\beta_{i^*} \leq 2^{q_2}$. The probability that ℓ divides β_{i^*} is bounded by the probability that a random prime in $\mathsf{Primes}(\lambda)$ divides a number less than 2^{q_2}. Any such a number has less than q_2 distinct prime factors and there are more than $2^\lambda/\lambda$ primes in $\mathsf{Primes}(\lambda)$. Therefore, the probability that ℓ divides β_{i^*} is at most $\frac{q_2\lambda}{2^\lambda}$. Overall, we obtain that a generic adversary can break the adaptive root subgroup assumption with probability at most $\frac{(q_1+q_2)^2}{A} + \frac{2(q_1+q_2)^3}{M} + \frac{q_2\lambda}{2^\lambda}$, which is negligible if $1/A$ and $1/|B-A|$ are negligible in λ and q_1, q_2 are bounded by some polynomials in λ. □

Corollary 2. *(Non-trivial order hardness). Let $G \in \mathcal{G}_{\mathsf{HSM}}$ be a generic group where $|G^q|$ is a uniformly chosen integer in $[A, B]$ such that $1/A$ and $1/|B-A|$ are negligible in λ. Any generic adversary $\mathcal{A}$ that performs a polynomial number of queries to oracle $\mathcal{O}_2$ succeeds in finding an element $h \neq 1 \in G$ and a positive integer d such that $h^d = 1$ and $d < q$ with at most negligible probability in λ.*[5]

Proof. Suppose that $\mathcal{B}$ an adaptive root adversary that is given G from its challenger. $\mathcal{B}$ gives G to $\mathcal{A}$. When $\mathcal{A}$ makes an oracle query, $\mathcal{B}$ forwards it to its challenger. $\mathcal{A}$ returns h and d to $\mathcal{B}$.

We claim that $h^q \neq 1$. Assume that on the contrary $h^q = 1$. We have $0 < d < q$, $h^d = 1$. Denote that $q' = q \bmod d$. Then $h^{q'} = 1$ and $0 < q' < d$. Since q is prime and $0 < d < q$, $\gcd(d, q) = 1$. By the Euclidean algorithm, we can apply the same computation recursively until we get $h^1 = 1$, which is a contradiction. Hence $h^q \neq 1$.

Since $h^q \neq 1$, $\mathcal{B}$ sends h to its challenger and receives a prime ℓ. With non-negligible probability, ℓ is relative prime to d. If so, $\mathcal{B}$ computes $c = \ell^{-1} \bmod d$. $\mathcal{B}$ returns $h^c = h^{1/\ell}$ to its challenger. Since the adaptive root assumption holds in the generic group model, $\mathcal{A}$ succeeds with negligible probability. □

4 ZK Proofs for HSM Group with Trustless Setup

In this section, we will give two different ZK proofs for HSM groups. The definition of an argument system is given in the Appendix A.1.

4.1 Argument of Knowledge for Exponentiation

We first construct an argument of knowledge for the following relation about exponentiation within a group G with order q subgroup F:

$$\mathcal{R}_{\mathsf{ExpS}} = \{w \in G; x \in \mathbb{Z} : w = g^x \neq 1\},$$

where g and G are the parameters in the CRS $\mathcal{G}_{\mathsf{HSM}}$. The ZK proof is given in Algorithm 3.

Lemma 5. *Protocol* PoKES *is an argument of knowledge of $\mathcal{R}_{\mathsf{ExpS}}$ in the generic group model.*

[5] Non-trivial order hardness is similar to the low order assumption in [5], except that their assumption did not rule out the trivial attack that $f^q = 1$.

Algorithm 3: Protocol PoKES for the relation $\mathcal{R}_{\mathsf{ExpS}}$

Param: $\mathcal{G}_{\mathrm{HSM}} \leftarrow \mathsf{GGen}_{\mathrm{HSM},q}(1^\lambda)$, $g \in G \setminus F$
Input: $w \in G$
Witness: $x \in \mathbb{Z}$

1. Prover finds $d \in \mathbb{Z}$ and $e \in [0, q-1]$ s.t. $x = dq + e$. Prover sends $D = g^d$ and e to the verifier.
2. If $e \in [0, q-1]$ and $D^q g^e = w$, verifier sends $\ell \xleftarrow{\$} \mathsf{Primes}(\lambda)$.
3. Prover finds $q' \in \mathbb{Z}$ and $r \in [0, \ell-1]$ s.t. $x = q'\ell + r$. Prover sends $Q = g^{q'}$ and r to the verifier.
4. Verifier accepts if $r \in [0, \ell-1]$ and $Q^\ell g^r = w$.

Proof. We describe the extractor Ext:

1. W.l.o.g. let $g_1 = g$ be encoded in the CRS.
2. Run $\mathcal{A}_0$ to get output (w, state).
3. Let $\mathcal{L} \leftarrow \{\}$.
4. Run Protocol PoKES with $\mathcal{A}_1$ on input (w, state), sampling fresh randomness for the verifier. If the transcript (D, e, ℓ, Q, r) is accepting set $\mathcal{L} \leftarrow \mathcal{L} \cup \{(r, \ell)\}$, and otherwise repeat this step.
5. Use the CRT algorithm to compute x such that $x = r_i \bmod \ell_i$ for each $(r_i, \ell_i) \in \mathcal{L}$. If $g^x = w$, output x and stop. Otherwise, return to Step 4.

It remains to argue that Ext succeeds with overwhelming probability in a poly(λ) number of rounds. Suppose that after some polynomial number of rounds the extractor has obtained M accepting transcripts $\{D, e, \ell_i, Q_i, r_i\}$ for independent values of $\ell_i \in \mathsf{Primes}(\lambda)$.

Consider an accepting transcripts (D, e, ℓ_1, Q_1, r_1) such that $w = Q_1^{\ell_1} g^{r_1} = D^q g^e$. By Lemma 2, we can write $Q_1 = f^\gamma \prod_{i=1}^m g_i^{\alpha_i}$[6], and $D = f^\nu \prod_{i=1}^m g_i^{\mu_i}$. Hence:

$$\begin{aligned} Q_1^{\ell_1} g^{r_1} &= f^{\gamma \ell_1} g^{r_1} \prod_{i=1}^m g_i^{\alpha_i \ell_1} = f^{\gamma \ell_1} g^{\alpha_1 \ell_1 + r_1} \prod_{i=2}^m g_i^{\alpha_i \ell_1} \\ &= D^q g^e = f^{\nu q} g^e \prod_{i=1}^m g_i^{\mu_i q} = g^{\mu_1 q + e} \prod_{i=2}^m g_i^{\mu_i q} \end{aligned}$$

By Lemma 4, $\gamma \ell_1 = 0 \bmod q$. Also, $\alpha_i \ell_1 = \mu_i q$ for all $i \in [2, m]$ with probability 1 - ϵ. Therefore ℓ_1 divides $\mu_i q$. Since $\ell_1 \neq q$, then ℓ_1 divides μ_i since ℓ_1 and q are relatively prime. However, $\mu_i \leq 2^{q_2}$ and μ_i is chosen before ℓ_1 is sampled. Hence the probability that ℓ_1 divides some non-zero μ_i is at most $\frac{q_2 \lambda \ln 2}{2^\lambda}$. We conclude that $\alpha_i = \mu_i = 0$ for $i \in [2, m]$ with probability 1 - $\epsilon - \frac{q_2 \lambda \ln 2}{2^\lambda}$. Hence, we can express $w = g^{\alpha_1 \ell_1 + r_1}$ for some integers α_1, r_1.

[6] Since $g = g_1$, if Q_1 is computed from f, g_i and $w = g^x = g_1^x$, we can write $Q_1 = f^\gamma \prod_{i=1}^m g_i^{\alpha_i}$.

Algorithm 4: Protocol $\mathsf{ZKPoKRepS}$ for the relation $\mathcal{R}_{\mathsf{RepS}}$

Param: $\mathcal{G}_{\text{HSM}} \leftarrow \mathsf{GGen}_{\text{HSM},q}(1^\lambda)$, $g_1, \ldots, g_n \in G \setminus F$, $B = n2^{\lambda+\epsilon_d+1}|G|$ where $\epsilon_d = 80$.
Input: $w \in G$.
Witness: $\boldsymbol{x} = (x_1, \ldots, x_n) \in \mathbb{Z}^n$.

1. Prover chooses $k_1, \ldots, k_n \xleftarrow{\$} [-B, B]$, $t \xleftarrow{\$} \mathbb{Z}_q$ and sends $R = \prod_{i=1}^n g_i^{k_i}$ to the verifier.
2. Verifier sends $c \xleftarrow{\$} [0, q-1]$ to the prover.
3. Prover computes $s_i = k_i + cx_i$ for $i \in [1, n]$. Prover finds $d_i \in \mathbb{Z}$, $e_i \in [0, q-1]$ s.t. $s_i = d_i q + e_i$ and sends $D = \prod_{i=1}^n g_i^{d_i}$ and $\boldsymbol{e} = (e_1, \ldots, e_n)$ to the verifier.
4. If $e_1, \ldots, e_n \in [0, q-1]$ and $D^q \prod_{i=1}^n g_i^{e_i} = Rw^c$, verifier sends $\ell \xleftarrow{\$} \mathsf{Primes}(\lambda)$.
5. Prover finds $q_i \in \mathbb{Z}$ and $r_i \in [0, \ell-1]$ s.t. $s_i = q_i \ell + r_i$ for $i \in [1, n]$. Prover sends $Q = \prod_{i=1}^n g_i^{q_i}$ and $\boldsymbol{r} = (r_1, \ldots, r_n)$ to the verifier.
6. Verifier accepts if $r_1, \ldots, r_n \in [0, \ell-1]$ and $Q^\ell \prod_{i=1}^n g_i^{r_i} = Rw^c$.

By the argument above, with overwhelming probability there exists $x \in \mathbb{Z}$ such that $x = r_i \bmod \ell_i$ and $g^x = w$ and $x < 2^{q_2}$. Hence, the CRT algorithm used in Step 5 will recover the required x once $|\mathcal{L}| > q_2$.

Since a single round of interaction with $\mathcal{A}_1$ results in an accepting transcript with probability $\epsilon \geq 1/\mathsf{poly}(\lambda)$, in expectation the extractor obtains $|\mathcal{L}| > q_2$ accepting transcripts for independent primes ℓ_i after $q_2 \cdot \mathsf{poly}(\lambda)$ rounds. Hence, Ext outputs x such that $g^x = w$ in expected polynomial time, as required. □

Note that there are more than $2^\lambda/\lambda$ primes in $\mathsf{Primes}(\lambda)$ and it can be instantiated by a hash to prime function [1]. The soundness error is about $1/2^{\lambda - \log_2 \lambda}$ if ℓ is λ bits.

4.2 ZK Proof for Multi-exponentiation

We now construct an argument of knowledge for the following relation:

$$\mathcal{R}_{\mathsf{RepS}} = \{w \in G; \boldsymbol{x} \in \mathbb{Z}^n : w = \prod_{i=1}^n g_i^{x_i}\},$$

where $g_1, \ldots, g_n \in G \setminus F$ are in the CRS $\mathcal{G}_{\mathsf{HSM}}$. The ZK proof is given in Algorithm 4.

Theorem 1. *Protocol* $\mathsf{ZKPoKRepS}$ *is an argument of knowledge for* $\mathcal{R}_{\mathsf{RepS}}$ *in the generic group model.*

Proof. We describe the extractor Ext:

1. Run $\mathcal{A}_0$ to get output (w, state).
2. Let $\mathcal{L} \leftarrow \{\}$. Run Step 1 of Protocol $\mathsf{ZKPoKRepS}$ with $\mathcal{A}_1$ on input (w, state).

3. Run Step 2–3 of Protocol ZKPoKRepS with $\mathcal{A}_1$, sampling fresh randomness c for the verifier.
4. Run Step 4–5 of Protocol ZKPoKRepS with $\mathcal{A}_1$, sampling fresh randomness ℓ for the verifier. If the transcript $(R, c, z, D, \boldsymbol{e}, \ell, Q, \boldsymbol{r})$ is accepting, set $\mathcal{L} \leftarrow \mathcal{L} \cup \{(\boldsymbol{r}, \ell)\}$, and otherwise repeat this step.
5. Use the CRT algorithm to compute $\boldsymbol{s} = (s_1, \ldots, s_n)$ such that $\boldsymbol{s} = \boldsymbol{r}_i \bmod \ell_i$ for each $(\boldsymbol{r}_i, \ell_i) \in \mathcal{L}$. If $\prod_{i=1}^n g_i^{s_i} \neq Rw^c$, return to Step 5.
6. Consider the intermediate transcript as $(R, c, D, \boldsymbol{e}, \boldsymbol{s})$. Run from Step 4 for the second time and obtain $(R, c', D', \boldsymbol{e}', \boldsymbol{s}')$.
7. Compute $\Delta_{s_i} = s_i - s'_i$ for $i \in [1, n]$ and $\Delta_c = c - c'$. Output $\boldsymbol{x} = (x_1, \ldots, x_n)$ for $x_i = \Delta_{s_i} / \Delta_c$.

Analysis for Step 5. This is a generalization of the protocol PoKES. We first argue that $\prod_{i=1}^n g_i^{s_i} = Rw^c$ with overwhelming probability in a poly(λ) number of rounds. Suppose that after some polynomial number of rounds the extractor has obtained M accepting transcripts $\{R, c, D, \boldsymbol{e}, \ell_i, Q_i, \boldsymbol{r}_i\}$ for independent values of $\ell_i \in \mathsf{Primes}(\lambda)$.

Consider an accepting transcripts $(R, c, D, \boldsymbol{e} = (e_1, \ldots, e_n), \ell_1, Q_1, \boldsymbol{r}_1 = (r_{1,1}, \ldots, r_{1,n}))$ such that $Rw^c = Q_1^{\ell_1} \prod_{i=1}^n g_i^{r_{1,i}} = D^q \prod_{i=1}^n g_i^{e_i}$. By Lemma 2, we can write $Q_1 = \prod_{i=1}^m g_i^{\alpha_i} \cdot f^\gamma$ and $D = \prod_{i=1}^m g_i^{\beta_i} \cdot f^\delta$. Hence:

$$Q_1^{\ell_1} \prod_{i=1}^n g_i^{r_{1,i}} = \prod_{i=1}^n g_i^{\alpha_i \ell_1 + r_{1,i}} \prod_{i=n+1}^m g_i^{\alpha_i \ell_1} \cdot f^{\gamma \ell_1} = D^q \prod_{i=1}^n g_i^{e_i}$$
$$= \prod_{i=1}^n g_i^{\beta_i q + e_i} \prod_{i=n+1}^m g_i^{\beta_i q} \cdot f^{\delta q} = \prod_{i=1}^n g_i^{\beta_i q + e_i} \prod_{i=n+1}^m g_i^{\beta_i q}.$$

By Lemma 4, $\alpha_i \ell_1 = \beta_i q$ for all $i \in [n+1, m]$ with overwhelming probability. Therefore ℓ_1 divides $\beta_i q$. Since $\ell_1 \neq q$, ℓ_1 and q are relatively prime and ℓ_1 divides β_i. However, $\beta_i \leq 2^{q_2}$ and β_i are chosen before ℓ_1 is sampled. Hence the probability that ℓ_1 divides some non-zero β_i is at most $\frac{q_2 \lambda \ln 2}{2^\lambda}$. We conclude that with overwhelming probability $\alpha_i = \beta_i = 0$ for $i \in [n+1, m]$. Also by Lemma 4, $\gamma \ell_1 = 0 \bmod q$. Hence, we can express $Rw^c = \prod_{i=1}^n g_i^{\alpha_i \ell_1 + r_{1,i}}$ for some integers $\alpha_i, r_{1,i}$.

By the argument above, with overwhelming probability there exists $\boldsymbol{s} \in \mathbb{Z}^n$ such that $\boldsymbol{s} = \boldsymbol{r}_i \bmod \ell_i$, $s_i < 2^{q_2}$ for all $s_i \in \boldsymbol{s}$ and $\prod_{i=1}^n g_i^{s_i} = Rw^c$. Hence, the CRT algorithm used in Step 5 will recover the required vector $\boldsymbol{s}$ once $|\mathcal{L}| > q_2$. Since a single round of interaction with $\mathcal{A}_1$ results in an accepting transcript with probability $\epsilon \geq 1/\mathsf{poly}(\lambda)$, in expectation the extractor obtains $|\mathcal{L}| > q_2$ accepting transcripts for independent primes ℓ_i after $q_2 \cdot \mathsf{poly}(\lambda)$ rounds. Hence, Ext outputs $\boldsymbol{s}$ such that $\prod_{i=1}^n g_i^{s_i} = Rw^c$ in expected polynomial time.

Analysis for Step 7. It remains to argue that Ext succeeds with overwhelming probability in Step 7. W.l.o.g., assume that $c > c'$, by Step 6, we have $\prod_{i=1}^n g_i^{s_i} \cdot w^{-c} = \prod_{i=1}^n g_i^{s'_i} \cdot w^{-c'}$. Then $\prod_{i=1}^n g_i^{\Delta_{s_i}} = w^{\Delta_c} = (\prod_{i=1}^m g_i^{\alpha'_i} \cdot f^{\gamma'})^{\Delta_c}$ for some $\alpha'_i \in \mathbb{Z}$ and $\gamma' \in \mathbb{Z}_q$ by Lemma 2. By Lemma 4, $\Delta_{s_i} = \alpha'_i \Delta_c$ for $i \in [1, n]$, $\alpha'_i = 0$ for $i \in [n+1, m]$ and $\gamma' = 0 \bmod q$ with overwhelming probability.

If $\mu = \prod_{i=1}^{n} g_i^{\Delta_{s_i}/\Delta_c} \neq w$, then $\mu^{\Delta_c} = w^{\Delta_c}$. It follows that μ/w is an element of order $1 < \Delta_c < q$. By Corollary 2, the probability of finding a non-trivial order of $\mu/w \neq 1$ is negligible. Hence, $\mu = w$ with overwhelming probability. It implies that $\Delta_{s_i}/\Delta_c \in \mathbb{Z}$ for all i. Hence, the witness $\boldsymbol{x} = (x_1, \ldots, x_n)$ can be extracted as in Step 7. □

Theorem 2. *The protocol* ZKPoKRepS *is an honest-verifier statistically zero-knowledge argument of knowledge for relation* $\mathcal{R}_{\mathsf{RepS}}$ *in the generic group model.*

Proof. The simulator Sim picks a random challenge $c' \xleftarrow{\$} [0, q-1]$ and $\ell' \xleftarrow{\$} \mathsf{Primes}(\lambda)$. It picks random $q'_1, \ldots, q'_n, \xleftarrow{\$} [0, B-1]$, $r'_1, \ldots, r'_n \xleftarrow{\$} [0, \ell-1]$. It finds $d'_i \in \mathbb{Z}$ and $e'_i \in [0, q-1]$ such that $d'_i q + e'_i = q'_i \ell' + r'_i$. It computes:

$$Q' = \prod_{i=1}^{n} g_i^{q'_i}, \quad D' = \prod_{i=1}^{n} g_i^{d'_i}, \quad R' = D'^q \prod_{i=1}^{n} g_i^{e'_i} \cdot w^{-c'}.$$

We argue that the transcript $(R', c', (D', \boldsymbol{e}' = (e'_1, \ldots, e'_n)), \ell', (Q', \boldsymbol{r}' = (r'_1, \ldots, r'_n)))$ is indistinguishable from a real transcript between a prover and a verifier. Sim chooses ℓ', c' identically to the honest verifier. It also solves $R', D', \boldsymbol{e}'$ uniquely from the other values such that the verification holds.

We must show that in the real protocol, independent of ℓ and c, the values in $\boldsymbol{r}$ have a negligible statistical distance from the uniform distribution over $[0, \ell-1]$ and each $g_i^{q_i}$ has a negligible statistical distance from uniform over G. In addition we must argue that Q and $\boldsymbol{r}$ are independent. For this we use the following facts, which are easy to verify:

1. Fact 1: If Z is a uniform random variable over N consecutive integers and $m < N$, then $Z \bmod m$ has a statistical distance at most m/N from the uniform distribution over $[0, m-1]$.
2. Fact 2: For independent random variables X_1, X_2, Y_1, Y_2, the distance between the joint distributions (X_1, X_2) and (Y_1, Y_2) is at most the sum of statistical distances of X_1 from Y_1 and X_2 from Y_2. Similarly, if these variables are group elements in G, the statistical distance between $X_1 \cdot X_2$ and $Y_1 \cdot Y_2$ is no greater than the sum of statistical distances of X_1 from Y_1 and X_2 from Y_2.
3. Fact 3: Consider random variables X_1, X_2, Y_1, Y_2 with statistical distances $s_1 = \Delta(X_1, Y_1)$ and $s_2 = \Delta(X_2, Y_2)$, where $\Pr(X_1 = a | X_2 = b) < \Pr(X_1 = a) + \epsilon_1$ and $\Pr(Y_1 = a | Y_2 = b) < \Pr(Y_1 = a) + \epsilon_2$ for all values a, b. Then the joint distributions (X_1, X_2) and (Y_1, Y_2) have a statistical distance at most $s_1 + s_2 + \epsilon_1 |\mathrm{supp}(X_2)| + \epsilon_2 |\mathrm{supp}(Y_2)|$, where supp is the support.

Consider fixed values of $c, x_1, \ldots, x_n$ and ℓ. In the real protocol, the prover computes $s_i = k_i + c x_i$, where k_i is uniform in $[-B, B]$ and t is uniform in $\mathbb{Z}_q$, and sets $r_i = s_i \bmod \ell$. By Fact 1, the value of s_i is distributed uniformly over a range of $2B+1$ consecutive integers, thus r_i has a statistical distance at most $\ell/(2B+1)$ from uniform over $[0, \ell-1]$. This bounds the distance between the real r_i and the simulated r'_i, which is uniform over $[0, \ell-1]$.

Next, we show that each $g_i^{q_i}$ is statistically indistinguishable from uniform in the subgroup generated by g_i (denoted as G_i). The distribution of $g_i^{q_i}$ over G_i is determined by the distribution of $q_i \bmod |G_i|$. Consider the distribution of $q_i = \lfloor \frac{s_i}{\ell} \rfloor$ over the consecutive integers in $[\lfloor \frac{cx_i - B}{\ell} \rfloor, \lfloor \frac{cx_i + B}{\ell} \rfloor]$. Denote this by the random variable Z. The probability that $q_i = z$ is the probability that s_i falls in the interval $[z\ell, (z+1)\ell - 1]$. Hence $\Pr[q_i = z] = \ell/(2B+1)$ for all $z \in Z$ if $z\ell \geq cx_i - B$ and $(z+1)\ell - 1 \leq cx_i + B$. This probability may or may not hold for the two endpoints $E_1 = \lfloor \frac{cx_i - B}{\ell} \rfloor$ and $E_2 = \lfloor \frac{cx_i + B}{\ell} \rfloor$. Denote Y as the set of points with $\Pr[q_i = z] = \ell/(2B+1)$ only. The distance of q_i from a uniform random variable U_Y over Y is largest when the number of possible s_i mapping to E_1 and E_2 are both $\ell - 1$, i.e., $cx_i - B = 1 \bmod \ell$ and $cx_i + B = \ell - 2 \bmod \ell$. In this case, q_i is one of the two endpoints outside Y with probability $\frac{2(\ell-1)}{2B+1}$. As $|Y| = \frac{2B+3}{\ell} - 3$, the statistical distance of q_i from U_Y is at most $\frac{1}{2}(|Y|(\frac{1}{|Y|} - \frac{\ell}{2B+1}) + \frac{2(\ell-1)}{2B+1}) = \frac{5\ell-4}{2(2B+1)} \leq \frac{2^{\lambda+1}}{B}$. Moreover, the statistical distance of $q_i \bmod |G_i|$ from $U_Y \bmod |G_i|$ is no larger.

By Fact 1, $U_Y \bmod |G_i|$ has a statistical distance at most $\frac{|G_i|}{|Y|} \leq \frac{2^\lambda |G|}{2B+3-3\cdot 2^\lambda} < \frac{2^{\lambda-1}|G|}{B+1-2^\lambda}$. By the triangle inequality, the statistical distance of $q_i \bmod |G_i|$ from uniform is at most $\frac{2^{\lambda+1}}{B} + \frac{2^{\lambda-1}|G|}{B+1-2^\lambda}$. This also bounds the distance of $g_i^{q_i}$ from uniform in G_i. The simulated value q_i' is uniformly chosen from a set of size B. Again by Fact 1, if $|G_i| < B$, then $q_i' \bmod |G_i|$ has a distance $|G_i|/B \leq |G|/B$ from uniform. The simulated value $g_i^{q_i'}$ has a distance at most $|G|/B$ from uniform in G_i. By the triangle inequality, the statistical distance of $g_i^{q_i}$ and $g_i^{q_i'}$ is at most:

$$\begin{aligned} \frac{2^{\lambda+1}}{B} + \frac{2^{\lambda-1}|G|}{B+1-2^\lambda} + \frac{|G|}{B} &< \frac{2^{\lambda-1}|G| + |G| + 2^{\lambda+2}}{B+1-2^\lambda} \\ &= \frac{(2^{\lambda-1}+1)|G| + 2^{\lambda+1}}{B+1-2^\lambda} \leq \frac{1}{n 2^{\epsilon_d+1}}, \end{aligned}$$

if $B \geq n2^{\epsilon_d+1}(2^{\lambda-1}+1)|G| + n2^{\epsilon_d+\lambda+2} + 2^\lambda - 1$ for some distance parameter ϵ_d.

Finally, we consider the joint distribution of $g_i^{r_i}$ and r_i. Consider the conditional distribution of $q_i|r_i$. Note that $q_i = z$ if $(s_i - r_i)/\ell = z$. We repeat a similar argument as above for bounding the distribution of q_i from uniform. For each possible value of z, there always exists a unique value of s_i such that $\lfloor \frac{s_i}{\ell} \rfloor = z$ and $s_i = 0 \bmod \ell$, except possibly at the two endpoints E_1, E_2 of the range of q_i. When r_i disqualifies the two points E_1 and E_2, then each of the remaining points $z \notin \{E_1, E_2\}$ still has an equal probability mass, and thus the probability $\Pr(q_i = z|r_i)$ increases by at most $\frac{1}{|Y|} - \frac{\ell}{2B+1}$. The same applies to the variable $q_i|r_i \bmod |G_i|$ and hence the variable $g^{q_i}|r_i$.

We can compare the joint distribution $X_i = (g_i^{q_i}, r_i)$ to the simulated distribution $Y_i = (g_i^{q_i'}, r_i')$ using Fact 3. Setting $\epsilon_1 = \frac{1}{|Y|} - \frac{\ell}{2B+1}$ and $\epsilon_2 = 0$, the distance between these joint distributions is at most $\frac{1}{n2^\lambda} + \frac{\ell}{2B+1} + \epsilon_1 \ell = \frac{1}{n2^\lambda} + \frac{1}{2B+3-3\ell} + \frac{\ell(1-\ell)}{2B+1}$. Moreover, as each X_i is independent from X_j for $i \neq j$, we use Fact 2 to bound the distance between joint distributions $(g_1^{q_1}, \ldots, g_n^{q_n}, r_1, \ldots, r_n)$

Table 1. Comparison of ZK Proofs of DL relation in HSM group for $x \in [0, \tilde{s} \cdot 2^{80}]$.

	Communication size (Bytes)				Remark
	$\lambda = 112$	$\lambda = 128$	$\lambda = 192$	$\lambda = 256$	
CCL + 19 [4]	21930	29120	55700	91300	
CCL + 20 [5] (*lcm* trick)	2211	2930	5588	9148	Modified relation
This paper	591	771	1467	2389	Generic group model

and $(g_1^{q_1'}, \ldots, g_n^{q_n'}, r_1', \ldots, r_n')$ by the sum of individual distances between each X_i and Y_i, which is at most:

$$\frac{1}{2^{\epsilon_d+1}} + \frac{n}{2B+3-3\ell} + \frac{n\ell(1-\ell)}{2B+1} < \frac{1}{2^{\epsilon_d+1}} + \frac{n}{2B+3-3\ell} < \frac{1}{2^{\epsilon_d}},$$

where the last equality holds if $B > n2^{\epsilon_d} + 2^{\lambda+1} - 1$. Finally, this also bounds the distance between $(Q, \boldsymbol{r})$ and $(Q', \boldsymbol{r'})$, where $Q = \prod_i g_i^{q_i}$ and $Q' = \prod_i g_i^{q_i'}$. Combining the two requirements on B, we can simplify the requirement as $B \geq n2^{\lambda+\epsilon_d+1}|G|$. $\square$

Comparison. We compare our scheme with the similar ZK proofs for DL relation in HSM group in [4] and [5]. However, there are some minor differences for the relation to be proven. In our case, we prove the knowledge of $x = \log_{g_1} w$ for some $g_1 \in G \setminus F$ and $x \in \mathbb{Z}$. In the other two schemes, $g_1 \in G^q$ and the range of x is restricted to $x \in [0, S]$ (where $S = \tilde{s} \cdot 2^{40}$ in [5] and $S = \tilde{s} \cdot 2^{\lambda-2}$ in [4]). More importantly, the ZK proof in [5] only proves the knowledge of x such that $h^y = g_1^x$ for some public value y. The relation proved is slightly modified. On the other hand, our proof uses the generic group model. We note that there are some ZK proofs for class group [1] using the generic group model as well.

We compare these schemes in Table 1 by setting $g_1 \in G^q \subset G \setminus F$ and fixing the range S as $\tilde{s} \cdot 2^{80}$. We use 2^{-80} for statistical distance and soundness error for fair comparison. In our scheme, we can set $B = 2^{\lambda+81}\tilde{s}$, where $\tilde{s} := \left\lceil \frac{1}{\pi} \log|\Delta_K|\sqrt{|\Delta_K|} \right\rceil$. Note that the communication size of our scheme does not change much for soundness error $\epsilon_s < \lambda - \log\lambda$ (only the size of ℓ and $\boldsymbol{r}$ are affected).

4.3 ZK Proof for the Well-Formedness of a CL Ciphertext

Consider a prover honestly generated his public key pk and encrypted a message $m \in \mathbb{Z}_q$ using a randomness $\rho \in [0, S]$. We present a zero-knowledge proof of knowledge of the following relation:

$$\mathcal{R}_{\mathsf{Enc}} = \{(\mathsf{pk}, C_1, C_2); (m, \rho) | \mathsf{pk} \in G^q, \rho \in [0, S] : C_1 = f^m \mathsf{pk}^\rho \wedge C_2 = g_q^\rho\}.$$

For the relation $\mathcal{R}_{\mathsf{Enc}}$, we cannot apply the protocol $\mathsf{ZKPoKRepS}$ directly since $f \in F$. We propose a new ZK proof $\mathsf{ZKPoKEnc}$ for $\mathcal{R}_{\mathsf{Enc}}$ in Algorithm 5.

Algorithm 5: Protocol ZKPoKEnc for the relation $\mathcal{R}_{\mathsf{Enc}}$

Param: $\mathcal{G}_{\text{HSM}} \leftarrow \mathsf{GGen}_{\text{HSM},q}(1^\lambda)$, $B = 2^{\lambda+\epsilon_d+2}\tilde{s}$, where $\epsilon_d = 80$.
Input: $C_1, C_2, \mathsf{pk} \in G^q$.
Witness: $\rho \in [0, S], m \in \mathbb{Z}_q$, where $S = \tilde{s} \cdot 2^{\epsilon_d}$.

1 Prover chooses $s_\rho \xleftarrow{\$} [-B, B]$, $s_m \xleftarrow{\$} \mathbb{Z}_q$ and computes:

$$S_1 = \mathsf{pk}^{s_\rho} f^{s_m}, \quad S_2 = g_q^{s_\rho}.$$

Prover sends (S_1, S_2) to the verifier.

2 Verifier sends $c \xleftarrow{\$} [0, q-1]$ to the prover.

3 Prover computes:

$$u_\rho = s_\rho + c\rho, \quad u_m = s_m + cm \mod q.$$

Prover finds $d_\rho \in \mathbb{Z}$ and $e_\rho \in [0, q-1]$ s.t. $u_\rho = d_\rho q + e_\rho$. Prover computes:

$$D_1 = \mathsf{pk}^{d_\rho}, \quad D_2 = g_q^{d_\rho}.$$

Prover sends (u_m, D_1, D_2, e_ρ) to the verifier.

4 The verifier checks if $e_\rho \in [0, q-1]$ and:

$$D_1^q \mathsf{pk}^{e_\rho} f^{u_m} = S_1 C_1^c, \quad D_2^q g_q^{e_\rho} = S_2 C_2^c.$$

If so, the verifier sends $\ell \xleftarrow{\$} \mathsf{Primes}(\lambda)$.

5 Prover finds $q_\rho \in \mathbb{Z}$ and $r_\rho \in [0, \ell-1]$ s.t. $u_\rho = q_\rho \ell + r_\rho$. Prover computes:

$$Q_1 = \mathsf{pk}^{q_\rho}, \quad Q_2 = g_q^{q_\rho}.$$

Prover sends (Q_1, Q_2, r_ρ) to the verifier.

6 Verifier accepts if $r_\rho \in [0, \ell-1]$ and:

$$Q_1^\ell \mathsf{pk}^{r_\rho} f^{u_m} = S_1 C_1^c, \quad Q_2^\ell g_q^{r_\rho} = S_2 C_2^c.$$

Theorem 3. *The protocol* ZKPoKEnc *is an argument of knowledge in the generic group model.*

Proof. We rewind the adversary on fresh challenges ℓ so that each accepting transcript outputs an (r_ρ, ℓ), where $s_\rho = r_\rho \mod \ell$ with overwhelming probability.

If $\mathsf{pk}^{s_\rho} \neq S_1 C_1^c f^{-u_m}$ and $(\mathsf{pk}^{s_\rho})^q \neq (S_1 C_1^c f^{-u_m})^q$, then we have:

$$\mathsf{pk}^{s_\rho} \neq S_1 C_1^c f^{-u_m} = Q_1^\ell \mathsf{pk}^{r_\rho} = D_1^q \mathsf{pk}^{e_\rho}.$$

Let $\gamma_\rho = \frac{r_\rho - s_\rho}{\ell}$. Then $Q_1 \mathsf{pk}^{\gamma_\rho}$ is an ℓ-th root of $(S_1 C_1^c f^{-u_m})/\mathsf{pk}^{s_\rho} \neq 1$. This would break the adaptive root subgroup assumption since

$(S_1 C_1^c f^{-u_m})^q / (\mathsf{pk}^{s_\rho})^q \neq 1$. If $\mathsf{pk}^{s_\rho} \neq S_1 C_1^c f^{-u_m}$ and $(\mathsf{pk}^{s_\rho})^q = (S_1 C_1^c f^{-u_m})^q$, then $S_1 C_1^c = \mathsf{pk}^{s_\rho} f^{\delta'}$ for some $\delta' \neq u_m \in \mathbb{Z}_q$. It is contradictory to $S_1 C_1^c f^{-u_m} = D_1^q \mathsf{pk}^{e_\rho}$ where $\mathsf{pk} \in G^q$. Hence by Corollary 1 it follows that $\mathsf{pk}^{s_\rho} f^{u_m} = S_1 C_1^c$ with overwhelming probability.

The extractor obtains a pair of accepting transcripts with (s_ρ, u_m, c) and (s'_ρ, u'_m, c'). The extractor can compute $\Delta_{s_\rho} = s_\rho - s'_\rho$ and $\Delta_{u_m} = u_m - u'_m$ mod q. We denote $\rho = \frac{\Delta_{s_\rho}}{\Delta_c}$ and $m = \frac{\Delta_{u_m}}{\Delta_c}$ mod q. Hence we have:

$$C_1^{\Delta_c} = (\mathsf{pk}^\rho f^m)^{\Delta_c}.$$

If $C_1 \neq \mathsf{pk}^\rho f^m$, then $\frac{\mathsf{pk}^\rho f^m}{C_1}$ is a non-trivial element of order $\Delta c < q$. It contradicts the hardness of computing a non-trivial element and its order in the generic group model (Corollary 2).

Note that our scheme includes a sub-protocol ZKPoKRepS on input C_2 w.r.t. bases $g_q \in G \setminus F$. Since ZKPoKRepS is an argument of knowledge, there exists an extractor to extract the same ρ such that $C_2 = g_q^\rho$. Hence the extractor can output (m, ρ, sk) such that $C_1 = \mathsf{pk}^\rho f^m$, $C_2 = g_q^\rho$. □

Theorem 4. *The protocol* ZKPoKEnc *is an honest-verifier statistically zero-knowledge argument of knowledge for relation* $\mathcal{R}_{\mathsf{Enc}}$ *in the generic group model.*

Proof. The simulator Sim randomly picks a challenge $c' \in [0, 2^\lambda]$ and a prime $\ell' \in \mathsf{Prime}(\lambda)$. It picks a random $u'_m \in \mathbb{Z}_q$, $q'_\rho \in [0, B-1]$ and $r'_\rho \in [0, \ell' - 1]$.

It finds $d'_\rho \in \mathbb{Z}$ and $e'_\rho, \in [0, q-1]$ such that

$$d'_\rho q + e'_\rho = q'_\rho \ell' + r'_\rho.$$

It computes:

$$D'_1 = \mathsf{pk}^{d'_\rho}, \quad D'_2 = g_q^{d'_\rho}, \quad Q'_1 = \mathsf{pk}^{q'_\rho}, \quad Q'_2 = g_q^{q'_\rho},$$
$$S'_1 = Q_1'^{\ell'} \mathsf{pk}^{r'_\rho} f^{u'_m} C_1^{-c'}, \quad S'_2 = Q_2'^{\ell'} g_q^{r'_\rho} C_2^{-c'}.$$

We argue that the simulated transcript $(S'_1, S'_2, c', u'_m, D'_1, D'_2, e'_\rho, \ell', Q'_1, Q'_2, r'_\rho)$ is indistinguishable from a real transcript $(S_1, S_2, c, u_m, D_1, D_2, e_\rho, \ell, Q_1, Q_2, r_\rho)$ between a prover and a verifier. Sim chooses (ℓ', c') identically to the honest verifier. Both u_m and u'_m are uniformly distributed in $\mathbb{Z}_q$. $(S'_1, S'_2, D'_1, D'_2, e'_\rho)$ is uniquely defined by the other values such that the verification holds.

For simulated transcript (Q'_1, Q'_2, r'_ρ) and real transcript (Q_1, Q_2, r_ρ), the same arguments as in the *Theorem* 2 apply. Namely, in the real protocol, independent of ℓ and c, the values r_ρ has a negligible statistical distance from the uniform distribution over $[0, \ell - 1]$ and each one of $\mathsf{pk}^{q_\rho}, g_q^{q_\rho}$ has negligible statistical from uniform over $G_k = \langle \mathsf{pk} \rangle, G^q$ respectively. In addition, Q_1, Q_2 and r_ρ are independent. Thus, the simulator produces statistically indistinguishable transcripts. The complete proof is as follows.

Consider fixed values of c, ρ and ℓ. In the real protocol, the prover computes $u_\rho = c\rho + s_\rho$ where s_ρ is uniform in $[-B, B]$ and sets $r_\rho = u_\rho$ mod ℓ. By Fact 1, the value of u_ρ is distributed uniformly over a range of $2B + 1$ consecutive integers, thus r_ρ has a statistical distance at most $\ell/(2B+1)$ from uniform over $[0,\ell-1]$. This bounds the distance between the real r_ρ and the simulated r'_ρ, which is uniform over $[0,\ell-1]$.

Next, we show that $g_q^{q_\rho}$ is statistically indistinguishable from uniform in G^q. The distribution of $g_q^{q_\rho}$ over G^q is determined by the distribution of q_ρ mod $|G^q|$. Consider the distribution of $q_\rho = \left\lfloor \frac{u_\rho}{\ell} \right\rfloor$ over the consecutive integers in $[\left\lfloor \frac{c\rho-B}{\ell} \right\rfloor, \left\lfloor \frac{c\rho+B}{\ell} \right\rfloor]$ Denote this by the random variable Z. The probability that $q_\rho = z$ is the probability that u_ρ falls in the interval $[z\ell,(z+1)\ell-1]$. This probability is $\ell/(2B+1)$ for all points where $z\ell \geq c\rho - B$ and $(z+1)\ell-1 \leq c\rho+B$, which includes all points except possibly the two endpoints $\left\lfloor \frac{c\rho-B}{\ell} \right\rfloor$ and $\left\lfloor \frac{c\rho+B}{\ell} \right\rfloor$. Call this set of points Y. The distance of q_ρ from a uniform random variable U_Y over Y is largest when $c\rho - B = 1 \bmod \ell$ and $c\rho + B = \ell - 2 \bmod \ell$. In this case, q_ρ is one of the two endpoints outside Y with probability $\frac{2(\ell-2)}{2B+1}$. For each $z \in Y$, $\Pr[q_\rho = z] = \ell/(2B+1)$. As $|Y| = \frac{2B+3}{\ell} - 3$, the statistical distance of q_ρ from U_Y is at most: $\frac{1}{2}[Y(\frac{1}{Y} - \frac{\ell}{2B+1}) + \frac{2(\ell-1)}{2B+1}] = \frac{5\ell-4}{2B+1} \leq \frac{2^{\lambda+2}}{B}$. Moreover, the statistical distance of q_ρ mod $|G^q|$ from U_Y mod $|G^q|$ is no larger. By Fact 1, U_Y mod $|G_i|$ has a statistical distance at most $\frac{|G_i|}{|Y|} \leq \frac{2^\lambda|G|}{2B+3-3\cdot 2^\lambda} < \frac{2^{\lambda-1}|G|}{B+1-2^\lambda}$. By the triangle inequality, the statistical distance of q_ρ mod $|G^q|$ from uniform is at most $\frac{2^{\lambda+1}}{B} + \frac{2^{\lambda-1}|G|}{B+1-2^\lambda}$. This also bounds the distance of $g_q^{q_\rho}$ from uniform in G^q. The simulated value q'_ρ is uniformly chosen from a set of size B. Again by Fact 1, if $|G^q| < B$, then q'_ρ mod $|G^q|$ has a distance $|G^q|/B$ from uniform. The simulated value $g_q^{q'_\rho}$ has a distance at most $|G^q|/B$ from uniform in G^q. By the triangle inequality, the statistical distance of $g_q^{q_\rho}$ and $g_q^{q'_\rho}$ is at most $\frac{2^{\lambda+1}}{B} + \frac{2^{\lambda-1}|G^q|}{B+1-2^\lambda} + \frac{|G^q|}{B} < \frac{1}{2^{\epsilon_d+2}}$, if $B \geq 2^{\epsilon_d+2}(2^{\lambda-1}+1)|G^q| + 2^{\lambda+\epsilon_d+3} + 2^\lambda - 1$. Similarly, the same argument holds for the distances of pk^{q_ρ} and $\mathsf{pk}^{q'_\rho}$. By using Fact 3, the distance between the joint distribution $X_\rho = (\mathsf{pk}^{q_\rho}, g_q^{q_\rho})$ and the simulated distribution $Y_\rho = (\mathsf{pk}^{q'_\rho}, g_q^{q'_\rho})$ is at most $\frac{1}{2^{\epsilon_d+1}}$.

Finally, we consider the joint distribution of $(\mathsf{pk}^{q_\rho}, g_q^{q_\rho})$ and r_ρ. Consider the conditional distribution of $q_\rho|r_\rho$. Note that $q_\rho = z$ if $(s_\rho - r_\rho)/\ell = z$. We repeat a similar argument as above for bounding the distribution of q_ρ from uniform. For each possible value of z, there always exists a unique value of s_ρ such that $\left\lfloor \frac{s_\rho}{\ell} \right\rfloor = z$ and $s_\rho = 0 \bmod \ell$, except possibly at the two endpoints E_1, E_2 of the range of q_ρ. When r_ρ disqualifies the two points E_1 and E_2, then each of the remaining points $z \notin \{E_1, E_2\}$ still have equal probability mass, and thus the probability $\Pr(q_\rho = z|r_\rho)$ increases by at most $\frac{1}{|Y|} - \frac{\ell}{2B+1}$. The same applies to the variable $(\mathsf{pk}^{q_\rho}, g_q^{q_\rho})|r_\rho$.

We can compare the joint distribution $X_\rho = (\mathsf{pk}^{q_\rho}, g_q^{q_\rho}, r_\rho)$ to the simulated distribution $Y_\rho = (\mathsf{pk}^{q'_\rho}, g_q^{q'_\rho}, r'_\rho)$ using Fact 3. Setting $\epsilon_1 = \frac{1}{|Y|} - \frac{\ell}{2B+1}$ and $\epsilon_2 = 0$, the distance between these joint distributions is at most $\frac{1}{2^{\epsilon_d+1}} + \frac{\ell}{2B+1} + \epsilon_1\ell = \frac{1}{2^{\epsilon_d+1}} + \frac{1}{2B+3-3\ell} + \frac{\ell(1-\ell)}{2B+1} < \frac{1}{2^{\epsilon_d}}$, where the last equality holds if $B > 2^{\epsilon_d} + 2^{\lambda+1} - 1$. This bounds the distance between (Q_1, Q_2, r_ρ) and (Q'_1, Q'_2, r'_ρ). Combining the two requirements on B, we can simplify the requirement as $B \geq 2^{\lambda+\epsilon_d+2}\tilde{s}$. $\square$

Table 2. Comparison of communication size for ZK proof of the well-formedness of CL ciphertext.

	Communication size (bytes)				Additional requirement
	$\lambda = 112$	$\lambda = 128$	$\lambda = 192$	$\lambda = 256$	
CCL + 19 [4]	37970	49950	95520	156130	$\times$
CCL + 20 [5]	495	645	1214	1972	Pick random $g_q \in G^q$
This paper	1129	1488	2864	4692	$\mathsf{pk} \in G^q$, generic group model

Comparison. We compare our scheme with the similar ZK proofs for the well-formedness of CL ciphertext in [4] and [5] in Table 2. We use the statistical distance 2^{-80} suggested for the CL encryption in [7]. We use the same statistical distance and soundness error of 2^{-80} for fair comparison.

We note that CCL + 20 [5] required that the generator g_q is randomly chosen in G^q prior to running the zero knowledge proof. In order to achieve trustless setup, it should be jointly generated by all participating parties according to [5]. It introduces some overheads in bandwidth as well as a few more rounds of communication. In our scheme, we additionally require that $\mathsf{pk} \in G^q$. It can be proved by the owner of the secret key separately (e.g., Sect. 5.2 scheme 1), or can be embedded into this ZK proof if the prover himself is also the owner of the secret key (e.g., Sect. 5.1).

5 Applications to Threshold ECDSA and Two-Party ECDSA

5.1 Two-Party ECDSA

The two-party ECDSA in [4] used a ZK proof for the CL ciphertext with a slightly different relation. Suppose that $\hat{P}$ is a generator in $\mathcal{G}_{\text{ECC}}$ included in the system parameter param. The two-party ECDSA in [4] used a ZK proof of plaintext and randomness used in the additive homomorphic encryption for the following relation:

$$\mathcal{R}_{\mathsf{EncECC}} = \{(m, \rho) : C_1 = f^m \mathsf{pk}^\rho \wedge C_2 = g_q^\rho \wedge \hat{Q} = \hat{P}^m\}.$$

This ZK proof is used in the interactive key generation $\mathsf{IKeyGen}$ phase of the two-party ECDSA.

For the relation $\mathcal{R}_{\mathsf{EncECC}}$, we cannot apply the protocol $\mathsf{ZKPoKRepS}$ directly since pk is not in the CRS. Moreover, pk may not be well-formed (e.g., $\mathsf{pk} = g_q^{\mathsf{sk}} f^\delta$ for some $\delta \in \mathbb{Z}_q$). Therefore, we change the relation to:

$$\mathcal{R}_{\mathsf{Enc}'} = \{(m, \rho, \mathsf{sk}) : C_1 = f^m \mathsf{pk}^\rho \wedge C_2 = g_q^\rho \wedge \hat{Q} = \hat{P}^m \wedge \mathsf{pk} = g_q^{\mathsf{sk}}\}.$$

It is because the knowledge of the secret key is known by the prover in the $\mathsf{IKeyGen}$ algorithm.

We propose a new ZK proof ZKPoKEnc' for $\mathcal{R}_{\mathsf{Enc}'}$ as shown in Algorithm 6. The security proofs are similar to the previous proof and are omitted due to the page limit.

Algorithm 6: Protocol ZKPoKEnc' for the relation $\mathcal{R}_{\mathsf{Enc}'}$

Param: $(\hat{G}, q, \hat{P}) \leftarrow \mathsf{GGen}_{\mathrm{ECC}}(1^\lambda)$, $\mathcal{G}_{\mathrm{HSM}} \leftarrow \mathsf{GGen}_{\mathrm{HSM},q}(1^\lambda)$, $B = 2^{\lambda+\epsilon_d+2}\tilde{s}$, $\epsilon_d = 80$.

Input: $C_1, C_2, \mathsf{pk} \in G, \hat{C} \in \hat{G}$.

Witness: $\rho, \mathsf{sk} \in [0, S], m \in \mathbb{Z}_q$, where $S = \tilde{s} \cdot 2^{\epsilon_d}$.

1 Prover chooses $s_\rho, s_k \xleftarrow{\$} [-B, B]$, $s_m \xleftarrow{\$} \mathbb{Z}_q$ and computes:

$$S_1 = \mathsf{pk}^{s_\rho} f^{s_m}, \quad S_2 = g_q^{s_\rho}, \quad S_3 = g_q^{s_k}, \quad \hat{S} = \hat{P}^{s_m}.$$

Prover sends $(S_1, S_2, S_3, \hat{S})$ to the verifier.

2 Verifier sends $c \xleftarrow{\$} [0, q-1]$ to the prover.

3 Prover computes:

$$u_\rho = s_\rho + c\rho, \quad u_k = s_k + c \cdot \mathsf{sk}, \quad u_m = s_m + cm \mod q.$$

Prover finds $d_\rho, d_k \in \mathbb{Z}$ and $e_\rho, e_k \in [0, q-1]$ s.t. $u_\rho = d_\rho q + e_\rho$ and $u_k = d_k q + e_k$. Prover computes:

$$D_1 = \mathsf{pk}^{d_\rho}, \quad D_2 = g_q^{d_\rho}, \quad D_3 = g_q^{d_k}.$$

Prover sends $(u_m, D_1, D_2, D_3, e_\rho, e_k)$ to the verifier.

4 The verifier checks if $e_\rho, e_k \in [0, q-1]$ and:

$$\hat{S}\hat{C}^c = \hat{P}^{u_m}, \quad D_1^q \mathsf{pk}^{e_\rho} f^{u_m} = S_1 C_1^c, \quad D_2^q g_q^{e_\rho} = S_2 C_2^c, \quad D_3^q g_q^{e_k} = S_3 \mathsf{pk}^c.$$

If so, the verifier sends $\ell \xleftarrow{\$} \mathsf{Primes}(\lambda)$.

5 Prover finds $q_\rho, q_k \in \mathbb{Z}$ and $r_\rho, r_k \in [0, \ell-1]$ s.t. $u_\rho = q_\rho \ell + r_\rho$ and $u_k = q_k \ell + r_k$. Prover computes:

$$Q_1 = \mathsf{pk}^{q_\rho}, \quad Q_2 = g_q^{q_\rho}, \quad Q_3 = g_q^{q_k}.$$

Prover sends $(Q_1, Q_2, Q_3, r_\rho, r_k)$ to the verifier.

6 Verifier accepts if $r_\rho, r_k \in [0, \ell-1]$ and:

$$Q_1^\ell \mathsf{pk}^{r_\rho} f^{u_m} = S_1 C_1^c, \quad Q_2^\ell g_q^{r_\rho} = S_2 C_2^c, \quad Q_3^\ell g_q^{r_k} = S_3 \mathsf{pk}^c.$$

Evaluation. We follow the evaluation methodology in [5]. For each scheme, the bandwidth used is the sum of the total input and output transmission for a single party. A broadcast message is only counted as one transmission only. All interactive zero-knowledge proofs are turned into a non-interactive one using

Table 3. Comparison for two-party ECDSA with different security levels.

	Security level	lKeyGen (Bytes)	lSign (Bytes)	Assumption
CCL + 19 [4]	$\lambda = 112$	38714	575	Hard subgroup membership
	$\lambda = 128$	50876	697	
	$\lambda = 192$	97230	1260	
	$\lambda = 256$	158850	1973	
CCL + 19-*lcm* [5]	$\lambda = 112$	4559	575	Hard subgroup membership
	$\lambda = 128$	5939	697	
	$\lambda = 192$	11280	1260	
	$\lambda = 256$	18351	1973	
Our two-party ECDSA	$\lambda = 112$	2453	575	Hard subgroup membership, adaptive root subgroup.
	$\lambda = 128$	3173	697	
	$\lambda = 192$	6030	1260	
	$\lambda = 256$	9789	1973	

the Fiat-Shamir transformation, such that the commit message can be omitted if possible.

We compare our scheme with the two-party ECDSA scheme in [4], which used a binary challenge in the ZK proof in the lKeyGen algorithm. As a result, the ZK proof has to be repeated for ϵ_s times for soundness error of $2^{-\epsilon_s}$. Recently, [5] proposed an *lcm* trick (CCL + 19-*lcm*) to replace a binary challenge with a challenge of 10 bits. Hence, the ZK proof has to be repeated for $\epsilon_s/10$ times. However, the relationship proved by the *lcm* trick is changed slightly, and hence the prover and the verifier have to additionally compute exponentiation of $y = lcm(1, \ldots, 2^{10})$, which is a 1479 bits integer, in lKeyGen and lSign respectively.

In our scheme, we only need to run the ZK proof for one time only and no extra exponentiation is needed. The comparison of communication size is shown in Table 3. For a soundness error and statistical distance of 2^{-80}, CCL + 19 [4] needs at least 10 times more bandwidth in lKeyGen than ours, while CCL + 19-*lcm* [5] needs about twice the bandwidth in lKeyGen than ours. Our scheme additionally relies on the adaptive root subgroup assumption in the generic group model. Note that the security of ECDSA is based on the DL assumption in the generic group model [2].

5.2 Threshold ECDSA

Our proposed ZK proofs can be used to improve the state-of-the-art bandwidth efficient threshold ECDSA CCL + 20 [5]. We give two threshold ECDSA schemes in this section. Our scheme 1 reduces the communication cost of lKeyGen in CCL + 20 and also reduces the computation time in both lKeyGen and lSign, at the price of having a larger communication cost for lSign. Our scheme 2 outperforms CCL + 20 [5] in the communication cost and computation time in lKeyGen, while having the same performance in lSign.

Our Scheme 1. We show how to use our protocols ZKPoKRepS and ZKPoKEnc to build a threshold ECDSA with fast trustless setup from the scheme in [5]. There are three main differences in the protocol (shown in Table 4):

Table 4. Scheme 1: Modifications to the threshold ECDSA in [5] are shown in the box.

	IKeyGen(param)	
P_i		All players $\{P_j\}_{j\neq i}$
$u_i \xleftarrow{\$} \mathbb{Z}_q$		
$(\mathsf{kgc}_i, \mathsf{kgd}_i) \leftarrow \mathsf{Com}(\hat{P}^{u_i})$		
$(\mathsf{sk}_i, \mathsf{pk}_i) \leftarrow \mathsf{CL.KeyGen}()$	$\xrightarrow{\mathsf{kgc}_i, \mathsf{pk}_i}$	
	$\xrightarrow{\mathsf{kgd}_i}$	
$\pi_k := \mathsf{ZKPoKRepS}(\mathsf{pk}_i; \mathsf{sk}_i : \mathsf{pk}_i = g_q^{\mathsf{sk}_i})$	$\xleftrightarrow{\pi_k}$	Abort if the proof fails.
Follow from line 5 of Fig. 4 in in [5].		
	ISign(param, m)	
P_i	Phase 1	All players $\{P_j\}_{j\neq i}$
$k_i, \gamma_i \xleftarrow{\$} \mathbb{Z}_q$, $r_i \xleftarrow{\$} [0, S]$		
$(\mathsf{c}_i, \mathsf{d}_i) \leftarrow \mathsf{Com}(\hat{P}^{\gamma_i})$		
$C_{k_i} \leftarrow \mathsf{CL.Enc}(\mathsf{pk}_i, k_i; r_i)$	$\xrightarrow{C_{k_i}, \mathsf{c}_i}$	
$\pi_C := \mathsf{ZKPoKEnc}((k_i, r_i) :$		
$((\mathsf{pk}_i, C_{k_i}); (k_i, r_i)) \in \mathcal{R}_{\mathsf{Enc}})$	$\xleftrightarrow{\pi_C}$	Abort if the proof fails.

1. IKeyGen:
   (a) We do not need to run the interactive ISetup algorithm in [5] to generate the generator g_q used in IKeyGen.
   (b) One of the main differences between our ZKPoKEnc protocol and with the argument of knowledge for CL ciphertext in [5] is that our ZKPoKEnc protocol requires that the public key pk is well-formed. This can be achieved by adding a zero-knowledge proof of the secret key sk with respect to pk in the key generation phase.
2. ISign: For the interactive signing phase, we only need to modify phase 1 of the signing protocol in [5]. All other phases remain the same.

The resulting scheme 1 is secure in the generic group model by assuming the hardness of the hard subgroup membership and the adaptive root subgroup assumption.

Our Scheme 2. If we make the extra adaptive root subgroup assumption, we can keep the ISign algorithm and the most of the IKeyGen algorithm in CCL + 20 [5]. We only need to modify the interactive ISetup algorithm in [5], such that the proof of knowledge of t_i for $g_i = g_q^{t_i}$ is replaced by our ZKPoKRepS protocol. The resulting scheme is the most bandwidth efficient for the total bandwidth used in the IKeyGen and the ISign algorithms, at the price of using one more assumption.

Evaluation. We compare our schemes with the state-of-the-art bandwidth efficient threshold ECDSA scheme [5] in Table 5. The total number of party is n and the threshold is t.

Table 5. Comparison for threshold ECDSA with different security levels.

	Security level	IKeyGen (bytes)	ISign (bytes)	Assumption
CCL + 20 [5]	$\lambda = 112$	$32tn + 2692n - 64$	$2397t - 1412$	Hard subgroup membership Strong root subgroup
	$\lambda = 128$	$32tn + 3479n - 64$	$3100t - 1891$	
	$\lambda = 192$	$32tn + 6518n - 96$	$5862t - 3694$	
	$\lambda = 256$	$32tn + 10535n - 128$	$9489t - 6099$	
Our threshold ECDSA scheme 1	$\lambda = 112$	$32tn + 797n - 64$	$3031t - 1412$	Hard subgroup membership Adaptive root subgroup
	$\lambda = 128$	$32tn + 979n - 64$	$3944t - 1891$	
	$\lambda = 192$	$32tn + 1779n - 96$	$7512t - 3694$	
	$\lambda = 256$	$32tn + 2805n - 128$	$12210t - 6099$	
Our threshold ECDSA scheme 2	$\lambda = 112$	$32tn + 1072n - 64$	$2397t - 1412$	Hard subgroup membership Adaptive root subgroup Strong root subgroup
	$\lambda = 128$	$32tn + 1319n - 64$	$3100t - 1891$	
	$\lambda = 192$	$32tn + 2397n - 96$	$5862t - 3694$	
	$\lambda = 256$	$32tn + 3775n - 128$	$9489t - 6099$	

The most common threshold signature P2SH transaction of Bitcoin is the case of (t, n) = (1,3), (2,4) and (2,5). By using this parameter, our scheme 1 is the most bandwidth efficient for the IKeyGen algorithm and it is about 69–74% less than CCL + 20. However, the bandwidth of the ISign algorithm of CCL + 20 and our scheme 2 is 20–22% less than our scheme 1. Our scheme 2 uses 59–65% less bandwidth than [5] in IKeyGen (as shown in Fig. 2), with the same

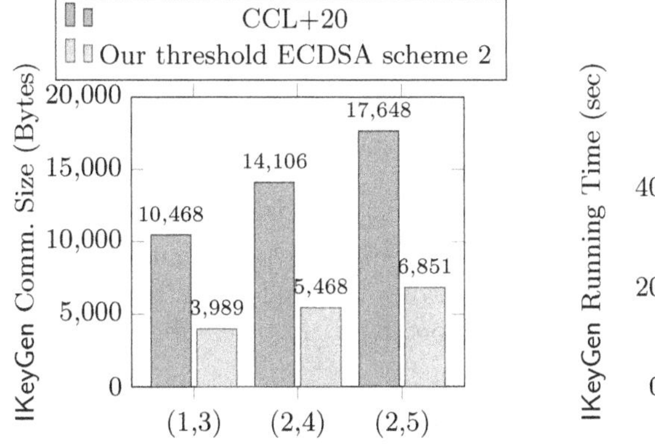

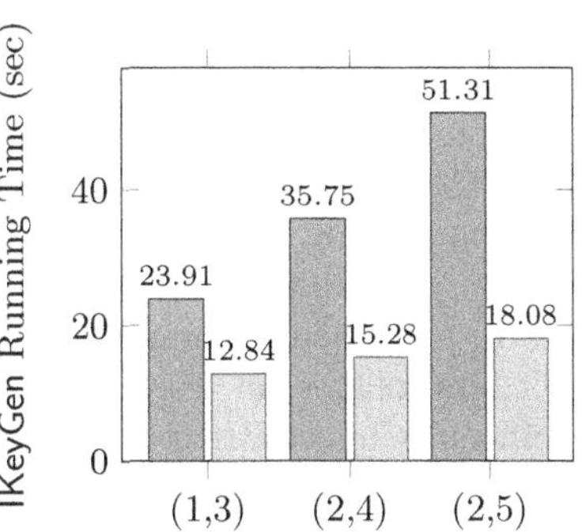

Fig. 2. (t, n)-Threshold ECDSA with 128-bit security.

bandwidth in ISign. Our schemes are proved secure in the generic group model. Note that the security of ECDSA is based on the DL assumption in the generic group model [2].

6 Implementation

Choices of Parameters. Various security parameters are used for soundness error and statistical distance in different threshold ECDSA papers which makes it difficult to compare the efficiency of different schemes. Lindell17 [13] used 2^{-40} for soundness error and statistical distance. LN18 [14] used 2^{-80} for these parameters. CCL + 19 [4] followed [13] to use 2^{-40} for comparison, but they suggested to use 2^{-60} in practice. GG18 [11] and GG20 [12] used a soundness error of 2^{-q} and a statistical distance of $2^{-\lambda}$. CCL + 20 [5] used $2^{-\lambda}$ for soundness error and 2^{-40} for statistical distance. For the two-party and threshold ECDSA based on oblivious transfer, DKLs18 [9] and DKLs19 [10] used 2^{-80} for statistical distance. In addition, the CL encryption [7] proposed to use 2^{-80} for statistical distance. In this paper, we take the middle ground of using 2^{-80} for soundness error and statistical distance for the ZK proofs as well as the CL encryption.

We only implement the schemes with 112-bit and 128-bit security due to the constraint in running time (it takes >66 s to run the IKeyGen of CCL + 19 for 128-bit security). We use the secp256k1 curve.

Testing Environment. We implemented our schemes, CCL + 19 [4] and CCL + 20 [5] using Rust. We tested the program in a MacBook with Intel Core i5 1.4 GHz, 16 GB RAM. The results are the median running time for running >100 times. The program is implemented in one single thread for comparing different settings.

During the testing, we do not consider the network conditions. We may further outperform existing schemes in terms of running time since our schemes use a smaller bandwidth.

6.1 Two-Party ECDSA

We show the running time for both IKeyGen and ISign for 112-bit and 128-bit security level in Fig. 3. As compared with the CCL + 19-*lcm* in [5], the running time of our IKeyGen is 35–65% times faster, and the running time of our ISign is 104–138% times faster.

In particular, the *lcm* trick has a non-obvious cost of doubling the running of ISign as compared with CCL + 19 [4] and our scheme. The prover and the verifier have to additionally compute exponentiation of $y = lcm(1, \dots, 2^{10})$, which is a 1479 bits integer, in IKeyGen and ISign respectively. It takes about 0.6 s and significantly affects the performance in ISign.

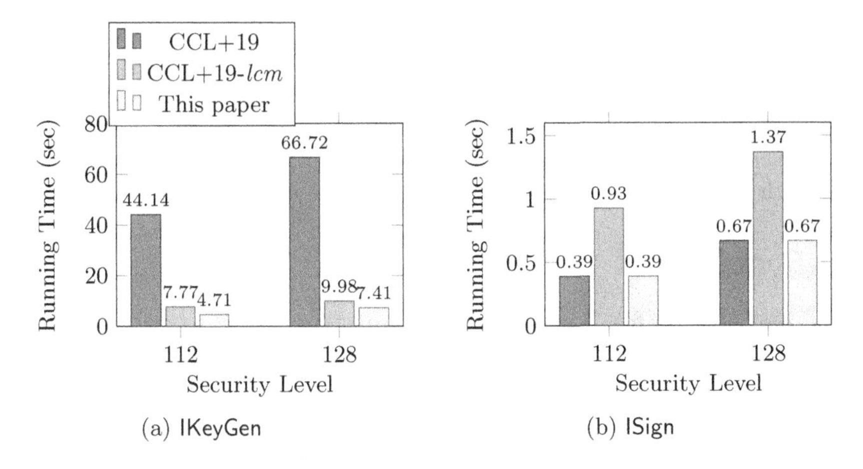

Fig. 3. Running time of two-party ECDSA.

6.2 Threshold ECDSA

We show the running time for both IKeyGen and ISign for 112-bit and 128-bit security level in Fig. 4. As compared with CCL + 20 [5], the running time of our scheme 1 is 85–90% faster in IKeyGen, with the price of a higher communication cost in ISign. If one wants to minimize the communication cost, our scheme 2 is still 46–65% faster in IKeyGen. For the running time in ISign, our scheme 1 is slightly slower than scheme 2/CCL + 20.

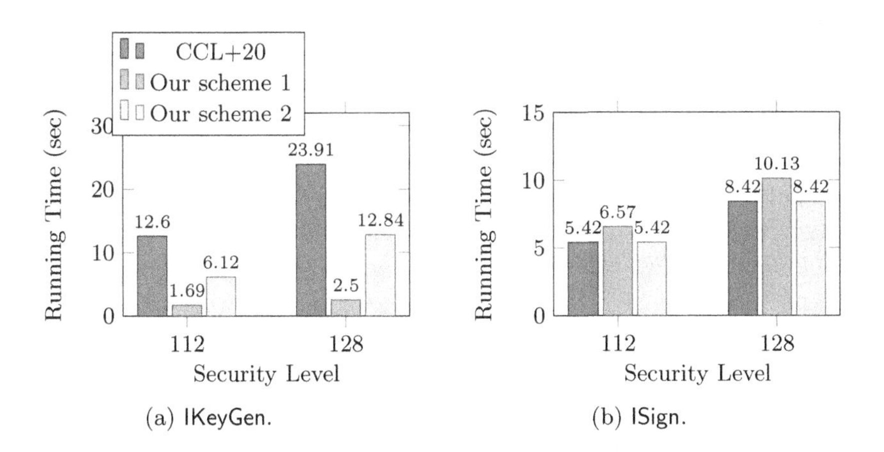

Fig. 4. Running time of threshold ECDSA with $t = 1, n = 3$.

7 Conclusion

In this paper, we propose a compact zero-knowledge proof for the DL relation in HSM groups and the CL ciphertext. When applied to two-party ECDSA and threshold ECDSA, it can significantly improve the performance in terms of bandwidth used in $\mathsf{IKeyGen}$, and the running time of $\mathsf{IKeyGen}$ and ISign.

A Background

A.1 Definitions for Argument Systems

An argument system for a relation $\mathcal{R} \subset \mathcal{X} \times \mathcal{W}$ is a triple of randomized polynomial time algorithms $(\mathsf{Setup}, \mathsf{P}, \mathsf{V})$, where:

- Setup takes a security parameter 1^λ and outputs a common reference string (CRS) crs.
- P takes as input the crs, a statement $x \in \mathcal{X}$ and a witness $w \in \mathcal{W}$. V takes as input the crs and x and after interaction with P outputs 0 or 1.

The transcript between the prover and the verifier is denoted as $\langle \mathsf{V}(\mathsf{crs}, x), \mathsf{P}(\mathsf{crs}, x, w) \rangle$, and it is equal to 1 if the verifier accepted the transcript.

Definition 1 (Completeness). *An argument system* $(\mathsf{Setup}, \mathsf{P}, \mathsf{V})$ *for a relation* $\mathcal{R}$ *is complete if for all* $(x, w) \in \mathcal{R}$*:*

$$\Pr[\langle \mathsf{V}(\mathsf{crs}, x), \mathsf{P}(\mathsf{crs}, x, w) \rangle = 1 : \mathsf{crs} \xleftarrow{\$} \mathsf{Setup}(1^\lambda)] = 1.$$

We follow the soundness definition for trapdoorless crs from [1].

Definition 2 (Soundness). *An argument system* $(\mathsf{Setup}, \mathsf{P}, \mathsf{V})$ *is sound if for all polynomial time adversaries* $\mathcal{A} = (\mathcal{A}_0, \mathcal{A}_1)$*:*

$$\Pr\left[\begin{array}{l} \langle \mathsf{V}(\mathsf{crs}, x), \mathcal{A}_1(\mathsf{crs}, x, \mathsf{state}) \rangle = 1 \\ \textit{and } \nexists w \textit{ s.t. } (x, w) \in \mathcal{R} \end{array} : \begin{array}{l} \mathsf{crs} \xleftarrow{\$} \mathsf{Setup}(1^\lambda) \\ (x, \mathsf{state}) \leftarrow \mathcal{A}_0(\mathsf{crs}) \end{array}\right] = \mathsf{negl}(\lambda).$$

Additionally, the argument system is an argument of knowledge if for all polynomial time adversaries $\mathcal{A}_1$ *there exists a polynomial time extractor* Ext *such that for all polynomial time adversaries* $\mathcal{A}_0$*:*

$$\Pr\left[\begin{array}{l} \langle \mathsf{V}(\mathsf{crs}, x), \mathcal{A}_1(\mathsf{crs}, x, \mathsf{state}) \rangle = 1 \\ \textit{and } (x, w') \notin \mathcal{R} \end{array} : \begin{array}{l} \mathsf{crs} \xleftarrow{\$} \mathsf{Setup}(1^\lambda) \\ (x, \mathsf{state}) \leftarrow \mathcal{A}_0(\mathsf{crs}) \\ w' \xleftarrow{\$} \mathsf{Ext}(\mathsf{crs}, x, \mathsf{state}) \end{array}\right] = \mathsf{negl}(\lambda).$$

Definition 3 (Zero Knowledge). *An argument system* $(\mathsf{Setup}, \mathsf{P}, \mathsf{V})$ *is statistical zero-knowledge if there exists a polynomial time simulator* Sim *such that for all* $(x, w) \in \mathcal{R}$*, the following two distributions are statistically indistinguishable:*

$$D_1 = \{\langle \mathsf{V}(\mathsf{crs}, x), \mathsf{P}(\mathsf{crs}, x, w) \rangle, \mathsf{crs} \xleftarrow{\$} \mathsf{Setup}(1^\lambda)\},$$

$$D_2 = \{\langle \mathsf{V}(\mathsf{crs}, x), \mathsf{Sim}(\mathsf{crs}, x) \rangle, \mathsf{crs} \xleftarrow{\$} \mathsf{Setup}(1^\lambda)\}.$$

A.2 Generalized Schnorr Proofs

The Sigma protocol based on Schnorrs proof can be generalized for proving DL in groups of unknown order [3]. It can be done by introducing appropriate range checking and using computations over the integers. The proof size is dominated by the response of size $(\epsilon_s + \epsilon_d)\cdot$ ord(G), and hence it is not practical. By taking $\epsilon_s = \epsilon_d = 80$, the proof size is in the order of MBytes.

B More Implementation Results for Threshold ECDSA

We also implemented the threshold ECDSA schemes for the setting of (t, n) = (2,4) and (2,5) and the security level of 112-bit and 128-bit. The complete comparison tables for these cases are given in Tables 6, 7, 8 and 9.

Table 6. (2, 4)-Threshold ECDSA for 112 bit security

	IKeyGen		ISign	
	Communication size (bytes)	Running time (sec)	Communication size (bytes)	Running time (sec)
CCL + 20	10958	19.34	3382	10.23
Our threshold scheme 1	3380	2.82	4650	11.70
Our threshold scheme 2	4478	8.33	3382	10.23

Table 7. (2, 4)-Threshold ECDSA for 128 bit security

	IKeyGen		ISign	
	Communication size (bytes)	Running time (sec)	Communication size (bytes)	Running time (sec)
CCL + 20	14106	35.75	4308	15.75
Our threshold scheme 1	4107	4.11	4650	17.54
Our threshold scheme 2	5468	15.28	4308	15.75

Table 8. (2, 5)-Threshold ECDSA for 112 bit security

	IKeyGen		ISign	
	Communication size (bytes)	Running time (sec)	Communication size (bytes)	Running time (sec)
CCL + 20	13714	28.70	3382	16.45
Our threshold scheme 1	4241	4.25	4650	18.28
Our threshold scheme 2	5614	11.00	3382	16.45

Table 9. (2, 5)-Threshold ECDSA for 128 bit security

	IKeyGen		ISign	
	Communication size (bytes)	Running time (sec)	Communication size (bytes)	Running time (sec)
CCL + 20	17468	51.31	4308	25.51
Our threshold scheme 1	5150	6.10	4650	27.23
Our threshold scheme 2	6851	18.08	4308	25.51

References

1. Boneh, D., Bünz, B., Fisch, B.: Batching techniques for accumulators with applications to IOPs and stateless blockchains. In: Boldyreva, A., Micciancio, D. (eds.) CRYPTO 2019. LNCS, vol. 11692, pp. 561–586. Springer, Cham (2019). https://doi.org/10.1007/978-3-030-26948-7_20
2. Brown, D.R.L.: Generic groups, collision resistance, and ECDSA. Des. Codes Cryptogr. **35**(1), 119–152 (2005)
3. Camenisch, J., Kiayias, A., Yung, M.: On the portability of generalized schnorr proofs. In: Joux, A. (ed.): EUROCRYPT 2009. Lecture Notes in Computer Science, vol. 5479, pp. 425–442. Springer (2009)
4. Castagnos, G., Catalano, D., Laguillaumie, F., Savasta, F., Tucker, I.: Two-party ECDSA from hash proof systems and efficient instantiations. In: Boldyreva, A., Micciancio, D. (eds.) CRYPTO 2019. LNCS, vol. 11694, pp. 191–221. Springer, Cham (2019). https://doi.org/10.1007/978-3-030-26954-8_7
5. Castagnos, G., Catalano, D., Laguillaumie, F., Savasta, F., Tucker, I.: Bandwidth-efficient threshold EC-DSA. In: Kiayias, A., Kohlweiss, M., Wallden, P., Zikas, V. (eds.) PKC 2020. Lecture Notes in Computer Science, vol. 12111, pp. 266–296. Springer (2020)
6. Castagnos, G., Laguillaumie, F.: On the security of cryptosystems with quadratic decryption: the nicest cryptanalysis. In: Joux, A. (ed.): EUROCRYPT 2009. Lecture Notes in Computer Science, vol. 5479, pp. 260–277. Springer (2009)
7. Castagnos, G., Laguillaumie, F.: Linearly homomorphic encryption from DDH. In: Nyberg, K. (ed.) CT-RSA 2015. Lecture Notes in Computer Science, vol. 9048, pp. 487–505. Springer (2015)

8. Damgård, I., Koprowski, M.: Generic lower bounds for root extraction and signature schemes in general groups. In: Knudsen, L.R. (ed.) EUROCRYPT 2002. LNCS, vol. 2332, pp. 256–271. Springer, Heidelberg (2002). https://doi.org/10.1007/3-540-46035-7_17
9. Doerner, J., Kondi, Y., Lee, E., Shelat, A.: Secure two-party threshold ECDSA from ECDSA assumptions. In: IEEE SP 2018, pp. 980–997. IEEE Computer Society (2018)
10. Doerner, J., Kondi, Y., Lee, E., Shelat, A.: Threshold ECDSA from ECDSA assumptions: the multiparty case. In: IEEE SP 2019, pp. 1051–1066. IEEE (2019)
11. Gennaro, R., Goldfeder, S.: Fast multiparty threshold ECDSA with fast trustless setup. In: Lie, D., Mannan, M., Backes, M., Wang, X. (eds.) CCS 2018, pp. 1179–1194. ACM (2018)
12. Gennaro, R., Goldfeder, S.: One round threshold ecdsa with identifiable abort. Cryptology ePrint Archive, Report 2020/540 (2020). https://eprint.iacr.org/2020/540
13. Lindell, Y.: Fast secure two-party ECDSA signing. In: Katz, J., Shacham, H. (eds.) CRYPTO 2017. LNCS, vol. 10402, pp. 613–644. Springer, Cham (2017). https://doi.org/10.1007/978-3-319-63715-0_21
14. Lindell, Y., Nof, A.: Fast secure multiparty ECDSA with practical distributed key generation and applications to cryptocurrency custody. In: Lie, D., Mannan, M., Backes, M., Wang, X. (eds.) CCS 2018, pp. 1837–1854. ACM (2018)
15. Shoup, V.: Lower bounds for discrete logarithms and related problems. In: Fumy, W. (ed.) EUROCRYPT 1997. LNCS, vol. 1233, pp. 256–266. Springer, Heidelberg (1997). https://doi.org/10.1007/3-540-69053-0_18

Universal Proxy Re-Encryption

Nico Döttling[1] and Ryo Nishimaki[2(✉)]

[1] CISPA Helmholtz Center for Information Security, Saarbrücken, Germany
doettling@cispa.saarland
[2] NTT Secure Platform Laboratories, Tokyo, Japan
ryo.nishimaki.zk@hco.ntt.co.jp

Abstract. We put forward the notion of universal proxy re-encryption (UPRE). A UPRE scheme enables a proxy to convert a ciphertext under a (delegator) public key of *any existing public-key encryption (PKE) scheme* into another ciphertext under a (delegatee) public key of *any existing PKE scheme (possibly different from the delegator one)*. The proxy has a re-encryption key generated from the delegator's secret key and the delegatee public key. Thus UPRE generalizes proxy re-encryption by supporting arbitrary PKE schemes and allowing to convert ciphertexts into ones of *possibly different PKE schemes*. In this work, we

- provide syntax and definitions for both UPRE and a variant we call relaxed UPRE. The relaxed variant means that decryption algorithms for re-encrypted ciphertexts are slightly modified but still only use the original delegatee secret keys for decryption.
- construct a UPRE based on probabilistic indistinguishability obfuscation (PIO). It allows us to re-encrypt ciphertexts polynomially many times.
- construct relaxed UPRE from garbled circuits (GCs). We provide two variants of this construction, one which allows us to re-encrypt ciphertexts polynomially many times, and a second one which satisfies a stronger security requirement but only allows us to re-encrypt ciphertexts a constant number of times.

Keywords: Universal proxy re-encrytion · Public-key encryption · Secret sharing

1 Introduction

1.1 Background

Constructing cryptographic systems from scratch is a challenging task. When migrating from a legacy cryptosystem to a new one with better security and functionality, it would be desirable to reuse existing public key infrastructures (PKI) to reduce the cost of migration. In this work, we explore a *universal* methodology to construct a new and easily deployable cryptographic system from existing cryptographic systems and PKI.

J. A. Garay (Ed.): PKC 2021, LNCS 12710, pp. 512–542, 2021.
https://doi.org/10.1007/978-3-030-75245-3_19

As a particular example of cryptographic systems, we consider proxy re-encryption (PRE) [BBS98]. PRE allows to convert a ciphertext under public key pk_f (we call delegator public key and f denotes "from") into another ciphertext under public key pk_t (we call delegatee public key and t denotes "to") by using a re-encryption key $\mathsf{rk}_{f \to t}$ without decrypting the original ciphertext by sk_f (we call delegator secret key). A third party, called proxy, owns the re-encryption key $\mathsf{rk}_{f \to t}$ and executes the re-encryption procedure. PRE thus enables delegation of re-encryption and several useful applications. It can be used to achieve encrypted email forwarding [BBS98, Jak99], key escrow [ID03], encrypted file storage [AFGH05], secure publish-subscribe operation [PRSV17], and secure payment systems for credit cards [GSL19].

However, all known PRE schemes only support conversions from ciphertexts under a public key generated by *their key generation algorithm* into other ones under another key generated by *the same key generation algorithm with the same parameter.* They *cannot* convert ciphertexts into ones under another key generated by *another key generation algorithm of another encryption scheme.* Moreover, almost all known PRE schemes were constructed from scratch by using specific cryptographic assumptions such as the decisional Diffie-Hellman (DDH) assumption and the learning with errors (LWE) assumption. The formats of their keys and ciphertexts are fixed in advance at the setup and can never be changed. Only a few PRE schemes use public-key encryption (PKE) schemes generically [HKK+12]. However, in such schemes, we cannot use a PKE scheme as it is (some additional conversion is needed). Moreover, only delegatees (receivers of converted ciphertexts) can select any PKE scheme and delegators (senders of original ciphertexts) cannot. From a practical point of view, this is unsatisfactory as we need to build a new system using a PRE scheme from scratch if we want to use applications of PRE described above. When we use a PRE scheme, we cannot use existing and widely used public-key cryptosystems to achieve the applications of PRE. Ideally, we would like to achieve a re-encryption mechanism that works for any pair of PKE schemes without any modification and setup.

Universal Proxy Re-Encryption. To resolve the problems above, we put forward the concept of *universal proxy re-encryption (UPRE).* UPRE enables us to convert ciphertexts under a public key of a scheme Σ_f (delegator scheme) into ciphertexts under another public key of *another scheme* Σ_t (delegatee scheme). *We can select arbitrary secure PKE schemes for* Σ_f, Σ_t. For example, we can use Goldwasser-Micali PKE [GM84] as Σ_f and ElGamal PKE [ElG85] as Σ_t. If a delegator and delegatee have key pairs $(\mathsf{pk}_f, \mathsf{sk}_f)$ and $(\mathsf{pk}_t, \mathsf{sk}_t)$ of schemes Σ_f and Σ_t, respectively, then a re-encryption key generation algorithm of UPRE can output a re-encryption key $\mathsf{rk}_{f \to t}$ from $(\Sigma_f, \Sigma_t, \mathsf{sk}_f, \mathsf{pk}_t)$. A proxy can generate a re-encrypted ciphertext rct from $\mathsf{rk}_{f \to t}$ and $\mathsf{Enc}_f(\mathsf{pk}_f, m)$ where Enc_f is the encryption algorithm of Σ_f. Of course, the re-encrypted ciphertext rct can be correctly decrypted to m by using sk_t.

Ideally, a re-encrypted ciphertext should be decrypted by the original decryption algorithm of the delegatee scheme (i.e., $\mathsf{Dec}_t(\mathsf{sk}_t, \cdot)$). However, we can also consider a relaxed variant where a re-encrypted ciphertext can be decrypted via a slightly modified decryption algorithm *with the original delegatee decryption key* sk_t. We call this variant *relaxed UPRE*. Here, we emphasize that the delegator uses only pk_f and Enc_f to encrypt a message and the delegatee uses only sk_t to decrypt a re-encrypted ciphertext (they do not need any additional keys) even if its decryption procedure is slightly modified. Our work is the first to explore such a universal methodology for proxy re-encryption.

UPRE enables us to build a re-encryption mechanism dynamically by using currently deployed cryptosystems. Users who have already used PKE schemes can convert ciphertexts into other ones by using a UPRE scheme. They do not need to setup a proxy re-encryption system from scratch. Therefore, UPRE offers more flexibility than standard PRE. In addition, UPRE has applications that PRE does not have, e.g. the following. UPRE enables us to delegate migration of encryption systems to a third party such as cloud-servers with many computational resources when an encryption scheme with some parameter settings becomes obsolete, or vulnerability is found in an encryption system. That is, we can outsource renewing encrypted storage to a third party.

UPRE can be seen as a generalized notion of PRE. Therefore, we can consider several analogies of the notions used in PRE. They are the notions of "direction" and "the number of hops". For directions, there are unidirectional and bidirectional, which means that a re-encryption key between pk_f and pk_t can be used for only one-way from f to t and both ways, respectively. For the number of hops, there are single-hop and multi-hop, which mean a re-encrypted ciphertext cannot be converted anymore and can be converted polynomially-many times, respectively. In particular, when only a constant number of conversions is possible, we call it constant-hop. We consider unidirectional single/constant/multi-hop but do not focus on bidirectional since the functionality of a bidirectional re-encryption key is simulated by two unidirectional re-encryption keys.

The main question addressed in this work is how to achieve UPRE. Regarding feasibility, it seems plausible that UPRE can be achieved from indistinguishability obfuscation (IO) [BGI+12, GGH+16] or multilinear maps [GGH13, CLT13, GGH15].[1] And in fact, we present a construction based on IO as an initial step, though we emphasize that formally proving security is not a trivial task even if we use IO. Consequently, the main focus of this work is concerned with the following question.

Is it possible to achieve a UPRE scheme without IO and multilinear maps?

We give a positive answer to this question.

1.2 Our Contributions

The main contributions of this study are the following.

[1] A.k.a. "heavy hammers".

1. We introduce the notion of UPRE and formally define its security.
2. We present a general construction of multi-hop UPRE for some class of PKE by using probabilistic IO (PIO).
3. We present a general construction of multi-hop relaxed UPRE for any PKE by using only garbled circuits (GC) and therefore need no additional assumptions.
4. By using our general constructions and known instantiations of tools above, we can obtain multi-hop (relaxed) UPRE schemes from IO, or generic standard assumptions.

The third contribution is notable since we introduce a new design idea and use only weak assumptions. We explain more details (tools, security levels, and so on) of these contributions below.

For UPRE, we can consider a natural analog of security against chosen plaintext attacks (CPA) for PRE (PRE-CPA), where adversaries execute CPA attacks with oracles that give re-encryption keys and re-encrypted ciphertexts. However, we do not focus on the definition of CPA-security for UPRE (UPRE-CPA) because Cohen introduced a better security notion called security against honest re-encryption attacks (HRA) for PRE [Coh19][2]. Thus, we define security against honest re-encryption attacks for UPRE (UPRE-HRA), which implies UPRE-CPA, instead of CPA-security. We also define security against corrupted-delegator re-encryption attacks (CRA) to consider the setting of migration of encryption system explained in Sect. 1.1. That is, even if a delegator is corrupted, once a ciphertext is re-encrypted for an honest delegatee, then the delegator cannot obtain information about a plaintext from the re-encrypted ciphertext.[3,4] See Sect. 2 for details.

We present three general constructions of UPRE. One is UPRE for some class of PKE based on PIO. PIO was introduced by Canetti, Lin, Tessaro, and Vaikuntanathan [CLTV15]. Another is relaxed UPRE for any PKE based on GC. The other is constant-hop and CRA-secure relaxed UPRE for any PKE based on GC. We emphasize that our relaxed UPRE is based on *generic* standard assumptions without relying on heavy tools. We look closer at what kind of (relaxed) UPRE is achieved below.

Our UPRE scheme based on PIO is a unidirectional multi-hop UPRE scheme. The required properties for PKE schemes depend on the security level of PIO. If we assume additional properties on PKE, then we can achieve UPRE from sub-exponentially secure IO (sub-exp IO) and sub-exponentially secure OWF

---

[2] Derler, Krenn, Lorünser, Ramacher, Slamanig, and Striecks also proposed a similar security notion in the forward secret setting as (fs)-RIND-CPA [DKL+18].

[3] Note that the corrupted delegator does not have a ciphertext to be re-encrypted here.

[4] Davidson, Deo, Lee, and Martin [DDLM19] independently introduced a stronger notion called strong post-compromised security in the *standard PRE setting*. Note that our work appeared before their publication. Our work appeared on September 7th in 2018 while their work [DDLM19] did on April 5th in 2019. (See the submission dates on Cryptology ePrint Archive.).

(sub-exp OWF). Most well-known CPA-secure PKE schemes such as ElGamal, Goldwasser-Micali PKE schemes satisfy the additional properties. However, if we use any PKE, we need PIO with the strongest security for specific circuits (refer to [CLTV15]). If we use the exponential DDH assumption, we can achieve UPRE from any PKE and polynomially secure IO. The advantage of the scheme based on PIO is that it is a multi-hop UPRE scheme and conceptually simple.

Our relaxed UPRE scheme based on garbled circuits (GC) is a unidirectional multi-hop *relaxed* UPRE scheme for any PKE scheme. This is a significant contribution since GC exist if one-way functions exist (a very weak cryptographic assumption). This relaxed UPRE scheme satisfies HRA-security. However, some meta information (all garbled circuits from the first delegator to the last delegatee) is directly preserved in all re-encrypted ciphertexts. Therefore, the number of hops cannot be hidden in the scheme based on GC. In particular, when a delegator is corrupted, we do not know how to prove that a re-encrypted ciphertext does not reveal information about the plaintext.

Our last UPRE scheme is a unidirectional constant-hop relaxed UPRE scheme for any PKE scheme based on GC. This scheme satisfies CRA-security unlike the multi-hop scheme above, but it can re-encrypt only constant times since its re-encryption procedure incurs polynomial blow-up.

In the GC-based schemes, we must use a slightly modified decryption algorithm (i.e., we achieve relaxed UPRE) though we can use the original delegatee decryption key as it is. While this is a small disadvantage of the GC-based constructions, we would like to emphasize that these are the first constructions of relaxed UPRE, achieved by the standard assumptions.

1.3 Technical Overview

In this section, we give a high-level overview of our UPRE schemes and techniques. To achieve the re-encryption mechanism, we use a circuit with a hard-wired secret key of a delegator PKE scheme to generate a re-encryption key. This is because UPRE supports *general PKE schemes* and we need to decrypt ciphertexts once to re-encrypt them. However, such a circuit should not be directly revealed to a proxy to guarantee security. Therefore, we must hide information about the secret-key in a re-encryption key. That is, to use CPA security of the delegator PKE scheme, we must erase information about the secret key embedded in a re-encryption key in security proofs. This is the most notable issue to prove the security of UPRE. When we succeed in erasing secret keys from re-encryption keys in our reductions, we can directly use the CPA-security of delegators to prove the security of a UPRE scheme.

Based on IO. IO is a promising tool to hide information about delegator secret keys since IO is a kind of compiler that outputs a functionally equivalent program that does not reveal information about the original program. We define a re-encryption circuit C_{re}, in which a delegator secret key sk_f and a delegatee public key pk_t are hard-wired in and which takes a delegator ciphertext ct_f as an input. The re-encryption circuit decrypts ct_f by using sk_f, obtains a plaintext m, and generates a ciphertext of m under pk_t. We can hide information about sk_f by using PIO (note that C_{re} is a randomized circuit). That is, a re-encryption key from delegator f to delegatee t is $pi\mathcal{O}(\mathsf{C}_{\mathsf{re}})$ where $pi\mathcal{O}$ is a PIO algorithm. A re-encrypted ciphertext is a fresh ciphertext under pk_t. Thus, we can achieve multi-hop UPRE. This construction is similar to the FHE scheme based on PIO presented by Canetti et al. [CLTV15]. However, we cannot directly use the result by Canetti et al. since the setting of unidirectional multi-hop UPRE is different from that of FHE.

The security proof proceeds as follows. To erase sk_f, we use a dummy re-encryption circuit that does not run the decryption algorithm of Σ_f with sk_f and just outputs a dummy ciphertext under pk_t (does not need plaintext m). We expect that adversaries cannot distinguish this change. This intuition is not false. However, to formally prove it, we cannot directly use the standard CPA-security of PKE since an obfuscated circuit of the re-encryption circuit generates ciphertexts under *hard-wired* pk_t. It means that we cannot use a target ciphertext of the CPA-security game and the common "punctured programming" approach unless the scheme has a kind of "puncturable" property for its secret key [CHN+18]. Therefore, we use trapdoor encryption introduced by Canetti et al. [CLTV15].

In trapdoor encryption, there are two modes for key generation. One is the standard key generation, and the other one is the trapdoor key generation, which does not output a secret key for decryption. The two modes are computationally indistinguishable. Ciphertexts under a trapdoor key are computationally/statistically/perfectly indistinguishable. Thus, we proceed as follows. First, we change the hard-wired public key pk_t into a trapdoor key tk_t. Second, we use the security of PIO. The indistinguishability under tk_t is used to satisfy the condition of PIO.

We can consider the relationships among keys as a directed acyclic graph (DAG). Each vertex is a user who has a key pair, and each edge means that a re-encryption key was generated between two vertices. To prove ciphertext indistinguishability under a target public-key, we repeat the two processes above from the farthest vertex connected to the target vertex to the target vertex. We gradually erase information about secret keys of vertices connected to the target vertex. At the final step, information about the target secret key is also deleted, and we can use security under the target public-key of the delegator's PKE scheme. Those processes are the notable differences from the security proof of FHE based on PIO by Canetti et al. [CLTV15]. The point is that one vertex can be connected to multiple vertices in the multi -hop (U)PRE setting.

Types of indistinguishability under trapdoor keys affect what kind of PIO can be used. The weakest indistinguishability under a trapdoor key, which is equivalent to the standard IND-CPA security, requires stronger security of PIO. If we use perfect indistinguishability under a trapdoor key, which is achieved by re-randomizable PKE schemes such as ElGamal PKE scheme, then we can use weaker PIO for circuits that are implied by sub-exp IO for circuits and sub-exp OWF. Finally, we can use doubly-probabilistic IO introduced by Agrikola, Couteau, and Hofheinz [ACH20] instead of PIO to achieve UPRE for IND-CPA

PKE. Agrikola et al. prove that we can achieve doubly-probabilistic IO by using polynomially secure IO and the exponential DDH assumption.

Based on GC. The most challenging task in this work is achieving a relaxed UPRE scheme without obfuscation. Surprisingly, we can achieve a relaxed UPRE scheme for any CPA-secure PKE scheme by using GC in combination with a secret sharing scheme. The idea is that a proxy and a delegatee are different entities and can separately use shares of a decryption key. We generate *shares of a decryption key*, and use a garbled circuit where one of the shares is hardwired to hide information about the decryption key.

Our re-encryption mechanism proceeds in the following two steps. First, we generate shares (s_1, s_2) of a delegator secret key sk_f by a secret sharing scheme. We encrypt share s_1 by using pk_t and obtain $\widetilde{\mathsf{ct}}_t \leftarrow \mathsf{Enc}(\mathsf{pk}_t, s_1)$. A re-encryption key from f to t is $\mathsf{rk}_{f\rightarrow t} := (s_2, \widetilde{\mathsf{ct}}_t)$. Roughly speaking, s_1 is hidden by the CPA-security of PKE, and s_2 does not reveal information about sk_f by the privacy property of secret sharing. We define a circuit $\mathsf{C}_{\mathsf{de}}^{\mathsf{re}}$ where s_2 and the delegator ciphertext ct_f are hard-wired. The circuit $\mathsf{C}_{\mathsf{de}}^{\mathsf{re}}$ takes as input s_1, reconstructs sk_f from (s_1, s_2), and computes $\mathsf{Dec}_f(\mathsf{sk}_f, \mathsf{ct}_f)$. Now, we garble $\mathsf{C}_{\mathsf{de}}^{\mathsf{re}}[s_2, \mathsf{ct}_f]$ and obtain a garbled circuit $\widetilde{\mathsf{C}_{\mathsf{de}}^{\mathsf{re}}}$ and labels $\{\mathsf{labels}_{i,b}\}_{i\in[|s_1|]b\in\{0,1\}}$. We set a re-encrypted ciphertext to $\mathsf{rct} := (\widetilde{\mathsf{ct}}_t, \widetilde{\mathsf{C}_{\mathsf{de}}^{\mathsf{re}}}, \{\mathsf{labels}_{i,b}\})$ (we omit $\{i \in [|s_1|], b \in \{0,1\}\}$ if it is clear from the context). The delegatee t can evaluate the garbled circuit and obtain decrypted value since the delegatee can obtain s_1 from $\widetilde{\mathsf{ct}}_t$. However, this does not work since sending $\{\mathsf{labels}_{i,b}\}$ breaks the security of GC and sk_f is revealed.

Before we move to the second step, we introduce the notion of weak batch encryption, which is a non-succinct variant of batch encryption [BLSV18] and easily constructed from standard CPA-secure PKE. A batch key pair $(\hat{\mathsf{pk}}, \hat{\mathsf{sk}})$ is generated from a choice string $s \in \{0,1\}^\lambda$. We can encrypt a pair of vector messages $(\{m_{i,0}\}_{i\in[\lambda]}, \{m_{i,1}\}_{i\in[\lambda]})$ by using $\hat{\mathsf{pk}}$. We can obtain $\{m_{i,s[i]}\}_{i\in[\lambda]}$ from a batch ciphertext and $\hat{\mathsf{sk}}$. A batch public-key $\hat{\mathsf{pk}}$ does not reveal any information about s. Adversaries cannot obtain any information about $\{m_{i,1-s[i]}\}_{i\in[\lambda]}$ from a batch ciphertext even if $\hat{\mathsf{sk}}$ is given. By using 2λ pairs of a public-key and secret-key of PKE, we can achieve weak batch encryption (we select a key pair based on each bit of s). Note that we can recycle $\hat{\mathsf{pk}}$ for many vectors of messages. See Sect. 3.1 for details.

Now, we move to the second step. To send only $\{\mathsf{labels}_{i,s_1[i]}\}_{i\in|s_1|}$ to the delegatee t, we use weak batch encryption. That is, we let s_1 be choice bits of a batch key pair and $\{\mathsf{labels}_{i,b}\}$ be messages of batch encryption. To achieve a re-encryption mechanism with this idea, at the re-encryption key generation phase, we generate a batch key pair $(\hat{\mathsf{pk}}, \hat{\mathsf{sk}}) \leftarrow \mathsf{BatchGen}(s_1)$. Moreover, we encrypt the batch secret-key $\hat{\mathsf{sk}}$ under pk_t. That is, we set $\mathsf{rk}_{f\rightarrow t} := (\hat{\mathsf{pk}}, s_2, \mathsf{Enc}(\mathsf{pk}_t, \hat{\mathsf{sk}}))$. At the re-encryption phase, we generate not only the garbled circuit $\widetilde{\mathsf{C}_{\mathsf{de}}^{\mathsf{re}}}$ of $\mathsf{C}_{\mathsf{de}}^{\mathsf{re}}[s_2, \mathsf{ct}_f]$ and $\{\mathsf{labels}_{i,b}\}_{i,b}$ but also the batch ciphertext

$\hat{\mathsf{ct}} \leftarrow \mathsf{BatchEnc}(\hat{\mathsf{pk}}, (\{\mathsf{labels}_{i,0}\}_i, \{\mathsf{labels}_{i,1}\}_i))$. That is, a re-encrypted ciphertext is $\mathsf{rct} := (\widetilde{\mathsf{ct}}_t, \hat{\mathsf{ct}}, \widetilde{\mathsf{C}}^{\mathsf{re}}_{\mathsf{de}})$, where $\widetilde{\mathsf{ct}}_t \leftarrow \mathsf{Enc}(\mathsf{pk}_t, \hat{\mathsf{sk}})$.

The delegatee t can obtain the plaintext m as follows. It obtains $\hat{\mathsf{sk}} \leftarrow \mathsf{Dec}_t(\mathsf{sk}_t, \widetilde{\mathsf{ct}}_t)$ by its secret key sk_t, recover selected messages $\{\mathsf{labels}_{i,s_1[i]}\}_i \leftarrow \mathsf{BatchDec}(\hat{\mathsf{sk}}, \hat{\mathsf{ct}})$, and $m' \leftarrow \mathsf{Eval}(\widetilde{\mathsf{C}}^{\mathsf{re}}_{\mathsf{de}}, \{\mathsf{labels}_{i,s_1[i]}\}_i)$. By the functionality of GC, it holds that $m' = \mathsf{C}^{\mathsf{re}}_{\mathsf{de}}[s_2, \mathsf{ct}_f](s_1) = m$. Thus, this construction works as relaxed UPRE for any PKE scheme if there exists GC.

Intuitively, the re-encryption key $\mathsf{rk}_{f \to t}$ does not reveal information about sk_f since the CPA-security of PKE and the receiver privacy of weak batch encryption hides information about s_1. Adversaries cannot obtain any information about sk_f from the other share s_2 by the privacy property of the secret sharing scheme. That is, we can erase information about sk_f and can use the CPA-security of pk_f. Here, the choice s_1 is fixed at the re-encryption key generation phase and recycled in many re-encryption phases. However, this is not an issue since the security of weak batch encryption holds for many batch ciphertexts under the same batch key pair.

We explain only the single-hop case. However, we can easily extend the idea above to a multi-hop construction. See Sect. 3 for the detail. We note that the secret sharing mechanism was used in previous (non-universal) PRE schemes [CWYD10,HKK+12]. (The technique is called token-controlled technique in some papers.) However, using garbled circuits and batch encryption is new in the PRE setting.

In the construction above, a delegator might obtain information about the plaintext since the re-encrypted ciphertext includes ct_f in the garbled circuit and the delegator has sk_f. We have no way to prove that the construction above satisfies CRA-security. This is a problem when we use a relaxed UPRE scheme for migration of encryption systems explained in Sect. 1.1. However, we can easily solve this problem by encrypting a garbled circuit under the delegatee's public key since we can hide ct_f by using the security of the delegatee's PKE scheme. Yet, this extension incurs polynomial blow-up of ciphertext size. Thus, we can apply the re-encryption procedure only constant times.

Summary of Our Results. We give a summary of our concrete instantiations in Table 1.

Table 1. Summary of our UPRE schemes. In "Type" column, rUPRE means relaxed UPRE. In "#Hop" column, const/multi means constant/multi-hop, respectively. In "Security" column, HRA and CRA means security against honest-re-encryption/corrupted-delegator-re-encryption attacks, respectively. In "Supported PKE" column, 0-hiding trapdoor means trapdoor encryption that satisfies 0-hiding security.

Instantiation	Type	#Hop	Security	Supported PKE	Assumptions
Ours from IO + [CLTV15]	UPRE	Multi	HRA & CRA	0-hiding trapdoor	Sub-exp IO and OWF
Ours from IO + [CLTV15]	UPRE	Multi	HRA & CRA	Any IND-CPA	di-PIO and OWF
Ours from IO + [ACH20]	UPRE	Multi	HRA & CRA	Any IND-CPA	IO and exp. DDH
Ours in Sect. 3	rUPRE	Multi	HRA	Any IND-CPA	PKE
Ours in Sect. 4	rUPRE	Const	HRA & CRA	Any IND-CPA	PKE

1.4 Related Work

Encryption switching protocol (ESP), which was introduced by Couteau, Peters, and Pointcheval [CPP16], is a related notion. It is an interactive two-party computation that enables us to transform a ciphertext of a PKE scheme into a ciphertext of another PKE scheme and vice versa. It has a similar functionality to that of UPRE. However, they are incomparable in the following sense. In an ESP, parties must interactively communicate each other though there does not exists a proxy (and no re-encryption key). UPRE does not need interactive communication. Moreover, the proposed ESPs are not universal, that is, the protocols work only for specific PKE schemes. Thus, the purpose of ESPs is different from that of UPRE and they are incomparable.

There is a universal methodology to construct a new cryptographic system from existing *signature* schemes. Hohenberger, Koppula, and Waters introduce the notion of universal signature aggregator (USA) [HKW15], which enables us to aggregate signatures under different secret keys of *different* signature schemes. Standard aggregate signatures enable us to compress multiple signatures under different secret keys of *the same* scheme into one compact signature that is verified by a set of multiple verification keys [BGLS03]. Thus, USA is a generalization of aggregate signatures. Hohenberger et al. [HKW15] constructed selectively (resp. adaptively) secure USA scheme from sub-exp IO, sub-exp OWF, and additive homomorphic encryption (resp. IO, OWF, homomorphic encryption, and universal samplers) in the standard (resp. random oracle) model.

Reconfigurable cryptography was introduced by Hesse, Hofheinz, and Rupp [HHR16]. It makes updating PKI easier by using long-term keys, short-term keys, and common reference strings. Reconfigurable encryption can update keys, but cannot update ciphertexts.

There is a long series of works on proxy re-encryption. After the introduction of proxy cryptography by Blaze, Bleumer, and Strauss [BBS98], improved constructions [ID03, AFGH05], CCA-secure constructions [CH07, LV08, DWLC08, SC09, HKK+12], key-private constructions [ABH09, ABPW13, NX15], obfuscation-based definition and constructions [HRsV11, CCV12, CCL+14] have been proposed. Note that this is not an exhaustive list.

Organization. The main body of this paper consists of the following parts. In Sect. 2, we introduce the syntax and security definitions of UPRE. In Sect. 3, we present our relaxed UPRE scheme based on GC, and prove its security. In Sect. 4, we present our CRA-secure relaxed UPRE scheme. We omit many contents (basic preliminaries) due to space limitations. In particular, we omit our UPRE scheme based on IO. See the full version of this paper for omitted contents.

2 Definition of Universal Proxy Re-Encryption

In this section, we present the definitions of universal proxy re-encryption (UPRE). In particular, we present the definition of UPRE for PKE and its security notions. A UPRE scheme enables us to convert ciphertexts of a PKE scheme Σ_f into ciphertexts of a (possibly) different PKE scheme Σ_t. A UPRE scheme does not need a setup for a system. That is, it can use existing PKE schemes with different parameters. UPRE can be seen as a generalization proxy re-encryption [BBS98]. Therefore, we borrow many terms of proxy re-encryption [AFGH05, CH07].

Notations. We consider multiple PKE schemes and key pairs, so we assume that every known PKE scheme is named by a number in $[N]$ (say, 1 is for Goldwasser-Micali PKE, 2 is for ElGamal PKE etc.). We also put a number in $[U]$ for a generated key pair. When we write $(\mathsf{pk}_i, \mathsf{sk}_i) \leftarrow \mathsf{Gen}_{\sigma_i}(1^\lambda)$, we mean that i-th key pair is generated by PKE scheme $\Sigma_{\sigma_i} = (\mathsf{Gen}_{\sigma_i}, \mathsf{Enc}_{\sigma_i}, \mathsf{Dec}_{\sigma_i})$ where $\sigma_i \in [N]$. In this paper, when we emphasize which user is a delegator or delegatee, we denote delegator and delegatee key pairs by $(\mathsf{pk}_f, \mathsf{sk}_f)$ and $(\mathsf{pk}_t, \mathsf{sk}_t)$, respectively ($f$ and t mean "from" and "to", respectively). That is, a ciphertext under pk_f will be converted into a ciphertext pk_t. We assume that in the description of Σ_{σ_i}, ciphertext space $\mathcal{C}_{\sigma_i}$ and message space $\mathcal{M}_{\sigma_i}$ are also included. When we use Σ_{σ_i} as an input for algorithms of UPRE, we interpret it as a description of algorithms (rather than Turing machines or circuits). Note that the length of such descriptions is polynomial since algorithms of PKE should be PPT.

2.1 Unidirectional UPRE

Definition 2.1 (Universal Proxy Re-Encryption for PKE: Syntax). *A universal re-encryption scheme* UPRE *consists of two PPT algorithms* (ReKeyGen, ReEnc).

- $\mathsf{ReKeyGen}(1^\lambda, \Sigma_{\sigma_f}, \Sigma_{\sigma_t}, \mathsf{sk}_f, \mathsf{pk}_t)$ *takes the security parameter, a pair of PKE scheme* $(\Sigma_{\sigma_f}, \Sigma_{\sigma_t})$*, a secret-key* sk_f *of* Σ_{σ_f}*, and a public-key* pk_t *of* Σ_{σ_t} *and outputs a re-encryption key* $\mathsf{rk}_{f\to t}$ *for ciphertexts under* pk_f*. The security parameter is often omitted.*
- $\mathsf{ReEnc}(\Sigma_{\sigma_f}, \Sigma_{\sigma_t}, \mathsf{rk}_{f\to t}, \mathsf{ct}_f)$ *takes a pair of PKE schemes* $(\Sigma_{\sigma_f}, \Sigma_{\sigma_t})$*, a re-encryption key* $\mathsf{rk}_{f\to t}$*, and a ciphertext* ct_f *under* pk_f *of* Σ_{σ_f}*, and outputs a re-encrypted ciphertext* ct_t *under* pk_t*.*

Definition 2.2 (Relaxed Universal Proxy Re-Encryption for PKE: Syntax). *A relaxed universal re-encryption scheme* UPRE *consists of two PPT and one deterministic polynomial-time algorithms* (ReKeyGen, ReEnc, mDec)*.*

- $\mathsf{ReKeyGen}(1^\lambda, \Sigma_{\sigma_f}, \Sigma_{\sigma_t}, \mathsf{sk}_f, \mathsf{pk}_t)$ *is the same as in Definition 2.1.*
- $\mathsf{ReEnc}(\Sigma_{\sigma_f}, \Sigma_{\sigma_t}, \mathsf{rk}_{f\to t}, \mathsf{ct}_f)$ *takes a pair of PKE schemes* $(\Sigma_{\sigma_f}, \Sigma_{\sigma_t})$*, a re-encryption key* $\mathsf{rk}_{f\to t}$*, and a ciphertext* ct_f *under* pk_f *of* Σ_{σ_f}*, and outputs a re-encrypted ciphertext* rct*. We implicitly assume that* rct *includes index* ℓ *which indicates how many times* ReEnc *was applied so far. When we write* $\mathsf{rct}^{(\ell)}$*, it means that* $\mathsf{rct}^{(\ell)}$ *was obtained by applying* ReEnc ℓ *times.*
- $\mathsf{mDec}(\Sigma_{\sigma_t}, \mathsf{sk}_t, \mathsf{rct}^{(\ell)}, \ell)$ *is a deterministic algorithm and takes a PKE scheme* Σ_{σ_t}*, a secret key* sk_t*, a re-encrypted ciphertext* $\mathsf{rct}^{(\ell)}$ *under* $\mathsf{rk}_{f\to t}$*, and index* ℓ *and outputs a message* m*. When* $\ell = 1$*, we omit the index.*

The difference between UPRE and relaxed UPRE is that we can use the decryption algorithm of Σ_{σ_t} as it is in UPRE. In relaxed UPRE, we need use a modified decryption algorithm though what we need for decryption is the original secret key sk_t. Note that re-encrypted ciphertext space $\mathcal{C}_{\sigma_f \to \sigma_t}$ potentially depends on $\mathcal{C}_{\sigma_f}$ and $\mathcal{C}_{\sigma_t}$ and possibly $\mathsf{rct} \notin \mathcal{C}_{\sigma_t}$ happens.

Hereafter, we focus only on the relaxed notion since we can easily replace $\mathsf{mDec}(\Sigma_{\sigma_t}, \mathsf{sk}_t, \mathsf{rct}^{(\ell)}, \ell)$ with $\mathsf{Dec}(\mathsf{sk}_t, \mathsf{ct}_t)$.

On Message Space. For simplicity, we consider messages in $\mathcal{M}_{\sigma_1} \cap \cdots \cap \mathcal{M}_{\sigma_N}$ where N is the number of considered PKE scheme in security games (described later). We can consider $\{0,1\}^{\ell}$ as a message space where ℓ is a polynomial of a security parameter and UPRE for such a message space by considering bit-by-bit encryption for all PKE scheme. However, this is cumbersome. Thus, hereafter, we consider messages in the intersection of all message spaces though we do not explicitly mention.

Bidirectional UPRE. We can consider bidirectional UPRE, where a re-encryption key generated from key pairs $(\mathsf{pk}_f, \mathsf{sk}_f)$ and $(\mathsf{pk}_t, \mathsf{sk}_t)$ can convert ciphertexts under pk_f (resp. pk_t) into ciphertexts that can be decrypted by sk_t (resp. sk_f). Although unidirectional UPRE can support the functionality of bidirectional UPRE by generating two re-encryption keys $\mathsf{rk}_{f \to t}$ and $\mathsf{rk}_{t \to f}$, it is not clear whether security is preserved. We focus on unidirectional UPRE in this study.

Functionality and Security. We introduce the correctness and a security notion of UPRE that we call security against *honest re-encryption attacks (HRA)* for UPRE. Correctness is easy to understand.

This HRA for UPRE is based on security against HRA of PRE introduced by Cohen [Coh19]. Roughly speaking, in the setting of HRA, adversaries are allowed to obtain an honestly encrypted ciphertext *via an honest encryption oracle* and can convert it into a re-encrypted ciphertext under a key of a *corrupted* user via a re-encryption oracle. In PRE-CPA security, adversaries cannot obtain such a re-encrypted ciphertext because it is *not allowed* to obtain a re-encryption key query *from an honest user to a corrupted user* via the re-encryption key oracle to prevent trivial attacks[5]. Cohen observes that PRE-CPA security is not sufficient for many applications of PRE. Therefore, we define HRA-security for UPRE (in fact, we also define a selective variant).

First, we consider *single-hop* UPRE, where if a ciphertext is converted into another ciphertext, then we cannot convert the re-encrypted one anymore.

Definition 2.3 (UPRE for PKE: Single-Hop Correctness). *A relaxed UPRE scheme* UPRE *for PKE is correct if for all pairs of PKE schemes* $(\Sigma_{\sigma_f}, \Sigma_{\sigma_t})$, $(\mathsf{pk}_f, \mathsf{sk}_f) \leftarrow \mathsf{Gen}_{\sigma_f}(1^{\lambda_f})$, $(\mathsf{pk}_t, \mathsf{sk}_t) \leftarrow \mathsf{Gen}_{\sigma_t}(1^{\lambda_t})$, $m \in \mathcal{M}_{\sigma_f} \cap \mathcal{M}_{\sigma_t}$,

[5] Of course, a re-encryption query from an honest user to a corrupted user is also prohibited in PRE-CPA security.

$\mathsf{ct}_f \leftarrow \mathsf{Enc}_{\sigma_f}(\mathsf{pk}_f, m)$, *it holds that*

$$\Pr[\mathsf{mDec}(\Sigma_{\sigma_t}, \mathsf{sk}_t, \mathsf{ReEnc}(\Sigma', \mathsf{ReKeyGen}(\Sigma', \mathsf{sk}_f, \mathsf{pk}_t), \mathsf{ct}_f)) = m] = 1,$$

where $\Sigma' := (\Sigma_{\sigma_f}, \Sigma_{\sigma_t})$. *In the case of UPRE,* $\mathsf{mDec}(\Sigma_{\sigma_t}, \cdot, \cdot) = \mathsf{Dec}_{\sigma_t}(\cdot, \cdot)$.

Before we present the definition of the HRA security for UPRE, we give an informal explanation about it. Readers who are familiar with PRE-HRA security [Coh19] may be able to skip explanations below and jump into the formal definition. Readers who are familiar with PRE-CPA security [ABH09, Coh19] may be able to skip explanations below except "Honest encryption and re-encryption query" part.

Challenge query: We consider a natural extension of the CPA security of PKE. The adversary selects a target public-key pk_{i^*} indexed by i^* and tries to distinguish whether a target ciphertext ct_{i^*} is an encryption of m_0 or m_1 that it selects. This will be modeled by the challenge oracle $\mathcal{O}_{\mathsf{cha}}$.
Key query: The adversary can be given public keys pk_i or key pairs $(\mathsf{pk}_i, \mathsf{sk}_i)$ by specifying a user and a PKE scheme at the setup phase since we consider multiple keys and schemes. When a secret key is given, it means its owner is corrupted.
Re-encryption key query: The most notable feature is that the adversary is given re-encryption keys by the re-encryption key oracle $\mathcal{O}_{\mathsf{rekey}}$. If the adversary specifies existing indices of keys, say (i, j), then it is given a corresponding re-encryption key from i to j. Here, we must restrict queries for some indices to prevent trivial attacks. If j is a corrupted user and i is the target user (queried to $\mathcal{O}_{\mathsf{cha}}$), then the adversary trivially wins the security game by converting the target ciphertext and decrypting with the corrupted key sk_j. Therefore, such queries must be prohibited.
Honest encryption and re-encryption query: If the adversary specifies keys and a ciphertext to the re-encryption oracle $\mathcal{O}_{\mathsf{reenc}}$, then it is given a re-encrypted ciphertext generated from queried values. One might think this oracle is redundant since it is simulatable by $\mathcal{O}_{\mathsf{rekey}}$. However, there is a subtle issue here since a re-encryption key query with a corrupted delegatee is prohibited as explained above. As Cohen observed [Coh19] in the setting of PRE, simply prohibiting such a query is not sufficient and considering re-encryption queries is meaningful.

Re-encrypted ciphertexts may leak information about a delegator key pair and help to attack a delegator ciphertext. As Cohen observed [Coh19], if a re-encryption key is $\mathsf{Enc}(\mathsf{pk}_t, \mathsf{sk}_f)$ and *it is included in a re-encrypted ciphertext*, then the delegatee easily breaks security. This is unsatisfactory when we consider applications of PRE and UPRE. However, in the setting of PRE, such a construction is secure under the standard CPA-security model since it prohibits queries (i, j) (resp. (i, j, ct_i)) to the re-encryption key generation (resp. re-encryption) oracle [Coh19]. Thus, we introduce the notion of derivative and the honest encryption oracle $\mathcal{O}_{\mathsf{enc}}$ in UPRE as Cohen did.

We say that a (re-encrypted) ciphertext is a derivative if it is the target ciphertext generated by the challenge oracle or a re-encrypted ciphertext from the target ciphertext. This is managed by a set Drv. The honest encryption oracle allows the adversary to obtain a re-encrypted ciphertext under a corrupted key from honest encryption. The re-encryption oracle does not accept queries whose delegatee is a corrupted user j and ciphertext is a derivative to prevent trivial attacks. Moreover, the re-encryption oracle does not accept ciphertexts that are not generated via the honest encryption oracle.

Definition 2.4 (Derivative). *We say that a (re-encrypted) ciphertext is a derivative when the (re-encrypted) ciphertext is a target ciphertext itself or obtained from a target ciphertext given by $\mathcal{O}_{\mathsf{cha}}$ by applying re-encryption.*

Definition 2.5 (UPRE for PKE: Single-Hop selective HRA Security). *We define the experiment $\mathsf{Exp}_{\mathcal{A}}^{\mathsf{upre\text{-}hra}}(1^\lambda, b)$ between an adversary $\mathcal{A}$ and a challenger. The experiment consists of three phases.*

Phase 1 (Setup): *This is the setup phase. All security parameters are chosen by the challenger.*

- *The challenger initializes $\#\mathsf{Keys} := 0, \mathsf{HList} := \emptyset, \mathsf{CList} := \emptyset$, $\#\mathsf{CT} := 0$, $\mathsf{KeyCTList} := \emptyset$, $\mathsf{Drv} := \emptyset$. Note that we assume that all indices are recorded with keys and corresponding schemes though we do not explicitly write for simplicity.*
- *For an honest key query (i, σ_i, λ_i) from $\mathcal{A}$, if the challenger already received $(i, *, *)$ before, it outputs $\bot$. Otherwise, the challenger generates uncorrupted keys $(\mathsf{pk}_i, \mathsf{sk}_i) \leftarrow \mathsf{Gen}_{\sigma_i}(1^{\lambda_i})$, sends $(\Sigma_{\sigma_i}, \mathsf{pk}_i)$ to $\mathcal{A}$, and sets $\mathsf{HList} := \mathsf{HList} \cup i$ and $\#\mathsf{Keys} := \#\mathsf{Keys} + 1$. If $\lambda_i < \lambda$, then the challenger ignores the query.*[6]
- *For a corrupted key query (i, σ_i, λ_i) from $\mathcal{A}$, if the challenger already received $(i, *, *)$ before, it outputs $\bot$. Otherwise, the challenger generates corrupted keys $(\mathsf{pk}_i, \mathsf{sk}_i) \leftarrow \mathsf{Gen}_{\sigma_i}(1^{\lambda_i})$, sends $(\Sigma_{\sigma_i}, \mathsf{pk}_i, \mathsf{sk}_i)$ to $\mathcal{A}$, and sets $\mathsf{CList} := \mathsf{CList} \cup i$ and $\#\mathsf{Keys} := \#\mathsf{Keys} + 1$.*

Let $\mathcal{M}_U$ be the intersection of all message spaces defined by $\mathsf{pk}_{i_1}, \ldots, \mathsf{pk}_{i_{\#\mathsf{Keys}}}$. At the end of Phase 1, we assume that the list $((1, \sigma_1), \ldots, (\#\mathsf{Keys}, \sigma_{\#\mathsf{Keys}}))$ is broadcasted and all entities know it.

Phase 2 (Oracle query): *This is the oracle query phase.*

$\mathcal{O}_{\mathsf{enc}}(i, m)$**:** *For an honest encryption query (i, m) where $i \leq \#\mathsf{Keys}$, the challenger generates $\mathsf{ct}_i \leftarrow \mathsf{Enc}_{\sigma_i}(\mathsf{pk}_i, m)$, sets $\#\mathsf{CT} := \#\mathsf{CT} + 1$, records $(\mathsf{ct}_i, \Sigma_{\sigma_i}, i, \#\mathsf{CT})$ in $\mathsf{KeyCTList}$, and gives $(\mathsf{ct}_i, \#\mathsf{CT})$ to $\mathcal{A}$.*

$\mathcal{O}_{\mathsf{rekey}}(i, j)$**:** *For a re-encryption key query (i, j) where $i, j \leq \#\mathsf{Keys}$, the challenger outputs $\bot$ if $i = j$ or $i \in \mathsf{HList} \wedge j \in \mathsf{CList}$. Otherwise, the challenger generates $\mathsf{rk}_{i \to j} \leftarrow \mathsf{ReKeyGen}(\Sigma_{\sigma_i}, \Sigma_{\sigma_j}, \mathsf{sk}_i, \mathsf{pk}_j)$ and gives $\mathsf{rk}_{i \to j}$ to $\mathcal{A}$.*

$\mathcal{O}_{\mathsf{reenc}}(i, j, k)$**:** *For a re-encryption query (i, j, k) where $i, j \leq \#\mathsf{Keys}$ and $k \leq \#\mathsf{CT}$, the challenger does the following.*

---

[6] If we prefer longer security parameters, then we can change the condition to $\lambda_i < c\lambda$ for some constant $c > 1$.

1. *If* $j \in \mathsf{CList} \wedge k \in \mathsf{Drv}$, *then returns* $\perp$.
2. *If there is no value* $(*, *, i, k)$ *in* $\mathsf{KeyCTList}$, *returns* $\perp$.
3. *Otherwise, retrieves* $\mathsf{rk}_{i \to j}$ *for* (i, j) *(if it does not exists, generates* $\mathsf{rk}_{i \to j} \leftarrow \mathsf{ReKeyGen}(\Sigma_{\sigma_i}, \Sigma_{\sigma_j}, \mathsf{sk}_i, \mathsf{pk}_j)$ *and stores it), generates* $\mathsf{rct} \leftarrow \mathsf{ReEnc}(\Sigma_{\sigma_i}, \Sigma_{\sigma_j}, \mathsf{rk}_{i \to j}, \mathsf{ct}_i)$ *from* ct_i *in* $\mathsf{KeyCTList}$, *sets* $\#\mathsf{CT} := \#\mathsf{CT} + 1$, *records* $(\mathsf{rct}, \Sigma_{\sigma_j}, j, \#\mathsf{CT})$ *in* $\mathsf{KeyCTList}$, *and gives* $(\mathsf{rct}, \#\mathsf{CT})$ *to* $\mathcal{A}$.

$\mathcal{O}_{\mathsf{cha}}(i^*, m_0, m_1)$: *This oracle is invoked only once. For a challenge query* (i^*, m_0, m_1) *where* $i^* \in \mathsf{HList}$ *and* $m_0, m_1, \in \mathcal{M}_U$ *(defined at the end of Phase 1), the challenger generates* $\mathsf{ct}^* \leftarrow \mathsf{Enc}_{\sigma_{i^*}}(pk_{i^*}, m_b)$, *gives it to* $\mathcal{A}$, *and sets* $\#\mathsf{CT} := \#\mathsf{CT} + 1$, $\mathsf{Drv} := \mathsf{Drv} \cup \{\#\mathsf{CT}\}$, $\mathsf{KeyCTList} := \mathsf{KeyCTList} \cup \{(\mathsf{ct}^*, \Sigma_{\sigma_{i^*}}, i^*, \#\mathsf{CT})\}$.

Phase 3 (Decision): *This is the decision phase.* $\mathcal{A}$ *outputs a guess* b' *for* b. *The experiment outputs* b'.

We say the UPRE *is single-hop UPRE-HRA secure if, for any* $\sigma_i \in [N]$, *for any PPT* $\mathcal{A}$, *it holds that*

$$\mathsf{Adv}_{\mathcal{A}}^{\mathsf{upre\text{-}hra}}(\lambda) := |\Pr[\mathsf{Exp}_{\mathcal{A}}^{\mathsf{upre\text{-}hra}}(1^\lambda, 0) = 1] - \Pr[\mathsf{Exp}_{\mathcal{A}}^{\mathsf{upre\text{-}hra}}(1^\lambda, 1) = 1]| \leq \mathsf{negl}(\lambda).$$

Discussion on Definition 2.5. (1) On security parameter: We can simply set $\forall i\ \lambda_i := \lambda$. Some λ_j may be longer than other λ_i (say, $\lambda_j = \mathrm{poly}(\lambda_i)$). (2) On adaptive corruption: The adversary is not allowed to adaptively corrupt users during the experiment. This is because, in general, it is difficult to achieve security against adaptive corruption. In particular, in our setting, $\mathcal{O}_{\mathsf{rekey}}$ cannot decide whether it should return $\perp$ or a valid re-encryption key if j may be corrupted later. This static security is standard in the PRE setting [AFGH05, CH07, LV08, ABH09]. One exception is the work by Fuchsbauer, Kamath, Klein, and Pietrzak [FKKP19]. We do not know whether the techniques by Fuchbauer et al. are applicable to the UPRE setting. This is an interesting future work. The honest and corrupted key generation queries could be moved to the oracle query phase, but it does not incur a significant difference. Thus, we select a simpler model as most works on re-encryption did [AFGH05, LV08, ABH09, Coh19].

Knowledgeable readers might think a UPRE definition based on the PRE definition by Chow et al. [CWYD10] is better than the definition above. In the PRE setting, the defition by Chow et al. might be stronger than that by Cohen. However, the relationship between them is not formally studied. Thus, which definition is better or not is out of scope of this paper.

2.2 Unidirectional Multi-hop UPRE

In this section, we introduce multi-hop UPRE, which is an extension of single-hop UPRE, where a re-encrypted ciphertext rct generated by $\mathsf{rk}_{f \to t}$ could be re-encrypted many times. Let $L = L(\lambda)$ be the maximum number of hops that a UPRE scheme can support.

Definition 2.6 (UPRE for PKE: L-hop Correctness). *A multi-hop UPRE scheme* mUPRE *for PKE is L-hop correct if for all PKE schemes* $(\Sigma_{\sigma_0}, \Sigma_{\sigma_1}, \ldots, \Sigma_{\sigma_L})$ *that satisfy correctness and* $\sigma_{i-1} \neq \sigma_i$ *for all* $i \in [L]$, $(\mathsf{pk}_i, \mathsf{sk}_i) \leftarrow \mathsf{Gen}_{\sigma_i}(1^{\lambda_i})$ *(for all* $i = 0, \ldots, L$*),* $m \in \mathcal{M}_{\sigma_0} \cap \cdots \cap \mathcal{M}_{\sigma_L}$, $\mathsf{ct}_0 \leftarrow \mathsf{Enc}_{\sigma_0}(\mathsf{pk}_0, m)$, *it holds that*

$$\Pr[\mathsf{mDec}(\Sigma_{\sigma_j}, \mathsf{sk}_j, \mathsf{rct}^{(j)}, j) = m] = 1$$

where $\mathsf{rct}^{(j)} \leftarrow \mathsf{ReEnc}(\Sigma'_j, \mathsf{ReKeyGen}(\Sigma'_j, \mathsf{sk}_{j-1}, \mathsf{pk}_j), \mathsf{rct}^{(j-1)})$, $\mathsf{rct}^{(0)} = \mathsf{ct}_0$, $\Sigma'_j := (\Sigma_{\sigma_{j-1}}, \Sigma_{\sigma_j})$ *and* $j \in [1, L]$.

The reason why mDec is indexed by j is that the decryption procedure for j-times re-encrypted ciphertexts might be different. See Sect. 3 as a concrete example.

The security notion of multi-hop UPRE is similar to that of single-hop one, but slightly more complex since we consider many intermediate keys from a delegator to a delegatee. In particular, we use a directed acyclic graph (DAG) to reflect the relationships among keys. A user is modeled as a vertex in a graph and if there exists a re-encryption key from vertex (user) i to vertex (user) j, then a directed edge (i, j) is assigned between the vertices (note that edge (i, j) is not equal to (j, i) since we consider DAGs). That is, a DAG $G = (V, E)$ denotes that V is a set of users and E is a set of index pairs whose re-encryption key was issued. We do not consider cyclic graphs in this study since it incurs an issue of circular security in our constructions[7].

We introduce the notion of *admissible edges* to exclude trivial attacks by using oracles. Roughly speaking, an admissible edge means that ciphertexts under a target public key will not be converted into ciphertexts under *corrupted* public keys in CList. We denote by $i \rightsquigarrow j$ there exists a path from vertex i to vertex j in G.

Definition 2.7 (Admissible edge). *We say that* (i, j) *is an admissible edge with respect to* $G = (V, E)$ *if, in* $E \cup (i, j)$*, there does not exist a path from any vertex* $i^* \in \mathsf{HList}$ *(honest user set fixed at the setup phase) to* $j^* \in \mathsf{CList}$ *such that the path includes edge* (i, j) *as an intermediate edge (this includes the case* $j = j^*$*). That is, no* $i^* \in \mathsf{HList}$, $j^* \in \mathsf{CList}$ *such that a path* $i^* \rightsquigarrow j^*$ *exists in* $G' = (V, E \cup (i, j))$.

We also introduce the notion of the *selective-graph model* as a weaker attack model. In the selective-graph model, the adversary must commit a graph $G^* = (V^*, E^*)$ at the beginning of an experiment. To formally define this model, we define a *deviating pair with respect to* G^* *and* G.

Definition 2.8 (deviating pair). *We say that* (i, j) *is a deviating pair with respect to* $G^* = (V^*, E^*)$ *and* $G = (V, E)$ *in the selective-graph model if* $i \in V^* \wedge j \in V$ *or* $j \in V^* \wedge i \in V$.

[7] The circular security issue arises in constructions that use general PKE schemes. If there exists a cycle, we have no way to use the CPA-security of a PKE scheme in the cycle since the information of each secret key in the cycle is in a re-encryption key in the cycle. This does not happen in concrete constructions based on some hard problems such as the DDH.

In the selective-graph model, the adversary must select $i^* \in V^*$ as the target vertex that will be queried to $\mathcal{O}_{\mathsf{cha}}$. Moreover, the adversary is not given re-encryption keys and re-encrypted ciphertexts from $\mathcal{O}_{\mathsf{rekey}}$ and $\mathcal{O}_{\mathsf{reenc}}$, respectively, if queried (i, j) is a deviating pair. That is, the structure of DAG that is connected to the target vertex must be determined at the beginning of the game. We focus on security in the selective-graph model in this study since it is what our schemes achieve. For admissible edges in the selective-graph model, we consider $i^* \in V^*_{\mathsf{h}}$ (defined below) instead of $i^* \in \mathsf{HList}$ (i.e., replacing HList with V^*_{h} in Definition 2.7).

Definition 2.9 (UPRE for PKE: Multi-Hop selective-graph HRA Security). *We define the experiment* $\mathsf{Exp}^{\mathsf{upre\text{-}msg\text{-}hra}}_{\mathcal{A}}(1^\lambda, b)$ *between an adversary* $\mathcal{A}$ *and a challenger. The experiment consists of three phases.*

Phase 1 (Setup): *This is the setup phase. All security parameters are chosen by the challenger.*

- *The challenger initializes* $\#\mathsf{Keys} := 0, \mathsf{HList} := \emptyset, \mathsf{CList} := \emptyset, \#\mathsf{CT} := 0, \mathsf{KeyCTList} := \emptyset, \mathsf{Drv} := \emptyset, V := \emptyset, E := \emptyset$.
- *At the beginning of this phase,* $\mathcal{A}$ *must commit a graph* $G^* = (V^* = (V^*_{\mathsf{h}}, V^*_{\mathsf{c}}), E^*)$. *We assume that* $V^* = \{1, \ldots, |V^*|\}$ *by using appropriate renaming. If there is an edge* $(i, j) \in E^*$ *such that* $i \in V^*_{\mathsf{h}} \wedge j \in V^*_{\mathsf{c}}$, *then the game aborts. The challenger generates keys* $(\mathsf{pk}_i, \mathsf{sk}_i) \leftarrow \mathsf{Gen}_{\sigma_i}(1^{\lambda_i})$ *for all* $i \in V^*$ *and sends* $\{\mathsf{pk}_i\}_{i \in V^*_{\mathsf{h}}}, \{(\mathsf{pk}_j, \mathsf{sk}_j)\}_{j \in V^*_{\mathsf{c}}}$ *to* $\mathcal{A}$. *We assume that* $\mathcal{A}$ *selects* (σ_i, λ_i) *for all* $i \in V^*$ *as the key generation queries below (if* $\lambda_i < \lambda$ *for* $i \in V^*_{\mathsf{h}}$, *then the game aborts). The challenger also generates* $\mathsf{rk}_{i \to j} \leftarrow \mathsf{ReKeyGen}(\Sigma_{\sigma_i}, \Sigma_{\sigma_j}, \mathsf{sk}_i, \mathsf{pk}_j)$ *for all* $(i, j) \in E^*$ *and sends them to* $\mathcal{A}$. *The challenger sets* $\mathsf{HList} := \mathsf{HList} \cup V^*_{\mathsf{h}}$, $\mathsf{CList} := \mathsf{CList} \cup V^*_{\mathsf{c}}$, *and* $\#\mathsf{Keys} := \#\mathsf{Keys} + |V^*|$.
- *For the i-th honest key generation query* (σ_i, λ_i) *from* $\mathcal{A}$, *if* $\lambda_i < \lambda$, *the challenger outputs* $\perp$. *Otherwise, the challenger generates uncorrupted keys* $(\mathsf{pk}_i, \mathsf{sk}_i) \leftarrow \mathsf{Gen}_{\sigma_i}(1^{\lambda_i})$, *sends* $(\Sigma_{\sigma_i}, \mathsf{pk}_i)$ *to* $\mathcal{A}$, *and sets* $\mathsf{HList} := \mathsf{HList} \cup i$, $\#\mathsf{Keys} := \#\mathsf{Keys} + 1$, *and* $V := V \cup \{i\}$.
- *For the j-th corrupted key generation query* (j, σ_j, λ_j) *from* $\mathcal{A}$, *the challenger generates corrupted keys* $(\mathsf{pk}_i, \mathsf{sk}_i) \leftarrow \mathsf{Gen}_{\sigma_i}(1^{\lambda_i})$, *sends* $(\Sigma_{\sigma_i}, \mathsf{pk}_i, \mathsf{sk}_i)$ *to* $\mathcal{A}$, *and sets* $\mathsf{CList} := \mathsf{CList} \cup i$, $\#\mathsf{Keys} := \#\mathsf{Keys} + 1$, *and* $V := V \cup \{i\}$.
- *The challenger maintains graph* $G := (V, E)$ *during the experiment. Note that we assume that all keys and schemes are recorded with vertices and edges though we do not explicitly write for simplicity.*

Phase 2 (Oracle query): *This is the oracle query phase.*

$\mathcal{O}_{\mathsf{enc}}(i, m)$**:** *For an honest encryption query* (i, m) *where* $i \le \#\mathsf{Keys}$, *the challenger generates* $\mathsf{ct}_i \leftarrow \mathsf{Enc}_{\sigma_i}(\mathsf{pk}_i, m)$, *sets* $\#\mathsf{CT} := \#\mathsf{CT} + 1$, *record* $(\mathsf{ct}_i, \Sigma_{\sigma_i}, i, \#\mathsf{CT})$ *in* $\mathsf{KeyCTList}$, *and gives* $(\mathsf{ct}_i, \#\mathsf{CT})$ *to* $\mathcal{A}$.

$\mathcal{O}_{\mathsf{rekey}}(i, j)$**:** *For a re-encryption key query* (i, j) *where* $i, j \le \#\mathsf{Keys}$, *the challenger does the following.*

1. *If* $i \in V^*$ *or* $j \in V^*$ *or* $i = j$, *then output* $\perp$.

2. *Otherwise, the challenger generates* $\mathsf{rk}_{i \to j} \leftarrow \mathsf{ReKeyGen}(\Sigma_{\sigma_i}, \Sigma_{\sigma_j}, \mathsf{sk}_i, \mathsf{pk}_j)$ *and updates* $E := E \cup (i, j)$ *and gives* $\mathsf{rk}_{i \to j}$ *to* $\mathcal{A}$.

$\mathcal{O}_{\mathsf{reenc}}(i, j, k)$: *For a re-encryption query* (i, j, k) *where* $i, j \leq \#\mathsf{Keys}$ *and* $k \leq \#\mathsf{CT}$, *the challenger does the following.*

1. *If (A)* (i, j) *is a deviating pair with respect to* G^* *and* G, *or (B)* (i, j) *is not an admissible edge with respect to* $G^* = (V^*, E^*)$ *and* $k \in \mathsf{Drv}$, *then returns* $\bot$.
2. *If there is no* $(*, *, i, k)$ *in* $\mathsf{KeyCTList}$, *then outputs* $\bot$.
3. *Otherwise, generates* $\mathsf{rk}_{i \to j} \leftarrow \mathsf{ReKeyGen}(\Sigma_{\sigma_i}, \Sigma_{\sigma_j}, \mathsf{sk}_i, \mathsf{pk}_j)$ *and* $\mathsf{rct}_j \leftarrow \mathsf{ReEnc}(\Sigma_{\sigma_i}, \Sigma_{\sigma_j}, \mathsf{rk}_{i \to j}, \mathsf{rct}_i)$ *from* rct_i *in* $\mathsf{KeyCTList}$, *sets* $\#\mathsf{CT} := \#\mathsf{CT}+1$, *records* $(\mathsf{rct}_j, \Sigma_{\sigma_j}, j, \#\mathsf{CT})$ *in* $\mathsf{KeyCTList}$, *and gives* $(\#\mathsf{CT}, \mathsf{rct}_j)$ *to* $\mathcal{A}$. *If* $k \in \mathsf{Drv}$, *then also sets* $\mathsf{Drv} := \mathsf{Drv} \cup \{\#\mathsf{CT}\}$.

$\mathcal{O}_{\mathsf{cha}}(i^*, m_0, m_1)$: *This oracle is invoked only once. For a challenge query* (i^*, m_0, m_1) *where* $i^* \in V^*_{\mathsf{h}}$ *and* $m_0, m_1, \in \mathcal{M}_U$ *(same as defined in Definition 2.5), the challenger generates* $\mathsf{ct}^* \leftarrow \mathsf{Enc}_{\sigma i^*}(pk_{i^*}, m_b)$ *and gives it to* $\mathcal{A}$. *The challenger also sets* $\#\mathsf{CT} := \#\mathsf{CT} + 1$, $\mathsf{Drv} := \mathsf{Drv} \cup \{\#\mathsf{CT}\}$, $\mathsf{KeyCTList} := \mathsf{KeyCTList} \cup \{(\mathsf{ct}^*, \Sigma_{\sigma_{i^*}}, i^*, \#\mathsf{CT})\}$.

Phase 3 (Decision): *This is the decision phase.* $\mathcal{A}$ *outputs a guess* b' *for* b. *The experiment outputs* b'.

We say the UPRE *is multi-hop selective-graph UPRE-HRA secure if, for any PPT* $\mathcal{A}$, *it holds that*

$$\begin{aligned}\mathsf{Adv}_{\mathcal{A}}^{\mathsf{upre\text{-}msg\text{-}hra}}(\lambda) :=| \Pr[\mathsf{Exp}_{\mathcal{A}}^{\mathsf{upre\text{-}msg\text{-}hra}}(1^\lambda, 0) = 1] \\ - \Pr[\mathsf{Exp}_{\mathcal{A}}^{\mathsf{upre\text{-}msg\text{-}hra}}(1^\lambda, 1) = 1]| \leq \mathsf{negl}(\lambda).\end{aligned}$$

UPRE-CPA Security. We can easily consider the CPA-security of UPRE. We can obtain the security experiment of the CPA-security if we employ the following items in the experiment of the HRA security.

1. The honest encryption oracle $\mathcal{O}_{\mathsf{enc}}$ is not used.
2. Neither the set Drv nor number $\#\mathsf{CT}$ is used.
3. The condition that $\mathcal{O}_{\mathsf{reenc}}$ outputs $\bot$ for a query (i, j) such that $i \in \mathsf{HList} \wedge j \in \mathsf{CList}$ (or (i, j) is not an admissible edge) is used instead of the first and second conditions of $\mathcal{O}_{\mathsf{reenc}}$ in the experiment of the HRA security.

2.3 Security Against Corrupted-Delegator Re-Encryption Attacks

Re-encrypted ciphertexts of relaxed UPRE schemes might include values that leak information about a plaintext to a delegator (that is, an entity that has a secret key for the original ciphertext). This is an important issue to use UPRE in migration of encryption systems explained in Sect. 1.1. We will see a concrete example in Sect. 3. To capture attacks on re-encrypted ciphertext by corrupted delegator, we define a new security notion for UPRE (and PRE), security against corrupted-delegator re-encryption attacks (CRA). We write the definition of the UPRE case. The PRE case is similarly defined as PRE-CRA security. We can also similarly define a single-hop variant.

Definition 2.10 (Selective-graph UPRE-CRA security). *The experiment* $\mathsf{Exp}_{\mathcal{A}}^{\mathsf{upre\text{-}msg\text{-}cra}}(1^\lambda, b)$ *of this security notion is the same as that of multi-hop selective-graph UPRE-HRA security except that the challenge oracle* $\mathcal{O}_{\mathsf{cha}}$ *is modified as follows.*

$\mathcal{O}_{\mathsf{cha}}(i_{\mathsf{c}}, i^*, m_0, m_1)$: *This oracle is invoked only once. For a challenge query* $(i_{\mathsf{c}}, i^*, m_0, m_1)$ *where* $i_{\mathsf{c}} \in V_{\mathsf{c}}^* \ \wedge \ i^* \in V_{\mathsf{h}}^*$ *and* $m_0, m_1, \in \mathcal{M}_U$ *(same as defined in Definition 2.5), the challenger does the following.*

1. *Generates* $\mathsf{ct}_{i_{\mathsf{c}}} \leftarrow \mathsf{Enc}_{\sigma_{i_{\mathsf{c}}}}(pk_{i_{\mathsf{c}}}, m_b)$.
2. *Generates* $\mathsf{rk}_{i_{\mathsf{c}} \to i^*} = \mathsf{ReKeyGen}(\Sigma_{\sigma_{i_{\mathsf{c}}}}, \Sigma_{\sigma_{i^*}}, \mathsf{sk}_{i_{\mathsf{c}}}, \mathsf{pk}_{i^*})$.
3. *Generates* $\mathsf{rct}^* \leftarrow \mathsf{ReEnc}(\Sigma_{\sigma_{i_{\mathsf{c}}}}, \Sigma_{\sigma_{i^*}}, \mathsf{rk}_{i_{\mathsf{c}} \to i^*}, \mathsf{ct}_{i_{\mathsf{c}}})$ *and gives* $(\mathsf{rct}^*, \mathsf{rk}_{i_{\mathsf{c}} \to i^*})$ *to* $\mathcal{A}$.

The challenger also sets $\#\mathsf{CT} := \#\mathsf{CT}+1$, $\mathsf{Drv} := \mathsf{Drv} \cup \{\#\mathsf{CT}\}$, $\mathsf{KeyCTList} := \mathsf{KeyCTList} \cup \{(\mathsf{ct}^*, \Sigma_{\sigma_{i^*}}, i^*, \#\mathsf{CT})\}$.

We say the UPRE *is multi-hop selective-graph UPRE-CRA secure if, for any PPT* $\mathcal{A}$, *it holds that*

$$\mathsf{Adv}_{\mathcal{A}}^{\mathsf{upre\text{-}msg\text{-}cra}}(\lambda) := \mid \Pr[\mathsf{Exp}_{\mathcal{A}}^{\mathsf{upre\text{-}msg\text{-}cra}}(1^\lambda, 0) = 1] - \Pr[\mathsf{Exp}_{\mathcal{A}}^{\mathsf{upre\text{-}msg\text{-}cra}}(1^\lambda, 1) = 1] \mid \leq \mathsf{negl}(\lambda).$$

This definition means that adversaries that have secret key $\mathsf{sk}_{i_{\mathsf{c}}}$ cannot break the security of the re-encrypted ciphertext rct^* generated from the ciphertext $\mathsf{ct}_{i_{\mathsf{c}}}$ under $\mathsf{pk}_{i_{\mathsf{c}}}$ if they are not given the original ciphertext $\mathsf{ct}_{i_{\mathsf{c}}}$ (even if re-encryption key $\mathsf{rk}_{i_{\mathsf{c}} \to i^*}$ is given). The fact that $\mathsf{ct}_{i_{\mathsf{c}}}$ is not given to $\mathcal{A}$ guarantees that $\mathcal{A}$ cannot trivially break the security.

2.4 On Re-Encryption Simulatability

Cohen introduced the notion of re-encryption simulatability for PRE to prove PRE-HRA security in a modular way [Coh19]. He proved that if a PRE scheme is PRE-CPA secure and satisfies re-encryption simulatability[8], then the scheme is PRE-HRA secure.

The re-encryption simulatability is sufficient to prove PRE-HRA security (if a PRE is PRE-CPA secure scheme) and useful. Thus, one might think it is better to use re-encryption simulatability for UPRE. However, it is a slightly stronger security notion. Our relaxed UPRE schemes in Sects. 3 and 4 are *UPRE-HRA secure*, yet *does not* satisfy re-encryption simulatability. Thus, we do not use re-encryption simulatability to prove UPRE-HRA security in this study[9].

[8] Note that Cohen *does not* use key-privacy of PRE [ABH09] to prove PRE-HRA security.

[9] We could define a weaker variant of re-encryption simulatability for UPRE (and PRE) that still implies HRA security. However, such a definition is not simple, and proofs are not simplified. Proving such a weak re-encryption simulatability takes almost the same efforts to prove HRA security directly. Thus, we do not use re-encryption simulatability.

2.5 UPRE for More Advanced Encryption

We give the basic definitions of UPRE for PKE in Sects. 2.1 and 2.2. We can consider more definitions for advanced encryption since UPRE is a general concept.

CCA-Security. First, we can consider CCA-security of UPRE for PKE. The definition of CCA-security of UPRE for PKE could be defined in a similar way to that of PRE [CH07,LV08,HKK+12] though it will be more complex. We leave giving a formal definition of CCA-security and concrete constructions as an open problem since they are not in the scope of this paper. The focus of this study is that we initiate the study of UPRE, present the basic definition, and construct concrete schemes from well-known cryptographic assumptions.

Beyond PKE. We can also consider not only UPRE for PKE but also UPRE for identity-based encryption (IBE), attribute-based encryption (ABE), and functional encryption (FE). Moreover, we can even consider UPRE from a primitive to another primitive such as from IBE to FE. It is easier to consider UPRE between the same primitive since additional inputs to encryption algorithms such as an attribute in a delegator ciphertext can be recycled in a re-encrypted ciphertext. Defining UPRE between different primitives is much challenging since we have issues about how to set such additional inputs at re-encryption phase and define security between different primitives. We leave these as open problems since they are not in the scope of this paper.

3 Multi-hop Construction Based on Garbled Circuits

In this section, we provide a UPRE scheme using garbled circuits. The main idea of the construction provided here is that the re-encryptor delegates decryption to the target node via garbled circuits. To achieve UPRE, we use weak batch encryption schemes, which are constructed from standard IND-CPA secure PKE schemes.

3.1 Weak Batch Encryption

Definition 3.1 (Weak Batch Encryption). *Let $\mathcal{M}$ be a message space. A weak batch encryption scheme is a tuple of algorithms* $(\mathsf{BatchGen}, \mathsf{BatchEnc}, \mathsf{BatchDec})$ *where*

- $\mathsf{BatchGen}(1^\lambda, s)$ *takes as input the security parameter and selection bits* $s \in \{0,1\}^\lambda$, *and outputs a pair* $(\hat{\mathsf{pk}}, \hat{\mathsf{sk}})$ *of public and secret keys.*
- $\mathsf{BatchEnc}(\hat{\mathsf{pk}}, \{(m_{i,0}, m_{i,1})\}_{i\in[\lambda]})$ *takes as input a public key* $\hat{\mathsf{pk}}$ *and* λ*-pairs of messages* $\{(m_{i,0}, m_{i,1})\}_{i\in[\lambda]}$ *where* $m_{i,b} \in \mathcal{M}$, *and outputs a ciphertext* $\hat{\mathsf{ct}}$.
- $\mathsf{BatchDec}(\hat{\mathsf{sk}}, \hat{\mathsf{ct}})$ *takes as input a secret key* $\hat{\mathsf{sk}}$ *and a ciphertext message* $\hat{\mathsf{ct}}$, *and outputs* $\{m'_i\}_{i\in[\lambda]}$, *or* $\bot$.

Correctness: *For any* λ, $s \in \{0,1\}^\lambda$, $m_{i,b} \in \mathcal{M}$, *we have that*

$$\Pr\left[\forall i\ m'_i = m_{i,s[i]} \;\middle|\; \begin{array}{r} (\hat{\mathsf{pk}}, \hat{\mathsf{sk}}) \leftarrow \mathsf{BatchGen}(1^\lambda, s), \\ \hat{\mathsf{ct}} \leftarrow \mathsf{BatchEnc}(\hat{\mathsf{pk}}, \{(m_{i,0}, m_{i,1})\}_{i\in[\lambda]}), \\ \{m'_i\}_{i\in[\lambda]} \leftarrow \mathsf{BatchDec}(\hat{\mathsf{sk}}, \hat{\mathsf{ct}}) \end{array}\right] > 1 - \mathsf{negl}(\lambda),$$

where $s[i]$ *denotes* i*-th bit of* s.

Receiver Privacy: *We require that public keys* $\hat{\mathsf{pk}}$ *are independent of the selection bits* $s \in \{0,1\}^\lambda$ *used to generate* $\hat{\mathsf{pk}}$. *That is, for all* s_1, s_2 *it holds that*

$$\hat{\mathsf{pk}}_1 \equiv \hat{\mathsf{pk}}_2$$

where $(\hat{\mathsf{pk}}_1, \hat{\mathsf{sk}}_1) \leftarrow \mathsf{BatchGen}(1^\lambda, s_1)$ *and* $(\hat{\mathsf{pk}}_2, \hat{\mathsf{sk}}_2) \leftarrow \mathsf{BatchGen}(1^\lambda, s_2)$ *and* $\equiv$ *means the statistical distance is equal to* 0.

Sender Privacy against Semi-honest Receiver: *We define the experiment* $\mathsf{Exp}^{\mathsf{wbe\text{-}cpa}}_{\mathcal{A}}(1^\lambda, \beta)$ *between an adversary* $\mathcal{A}$ *and challenger as follows.*

1. $\mathcal{A}$ *chooses* $s \in \{0,1\}^\lambda$ *and sends it to the challenger.*
2. *The challenger computes* $(\hat{\mathsf{pk}}, \hat{\mathsf{sk}}) \leftarrow \mathsf{BatchGen}(1^\lambda, s)$ *and sends* $\hat{\mathsf{pk}}$ *to* $\mathcal{A}$.
3. $\mathcal{A}$ *sends* $\{(m_{i,0}, m_{i,1})\}_{i\in[\lambda]}$ *to the challenger and:*
   - *If* $\beta = 0$, *the challenger computes* $\hat{\mathsf{ct}}^* \leftarrow \mathsf{BatchEnc}(\hat{\mathsf{pk}}, \{(m_{i,0}, m_{i,1})\})$.
   - *Else if* $\beta = 1$, *the challenger computes* $\hat{\mathsf{ct}}^* \leftarrow \mathsf{BatchEnc}(\hat{\mathsf{pk}}, \{(m_{i,s[i]}, m_{i,s[i]})\})$.
4. *The challenger sends* $(\hat{\mathsf{sk}}, \hat{\mathsf{ct}}^*)$ *to* $\mathcal{A}$.
5. $\mathcal{A}$ *outputs a guess* β' *for* β. *The experiment outputs* β'.

We say $(\mathsf{BatchGen}, \mathsf{BatchEnc}, \mathsf{BatchDec})$ *is WBE-CPA secure against semi-honest receiver if for any PPT adversary* $\mathcal{A}$, *it holds that*

$$\mathsf{Adv}^{\mathsf{wbe\text{-}cpa}}_{\mathcal{A}}(\lambda) := |\Pr[\mathsf{Exp}^{\mathsf{wbe\text{-}cpa}}_{\mathcal{A}}(1^\lambda, 0) = 1] - \Pr[\mathsf{Exp}^{\mathsf{wbe\text{-}cpa}}_{\mathcal{A}}(1^\lambda, 1) = 1]| \leq \mathsf{negl}(\lambda).$$

We can consider a multi-challenge variant. That is, $\mathcal{A}$ *can send* $\{(m^{(j)}_{i,0}, m^{(j)}_{i,1})\}_{i\in[\lambda]}$ *and obtain many target ciphertexts after* $(\hat{\mathsf{pk}}, \hat{\mathsf{sk}})$ *is given for* $j = 1, \ldots, \mathrm{poly}(\lambda)$.

IND-CPA Security: *The experiment* $\mathsf{Exp}^{\mathsf{ind\text{-}cpa}}_{\mathcal{A}}(1^\lambda, \beta)$ *is the same as* $\mathsf{Exp}^{\mathsf{wbe\text{-}cpa}}_{\mathcal{A}}(1^\lambda, \beta)$ *above except that*

1. $\mathcal{A}$ *is not given* $\hat{\mathsf{sk}}$.
2. *If* $\beta = 1$, *then* $\hat{\mathsf{ct}}^* \leftarrow \mathsf{BatchEnc}(\hat{\mathsf{pk}}, \{(\mathbf{0}, \mathbf{0})\})$ *where* $\mathbf{0}$ *is a fixed special message (considered as all zero) that does not depend on* β.

If $\Pr[\mathsf{Exp}^{\mathsf{ind\text{-}cpa}}_{\mathcal{A}}(1^\lambda, 0) = 1] - \Pr[\mathsf{Exp}^{\mathsf{ind\text{-}cpa}}_{\mathcal{A}}(1^\lambda, 1) = 1]$ *is negligible, then the weak batch encryption is IND-CPA secure.*

The difference between weak batch encryption and batch encryption proposed by Brakerski, Lombardi, Segev, and Vaikuntanathan [BLSV18] is that there is no efficiency requirement on the size of the batch public-key $\hat{\mathsf{pk}}$. Thus, it is easy to achieve weak batch encryption.

Theorem 3.1 (Weak Batch Encryption from IND-CPA PKE). *If there exists IND-CPA secure PKE, then there exists weak batch encryption.*

Proof. Let $\Sigma = (\mathsf{Gen}, \mathsf{Enc}, \mathsf{Dec})$ be an IND-CPA secure PKE scheme.

$\mathsf{BatchGen}(1^\lambda, s)$**:** It generates $(\mathsf{pk}_{i,b}, \mathsf{sk}_{i,b}) \leftarrow \mathsf{Gen}(1^\lambda)$ for all $i \in [\lambda]$ and $b \in \{0,1\}$ and outputs $\hat{\mathsf{pk}} := \{\mathsf{pk}_{i,b}\}_{i \in [\lambda], b \in \{0,1\}}$ and $\hat{sk} := \{sk_{i,s[i]}\}_{i \in [\lambda]}$.

$\mathsf{BatchEnc}(\hat{\mathsf{pk}}, \{(m_{i,0}, m_{i,1})\}_{i \in [\lambda]})$**:** It generates $\mathsf{ct}_{i,b} \leftarrow \mathsf{Enc}(\mathsf{pk}_{i,b}, m_{i,b})$ for all $i \in [\lambda]$ and $b \in \{0,1\}$. It outputs $\hat{\mathsf{ct}} := \{\mathsf{ct}_{i,b}\}_{i \in [\lambda], b \in \{0,1\}}$.

$\mathsf{BatchDec}(\hat{\mathsf{sk}}, \hat{\mathsf{ct}})$**:** It parses $\hat{sk} = (\mathsf{sk}_1, \ldots, \mathsf{sk}_\lambda)$ and $\hat{\mathsf{ct}} = \{\mathsf{ct}_{i,b}\}_{i \in [\lambda], b \in \{0,1\}}$. It computes $m_i' \leftarrow \mathsf{Dec}(\mathsf{sk}_i, \mathsf{ct}_{i,b})$ for $b \in \{0,1\}$ and sets $m_i := m_{i,b}'$ if $m_{i,b}' \neq \bot$. It outputs $\{m_i\}_{i \in [\lambda]}$.

The receiver privacy trivially holds since $\hat{\mathsf{pk}}$ does not include any information about s. The sender privacy follows from the IND-CPA security of Σ and the standard hybrid argument because $\{sk_{i,1-s[i]}\}_{i \in [\lambda]}$ are never used. Moreover, it is easy to see that the scheme satisfies the multi-challenge version by the standard hybrid argument. The IND-CPA security trivially holds. ■

3.2 Our Multi-Hop Scheme from GC

Our scheme $\mathsf{UPRE_{gc}}$ is based on a garbling scheme $(\mathsf{Garble}, \mathsf{Eval})$, a weak batch-encryption scheme $(\mathsf{BatchGen}, \mathsf{BatchEnc}, \mathsf{BatchDec})$ and a 2-player secret-sharing scheme $(\mathsf{Share}, \mathsf{Reconstruct})$. We overload the notation $\Sigma_{\sigma_i} = (\mathsf{Gen}_{\sigma_i}, \mathsf{Enc}_{\sigma_i}, \mathsf{Dec}_{\sigma_i})$ by $\Sigma_i = (\mathsf{Gen}_i, \mathsf{Enc}_i, \mathsf{Dec}_i)$ for ease of notation. Moreover, we sometimes write labels instead of $\{\mathsf{labels}_{k,b}\}_{k \in [n], b \in \{0,1\}}$ if it is clear from the context for ease of notation. We also denote by labels_s labels selected by s, that is, $\{\mathsf{labels}_{i,s_i}\}_{i \in [\lambda]}$. Moreover, $\widetilde{\mathsf{labels}}$ basically denotes selected labels output by $\mathsf{BatchDec}$.

- $\mathsf{ReKeyGen}(1^\lambda, \Sigma_f, \Sigma_t, \mathsf{sk}_f, \mathsf{pk}_t)$:
  - Compute $(s_1, s_2) \leftarrow \mathsf{Share}(\mathsf{sk}_f)$
  - $(\hat{\mathsf{pk}}, \hat{\mathsf{sk}}) \leftarrow \mathsf{BatchGen}(1^\lambda, s_1)$
  - Compute $\widetilde{\mathsf{ct}}_t \leftarrow \mathsf{Enc}_t(\mathsf{pk}_t, \hat{\mathsf{sk}})$
  - Output $\mathsf{rk}_{f \to t} := (\hat{\mathsf{pk}}, s_2, \widetilde{\mathsf{ct}}_t)$.
- $\mathsf{ReEnc}(\Sigma_f, \Sigma_t, \mathsf{rk}_{f \to t}, \mathsf{ct}_f)$:
  - Parse $\mathsf{rk}_{f \to t} = (\hat{\mathsf{pk}}, s_2, \widetilde{\mathsf{ct}}_t)$.
  - If ct_f is in the ciphertext space of Σ_f (1st level), set $\mathsf{C} \leftarrow \mathsf{P}[s_2, \mathsf{ct}_f]$ (Fig. 1); Else if (level $i > 1$), parse $\mathsf{ct}_f = (\hat{\mathsf{ct}}', \widetilde{\mathsf{ct}}_f, \tilde{\mathsf{C}}_{i-1}, \ldots, \tilde{\mathsf{C}}_1)$ and set $\mathsf{C} \leftarrow \mathsf{Q}[s_2, \hat{\mathsf{ct}}', \widetilde{\mathsf{ct}}_f]$ (Fig. 2)
  - Compute $(\tilde{\mathsf{C}}_i, \mathsf{labels}) \leftarrow \mathsf{Garble}(\mathsf{C})$.
  - Compute $\hat{\mathsf{ct}} \leftarrow \mathsf{BatchEnc}(\hat{\mathsf{pk}}, \mathsf{labels})$
  - Output $(\hat{\mathsf{ct}}, \widetilde{\mathsf{ct}}_t, \tilde{\mathsf{C}}_i, \ldots, \tilde{\mathsf{C}}_1)$
- $\mathsf{mDec}(\Sigma_t, \mathsf{sk}_t, \mathsf{rct}, i)$: Parse $\mathsf{rct} = (\hat{\mathsf{ct}}, \widetilde{\mathsf{ct}}_t, \tilde{\mathsf{C}}_i, \ldots, \tilde{\mathsf{C}}_1)$.
  - Compute $\hat{\mathsf{sk}}' \leftarrow \mathsf{Dec}(\mathsf{sk}_t, \widetilde{\mathsf{ct}}_t)$.

First Level Re-Encryption Circuit $\mathsf{P}[s_2, \mathsf{ct}_f](s_1)$

Hardwired: s_2, ct_f.
Input: A share s_1.

- Compute $\mathsf{sk}'_f \leftarrow \mathsf{Reconstruct}(s_1, s_2)$.
- Compute and output $m' \leftarrow \mathsf{Dec}_f(\mathsf{sk}'_f, \mathsf{ct}_f)$.

Fig. 1. The description of the first level re-encryption circuit P

Higher Level Re-Encryption Circuit $\mathsf{Q}[s_2, \hat{\mathsf{ct}}', \tilde{\mathsf{ct}}_f](s_1)$

Hardwired: s_2, $\hat{\mathsf{ct}}'$, $\tilde{\mathsf{ct}}_f$.
Input: A share s_1.

- Compute $\mathsf{sk}'_f \leftarrow \mathsf{Reconstruct}(s_1, s_2)$.
- Compute $\hat{\mathsf{sk}}' \leftarrow \mathsf{Dec}(\mathsf{sk}'_f, \tilde{\mathsf{ct}}_f)$.
- Compute and output $\widetilde{\mathsf{labels}} \leftarrow \mathsf{BatchDec}(\hat{\mathsf{sk}}', \hat{\mathsf{ct}}')$.

Fig. 2. The description of the higher level re-encryption circuit Q

- Compute $\widetilde{\mathsf{labels}}_i \leftarrow \mathsf{BatchDec}(\hat{\mathsf{sk}}', \hat{\mathsf{ct}})$
- For $j = i, \ldots, 2$ do: Compute $\widetilde{\mathsf{labels}}_{j-1} \leftarrow \mathsf{Eval}(\tilde{\mathsf{C}}_j, \widetilde{\mathsf{labels}}_j)$.
- Compute and output $m' \leftarrow \mathsf{Eval}(\tilde{\mathsf{C}}_1, \widetilde{\mathsf{labels}}_1)$.

Correctness. We now turn to the correctness of $(\mathsf{ReKeyGen}, \mathsf{ReEnc}, \mathsf{mDec})$. We will show correctness via induction.

We will first show correctness for level 1 ciphertexts. Let thus $\mathsf{rct} = (\hat{\mathsf{ct}}, \tilde{\mathsf{ct}}_t, \tilde{\mathsf{C}}_1)$ be a level 1 ciphertext, where $(\tilde{\mathsf{C}}_1, \mathsf{labels}) \leftarrow \mathsf{Garble}(\mathsf{P}[s_2, \mathsf{ct}_f])$, $\hat{\mathsf{ct}} = \mathsf{BatchEnc}(\hat{\mathsf{pk}}, \mathsf{labels})$ and $\tilde{\mathsf{ct}}_t = \mathsf{Enc}_t(\mathsf{pk}_t, \hat{\mathsf{sk}})$. Consider the computation of $\mathsf{mDec}(\Sigma_t, \mathsf{sk}_t, \mathsf{rct})$. By the correctness of Σ_t it holds that $\hat{\mathsf{sk}}' = \mathsf{Dec}(\mathsf{sk}_t, \tilde{\mathsf{ct}}_t) = \hat{\mathsf{sk}}$. Next, by the correctness of the batch public key encryption $(\mathsf{BatchGen}, \mathsf{BatchEnc}, \mathsf{BatchDec})$ it holds that that $\widetilde{\mathsf{labels}} = \mathsf{BatchDec}(\hat{\mathsf{sk}}, \hat{\mathsf{ct}}) = \mathsf{labels}_{s_1}$. Thus, by the correctness of the garbling scheme $(\mathsf{Garble}, \mathsf{Eval})$ it holds that $\mathsf{Eval}(\tilde{\mathsf{C}}_1, \widetilde{\mathsf{labels}}) = \mathsf{Eval}(\tilde{\mathsf{C}}_1, \mathsf{labels}_{s_1}) = \mathsf{P}[s_2, \mathsf{ct}_f](s_1)$. By the definition of P, $\mathsf{P}[s_2, \mathsf{ct}_f](s_1)$ computes $\mathsf{sk}_f \leftarrow \mathsf{Reconstruct}(s_1, s_2)$ and outputs $m' \leftarrow \mathsf{Dec}_f(\mathsf{sk}'_f, \mathsf{ct}_f)$. Thus, by the correctness of $(\mathsf{Share}, \mathsf{Reconstruct})$ it holds that $\mathsf{sk}'_f = \mathsf{sk}_f$ and finally by the correctness of Σ_f we get that $m' = m$.

Now assume that decryption is correct for level $(i-1)$ ciphertexts and consider a ciphertext $\mathsf{rct} = (\hat{\mathsf{ct}}, \tilde{\mathsf{ct}}_t, \tilde{\mathsf{C}}_i, \ldots, \tilde{\mathsf{C}}_1)$ at level $i > 1$. As before, it holds that $(\tilde{\mathsf{C}}_i, \mathsf{labels}) \leftarrow \mathsf{Garble}(\mathsf{Q}[s_2, \hat{\mathsf{ct}}', \tilde{\mathsf{ct}}_f])$, $\hat{\mathsf{ct}} = \mathsf{BatchEnc}(\hat{\mathsf{pk}}, \mathsf{labels})$ and

$\widetilde{\mathsf{ct}}_t = \mathsf{Enc}_t(\mathsf{pk}_t, \hat{\mathsf{sk}})$. Again consider the computation of $\mathsf{mDec}(\Sigma_t, \mathsf{sk}_t, \mathsf{rct})$. By the correctness of Σ_t it holds that $\hat{\mathsf{sk}}' = \mathsf{Dec}(\mathsf{sk}_t, \widetilde{\mathsf{ct}}_t) = \hat{\mathsf{sk}}$. Next, by the correctness of the batch public key encryption scheme (BatchGen, BatchEnc, BatchDec) it holds that that $\widetilde{\mathsf{labels}} = \mathsf{BatchDec}(\hat{\mathsf{sk}}, \hat{\mathsf{ct}}) = \mathsf{labels}_{s_1}$. Thus, by the correctness of the garbling scheme (Garble, Eval) it holds that $\mathsf{Eval}(\tilde{\mathsf{C}}_i, \widetilde{\mathsf{labels}}_i) = \mathsf{Eval}(\tilde{\mathsf{C}}_i, \widetilde{\mathsf{labels}}_{s_1}) = \mathsf{Q}[s_2, \hat{\mathsf{ct}}', \widetilde{\mathsf{ct}}_f](s_1)$.

Notice now that we can substitute $\mathsf{Q}[s_2, \hat{\mathsf{ct}}', \widetilde{\mathsf{ct}}_f](s_1)$ by

- Compute $\mathsf{sk}'_f \leftarrow \mathsf{Reconstruct}(s_1, s_2)$.
- Compute $\hat{\mathsf{sk}} \leftarrow \mathsf{Dec}(\mathsf{sk}_f, \widetilde{\mathsf{ct}}_f)$.
- Compute $\widetilde{\mathsf{labels}} \leftarrow \mathsf{BatchDec}(\hat{\mathsf{sk}}, \hat{\mathsf{ct}}')$.

By the correctness of (Share, Reconstruct) it holds that $\mathsf{sk}'_f = \mathsf{Reconstruct}(s_1, s_2) = \mathsf{sk}_f$. By inspection we see that the remaining steps of the computation are identical to the decryption of a level $(i-1)$ ciphertext. The induction hypothesis provides that decryption is correct for level $(i-1)$ ciphertexts and we are done.

3.3 Security Proof

Theorem 3.2 (UPRE-HRA security). *Assume that* $\mathsf{gc} = (\mathsf{Garble}, \mathsf{Eval})$ *is a selectively secure garbling scheme,* (Share, Reconstruct) *is a 2-out-of-2 secret sharing scheme and* (BatchGen, BatchEnc, BatchDec) *is a weak batch encryption scheme in the sense of Definition 3.1, and both* Σ_f *and* Σ_t *are IND-CPA secure PKE, then* $\mathsf{UPRE}_{\mathsf{gc}}$ *is selective-graph UPRE-HRA secure.*

Proof. We define a sequence of hybrid experiments $\mathsf{Hyb}^x_{\mathcal{A}}(b)$. We emphasize differences among hybrid experiments by using red underlines. Hereafter, $\mathsf{Hyb}^x_{\mathcal{A}}(b) \approx \mathsf{Hyb}^y_{\mathcal{A}}(b)$ denotes $|\Pr[\mathsf{Hyb}^x_{\mathcal{A}}(b) = 1] - \Pr[\mathsf{Hyb}^y_{\mathcal{A}}(b) = 1]| \leq \mathsf{negl}(\lambda)$. We say that a ciphertext ct is a level i re-encryption, if ct is of the form $\mathsf{ct} = (\hat{\mathsf{ct}}, \widetilde{\mathsf{ct}}_t, \tilde{\mathsf{C}}_i, \ldots, \tilde{\mathsf{C}}_1)$, i.e. ct is the result of i re-encryptions.

$\mathsf{Hyb}^0_{\mathcal{A}}(b)$: The first experiment is the original security experiment for b, $\mathsf{Exp}^{\mathsf{upre\text{-}msg\text{-}hra}}_{\mathcal{A}}(1^\lambda, b)$. That is, it holds that $\mathsf{Hyb}^0_{\mathcal{A}}(b) = \mathsf{Exp}^{\mathsf{upre\text{-}msg\text{-}hra}}_{\mathcal{A}}(1^\lambda, b)$. Note that in the successive experiments, we can easily simulate all keys in $G = (V, E)$ since vertices in V are not connected to the target vertex in G^* and simulators can generate keys for them by itself.

$\mathsf{Hyb}^{0'}_{\mathcal{A}}(b)$: This experiment is the same as $\mathsf{Hyb}^0_{\mathcal{A}}(b)$ except that we guess the target vertex i^* that will be queried to challenge oracle $\mathcal{O}_{\mathsf{cha}}$ and abort if the guess is incorrect. The guess is correct with probability $1/|V^*_{\mathsf{h}}|$, so $\Pr[\mathsf{Hyb}^{0'}_{\mathcal{A}}(b) = 1] = \frac{1}{|V^*_{\mathsf{h}}|} \cdot \Pr[\mathsf{Hyb}^0_{\mathcal{A}}(b) = 1]$.

$\mathsf{Hyb}^1_{\mathcal{A}}(b)$: In this hybrid we record not only $(\mathsf{rct}_i, \Sigma_i, i, \#\mathsf{CT})$ but also m in KeyCTList for encryption query (i, m).

Moreover, for each re-encryption query, store the value $\widetilde{\mathsf{labels}} = \mathsf{labels}_{s_1}$.

The modification between $\mathsf{Hyb}_{\mathcal{A}}^{0'}(b)$ and $\mathsf{Hyb}_{\mathcal{A}}^{1}(b)$ is merely syntactic, thus it holds that $\Pr[\mathsf{Hyb}_{\mathcal{A}}^{0'}(b) = 1] = \Pr[\mathsf{Hyb}_{\mathcal{A}}^{1}(b) = 1]$.

We will now replace re-encrypted ciphertexts by simulated re-encrypted ciphertexts. For re-encryption query $(\widehat{i}, j, k)$ such that $(\widehat{i}, j)$ is not an admissible edge with respect to $G^* = (V^*, E^*)$ and $k \notin \mathsf{Drv}$, the re-encrypted ciphertext is differently generated by a modified re-encryption procedure. We can assume $\widehat{i}$ is honest since we do not need guarantee anything if $\widehat{i}$ is not honest. The goal of the processes below is erasing secret keys of honest vertices queried by re-encryption queries. Note that $\widehat{i} = i^*$ is possible due to the restriction $k \notin \mathsf{Drv}$ though $(\widehat{i}, j)$ is not admissible. We repeat the processes below for $u = 1, \ldots, Q_{\mathsf{reenc}}$ where Q_{reenc} is the total number of tuples $(\widehat{i}, j, k)$ such that $(\widehat{i}, j)$ is not an admissible edge with respect to $G^* = (V^*, E^*)$ and $k \notin \mathsf{Drv}$. Without loss of generality, we can assume that each $\widehat{i}$ is different for each such re-encryption query.[10] The changes in experiments below are for re-encryption query for u-th tuple $(\widehat{i}, j, k)$ such that $(\widehat{i}, j)$ is not an admissible edge with respect to $G^* = (V^*, E^*)$ and $k \notin \mathsf{Drv}$.

$\mathsf{Hyb}_{\mathcal{A}}^{1,u,1}(b)$: This is the same as $\mathsf{Hyb}_{\mathcal{A}}^{1,(u-1),3}$ except that: Retrieve s_1 of $\widehat{i}$,
- Parse $\mathsf{rk}_{\widehat{i} \to j} = (\hat{\mathsf{pk}}, s_2, \widetilde{\mathsf{ct}}_j)$.
- If ct_f is in the ciphertext space of Σ_f, set $\mathsf{C} \leftarrow \mathsf{P}[s_2, \mathsf{ct}_{\widehat{i}}]$; Else if, parse $\mathsf{ct}_f = (\hat{\mathsf{ct}}', \widetilde{\mathsf{ct}}_f, \tilde{\mathsf{C}}_{i-1}, \ldots, \tilde{\mathsf{C}}_1)$ and set $\mathsf{C} \leftarrow \mathsf{Q}[s_2, \hat{\mathsf{ct}}', \widetilde{\mathsf{ct}}_{\widehat{i}}]$.
- Compute $(\tilde{\mathsf{C}}_{\iota}, \mathsf{labels}) \leftarrow \mathsf{Garble}(\mathsf{C})$.
- Compute $\underline{\mathsf{labels}^* \leftarrow \{(\mathsf{labels}_{i,s_1[i]}, \mathsf{labels}_{i,s_1[i]})\}_{i \in [\lambda]}}$
- Compute $\underline{\hat{\mathsf{ct}} \leftarrow \mathsf{BatchEnc}(\hat{\mathsf{pk}}, \mathsf{labels}^*)}$.
- Output $(\hat{\mathsf{ct}}, \widetilde{\mathsf{ct}}_j, \tilde{\mathsf{C}}_{\iota}, \ldots, \tilde{\mathsf{C}}_1)$.

That is, we compute $\hat{\mathsf{ct}}$ via $\mathsf{BatchEnc}(\hat{\mathsf{pk}}, \mathsf{labels}^*)$ instead of $\mathsf{BatchEnc}(\hat{\mathsf{pk}}, \mathsf{labels})$.

$\mathsf{Hyb}_{\mathcal{A}}^{1,u,2}(b)$: This is the same as $\mathsf{Hyb}_{\mathcal{A}}^{1,u,1}$ except that: Retrieve s_1 of $\widehat{i}$,
- Parse $\mathsf{rk}_{\widehat{i} \to j} = (\hat{\mathsf{pk}}, s_2, \widetilde{\mathsf{ct}}_j)$.
- If ct_f is in the ciphertext space of Σ_f, set $\mathsf{C} \leftarrow \mathsf{P}[s_2, \mathsf{ct}_{\widehat{i}}]$; Else if, parse $\mathsf{ct}_f = (\hat{\mathsf{ct}}', \widetilde{\mathsf{ct}}_f, \tilde{\mathsf{C}}_{i-1}, \ldots, \tilde{\mathsf{C}}_1)$ and set $\mathsf{C} \leftarrow \mathsf{Q}[s_2, \hat{\mathsf{ct}}', \widetilde{\mathsf{ct}}_{\widehat{i}}]$.
- Compute $\underline{(\tilde{\mathsf{C}}_{\iota}, \widetilde{\mathsf{labels}}) \leftarrow \mathsf{GCSim}(\mathsf{C}(s_1))}$.
- Compute $\underline{\mathsf{labels}^* \leftarrow (\widetilde{\mathsf{labels}}, \widetilde{\mathsf{labels}})}$.
- Compute $\hat{\mathsf{ct}} \leftarrow \mathsf{BatchEnc}(\hat{\mathsf{pk}}, \mathsf{labels}^*)$.
- Output $(\hat{\mathsf{ct}}, \widetilde{\mathsf{ct}}_j, \tilde{\mathsf{C}}_{\iota}, \ldots, \tilde{\mathsf{C}}_1)$.

$\mathsf{Hyb}_{\mathcal{A}}^{1,u,3}(b)$: This is the same as $\mathsf{Hyb}_{\mathcal{A}}^{1,u,2}(b)$ except that: Retrieve m and labels $\widetilde{\mathsf{labels}}'$ (corresponding to $\hat{\mathsf{ct}}'$),
- Parse $\mathsf{rk}_{\widehat{i} \to j} = (\hat{\mathsf{pk}}, s_2, \widetilde{\mathsf{ct}}_j)$.

[10] If there exists $(\widehat{i}, j_1, k_1)$ and $(\widehat{i}, j_2, k_2)$ such that $(\widehat{i}, j_1)$ and $(\widehat{i}, j_2)$ are not admissible and $k_1, k_2 \notin \mathsf{Drv}$, then we can use the same simulation process described in hybrid experiments for those queries.

- If $\widetilde{\mathsf{ct}_f}$ is in the ciphertext space of Σ_f, set compute $(\tilde{\mathsf{C}}_\iota, \widetilde{\mathsf{labels}}) \leftarrow \mathsf{GCSim}(m)$; Else if, parse $\mathsf{ct}_f = (\hat{\mathsf{ct}}', \tilde{\mathsf{ct}}_f, \tilde{\mathsf{C}}_{i-1}, \ldots, \tilde{\mathsf{C}}_1)$ and compute $(\tilde{\mathsf{C}}_\iota, \widetilde{\mathsf{labels}}) \leftarrow \mathsf{GCSim}(\widetilde{\mathsf{labels}}')$.
- Compute $\mathsf{labels}^* \leftarrow (\widetilde{\mathsf{labels}}, \widetilde{\mathsf{labels}})$.
- Compute $\hat{\mathsf{ct}} \leftarrow \mathsf{BatchEnc}(\hat{\mathsf{pk}}, \mathsf{labels}^*)$.
- Output $(\hat{\mathsf{ct}}, \tilde{\mathsf{ct}}_j, \tilde{\mathsf{C}}_\iota, \ldots, \tilde{\mathsf{C}}_1)$.

For syntactic convention, we let $\mathsf{Hyb}_{\mathcal{A}}^{1,0,3}(b) := \mathsf{Hyb}_{\mathcal{A}}^{1}(b)$. Moreover, notice that at hybrid $\mathsf{Hyb}_{\mathcal{A}}^{1,Q_{\mathsf{reenc}},3}(b)$ all re-encryption queries are simulated with garbled circuits and their labels that do not depends on secret keys (or more specifically, without values that depend on secret keys). That is, we do not explicitly use sk_{i^*} to compute re-encrypted ciphertexts as above. However, in $\hat{\mathsf{pk}}$ and s_2, information about sk_{i^*} still remains. We will handles these issues in the following process.

Process for removing sk_{i^*} *of the target vertex.* Now, we focus on vertices in V^* connected via admissible edges. To use the security of Σ_{i^*}, we need remove information about sk_{i^*} from all re-encryption keys in $G^* = (V^*, E^*)$ possibly connected to i^*. Let Q be the total number of admissible edges connected to target vertex i^*. We call the following procedure a depth-search from vertex i: We seek a vertex that is connected to i and does not have an outgoing edge in a forward direction. If there is a vertex i' (possibly $i' = i$) that has two or more than two edges during the search, then we select a vertex i_1' that is not searched yet and is numbered by the smallest number, and set a flag such that the vertex is already searched to i_1'. We scan $G^* = (V^*, E^*)$ by the depth-search as follows.

First, we do a depth-search from i^* and find a vertex j such that j does not have an outgoing edge.

Repeat the following process.

1. (Backward scan process) Go back to the vertex i' that has two or more than two edges. If there is no such a vertex, then we end. If an edge was scanned by this backward scan, then we set a "scanned" flag to the edge.
2. Do the depth-search from i'.

During the backward scan process above, we repeat the hybrid transitions $\mathsf{Hyb}_{\mathcal{A}}^{2,v,1}$, $\mathsf{Hyb}_{\mathcal{A}}^{2,v,2}$, and $\mathsf{Hyb}_{\mathcal{A}}^{2,v,3}$ below whenever we move on a edge where $v = 1, \ldots, Q$. We let Dlist be the list of vertices whose re-encryption key consists of a simulated and dummy values. That is, if $j \in \mathsf{Dlist}$, then $\mathsf{rk}_{i \to j} = (\hat{\mathsf{pk}}, s_2, \mathsf{Enc}(\mathsf{pk}_j, 0^n))$ where $(\hat{\mathsf{pk}}, \hat{\mathsf{sk}}) \leftarrow \mathsf{BatchGen}(0^n)$ and $(s_1, s_2) \leftarrow \mathsf{Share}(0^n)$ for any i. We initialize $\mathsf{Dlist} := \emptyset$ and maintain Dlist during the repeated processes below.

In the following hybrids we modify the key-generation for honest vertices. That is, all changes in the experiments are in the computation of $\mathsf{rk}_{i \to j}$.

$\mathsf{Hyb}_{\mathcal{A}}^{2,v,1}(b)$: At this point, we are at vertex i and edge (i, j) was just scanned.
- Compute $(s_1, s_2) \leftarrow \mathsf{Share}(\mathsf{sk}_i)$

- Compute $(\hat{\mathsf{pk}}, \hat{\mathsf{sk}}) \leftarrow \mathsf{BatchGen}(s_1)$.
- Compute $\widetilde{\mathsf{ct}}_j \leftarrow \underline{\mathsf{Enc}_j(\mathsf{pk}_j, 0^n)}$
- Output $\mathsf{rk}_{i \to j} := (\hat{\mathsf{pk}}, s_2, \widetilde{\mathsf{ct}}_j)$.

That is, we compute $\widetilde{\mathsf{ct}}_j \leftarrow \mathsf{Enc}_j(\mathsf{pk}_j, 0^n)$ instead of $\widetilde{\mathsf{ct}}_j \leftarrow \mathsf{Enc}_j(\mathsf{pk}_j, (s_1, \hat{\mathsf{sk}}))$.

$\mathsf{Hyb}_{\mathcal{A}}^{2,v,2}(b)$:
- Compute $(s_1, s_2) \leftarrow \mathsf{Share}(\mathsf{sk}_i)$
- Compute $(\hat{\mathsf{pk}}, \hat{\mathsf{sk}}) \leftarrow \underline{\mathsf{BatchGen}(0^n)}$.
- Compute $\widetilde{\mathsf{ct}}_j \leftarrow \mathsf{Enc}_j(\mathsf{pk}_j, 0^n)$
- Output $\mathsf{rk}_{i \to j} := (\hat{\mathsf{pk}}, s_2, \widetilde{\mathsf{ct}}_j)$.

$\mathsf{Hyb}_{\mathcal{A}}^{2,v,3}(b)$:
- Compute $(s_1, s_2) \leftarrow \underline{\mathsf{Share}(0^n)}$
- Compute $(\hat{\mathsf{pk}}, \hat{\mathsf{sk}}) \leftarrow \mathsf{BatchGen}(0^n)$.
- Compute $\widetilde{\mathsf{ct}}_j \leftarrow \mathsf{Enc}_j(\mathsf{pk}_j, 0^n)$
- Output $\mathsf{rk}_{i \to j} := (\hat{\mathsf{pk}}, s_2, \widetilde{\mathsf{ct}}_j)$ and renew $\mathsf{Dlist} := \mathsf{Dlist} \cup \{j\}$.

For syntactic convention, we let $\mathsf{Hyb}_{\mathcal{A}}^{2,0,3}(b) := \mathsf{Hyb}_{\mathcal{A}}^{1,Q_{\mathsf{reenc}},3}(b)$.

Now, we prove indistinguishability of hybrid games. First notice that by correctness of $(\mathsf{Share}, \mathsf{Reconstruct})$ and $(\mathsf{BatchGen}, \mathsf{BatchEnc}, \mathsf{BatchDec})$ the modification between $\mathsf{Hyb}_{\mathcal{A}}^{1,u,2}(b)$ and $\mathsf{Hyb}_{\mathcal{A}}^{1,u,3}(b)$ is merely syntactic and the following lemma holds.

Lemma 3.1. *It holds that* $\mathsf{Hyb}_{\mathcal{A}}^{1,u,2}(b) = \mathsf{Hyb}_{\mathcal{A}}^{1,u,3}(b)$.

Proof. This immediately holds since m and $\widetilde{\mathsf{labels}}'$ are outputs of $\mathsf{C}(s_1)$ when $\mathsf{C} = \mathsf{P}$ and $\mathsf{C} = \mathsf{Q}$, respectively. ∎

Indistinguishability of $\mathsf{Hyb}_{\mathcal{A}}^{1,(u-1),3}(b)$ and $\mathsf{Hyb}_{\mathcal{A}}^{1,u,1}(b)$is shown in Lemma 3.2, whereas indistinguishability of $\mathsf{Hyb}_{\mathcal{A}}^{1,u,1}(b)$ and $\mathsf{Hyb}_{\mathcal{A}}^{1,u,2}(b)$is shown in Lemma 3.3.

Lemma 3.2. *If* $(\mathsf{BatchGen}, \mathsf{BatchEnc}, \mathsf{BatchDec})$ *is WBE-CPA secure, then it holds that* $\mathsf{Hyb}_{\mathcal{A}}^{1,u,1}(b) \approx \mathsf{Hyb}_{\mathcal{A}}^{1,(u-1),3}(b)$.

Proof of Lemma 3.2. We will construct a reduction $\mathcal{B}$ which breaks the sender privacy of $(\mathsf{BatchGen}, \mathsf{BatchEnc}, \mathsf{BatchDec})$. The reduction $\mathcal{B}$ answers re-encryption queries as follows. From the first to $(u-1)$-th re-encryption queries are handled as in $\mathsf{Hyb}_{\mathcal{A}}^{1,u,1}(b)$. From the $(u+1)$-th to Q_{reenc}-th re-encryption queries are handled as in $\mathsf{Hyb}_{\mathcal{A}}^{1,(u-1),3}(b)$. $\mathcal{B}$ can simulate all oracles since $\mathcal{B}$ can generate secret keys by itself. For the u-th query $(\widehat{i}, j, k)$ such that $(\widehat{i}, j)$ is not an admissible edge with respect to G^* and $k \notin \mathsf{Drv}$, $\mathcal{B}$ embeds its own challenge. That is, $\mathcal{B}$ sends s_1 and labels to the experiment and obtains $(\hat{\mathsf{pk}}, \hat{\mathsf{sk}}, \hat{\mathsf{ct}})$. It then uses these values in its own simulation. Clearly, if $\hat{\mathsf{ct}} = \mathsf{BatchEnc}(\hat{\mathsf{pk}}, \mathsf{labels})$, then this query is handled as in $\mathsf{Hyb}_{\mathcal{A}}^{1,(u-1),3}(b)$. On the other hand, if $\hat{\mathsf{ct}} = \mathsf{BatchEnc}(\hat{\mathsf{pk}}, \mathsf{labels}^*)$, then the query is handled as in $\mathsf{Hyb}_{\mathcal{A}}^{1,u,1}(b)$. ∎

Lemma 3.3. *If* $\mathsf{gc} = (\mathsf{Garble}, \mathsf{Eval})$ *is a selectively secure garbling scheme, then it holds that* $\mathsf{Hyb}_{\mathcal{A}}^{1,u,2}(b) \approx \mathsf{Hyb}_{\mathcal{A}}^{1,u,1}(b)$.

Proof of Lemma 3.3. We will construct a reduction $\mathcal{B}$ which breaks the security of $(\mathsf{Garble}, \mathsf{Eval})$. As in the proof of Lemma 3.2, from the first to $(u-1)$-th re-encryption queries are handled as in $\mathsf{Hyb}_{\mathcal{A}}^{1,u,2}(b)$ and from the $(u+1)$-th to Q_{reenc}-th re-encryption queries are handled as in $\mathsf{Hyb}_{\mathcal{A}}^{1,u,1}(b)$. $\mathcal{B}$ can simulate all oracles since $\mathcal{B}$ can generate secret keys by itself. $\mathcal{B}$ will embed its challenge in the u-th re-encryption query $(\widehat{i}, j, k)$ such that $(\widehat{i}, j)$ is not an admissible edge with respect to G^* and $k \notin \mathsf{Drv}$. That is, $\mathcal{B}$ sends (C, s_1) to the experiment and obtains $(\tilde{\mathsf{C}}, \widetilde{\mathsf{labels}})$. It then uses these values in its own simulation. Clearly, if $(\tilde{\mathsf{C}}, \mathsf{labels}) = \mathsf{Grbl}(\mathsf{C})$ and $\widetilde{\mathsf{labels}} = \mathsf{labels}_{s_1}$, then this query is handled as in $\mathsf{Hyb}_{\mathcal{A}}^{1,u,1}(b)$. On the other hand, if $(\tilde{\mathsf{C}}, \widetilde{\mathsf{labels}}) = \mathsf{GCSim}(\mathsf{C}(s_1))$, then the query is handled as in $\mathsf{Hyb}_{\mathcal{A}}^{1,u,2}(b)$. ■

Lemma 3.4. *If* Σ_j *is CPA-secure, then it holds that* $\mathsf{Hyb}_{\mathcal{A}}^{2,(v-1),3} \stackrel{\mathsf{c}}{\approx} \mathsf{Hyb}_{\mathcal{A}}^{2,v,1}$.

Proof. First, at this point, honest vertex j does not have any not-scanned edge. That is, we never use sk_j for simulation at this point. We can construct an adversary $\mathcal{B}$ that is given pk_j. $\mathcal{B}$ sends $(\hat{\mathsf{sk}}, 0^n)$ as a challenge message pair and receive a target ciphertext $\widetilde{\mathsf{ct}}_j^*$. $\mathcal{B}$ uses $\widetilde{\mathsf{ct}}_j^*$ as a part of $\mathsf{rk}_{i \to j}$. Thus, the lemma immediately follows from the CPA-security of Σ_j. ■

Lemma 3.5. *It holds that* $\mathsf{Hyb}_{\mathcal{A}}^{2,v,2}(b) \equiv \mathsf{Hyb}_{\mathcal{A}}^{2,v,1}(b)$

Proof. This follows from the fact that the distribution of $\hat{\mathsf{pk}}$ is independent of s_1 ■

Lemma 3.6. *If* $(\mathsf{Share}, \mathsf{Reconstruct})$ *is 2-out-of-2 secrete sharing scheme, then it holds that* $\mathsf{Hyb}_{\mathcal{A}}^{2,v,2}(b) \stackrel{\mathsf{s}}{\approx} \mathsf{Hyb}_{\mathcal{A}}^{2,v,3}(b)$.

Proof. This immediately follows from the security of $(\mathsf{Share}, \mathsf{Reconstruct})$ since s_1 is not used anywhere at this point. ■

In $\mathsf{Hyb}_{\mathcal{A}}^{2,Q,3}(b)$, sk_{i^*} is neither written in any re-encryption key nor used to generate a re-encrypted ciphertext. Thus, we can use the security of Σ_{i^*}. We can prove that $\mathsf{Hyb}_{\mathcal{A}}^{2,Q,3}(0) \stackrel{\mathsf{c}}{\approx} \mathsf{Hyb}_{\mathcal{A}}^{2,Q,3}(1)$ holds due to the CPA-security of Σ_{i^*}. Therefore, it holds that $\mathsf{Hyb}_{\mathcal{A}}^{0}(0) \stackrel{\mathsf{c}}{\approx} \mathsf{Hyb}_{\mathcal{A}}^{0}(1)$ since Q_{reenc}, Q and $|V_{\mathsf{h}}^*|$ are polynomials. ■

4 Constant-Hop Construction Secure Against CRA

In this section, we present constant-hop and CRA-secure UPRE schemes for PKE based on GC. The design is almost the same as that of the scheme in Sect. 3 except that we encrypt the garbled circuit $\tilde{\mathsf{C}}$ by using the delegatee's public key to hide information about the delegator's ciphertext.

4.1 Our Constant-Hop Scheme from GC

Our scheme $\mathsf{UPRE}_{\mathsf{cra}}$ is based on a on a garbling scheme $(\mathsf{Garble}, \mathsf{Eval})$, a weak batch encryption scheme $(\mathsf{BatchGen}, \mathsf{BatchEnc}, \mathsf{BatchDec})$ and a 2-player secret-sharing scheme $(\mathsf{Share}, \mathsf{Reconstruct})$. As in Sect. 3, we overload the notation $\Sigma_{\sigma_i} = (\mathsf{Gen}_{\sigma_i}, \mathsf{Enc}_{\sigma_i}, \mathsf{Dec}_{\sigma_i})$ by $\Sigma_i = (\mathsf{Gen}_i, \mathsf{Enc}_i, \mathsf{Dec}_i)$ for ease of notation (Fig. 4).

- $\mathsf{ReKeyGen}(1^\lambda, \Sigma_f, \Sigma_t, \mathsf{sk}_f, \mathsf{pk}_t)$:
  - Compute $(s_1, s_2) \leftarrow \mathsf{Share}(\mathsf{sk}_f)$
  - $(\hat{\mathsf{pk}}, \hat{\mathsf{sk}}) \leftarrow \mathsf{BatchGen}(1^\lambda, s_1)$
  - Compute $\tilde{\mathsf{ct}}_t \leftarrow \mathsf{Enc}_t(\mathsf{pk}_t, \hat{\mathsf{sk}})$
  - Output $\mathsf{rk}_{f \to t} := (\hat{\mathsf{pk}}, s_2, \tilde{\mathsf{ct}}_t)$.
- $\mathsf{ReEnc}(\Sigma_f, \Sigma_t, \mathsf{rk}_{f \to t}, \mathsf{ct}_f)$:
  - Parse $\mathsf{rk}_{f \to t} = (\hat{\mathsf{pk}}, s_2, \tilde{\mathsf{ct}}_t)$.
  - Parse $\mathsf{ct}_f = (\hat{\mathsf{ct}}', \tilde{\mathsf{ct}}_f, \tilde{\mathsf{ct}}'_f)$.
  - If this is the first re-encryption (1st level), set $\mathsf{C} \leftarrow \mathsf{P}[s_2, \mathsf{ct}_f]$ (Fig. 3); Else if (level $i > 1$), set $\mathsf{C} \leftarrow \mathsf{Q}[s_2, \hat{\mathsf{ct}}', \tilde{\mathsf{ct}}_f, \tilde{\mathsf{ct}}'_f]$ (Fig. 2)
  - Compute $(\tilde{\mathsf{C}}, \mathsf{labels}) \leftarrow \mathsf{Garble}(\mathsf{C})$.
  - Compute $\hat{\mathsf{ct}} \leftarrow \mathsf{BatchEnc}(\hat{\mathsf{pk}}, \mathsf{labels})$.
  - Compute $\tilde{\mathsf{ct}}'_t \leftarrow \mathsf{Enc}_t(\mathsf{pk}_t, \tilde{\mathsf{C}})$.
  - Output $(\hat{\mathsf{ct}}, \tilde{\mathsf{ct}}_t, \tilde{\mathsf{ct}}'_t)$.
- $\mathsf{mDec}(\Sigma_t, \mathsf{sk}_t, \mathsf{rct}, i)$: Parse $\mathsf{rct} = (\hat{\mathsf{ct}}, \tilde{\mathsf{ct}}_t, \tilde{\mathsf{ct}}'_t)$.
  - Compute $\hat{\mathsf{sk}}' \leftarrow \mathsf{Dec}(\mathsf{sk}_t, \tilde{\mathsf{ct}}_t)$.
  - Compute $\widetilde{\mathsf{labels}}_i \leftarrow \mathsf{BatchDec}(\hat{\mathsf{sk}}', \hat{\mathsf{ct}})$.
  - Compute $\tilde{\mathsf{C}}_i := \tilde{\mathsf{C}} \leftarrow \mathsf{Dec}_t(\mathsf{sk}_t, \tilde{\mathsf{ct}}'_t)$.
  - For $j = i, \ldots, 2$ do: Compute $(\tilde{\mathsf{C}}_{j-1}, \widetilde{\mathsf{labels}}_{j-1}) \leftarrow \mathsf{Eval}(\tilde{\mathsf{C}}_j, \widetilde{\mathsf{labels}}_j)$.
  - Compute and output $m' \leftarrow \mathsf{Eval}(\tilde{\mathsf{C}}_1, \widetilde{\mathsf{labels}}_1)$.

First Level Re-Encryption Circuit $\mathsf{P}[s_2, \mathsf{ct}_f](s_1)$

Hardwired: s_2, ct_f.
Input: A share s_1.

- Compute $\mathsf{sk}'_f \leftarrow \mathsf{Reconstruct}(s_1, s_2)$.
- Compute and output $m' \leftarrow \mathsf{Dec}_f(\mathsf{sk}'_f, \mathsf{ct}_f)$.

Fig. 3. The description of the first level re-encryption circuit P

Higher Level Re-Encryption Circuit $\mathsf{Q}[s_2, \hat{\mathsf{ct}}', \widetilde{\mathsf{ct}}_f, \widetilde{\mathsf{ct}}'_f](s_1)$

Hardwired: s_2, $\hat{\mathsf{ct}}'$, $\widetilde{\mathsf{ct}}_f$, $\widetilde{\mathsf{ct}}'_f$.
Input: A share s_1.

- Compute $\mathsf{sk}'_f \leftarrow \mathsf{Reconstruct}(s_1, s_2)$.
- Compute $\hat{\mathsf{sk}}' \leftarrow \mathsf{Dec}(\mathsf{sk}'_f, \widetilde{\mathsf{ct}}_f)$.
- Compute and output $\tilde{\mathsf{C}} \leftarrow \mathsf{Dec}_f(\mathsf{sk}'_f, \widetilde{\mathsf{ct}}'_f)$ and $\widetilde{\mathsf{labels}} \leftarrow \mathsf{BatchDec}(\hat{\mathsf{sk}}', \hat{\mathsf{ct}}')$.

Fig. 4. The description of the higher level re-encryption circuit Q

Theorem 4.1 (UPRE-CRA security). *Assume that* $\mathsf{gc} = (\mathsf{Garble}, \mathsf{Eval})$ *is a selectively secure garbling scheme,* $(\mathsf{Share}, \mathsf{Reconstruct})$ *is a 2-out-of-2 secret sharing scheme and* $(\mathsf{BatchGen}, \mathsf{BatchEnc}, \mathsf{BatchDec})$ *is a weak batch encryption scheme in the sense of Definition 3.1, and both* Σ_f *and* Σ_t *are IND-CPA secure PKE, then* $\mathsf{UPRE}_{\mathsf{cra}}$ *is a selective-graph UPRE-CRA secure UPRE scheme.*

We omit the proof due to the space limit.

References

[ABH09] Ateniese, G., Benson, K., Hohenberger, S.: Key-private proxy re-encryption. In: Fischlin, M. (ed.) CT-RSA 2009. LNCS, vol. 5473, pp. 279–294. Springer, Heidelberg (2009). https://doi.org/10.1007/978-3-642-00862-7_19

[ABPW13] Aono, Y., Boyen, X., Phong, L.T., Wang, L.: Key-private proxy re-encryption under LWE. In: Paul, G., Vaudenay, S. (eds.) INDOCRYPT 2013. LNCS, vol. 8250, pp. 1–18. Springer, Cham (2013). https://doi.org/10.1007/978-3-319-03515-4_1

[ACH20] Agrikola, T., Couteau, G., Hofheinz, D.: The usefulness of sparsifiable inputs: how to avoid subexponential iO. In: Kiayias, A., Kohlweiss, M., Wallden, P., Zikas, V. (eds.) PKC 2020. LNCS, vol. 12110, pp. 187–219. Springer, Cham (2020). https://doi.org/10.1007/978-3-030-45374-9_7

[AFGH05] Ateniese, G., Fu, K., Green, M., Hohenberger, S.: Improved Proxy re-encryption schemes with applications to secure distributed storage. In: NDSS 2005 (2005)

[BBS98] Blaze, M., Bleumer, G., Strauss, M.: Divertible protocols and atomic proxy cryptography. In: Nyberg, K. (ed.) EUROCRYPT 1998. LNCS, vol. 1403, pp. 127–144. Springer, Heidelberg (1998). https://doi.org/10.1007/BFb0054122

[BGI+12] Barak, B., et al.: On the (im)possibility of obfuscating programs. J. ACM **59**(2), 6 (2012)

[BGLS03] Boneh, D., Gentry, C., Lynn, B., Shacham, H.: Aggregate and verifiably encrypted signatures from bilinear maps. In: Biham, E. (ed.) EUROCRYPT 2003. LNCS, vol. 2656, pp. 416–432. Springer, Heidelberg (2003). https://doi.org/10.1007/3-540-39200-9_26

[BLSV18] Brakerski, Z., Lombardi, A., Segev, G., Vaikuntanathan, V.: Anonymous IBE, leakage resilience and circular security from new assumptions. In: Nielsen, J.B., Rijmen, V. (eds.) EUROCRYPT 2018. LNCS, vol. 10820, pp. 535–564. Springer, Cham (2018). https://doi.org/10.1007/978-3-319-78381-9_20
[CCL+14] Chandran, N., Chase, M., Liu, F.-H., Nishimaki, R., Xagawa, K.: Re-encryption, functional re-encryption, and multi-hop re-encryption: a framework for achieving obfuscation-based security and instantiations from lattices. In: Krawczyk, H. (ed.) PKC 2014. LNCS, vol. 8383, pp. 95–112. Springer, Heidelberg (2014). https://doi.org/10.1007/978-3-642-54631-0_6
[CCV12] Chandran, N., Chase, M., Vaikuntanathan, V.: Functional re-encryption and collusion-resistant obfuscation. In: Cramer, R. (ed.) TCC 2012. LNCS, vol. 7194, pp. 404–421. Springer, Heidelberg (2012). https://doi.org/10.1007/978-3-642-28914-9_23
[CH07] Canetti, R., Hohenberger, S.: Chosen-ciphertext secure proxy re-encryption. ACM CCS **2007**, 185–194 (2007)
[CHN+18] Cohen, A., Holmgren, J., Nishimaki, R., Vaikuntanathan, V., Wichs, D.: Watermarking cryptographic capabilities. SIAM J. Comput. **47**(6), 2157–2202 (2018)
[CLT13] Coron, J.-S., Lepoint, T., Tibouchi, M.: Practical multilinear maps over the integers. In: Canetti, R., Garay, J.A. (eds.) CRYPTO 2013. LNCS, vol. 8042, pp. 476–493. Springer, Heidelberg (2013). https://doi.org/10.1007/978-3-642-40041-4_26
[CLTV15] Canetti, R., Lin, H., Tessaro, S., Vaikuntanathan, V.: Obfuscation of probabilistic circuits and applications. In: Dodis, Y., Nielsen, J.B. (eds.) TCC 2015. LNCS, vol. 9015, pp. 468–497. Springer, Heidelberg (2015). https://doi.org/10.1007/978-3-662-46497-7_19
[Coh19] Cohen, A.: What about bob? the inadequacy of CPA security for proxy reencryption. In: PKC 2019, Part II. LNCS, vol. 11443, pp. 287–316 (2019)
[CPP16] Couteau, G., Peters, T., Pointcheval, D.: Encryption switching protocols. In: Robshaw, M., Katz, J. (eds.) CRYPTO 2016. LNCS, vol. 9814, pp. 308–338. Springer, Heidelberg (2016). https://doi.org/10.1007/978-3-662-53018-4_12
[CWYD10] Chow, S.S.M., Weng, J., Yang, Y., Deng, R.H.: Efficient unidirectional proxy re-encryption. In: AFRICACRYPT 10. LNCS, vol. 6055, pp. 316–332 (2010)
[DDLM19] Davidson, A., Deo, A., Lee, E., Martin, K.: Strong post-compromise secure proxy re-encryption. In: Jang-Jaccard, J., Guo, F. (eds.) ACISP 2019. LNCS, vol. 11547, pp. 58–77. Springer, Cham (2019). https://doi.org/10.1007/978-3-030-21548-4_4
[DKL+18] Derler, D., Krenn, S., Lorünser, T., Ramacher, S., Slamanig, D., Striecks, C.: Revisiting proxy re-encryption: forward secrecy, improved security, and applications. In: Abdalla, M., Dahab, R. (eds.) PKC 2018. LNCS, vol. 10769, pp. 219–250. Springer, Cham (2018). https://doi.org/10.1007/978-3-319-76578-5_8
[DWLC08] Deng, R.H., Weng, J., Liu, S., Chen, K.: Chosen-ciphertext secure proxy re-encryption without pairings. In: Franklin, M.K., Hui, L.C.K., Wong, D.S. (eds.) CANS 2008. LNCS, vol. 5339, pp. 1–17. Springer, Heidelberg (2008). https://doi.org/10.1007/978-3-540-89641-8_1
[ElG85] ElGamal, T.: A public key cryptosystem and a signature scheme based on discrete logarithms. IEEE Trans. Inf. Theor. **31**, 469–472 (1985)

[FKKP19] Fuchsbauer, G., Kamath, C., Klein, K., Pietrzak, K.: Adaptively secure proxy re-encryption. In: Lin, D., Sako, K. (eds.) PKC 2019. LNCS, vol. 11443, pp. 317–346. Springer, Cham (2019). https://doi.org/10.1007/978-3-030-17259-6_11

[GGH13] Garg, S., Gentry, C., Halevi, S.: Candidate multilinear maps from ideal lattices. In: Johansson, T., Nguyen, P.Q. (eds.) EUROCRYPT 2013. LNCS, vol. 7881, pp. 1–17. Springer, Heidelberg (2013). https://doi.org/10.1007/978-3-642-38348-9_1

[GGH15] Gentry, C., Gorbunov, S., Halevi, S.: Graph-induced multilinear maps from lattices. In: Dodis, Y., Nielsen, J.B. (eds.) TCC 2015. LNCS, vol. 9015, pp. 498–527. Springer, Heidelberg (2015). https://doi.org/10.1007/978-3-662-46497-7_20

[GGH+16] Garg, S., Gentry, C., Halevi, S., Raykova, M., Sahai, A., Waters, B.: Candidate indistinguishability obfuscation and functional encryption for all circuits. SIAM J. Comput. **45**(3), 882–929 (2016)

[GM84] Goldwasser, S., Micali, S.: Probabilistic encryption. J. Comput. Syst. Sci. **28**(2), 270–299 (1984)

[GSL19] Gaddam, S., Sinha, R., Luykx, A.: Applying proxy-re-encryption to payments. Real World Crypto 2019 (2019). https://rwc.iacr.org/2019/slides/Applying_PRE_Payments.pdf

[HHR16] Hesse, J., Hofheinz, D., Rupp, A.: Reconfigurable cryptography: a flexible approach to long-term security. In: Kushilevitz, E., Malkin, T. (eds.) TCC 2016. LNCS, vol. 9562, pp. 416–445. Springer, Heidelberg (2016). https://doi.org/10.1007/978-3-662-49096-9_18

[HKK+12] Hanaoka, G., Kawai, Y., Kunihiro, N., Matsuda, T., Weng, J., Zhang, R., Zhao, Y.: Generic construction of chosen ciphertext secure proxy re-encryption. In: Dunkelman, O. (ed.) CT-RSA 2012. LNCS, vol. 7178, pp. 349–364. Springer, Heidelberg (2012). https://doi.org/10.1007/978-3-642-27954-6_22

[HKW15] Hohenberger, S., Koppula, V., Waters, B.: Universal signature aggregators. In: Oswald, E., Fischlin, M. (eds.) EUROCRYPT 2015. LNCS, vol. 9057, pp. 3–34. Springer, Heidelberg (2015). https://doi.org/10.1007/978-3-662-46803-6_1

[HRsV11] Hohenberger, S., Rothblum, G.N., Shelat, A., Vaikuntanathan, V.: Securely obfuscating re-encryption. J. Cryptol. **24**(4), 694–719 (2010). https://doi.org/10.1007/s00145-010-9077-7

[ID03] Ivan, A., Dodis, Y.: Proxy cryptography revisited. In: NDSS 2003 (2003)

[Jak99] Jakobsson, M.: On quorum controlled asymmetric proxy re-encryption. In: Imai, H., Zheng, Y. (eds.) PKC 1999. LNCS, vol. 1560, pp. 112–121. Springer, Heidelberg (1999). https://doi.org/10.1007/3-540-49162-7_9

[LV08] Libert, B., Vergnaud, D.: Unidirectional chosen-ciphertext secure proxy re-encryption. In: PKC 2008. LNCS, vol. 4939, pp. 360–379 (2008)

[NX15] Nishimaki, R., Xagawa, K.: Key-private proxy re-encryption from lattices, revisited. IEICE Trans. **98-A**(1), 100–116 (2015)

[PRSV17] Polyakov, Y., Rohloff, K., Sahu, G., Vaikuntanathan, V.: Fast proxy re-encryption for publish/subscribe systems. ACM Trans. Priv. Secur. **20**(4), 14:1–14:31 (2017)

[SC09] Shao, J., Cao, Z.: CCA-secure proxy re-encryption without pairings. In: PKC 2009. LNCS, vol. 5443, pp. 357–376 (2009)

Master-Key KDM-Secure ABE via Predicate Encoding

Shengyuan Feng, Junqing Gong(✉), and Jie Chen(✉)

East China Normal University, Shanghai, China
51184506007@stu.ecnu.edu.cn, jqgong@sei.ecnu.edu.cn, s080001@e.ntu.edu.sg

Abstract. In this paper, we propose the first generic framework for attribute-based encryptions (ABE) with master-secret-key-dependent-message security (mKDM security) for affine functions via predicate encodings by Chen, Gay and Wee [Eurocrypt 2015]. The construction is adaptively secure under standard k-Lin assumption in prime-order bilinear groups. By this, we obtain a set of new mKDM-secure ABE schemes with high expressiveness that have never been reached before: we get the first hierarchical IBE (HIBE) scheme and the first ABE scheme for arithmetic branching program (ABP) with mKDM security for affine functions. Thanks to the expressiveness (more concretely, delegability like HIBE), we can obtain mKDM-secure ABE against chosen-ciphertext attack (i.e., CCA security) via a classical CPA-to-CCA transformation that works well in the context of mKDM.

1 Introduction

Semantic security of public-key encryption (PKE) ensures a ciphertext does not leak any information on the message without corresponding secret key. However this might not be true when the message depends on the secret key [ABBC10, CGH12]. The notion of key-dependent message (KDM) security is established to capture this situation [CL01, BRS03]. Specifically, given pk whose corresponding secret key is sk, KDM security means it remains semantically secure even when the message is $f(\mathsf{sk})$ for f from some a-priori function family $\mathcal{F}$.

Although much progress has been made on building KDM-secure PKE [CCS09, Hof13, LLJ15, HLL16, KT18, DGHM18, KM19, KMT19] and even analogous enhancement of other cryptographic primitives [HK07], the study of KDM security in the context of attribute-based encryption

S. Feng—Supported by National Natural Science Foundation of China (61972156).
J. Gong—Supported by National Natural Science Foundation of China (62002120), NSFC-ISF Joint Scientific Research Program (61961146004) and Innovation Program of Shanghai Municipal Education Commission (2021-01-07-00-08-E00101).
J. Chen—Supported by National Natural Science Foundation of China (61972156, U1705264, 61632012), NSFC-ISF Joint Scientific Research Program (61961146004) and National Key Research and Development Program of China (2018YFA0704701). The author would like to thank Ant Group for its support and assistance with this work.

J. A. Garay (Ed.): PKC 2021, LNCS 12710, pp. 543–572, 2021.
https://doi.org/10.1007/978-3-030-75245-3_20

(ABE) [SW05, GPSW06], a generalization of PKE, lags behind. In an ABE for predicate P under master key pair $(\mathsf{mpk}, \mathsf{msk})$, a ciphertext encrypts message m under mpk with an attribute x, a user key sk is issued for a policy y by msk; decryption recovers m when $P(x, y) = 1$. The semantic security requires that a key holder cannot get any information on m when $P(x, y) = 0$; typically, we need this to hold even when multiple key holders collude with each other.

State-of-the-art: KDM Security in IBE. To our best knowledge, all existing results on KDM security in ABE only concern the simplest case—identity-based encryption (IBE) [Sha84, BF01]. Here both attribute x and policy y belong to the same domain (say, binary strings of fixed length) and $P(x, y) = 1$ if and only if $x = y$. Due to the presence of two types of secret keys in IBE, two flavors of KDM securities are considered: master-key-dependent-message (mKDM) security [GHV12] and user-key-dependent-message (uKDM) security [AP12]. In this work, we focus on the former one: given mpk whose corresponding master secret key is msk, it remains semantically secure even when the message is $f(\mathsf{msk})$ for f from some a-priori function family $\mathcal{F}$.

The first mKDM-secure IBE scheme [GHV12] has several limitations: the scheme is selectively secure and bounded in the sense that the size of mpk is proportional to the number of encryptions of key-dependent messages. Recently, Garg *et al.* [GGH20] discovered a surprising connection between mKDM security and tight reduction technique in the context of IBE and avoided the above limitations. As a bonus, their scheme also enjoys tight reduction.

This Work: KDM Security in Expressive ABE. We initiate the study of KDM security in the context of ABE beyond IBE. A classical application and motivation of ABE is to support fine-grained access control. A more expressive ABE (i.e., supporting larger class of policies) means a more flexible and powerful access control system. Apart from this, higher expressiveness may also help us to achieve higher security level. For instance, one can get chosen-ciphertext secure IBE from chosen-plaintext secure HIBE [CHK04] and follow-up works extended the method to the ABE setting [YAHK11, BL16, CMP17].

1.1 Results

This work proposes the first generic framework for ABE with mKDM-security for affine functions via predicate encodings [Wee14, CGW15]. Our construction is adaptively secure under standard k-Lin assumption in the prime-order bilinear group. Thanks to various concrete instantiations of predicate encodings, we can derive a set of new mKDM-secure ABE schemes; they support more complex policies than IBE, which have never been reached since the first KDM-secure IBE was proposed [GHV12, AP12]. In particular, as examples, we obtain

- the first HIBE scheme with mKDM-security for affine functions; users are organized in a tree-based structure and can partially delegate the decryption power (i.e., user secret key) to its children;

– the first ABE for arithmetic branching program (ABP) with mKDM-security for affine functions; note that, ABP covers **NC1**, **LOGSPACE** and the class of arithmetic circuits.

With the high expressiveness (more concretely, delegability like HIBE), we upgrade the generic framework to resist the chosen-ciphertext attack (i.e., achieve CCA security) and obtain CCA-secure variants of all above concrete ABE schemes. We summarize existing KDM-secure ABE (for affine functions) in Table 1.

Table 1. Comparison among existing KDM-secure ABE for affine functions.

Reference	Policy	KDM	CCA?
[GHV12]	IBE	mKDM	✗
[AP12]	IBE	uKDM	✗
[GGH20]	IBE	mKDM	✗
Sect. 6.1	(H)IBE	mKDM	✔
Sect. 6.2	ABE for ABP	mKDM	✔

A Brief Technical Overview. Our generic framework (with CPA security) is obtained by extending Garg *et al.*'s mKDM-secure IBE scheme [GGH20]. Recall that their IBE can be viewed as a combination of the KDM-secure PKE scheme from [BHHO08] and tightly-secure IBE from [AHY15,GDCC16]. The latter ingredient is aimed to handle leakage of master secret key in user secret keys in the presence of multiple challenge ciphertexts. We achieve this *in the context of ABE* by combining Chen *et al.*'s dual-system ABE via predicate encodings and nested dual-system technique that has been widely used to achieve unbounded ABE [LW11,OT12,KL15,CGKW18]. The first idea is to handle the afore-mentioned leakage while the second one ensures that this works well with multiple ciphertexts. See Sect. 1.2 for a more detailed technical overview. To get their CCA variant, we simply employ the classical CPA-to-CCA transformation [CHK04] which relies on delegation and is proved to work in the setting of mKDM security. For those predicates without delegation, we provide a generic way to extend their predicate encodings with a special delegation layer that is sufficient for the CPA-to-CCA transformation; this basically follows [YAHK11,BL16,CMP17]. See the full paper for more details.

Discussion in the Scope of IBE. Our generic framework gives us a new IBE scheme with mKDM-security (see Sect. 6.1) as [GHV12,GGH20], we make a comparison among them in Table 2 before we move to more technical details. We highlight that, Garg *et al.*'s scheme is the unique one with tight security but the master public key size is linear in λ; on the other hand, our scheme enjoys constant-size master public key but the security loss is related to the number of queries. It is, of course, the ideal case to have a tightly secure scheme with constant-size master public key. However this has been an open problem in the context of *standard* semantic security for IBE. The only exception is the scheme in [CGW17] over composite-order bilinear groups, but this can only be considered as a partial solution due to the lack of realization of Déjà Q technique [CM14,CMM16] in prime-order bilinear groups. We finally note that our IBE scheme is the unique one with mKDM-security against *chosen-ciphertext attack*; this benefits from the high expressiveness of our generic framework that is able to lead to the first mKDM-secure HIBE (against chosen-plaintext attack).

Table 2. Comparison among existing mKDM-secure IBE. Here, λ is the security parameter and Q_C is the number of ciphertexts.

Reference	Adaptive?	$\lvert\mathsf{mpk}\rvert$	CCA?	Tight?	Assumption
[GHV12]	✘	$O(Q_C)$	✘	✘	DLIN
[GGH20]	✔	$O(\lambda)$	✘	✔	SXDH
Sect. 6.1	✔	$O(1)$	✔	✘	SXDH

1.2 Technical Overview

Garg *et al.*'s Scheme [GGH20]. We start from the unique mKDM-secure IBE (with adaptive security against unbounded collusion) by Garg *et al.* [GGH20]. Let (p, G_1, G_2, G_T, e) be asymmetric bilinear groups of prime order p; we use g_1, g_2, g_T to denote random generators of G_1, G_2, G_T and employ the implicit representation of group elements: for a matrix $\mathbf{M}$ over $\mathbb{Z}_p$, we write $[\mathbf{M}]_s := g_s^{\mathbf{M}}$ where $s \in \{1, 2, T\}$ and the exponentiation is carried out component-wise. Garg *et al.*'s scheme uses the basis:

$$(\mathbf{A}_1, \mathbf{A}_2, \mathbf{A}_3) \leftarrow \mathbb{Z}_p^{\ell \times \ell_1} \times \mathbb{Z}_p^{\ell \times \ell_2} \times \mathbb{Z}_p^{\ell \times \ell_3} \tag{1}$$

and its dual basis $(\mathbf{A}_1^\dagger, \mathbf{A}_2^\dagger, \mathbf{A}_3^\dagger) \in \mathbb{Z}_p^{\ell \times \ell_1} \times \mathbb{Z}_p^{\ell \times \ell_2} \times \mathbb{Z}_p^{\ell \times \ell_3}$ where $\ell = \ell_1 + \ell_2 + \ell_3 = \Theta(\log p)$ is much larger than k and $\ell_1, \ell_2, \ell_3 \geq k$; this satisfies orthogonality (i.e., $\mathbf{A}_i^\top \mathbf{A}_j^\dagger = \mathbf{0}$ for $i \neq j$) and non-degeneracy (i.e., $\mathbf{A}_i^\top \mathbf{A}_i^\dagger = \mathbf{I}$ for all $i = 1, 2, 3$).

We review Garg *et al.*'s IBE scheme from k-Lin assumption (with identity space $\{0,1\}^n$) as follows:

$$\begin{aligned}
\mathsf{mpk} &:= \boxed{[\mathbf{A}_1^\top]_1,\ [\mathbf{A}_1^\top \mathbf{k}]_T},\ [\mathbf{B}]_2,\ \{\, [\mathbf{A}_1^\top \mathbf{W}_{i,b}]_1,\ [\mathbf{W}\mathbf{B}_{i,b}]_2 \,\}_{i \in [n], b \in \{0,1\}} \\
\mathsf{msk} &:= \boxed{[\mathbf{k}]_T} \\
\mathsf{sk}_{\mathsf{id}} &:= \boxed{[\mathbf{k}]_2} \cdot\ [(\mathbf{W}_{1,\mathsf{id}[1]} + \cdots + \mathbf{W}_{n,\mathsf{id}[n]})\mathbf{B}\mathbf{r}]_2,\ [\mathbf{B}\mathbf{r}]_2 \\
\mathsf{ct}_{\mathsf{id}} &:= \boxed{[\mathbf{s}^\top \mathbf{A}_1^\top]_1,\ [\mathbf{s}^\top \mathbf{A}_1^\top \mathbf{k}]_T \cdot m},\ [\mathbf{s}^\top \mathbf{A}_1^\top (\mathbf{W}_{1,\mathsf{id}[1]} + \cdots + \mathbf{W}_{n,\mathsf{id}[n]})]_1
\end{aligned} \tag{2}$$

where $\mathsf{id} \in \{0,1\}^n$, $\mathbf{k} \leftarrow \{0,1\}^\ell$, $\mathbf{W}_{i,b} \leftarrow \mathbb{Z}_p^{\ell \times (k+1)}$, $\mathbf{B} \leftarrow \mathbb{Z}_p^{(k+1) \times k}$, $\mathbf{s} \leftarrow \mathbb{Z}_p^{\ell_1}$, $\mathbf{r} \leftarrow \mathbb{Z}_p^k$. Recall that the above scheme is a clever combination of the KDM-secure

PKE scheme from [BHHO08] and tightly-secure IBE from [AHY15,GDCC16]; we highlight the two ingredients by solid boxes and gray boxes, respectively. Accordingly, the proof roughly consists of two phases: (a) One first changes all keys and ciphertexts to the following forms by the tight reduction technique [AHY15,GDCC16] using the parts in gray boxes. We highlight the differences by dashed boxes. (Note that the distribution here is slightly different from that in [GGH20]; one more computational transition can fill the gap.)

$$
\begin{aligned}
\mathsf{sk_{id}} &:= \boxed{[\mathbf{k} + \boxed{\mathbf{A}_2^{\dagger}\widehat{\mathbf{k}}}]_2} \cdot \boxed{[(\mathbf{W}_{1,\mathsf{id}[1]} + \cdots + \mathbf{W}_{n,\mathsf{id}[n]})\mathbf{Br}]_2,\ [\mathbf{Br}]_2}, & \widehat{\mathbf{k}} \leftarrow \mathbb{Z}_p^{\ell_2} \\
\mathsf{ct_{id}} &:= \boxed{[\mathbf{s}^{\top}\mathbf{A}_1^{\top} + \boxed{\widehat{\mathbf{s}}^{\top}\mathbf{A}_2^{\top}}]_1,\ [(\mathbf{s}^{\top}\mathbf{A}_1^{\top} + \boxed{\widehat{\mathbf{s}}^{\top}\mathbf{A}_2^{\top}})\mathbf{k}]_T \cdot m}, & \widehat{\mathbf{s}} \leftarrow \mathbb{Z}_p^{\ell_2} \quad (3) \\
&\quad \boxed{[(\mathbf{s}^{\top}\mathbf{A}_1^{\top} + \boxed{\widehat{\mathbf{s}}^{\top}\mathbf{A}_2^{\top}})(\mathbf{W}_{1,\mathsf{id}[1]} + \cdots + \mathbf{W}_{n,\mathsf{id}[n]})]_1},
\end{aligned}
$$

(b) One then carries out the KDM argument for PKE from [BHHO08] using the parts in solid boxes; this benefits from the fact that $\mathbf{A}_2^{\dagger}\widehat{\mathbf{k}}$ introduced in the first phase "controls" the leakage of $\mathbf{k}$ via $\mathsf{sk_{id}}$.

Strategy. In order to extend scheme (2) to more expressive ABE, a natural idea is to follow the high-level idea of [GGH20] reviewed above but employ a tightly secure ABE scheme in the parts with gray boxes. However this strategy has two issues. First, to our best knowledge, there only exist tightly secure IBE [AHY15,GDCC16] and HIBE [LP20] in the multiple ciphertexts setting while no known result on the tight reduction for ABE even in the single ciphertext setting. Second, even with the recent progress on tightly secure HIBE [LP20], the construction of mKDM-secure HIBE is not modular, one has to go into the detail of the proof as in [LP20]. To circumvent the issues, we start from the following warm-up scheme presented in [GGH20]:

$$
\begin{aligned}
\mathsf{mpk} &:= \boxed{[\mathbf{A}_1^{\top}]_1,\ [\mathbf{A}_1^{\top}\mathbf{k}]_T},\ \boxed{[\mathbf{B}]_2,\ [\mathbf{A}_1^{\top}\mathbf{W}]_1,\ [\mathbf{A}_1^{\top}\mathbf{V}]_1, [\mathbf{WB}]_2,\ [\mathbf{VB}]_2} \\
\mathsf{msk} &:= \boxed{[\mathbf{k}]_T} \\
\mathsf{sk_{id}} &:= \boxed{[\mathbf{k}]_2} \cdot \boxed{[(\mathbf{W} + \mathsf{id} \cdot \mathbf{V})\mathbf{Br}]_2,\ [\mathbf{Br}]_2} \\
\mathsf{ct_{id}} &:= \boxed{[\mathbf{s}^{\top}\mathbf{A}_1^{\top}]_1,\ [\mathbf{s}^{\top}\mathbf{A}_1^{\top}\mathbf{k}]_T \cdot m},\ \boxed{[\mathbf{s}^{\top}\mathbf{A}_1^{\top}(\mathbf{W} + \mathsf{id} \cdot \mathbf{V})]_1}
\end{aligned}
\qquad (4)
$$

where the gray boxes involve a *non-tightly* secure IBE scheme from [CGW15] with $\mathsf{id} \in \mathbb{Z}_p$. As reported in [GGH20], the scheme is mKDM-secure with respect to affine functions in the *single*-ciphertext setting. Our strategy is to

> upgrade the proof to the *multi-ciphertexts* setting *without* tight reduction technique.

The advantage of this strategy is that we can immediately generalize scheme (4) to more expressive ABE via predicate encodings [CGW15]; this allows us to derive mKDM-secure *ABE for various policies* in an *modular* way. As [GGH20], the proof consists of two phases: in the first phase, we will prove[1]

$$\begin{pmatrix} \mathsf{mpk}: [\mathbf{A}_1^\top]_1, [\mathbf{A}_1^\top\mathbf{W}]_1, [\mathbf{A}_1^\top\mathbf{V}]_1, [\mathbf{B}]_2, [\mathbf{WB}]_2, [\mathbf{VB}]_2 \\ \mathsf{sk}_{\mathsf{id}_i}: [\mathbf{Br}_i]_2, [(\mathbf{W} + \mathsf{id}_i \cdot \mathbf{V})\mathbf{Br}_i]_2, \quad \mathbf{r}_i \leftarrow \mathbb{Z}_p^k \\ \mathsf{ct}^*_{\mathsf{id}'_j}: [\mathbf{s}_j^\top\mathbf{A}_1^\top]_1, [\mathbf{s}_j^\top\mathbf{A}_1^\top(\mathbf{W} + \mathsf{id}'_j \cdot \mathbf{V})]_1, \quad \mathbf{s}_j \leftarrow \mathbb{Z}_p^{\ell_1} \end{pmatrix}$$

$$\approx_c \begin{pmatrix} \mathsf{mpk}: [\mathbf{A}_1^\top]_1, [\mathbf{A}_1^\top\mathbf{W}]_1, [\mathbf{A}_1^\top\mathbf{V}]_1, [\mathbf{B}]_2, [\mathbf{WB}]_2, [\mathbf{VB}]_2 \\ \mathsf{sk}_{\mathsf{id}_i}: [\mathbf{Br}_i]_2, [\boxed{\mathbf{A}_2^\dagger\widehat{\mathbf{k}}_i} + (\mathbf{W} + \mathsf{id}_i \cdot \mathbf{V})\mathbf{Br}_i]_2, \quad \mathbf{r}_i \leftarrow \mathbb{Z}_p^k, \ \widehat{\mathbf{k}}_i \leftarrow \mathbb{Z}_p^{\ell_2} \\ \mathsf{ct}^*_{\mathsf{id}'_j}: [\mathbf{s}_j^\top\mathbf{A}_1^\top + \boxed{\widehat{\mathbf{s}}_j^\top\mathbf{A}_2^\top}]_1, \quad \mathbf{s}_j \leftarrow \mathbb{Z}_p^{\ell_1}, \widehat{\mathbf{s}}_j \leftarrow \mathbb{Z}_p^{\ell_2} \\ \quad [(\mathbf{s}_j^\top\mathbf{A}_1^\top + \boxed{\widehat{\mathbf{s}}_j^\top\mathbf{A}_2^\top})(\mathbf{W} + \mathsf{id}'_j \cdot \mathbf{V})]_1, \end{pmatrix} \quad (5)$$

where $\mathsf{id}_1, \ldots, \mathsf{id}_{Q_K}$ and $\mathsf{id}'_1, \ldots, \mathsf{id}'_{Q_C}$ are key and ciphertext queries, respectively, this is analogous to the first phase in Garg *et al.*'s proof that changes the key and ciphertext distributions to (3); the second phase is essentially identical to that in Garg *et al.*'s proof with $\widehat{\mathbf{k}}_i$ and $\widehat{\mathbf{s}}_j$. Note that the key and ciphertext structures do not allow us to use known tight reduction techniques as in [GGH20].

Solution: Nested Dual-System Method. To carry out the strategy, we will prove (5) using the so-called *nested dual-system method* [LW11] that was developed to realize *unbounded* HIBE and ABE. To see why this can be useful, we consider unbounded HIBE built from IBE [LW11] as an example: a HIBE ciphertext is composed of a set of IBE ciphertexts while a HIBE key is composed of a set of IBE keys. To get standard semantic security of the unbounded HIBE, one has already been required to handle multiple keys and multiple ciphertexts of underlying IBE; this is essentially the same situation as in (5).

From a high level, the nested dual-system argument works as the standard dual-system argument [Wat09]: we **(i)** change all challenge ciphertexts into semi-functional form and **(ii)** change all keys into the semi-functional form one-by-one. The "nested" means that step **(ii)** employs another dual-system argument where the roles of ciphertexts and keys are exchanged; namely, we are handling a single key in the presence of multiple ciphertexts.

However this method is not compatible with predicate encodings in general. Roughly, the security of predicate encoding [Wee14, CGW15] ensures that, given a ciphertext, a secret key that is not authorized to decrypt has an extra computational entropy such as $\widehat{\mathbf{k}}_i$ in (5) that will be used to hide the master secret. This is compatible with the standard dual-system argument [Wat09, Wee14, CGW15] where we have a single ciphertext and multiple keys and the proof adds entropy to each key one by one and always keeps the unique ciphertext "unchanged". However step **(ii)** involves multiple *ciphertexts* and a single *key*; we can not add

[1] In Sects. 3.3 and 3.4 where we describe our formal proof, $\widehat{\mathbf{k}}_i$ indicates a random vector from a subspace of $\mathbb{Z}_p^{\ell}$, say $\mathsf{span}(\mathbf{A}_2^\dagger)$.

extra entropy to ciphertexts while keeping the unique key "changed" via predicate encodings. One can circumvent this issue by simply introducing an extra subspace into basis (1) but this complicates the proof. (Note that, even though, this will not hurt the efficiency too much since ℓ is independent of the number of subspaces in our context.).

In this work, we will rely on a variant of nested dual-system argument implicitly used in the proof of entropy expansion lemma from [CGKW18] where they exchanged the roles of ciphertexts and keys at the very beginning in step **(i)**. By this, when step **(ii)** reverses the roles again, we are facing a single ciphertext and multiple keys that is compatible with predicate encodings and can avoid the extra subspace in the aforementioned trivial countermeasure. In particular, we can continue to use the basis (1) as [GGH20] although the proof is different. Note that, even with this special arrangement, [CGKW18] essentially works with IBE (an attribute $i \in \mathbb{Z}_p$ is encoded in an IBE form: $\mathbf{W} + i \cdot \mathbf{V}$); this is the first time to highlight this property and apply this to general ABE via predicate encodings.

Proof Overview. For simplicity, we will illustrate our proof of (5) for the *IBE* functionality in asymmetric *composite*-order bilinear groups (N, G_N, H_N, G_T, e) whose order N is a product of three primes p_1, p_2, p_3. Let g_i, h_i be random generators of subgroups of order p_i in G_N, H_N for $i \in \{1, 2, 3\}$, respectively. The switch between composite- and prime-order groups will rely on the following classical correspondence in [CGKW18]:

$$\begin{array}{rrcl}
 & g_1, h_{123} & \leftrightarrow & [\mathbf{A}^\top]_1, [\mathbf{B}]_2 \\
w, v \leftrightarrow \mathbf{W}, \mathbf{V} & g_1^w, g_1^v, h_{123}^w, h_{123}^v & \leftrightarrow & [\mathbf{A}_1^\top \mathbf{W}]_1, [\mathbf{A}_1^\top \mathbf{V}]_1, [\mathbf{WB}]_2, [\mathbf{VB}]_2 \\
s \leftrightarrow \mathbf{s} & g_1^s, g_1^{sw}, g_1^{sv} & \leftrightarrow & [\mathbf{s}^\top \mathbf{A}_1^\top]_1, [\mathbf{s}^\top \mathbf{A}_1^\top \mathbf{W}]_1, [\mathbf{s}^\top \mathbf{A}_1^\top \mathbf{V}]_1 \\
\hat{s} \leftrightarrow \widehat{\mathbf{s}} & g_2^{\hat{s}}, g_2^{\hat{s}w}, g_2^{\hat{s}v} & \leftrightarrow & [\widehat{\mathbf{s}}^\top \mathbf{A}_2^\top]_1, [\widehat{\mathbf{s}}^\top \mathbf{A}_2^\top \mathbf{W}]_1, [\widehat{\mathbf{s}}^\top \mathbf{A}_2^\top \mathbf{V}]_1 \\
\hat{\alpha}, r \leftrightarrow \widehat{\mathbf{k}}, \mathbf{r} & h_{123}^r, h_{123}^{wr}, h_{123}^{vr}, h_2^{\hat{\alpha}} & \leftrightarrow & [\mathbf{Br}]_2, [\mathbf{WBr}]_2, [\mathbf{VBr}]_2, [\mathbf{A}_2^\dagger \widehat{\mathbf{k}}]_2
\end{array}$$

by which the statement (5) can be translated into composite-order groups as:

$$\begin{pmatrix} \mathsf{mpk} : g_1,\, g_1^w,\, g_1^v,\, h_{123},\, h_{123}^w,\, h_{123}^v \\ \mathsf{sk}_{\mathsf{id}_i} : h_{123}^{r_i},\, h_{123}^{(w+\mathsf{id}_i \cdot v) r_i} \\ \mathsf{ct}^*_{\mathsf{id}'_j} : g_1^{s_j},\, g_1^{s_j(w+\mathsf{id}'_j \cdot v)} \end{pmatrix} \approx_c \begin{pmatrix} \mathsf{mpk} : g_1,\, g_1^w,\, g_1^v,\, h_{123},\, h_{123}^w,\, h_{123}^v \\ \mathsf{sk}_{\mathsf{id}_i} : h_{123}^{r_i},\, \boxed{h_2^{\hat{\alpha}_i}} \cdot h_{123}^{(w+\mathsf{id}_i \cdot v) r_i} \\ \mathsf{ct}^*_{\mathsf{id}'_j} : g_1^{s_j} \cdot \boxed{g_2^{\hat{s}_j}},\, g_1^{s_j(w+\mathsf{id}'_j \cdot v)} \cdot \boxed{g_2^{\hat{s}_j(w+\mathsf{id}'_j \cdot v)}} \end{pmatrix} \tag{6}$$

where $w, v \leftarrow \mathbb{Z}_N$ and $\hat{\alpha}_i, r_i, s_j, \hat{s}_j \leftarrow \mathbb{Z}_N$ for $i \in [Q_K], j \in [Q_C]$. Following [CGKW18], our proof consists of two steps.

1. We change all secret keys into the following form that is analogous to so-called semi-functional keys in standard (nested) dual-system argument [Wat09, LW11]:

$$\mathsf{sk}_{\mathsf{id}_i} = (h_{123}^{r_i}, \boxed{h_2^{\hat{\alpha}_i}} \cdot h_{123}^{(w+\mathsf{id}_i \cdot v) r_i}).$$

   This is basically the step that changes normal keys to semi-functional keys in the standard dual-system argument [Wat09, CGW15]. The indistinguishability employs a standard hybrid argument going through every keys based on (a) subgroup decision assumption: $h_{12}^{r_i} \approx_c h_1^{r_i}$ given g_1, h_{123} and (b) statistical argument: for all $\hat{\alpha}_i, r_i \in \mathbb{Z}_N$, we have $w \bmod p_2 \approx_s w + \hat{\alpha}_i / r_i \bmod p_2$ when $w \leftarrow \mathbb{Z}_N$.
2. We change all ciphertexts into the following form that is analogous to so-called semi-functional ciphertexts in the standard dual-system argument [Wat09]:

$$\mathsf{ct}_{\mathsf{id}_j}^* = (g_1^{s_j} \cdot \boxed{g_2^{\hat{s}_j}}, g_1^{s_j(w+\mathsf{id}_j' \cdot v)} \cdot \boxed{g_2^{\hat{s}_j(w+\mathsf{id}_j' \cdot v)}}).$$

   Again, we will make the change in a one-by-one manner. However, we cannot simply use subgroup decision assumption for each transition. Instead, we will employ a game sequence with the help of the p_3-subgroup. Let us show how to change the $\hat{\jmath}$-th ciphertext as an example. Given

$$\mathsf{mpk} = (g_1, g_1^w, g_1^v, h_{123}, h_{123}^w, h_{123}^v)$$

   and ciphertexts that has been changed (with index $j < \hat{\jmath}$) and has not been changed (with index $j > \hat{\jmath}$):

$$\begin{aligned} \mathsf{ct}_{\mathsf{id}_j'}^* (j < \hat{\jmath}) &: g_1^{s_j} \cdot g_2^{\hat{s}_j}, \ g_1^{s_j(w+\mathsf{id}_j' \cdot v)} \cdot g_2^{\hat{s}_j(w+\mathsf{id}_j' \cdot v)} \\ \mathsf{ct}_{\mathsf{id}_j'}^* (j > \hat{\jmath}) &: g_1^{s_j}, \qquad g_1^{s_j(w+\mathsf{id}_j' \cdot v)} \end{aligned}$$

   we change the $\hat{\jmath}$-th ciphertext along with *all* secret keys via the following hybrid argument:

$$\begin{aligned} & \begin{pmatrix} \mathsf{sk}_{\mathsf{id}_i} : h_{123}^{r_i}, \ h_2^{\hat{\alpha}_i} \cdot h_{123}^{(w+\mathsf{id}_i \cdot v) r_i}, \quad \forall i \in [Q_K] \\ \mathsf{ct}_{\mathsf{id}_{\hat{\jmath}}'}^* : g_1^{s_{\hat{\jmath}}}, \ g_1^{s_{\hat{\jmath}}(w+\mathsf{id}_{\hat{\jmath}}' \cdot v)} \end{pmatrix} \\ \approx_c & \begin{pmatrix} \mathsf{sk}_{\mathsf{id}_i} : h_{123}^{r_i}, \ h_2^{\hat{\alpha}_i} \cdot h_{123}^{(w+\mathsf{id}_i \cdot v) r_i}, \quad \forall i \in [Q_K] \\ \mathsf{ct}_{\mathsf{id}_{\hat{\jmath}}'}^* : g_1^{s_{\hat{\jmath}}} \cdot \boxed{g_3^{\tilde{s}_{\hat{\jmath}}}}, \ g_1^{s_{\hat{\jmath}}(w+\mathsf{id}_{\hat{\jmath}}' \cdot v)} \cdot \boxed{g_3^{\tilde{s}_{\hat{\jmath}}(w+\mathsf{id}_{\hat{\jmath}}' \cdot v)}} \end{pmatrix} \\ \approx_c & \begin{pmatrix} \mathsf{sk}_{\mathsf{id}_i} : h_{123}^{r_i}, \ h_2^{\hat{\alpha}_i} \cdot \boxed{h_3^{\tilde{\alpha}_i}} \cdot h_{123}^{(w+\mathsf{id}_i \cdot v) r_i}, \quad \forall i \in [Q_K] \\ \mathsf{ct}_{\mathsf{id}_{\hat{\jmath}}'}^* : g_1^{s_{\hat{\jmath}}} \cdot g_3^{\tilde{s}_{\hat{\jmath}}}, \ g_1^{s_{\hat{\jmath}}(w+\mathsf{id}_{\hat{\jmath}}' \cdot v)} \cdot g_3^{\tilde{s}_{\hat{\jmath}}(w+\mathsf{id}_{\hat{\jmath}}' \cdot v)} \end{pmatrix} \\ \approx_c & \begin{pmatrix} \mathsf{sk}_{\mathsf{id}_i} : h_{123}^{r_i}, \ h_2^{\hat{\alpha}_i} \cdot h_3^{\tilde{\alpha}_i} \cdot h_{123}^{(w+\mathsf{id}_i \cdot v) r_i}, \quad \forall i \in [Q_K] \\ \mathsf{ct}_{\mathsf{id}_{\hat{\jmath}}'}^* : g_1^{s_{\hat{\jmath}}} \cdot \boxed{g_2^{\hat{s}_{\hat{\jmath}}}}, \ g_1^{s_{\hat{\jmath}}(w+\mathsf{id}_{\hat{\jmath}}' \cdot v)} \cdot \boxed{g_2^{\hat{s}_{\hat{\jmath}}(w+\mathsf{id}_{\hat{\jmath}}' \cdot v)}} \end{pmatrix} \end{aligned}$$

$$\approx_c \begin{pmatrix} \mathsf{sk}_{\mathsf{id}_i} : h_{123}^{r_i}, h_2^{\hat{\alpha}_i} \cdot \cancel{h_3^{\tilde{\alpha}_i}} \cdot h_{123}^{(w+\mathsf{id}_i \cdot v)r_i}, \quad \forall i \in [Q_K] \\ \mathsf{ct}^*_{\mathsf{id}'_{\hat{\jmath}}} : g_1^{s_{\hat{\jmath}}} \cdot g_2^{\hat{s}_{\hat{\jmath}}}, g_1^{s_{\hat{\jmath}}(w+\mathsf{id}'_{\hat{\jmath}} \cdot v)} \cdot g_2^{\hat{s}_{\hat{\jmath}}(w+\mathsf{id}'_{\hat{\jmath}} \cdot v)} \end{pmatrix}$$

where $\tilde{\alpha}_i, \tilde{s}_{\hat{\jmath}} \leftarrow \mathbb{Z}_N$ for all $i \in [Q_K]$. Here

- the first $\approx_c$ follows from subgroup decision assumption: $g_1^{s_{\hat{\jmath}}} \approx_c g_1^{s_{\hat{\jmath}}} \cdot g_3^{\tilde{s}_{\hat{\jmath}}}$ given g_1, g_2, h_{123}, h_2.
- the second $\approx_c$ is similar to the first step of our proof with (a) subgroup decision assumption: $h_{13}^{r_i} \approx_c h_1^{r_i}$ given g_1, g_2, h_2, h_{123} and (b) statistical argument over p_3-subgroup for a fixed $i \in [Q_K]$: for all $\tilde{\alpha}_i, r_i \in \mathbb{Z}_N$,

$$\overbrace{w + \mathsf{id}_i \cdot v}^{\mathsf{sk}_{\mathsf{id}_i}}, \overbrace{w + \mathsf{id}'_{\hat{\jmath}} \cdot v}^{\mathsf{ct}^*_{\mathsf{id}'_{\hat{\jmath}}}} \approx_s \boxed{\tilde{\alpha}_i / r_i} + w + \mathsf{id}_i \cdot v, w + \mathsf{id}'_{\hat{\jmath}} \cdot v \mod p_3$$

  when $w, v \leftarrow \mathbb{Z}_N$.
- the third $\approx_c$ follows from subgroup decision assumption: $g_3^{\tilde{s}_{\hat{\jmath}}} \approx_c g_2^{\hat{s}_{\hat{\jmath}}}$ given $g_1, g_2, h_{123}, h_{23}$; h_{23} is a random generator of subgroup of order $p_2 p_3$ that is used to simulate term $\{h_2^{\hat{\alpha}_i} \cdot h_3^{\tilde{\alpha}_i}\}_{i \in [Q_K]}$.
- the last $\approx_c$ is analogous to the second one except that statistical argument becomes: for all $\tilde{\alpha}_i, r_i \in \mathbb{Z}_N$, we have $w \mod p_3 \approx_s w + \tilde{\alpha}_i / r_i \mod p_3$ when $w \leftarrow \mathbb{Z}_N$.

In the final proof with *predicate encodings* in *prime-order* bilinear groups, we translate

- subgroup decision assumption over G_N into the prime-order version in [CGKW18] w.r.t. basis (1), cf. Lemma 1;
- subgroup decision assumption over H_N into the MDDH assumption w.r.t. $\mathbf{B}$, see Assumption 1;
- the statistical arguments into the so-called α-privacy of predicate encoding, cf. Sect. 2.3.

1.3 Discussions and Open Problems

Towards Framework via Pair Encoding. Pair encoding [Att14, AC17] is a primitive similar to the predicate encoding [Wee14, CGW15]. It is also feasible to generalize (4) via pair encodings. Although this will give us even more expressive mKDM-secure ABE, the security would rely on complex q-type assumptions. In this paper, we restrict us to the security based on static assumption notably k-Lin assumption. We leave this as an open problem to get even more expressive ABE that goes beyond predicate encoding.

Towards Multi-instance Setting. As [GGH20], we only study the mKDM-security in the single instance setting. We believe both constructions can be extended to multiple instance setting, as [GHV12], where the message can be

$f(\mathsf{msk}_1, \ldots, \mathsf{msk}_N)$ with msk_i are master secret keys of N independent instances. We leave this as one of future works. In fact, [GHV12] reported that they can reduce the mKDM-security of their IBE scheme in the multiple instance setting to that in the single instance setting. However we point out that this might not be straightforward in the context of ABE: each instance can support different policies which makes the above reduction quite hard.

More Open Problems. We leave several open problems:

- As we have discussed, it is desirable to have a mKDM-secure IBE with tight security under constant-size master public key in the prime-order bilinear group. This will be a breakthrough even for the standard semantic security.
- It would be interesting to build a mKDM-secure ABE from various assumptions such as learning with error (LWE) assumption. Note that, to our best knowledge, there is no LWE-based construction with such security property.
- A formal study of the relation of uKDM-security and mKDM-security is also appealing. For now, we can conjecture that mKDM-security is strictly stronger than uKDM-security. However there's no formal implication and/or separation results on this.

Organization. We describe some background knowledge in Sect. 2. In Sect. 3, we present our generic ABE scheme via predicate encoding and prove its mKDM security from k-Lin assumption in the prime-order biliear group. We show how to add delegation and revisit the CPA-to-CCA transformation with mKDM security in Sect. 4 and Sect. 5. Several concrete schemes derived from previous generic results will be given out in Sect. 6.

2 Preliminaries

Notation. We use $s \leftarrow S$ to indicate that s is selected uniformly from finite set S. PPT stands for probabilistic polynomial time. For a matrix $\mathbf{A}$ over $\mathbb{Z}_p$, we use $\mathsf{span}(\mathbf{A})$ to denote the column span of $\mathbf{A}$, and we use $\mathsf{basis}(\mathbf{A})$ to denote a basis of $\mathsf{span}(\mathbf{A})$. We use $\langle \mathsf{G}, \mathcal{A} \rangle = 1$ to denote that adversary $\mathcal{A}$ wins game G. We use $\approx_c$ and $\approx_s$ to denote two distributions being computationally and statistically indistinguishable, respectively.

2.1 Attribute-Based Encryption

Syntax. An attribute-based encryption (ABE) scheme for predicate $P : \mathcal{X} \times \mathcal{Y} \rightarrow \{0, 1\}$ consists of the following PPT algorithms:

- $\mathsf{Setup}(1^\lambda, P) \rightarrow (\mathsf{mpk}, \mathsf{msk})$. The setup algorithm takes as input the security parameter 1^λ and a description of predicate P, outputs a master public/secret key pair $(\mathsf{mpk}, \mathsf{msk})$. We assume that mpk contains the description of domains $\mathcal{X}$, $\mathcal{Y}$ of P as well as message space $\mathcal{M}$.

- $\mathsf{Enc}(\mathsf{mpk}, x, m) \to \mathsf{ct}_x$. The encryption algorithm takes as input the master public key mpk, an index $x \in \mathcal{X}$ and a message $m \in \mathcal{M}$, outputs a ciphertext ct_x.
- $\mathsf{KeyGen}(\mathsf{mpk}, \mathsf{msk}, y) \to \mathsf{sk}_y$. The key generation algorithm takes as input the master public/secret key pair $(\mathsf{mpk}, \mathsf{msk})$ and an index $y \in \mathcal{Y}$, outputs a secret key sk_y.
- $\mathsf{Dec}(\mathsf{mpk}, \mathsf{sk}_y, \mathsf{ct}_x) \to m$. The decryption algorithm takes as input the master public key mpk, a secret key sk_y and a ciphertext ct_x, outputs a message m or a symbol $\perp$ indicating the ciphertext is invalid.

Correctness. For all $(x, y) \in \mathcal{X} \times \mathcal{Y}$ such that $P(x, y) = 1$ and $m \in \mathcal{M}$, it is required that

$$\Pr\left[m = \mathsf{Dec}(\mathsf{mpk}, \mathsf{sk}_y, \mathsf{ct}_x) \;\middle|\; \begin{array}{c} (\mathsf{mpk}, \mathsf{msk}) \leftarrow \mathsf{Setup}(1^\lambda, P) \\ \mathsf{ct}_x \leftarrow \mathsf{Enc}(\mathsf{mpk}, x, m) \\ \mathsf{sk}_y \leftarrow \mathsf{KeyGen}(\mathsf{mpk}, \mathsf{msk}, y) \end{array} \right] = 1.$$

$\mathcal{F}$-mKDM Security. Let $\mathcal{F}$ be a function family. For all stateful PPT adversaries $\mathcal{A}$, the advantage function is defined as

$$\mathsf{mKDMAdv}^{\text{CPA}}_{\mathcal{A},\mathcal{F}}(\lambda) := \left| \Pr\left[b = b' \;\middle|\; \begin{array}{c} b \leftarrow \{0,1\} \\ (\mathsf{mpk}, \mathsf{msk}) \leftarrow \mathsf{Setup}(1^\lambda, P) \\ b' = \mathcal{A}^{\mathsf{O}^b_{\mathsf{Enc}}(\cdot,\cdot), \mathsf{O}_{\mathsf{KeyGen}}(\cdot)}(\mathsf{mpk}) \end{array} \right] - \frac{1}{2} \right|$$

where the oracles work as follows:

- $\mathsf{O}^b_{\mathsf{Enc}}(x, F)$, on input $x \in \mathcal{X}$ and $F \in \mathcal{F}$, picks $m \leftarrow \mathcal{M}$, returns ct^b where

$$\mathsf{ct}^0 \leftarrow \mathsf{Enc}(\mathsf{mpk}, x, F(\mathsf{msk})) \quad \text{and} \quad \mathsf{ct}^1 \leftarrow \mathsf{Enc}(\mathsf{mpk}, x, m);$$

- $\mathsf{O}_{\mathsf{KeyGen}}(y)$, on input $y \in \mathcal{Y}$, returns sk_y where

$$\mathsf{sk}_y \leftarrow \mathsf{KeyGen}(\mathsf{mpk}, \mathsf{msk}, y);$$

with the restriction that all queries $(x, \cdot)$ and y satisfy $P(x, y) = 0$. An ABE scheme is *master-key-dependent-message* secure with respect to function family $\mathcal{F}$ against *chosen-plaintext attack* if $\mathsf{mKDMAdv}^{\text{CPA}}_{\mathcal{A},\mathcal{F}}(\lambda)$ is negligible in λ. In the following, we use $\mathbf{mKDM}_b$ to denote the above game parameterized by b. We can also define the variant against *chosen-ciphertext attack* analogously by providing $\mathcal{A}$ with a decryption oracle that works as below:

- $\mathsf{O}_{\mathsf{Dec}}(y, \mathsf{ct})$, on input $y \in \mathcal{Y}$ and a ciphertext ct, generates $\mathsf{sk}_y \leftarrow \mathsf{KeyGen}(\mathsf{mpk}, \mathsf{msk}, y)$ and returns

$$m' \leftarrow \mathsf{Dec}(\mathsf{mpk}, \mathsf{sk}_y, \mathsf{ct})$$

with the restriction that ct is not produced by $\mathsf{O}^b_{\mathsf{Enc}}$. In this work, we will always consider $\mathcal{F}$ being an affine function and call $\mathcal{F}$-mKDM as mKDM when the context is clear.

2.2 Prime-Order Bilinear Groups

We assume a group generator $\mathcal{G}$ which takes as input a security parameter 1^λ and outputs a group description $\mathbb{G} := (p, G_1, G_2, G_T, e)$. Here G_1, G_2, G_T are cyclic groups of prime order p of $\Theta(\lambda)$ bits and $e : G_1 \times G_2 \to G_T$ is a non-degenerated bilinear map. Typically, the descriptions of G_1, G_2 contain respective generators g_1, g_2. We employ the implicit representation of group elements: for any matrix $\mathbf{A}$ over $\mathbb{Z}_p$ and $s \in \{1, 2, T\}$, we define $[\mathbf{A}]_s := g_s^{\mathbf{A}}$ where the exponentiation is carried out component-wise. Given $[\mathbf{A}]_1$ and $[\mathbf{B}]_2$, we define $[\mathbf{AB}]_T = e([\mathbf{A}]_1, [\mathbf{B}]_2)$.

Matrix Decisional Diffie-Hellman Assumption. We revisit the matrix decisional Diffie-Hellman (MDDH) assumption in the prime-order bilinear group that is a generalization of k-Linear assumption.

Assumption 1 ($\mathbf{MDDH}_{k,\ell}$, [EHK+13]) *Let $k, \ell \in \mathbb{N}$, $s \in \{1, 2, T\}$. For all PPT adversaries $\mathcal{A}$, the advantage function*

$$\mathsf{Adv}_{\mathcal{A}}^{\mathbf{MDDH}_{k,\ell}}(\lambda) := |\Pr[\mathcal{A}(\mathbb{G}, [\mathbf{A}]_s, [\mathbf{As}]_s) = 1] - \Pr[\mathcal{A}(\mathbb{G}, [\mathbf{A}]_s, [\mathbf{u}]_s) = 1]|$$

is negligible in λ where $\mathbf{A} \leftarrow \mathbb{Z}_p^{\ell \times k}$, $\mathbf{s} \leftarrow \mathbb{Z}_p^k$ and $\mathbf{u} \leftarrow \mathbb{Z}_p^\ell$.

We write $\mathbf{MDDH}_k = \mathbf{MDDH}_{k,k+1}$ and have $\mathbf{MDDH}_k \Rightarrow \mathbf{MDDH}_{k,\ell}$ for $\ell > k$. Note that the assumption unconditionally holds when $\ell \leq k$.

2.3 Predicate Encoding

Syntax. A $\mathbb{Z}_p$-linear predicate encoding [Wee14, CGW15] for $P : \mathcal{X} \times \mathcal{Y} \to \{0, 1\}$ consists of five deterministic algorithms:

$$\begin{aligned} &\mathsf{sE} : \mathcal{X} \times \mathbb{Z}_p^n \to \mathbb{Z}_p^{n_s} && && \mathsf{sD} : \mathcal{X} \times \mathcal{Y} \times \mathbb{Z}_p^{n_s} \to \mathbb{Z}_p \\ &\mathsf{rE} : \mathcal{Y} \times \mathbb{Z}_p^n \to \mathbb{Z}_p^{n_r} && \mathsf{kE} : \mathcal{Y} \times \mathbb{Z}_p \to \mathbb{Z}_p^{n_r} && \mathsf{rD} : \mathcal{X} \times \mathcal{Y} \times \mathbb{Z}_p^{n_r} \to \mathbb{Z}_p \end{aligned}$$

for some $n, n_s, n_r \in \mathbb{N}$ with the following features:

(linearity). For all $(x, y) \in \mathcal{X} \times \mathcal{Y}$, $\mathsf{sE}(x, \cdot)$, $\mathsf{rE}(y, \cdot)$, $\mathsf{kE}(y, \cdot)$, $\mathsf{sD}(x, y, \cdot)$, $\mathsf{rD}(x, y, \cdot)$ are $\mathbb{Z}_p$-linear. A $\mathbb{Z}_p$-linear function $L : \mathbb{Z}_p^n \to \mathbb{Z}_p^{n'}$ can be encoded as a matrix $\mathbf{L} = (l_{i,j}) \in \mathbb{Z}_p^{n \times n'}$ such that

$$L : (w_1, \ldots, w_n) \to (\textstyle\sum_{i=1}^n l_{i,1} w_i, \ldots, \sum_{i=1}^n l_{i,n'} w_i). \tag{7}$$

(restricted α-reconstruction). For all $(x, y) \in \mathcal{X} \times \mathcal{Y}$ such that $P(x, y) = 1$, $\alpha \in \mathbb{Z}_p$ and $\mathbf{w} \in \mathbb{Z}_p^n$, we have

$$\mathsf{sD}(x, y, \mathsf{sE}(x, \mathbf{w})) = \mathsf{rD}(x, y, \mathsf{rE}(y, \mathbf{w})) \quad \text{and} \quad \mathsf{rD}(x, y, \mathsf{kE}(y, \alpha)) = \alpha. \tag{8}$$

(α-privacy). For all $(x, y) \in \mathcal{X} \times \mathcal{Y}$ such that $P(x, y) = 0$, $\alpha \in \mathbb{Z}_p$ and $\mathbf{w} \leftarrow \mathbb{Z}_p^n$, the following distributions are identical:

$$\begin{aligned} &\{\, x, y, \alpha, \mathsf{sE}(x, \mathbf{w}), \mathsf{kE}(y, \alpha) + \mathsf{rE}(y, \mathbf{w}) \,\} \\ \text{and} \quad &\{\, x, y, \alpha, \mathsf{sE}(x, \mathbf{w}), \mathsf{rE}(y, \mathbf{w}) \,\}. \end{aligned} \tag{9}$$

Notations and Facts. For $s \in \{1, 2, T\}$, we can define an extension of linear function (7) where we replace scalars $w_i \in \mathbb{Z}_p$ with (column) vector $\mathbf{w}_i \in \mathbb{Z}_p^k$ "in the exponent":

$$\begin{array}{cccc} L: & (G_s^k)^n & \to & (G_s^k)^{n'} \\ & ([\mathbf{w}_1]_s, \ldots, [\mathbf{w}_n]_s) & \mapsto & (\prod_{i=1}^n [l_{i,1}\mathbf{w}_i]_s, \ldots, \prod_{i=1}^n [l_{i,n'}\mathbf{w}_i]_s) \end{array} \tag{10}$$

For simplicity, we use the same notation L since they correspond to the same $\mathbf{L}$. Moreover, this works with row vectors and matrices analogously. We conclude this part with some properties of (10):

($L(\cdot)$ and pairing e are commutative). Let $n' = 1$. For all $\mathbf{a}, \mathbf{b}_1, \ldots, \mathbf{b}_n \in \mathbb{Z}_p^k$, we have

$$e([\mathbf{a}^\top]_1, L([\mathbf{b}_1]_2, \ldots, [\mathbf{b}_n]_2)) = L([\mathbf{a}^\top \mathbf{b}_1]_T, \ldots, [\mathbf{a}^\top \mathbf{b}_n]_T), \tag{11}$$

$$e(L([\mathbf{b}_1^\top]_1, \ldots, [\mathbf{b}_n^\top]_1), [\mathbf{a}]_2) = L([\mathbf{b}_1^\top \mathbf{a}]_T, \ldots, [\mathbf{b}_n^\top \mathbf{a}]_T). \tag{12}$$

($L(\cdot)$ and $[\cdot]_s$ are commutative). For all $(\mathbf{w}_1, \ldots, \mathbf{w}_n) \in (\mathbb{Z}_p^k)^n$, we have

$$L([\mathbf{w}_1]_s, \ldots, [\mathbf{w}_n]_s) = [L(\mathbf{w}_1, \ldots, \mathbf{w}_n)]_s. \tag{13}$$

3 Master-Key KDM ABE

In this section, we present our generic ABE via predicate encodings in the prime-order bilinear group. The scheme is adaptively mKDM-CPA secure (with respect to affine functions) against unbounded collusion under k-Lin assumption.

3.1 Basis

Our ABE scheme based on $\mathbf{MDDH}_k$ assumption uses the following basis

$$(\mathbf{A}_1, \mathbf{A}_2, \mathbf{A}_3) \leftarrow \mathbb{Z}_p^{\ell \times \ell_1} \times \mathbb{Z}_p^{\ell \times \ell_2} \times \mathbb{Z}_p^{\ell \times \ell_3} \tag{14}$$

where $\ell = \ell_1 + \ell_2 + \ell_3 \geq 2(\lambda + k \log p)$ and $\ell_1 = \ell_2 = k$, $\ell_3 \geq k$. We denote their dual basis by $(\mathbf{A}_1^\dagger, \mathbf{A}_2^\dagger, \mathbf{A}_3^\dagger)$ such that $\mathbf{A}_i^\top \mathbf{A}_j^\dagger = \mathbf{0}$ when $i \neq j$ and $\mathbf{A}_i^\top \mathbf{A}_i^\dagger = \mathbf{I}$. We write horizontal concatenation $\mathbf{A}_{ij} = (\mathbf{A}_i | \mathbf{A}_j)$, $\mathbf{A}_{ij}^\dagger = (\mathbf{A}_i^\dagger | \mathbf{A}_j^\dagger)$ for short.

Subgroup Decision Assumption. We describe a three-subgroup variant of prime-order $(\mathbf{A}_1 \mapsto \mathbf{A}_{12})$-subgroup decision assumption [CGKW18], denoted by $\mathbf{SD}_{\mathbf{A}_1 \mapsto \mathbf{A}_{12}}$. By symmetry, we can permute the indices for $\mathbf{A}_1$, $\mathbf{A}_2$, $\mathbf{A}_3$. One can define the assumption over dual bases $\mathbf{A}_1^\dagger$, $\mathbf{A}_2^\dagger$, $\mathbf{A}_3^\dagger$ analogously.

Lemma 1 ($\mathbf{MDDH}_{\ell_1, \ell_1+\ell_2} \Rightarrow \mathbf{SD}_{\mathbf{A}_1 \mapsto \mathbf{A}_{12}}$). *Under $\mathbf{MDDH}_{\ell_1, \ell_1+\ell_2}$ assumption in G_1, there exists an efficient sampler outputting random $([\mathbf{A}_1]_1, [\mathbf{A}_2]_1, [\mathbf{A}_3]_1)$ along with bases* $\mathsf{basis}(\mathbf{A}_1^\dagger)$, $\mathsf{basis}(\mathbf{A}_1^\dagger, \mathbf{A}_2^\dagger)$, $\mathsf{basis}(\mathbf{A}_3^\dagger)$ *(of arbitrary choice) such that the advantage function*

$$\mathsf{Adv}_{\mathcal{A}}^{\mathrm{SD}_{\mathbf{A}_1 \mapsto \mathbf{A}_{12}}}(\lambda) := |\Pr[\mathcal{A}(D, [\mathbf{t}_0]_1) = 1] - \Pr[\mathcal{A}(D, [\mathbf{t}_1]_1) = 1]|$$

is negligible in λ *where*

$$D := (\,[\mathbf{A}_1]_1, [\mathbf{A}_2]_1, [\mathbf{A}_3]_1, \mathsf{basis}(\mathbf{A}_1^\dagger), \mathsf{basis}(\mathbf{A}_1^\dagger, \mathbf{A}_2^\dagger), \mathsf{basis}(\mathbf{A}_3^\dagger)\,),$$
$$\mathbf{t}_0 \leftarrow \mathsf{span}(\mathbf{A}_1) \quad \textit{and} \quad \mathbf{t}_1 \leftarrow \mathsf{span}(\mathbf{A}_1, \mathbf{A}_2).$$

3.2 Scheme

Construction. Our ABE scheme via predicate encoding is as follows:

- $\mathsf{Setup}(1^\lambda, P)$: Let n be parameter size of predicate encoding $(\mathsf{sE}, \mathsf{rE}, \mathsf{kE}, \mathsf{sD}, \mathsf{rD})$ for P. Run $\mathbb{G} \leftarrow \mathcal{G}(1^\lambda)$, sample $\mathbf{A}_1 \leftarrow \mathbb{Z}_p^{\ell \times k}$ as in (14), $\mathbf{B} \leftarrow \mathbb{Z}_p^{(k+1)\times k}$, pick $\mathbf{W}_1, \ldots, \mathbf{W}_n \leftarrow \mathbb{Z}_p^{\ell \times (k+1)}$ and $\mathbf{k} \leftarrow \{0,1\}^\ell$. Output

$$\mathsf{mpk} := \begin{pmatrix} \mathbb{G}, [\mathbf{A}_1^\top]_1, [\mathbf{A}_1^\top \mathbf{W}_1]_1, \ldots, [\mathbf{A}_1^\top \mathbf{W}_n]_1, \\ [\mathbf{B}]_2,\ [\mathbf{W}_1\mathbf{B}]_2,\ \ldots, [\mathbf{W}_n\mathbf{B}]_2,\ [\mathbf{A}_1^\top \mathbf{k}]_T \end{pmatrix}, \quad \mathsf{msk} := [\mathbf{k}]_T.$$

- $\mathsf{Enc}(\mathsf{mpk}, x, m)$: Pick $\mathbf{s} \leftarrow \mathbb{Z}_p^k$ and output

$$\mathsf{ct}_x := (\,\overbrace{[\mathbf{s}^\top \mathbf{A}_1^\top]_1}^{C_0}, \overbrace{\mathsf{sE}(x, [\mathbf{s}^\top \mathbf{A}_1^\top \mathbf{W}_1]_1, \ldots, [\mathbf{s}^\top \mathbf{A}_1^\top \mathbf{W}_n]_1)}^{\vec{C}_1}, \overbrace{[\mathbf{s}^\top \mathbf{A}_1^\top \mathbf{k}]_T \cdot m}^{C}\,).$$

- $\mathsf{KeyGen}(\mathsf{mpk}, \mathsf{msk}, y)$: Recover $\mathbf{k} \in \{0,1\}^\ell$ from $\mathsf{msk} = [\mathbf{k}]_T$. Pick $\mathbf{r} \leftarrow \mathbb{Z}_p^k$ and output

$$\mathsf{sk}_y := (\,\overbrace{[\mathbf{Br}]_2}^{K_0}, \overbrace{\mathsf{kE}(y, [\mathbf{k}]_2) \cdot \mathsf{rE}(y, [\mathbf{W}_1\mathbf{Br}]_2, \ldots, [\mathbf{W}_n\mathbf{Br}]_2)}^{\vec{K}_1}\,).$$

- $\mathsf{Dec}(\mathsf{mpk}, \mathsf{sk}_y, \mathsf{ct}_x)$: Parse $\mathsf{sk}_y = (K_0, \vec{K}_1)$ and $\mathsf{ct}_x = (C_0, \vec{C}_1, C)$, and output

$$m' = C \cdot e(C_0, \mathsf{rD}(x, y, \vec{K}_1))^{-1} \cdot e(\mathsf{sD}(x, y, \vec{C}_1), K_0).$$

The correctness follows from properties in Sect. 2.3 as in [CGW15]. See the full paper for more details.

Security. We have the following theorem for the above scheme.

Theorem 1 (Main Theorem). *Under* $\mathbf{MDDH}_k$ *assumption (cf. Sect. 3.1), our ABE scheme described in this section is master-key-dependent-message secure for affine functions mapping* G_T^ℓ *to* G_T *against chosen-plaintext attack.*

3.3 Useful Lemmas

We prepare two lemmas with respect to the basis (14) in Sect. 3.1 which will be used throughout the proof. The first lemma (Lemma 2) is a variant of "$\mathbf{c} \approx_s \mathbf{c} - \mathbf{f}$" where $\mathbf{c} \leftarrow \mathbb{Z}_p^\ell$ and $\mathbf{f} \in \mathbb{Z}_p^\ell$; here we allow $\mathbf{c}$ to live in a subspace and work with groups. The second lemma (Lemma 3) is an extension of leftover hash lemma which additionally gives out an extra term randomly picked from the coset $\mathbf{k} + \mathsf{span}(\mathbf{A}_{23}^\dagger)$. We present the lemmas without proofs.

Lemma 2. *Let* $Q \in \mathbb{N}$. *For any* $\{\mathbf{f}_j\}_{j\in[Q]} \in (\mathbb{Z}_p^\ell)^Q$, *we have*

$$\{[\mathbf{c}_j]_1\}_{j\in[Q]} \approx_c \{[\mathbf{c}_j - \mathbf{f}_j]_1\}_{j\in[Q]} \quad \textit{given} \quad \mathbf{A}_1, [\mathbf{A}_2]_1, [\mathbf{A}_3]_1, \mathbf{A}_1^\dagger, \mathsf{basis}(\mathbf{A}_2^\dagger, \mathbf{A}_3^\dagger)$$

where $\mathbf{c}_j \leftarrow \mathsf{span}(\mathbf{A}_1, \mathbf{A}_2)$. *The distinguishing advantage* $\mathsf{Adv}_{\mathcal{A}}^{\text{CompHide}_Q}(\lambda)$ *is bounded by* $2Q \cdot \mathsf{Adv}_{\mathcal{B}}^{\mathbf{MDDH}_{k,\ell}}(\lambda)$ *for all PPT adversaries* $\mathcal{B}$.

Lemma 3. *Within probability* $1 - 1/2^\lambda$, *we have*

$$(\mathbf{A}_1^\top, \mathbf{A}_2^\top, \mathbf{A}_{23}^\dagger, \mathbf{A}_1^\top\mathbf{k}, \mathbf{k} + \widehat{\mathbf{k}}, \boxed{\mathbf{A}_2^\top\mathbf{k}}) \approx_s (\mathbf{A}_1^\top, \mathbf{A}_2^\top, \mathbf{A}_{23}^\dagger, \mathbf{A}_1^\top\mathbf{k}, \mathbf{k} + \widehat{\mathbf{k}}, \mathbf{u})$$

where $\mathbf{k} \leftarrow \{0,1\}^\ell$, $\mathbf{u} \leftarrow \mathbb{Z}_p^k$ *and* $\widehat{\mathbf{k}} \leftarrow \mathsf{span}(\mathbf{A}_{23}^\dagger)$.

3.4 Proof

We prove the following technical lemma that implies Theorem 1 (see Sect. 2.2 and Lemma 1).

Lemma 4. *For all PPT adversaries* $\mathcal{A}$ *making at most* Q_C *and* Q_K *queries to* $\mathsf{O}_{\mathsf{Enc}}$ *and* $\mathsf{O}_{\mathsf{KeyGen}}$, *respectively, there exist* $\mathcal{B}_1$, $\mathcal{B}_2$, $\mathcal{B}_3$ *with* $\mathsf{Time}(\mathcal{B}_1), \mathsf{Time}(\mathcal{B}_2), \mathsf{Time}(\mathcal{B}_3) \approx \mathsf{Time}(\mathcal{A})$ *such that*

$$\begin{aligned}\mathsf{mKDMAdv}_{\mathcal{A}}^{\text{CPA}}(\lambda) \le\ & \mathsf{poly}(\ell, Q_C, Q_K) \cdot \mathsf{Adv}_{\mathcal{B}_1}^{\mathbf{MDDH}_k}(\lambda) \\ & + 2 \cdot \mathsf{Adv}_{\mathcal{B}_2}^{\text{CompHide}_{Q_C}}(\lambda) + \mathsf{Adv}_{\mathcal{B}_3}^{\mathbf{MDDH}_{k,Q_C}}(\lambda) + 1/2^\lambda.\end{aligned}$$

We prove the lemma via the following game sequence, summarized in Fig. 1. For each query (x, F) to $\mathsf{O}_{\mathsf{Enc}}$, we represent the affine function F as $(\mathbf{f}, f) \in \mathbb{Z}_p^\ell \times \mathbb{Z}_p$ and define $F([\mathbf{k}]_T) = [\mathbf{f}^\top\mathbf{k} + f]_T$. Similar to our notation of linear function in Sect. 2.3, we also use F to indicate the corresponding affine function over $\mathbb{Z}_p$, namely, $F(\mathbf{k}) = \mathbf{f}^\top\mathbf{k} + f$.

Game G_0. This game is the mKDM-CPA security game $\mathbf{mKDM}_0$. Under

$$\mathsf{mpk} = ([\mathbf{A}_1^\top]_1, [\mathbf{A}_1^\top\mathbf{W}_1]_1, \ldots, [\mathbf{A}_1^\top\mathbf{W}_n]_1, [\mathbf{B}]_2, [\mathbf{W}_1\mathbf{B}]_2, \ldots, [\mathbf{W}_n\mathbf{B}]_2, [\mathbf{A}_1^\top\mathbf{k}]_T)$$

where $\mathbf{A}_1 \leftarrow \mathbb{Z}_p^{\ell\times k}$, $\mathbf{B} \leftarrow \mathbb{Z}_p^{(k+1)\times k}$, $\mathbf{W}_1, \ldots, \mathbf{W}_n \leftarrow \mathbb{Z}_p^{\ell\times(k+1)}$ and $\mathbf{k} \leftarrow \{0,1\}^\ell$, the oracles work as follows:

- on the i-th query y_i, with $i \in [Q_K]$, $\mathsf{O}_{\mathsf{KeyGen}}$ outputs

$$\mathsf{sk}_i = ([\mathbf{d}_i]_2, \mathsf{kE}(y_i, [\mathbf{k}]_2) \cdot \mathsf{rE}(y_i, [\mathbf{W}_1\mathbf{d}_i]_2, \ldots, [\mathbf{W}_n\mathbf{d}_i]_2)), \qquad \mathbf{d}_i \leftarrow \mathsf{span}(\mathbf{B}),$$

- on the j-th query (x_j, F_j), with $j \in [Q_C]$, $\mathsf{O}_{\mathsf{Enc}}$ parses F_j as $(\mathbf{f}_j, f_j)$ and outputs

$$\mathsf{ct}_j^* = ([\mathbf{c}_j^\top]_1, \mathsf{sE}(x_j, [\mathbf{c}_j^\top\mathbf{W}_1]_1, \ldots, [\mathbf{c}_j^\top\mathbf{W}_n]_1), [\mathbf{c}_j^\top\mathbf{k} + \overbrace{\mathbf{f}_j^\top\mathbf{k} + f_j}^{F_j(\mathbf{k})}]_T),$$
$$\mathbf{c}_j \leftarrow \mathsf{span}(\mathbf{A}_1).$$

Game	sk_i	ct_j^*		Remark	Justification
	$\mathsf{kE}(y_i, ?)$	$C_{0,j}$	C_j		
0	$\mathbf{k}$	$\mathbf{c}_j^\top$	$\mathbf{c}_j^\top\mathbf{k} + \mathbf{f}_j^\top\mathbf{k} + f_j$	$\mathbf{c}_j \leftarrow \mathsf{span}(\mathbf{A}_1)$	$\mathbf{mKDM}_0$, $F_j(\mathbf{k}) = \mathbf{f}_j^\top\mathbf{k} + f_j$
1	$\mathbf{k} + \boxed{\widehat{\mathbf{k}}_i}$	$\mathbf{c}_j^\top$	$(\mathbf{c}_j^\top + \mathbf{f}_j^\top)\mathbf{k} + f_j$	$\mathbf{c}_j \leftarrow \mathsf{span}(\mathbf{A}_1, \boxed{\mathbf{A}_2})$ $\widehat{\mathbf{k}}_i \leftarrow \mathsf{span}(\mathbf{A}_2^\dagger, \mathbf{A}_3^\dagger)$	Nested dual-system argument, see Fig. 2
2	$\mathbf{k} + \widehat{\mathbf{k}}_i$	$\boxed{\mathbf{c}_j^\top - \mathbf{f}_j^\top}$	$\boxed{\mathbf{c}_j^\top}\mathbf{k} + f_j$		Lemma 2
3	$\mathbf{k} + \widehat{\mathbf{k}}_i$	$\mathbf{c}_j^\top - \mathbf{f}_j^\top$	$\overline{\mathbf{s}}_j^\top\mathbf{A}_1^\top\mathbf{k} +$ $\underline{\mathbf{s}}_j^\top\boxed{\mathbf{u}} + f_j$	$\mathbf{u}, \overline{\mathbf{s}}_j, \underline{\mathbf{s}}_j \leftarrow \mathbb{Z}_p^k$ $\mathbf{c}_j = \mathbf{A}_1\overline{\mathbf{s}}_j + \mathbf{A}_2\underline{\mathbf{s}}_j$	Lemma 3
4	$\mathbf{k} + \widehat{\mathbf{k}}_i$	$\mathbf{c}_j^\top - \mathbf{f}_j^\top$	$\boxed{m_j}$	$m_j \leftarrow \mathbb{Z}_p$	$([\underline{\mathbf{s}}_j^\top]_1, [\overline{\mathbf{s}}_j^\top\mathbf{A}_1^\top\mathbf{k} +$ $\underline{\mathbf{s}}_j^\top\mathbf{u} + f_j]_T) \approx_c$ $([\underline{\mathbf{s}}_j^\top]_1, [m_j]_T)$
5	$\mathbf{k} + \widehat{\mathbf{k}}_i$	$\mathbf{c}_j^\top - \cancel{\mathbf{f}_j^\top}$	m_j		Lemma 2
6	$\mathbf{k} + \widehat{\mathbf{k}}_i$	$\mathbf{c}_j^\top$	$\boxed{\mathbf{c}_j^\top\mathbf{k}} + m_j$		$m_j \approx_s m_j + \mathbf{c}_j^\top\mathbf{k}$
7	$\mathbf{k} + \cancel{\widehat{\mathbf{k}}_i}$	$\mathbf{c}_j^\top$	$\mathbf{c}_j^\top\mathbf{k} + m_j$	$\mathbf{c}_j \leftarrow \mathsf{span}(\mathbf{A}_1, \cancel{\mathbf{A}_2})$	$\mathbf{mKDM}_1$, analogous to G_1

Fig. 1. mKDM-CPA security proof of our ABE scheme. In column "sk_i", we let $\mathsf{sk}_i = (K_{0,i}, \vec{K}_{1,i})$ and only present the kE-part in $K_{0,i}$ and omit $[\cdot]_2$; in column "ct_j^*", we let $\mathsf{ct}_j^* = (C_{0,j}, \vec{C}_{1,j}, C_j)$, only show $C_{0,j}$, C_j and omit $[\cdot]_1$, $[\cdot]_T$, respectively. We also note that $\vec{C}_{1,j}$ in ct_j^* depends on $C_{0,j}$ in an obvious way, we do not show it in this figure.

By the definition, for all PPT adversaries $\mathcal{A}$, we have

$$\Pr[\langle \mathbf{mKDM}_0, \mathcal{A}\rangle = 1] = \Pr[\langle \mathsf{G}_0, \mathcal{A}\rangle = 1].$$

Game G_1. We modify the distribution of all $\{\mathsf{sk}_i\}_{i\in[Q_K]}$ and $\{\mathsf{ct}_j^*\}_{j\in[Q_C]}$ as follows:

$$\mathsf{sk}_i = ([\mathbf{d}_i]_2, \mathsf{kE}(y_i, [\mathbf{k} + \boxed{\widehat{\mathbf{k}}_i}]_2) \cdot \mathsf{rE}(y_i, [\mathbf{W}_1\mathbf{d}_i]_2, \ldots, [\mathbf{W}_n\mathbf{d}_i]_2)),$$
$$\mathbf{d}_i \leftarrow \mathsf{span}(\mathbf{B}), \boxed{\widehat{\mathbf{k}}_i \leftarrow \mathsf{span}(\mathbf{A}_2^\dagger, \mathbf{A}_3^\dagger)},$$
$$\mathsf{ct}_j^* = ([\mathbf{c}_j^\top]_1, \mathsf{sE}(x_j, [\mathbf{c}_j^\top\mathbf{W}_1]_1, \ldots, [\mathbf{c}_j^\top\mathbf{W}_n]_1), [(\mathbf{c}_j^\top + \mathbf{f}_j^\top)\mathbf{k} + f_j]_T),$$
$$\mathbf{c}_j \leftarrow \mathsf{span}(\mathbf{A}_1, \boxed{\mathbf{A}_2}).$$

We claim that $\mathsf{G}_0 \approx_c \mathsf{G}_1$ via nested dual system argument. In more detail, we have the following lemma and the detail will be given out in Sect. 3.5.

Lemma 5 ($\mathsf{G}_0 \approx_c \mathsf{G}_1$). *For all PPT adversaries $\mathcal{A}$, there exists $\mathcal{B}$ with* $\mathsf{Time}(\mathcal{B}) \approx \mathsf{Time}(\mathcal{A})$ *such that*

$$|\Pr[\langle \mathsf{G}_0, \mathcal{A}\rangle = 1] - \Pr[\langle \mathsf{G}_1, \mathcal{A}\rangle = 1]| \le \mathsf{poly}(\ell, Q_C, Q_K) \cdot \mathsf{Adv}_{\mathcal{B}}^{\mathbf{MDDH}_k}(\lambda).$$

Game G_2. We modify the distribution of all $\{\mathsf{ct}_j^*\}_{j\in[Q_C]}$ as follows:

$$\mathsf{ct}_j^* = ([\boxed{\mathbf{c}_j^\top - \mathbf{f}_j^\top}]_1, \mathsf{sE}(x_j, [(\boxed{\mathbf{c}_j^\top - \mathbf{f}_j^\top})\mathbf{W}_1]_1, \ldots, [(\boxed{\mathbf{c}_j^\top - \mathbf{f}_j^\top})\mathbf{W}_n]_1), [\boxed{\mathbf{c}_j^\top}\mathbf{k} + f_j]_T).$$

We claim that $\mathsf{G}_1 \approx_c \mathsf{G}_2$. This follows from Lemma 2 which states that for any $\{\mathbf{f}_j\}_{j\in[Q_C]} \in (\mathbb{Z}_p^\ell)^{Q_C}$, we have

$$\{[\mathbf{c}_j]_1\}_{j\in[Q_C]} \approx_c \{[\mathbf{c}_j - \mathbf{f}_j]_1\}_{j\in[Q_C]} \quad \text{given} \quad \mathbf{A}_1, [\mathbf{A}_2]_1, \mathsf{basis}(\mathbf{A}_2^\dagger, \mathbf{A}_3^\dagger)$$

where $\mathbf{c}_j \leftarrow \mathsf{span}(\mathbf{A}_1, \mathbf{A}_2)$. In more detail, we have the following lemma and the proof is deferred to the full paper.

Lemma 6 ($\mathsf{G}_1 \approx_c \mathsf{G}_2$)**.** *For all PPT adversaries $\mathcal{A}$, there exists $\mathcal{B}$ with* $\mathsf{Time}(\mathcal{B}) \approx \mathsf{Time}(\mathcal{A})$ *such that*

$$|\Pr[\langle \mathsf{G}_1, \mathcal{A}\rangle = 1] - \Pr[\langle \mathsf{G}_2, \mathcal{A}\rangle = 1]| \le \mathsf{Adv}_{\mathcal{B}}^{\text{COMPHIDE}_{Q_C}}(\lambda).$$

Game G_3. We modify the distribution of all $\{\mathsf{ct}_j^*\}_{j\in[Q_C]}$ as follows:

$$\mathsf{ct}_j^* = ([\mathbf{c}_j^\top - \mathbf{f}_j^\top]_1, \mathsf{sE}(x_j, [(\mathbf{c}_j^\top - \mathbf{f}_j^\top)\mathbf{W}_1]_1, \ldots, [(\mathbf{c}_j^\top - \mathbf{f}_j^\top)\mathbf{W}_n]_1), [\bar{\mathbf{s}}_j^\top \mathbf{A}_1^\top \mathbf{k} + \underline{\mathbf{s}}_j^\top \boxed{\mathbf{u}} + f_j]_T)$$

where $\mathbf{u}, \bar{\mathbf{s}}_j, \underline{\mathbf{s}}_j \leftarrow \mathbb{Z}_p^k$ and $\mathbf{c}_j = \mathbf{A}_1\bar{\mathbf{s}}_j + \mathbf{A}_2\underline{\mathbf{s}}_j$. We claim that $\mathsf{G}_2 \approx_s \mathsf{G}_3$. This follows from Lemma 3 which asserts that, with probability $1 - 1/2^\lambda$, it holds that

$$(\underbrace{\overbrace{\mathbf{A}_1^\top, \mathbf{A}_1^\top\mathbf{k}}^{\mathsf{mpk}}, \mathbf{A}_2^\top, \boxed{\mathbf{A}_2^\top\mathbf{k}}}_{\mathsf{ct}_j^*}, \overbrace{\mathbf{A}_{23}^\dagger, \mathbf{k} + \widehat{\mathbf{k}}}^{\mathsf{sk}_i}) \approx_s (\mathbf{A}_1^\top, \mathbf{A}_1^\top\mathbf{k}, \mathbf{A}_2^\top, \mathbf{u}, \mathbf{A}_{23}^\dagger, \mathbf{k} + \widehat{\mathbf{k}})$$

where $\mathbf{k} \leftarrow \{0,1\}^\ell$, $\mathbf{u} \leftarrow \mathbb{Z}_p^k$ and $\widehat{\mathbf{k}} \leftarrow \mathsf{span}(\mathbf{A}_{23}^\dagger)$. Here we use $\mathbf{A}_1^\top$, $\mathbf{A}_1^\top\mathbf{k}$ to simulate mpk; all $\{\mathsf{ct}_j^*\}_{j\in[Q_C]}$ are simulated additionally with $\mathbf{A}_2^\top$, $\mathbf{A}_2^\top\mathbf{k}$ or $\mathbf{u}$; all $\{\mathsf{sk}_i\}_{i\in[Q_K]}$ are simulated using $(\mathbf{k} + \widehat{\mathbf{k}}) + \widetilde{\mathbf{k}}_i$ with $\widetilde{\mathbf{k}}_i \leftarrow \mathsf{span}(\mathbf{A}_{23}^\dagger)$, namely we implicitly set $\widehat{\mathbf{k}}_i = \widehat{\mathbf{k}} + \widetilde{\mathbf{k}}_i$. In more detail, we have the following lemma and the proof is deferred to the full paper.

Lemma 7 ($\mathsf{G}_2 \approx_s \mathsf{G}_3$)**.** *For all PPT adversaries $\mathcal{A}$,*

$$|\Pr[\langle \mathsf{G}_2, \mathcal{A}\rangle = 1] - \Pr[\langle \mathsf{G}_3, \mathcal{A}\rangle = 1]| \le 1/2^\lambda.$$

Game G_4. We modify the distribution of all $\{\mathsf{ct}_j^*\}_{j\in[Q_C]}$ as follows:

$$\mathsf{ct}_j^* = ([\mathbf{c}_j^\top - \mathbf{f}_j^\top]_1, \mathsf{sE}(x_j, [(\mathbf{c}_j^\top - \mathbf{f}_j^\top)\mathbf{W}_1]_1, \ldots, [(\mathbf{c}_j^\top - \mathbf{f}_j^\top)\mathbf{W}_n]_1), [\boxed{m_j}]_T), \qquad m_j \leftarrow \mathbb{Z}_p,$$

where $\mathbf{c}_j \leftarrow \mathsf{span}(\mathbf{A}_1, \mathbf{A}_2)$. We claim that $\mathsf{G}_3 \approx_c \mathsf{G}_4$. This follows from $\mathbf{MDDH}_{k,Q_C}$ which implies that, for all $\{\bar{\mathbf{s}}_j^\top\mathbf{A}_1^\top\mathbf{k} + f_j\}_{j\in[Q_C]} \in \mathbb{Z}_p^{Q_C}$ with $\bar{\mathbf{s}}_j \in \mathbb{Z}_p^k$, we have

$$\{[\underline{\mathbf{s}}_j^\top]_1, [\bar{\mathbf{s}}_j^\top\mathbf{A}_1^\top\mathbf{k} + \underline{\mathbf{s}}_j^\top\mathbf{u} + f_j]_T\}_{j\in[Q_C]} \approx_c \{[\underline{\mathbf{s}}_j^\top]_1, [m_j]_T\}_{j\in[Q_C]}$$

where $\mathbf{u}, \underline{\mathbf{s}}_j \leftarrow \mathbb{Z}_p^k$ and $m_j \leftarrow \mathbb{Z}_p$. Note that we will set $\mathbf{c}_j = \mathbf{A}_1\bar{\mathbf{s}}_j + \mathbf{A}_2\underline{\mathbf{s}}_j$. In more detail, we have the following lemma and the proof is deferred to the full paper.

Lemma 8 ($\mathsf{G}_3 \approx_c \mathsf{G}_4$). *For all PPT adversaries $\mathcal{A}$, there exists $\mathcal{B}$ with* $\mathsf{Time}(\mathcal{B}) \approx \mathsf{Time}(\mathcal{A})$ *such that*

$$|\Pr[\langle \mathsf{G}_3, \mathcal{A}\rangle = 1] - \Pr[\langle \mathsf{G}_4, \mathcal{A}\rangle = 1]| \leq \mathsf{Adv}_{\mathcal{B}}^{\mathbf{MDDH}_{k,Q_C}}(\lambda).$$

Game G_5. We modify the distribution of all $\{\mathsf{ct}_j^*\}_{j\in[Q_C]}$ as follows:

$$\mathsf{ct}_j^* = ([\mathbf{c}_j^\top - \cancel{\mathbf{f}_j^\top}]_1, \mathsf{sE}(x_j, [(\mathbf{c}_j^\top - \cancel{\mathbf{f}_j^\top})\mathbf{W}_1]_1, \ldots, [(\mathbf{c}_j^\top - \cancel{\mathbf{f}_j^\top})\mathbf{W}_n]_1), [m_j]_T), \qquad m_j \leftarrow \mathbb{Z}_p.$$

We claim that $\mathsf{G}_4 \approx_c \mathsf{G}_5$ via Lemma 2 that is analogous to $\mathsf{G}_1 \approx_c \mathsf{G}_2$. In more detail, we have the following lemma and the proof is deferred to the full paper.

Lemma 9 ($\mathsf{G}_4 \approx_c \mathsf{G}_5$). *For all PPT adversaries $\mathcal{A}$, there exists $\mathcal{B}$ with* $\mathsf{Time}(\mathcal{B}) \approx \mathsf{Time}(\mathcal{A})$ *such that*

$$|\Pr[\langle \mathsf{G}_4, \mathcal{A}\rangle = 1] - \Pr[\langle \mathsf{G}_5, \mathcal{A}\rangle = 1]| \leq \mathsf{Adv}_{\mathcal{B}}^{\textsc{CompHide}_{Q_C}}(\lambda).$$

Game G_6. We modify the distribution of all $\{\mathsf{ct}_j^*\}_{j\in[Q_C]}$ as follows:

$$\mathsf{ct}_j^* = ([\mathbf{c}_j^\top]_1, \mathsf{sE}(x_j, [\mathbf{c}_j^\top \mathbf{W}_1]_1, \ldots, [\mathbf{c}_j^\top \mathbf{W}_n]_1), [\boxed{\mathbf{c}_j^\top \mathbf{k}} + m_j]_T).$$

We claim that $\mathsf{G}_5 \approx_s \mathsf{G}_6$. This follows from the fact that, for all $\mathbf{c}_j \leftarrow \mathsf{span}(\mathbf{A}_1, \mathbf{A}_2)$ and $\mathbf{k} \leftarrow \{0,1\}^\ell$, it holds that

$$\{m_j\}_{j\in[Q_C]} \approx_s \{m_j + \mathbf{c}_j^\top \mathbf{k}\}_{j\in[Q_C]}$$

where $m_j \leftarrow \mathbb{Z}_p$. In more detail, we have the following lemma and the proof is deferred to the full paper.

Lemma 10 ($\mathsf{G}_5 \approx_s \mathsf{G}_6$). *For all PPT adversaries $\mathcal{A}$,*

$$\Pr[\langle \mathsf{G}_5, \mathcal{A}\rangle = 1] = \Pr[\langle \mathsf{G}_6, \mathcal{A}\rangle = 1].$$

Game G_7. We modify the distribution of all $\{\mathsf{sk}_i\}_{i\in[Q_K]}$ and $\{\mathsf{ct}_j^*\}_{j\in[Q_C]}$ as follows:

$$\mathsf{sk}_i = ([\mathbf{d}_i]_2, \mathsf{kE}(y_i, [\mathbf{k} + \cancel{\widehat{\mathbf{k}}_i}]_2) \cdot \mathsf{rE}(y_i, [\mathbf{W}_1\mathbf{d}_i]_2, \ldots, [\mathbf{W}_n\mathbf{d}_i]_2)),$$
$$\mathsf{ct}_j^* = ([\mathbf{c}_j^\top]_1, \mathsf{sE}(x_j, [\mathbf{c}_j^\top \mathbf{W}_1]_1, \ldots, [\mathbf{c}_j^\top \mathbf{W}_n]_1), [\mathbf{c}_j^\top \mathbf{k} + m_j]_T), \qquad \mathbf{c}_j \leftarrow \mathsf{span}(\mathbf{A}_1, \cancel{\mathbf{A}_2}).$$

We claim that $\mathsf{G}_6 \approx_c \mathsf{G}_7$ via nested dual system argument that is analogous to $\mathsf{G}_0 \approx_c \mathsf{G}_1$. In more detail, we have the following lemma and the detail will be given out in Sect. 3.5.

Lemma 11 ($\mathsf{G}_6 \approx_c \mathsf{G}_7$). *For all PPT adversaries $\mathcal{A}$, there exists $\mathcal{B}$ with* $\mathsf{Time}(\mathcal{B}) \approx \mathsf{Time}(\mathcal{A})$ *such that*

$$|\Pr[\langle \mathsf{G}_6, \mathcal{A}\rangle = 1] - \Pr[\langle \mathsf{G}_7, \mathcal{A}\rangle = 1]| \leq \mathsf{poly}(\ell, Q_C, Q_K) \cdot \mathsf{Adv}_{\mathcal{B}}^{\mathbf{MDDH}_k}(\lambda).$$

Furthermore, G_7 is exactly the same as mKDM-CPA security game $\mathbf{mKDM}_1$. By the definition, for all PPT adversaries $\mathcal{A}$, we have

$$\Pr[\langle \mathsf{G}_7, \mathcal{A}\rangle = 1] = \Pr[\langle \mathbf{mKDM}_1, \mathcal{A}\rangle = 1].$$

This completes the proof of Lemma 4 that implies Theorem 1.

3.5 Nested Dual-System Argument

Overview. This section proves Lemma 5 ($\mathsf{G}_0 \approx_c \mathsf{G}_1$) and Lemma 11 ($\mathsf{G}_6 \approx_c \mathsf{G}_7$). As both arguments are irrelevant to $\mathbf{k}$, we will neglect $\mathbf{k}$-related terms $[(\mathbf{c}_j^\top + \mathbf{f}_j^\top)\mathbf{k} + f_j]_T$ or $[\mathbf{c}_j^\top \mathbf{k} + m_j]_T$ in ct_j^* and $\mathsf{kE}(y_i, [\mathbf{k}]_2)$ in sk_i for now. More concretely, we will focus on the following statement that allows us to simulate the actual ciphertexts and secret keys in Lemma 5 and Lemma 11.

$$\begin{pmatrix} \mathsf{mpk}: [\mathbf{A}_1^\top]_1, [\mathbf{A}_1^\top \mathbf{W}_1]_1, \ldots, [\mathbf{A}_1^\top \mathbf{W}_n]_1, [\mathbf{B}]_2, [\mathbf{W}_1 \mathbf{B}]_2, \ldots, [\mathbf{W}_n \mathbf{B}]_2 \\ \mathsf{sk}_i : [\mathbf{d}_i]_2, \boxed{\mathsf{rE}(y_i, [\mathbf{W}_1 \mathbf{d}_i]_2, \ldots, [\mathbf{W}_n \mathbf{d}_i]_2)}, \quad \mathbf{d}_i \leftarrow \mathsf{span}(\mathbf{B}) \\ \mathsf{ct}_j^* : [\mathbf{c}_j^\top]_1, \mathsf{sE}(x_j, [\mathbf{c}_j^\top \mathbf{W}_1]_1, \ldots, [\mathbf{c}_j^\top \mathbf{W}_n]_1), \quad \boxed{\mathbf{c}_j \leftarrow \mathsf{span}(\mathbf{A}_1)} \end{pmatrix} \approx_c$$
$$\begin{pmatrix} \mathsf{mpk}: [\mathbf{A}_1^\top]_1, [\mathbf{A}_1^\top \mathbf{W}_1]_1, \ldots, [\mathbf{A}_1^\top \mathbf{W}_n]_1, [\mathbf{B}]_2, [\mathbf{W}_1 \mathbf{B}]_2, \ldots, [\mathbf{W}_n \mathbf{B}]_2 \\ \mathsf{sk}_i : [\mathbf{d}_i]_2, \mathsf{kE}(y_i, [\widehat{\mathbf{k}}_i]_2) \cdot \mathsf{rE}(y_i, [\mathbf{W}_1 \mathbf{d}_i]_2, \ldots, [\mathbf{W}_n \mathbf{d}_i]_2), \quad \mathbf{d}_i \leftarrow \mathsf{span}(\mathbf{B}) \\ \mathsf{ct}_j^* : [\mathbf{c}_j^\top]_1, \mathsf{sE}(x_j, [\mathbf{c}_j^\top \mathbf{W}_1]_1, \ldots, [\mathbf{c}_j^\top \mathbf{W}_n]_1), \quad \mathbf{c}_j \leftarrow \mathsf{span}(\mathbf{A}_{12}) \end{pmatrix} \tag{15}$$

where indices i and j go over $[Q_K]$ and $[Q_C]$, respectively; $\mathbf{W}_1, \ldots, \mathbf{W}_n \leftarrow \mathbb{Z}_p^{\ell \times (k+1)}$, $\widehat{\mathbf{k}}_i \leftarrow \mathsf{span}(\mathbf{A}_2^\dagger, \mathbf{A}_3^\dagger)$. Observe that

- for Lemma 5, LHS and RHS in (15) correspond to G_0 and G_1, respectively; we can simulate the omitted terms $[(\mathbf{c}_j^\top + \mathbf{f}_j^\top)\mathbf{k} + f_j]_T$ and $\mathsf{kE}(y_i, [\mathbf{k}]_2)$ by sampling $\mathbf{k} \leftarrow \{0,1\}^\ell$ by ourselves;
- for Lemma 11, LHS and RHS in (15) correspond to G_7 and G_6, respectively; we can simulate the omitted terms $[\mathbf{c}_j^\top \mathbf{k} + m_j]_T$ and $\mathsf{kE}(y_i, [\mathbf{k}]_2)$ by sampling $\mathbf{k} \leftarrow \{0,1\}^\ell$ and $m_j \leftarrow \mathbb{Z}_p$ by ourselves;

More formally, let $\mathsf{Adv}^{\text{NesDualSys}}(\lambda)$ be the advantage function of distinguishing LHS and RHS in (15).

Bounding $\mathsf{Adv}^{\text{NesDualSys}}(\lambda)$. In the remaining of this section, we bound $\mathsf{Adv}^{\text{NesDualSys}}(\lambda)$ as follow:

Lemma 12. *For all PPT adversaries $\mathcal{A}$, there exists $\mathcal{B}$ with $\mathsf{Time}(\mathcal{B}) \approx \mathsf{Time}(\mathcal{A})$ such that*

$$\begin{aligned} \mathsf{Adv}_{\mathcal{A}}^{\text{NesDualSys}}(\lambda) &\leq 4Q_K \cdot \mathsf{Adv}^{\mathbf{MDDH}_k}(\lambda) + Q_C \cdot \Big(\mathsf{Adv}^{\mathbf{SD}_{\mathbf{A}_1 \mapsto \mathbf{A}_{13}}}(\lambda) \\ &\quad + 4Q_K \cdot \mathsf{Adv}^{\mathbf{MDDH}_k}(\lambda) + \mathsf{Adv}^{\mathbf{SD}_{\mathbf{A}_3 \mapsto \mathbf{A}_2}}(\lambda)\Big) \\ &\leq \mathsf{poly}(\ell, Q_K, Q_C) \cdot \mathsf{Adv}_{\mathcal{B}}^{\mathbf{MDDH}_k}(\lambda). \end{aligned}$$

This readily proves Lemma 5 and Lemma 11. To prove the lemma, we use the following game sequence, summarized in Fig. 2, and prove that

$$\mathsf{H}_0 \approx_c \mathsf{H}_{1.0} \approx_c \cdots \approx_c \mathsf{H}_{1.4} = \mathsf{H}_{2.0} \approx_c \cdots \approx_c \mathsf{H}_{Q_C.4} \approx_c \mathsf{H}_{Q_C+1}$$

Game	sk_i	ct_j^*			Justification
	$\widehat{\mathbf{k}}_i \leftarrow \mathsf{span}(?)$	$\mathbf{c}_j \leftarrow \mathsf{span}(\mathbf{A}_1, ?)$			
		$j < \jmath$	$j = \jmath$	$j > \jmath$	
0	—	—			LHS in (15)
$\jmath.0$	$\mathbf{A}_2^{\dagger}$	$\mathbf{A}_2$	—		α-privacy, cf. [CGW15] for $\jmath = 1$; $\mathsf{H}_{\jmath.0} = \mathsf{H}_{\jmath-1.4}$ for $\jmath > 1$
$\jmath.1$	$\mathbf{A}_2^{\dagger}$	$\mathbf{A}_2$	$\mathbf{A}_3$	—	$(\mathbf{A}_2^{\dagger}, [\mathsf{span}(\mathbf{A}_1)]_1) \approx_c (\mathbf{A}_2^{\dagger}, [\mathsf{span}(\mathbf{A}_1, \mathbf{A}_3)]_1)$
$\jmath.2$	$\mathbf{A}_2^{\dagger}, \mathbf{A}_3^{\dagger}$	$\mathbf{A}_2$	$\mathbf{A}_3$	—	α-privacy, cf. [CGW15]
$\jmath.3$	$\mathbf{A}_2^{\dagger}, \mathbf{A}_3^{\dagger}$	$\mathbf{A}_2$	$\mathbf{A}_2$	—	$(\mathsf{basis}(\mathbf{A}_2^{\dagger}, \mathbf{A}_3^{\dagger}), [\mathsf{span}(\mathbf{A}_3)]_1) \approx_c (\mathsf{basis}(\mathbf{A}_2^{\dagger}, \mathbf{A}_3^{\dagger}), [\mathsf{span}(\mathbf{A}_2)]_1)$
$\jmath.4$	$\mathbf{A}_2^{\dagger}$	$\mathbf{A}_2$		—	analogous to $\mathsf{H}_{\jmath.2}$
$Q_C + 1$	$\mathbf{A}_2^{\dagger}, \mathbf{A}_3^{\dagger}$	$\mathbf{A}_2$			RHS in (15), analogous to $\mathsf{H}_{\jmath.2}$

Fig. 2. Game sequence for nested dual-system argument ($\jmath \in [Q_C]$)

where "=" and "$\approx_c$" mean two games are exactly identical and computationally indistinguishable, respectively.

Game H_0. In this game, the adversary $\mathcal{A}$ is given LHS in (15).

Game $\mathsf{H}_{\jmath.0}(\jmath \in [Q_C])$. In this game, the distribution of all $\{\mathsf{sk}_i\}_{i \in [Q_K]}$ and $\{\mathsf{ct}_j^*\}_{j \in [Q_C]}$ is as follows:

$$\mathsf{sk}_i : [\mathbf{d}_i]_2, \boxed{\mathsf{kE}(y_i, [\widehat{\mathbf{k}}_i]_2)} \cdot \mathsf{rE}(y_i, [\mathbf{W}_1\mathbf{d}_i]_2, \ldots, [\mathbf{W}_n\mathbf{d}_i]_2),$$
$$\mathbf{d}_i \leftarrow \mathsf{span}(\mathbf{B}),\ \widehat{\mathbf{k}}_i \leftarrow \mathsf{span}(\mathbf{A}_2^{\dagger}),$$
$$\mathsf{ct}_j^*(j < \jmath) : [\mathbf{c}_j^{\top}]_1, \mathsf{sE}(x_j, [\mathbf{c}_j^{\top}\mathbf{W}_1]_1, \ldots, [\mathbf{c}_j^{\top}\mathbf{W}_n]_1), \qquad \mathbf{c}_j \leftarrow \mathsf{span}(\mathbf{A}_1, \mathbf{A}_2),$$
$$\mathsf{ct}_j^*(j = \jmath) : [\mathbf{c}_j^{\top}]_1, \mathsf{sE}(x_j, [\mathbf{c}_j^{\top}\mathbf{W}_1]_1, \ldots, [\mathbf{c}_j^{\top}\mathbf{W}_n]_1), \qquad \mathbf{c}_j \leftarrow \mathsf{span}(\mathbf{A}_1),$$
$$\mathsf{ct}_j^*(j > \jmath) : [\mathbf{c}_j^{\top}]_1, \mathsf{sE}(x_j, [\mathbf{c}_j^{\top}\mathbf{W}_1]_1, \ldots, [\mathbf{c}_j^{\top}\mathbf{W}_n]_1), \qquad \mathbf{c}_j \leftarrow \mathsf{span}(\mathbf{A}_1).$$

We note that $\mathsf{H}_{\jmath.0} = \mathsf{H}_{\jmath-1.4}$ for $\jmath > 1$. Furthermore, we claim that $\mathsf{H}_0 \approx_c \mathsf{H}_{1.0}$. This follows from the dual-system argument in [CGW15]: first switch $\mathbf{d}_i$ to $\mathbb{Z}_p^{k+1}$ by $\mathbf{MDDH}_k$ assumption stating that

$$([\mathbf{B}]_2, [\mathsf{span}(\mathbf{B})]_2) \approx_c ([\mathbf{B}]_2, [\mathbb{Z}_p^{k+1}]_2),$$

program $\mathbf{W}_t$ for all $t \in [n]$ via the change of variable

$$\mathbf{W}_t \mapsto \mathbf{W}_t + \mathbf{A}_2^{\dagger}\mathbf{w}_t(\mathbf{b}^{\dagger})^{\top} \quad \text{where} \quad \mathbf{w}_t \leftarrow \mathbb{Z}_p^{\ell_2}$$

ensuring $\mathbf{w}_t$ only leaked by sk_i, then use α-privacy of predicate encoding with $\mathbf{w}_t$ (cf. (9)), finally switch $\mathbf{d}_i$ back by $\mathbf{MDDH}_k$ assumption again. In more detail, we have the following lemma and the proof is deferred to the full paper.

Lemma 13 ($\mathsf{H}_0 \approx_c \mathsf{H}_{1.0}$). *For all PPT adversaries $\mathcal{A}$, there exists $\mathcal{B}$ with* $\mathsf{Time}(\mathcal{B}) \approx \mathsf{Time}(\mathcal{A})$ *such that*

$$|\Pr[\langle \mathsf{H}_0, \mathcal{A}\rangle = 1] - \Pr[\langle \mathsf{H}_{1.0}, \mathcal{A}\rangle = 1]| \leq 2Q_K \cdot \mathsf{Adv}^{\mathbf{MDDH}_k}(\lambda).$$

Game $\mathsf{H}_{\hat{\jmath}.1}(\hat{\jmath} \in [Q_C])$. We change the distribution of ct_j^* for $j = \hat{\jmath}$ as follows:

$$\mathsf{ct}_j^*(j = \hat{\jmath}) : [\mathbf{c}_j^\top]_1, \mathsf{sE}(x_j, [\mathbf{c}_j^\top \mathbf{W}_1]_1, \ldots, [\mathbf{c}_j^\top \mathbf{W}_n]_1), \qquad \mathbf{c}_j \leftarrow \mathsf{span}(\mathbf{A}_1, \boxed{\mathbf{A}_3}).$$

We claim that $\mathsf{H}_{\hat{\jmath}.0} \approx_c \mathsf{H}_{\hat{\jmath}.1}$ for all $\hat{\jmath} \in [Q_C]$ by $\mathbf{SD}_{\mathbf{A}_1 \mapsto \mathbf{A}_{13}}$ assumption (cf. Lemma 1). In more detail, we have the following lemma and the proof is deferred to the full paper.

Lemma 14 ($\mathsf{H}_{\hat{\jmath}.0} \approx_c \mathsf{H}_{\hat{\jmath}.1}$). *For all PPT adversaries $\mathcal{A}$, there exists $\mathcal{B}$ with* $\mathsf{Time}(\mathcal{B}) \approx \mathsf{Time}(\mathcal{A})$ *such that*

$$|\Pr[\langle \mathsf{H}_{\hat{\jmath}.0}, \mathcal{A}\rangle = 1] - \Pr[\langle \mathsf{H}_{\hat{\jmath}.1}, \mathcal{A}\rangle = 1]| \leq \mathsf{Adv}_{\mathcal{B}}^{\mathbf{SD}_{\mathbf{A}_1 \mapsto \mathbf{A}_{13}}}(\lambda).$$

Game $\mathsf{H}_{\hat{\jmath}.2}(\hat{\jmath} \in [Q_C])$. We change the distribution of all $\{\mathsf{sk}_i\}_{i \in [Q_K]}$ as follows:

$$\mathsf{sk}_i : [\mathbf{d}_i]_2, \mathsf{kE}(y_i, [\widehat{\mathbf{k}}_i]_2) \cdot \mathsf{rE}(y_i, [\mathbf{W}_1 \mathbf{d}_i]_2, \ldots, [\mathbf{W}_n \mathbf{d}_i]_2), \qquad \widehat{\mathbf{k}}_i \leftarrow \mathsf{span}(\mathbf{A}_2^\dagger, \boxed{\mathbf{A}_3^\dagger}).$$

We claim that $\mathsf{H}_{\hat{\jmath}.1} \approx_c \mathsf{H}_{\hat{\jmath}.2}$ for all $\hat{\jmath} \in [Q_C]$. This is analogous to $\mathsf{H}_0 \approx_c \mathsf{H}_{1.0}$ except that we ensure $\mathbf{w}_t$ only leaked by sk_i and $\mathsf{ct}_{\hat{\jmath}}$ and then use α-privacy of predicate encoding with $\mathbf{w}_t$ (cf. (9)). In more detail, we have the following lemma and the proof is deferred to the full paper.

Lemma 15 ($\mathsf{H}_{\hat{\jmath}.1} \approx_c \mathsf{H}_{\hat{\jmath}.2}$). *For all PPT adversaries $\mathcal{A}$, there exists $\mathcal{B}$ with* $\mathsf{Time}(\mathcal{B}) \approx \mathsf{Time}(\mathcal{A})$ *such that*

$$|\Pr[\langle \mathsf{H}_{\hat{\jmath}.1}, \mathcal{A}\rangle = 1] - \Pr[\langle \mathsf{H}_{\hat{\jmath}.2}, \mathcal{A}\rangle = 1]| \leq 2Q_K \cdot \mathsf{Adv}_{\mathcal{B}}^{\mathbf{MDDH}_k}(\lambda).$$

Game $\mathsf{H}_{\hat{\jmath}.3}(\hat{\jmath} \in [Q_C])$. We change the distribution of ct_j^* for $j = \hat{\jmath}$ as follows:

$$\mathsf{ct}_j^*(j = \hat{\jmath}) : [\mathbf{c}_j^\top]_1, \mathsf{sE}(x_j, [\mathbf{c}_j^\top \mathbf{W}_1]_1, \ldots, [\mathbf{c}_j^\top \mathbf{W}_n]_1), \qquad \mathbf{c}_j \leftarrow \mathsf{span}(\mathbf{A}_1, \boxed{\mathbf{A}_2}).$$

We claim that $\mathsf{H}_{\hat{\jmath}.2} \approx_c \mathsf{H}_{\hat{\jmath}.3}$ for all $\hat{\jmath} \in [Q_C]$ by $\mathbf{SD}_{\mathbf{A}_3 \mapsto \mathbf{A}_2}$ assumption (cf. Lemma 1). In more detail, we have the following lemma and the proof is deferred to the full paper.

Lemma 16 ($\mathsf{H}_{\hat{\jmath}.2} \approx_c \mathsf{H}_{\hat{\jmath}.3}$). *For all PPT adversaries $\mathcal{A}$, there exists $\mathcal{B}$ with* $\mathsf{Time}(\mathcal{B}) \approx \mathsf{Time}(\mathcal{A})$ *such that*

$$|\Pr[\langle \mathsf{H}_{\hat{\jmath}.2}, \mathcal{A}\rangle = 1] - \Pr[\langle \mathsf{H}_{\hat{\jmath}.3}, \mathcal{A}\rangle = 1]| \leq \mathsf{Adv}_{\mathcal{B}}^{\mathbf{SD}_{\mathbf{A}_3 \mapsto \mathbf{A}_2}}(\lambda).$$

Game $\mathsf{H}_{\jmath.4}(\jmath \in [Q_C])$. We change the distribution of all $\{\mathsf{sk}_i\}_{i\in[Q_K]}$ as follows:

$$\mathsf{sk}_i : [\mathbf{d}_i]_2, \mathsf{kE}(y_i, [\widehat{\mathbf{k}}_i]_2) \cdot \mathsf{rE}(y_i, [\mathbf{W}_1\mathbf{d}_i]_2, \ldots, [\mathbf{W}_n\mathbf{d}_i]_2), \qquad \widehat{\mathbf{k}}_i \leftarrow \mathsf{span}(\mathbf{A}_2^\dagger, \cancel{\mathbf{A}_3^\dagger}).$$

We claim that $\mathsf{H}_{\jmath.3} \approx_c \mathsf{H}_{\jmath.4}$ for all $\jmath \in [Q_C]$. This is analogous to $\mathsf{H}_{\jmath.1} \approx_c \mathsf{H}_{\jmath.2}$. In more detail, we have the following lemma and the proof is deferred to the full paper. We note that $\mathsf{H}_{\jmath.4}$ is exactly the same as $\mathsf{H}_{\jmath+1.1}$ for all $\jmath \in [Q_C - 1]$.

Lemma 17 ($\mathsf{H}_{\jmath.3} \approx_c \mathsf{H}_{\jmath.4}$). *For all PPT adversaries $\mathcal{A}$, there exists $\mathcal{B}$ with* $\mathsf{Time}(\mathcal{B}) \approx \mathsf{Time}(\mathcal{A})$ *such that*

$$|\Pr[\langle \mathsf{H}_{\jmath.3}, \mathcal{A}\rangle = 1] - \Pr[\langle \mathsf{H}_{\jmath.4}, \mathcal{A}\rangle = 1]| \leq 2Q_K \cdot \mathsf{Adv}_{\mathcal{B}}^{\mathbf{MDDH}_k}(\lambda).$$

Game H_{Q_C+1}. We change the distribution of all $\{\mathsf{sk}_i\}_{i\in[Q_K]}$ as follows:

$$\mathsf{sk}_i : [\mathbf{d}_i]_2, \mathsf{kE}(y_i, [\widehat{\mathbf{k}}_i]_2) \cdot \mathsf{rE}(y_i, [\mathbf{W}_1\mathbf{d}_i]_2, \ldots, [\mathbf{W}_n\mathbf{d}_i]_2), \qquad \widehat{\mathbf{k}}_i \leftarrow \mathsf{span}(\mathbf{A}_2^\dagger, \boxed{\mathbf{A}_3^\dagger}).$$

We claim that $\mathsf{H}_{Q_C.4} \approx_c \mathsf{H}_{Q_C+1}$. This is analogous to $\mathsf{H}_{\jmath.1} \approx_c \mathsf{H}_{\jmath.2}$. In more detail, we have the following lemma and the proof is deferred to the full paper.

Lemma 18 ($\mathsf{H}_{Q_C.4} \approx_c \mathsf{H}_{Q_C+1}$). *For all PPT adversaries $\mathcal{A}$, there exists $\mathcal{B}$ with* $\mathsf{Time}(\mathcal{B}) \approx \mathsf{Time}(\mathcal{A})$ *such that*

$$|\Pr[\langle \mathsf{H}_{Q_C.4}, \mathcal{A}\rangle = 1] - \Pr[\langle \mathsf{H}_{Q_C+1}, \mathcal{A}\rangle = 1]| \leq 2Q_K \cdot \mathsf{Adv}_{\mathcal{B}}^{\mathbf{MDDH}_k}(\lambda).$$

We note that H_{Q_C+1} is exactly the same as RHS in (15). This is sufficient to bound $\mathsf{Adv}^{\textsc{NesDualSys}}(\lambda)$.

4 Delegation

In this section, we will show how to support delegable predicates. A predicate $P : \mathcal{X} \times \mathcal{Y} \to \{0,1\}$ is said to be delegable if there exists a *strong partial ordering* $\prec$ on $\mathcal{Y}$ such that

$$(y' \prec y) \wedge P(x, y') = 1 \implies P(x, y) = 1 \qquad \forall x \in \mathcal{X}.$$

Delegation in ABE. An ABE scheme for a delegable predicate $P : \mathcal{X} \times \mathcal{Y} \to \{0,1\}$ consists of algorithms Setup, KeyGen, Enc, Dec as defined in Sect. 2.1 and an extra delegation algorithm:

- $\mathsf{Del}(\mathsf{mpk}, \mathsf{sk}_y, y') \to \mathsf{sk}_{y'}$. The delegation algorithm takes as input the master public key mpk, a secret key sk_y for $y \in \mathcal{Y}$ and a $y' \in \mathcal{Y}$ satisfying $y' \prec y$, outputs a secret key $\mathsf{sk}_{y'}$ for y'.

We further require that, for all $y, y' \in \mathcal{Y}$ satisfying $y' \prec y$, it holds that

$$\{\,\mathsf{sk}_{y'} \leftarrow \mathsf{Del}(\mathsf{mpk}, \mathsf{KeyGen}(\mathsf{mpk}, \mathsf{msk}, y), y')\,\} \equiv \{\,\mathsf{sk}_{y'} \leftarrow \mathsf{KeyGen}(\mathsf{mpk}, \mathsf{msk}, y')\,\}$$

If it does not hold, one should turn to the security model described in [SW08].

Delegable Predicate Encoding. A $\mathbb{Z}_p$-linear predicate encoding for delegable predicate P is composed of algorithms $\mathsf{sE}, \mathsf{sD}, \mathsf{rE}, \mathsf{kE}, \mathsf{rD}$ and an extra algorithm

$$\mathsf{dE} : \mathcal{Y} \times \mathcal{Y} \times \mathbb{Z}_p^{n_r} \to \mathbb{Z}_p^{n'_r}$$

with the following features:

(linearity). For all $y, y' \in \mathcal{Y}$, $\mathsf{dE}(y, y', \cdot)$ is $\mathbb{Z}_p$-linear (see Eq. (7)).
(delegability). For all $y, y' \in \mathcal{Y}$ with $y' \prec y$, $\alpha \in \mathbb{Z}_p$ and $\mathbf{w} \leftarrow \mathbb{Z}_p^n$, it holds

$$\mathsf{dE}(y, y', \mathsf{kE}(y, \alpha) + \mathsf{rE}(y, \mathbf{w})) = \mathsf{kE}(y', \alpha) + \mathsf{rE}(y', \mathbf{w}). \tag{16}$$

Example for n-level HIBE [BBG05]**.** In a n-level HIBE with $\mathcal{X} = \mathcal{Y} = \mathbb{Z}_p^n$, if $\mathbf{y}$ is a prefix of $\mathbf{y}'$ then we say $\mathbf{y}' \prec \mathbf{y}$. Let $\mathbf{x} = (x_1, \dots, x_{n_x})$, $\mathbf{y} = (y_1, \dots, y_{n_y})$, $\mathbf{y}' = (y_1, \dots, y_{n'_y})$ for $n_x, n_y, n'_y \le n$ and $\mathbf{y}' \prec \mathbf{y}$. Let $\mathbf{w} \leftarrow \mathbb{Z}_p^{1\times(n+1)}$, we have

$$\mathsf{sE}(\mathbf{x}, \mathbf{w}) := \mathbf{w} \left(1 \ \mathbf{x} \ \mathbf{0}_{n-n_x}\right)^\top \qquad \mathsf{sD}(\mathbf{x}, \mathbf{y}, c) := c$$

$$\mathsf{rE}(\mathbf{y}, \mathbf{w}) := \mathbf{w} \begin{pmatrix} 1 \ \mathbf{y} & \\ & \mathbf{I}_{n-n_y} \end{pmatrix}^\top \qquad \mathsf{rD}(\mathbf{x}, \mathbf{y}, \mathbf{k}) := \mathbf{k} \left(1 \ x_{n_y+1} \ \cdots \ x_{n_x} \ \mathbf{0}_{n-n_x}\right)^\top$$

$$\mathsf{kE}(\mathbf{y}, \alpha) := \left(\alpha \ \mathbf{0}_{n-n_y}\right) \qquad \mathsf{dE}(\mathbf{y}, \mathbf{y}', \mathbf{k}') := \mathbf{k}' \begin{pmatrix} 1 \ y_{n_y} \ \cdots \ y_{n'_y} & \\ & \mathbf{I}_{n-n'_y} \end{pmatrix}^\top$$

Scheme. Our delegable ABE scheme is basically the ABE scheme in Sect. 3.2 equipped with an additional algorithm Del that works as follows:

– $\mathsf{Del}(\mathsf{mpk}, \mathsf{sk}_y, y')$: Parse $\mathsf{sk}_y = (K_0, \overrightarrow{K}_1)$, pick $\mathbf{r}' \leftarrow \mathbb{Z}_p^k$ and output

$$\mathsf{sk}_{y'} := (K_0 \cdot [\mathbf{B}\mathbf{r}']_2, \mathsf{dE}(y, y', \overrightarrow{K}_1) \cdot \mathsf{rE}(y', [\mathbf{W}_1\mathbf{B}\mathbf{r}']_2, \dots, [\mathbf{W}_n\mathbf{B}\mathbf{r}']_2)).$$

As secret keys generated by KeyGen and Del are indistinguishable, the proof in Sect. 3.4 is sufficient to prove that our scheme for delegable predicates can also achieve mKDM-CPA security.

5 CPA-to-CCA Transformation

This section revisits the classical CPA-to-CCA transformation by Canetti, Halevi and Katz [CHK04] (CHK transformation). We remark that the basic idea is not new which is also used in previous work for CCA secure ABE [YAHK11,BL16, CMP17]; this section is to show that the idea indeed works for mKDM security.

IBE-Enhanced Predicate. Given a delegable predicate $P : \mathcal{X} \times \mathcal{Y} \to \{0, 1\}$ with partial ordering $\prec$ on $\mathcal{Y}$, we define its IBE-enhanced version $\overline{P} : \overline{\mathcal{X}} \times \overline{\mathcal{Y}} \to \{0, 1\}$ as

$$\overline{\mathcal{X}} = \mathcal{X} \times \mathbb{Z}_p,$$

$$\overline{\mathcal{Y}} = \mathcal{Y} \times (\mathbb{Z}_p \cup \{\star\}),$$

$$\overline{P}((x, \mathsf{id}), (y, \mathsf{id}')) = \begin{cases} P(x, y) \wedge (\mathsf{id} = \mathsf{id}') & \mathsf{id}' \neq \star \\ P(x, y) & \mathsf{id}' = \star \end{cases}$$

along with strong partial ordering $\overline{\prec}$ on $\overline{\mathcal{Y}}$ is defined as follows:

$$(y', \mathsf{id}) \,\overline{\prec}\, (y', \star) \,\overline{\prec}\, (y, \star), \quad \forall y' \prec y \in \mathcal{Y},\ \mathsf{id} \in \mathbb{Z}_p$$

where $\star$ is a special symbol. Here the first $\overline{\prec}$ involves IBE-part that is used to embed verification key of an one-time signature scheme as CHK transformation; the second $\overline{\prec}$ preserves the delegation in P. Note that we consider *delegable* predicate and all discussions naturally cover the case *without* delegation.

Transformation (Informal). Assuming a predicate encoding for $\overline{P} : \overline{\mathcal{X}} \times \overline{\mathcal{Y}} \to \{0,1\}$ as defined above for $P : \mathcal{X} \times \mathcal{Y} \to \{0,1\}$, Sect. 4 gives us a mKDM-CPA secure scheme $(\overline{\mathsf{Setup}}, \overline{\mathsf{Enc}}, \overline{\mathsf{KeyGen}}, \overline{\mathsf{Dec}}, \overline{\mathsf{Del}})$ for $\overline{P}$. Our mKDM-CCA secure ABE $(\mathsf{Setup}, \mathsf{Enc}, \mathsf{KeyGen}, \mathsf{Dec}, \mathsf{Del})$ for P follows the CHK transformation:

- $\mathsf{Setup}(1^\lambda, P) = \overline{\mathsf{Setup}}(1^\lambda, \overline{P})$ outputs $(\mathsf{mpk}, \mathsf{msk})$;
- $\mathsf{Enc}(\mathsf{mpk}, x, m)$ outputs $(\mathsf{vk}, \overline{\mathsf{ct}} = \overline{\mathsf{Enc}}(\mathsf{mpk}, (x, \mathsf{vk}), m), \sigma = \mathsf{Sign}(\mathsf{sigk}, \overline{\mathsf{ct}}))$ where $(\mathsf{sigk}, \mathsf{vk})$ is a fresh key pair of a strong one-time signature scheme;
- $\mathsf{KeyGen}(\mathsf{msk}, y) = \overline{\mathsf{KeyGen}}(\mathsf{msk}, (y, \star))$ outputs sk_y;
- $\mathsf{Del}(\mathsf{msk}, \mathsf{sk}_y, y') = \overline{\mathsf{Del}}(\mathsf{msk}, \mathsf{sk}_y, (y', \star))$ outputs $\mathsf{sk}_{y'}$;
- $\mathsf{Dec}(\mathsf{mpk}, \mathsf{sk}_y, \mathsf{ct}_x)$ outputs $\overline{\mathsf{Dec}}(\mathsf{mpk}, \overline{\mathsf{Del}}(\mathsf{mpk}, \mathsf{sk}_y, (y, \mathsf{vk})), \overline{\mathsf{ct}})$ if σ is a valid signature for $\overline{\mathsf{ct}}$ under vk.

See the full paper for formal transformation and security analysis.

Generic Construction. Given a predicate encoding $(\mathsf{sE}, \mathsf{rE}, \mathsf{kE}, \mathsf{sD}, \mathsf{rD}, \mathsf{dE})$ for $P : \mathcal{X} \times \mathcal{Y} \to \{0,1\}$ with parameter n, n_s, n_r, the predicate encoding $(\overline{\mathsf{sE}}, \overline{\mathsf{rE}}, \overline{\mathsf{kE}}, \overline{\mathsf{sD}}, \overline{\mathsf{rD}}, \overline{\mathsf{dE}})$ for $\overline{P} : \overline{\mathcal{X}} \times \overline{\mathcal{Y}} \to \{0,1\}$ has parameter

$$\overline{n} = n + 2, \quad \overline{n}_s = n_s + 1, \quad \overline{n}_r = \begin{cases} n_r + 1 & \mathsf{id}' \neq \star \\ n_r + 2 & \mathsf{id}' = \star \end{cases}$$

and is defined as follows: for $(x, y) \in \mathcal{X} \times \mathcal{Y}$ and $\mathsf{id}, \mathsf{id}' \in \mathbb{Z}_p \cup \{\star\}$,

$$\overline{\mathsf{sE}}((x, \mathsf{id}), (\mathbf{w}, w_1, w_2)) := (\mathsf{sE}(x, \mathbf{w}), w_1 + \mathsf{id} \cdot w_2) \quad (\mathsf{id} \neq \star)$$

$$\overline{\mathsf{rE}}((y, \mathsf{id}), (\mathbf{w}, w_1, w_2)) := \begin{cases} (\mathsf{rE}(y, \mathbf{w}), w_1 + \mathsf{id} \cdot w_2) & \mathsf{id} \neq \star \\ (\mathsf{rE}(y, \mathbf{w}), w_1, w_2) & \mathsf{id} = \star \end{cases}$$

$$\overline{\mathsf{kE}}((y, \mathsf{id}), \alpha) := \begin{cases} (\mathsf{kE}(y, \alpha - \delta), \delta) & \mathsf{id} \neq \star \\ (\mathsf{kE}(y, \alpha - \delta), \delta, 0) & \mathsf{id} = \star \end{cases}$$

$$\overline{\mathsf{sD}}((x, \mathsf{id}), (y, \mathsf{id}'), (\mathbf{c}, c)) := \mathsf{sD}(x, y, \mathbf{c}) + c \quad (\mathsf{id} \neq \star,\ \mathsf{id}' \neq \star)$$

$$\overline{\mathsf{rD}}((x,\mathsf{id}),(y,\mathsf{id}'),(\mathbf{k},k)) := \mathsf{rD}(x,y,\mathbf{k})+k \quad (\mathsf{id}\neq\star,\ \mathsf{id}'\neq\star)$$

$$\overline{\mathsf{dE}}((y,\mathsf{id}),(y',\mathsf{id}'),(\mathbf{k},k_1,k_2)) := \begin{cases}(\mathbf{k},k_1+\mathsf{id}'\cdot k_2) & y'=y, \mathsf{id}=\star, \mathsf{id}'\neq\star\\ (\mathsf{dE}(y,y',\mathbf{k}),(k_1,k_2)) & y'\prec y,\ \mathsf{id}=\star,\ \mathsf{id}'=\star\end{cases}$$

where $(\mathbf{w},w_1,w_2)\leftarrow\mathbb{Z}_p^{\overline{n}}$ and $\alpha,\delta\leftarrow\mathbb{Z}_p$. Note that we only give out $\overline{\mathsf{rD}}$ for the case "$\mathsf{id}\neq\star$, $\mathsf{id}'\neq\star$"; for the case "$\mathsf{id}\neq\star$, $\mathsf{id}'=\star$" where the encoding is in the form $(\mathbf{k},k_1,k_2)$, we apply $\overline{\mathsf{dE}}$ first.

6 Concrete Schemes

6.1 Concrete mKDM-secure Hierarchical IBE

This section presents a concrete mKDM-CCA secure n-level HIBE scheme derived from our generic construction via predicate encoding in Sect. 4.

Construction. Assuming (Gen, Sign, Verify) is a strongly unforgeable one-time signature scheme against chosen-message attack in the multi-user setting (MU-sUF-CMA security), our mKDM-CCA secure HIBE scheme is as follows:

- $\mathsf{Setup}(1^\lambda,n)$: Run $\mathbb{G}\leftarrow\mathcal{G}(1^\lambda)$, sample $\mathbf{A}_1\leftarrow\mathbb{Z}_p^{\ell\times k}$, $\mathbf{B}\leftarrow\mathbb{Z}_p^{(k+1)\times k}$, pick $\mathbf{W},\mathbf{W}_1,\ldots,\mathbf{W}_{n+1}\leftarrow\mathbb{Z}_p^{\ell\times(k+1)}$ and $\mathbf{k}\leftarrow\{0,1\}^\ell$. Output

$$\mathsf{mpk} := \begin{pmatrix}[\mathbf{A}_1^\top]_1, [\mathbf{A}_1^\top\mathbf{W}]_1, [\mathbf{A}_1^\top\mathbf{W}_1]_1, \ldots, [\mathbf{A}_1^\top\mathbf{W}_{n+1}]_1,\\ [\mathbf{B}]_2,\ [\mathbf{W}\mathbf{B}]_2,\ [\mathbf{W}_1\mathbf{B}]_2,\ \ldots, [\mathbf{W}_{n+1}\mathbf{B}]_2,\ [\mathbf{A}_1^\top\mathbf{k}]_T\end{pmatrix}, \quad \mathsf{msk}:=[\mathbf{k}]_T.$$

  We assume that group description $\mathbb{G}$ is always contained in mpk.
- $\mathsf{Enc}(\mathsf{mpk},\mathsf{id},m)$: Parse $\mathsf{id}=(\mathsf{id}_1,\ldots,\mathsf{id}_t)$ where $t\leq n$, run $(\mathsf{sigk},\mathsf{vk})\leftarrow\mathsf{Gen}(1^\lambda)$, pick $\mathbf{s}\leftarrow\mathbb{Z}_p^k$ and compute

$$\overline{\mathsf{ct}} := (\,[\mathbf{s}^\top\mathbf{A}_1^\top]_1,\ [\mathbf{s}^\top(\mathbf{A}_1^\top\mathbf{W}+\textstyle\sum_{i=1}^t \mathsf{id}_i\mathbf{A}_1^\top\mathbf{W}_i+\mathsf{vk}\mathbf{A}_1^\top\mathbf{W}_{n+1})]_1,\ [\mathbf{s}^\top\mathbf{A}_1^\top\mathbf{k}]_T\cdot m\,).$$

  Output

$$\mathsf{ct}_{\mathsf{id}} := (\mathsf{vk},\overline{\mathsf{ct}},\mathsf{Sign}(\mathsf{sigk},\overline{\mathsf{ct}})).$$

- $\mathsf{KeyGen}(\mathsf{mpk},\mathsf{msk},\mathsf{id})$: Recover $\mathbf{k}\in\{0,1\}^\ell$ from $\mathsf{msk}=[\mathbf{k}]_T$. Parse $\mathsf{id}=(\mathsf{id}_1,\ldots,\mathsf{id}_t)$ where $t\leq n$, pick $\mathbf{r}\leftarrow\mathbb{Z}_p^k$ and output

$$\mathsf{sk}_{\mathsf{id}} := (\,[\mathbf{B}\mathbf{r}]_2,\ [\mathbf{k}+(\mathbf{W}\mathbf{B}+\textstyle\sum_{i=1}^t\mathsf{id}_i\mathbf{W}_i\mathbf{B})\mathbf{r}]_2,\ [\mathbf{W}_{t+1}\mathbf{B}\mathbf{r}]_2,\ \ldots,\ [\mathbf{W}_{n+1}\mathbf{B}\mathbf{r}]_2\,).$$

- $\mathsf{Del}(\mathsf{mpk},\mathsf{sk}_{\mathsf{id}},\mathsf{id}')$: Parse $\mathsf{sk}_{\mathsf{id}}=(K_0,K_1,K_{t+1},\ldots,K_{n+1})$ for $\mathsf{id}=(\mathsf{id}_1,\ldots,\mathsf{id}_t)$ and $\mathsf{id}'=(\mathsf{id},\mathsf{id}_{t+1})$ where $t<n$, pick $\mathbf{r}'\leftarrow\mathbb{Z}_p^k$ and output

$$\mathsf{sk}_{\mathsf{id}'} := \begin{pmatrix}K_0\cdot[\mathbf{B}\mathbf{r}']_2,\ K_1\cdot K_{t+1}^{\mathsf{id}_{t+1}}\cdot[(\mathbf{W}\mathbf{B}+\sum_{i=1}^{t+1}\mathsf{id}_i\mathbf{W}_i\mathbf{B})\mathbf{r}']_2,\\ K_{t+2}\cdot[\mathbf{W}_{t+2}\mathbf{B}\mathbf{r}']_2,\ldots,K_{n+1}\cdot[\mathbf{W}_{n+1}\mathbf{B}\mathbf{r}']_2\end{pmatrix}.$$

- $\mathsf{Dec}(\mathsf{mpk},\mathsf{sk}_{\mathsf{id}},\mathsf{ct}_{\mathsf{id}})$: Parse $\mathsf{ct}_{\mathsf{id}}=(\mathsf{vk},\overline{\mathsf{ct}},\sigma)$, output $\perp$ if $\mathsf{Verify}(\mathsf{vk},\overline{\mathsf{ct}},\sigma)=0$. Otherwise, parse $\mathsf{sk}_{\mathsf{id}}=(K_0,K_1,K_{t+1},\ldots,K_{n+1})$ and $\overline{\mathsf{ct}}=(C_0,C_1,C)$. Output

$$m' = C\cdot e(C_0,K_1\cdot K_{n+1}^{\mathsf{vk}})^{-1}\cdot e(C_1,K_0).$$

6.2 Concrete mKDM-secure ABE for ABP

This section presents a concrete mKDM-CCA secure ABE for arithmetic branching programs (ABP) derived from our generic construction. We work with arithmetic span programs (ASP) that captures ABP [IW14] and use the predicate encoding from [CGW15].

Arithmetic Span Program [IW14]**.** An arithmetic span program $(\mathcal{V}, \rho)$ is a collection of row vectors $\mathcal{V} = \{(\mathbf{y}_j, \mathbf{z}_j)\}_{j\in[n']} \in (\mathbb{Z}_p^{\ell'} \times \mathbb{Z}_p^{\ell'})^{n'}$ and $\rho : [n'] \to [n]$. We say that

$$\mathbf{x} \in \mathbb{Z}_p^n \text{ satisfies } (\mathcal{V}, \rho) \quad \text{if} \quad \mathbf{1} \in \mathsf{span}(\mathbf{y}_j + x_{\rho(j)}\mathbf{z}_j),$$

where $\mathbf{1} := (1, 0, \dots, 0)^\top \in \mathbb{Z}_p^{\ell'}$. That is, $\mathbf{x}$ satisfies $(\mathcal{V}, \rho)$ if there exist constants $\omega_1, \dots, \omega_{n'} \in \mathbb{Z}_p$ such that

$$\textstyle\sum_{j\in[n']} \omega_j(\mathbf{y}_j + x_{\rho(j)}\mathbf{z}_j) = \mathbf{1}.$$

We impose a one-use restriction, that is, ρ is a permutation and $n' = n$. By re-ordering the coordinates in $\mathcal{V}$, we may assume that ρ is the identity map.

Predicate Encodings from [CGW15]**.** Let $(\mathbf{w}, \mathbf{v}, \mathbf{u}) \leftarrow \mathbb{Z}_p^n \times \mathbb{Z}_p^n \times \mathbb{Z}_p^{\ell'-1}$. Define

$$\begin{aligned}
\mathsf{sE}(\mathbf{x}, (\mathbf{w}, \mathbf{v}, \mathbf{u})) &:= \big(w_1 + x_1 v_1 \ \dots\ w_n + x_n v_n\big) \in \mathbb{Z}_p^n \\
\mathsf{rE}(\mathcal{V}, (\mathbf{w}, \mathbf{v}, \mathbf{u})) &:= \begin{pmatrix} \mathbf{y}_1^\top \binom{0}{\mathbf{u}} + w_1 \ \dots\ \mathbf{y}_n^\top \binom{0}{\mathbf{u}} + w_n \\ \mathbf{z}_1^\top \binom{0}{\mathbf{u}} + v_1 \ \dots\ \mathbf{z}_n^\top \binom{0}{\mathbf{u}} + v_n \end{pmatrix} \in \mathbb{Z}_p^{2n} \\
\mathsf{kE}(\mathcal{V}, \alpha) &:= \begin{pmatrix} \mathbf{y}_1^\top \binom{\alpha}{\mathbf{0}} \ \dots\ \mathbf{y}_n^\top \binom{\alpha}{\mathbf{0}} \\ \mathbf{z}_1^\top \binom{\alpha}{\mathbf{0}} \ \dots\ \mathbf{z}_n^\top \binom{\alpha}{\mathbf{0}} \end{pmatrix} \in \mathbb{Z}_p^{2n} \\
\mathsf{sD}(\mathbf{x}, \mathcal{V}, \mathbf{c}) &:= \textstyle\sum_{j\in[n]} \omega_j c_j \\
\mathsf{rD}(\mathbf{x}, \mathcal{V}, (\mathbf{d}, \mathbf{d}')) &:= \textstyle\sum_{j\in[n]} \omega_j (d_j + x_j d'_j)
\end{aligned}$$

Construction. Assuming $(\mathsf{Gen}, \mathsf{Sign}, \mathsf{Verify})$ is a strongly unforgeable one-time signature scheme against chosen-message attack in the multi-user setting (MU-sUF-CMA security), our mKDM-CCA secure ABE scheme for ABP is as follows:

- $\mathsf{Setup}(1^\lambda, n)$: Run $\mathbb{G} \leftarrow \mathcal{G}(1^\lambda)$, sample $\mathbf{A}_1 \leftarrow \mathbb{Z}_p^{\ell\times k}$, $\mathbf{B} \leftarrow \mathbb{Z}_p^{(k+1)\times k}$, pick $\mathbf{W}, \mathbf{W}_1, \dots, \mathbf{W}_n, \mathbf{V}, \mathbf{V}_1, \dots, \mathbf{V}_n \leftarrow \mathbb{Z}_p^{\ell\times(k+1)}$ and $\mathbf{k} \leftarrow \{0,1\}^\ell$. Output

$$\mathsf{mpk} := \begin{pmatrix} [\mathbf{A}_1^\top]_1, [\mathbf{A}_1^\top\mathbf{W}]_1, [\mathbf{A}_1^\top\mathbf{W}_1]_1, \dots, [\mathbf{A}_1^\top\mathbf{W}_n]_1, \\ [\mathbf{A}_1^\top\mathbf{V}]_1, [\mathbf{A}_1^\top\mathbf{V}_1]_1, \dots, [\mathbf{A}_1^\top\mathbf{V}_n]_1, \\ [\mathbf{B}]_2, [\mathbf{W}\mathbf{B}]_2, [\mathbf{W}_1\mathbf{B}]_2, \dots, [\mathbf{W}_n\mathbf{B}]_2, \\ [\mathbf{V}\mathbf{B}]_2, [\mathbf{V}_1\mathbf{B}]_2, \dots, [\mathbf{V}_n\mathbf{B}]_2, [\mathbf{A}_1^\top\mathbf{k}]_T \end{pmatrix}, \quad \mathsf{msk} := [\mathbf{k}]_T.$$

  We assume that group description $\mathbb{G}$ is always contained in mpk.

- $\mathsf{Enc}(\mathsf{mpk}, \mathbf{x}, m)$: Parse $\mathbf{x} = (x_1, \ldots, x_n)$, run $(\mathsf{sigk}, \mathsf{vk}) \leftarrow \mathsf{Gen}(1^\lambda)$, pick $\mathbf{s} \leftarrow \mathbb{Z}_p^k$ and compute

$$\overline{\mathsf{ct}} := \begin{pmatrix} [\mathbf{s}^\top \mathbf{A}_1^\top]_1, \ [\mathbf{s}^\top (\mathbf{A}_1^\top \mathbf{W} + \mathsf{vk} \cdot \mathbf{A}_1^\top \mathbf{V})]_1, \\ \{[\mathbf{s}^\top (\mathbf{A}_1^\top \mathbf{W}_j + x_j \cdot \mathbf{A}_1^\top \mathbf{V}_j)]_1\}_{j \in [n]}, \ [\mathbf{s}^\top \mathbf{A}_1^\top \mathbf{k}]_T \cdot m \end{pmatrix}.$$

Output

$$\mathsf{ct}_\mathbf{x} := (\mathsf{vk}, \overline{\mathsf{ct}}, \mathsf{Sign}(\mathsf{sigk}, \overline{\mathsf{ct}})).$$

- $\mathsf{KeyGen}(\mathsf{mpk}, \mathsf{msk}, \mathcal{V})$: Recover $\mathbf{k} \in \{0,1\}^\ell$ from $\mathsf{msk} = [\mathbf{k}]_T$. Parse $\mathcal{V} = \{(\mathbf{y}_j, \mathbf{z}_j)\}_{j \in [n]}$, pick $\mathbf{k}' \leftarrow \mathbb{Z}_p^\ell$, $\mathbf{K}' \leftarrow \mathbb{Z}_p^{\ell \times (\ell' - 1)}$, $\mathbf{r}, \mathbf{r}_j \leftarrow \mathbb{Z}_p^k$ for all $j \in [n]$ and output

$$\mathsf{sk}_\mathcal{V} := \left(\begin{matrix} [\mathbf{Br}]_2, [\mathbf{k}' + \mathbf{WBr}]_2, \\ [\mathbf{VBr}]_2, \end{matrix} \left\{ \begin{matrix} [\mathbf{Br}_j]_2, [((\mathbf{k} - \mathbf{k}')|\mathbf{K}')\mathbf{y}_j + \mathbf{W}_j \mathbf{Br}_j]_2, \\ [((\mathbf{k} - \mathbf{k}')|\mathbf{K}')\mathbf{z}_j + \mathbf{V}_j \mathbf{Br}_j]_2 \end{matrix} \right\}_{j \in [n]} \right).$$

- $\mathsf{Dec}(\mathsf{mpk}, \mathsf{sk}_\mathcal{V}, \mathsf{ct}_\mathbf{x})$: Parse $\mathsf{ct}_\mathbf{x} = (\mathsf{vk}, \overline{\mathsf{ct}}, \sigma)$, output $\perp$ if $\mathsf{Verify}(\mathsf{vk}, \overline{\mathsf{ct}}, \sigma) = 0$. Otherwise, parse $\mathsf{sk}_\mathcal{V} = (K_0, K_1, K_2, \{K_{0,j}, K_{1,j}, K_{2,j}\}_{j \in [n]})$ and $\overline{\mathsf{ct}} = (C_0, C_1, \{C_{1,j}\}_{j \in [n]}, C)$. If $\mathbf{x}$ satisfies $\mathcal{V}$, one can compute $\omega_1, \ldots, \omega_n \in \mathbb{Z}_p$ such that $\sum_{j \in [n]} \omega_j (\mathbf{y}_j + x_j \cdot \mathbf{z}_j) = \mathbf{1}$. Output

$$m' = C \cdot \left(e(C_0, K_1 \cdot K_2^{\mathsf{vk}})^{-1} \cdot e(C_1, K_0)\right) \cdot \prod_{j \in [n]} \left(e(C_0, K_{1,j} \cdot K_{2,j}{}^{x_j})^{-1} \cdot e(C_{1,j}, K_{0,j})\right)^{\omega_j}.$$

References

[ABBC10] Acar, T., Belenkiy, M., Bellare, M., Cash, D.: Cryptographic agility and its relation to circular encryption. In: Gilbert, H. (ed.) EUROCRYPT 2010. LNCS, vol. 6110, pp. 403–422. Springer, Heidelberg (2010). https://doi.org/10.1007/978-3-642-13190-5_21

[AC17] Agrawal, S., Chase, M.: Simplifying design and analysis of complex predicate encryption schemes. In: Coron, J.-S., Nielsen, J.B. (eds.) EUROCRYPT 2017. LNCS, vol. 10210, pp. 627–656. Springer, Cham (2017). https://doi.org/10.1007/978-3-319-56620-7_22

[AHY15] Attrapadung, N., Hanaoka, G., Yamada, S.: A framework for identity-based encryption with almost tight security. In: Iwata, T., Cheon, J.H. (eds.) ASIACRYPT 2015. LNCS, vol. 9452, pp. 521–549. Springer, Heidelberg (2015). https://doi.org/10.1007/978-3-662-48797-6_22

[AP12] Alperin-Sheriff, J., Peikert, C.: Circular and KDM security for identity-based encryption. In: Fischlin, M., Buchmann, J., Manulis, M. (eds.) PKC 2012. LNCS, vol. 7293, pp. 334–352. Springer, Heidelberg (2012). https://doi.org/10.1007/978-3-642-30057-8_20

[Att14] Attrapadung, N.: Dual system encryption via doubly selective security: framework, fully secure functional encryption for regular languages, and more. In: Nguyen, P.Q., Oswald, E. (eds.) EUROCRYPT 2014. LNCS, vol. 8441, pp. 557–577. Springer, Heidelberg (2014). https://doi.org/10.1007/978-3-642-55220-5_31

[BBG05] Boneh, D., Boyen, X., Goh, E.-J.: Hierarchical identity based encryption with constant size ciphertext. In: Cramer, R. (ed.) EUROCRYPT 2005. LNCS, vol. 3494, pp. 440–456. Springer, Heidelberg (2005). https://doi.org/10.1007/11426639_26

[BF01] Boneh, D., Franklin, M.: Identity-based encryption from the weil pairing. In: Kilian, J. (ed.) CRYPTO 2001. LNCS, vol. 2139, pp. 213–229. Springer, Heidelberg (2001). https://doi.org/10.1007/3-540-44647-8_13

[BHHO08] Boneh, D., Halevi, S., Hamburg, M., Ostrovsky, R.: Circular-secure encryption from decision Diffie-Hellman. In: Wagner, D. (ed.) CRYPTO 2008. LNCS, vol. 5157, pp. 108–125. Springer, Heidelberg (2008). https://doi.org/10.1007/978-3-540-85174-5_7

[BL16] Blömer, J., Liske, G.: Construction of fully CCA-secure predicate encryptions from pair encoding schemes. In: Sako, K. (ed.) CT-RSA 2016. LNCS, vol. 9610, pp. 431–447. Springer, Heidelberg (2016)

[BRS03] Black, J., Rogaway, P., Shrimpton, T.: Encryption-scheme security in the presence of key-dependent messages. In: Nyberg, K., Heys, H. (eds.) SAC 2002. LNCS, vol. 2595, pp. 62–75. Springer, Heidelberg (2003). https://doi.org/10.1007/3-540-36492-7_6

[CCS09] Camenisch, J., Chandran, N., Shoup, V.: A public key encryption scheme secure against key dependent chosen plaintext and adaptive chosen ciphertext attacks. In: Joux, A. (ed.) EUROCRYPT 2009. LNCS, vol. 5479, pp. 351–368. Springer, Heidelberg (2009). https://doi.org/10.1007/978-3-642-01001-9_20

[CGH12] Cash, D., Green, M., Hohenberger, S.: New definitions and separations for circular security. In: Fischlin, M., Buchmann, J., Manulis, M. (eds.) PKC 2012. LNCS, vol. 7293, pp. 540–557. Springer, Heidelberg (2012). https://doi.org/10.1007/978-3-642-30057-8_32

[CGKW18] Chen, J., Gong, J., Kowalczyk, L., Wee, H.: Unbounded ABE via bilinear entropy expansion, revisited. In: Nielsen, J.B., Rijmen, V. (eds.) EUROCRYPT 2018. LNCS, vol. 10820, pp. 503–534. Springer, Cham (2018). https://doi.org/10.1007/978-3-319-78381-9_19

[CGW15] Chen, J., Gay, R., Wee, H.: Improved dual system ABE in prime-order groups via predicate encodings. In: Oswald, E., Fischlin, M. (eds.) EUROCRYPT 2015. LNCS, vol. 9057, pp. 595–624. Springer, Heidelberg (2015). https://doi.org/10.1007/978-3-662-46803-6_20

[CGW17] Chen, J., Gong, J., Weng, J.: Tightly secure IBE under constant-size master public key. In: Fehr, S. (ed.) PKC 2017. Part I, volume 10174 of LNCS, pp. 207–231. Springer, Heidelberg (2017)

[CHK04] Canetti, R., Halevi, S., Katz, J.: Chosen-ciphertext security from identity-based encryption. In: Cachin, C., Camenisch, J.L. (eds.) EUROCRYPT 2004. LNCS, vol. 3027, pp. 207–222. Springer, Heidelberg (2004). https://doi.org/10.1007/978-3-540-24676-3_13

[CL01] Camenisch, J., Lysyanskaya, A.: An efficient system for non-transferable anonymous credentials with optional anonymity revocation. In: Pfitzmann, B. (ed.) EUROCRYPT 2001. LNCS, vol. 2045, pp. 93–118. Springer, Heidelberg (2001). https://doi.org/10.1007/3-540-44987-6_7

[CM14] Chase, M., Meiklejohn, S.: Déjà Q: using dual systems to revisit q-type assumptions. In: Nguyen, P.Q., Oswald, E. (eds.) EUROCRYPT 2014. LNCS, vol. 8441, pp. 622–639. Springer, Heidelberg (2014). https://doi.org/10.1007/978-3-642-55220-5_34

[CMM16] Chase, M., Maller, M., Meiklejohn, S.: Déjà Q all over again: tighter and broader reductions of q-type assumptions. In: Cheon, J.H., Takagi, T. (eds.) ASIACRYPT 2016. LNCS, vol. 10032, pp. 655–681. Springer, Heidelberg (2016). https://doi.org/10.1007/978-3-662-53890-6_22

[CMP17] Chatterjee, S., Mukherjee, S., Pandit, T.: CCA-secure predicate encryption from pair encoding in prime order groups: generic and efficient. In: Patra, A., Smart, N.P. (eds.) INDOCRYPT 2017. LNCS, vol. 10698, pp. 85–106. Springer, Cham (2017). https://doi.org/10.1007/978-3-319-71667-1_5

[DGHM18] Döttling, N., Garg, S., Hajiabadi, M., Masny, D.: New constructions of identity-based and key-dependent message secure encryption schemes. In: Abdalla, M., Dahab, R. (eds.) PKC 2018. LNCS, vol. 10769, pp. 3–31. Springer, Cham (2018). https://doi.org/10.1007/978-3-319-76578-5_1

[EHK+13] Escala, A., Herold, G., Kiltz, E., Ràfols, C., Villar, J.: An algebraic framework for Diffie-Hellman assumptions. In: Canetti, R., Garay, J.A. (eds.) CRYPTO 2013. LNCS, vol. 8043, pp. 129–147. Springer, Heidelberg (2013). https://doi.org/10.1007/978-3-642-40084-1_8

[GDCC16] Gong, J., Dong, X., Chen, J., Cao, Z.: Efficient IBE with tight reduction to standard assumption in the multi-challenge setting. In: Cheon, J.H., Takagi, T. (eds.) ASIACRYPT 2016. LNCS, vol. 10032, pp. 624–654. Springer, Heidelberg (2016). https://doi.org/10.1007/978-3-662-53890-6_21

[GGH20] Garg, S., Gay, R., Hajiabadi, M.: Master-key KDM-secure IBE from pairings. In: Kiayias, A., Kohlweiss, M., Wallden, P., Zikas, V. (eds.) Part I: PKC 2020. LNCS, vol. 12110, pp. 123–152. Springer, Heidelberg (2020)

[GHV12] Galindo, D., Herranz, J., Villar, J.: Identity-based encryption with master key-dependent message security and leakage-resilience. In: Foresti, S., Yung, M., Martinelli, F. (eds.) ESORICS 2012. LNCS, vol. 7459, pp. 627–642. Springer, Heidelberg (2012). https://doi.org/10.1007/978-3-642-33167-1_36

[GPSW06] Goyal, V., Pandey, O., Sahai, A., Waters, B.: Attribute-based encryption for fine-grained access control of encrypted data. In: Juels, A., Wright, R.N., De Capitani di Vimercati, S. (eds.) ACM CCS 2006, pp. 89–98. ACM Press (2006). Cryptology ePrint Archive Report 2006/309

[HK07] Halevi, S., Krawczyk, H.: Security under key-dependent inputs. In: Ning, P., De Capitani di Vimercati, S., Syverson, P.F. (eds.) ACM CCS 2007, pp. 466–475. ACM Press (2007)

[HLL16] Han, S., Liu, S., Lyu, L.: Efficient KDM-CCA secure public-key encryption for polynomial functions. In: Cheon, J.H., Takagi, T. (eds.) ASIACRYPT 2016. LNCS, vol. 10032, pp. 307–338. Springer, Heidelberg (2016). https://doi.org/10.1007/978-3-662-53890-6_11

[Hof13] Hofheinz, D.: Circular chosen-ciphertext security with compact ciphertexts. In: Johansson, T., Nguyen, P.Q. (eds.) EUROCRYPT 2013. LNCS, vol. 7881, pp. 520–536. Springer, Heidelberg (2013). https://doi.org/10.1007/978-3-642-38348-9_31

[IW14] Ishai, Y., Wee, H.: Partial garbling schemes and their applications. In: Esparza, J., Fraigniaud, P., Husfeldt, T., Koutsoupias, E. (eds.) ICALP 2014. LNCS, vol. 8572, pp. 650–662. Springer, Heidelberg (2014). https://doi.org/10.1007/978-3-662-43948-7_54

[KL15] Kowalczyk, L., Lewko, A.B.: Bilinear entropy expansion from the decisional linear assumption. In: Gennaro, R., Robshaw, M. (eds.) CRYPTO 2015. LNCS, vol. 9216, pp. 524–541. Springer, Heidelberg (2015). https://doi.org/10.1007/978-3-662-48000-7_26

[KM19] Kitagawa, F., Matsuda, T.: CPA-to-CCA transformation for KDM security. In: Hofheinz, D., Rosen, A. (eds.) Part II: TCC 2019. LNCS, vol. 11892, pp. 118–148. Springer, Heidelberg (2019)

[KMT19] Kitagawa, F., Matsuda, T., Tanaka, K.: CCA security and trapdoor functions via key-dependent-message security. In: Boldyreva, A., Micciancio, D. (eds.) Part III: CRYPTO 2019. LNCS, vol. 11694, pp. 33–64. Springer, Heidelberg (2019)

[KT18] Kitagawa, F., Tanaka, K.: A framework for achieving KDM-CCA secure public-key encryption. In: Peyrin, T., Galbraith, S. (eds.) ASIACRYPT 2018. LNCS, vol. 11273, pp. 127–157. Springer, Cham (2018). https://doi.org/10.1007/978-3-030-03329-3_5

[LLJ15] Xianhui, L., Li, B., Jia, D.: KDM-CCA security from RKA secure authenticated encryption. In: Oswald, E., Fischlin, M. (eds.) Part I: EUROCRYPT 2015. LNCS, vol. 9056, pp. 559–583. Springer, Heidelberg (2015)

[LP20] Langrehr, R., Pan, J.: Hierarchical identity-based encryption with tight multi-challenge security. In: Kiayias, A., Kohlweiss, M., Wallden, P., Zikas, V. (eds.) PKC 2020. LNCS, vol. 12110, pp. 153–183. Springer, Cham (2020). https://doi.org/10.1007/978-3-030-45374-9_6

[LW11] Lewko, A., Waters, B.: Unbounded HIBE and attribute-based encryption. In: Paterson, K.G. (ed.) EUROCRYPT 2011. LNCS, vol. 6632, pp. 547–567. Springer, Heidelberg (2011). https://doi.org/10.1007/978-3-642-20465-4_30

[OT12] Okamoto, T., Takashima, K.: Fully secure unbounded inner-product and attribute-based encryption. In: Wang, X., Sako, K. (eds.) ASIACRYPT 2012. LNCS, vol. 7658, pp. 349–366. Springer, Heidelberg (2012). https://doi.org/10.1007/978-3-642-34961-4_22

[Sha84] Shamir, A.: Identity-based cryptosystems and signature schemes. In: Blakley, G.R., Chaum, D. (eds.) CRYPTO'84. LNCS, vol. 196, pp. 47–53. Springer, Heidelberg (1984)

[SW05] Sahai, A., Waters, B.: Fuzzy identity-based encryption. In: Cramer, R. (ed.) EUROCRYPT 2005. LNCS, vol. 3494, pp. 457–473. Springer, Heidelberg (2005). https://doi.org/10.1007/11426639_27

[SW08] Shi, E., Waters, B.: Delegating capabilities in predicate encryption systems. In: Aceto, L., Damgård, I., Goldberg, L.A., Halldórsson, M.M., Ingólfsdóttir, A., Walukiewicz, I. (eds.) ICALP 2008. LNCS, vol. 5126, pp. 560–578. Springer, Heidelberg (2008). https://doi.org/10.1007/978-3-540-70583-3_46

[Wat09] Waters, B.: Dual system encryption: realizing fully secure IBE and HIBE under simple assumptions. In: Halevi, S. (ed.) CRYPTO 2009. LNCS, vol. 5677, pp. 619–636. Springer, Heidelberg (2009). https://doi.org/10.1007/978-3-642-03356-8_36

[Wee14] Wee, H.: Dual system encryption via predicate encodings. In: Lindell, Y. (ed.) TCC 2014. LNCS, vol. 8349, pp. 616–637. Springer, Heidelberg (2014). https://doi.org/10.1007/978-3-642-54242-8_26

[YAHK11] Yamada, S., Attrapadung, N., Hanaoka, G., Kunihiro, N.: Generic constructions for chosen-ciphertext secure attribute based encryption. In: Catalano, D., Fazio, N., Gennaro, R., Nicolosi, A. (eds.) PKC 2011. LNCS, vol. 6571, pp. 71–89. Springer, Heidelberg (2011). https://doi.org/10.1007/978-3-642-19379-8_5

Exact Lattice Sampling from Non-Gaussian Distributions

Maxime Plançon[1(✉)] and Thomas Prest[2]

[1] IBM Research and ETH Zurich, Zürich, Switzerland
mpl@zurich.ibm.com
[2] PQShield, Oxford, UK
thomas.prest@pqshield.com

Abstract. We propose a new framework for (trapdoor) sampling over lattices. Our framework can be instantiated in a number of ways. It allows for example to sample from uniform, affine and "product affine" distributions. Another salient point of our framework is that the output distributions of our samplers are perfectly indistinguishable from ideal ones, in contrast with classical samplers that are statistically indistinguishable. One caveat of our framework is that all our current instantiations entail a rather large standard deviation.

Keywords: Trapdoor sampling · Lattice trapdoors · Squaremonic functions · Regular algorithms

1 Introduction

Sampling over a lattice – usually using a trapdoor – is a fundamental building block in lattice-based cryptography. Since its inception [21,23], it has seen a myriad of applications such as full-domain hash signature schemes [21], identity-based encryption or IBE [21], hierarchical IBE [3,4,12], attribute-based encryption [10], standard model signatures and so on.

Given its importance, surprisingly few sampling methods have been proposed. The most prominent is arguably the Klein/GPV sampler [21,23], a randomized variant of Babai's nearest plane algorithm. Analogously, Peikert's sampler [28] randomizes Babai's round-off algorithm. Both samplers can sample over any lattice, provided a (preferably) short basis. The Micciancio-Peikert framework [26] and its variations operate at a slightly different level by constructing pseudorandom lattices along with trapdoors that allow to sample efficiently.

These proposals share two notable common points. First, they all sample from discrete *Gaussian* distributions. Gaussians come with their share of challenges in terms of implementation, precision analysis and side-channel analysis, and have often been replaced with simpler distributions whenever possible [6,9,16]. To the best of our knowledge, the only attempt [25] to rely on other distributions

Most of this work was done while Maxime Plançon was an intern at PQShield.

J. A. Garay (Ed.): PKC 2021, LNCS 12710, pp. 573–595, 2021.
https://doi.org/10.1007/978-3-030-75245-3_21

than discrete Gaussians was restricted to the Micciancio-Peikert framework. A second common point is that they do not sample perfectly from a discretized ideal distribution, but statistically close to it. A blueprint for performing exact lattice sampling is proposed at the end of [11]; it is rather involved as it entails infinite sums of transcendental functions. To the best of our knowledge, neither [25] nor [11] have been implemented.

The motivation of this work is to propose alternative trapdoor samplers that lift the two aforementioned limitations: (a) being restricted to Gaussian distributions, (b) achieving only statistical correctness instead of the stronger notion of perfect correctness. In itself, lifting these limitations is conceptually interesting, and may further our theoretic comprehension of lattice sampling. From a practical perspective, a new approach with different strengths and weaknesses provides more avenues for optimization.

1.1 Our Contribution

We propose a new framework for lattice (trapdoor) sampling. At a high level, it requires two components. First, we require an $\mathcal{L}$-regular algorithm; intuitively, a regular algorithm maps the ambient space to a lattice $\mathcal{L}$ in a way that defines a $\mathcal{L}$-regular tiling of the space. This notion provides a natural abstraction of Babai's nearest plane and round-off algorithms, as well as any exact closest vector problem (or CVP) solver.

The second component is a $\mathcal{T}$-squaremonic function; the term *squaremonic* is a portmanteau of *square* and *harmonic*. This notion is a variation of harmonic functions over lattice tiles instead of balls. The key property of squaremonic functions is that rounding them over a lattice is equivalent (by translation) to discretizing them over the same lattice. The interplay between regular algorithms and squaremonic functions gives us a class of lattice samplers, corresponding to various instances of our framework. Our framework and its instantiations have two interesting properties.

- **Non-Gaussian distributions.** We can sample from uniform, affine and "product affine" distributions, discretized over a subset of a lattice – typically, its intersection with a L_p ball. This contrasts with classical lattice sampling algorithms, which are restricted to Gaussian distributions – with the exception of [25] in the setting of [26].
- **Exact sampling.** The output distribution of our algorithms are *exact* discrete distributions over a lattice, perfectly independent of the basis used. In comparison, existing lattice (trapdoor) samplers [21,26,28], entail a trade-off between the standard deviation of the (Gaussian) distribution and the correctness of the sampler (i.e. the divergence of its output from an ideal distribution), see [18,21,29]. In our case, there is a trade-off between the standard deviation of the distribution and the *running time* of the sampler. While the practical impact of this exactness is unclear, we believe it is conceptually interesting.

At a technical level, our approach is simple; one possible instantiation is to sample $\mathbf{x} \leftarrow f$ from a continuous distribution f, compute $\mathbf{B} \lfloor \mathbf{B}^{-1}\mathbf{x} \rceil$ and apply a simple rejection sampling step. We note that works by Regev [31] and Gentry, Peikert and Vaikuntanathan [21] considered doing exactly this. However, both works took f to be a continuous Gaussian; achieving statistical closeness then required an exponential standard deviation, and this approach was deemed non-viable by [21]. What allows us to unlock this situation is to rely on different distributions; the ones we choose are naturally more amenable to this approach.

One current drawback in our approach is that it entails standard deviations that are higher than the state of the art. Compared to the "classical" samplers of [21,28], the Euclidean norm can be larger by a factor $O(n^{1.5})$. We therefore consider reducing this standard deviation as a relevant and important open question.

We are not aware of any straightforward way to apply our approach with Gaussians or, conversely, to adapt the [21] sampler to the distributions we have chosen. Again, we see future results in either direction (either positive or negative) as interesting open questions.

Finally, we note that our main motivation for this work was the constructive side of lattice sampling (e.g. trapdoor sampling), and this is reflected in this document. However, *Gaussian* sampling over lattices has also been studied in the context of theoretical cryptanalysis and computational complexity theory [1,2,23,32].

1.2 Related Works

A few lattice sampling frameworks have been proposed; foundational algorithmic works are [21,23,28], which first proposed trapdoor samplers. The Micciancio-Peikert framework [26] and its follow-up works [13] directly construct lattices that can easily be sampled from using [21,28]. Note that unlike our work, these works only considered statistically correct sampling and Gaussian distributions. This is also true for their follow-up works, with the exception of the ones discussed below.

Sampling from non-Gaussian distributions in the Micciancio-Peikert framework was considered by [25], and sampling exactly via analytical techniques was studied by [11]. We note that [21,31] considered a similar idea to ours. Unfortunately, both works consider instantiating it with Gaussians, leading to statistical correctness and exponential standard deviation.

2 Preliminaries

2.1 Lattices

Linear Algebra. We use the column convention for vectors, which are written in bold lower case letters $\mathbf{v}$. Matrices are written in bold upper case letters $\mathbf{M}$. The notation $\mathbf{M} = (\mathbf{b}_1 \ldots, \mathbf{b}_n)$ means that the i-th column of the matrix

$\mathbf{M}$ is $\mathbf{b}_i$. The identity matrix of rank n is written $\mathbf{I}_n$ and the set of $n \times n$ invertible matrices with coefficients in a ring R is written $\mathrm{GL}_n(R)$.

Given a matrix $\mathbf{B} \in \mathbb{R}^{n\times n}$, its Gram-Schmidt orthogonalization (GSO) is the unique decomposition $\mathbf{B} = \widetilde{\mathbf{B}} \cdot \mathbf{U}$ such that $\mathbf{U} \in \mathbb{R}^{n\times n}$ is upper-triangular with ones on the diagonal and the colmuns of $\widetilde{\mathbf{B}}$ are pairwise orthogonal. For $n \in \mathbb{N}$, $r \in \mathbb{R}_+$ and $p \in \{1, 2, \infty\}$, we define the centered ℓ_p hyperball of radius r as $\mathcal{B}_p^n(r) = \{\mathbf{x} \in \mathbb{R}^n \mid \|\mathbf{x}\|_p \leq r\}$. We introduce $s_1(\mathbf{B}) = \max_{\mathbf{x}\in\mathbb{R}^n\backslash 0^n} \frac{\|\mathbf{Bx}\|}{\|\mathbf{x}\|}$ to be the operator norm of a matrix $\mathbf{B}$ as an endomorphism of $(\mathbb{R}^n, \|\cdot\|_2)$, also known as spectral norm. The value of $s_1(\mathbf{B})$ is also the largest eigenvalue of $\mathbf{B}^t\mathbf{B}$. The fundamental parallelepiped associated to $\mathbf{B} \in \mathbb{R}^{m\times n}$ is $\mathcal{P}(\mathbf{B}) = \mathbf{B} \cdot [-1/2, 1/2]^n$.

Lattices. A lattice is a discrete subgroup of $\mathbb{R}^m$. Given a set $\mathbf{B} = (\mathbf{b}_1, \ldots, \mathbf{b}_n) \in \mathbb{R}^{m\times n}$ of linearly independent vectors in $\mathbb{R}^m$, we note $\mathcal{L}(\mathbf{B})$ the lattice generated by $\mathbf{B}$, that is

$$\mathcal{L}(\mathbf{B}) = \{\sum_{i=1}^{n} c_i \mathbf{b}_i,\ \mathbf{c} \in \mathbb{Z}^m\}.$$

In such a case, we say that $\mathbf{B}$ is a basis of $\mathcal{L}(\mathbf{B})$. In this document, we only consider full-rank lattices; for lattices of the form $\mathcal{L} = \mathcal{L}(\mathbf{B})$, it implies that $\mathbf{B}$ is a square invertible matrix. While our arguments readily extend to the general case, this choice makes their exposition simpler. Given a lattice $\mathcal{L}$, we note $\mathrm{Vol}(\mathcal{L})$ its volume, that is the absolute value of the determinant of any basis $\mathbf{B}$ of $\mathcal{L}$: $\mathrm{Vol}(\mathcal{L}) = |\det \mathbf{B}|$. One can check that all the bases of $\mathcal{L}$ have the same determinant (in absolute value), and this definition is therefore consistent. We call a *trapdoor* of a lattice $\mathcal{L}$ any set τ that characterizes the lattice, and write $\mathcal{L}(\tau)$ the lattice characterized by the trapdoor τ. When the trapdoor is a basis $\mathbf{B}$, the notation $\mathcal{L}(\mathbf{B})$ is consistent. Finally, the Voronoi cell of a lattice can be defined as follows :

$$\mathcal{V}(\mathcal{L}) = \{\mathbf{z} \in \mathbb{R}^n \mid \forall \mathbf{x} \in \mathcal{L},\ \|\mathbf{z}\|_2 \leq \|\mathbf{x} - \mathbf{z}\|_2\}.$$

Informally, the Voronoi cell of a lattice is the set of vectors that are closer to the origin than to any other lattice point (see [14] for further information).

Lattice Tilings. A family $\{\mathcal{T}_i\}_{i\in I}$ of sets in $\mathbb{R}^n$ is a tiling or a tessellation of $\mathbb{R}^n$ and the sets are called tiles if the union of sets covers $\mathbb{R}^n$ and the set interiors are mutually disjoint. We focus our study on *lattice tilings*, which are tilings of the form $\mathcal{T} + \mathcal{L} = \{\mathcal{T} + x\}_{x\in\mathcal{L}}$ for some lattice $\mathcal{L}$. For such tilings, $\mathcal{T}$ is called a *prototile* of the tiling. We note that if $\mathcal{T}$ is a prototile of $\mathcal{L}$, then $\mathrm{Vol}(\mathcal{T}) = \mathrm{Vol}(\mathcal{L})$. A tiling is called convex if all the tiles are compact convex bodies. The prototile of a convex lattice tiling is called a *parallelohedron*.[1] Figure 1 displays a few example of convex lattice tilings, for a fixed lattice but different parallelohedra.

[1] It has been conjectured by Voronoi [35] that every parallelohedron $\mathcal{T} \subset \mathcal{R}^n$ is affine equivalent to the Voronoi cell of some lattice $\mathcal{L}' \subset \mathcal{R}^n$.

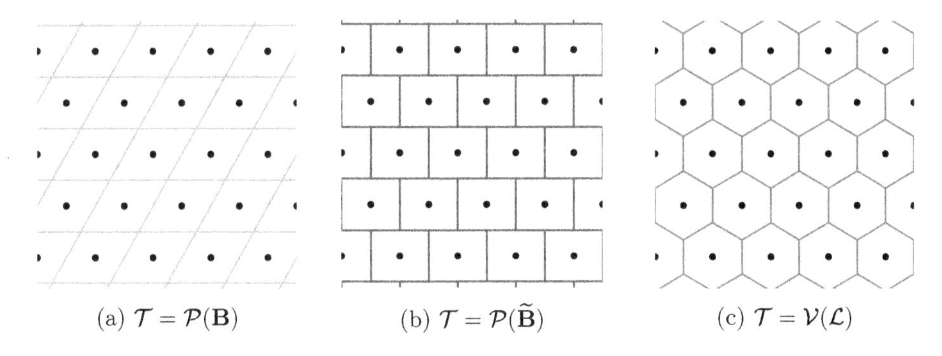

(a) $\mathcal{T} = \mathcal{P}(\mathbf{B})$ (b) $\mathcal{T} = \mathcal{P}(\widetilde{\mathbf{B}})$ (c) $\mathcal{T} = \mathcal{V}(\mathcal{L})$

Fig. 1. A few examples of convex lattice tilings $\mathcal{L}(\mathbf{B}) + \mathcal{T}$, for different values of the prototile $\mathcal{T}$: the fundamental parallelelepiped associated to $\mathbf{B}$, $\widetilde{\mathbf{B}}$ or the Voronoi cell of $\mathcal{L}$.

In this document, we almost exclusively work with the tile $\mathcal{T} = \mathcal{P}(\mathbf{B})$, so we introduce the notation $M_p(\mathbf{B}) = \sup\{\|\mathbf{x}\|_p \mid \mathbf{x} \in \mathcal{P}(\mathbf{B})\}$, which is also half the operator norm of $\mathbf{B}$ as a linear operator from $(\mathbb{R}^n, \|\cdot\|_\infty)$ to $(\mathbb{R}^n, \|\cdot\|_p)$. For $a \in \mathbb{R}$, we also note $\overrightarrow{a} = (a, \ldots, a)$.

$\mathcal{L}$-regular algorithms. The first of the two ingredients in our framework is the notion of ($\mathcal{L}$-)regular algorithms.

Definition 1 (Regular algorithm). *Let $\mathbf{T}$ be a set of trapdoors. Let $\mathcal{A} : \mathbf{T} \times \mathbb{R}^n \to \mathbb{R}^n$ be a deterministic algorithm taking as an input a trapdoor τ of a lattice $\mathcal{L}$, a target vector $\mathbf{t}$, and outputting a lattice point $\mathbf{v}$.*[2]

We say that $\mathcal{A}$ is $\mathcal{L}$-regular if for all $\tau \in \mathbf{T}$ such that $\mathcal{L} = \mathcal{L}(\tau)$, $\mathcal{A}(\tau, \mathbf{0}) = \mathbf{0}$ and if the set of points $\mathbf{y}$ such that the following equality holds:

$$\forall \mathbf{x} \in \mathbb{R}^n, \mathcal{A}(\tau, \mathbf{x} + \mathbf{y}) = \mathcal{A}(\tau, \mathbf{x}) + \mathbf{y}, \tag{1}$$

is exactly the lattice $\mathcal{L}$. If $\mathcal{A}$ is $\mathcal{L}$-regular for any lattice $\mathcal{L} \in \mathrm{GL}_n(\mathbb{R})/\mathrm{GL}_n(\mathbb{Z})$, i.e. for any couple $(\tau, \mathcal{L}(\tau))$, (1) holds for exactly $\mathbf{y} \in \mathcal{L}(\tau)$, we simply say that $\mathcal{A}$ is regular.

If $\mathcal{A}$ is $\mathcal{L}$-regular, then $\mathbf{x} \mapsto \mathcal{A}(\tau, \mathbf{x}) - \mathbf{x}$ is $\mathcal{L}$-periodic and admits $\mathbf{0}$ as a fixed point. Any $\mathcal{L}$-regular algorithm induces a $\mathcal{L}$-tiling. Indeed, for $\mathbf{v} \in \mathcal{L}$, let:

$$\mathcal{T}_{\mathbf{v}} = \{\mathbf{x} \in \mathbb{R}^n | \mathcal{A}(\tau, \mathbf{x}) = \mathbf{v}\}.$$

One can easily show that $\{\mathcal{T}_{\mathbf{v}}\}_{\mathbf{v} \in \mathcal{L}}$ is a $\mathcal{L}$-tiling. Finally, it is easy to show that the image of $\mathbf{x} \mapsto \mathcal{A}(\tau, \mathbf{x})$ is exactly the lattice $\mathcal{L}(\tau)$.

Examples of $\mathcal{L}$-regular algorithms include Babai's algorithms [7]. The round-off algorithm (Algorithm 1) induces the lattice tiling illustrated in Fig. 1a.

[2] From a practical viewpoint, one can think of the trapdoor as a short basis. The trapdoor can contain more information, such as the Gram-Schmidt orthogonalization (or GSO) of the basis, or any precomputation on the lattice.

The nearest plane algorithm (Algorithm 2) induces the lattice tiling illustrated in Fig. 1b. Any exact CVP solver (*i.e.* any algorithm that outputs a closest lattice point to the target) is also a valid example of $\mathcal{L}$-regular algorithm, and its induced tiling is the Voronoi diagram of $\mathcal{L}$, illustrated in Fig. 1c.

Algorithm 1: Babai round-off algorithm

Require: A basis $\mathbf{B} \in \mathbb{R}^{n\times n}$ of $\mathcal{L}$, a target $\mathbf{x} \in \mathbb{R}^n$
Ensure: $\mathbf{v} \in \mathcal{L} \cap \{\mathbf{x} + \mathcal{P}(\mathbf{B})\}$
1: $\mathbf{t} \leftarrow \mathbf{B}^{-1} \cdot \mathbf{x}$
2: **for** $i = 1, \ldots, n$ **do**
3: $z_i = \lfloor t_i \rceil$
4: **end for**
5: **return** $\mathbf{v} = \mathbf{B} \cdot \mathbf{z}$

Algorithm 2: Babai nearest plane algorithm

Require: A basis $\mathbf{B} \in \mathbb{R}^{n\times n}$ of $\mathcal{L}$, its GSO $\mathbf{B} = \widetilde{\mathbf{B}} \cdot \mathbf{U}$, a target $\mathbf{x} \in \mathbb{R}^n$
Ensure: $\mathbf{v} \in \mathcal{L} \cap \{\mathbf{x} + \mathcal{P}(\widetilde{\mathbf{B}})\}$
1: $\mathbf{t} \leftarrow \mathbf{B}^{-1} \cdot \mathbf{x}$
2: **for** $i = n, \ldots, 1$ **do**
3: $z_i \leftarrow \left\lfloor t_i + \sum_{j>i} (t_j - z_j) U_{ij} \right\rceil$
4: **end for**
5: **return** $\mathbf{v} = \mathbf{B} \cdot \mathbf{z}$

2.2 Distributions

Let $\mathcal{D}$ be a distribution of density f over $\mathbb{R}^n$. With $\mathcal{L}$ a lattice of $\mathbb{R}^n$, we define the discretization of $\mathcal{D}$ over $\mathcal{L}$, and we write $\mathcal{D}_{\mathcal{L}}$ the distribution of density

$$f_{\mathcal{L}} : \mathbf{x} \in \mathcal{L} \longmapsto \frac{f(\mathbf{x})}{f(\mathcal{L})},$$

where $f(\mathcal{L}) = \sum_{y\in\mathcal{L}} f(\mathbf{y})$. Let X be a real random variable, we write respectively $\mathbb{E}(X)$ and $\mathbb{V}(X)$ respectively the expected value and the variance of X. Both notations extend to vectors by coordinate-wise application. For a subset $\Omega \subset \mathbb{R}^n$, we write its indicator function $\mathbf{1}_{\Omega}$.

Let f be the density of a probability distribution $\mathcal{D}$ over $\mathbb{R}$ that we want to sample from. We define the Inverse Cumulative Density Function (after $\mathrm{ICDF}_{\mathcal{D}}$) as the reciprocal of the cumulative density function

$$\mathrm{ICDF}_{\mathcal{D}} = \left(x \longmapsto \int_{-\infty}^{x} f(t)\mathrm{d}t \right)^{-1}.$$

Proposition 1. *If the random variable U has a uniform distribution on $[0, 1]$, then the distribution of $\mathrm{ICDF}_{\mathcal{D}}(U)$ is $\mathcal{D}$.*

If evaluating the ICDF of a given distribution $\mathcal{D}$ is possible, one can use Proposition 1 to sample from $\mathcal{D}$.

2.3 Squaremonic Functions

In this subsection, we introduce the second ingredient of our framework: a class of functions that behave nicely when discretized over a lattice.

Definition 2 (Squaremonicity). *Let $\mathcal{T}$ be a prototile of a $\mathcal{L}$-regular tiling. We say that a function $f : \Omega \subset \mathbb{R}^n \longmapsto \mathbb{R}$ is $\mathcal{T}$-squaremonic if*

$$\forall \mathbf{x} \in \mathbb{R}^n \text{ such that } \mathcal{T} + \mathbf{x} \subset \Omega, \quad \frac{1}{\mathrm{Vol}(\mathcal{T})} \int_{\mathcal{T}+\mathbf{x}} f = f(\mathbf{x}). \tag{2}$$

We will refer to (2) as the squaremonic equation or the squaremonic property, and $\mathcal{T}$ is called a squaremonic tile of f. In addition, we say that a distribution is squaremonic if its density is squaremonic.

Notice that due to the linearity of the integral, for a given prototile $\mathcal{T}$, the set of $\mathcal{T}$-squaremonic functions is a linear space. We stress that these squaremonic functions are not only a theoretical object. Indeed, constant functions, linear functions (hence affine functions) and affine product functions admit squaremonic tiles. More details are given in Sect. 4.

The name *square-harmonic* or squaremonic is a portmanteau of *square* and *harmonic*. This name stems from a similarity between these squaremonic functions and harmonic functions. Harmonic functions on an open subset $\Omega \subset \mathbb{R}^n$ are the solutions of the equation $\Delta f = 0$, where $\Delta = \sum \partial_i^2$ is the Laplacian operator. Harmonicity is equivalent to the *Mean Value Property*, that is

$$\forall \mathbf{x} \in \Omega, \ \forall r > 0 \text{ such that } B_2^n(\mathbf{x}, r) \subset \Omega, \quad \frac{1}{\mathrm{Vol}(B_2^n(\mathbf{x}, r))} \int_{B_2^n(\mathbf{x},r)} f = f(\mathbf{x}). \tag{3}$$

Informally, the mean value of a harmonic function over a Euclidean ball of center $\mathbf{x}$ and radius r is the value of f in the center $\mathbf{x}$. The property (2) verified by squaremonic functions is similar to (3): the mean value of f over a fundamental domain of a lattice is the value of f in a fixed point of the fundamental domain. The scalability of the radius of the ball for harmonic functions makes a substantial difference with the mean value property for squaremonic functions. Indeed, the tile over which the mean value is calculated cannot, in general, be stretched out, which seems to provide less rich properties. Nonetheless, this resemblance between harmonic and squaremonic functions extends to the maximum principle, that is, the maximum of a harmonic function over the topologic closure of an open set Ω is the maximum over its boundary $\partial\Omega$. A similar yet weaker property holds for squaremonic functions : the maximum of a squaremonic function over the topologic closure of an open set Ω is the maximum over its thickened boundary $\{\mathbf{x} \in \Omega \mid \mathcal{T} + \mathbf{x} \subset \Omega\}$. To our knowledge, a few other properties of harmonic functions can be translated similarly into a squaremonic equivalent. Harmonic analysis is a vastly studied subject, the interested reader can refer to [5,24,27,34]. A crucial setup for squaremonicity in dimension n is the prototile $\mathcal{H}_n = [0,1]^n$ of the lattice $\mathbb{Z}^n$.

3 Our Framework

In this section we introduce the sampler framework, prove its correctness and give an analysis on how to set the parameters from a theoretical point of view.

3.1 Framework Description

As mentioned in the previous sections, the main idea of the sampler is to discretize a continuous distribution over a chosen lattice $\mathcal{L}$. The sampler needs to be provided with two algorithms : $\mathsf{Sample}\mathcal{D}$ to sample from the continuous distribution $\mathcal{D}$, and an $\mathcal{L}$-regular CVP algorithm $\mathcal{A}$ to discretize the distribution over the lattice. The conditions for the sampler to be correct and its running time are specified in Theorem 1.

Algorithm 3: Squaremonic Sampler

Require: A trapdoor τ of a lattice $\mathcal{L}$, a target $\mathbf{c}$
Ensure: $\mathbf{x}$ sampled from $\mathcal{D}_{\mathcal{L}}$ of support $\Omega_{\mathbf{c}} \subset \mathbb{R}^n$
1: **while** True **do**
2: $\quad\mathbf{y} \leftarrow \mathsf{Sample}\mathcal{D}$ $\quad\{\mathsf{Sample}\mathcal{D}$ samples from $\mathcal{D}\}$
3: $\quad\mathbf{x} = \mathcal{A}(\tau, \mathbf{c} + \mathbf{y})$
4: $\quad$**if** $\mathbf{x} - \mathbf{c} \in \Omega$ **then**
5: $\quad\quad$Return $\mathbf{x}$
6: $\quad$**end if**
7: **end while**

Theorem 1. *Let τ be a trapdoor of a lattice $\mathcal{L}$ and $\mathcal{A} : \mathbf{T} \times \mathbb{R}^n \longrightarrow \mathbb{R}^n$ be a deterministic algorithm with $\tau \in \mathbf{T}$. Let $\mathcal{D}$ be a distribution of density f over some subset $\Omega' \subset \mathbb{R}^n$. Let $\Omega \subset \Omega'$ be a measurable set, and $\mathbf{c} \in \mathbb{R}^n$. Suppose that:*

1. *$\mathcal{D}$ is sampleable in polynomial time.*
2. *$\mathcal{A}$ is an $\mathcal{L}$-regular algorithm inducing a tiling of prototile $\mathcal{T} = \mathcal{T}_{\mathbf{0}}$.*
3. *The density f is $\mathcal{T}$-squaremonic.*
4. *The set Ω is such that $\Omega \subset \{\mathbf{x} \mid \mathbf{x} + \mathcal{T} \subset \Omega'\} \subset \Omega'$. We moreover require that testing that some vector $\mathbf{x}$ is in Ω can be done efficiently.*

Then the output $\mathbf{x}$ of Algorithm 3 is distributed as follows:

$$\mathbf{x} \sim \{(\mathbf{c} + \mathcal{D})\mathbf{1}_{\Omega_{\mathbf{c}}}\}_{\mathcal{L}}, \tag{4}$$

where $\Omega_{\mathbf{c}} = \Omega + \mathbf{c}$. In addition, the expected number of iterations of the **while** *loop is $\mathcal{D}((\mathcal{L} - \mathbf{c}) \cap \Omega + \mathcal{T})^{-1}$.*

Proof. We prove separately correctness and the number of iterations.

Correctness. First, we note that the output $\mathbf{x}$ of Algorithm 3 is necessarily in $\mathcal{L} \cap \Omega_{\mathbf{c}}$. On one hand, it follows from the $\mathcal{L}$-regularity of $\mathcal{A}$ that $\mathbb{P}[\mathbf{x} = \mathbf{v}] = 0$ for any $\mathbf{v} \notin \mathcal{L}$. On the other hand, $\mathbf{x}$ is rejected at step 4 if and only if $\mathbf{x} - \mathbf{c} \notin \Omega$.

Now, we study the probability that $\mathbf{v} \in \mathcal{L} \cap \Omega_{\mathbf{c}}$ is output. The random variable $\mathbf{y}$ follows the distribution $\mathcal{D}$, hence $\mathbf{c}+\mathbf{y}$ follows the distribution $\mathbf{c}+\mathcal{D}$. At the end of step 3:

$$\begin{aligned} \mathbb{P}[\mathbf{x}=\mathbf{v}] &= \mathbb{P}_{\mathbf{y}\leftarrow\mathcal{D}}[\mathbf{c}+\mathbf{y}\in\mathcal{T}_{\mathbf{v}}] & (5)\\ &= \int_{\mathcal{T}_{\mathbf{v}}} f(\mathbf{t}-\mathbf{c})\mathrm{d}\mathbf{t} & (6)\\ &= \int_{(\mathbf{v}-\mathbf{c})+\mathcal{T}} f(\mathbf{t})\mathrm{d}\mathbf{t} & (7)\\ &= \mathrm{Vol}(\mathcal{T})\cdot f(\mathbf{v}-\mathbf{c}) & (8) \end{aligned}$$

(5) follows from the fact that $\mathbf{v}$ is output if and only if $\mathbf{c}+\mathbf{v}$ is in $\mathcal{T}_{\mathbf{v}}$. Since $\Omega+\mathcal{T}\subseteq\Omega'$ and $\mathbf{v}\in\Omega_{\mathbf{c}}$, it implies that $\mathcal{T}_{\mathbf{v}}\subseteq\Omega'_{\mathbf{c}}$ and (6) is therefore valid. (7) is a simple change of variable (translation by $\mathbf{c}$). Finally, and most crucially, (8) follows from the $\mathcal{T}$-squaremonicity of f. Therefore the distribution of $\mathbf{x}$ is proportional to $f(\mathbf{v}-\mathbf{c})$, and its support is exactly $\mathcal{L}\cap\Omega_{\mathbf{c}}$. The result follows.

Number of Iterations. The support of the output of Algorithm 3 is exactly $\mathcal{L}\cap\Omega_{\mathbf{c}}$. Combining this fact with (6), the probability that Algorithm 3 terminates at a given iteration is:

$$P := \sum_{\mathbf{v}\in\mathcal{L}\cap\Omega_{\mathbf{c}}} \int_{\mathcal{T}_{\mathbf{v}}} f(\mathbf{t}-\mathbf{c})\mathrm{d}\mathbf{t} = \sum_{\mathbf{v}\in(\mathcal{L}-\mathbf{c})\cap\Omega} \int_{\mathcal{T}_{\mathbf{v}}} f(\mathbf{t})\mathrm{d}\mathbf{t} = \mathcal{D}((\mathcal{L}-\mathbf{c})\cap\Omega+\mathcal{T}) \quad (9)$$

and the expected number of iterations is $1/P$. □

Figure 2 provides a visual illustration of our framework. A continuous distribution is sampled (Fig. 2a) and discretized (Fig. 2b) via a regular algorithm (here, the round-off algorithm). Finally, a rejection step (Fig. 2c) discards all points outside $\Omega_{\mathbf{c}}$ since these might leak information about the basis used.

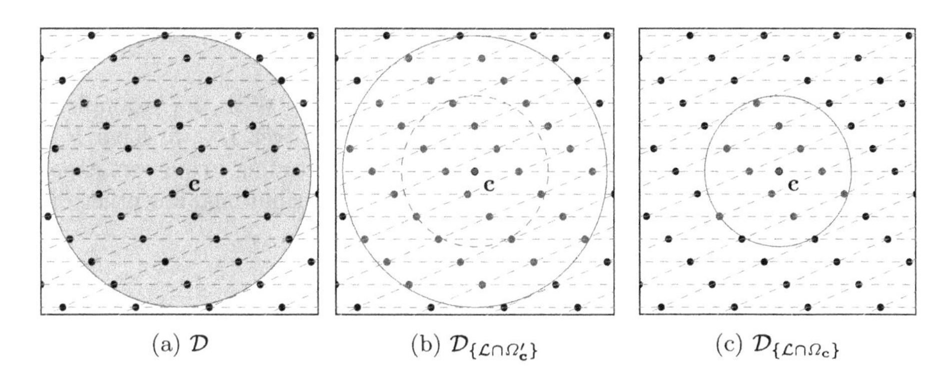

Fig. 2. Visual illustration of Algorithm 3. A continuous distribution is sampled (a), then discretized (b), and finally rejection sampling is applied (c).

Security. The security of our framework is given by the independance between the trapdoor used in the regular algorithm and the output distribution. The security of our framework is therefore immediate from Theorem 1. Indeed, the output distribution of the proposed sampler is *perfectly* indistinguishable from the ideal distribution $\{\mathbf{c}+\mathcal{D}\}_{\mathcal{L}\cap\Omega_\mathbf{c}}$. There is therefore no leakage of information as long as Ω is independent from the trapdoor. In the instantiations we propose, this is indeed the case. This differs from classical samplers, which are only *statistically* indistinguishable from ideal distributions.

Using our sampler in a specific cryptographic scheme may mandate additional context-specific requirements. For example, using it in a signature scheme *à la* [21] requires the distribution to satisfy something analog to their leftover hash lemma [21, Lemma 5.1], but this will be verified easily for the (currently) large distributions that our framework samples from.

3.2 Rejection Rate and Parameter Analysis

The acceptance rate P is the weight of the discretization $\mathcal{D}_\mathcal{L}$ over $\Omega + \mathbf{c}$, which by squaremonicity of f is given by $P = \mathcal{D}(\mathcal{L} \cap (\Omega + \mathbf{c}) + \mathcal{T})$. While the concrete value of P seems hard to calculate, we have two strategies to give an estimate. The first strategy is to lower bound the probability P by considering the set

$$\Omega'' = \bigcup_{\substack{A \subset \Omega' \\ A - \mathcal{T} \subset \Omega}} A.$$

Indeed, it follows from the definition that $\mathbf{y} \in \Omega''$ implies $\mathbf{x} \in \Omega + \mathbf{c}$, hence the sample is accepted, therefore we have $P \geq P'' := \mathcal{D}(\Omega'')$. Using this conservative bound in our implementation to choose the parameters of the distribution underestimates the actual empirical acceptance rate by a constant factor. The second strategy is to use the so-called Gaussian heuristic, that is a prediction of the number of lattice points in a measurable convex body of $\mathbb{R}^n$.

Heuristic 1 (Gaussian Heuristic). *Let $\mathcal{L}$ be a full rank lattice of $\mathbb{R}^n$. For a convex body $K \subset \mathbb{R}^n$, we have*

$$|\mathcal{L} \cap K| \simeq \frac{\mathrm{Vol}(K)}{\mathrm{Vol}(\mathcal{L})}.$$

Under Heuristic 1, we have $|\mathcal{L} \cap \Omega| = \mathrm{Vol}(\Omega)/\mathrm{Vol}(\mathcal{L})$. With, for example, f constant (corresponding to the uniform distribution) over Ω', we have $P = \mathrm{Vol}(\Omega)/\mathrm{Vol}(\mathcal{L}) \cdot \mathrm{Vol}(\mathcal{L})/\mathrm{Vol}(\Omega') = \mathrm{Vol}(\Omega)/\mathrm{Vol}(\Omega')$. According to our own experiments, this estimate is very accurate for constant distributions. For other distributions, we extrapolate the previous formula to

$$P = \mathcal{D}(\Omega).$$

While this estimate is unlikely to be accurate[3], it matches with our experiments on uniform and affine distributions for reasonable (constant) acceptance rates.

[3] The difference with uniform is that in general the integrals of f over $\Omega \backslash (\mathcal{L} \cap \Omega + \mathcal{T})$ and $(\mathcal{L} \cap \Omega + \mathcal{T}) \cap (\Omega' \backslash \Omega)$ do not compensate each other.

Heuristic 2. *With notations from Theorem 1, the probability* $P = \mathcal{D}((\mathcal{L} - c) \cap \Omega + \mathcal{T})$ *is* $\mathcal{D}(\Omega)$.

We note that as we narrow the support Ω_c of the final distribution, the acceptance rate of our algorithm will become increasingly lower. In practice, lowering the standard deviations given in Table 1 even by a constant factor can result in an huge blow-up in the running time.

4 Instantiations of Our Framework

In this section, we instantiate the framework described in Sect. 3 with various examples of distributions and the RoundOff algorithm. The first subsection presents properties of squaremonic functions. We give a partial study of their properties and examples.

Instantiating our framework implies setting four components: a continuous support Ω', a probability distribution $\mathcal{D}$ over Ω', an $\mathcal{L}$-regular algorithm of prototile $\mathcal{T}$ and a set Ω[4] such that the support of the sampled distribution is $\mathcal{L} \cap \Omega$. We only consider the RoundOff algorithm for explicit examples and explain how to extend the results to both the NearestPlane algorithm, and the ExactCVP when it is possible.

Table 1 sums up the standard deviation (up to a constant factor that we omit) of the distribution that can be sampled with our framework for a constant acceptance rate (independent of the dimension n). A ✗ mark means that the distribution is in general not squaremonic over the tile of the regular algorithm.

Table 1. Standard deviation achieved in constant acceptance rate for the regular algorithm/distribution couple by Algorithm 3.

	ℓ_∞ Uniform	ℓ_2 Uniform	Affine	Affine product
RoundOff	$n^{1.5} s_1(\mathbf{B})$	$n s_1(\mathbf{B})$	$n^{1.5} s_1(\mathbf{B})$	$n^{1.5} s_1(\mathbf{B})$
NearestPlane	$n^{1.5} s_1(\widetilde{\mathbf{B}})$	$n s_1(\widetilde{\mathbf{B}})$	$n^{1.5} s_1(\widetilde{\mathbf{B}})$	$n^{1.5} s_1(\widetilde{\mathbf{B}})$
ExactCVP	$n^{1.5} \rho_\infty(\mathcal{L})$	$n^{1.5} \rho_2(\mathcal{L})$	$n^{1.5} \rho_1(\mathcal{L})$	✗

4.1 Mean Value Property over Regular Tilings

In this section, we provide two interpretations of squaremonicity which may be more intuitive than the arguably abstract Definition 2. We also explain how in many cases, we can reduce the study of a $\mathcal{T}$-squaremonic function (for an arbitrary tile $\mathcal{T}$), to studying a $\mathcal{H}_n$-squaremonic function (for the hypercube $\mathcal{H}_n = [0,1]^n$), then to studying n $[0,1]$-squaremonic functions. This simplifies many subsequent proofs and arguments.

[4] Remind that testing that a vector is in the set Ω has to be easy. In the examples we develop, such a test reduces to computing an ℓ_p norm for p in $\{1, 2, \infty\}$, and an inequality.

Intuitive Interpretations. There are at least two geometric interpretations of the notion of squaremonic distributions. The first one is as follows. Consider a distribution $\mathcal{D}$ and a $\mathcal{L}$-regular tiling $\mathcal{L} + \mathcal{T}$ of the space, of prototile $\mathcal{T}$. We define $\mathcal{D}_1$ as the discretization of $\mathcal{D}$ over $\mathcal{L}$. In addition, we define $\mathcal{D}_2$ as a $\mathcal{T}$-rounding of $\mathcal{D}$ over $\mathcal{L}$; more precisely, given a point $\mathbf{v} \in \mathcal{L}$, we set $\mathcal{D}_2(\mathbf{v})$ as the integral of the density function of $\mathcal{D}$ over the compact set $\mathbf{v} + \mathcal{T}$. Saying that $\mathcal{D}$ is $\mathcal{T}$-squaremonic implies that $\mathcal{D}_1$ and $\mathcal{D}_2$ are the same distribution. Note that when $\mathcal{D}$ is a continuous Gaussian, $\mathcal{D}_1$ and $\mathcal{D}_2$ are what is commonly called a *discrete Gaussian* and *rounded Gaussian*, respectively. For Gaussians, $\mathcal{D}_1$ and $\mathcal{D}_2$ are in general *not* equal.

For an interpretation more oriented towards mathematical analysis, consider a continuous function $f : \mathbb{R} \longrightarrow \mathbb{R}$. For all $x \in \mathbb{R}$, via the intermediate value theorem, there exists a number $0 < a < 1$ such that

$$\int_{x}^{x+1} f(t)\mathrm{d}t = f(x+a).$$

If f is monotonic, then $a(x)$ is unique; we then abusively note $a : x \mapsto a(x)$ the continuous function mapping x to $a(x)$. Here, saying that f is squaremonic with respect to the tile $\mathcal{T} = [0, 1)$ is equivalent to saying that a is constant.

Separable Squaremonic Functions. In this paragraph, we split the set of squaremonic functions in two: those that satisfy a $\mathrm{GL}_n(\mathbb{R})$ stability condition, and those that have separated variables (both sets are not disjoint). This simplifies proofs and makes arguments clearer.

We assume for this discussion that the regular algorithm we use is $\mathsf{RoundOff} \circ t_{\mathbf{Ba}}$ with $t_{\mathbf{Ba}}$ the translation by $\mathbf{Ba}$, so $\mathcal{T} = \mathcal{P}(\mathbf{M}) - \mathbf{Ma}$ for some matrix $\mathbf{M}$ and some vector $\mathbf{a} \in \mathcal{H}_n$. Let $\mathcal{C}$ be a set of functions such that $\forall f \in \mathcal{C}$, $\forall \mathbf{M} \in \mathrm{GL}_n(\mathbb{R})$, $f \circ \mathbf{M} \in \mathcal{C}$. All the examples we develop in this paper (namely constant, affine and affine product) share this $\mathrm{GL}_n(\mathbb{R})$ stability property. Let f be a function from such a set $\mathcal{C}$. The study of the squaremonic equation of f relatively to $\mathcal{P}(\mathbf{M}) - \mathbf{Ba}$ reduces via a substitution to the study of $f \circ \mathbf{M}^{-1}$'s squaremonicity over a translation of $\mathcal{H}_n$, the canonical tile. This fact suggests that for such classes of functions, we study the squaremonicity in the canonical setup first, and extend the result to any basis of any lattice.

Let us consider a lattice $\mathcal{L} = \mathcal{L}(\mathbf{B})$, together with the translated $\mathsf{RoundOff}$ tile $\mathcal{P}(\mathbf{B}) - \mathbf{Ba}$. As argued in the previous paragraph, we first study the squaremonicity of some function f over the canonical tile $\mathcal{H}_n$. In this paragraph, we study squaremonic functions with separated variables, that is squaremonic functions f such that $f(\mathbf{x}) = \prod_{i=1}^{n} f_i(x_i)$ (which correspond to all our instantiations, except affine and ℓ_2 uniform). Then, the squaremonicity of f relatively to $\mathcal{H}_n - \mathbf{a}$ is equivalent to $\forall\ 1 \le i \le n,\ f_i$ is squaremonic relatively to $\mathcal{H}_1 - a_i$. This fact comes from the factorization of the squaremonic integral into 1-dimensional integrals. Assume, all f_i's are squaremonic relatively to $\mathcal{H}_1 - a_i$, then

$$\begin{aligned}\int_{\mathcal{H}_n-\mathbf{a}+\mathbf{x}} f(\mathbf{t})\mathrm{d}\mathbf{t} &= \int_{\mathcal{H}_n-\mathbf{a}+\mathbf{x}} \prod_{i=1}^{n} f_i(t_i)\mathrm{d}t_i \\ &= \prod_{i=1}^{n} \int_{[-a_i,1-a_i]+x_i} f(t_i)\mathrm{d}t_i \\ &= \prod_{i=1}^{n} f_i(x_i) \\ &= f(\mathbf{x}),\end{aligned}$$

and f is squaremonic relatively to the canonical tile (with an offset parameter $\mathbf{a}$ for the unit hypercube), and vice-versa. Constant distributions (over a hypercube) and affine product distributions (functions of the type $\mathbf{x} \longmapsto \prod_i (a_i x_i + b_i)$, for some vectors $\mathbf{a}, \mathbf{b} \in \mathbb{R}^n$) share this property that their variables are separated, therefore their n-dimensional squaremonicity reduces to n times 1-dimensional squaremonicity. Moreover, sampling from a separated variables density can be done coordinate-wise in parallel (as each coordinate is independent from the others), which is algorithmic-wise convenient.

4.2 Uniform Distributions with the RoundOff Algorithm

Let Ω be a compact subset of $\mathbb{R}^n$. We define the (continuous) uniform distribution over Ω as the distribution of density proportional to $\mathbf{1}_\Omega$, and write it $\mathcal{U}(\Omega)$. We will consider two different shapes for Ω : the ℓ_2 balls, to optimize the shortness of the output and the ℓ_∞ balls to optimize the speed and simplicity of the sampler. Because constant functions are squaremonic for any prototile, any regular algorithm would work.

Uniform Distribution over a Hypercube. The first example of uniform distribution over a lattice we give is the uniform distribution over a hypercube. The reason for this choice is that over a hypercube, the coordinates of the random vector are independent, which makes the continuous sampling very easy.

Proposition 2 (ℓ_∞ Uniform with RoundOff instantiation). *Let $\mathbf{B}$ be a basis of a lattice $\mathcal{L}$ and $\mathbf{c} \in \mathbb{R}^n$. The instantiation of Algorithm 3 with*

1. $\Omega' = [-nM_\infty(\mathbf{B}), nM_\infty(\mathbf{B})]^n$
2. $\Omega = [-(n-1)M_\infty(\mathbf{B}), (n-1)M_\infty(\mathbf{B})]^n$
3. $\mathcal{D} = \mathcal{U}(\Omega')$
4. $\mathcal{A} = \mathsf{RoundOff}(\mathbf{B}, \cdot)$

satisfies the requirements of Theorem 1 and its acceptance rate is heuristically and asymptotically $P \longrightarrow 1/e$. In other words, the uniform distribution over the hypercube of radius $(n-1)M_\infty(\mathbf{B})$ and center $\mathbf{c}$ is sampleable in polynomial time using Algorithm 3.

Proof. Correctness. We check the requirements of Theorem 1. For Item 1, sampling from $\mathcal{D}$ is done easily by sampling uniformly over $[0, 1]^n$ and applying an affine transformation. For Item 2, the RoundOff algorithm is indeed $\mathcal{L}$-regular of prototile $\mathcal{P}(\mathbf{B})$. For Item 3, the density $\mathbf{1}_{\Omega'}$ is trivially $\mathcal{P}(\mathbf{B})$-squaremonic. Finally, for Item 4, by triangle inequality, if $\mathbf{y} = \mathbf{x}+\mathbf{t} \in \Omega+\mathcal{P}(\mathbf{B})$, $\|\mathbf{y}\|_\infty \leq (n-1)M_\infty(\mathbf{B}) + M_\infty(\mathbf{B})$, so $\Omega + \mathcal{P}(\mathbf{B}) \subset \Omega'$, and the instantiation is correct.

Expected Running Time and Radius. Under Heuristic 1, the probability of a sample to be accepted is given by

$$P \simeq \frac{\mathrm{Vol}(\Omega)}{\mathrm{Vol}\,\Omega'} = \left(\frac{(n-1)M_\infty(\mathbf{B})}{nM_\infty(\mathbf{B})}\right)^n = \left(1 - \frac{1}{n}\right)^n.$$

□

Proposition 3. *Let X be a random variable following the discrete uniform distribution $\mathcal{U}([-R, R]^n)_\mathcal{L}$. Then, the expected ℓ_2 norm of X is bounded by*

$$\|X\|_2 \leq \frac{n^2}{2} s_1(\mathbf{B}).$$

Proof. With notations from Proposition 2 and using inequalities between ℓ_2 and ℓ_∞ norms, we have

$$\|X\|_2 \leq \sqrt{n}\|X\|_\infty \leq n^{1.5}M_\infty/2 \leq \frac{n^2}{2} s_1(\mathbf{B})$$

This completes the proof. □

Uniform Distribution Over an ℓ_2 Hyperball. In this paragraph we give a second example of uniform distribution, this time over a ℓ_2 ball of dimension n. Although sampling uniformly random from this set seems more complicated than a hypercube, the ℓ_2 norm of the output random variable with parameter associated to a constant acceptance rate is in average $\sqrt{n}$ lower in the hyperball than in the hypercube (Propositions 3 and 5). As in the previous example, we chose the usual RoundOff algorithm, but any regular CVP algorithm would work.

Proposition 4 (ℓ_2 Uniform with RoundOff instantiation). *The instantiation of Algorithm 3 with*

1. $\Omega' = \mathcal{B}_2^n(nM_2(\mathbf{B}))$
2. $\Omega = \mathcal{B}_2^n((n-1)M_2(\mathbf{B}))$
3. $\mathcal{D} = \mathcal{U}(\Omega')$
4. $\mathcal{A} = \mathsf{RoundOff}(\mathbf{B}, \cdot)$

satisfies the requirements of Theorem 1 and its rejection rate is heuristically and asymptotically $P \longrightarrow 1/e$. In other words, for any center $\mathbf{c} \in \mathbb{R}^n$, the distribution $\mathcal{U}_{\mathcal{L},\mathbf{c}}(nM_2(\mathbf{B}))$ is sampleable in polynomial time.

Proof. Correctness. We check the requirements of Theorem 1. For Item 1, there are several polynomial-time algorithms that sample from the continuous uniform distribution over ℓ_2 balls, for example an ICDF-like algorithm using the identity $\mathcal{U}([0,1])^{1/n} \cdot \mathcal{U}(\mathcal{S}_{n-1}) \sim \mathcal{U}(\mathcal{B}_2^n(1))$ (sampling from the unit sphere $\mathcal{S}_{n-1}$ can be done using results from [15,33], or normalizing spherical Gaussian distributions), using the algorithm from [8], etc. For Item 2, the RoundOff is $\mathcal{L}$ regular for any basis and has prototile $\mathcal{T} = \mathcal{P}(\mathbf{B})$. For Item 3, the distribution $\mathcal{D}$ has density $\mathbf{1}_{\Omega'}$ which is trivially squaremonic over $\mathcal{P}(\mathbf{B})$. Finally, for Item 4, with $M_2(\mathbf{B}) = \max\{\|\mathbf{x}\| \mid \mathbf{x} \in \mathcal{P}(\mathbf{B})\}$, we have $\Omega' \subset \Omega + \mathcal{T}$ via the triangular inequality of $\|.\|_2$.

Expected Running Time and Radius. Under Heuristic 1, the probability of a sample to be accepted is given by

$$P \simeq \frac{\mathrm{Vol}(\Omega)}{\mathrm{Vol}(\Omega')}.$$

The volume of a n-hyperball is homogeneous to the n-th power of its radius. Otherly said, $P \simeq ((n-1)M_2(\mathbf{B})/(nM_2(\mathbf{B})))^n$, which completes the proof. □

Proposition 5. *Let $\mathcal{L}$ be a lattice of basis $\mathbf{B}$. Let X be the output of the instantiation of Proposition 4 (X follows $\mathcal{U}((n-1)M_2(\mathbf{B}))_{\mathcal{L}}$). Then we have*

$$\|X\|_2 \leq \frac{n^{1.5}}{2} s_1(\mathbf{B}).$$

Proof. We have $X \in \mathcal{B}_2^n((n-1)M_2)$, therefore $\|X\|_2 \leq (n-1)M_2$. Moreover, we have $M_2 \leq \frac{\sqrt{n}}{2} s_1(\mathbf{B})$, which completes the proof. □

In both uniform examples above, using the NearestPlane (respectively an ExactCVP) instead of the RoundOff is also valid and yields similar results, substituting $\mathcal{P}(\mathbf{B})$ by $\mathcal{P}(\widetilde{\mathbf{B}})$ (respectively the Voronoi cell of the lattice), and $M_p(\mathbf{B})$ by $M_p(\widetilde{\mathbf{B}})$ (respectively $\rho_p(\mathcal{L})$, the *covering radius* of the lattice, relatively to the ℓ_p norm).

4.3 Affine Distributions with the RoundOff Algorithm

Let $R > 0$ and $\mathcal{B}_{1+}^n(R) = \mathcal{B}_1^n(R) \cap \mathbb{R}_+^n$. We define the affine distribution $\mathcal{A}_n(R, R')$ of parameters R and $R' \geq R$ over $\mathcal{B}_{1+}^n(R)$ as the distribution of density $\mathbf{x} \longmapsto (R' - \|\mathbf{x}\|_1)\, \mathbf{1}_{\mathcal{B}_{1+}^n(R)}$. We define numbers $m_1^i(\mathbf{B}) = \max\{|x_i| \mid \mathbf{x} \in \mathcal{P}(\mathbf{B})\}$, and the point $\mathbf{m}_1(\mathbf{B})$ which coordinates are the $m_1^i(\mathbf{B})$'s.

Proposition 6 (Affine distribution with RoundOff instantiation). *Let $\mathbf{B}$ be a basis of a lattice $\mathcal{L}$ and $\mathbf{c} \in \mathbb{R}^n$. The instantiation of Algorithm 3 with*

1. $\Omega' = \mathcal{B}_{1+}^n(R') - \mathbf{m}_1(\mathbf{B})$, *with* $R' = (n+1)(M_1(\mathbf{B}) + \|\mathbf{m}_1(\mathbf{B})\|_1)$
2. $\Omega = \mathcal{B}_{1+}^n(R)$, *with* $R = n(M_1(\mathbf{B}) + \|\mathbf{m}_1(\mathbf{B})\|_1)$
3. $\mathcal{D} = \mathcal{A}_n(R', R') - \mathbf{m}_1(\mathbf{B})$
4. $\mathcal{A} = \mathsf{RoundOff}(\mathbf{B}, \cdot)$

is correct and its acceptance rate is heuristically and asymptotically $P \longrightarrow 1/e$. In other words, the distribution $\mathcal{A}(R, R')_{\mathcal{L},\mathbf{c}}$ is sampleable in polynomial time.

Proof. Correctness. We check the requirements of Theorem 1. For Item 1, Algorithm 4 is an example of such polynomial time continuous sampler, which correctness is stated by Lemma 1. For Item 2, the RoundOff algorithm is $\mathcal{L}$-regular, with prototile $\mathcal{P}(\mathbf{B})$. For Item 3, we want to prove that $f : \mathbf{x} \longmapsto R - \|\mathbf{x}\|_1$ is squaremonic for $\mathcal{P}(\mathbf{B})$. Notice that f is affine, that is $f = R + u$, with R constant and $u : \mathbb{R}^n \longrightarrow \mathbb{R}$ linear. With $\mathcal{H}_n^- = \{\mathbf{x} \in \mathcal{H}_n - \mathbf{1/2} \;/\; x_1 \leq 0\}$ and $\mathcal{H}_n^+ = -\mathcal{H}_n^-$, we have the following :

$$\int_{\mathcal{P}(\mathbf{B})+\mathbf{x}} f(\mathbf{y})\mathrm{d}\mathbf{y} = \int_{\mathcal{P}(\mathbf{B})+\mathbf{x}} (R + u(\mathbf{y}))\,\mathrm{d}\mathbf{y} \tag{10}$$

$$= \int_{\mathcal{P}(\mathbf{B})} (R + u(\mathbf{z}) + u(\mathbf{x}))\,\mathrm{d}\mathbf{z} \tag{11}$$

$$= \mathrm{Vol}(\mathcal{P}(\mathbf{B}))f(\mathbf{x}) + \int_{\mathcal{P}(\mathbf{B})} u(\mathbf{z})\mathrm{d}\mathbf{z} \tag{12}$$

$$= \det \mathcal{L} f(\mathbf{x}) + \det \mathcal{L} \left(\int_{\mathcal{H}_n^-} u + \int_{\mathcal{H}_n^+} u \right) \tag{13}$$

$$= \det \mathcal{L} f(\mathbf{x}) \tag{14}$$

where (11) comes from the substitution $\mathbf{y} = \mathbf{z} + \mathbf{x}$, (12) comes from the linearity of the integral, (13) comes from the substitution $\mathbf{B}\mathbf{w} = \mathbf{z}$ and splitting the integral over $\mathcal{H}_n$ into the positive and negative part, and (14) comes from the fact that as u is linear, it is odd and the two integrals cancel each other. Finally, for Item 4, by the triangular inequality, if $\mathbf{x} = \mathbf{y} + \mathbf{t} \in \Omega + \mathcal{P}(\mathbf{B})$, then $\mathbf{x} + \mathbf{m}_1(\mathbf{B}) \in \mathbb{R}_+^n$ and $\|\mathbf{x}\|_1 \leq nM_1(\mathbf{B}) + M_1(\mathbf{B})$, so $\Omega + \mathcal{T} \subset \Omega'$.

Expected Running Time and Radius. According to Heuristic 2, the acceptance rate P is given by

$$P = \int_{\Omega} f.$$

Let R be the radius of Ω. First, f is proportional to $\mathbf{x} \longmapsto R + M_1(\mathbf{B}) + \|\mathbf{m}_1(\mathbf{B})\|_1 - \|\mathbf{x} + \mathbf{m}_1(\mathbf{B})\|_1$. The graph of the latter function describes the $n+1$ dimensional ℓ_1 ball over the all-positive quadrant $\mathbb{R}_+^n$ of $\mathbb{R}^n$, so the normalization factor is $1/2^n$ times the volume of the ℓ_1 ball of dimension $n+1$ and radius $R + M_1(\mathbf{B}) + \|\mathbf{m}_1(\mathbf{B})\|_1$. In the end,

$$f(\mathbf{x}) = \frac{(n+1)!}{(R + M_1(\mathbf{B}) + \|\mathbf{m}_1(\mathbf{B})\|_1)^{n+1}} \cdot (R + M_1(\mathbf{B}) + \|\mathbf{m}_1(\mathbf{B})\|_1 - \|\mathbf{x}\|_1).$$

Now, we calculate the acceptance rate, writing M_1 instead of $M_1(\mathbf{B})$ and $\mathbf{m}_1$ instead of $\mathbf{m}_1(\mathbf{B})$ to save space.

$$P = \int_{\mathcal{B}_{1+}^n(R)} f(\mathbf{t})\mathrm{d}\mathbf{t} \tag{15}$$

$$= \frac{(n+1)!}{(R + M_1 + \|\mathbf{m}_1\|_1)^{n+1}} \int_{\mathcal{B}_{1+}^n(R)} (R + M_1 + \|\mathbf{m}_1\|_1 - \|\mathbf{x} + \mathbf{m}_1\|_1)\, \mathrm{d}\mathbf{x} \tag{16}$$

$$= \frac{(n+1)!}{(R + M_1 + \|\mathbf{m}_1\|_1)^{n+1}} \cdot \int_{\mathcal{B}_{1+}^n(R)} (R + M_1 - \|\mathbf{x}\|_1)\, \mathrm{d}\mathbf{x} \tag{17}$$

$$= \frac{(n+1)!}{(R + M_1 + \|\mathbf{m}_1\|_1)^{n+1}} \left(\mathrm{Vol}(\mathcal{B}_{1+}^{n+1}(R)) + M_1 \mathrm{Vol}(\mathcal{B}_{1+}^n(R))\right) \tag{18}$$

$$= \left(1 - \frac{M_1 + \|\mathbf{m}_1\|_1}{R + M_1 + \|\mathbf{m}_1\|_1}\right)^{n+1} + \frac{(n+1)M_1}{R}\left(1 - \frac{M_1 + \|\mathbf{m}_1\|_1}{R + M_1 + \|\mathbf{m}_1\|_1}\right)^{n+1} \tag{19}$$

$$= \left(1 - \frac{M_1 + \|\mathbf{m}_1\|_1}{R + M_1 + \|\mathbf{m}_1\|_1}\right)^{n+1} \left(1 + \frac{(n+1)M_1}{R}\right), \tag{20}$$

where (15) is the estimate Sect. 3.2, (17) follows from the fact that $\|\mathbf{x} - \mathbf{m}_1\|_1 = \|\mathbf{x}\|_1 + \|\mathbf{m}_1\|_1$, (18) follows from the linearity of the integral and from the fact that the graph of $\mathbf{x} \longmapsto R - \|\mathbf{x}\|_1$ over $\mathcal{B}_{1+}^n(R)$ describes the set $\mathcal{B}_{1+}^{n+1}(R) \cap \mathbb{R}_+^n$, and (19) follows from the fact that $\mathrm{Vol}(\mathcal{B}_{1+}^n(r)) = \frac{r^n}{(n+1)!}$. Finally, one can check that if the radius of Ω verifies $R = n(M_1 + \|\mathbf{m}_1\|_1)$, then P converges to $1/e$. □

Lemma 1. *There is a polynomial time algorithm, that on input a dimension n and a radius R' outputs a sample from $\mathcal{A}_n(R', R')$.*

Proof. Algorithm 4 is such an algorithm, its proof of correctness is deferred to Appendix A. □

Algorithm 4: Continuous affine sampler

Require: Dimension n, radius R'
Ensure: A sample from $\mathcal{A}_n(R', R')$
1: $\mathbf{x} = \mathbf{0}$
2: $\mathbf{u} \leftarrow^{\$} \mathcal{H}_n$ {Here, $\leftarrow^{\$}$ means sampled uniformly at random}
3: **for** $i = n, \ldots, 1$ **do**
4: $\quad x_i = \left(R' - \sum_{j=i+1}^{n} x_j\right)\left(1 - (1 - u_i)^{1/(i+1)}\right)$
5: **end for**
6: **return** $\mathbf{x}$

Proposition 7. *Let $n \in \mathbb{N}$. Let X be a random variable following the distribution $\mathcal{A}_n(R, R')$, $R = n\,(M_1(\mathbf{B}) + \|\mathbf{m}_1(\mathbf{B})\|_1)$. Then, we have*

$$\mathbb{E}(\|X\|_2) \le 2n^2 s_1(\mathbf{B}).$$

Proof. Let Y be a random variable following $\mathcal{A}(R', R')$. We have $\mathbb{E}(\|X\|_2) \le \mathbb{E}(\|Y\|_2)$, and we use Jensen's inequality :

$$\mathbb{E}(\|X\|_2) \le \sqrt{\mathbb{E}(\|Y\|_2^2)}.$$

One can check that the variance of Y_1 is asymptotically equal to $\left(\frac{R'}{n}\right)^2$.

$$\begin{aligned}\mathbb{E}(\|Y\|_2^2) &= n\mathbb{E}(Y_1^2)\\ &\sim n(M_1 + \|\mathbf{m}_1\|_1)^2\end{aligned}$$

Now, notice that $M_1(\mathbf{B}) \le \|\mathbf{m}_1\|_1 \le n^{1.5} s_1(\mathbf{B})$, which completes the proof. □

Proposition 7 bounds the expected ℓ_2 norm of a random variable following the continuous affine distribution. While the instantiation of Algorithm 3 would sample from the discretization of the latter distribution, we expect the discrete distribution to have similar moments as the continuous one. This similarity can be quantified using Riemann-sum-like arguments. Using the NearestPlane (respectively an ExactCVP) instead of the RoundOff is also valid (as long as the prototile of the algorithm is symmetrical, which is the case for the NearestPlane and the ExactCVP) and yields similar results, substituting $\mathcal{P}(\mathbf{B})$ by $\mathcal{P}(\widetilde{\mathbf{B}})$ (respectively the Voronoi cell of the lattice).

5 Open Problems

Better Efficiency. The main drawback of our framework is that our instantiations suffer large standard deviations. The $O(n^{1.5})$ overhead factor roughly comes from two different problems. The first one is that we measure the size of the output of our algorithms with the ℓ_2 norm, but the distributions sometimes have shapes more amenable to the ℓ_1 or ℓ_∞ norm. We usually lose a $\sqrt{n}$ factor due to the norm inequalities, but measuring the ℓ_∞ norm of the output, for example, can be relevant in cryptography.[5]

The second reason is that, informally, when the support of the distribution is an ℓ_p ball, the radius of the ball increases as the standard deviation increases, but its volume increases as its radius to the power n. The acceptance rates of the distributions defined over ℓ_p balls of radius r have the following form:

[5] For example, although it does not use trapdoor sampling, the signature scheme Dilithium [17] relies for its security on the MSIS problem with the ℓ_∞ norm.

$$\left(1 - \frac{M_p(\mathbf{B})}{r + M_p(\mathbf{B})}\right)^n$$

and we lose a factor $O(n)$ by setting $r = nM_p(\mathbf{B})$.

While this seems to prevent the framework from being practically efficient, there are several ways to improve its performance. First, it seems that by being more permissive on the rejection sampling step in our sampler framework, one can find a precision/size trade-off, trading perfect indistinguishability for statistical indistinguishability. As mentioned in the introduction, the idea of using a regular algorithm to round a continuous distribution was, to our knowledge, only attempted on Gaussian distributions, yielding a very large standard deviation to compensate the lack of squaremonicity of the Gaussian density function. We leave for future work to study the behaviour of the standard deviation when the density function is only "ϵ-$\mathcal{T}$-squaremonic". In addition, our proofs use inequalities on the quality of the basis in a *worse-case* scenario. In a cryptographic context, it is likely that we will obtain outputs with shorter norms.

More Instantiations. There are likely more squaremonic functions than the ones we exhibited. Harmonic functions are at the core of a vastly studied domain in mathematics, and we believe that squaremonic functions may enjoy similarly rich properties. We tried – unsuccessfully – to find a partial differential equation equivalent to the squaremonic mean value property, which eventually may lead to finding more squaremonic functions. The more squaremonic functions we find, the more sampleable distributions we have, with potentially improved instantiations.

Precision of Floating-Point Arithmetic. We make an extensive use of continuous distributions in this work. This raises the question of the necessary precision for floating-point arithmetic operations. Solving this question will be key to efficiently and securely instantiating our algorithms.

Secure Implementation. Finally, our algorithms may require to sample from non-uniform distributions. This sampling should be performed in a manner that does not leak side-channel information (e.g. timing). Indeed, several attacks [19] have been mounted against implementations of lattice-based signature schemes that leaked such information. In addition, a secure implementation would need to ensure that the acceptance probability does not depend of the private key, in order to prevent timing attacks in the line of [20].

Acknowledgements. Thomas Prest is supported by the Innovate UK Research Grant 104423 (PQ Cybersecurity).

A Appendix

Proof. [Proof of Lemma 1] Let X be a random variable following $\mathcal{A}_n(R, R)$. The variable X has a density, which is given by $f : \mathbf{x} \longmapsto \frac{1}{\mathsf{Vol}(\mathcal{B}_1^{n+1}(R))}(R - \|\mathbf{x}\|_1)$. We write $A = \frac{1}{\mathsf{Vol}(\mathcal{B}_1^{n+1})}$, and calculate the density g of X_n.

$$\begin{aligned}
g(x_n) &= A \int_{\mathbb{R}^{n-1}} f(t_1, \ldots, t_{n-1}, x_n)\mathrm{d}t_1 \ldots \mathrm{d}t_{n-1} \\
&= A \int_{\mathbb{R}^{n-1}} \left(R - x_n - \sum_{i=1}^{n-1} t_i\right) \mathrm{d}t_1 \ldots \mathrm{d}t_{n-1}. \\
&= A\frac{1}{2} \int_{\mathbb{R}^{n-2}} \left[-\left(R - x_n - \sum_{i=1}^{n-2} t_i\right)^2\right]_{t_1=0}^{R-x_n-\sum_{i=2}^{n-1} t_i} \mathrm{d}t_2 \ldots t_{n-1} \\
&= A\frac{1}{2} \int_{\mathbb{R}^{n-2}} \left(R - x_n - \sum_{i=2}^{n-2} t_i\right)^2 \mathrm{d}t_2 \ldots t_{n-1} \\
&\;\vdots \\
&= \frac{A}{n!} (R - x_n)^n
\end{aligned}$$

Finally, the density of X_n is

$$\boxed{g(x_n) = \frac{(n+1)}{R^{n+1}}(R - x_n)^n.}$$

Now, we compute the cumulative density function:

$$\begin{aligned}
G(x_n) &= \int_0^{x_n} g(t_n)\mathrm{d}t_n \\
&= \frac{1}{R^{n+1}} \left[-(R - t_n)^{n+1}\right]_0^{R-x_n} \\
&= \frac{1}{R^{n+1}} \left(R^{n+1} - (R - x_n)^{n+1}\right).
\end{aligned}$$

Finally,

$$\boxed{G(x_n) = 1 - (1 - \frac{x_n}{R})^{n+1}.}$$

The function ICDF_{x_n} is the reciprocal of G, and the result follows from Proposition 1. □

References

1. Aggarwal, D., Dadush, D., Regev, O., Stephens-Davidowitz, N.: Solving the shortest vector problem in 2^n time using discrete Gaussian sampling: Extended abstract. In: Servedio, R.A., Rubinfeld, R., (eds.) 47th ACM STOC, pp. 733–742. ACM Press (2015)
2. Aggarwal, D., Dadush, D., Stephens-Davidowitz, N.: Solving the closest vector problem in 2^n time - the discrete Gaussian strikes again! In: Guruswami, V. (eds.) 56th FOCS, pp. 563–582. IEEE Computer Society Press (2015)
3. Agrawal, S., Boneh, D., Boyen, X.: Efficient lattice (H)IBE in the standard model. In: Gilbert, H. (ed.) EUROCRYPT 2010, vol. 6110, pp. 553–572. Springer, Heidelberg (2010). https://doi.org/10.1007/978-3-642-13190-5_28
4. Agrawal, S., Boneh, D., Boyen, X.: Lattice basis delegation in fixed dimension and shorter-ciphertext hierarchical IBE. In: Rabin, T. (ed.) CRYPTO 2010. LNCS, vol. 6223, pp. 98–115. Springer, Heidelberg (2010). https://doi.org/10.1007/978-3-642-14623-7_6
5. Alazard, T.: Analyse et équations aux dérivées partielles (2017)
6. Alkim, E., Ducas, L., Pöppelmann, T., Schwabe, P.: Post-quantum key exchange - a new hope. In: Holz, T., Savage, S. (eds.) USENIX Security 2016, pp. 327–343. USENIX Association (2016)
7. Babai, L.: On lovász'lattice reduction and the nearest lattice point problem. Combinatorica **6**(1), 1–13 (1986)
8. Barthe, F., Guédon, O., Mendelson, S., Naor, A., et al.: A probabilistic approach to the geometry of the pn-ball. Ann. Probabil. **33**(2), 480–513 (2005)
9. Bos, J.W., et al.: Frodo: take off the ring! practical, quantum-secure key exchange from LWE. In: Weippl, E.R., Katzenbeisser, S., Kruegel, C., Myers, A.C., Halevi, S. (eds.) ACM CCS 2016, pp. 1006–1018. ACM Press (2016)
10. Boyen, X.: Attribute-based functional encryption on lattices. In: Sahai, A. (ed.) TCC 2013. LNCS, vol. 7785, pp. 122–142. Springer, Heidelberg (2013). https://doi.org/10.1007/978-3-642-36594-2_8
11. Brakerski, Z., Langlois, A., Peikert, C., Regev, O., Stehlé, D.: Classical hardness of learning with errors. In: Boneh, D., Roughgarden, T., Feigenbaum, J. (eds.) 45th ACM STOC, pp. 575–584. ACM Press (2013)
12. Cash, D., Hofheinz, D., Kiltz, E., Peikert, C.: Bonsai trees, or how to delegate a lattice basis. In: Gilbert, H. (ed.) EUROCRYPT 2010. LNCS, vol. 6110, pp. 523–552. Springer, Berlin, Heidelberg (2010). https://doi.org/10.1007/978-3-642-13190-5_27
13. Chen, Y., Genise, N., Mukherjee, P.: Approximate trapdoors for lattices and smaller hash-and-sign signatures. In: Galbraith, S.D., Moriai, S. (eds.) ASIACRYPT 2019. LNCS, vol. 11923, pp. 3–32. Springer, Heidelberg (2019). https://doi.org/10.1007/978-3-030-34618-8_1
14. Conway, J.H., Sloane, N.J.A.: Low-dimensional lattices. vi. voronoi reduction of three-dimensional lattices. Proc. R. Soc. Lond. Ser. A: Math. Phys. Sci. **436**(1896), 55–68 (1992)
15. Cumbus, C.: Uniform sampling in the hypersphere via latent variables and the Gibbs sampler (1996)
16. Ducas, L., Kiltz, E., Lepoint, T., Lyubashevsky, V., Schwabe, P., Seiler, G., Stehlé, D.: CRYSTALS-Dilithium: a lattice-based digital signature scheme. IACR TCHES **2018**(1), 238–268 (2018). https://tches.iacr.org/index.php/TCHES/article/view/839

17. Ducas, L., Lepoint, T., Lyubashevsky, V., Schwabe, P., Seiler, G., Stehlé, D: Crystals-dilithium: Digital signatures from module lattices (2018)
18. Ducas, L., Nguyen, P.Q.: Faster Gaussian lattice sampling using lazy floating-point arithmetic. In: Wang, X., Sako, K. (eds.) ASIACRYPT 2012. LNCS, vol. 7658, pp. 415–432. Springer, Heidelberg (2012). https://doi.org/10.1007/978-3-642-34961-4_26
19. Espitau, T., Fouque, P.-A., Gérard, B., Tibouchi, M.: Side-channel attacks on BLISS lattice-based signatures: exploiting branch tracing against strongSwan and electromagnetic emanations in microcontrollers. In: Thuraisingham, B.M., Evans, D., Malkin, T., Xu, D. (eds.) ACM CCS 2017, pp. 1857–1874. ACM Press (2017)
20. Fouque, P.-A., Kirchner, P., Tibouchi, M., Wallet, A., Yang, Yu.: Key recovery from Gram-Schmidt norm leakage in hash-and-sign signatures over NTRU lattices. In: Canteaut, A., Ishai, Y. (eds.) EUROCRYPT 2020. Lecture Notes in Computer Science, vol. 12107, pp. 34–63. Springer, Heidelberg (2020). https://doi.org/10.1007/978-3-030-45727-3_2
21. Gentry, C., Peikert, C., Vaikuntanathan, V.: Trapdoors for hard lattices and new cryptographic constructions. In: Ladner, R.E., Dwork, C. (eds.) 40th ACM STOC, pp. 197–206. ACM Press (2008)
22. Gilbert, H. (ed.): Advances in Cryptology – EUROCRYPT 2010. LNCS, vol. 6110. Springer, Heidelberg (2010). https://doi.org/10.1007/978-3-642-13190-5
23. Klein, P.N.: Finding the closest lattice vector when it's unusually close. In: Shmoys, D.B. (ed.) 11th SODA, pp. 937–941. ACM-SIAM (2000)
24. Lieb, E.H., Loss, M., Loss, M.A., American Mathematical Society: Analysis. Crm Proceedings & Lecture Notes. American Mathematical Society (2001)
25. Lyubashevsky, V., Wichs, D.: Simple lattice trapdoor sampling from a broad class of distributions. In: Katz, J. (ed.) PKC 2015. LNCS, vol. 9020, pp. 716–730. Springer, Heidelberg (2015). https://doi.org/10.1007/978-3-662-46447-2_32
26. Micciancio, D., Peikert, C.: Trapdoors for lattices: simpler, tighter, faster, smaller. In: Pointcheval, D., Johansson, T. (eds.) EUROCRYPT 2012. LNCS, vol. 7237, pp. 700–718. Springer, Heidelberg (2012)
27. Muscalu, C., Schlag, W.: Harmonic functions; poisson kernel. Cambridge Studies in Advanced Mathematics, vol. 1, pp. 28–51. Cambridge University Press (2013)
28. Peikert, C.: An efficient and parallel Gaussian sampler for lattices. In: Rabin, T. (ed.) CRYPTO 2010. LNCS, vol. 6223, pp. 80–97. Springer, Heidelberg (2010). https://doi.org/10.1007/978-3-642-14623-7_5
29. Prest, T.: Sharper bounds in lattice-based cryptography using the Rényi divergence. In: Takagi, T., Peyrin, T. (eds.) ASIACRYPT 2017, Part I. LNCS, vol. 10624, pp. 347–374. Springer, Heidelberg (2017). https://doi.org/10.1007/978-3-319-70694-8_13
30. Rabin, T. (ed.): CRYPTO 2010. LNCS, vol. 6223. Springer, Heidelberg (2010). https://doi.org/10.1007/978-3-642-14623-7
31. Regev, O.: On lattices, learning with errors, random linear codes, and cryptography. In: Gabow, H.N., Fagin, R. (eds.) 37th ACM STOC, pp. 84–93. ACM Press (2005)
32. Regev, O.: On lattices, learning with errors, random linear codes, and cryptography. J. ACM **56**(6), 34:1–34:40 (2009)
33. Shao, M.-Z., Badler, N.: Spherical sampling by archimedes' theorem. Technical reports (CIS), pp. 184 (1996)

34. Stein, E.M., Murphy, T.S., Princeton University Press: Harmonic Analysis: Real-variable Methods, Orthogonality, and Oscillatory Integrals. Monographs in harmonic analysis. Princeton University Press (1993)
35. Voronoi, G.: Nouvelles applications des paramètres continus à la théorie des formes quadratiques. deuxième mémoire. recherches sur les parallélloèdres primitifs. Journal für die reine und angewandte Mathematik **134**, 198–287 (1908)

Efficient Adaptively-Secure IB-KEMs and VRFs via Near-Collision Resistance

Tibor Jager[1], Rafael Kurek[1], and David Niehues[2(✉)]

[1] Bergische Universität Wuppertal, Wuppertal, Germany
tibor.jager@uni-wuppertal.de, rafael.kurek@rub.de
[2] Paderborn University, Paderborn, Germany
david.niehues@upb.de

Abstract. We construct more efficient cryptosystems with provable security against *adaptive* attacks, based on simple and natural hardness assumptions in the standard model. Concretely, we describe:

– An adaptively-secure variant of the efficient, selectively-secure LWE-based identity-based encryption (IBE) scheme of Agrawal, Boneh, and Boyen (EUROCRYPT 2010). In comparison to the previously most efficient such scheme by Yamada (CRYPTO 2017) we achieve smaller lattice parameters and shorter public keys of size $\mathcal{O}(\log \lambda)$, where λ is the security parameter.
– Adaptively-secure variants of two efficient selectively-secure pairing-based IBEs of Boneh and Boyen (EUROCRYPT 2004). One is based on the DBDH assumption, has the same ciphertext size as the corresponding BB04 scheme, and achieves full adaptive security with public parameters of size only $\mathcal{O}(\log \lambda)$. The other is based on a q-type assumption and has public key size $\mathcal{O}(\lambda)$, but a ciphertext is only a single group element and the security reduction is quadratically tighter than the corresponding scheme by Jager and Kurek (ASIACRYPT 2018).
– A very efficient adaptively-secure verifiable random function where proofs, public keys, and secret keys have size $\mathcal{O}(\log \lambda)$.

As a technical contribution we introduce *blockwise partitioning*, which leverages the assumption that a cryptographic hash function is *weak near-collision resistant* to prove full adaptive security of cryptosystems.

1 Introduction

A very fundamental question in cryptography is to which extent idealizations like the random oracle model [7] are necessary to obtain practical constructions of cryptosystems. By advancing our techniques to prove security of schemes, we may

This work was partially supported by the German Research Foundation (DFG) within the Collaborative Research Centre On-The-Fly Computing (GZ: SFB 901/3) under the project number 160364472 and the European Research Council (ERC) under the European Union's Horizon 2020 research and innovation programme, grant agreement 802823.

J. A. Garay (Ed.): PKC 2021, LNCS 12710, pp. 596–626, 2021.
https://doi.org/10.1007/978-3-030-75245-3_22

eventually be able to obtain standard-model schemes that are about as efficient as corresponding schemes with security proofs in the ROM. From a practical perspective, it would be preferable to have security guarantees that are not based on an uninstantiable model [20]. From a theoretical perspective, it allows us to understand when a random oracle is necessary, and when not. For some primitives it is known that a programmable random oracle is indeed inherently necessary [25,27,31,46]. But for many others, including those considered in this paper, there are no such impossibility results.

In the context of identity-based encryption the established standard security notion [16] considers an adversary which is able to choose the identities for which it requests secret keys or a challenge ciphertext *adaptively* in the security experiment. This yields much stronger security guarantees than so-called *selective* security definitions [14], where the adversary has to announce the "target identity" associated with a challenge ciphertext at the beginning of the security experiment, even before seeing the public parameters.

"Selective" security is much easier to achieve and therefore yields more efficient constructions. The random oracle model is then a useful tool to generically convert a selectively-secure scheme into an adaptively-secure one. This has negligible performance overhead, and thus yields an efficient and adaptively-secure construction. This generic construction is based on the fact that a random oracle is "programmable", which essentially means that it is possible to adaptively modify the mapping of function inputs to outputs in a way that is convenient for the security proof. While this is very useful to achieve efficient and adaptively-secure constructions, it is often considered a particularly unnatural property of the random oracle model, due to the fact that no fixed function can be as freely adaptively programmed as a random oracle.

There exist techniques to achieve adaptive security in the standard model by realizing certain properties of a random oracle with a concrete construction (i.e., in the standard model). This includes *admissible hash functions* [15], *programmable hash functions* [22,28,33,34,51], and *extremely lossy functions* [55]. However, these typically yield significantly less efficient constructions and are therefore less interesting for practical applications than corresponding constructions in the random oracle model.

A recent, quite different approach that addresses this issue is to use *truncation collision resistance* [37] of a cryptographic hash function to achieve adaptive security. In contrast to the aforementioned approaches, this does not introduce a new "algebraic" construction of a hash function. Instead, their idea is to formulate a concrete hardness assumption that on the one hand is "weak enough" to appear reasonable for *standard* cryptographic hash functions, such as SHA-3, but which at the same time is "strong enough" to be used to achieve adaptive security. It is shown that this indeed yields very efficient and adaptively-secure constructions, such as identity-based encryption with a single group element overhead and digital signatures that consist of a single group element. Notably, truncation collision resistance is also achieved by a non-programmable random oracle, even though this security notions is considered as a (non-standard, but seemingly reasonable) security notion for standard-model cryptographic hash functions. However, the main disadvantages of the constructions in [37] are that very strong computational hardness assumptions (so-called q-type assumptions with very large q) are required, and that the reductions are extremely non-tight.

Table 1. Comparison of adaptively secure IBEs based on LWE in the standard model

Schemes	|mpk| # of $\mathbb{Z}_q^{n\times m}$ matr.	|usk|, |ct| # of $\mathbb{Z}_q^m$ vec.	LWE param $1/\alpha$	Reduction Cost	Remarks
[21]	$\mathcal{O}(\lambda)$	$\mathcal{O}(\lambda)$	$\tilde{\mathcal{O}}(n^{1.5})$	$\mathcal{O}(\varepsilon^{\nu+1}/Q^{\nu})^{\ddagger}$	
[2]+[18]	$\mathcal{O}(\lambda)$	$\mathcal{O}(1)$	$\tilde{\mathcal{O}}(n^{5.5})$	$\mathcal{O}(\varepsilon^2/qQ)$	
[52]	$\mathcal{O}(\lambda^{1/\mu})^{\dagger}$	$\mathcal{O}(1)$	$n^{\omega(1)}$	$\mathcal{O}(\varepsilon^{\mu+1}/kQ^{\mu})^{\dagger}$	
[56]	$\mathcal{O}(\log Q)$	$\mathcal{O}(1)$	$\tilde{\mathcal{O}}(Q^2 n^{6.5})$	$\mathcal{O}(\varepsilon/kQ^2)$	Q-bounded
[4]*	$\mathcal{O}(\lambda/\log^2\lambda)$	$\mathcal{O}(1)$	$\tilde{\mathcal{O}}(n^6)$	$\mathcal{O}(\varepsilon^2/qQ)$	
[19]	$\mathcal{O}(\lambda)$	$\mathcal{O}(1)$	superpoly(n)	$\mathcal{O}(\lambda)$	
[41]	$\mathcal{O}(\lambda^{1/\mu})^{\dagger}$	$\mathcal{O}(1)$	$\mathcal{O}(n^{2.5+2\mu})^{\dagger}$	$\mathcal{O}((\lambda^{\mu-1}\varepsilon^{\mu}/Q^{\mu})^{\mu+1})^{\dagger}$	Ring-based
[53] + $\mathsf{F}_{\mathsf{MAH}}$ §	$\mathcal{O}(\log^3\lambda)$	$\mathcal{O}(1)$	$\tilde{\mathcal{O}}(n^{11})$	$\mathcal{O}(\varepsilon^{\nu+1}/Q^{\nu})^{\ddagger}$	
[53] + $\mathsf{F}_{\mathsf{AFF}}$ §	$\mathcal{O}(\log^2\lambda)$	$\mathcal{O}(1)$	poly(λ)	$\mathcal{O}(\varepsilon^2/k^2 Q)$	Expensive offline phase
Sec. 3	$\mathcal{O}(\log\lambda)$	$\mathcal{O}(1)$	$\tilde{\mathcal{O}}(n^6)$	$\mathcal{O}(\varepsilon^2/t^2)$	

We compare adaptively secure IBE schemes under the LWE assumption that do not use random oracles. We measure the size of ct and usk in the number of $\mathbb{Z}_q^m$ vectors and the size of mpk in the number of $\mathbb{Z}_q^{n\times m}$ matrices. Q, ε and t, respectively, denote the number of queries, the advantage against the security of the respective IBE, and the runtime of an adversary. We measure the reduction cost by the advantage of the algorithm solving the LWE problem that is constructed from the adversary against the IBE scheme. All reduction costs were computed using the technique of Bellare and Ristenpart [6].

† The constant $\mu \in \mathbb{N}$ can be chosen arbitrarily. However, the reduction cost degrades exponentially in μ and hence it should be chosen rather small.

‡ $\nu > 1$ is the constant satisfying $c = 1 - 2^{-1/\nu}$, where c is the relative distance of an underlying error correcting code. ν can be chosen arbitrarily close to one by choosing c closer to $1/2$ [30]. However, this comes with larger public keys as shown in [39].

∗ The authors also propose an additional scheme that we do not include, because it relies on much stronger complexity assumptions.

§Yamada [53] provides two instantiations of his IBE, one based on a modified admissible hash function ($\mathsf{F}_{\mathsf{MAH}}$) and one based on affine functions ($\mathsf{F}_{\mathsf{AFF}}$). When Yamada's scheme is used with the second instantiation, the key generation and encryption need to compute the description of a branching program that computes the division. This makes the construction less efficient.

Our Contributions. We introduce *blockwise partitioning* as a new approach to leverage the assumption that a cryptographic hash function is *weak near-collision resistant.* We informally say that a hash functions is weak near-collision resistant if the generic birthday attack is the fastest algorithm to find collisions on a subset of the output bits, where the subset has to be stated in advance. We formally introduce weak near-collision resistance in Definition 1. It can be seen as a new variant of truncation collision resistance [37], which essentially captures the same intuition and therefore can be considered equally reasonable. However, we will show that our technique yields more efficient and tighter constructions of identity-based encryption, based on lattices and on pairings, and a highly efficient new verifiable random function. We give a more detailed comparison between blockwise partitioning based on weak near-collision resistance and the results from [37] in Sect. 2.

Near-Collision Resistance of Standardized Hash Functions. The near-collision resistance of hash functions has been studied in several works and has been shown to be an important property of hash functions [10,11,48]. Further, the Handbook of Applied Cryptography [44, Remark 9.22] lists near-collision resistance as a desired property of hash functions and a potential *certificational property.* Moreover, the sponge construction for hash functions, which SHA-3 is based on, has been shown to be indifferentiable from a random oracle [9], in a slightly idealized model. This immediately implies the near-collision resistance of the sponge construction in this model. Since weak near-collision resistance is an even weaker property, we view it as a natural property of modern hash functions.

Lattice-Based IB-KEM. We apply our approach to construct a lattice-based IB-KEM with constant size ciphertexts and public keys of size $O(\log \lambda)$. This scheme has efficiency close to existing selectively-secure ones, which makes progress towards answering an open problem posed in Peikert's survey on lattice cryptography [47] on the existence of adaptively-secure schemes whose efficiency is comparable to selectively-secure ones. We compare the efficiency of existing schemes in Table 1, which is based on the respective table by Yamada [53], and discuss the used techniques in the full version [38].

Pairing-Based IB-KEM. We also construct two new variants of the pairing-based identity-based encryption schemes of Boneh and Boyen [14] and Waters [51]. In comparison to [14] we achieve adaptive security instead of selective security. In comparison to [51] we have public parameters of size $O(\log \lambda)$ instead of $O(\lambda)$. Security is based on the same algebraic complexity assumption as the original schemes plus weak near-collision resistance. The security analysis is also much simpler than in [51] or the simplified proof by Bellare and Ristenpart [6] and does not require an "artificial abort" [51]. To our best knowledge, this is the first adaptively-secure IBE scheme where ciphertexts consist only of *two* elements of a prime order algebraic group with logarithmic-size public parameters. The scheme also gives rise to an adaptively-secure (EUF-CMA) CDH-based digital signature scheme with logarithmic-size keys. See Table 2.

We also describe a new *adaptively-secure* variant of a scheme by Boneh and Boyen [14] based on a q-type assumption where a ciphertext consists only of a *single* group element. In comparison to the corresponding construction from [37], the q of the required q-type assumption is reduced *quadratically*, while the tightness of the reduction is improved *quadratically*, too. This scheme also gives rise to a signature scheme with adaptive security in the standard model, where a signature is only a single element from a prime-order group, which achieves the same quadratic improvement over a construction from [37].

Table 2. Comparison of IB-KEMs based on pairings with prime order groups and short ciphertexts. $|\mathsf{mpk}|$ is the number of group elements in public keys (descriptions of groups and hash functions not included), λ the security parameter. All public keys include at least one element from the target group of the pairing, except for [16]. $|\mathsf{usk}|$ and $|\mathsf{ct}|$ are the respective numbers of group elements in the user secret keys and ciphertexts when viewed as a KEM. "adap." means adaptive IND-ID-CPA security as defined below, "selec." is selective security in the sense of [14]. The security loss is defined as the value L that satisfies $t_{\mathcal{B}}/\varepsilon_{\mathcal{B}} = L \cdot t_{\mathcal{A}}/\varepsilon_{\mathcal{A}}$, where $t_{\mathcal{A}}$,$\varepsilon_{\mathcal{A}}$ and $t_{\mathcal{B}}$,$\varepsilon_{\mathcal{B}}$ are the respective running time and advantage of the adversary and reduction, and we ignored negligible terms in the security loss. q_{key} is the number of identity key queries.

Scheme	$\|\mathsf{mpk}\|$	$\|\mathsf{usk}\|$	$\|\mathsf{ct}\|$	Security	Assumption	ROM	Security Loss
[16]	2	1	1	adap.	DBDH	Yes	$O(q_{key})$
[51]	$\mathcal{O}(\lambda)$	2	2	adap.	DBDH	No	$O(t^2 + (\lambda \cdot q_{key} \cdot \varepsilon^{-1})^2)$
[50]	13	9	10	adap.	DLIN+DBDH	No	$O(q_{key})$
[43]	25	6	6	adap.	DLIN	No	$O(q_{key})$
[23]	9	4	4	adap.	SXDH	No	$O(q_{key})$
[5]	$O(\lambda)$	8	8	adap.	DLIN	No	$O(\log(\lambda))$
Sec. 4.1	$O(\log \lambda)$	2	2	adap.	DBDH	No	$O(t_{\mathcal{A}}^2/\varepsilon_{\mathcal{A}})$
[14]	4	2	2	selec.	qDBDHI	No	$O(1)$
[29]	3	2	3	adap.	qABDHE	No	$1 + \mathcal{O}(q_{key}^2)/t_{\mathcal{A}}$
[37]	$O(\lambda)$	1	1	adap.	qDBDHI	No	$O(t_{\mathcal{A}}^7/\varepsilon_{\mathcal{A}}^4)$
Sec. 4.2	$O(\lambda)$	1	1	adap.	qDBDHI	No	$O(t_{\mathcal{A}}^3/\varepsilon_{\mathcal{A}}^2)$

Pairing-Based VRF. As our last contribution, we construct a new VRF based on the q-DBDHI assumption by using blockwise partitioning and techniques of Yamada's VRF [53]. Our VRF is the first to achieve both small public keys and small proofs at the same time. Furthermore, the size of the keys and proofs is not only asymptotically small but also concretely: for $\lambda = 128$, public keys of our VRF consist of only 10 group elements and proofs of only 9 group elements. We compare the efficiency of existing schemes in Table 3, which is based on the respective table by Kohl [42], and discuss the used techniques in the full version [38].

2 Blockwise Partitioning via Near-Collision Resistance

High-Level Approach. *Confined guessing* [12,13] is a semi-generic technique to construct efficient and adaptively-secure digital signature schemes. It has been used for instance in [3,24]. Unfortunately, it is only applicable to signatures,

Table 3. Comparison of adaptively secure VRFs in the standard model

Schemes	$\lvert\mathsf{vk}\rvert$	$\lvert\pi\rvert$	Assumption	Security loss
[35]	$\mathcal{O}(\lambda)$	$\mathcal{O}(\lambda)$	$\mathcal{O}(\lambda \cdot Q)$-DDHE	$\mathcal{O}(\lambda Q/\varepsilon)$
[17]	$\mathcal{O}(\lambda)$	$\mathcal{O}(\lambda)$	$\mathcal{O}(\lambda)$-DDH	$\mathcal{O}(\lambda)$
[36]	$\mathcal{O}(\lambda)$	$\mathcal{O}(\lambda)$	$\mathcal{O}(\log(Q/\varepsilon))$-DDH	$\mathcal{O}(Q^{\nu}/\varepsilon^{\nu+1})$
[32]	$\mathcal{O}(\lambda)$	$\mathcal{O}(\lambda)$	DLIN	$\mathcal{O}(\lambda\log(\lambda)Q^{2/c}/\varepsilon^{3})$
[53] Sec. 6.1	$\omega(\lambda\log^{2}\lambda)^{\dagger}$	$\omega(\log^{2}\lambda)^{\dagger}$	$\tilde{\mathcal{O}}(\lambda)$-DDH	$\mathcal{O}(Q^{\nu}/\varepsilon^{\nu+1})$
[53] Sec. 6.2	$\omega(\log^{2}\lambda)^{\dagger}$	$\omega(\sqrt{\lambda}\log^{2}\lambda)^{\dagger}$	$\tilde{\mathcal{O}}(\lambda)$-DDH	$\mathcal{O}(Q^{\nu}/\varepsilon^{\nu+1})$
[54] App. C.	$\omega(\log^{2}\lambda)^{\dagger}$	$\mathsf{poly}(\lambda)$	$\mathsf{poly}(\lambda)$-DDH	$\mathcal{O}(\lambda^{2}Q/\varepsilon^{2})$
[40] Sec. 5.1	$\omega(\log^{2}\lambda)^{\dagger}$	$\omega(\lambda\log^{2}\lambda)^{\dagger}$	$\omega(\log^{2}\lambda)^{\dagger}$-DDH	$\mathcal{O}(Q^{\nu}/\varepsilon^{\nu+1})$
[40] Sec. 5.3	$\omega(\sqrt{\lambda}\log\lambda)^{\dagger}$	$\omega(\log\lambda)^{\dagger}$	$\omega(\log^{2}\lambda)^{\dagger}$-DDH	$\mathcal{O}(Q^{\nu}/\varepsilon^{\nu+1})$
[49]	$\mathcal{O}(\lambda)$	$\mathcal{O}(\lambda)$	DLIN	$\mathcal{O}(\lambda\log(\lambda)Q^{2/c}/\varepsilon^{3})$
[42]	$\omega(\lambda\log\lambda)^{\dagger}$	$\omega(\log\lambda)^{\dagger}$	DLIN	$\mathcal{O}(\lvert\pi\rvert\log(\lambda)Q^{2/\nu}/\varepsilon^{3})$
[42]	$\omega(\lambda^{2+2\eta})$	$\omega(1)^{\dagger}$	DLIN	$\mathcal{O}(\lvert\pi\rvert\log(\lambda)Q^{2+2/\nu}/\varepsilon^{3})$
[39]	$\mathcal{O}(\lambda)$	$\mathcal{O}(\lambda)$	$\mathcal{O}(t^{2}/\varepsilon)$-DDH	$\mathcal{O}(t^{3}/\varepsilon^{2})$
Sec. 5	$\mathcal{O}(\log\lambda)$	$\mathcal{O}(\log\lambda)$	$\mathcal{O}(t^{2}/\varepsilon)$-DDH	$\mathcal{O}(t^{2}/\varepsilon^{2})$

We compare adaptively secure VRF schemes in the standard model. We measure the size of vk and π in the number of the respective group. Q, ε and t respectively denote the number of queries an adversary makes, the adversaries advantage against the security of the respective VRF and the adversaries runtime. Most of the constructions use an error correcting code $C : \{0,1\}^{\lambda} \rightarrow \{0,1\}^{n}$ with constant relative minimal distance $c \leq 1/2$, where $n,\nu > 1$ can be chosen arbitrarily close to 1 by choosing c arbitrarily close to $1/2$ [30, Appendix E.1]. However, this leads to larger n and by that to larger public keys and/or proofs as shown in [39].
† Note that these terms only hold for "λ large enough" and therefore, key and proof sizes might have to be adapted with larger constants in order to guarantee adequate security.

but neither to identity-based schemes such as identity-based key encapsulation mechanisms (IB-KEMs), nor to verifiable random functions (VRFs).

We propose *blockwise partitioning* as a new semi-generic technique, and show how it can be used to construct efficient IB-KEMs and VRFs with adaptive security. It is based on the *near-collision resistance* of a cryptographic hash function and similar in spirit to the closely related notion of *truncation collision resistance* [37].

Explained on an informal level using IB-KEMs as example, our approach is to let the reduction guess $n' = \mathcal{O}(\log\lambda)$, many bits of $H(\mathsf{id}^*)$, where λ is the security parameter, H is a collision resistant hash function and id^* is the challenge identity chosen by the adversary. Then, the reduction is successful if the guess matches $H(\mathsf{id}^*)$ on all n' guessed bits and the hash of every identity queried by the adversary differs in at least one bit from the guess. For this approach to yield a reduction with non-negligible loss, we have to choose n' such that it fulfills the following two conflicting goals: n' has to be small enough for the probability of guessing n' bits of $H(\mathsf{id}^*)$ correctly to be non-negligible, but we also have to choose n' large enough to ensure that it is unlikely, relative to the adversaries advantage, for the adversary to make a query id whose hash also matches on the n' guessed bits. Like [12,13,37], we balance these two goals by choosing n' depending on the runtime and advantage of the adversary. Following this approach thus yields an ideal choice of n' for each adversary. Constructions like [12,13,37], however, do not use this ideal choice but the next largest power of two as n' and then guess the first n' bits of $H(\mathsf{id}^*)$. This has the advantage that it leaves only $\mathcal{O}(\log \lambda)$ many possibilities for n' and hence yields small key sizes. Unfortunately, this comes at the cost of a larger security loss in the reduction because n' can be almost double the size of the ideal choice. Furthermore, choosing n' in this sub-optimal manner also requires stronger q-type assumptions and a hash function with longer outputs.

We address this issue by viewing the output of the hash function as the concatenation of blocks of exponentially growing length, i.e. the first bit is the first block, bits two and three are the second block, bits four, five, six and seven are the third block and so on. Our reduction then uses the ideal choice for n' and guesses the bits in the blocks whose lengths sum up to exactly n'. This more fine-grained guessing yields constructions with tighter security from weaker assumptions. Furthermore, it reduces the required output length of the hash function from $4(\lambda+1)$ bits in [37] to only $2\lambda+3$ bits. Note that this is essentially optimal for a collision-resistant hash function. In particular, for many practical constructions one would probably use a collision resistant hash function, anyway, to map long identities to short strings. We compare our techniques to the ones of [37] in more detail after formally introducing blockwise partitioning.

In the remainder of this section we will describe the framework and assumptions for blockwise partitioning, give some more technical intuition, and state and prove a technical lemma that will be useful to use blockwise partitioning as modular as possible in security proofs.

Blockwise Partitioning. Let $H : \{0,1\}^* \to \{0,1\}^n$ be a hash function. We will assume in the sequel that $n = \sum_{i=0}^{\ell} 2^i$ for simplicity and ease of exposition. One can generalize this to arbitrary n, but this would make the notation rather cumbersome without providing additional insight or clarity. Then we can view the output space $\{0,1\}^n$ of the hash function as a direct product of sets of exponentially-increasing size

$$\{0,1\}^n = \{0,1\}^{2^0} \times \cdots \times \{0,1\}^{2^\ell}.$$

For a hash function H we define functions $H_0, \ldots, H_\ell$ such that

$$H_i : \{0,1\}^* \to \{0,1\}^{2^i} \qquad \text{and} \qquad H(x) = H_0(x)||\cdots||H_\ell(x).$$

One can consider each $H_i(x)$ as one "block" of $H(x)$. Note that blocks have exponentially increasing size and there are $\lfloor \log n \rfloor + 1$ blocks in total.

Using Blockwise Partitioning. Let $t = t(\lambda)$ be a polynomial and let $\varepsilon = \varepsilon(\lambda)$ be a non-negligible function such that $\varepsilon > 0$ and $t/\varepsilon < 2^\lambda$ for all λ. Think of t and ε as (approximations of) the running time and advantage of an adversary in a security experiment. We define an integer n' depending on (t, ε) as

$$n' := \lceil \log(4t \cdot (2t - 1)/\varepsilon) \rceil. \tag{1}$$

Note that if $n \geq 2\lambda + 3$, then we have $0 \leq n' \leq n$ as we show in Lemma 2 below.

The value n' uniquely determines an index set $\mathcal{I} = \{i_1, \ldots, i_\omega\} \subseteq \{0, \ldots, \ell\}$ such that $n' = \sum_{i \in \mathcal{I}} 2^i$, where $\ell := \lfloor \log n \rfloor$. The key point in defining n' as in Eq. (1) is that it provides the following two properties simultaneously:

Guessing from a Polynomially-Bounded Range. In order to enable a reduction from adaptive to selective security, we will later have to "predict" a certain hash values $H(x^*)$. Think of x^* as the challenge identity in an IB-KEM security experiment, or the message from the forgery in a signature security experiment. Blockwise partitioning enables this as follows.

Consider the following probabilistic algorithm BPSmp, which takes as input λ, t, and ε, computes n' as in Eq. (1), chooses $K_i \xleftarrow{\$} \{0,1\}^{2^i}$ uniformly random for $i \in \mathcal{I}$ and defines $K_i = \perp$ for all $i \notin \mathcal{I}$. Then it outputs

$$(K_0, \ldots, K_\ell) \xleftarrow{\$} \mathsf{BPSmp}(1^\lambda, t, \varepsilon).$$

The joint range of all hash functions H_i with $i \in \mathcal{I}$ is $\{0,1\}^{2^{i_1}} \times \cdots \times \{0,1\}^{2^{i_{|\mathcal{I}|}}}$, which has size

$$2^{n'} = 2^{\sum_{i \in \mathcal{I}} 2^i}.$$

Hence, we have that

$$\Pr\left[H_i(x^*) = K_i \text{ for all } i \in \mathcal{I}\right] = 2^{-n'}.$$

Note that $2^{n'}$ is *polynomially bounded*, due to the definition of n' in Eq. (1).

Upper Bound on the Collision Probability. In Lemma 2 below we will show that near-collision resistance of H guarantees that the probability that an adversary running in time t outputs any two values $x \neq x'$ such that

$$H_i(x) = H_i(x') \qquad \text{for all } i \in \mathcal{I} \tag{2}$$

is at most $\varepsilon/2$. Think of x and x' as values chosen adaptively by an adversary in a security experiment. In the context of IB-KEMs this would be chosen identities, in context of digital signatures chosen messages, for instance. Note that we do not argue that there is a *negligible* collision probability. This is not possible, because we consider a polynomially-bounded space, where an adversary will always be able to find collisions with non-negligible probability. However, we can guarantee that there will be no collision with probability at least $\varepsilon/2$. This means that an adversary that runs in some time t and has some advantage ε will sufficiently often be successful *without* finding a collision.

Hence, similar to confined guessing [12,13] and truncation collision resistance [37], blockwise partitioning enables us to guess challenge identities from a *polynomially bounded* space. At the same time, it ensures that the space is large enough such that collisions are sufficiently unlikely, such that any adversary breaking a considered cryptosystem with some advantage ε must "sufficiently often" be successful without finding a collision.

Blockwise Partitioning via Weak Near-Collision Resistance. We will now give a formal definition of weak near-collision resistance and then provide a technical lemma, which will be useful for security proofs based on blockwise partitioning of hash function outputs. Note that weak near-collision resistance is only required for the security of our constructions and we hence only require this property in the respective theorems and not in the constructions themselves.

Definition 1 (Weak near-collision resistance). *Let $\mathcal{H} = \{H : \{0,1\}^* \to \{0,1\}^n\}$ be a family of hash functions. For $n' \in \{1, \ldots, n\}$, we say that an adversary $\mathcal{A} = (\mathcal{A}_1, \mathcal{A}_2)$ breaks the weak n'-near-collision resistance of $\mathcal{H}$, if it runs in time $t_\mathcal{A}$, and it holds that*

$$\Pr\left[n'\text{-wNCR}_\mathcal{A}^\mathcal{H} = 1\right] \geq t_\mathcal{A}(t_\mathcal{A} - 1)/2^{n'+1},$$

where n'-wNCR is the experiment defined in Fig. 1 and the probability is over the randomness of $\mathcal{A}$ and choosing H. We say that $\mathcal{H}$ is weak near-collision resistant, *if there exists no adversary $\mathcal{A}$ breaking the weak n'-near-collision resistance of $\mathcal{H}$ for any $n' \in \{1, \ldots, n\}$.*

$n'\text{-wNCR}_\mathcal{A}^\mathcal{H}$

$(\mathcal{J}, st) \xleftarrow{\$} \mathcal{A}_1(n')$
$H \xleftarrow{\$} \mathcal{H}$
$(X^{(1)}, \ldots, X^{(Q+1)}) \xleftarrow{\$} \mathcal{A}_2(H, st)$
If $|\mathcal{J}| = n'$ and $\exists x \neq y \in \{X^{(1)}, \ldots, X^{(Q+1)}\}$ with $H(x)[i] = H(y)[i]$ for all $i \in \mathcal{J}$:
  return 1, else 0

Fig. 1. The security experiment for weak near-collision resistance, executed with a family of hash functions $\mathcal{H}$ and adversary $\mathcal{A} = (\mathcal{A}_1, \mathcal{A}_2)$, where $\mathcal{A}_1$ outputs an index set $\mathcal{J} \subseteq [n]$ and $\mathcal{H} \subseteq \{h : \{0,1\}^* \to \{0,1\}^n\}$. We restrict $\mathcal{A}_1$ to only output index sets $\mathcal{J}$ with $|\mathcal{J}| = n'$. Note that $H(x)[i]$ denotes the i-th bit of $H(x)$.

The following lemma will be useful to apply blockwise partitioning in security proofs.

Lemma 2. *Let $H : \{0,1\}^* \to \{0,1\}^n$ be a hash function, t be a polynomial, and let ε be a non-negligible function such that $\varepsilon > 0$ and $t/\varepsilon < 2^\lambda$ for all λ.*

Let $n' := \lceil \log(4t \cdot (2t-1)/\varepsilon) \rceil$ *as in Eq. (1) and define set* $\mathcal{I}$ *such that* $n' = \sum_{i \in \mathcal{I}} 2^i$. *Let* $\mathcal{A}$ *be an algorithm that outputs* $(X^{(1)}, \ldots, X^{(Q)}, X^*)$ *and runs in time* t *and let*

$$(K_0, \ldots, K_\ell) \xleftarrow{\$} \mathsf{BPSmp}(1^\lambda, t, \varepsilon),$$

where BPSmp *is the algorithm described above. Then, we have that* $1 \leq n' \leq 2\lambda + 3$ *and the following statements hold.*

1. *Let* coll *be the event that there exists* $x, x' \in \{X^{(1)}, \ldots, X^{(Q)}, X^*\}$ *such that*

$$H_i(x) = H_i(x') \text{ for all } i \in \mathcal{I}. \tag{3}$$

Let badChal *be the event that there exists* $i \in \mathcal{I}$ *such that* $\Pr[H_i(X^*) \neq K_i]$. *If* H *is drawn uniformly at random from a family of weak near-collision resistant hash functions in the sense of Definition 1, then we have*

$$(\varepsilon - \Pr[\mathsf{coll}]) \cdot \Pr[\neg \mathsf{badChal}] \geq \varepsilon^2/(32t^2 - 16t).$$

Moreover, coll *and* badChal *are independent of each other.*

2. *Let* badEval *be the event that there exists* $x \in \{X^{(1)}, \ldots, X^{(Q)}\}$ *with* $x \neq X^*$ *such that* $H_i(x) = K_i$ *for all* $i \in \mathcal{I}$. *Then we have*

$$\mathsf{badEval} \implies \mathsf{coll} \vee \mathsf{badChal}.$$

Proof. The proof uses the following inequalities and identities from [37,39] and we therefore refer to [37,39] and the full version [38] for the proof.

$$n' \in \{1, \ldots, 2\lambda + 3\}, \qquad \frac{2t(2t-1)}{2^{n'}} \leq \frac{\varepsilon}{2}, \text{ and } \qquad \frac{1}{2^{n'}} \geq \frac{\varepsilon}{16t^2 - 8t} \tag{4}$$

The statement that $1 \leq n' \leq 2\lambda + 3$ holds immediately follows from the first of the above equations. We start to prove Property 1 by showing $\Pr[\mathsf{coll}] < \varepsilon/2$. Assume an algorithm $\mathcal{A}$ running in time $t_\mathcal{A}$ that outputs $(X^{(1)}, \ldots, X^{(Q)}, X^*)$ such that there exist $x, x' \in \{X^{(1)}, \ldots, X^{(Q)}, X^*\}$ such that Eq. (3) holds with probability at least $\varepsilon/2$. By the definition of $\mathcal{I}$ and the functions H_i, this yields that $H(x)$ and $H(x')$ agree on at least n' positions. We construct an algorithm $\mathcal{B} = (\mathcal{B}_1, \mathcal{B}_2)$ that uses $\mathcal{A}$ to break the weak n'-near-collision resistance of $\mathcal{H}$. Note that the choice of $\mathcal{I}$ is independent of $H \in \mathcal{H}$. $\mathcal{B}_1$ therefore just encodes $K = (K_0, \ldots, K_\ell)$ to $\mathcal{J} \subseteq \{1, \ldots, n\}$ with $|\mathcal{J}| = n'$. $\mathcal{B}_2$ simply relays $\mathcal{A}$'s output $(X^{(1)}, \ldots, X^{(Q)}, X^*)$. The runtime $t_\mathcal{B}$ of $\mathcal{B}$ is at most $2t_\mathcal{A}$, since $\mathcal{B}$ does nothing more than executing $\mathcal{A}$ and relaying its outputs. Therefore, we get

$$\Pr[\mathsf{coll}] > \varepsilon_\mathcal{A}/2 \geq \frac{2t_\mathcal{A}(2t_\mathcal{A} - 1)}{2^{n'}} \geq \frac{t_\mathcal{B}(t_\mathcal{B} - 1)}{2^{n'+1}},$$

where the second inequality follows from Eq. (4). This contradicts the weak near-collision resistance of $\mathcal{H}$. Next, we determine $\Pr[\neg \mathsf{badChal}]$. We have that the events coll and badChal are independent of each other because $(K_0, \ldots, K_\ell)$ is chosen independently of $(X^{(1)}, \ldots, X^{(Q)}, X^*)$. Moreover, each K_i with $i \in \mathcal{I}$ is chosen uniformly at random from $\{0,1\}^{2^{2^i}}$ and thus we have

$$\Pr[\neg\mathsf{badChal}] = \Pr[H_i(X^*) = K_i \text{ for all } i \in \mathcal{I}] = \frac{1}{2^{\sum_{i \in \mathcal{I}} 2^i}} = 2^{-n'},$$

where the last equation follows by definition of n'. To prove Property 1, we then calculate

$$(\varepsilon_{\mathcal{A}} - \Pr[\mathsf{coll}])2^{-n'} \geq \left(\varepsilon_{\mathcal{A}} - \frac{\varepsilon_{\mathcal{A}}}{2}\right) \frac{\varepsilon_{\mathcal{A}}}{16t_{\mathcal{A}}^2 - 8t_{\mathcal{A}}} = \frac{\varepsilon_{\mathcal{A}}^2}{32t_{\mathcal{A}}^2 - 16t_{\mathcal{A}}},$$

where the first inequality follows from Eq. (4). Finally, to show Property 2, we explain that if $\mathsf{badEval}$ occurs, then either $\mathsf{badChal}$ or coll *must occur*. This is because if there exists $x \in \{X^{(1)}, \ldots, X^{(Q)}\}$ with $x \neq X^*$ and $H_i(x) = K_i$ for all $i \in \mathcal{I}$, then we have either that also $H_i(X^*) = K_i$ for all $i \in \mathcal{I}$ and then coll occurs, or we have that there exists an index $i \in \mathcal{I}$ such that $H_i(X^*) \neq K_i$ and then $\mathsf{badChal}$ occurs. This concludes the proof.

Near-Collision Resistance and the Non-programmable Random Oracle Model. Near-collision resistance holds *unconditionally* in the non-programmable random oracle model [27]. Hence, all our results can also be viewed as a generic technique to obtain adaptively-secure cryptosystems in the non-programmable random oracle model without any additional assumptions. In this sense, our paper is in line with recent works that aim to avoid programmability, such as [26].

Relation to ELFs. Extremely lossy functions (ELFs), which were introduced by Zhandry in [55], are hash functions that allow the reductions to choose the hash function's image size depending on the adversary. For the adversary, the function with a small image is indistinguishable from the injective version. Blockwise partitioning uses the weak near-collision resistance of standard hash functions similarly by selecting the blocks the guess in depending on the adversaries runtime and advantage. Hence, ELFs might potentially enable constructions similar to ours. However, the known ELF construction from [55] relies on (exponential hardness of) DDH, and thus seems tied to a group based setting. Also, our approach can be seen as partially addressing the open problem from [55] of constructing ELFs based on symmetric key techniques.

Comparison to Confined Guessing and Truncation Collision Resistance. Note that the index set $\mathcal{I}$ defined above may contain *multiple* indices. This is a major difference of our approach to confined guessing and truncation collision resistance, where always only *single* blocks are guessed.

The advantage of being able to guess multiple blocks is that we are now able to define n' in a much more fine-grained way, as *any* integer between 0 and n.

In contrast, [12,13] and [37] were only able to pick values n' of exponentially increasing size, such that $n' = 2^{2^j}$ for some j, which is the reason why our reductions can improve tightness and the strength of the required assumptions quadratically.

However, we cannot replace the approach of [12,13] and [37] with blockwise partitioning in a black-box manner. Instead, we have to provide a new security analysis for cryptosystems, and show that there are reductions which are compatible with guessing multiple blocks.

3 Lattice-Based IB-KEM

We describe how blockwise partitioning can be applied in the context of lattice based cryptography, using an *Identity-Based Key-Encapsulation-Mechanism* (IB-KEM) based on LWE as example. We build our IB-KEM from Yamada's IBE [53], for which we describe how blockwise partitioning can be embedded into lattice trapdoors by describing "compatible algorithms" for blockwise partitioning in the lattice context. The notion is inspired by [53] and we use it as a generic building block to instantiate the IB-KEM. The instantiation then has ciphertexts and secret keys consisting of a constant number of matrices and vectors and public keys consisting of only $\mathcal{O}(\log(\lambda))$ many matrices and vectors. Furthermore, we are able to achieve better LWE-parameters. We provide preliminaries on lattices in the full version [38].

Definition 3. *An IB-KEM consists of the following four PPT algorithms:*

- $(\mathsf{mpk}, \mathsf{msk}) \xleftarrow{\$} \mathsf{Setup}(1^\lambda)$ *takes as input the security parameter and outputs the public parameters* mpk *and the master secret key* msk.
- $\mathsf{usk}_{\mathsf{id}} \xleftarrow{\$} \mathsf{KeyGen}(\mathsf{msk}, \mathsf{id})$ *returns the user secret key* $\mathsf{usk}_{\mathsf{id}}$ *for identity* $\mathsf{id} \in \{0,1\}^*$.
- $(\mathsf{ct}, K) \xleftarrow{\$} \mathsf{Encap}(\mathsf{mpk}, \mathsf{id})$ *returns a tuple* (ct, K), *where* ct *is ciphertext encapsulating* K *with respect to identity* id.
- $K = \mathsf{Decap}(\mathsf{usk}_{\mathsf{id}}, \mathsf{ct}, \mathsf{id})$ *returns the decapsulated key* K *or an error symbol* $\perp$.

For correctness we require that for all $\lambda \in \mathbb{N}$, *all pairs* $(\mathsf{mpk}, \mathsf{msk})$ *generated by* $\mathsf{Setup}(1^\lambda)$, *all identities* $\mathsf{id} \in \{0,1\}^*$, *all* (K, ct) *output by* $\mathsf{Encap}(\mathsf{mpk}, \mathsf{id})$ *and all* $\mathsf{usk}_{\mathsf{id}}$ *generated by* $\mathsf{KeyGen}(\mathsf{msk}, \mathsf{id})$*:*

$$\Pr[\mathsf{Decap}(\mathsf{usk}_{\mathsf{id}}, \mathsf{ct}, \mathsf{id}) = K] \geq 1 - \mathsf{negl}(\lambda).$$

We use the standard IND-CPA-security notion for IB-KEMs from [8].

Definition 4. *Consider an adversary* $\mathcal{A}$ *with access (via oracle queries) to the procedures defined Fig. 2. We say that* $\mathcal{A}$ *is* legitimate, *if* $\mathcal{A}$ *never queries* $\mathsf{KeyGen}(\mathsf{msk}, \mathsf{id}^*)$, *where* id^* *is the output of* $\mathcal{A}_1$. *We define the advantage of* $\mathcal{A}$ *in breaking the* $\mathsf{IND\text{-}ID\text{-}CPA}$ *security of IB-KEM* Π *as*

$$\mathsf{Adv}_{\mathcal{A}}^{\mathsf{IND\text{-}ID\text{-}CPA}}(\lambda) := \left|\Pr[\mathsf{IND\text{-}ID\text{-}CPA}_{\mathcal{A}}^{\Pi}(\lambda) = 1] - 1/2\right|$$

$\mathsf{IND\text{-}ID\text{-}CPA}_{\mathcal{A}}^{\Pi}(\lambda)$

$b \xleftarrow{\$} \{0,1\}$
$(\mathsf{mpk}, \mathsf{msk}) \xleftarrow{\$} \mathsf{Setup}(1^\lambda)$
$(\mathsf{id}^*, st) \leftarrow \mathcal{A}_1^{\mathsf{KeyGen}(\mathsf{mpk},\mathsf{msk},\cdot)}(1^k, \mathsf{mpk})$
$K_0 \xleftarrow{\$} \mathcal{K}$; $(\mathsf{ct}, K_1) \xleftarrow{\$} \mathsf{Encap}(\mathsf{mpk}, \mathsf{id}^*)$
$b' \leftarrow \mathcal{A}_2^{\mathsf{KeyGen}(\mathsf{mpk},\mathsf{msk},\cdot)}(st, \mathsf{ct}, K_b)$
If $(b' == b)$ return 1, else 0

Fig. 2. The security experiment for IB-KEMs, executed with scheme Π = $(\mathsf{Setup}, \mathsf{KeyGen}, \mathsf{Encap}, \mathsf{Decap})$ and adversary $\mathcal{A} = (\mathcal{A}_1, \mathcal{A}_2)$. The oracle $\mathsf{KeyGen}(\mathsf{msk}, \mathsf{id})$ returns $\mathsf{usk}_{\mathsf{id}} \xleftarrow{\$} \mathsf{KeyGen}(\mathsf{msk}, \mathsf{id})$ with the restriction that $\mathcal{A}$ is not allowed to query oracle $\mathsf{KeyGen}(\mathsf{msk}, \cdot)$ for the target identity id^*.

We include the running time of the security experiment into the running time $t_{\mathcal{A}}$ *of* $\mathcal{A}$*. This will later allow us to simplify our security analysis and the statement of theorems.*

Our construction is based on $\mathsf{dLWE}_{n,m+1,q,\alpha}$. The construction follows Yamada's construction of a lattice IBE [53] and requires "compatible algorithms" to be instantiated. We first define properties required from these compatible algorithms and then define our IB-KEM. We provide a concrete instantiation of compatible algorithms based on blockwise partitioning in Sect. 3.2.

Compatible Algorithms. Let $\mathbf{G} \in \mathbb{Z}_q^{n \times m}$ be the gadget matrix as introduced in [45, Theorem 1]. That is, $\mathbf{G}$ is a full rank matrix for which there is an efficient algorithm $\mathbf{G}^{-1}$ that on input $\mathbf{U} \in \mathbb{Z}_q^{n \times m}$ outputs a matrix $\mathbf{V} \in \{-1,1\}^{m \times m}$ such that $\mathbf{GV} = \mathbf{U}$. We do not provide a formal definition of $\mathbf{G}$ due to space limitations and instead refer to [45] or the full version [38] for a formal definition. We then say that the algorithms $\mathsf{Encode}, \mathsf{PubEval}$ and $\mathsf{TrapEval}$ are *compatible with blockwise partitioning* if they combine the *vanishing trapdoors technique* from [1,18] with blockwise partitioning. That is, that Encode encodes $(K_0, \ldots, K_\ell) \xleftarrow{\$} \mathsf{BPSmp}(1^\lambda, t(\lambda), \varepsilon(\lambda))$ into matrices $\mathbf{B}, (\mathbf{B}_i)_{0 \le i \le \ell}$ and trapdoors $\mathbf{R}, (\mathbf{R})_{0 \le i \le \ell}$ such that $\mathsf{PubEval}(H, \mathsf{id}, \mathbf{B}, (\mathbf{B}_i)_{0 \le i \le \ell})$ computes $\mathbf{B}_{\mathsf{id}}$ with

$$\mathbf{B}_{\mathsf{id}} = \begin{matrix} \mathbf{AR}_{\mathsf{id}} + \mathbf{H}_{\mathsf{id}}\mathbf{G} \text{ if } H_i(\mathsf{id}) = K_i \text{ for all } i \in \mathcal{I} \\ \mathbf{AR}_{\mathsf{id}} \qquad\qquad \text{otherwise,} \end{matrix}$$

where $\mathbf{R}_{\mathsf{id}}$ is a matrix of small maximum norm that can be computed from the trapdoors using $\mathsf{TrapEval}$ and $\mathbf{H}_{\mathsf{id}}$ is a invertible matrix that depends on id. Note that we denote the infinity norm of a matrix $\mathbf{R}$ by $\|\mathbf{R}\|_\infty$.

Given these properties, the reduction can generate user secret keys for all identities id with $H_i(\mathsf{id}) \neq K_i$ for some $i \in \mathcal{I}$ by using a gadget trapdoor described in the full version [38]. At the same time, if id^* is such that $H_i(\mathsf{id}^*) = K_i$ for all $i \in \mathcal{I}$, then the reduction can extract a solution to its

LWE instance using the adversary. By this, compatible algorithms allow us to apply blockwise partitioning in the context of lattices. We formally define these conditions as follows.

Definition 5. *We say that the algorithms* (Encode, PubEval, TrapEval) *are δ-compatible with blockwise partitioning using a family of hash functions $\mathcal{H}$, if they are efficient and for all $\lambda \in \mathbb{N}, t = t(\lambda) = \mathsf{poly}(\lambda)$ and $\varepsilon = \varepsilon(\lambda)$ non-negligible in λ with $t(\lambda)/\varepsilon(\lambda) \leq 2^{\lambda}$, they satisfy the following properties:*

- *For some matrix $\mathbf{A} \in \mathbb{Z}_q^{n \times m}$, $(K_i)_{0 \leq i \leq \ell} \xleftarrow{\$} \mathsf{BPSmp}(1^{\lambda}, t(\lambda), \varepsilon(\lambda))$ we have that $\mathsf{Encode}(\mathbf{A}, (K_i)_{0 \leq i \leq \ell}) = ((\mathbf{B}, \mathbf{R}), (\mathbf{B}_i, \mathbf{R}_i)_{0 \leq i \leq \ell})$ with $\mathbf{B}, \mathbf{B}_i \in \mathbb{Z}_q^{n \times m}$ and $\mathbf{R}, \mathbf{R}_i \in \{-1, 1\}^{m \times m}$ for all $1 \leq i \leq \ell$.*
- *For $H \in \mathcal{H}$, $\mathsf{id} \in \{0,1\}^*$ and $(\mathbf{B}, (\mathbf{B}_i)_{0 \leq i \leq \ell})$ with $\mathbf{B}_i \in \mathbb{Z}_q^{n \times m}$ for all $0 \leq i \leq \ell$ it holds that $\mathsf{PubEval}(H, \mathsf{id}, \mathbf{B}, (\mathbf{B}_i)_{0 \leq i \leq \ell}) = \mathbf{B}_{\mathsf{id}} \in \mathbb{Z}_q^{n \times m}$.*
- *For $H \in \mathcal{H}, \mathbf{A} \in \mathbb{Z}_q^{n \times m}$, $\mathbf{R}_i \in \mathbb{Z}_q^{m \times m}$ for all $0 \leq i \leq \ell$, and all $\mathsf{id} \in \{0,1\}^*$ it holds that $\mathsf{TrapEval}(H, \mathsf{id}, \mathbf{R}, (\mathbf{R}_i)_{0 \leq i \leq \ell}) = \mathbf{R}_{\mathsf{id}} \in \mathbb{Z}^{m \times m}$.*

We require that for all $\mathsf{id} \in \{0,1\}^*, \mathbf{A} \in \mathbb{Z}_q^{n \times m}$ and $H \in \mathcal{H}$ it holds that

$$\mathsf{PubEval}(H, \mathsf{id}, (\mathbf{B}_i)_{0 \leq i \leq \ell}) \begin{cases} \mathbf{A}\mathbf{R}_{\mathsf{id}} & \text{if } H_i(\mathsf{id}) = K_i \text{ for all } i \in \mathcal{I} \\ \mathbf{A}\mathbf{R}_{\mathsf{id}} + \mathbf{H}_{\mathsf{id}}\mathbf{G} & \text{otherwise} \end{cases}$$

for some invertible matrix $\mathbf{H}_{\mathsf{id}} \in \mathbb{Z}_q^{n \times n}$ and that

$$||\mathbf{R}_{\mathsf{id}}||_{\infty} \leq \delta,$$

where $(K_i)_{0 \leq i \leq \ell}$ is sampled as $(K_i)_{0 \leq i \leq \ell} \xleftarrow{\$} \mathsf{BPSmp}(1^{\lambda}, t, \varepsilon)$ and we have that $\mathsf{Encode}(\mathbf{A}, (K_i)_{0 \leq i \leq \ell}) = ((\mathbf{B}, \mathbf{R}), (\mathbf{B}_i, \mathbf{R}_i)_{0 \leq i \leq \ell})$. Further $\mathbf{R}_{\mathsf{id}}$ is computed as $\mathbf{R}_{\mathsf{id}} = \mathsf{TrapEval}(H, \mathsf{id}, \mathbf{R}, (\mathbf{R}_i)_{0 \leq i \leq \ell})$. Finally, we require, that for $\mathbf{A}, \mathbf{A}' \xleftarrow{\$} \mathbb{Z}_q^{n \times m}$ and all $0 \leq i \leq \ell$ the distributions $(\mathbf{A}, \mathbf{A}')$ and $(\mathbf{A}, \mathbf{B}_i)$ and the distributions $(\mathbf{A}, \mathbf{A}')$ and $(\mathbf{A}, \mathbf{B})$ have only negligible statistical difference in λ.

The Construction. Let $\mathcal{H} = \{H : \{0,1\}^* \rightarrow \{0,1\}^{2\lambda+3}\}$ be a family of hash functions, let $\ell = \lfloor \log(2\lambda + 3) \rfloor$. Further, let $D_{\mathbb{Z}^m, \sigma}$ be the Gaussian distribution over $\mathbb{Z}^m$ with parameter $\sigma > 0$. Moreover, let $\mathsf{GenTrap}(1^n, 1^m, q)$ be an algorithm that outputs a matrix $\mathbf{A} \in \mathbb{Z}_q^{n \times m}$ that is indistinguishable from a random matrix and a trapdoor $\mathbf{A}_{\sigma_0}^{-1}$ for $\sigma_0 = \omega(n \log q \log m)$. Note that for arbitrary $m' \geq m$, $\mathbf{u} \in \mathbb{Z}_q^n$ and $\mathbf{B} \in \mathbb{Z}_q^{n \times (m'-m)}$, the trapdoor $\mathbf{A}_{\sigma_0}^{-1}$ allows sampling vectors $\mathbf{v} \in \mathbb{Z}_q^{m'}$ from $D_{\mathbb{Z}^{m'}, \sigma}$ conditioned on $[\mathbf{A} \mid \mathbf{B}]\mathbf{v} = \mathbf{u}$ for $\sigma' > \sigma_0$. We denote this as sampling from $[\mathbf{A} \mid \mathbf{B}]_{\sigma}^{-1}(\mathbf{u})$ and formalize it in the full version [38].

We now construct our IB-KEM scheme Π = (Setup, KeyGen, Encap, Decap) similar to [53] and based on LWE as follows.

Setup. $\mathsf{Setup}(1^{\lambda})$ chooses parameters $n, m, q, \ell, \sigma, \alpha$ and α' as specified in Remark 6, where q is a prime. It runs $(\mathbf{A}, \mathbf{A}_{\sigma_0}^{-1}) \xleftarrow{\$} \mathsf{GenTrap}(1^n, 1^m, q)$ such that $\mathbf{A} \in$

$\mathbb{Z}_q^{n \times m}$ and $\sigma_0 = \omega(\sqrt{n \log(q) \log(m)})$ and then samples $\mathbf{u} \xleftarrow{\$} \mathbb{Z}_q^n$. Finally, it samples $H \xleftarrow{\$} \mathcal{H}$ and $\mathbf{B}, (\mathbf{B}_i)_{0, \leq i \leq \ell}, \mathbf{C} \xleftarrow{\$} \mathbb{Z}_q^{m \times m}$ and then outputs

$$\mathsf{mpk} = (H, \mathbf{A}, \mathbf{B}, (\mathbf{B}_i)_{0 \leq i \leq \ell}, \mathbf{C}, \mathbf{u}) \text{and} \qquad \mathsf{msk} := \mathbf{A}_{\sigma_0}^{-1}.$$

Key Generation. The algorithm KeyGen receives (mpk, msk, id) as input and computes $\mathbf{B}_{\mathsf{id}} := \mathsf{PubEval}(H, \mathsf{id}, \mathbf{B}, (\mathbf{B}_i)_{0 \leq i \leq \ell})$ such that $\mathbf{B} \in \mathbb{Z}_q^{m \times m}$. It then computes $[\mathbf{A} \mid \mathbf{C} + \mathbf{B}_{\mathsf{id}}]_\sigma^{-1}$ from $\mathbf{A}_{\sigma_0}^{-1}$ and samples $\mathbf{e} \xleftarrow{\$} [\mathbf{A} \mid \mathbf{C} + \mathbf{B}_{\mathsf{id}}]_\sigma^{-1}(\mathbf{u})$. It then outputs $\mathsf{usk}_{\mathsf{id}} := \mathbf{e} \in \mathbb{Z}^{2m}$.

Encapsulation. The Encap algorithm receives an identity $\mathsf{id} \in \{0,1\}^*$ and mpk as input. It computes $\mathbf{B}_{\mathsf{id}} := \mathsf{PubEval}(H, \mathsf{id}, \mathbf{B}, (\mathbf{B}_i)_{0 \leq i \leq \ell})$ such that $\mathbf{B}_{\mathsf{id}} \in \mathbb{Z}_q^{n \times m}$. It then samples $\mathbf{s} \xleftarrow{\$} \mathbb{Z}_q^n, x_0 \xleftarrow{\$} D_{\mathbb{Z}, \alpha q}, \mathbf{x}_1, \mathbf{x}_2 \xleftarrow{\$} D_{\mathbb{Z}^m, \alpha' q}$ and $K \xleftarrow{\$} \{0,1\}$ and computes

$$c_0 = \mathbf{s}^\mathsf{T} \mathbf{u} + x_0 + K \cdot \lceil q/2 \rceil \in \mathbb{Z}_q, \quad \mathbf{c}_1^\mathsf{T} = \mathbf{s}^\mathsf{T} [\mathbf{A} \mid \mathbf{C} + \mathbf{B}_{\mathsf{id}}] + [\mathbf{x}_1^\mathsf{T} \mid \mathbf{x}_2^\mathsf{T}] \in \mathbb{Z}_q^{2m}.$$

It then returns $(\mathsf{ct} = (c_0, \mathbf{c}_1), K)$.

Decapsulation. In order to decapsulate a ciphertext $\mathsf{ct} = (c_0, \mathbf{c}_1)$, the algorithm Decap receives the user secret key $\mathsf{usk}_{\mathsf{id}} = \mathbf{e}$ and computes $w = c_0 - \mathbf{c}_1^\mathsf{T} \cdot \mathbf{e} \in \mathbb{Z}_q$. It then returns $K := 1$ if $|w - \lceil q/2 \rceil| < \lceil q/4 \rceil$ and $K := 0$ otherwise.

Error Term. We deduce the error term as Yamada in [54]. We have

$$w = c_0 - \mathbf{c}_1^\mathsf{T} \cdot \mathbf{e} = K \cdot \lceil q/2 \rceil + x_0 - \left[\mathbf{x}_1^\mathsf{T} \mid \mathbf{x}_2^\mathsf{T}\right] \cdot \mathbf{e},$$

where $x_0 - \left[\mathbf{x}_1^\mathsf{T} \mid \mathbf{x}_2^\mathsf{T}\right] \cdot \mathbf{e}$ is the error term. Assuming $\alpha' \geq \alpha$, the error term is then bounded as follows

$$\begin{aligned} \left|x_0 - \left[\mathbf{x}_1^\mathsf{T} \mid \mathbf{x}_2^\mathsf{T}\right] \mathbf{e}\right| &\leq |x_0| + \left|\left[\mathbf{x}_1^\mathsf{T} \mid \mathbf{x}_2^\mathsf{T}\right] \cdot \mathbf{e}\right| \\ &\leq |x_0| + \left\|\left[\mathbf{x}_1^\mathsf{T} \mid \mathbf{x}_2^\mathsf{T}\right]\right\|_2 \cdot \|\mathbf{e}\|_2 \\ &\leq \alpha q \sqrt{m} + (\alpha' \sqrt{2m}) \cdot \sigma \sqrt{2m} \\ &= \mathcal{O}(\alpha' \sigma m q) \end{aligned}$$

with overwhelming probability, where the first inequality follows from the triangle inequality, the second one follows from the Cauchy-Schwartz inequality, and the third follows from properties of the algorithm GenTrap and the fact that for $x_0 \xleftarrow{\$} D_{\mathbb{Z}, \alpha q}$ it holds that $|x_0| \leq \alpha q \sqrt{m}$ with overwhelming probability. We provide formal theorems for both of these claims in the full version [38]. This then implies the correctness of the scheme.

Remark 6. We select the parameters as described by Yamada (only in the full version [54]) with the additional constraint of n to be large enough to allow for blockwise partitioning. That is, we require

- that n' as chosen in Lemma 2 is at most n, that is $n \geq 2\lambda + 3$ as explained in Sect. 2,

- $\ell = \lfloor \log(n) \rfloor$ in order to use blockwise partitioning.
- the error term is less than $q/5$ with overwhelming probability, that is $q > \Omega(\alpha' \sigma m q)$,
- that $\mathsf{GenTrap}$ can operate, that is $m > 6n \lceil \log q \rceil$,
- that the leftover hash lemma can be applied, meaning $m \geq (n+1)\log(q) + \omega(\log(n))$ (we provide a formal definition of the leftover hash lemma in the full version [38]),
- σ has to be large enough such that the distribution of private keys in the actual scheme and in the reduction is the same, that is $\sigma > \sigma_0 = \omega(\sqrt{n \log(q) \log(m)})$ and $\sigma > m(1+\delta)\omega(\sqrt{\log(m)})$,
- that the ReRand algorithm can operate in the reduction, that is $\alpha'/2\alpha > \sqrt{2} \cdot m(\delta+1)$ and $\alpha q > \omega(\sqrt{\log(m)})$. We formally define the ReRand algorithm and the requirements for its application in the full version [38].
- that the worst to average case reduction works, that is $\alpha q > 2\sqrt{2n}$.

To satisfy the above requirements, we set the parameters as follows:

$$n = 2\lambda + 3, \qquad m = \mathcal{O}(n \log(q)), \qquad q = n^{7/2} \cdot \delta^2 \omega(\log^{7/2}(n))$$
$$\sigma = m \cdot \delta \cdot \omega(\sqrt{\log(m)}) \qquad \alpha q = 3\sqrt{n}, \qquad \alpha' q = 5\sqrt{n} \cdot m \cdot \delta$$

Note that our compatible algorithms have $\delta = 1 + (\ell+1)m$ compared to $\delta' = m^3 \mathcal{O}(\log^2(\lambda))(\mathcal{O}(\lambda)+1)$ for Yamada's compatible algorithms for the modified admissible hash function and $\delta'' = \mathsf{poly}(\lambda)$ for his partitioning based on affine functions. This allows us to use much smaller q and σ.

3.1 Security of the IB-KEM

Our construction is secure when used in conjunction with the compatible algorithms we describe below in Sect. 3.2 under the $\mathsf{dLWE}_{n,m+1,q,\alpha}$ assumption.

Theorem 7. *If* $\Pi :=$ $(\mathsf{Setup}, \mathsf{KeyGen}, \mathsf{Encap}, \mathsf{Decap})$ *from above is instantiated with a family* $\mathcal{H}$ *of weak near-collision resistant hash functions in the sense of Definition 1, then for any legitimate attacker* $\mathcal{A}$ *that breaks the* $\mathsf{IND\text{-}ID\text{-}CPA}$ *security of* Π *in time* $t_{\mathcal{A}}$ *with advantage* $\varepsilon_{\mathcal{A}} := \mathsf{Adv}_{\mathcal{A}}^{\Pi}(\lambda)$*, there exists an algorithm* $\mathcal{B}$ *that, given (sufficiently close approximations of)* $t_{\mathcal{A}}$ *and* $\varepsilon_{\mathcal{A}}$*, breaks the* $\mathsf{dLWE}_{n,m+1,q,\alpha}$ *assumption in time* $t_{\mathcal{B}} \approx t_{\mathcal{A}}$ *and with*

$$\mathsf{Adv}_{\mathcal{B}}^{\mathsf{dLWE}_{n,m+1,q,\alpha}}(\lambda) \geq \varepsilon_{\mathcal{A}}^2/(32t_{\mathcal{A}}^2 - 16t_{\mathcal{A}}) - \mathsf{negl}(\lambda),$$

for some negligible term negl.

The proof of Theorem 7 mostly follows the proof from [54]. We therefore only provide it in the full version [38] for completeness.

3.2 Compatibility of Blockwise Partitioning and Lattice IBE

In this section we describe the main technical novelty of our lattice based construction: how blockwise partitioning can be applied in the context of lattices. We first discuss how a hash function output $H_i(X)$ is encoded as a matrix using the full-rank-difference encoding from Agrawal *et al.* [1] and adapt it to our needs. We then proceed to describe compatible algorithms using this encoding that fulfill all requirements of Definition 5 and can thus be used to instantiate our IB-KEM.

Encoding Identities as Full Rank Difference Matrices. In our construction, we will first hash each $\mathsf{id} \in \{0,1\}^*$ with a weak near-collision resistant hash function $H \xleftarrow{\$} \mathcal{H}$ and then encode each $H_i(\mathsf{id})$ as an invertible matrix as described by Agrawal *et al.* [1]. In the following, we define the *full rank difference encoding function* of [1] and show how it can be adopted to fit blockwise partitioning. Informally, for a binary string $a \in \{0,1\}^{2^i}$, meaning a is a potential output of H_i, we pad a with zeros to be of length n by first padding it $\sum_{j=0}^{i-1} 2^j$ zeros in the front and with $\sum_{j=i+1}^{\ell} 2^j$ zeros in the end. We then canonically interpret it as a vector in $\mathbb{Z}_q^n$ and encode it with the full-rank difference encoding of [1]. We formalize this process in the following definition.

Definition 8. *Let $f(\mathsf{Z})$ be an irreducible polynomial of degree n in $\mathbb{Z}_q^n[\mathsf{Z}]$ and for $\mathbf{a} \in \mathbb{Z}_q^n$, let $g_{\mathbf{a}}(\mathsf{Z}) := \sum_{k=0}^{n-1} a_{k+1}\mathsf{Z}^k \in \mathbb{Z}_q^n[\mathsf{Z}]$. Then the function $\mathsf{FRD}(\mathbf{a}) : \mathbb{Z}_q^n \to \mathbb{Z}_q^{n\times n}$ from [1] is defined as*

$$\mathsf{FRD}(\mathbf{a}) := \begin{bmatrix} \mathsf{coeffs}(g_{\mathbf{a}} \bmod f) \\ \mathsf{coeffs}(\mathsf{Z}\cdot g_{\mathbf{a}} \bmod f) \\ \mathsf{coeffs}(\mathsf{Z}^2\cdot g_{\mathbf{a}} \bmod f) \\ \vdots \\ \mathsf{coeffs}(\mathsf{Z}^{n-1}\cdot g_{\mathbf{a}} \bmod f) \end{bmatrix} \in \mathbb{Z}_q^{n\times n},$$

where coeffs *denotes the coefficients of a polynomial in $\mathbb{Z}_q^n[\mathsf{Z}]$. For all $0 \le i \le \ell$ we define $\mathsf{FRD}_i : \{0,1\}^{2^i} \to \mathbb{Z}_q^{n\times n}$ to be the function that behaves as follows.*

1. *For an input $(a_1,\ldots,a_{2^i}) \in \{0,1\}^{2^i}$, FRD_i lets $\mathsf{offset}_i := \sum_{j=0}^{i-1} 2^j$ and sets $\mathbf{b}^T := [b_1,\ldots,b_n] \in \mathbb{Z}_q^n$, where*

$$b_k := \begin{cases} a_{k-\mathsf{offset}_i} & \text{if } \mathsf{offset}_i < k \le \mathsf{offset}_i + 2^i \\ 0 & \text{otherwise} \end{cases}$$

   for all $1 \le k \le n$.
2. *It then outputs $\mathsf{FRD}_i(a) := \mathsf{FRD}(\mathbf{b})$.*

Agrawal *et al.* [1] prove some properties of FRD that immediately imply the following properties of FRD_i.

Lemma 9 (Sect. 5 in [1]). *Let* $\mathsf{FRD}_i : \{0,1\}^{2^i} \to \mathbb{Z}_q^{n\times n}$ *be as defined in Definition 8, then the following holds:*

1. FRD_i *is injective.*
2. *There is an additive group* $\mathbb{G} \subset \mathbb{Z}_q^{n\times n}$ *such that each* $\mathbf{H} \in \mathbb{G}\setminus\{0\}$ *is invertible and the range of* FRD_i *is a subset of* $\mathbb{G}$ *for all* $1 \le i \le \ell$.

We refer to [1, Sect. 5] for the proofs of the underlying facts used in Lemma 9. Our definition of FRD_i serves some further purposes that allows us to use it in conjunction with blockwise partitioning. We detail these properties in the following lemma.

Lemma 10. *Let* BPSmp *be as defined in Sect. 2 and let* $t \in \mathbb{N}, \varepsilon \in (0,1]$ *with* $t/\varepsilon < 2^\lambda$. *Then for* $(K_0,\dots,K_\ell) \xleftarrow{\$} \mathsf{BPSmp}(1^\lambda,t,\varepsilon)$, $\mathcal{I} = \{i : K_i \ne \bot\} \subseteq \{0,\dots,\ell\}$ *and* $X \in \{0,1\}^*$ *it holds that*

$$-\left(\sum_{i\in\mathcal{I}} \mathsf{FRD}_i(K_i)\right) + \left(\sum_{i\in\mathcal{I}} \mathsf{FRD}_i(H_i(X))\right) = 0 \Leftrightarrow K_i = H_i(X) \text{ for all } i \in \mathcal{I}.$$

We do not present the proof here due to space limitations. However, we present it in the full version [38]. Next, we describe the algorithms ($\mathsf{Encode}, \mathsf{PubEval}, \mathsf{TrapEval}$) and how they use FRD_i. Afterwards, we prove that the algorithms are compatible and can thus be used in our IB-KEM. The algorithms behave as follows:

$\mathsf{Encode}(\mathbf{A}, K_0,\dots,K_\ell)$: The algorithm samples $\mathbf{R}, \mathbf{R}_i \xleftarrow{\$} \{-1,1\}^{m\times m}$ for all $0 \le i \le \ell$ and sets

$$\mathbf{B}_i := \begin{cases} \mathbf{A}\mathbf{R}_i + \mathbf{G} & \text{if } K_i \ne \bot \\ \mathbf{A}\mathbf{R}_i & \text{if } K_i = \bot \end{cases}$$

and $\mathbf{B} := \mathbf{A}\mathbf{R} - \left(\sum_{i\in\mathcal{I}} \mathsf{FRD}_i(K_i)\mathbf{G}\right)$. It then outputs the matrices $((\mathbf{B},\mathbf{R}), (\mathbf{B}_i,\mathbf{R}_i)_{0\le i\le \ell})$.

$\mathsf{PubEval}(H, \mathsf{id}, \mathbf{B}, (\mathbf{B}_i)_{0,\le i\le\ell})$: The algorithm computes $\mathbf{H}_i := \mathsf{FRD}_i(H_i(\mathsf{id}))$ for all $0 \le i \le \ell$ and sets $\mathbf{B}'_i := \mathbf{B}_i\mathbf{G}^{-1}(\mathbf{H}_i\mathbf{G})$. It then outputs $\mathbf{B}_{\mathsf{id}} := \mathbf{B} + \sum_{i=0}^{\ell} \mathbf{B}'_i$.

$\mathsf{TrapEval}(H, \mathsf{id}, \mathbf{R}, (\mathbf{R}_i)_{0\le i\le\ell})$: The algorithm computes $\mathbf{H}_i := \mathsf{FRD}_i(H_i(\mathsf{id}))$ for all $0 \le i \le \ell$ and sets $\mathbf{R}'_i := \mathbf{R}_i\mathbf{G}^{-1}(\mathbf{H}_i\mathbf{G})$. It then outputs $\mathbf{R}_{\mathsf{id}} := \mathbf{R} + \sum_{i=0}^{\ell} \mathbf{R}'_i$.

Lemma 11. *The algorithms* ($\mathsf{Encode}, \mathsf{PubEval}, \mathsf{TrapEval}$) *above are* $\delta = 1 + (\ell+1)m$*-compatible with blockwise partitioning using the family of weak near-collision resistant hash functions* $\mathcal{H}$ *described in Sect. 2.*

Proof. We first observe that the algorithms described above fulfill the syntactical requirements. We next show that

$$\mathsf{PubEval}(H, \mathsf{id}, (\mathbf{B}_i)_{0\le i\le\ell}) \begin{cases} \mathbf{A}\mathbf{R}_{\mathsf{id}} & \text{if } H_i(\mathsf{id}) = K_i \text{ for all } i \in \mathcal{I} \\ \mathbf{A}\mathbf{R}_{\mathsf{id}} + \mathbf{H}_{\mathsf{id}}\mathbf{G} & \text{otherwise} \end{cases}$$

for some invertible matrix $\mathbf{H}_{\mathsf{id}} \in \mathbb{Z}_q^{n\times n}$. For $\mathbf{H}_i := \mathsf{FRD}_i(H_i(\mathsf{id}))$ and $\mathbf{B}_i = \mathbf{AR}_i + x_i\mathbf{HG}$, where $x_i = 1$ if $i \in \mathcal{I}$ and 0 otherwise, we observe that $\mathbf{B}'_i = \mathbf{B}_i\mathbf{G}^{-1}(\mathbf{H}_i\mathbf{G}) = \mathbf{AR}_i\mathbf{G}^{-1}(\mathbf{H}_i\mathbf{G}) + x_i \cdot \mathbf{H}_i\mathbf{G} = \mathbf{AR}'_i + x_i\mathbf{H}_i\mathbf{G}$, where $\mathbf{R}'_i$ is as defined by $\mathsf{TrapEval}$. We then have that

$$\begin{aligned}\mathbf{B}_{\mathsf{id}} = \mathbf{B} + \sum_{i=0}^{\ell}\mathbf{B}'_i &= \mathbf{AR} - \left(\sum_{i\in\mathcal{I}}\mathsf{FRD}_i(K_i)\mathbf{G}\right) + \left(\sum_{i=0}^{\ell}\mathbf{AR}'_i + x_i\mathbf{H}_i\mathbf{G}\right)\\ &= \mathbf{A}\left(\mathbf{R} + \sum_{i=0}^{\ell}\mathbf{R}'_i\right) - \left(\sum_{i\in\mathcal{I}}\mathsf{FRD}_i(K_i)\mathbf{G}\right) + \left(\sum_{i\in\mathcal{I}}\mathsf{FRD}_i(H_i(\mathsf{id}))\mathbf{G}\right)\\ &= \mathbf{AR}_{\mathsf{id}} - \mathbf{H}_{\mathsf{id}}\mathbf{G},\end{aligned}$$

where $\mathbf{R}_{\mathsf{id}}$ is as in the description of $\mathsf{TrapEval}$ and $\mathbf{H}_{\mathsf{id}} = -\left(\sum_{i\in\mathcal{I}}\mathsf{FRD}_i(K_i)\right) + \left(\sum_{i\in\mathcal{I}}\mathbf{H}_i\right)$. Observe that $\mathbf{H}_{\mathsf{id}} = 0$ is equivalent to $K_i = H_i(\mathsf{id})$ for all $i \in \mathcal{I}$ by Lemma 10. Furthermore, we have by Lemma 9 that if $\mathbf{H}_{\mathsf{id}} \neq 0$, then $\mathbf{H}_{\mathsf{id}}$ is invertible. We proceed by proving the upper bound on $\|\mathbf{R}_{\mathsf{id}}\|_\infty$. First, observe $\|\mathbf{R}'_i\|_\infty = \|\mathbf{R}_i\mathbf{G}^{-1}(\mathbf{H}_i G)\|_\infty \leq m$ since $\mathbf{R}_i, \mathbf{G}^{-1}(\mathbf{H}_i\mathbf{G}) \in \{-1,1\}^{m\times m}$ and therefore their product $\mathbf{R}'_i \in \mathbb{Z}_q^{m\times m}$ can not contain any element of absolute value larger than m. We then have

$$\|\mathbf{R}_{\mathsf{id}}\|_\infty = \left\|\mathbf{R} + \sum_{i=0}^{\ell}\mathbf{R}'_i\right\|_\infty \leq \|\mathbf{R}\|_\infty + \sum_{i=0}^{\ell}\|\mathbf{R}'_i\|_\infty \leq 1 + (\ell+1)m = \delta,$$

where the last inequality follows from $\mathbf{R} \in \{-1,1\}^{m\times m}$ and $\|\mathbf{R}'_i\|_\infty \leq m$. Finally, we have that for $\mathbf{A}, \mathbf{A}' \xleftarrow{\$} \mathbb{Z}_q^{n\times m}$ it holds that for all $0 \leq i \leq \ell$ the distributions $(\mathbf{A}, \mathbf{A}')$ and $(\mathbf{A}, \mathbf{B}_i)$ have only negligible statistical difference by the leftover hash lemma, which we formally provide in the full version [38]. The same holds for the distributions $(\mathbf{A}, \mathbf{A}')$ and $(\mathbf{A}, \mathbf{B})$.

4 IB-KEMs from Pairings

In this section, we show how to use blockwise partitioning to create two variants of the IB-KEMs of Boneh and Boyen [14] and Waters [51], respectively. In comparison to [14], we achieve adaptive security instead of selective security. Additionally, we get ciphertexts of only a *single* element. In comparison to the corresponding construction from [37], the q of the required q-type assumption is reduced *quadratically*, while the tightness of the reduction is improved *quadratically*. In comparison to [51], we have public parameters of size $O(\log\lambda)$ instead of $O(\lambda)$. The security analysis is also much simpler than in [51] or the simplified proof by Bellare and Ristenpart [6]. To our best knowledge, this is the first adaptively-secure IBE scheme where ciphertexts consist only of *two* elements of a prime order algebraic group with logarithmic-size public parameters. For a better understanding we instantiate both constructions with symmetric pairings. However, asymmetric pairings work as well as it can be seen in [37].

Definition 12 (Definition 1 from [32]). *A* Bilinear Group Generator *is a probabilistic polynomial-time algorithm* GrpGen *that takes as input a security parameter* λ *(in unary) and outputs* $\mathcal{BG} = (p, \mathbb{G}, \mathbb{G}_T, \circ, \circ_T, e, \phi(1)) \stackrel{\$}{\leftarrow} \mathsf{GrpGen}(1^\lambda)$ *such that the following requirements are satisfied.*

1. *p is a prime and* $\log(p) \in \Omega(\lambda)$
2. *$\mathbb{G}$ and $\mathbb{G}_T$ are subsets of* $\{0,1\}^*$*, defined by algorithmic descriptions of maps* $\phi : \mathbb{Z}_p \to \mathbb{G}$ *and* $\phi_T : \mathbb{Z}_p \to \mathbb{G}_T$.
3. *$\circ$ and $\circ_T$ are algorithmic descriptions of efficiently computable (in the security parameter) maps* $\circ : \mathbb{G} \times \mathbb{G} \to \mathbb{G}$ *and* $\circ_T : \mathbb{G}_T \times \mathbb{G}_T \to \mathbb{G}_T$*, such that*
   a) $(\mathbb{G}, \circ)$ *and* $(\mathbb{G}_T, \circ_T)$ *form algebraic groups,*
   b) ϕ *is a group isomorphism from* $(\mathbb{Z}_p, +)$ *to* $(\mathbb{G}, \circ)$ *and*
   c) ϕ_T *is a group isomorphism from* $(\mathbb{Z}_p, +)$ *to* $(\mathbb{G}_T, \circ_T)$.
4. *e is an algorithmic description of an efficiently computable (in the security parameter) bilinear map* $e : \mathbb{G} \times \mathbb{G} \to \mathbb{G}_T$*. We require that e is non-degenerate, that is,*

$$x \neq 0 \Rightarrow e(\phi(x), \phi(x)) \neq \phi_T(0).$$

Encoding Elements of $\{0,1\}^{2\lambda+3}$ *as* $\mathbb{Z}_p$*-elements.* Furthermore, in order to simplify the notation and description of the construction and its security analysis, we assume that elements of $\{0,1\}^{2\lambda+3}$ can be injectively encoded as elements of $\mathbb{Z}_p$.

4.1 Compact IB-KEM from Decisional Bilinear Diffie-Hellman

In this section we describe a variant of the IBE scheme of Waters [51], which has public parameters of size $O(\log \lambda)$ instead of $O(\lambda)$.

The Construction. Let $\mathcal{H} = \{H : \{0,1\}^* \to \{0,1\}^{2\lambda+3}\}$ be a family of hash functions, let $\ell = \lfloor \log(2\lambda + 3) \rfloor$, and let GrpGen be a bilinear group generator. We construct IB-KEM scheme $\Pi = (\mathsf{Setup}, \mathsf{KeyGen}, \mathsf{Encap}, \mathsf{Decap})$ as follows.

Setup. Choose a group description $\mathcal{BG} \stackrel{\$}{\leftarrow} \mathsf{GrpGen}(1^\lambda)$, a random hash function $H \stackrel{\$}{\leftarrow} \mathcal{H}$, random generators $[1], [h] \in \mathbb{G}$, $\ell + 2$ random group elements $[u'], [u_0], \ldots, [u_\ell]$, and $x \stackrel{\$}{\leftarrow} \mathbb{Z}_p$. Compute $e([1], [hx]) = [hx]_T$ The master secret key is $\mathsf{msk} := [hx]$. The public parameters are defined as

$$\mathsf{mpk} = ([1], [u'], [u_0], \ldots, [u_\ell], [hx]_T).$$

Key Generation. Let

$$[u(\mathsf{id})] := [u'] \prod_{i=0}^{\ell} [u_i]^{H_i(\mathsf{id})} = \left[u' + \sum_{i=0}^{\ell} u_i H_i(\mathsf{id}) \right]$$

To compute the private key for identity id, choose $s \stackrel{\$}{\leftarrow} \mathbb{Z}_p$ and compute and return

$$\mathsf{usk}_{\mathsf{id}} = ([s], [hx] \cdot [u(\mathsf{id})]^s = [hx + u(\mathsf{id})s])$$

Encapsulation. To encapsulate a key, choose $r \xleftarrow{\$} \mathbb{Z}_p$ and compute and return

$$\mathsf{ct} := ([r], [u(\mathsf{id})]^r = [u(\mathsf{id})r]) \in \mathbb{G}^2 \quad \text{and} \quad K := [hx]_T^r = [hxr]_T$$

Decapsulation. To recover K from a ciphertext $\mathsf{ct} = ([r], [u(\mathsf{id})r])$ and a matching user secret key $([s], [hx + u(\mathsf{id})s])$, compute and output

$$\frac{e([hx + u(\mathsf{id})s], [r])}{e([u(\mathsf{id})r], [s])} = \frac{[hxr + u(\mathsf{id})sr]_T}{[u(\mathsf{id})sr]_T} = [hxr]_T$$

Security Analysis. The security of this construction is based on the Decisional Bilinear Diffie-Hellman assumption, which is the same assumption as for schemes of [14,51]. In addition, we assume that the hash function H is weak near-collision resistant.

Definition 13 (Decisional Bilinear Diffie-Hellman [14]). *The advantage of an adversary $\mathcal{A}$ in solving the* Decisional Bilinear Diffie-Hellman Problem *(*DBDH*) with respect to a Bilinear Group Generator* GrpGen *is*

$$\mathsf{Adv}_{\mathcal{A},\mathcal{BG}}^{\mathsf{DBDH}}(\lambda) := |\Pr[\mathcal{A}([\alpha], [\beta], [\gamma], V_0) = 1] - \Pr[\mathcal{A}([\alpha], [\beta], [\gamma], V_1) = 1]|,$$

where $\mathcal{BG} \xleftarrow{\$} \mathsf{GrpGen}(1^\lambda), \alpha, \beta, \gamma \xleftarrow{\$} \mathbb{Z}_p, V_0 = [\alpha\beta\gamma]_T$ and $V_1 \xleftarrow{\$} \mathbb{G}_T$. We say that the DBDH *assumption holds with respect to* GrpGen, *if $\mathsf{Adv}_{\mathcal{A}}^{\mathsf{DBDH}}(\lambda)$ is negligible for every PPT $\mathcal{A}$.*

Theorem 14. *If Π is instantiated with a family $\mathcal{H}$ of weak near-collision resistant hash functions in the sense of Definition 1, then for any legitimate attacker $\mathcal{A}$ that breaks the* IND-ID-CPA *security of Π in time $t_\mathcal{A}$ with advantage $\varepsilon_\mathcal{A} := \mathsf{Adv}_\mathcal{A}^\Pi(\lambda)$, there exists an algorithm $\mathcal{B}$ that, given (sufficiently close approximations of) $t_\mathcal{A}$ and $\varepsilon_\mathcal{A}$, breaks the* DBDH *assumption in time $t_\mathcal{B} \approx t_\mathcal{A}$ and with*

$$\mathsf{Adv}_{\mathcal{B}}^{\mathsf{DBDH}}(\lambda) \geq \frac{\ell}{\ell+1} \cdot \frac{\varepsilon_\mathcal{A}^2}{32t_\mathcal{A}^2 - 16t_\mathcal{A}} - \mathsf{negl}(\lambda)$$

for some negligible term negl.

Proof. Consider the following sequence of games, where we denote with G_i the event that Game i outputs 1 and with $E_i = \Pr\left[1 \xleftarrow{\$} G_i\right] - 1/2$ the advantage of $\mathcal{A}$ in Game i.

Game 0. This is the original $\mathsf{IND\text{-}ID\text{-}CPA}_\mathcal{A}^\Pi(\lambda)$ security experiment. By definition, we have

$$E_0 = \Pr[\mathsf{IND\text{-}ID\text{-}CPA}_\mathcal{A}^\Pi(\lambda) = 1] - 1/2 = \varepsilon_\mathcal{A}$$

Game 1. In this game, we additionally run algorithm

$$(K_0, \ldots, K_\ell) \xleftarrow{\$} \mathsf{BPSmp}(1^\lambda, t_\mathcal{A}, \varepsilon_\mathcal{A})$$

at the beginning of the experiment, where algorithm BPSmp is from Lemma 2.

Furthermore, we define $\mathcal{I} := \{i : K_i \neq \perp\}$. Let $\mathcal{Q}$ be the set of all identities that the adversary queries to $\mathsf{KeyGen}(\mathsf{mpk}, msk, \cdot)$, and let $\mathcal{Q}^* := \mathcal{Q} \cup \{\mathsf{id}^*\}$, where id^* is the identity of the challenge ciphertext. We raise event coll, abort the experiment, and output a random bit, if there exists $i \in \mathcal{I}$ and $\mathsf{id}, \mathsf{id}' \in \mathcal{Q}^*$ such that $\mathsf{id} \neq \mathsf{id}'$, but $H_i(\mathsf{id}) = H_i(\mathsf{id}')$ for all $i \in \mathcal{I}$. Note that coll is defined exactly as in Lemma 2 and that we have

$$E_1 \geq E_{-2} - \Pr[\mathsf{coll}] = \varepsilon_{\mathcal{A}} - \Pr[\mathsf{coll}].$$

Game 2. We raise event $\mathsf{badChal}$, output a random bit, and abort the game, if there exist $i \in \mathcal{I}$ such that $K_i \neq H(\mathsf{id}^*)$. Note that $\mathsf{badChal}$ is defined exactly as in Lemma 2 and that we have

$$E_2 = E_1 \cdot \Pr[\neg\mathsf{badChal}] = (\varepsilon_{\mathcal{A}} - \Pr[\mathsf{coll}]) \cdot \Pr[\neg\mathsf{badChal}] \geq \varepsilon_{\mathcal{A}}^2/(32t_{\mathcal{A}}^2 - 16t_{\mathcal{A}})$$

where the last inequality is from Property 1 of Lemma 2.

Game 3. This game deviates from the security proofs of other constructions in this paper. We need to deal with an event dlog, which is defined below, in order to apply blockwise partitioning to the Boneh-Boyen/Waters scheme.

First, we modify the way how the experiment samples the group elements that determine the function $[u(\mathsf{id})]$. The experiment first chooses a generator $[\alpha] \xleftarrow{\$} \mathbb{G}$ and $r', r_1, \ldots, r_\ell \xleftarrow{\$} \mathbb{Z}_p$ uniformly random. Then it sets

$$[u_i] := \begin{matrix} [\alpha r_i] \text{ if } K_i \neq \perp \\ [r_i] \text{ if } K_i = \perp \end{matrix} \qquad \text{and} \qquad [u'] := \left[r' - \sum_{i \in \mathcal{I}} \alpha r_i K_i\right] \tag{5}$$

Note that the distribution of these values is still uniform, and therefore identical to Game 2. Game 3 now raises event dlog and aborts, if there exists $\mathsf{id} \in \mathcal{Q}$ such that

$$\sum_{i \in \mathcal{I}} \alpha r_i K_i = \sum_{i \in \mathcal{I}} \alpha r_i H_i(\mathsf{id}) \iff \sum_{i \in \mathcal{I}} r_i(K_i - H_i(\mathsf{id})) = 0 \tag{6}$$

We claim that there exists an algorithm $\mathcal{B}_1$ that breaks the Decisional Bilinear Diffie-Hellman assumption with success probability $\Pr[\mathsf{dlog}]/|\mathcal{I}|$. $\mathcal{B}_1$ receives as input $(\mathcal{BG}, [r], [\beta], [\gamma], V)$. It will compute the discrete logarithm r and use this to break the DBDH assumption.[1]

$\mathcal{B}_1$ picks $j \xleftarrow{\$} \mathcal{I}$ at random and defines $[r_j] := [r]$. Then it proceeds exactly like Game 3. If dlog occurs, then Eq. (6) holds. Due to Game 2 we can be certain that $K_i = H_i(\mathsf{id}^*)$ holds for all $i \in \mathcal{I}$, and due to Game 1 we know that for any $\mathsf{id} \in \mathcal{Q}$ there must be at least one $i \in \mathcal{I}$ such that $H_i(\mathsf{id}) \neq H_i(\mathsf{id}^*)$. These two together yield that for any $\mathsf{id} \in \mathcal{Q}$ there must exist at least one $i \in \mathcal{I}$ such that $H_i(\mathsf{id}) \neq K_i$.

[1] We could alternatively reduce to the weaker discrete logarithm problem, but we will later reduce to DBDH anyway, so omitting the additional definition saves trees.

Let id be the first identity for which Eq. (6) holds. With probability at least $1/|\mathcal{I}|$ we have $j = i$. In this case $\mathcal{B}_1$ is able to compute

$$r = r_j = \frac{\sum_{i \in \mathcal{I} \setminus \{j\}} r_i(K_i - H_i(\mathsf{id}))}{H_j(\mathsf{id}) - K_j}$$

which immediately enables $\mathcal{B}_1$ to test whether $V = e([\beta], [\gamma])^r$ holds. With $|\mathcal{I}| \leq \ell$ we thus get

$$E_3 \geq E_2 - \mathsf{Adv}^{\mathsf{DBDH}}_{\mathcal{B}_1}(\lambda)/\ell$$

Reduction. Now we are able to describe our final reduction $\mathcal{B}_2$ to the Decisional Bilinear Diffie-Hellman assumption. $\mathcal{B}_2$ that receives $(\mathcal{BG}, [\alpha], [\beta], [\gamma], V)$ and simulates the IND-ID-CPA experiment as follows.

Setup. $\mathcal{B}_2$ defines $[x] := [\alpha]$, $[h] := [\beta]$, and uses $[\alpha]$ to compute $[u'], [u_0], \ldots, [u_\ell]$ exactly as in Game 3, Eq. (5). The master public parameters are defined as

$$\mathsf{mpk} = ([1], [u'], [u_0], \ldots, [u_\ell], e([\alpha], [\beta]))$$

note that this is a correctly distributed master public key. The secret key is implicitly defined as $[\alpha\beta]$.

Key Generation. In the sequel let us write

$$a(\mathsf{id}) := \sum_{i \in \mathcal{I}} r_i(H_i(\mathsf{id}) - K_i) \qquad \text{and} \qquad b(\mathsf{id}) := r' + \sum_{i \notin \mathcal{I}} r_i H_i(\mathsf{id})$$

such that we have $[u(\mathsf{id})] = [\alpha a(\mathsf{id}) + b(\mathsf{id})]$.
$\mathcal{B}_2$ needs to compute a secret key of the form

$$[s], [\alpha\beta + u(\mathsf{id})s]$$

such that s is uniform over $\mathbb{Z}_p$. To this end, it picks $s' \xleftarrow{\$} \mathbb{Z}_p$ and computes

$$[s] := [\beta]^{-1/a(\mathsf{id})} \cdot [s'],$$

which is correctly distributed and implicitly defines $s := -\beta/a(\mathsf{id}) + s'$. Then it computes

$$\begin{aligned} [z] &:= [\beta]^{-b(\mathsf{id})/a(\mathsf{id})} \cdot [\alpha]^{a(\mathsf{id})s'} \cdot [b(\mathsf{id})s'] \\ &= [\alpha\beta - \alpha\beta - \beta b(\mathsf{id})/a(\mathsf{id}) + \alpha a(\mathsf{id})s' + b(\mathsf{id})s'] \\ &= [\alpha\beta + (\alpha a(\mathsf{id}) + b(\mathsf{id}))(-\beta/a(\mathsf{id}) + s')] \\ &= [\alpha\beta + u(\mathsf{id})s] \end{aligned}$$

Note here that we have $a(\mathsf{id}) \neq 0$ for all $\mathsf{id} \in \mathcal{Q}$, as otherwise we raise event dlog and abort due to Game 3, Eq. (6). Then it returns $([s], [z])$.

Encapsulation. Given a challenge identity id^*, $\mathcal{B}_2$ has to create a challenge ciphertext of the form

$$\mathsf{ct} := ([r], [u(\mathsf{id}^*)r])$$

$\mathcal{B}_2$ sets $[r] := [\gamma]$, where $[\gamma]$ is from the DBDH challenge. Note that we have $a(\mathsf{id}^*) = 0$, as otherwise we raise event guess and abort due to Game 2, and thus

$$[u(\mathsf{id}^*)\gamma] = [b(\mathsf{id}^*)\gamma] = [\gamma]^{b(\mathsf{id}^*)}$$

such that $\mathsf{ct}^* = ([\gamma], [\gamma]^{b(\mathsf{id}^*)})$ is a consistent ciphertext.
Finally, it sets $K^* := T$ and returns (ct^*, K^*).

Note that if $T = [\alpha\beta\gamma]_T$, then this is a correct key, since for any valid user key $([s], [hx + u(\mathsf{id}^*)s])$ for the challenge identity id^* we have

$$\frac{e([\alpha\beta + u(\mathsf{id})s], [\gamma])}{e([u(\mathsf{id})\gamma], [s])} = \frac{[\alpha\beta\gamma + u(\mathsf{id})s\gamma]_T}{[u(\mathsf{id})s\gamma]_T} = [\alpha\beta\gamma]_T$$

while if T is random, then so is K^*. Hence, $\mathcal{B}_2$ provides a perfect simulation of Game 3. It returns whatever $\mathcal{A}$ returns, and thus we have that

$$\mathsf{Adv}^{\mathsf{DBDH}}_{\mathcal{B}_2}(\lambda) \geq E_3.$$

By collecting probability across all games, we get

$$\frac{\mathsf{Adv}^{\mathsf{DBDH}}_{\mathcal{B}_1}(\lambda)}{\ell} + \mathsf{Adv}^{\mathsf{DBDH}}_{\mathcal{B}_2}(\lambda) \geq \frac{\varepsilon^2_{\mathcal{A}}}{32t^2_{\mathcal{A}} - 16t_{\mathcal{A}}}.$$

4.2 IB-KEM with Short Ciphertexts

In this section, we present a new IB-KEM that is adaptively secure and where the ciphertext consists of only a *single* element. Compared to the only other construction with these properties ([37]), the q of the required q-type assumption is reduced *quadratically*, while the tightness of the reduction is improved *quadratically*, as well. Due to weak near-collision resistance, we are also able to reduce the output length of the hash function to roughly half of the output length required in [37], which reduces computational costs while guaranteeing the same level of security. **The construction.** Let $\mathcal{H} = \{H : \{0,1\}^* \to \{0,1\}^{2\lambda+3}\}$ be a family of hash functions, let $\ell = \lfloor \log(2\lambda + 3) \rfloor$, and let GrpGen be a bilinear group generator. We construct the IB-KEM scheme $\Pi = (\mathsf{Setup}, \mathsf{KeyGen}, \mathsf{Encap}, \mathsf{Decap})$ as follows.

Setup. Choose a group description $\mathcal{BG} \xleftarrow{\$} \mathsf{GrpGen}(1^\lambda)$, a random hash function $H \xleftarrow{\$} \mathcal{H}$, a random generator $[1] \in \mathbb{G}_1$, and random elements $x_0, \ldots, x_\ell \in \mathbb{Z}_p^*$. Define the master secret key msk as

$$\mathsf{msk} = (x_0, \ldots, x_\ell) \in \mathbb{Z}_p^{\ell+1}.$$

For $i \in \mathbb{N}$ and $m \in \mathbb{N}_0$ define $b_i(m)$ as the function that, on input of integer m, outputs the i-th bit of the binary representation of m. For $\mathsf{msk} = (x_0, \ldots, x_\ell)$ and $m = 0, \ldots, 2^{\ell+1} - 1$ define

$$F(\mathsf{msk}, m) := \prod_{i=0}^{\ell} x_i^{b_i(m)}. \tag{7}$$

The public parameters are defined as

$$\mathsf{mpk} = ([F(\mathsf{msk}, 0)], \ldots, [F(\mathsf{msk}, 2^{\ell+1} - 1]).$$

Key Generation. Let

$$u(\mathsf{id}) = \prod_{i=0}^{\ell} (H_i(\mathsf{id}) + x_i) \in \mathbb{Z}_p. \tag{8}$$

Then the private key for identity id is computed as $\mathsf{usk}_{\mathsf{id}} = [1/u(\mathsf{id})]$.
Encapsulation. Observe that

$$u(\mathsf{id}) = \prod_{i=0}^{\ell} (H_i(\mathsf{id}) + x_i) = d_0 + \sum_{m=1}^{2^\ell - 1} \left(d_m \prod_{i=0}^{\ell} x_i^{b_i(n)}\right),$$

where the constants d_i are efficiently computable from $H(\mathsf{id})$. Using $H(\mathsf{id})$ and mpk first $[u(\mathsf{id})]$ is computed as

$$[u(\mathsf{id})] = \left[d_0 + \sum_{m=1}^{2^\ell - 1} \left(d_m \prod_{i=0}^{\ell} x_i^{b_i(n)}\right)\right] = [d_0] \cdot \prod_{m=1}^{2^\ell - 1} [F(\mathsf{msk}, m)]^{d_m}.$$

Note that this does not require knowledge of $x_0, \ldots, x_\ell$ explicitly.
Finally, the ciphertext and key are computed as

$$(\mathsf{ct}, K) = ([u(\mathsf{id})]^r, e([1], [1])^r) \in \mathbb{G}_1 \times \mathbb{G}_T.$$

for a uniformly random $r \stackrel{\$}{\leftarrow} \mathbb{Z}_p$.
Decapsulation. To recover K from a ciphertext ct for identity id and a matching user secret key $[1/(u(\mathsf{id}))]$, compute and output $e(C, \mathsf{usk}_{\mathsf{id}})$.

Security Analysis. The security of this construction is based on the q-DBDHI assumption, which is the same assumption as for the scheme of [14]. In addition, we assume that the hash function H is weak near-collision resistant.

Definition 15 (q-Decision Bilinear Diffie-Hellman Inversion Assumption [14]). *For a PPT algorithm $\mathcal{A}$, the advantage of $\mathcal{A}$ in solving the q* -Decision Bilinear Diffie-Hellman Inversion Problem *(q-DBDHI) with respect to a Bilinear Group Generator* GrpGen *is*

$$\begin{aligned}\mathsf{Adv}_{\mathcal{A}}^{q\text{-DBDHI}}(\lambda) := \big|&\Pr\left[\mathcal{A}\left(\mathcal{BG}, [y], [y\alpha], [y\alpha^2], \ldots, [y\alpha^q], V_0\right) = 1\right] \\ &- \Pr\left[\mathcal{A}\left(\mathcal{BG}, [y], [y\alpha], [y\alpha^2], \ldots, [y\alpha^q], V_1\right) = 1\right]\big|,\end{aligned}$$

where $\mathcal{BG} \xleftarrow{\$} \mathsf{GrpGen}(1^\lambda), \alpha \xleftarrow{\$} \mathbb{Z}_p^*, [y] \xleftarrow{\$} \mathbb{G}, V_0 = e([y],[y])^{1/\alpha}$ *and* $V_1 \xleftarrow{\$} \mathbb{G}_T$. *The probability is over the randomness of* $\mathcal{A}$, GrpGen *and sampling* $\alpha, \tilde{g}, h$ *and* V_1. *We say that the* q-DBDHI *assumption holds with respect to* GrpGen *if* $\mathsf{Adv}_{\mathcal{A}}^{q\text{-DBDHI}}(\lambda)$ *is negligible for every PPT* $\mathcal{A}$.

We start by defining the strength of the q-DBDHI assumption and set $q := 4\lambda + 7 + j + 2\sum_{i \in [\lfloor \log(2\lambda+3) \rfloor]_0, K_i \neq \perp} \left(2^{2^i} - 1\right)$. Using the following lemma, we immediately obtain $q \leq 4\lambda + 8 + \lfloor \log(2\lambda+3) \rfloor + 32t_{\mathcal{A}}^2/\varepsilon_{\mathcal{A}}$ because $j \leq \lfloor \log(2\lambda+3) \rfloor + 1$.

Lemma 16. *Let* $\mathcal{I} = \{i : K_i \neq \perp\}$ *be as above, then*

$$2 \cdot \sum_{\substack{i \in [\lfloor \log(2\lambda+3) \rfloor]_0 \\ i \in \mathcal{I}}} \left(2^{2^i} - 1\right) \leq \frac{32t_{\mathcal{A}}^2}{\varepsilon_{\mathcal{A}}}.$$

The proof of Lemma 16 consists only of simple arithmetic and we therefore provide it in the full version [38].

Theorem 17. *If* Π *is instantiated with a family* $\mathcal{H}$ *of weak near-collision resistant hash functions in the sense of Definition 1, then for any legitimate attacker* $\mathcal{A}$ *that breaks the* IND-ID-CPA *security of* Π *in time* $t_{\mathcal{A}}$ *with advantage* $\varepsilon_{\mathcal{A}} := \mathsf{Adv}_{\mathcal{A}}^{\Pi}(\lambda)$, *there exists an algorithm* $\mathcal{B}$ *that, given (sufficiently close approximations of)* $t_{\mathcal{A}}$ *and* $\varepsilon_{\mathcal{A}}$, *breaks the* q-DBDHI *assumption with* $q \leq 4\lambda + 9 + \lfloor \log(2\lambda+3) \rfloor + 32t_{\mathcal{A}}^2/\varepsilon_{\mathcal{A}}$ *in time* $t_{\mathcal{B}} = O(32t_{\mathcal{A}}^2/\varepsilon_{\mathcal{A}})$ *and with*

$$\mathsf{Adv}_{\mathcal{B}}^{q\text{-DBDHI}}(\lambda) \geq \varepsilon_{\mathcal{A}}^2/(32t_{\mathcal{A}}^2 - 16t_{\mathcal{A}}) - \mathsf{negl}(\lambda),$$

for some negligible term negl.

The proof of Theorem 17 adapts the techniques from the poof of Theorem 14 to the q-DBDHI assumption. For a complete overview, we provide the proof in the full version [38].

5 Verifiable Random Functions from Pairings

In this section, we use blockwise partitioning in order to construct the first verifiable random function without random oracles that has both, short proofs and short public keys. Compared to previous VRF constructions that also achieve small proof sizes, like [40,42], we achieve much better concrete proof sizes or much smaller public keys. We provide preliminaries to VRFs in the full version [38]. The construction of the VRF roughly follows the construction of the IB-KEM. The major difference is that including group elements in the proof of the VRF allows us to only include the group elements $[x_i]$ instead of all possible combinations $F(\mathsf{msk}, m)$, as in the IB-KEM, in the public keys. Instead of viewing the VRF as an adaptation of our previous IB-KEM in Sect. 4.2, it can also be viewed as an adaptation of Yamada's VRF [53] to blockwise partitioning.

The construction. Let $\mathcal{H}_\lambda = \{H : \{0,1\}^* \to \{0,1\}^{2\lambda+3}\}$ be a family of hash functions, let $\ell = \lfloor \log(2\lambda+3) \rfloor$, let GrpGen be a certified bilinear group generator, and let $\mathcal{VRF} = (\mathsf{Gen}, \mathsf{Eval}, \mathsf{Vfy})$ be the following algorithms.

Key generation. $\mathsf{Gen}(1^\lambda)$ chooses a group description $\mathcal{BG} \xleftarrow{\$} \mathsf{GrpGen}(1^\lambda)$, a random hash function $H \xleftarrow{\$} \mathcal{H}_\lambda$, a random generator $[1] \xleftarrow{\$} \mathbb{G}^*$. Then it samples $w_i \xleftarrow{\$} \mathbb{Z}_p^*$ and sets $W_i := [w_i]$ for all $i = 0, \dots, \ell$. It returns

$$\mathsf{vk} := ([1], \mathcal{BG}, W_0, \dots, W_\ell, H) \qquad \text{and} \qquad \mathsf{sk} := (w_0, \dots, w_\ell).$$

Evaluation. $\mathsf{Eval}(\mathsf{sk}, X)$ computes for $i = 0, \dots, \ell$

$$\Theta_i(X) := \prod_{i'=0}^{i} (w_{i'} + H_{i'}(X)).$$

If there is an index $0 \leq i \leq \ell$ such that $\Theta_i(X) \equiv 0 \bmod p$ it sets $Y := 1_{\mathbb{G}_T}$ and $\pi_i = 1_{\mathbb{G}}$ for all $i = 0, \dots, \ell$. Otherwise, it computes

$$Y := e([1],[1])^{1/\Theta_\ell(X)} \qquad \text{and} \qquad \pi_i := g^{1/\Theta_i(X)}$$

for all $i = 0, \dots, \ell$. It outputs $(Y, \pi = (\pi_0, \dots, \pi_\ell))$.

Verification. $\mathsf{Vfy}(\mathsf{vk}, X, Y, \pi)$ checks if the following conditions are met and outputs 0 if not, otherwise it outputs 1.

1. We have that $X \in \{0,1\}^*$.
2. vk has the form $([1], \mathcal{BG}, W_0, \dots, W_\ell, H)$ and $\mathsf{sk} = (w_0, \dots, w_\ell)$.
3. $\mathcal{BG}$ is a certified encoding of a bilinear group: $\mathsf{GrpVfy}(1^\lambda, \mathcal{BG}) = 1$ Further, all group elements can be verified $\mathsf{GrpElemVfy}(1^\lambda, \mathcal{BG}, [1]) = 1$, $\mathsf{GrpElemVfy}(1^\lambda, \mathcal{BG}, h) = 1$, $\mathsf{GrpElemVfy}(1^\lambda, \mathcal{BG}, W_i) = 1$ and also $\mathsf{GrpElemVfy}(1^\lambda, \mathcal{BG}, \pi_i) = 1$ for all $0 \leq i \leq \ell$.
4. If there is an index $\leq i \leq \ell$ such that $W_i \cdot [H_i(X)] = 1_{\mathbb{G}}$, then it holds that $Y = 1_{\mathbb{G}_T}$ and $\pi_i = 1_{\mathbb{G}}$ for all $i = 0, \dots, \ell$.
5. If we have $W_i \cdot [H_i(X)] \neq 1_{\mathbb{G}}$ for all $i = 0, \dots, \ell$, then for all of these i it holds that $e(\pi_i, W_i \cdot [H_i(X)]) = e([1], \pi_{i-1})$.
6. It holds that $e(\pi_\ell, [1]) = Y$.

$\mathcal{VRF}$ as specified above is correct and fulfills the unique provability requirements as can be proven with standard arguments. Also note that using a hash function does not affect unique provability because the hash function deterministically maps each input to an output. Like the IB-KEM we present in Sect. 4.2, our VRF is based on the q-DBDHI assumption. We set $q := \log(2\lambda+3) + 2 + 2\sum_{\substack{i \in [\lfloor \log(2\lambda+3) \rfloor]_0 \\ K_i \neq \perp}} \left(2^{2^i} - 1\right)$ which is at most $\log(2\lambda+3) + 2 + \frac{32t - \mathcal{A}^2}{\varepsilon_\mathcal{A}}$ by Lemma 16.

Theorem 18. *If $\mathcal{VRF}$ is instantiated with a family $\mathcal{H} = \{H : \{0,1\}^* \to \{0,1\}^{2\lambda+3}\}$ of weak near-collision resistant hash functions from Definition 1, then for any legitimate attacker $\mathcal{A}$ that breaks the pseudorandomness of $\mathcal{VRF}$ in* *time* $t_{\mathcal{A}}$ *with advantage* $\varepsilon_{\mathcal{A}} := \mathsf{Adv}_{\mathcal{A}}^{\mathsf{RoR}}(\lambda)$, *there exists an algorithm* $\mathcal{B}$ *that, given (sufficiently close approximations of)* $t_{\mathcal{A}}$ *and* $\varepsilon_{\mathcal{A}}$, *breaks the* q-DBDHI *assumption with* $q \leq \ell + 2 + 32t_{\mathcal{A}}^2/\varepsilon_{\mathcal{A}}$ *in time* $t_{\mathcal{B}} = O(t_{\mathcal{A}}^2/\varepsilon_{\mathcal{A}})$ *and with*

$$\mathsf{Adv}_{\mathcal{A}}^{q\text{-}\mathsf{DBDHI}}(\lambda) \geq \varepsilon_{\mathcal{A}}^2/(32t_{\mathcal{A}}^2 - 16t_{\mathcal{A}}) - \mathsf{negl}(\lambda),$$

for some negligible term negl.

The proof of Theorem 18 follows the proof of Theorem 17 and we thus provide it in the full version [38].

References

1. Agrawal, S., Boneh, D., Boyen, X.: Efficient lattice (H)IBE in the standard model. In: Gilbert, H. (ed.) EUROCRYPT 2010. LNCS, vol. 6110, pp. 553–572. Springer, Heidelberg (2010). https://doi.org/10.1007/978-3-642-13190-5_28
2. Agrawal, S., Boneh, D., Boyen, X.: Lattice basis delegation in fixed dimension and shorter-ciphertext hierarchical IBE. In: Rabin, T. (ed.) CRYPTO 2010. LNCS, vol. 6223, pp. 98–115. Springer, Heidelberg (2010). https://doi.org/10.1007/978-3-642-14623-7_6
3. Alperin-Sheriff, J.: Short signatures with short public keys from homomorphic trapdoor functions. In: Katz, J. (ed.) PKC 2015. LNCS, vol. 9020, pp. 236–255. Springer, Heidelberg (2015). https://doi.org/10.1007/978-3-662-46447-2_11
4. Apon, D., Fan, X., Liu, F.H.: Compact identity based encryption from LWE. Cryptology ePrint Archive, Report 2016/125. http://eprint.iacr.org/2016/125
5. Attrapadung, N., Hanaoka, G., Yamada, S.: A framework for identity-based encryption with almost tight security. In: Iwata, T., Cheon, J.H. (eds.) ASIACRYPT 2015. LNCS, vol. 9452, pp. 521–549. Springer, Heidelberg (2015). https://doi.org/10.1007/978-3-662-48797-6_22
6. Bellare, M., Ristenpart, T.: Simulation without the artificial abort: simplified proof and improved concrete security for waters' IBE scheme. In: Joux, A. (ed.) EUROCRYPT 2009. LNCS, vol. 5479, pp. 407–424. Springer, Heidelberg (2009). https://doi.org/10.1007/978-3-642-01001-9_24
7. Bellare, M., Rogaway, P.: Random oracles are practical: a paradigm for designing efficient protocols. In: ACM CCS 93 (1993)
8. Bentahar, K., Farshim, P., Malone-Lee, J., Smart, N.P.: Generic constructions of identity-based and certificateless KEMs. J. Cryptol. **21**, 178–199 (2007)
9. Bertoni, G., Daemen, J., Peeters, M., Van Assche, G.: On the indifferentiability of the sponge construction. In: Smart, N. (ed.) EUROCRYPT 2008. LNCS, vol. 4965, pp. 181–197. Springer, Heidelberg (2008). https://doi.org/10.1007/978-3-540-78967-3_11
10. Biham, E., Chen, R.: Near-collisions of SHA-0. In: Franklin, M. (ed.) CRYPTO 2004. LNCS, vol. 3152, pp. 290–305. Springer, Heidelberg (2004). https://doi.org/10.1007/978-3-540-28628-8_18
11. Biham, E., Chen, R., Joux, A., Carribault, P., Lemuet, C., Jalby, W.: Collisions of SHA-0 and reduced SHA-1. In: Cramer, R. (ed.) EUROCRYPT 2005. LNCS, vol. 3494, pp. 36–57. Springer, Heidelberg (2005). https://doi.org/10.1007/11426639_3

12. Böhl, F., Hofheinz, D., Jager, T., Koch, J., Seo, J.H., Striecks, C.: Practical signatures from standard assumptions. In: Johansson, T., Nguyen, P.Q. (eds.) EUROCRYPT 2013. LNCS, vol. 7881, pp. 461–485. Springer, Heidelberg (2013). https://doi.org/10.1007/978-3-642-38348-9_28
13. Böhl, F., Hofheinz, D., Jager, T., Koch, J., Striecks, C.: Confined guessing: new signatures from standard assumptions. J. Cryptol. **28**, 176–208 (2014)
14. Boneh, D., Boyen, X.: Efficient selective-ID secure identity-based encryption without random Oracles. In: Cachin, C., Camenisch, J.L. (eds.) EUROCRYPT 2004. LNCS, vol. 3027, pp. 223–238. Springer, Heidelberg (2004). https://doi.org/10.1007/978-3-540-24676-3_14
15. Boneh, D., Boyen, X.: Secure identity based encryption without random Oracles. In: Franklin, M. (ed.) CRYPTO 2004. LNCS, vol. 3152, pp. 443–459. Springer, Heidelberg (2004). https://doi.org/10.1007/978-3-540-28628-8_27
16. Boneh, D., Franklin, M.: Identity-based encryption from the weil pairing. In: Kilian, J. (ed.) CRYPTO 2001. LNCS, vol. 2139, pp. 213–229. Springer, Heidelberg (2001). https://doi.org/10.1007/3-540-44647-8_13
17. Boneh, D., Montgomery, H.W., Raghunathan, A.: Algebraic pseudorandom functions with improved efficiency from the augmented cascade. In: ACM CCS (2010)
18. Boyen, X.: Lattice mixing and vanishing trapdoors: a framework for fully secure short signatures and more. In: PKC 2010 (2010)
19. Boyen, X., Li, Q.: Towards tightly secure lattice short signature and Id-based encryption. In: Cheon, J.H., Takagi, T. (eds.) ASIACRYPT 2016. LNCS, vol. 10032, pp. 404–434. Springer, Heidelberg (2016). https://doi.org/10.1007/978-3-662-53890-6_14
20. Canetti, R., Goldreich, O., Halevi, S.: The random oracle methodology, revisited (preliminary version). In: 30th ACM STOC (1998)
21. Cash, D., Hofheinz, D., Kiltz, E., Peikert, C.: Bonsai trees, or how to delegate a lattice basis. In: Gilbert, H. (ed.) EUROCRYPT 2010. LNCS, vol. 6110, pp. 523–552. Springer, Heidelberg (2010). https://doi.org/10.1007/978-3-642-13190-5_27
22. Catalano, D., Fiore, D., Nizzardo, L.: Programmable hash functions go private: constructions and applications to (homomorphic) signatures with shorter public keys. In: Gennaro, R., Robshaw, M. (eds.) CRYPTO 2015. LNCS, vol. 9216, pp. 254–274. Springer, Heidelberg (2015). https://doi.org/10.1007/978-3-662-48000-7_13
23. Chen, J., Lim, H.W., Ling, S., Wang, H., Wee, H.: Shorter IBE and signatures via asymmetric pairings. In: Abdalla, M., Lange, T. (eds.) Pairing 2012. LNCS, vol. 7708, pp. 122–140. Springer, Heidelberg (2013). https://doi.org/10.1007/978-3-642-36334-4_8
24. Ducas, L., Micciancio, D.: Improved short lattice signatures in the standard model. In: Garay, J.A., Gennaro, R. (eds.) CRYPTO 2014. LNCS, vol. 8616, pp. 335–352. Springer, Heidelberg (2014). https://doi.org/10.1007/978-3-662-44371-2_19
25. Fischlin, M., Fleischhacker, N.: Limitations of the meta-reduction technique: the case of Schnorr signatures. In: Johansson, T., Nguyen, P.Q. (eds.) EUROCRYPT 2013. LNCS, vol. 7881, pp. 444–460. Springer, Heidelberg (2013). https://doi.org/10.1007/978-3-642-38348-9_27
26. Fischlin, M., Harasser, P., Janson, C.: Signatures from sequential-OR proofs. In: Canteaut, A., Ishai, Y. (eds.) EUROCRYPT 2020. LNCS, vol. 12107, pp. 212–244. Springer, Cham (2020). https://doi.org/10.1007/978-3-030-45727-3_8
27. Fischlin, M., Lehmann, A., Ristenpart, T., Shrimpton, T., Stam, M., Tessaro, S.: Random Oracles with(out) programmability. In: Abe, M. (ed.) ASIACRYPT

2010. LNCS, vol. 6477, pp. 303–320. Springer, Heidelberg (2010). https://doi.org/10.1007/978-3-642-17373-8_18
28. Freire, E.S.V., Hofheinz, D., Paterson, K.G., Striecks, C.: Programmable hash functions in the multilinear setting. In: Canetti, R., Garay, J.A. (eds.) CRYPTO 2013. LNCS, vol. 8042, pp. 513–530. Springer, Heidelberg (2013). https://doi.org/10.1007/978-3-642-40041-4_28
29. Gentry, C.: Practical identity-based encryption without random oracles. In: Vaudenay, S. (ed.) EUROCRYPT 2006. LNCS, vol. 4004, pp. 445–464. Springer, Heidelberg (2006). https://doi.org/10.1007/11761679_27
30. Goldreich, O.: Computational Complexity - A Conceptual Perspective. Cambridge University Press, New York (2008)
31. Hanaoka, G., Matsuda, T., Schuldt, J.C.N.: On the impossibility of constructing efficient key encapsulation and programmable hash functions in prime order groups. In: Safavi-Naini, R., Canetti, R. (eds.) CRYPTO 2012. LNCS, vol. 7417, pp. 812–831. Springer, Heidelberg (2012). https://doi.org/10.1007/978-3-642-32009-5_47
32. Hofheinz, D., Jager, T.: Verifiable random functions from standard assumptions. In: Kushilevitz, E., Malkin, T. (eds.) TCC 2016. LNCS, vol. 9562, pp. 336–362. Springer, Heidelberg (2016). https://doi.org/10.1007/978-3-662-49096-9_14
33. Hofheinz, D., Jager, T., Kiltz, E.: Short signatures from weaker assumptions. In: Lee, D.H., Wang, X. (eds.) ASIACRYPT 2011. LNCS, vol. 7073, pp. 647–666. Springer, Heidelberg (2011). https://doi.org/10.1007/978-3-642-25385-0_35
34. Hofheinz, D., Kiltz, E.: Programmable hash functions and their applications. In: Wagner, D. (ed.) CRYPTO 2008. LNCS, vol. 5157, pp. 21–38. Springer, Heidelberg (2008). https://doi.org/10.1007/978-3-540-85174-5_2
35. Hohenberger, S., Waters, B.: Constructing verifiable random functions with large input spaces. In: Gilbert, H. (ed.) EUROCRYPT 2010. LNCS, vol. 6110, pp. 656–672. Springer, Heidelberg (2010). https://doi.org/10.1007/978-3-642-13190-5_33
36. Jager, T.: Verifiable random functions from weaker assumptions. In: Dodis, Y., Nielsen, J.B. (eds.) TCC 2015. LNCS, vol. 9015, pp. 121–143. Springer, Heidelberg (2015). https://doi.org/10.1007/978-3-662-46497-7_5
37. Jager, T., Kurek, R.: Short digital signatures and ID-KEMs via truncation collision resistance. In: Peyrin, T., Galbraith, S. (eds.) ASIACRYPT 2018. LNCS, vol. 11273, pp. 221–250. Springer, Cham (2018). https://doi.org/10.1007/978-3-030-03329-3_8
38. Jager, T., Kurek, R., Niehues, D.: Efficient adaptively-secure ib-kems and vrfs via near-collision resistance (full version of this publication). Cryptology ePrint Archive, Report 2021/160. https://eprint.iacr.org/2021/160
39. Jager, T., Niehues, D.: On the real-world instantiability of admissible hash functions and efficient verifiable random functions. In: Paterson, K.G., Stebila, D. (eds.) SAC 2019. LNCS, vol. 11959, pp. 303–332. Springer, Cham (2020). https://doi.org/10.1007/978-3-030-38471-5_13
40. Katsumata, S.: On the untapped potential of encoding predicates by arithmetic circuits and their applications. In: Takagi, T., Peyrin, T. (eds.) ASIACRYPT 2017. LNCS, vol. 10626, pp. 95–125. Springer, Cham (2017). https://doi.org/10.1007/978-3-319-70700-6_4
41. Katsumata, S., Yamada, S.: Partitioning via non-linear polynomial functions: more compact IBEs from ideal lattices and bilinear maps. In: Cheon, J.H., Takagi, T. (eds.) ASIACRYPT 2016. LNCS, vol. 10032, pp. 682–712. Springer, Heidelberg (2016). https://doi.org/10.1007/978-3-662-53890-6_23

42. Kohl, L.: Hunting and gathering – verifiable random functions from standard assumptions with short proofs. In: Lin, D., Sako, K. (eds.) PKC 2019. LNCS, vol. 11443, pp. 408–437. Springer, Cham (2019). https://doi.org/10.1007/978-3-030-17259-6_14
43. Lewko, A.: Tools for simulating features of composite order bilinear groups in the prime order setting. In: Pointcheval, D., Johansson, T. (eds.) EUROCRYPT 2012. LNCS, vol. 7237, pp. 318–335. Springer, Heidelberg (2012). https://doi.org/10.1007/978-3-642-29011-4_20
44. Menezes, A.J., van Oorschot, P.C., Vanstone, S.A.: Handbook of Applied Cryptography. 5th edn. CRC Press, Boca Raton (1996)
45. Micciancio, D., Peikert, C.: Trapdoors for lattices: simpler, tighter, faster, smaller. In: Pointcheval, D., Johansson, T. (eds.) EUROCRYPT 2012. LNCS, vol. 7237, pp. 700–718. Springer, Heidelberg (2012). https://doi.org/10.1007/978-3-642-29011-4_41
46. Nielsen, J.B.: Separating random oracle proofs from complexity theoretic proofs: The non-committing encryption case. In: CRYPTO 2002
47. Peikert, C.: A decade of lattice cryptography. Cryptology ePrint Archive, Report 2015/939. http://eprint.iacr.org/2015/939
48. Polak, I., Shamir, A.: Using random error correcting codes in near-collision attacks on generic hash-functions. In: Meier, W., Mukhopadhyay, D. (eds.) INDOCRYPT 2014. LNCS, vol. 8885, pp. 219–236. Springer, Cham (2014). https://doi.org/10.1007/978-3-319-13039-2_13
49. Roşie, R.: Adaptive-secure VRFs with shorter keys from static assumptions. In: Camenisch, J., Papadimitratos, P. (eds.) CANS 2018. LNCS, vol. 11124, pp. 440–459. Springer, Cham (2018). https://doi.org/10.1007/978-3-030-00434-7_22
50. Waters, B.: Dual system encryption: realizing fully secure IBE and HIBE under simple assumptions. In: Halevi, S. (ed.) CRYPTO 2009. LNCS, vol. 5677, pp. 619–636. Springer, Heidelberg (2009). https://doi.org/10.1007/978-3-642-03356-8_36
51. Waters, B.: Efficient identity-based encryption without random oracles. In: Cramer, R. (ed.) EUROCRYPT 2005. LNCS, vol. 3494, pp. 114–127. Springer, Heidelberg (2005). https://doi.org/10.1007/11426639_7
52. Yamada, S.: Adaptively secure identity-based encryption from lattices with asymptotically shorter public parameters. In: Fischlin, M., Coron, J.-S. (eds.) EUROCRYPT 2016. LNCS, vol. 9666, pp. 32–62. Springer, Heidelberg (2016). https://doi.org/10.1007/978-3-662-49896-5_2
53. Yamada, S.: Asymptotically compact adaptively secure lattice IBEs and verifiable random functions via generalized partitioning techniques. In: Katz, J., Shacham, H. (eds.) CRYPTO 2017. LNCS, vol. 10403, pp. 161–193. Springer, Cham (2017). https://doi.org/10.1007/978-3-319-63697-9_6
54. Yamada, S.: Asymptotically compact adaptively secure lattice IBEs and verifiable random functions via generalized partitioning techniques. Cryptology ePrint Archive, Report 2017/096. http://eprint.iacr.org/2017/096
55. Zhandry, M.: The magic of ELFs. In: Robshaw, M., Katz, J. (eds.) CRYPTO 2016. LNCS, vol. 9814, pp. 479–508. Springer, Heidelberg (2016). https://doi.org/10.1007/978-3-662-53018-4_18
56. Zhang, J., Chen, Yu., Zhang, Z.: Programmable hash functions from lattices: short signatures and IBEs with small key sizes. In: Robshaw, M., Katz, J. (eds.) CRYPTO 2016. LNCS, vol. 9816, pp. 303–332. Springer, Heidelberg (2016). https://doi.org/10.1007/978-3-662-53015-3_11

Subversion-Resilient Public Key Encryption with Practical Watchdogs

Pascal Bemmann[1(✉)], Rongmao Chen[2], and Tibor Jager[1]

[1] University of Wuppertal, Wuppertal, Germany
{bemmann,tibor.jager}@uni-wuppertal.de
[2] School of Computer, National University of Defense Technology, Changsha, China
chromao@nudt.edu.cn

Abstract. Restoring the security of maliciously implemented cryptosystems has been widely considered challenging due to the fact that the subverted implementation could arbitrarily deviate from the official specification. Achieving security against adversaries that can arbitrarily subvert implementations seems to inherently require trusted component assumptions and/or architectural properties. At ASIACRYPT 2016, Russell *et al.* proposed an attractive model where a watchdog is used to test and approve individual components of an implementation before or during deployment. Such a detection-based strategy has been useful for designing various cryptographic schemes that are provably resilient to subversion.

We consider Russell *et al.*'s watchdog model from a practical perspective regarding watchdog efficiency. We find that the asymptotic definitional framework, while permitting strong positive theoretical results, does not yet guarantee practical watchdogs, due to the fact that the running time of a watchdog is only bounded by an abstract polynomial. Hence, in the worst case, the running time of the watchdog might exceed the running time of the adversary, which seems impractical for most applications. We adopt Russell *et al.*'s watchdog model to the concrete security setting and design the first subversion-resilient public-key encryption scheme which allows for extremely efficient watchdogs with only *linear* running time.

At the core of our construction is a new variant of a combiner for key encapsulation mechanisms (KEMs) by Giacon *et al.* (PKC'18). We combine this construction with a new subversion-resilient randomness generator that also can be checked by an efficient watchdog, even in *constant* time, which could be of independent interest for the design of other

The first author was supported by the research training group "Human Centered Systems Security" (NERD.NRW) sponsored by the state of North-Rhine Westphalia. The second author was supported by the National Natural Science Foundation of China (Grant No. 62032005, No. 61702541, No. 61872087, No. 61872089) and the Young Elite Scientists Sponsorship Program by China Association for Science and Technology (No. YESS20170128). The third author was supported by the European Research Council (ERC) under the European Union's Horizon 2020 research and innovation programme, grant agreement 802823.

J. A. Garay (Ed.): PKC 2021, LNCS 12710, pp. 627–658, 2021.
https://doi.org/10.1007/978-3-030-75245-3_23

subversion-resilient cryptographic schemes. Our work thus shows how to apply Russell *et al.*'s watchdog model to design subversion-resilient cryptography with efficient watchdogs. We insist that this work does not intend to show that the watchdog model outperforms other defense approaches, but to demonstrate that practical watchdogs are practically achievable.

Keywords: Subversion-resilience · Watchdog · Randomness generator · Public key encryption

1 Introduction

Modern cryptography has been a tremendous success due to its remarkable functionalities and security guarantees. Nevertheless, it has been of increasing concern that the robustness of security guarantees provided by cryptographic tools in practice may be weaker than thought. In particular, cryptosystems in the real world could be stealthily weakened by attackers who have the capability of tampering with the actual algorithm implementation for exfiltrating secret information while keeping it indistinguishable—in black-box testing—from a truthful one. Such a powerful adversary was originally considered in the *kleptographic* setting by Young and Yung [31,32] over two decades ago while the striking Snowden revelations (in 2013) of massive surveillance of encrypted communication attracted renewed attention worldwide. News reports [14] have recently confirmed that a spying agency subverted a widely-used implementation of the Dual EC pseudorandom number generator, which was then also exploited by another government. This provides a concrete real-world example showing the demand for subversion-resilient cryptosystems.

Recent research showed that such impactful subversion attacks could be mounted on a large class of cryptographic primitives, including encryption schemes [5,6,11,15], digital signatures [2] and non-interactive zero-knowledge proofs [3,20]. More generally, Berndt and Liśkiewicz [7] proved that there exist universal algorithm substitution attacks on any cryptographic algorithm with sufficiently large min-entropy. These negative results, in turn, significantly increased the awareness of the research community and consequently, extensive efforts have been made towards effective approaches to subversion-resilient cryptography.

Since subversion attacks consider a much stronger adversary than many classical security models, it turns out that further reasonable assumptions are generally needed, since otherwise there is no much hope to achieve meaningful security guarantees [1,2,4–6,12,13,15,17,19,25,27–29]. All the different assumptions considered in these works be they trusted components [2,10,12,17,25] or architectural requirements [13,27–29], have their own plausibility, and thus are generally incomparable, as they rely on different assumptions and may be useful in different application contexts. Nevertheless, it is still widely considered meaningful to weaken the specific assumptions adopted within each model for more practical and/or broadly realizable subversion-resilience. As we will explain below, this is the main motivation of our work.

Subversion-Resilience in the Watchdog Model. In this work, we consider the watchdog model introduced by Russell *et al.* [27] at ASIACRYPT 2016. This model has been useful to design a broad class of cryptographic tools secure against subversion attacks. The watchdog model is based on an architectural assumption, namely the *split-program methodology*, where an algorithm is decomposed into several functional components. The adversary supplies implementations of all components to a so-called "watchdog", which performs a black-box test to decide whether the (possibly subverted) implementation of each component is sufficiently compliant with the specification to provide the expected security properties. A cryptographic scheme is said to be subversion-resilient, if *either* there exists a watchdog that can detect the subversion of components with *non-negligible* probability; *or* the security of the cryptographic scheme is preserved even if the subverted implementation is used. It is shown that, under the aforementioned architectural assumption, such a watchdog-based approach is able to resist even complete subversion, where all algorithms are implemented by the adversary, including the key generation algorithm. Concretely, it is possible to construct various subversion-resilient primitives, including one-way-permutations [27], pseudorandom generators [27], randomness generators [28], semantically secure encryption schemes [28], random oracles [29] and signature schemes [13].

Weaker Watchdogs Imply Stronger Security. Generally, the stronger a watchdog is, the better it can prevent subversion attacks. As an extreme example, imagine a "super" watchdog with unlimited running time, which would be able to exhaustively test whether a given cryptographic algorithm perfectly meets the specification on all possible inputs, even if the input space is exponential (as common for the randomness space of a key generation algorithm, or the message and randomness space of an encryption algorithm, for instance). Such a watchdog would be able to detect and reject any subverted implementation that deviates from the specification, and thus trivially imply security in the subversion setting, since no subversion is permitted. However, such an ideal watchdog is too strong to be efficiently constructable in practice.

Russell *et al.* [27] considered various notions of watchdogs:

- An *offline watchdog* performs a one-time check of the supplied implementations prior to deployment;
- An *online watchdog* is executed in parallel to the deployment of the scheme, and able to access the full transcript of cryptographic protocols by monitoring public interactions between users;
- An *omniscient watchdog* is in addition also aware of the entire internal state (*e.g.*, secret keys) of the implementation.

Note that among all of the above, the offline watchdog is the weakest and thus the most desirable that one might want to use for achieving subversion resilience in the watchdog model. In particular, recent efforts have been made to construct subversion-resistant primitives in the offline watchdog model, including encryption schemes [28] and signature schemes [13]. We emphasize that an offline watchdog can not defend against *stateful* subversions, which are out of scope of this work (for more explanations see Sect. 3).

Our Motivation: Subversion-Resilience with Efficient Watchdogs. The offline watchdog is particularly attractive from a practical perspective, as only a "one-time" check is required. However, it turns out that such a one-time check can require very extensive testing in order to achieve some desirable security guarantee in practice. Concretely, the current approach [27] considers a watchdog already successful if it has a *non-negligible* probability of detecting a malicious subversion. To obtain some *concrete* acceptable detection probability, this could require the offline watchdog to do a *polynomial* amount of testing, where in the worst case the running time of the watchdog might even have to exceed the running time of the adversary, which seems not very practical. As pointed out by Russell *et al.* in [28], amplifying a non-negligible detection probability ϵ to an overwhelming detection probability $1 - \delta$ would require $\epsilon^{-1} \log(\delta^{-1})$ repetitions of testing. Also, due to the asymptotic definition, it is unclear how long the watchdog would need to be run *concretely* in practice before it could state with high confidence whether a given component is considered sufficiently secure or not.

In the theory of self-testing/correcting programs by Blum, Luby and Rubinfeld [8], limited testing by the tester/corrector is also considered as a central design goal. Therefore we are interested in constructing subversion-resilient cryptosystems in the watchdog model, such that we can construct extremely efficient watchdog algorithms, that are guaranteed to run significantly faster than an adversary, ideally in *linear* or even in *constant* time. We believe that this is a necessary step towards making Russell *et al.*'s [27] watchdog model applicable in real-world applications. In particular, we are interested in techniques to construct cryptographic schemes that allow for watchdogs with a concretely-bounded running time that only need to perform a very limited number of tests in order to achieve strong security guarantees.

Remark. We stress that we do not intend to show that the watchdog model outperforms other approaches in defending against subversion attacks, but mainly aim at exploring the possibility of achieving security against subversion attacks in this model using watchdogs with minimal running time. In fact, as mentioned above, all the existing models are generally incomparable, due to the adoption of different specific approaches and assumptions.

1.1 Our Results

Motivated by the aforementioned practical concerns, in this work, we design the first random number generator and public key encryption scheme with offline watchdogs that perform only limited testing, but still achieve strong standard security guarantees. In particular, we make the following contributions.

- The main theoretical contribution of our work is a parameterized refinement of Russell *et al.*'s watchdog model. More precisely, we present a generic model to capture the goal of subversion-resilience with a universal offline watchdog and trusted amalgamation for any cryptographic primitive. The model is defined with concrete security parameters so that specific bounds on the runtime of the watchdog are explicitly given. This requires a conceptual modification of the joint security experiment involving the watchdog and the adversary.
- As the first contribution, we then construct an extremely simple randomness generator that is guaranteed to output *uniformly* random bits even if the watchdog only tests the underlying component for a *constant* time. Note that this randomness generator could also be used to design other subversion-resilient cryptographic schemes with runtime-constrained watchdogs.
- Based on this randomness generator as well as an additional trusted XOR operation[1], we design a subversion-resilient key encapsulation mechanism (KEM) using watchdogs running in *linear* time. This KEM then implies a subversion-resilient public key encryption scheme that has a watchdog with practical running time. The size of public keys and ciphertexts of this scheme are linear in the security parameter.

Below we elaborate on the proposed techniques in more detail.

1.2 Technical Overview

At the core of our proposed PKE scheme is the subversion-resilient KEM using offline watchdogs doing constant-time testing. As mentioned above, such a construction is challenging as we now only rely on watchdogs that do less testing. Below we first present the intuition why this is a non-trivial task and then the idea behind our construction.

The Difficulty of Recognizing a Subverted KEM with a Watchdog. Let $\mathsf{KEM} = (\mathsf{Gen}, \mathsf{Encaps}, \mathsf{Decaps})$ be the specification of a legitimate (*i.e.*, not subverted) KEM. Let $R_{\mathsf{gen}}, R_{\mathsf{enc}}$ be the randomness spaces of Gen and Encaps. Let F be the deterministic function parameterized by a KEM which takes as input randomness $(r, s) \in R_{\mathsf{gen}} \times R_{\mathsf{enc}}$ for Gen and Encaps, respectively, and then computes

$$(pk, sk, C, K) = F_{\mathsf{KEM}}(r, s)$$

with

$$(pk, sk) \leftarrow \mathsf{Gen}(1^\lambda; r) \ , \ (C, K) \leftarrow \mathsf{Encaps}(pk; s).$$

Now let $\widetilde{\mathsf{KEM}} = (\widetilde{\mathsf{Gen}}, \widetilde{\mathsf{Encaps}}, \widetilde{\mathsf{Decaps}})$ be a (possibly subverted) implementation of the algorithms of KEM. We observe that if

$$F_{\mathsf{KEM}}(r, s) = F_{\widetilde{\mathsf{KEM}}}(r, s) \tag{1}$$

[1] Such a trusted operation is also required in the PKE construction by Russell *et al.*. in [28].

on all $(r,s) \in R_{\mathsf{gen}} \times R_{\mathsf{enc}}$, then the security of the originally specified scheme KEM implies security of $\widetilde{\mathsf{KEM}}$, if (r,s) are indeed chosen randomly. If Eq. (1) holds, then the implementations $\widetilde{\mathsf{Gen}}$ and $\widetilde{\mathsf{Encaps}}$ agree with the specification on all inputs, and these are the only algorithms of $\widetilde{\mathsf{KEM}}$ used in the security experiment. The same holds if Eq. (1) holds for all but a *negligible* fraction of all r, s, since the probability that a security experiment chose (r,s) such that Eq. (1) does *not* hold would be negligible.

Unfortunately, we are not able to test efficiently whether Eq. (1) holds for all but a negligible fraction of all r, s. Let

$$\mathsf{Neq} := \{(r,s) : F_{\mathsf{KEM}}(r,s) \neq F_{\widetilde{\mathsf{KEM}}}(r,s)\} \tag{2}$$

and

$$\mathsf{Eq} := \{(r,s) : F_{\mathsf{KEM}}(r,s) = F_{\widetilde{\mathsf{KEM}}}(r,s)\}. \tag{3}$$

That is, Neq contains all "bad" randomness values such that Eq. (1) does *not* hold with respect to $(\mathsf{KEM}, \widetilde{\mathsf{KEM}})$. Analogously, Eq contains all "good" randomness values for which Eq. (1) does hold. Since Neq and Eq are disjoint sets, we have

$$\mathsf{Neq} \cup \mathsf{Eq} = R_{\mathsf{gen}} \times R_{\mathsf{enc}} \quad \text{and} \quad \mathsf{Neq} \cap \mathsf{Eq} = \emptyset.$$

Note that testing whether $|\mathsf{Neq}|/2^{\lambda}$ is negligible by repeatedly running F on different inputs takes exponential time. Even if we granted the watchdog a very large running time, by allowing it to evaluate F a polynomial $P(\lambda)$ of times, where $P(\lambda)$ is large, this watchdog could still fail to recognize that $|\mathsf{Neq}|$ is non-negligible with very high probability.

For instance, suppose that $\mathsf{Neq} \subset \{0,1\}^{\lambda} \times \{0,1\}^{\lambda}$ were a random subset of size $|\mathsf{Neq}| = |R_{\mathsf{gen}} \times R_{\mathsf{enc}}|/P^2(\lambda)$. Then a watchdog running in time P would fail to detect the subversion only with probability $1 - 1/P(\lambda)$. At the same time, the scheme would be insecure, since we have

$$\frac{|R_{\mathsf{gen}} \times R_{\mathsf{enc}}|/P^2(\lambda)}{|R_{\mathsf{gen}} \times R_{\mathsf{enc}}|} = \frac{1}{P^2(\lambda)}$$

and thus the security experiment would choose "bad" randomness $(r,s) \in \mathsf{Neq}$ with significant probability $\frac{1}{P^2(\lambda)}$.

Our Approach to Overcoming the Technical Difficulties. We build a subversion-resilient KEM $\mathsf{KEMSR} = (\mathsf{GenSR}, \mathsf{EncapsSR}, \mathsf{DecapsSR})$ based on a regular $\mathsf{KEM} = (\mathsf{Gen}, \mathsf{Encaps}, \mathsf{Decaps})$ in the following way. For ease of exposition, we describe a less efficient scheme here. Our actual scheme can be instantiated much more efficiently, by trading the size of keys and ciphertexts for reasonably increased running time of the watchdog. See Sect. 5.3.

A key pair $(pk, sk) = ((pk_i)_{i \in [\lambda]}, (sk_i)_{i \in [\lambda]})$ of KEMSR consists of λ many public keys

$$(pk_1, sk_1), \ldots, (pk_{\lambda}, sk_{\lambda}) \xleftarrow{\$} \mathsf{Gen}(1^{\lambda})$$

of KEM. In order to generate an encapsulated key, we run $(C_i, K_i) \leftarrow \mathsf{Encaps}(pk_i)$ for all $i \in [\lambda]$, and return

$$(C, K) := ((C_1, \ldots, C_\lambda), K_1 \oplus \cdots \oplus K_\lambda).$$

Here the $\oplus$ is part of the trusted amalgamation function.

The security proof against subversion in the watchdog model of this construction is based on the following idea. Let $\widetilde{\mathsf{KEM}}$ be a subverted implementation of KEM[2] and let Neq be as in Eq. (6). We construct a reduction to the security of the underlying KEM that goes through if the simulated security experiment generates *at least one* pair (pk_i, C_i) using "good" randomness, that is, choosing $(r, s) \xleftarrow{\$} R_{\mathsf{gen}} \times R_{\mathsf{enc}}$ such that $(r, s) \in \mathsf{Eq}$.

Note that even if the underlying KEM is heavily subverted, for instance such that half of all randomness tuples (r, s) are "bad" and we have

$$|\mathsf{Neq}| = \frac{|R_{\mathsf{gen}} \times R_{\mathsf{enc}}|}{2} \tag{4}$$

we would still have

$$\Pr\left[(r, s) \notin \mathsf{Neq} : (r, s) \xleftarrow{\$} R_{\mathsf{gen}} \times R_{\mathsf{enc}}\right] = 1/2.$$

Therefore, the probability that the experiment generates at least one pair (pk_i, C_i) using "good" randomness is $1 - 2^{\lambda}$, which is almost certain, up to a negligibly small probability.

If the adversary produces a subverted implementation where $|\mathsf{Neq}|$ is larger than in Eq. (4), then of course it becomes less likely that the experiment chooses "good" randomness. However, already for $|\mathsf{Neq}|$ as in Eq. (4) we are able to detect the subversion almost certainly, and with a very efficient watchdog. Concretely, a watchdog running F λ times and comparing the output to the specification is able to detect the subversion with overwhelming probability $1 - 2^{-\lambda}$. This detection probability increases with larger $|\mathsf{Neq}|$.

In order to ease the notation and make our approach clear, the above sketch of our construction uses λ many executions of the KEM procedures as well as a watchdog which tests each algorithm λ many times. As we will see later, in our construction these parameters can be adjusted to allow for tradeoffs between ciphertext (and key) size and runtime of the watchdog.

On the KEM Combiner. Note that a similar idea of using a KEM combiner was also used by Giacon *et al.* [21]. However, the work by Giacon *et al.* considers a different setting from our work. In their work, it is assumed that there are different KEMs with different security properties, in a situation where it is unclear which one is the most suitable candidate for establishing security (*e.g.*, since they are based on different hardness assumptions). Instead, we primarily address the problem of using a possibly subverted KEM to realize secure key

[2] In our model the adversary provides an implementation of each building block instead of an implementation of KEMSR.

encapsulation. Our main approach is to use the watchdog doing limited testing to ensure that the subverted KEM is consistent with its official specification at some points, based on which we are able to have desirable security guarantee via amplification.

One may wonder whether we could use combiners for public key encryption directly to obtain a subversion-resilient PKE scheme. The answer is negative. From a syntax level, most of the currently known combiners would be considered as part of the trusted amalgamation in our model. However, since we consider a runtime-constrained watchdog, we can not rule out the possibility that the PKE scheme would, for instance, simply output the message instead of a ciphertext for a specified message m. Such an attack is known as an "input trigger attack" [15] and prevents us from directly using most of the existing combiners/amplifiers in our setting.

Russell *et al.* [28] argued that subverted encryption algorithms can not have direct access to the input message in order to rule out input trigger attacks. Thus, they blind the message with a random coin which is output as part of the ciphertext. We remark that this approach does not work in our setting, since this still requires polynomial time testing by the watchdog in order to obtain an overwhelming detection probability. In our construction, we bypass this type of attacks by directly performing the XOR operation on the message with the output key of our designed subversion-resilient KEM.

Limitations of Our Approach. Note that while our construction allows for watchdogs with limited runtime, it comes with some limitations. Following Russel *et al.* [28], we proved our results under the assumption that trusted amalgamation is feasible. This means that all components of a cryptographic scheme can be split into multiple smaller parts, which can be tested individually by the watchdog. During the security experiment the amalgamation then assembles the building blocks without adversarial interference. Further, in our model we only account for *stateless* subversions, as we only rely on offline watchdogs with bounded runtime. If *stateful* subversions are allowed, a subverted algorithm could behave honestly until the watchdogs stop testing and then arbitrarily break security. For further discussion on alternative models, we refer to the following section. Furthermore, note that our proposed PKE scheme uses the key produced by our constructed subversion-resilient KEM to (in a trusted manner) XOR the message, thus limiting the message length to be encrypted.

2 Related Work

Since the Snowden revelations in 2013, extensive efforts have explored the feasibility results in the subversion setting, relying on different assumptions regarding trusted components and architectural requirements [1,2,4–6,12,13,15,17,19,25, 27–29].

2.1 Existing Constructions in the Watchdog Model

There have been various constructions in the typical watchdog model by [27]. Based on the split-program methodology [27], several cryptographic schemes were proposed and proved to be subversion-resilient in the complete subversion setting [13,27–29]. Particularly, in [27], Russell *et al.* constructed subversion-resilient (trapdoor) one way permutations (TDOWP) in the offline watchdog model (assuming fixed public input distributions). The main idea is to use a standard hash function (modeled as a random oracle) to disable the ability of an adversary to embed any potential backdoors in the function. Further, based on this general sanitizing strategy, they built a subversion-resilient signature scheme with online watchdogs, and subversion-resilient pseudorandom generators (PRG) with offline watchdogs. To generically eliminate subliminal channels in randomized algorithms, Russell *et al.* [28] proposed a "double-splitting" strategy where the randomness generation is carried out by mixing the output of two independent components with an immunization function. Based on this they showed how to further immunize each algorithm of an encryption scheme, including symmetric-key encryption and public-key encryption, with offline watchdogs. In [11], Chen *et al.* also discussed how to construct subversion-resilient key encapsulation mechanisms by using this useful strategy. Russell *et al.* also considered how to correct subverted random oracles in [29] and Chow *et al.* [13] further extended their results to construct subversion-resilient signature schemes in the offline watchdog model. In [1], by relying on an additional independent (untamperable) source of public randomness, Ateniese *et al.* proposed a subversion-secure immunizer in the plain model for a broad class of deterministic primitives.

There are some other constructions which also implicitly rely on the (polynomial-testing) watchdog to achieve subversion-resilience. In [6], Bellare, Patterson and Rogaway showed that symmetric encryption producing unique ciphertexts could resist subversion attacks, assuming that all subverted ciphertext are decryptable. This decryptability condition was further relaxed by [15] for considering the possibility of input-trigger attacks. Note that both of them require an omniscient watchdog that needs to access the decryption key for verifying the ciphertext decryptability produced by the supplied implementation of encryption algorithm. Similarly, Ateniese, Magri and Venturi [2] showed that unique signatures are subversion-resilient on the condition that all subverted signatures are valid. They also proved the unforgeability of unique signatures still hold against random message attacks when the verifiability condition is relaxed in a way similar to what considered by [15]. Note that their constructions require an online watchdog as the signature scheme is publicly verifiable.

2.2 Combiner and Amplification

As mentioned earlier, Giacon *et al.* [21] also proposed the XOR combiner for KEMs but in a different setting from ours. Roughly, a combiner is an algorithm that takes as input several instantiations of the same primitive and then combines these into a single scheme, aiming at achieving desirable security on the condition that at least one of the underlying "building blocks" is secure. There have been several works constructing combiners for different primitives such as KEMs [21], authenticated encryption with associated data (AEAD) [26] and functional encryption [24].

The watchdog model generally relies on trusted amplification to build fully functional implementation from individual "secure enough" components for strong security. In fact, amplification is strongly related to cryptographic combiners. Roughly speaking, given a cryptographic scheme with some "weak" security guarantee, the amplifier can construct a scheme with stronger security guarantees (for example simply by repeated executions). Amplification has been applied to different primitives like functional encryption [23], interactive cryptographic protocols [16] and CCA-secure public key encryption [22].

2.3 Cryptographic Reverse Firewalls

Note that the watchdog model essentially relies on testing, combined with the split-program methodology, to achieve feasibility results in the subversion setting. Alternatively, one may consider other models relying on different assumptions, such as trusted components. In particular, Mironov and Stephens-Davidowitz [25] introduced the notion of *cryptographic reverse firewalls*, which permits quite extensive results [2,9,10,12,17]. A reverse firewall is an independent trusted on-line party, which could be viewed as a proxy located between a (potentially) subverted machine and the outside world. It is assumed that the reverse firewall has access to a source of trusted randomness and could faithfully re-randomize all incoming/outgoing communication generated by the subverted algorithm, so that subversion-resilience is achieved even if the full implementation has been tampered with by the adversary. It is worth mentioning that the reverse firewall is not assumed to be a trusted party to achieve security in absence of subversion. In particular, it has no access to any secret information, such as secret keys. Note that similar to the online watchdog model, an (active) reverse firewall is able to defend against *stateful* subversion, which is inherently not captured by the offline watchdog model. Furthermore, many constructions using the reverse firewall model, such as [2,10,12,17,25], require some form of "re-randomizability" of the algorithm outputs provided to an adversary, which limits their applicability to non-rerandomizable primitives. Two notable exceptions are due to Mironov and Stephens-Davidowitz [25], who proposed a generic approach to convert any protocol into a protocol that is compatible with reverse firewalls, and Bossuat *et al.* [9], where the reverse firewall is in possession of a public key which allows it to sanitize protocol messages without requiring rerandomizability of the underlying primitives.

2.4 Self-guarding Mechanisms

Another alternative model is the so-called self-guarding mechanism, which was introduced by Fischlin and Mazaheri [19]. This model assumes that there exists an honest initialization phase where the algorithm is not subverted and thus produce a "clean" output. Thus, during this phase, one could gather a collection of samples by executing the honest implementation. After the implementation was tampered with, the output would be sanitized by the honest samples to resist any possible secret exfiltration. The main advantage of this model is that it does not require an active party (such as the reverse firewall or the watchdog) but rather constructs primitives that are "inherently" immune to subversion attacks. A limitation of this approach is the bounded security which depends on the number of samples collected during the good initial phase. Also, such a strategy only considers attacks that wake up at a later point in time, *e.g.*, due to the software update, while the watchdog model considers long-term subversion attacks that might be active during the whole life cycle of the cryptosystem.

3 A Definitional Framework for Subversion-Resilient Cryptography

In this section, we present a variant of the security definitions from [27] which is similar in spirit to theirs but captures our security goals for watchdogs with bounded running time better.

3.1 Notations

Before we present our model, we first introduce the notations used in this work. We will use $x \xleftarrow{\$} X$ to denote sampling x uniformly at random from the set X. Further, let $\mathcal{A}$ be a randomized algorithm. In order to explicitly reference the random coins used by $\mathcal{A}$, we will use $y \leftarrow \mathcal{A}(x; r)$ to denote assigning y to the output of $\mathcal{A}$ running on input x using the random coins r. $[1, n]$ will denote the set of natural numbers from 1 to n, *i.e.* $\{1, 2, \ldots, n-1, n\}$. To denote an implementation (provided by some adversary) of some algorithm $\mathcal{B}$, we will use $\widetilde{\mathcal{B}}$. Finally, we will use $\widehat{\Pi}$ to denote the specification of a scheme.

3.2 A General Security Definition for Cryptographic Schemes

We define a *cryptographic scheme* Π as a tuple of n algorithms

$$\Pi = (\Pi_1, \ldots, \Pi_n).$$

Note that for a specific primitive, n is a fixed number and is usually small. For example, for a public-key encryption scheme, which is typically defined as a tuple of algorithms $(\mathsf{Gen}, \mathsf{Encrypt}, \mathsf{Decrypt})$, we have $n = 3$ and

$$(\Pi_1, \Pi_2, \Pi_3) = (\mathsf{Gen}, \mathsf{Encrypt}, \mathsf{Decrypt}).$$

Security of Π is defined via a *security experiment* $\mathsf{Exp}^{\Pi}_{\mathcal{A}}(1^\lambda)$ which involves Π and an adversary $\mathcal{A}$ and outputs a bit $b \in \{0, 1\}$. In the sequel, we will focus on security experiments based on the *indistinguishability* of two distributions.[3] Then we can generically define the *advantage function* of $\mathcal{A}$ with respect to Π and experiment Exp as

$$\mathsf{Adv}_{\mathcal{A}}^{\Pi}(1^\lambda) := \left|\Pr\left[\mathsf{Exp}_{\mathcal{A}}^{\Pi}(1^\lambda) = 1\right] - 1/2\right|.$$

In the concrete security setting, we say the scheme Π is (t, ϵ)-*secure*, if $\mathsf{Adv}_{\mathcal{A}}^{\Pi}(1^\lambda) \leq \epsilon$ for all $\mathcal{A}$ running in time at most t.

3.3 Subversion-Resilience with an Offline Watchdog

To define security against subversion attacks (adversarial implementations), we follow Russell *et al.*'s approach [27] and consider a setting where *the adversary itself* provides the implementation used in the security experiment of the considered scheme. More precisely, we consider an adversary $\mathcal{A}$ that consists of two parts $(\mathcal{A}_0, \mathcal{A}_1)$, where $\mathcal{A}_0$ produces a (possibly subverted) *implementation* and a state *st*

$$(\widetilde{\Pi}_1, \ldots, \widetilde{\Pi}_n, st) \xleftarrow{\$} \mathcal{A}_0(1^\lambda).$$

Then $\mathcal{A}_1(st)$ engages in the security experiment Exp, which uses $\widetilde{\Pi} = (\widetilde{\Pi}_1, \ldots, \widetilde{\Pi}_n)$. Note that in such a strong adversarial setting it is impossible to achieve meaningful security without further assumptions. Therefore, based on the fact that in the real world implementations of algorithms can be tested before deployment in an application, Russell *et al.* [27] introduced an additional party called the *watchdog*. The watchdog aims to detect a possible subversion in the implementation supplied by the adversary. The watchdog WD is aware of an "honest" (not subverted) *specification* of the scheme, denoted by

$$\widehat{\Pi} = (\Pi_1, \ldots, \Pi_n),$$

and has oracle access to the implementation $\widetilde{\Pi} = (\widetilde{\Pi}_1, \ldots, \widetilde{\Pi}_n)$ produced by $\mathcal{A}_0$. The adversary $\mathcal{A}$ is only considered successful if it breaks the security of the scheme and the subverted implementation *evades detection* by the watchdog. Hence, we consider the *subversion-resilience* security experiment $\overline{\mathsf{SR}}_{\mathsf{Exp},\Pi}^{\mathcal{A},\mathsf{WD}}(1^\lambda)$ from Fig. 1 (a), which involves a subversion adversary $\mathcal{A} = (\mathcal{A}_0, \mathcal{A}_1)$, a watchdog WD, a protocol specification $\widehat{\Pi}$ and an underlying standard (indistinguishability-based) experiment Exp.

At the beginning of the experiment, adversary $\mathcal{A}_0$ produces a (subverted) implementation $\widetilde{\Pi}$ and a state *st*. The watchdog is provided oracle access to $\widetilde{\Pi}$. If WD outputs `true`, which means that the watchdog has detected a subverted implementation, the experiment outputs a random bit. This implies that

[3] Even though it is straightforward to extend our description to the general case capturing both classical cases of "indistinguishability" and "search problems", we refrain from introducing additional notation to achieve this. We will only consider indistinguishability in this paper.

$\overline{\mathsf{SR}}^{\mathcal{A},\mathsf{WD}}_{\mathsf{Exp},\widehat{\Pi}}(1^\lambda)$	$\mathsf{SR}^{\mathcal{A},\mathsf{WD}}_{\mathsf{Exp},\widehat{\Pi}}(1^\lambda)$
$(\widetilde{\Pi}, st) \leftarrow \mathcal{A}_0(1^\lambda)$	$(\widetilde{\Pi}, st) \leftarrow \mathcal{A}_0(1^\lambda)$
If $\mathsf{WD}^{\widetilde{\Pi}}(1^\lambda)$ **then**	**If** $\mathsf{WD}^{\widetilde{\Pi}}(1^\lambda)$ **then**
$b \xleftarrow{\$} \{0,1\}$	$b \xleftarrow{\$} \{0,1\}$
Return b	**Return** b
Return $\mathsf{Exp}^{\mathcal{A}_1(st)}_{\widetilde{\Pi}}(1^\lambda)$	**Return** $\mathsf{Exp}^{\mathcal{A}_1(st)}_{\mathsf{Am}(\widetilde{\Pi})}(1^\lambda)$
(a) Without trusted amalgamation and with $\widehat{\Pi} = (\Pi_1, \ldots, \Pi_n)$	(b) With trusted amalgamation and $\widehat{\Pi} = (\mathsf{Am}, \Pi_1, \ldots, \Pi_n)$

Fig. 1. Security experiments with watchdog and subverted implementation.

$\mathcal{A}$ has zero advantage, if it outputs an implementation that WD recognizes as subverted. If $\mathsf{WD}^{\widetilde{\Pi}} = \mathtt{false}$, then the security experiment Exp is executed, using the *adversarially-provided* implementation $\widetilde{\Pi}$ of $\widehat{\Pi}$ and with an adversary $\mathcal{A}_1(st)$ that may depend on the state produced by $\mathcal{A}_0$.

In order to avoid trivial watchdogs that always output `true`, such that any scheme would be provably secure, we require that the watchdog is "correct" in the sense that it *always* outputs `false` when provided with oracle access to the actual protocol. Formally:

Definition 1. *We say that* WD *is a* correct *watchdog for protocol specification* $\widehat{\Pi}$, *if*

$$\Pr\left[\mathsf{WD}^{\widehat{\Pi}} = \mathtt{false}\right] = 1.$$

All watchdogs in this work will trivially fulfill this property. As one would intuitively expect, our watchdogs simply compare the output of the oracle with the expected results of the specification. Thus, our watchdogs will never reject the protocol specification.

Note that in the above security experiment (Fig. 1), WD verifies $\widetilde{\Pi}$ prior to the experiment Exp. That is, our definition only considers offline watchdogs that simply check the supplied implementations by the adversary with no access to the full transcript of the experiment Exp. As discussed in [27,28], such a watchdog is preferable over online watchdogs in the sense that it only carries out a one-time check on the implementation and does not require constant monitoring of all communication. We also remark that in this work we will only consider a *universal* watchdog, which means it is quantified before the adversary in the security definition. Thus, for a secure scheme there exists a *single* watchdog that defends against all considered adversaries.

Stateless Subversion. We also remark here that we only consider *stateless* subversion in this work. That is, the subverted implementation does not hold any state between different executions. Note that we are mainly interested in offline watchdogs which run in bounded time for testing. A trivial attack to evade such a detection is the so-called *time bomb* attack which only becomes active when the underlying algorithm is at some specific state. Specifically, the implementations would behave honestly when they are under testing by the offline watchdog, and at a later point in time the malicious behavior would be triggered to wake up. It is clear that such a tricky attack is impossible to be detected by our considered (*i.e.* bounded running time) watchdog. In fact, to prevent such an attack in hardware tokens, some previous work requires a semi-online watchdog to perform testing regularly [18]. Therefore, we insist that stateful subversion is not captured by our considered model. Another approach to consider stateful subversion are reverse firewalls, as discussed in Sect. 2.3.

3.4 The Split-Program Model and Trusted Amalgamation

The above offline watchdog model is meaningful and was used to establish security for some specific cryptographic primitives [27]. However, it turns out that it is still not generic enough to achieve subversion-resilience for many other primitives. Particularly, it is known that if the user makes only black-box use of the subverted implementation of randomized algorithms, it is hopeless to eliminate a steganographic channel built on the output of algorithms [28]. Therefore a non-black-box model is required for general feasibility results.

Motivated by the above, Russell *et al.* [28] proposed the *split-program model*, where the specification of each algorithm is split into a constant number of components. Precisely, a scheme Π is still represented by a tuple of algorithms $(\Pi_1, \ldots, \Pi_n)$, but n may be larger than the actual number of algorithms of a protocol. The actual algorithms are then "amalgamated" by combining these underlying building blocks in a trusted way that cannot be influenced by the adversary. Using such a somewhat relaxed model, Russell *et al.* [28] showed how to generically design stego-free specifications for randomized algorithms which play a crucial role in constructing subversion-resilient encryption schemes (in their offline watchdog model). Basically, they further split the specification of any probabilistic algorithm into two parts: the randomized component and the deterministic component, that are tested individually by the watchdog. The randomized component generates random coins which (perhaps together with other inputs drawn from public distributions) are taken as input by the deterministic component to generate the output of the composed algorithm.

Note that for a meaningful construction of a subversion-resilient cryptosystem, the amalgamation should be *as-simple-as-possible*, such that most of the complexity of the involved algorithms is contained in the algorithms $\Pi = (\Pi_1, \ldots, \Pi_n)$ that may be subject to subversion. To make this approach more precise, we explicitly define an *amalgamation function* Am and include it in the specification of the scheme. For instance, for a public-key encryption scheme we would have the specification

$$\widehat{\Pi} = (\mathsf{Am}, \Pi) = (\mathsf{Am}, (\Pi_1, \ldots, \Pi_n))$$

for which

$$\mathsf{Am}(\Pi_1, \ldots, \Pi_n) = (\mathsf{Gen}, \mathsf{Encrypt}, \mathsf{Decrypt})$$

holds.

As depicted in Fig. 1 (b), the subversion-resilience security experiment with trusted amalgamation proceeds exactly as the basic experiment described above, except that the watchdog has access to all procedures

$$(\widetilde{\Pi}_1, \ldots, \widetilde{\Pi}_n, st) \xleftarrow{\$} \mathcal{A}_0(1^\lambda)$$

produced by $\mathcal{A}_0$ *individually.* The security experiment is then executed with the amalgamated primitive

$$\mathsf{Am}(\widetilde{\Pi}_1, \ldots, \widetilde{\Pi}_n).$$

Following our example for public key encryption, this would correspond to

$$\mathsf{Am}(\widetilde{\Pi}_1, \ldots, \widetilde{\Pi}_n) = (\widetilde{\mathsf{Gen}}, \widetilde{\mathsf{Encrypt}}, \widetilde{\mathsf{Decrypt}}).$$

With our security model set up, we can now define the advantage of a subversion adversary in the split program model with offline watchdog as

$$\mathsf{AdvSR}^{\mathcal{A},\mathsf{WD}}_{\mathsf{Exp},\widehat{\Pi}}(1^\lambda) := \left|\Pr\left[\mathsf{SR}^{\mathcal{A},\mathsf{WD}}_{\mathsf{Exp},\widehat{\Pi}}(1^\lambda)\right] - 1/2\right|.$$

This allows to present our formal definition of subversion-resilience.

Definition 2. *A specification of a cryptographic protocol* $\widehat{\Pi} = (\mathsf{Am}, \Pi)$ *is* $(t_{\mathsf{WD}}, t_{\mathcal{A}}, \varepsilon)$-subversion-resilient in the offline watchdog model with trusted amalgamation, *if one can efficiently construct a* correct *watchdog algorithm* WD *running in time at most* t_{WD} *such that for any adversary* $\mathcal{A} = (\mathcal{A}_0, \mathcal{A}_1)$ *running in time at most* $t_{\mathcal{A}}$ *it holds that*

$$\mathsf{AdvSR}^{\mathcal{A},\mathsf{WD}}_{\mathsf{Exp},\widehat{\Pi}}(1^\lambda) \leq \varepsilon$$

using the experiment shown in Fig. 1 (b).

Here it might seem counterintuitive to define security with regards to the *specification*, if the underlying security experiment is executed with the *subverted* implementation. Our definition can be interpreted in the following way. While the security experiment is executed with the subverted implementation provided by the adversary, the watchdog (which is also executed in the experiment) tests the implementation with respect to that specification, and the adversary outputs subverted algorithms that syntactically follow the specification of the trusted amalgamation. Following Russell *et al.* [28], we split randomized algorithms into a probabilistic part (the randomness generation) and a deterministic part, where all parts can be tested individually. The trusted amalgamation then feeds the generated randomness into the deterministic algorithms. Since we are considering universal *offline* watchdogs, we have to make the assumption that a subverted implementation of a deterministic primitive also is deterministic. Otherwise, a subverted implementation could probabilistically deviate from the specification with some probability, where this probability could possibly be chosen depending on the watchdog and its bounded running time, so that the watchdog might fail to detect the subversion. (Note that is very closely connected to the reason why offline watchdogs cannot consider *stateful* subversion).

3.5 Comparisons with Previous Watchdog Models

The security model presented in this section is a refinement of the security models from [27,28]. We follow the "concrete security" approach instead of considering asymptotic definitions and assume the specification could be divided into an arbitrary number of components. Similarly to [28], we consider a single security experiment that can be separated in a "detection phase" and a "surveillance phase". Note that in [28] two advantage functions are defined: one for the watchdog and another for the adversary. Security then holds if either the detection advantage of the watchdog is non-negligible or the adversaries' advantage is negligible. We change the model in the regard that we enforce that the adversary "loses" the security experiment in case the watchdog detects subversion, by outputting a random bit instead of executing the experiment. In this way, we simplify the security definition by using a single advantage function. We remark that our refined model is inherently incomparable with previous models [27,28] but has notational advantages for our goal of achieving subversion-resilience with efficient watchdogs.

4 Subversion-Resilient Randomness Generators

After presenting our security model we will now show how to generate randomness in a way that allows a watchdog to guarantee in *constant* time (also independent from an adversary's runtime), that the outputs of our construction are *uniformly random* (*i.e.*, not just indistinguishable from random, but truly random). This randomness generator will then later be used to generate the random coins for our subversion-resilient KEM and PKE scheme. Additionally, this construction is of independent interest as it is a general and efficient tool to provide uniformly random coins to any cryptographic primitives in our model.

A randomness generator is a randomized algorithm which on input of a security parameter outputs some strings. We consider a randomness generator secure if its outputs are indistinguishable from uniformly random strings.

Definition 3. *We say that a randomness generator* RG *is* (t,ε)*-indistinguishable if for any adversary* $\mathcal{A}$ *running in time* t *it holds that*

$$\mathsf{Adv}_{\mathcal{A}}^{\mathsf{RG}} = |\Pr[\mathsf{RGIND}_{\mathsf{RG}}^{\mathcal{A}}(1^\lambda) - 1/2]| \leq \varepsilon$$

with $\mathsf{RGIND}_{\mathsf{RG}}^{\mathcal{A}}(1^\lambda)$ *displayed in Fig. 2 (a).*

Following Definition 2, we say that a randomness generator is *subversion-resilient under trusted amalgamation* if the randomness generator produces outputs that are indistinguishable from random, even in a security experiment which uses a trusted amalgamation of a subverted implementation.

Definition 4. *We say the specification of a randomness generator* $\widehat{\mathsf{RGSR}} = (\mathsf{Am}_{\mathsf{RG}}, \mathsf{RGSR})$ *is* $(t_{\mathsf{WD}}, t_{\mathcal{A}}, \varepsilon)$-subversion-resilient in the offline watchdog model with trusted amalgamation, *if one can efficiently construct a* correct *watchdog*

$\mathsf{RGIND}^{\mathcal{A}}_{\mathsf{RG}}(1^\lambda)$

$b \xleftarrow{\$} \{0,1\}$
If $b == 0$ **then**
  return $\mathcal{A}^{\mathcal{O}}(1^\lambda) == b$
If $b == 1$ **then**
  return $\mathcal{A}^{\mathsf{RG}}(1^\lambda) == b$

(a) Experiment for a randomness generator RG. Oracle $\mathcal{O}$ returns uniformly random strings.

$\mathsf{SR}^{\mathcal{A},\mathsf{WD}}_{\mathsf{RGIND},\widetilde{\mathsf{RGSR}}}(1^\lambda)$

$(\widetilde{\mathsf{RGSR}}, st) \leftarrow \mathcal{A}_0(1^\lambda)$
If $\mathsf{WD}^{\widetilde{\mathsf{RGSR}}}(1^\lambda)$ **then**
  $b \xleftarrow{\$} \{0,1\}$
  Return b
Return $\mathsf{RGIND}^{\mathcal{A}_1(st)}_{\mathsf{Am}(\widetilde{\mathsf{RGSR}})}(1^\lambda)$

(b) Subversion-resilience experiment for randomness generators.

Fig. 2. Security experiments with watchdog and subverted implementation.

WD *running in time at most* t_{WD}*, such that for any adversary* $\mathcal{A} = (\mathcal{A}_0, \mathcal{A}_1)$ *running in time at most* $t_{\mathcal{A}}$ *it holds that:*

$$\mathsf{AdvSR}^{\mathcal{A},\mathsf{WD}}_{\mathsf{RGIND},\widetilde{\mathsf{RGSR}}}(1^\lambda) \leq \varepsilon$$

with the used experiments shown in Fig. 2 (a) and (b).

Known Impossibilities. Russell *et al.* [28] showed that it is impossible to immunize a *single* randomness generator against subversion with an immunizing function. Essentially, they adopt the approach of subverting algorithms from [5,6] to randomness generators, showing that one can easily introduce a bias into a single source via rejection sampling. This bias can then be maintained by a subverted immunizing function. This bias may furthermore be "hidden", in the sense that detecting it requires knowledge of a secret key only known to the adversary to compute some predicate, such that a watchdog would not be able to efficiently detect it, while a subverting adversary may easily distinguish the subverted RG from random.

In order to overcome this general impossibility, Russel *et al.* [28] introduce the *"double splitting"* approach. Here, two RNGs are run independently in parallel. The outputs of these two RNGs are then fed into an immunization function, which may also be subverted. Russel *et al.* showed that if the immunization function is modeled as a random oracle, then this yields a randomness generator whose output is indistinguishable from outputs of a non-subverted randomness generator, even for the subverting adversary. They provide a standard-model construction of a randomness generator that outputs a single bit and a watchdog which tests whether one bit appears significantly more often than the other. Using the Chernoff bound, they argue that the watchdog will notice a bias after gathering enough samples. The randomness generator would then be run n times independently to obtain a n bit output.

We describe a new construction, which applies the "two independent RNG" approach of [28] in a different way. Our construction is extremely simple and efficient to test, yet provides *perfect* random bits and does not require a random oracle.

$\mathsf{Am}_{\mathsf{RG}}(1^\lambda, \mathsf{RG}, \mathsf{VN})$

$b := \perp$
While $b = \perp$ **do**
  $b_0 \leftarrow \mathsf{RG}(1^\lambda)$; $b_1 \leftarrow \mathsf{RG}(1^\lambda)$; $b := \mathsf{VN}(b_0, b_1)$
Return b

Fig. 3. The trusted amalgamation function $\mathsf{Am}_{\mathsf{RG}}$ for a randomness generator RG and a von Neumann extractor VN.

4.1 Construction

The specification $\widehat{\mathsf{RGSR}} = (\mathsf{Am}, \mathsf{RG}, \mathsf{VN})$ of our randomness generator consists of the following building blocks:

- A probabilistic algorithm RG that on input 1^λ outputs a bit $\mathsf{RG}(1^\lambda) \in \{0,1\}$.
- A simple binary and deterministic immunization function $\mathsf{VN} : \{0,1\} \times \{0,1\} \rightarrow \{0,1\}$, which is defined as follows:

$$\mathsf{VN}(b_0, b_1) := \begin{cases} 0 \text{ if } b_0 < b_1, \\ 1 \text{ if } b_0 > b_1, \\ \perp \text{ else.} \end{cases}$$

  Note that this function is the classical von Neumann extractor [30].

The von Neumann extractor takes as input two bits with some (arbitrary and unknown but fixed) bias and outputs a uniformly random bit, as long as the two input bits are distinct from each other.

Using these two building blocks, we construct an algorithm that on input 1^λ outputs a single bit using trusted amalgamation. The amalgamation is essentially a very simple while-loop, given in Fig. 3. It can be easily generalized to output n bits by calling it n times.

The amalgamation function $\mathsf{Am}_{\mathsf{RG}}$ is extremely simple, it runs RG twice independently and applies VN to the output. This is repeated in a while-loop, until the output of VN is not the error symbol $\perp$, but a bit $b \in \{0,1\}$.

Correctness. Since we have $\mathsf{VN}(b_0, b_1) = \perp \iff b_0 = b_1$, the correctness of this algorithm depends on the probability that the two executions of RG computing b_0 and b_1 in the while-loop yield $b_0 \neq b_1$. Let $p := \Pr\left[\mathsf{RG}(1^\lambda) = 1\right]$, then we have

$$\Pr\left[b_0 \neq b_1\right] = 2p(1-p).$$

Hence, it takes an expected $(p(1-p))^{-1}$ executions of RG and $(2p(1-p))^{-1}$ executions of VN to generate an output bit. For instance, if RG is truly random, then we would have 4 expected executions of RG and 2 of VN. Even if RG is a rather bad random number generator, say with $p = 1/4$, then one would expect about $5 + 1/3$ executions of RG and $2 + 2/3$ of VN.

4.2 Security

The proof that $\widehat{\mathsf{RGSR}}$ is a subversion-resilient randomness generator uses the fact that the adversary provides a *single* implementation $\widetilde{\mathsf{RG}}$ which is then queried twice by the trusted amalgamation. Therefore, the two bits b_0, b_1 are computed *independently* in every while loop and are identically distributed. The watchdog only has to test the implementation of the von Neumann extractor on all four possible inputs. It is not necessary to test the implementation of the randomness generator at all to achieve security.

Theorem 1. *The specification* $\widehat{\mathsf{RGSR}}$ *as defined above is* $(\mathcal{O}(1), t_{\mathcal{A}}, 0)$*-subversion-resilient in the offline watchdog model with trusted amalgamation.*

Note that the theorem asserts that we can construct a *constant-time* watchdog. It will be independent of the runtime of the adversary or any bias possibly embedded in the subverted implementation of RG.

Proof. The only component that we test is the implementation of $\mathsf{VN} : \{0,1\} \times \{0,1\} \rightarrow \{0,1\}$, which is a very simple function with only four possible inputs. Therefore it can be checked on all possible inputs in constant time. The watchdog WD runs a given implementation $\widetilde{\mathsf{VN}}$ on all four possible inputs and checks the correctness of the output with the specification.

In case $\widetilde{\mathsf{VN}}$ deviates from the specification on any input, the watchdog will detect this with probability 1. Thus, this would immediately lead to an advantage of 0 for the adversary.

Provided that $\widetilde{\mathsf{VN}}$ implements VN correctly and using the fact that the two bits $b_0, b_1 \leftarrow \widetilde{\mathsf{RG}}(1^\lambda)$ are computed *independently* in every while loop, we obtain that when $\widetilde{\mathsf{RG}}$ outputs a bit b then we have

$$\begin{aligned} \Pr[b=0] = \Pr[b_0 = 0 \wedge b_1 = 1] &= \Pr[b_0 = 1 \wedge b_1 = 0] \\ &= \Pr[b=1], \end{aligned}$$

and thus $\Pr[b=0] = \Pr[b=1] = 1/2$, again leading to an advantage of 0 for the adversary. □

4.3 Discussions

The main advantage of our proposed RG is that it achieves perfect security using a *constant*-time watchdog. Note that Russell *et al.* [28] also described several alternative approaches to purify randomness in the standard model. Below we provide more discussion about their approaches. It is worth mentioning that in [1], Ateniese *et al.* proposed a different approach to eliminating the requirement of random oracles by essentially relying on an additional independent and untamperable source of public randomness.

Simple Multi-splitting. The first approach proposed in [28] is simple multi-splitting, which means that n copies of RG (each outputting a single bit) are run and all outputs are concatenated and output. The main problem with this approach is that RG has to be tested very many times, otherwise the watchdog is unable to notice a small, but non-negligible bias.

More Efficient Construction Using Randomness Extractors. The second approach is to use randomness extractors, but in a totally different way. Precisely, it is observed that a watchdog making $\mathcal{O}(n^{2c})$ queries can verify that the output of each RG has at least $c \log n$ bits of entropy (for some constant c). Thus, Russell *et al.* [28] proposed to run RG for $\log n$ times to obtain a random string of length $\log n$, which is then used as a seed for a randomness extractor. This extractor can then be used to obtain more random bits from RG, which afterward can be expanded with a pseudorandom generator (PRG). Note that in this case a watchdog would not only have to check RG for entropy but also recompute all calculations of the extractor and the PRG to check if these components follow their specifications.

A disadvantage of our construction of RG is that we do not have a strict upper bound on its running time, but only expected bounds. We consider this a minor disadvantage, though, since lack of functionality will serve as an automated way to detect subversion that introduces a too heavy bias in RG. The efficiency can be improved if one is willing to do a little bit more testing. For instance, the watchdog could also test RG and check for a too heavy bias p that would significantly harm performance. Note however that even a particularly bad underlying randomness generator RG, which always outputs a constant 0, for instance, would only harm correctness, but not the security of RG.

5 Subversion-Resilient Key Encapsulation Mechanisms

In this chapter, we will construct a (t, ε)-indistinguishable key encapsulation mechanism that is subversion-resilient even if *all* the algorithms are subject to subversion, provided that we have a very simple trusted amalgamation function. Our construction achieves subversion-resilience with a watchdog whose running time is only *linear* in the security parameter, while also allowing for tradeoffs between ciphertext size and the watchdog's runtime.

5.1 Key Encapsulation Mechanisms and Security Definitions

We define *subversion-resilient* KEMs by adapting Definition 2 to KEMs.

Definition 5. *We say that the specification* $\widehat{\mathsf{KEMSR}} = (\mathsf{Am}_{\mathsf{KEM}}, \mathsf{KEMSR})$ *of a key encapsulation mechanism is* $(t_{\mathsf{WD}}, t_{\mathcal{A}}, \varepsilon)$ subversion-resilient in the offline watchdog model with trusted amalgamation, *if one can efficiently construct a correct watchdog* WD *running in time at most* t_{WD} *such that for any adversary* $\mathcal{A} = (\mathcal{A}_0, \mathcal{A}_1)$ *running in time at most* $t_{\mathcal{A}}$ *it holds that:*

$$\mathsf{AdvSR}^{\mathcal{A},\mathsf{WD}}_{\mathsf{KEMIND},\widehat{\mathsf{KEMSR}}}(1^\lambda) \leq \varepsilon$$

with the used experiments shown in Fig. 4 (a) and (b).

Key encapsulation mechanisms are techniques to securely transport symmetric cryptographic key material using public key cryptography. We will use the following standard definitions for key encapsulation mechanisms and their security.

Definition 6. *A* key encapsulation mechanism *(or KEM) consists of three algorithms* $\mathsf{KEM} = (\mathsf{Gen}, \mathsf{Encaps}, \mathsf{Decaps})$ *with the following syntax.*

- $\mathsf{Gen}(1^\lambda)$*: The randomized key generation algorithm takes as input a security parameter* $\lambda \in \mathbb{N}$ *and outputs a key pair* (sk, pk)*.*
- $\mathsf{Encaps}(pk)$*: The randomized encryption algorithm takes as input a public key* pk*. It outputs a key* $K \in \mathcal{KS}$*, where* $\mathcal{KS}$ *is called the* key space *defined by* pk *(either implicitly or explicitly), and a ciphertext* C*.*
- $\mathsf{Decaps}(sk, C)$ *: The deterministic decapsulation algorithm takes a secret key* sk *and a ciphertext* C*. It outputs a key* $K \in \mathcal{KS}$ *or a distinguished error symbol* $\perp$*.*

Definition 7. *We say that* $\mathsf{KEM} = (\mathsf{Gen}, \mathsf{Encaps}, \mathsf{Decaps})$ *is* $(t_\mathcal{A}, \varepsilon)$-indistinguishable *if for any adversary* $\mathcal{A}$ *running in time at most* $t_\mathcal{A}$ *it holds that*

$$\mathsf{Adv}_{\mathcal{A}}^{\mathsf{KEM}}(1^\lambda) := |\Pr[\mathsf{KEMIND}_{\mathsf{KEM}}^{\mathcal{A}}(1^\lambda)] - 1/2| \leq \varepsilon$$

with KEMIND *as defined in Fig. 4 (a).*

$\mathsf{KEMIND}_{\mathsf{KEM}}^{\mathcal{A}}(1^\lambda)$

$(sk, pk) \leftarrow \mathsf{Gen}(1^\lambda)$
$K_0 \xleftarrow{\$} \mathcal{KS}$
$(C^*, K_1) \leftarrow \mathsf{Encaps}(pk)$
$b \xleftarrow{\$} \{0,1\}$
$b_\mathcal{A} \leftarrow \mathcal{A}(1^\lambda, pk, K_b, C^*)$
If $b_\mathcal{A} == b$ **then return** 1
Else return 0

(a) Indistinguishability experiment for key encapsulation mechanisms.

$\mathsf{SR}_{\mathsf{KEMIND}, \widetilde{\mathsf{KEMSR}}}^{\mathcal{A}, \mathsf{WD}}(1^\lambda)$

$(\widetilde{\mathsf{KEMSR}}, st) \leftarrow \mathcal{A}_0(1^\lambda)$
If $\mathsf{WD}^{\widetilde{\mathsf{KEMSR}}}(1^\lambda)$ **then**
  $b \xleftarrow{\$} \{0,1\}$
  Return b
Return $\mathsf{KEMIND}_{\mathsf{Am}(\widetilde{\mathsf{KEMSR}})}^{\mathcal{A}_1(st)}(1^\lambda)$

(b) Subversion-resilience experiment for key encapsulation mechanisms.

Fig. 4. Security experiments with watchdog and subverted implementation.

5.2 Our Proposed KEM

Idea Overview. Before we present the technical details of our construction, let us illustrate our approach. In order to obtain random coins for our scheme, we will use the subversion-resilient randomness generator from the previous chapter. Overall, we will use n instantiations of a KEM in parallel, where n is a parameter that can be chosen appropriately depending on the application. This means, we run the key generation algorithm n times in parallel to obtain n key pairs. To encapsulate a key, we will also run the Encaps algorithm n times in parallel, each time using a public key that was previously generated. This gives us n ciphertext/key pairs. While all ciphertexts are just output as the final ciphertext, the amalgamation executes an XOR function on all keys. As we will see later in the security analysis, as long as one public key and the ciphertext under that public key were executed honestly, the resulting key pair will be indistinguishable from random.

Construction. With these definitions in place, we are now ready to describe our construction. Let $\widehat{\mathsf{RGSR}} = (\mathsf{Am}_{\mathsf{RG}}, \mathsf{RGSR})$ be the specification of a subversion-resilient randomness generator. Further, let $n > 0$ be an arbitrary constant which allows us to adjust the construction. Since we focus on the key encapsulation mechanism in this section, we will use

$$\mathsf{RG}(1^\lambda) := \mathsf{Am}_{\mathsf{RG}}(1^\lambda, \mathsf{RGSR})$$

to simplify notation. Let $(\mathsf{Gen}, \mathsf{Encaps}, \mathsf{Decaps})$ be a key encapsulation mechanism. From these building blocks we define a specification of a subversion-resilient key encapsulation mechanism

$$\widehat{\mathsf{KEMSR}} = (\mathsf{Am}_{\mathsf{KEM}}, \mathsf{KEMSR}) = (\mathsf{Am}_{\mathsf{KEM}}, (\mathsf{RGSR}, \mathsf{Gen}, \mathsf{Encaps}, \mathsf{Decaps}))$$

where the trusted amalgamation $\mathsf{Am}_{\mathsf{KEM}}$ defines algorithms $(\mathsf{GenSR}, \mathsf{EncapsSR}, \mathsf{DecapsSR})$ as follows.

- $\mathsf{GenSR}(1^\lambda)$: Compute $r_i \leftarrow \mathsf{RG}(1^\lambda)$ and $(sk_i, pk_i) \leftarrow \mathsf{Gen}(1^\lambda; r_i)$ for all $i \in [n]$ and output
$$pk := (pk_i)_{i \in [n]} \quad \text{and} \quad sk := (sk_i)_{i \in [n]}.$$
See Fig. 5 for an illustration.
- $\mathsf{EncapsSR}(pk)$: On input $pk = (pk_1, \ldots, pk_n)$ compute $r_i \leftarrow \mathsf{RG}(1^\lambda)$ and $(C_i, K_i) \leftarrow \mathsf{Encaps}(pk_i; r_i)$ for all $i \in [n]$ and output
$$C := (C_1, \ldots, C_n) \quad \text{and} \quad K := K_1 \oplus \cdots \oplus K_n.$$
See Fig. 6 for an illustration.
- $\mathsf{DecapsSR}(C, sk)$: On input $sk = (sk_1, \ldots, sk_n)$ and $C = (C_1, \ldots, C_n)$ compute $K_i = \mathsf{Decaps}(sk_i, C_i)$ for all $i \in [n]$. If there exists $i \in [n]$ such that $K_i = \perp$, then output $\perp$. Otherwise output
$$K = K_1 \oplus \cdots \oplus K_n.$$

The trusted amalgamation function $\mathsf{Am}_{\mathsf{KEM}}$ essentially consists of simple loops with n independent iterations of calls to the underlying RG and KEM procedures, plus a simple $\oplus$ function. Note that a trusted $\oplus$ was also used in [27] in order to handle large message spaces for public key encryption.

Security Analysis

Theorem 2. *Let* KEM *be a* $(t_{\mathcal{A}}, \varepsilon)$ *indistinguishable key encapsulation mechanism and* $\widehat{\mathsf{RGSR}}$ *be the specification of a* $(\mathcal{O}(1), t_{\mathcal{B}}, 0)$ *subversion-resilient randomness generator. Then* $\widehat{\mathsf{KEMSR}}$ *as defined above with parameters* $n, n_{\mathsf{WD}} > 0 \in \mathbb{N}$ *is* $(t_{\mathsf{WD}}, t'_{\mathcal{A}}, \varepsilon')$ *subversion-resilient in the offline watchdog model with trusted amalgamation with*

$$t_{\mathsf{WD}} \in \mathcal{O}(n_{\mathsf{WD}}), \qquad t'_{\mathcal{A}} \in \mathcal{O}(t_{\mathcal{A}} + t_{\mathcal{B}} + n),$$

$$\varepsilon' \leq \varepsilon + \left(\frac{n_{\mathsf{WD}}}{n_{\mathsf{WD}} + n}\right)^{n_{\mathsf{WD}}} \cdot \left(1 - \frac{n_{\mathsf{WD}}}{n_{\mathsf{WD}} + n}\right)^{n}.$$

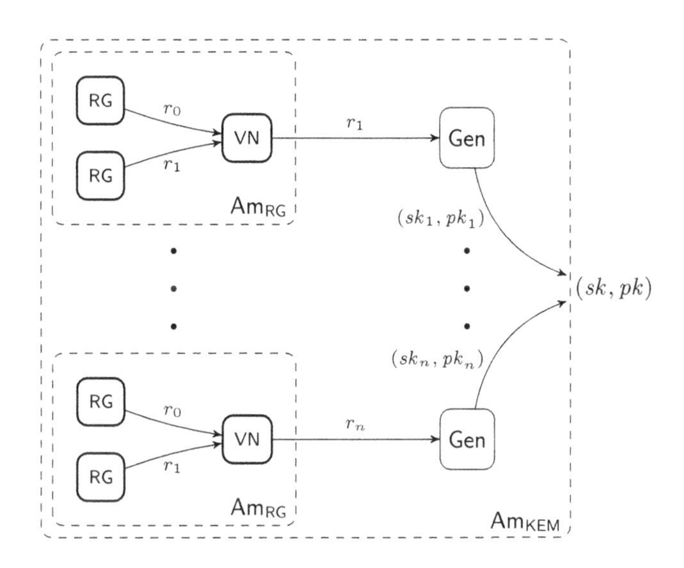

Fig. 5. Subversion-resilient KEM: key generation algorithm.

Proof. The following notation and helper functions will be useful for the proof. Let $R_{\mathsf{gen}}, R_{\mathsf{enc}}$ denote the randomness space of the algorithms Gen and Encaps, respectively. Let F_{KEM} be the deterministic function parameterized by a key encapsulation mechanism KEM = (Gen, Encaps, Decaps) which takes as input randomness $(r, s) \in R_{\mathsf{gen}} \times R_{\mathsf{enc}}$ for Gen and Encaps, respectively, and then computes

$$(pk, sk, C, K) = F_{\mathsf{KEM}}(r, s) \tag{5}$$

with

$$(pk, sk) \leftarrow \mathsf{Gen}(1^{\lambda}; r) \quad \text{and} \quad (C, K) \leftarrow \mathsf{Encaps}(pk; s).$$

For KEM (which is part of the specification $\widehat{\mathsf{KEMSR}}$) and a corresponding implementation $\widetilde{\mathsf{KEM}}$ we can now define sets Neq and Eq as

$$\mathsf{Neq} := \left\{(r,s) : F_{\mathsf{KEM}}(r,s) \neq F_{\widetilde{\mathsf{KEM}}}(r,s)\right\} \tag{6}$$

and

$$\mathsf{Eq} := \left\{(r,s) : F_{\mathsf{KEM}}(r,s) = F_{\widetilde{\mathsf{KEM}}}(r,s)\right\}. \tag{7}$$

Hence, set Neq contains all "bad" randomness values where the implementation deviates from the specification, and Eq contains all "good" randomness values where specification and implementation match. Since Neq and Eq are disjoint sets, we have

$$\mathsf{Neq} \cup \mathsf{Eq} = R_{\mathsf{gen}} \times R_{\mathsf{enc}} \quad \text{and} \quad \mathsf{Neq} \cap \mathsf{Eq} = \emptyset.$$

Watchdog Construction. We construct a universal offline watchdog WD which proceeds as follows.

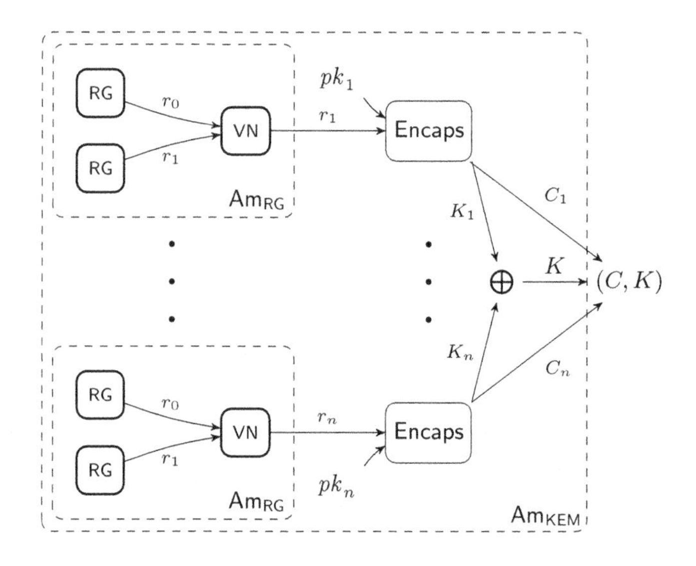

Fig. 6. Subversion-resilient KEM: encapsulation algorithm.

1. First WD runs the watchdog for $\widehat{\mathsf{RGSR}}$ as a subroutine. If this algorithm outputs `true`, then WD outputs `true`. Otherwise, WD proceeds.
2. Then, for $i \in [1, n_{\mathsf{WD}}]$, WD picks $(r_i, s_i) \xleftarrow{\$} R_{\mathsf{gen}} \times R_{\mathsf{enc}}$ uniformly at random and checks whether

$$F_{\mathsf{KEM}}(r_i, s_i) = F_{\widetilde{\mathsf{KEM}}}(r_i, s_i)$$

holds where F is as defined in Eq. (5). If any of these checks fails, then the watchdog outputs `true`. Otherwise, it outputs `false`.

Note that the above watchdog performs only a constant number of queries to check RG plus n_{WD} many evaluations of each Gen and Encaps.

Security Analysis. In order to analyze the security of our scheme with respect to this watchdog, consider the following sequence of games.
Game 0. This Game is the $\mathsf{SR}^{\mathcal{A},\mathsf{WD}}_{\mathsf{KEMIND},\widehat{\mathsf{KEMSR}}}(1^\lambda)$ experiment.

Game 1. This game is identical to Game 0, except that all invocations of $\widetilde{\mathsf{RG}}$ are replaced with uniformly random bits.

Since WD runs the watchdog for $\widehat{\mathsf{RGSR}}$ as a subroutine it outputs `true` only if the watchdog for $\widehat{\mathsf{RGSR}}$ does. By the $(\mathcal{O}(1), t_{\mathcal{B}}, 0)$-subversion-resilience of RG this game is therefore perfectly indistinguishable from Game 0.
Game 2. This game is identical to Game 1, except that the execution of game $\mathsf{KEMIND}^{\mathcal{A}}_{\mathsf{KEM}}$ is changed in the following way. After computing

$$(sk, pk) = ((pk_i)_{i\in[n]}, (sk_i)_{i\in[n]})$$

for $(sk_i, pk_i) = \widetilde{\mathsf{Gen}}(1^\lambda; r_i)$, and then

$$(C^*, K_1) = ((C_1^*, \ldots, C_n^*), (K_{11} \oplus \ldots \oplus K_{1n}))$$

with $(C_i^*, K_{1i}) = \widetilde{\mathsf{Encaps}}(pk_i; s_i)$ and uniform r_i, s_i, the experiment checks whether $\exists i \in [1, n]$ such that

$$F_{\mathsf{KEM}}(r_i, s_i) = (pk_i, sk_i, C_i, K_i) = F_{\widetilde{\mathsf{KEM}}}(r_i, s_i).$$

Thus, the experiment ensures that at least one ciphertext was computed according to the specification, with a public key that was also computed according to the specification. If such a ciphertext was not output, then the game simply aborts.

Note that Game 2 and Game 1 only differ if an abort occurs *after* the watchdog has approved the implementation. Therefore, the probability for this event is

$$\begin{aligned}
\Pr[\text{Abort}] &= \Pr\left[\begin{array}{c}\mathsf{WD}^{\widetilde{\mathsf{KEM}}} = \text{false} \wedge \\ \text{Challenger aborts } \mathsf{KEMIND}^{\mathcal{A}}_{\mathsf{KEM}}(1^\lambda)\end{array}\right] \\
&\overset{(*)}{=} \Pr\left[\mathsf{WD}^{\widetilde{\mathsf{KEM}}} = \text{false}\right] \cdot \Pr\left[\text{Challenger aborts } \mathsf{KEMIND}^{\mathcal{A}}_{\mathsf{KEM}}(1^\lambda)\right] \\
&\leq \left(\frac{|\mathsf{Eq}|}{|R_{\mathsf{gen}} \times R_{\mathsf{enc}}|}\right)^{n_{\mathsf{WD}}} \cdot \left(\frac{|\mathsf{Neq}|}{|R_{\mathsf{gen}} \times R_{\mathsf{enc}}|}\right)^{n} \\
&\overset{(**)}{\leq} \left(\frac{n_{\mathsf{WD}}}{n_{\mathsf{WD}} + n}\right)^{n_{\mathsf{WD}}} \cdot \left(1 - \frac{n_{\mathsf{WD}}}{n_{\mathsf{WD}} + n}\right)^{n}
\end{aligned}$$

with Neq and Eq as defined in Eq. (6) and Eq. (7), respectively. Note here that the equation marked with $(*)$ holds because the two events are independent, since they only depend on the used randomness and the watchdog samples its randomness independently from the experiment. The following inequality holds by definition of the watchdog and the abort condition. The bound marked with (**) holds since the previous line can be written as $p^\lambda \cdot (1-p)^\lambda$ for some $p \in [0,1]$. Calculating the derivative of this function and computing the root yields that the term is maximized for

$$p = \left(\frac{|\mathsf{Eq}|}{|R_{\mathsf{gen}} \times R_{\mathsf{enc}}|}\right) = \frac{n_{\mathsf{WD}}}{n_{\mathsf{WD}} + n}.$$

Thus, if we fix n_{WD} and n, the above term states the best bound any adversary can achieve.

Now we are ready to argue that security in Game 2 is implied by the security of the underlying KEM. To this end, consider a $(t_\mathcal{A}, \varepsilon_2)$ adversary $\mathcal{A}_2$ which breaks the security of Game 2. From this, we construct a $(t_\mathcal{B}, \varepsilon)$ adversary $\mathcal{B}$ breaking the security of the underlying KEM.

Construction of $\mathcal{B}$. Adversary $\mathcal{B}$ receives as input $(1^\lambda, pk, K_b, C^*)$ for a uniformly chosen $b \in \{0,1\}$ and then simulates Game 2 as follows.

First, it obtains an implementation $\widetilde{\mathsf{KEMSR}}$ and state st from $\mathcal{A}_0$. It runs the watchdog for $\widehat{\mathsf{KEMSR}}$ as specified above. In case that watchdog outputs false, $\mathcal{B}$ outputs a uniformly random bit, just like the original security experiment. Otherwise, $\mathcal{B}$ continues to simulate Game 2.

If this is the case, then $\mathcal{B}$ generates keys $(sk, pk) = ((sk_1, \ldots, sk_n), (pk_1, \ldots, pk_n))$ using the amalgamated algorithm $\widetilde{\mathsf{Gen}}$, based on the implementation provided by $\mathcal{A}_0$. In order to compute the challenge ciphertexts, $\mathcal{B}$ computes ciphertexts C_i and keys K_i for $i \in [1,n]$ by running $\widetilde{\mathsf{Encaps}}$ using uniformly random coins. As in Game 2, $\mathcal{B}$ checks whether there exist (sk_i, pk_i, C_i, K_i) for some $i \in [1,n]$ which were computed according to the specification. In case no such pair is found, $\mathcal{B}$ aborts.

Otherwise, let i denote the smallest index for which this condition is fulfilled. $\mathcal{B}$ then computes the challenge ciphertext for $\mathcal{A}$ by replacing (C_i, K_i) (which are guaranteed to be "honestly" generated, according to the specification) by its own challenge $(C^*, K_b,)$. More formally, $\mathcal{B}$ outputs $(1^\lambda, st, pk, K, C)$ with $K = (K_1 \oplus \ldots \oplus K_n)$ and $C = (C_1, \ldots, C_n)$ to $\mathcal{A}_1$, where $(C_i, K_i) = (C^*, K_b)$. Finally $\mathcal{B}$ outputs whatever $\mathcal{A}$ outputs.

Now observe that if $b = 0$, then K_0 was chosen uniformly from the key space $\mathcal{KS}$ and therefore the key K is uniformly random in $\mathcal{KS}$. Otherwise, if $b = 1$, then K_1 is the key encapsulated in the ciphertext C^*.

It remains to analyze the advantage of $\mathcal{B}$. Since $\mathcal{B}$ simulates Game 2 perfectly, $\mathcal{B}$ "wins" if and only if $\mathcal{A}$ wins in Game 2, *i.e.* $\varepsilon = \varepsilon_2$. Since Game 2 and Game 1 only differ by the abort condition, we obtain that

$$\varepsilon_2 = \varepsilon_1 - \Pr[\text{ Abort}] \geq \varepsilon_1 - \left(\frac{n_{\mathsf{WD}}}{n_{\mathsf{WD}} + n}\right)^{n_{\mathsf{WD}}} \cdot \left(1 - \frac{n_{\mathsf{WD}}}{n_{\mathsf{WD}} + n}\right)^n.$$

Finally, Game 1 and Game 0 are perfectly indistinguishable due to the $(\mathcal{O}(1), t_\mathcal{B}, 0)$-subversion-resilience of $\widehat{\mathsf{RG}}$. Since Game 0 is the original subversion-resilience Game $\mathsf{SR}^{\mathcal{A},\mathsf{WD}}_{\mathsf{KEMIND},\widehat{\mathsf{KEMSR}}}(1^\lambda)$, we obtain that

$$\varepsilon_0 \leq \varepsilon + \left(\frac{n_{\mathsf{WD}}}{n_{\mathsf{WD}}+n}\right)^{n_{\mathsf{WD}}} \cdot \left(1 - \frac{n_{\mathsf{WD}}}{n_{\mathsf{WD}}+n}\right)^{n}$$

which completes the proof. □

5.3 Efficient Instantiation of the Subversion-Resilient KEM and the Watchdog

The variable n determines the efficiency of the constructed scheme in terms of the number of parallel instances of the underlying KEM (note that this has direct impact on the size of keys and ciphertexts), while n_{WD} determines the number of tests performed by the watchdog. Both together determine the overall security guarantee inherited from the underlying KEM.

Table 1. Instantiating our construction and the watchdog with different values n and n_{WD}. Recall that n is the number of parallel KEM instances used in our construction and n_{WD} is the number of tests (on each Gen and Encaps) done by the watchdog.

Security parameter λ	n	$\lceil \log_2(n_{\mathsf{WD}}) \rceil$
128	32	8
128	16	11
128	8	18
128	4	33
256	64	9
256	32	12
256	16	19
256	8	34

Defining n_{WD} and n as variables yields interesting tradeoffs between the watchdog's runtime, the size of ciphertexts and keys, and the obtained security bounds.

In Table 1 we consider different choices of n and n_{WD} for $\lambda \in \{128, 256\}$, *i.e.*, “128-bit” and “256-bit” security. For different values of n, we compute the number n_{WD} of tests performed by the watchdog in order to achieve that

$$\left(\frac{n_{\mathsf{WD}}}{n_{\mathsf{WD}}+n}\right)^{n_{\mathsf{WD}}} \cdot \left(1 - \frac{n_{\mathsf{WD}}}{n_{\mathsf{WD}}+n}\right)^{n} \leq 2^{-\lambda}$$

holds. Note that together with the assumption that the underlying KEM is instantiated such that it provides $\varepsilon \leq 2^{-\lambda}$, we thus obtain a security bound on the subversion-resilient KEM of

$$\varepsilon_0 \leq \varepsilon + \left(\frac{n_{\mathsf{WD}}}{n_{\mathsf{WD}}+n}\right)^{n_{\mathsf{WD}}} \cdot \left(1 - \frac{n_{\mathsf{WD}}}{n_{\mathsf{WD}}+n}\right)^{n} \leq 2^{-\lambda+1}.$$

Table 1 shows how our subversion-resilient KEM can be instantiated. For instance, for $\lambda = 128$ and with $n = 8$, the watchdog only needs to test the Gen and Encaps algorithm only 2^{18} times, which can be practically accomplished for many underlying KEM constructions within a short time on moderate hardware. Even for $\lambda = 128$ and with n as small as $n = 4$ only 2^{33} tests are already sufficient, which also seems practically feasible, since it can be accomplished for most underlying KEMs within minutes or at most few hours on standard hardware such as a laptop computer.

6 Subversion-Resilient Public-Key Encryption

After successfully constructing a subversion-resilient KEM, we now proceed to construct a subversion-resilient public key encryption scheme. We will show that the standard way to construct public-key encryption from a KEM also preserves subversion-resilience, provided that a trusted XOR operation is given.

$\mathsf{PKEIND}^{\mathcal{A}}_{\mathsf{PKE}}(1^\lambda)$

$(sk, pk) \leftarrow \mathsf{Gen}_{\mathsf{PKE}}(1^\lambda)$
$(m_0, m_1) \leftarrow \mathcal{A}(1^\lambda, pk)$
$b \xleftarrow{\$} \{0,1\}$
$C^* \leftarrow \mathsf{Encrypt}(pk, m_b)$
$b_{\mathcal{A}} \leftarrow \mathcal{A}(1^\lambda, C^*)$
If $b == b_{\mathcal{A}}$ **then Return** 1
Else Return 0

(a) Indistinguishability experiment for public key encryption schemes.

$\mathsf{SR}^{\mathcal{A},\mathsf{WD}}_{\mathsf{PKEIND},\widetilde{\mathsf{PKESR}}}(1^\lambda)$

$(\widetilde{\mathsf{PKESR}}, st) \leftarrow \mathcal{A}_0(1^\lambda)$
If $\mathsf{WD}^{\widetilde{\mathsf{PKESR}}}(1^\lambda)$ **then**
  $b \xleftarrow{\$} \{0,1\}$
  Return b
Return $\mathsf{PKEIND}^{\mathcal{A}_1(st)}_{\mathsf{Am}(\widetilde{\mathsf{PKESR}})}(1^\lambda)$

(b) Subversion-resilience experiment for public key encryption schemes.

Fig. 7. Security experiments for public key encryption schemes.

6.1 Definitions and Construction

We begin by recalling the standard definition for public key encryption and its standard IND-CPA-style security definition.

Definition 8. *Let* $\mathsf{PKE} = (\mathsf{Gen}_{\mathsf{PKE}}, \mathsf{Encrypt}, \mathsf{Decrypt})$ *be a public key encryption scheme with the following syntax:*

- $\mathsf{Gen}_{\mathsf{PKE}}(1^\lambda)$: *The randomized key-generation algorithm takes as input a security parameter* $\lambda \in \mathbb{N}$ *and outputs a key pair* (sk, pk).
- $\mathsf{Encrypt}(pk, m)$: *The randomized encrypt algorithm takes as input the public key* pk *and a message* m *and outputs the ciphertext* C.
- $\mathsf{Decrypt}(sk, C)$: *The deterministic decryption algorithm takes as input the secret key* sk *and the ciphertext* C. *It outputs a message* m *or the error symbol* $\perp$.

Definition 9. *We say that* $\mathsf{PKE} = (\mathsf{Gen}_{\mathsf{PKE}}, \mathsf{Encrypt}, \mathsf{Decrypt})$ *is* $(t_{\mathcal{A}}, \varepsilon)$-indistinguishable *if for any adversary* $\mathcal{A}$ *running in time at most* $t_{\mathcal{A}}$ *it holds that*

$$\mathsf{Adv}_{\mathcal{A}}^{\mathsf{PKE}}(1^\lambda) := |\Pr[\mathsf{PKEIND}_{\mathsf{PKE}}^{\mathcal{A}}(1^\lambda)] - 1/2| \leq \varepsilon$$

with $\mathsf{PKEIND}_{\mathsf{PKE}}^{\mathcal{A}}(1^\lambda)$ *shown in Fig. 7 (a).*

Definition 10. *We say that a specification of a public key encryption scheme* $\widehat{\mathsf{PKESR}} = (\mathsf{Am}_{\mathsf{PKE}}, \mathsf{PKESR})$ *is* $(t_{\mathsf{WD}}, t_{\mathcal{A}}, \varepsilon)$-subversion-resilient in the offline watchdog model with trusted amalgamation *if one can efficiently construct a* correct *watchdog* WD *running in time at most* t_{WD} *such that for any adversary* $\mathcal{A} = (\mathcal{A}_0, \mathcal{A}_1)$ *running in time* $t_{\mathcal{A}}$ *it holds that*

$$\mathsf{AdvSR}_{\mathsf{PKEIND}, \widehat{\mathsf{PKESR}}}^{\mathcal{A}, \mathsf{WD}}(1^\lambda) \leq \varepsilon$$

with the used experiments shown in Fig. 7 (a) and (b).

Description of the Construction. Let $\widehat{\mathsf{KEMSR}} = (\mathsf{Am}_{\mathsf{KEM}}, \mathsf{KEMSR})$ be the specification of a subversion-resilient key encapsulation mechanism with

$$\mathsf{Am}_{\mathsf{KEM}}(\widehat{\mathsf{KEMSR}}) = (\mathsf{GenSR}_{\mathsf{KEM}}, \mathsf{EncapsSR}, \mathsf{DecapsSR}).$$

We then construct the specification of a public key encryption scheme $\widehat{\mathsf{PKESR}} = (\mathsf{Am}_{\mathsf{PKESR}}, \mathsf{KEMSR})$ with

$$\mathsf{Am}_{\mathsf{PKESR}}(\mathsf{KEMSR}) = (\mathsf{GenSR}_{\mathsf{PKE}}, \mathsf{EncryptSR}, \mathsf{DecryptSR})$$

where each algorithm is defined as follows:

- $\mathsf{GenSR}_{\mathsf{PKE}}(1^\lambda)$: Output $(sk, pk) = \mathsf{GenSR}_{\mathsf{KEM}}(1^\lambda)$.
- $\mathsf{EncryptSR}(pk, m)$: Compute $(C, K) \leftarrow \mathsf{EncapsSR}(pk)$ and output $(C, K \oplus m)$.
- $\mathsf{DecryptSR}(sk, C)$: Parse $C = (C_0, C_1)$. Compute $K \leftarrow \mathsf{DecapsSR}(sk, C_0)$. Output $m = C_1 \oplus K$.

Thus, the specification of our public key encryption scheme is basically the specification of the underlying subversion-resilient key encapsulation mechanism. Thus, the amalgamation $\mathsf{Am}_{\mathsf{PKESR}}$ is almost identical to $\mathsf{Am}_{\mathsf{KEM}}$. the only difference is that during encrypt, the message is additionally XOR'ed to the key K.

Security Analysis. Subversion-resilience of the new public key encryption scheme follows directly from the security of the underlying KEM and the usage of a trusted $\oplus$.

Theorem 3. *Let* $\widehat{\mathsf{KEMSR}} = (\mathsf{Am}_{\mathsf{KEM}}, \mathsf{KEMSR})$ *be the specification of a* $(t_{\mathsf{WD}}, t_{\mathcal{A}}, \epsilon)$ *subversion-resilient KEM. Then* $\widehat{\mathsf{PKESR}}$ *as described above is* $(t_{\mathsf{WD}}, t_{\mathcal{A}}, \epsilon)$ *subversion-resilient under a trusted* $\oplus$ *operation.*

Proof Sketch. The watchdog for PKE simply runs the watchdog for $\widehat{\mathsf{KEMSR}}$ as a subroutine. Thus, either the watchdog detects subversion or the ciphertext-key-pair output is ε-indistinguishable. Since the $\oplus$ operation is trusted, the resulting ciphertexts of PKE are also ε-indistinguishable. Therefore PKE is subversion-resilient iff $\widehat{\mathsf{KEMSR}}$ is subversion-resilient.

Note that while the adversary can freely choose the messages in the experiment, input trigger attacks are not possible. This is because no subverted algorithm has direct access to the message m_b, since the XOR operation used to encrypt the message with the KEM key is part of the trusted amalgamation.

Acknowledgments. We would like to thank Moti Yung and the anonymous reviewers of PKC 2021 for their helpful comments and suggestions, and in particular Cristina Onete for shepherding this paper and providing very detailed and valuable inputs.

References

1. Ateniese, G., Francati, D., Magri, B., Venturi, D.: Public immunization against complete subversion without random Oracles. In: Deng, R.H., Gauthier-Umaña, V., Ochoa, M., Yung, M. (eds.) ACNS 2019. LNCS, vol. 11464, pp. 465–485. Springer, Cham (2019). https://doi.org/10.1007/978-3-030-21568-2_23
2. Ateniese, G., Magri, B., Venturi, D.: Subversion-resilient signature schemes. In: Ray, I., Li, N., Kruegel, C. (eds.) ACM CCS 2015, pp. 364–375. ACM Press, October 2015
3. Bellare, M., Fuchsbauer, G., Scafuro, A.: NIZKs with an untrusted CRS: security in the face of parameter subversion. In: Cheon, J.H., Takagi, T. (eds.) ASIACRYPT 2016. LNCS, vol. 10032, pp. 777–804. Springer, Heidelberg (2016). https://doi.org/10.1007/978-3-662-53890-6_26
4. Bellare, M., Hoang, V.T.: Resisting randomness subversion: fast deterministic and hedged public-key encryption in the standard model. In: Oswald, E., Fischlin, M. (eds.) EUROCRYPT 2015. LNCS, vol. 9057, pp. 627–656. Springer, Heidelberg (2015). https://doi.org/10.1007/978-3-662-46803-6_21
5. Bellare, M., Jaeger, J., Kane, D.: Mass-surveillance without the state: strongly undetectable algorithm-substitution attacks. In: Ray, I., Li, N., Kruegel, C. (eds.) ACM CCS 2015, pp. 1431–1440. ACM Press, October 2015
6. Bellare, M., Paterson, K.G., Rogaway, P.: Security of symmetric encryption against mass surveillance. In: Garay, J.A., Gennaro, R. (eds.) CRYPTO 2014. LNCS, vol. 8616, pp. 1–19. Springer, Heidelberg (2014). https://doi.org/10.1007/978-3-662-44371-2_1
7. Berndt, S., Liskiewicz, M.: Algorithm substitution attacks from a steganographic perspective. In: Thuraisingham, B.M., Evans, D., Malkin, T., Xu, D. (eds.) ACM CCS 2017, pp. 1649–1660. ACM Press, October/November 2017
8. Blum, M., Luby, M., Rubinfeld, R.: Self-testing/correcting with applications to numerical problems. In: 22nd ACM STOC, pp. 73–83. ACM Press, May 1990
9. Bossuat, A., Bultel, X., Fouque, P.-A., Onete, C., van der Merwe, T.: Designing reverse firewalls for the real world. In: Chen, L., Li, N., Liang, K., Schneider, S. (eds.) ESORICS 2020. LNCS, vol. 12308, pp. 193–213. Springer, Cham (2020). https://doi.org/10.1007/978-3-030-58951-6_10

10. Chakraborty, S., Dziembowski, S., Nielsen, J.B.: Reverse firewalls for actively secure MPCs. In: Micciancio, D., Ristenpart, T. (eds.) CRYPTO 2020. LNCS, vol. 12171, pp. 732–762. Springer, Cham (2020). https://doi.org/10.1007/978-3-030-56880-1_26
11. Chen, R., Huang, X., Yung, M.: Subvert KEM to break DEM: practical algorithm-substitution attacks on public-key encryption. In: Moriai, S., Wang, H. (eds.) ASIACRYPT 2020. LNCS, vol. 12492, pp. 98–128. Springer, Cham (2020). https://doi.org/10.1007/978-3-030-64834-3_4
12. Chen, R., Mu, Y., Yang, G., Susilo, W., Guo, F., Zhang, M.: Cryptographic reverse firewall via malleable smooth projective hash functions. In: Cheon, J.H., Takagi, T. (eds.) ASIACRYPT 2016. LNCS, vol. 10031, pp. 844–876. Springer, Heidelberg (2016). https://doi.org/10.1007/978-3-662-53887-6_31
13. Chow, S.S.M., Russell, A., Tang, Q., Yung, M., Zhao, Y., Zhou, H.-S.: Let a non-barking watchdog bite: cliptographic signatures with an offline watchdog. In: Lin, D., Sako, K. (eds.) PKC 2019. LNCS, vol. 11442, pp. 221–251. Springer, Cham (2019). https://doi.org/10.1007/978-3-030-17253-4_8
14. Claburn, T.: NSA: we've learned our lesson after foreign spies used one of our crypto backdoors - but we can't say how exactly. The Register (2020). https://www.theregister.com/2020/10/28/nsa_backdoor_wyden/
15. Degabriele, J.P., Farshim, P., Poettering, B.: A more cautious approach to security against mass surveillance. In: Leander, G. (ed.) FSE 2015. LNCS, vol. 9054, pp. 579–598. Springer, Heidelberg (2015). https://doi.org/10.1007/978-3-662-48116-5_28
16. Dodis, Y., Impagliazzo, R., Jaiswal, R., Kabanets, V.: Security amplification for *Interactive* cryptographic primitives. In: Reingold, O. (ed.) TCC 2009. LNCS, vol. 5444, pp. 128–145. Springer, Heidelberg (2009). https://doi.org/10.1007/978-3-642-00457-5_9
17. Dodis, Y., Mironov, I., Stephens-Davidowitz, N.: Message transmission with reverse firewalls—secure communication on corrupted machines. In: Robshaw, M., Katz, J. (eds.) CRYPTO 2016. LNCS, vol. 9814, pp. 341–372. Springer, Heidelberg (2016). https://doi.org/10.1007/978-3-662-53018-4_13
18. Dziembowski, S., Faust, S., Standaert, F.X.: Private circuits III: hardware trojan-resilience via testing amplification. In: Weippl, E.R., Katzenbeisser, S., Kruegel, C., Myers, A.C., Halevi, S. (eds.) ACM CCS 2016, pp. 142–153. ACM Press, October 2016
19. Fischlin, M., Mazaheri, S.: Self-guarding cryptographic protocols against algorithm substitution attacks. In: CSF, pp. 76–90. IEEE Computer Society (2018)
20. Fuchsbauer, G.: Subversion-zero-knowledge SNARKs. In: Abdalla, M., Dahab, R. (eds.) PKC 2018. LNCS, vol. 10769, pp. 315–347. Springer, Cham (2018). https://doi.org/10.1007/978-3-319-76578-5_11
21. Giacon, F., Kiltz, E., Poettering, B.: Hybrid encryption in a multi-user setting, revisited. In: Abdalla, M., Dahab, R. (eds.) PKC 2018. LNCS, vol. 10769, pp. 159–189. Springer, Cham (2018). https://doi.org/10.1007/978-3-319-76578-5_6
22. Holenstein, T., Renner, R.: One-way secret-key agreement and applications to circuit polarization and immunization of public-key encryption. In: Shoup, V. (ed.) CRYPTO 2005. LNCS, vol. 3621, pp. 478–493. Springer, Heidelberg (2005). https://doi.org/10.1007/11535218_29
23. Jain, A., Korb, A., Manohar, N., Sahai, A.: Amplifying the security of functional encryption, unconditionally. In: Micciancio, D., Ristenpart, T. (eds.) CRYPTO 2020. LNCS, vol. 12170, pp. 717–746. Springer, Cham (2020). https://doi.org/10.1007/978-3-030-56784-2_24

24. Jain, A., Manohar, N., Sahai, A.: Combiners for functional encryption, unconditionally. In: Canteaut, A., Ishai, Y. (eds.) EUROCRYPT 2020. LNCS, vol. 12105, pp. 141–168. Springer, Cham (2020). https://doi.org/10.1007/978-3-030-45721-1_6
25. Mironov, I., Stephens-Davidowitz, N.: cryptographic reverse firewalls. In: Oswald, E., Fischlin, M. (eds.) EUROCRYPT 2015. LNCS, vol. 9057, pp. 657–686. Springer, Heidelberg (2015). https://doi.org/10.1007/978-3-662-46803-6_22
26. Poettering, B., Rösler, P.: Combiners for AEAD. IACR Trans. Symmetric Cryptol. **2020**(1), 121–143 (2020)
27. Russell, A., Tang, Q., Yung, M., Zhou, H.-S.: Cliptography: clipping the power of kleptographic attacks. In: Cheon, J.H., Takagi, T. (eds.) ASIACRYPT 2016. LNCS, vol. 10032, pp. 34–64. Springer, Heidelberg (2016). https://doi.org/10.1007/978-3-662-53890-6_2
28. Russell, A., Tang, Q., Yung, M., Zhou, H.S.: Generic semantic security against a kleptographic adversary. In: Thuraisingham, B.M., Evans, D., Malkin, T., Xu, D. (eds.) ACM CCS 2017, pp. 907–922. ACM Press, October/November 2017
29. Russell, A., Tang, Q., Yung, M., Zhou, H.-S.: Correcting subverted random oracles. In: Shacham, H., Boldyreva, A. (eds.) CRYPTO 2018. LNCS, vol. 10992, pp. 241–271. Springer, Cham (2018). https://doi.org/10.1007/978-3-319-96881-0_9
30. von Neumann, J.: Various techniques used in connection with random digits. In: Householder, A., Forsythe, G., Germond, H. (eds.) Monte Carlo Method, pp. 36–38. National Bureau of Standards Applied Mathematics Series, 12, U.S. Government Printing Office, Washington, D.C (1951)
31. Young, A., Yung, M.: The dark side of "Black-Box" cryptography or: should we trust capstone? In: Koblitz, N. (ed.) CRYPTO 1996. LNCS, vol. 1109, pp. 89–103. Springer, Heidelberg (1996). https://doi.org/10.1007/3-540-68697-5_8
32. Young, A., Yung, M.: Kleptography: using cryptography against cryptography. In: Fumy, W. (ed.) EUROCRYPT 1997. LNCS, vol. 1233, pp. 62–74. Springer, Heidelberg (1997). https://doi.org/10.1007/3-540-69053-0_6

Non-interactive CCA2-Secure Threshold Cryptosystems: Achieving Adaptive Security in the Standard Model Without Pairings

Julien Devevey[1(✉)], Benoît Libert[1,2], Khoa Nguyen[3], Thomas Peters[4], and Moti Yung[5]

[1] ENS de Lyon, Laboratoire LIP (U. Lyon, CNRS, ENSL, Inria, UCBL), Lyon, France
julien.devevey@ens-lyon.fr
[2] CNRS, Laboratoire LIP, Lyon, France
[3] SPMS, Nanyang Technological University, Singapore, Singapore
[4] FNRS & UCLouvain, ICTEAM, Louvain-la-Neuve, Belgium
[5] Google and Columbia University, New York, USA

Abstract. We consider threshold public-key encryption, where the decryption servers distributively hold the private key shares, and we need a threshold of these servers to decrypt the message (while the system remains secure when less than the threshold is corrupt). We investigate the notion of chosen-ciphertext secure threshold systems which has been historically hard to achieve. We further require the systems to be, both, adaptively secure (i.e., secure against a strong adversary making corruption decisions dynamically during the protocol), and non-interactive (i.e., where decryption servers do not interact amongst themselves but rather efficiently contribute, each, a single message). To date, only pairing-based implementations were known to achieve security in the standard security model without relaxation (i.e., without assuming the random oracle idealization) under the above stringent requirements. Here, we investigate how to achieve the above using other assumptions (in order to understand what other algebraic building blocks and mathematical assumptions are needed to extend the domain of encryption methods achieving the above). Specifically, we show realizations under the Decision Composite Residuosity (DCR) and Learning-With-Errors (LWE) assumptions.

Keywords: Threshold cryptography · Adaptive security · Non-interactive schemes · Standard model · Chosen-ciphertext security · DCR · LWE

1 Introduction

Threshold cryptography [17,36,38,39] avoids a single point of failure by splitting the secret key into $\ell > 1$ shares and handing them over to different servers.

J. A. Garay (Ed.): PKC 2021, LNCS 12710, pp. 659–690, 2021.
https://doi.org/10.1007/978-3-030-75245-3_24

This is done in such a way that any set of size at least $t \leq \ell$ servers can jointly compute private key operations whereas no subset of up to $t-1$ servers can similarly compute or otherwise compromise the cryptosystem's security.

Chosen-ciphertext (IND-CCA) security [69,74] is recognized as the *de facto* security notion for public-key encryption. Designing threshold IND-CCA2-secure cryptosystems is non-trivial, and particularly challenging when we aim to combine all desirable properties. In this paper, we are interested in CCA2-secure threshold public-key encryption schemes that are simultaneously: secure under adaptive corruptions (namely, where adversaries can choose whom to corrupt based on the previously obtained information during the protocol), and non-interactive. By "non-interactive" we mean that decryption servers do not communicate with one another in a time consuming protocol, but rather only send a single message to a combiner which gathers these partial decryptions to produce the cleartext. In addition, our goal is to prove security in the standard model (i.e., without the random oracle idealization) and without assuming reliable erasures on behalf of decryption servers. Finally, we also wish to achieve robustness and prevent corrupted servers from hindering the decryption process.

We re-emphasize that we aim at simple non-interactive client/servers protocols where, in order to decrypt a message, a client sends a ciphertext to a decryption server that responds with a decryption share (along with a non-interactive proof of share correctness) without having to talk to other servers. As advocated in [78], such non-interactive protocols are attractive as they require no synchronization among servers, and do not rely on network latency guarantees.

To our knowledge, all solutions that combine all the aforementioned properties [62,65] rely on bilinear maps. In this paper, we consider the problem of schemes realizing the above under other well-established and non-pairing-related standard assumptions.

Non-interactive Schemes. When we aim to avoid interaction during the decryption process in the design of threshold CCA2 schemes, the common stumbling block is that decryption servers often need to know whether an incoming ciphertext is valid or not before releasing their partial decryption result. The early solutions to this problem involved non-interactive zero-knowledge (NIZK) proofs [46,77] of ciphertext well-formedness in the random oracle model. In the standard model, Canetti and Goldwasser [23] thresholdized the Cramer-Shoup cryptosystem [31] by means of a randomized decryption protocol. Their approach involves shared randomizers in order to prevent partial decryptions on invalid ciphertexts from leaking information on the secret key shares. To remove interaction from the process, shareholders have to store a large number of pre-shared randomizers, which entails a prohibitively large storage cost. Cramer, Damgård and Ishai suggested [28] a non-interactive distributed randomization technique but it only supports a small number of servers. Boneh *et al.* [16] observed that, at least for static adversaries, these limitations can be avoided if shared randomizers are generated using non-interactive distributed pseudorandom functions.

In the static corruption setting, generic or partially generic CCA2-secure threshold constructions were proposed in [14,15,42,81]. Boneh, Boyen and Halevi [14] notably came up with the first fully non-interactive realization in the standard model. Their scheme crucially relies on pairings to publicly check the validity of ciphertexts, which drastically simplifies the problem of proving security in the threshold setting. Bilinear maps also provide robustness essentially for free, by making the validity of decryption shares publicly verifiable. Similar applications of the Canetti-Halevi-Katz [24] methodology to threshold cryptography were considered in [18,58]. Wee [81] subsequently laid out a framework for the design of non-interactive threshold signatures and CCA2-secure cryptosystems in the random oracle model under static corruptions.

More recently, Boneh *et al.* [15] introduced a tool, called *universal thresholdizer*, that essentially turns any non-interactive cryptographic scheme (such as public-key encryption, digital signatures or pseudorandom functions) into a threshold variant of the same primitive. Their compiler builds on fully homomorphic encryption (FHE) [50] and notably implies CCA2-secure non-interactive threshold encryption schemes in the static corruption setting.

Adaptive Corruptions. Most threshold cryptosystems (e.g., [14,23,42,46, 77]) have been analyzed in a static corruption model, where the adversary commits to the set of corrupted servers *before* the protocol execution. Unfortunately, security under static corruptions does not imply security against more realistic adversaries that can adaptively corrupt servers based on previously and dynamically collected information. Canetti *et al.* [22] put forth adaptively secure key generation protocols for the distributed generation of discrete-log-based keys as well as adaptively secure threshold DSA signatures. Frankel, MacKenzie and Yung [47,48] independently showed different methods to achieve adaptive security. Their techniques were extended [5] to obtain proactive [70] RSA signatures.

The constructions of [22,47,48] inherently require interaction as they rely on the so-called "single inconsistent player" (SIP) technique. The latter consists of transforming a t-out-of-ℓ secret sharing into an additive t-out-of-t sharing of the same secret. In the latter case, only one server (which is randomly chosen ahead of time by the simulator among the ℓ severs) has an inconsistent internal state that causes the simulation to fail if it gets corrupted. Since this occurs with probability $\approx 1/2$, the stuck simulator can rewind the adversary and use different random coins with the hope of avoiding a new corruption of the inconsistent player. The threshold schemes of [47,48] thus proceed by switching from a (t, ℓ) polynomial secret sharing to a (t, t) additive secret sharing by first choosing a set of t participants. If a single participant fails to provide a valid contribution, the whole protocol must restart from scratch.[1] Jarecki and Lysyanskaya [55] extended the SIP technique to eliminate the need for erasures and described an adaptively secure variant of the Canetti-Goldwasser scheme [23]. Abe and Fehr

[1] An alternative approach, suggested in [5,73], requires each participant to store backup shares of other participant's shares in such a way that the missing contributions of faulty servers can be reconstructed. However, it still requires additional interaction.

[2] removed zero-knowledge proofs from the Jarecki-Lysyanskaya construction and proved it secure in (a variant of) the universal composability framework. However, [2,55] both require interaction during the decryption protocol. As in previous threshold variants of Cramer-Shoup, it requires either a large amount of synchronized interaction or a storage of a large number (i.e., proportional to the total number of decryption queries over the lifetime of the system) of pre-shared secrets. As argued in [78], none of the schemes in [1,2,23,55] is a simple, non-interactive, client/server protocol.

An adaptively secure extension of the Boneh-Boyen-Halevi construction [14] was proposed by Libert and Yung [64] using bilinear maps in composite order groups. It was subsequently shown [62,65] that pairing-based NIWI/NIZK arguments [53,56] can be used to remove interaction from threshold variants of Cramer-Shoup while proving security under adaptive corruptions in the standard model. A natural question to ask (from an algebraic perspective aiming not to put all one's eggs in the same [pairing] basket) is whether similarly simple non-interactive adaptively secure systems can be realized in the standard model outside the world of pairing-based cryptography.

OUR CONTRIBUTION. In this paper, we provide IND-CCA-secure non-interactive threshold cryptosystems proven secure in the sense of a game-based definition of *adaptive security* under the Decision Composite Residuosity assumption [71] (DCR) and the Learning-With-Errors (LWE) assumption [75].

Our first construction relies on both assumptions and features ciphertexts that are about as short as in standard (i.e., non-threshold) DCR-based CCA2-secure encryption schemes based on the Cramer-Shoup paradigm [20,32]. Indeed, ciphertexts are only roughly 3 times as large as those of [20]. Our scheme offers at least two advantages over the DCR-based system obtained by applying universal thresholdizers [15] to, e.g., the Camenisch-Shoup cryptosystem [20, Section 3.2]. First, in line with our goal, we can prove adaptive security under a polynomial reduction for $t, \ell = \mathsf{poly}(\lambda)$ without relying on complexity leveraging.[2] Indeed, universal thresholdizers are not known to enable adaptive security under our definition. Second, the scheme implies a more efficient *voting-friendly* threshold cryptosystem [12] in the sense that its ciphertexts can be publicly "downgraded" (by discarding the ciphertext components that ensure CCA2 security) into an additively homomorphic encryption scheme which is much more efficient than the voting-friendly scheme derived from [15,20]. The reason is that the shared decryption algorithm of [15] would proceed by homomorphically evaluating the decryption circuit of the standard Paillier-based scheme [20] over FHE-encrypted Paillier secret keys.

Our second construction relies on the sole LWE assumption. To our knowledge, it is the first adaptively secure non-interactive threshold cryptosystem with CCA2 security in the standard model under a quantum-safe assumption. One caveat is that, analogously to previous LWE-based threshold cryptosystems, it

[2] When $t, \ell = O(\log \lambda)$, statically secure schemes can be proven adaptively secure by guessing the set of corrupted servers upfront.

relies on an LWE assumption with super-polynomial approximation factor. The reason is that, as in all earlier threshold LWE-based constructions [10,15], decryption servers need to add a noise flooding term (which requires a super-polynomial modulus-to-noise ratio) in order to not leak their secret key shares when computing partial decryptions. It remains an open problem to prove adaptive security under a more common LWE assumption with polynomial approximation factor.

Technical Overview. Our schemes build on hash proof systems [32] and can be seen as pairing-free adaptation of constructions proposed by Libert and Yung [65]. In [65], they exploit the property that, in the security proofs of encryption schemes built upon hash proof systems, the simulator always knows the secret keys, which makes it easier to answer adaptive corruption queries (a similar observation was made by Dodis and Fazio [41] in the context of trace-and-revoke schemes). In the threshold setting, the reduction knows all secret key shares and can always provide a consistent internal state for adaptively corrupted servers.

To address the difficulty that valid ciphertexts are not publicly recognizable, [62,65] replaced the designated-verifier NIZK proofs of ciphertext validity [31,32] by publicly verifiable pairing-based NIZK arguments. This eliminates the need for randomized decryption – which was the culprit of interaction in [23,55] – since the shared decryption oracle can just reject invalid ciphertexts. This, in turn, preserves the entropy of the centralized secret key (which is used to create the challenge ciphertext in [31,32]) as decryption queries on valid ciphertexts do not decrease the entropy of secret keys conditionally on the adversary's view. In the challenge ciphertext, the reduction must be able to simulate a fake argument of ciphertext validity while making sure that the adversary cannot come up with such a fake argument in decryption queries. For this purpose, the underlying NIZK argument has to provide one-time simulation-soundness [76].

Our first scheme is a threshold version of (a variant of) an Elgamal-Paillier combination proposed in [20]. The public key contains $h = g^{4N \cdot x} \bmod N^2$, where N is a safe-prime product and $x \in \mathbb{Z}$ is the secret key. Messages $\mathsf{Msg} \in \mathbb{Z}_N$ are encrypted as $(C_0, C_1) = (g^{2N \cdot r}, (1+N)^{\mathsf{Msg}} \cdot h^r) \in (\mathbb{Z}_{N^2}^*)^2$ and can be decrypted using x. The security proof of [20] involves a hybrid game where C_0 is sampled as a random quadratic residue (instead of a $2N$-th residue) in $\mathbb{Z}_{N^2}^*$ before computing $C_1 = (1+N)^{\mathsf{Msg}} \cdot C_0^{2x} \bmod N^2$. In order to exploit the entropy of $x \bmod N$ in the challenge phase, each ciphertext (C_0, C_1) should come with a simulation-sound NIZK proof/argument that C_0 is an N-th residue in $\mathbb{Z}_{N^2}^*$.

This NIZK component can be realized from recent results [21,25,72] on the standard-model instantiability of the Fiat-Shamir paradigm [45]. In our setting, we can use an argument of composite residuosity described by Libert *et al.* [61], which argues soundness in one shot (i.e., without parallel repetitions). However, the latter construction is somewhat an overkill for our purposes as it provides *unbounded* simulation-soundness (USS) while we only need *one-time* simulation-soundness in the context of threshold CCA2 security. We, thus, construct an optimized version of the NIZK argument of [61], where the common reference string (CRS) only contains $O(1)$ Paillier ciphertexts, instead of $O(\lambda)$ in [61].

This new optimized NIZK argument suffices for all applications that only need one-time simulation soundness.[3]

Like its unbounded counterpart [61], our one-time simulation-sound argument adapts a compiler from [60], which builds USS arguments from trapdoor Σ-protocols. In short, these are Σ-protocols in the CRS model where an efficiently computable function $\mathsf{BadChallenge}$ uses a trapdoor to compute the only challenge Chall admitting a valid response z for a given false statement $x \notin \mathcal{L}$ and a given first prover message a. The USS argument of [60] uses a technique due to Damgård [33] that consists of having the prover first send an equivocable commitment to its first Σ-protocol message before opening the commitment in the response z. In [60], the equivocable commitment was replaced by a strengthened version of the $\mathcal{R}$-lossy encryption primitive of Boyle *et al.* [19]. In a nutshell, an $\mathcal{R}$-lossy PKE scheme is a tag-based encryption scheme where ciphertexts are injective for all tags t satisfying some relation $R(K,t)$ (where K is an initialization value chosen at key generation time) and equivocable when $R(K,t) = 0$. By equivocating the ciphertext in all simulated proofs while keeping it extractable in the adversary's fake proof, we can use the extraction trapdoor to compute the $\mathsf{BadChallenge}$ function (in order to ensure soundness via the techniques of [25]), even after having simulated proofs by means of ciphertext equivocation. This can be seen as applying the simulation-sound zero-knowledge techniques of Garay *et al.* [49] in the context of the $\mathsf{BadChallenge}$ function methodology [25].

In [60], it was shown that the underlying equivocable $\mathcal{R}$-lossy PKE scheme can be instantiated from the DCR assumption using public keys comprised of $O(\lambda)$ Paillier ciphertexts. In Sect. 3, we show that, if we only need to simulate *one* argument of a false statement, we can use a more efficient $\mathcal{R}$-lossy PKE scheme for a different relation allowing for constant-size public keys. While [61] uses the bit-matching relation of [19] which incurs long public keys as it must be combined with admissible hash functions [13], we can simply use the inequality relation where $R(K,t) = 1$ if and only if $K \neq t$. In our DCR-based instantiation, we can thus encrypt/commit to $\mathsf{Msg} \in \mathbb{Z}_N$ under the tag t by computing $\mathsf{ct} = (u^t \cdot v)^{\mathsf{Msg}} \cdot r^N \bmod N^2$, which can be decrypted as a standard Paillier ciphertext when N divides the order of $u^t \cdot v$. When $u^t \cdot v$ is an N-th residue, we can equivocate ct by finding $r \in \mathbb{Z}_N^*$ that explains ct as an encryption of an arbitrary plaintext. By suitably programming $u, v \in \mathbb{Z}_{N^2}^*$, we can make sure that $u^t \cdot v$ is an N-th residue for one specific tag $t = K$. Importantly, we need to equivocate without knowing the factorization of N since, in our application to simulation-soundness, we rely on the DCR assumption to switch between settings where either only one tag is equivocable or all tags are equivocable.

We note that the above tools do not quite make valid ciphertexts publicly recognizable because the NIZK argument only guarantees that C_0 is a composite residue without proving that it is also a square in $\mathbb{Z}_{N^2}^*$. However, it does not affect the application to CCA2 security since decryption servers can simply square C_0

[3] Faust *et al.* [43] showed that Fiat-Shamir provides simulation-soundness "for free" in the ROM. However, their proof crucially relies on the random oracle modeling of hash functions and it is not known to immediately carry over to the standard model.

themselves to make sure that C_0^2 lives in the subgroup of $2N$-th residues before releasing decryption shares $C_0^{2 \cdot \mathsf{sk}_i}$.

Our LWE-based construction relies on the dual Regev cryptosystem [51], where public keys contain random matrices $\mathbf{A} \in \mathbb{Z}_q^{n \times m}$ and $\mathbf{U} = \mathbf{A} \cdot \mathbf{R} \in \mathbb{Z}_q^{n \times L}$, for some $n, m, L \in \mathsf{poly}(\lambda)$ such that $n < m$, and secret keys are small-norm integer matrices $\mathbf{R} \in \mathbb{Z}^{m \times L}$. Since the columns of $\mathbf{R}$ have a lot of entropy conditionally on $(\mathbf{A}, \mathbf{U})$, it is tempting to adapt the approach of our DCR-based system and use LWE in an hash-proof-like fashion (as previously done in, e.g., [6]). However, this requires preventing the adversary from inferring information on $\mathbf{R}$ by making decryption queries on ill-formed ciphertexts. This cannot be achieved via designated-verifier NIZK proofs [32] since known LWE-based hash proof systems (e.g., [57,82]) do not provide smoothness in the worst-case. Namely, nothing is guaranteed on the unpredictability of $\mathbf{R}^\top \mathbf{c}_0$ when $\mathbf{c}_0$ is neither a vector of LWE samples for $\mathbf{A} \in \mathbb{Z}_q^{n \times m}$ nor a uniform vector over $\mathbb{Z}_q^m$, but something in between (e.g., a vector $\mathbf{c}_0 = \mathbf{A}^\top \cdot \mathbf{s} + \mathbf{e}_0$ where $\mathbf{e}_0 \in \mathbb{Z}^m$ is slightly too large).

To address the problem of showing that $\mathbf{c}_0$ is well-formed (i.e., of the form $\mathbf{c}_0 = \mathbf{A}^\top \cdot \mathbf{s} + \mathbf{e}_0$ for a small enough $\mathbf{e}_0 \in \mathbb{Z}^m$), we replace the designated-verifier NIZK proof by a Fiat-Shamir-based [45] publicly verifiable NIZK argument, which is known to provide soundness in the standard model under the LWE assumption [72]. To avoid relying on a generic Karp reduction to the Graph Hamiltonicity language used in [25], we rely on the simulation-sound NIZK argument of Libert *et al.* [60, Appendix G] which allows showing that a vector $\mathbf{c}_0$ is indeed of the form $\mathbf{c}_0 = \mathbf{A}^\top \cdot \mathbf{s} + \mathbf{e}_0$ for a small $\mathbf{e}_0 \in \mathbb{Z}^m$. Since their construction provides publicly verifiable arguments, its soundness property does not rely on the entropy of a verifier's secret key and bypasses the difficulties arising from the use of designated-verifier NIZK proofs. In particular, it keeps the verifier from accepting proofs for vectors $\mathbf{c}_0 = \mathbf{A}^\top \cdot \mathbf{s} + \mathbf{e}_0$ where $\mathbf{e}_0$ is only slightly too large, which preserves the entropy of the centralized secret key $\mathbf{R} \in \mathbb{Z}^{m \times \ell}$.

In the threshold setting, both schemes share their secret keys using the linear integer secret sharing (LISS) primitive of Damgård and Thorbek [35], which are similar to linear secret sharing schemes except that they work over $\mathbb{Z}$. In our LWE-based construction, we crucially exploit the fact that LISS schemes have small linear reconstruction coefficients that can multiply decryption shares without blowing up the underlying noise terms. We could have alternatively used $\{0, 1\}$-linear secret sharing (which can also express monotone Boolean formulas [59]) as in [15]. However, as observed in [63] in the adaptive corruption setting, LISS nicely interact with discrete Gaussian distributions and make it easier to analyze the remaining entropy of shared secret keys after all decryption queries and corruption queries. Indeed, our DCR-based TPKE bears similarities to the inner product functional encryption scheme of Agrawal *et al.* [4] in that it samples secret keys $x \in \mathbb{Z}$ from a Gaussian distribution over the integers. By sharing them with a LISS, we can adapt arguments used in [4,63] in order to assess the entropy of secret keys after all queries.

Related Work. Back in 2001, Fouque and Pointcheval [46] used the Naor-Yung paradigm [69] to construct a CCA2-secure threshold cryptosystem under the DCR assumption in the random oracle model. In the full version of the paper, we show, as a comment, that the proof of IND-CCA security of [46] is actually incorrect as an adversary can break the soundness of the proof of plaintext equalities between Paillier ciphertexts with different moduli. It can be fixed by having the encryptor prove that the plaintext is a positive integer smaller than both moduli.

The first LWE-based threshold encryption scheme was proposed by Bendlin and Damgård [10] who showed a threshold version of Regev's cryptosystem [75]. Xie *et al.* [83] gave a threshold CCA-secure realization where the size of public keys and ciphertexts grows at least linearly with the number of servers. Boneh *et al.* gave a compiler [15] that turns any IND-CCA secure into a non-interactive threshold variant thereof using fully homomorphic encryption. Bendlin *et al.* [11] considered lattice-based threshold signatures and IBE schemes. However, the servers can only compute an a priori bounded number of non-interactive private key operations without using interaction. Libert *et al.* [63] described non-interactive threshold pseudorandom functions from LWE. Our LWE-based TPKE and its security proof are actually inspired by their use of LISS schemes.

Organization. In Sect. 2, we first recall some definitions and tools that will be used in our constructions. Section 3 then presents our one-time simulation-sound NIZK arguments, which builds on our DCR-based $\mathcal{R}$-lossy PKE scheme described in Sect. 3.1. Our DCR-based threshold cryptosystem is explained in Sect. 4. Its variant based on the sole LWE assumption is given in the full version of the paper. For simplicity, we first present non-robust variants of both schemes. In the full version of the paper [40], we show that standard techniques can be applied to achieve robustness against malicious adversaries.

2 Background and Definitions

2.1 Lattices

For any $q \geq 2$, $\mathbb{Z}_q$ denotes the ring of integers with addition and multiplication modulo q. If $\mathbf{x} \in \mathbb{R}^n$ is a vector, $\|\mathbf{x}\| = \sqrt{\sum_{i=1}^n x_i^2}$ denotes its Euclidean norm and $\|\mathbf{x}\|_\infty = \max_i |x_i|$ its infinity norm. If $\mathbf{M}$ is a matrix over $\mathbb{R}$, then $\|\mathbf{M}\| := \sup_{\mathbf{x}\neq 0} \frac{\|\mathbf{Mx}\|}{\|\mathbf{x}\|}$ and $\|\mathbf{M}\|_\infty := \sup_{\mathbf{x}\neq 0} \frac{\|\mathbf{Mx}\|_\infty}{\|\mathbf{x}\|_\infty}$ denote its induced norms. For a finite set S, $U(S)$ stands for the uniform distribution over S. If X and Y are distributions over the same domain, $\Delta(X, Y)$ denotes their statistical distance.

Let $\mathbf{\Sigma} \in \mathbb{R}^{n\times n}$ be a symmetric positive-definite matrix, and $\mathbf{c} \in \mathbb{R}^n$. We define the Gaussian function on $\mathbb{R}^n$ by $\rho_{\mathbf{\Sigma},\mathbf{c}}(\mathbf{x}) = \exp(-\pi(\mathbf{x}-\mathbf{c})^\top \mathbf{\Sigma}^{-1}(\mathbf{x}-\mathbf{c}))$ and if $\mathbf{\Sigma} = \sigma^2 \cdot \mathbf{I}_n$ and $\mathbf{c} = \mathbf{0}$ we denote it by ρ_σ. For an n dimensional lattice $\Lambda \subset \mathbb{R}^n$ and for any lattice vector $\mathbf{x} \in \Lambda$ the discrete Gaussian is defined by $\rho_{\Lambda,\mathbf{\Sigma},\mathbf{c}}(\mathbf{x}) = \frac{\rho_{\mathbf{\Sigma},\mathbf{c}}}{\rho_{\mathbf{\Sigma},\mathbf{c}}(\Lambda)}$.

For an n-dimensional lattice Λ, we define $\eta_\varepsilon(\Lambda)$ as the smallest $r > 0$ such that $\rho_{1/r}(\widehat{\Lambda} \setminus \mathbf{0}) \leq \varepsilon$ with $\widehat{\Lambda}$ denoting the dual of Λ, for any $\varepsilon \in (0,1)$.

For a matrix $\mathbf{A} \in \mathbb{Z}_q^{n \times m}$, we define $\Lambda^{\perp}(\mathbf{A}) = \{\mathbf{x} \in \mathbb{Z}^m : \mathbf{A} \cdot \mathbf{x} = \mathbf{0} \bmod q\}$ and $\Lambda(\mathbf{A}) = \mathbf{A}^\top \cdot \mathbb{Z}^n + q\mathbb{Z}^m$. For an arbitrary vector $\mathbf{u} \in \mathbb{Z}_q^n$, we also define the shifted lattice $\Lambda^{\mathbf{u}}(\mathbf{A}) = \{\mathbf{x} \in \mathbb{Z}^m : \mathbf{A} \cdot \mathbf{x} = \mathbf{u} \bmod q\}$.

We now recall the definition of the Learning-With-Errors (LWE) assumption introduced by Regev [75].

Definition 2.1 **(LWE assumption).** *Let $m \geq n \geq 1$, $q \geq 2$ and $\alpha \in (0,1)$ be functions of a security parameter λ. The LWE problem consists in distinguishing between the distributions $(\mathbf{A}, \mathbf{A}\mathbf{s}+\mathbf{e})$ and $U(\mathbb{Z}_q^{m \times n} \times \mathbb{Z}_q^m)$, where $\mathbf{A} \sim U(\mathbb{Z}_q^{m \times n})$, $\mathbf{s} \sim U(\mathbb{Z}_q^n)$ and $\mathbf{e} \sim D_{\mathbb{Z}^m, \alpha q}$.*

Lemma 2.2 ([51, Theorem 4.1]). *There is a PPT algorithm that, given a basis $\mathbf{B}$ of an n-dimensional $\Lambda = \Lambda(\mathbf{B})$, a parameter $s > \|\widetilde{\mathbf{B}}\| \cdot \omega(\sqrt{\log n})$, and a center $\mathbf{c} \in \mathbb{R}^n$, outputs a sample from a distribution statistically close to $D_{\Lambda,s,\mathbf{c}}$.*

Lemma 2.3 ([68], **Lemma 4.4).** *For $\sigma = \omega(\sqrt{\log n})$, there exists a negligible function $\epsilon = \epsilon(n)$ such that $\Pr_{\mathbf{x} \hookleftarrow D_{\mathbb{Z}^n,\sigma}}[\|\mathbf{x}\| > \sigma\sqrt{n}] \leq \frac{1+\epsilon}{1-\epsilon} \cdot 2^{-n}$.*

Lemma 2.4 ([63, Lemma 2.6]). *Let $\epsilon \in (0,1), c \in \mathbb{R}$ and $\sigma > 0$, such that $\sigma \geq \sqrt{\ln 2(1+1/\epsilon)/\pi}$. Then $H_\infty(D_{\mathbb{Z},\sigma,c}) \geq \log \sigma - \log\left(1 + \frac{2\epsilon}{1-\epsilon}\right)$. For $\sigma = \Omega(\sqrt{n})$, we get $H_\infty(D_{\mathbb{Z},\sigma,c}) \geq \log(\sigma) - 2^{-n}$.*

Lemma 2.5 ([44]). *Let $\beta > 0, q \in \mathbb{Z}$ and $y \in \mathbb{Z}$. Then, the following holds: $\Delta(D_{\mathbb{Z}_q,\beta \cdot q,0}, D_{\mathbb{Z}_q,\beta \cdot q,y}) \leq \frac{|y|}{\beta q}$.*

Lemma 2.6 ([67, Theorem 2]). *There exists an efficient randomized algorithm $\mathsf{TrapGen}(1^n, 1^m, q)$ that given any integers $n \geq 1, q \geq 2$ and sufficiently large $m = O(n \log q)$ outputs a matrix $\mathbf{A} \in \mathbb{Z}_q^{n \times m}$ and a trapdoor $\mathbf{T}_{\mathbf{A}}$ such that the distribution of $\mathbf{A}$ is statistically close to uniform.*

Lemma 2.7 **(Adapted from** [51, corollary 2.8]). *Let $\Lambda' \subseteq \Lambda \subseteq \mathbb{R}^n$ be two lattices with the same dimension. Let $\epsilon \in (0,1/2)$. Then, for any $c \in \mathbb{R}^n$ and any $\sigma \geq \eta_\epsilon(\Lambda')$, the distribution $D_{\Lambda,\sigma,c} \bmod \Lambda'$ is within statistical distance 2ϵ from the uniform distribution over Λ/Λ'.*

2.2 Composite Residuosity Assumption

We now recall Paillier's Composite Residuosity assumption and its variant considered by Damgård and Jurik.

Definition 2.8 ([34,71]). *Let integers $N = pq$ and $s > 1$ for primes p, q. The* s-**Decision Composite Residuosity** (s-DCR) *assumption states that the distributions $\{x = w^{N^s} \bmod N^{s+1} \mid w \leftarrow U(\mathbb{Z}_N^\star)\}$ and $\{x \mid x \leftarrow U(\mathbb{Z}_{N^{s+1}}^\star)\}$ are computationally indistinguishable.*

It is known [34] that the s-DCR assumption is equivalent to the standard 1-DCR of [71] for any $s > 1$.

2.3 Linear Integer Secret Sharing

This section recalls the concept of linear integer secret sharing (LISS), as defined by Damgård and Thorbek [35]. Definitions below are taken from [79] where the secret to be shared lives in an interval $[-2^l, 2^l]$ centered in 0, for some $l \in \mathbb{N}$.

Definition 2.9. *A* ***monotone*** *access structure on* $[\ell]$ *is a non-empty collection* $\mathbb{A}$ *of sets* $A \subseteq [\ell]$ *such that* $\emptyset \notin \mathbb{A}$ *and, for all* $A \in \mathbb{A}$ *and all sets* B *such that* $A \subseteq B \subseteq [\ell]$*, we have* $B \in \mathbb{A}$*. For an integer* $t \in [\ell]$*, the* ***threshold-****t access structure* $T_{t,\ell}$ *is the collection of sets* $A \subseteq [\ell]$ *such that* $|A| \geq t$*. Sets* $A \in \mathbb{A}$ *are called qualified and sets* $B \notin \mathbb{A}$ *are called forbidden.*

Let $P = [\ell]$ be a set of shareholders. In a LISS scheme, a dealer D wants to share a secret s in a publicly known interval $[-2^l, 2^l]$. To this end, D uses a share generating matrix $\mathbf{M} \in \mathbb{Z}^{d \times e}$ and a random vector $\boldsymbol{\rho} = (s, \rho_2, \ldots, \rho_e)^\top$, where s is the secret to be shared and $\{\rho_i\}_{i=2}^{e}$ are randomly sampled in $[-2^{l_0+\lambda}, 2^{l_0+\lambda}]^{e-1}$, for some $l_0 \geq l \in \ell$. Usually, the distribution of the ρ_i is uniform but, in the following, we will set $l_0 = l$ and $\rho_i \hookleftarrow D_{\mathbb{Z},\sigma}$. The dealer D computes a vector $\boldsymbol{s} = (s_1, \ldots, s_d)^\top$ of share units as $\boldsymbol{s} = (s_1, \ldots, s_d)^\top = \mathbf{M} \cdot \boldsymbol{\rho} \in \mathbb{Z}^d$. Each party in $P = \{1, \ldots, \ell\}$ is assigned a set of share units. Letting $\psi : \{1, \ldots, d\} \to P$ be a surjective function, the i-th share unit s_i is assigned to the shareholder $\psi(i) \in P$, in which case player $\psi(i)$ is said to own the i-th row of $\mathbf{M}$. If $A \subseteq P$ is a set of shareholders, $\mathbf{M}_A \in \mathbb{Z}^{d_A \times e}$ denotes the set of rows jointly owned by A. Likewise, $\boldsymbol{s}_A \in \mathbb{Z}^{d_A}$ denotes the restriction of $\boldsymbol{s} \in \mathbb{Z}^d$ to the coordinates jointly owned by the parties in A. The j-th shareholder's share consists of $\boldsymbol{s}_{\psi^{-1}(j)} \in \mathbb{Z}^{d_j}$, so that it receives $d_j = |\psi^{-1}(j)|$ out of the $d = \sum_{j=1}^{\ell} d_j$ share units. The *expansion rate* $\mu = d/\ell$ is defined to be the average number of share units per player.

There exist security notions for LISS schemes but, since we do not explicitly rely on them, we omit their exposition for conciseness.

To construct LISS schemes, Damgård and Thorbek [35] used integer span programs [30].

Definition 2.10 ([30])**.** *An integer span program (ISP) is a tuple formed by three elements* $\mathcal{M} = (\mathbf{M}, \psi, \boldsymbol{\varepsilon})$*, where* $\mathbf{M} \in \mathbb{Z}^{d \times e}$ *is an integer matrix whose rows are labeled by a surjective function* $\psi : \{1, \ldots, d\} \to \{1, \ldots, \ell\}$ *and* $\boldsymbol{\varepsilon} = (1, 0, \ldots, 0)$ *is called target vector. The size of* $\mathcal{M}$ *is the number of rows* d *in* $\mathbf{M}$*.*

Definition 2.11. *Let* Γ *be a monotone access structure and let* $\mathcal{M} = (\mathbf{M}, \psi, \boldsymbol{\varepsilon})$ *an integer span program. Then,* $\mathcal{M}$ *is an ISP for* Γ *if it computes* Γ*: namely, for all* $A \subseteq \{1, \ldots, \ell\}$*, the following conditions hold:*

1. *If* $A \in \Gamma$*, there is a reconstruction vector* $\boldsymbol{\lambda} \in \mathbb{Z}^{d_A}$ *such that* $\boldsymbol{\lambda}^\top \cdot \mathbf{M}_A = \boldsymbol{\varepsilon}^\top$*.*
2. *If* $A \notin \Gamma$*, there exists* $\boldsymbol{\kappa} = (\kappa_1, \ldots, \kappa_e)^\top \in \mathbb{Z}^e$ *such that* $\mathbf{M}_A \cdot \boldsymbol{\kappa} = \mathbf{0} \in \mathbb{Z}^d$ *and* $\boldsymbol{\kappa}^\top \cdot \boldsymbol{\varepsilon} = 1$*. In this case,* $\boldsymbol{\kappa}$ *is called a sweeping vector for* A*.*

We also define $\kappa_{\max} = \max\{|a| \mid a$ *is an entry in some sweeping vector*$\}$*.*

Damgård and Thorbek [35] observed that a LISS can be built by setting the share generating matrix to be the matrix $\mathbf{M}$ of an ISP $\mathcal{M} = (\mathbf{M}, \psi, \varepsilon)$ that computes the access structure Γ. We may then specify a LISS scheme $\mathcal{L} = (\mathcal{M} = (\mathbf{M}, \psi, \varepsilon), \Gamma, \mathcal{R}, \mathcal{K})$ by an ISP for the access structure Γ, a space $\mathcal{R}$ of reconstruction vectors satisfying Condition 1 of Definition 2.11, and a space $\mathcal{K}$ of sweeping vectors satisfying Condition 2.

The last step is building an ISP for any access structure with small reconstruction vectors and small sweeping vectors. Damgård and Thorbek showed in [35] that LISS schemes can be obtained from [9,30]. While the Benaloh-Leichter (BL) secret sharing [9] was designed to work over finite groups, it was generalized in [35] to share integers using access structures consisting of monotone Boolean formulas. In turn, this implies a LISS scheme for any threshold access structure by applying a result of Valiant [52,80]. Their LISS scheme built upon Benaloh-Leichter [9] satisfies what we want: as can be observed from [35, Lemma 4], every coefficient of any reconstruction vector $\boldsymbol{\lambda}$ lives in $\{-1, 0, 1\}$ and [35, Lemma 5] shows that $\kappa_{\max} = 1$. Let a monotone Boolean formula f, then the BL-based technique allows us to build binary share distribution matrices $\mathbf{M} \in \{0,1\}^{d \times e}$ such that $d, e = O(\text{size}(f))$. Moreover they have at most $\text{depth}(f) + 1$ non-zero entries, so that each share unit s_i has magnitude $O(2^{l_0+\lambda} \cdot \text{depth}(f))$.

Finally, Valiant's result [80] implies the existence of a monotone Boolean formula of the threshold-t function $T_{t,\ell}$, which has size $d = O(\ell^{5.3})$ and depth $O(\log \ell)$. Recall that each player will receive about d/ℓ rows of $\mathbf{M}$ on average, then the average share size is $O(\ell^{4.3} \cdot (l_0 + \lambda + \log\log \ell))$ bits. Valiant's construction was improved by Hoory *et al.* [54] who gave a monotone formula of size $O(\ell^{1+\sqrt{2}})$ and depth $O(\log \ell)$ for the majority function.[4] This in turn reduces the average share size to $O(\ell^{\sqrt{2}} \cdot (l_0 + \lambda + \log\log \ell))$ bits.

2.4 Threshold PKE

In this section, we recall the TPKE syntax defined by Boneh *et al.* [15].

Definition 2.12 (Threshold PKE). *Let P be a party of ℓ servers and $\mathbb{S}$ be a class of efficient monotone access structure on P. A Threshold PKE scheme (TPKE) for some message space $\mathcal{M}$ is then a tuple of efficient* PPT *algorithms* (Keygen, Encrypt, PartDec, PartVerify, Combine) *with the following specifications:*

- $\mathsf{Keygen}(1^\lambda, \mathbb{A}) \to (\mathsf{pp}, \mathsf{ek}, \mathsf{sk}_1, \mathsf{sk}_2, \ldots, \mathsf{sk}_\ell)$*: On input a security parameter λ, $\mathbb{A} \in \mathbb{S}$ an access structure, the algorithm outputs a set of public parameters* pp *(which are implicit in the inputs of all other algorithms), a public key* pk *and a set of secret key shares* $\mathsf{sk}_1, \mathsf{sk}_2, \ldots, \mathsf{sk}_\ell$.
- $\mathsf{Encrypt}(\mathsf{pk}, \mathsf{Msg}) \to \mathsf{ct}$*: On input the public parameters* pp*, the encryption key* ek *and a message* $\mathsf{Msg} \in \mathcal{M}$*, the algorithm outputs a ciphertext* ct.

[4] Note that a threshold-t function can be obtained from the majority function by fixing the desired number of input bits, so that we need a majority function of size $\leq 2\ell$ to construct a threshold function $T_{t,\ell}$.

- $\mathsf{PartDec}(\mathsf{pk}, \mathsf{ct}, \mathsf{sk}_i) \to \mu_i$: *Given public parameters* pp, *a ciphertext* ct *and a secret key share* sk_i, *this algorithm outputs a partial decryption* μ_i.
- $\mathsf{PartVerify}(\mathsf{pk}, \mathsf{ct}, \mu_i) \to \mathsf{b} \in \{0,1\}$: *On input of public parameters* pp, *a ciphertext* ct *and a partial decryption* μ_i, *this algorithm outputs a bit* b.
- $\mathsf{Combine}\left(\mathsf{pk}, B = (\mathcal{S}, \{\phi(\mu_i)\}_{i \in \mathcal{S}}), \mathsf{ct}\right) \to \mathsf{Msg}'$: *Given public parameters and a set of images of* ϕ *of partial decryptions, the algorithm outputs a message* $\mathsf{Msg}' \in \mathcal{M}$. *The function* ϕ *is public and deterministic.*[5]

The goal is now to construct a TPKE scheme that satisfies the following compactness, correctness and requirements.

Definition 2.13 (Compactness [15]). *A TPKE scheme satisfies compactness if there exist polynomials* P *and* Q *such that* $\forall \lambda, \forall \mathbb{A} \in \mathbb{S}, |\mathsf{pk}| \leq P(\lambda) \wedge |\mathsf{ct}| \leq Q(\lambda)$, *where* $(\mathsf{pp}, \mathsf{pk}, \mathsf{sk}_1, \mathsf{sk}_2, \ldots, \mathsf{sk}_\ell) \leftarrow \mathsf{Keygen}(1^\lambda, \mathbb{A})$ *and the ciphertext is generated with* $\mathsf{ct} \leftarrow \mathsf{Encrypt}(\mathsf{pk}, \mathsf{Msg})$ *for any* $\mathsf{Msg} \in \mathcal{M}$.

Definition 2.14 (Decryption Correctness). *A TPKE provides decryption correctness if the following holds. For any* $\lambda \in \mathbb{N}$, *any access structure* $\mathbb{A} \in \mathbb{S}$, *any set* $\mathcal{S} \in \mathbb{A}$ *and any message* $\mathsf{Msg} \in \mathcal{M}$, *if we run* $(\mathsf{pp}, \mathsf{pk}, \mathsf{sk}_1, \mathsf{sk}_2, \ldots, \mathsf{sk}_\ell) \leftarrow \mathsf{Keygen}(1^\lambda, \mathbb{A})$, $\mathsf{ct} \leftarrow \mathsf{Encrypt}(\mathsf{pk}, \mathsf{Msg})$ *and then* $\mu_i \leftarrow \mathsf{PartDec}(\mathsf{pp}, \mathsf{sk}_i, \mathsf{ct}), \forall i \in \mathcal{S}$, *we have* $\Pr[\mathsf{Combine}\left(\mathsf{pk}, (\mathcal{S}, \{\phi(\mu_i)\}_{i \in \mathcal{S}}), \mathsf{ct}\right) = \mathsf{Msg}] = 1 - \mathrm{negl}(\lambda)$.

Definition 2.15 (Partial Verification Correctness). *A TPKE provides partial verification correctness if the following holds. For any* $\lambda \in \mathbb{N}$, *any* $\mathbb{A} \in \mathbb{S}$, *any* $\mathcal{S} \in \mathbb{A}$ *and any message* $\mathsf{Msg} \in \mathcal{M}$, *if we run* $(\mathsf{pp}, \mathsf{pk}, \mathsf{sk}_1, \mathsf{sk}_2, \ldots, \mathsf{sk}_\ell) \leftarrow \mathsf{Keygen}(1^\lambda, \mathbb{A})$, $\mathsf{ct} \leftarrow \mathsf{Encrypt}(\mathsf{pk}, \mathsf{Msg})$ *and* $\mu_i \leftarrow \mathsf{PartDec}(\mathsf{pp}, \mathsf{sk}_i, \mathsf{ct}), \forall i \in \mathcal{S}$, *then* $\Pr[\mathsf{PartVerify}(\mathsf{pk}, \mathsf{ct}, \mu_i) = 1] = 1 - \mathrm{negl}(\lambda)$.

We can now define chosen-ciphertext security in a model allowing the adversary to adaptively corrupt decryption servers.

Definition 2.16 (Adaptive-CCA security for TPKE). *A TPKE scheme provides chosen-ciphertext security under adaptive corruptions if no PPT adversary* $\mathcal{A}$ *has non-negligible advantage in the following game.*

1. *On input the the security parameter* λ, $\mathcal{A}$ *chooses an access structure* $\mathbb{A}$.
2. *The challenger generates* $(\mathsf{pp}, \mathsf{pk}, \mathsf{sk}_1, \mathsf{sk}_2, \ldots, \mathsf{sk}_\ell) \leftarrow \mathsf{Keygen}(1^\lambda, \mathbb{A})$. *It sends* $(\mathsf{pp}, \mathsf{pk})$ *to* $\mathcal{A}$ *and initializes an empty set* $\mathcal{C} = \emptyset$.
3. $\mathcal{A}$ *can adaptively interleave the following queries:*
   - ***Corruption:*** $\mathcal{A}$ *sends the challenger an index* $i \in [\ell]$. *The challenger replies by returning the share* sk_i *and updating the set* $\mathcal{C} = \mathcal{C} \cup \{i\}$.
   - ***Partial Decryption:*** $\mathcal{A}$ *chooses an index* $i \in [\ell]$ *and a ciphertext* ct *and the challenger returns a partial decryption* $\mu_i \leftarrow \mathsf{PartDec}(\mathsf{pk}, \mathsf{sk}_i, \mathsf{ct})$.
4. $\mathcal{A}$ *chooses* $\mathsf{Msg}_0^\star, \mathsf{Msg}_1^\star \in \mathcal{M}$. *The challenger replies with a challenge ciphertext* $\mathsf{ct}^* \leftarrow \mathsf{Encrypt}(\mathsf{pk}, \mathsf{Msg}_b^\star)$, *where* $b \hookleftarrow U(\{0,1\})$ *is a random bit.*

[5] It helps defining robustness. For non-robust TPKE, ϕ is the identity function.

5. *$\mathcal{A}$ makes more corruption and partial decryption queries subject to the following condition which must be satisfied at any time. Let $\mathcal{C} \subset [\ell]$ the set of corrupted servers and let $\mathcal{C}^*$ the subset of indexes $j \in [\ell]$ such that $\mathcal{A}$ made a decryption query of the form (j, ct^*). Then, it is required that $\mathcal{C} \cup \mathcal{C}^* \notin \mathbb{A}$.*
6. *The experiment ends with $\mathcal{A}$ outputting a bit $b' \in \{0,1\}$.*

The advantage of $\mathcal{A}$ is defined as $\mathbf{Adv}^{\text{ind-cca}}(\mathcal{A}) := \left| \Pr[b' = b] - \frac{1}{2} \right|$.

We now recall the notion of *robustness*, which informally captures that no malicious adversary can prevent a honest majority from decrypting a valid ciphertext.

Definition 2.17 ([15]). *A TPKE scheme satisfies* **robustness** *if no PPT adversary $\mathcal{A}$ can cause the following experiment $\mathsf{Expt}^{\text{robust}}_{\mathcal{A},\mathsf{TPKE}}(1^\lambda)$ to output 1 with non-negligible probability.*

1. *On input the security parameter λ, $\mathcal{A}$ chooses an access structure $\mathbb{A}$.*
2. *The challenger samples $(\mathsf{pp}, \mathsf{pk}, \mathsf{sk}_1, \mathsf{sk}_2, \ldots, \mathsf{sk}_\ell) \leftarrow \mathsf{Keygen}(1^\lambda, \mathbb{A})$ and provides $(\mathsf{pp}, \mathsf{pk}, \mathsf{sk}_1, \mathsf{sk}_2, \ldots, \mathsf{sk}_\ell)$ to $\mathcal{A}$.*
3. *$\mathcal{A}$ outputs a partial decryption forgery $\big(\mathsf{ct}^\star, \mu_i^\star, i\big)$, where $i \in [\ell]$.*
4. *The experiment outputs 1 if we have $\phi(\hat{\mu}_i^\star) \neq \phi(\mathsf{PartDec}(\mathsf{pk}, \mathsf{sk}_i, \mathsf{ct}^\star))$ while $\mathsf{PartVerify}(\mathsf{pk}, \mathsf{ct}^\star, \mu_i^\star) = 1$.*

We note that the function ϕ allows considering as robust a TPKE such that $\mu_i^\star = (\hat{\mu}_i^\star, \pi_i^\star)$ and where $\mathsf{Combine}$ only runs on $\hat{\mu}_i^\star$ and not on $\pi_i^\star$. While, given $(\hat{\mu}_i^\star, \pi_i^\star)$, $\mathsf{Combine}$ could have simply striped $\pi_i^\star$, such formalization would prevent showing as robust a TPKE where $\hat{\mu}_i^\star$ is a word in an admissible language and $\pi_i^\star$ is a probabilistic membership argument whose validity, moreover, does not necessarily ensure that $\pi_i^\star$ is in the range of honestly computed arguments. Thanks to ϕ, such case will not be artificially discarded.

A weaker robustness notion, a.k.a. consistency [14], captures the robustness of schemes where the word $\hat{\mu}_i^\star$ itself is probabilistic and whose validity tolerates a gap with respect to honestly computed statements. Here, we will focus on the (stronger) notion of robustness.

2.5 Correlation Intractable Hash Functions

We consider unique-output efficiently searchable relations [21].

Definition 2.18. *A relation $R \subseteq \mathcal{X} \times \mathcal{Y}$ is* **searchable** *in time T if there exists a function $f : \mathcal{X} \to \mathcal{Y}$ which is computable in time T and such that, if there exists y such that $(x, y) \in R$, then $f(x) = y$.*

Let $\lambda \in \mathbb{N}$ a security parameter. A hash family with input length $n(\lambda)$ and output length $m(\lambda)$ is a collection $\mathcal{H} = \{h_\lambda : \{0,1\}^{s(\lambda)} \times \{0,1\}^{n(\lambda)} \to \{0,1\}^{m(\lambda)}\}$ of keyed functions induced by efficient algorithms $(\mathsf{Gen}, \mathsf{Hash})$, where $\mathsf{Gen}(1^\lambda)$ outputs a key $k \in \{0,1\}^{s(\lambda)}$ and $\mathsf{Hash}(k, x)$ computes $h_\lambda(k, x) \in \{0,1\}^{m(\lambda)}$.

Definition 2.19. *For a relation ensemble* $\{R_\lambda \subseteq \{0,1\}^{n(\lambda)} \times \{0,1\}^{m(\lambda)}\}$*, a hash function family* $\mathcal{H} = \{h_\lambda : \{0,1\}^{s(\lambda)} \times \{0,1\}^{n(\lambda)} \to \{0,1\}^{m(\lambda)}\}$ *is* R**-correlation intractable** *if, for any probabilistic polynomial time (PPT) adversary* $\mathbb{A}$*, we have* $\Pr\left[k \leftarrow \mathsf{Gen}(1^\lambda)),\ x \leftarrow \mathcal{A}(k) : (x, h_\lambda(k,x)) \in R\right] = \mathsf{negl}(\lambda)$.

Peikert and Shiehian [72] described a correlation-intractable hash family for any searchable relation (in the sense of Definition 2.18) defined by functions f of bounded depth. When f is computable by a branching program, their construction relies on the standard SIS assumption with polynomial approximation factors. Under the LWE assumption with polynomial approximation factors, their bootstrapping theorem allows handling arbitrary bounded-depth functions.

2.6 Trapdoor Σ-protocols

Canetti *et al.* [25] considered a definition of Σ-protocols that slightly differs from the usual formulation [27,29].

Definition 2.20 (Adapted from [7,25]). *Let a language* $\mathcal{L} = (\mathcal{L}_{\mathsf{zk}}, \mathcal{L}_{\mathsf{sound}})$ *associated with two NP relations* $R_{\mathsf{zk}}, R_{\mathsf{sound}}$*. A 3-move interactive proof system* $\Pi = (\mathsf{Gen}_{\mathsf{par}}, \mathsf{Gen}_{\mathcal{L}}, \mathsf{P}, \mathsf{V})$ *in the common reference string model is a Gap* Σ*-protocol for* $\mathcal{L}$ *if it satisfies the following conditions:*

- **3-Move Form:** P *and* V *both take as input* $\mathsf{crs} = (\mathsf{par}, \mathsf{crs}_{\mathcal{L}})$*, with* $\mathsf{par} \leftarrow \mathsf{Gen}_{\mathsf{par}}(1^\lambda)$ *and* $\mathsf{crs}_{\mathcal{L}} \leftarrow \mathsf{Gen}_{\mathcal{L}}(\mathsf{par}, \mathcal{L})$*, and a statement* x *and proceed as follows: (i)* P *takes in* $w \in R_{\mathsf{zk}}(x)$*, computes* $(\mathbf{a}, st) \leftarrow \mathsf{P}(\mathsf{crs}, x, w)$ *and sends* $\mathbf{a}$ *to the verifier; (ii)* V *sends back a random challenge* Chall *from the challenge space* $\mathcal{C}$*; (iii)* P *finally sends a response* $\mathbf{z} = \mathsf{P}(\mathsf{crs}, x, w, \mathbf{a}, \mathsf{Chall}, st)$ *to* V*; (iv) On input of* $(\mathbf{a}, \mathsf{Chall}, \mathbf{z})$*,* V *outputs* 1 *or* 0.
- **Completeness:** *If* $(x, w) \in R_{\mathsf{zk}}$ *and* P *honestly computes* $(\mathbf{a}, \mathbf{z})$ *for a challenge* Chall*,* $\mathsf{V}(\mathsf{crs}, x, (\mathbf{a}, \mathsf{Chall}, \mathbf{z}))$ *outputs* 1 *with probability* $1 - \mathsf{negl}(\lambda)$.
- **Special zero-knowledge:** *There is a PPT simulator* ZKSim *that inputs* crs*,* $x \in \mathcal{L}_{\mathsf{zk}}$ *and a challenge* $\mathsf{Chall} \in \mathcal{C}$*. It outputs* $(\mathbf{a}, \mathbf{z}) \leftarrow \mathsf{ZKSim}(\mathsf{crs}, x, \mathsf{Chall})$ *such that* $(\mathbf{a}, \mathsf{Chall}, \mathbf{z})$ *is computationally indistinguishable from a real transcript with challenge* Chall *(for* $w \in R_{zk}(x)$*).*
- **Special soundness:** *For any CRS* $\mathsf{crs} = (\mathsf{par}, \mathsf{crs}_{\mathcal{L}})$ *obtained as* $\mathsf{par} \leftarrow \mathsf{Gen}_{\mathsf{par}}(1^\lambda)$*,* $\mathsf{crs}_{\mathcal{L}} \leftarrow \mathsf{Gen}_{\mathcal{L}}(\mathsf{par}, \mathcal{L})$*, any* $x \notin \mathcal{L}_{\mathsf{sound}}$*, and any first message* $\mathbf{a}$ *sent by* P*, there is at most one challenge* $\mathsf{Chall} = f(\mathsf{crs}, x, \mathbf{a})$ *for which an accepting transcript* $(\mathsf{crs}, x, \mathbf{a}, \mathsf{Chall}, \mathbf{z})$ *exists for some third message* $\mathbf{z}$*. The function* f *is called the "bad challenge function" of* Π*. That is, if* $x \notin \mathcal{L}_{\mathsf{sound}}$ *and the challenge differs from the bad challenge, the verifier never accepts.*

Definition 2.20 is taken from [25] and relaxes the standard special soundness property in that extractability is not required. Instead, it considers a bad challenge function f, which may not be efficiently computable. Canetti *et al.* [25] define *trapdoor* Σ-protocols as Σ-protocols where the bad challenge function is efficiently computable using a trapdoor. Here, we use a definition where the CRS and the trapdoor may depend on the language.

The common reference string $\mathsf{crs} = (\mathsf{par}, \mathsf{crs}_{\mathcal{L}})$ consists of a fixed part par and a language-dependent part $\mathsf{crs}_{\mathcal{L}}$ which is generated as a function of par and a language parameter $\mathcal{L} = (\mathcal{L}_{\mathsf{zk}}, \mathcal{L}_{\mathsf{sound}})$.

Definition 2.21 (Adapted from [25]). *A Σ-protocol $\Pi = (\mathsf{Gen}_{\mathsf{par}}, \mathsf{Gen}_{\mathcal{L}}, \mathsf{P}, \mathsf{V})$ with bad challenge function f for a trapdoor language $\mathcal{L} = (\mathcal{L}_{\mathsf{zk}}, \mathcal{L}_{\mathsf{sound}})$ is a* **trapdoor Σ-protocol** *if it satisfies the properties of Definition 2.20 and there exist PPT algorithms* $(\mathsf{TrapGen}, \mathsf{BadChallenge})$ *with the following properties.*

- $\mathsf{Gen}_{\mathsf{par}}$ *inputs $\lambda \in \mathbb{N}$ and outputs public parameters* $\mathsf{par} \leftarrow \mathsf{Gen}_{\mathsf{par}}(1^\lambda)$.
- $\mathsf{Gen}_{\mathcal{L}}$ *is a randomized algorithm that, on input of public parameters* par, *outputs the language-dependent part* $\mathsf{crs}_{\mathcal{L}} \leftarrow \mathsf{Gen}_{\mathcal{L}}(\mathsf{par}, \mathcal{L})$ *of* $\mathsf{crs} = (\mathsf{par}, \mathsf{crs}_{\mathcal{L}})$.
- $\mathsf{TrapGen}(\mathsf{par}, \mathcal{L}, \tau_{\mathcal{L}})$ *takes as input public parameters* par *and a membership-testing trapdoor $\tau_{\mathcal{L}}$ for the language $\mathcal{L}_{\mathsf{sound}}$. It outputs a common reference string* $\mathsf{crs}_{\mathcal{L}}$ *and a trapdoor $\tau_\Sigma \in \{0,1\}^{\ell_\tau}$, for some $\ell_\tau(\lambda)$.*
- $\mathsf{BadChallenge}(\tau_\Sigma, \mathsf{crs}, x, \mathbf{a})$ *takes in a trapdoor τ_Σ, a CRS* $\mathsf{crs} = (\mathsf{par}, \mathsf{crs}_{\mathcal{L}})$, *an instance x, and a first prover message* $\mathbf{a}$. *It outputs a challenge* Chall.

In addition, the following properties are required.

- **CRS indistinguishability:** *For any* $\mathsf{par} \leftarrow \mathsf{Gen}_{\mathsf{par}}(1^\lambda)$, *and any trapdoor $\tau_{\mathcal{L}}$ for the language $\mathcal{L}$, an honestly generated* $\mathsf{crs}_{\mathcal{L}}$ *is computationally indistinguishable from a CRS produced by* $\mathsf{TrapGen}(\mathsf{par}, \mathcal{L}, \tau_{\mathcal{L}})$. *Namely, for any* aux *and any PPT distinguisher $\mathcal{A}$, we have*

$$\begin{aligned}\mathbf{Adv}_{\mathcal{A}}^{\text{indist-}\Sigma}(\lambda) := |\Pr[\mathsf{crs}_{\mathcal{L}} \leftarrow \mathsf{Gen}_{\mathcal{L}}(\mathsf{par}, \mathcal{L}) : \mathcal{A}(\mathsf{par}, \mathsf{crs}_{\mathcal{L}}) = 1] \\ - \Pr[(\mathsf{crs}_{\mathcal{L}}, \tau_\Sigma) \leftarrow \mathsf{TrapGen}(\mathsf{par}, \mathcal{L}, \tau_{\mathcal{L}}) : \mathcal{A}(\mathsf{par}, \mathsf{crs}_{\mathcal{L}}) = 1]| \leq \mathsf{negl}(\lambda).\end{aligned}$$

- **Correctness:** *There exists a language-specific trapdoor $\tau_{\mathcal{L}}$ such that, for any instance $x \notin \mathcal{L}_{\mathsf{sound}}$ and all pairs* $(\mathsf{crs}_{\mathcal{L}}, \tau_\Sigma) \leftarrow \mathsf{TrapGen}(\mathsf{par}, \mathcal{L}, \tau_{\mathcal{L}})$, *we have* $\mathsf{BadChallenge}(\tau_\Sigma, \mathsf{crs}, x, \mathbf{a}) = f(\mathsf{crs}, x, \mathbf{a})$.

Note that the $\mathsf{TrapGen}$ algorithm does not take a specific statement x as input, but only a trapdoor $\tau_{\mathcal{L}}$ allowing to recognize elements of $\mathcal{L}_{\mathsf{sound}}$.

2.7 $\mathcal{R}$-Lossy Public-Key Encryption with Efficient Opening

In [60], Libert *et al.* formalized a generalization of the notion of $\mathcal{R}$-lossy encryption introduced by Boyle *et al.* [19]. The primitive is a tag-based encryption scheme [58] where the tag space $\mathcal{T}$ is partitioned into *injective* tags and *lossy* tags. When ciphertexts are generated for an injective tag, the decryption algorithm correctly recovers the underlying plaintext. When messages are encrypted under lossy tags, the ciphertext is statistically independent of the plaintext. In $\mathcal{R}$-lossy PKE schemes, the tag space is partitioned according to a binary relation $\mathcal{R} \subseteq \mathcal{K} \times \mathcal{T}$. The key generation algorithm takes as input an initialization value $K \in \mathcal{K}$ and partitions $\mathcal{T}$ in such a way that injective tags $t \in \mathcal{T}$ are exactly those for which $(K, t) \in \mathcal{R}$ (i.e., all tags t for which $(K, t) \notin \mathcal{R}$ are lossy).

From a security standpoint, the definitions of [19] require the initialization value K to be computationally hidden by the public key. The definition of [60] requires the existence of a lossy key generation algorithm LKeygen which outputs public keys with respect to which all tags t are lossy (in contrast with injective keys where the only lossy tags are those for which $(K, t) \notin \mathcal{R}$). In addition, [60] also asks that the secret key allows equivocating lossy ciphertexts (a property called *efficient opening* by Bellare *et al.* [8]) using an algorithm called Opener. For the purpose of constructing simulation-sound arguments, [60] uses two distinct opening algorithms Opener and LOpener. The former operates over injective public keys for lossy tags while the latter can equivocate ciphertexts encrypted under lossy keys for any tag.

Definition 2.22. *Let $\mathcal{R} \subseteq \mathcal{K}_\lambda \times \mathcal{T}_\lambda$ be an efficiently computable binary relation. An $\mathcal{R}$-lossy PKE scheme with efficient opening is a 7-uple of PPT algorithms* (Par-Gen, Keygen, LKeygen, Encrypt, Decrypt, Opener, LOpener) *such that:*

Parameter generation: *On input of a security parameter λ, a desired length of of initialization values $L \in \mathsf{poly}(\lambda)$ and a lower bound $B \in \mathsf{poly}(\lambda)$ on the message length,* $\mathsf{Par\text{-}Gen}(1^\lambda, 1^L, 1^B)$ *outputs public parameters Γ that specify a tag space $\mathcal{T}$, a space of initialization values $\mathcal{K}$, a public key space $\mathcal{PK}$, a secret key space $\mathcal{SK}$ and a trapdoor space $\mathcal{TK}$.*

Key generation: *For an initialization value $K \in \mathcal{K}$ and public parameters Γ, algorithm* $\mathsf{Keygen}(\Gamma, K)$ *outputs an injective public key $\mathsf{pk} \in \mathcal{PK}$, a decryption key $\mathsf{sk} \in \mathcal{SK}$ and a trapdoor key $\mathsf{tk} \in \mathcal{TK}$. The public key specifies a ciphertext space* CtSp *and a randomness space R^{LPKE}.*

Lossy Key generation: *Given an initialization value $K \in \mathcal{K}$ and public parameters Γ, the lossy key generation algorithm* $\mathsf{LKeygen}(\Gamma, K)$ *outputs a lossy public key $\mathsf{pk} \in \mathcal{PK}$, a lossy secret key $\mathsf{sk} \in \mathcal{SK}$ and a trapdoor key $\mathsf{tk} \in \mathcal{TK}$.*

Decryption under injective tags: *For any $\Gamma \leftarrow \mathsf{Par\text{-}Gen}(1^\lambda, 1^L, 1^B)$, any initialization value $K \in \mathcal{K}$, any tag $t \in \mathcal{T}$ such that $(K, t) \in \mathcal{R}$, and any message* $\mathsf{Msg} \in \mathsf{MsgSp}$, *we have*

$$\Pr\left[\exists r \in R^{\mathsf{LPKE}} : \mathsf{Decrypt}(\mathsf{sk}, t, \mathsf{Encrypt}(\mathsf{pk}, t, \mathsf{Msg}; r)) \neq \mathsf{Msg}\right] < \nu(\lambda) ,$$

for some negligible function $\nu(\lambda)$, where $(\mathsf{pk}, \mathsf{sk}, \mathsf{tk}) \leftarrow \mathsf{Keygen}(\Gamma, K)$ and the probability is taken over the randomness of Keygen.

Indistinguishability: *For any $\Gamma \leftarrow \mathsf{Par\text{-}Gen}(1^\lambda, 1^L, 1^B)$, the key generation algorithms* LKeygen *and* Keygen *satisfy the following:*

(i) For any $K \in \mathcal{K}$, the distributions $D_{\text{inj}} = \{(\mathsf{pk}, \mathsf{tk}) \mid (\mathsf{pk}, \mathsf{sk}, \mathsf{tk}) \leftarrow \mathsf{Keygen}(\Gamma, K)\}$ and $D_{\text{loss}} = \{(\mathsf{pk}, \mathsf{tk}) \mid (\mathsf{pk}, \mathsf{sk}, \mathsf{tk}) \leftarrow \mathsf{LKeygen}(\Gamma, K)\}$ are computationally indistinguishable. Namely, for any PPT adversary $\mathcal{A}$, we have $\mathbf{Adv}_{\mathcal{A}}^{\mathsf{indist\text{-}LPKE}}(\lambda) \leq \mathsf{negl}(\lambda)$, where

$$\begin{aligned} \mathbf{Adv}_{\mathcal{A}}^{\mathsf{indist\text{-}LPKE}}(\lambda) := \ & |\Pr[(\mathsf{pk}, \mathsf{tk}) \hookleftarrow D_{\text{inj}} : \mathcal{A}(\mathsf{pk}, \mathsf{tk}) = 1] \\ & - \Pr[(\mathsf{pk}, \mathsf{tk}) \hookleftarrow D_{\text{loss}} : \mathcal{A}(\mathsf{pk}, \mathsf{tk}) = 1]| . \end{aligned}$$

(ii) For any initialization values $K, K' \in \mathcal{K}$, the two distributions $\{\mathsf{pk} \mid (\mathsf{pk}, \mathsf{sk}, \mathsf{tk}) \leftarrow \mathsf{LKeygen}(\Gamma, K)\}$ and $\{\mathsf{pk} \mid (\mathsf{pk}, \mathsf{sk}, \mathsf{tk}) \leftarrow \mathsf{LKeygen}(\Gamma, K')\}$

are statistically indistinguishable. We require them to be $2^{-\Omega(\lambda)}$-close in terms of statistical distance.

Lossiness: *For any* $\Gamma \leftarrow \mathsf{Par\text{-}Gen}(1^\lambda, 1^L, 1^B)$*, any initialization value* $K \in \mathcal{K}$ *and tag* $t \in \mathcal{T}$ *such that* $(K,t) \notin \mathcal{R}$*, any* $(\mathsf{pk}, \mathsf{sk}, \mathsf{tk}) \leftarrow \mathsf{Keygen}(\Gamma, K)$*, and any* $\mathsf{Msg}_0, \mathsf{Msg}_1 \in \mathsf{MsgSp}$*, the following distributions are statistically close:*

$$\{C \mid C \leftarrow \mathsf{Encrypt}(\mathsf{pk}, t, \mathsf{Msg}_0)\} \quad \approx_s \quad \{C \mid C \leftarrow \mathsf{Encrypt}(\mathsf{pk}, t, \mathsf{Msg}_1)\}.$$

For any $(\mathsf{pk}, \mathsf{sk}, \mathsf{tk}) \leftarrow \mathsf{LKeygen}(\Gamma, K)$*, the above holds for any tag* t *(and not only those for which* $(K,t) \notin \mathcal{R}$*).*

Equivocation under lossy tags: *For any* $\Gamma \leftarrow \mathsf{Par\text{-}Gen}(1^\lambda, 1^L, 1^B)$*, any* $K \in \mathcal{K}$*, any keys* $(\mathsf{pk}, \mathsf{sk}, \mathsf{tk}) \leftarrow \mathsf{Keygen}(\Gamma, K)$ *let* D_R *denote the distribution, defined over the randomness space* R^{LPKE}*, from which the random coins used by* $\mathsf{Encrypt}$ *are sampled. For any message* $\mathsf{Msg} \in \mathsf{MsgSp}$ *and ciphertext* C*, let* $D_{\mathsf{pk},\mathsf{Msg},C,t}$ *denote the probability distribution on* R^{LPKE} *with support*

$$S_{\mathsf{pk},\mathsf{Msg},C,t} = \{\overline{r} \in R^{\mathsf{LPKE}} \mid \mathsf{Encrypt}(\mathsf{pk}, t, \mathsf{Msg}, \overline{r}) = C\} \ ,$$

and such that, for each $\overline{r} \in S_{PK,\mathsf{Msg},C,t}$*, we have*

$$D_{\mathsf{pk},\mathsf{Msg},C,t}(\overline{r}) = \Pr_{r' \hookleftarrow D_R}[r' = \overline{r} \mid \mathsf{Encrypt}(\mathsf{pk}, t, \mathsf{Msg}, r') = C] \ . \qquad (1)$$

For any random coins $r \hookleftarrow D_R$*, any tag* $t \in \mathcal{T}_\lambda$ *such that* $(K,t) \notin \mathcal{R}$*, and any messages* $\mathsf{Msg}_0, \mathsf{Msg}_1 \in \mathsf{MsgSp}$*, algorithm* Opener *takes as inputs* $\mathsf{pk}, C = \mathsf{Encrypt}(\mathsf{pk}, t, \mathsf{Msg}_0, r)$*,* r t*, and* tk*. It outputs a sample* $\overline{r}$ *from a distribution statistically close to* $D_{\mathsf{pk},\mathsf{Msg}_1,C,t}$*.*

Equivocation under lossy keys: *For any initialization value* $K \in \mathcal{K}_\lambda$*, any keys* $(\mathsf{pk}, \mathsf{sk}, \mathsf{tk}) \leftarrow \mathsf{LKeygen}(\Gamma, K)$*, any random coins* $r \hookleftarrow D_R$*, any tag* $t \in \mathcal{T}_\lambda$*, and any distinct messages* $\mathsf{Msg}_0, \mathsf{Msg}_1 \in \mathsf{MsgSp}$*, algorithm* $\mathsf{LOpener}$ *takes as input* $C = \mathsf{Encrypt}(\mathsf{pk}, t, \mathsf{Msg}_0, r)$*,* r*,* t *and* sk*. It outputs* $\overline{r} \in R^{\mathsf{LPKE}}$ *such that* $C = \mathsf{Encrypt}(\mathsf{pk}, t, \mathsf{Msg}_1, \overline{r})$*. We require that, for any* $t \in \mathcal{T}_\lambda$ *such that* $(K,t) \notin \mathcal{R}$*, the distributions*

$$\{\bar{r} \leftarrow \mathsf{LOpener}(\mathsf{pk}, \mathsf{sk}, t, \mathsf{ct}, \mathsf{Msg}_0, \mathsf{Msg}_1, r) \mid r \hookleftarrow D_R\}$$

and $\{\bar{r} \leftarrow \mathsf{Opener}(\mathsf{pk}, \mathsf{tk}, t, \mathsf{ct}, \mathsf{Msg}_0, \mathsf{Msg}_1, r) \mid r \hookleftarrow D_R\}$ *be statistically close.*

The above definition is slightly weaker than the one of [60] in the property of equivocation under lossy keys. Here, we do not require that the outputs of Opener and $\mathsf{LOpener}$ be statistically close to $D_{\mathsf{pk},\mathsf{Msg}_1,C,t}$ as defined in (1): We only require that, on lossy keys and lossy tags, Opener and $\mathsf{LOpener}$ sample random coins from statistically close distributions. In fact, the first indistinguishability property implies (since the distinguisher is given tk) that the outputs of both algorithms will be *computationally* indistinguishable from $D_{\mathsf{pk},\mathsf{Msg}_1,C,t}$. Our definition turns out to be sufficient for the purpose of simulation-sound arguments and will allow us to obtain a construction from the DCR assumption.

We note that the property of decryption under injective tags does not assume that random coins are honestly sampled, but only that they belong to some predefined set R^{LPKE}.

2.8 Trapdoor Σ-Protocol Showing Composite Residuosity

We recall the trapdoor Σ-protocols of [61], which allows proving that an element of $\mathbb{Z}_{N^2}^*$ is a composite residue (i.e., a Paillier encryption of 0).

Namely, let $N = pq$ be an RSA modulus and let an integer $\zeta > 1$. We describe a trapdoor Σ-protocol for the language

$$\mathcal{L}^{\mathsf{DCR}} := \{x \in \mathbb{Z}_{N^{\zeta+1}}^* \mid \exists w \in \mathbb{Z}_N^\star : x = w^{N^\zeta} \bmod N^{\zeta+1}\}.$$

We assume that the challenge space is $\{0, \ldots, 2^\lambda - 1\}$ and that $p, q > 2^{l(\lambda)}$, for some polynomial $l : \mathbb{N} \to \mathbb{N}$ such that $l(\lambda) > \lambda$ for any sufficiently large $\lambda \in \mathbb{N}$. The condition $p, q > 2^\lambda$ will ensure that the difference between any two challenges be co-prime with N.

In order to obtain a $\mathsf{BadChallenge}$ function that identifies bad challenges for elements $x \notin \mathcal{L}^{\mathsf{DCR}}$, one difficulty is the case of elements $x \in \mathbb{Z}_{N^{\zeta+1}}^*$ that are encryptions of an element $\alpha_x \in \mathbb{Z}_N$ such that $1 < \gcd(\alpha_x, N^\zeta) < N^\zeta$. Indeed, we cannot immediately identify a unique bad challenge by inverting α_x in $\mathbb{Z}_{N^\zeta}$. However, a closer analysis shows that, even when $\zeta > 1$ and $\gcd(\alpha_x, N^\zeta) > 1$, at most one bad challenge can exist in the set $\{0, 1, \ldots, 2^\lambda - 1\}$.

$\mathsf{Gen}_{\mathsf{par}}(1^\lambda)$: Given the security parameter λ, define $\mathsf{par} = \{\lambda\}$.

$\mathsf{Gen}_{\mathcal{L}}(\mathsf{par}, \mathcal{L}^{\mathsf{DCR}})$: Given public parameters par as well as a description of a language $\mathcal{L}^{\mathsf{DCR}}$, consisting of an RSA modulus $N = pq$ with p and q prime satisfying $p, q > 2^{l(\lambda)}$, for some polynomial $l : \mathbb{N} \to \mathbb{N}$ such that $l(\lambda) > \lambda$, define the language-dependent $\mathsf{crs}_{\mathcal{L}} = \{N\}$. The global CRS is

$$\mathsf{crs} = (\{\lambda\}, \mathsf{crs}_{\mathcal{L}}).$$

$\mathsf{TrapGen}(\mathsf{par}, \mathcal{L}^{\mathsf{DCR}}, \tau_{\mathcal{L}})$: Given par, the description of a language $\mathcal{L}^{\mathsf{DCR}}$ that specifies an RSA modulus N and a membership-testing trapdoor $\tau_{\mathcal{L}} = (p, q)$ consisting of the factorization of $N = pq$, output the language-dependent $\mathsf{crs}_{\mathcal{L}} = \{N\}$ which defines $\mathsf{crs} = (\{\lambda\}, \mathsf{crs}_{\mathcal{L}})$ and the trapdoor $\tau_\Sigma = (p, q)$.

$\mathsf{P}(\mathsf{crs}, x, w) \leftrightarrow \mathsf{V}(\mathsf{crs}, x)$: Given a crs, a statement $x = w^{N^\zeta} \bmod N^{\zeta+1}$, P (who has the witness $w \in \mathbb{Z}_N^\star$) and V interact as follows:

1. P chooses a random $r \hookleftarrow U(\mathbb{Z}_N^\star)$ and sends $a = r^{N^\zeta} \bmod N^{\zeta+1}$ to V.
2. V sends a random challenge $\mathsf{Chall} \hookleftarrow U(\{0, \ldots, 2^\lambda - 1\})$ to P.
3. P computes the response $z = r \cdot w^{\mathsf{Chall}} \bmod N$ and sends it to V.
4. V checks if $a \cdot x^{\mathsf{Chall}} \equiv z^{N^\zeta} \pmod{N^{\zeta+1}}$ and returns 0 if this condition is not satisfied.

$\mathsf{BadChallenge}(\mathsf{par}, \tau_\Sigma, \mathsf{crs}, x, a)$: Given $\tau_\Sigma = (p, q)$, decrypt x and a to obtain $\alpha_x = \mathcal{D}_{\tau_\Sigma}(x) \in \mathbb{Z}_{N^\zeta}$, $\alpha_a = \mathcal{D}_{\tau_\Sigma}(a) \in \mathbb{Z}_{N^\zeta}$.

1. If $\alpha_a = 0$, return $\mathsf{Chall} = 0$.
2. If $\alpha_a \neq 0$, let $d_x = \gcd(\alpha_x, N^\zeta)$, which lives in the set

$$\{p^i q^j \mid 0 \le i < \zeta,\ 0 \le j < \zeta\} \cup \{p^i q^\zeta \mid 0 \le i < \zeta\} \cup \{p^s q^j \mid 0 \le j < \zeta\}.$$

Then, do the following:

a. If $1 < d_x < N^\zeta$, return $\perp$ if d_x does not divide $N^\zeta - \alpha_a$.
b. Otherwise, the congruence $\alpha_a + \mathsf{Chall} \cdot \alpha_x \equiv 0 \pmod{\frac{N^\zeta}{d_x}}$ has a unique solution $\mathsf{Chall}' = -\alpha_x^{-1} \cdot \alpha_a \in \mathbb{Z}_{N^\zeta/d_x}$ since $\gcd(\alpha_x, N^\zeta/d_x) = 1$. If $\mathsf{Chall}' \in \mathbb{Z}_{N^\zeta/d_x} \setminus \{0, \ldots, 2^\lambda - 1\}$, return $\perp$. Else, return $\mathsf{Chall} = \mathsf{Chall}'$.

In [61], it is shown that the above construction is a trapdoor Σ-protocol with large challenge space. By applying [72], this implies compact NIZK arguments (i.e., without using parallel repetitions to achieve negligible soundness error) for the language $\mathcal{L}^{\mathsf{DCR}}$ assuming that the LWE assumption holds.

Lemma 2.23 ([61]). *The above protocol is a trapdoor Σ-protocol for the language $\mathcal{L}^{\mathsf{DCR}}$.*

3 NIZK Arguments with One-Time Simulation-Soundness

Libert *et al.* [60] gave a method that directly compiles (i.e., without relying on generic NIZK techniques [37]) any trapdoor Σ-protocol for a trapdoor language into an unbounded simulation-sound NIZK argument for the *same* language. As a building block, their construction uses an LWE-based equivocable $\mathcal{R}$-lossy PKE scheme for the bit-matching relation. Under the DCR assumption, a more efficient $\mathcal{R}$-lossy PKE scheme was described in [61]. In this section, we show that, in applications that only require *one-time* simulation-soundness, we can use an $\mathcal{R}$-lossy PKE scheme with a constant-size public key. In contrast, the $\mathcal{R}$-lossy PKE system of [61] has a large public key comprised of $\Theta(\lambda)$ Paillier ciphertexts.

In our *one-time* simulation-sound arguments, we use an $\mathcal{R}$-lossy PKE scheme for the inequality relation.

Definition 3.1. *Let $\mathcal{K} = \{0,1\}^\ell$ and $\mathcal{T} = \{0,1\}^\ell$, for some $\ell \in \mathsf{poly}(\lambda)$. The* **inequality relation** *$\mathcal{R}_{\mathsf{NEQ}} : \mathcal{K} \times \mathcal{T} \to \{0,1\}$ is the relation where $\mathcal{R}_{\mathsf{NEQ}}(K,t) = 1$ if and only if $K \neq t$.*

3.1 An $\mathcal{R}_{\mathsf{NEQ}}$-Lossy PKE Scheme from DCR

Our DCR-based $\mathcal{R}_{\mathsf{NEQ}}$-lossy PKE scheme goes as follows.

Par-Gen$(1^\lambda, 1^L, 1^B)$**:** Define $\mathcal{K} = \mathcal{T} = \{0,1\}^L$, so that the tag and initialization value spaces coincide. Define public parameters as $\Gamma = (1^\lambda, 1^L, 1^B)$.

Keygen(Γ, K)**:** On input of public parameters Γ and $K \in \mathcal{K}$, generate a key pair as follows.
1. Choose an RSA modulus $N = pq$ such that $p, q > 2^{l(\lambda)}$, for some polynomial $l : \mathbb{N} \to \mathbb{N}$ such that $l(\lambda) > L(\lambda)$ for any sufficiently large λ, and an integer $\zeta \in \mathsf{poly}(\lambda)$ such that $N^\zeta > 2^B$.
2. Pick $u \hookleftarrow U(\mathbb{Z}_{N^{\zeta+1}}^*)$, $\bar{v} \hookleftarrow U(\mathbb{Z}_N^*)$ and compute $v = u^{-K} \cdot \bar{v}^{N^\zeta} \bmod N^{\zeta+1}$, where K is interpreted as an element of $\mathbb{Z}_{N^\zeta}$.

Define $R^{\mathsf{LPKE}} = \mathbb{Z}_N^*$ and output $\mathsf{sk} = (p, q, K)$ as well as

$$\mathsf{pk} := \Big(N, \zeta, u, v\Big), \qquad \mathsf{tk} = (\bar{v}, K).$$

LKeygen(Γ, K): On input of public parameters Γ and an initialization value $K \in \mathcal{K}$, generate a key pair as follows.

1. Choose an RSA modulus $N = pq$ such that $p, q > 2^{l(\lambda)}$, for some polynomial $l : \mathbb{N} \to \mathbb{N}$ such that $l(\lambda) > L(\lambda)$ for any sufficiently large λ, and an integer $\zeta \in \mathsf{poly}(\lambda)$ such that $N^\zeta > 2^B$.
2. Choose $\bar{u}, \bar{v} \hookleftarrow U(\mathbb{Z}_N^*)$ uniformly. Compute $u = \bar{u}^{N^\zeta} \bmod N^{\zeta+1}$ and $v = u^{-K} \cdot \bar{v}^{N^\zeta} \bmod N^{\zeta+1}$, where K is interpreted as an element of $\mathbb{Z}_{N^\zeta}$.

Define $R^{\mathsf{LPKE}} = \mathbb{Z}_N^*$ and output $\mathsf{sk} = (\bar{u}, \bar{v}, K)$ as well as $\mathsf{pk} := \big(N, \zeta, u, v\big)$ and $\mathsf{tk} = (\bar{v}, K)$.

Encrypt$(\mathsf{pk}, t, \mathsf{Msg})$: To encrypt $\mathsf{Msg} \in \mathbb{Z}_{N^\zeta}$ for the tag $t \in \{0,1\}^L$, interpret t as an element of $\mathbb{Z}_{N^\zeta}$. Pick $r \hookleftarrow U(\mathbb{Z}_N^*)$ and compute

$$\mathsf{ct} = (u^t \cdot v)^{\mathsf{Msg}} \cdot r^{N^\zeta} \bmod N^{\zeta+1}.$$

Decrypt$(\mathsf{sk}, t, \mathsf{ct})$: Given $sk = (p, q, t^\star)$ and the tag $t \in \{0,1\}^L$, interpret t as an element of $\mathbb{Z}_{N^\zeta}$. Then, do the following:

1. Letting $\lambda(N) = \mathrm{lcm}(p-1, q-1)$, compute $h_t = (u^t \cdot v)^{\lambda(N)} \bmod N^{\zeta+1}$, which can be written $h_t = 1 + g_t N \bmod N^{\zeta+1}$, for some $g_t \in \mathbb{Z}_{N^\zeta}$, since its order is at most N^ζ. Return $\perp$ if $g_t = 0$ or $\gcd(g_t, N^\zeta) > 1$.
2. Otherwise, compute $\mathsf{Msg} = \frac{(\mathsf{ct}^{\lambda(N)} \bmod N^{\zeta+1}) - 1}{N} \cdot g_t^{-1} \bmod N^\zeta$, where the division is computed over $\mathbb{Z}$, and output $\mathsf{Msg} \in \mathbb{Z}_{N^\zeta}$.

Opener$(\mathsf{pk}, \mathsf{tk}, t, \mathsf{ct}, \mathsf{Msg}_0, \mathsf{Msg}_1, r)$: Given $\mathsf{tk} = (\bar{v}, K)$ and $t \in \{0,1\}^L$, return $\perp$ if $t \neq K$ when they are interpreted as elements of $\mathbb{Z}_{N^\zeta}$. Otherwise, given $\mathsf{Msg}_0, \mathsf{Msg}_1 \in \mathbb{Z}_{N^\zeta}$ and $r \in \mathbb{Z}_N^*$ such that

$$\mathsf{ct} = (u^t \cdot v)^{\mathsf{Msg}_0} \cdot r^{N^\zeta} = (\bar{v}^N)^{\mathsf{Msg}_0} \cdot r^{N^\zeta} \bmod N^{\zeta+1}, \tag{2}$$

output $\bar{r} = r \cdot \bar{v}^{\mathsf{Msg}_0 - \mathsf{Msg}_1} \bmod N$, so that $\mathsf{ct} = (u^t \cdot v)^{\mathsf{Msg}_1} \cdot \bar{r}^{N^\zeta} \bmod N^{\zeta+1}$.

LOpener$(\mathsf{sk}, t, \mathsf{ct}, \mathsf{Msg}_0, \mathsf{Msg}_1, r)$: Given $\mathsf{sk} = (\bar{u}, \bar{v}, K)$ and $t \in \{0,1\}^L$, interpret t as an element of $\mathbb{Z}_{N^\zeta}$. Given $\mathsf{Msg}_0, \mathsf{Msg}_1 \in \mathbb{Z}_{N^\zeta}$ and $r \in \mathbb{Z}_N^*$ such that

$$\mathsf{ct} = (u^t \cdot v)^{\mathsf{Msg}_0} \cdot r^{N^\zeta} = (\bar{u}^{t-K} \cdot \bar{v})^{N \cdot \mathsf{Msg}_0} \cdot r^{N^\zeta} \bmod N^{\zeta+1}, \tag{3}$$

output $\bar{r} = r \cdot (\bar{u}^{t-K} \cdot \bar{v})^{\mathsf{Msg}_0 - \mathsf{Msg}_1} \bmod N$, which satisfies

$$\mathsf{ct} = (u^t \cdot v)^{\mathsf{Msg}_1} \cdot \bar{r}^{N^\zeta} \bmod N^{\zeta+1}.$$

The scheme enables decryption under injective tags because, with high probability over the randomness of Keygen, the order of u is a multiple of N^ζ since u is sampled uniformly in $\mathbb{Z}_{N^{\zeta+1}}^*$ at step 2. Since $t, K \in \{0,1\}^L$ and $p, q > 2^L$, we have $\gcd(t-K, N^\zeta) = 1$, so that N^ζ divides the order of $u^{t-K} \cdot \bar{v}^{N^\zeta}$ when $t \neq K$. This ensures that h_t has order N^ζ and $\gcd(g_t, N^\zeta) = 1$ at step 1 of Decrypt.

We now prove that the scheme satisfies all the properties of Definition 2.22. The first indistinguishability property crucially imposes that lossy and injective keys be indistinguishable even when the equivocation trapdoor tk of Opener is given. This is important for our proof of one-time simulation-soundness, which requires that Opener be able to equivocate lossy ciphertexts given only tk and without knowing the factorization of N (otherwise, we could not meaningfully rely on the DCR assumption to switch from lossy to injective keys).

Theorem 3.2. *The above construction is an $\mathcal{R}_{\mathsf{NEQ}}$-lossy PKE scheme under the* DCR *assumption.* (The proof is available in the full version of the paper [40]).

3.2 The Argument System

Our one-time simulation-sound argument is very similar to the one of [60] which provides unbounded simulation-soundness using a more expensive $\mathcal{R}$-lossy PKE scheme. The construction relies on the following ingredients.

- A trapdoor Σ-protocol $\Pi' = (\mathsf{Gen}'_{\mathsf{par}}, \mathsf{Gen}'_{\mathcal{L}}, \mathsf{P}', \mathsf{V}')$ for an NP language $\mathcal{L}$. This protocol should satisfy the properties of Definition 2.21. In addition, the function $\mathsf{BadChallenge}(\tau_\Sigma, \mathsf{crs}, x, a)$ should be computable within time $T \in \mathsf{poly}(\lambda)$ for any input $(\tau, \mathsf{crs}, x, a)$. Let also $B \in \mathsf{poly}(\lambda)$ the maximal length of the first prover message sent by P'.
- A strongly unforgeable one-time signature scheme $\mathsf{OTS} = (\mathcal{G}, \mathcal{S}, \mathcal{V})$ with verification keys in $\{0,1\}^L$, where $L \in \mathsf{poly}(\lambda)$.
- An $\mathcal{R}_{\mathsf{NEQ}}$-lossy PKE scheme $\Pi^{\mathsf{LPKE}} = (\mathsf{Par\text{-}Gen}, \mathsf{Keygen}, \mathsf{LKeygen}, \mathsf{Encrypt}, \mathsf{Decrypt}, \mathsf{Opener}, \mathsf{LOpener})$ with space $\mathcal{K} = \mathcal{T} = \{0,1\}^L$. We assume that its decryption algorithm is computable within time T.
- A correlation intractable hash family $\mathcal{H} = (\mathsf{Gen}, \mathsf{Hash})$ for the class $\mathcal{R}_{\mathsf{CI}}$ of relations that are efficiently searchable within time T.

$\mathsf{Gen}_{\mathsf{par}}(1^\lambda)$: Run $\mathsf{par} \leftarrow \mathsf{Gen}'_{\mathsf{par}}(1^\lambda)$ and output par.

$\mathsf{Gen}_{\mathcal{L}}(\mathsf{par}, \mathcal{L})$: Given public parameters par and a language $\mathcal{L}$, the CRS is generated as follows.

1. Generate a CRS $\mathsf{crs}'_{\mathcal{L}} \leftarrow \mathsf{Gen}'_{\mathcal{L}}(\mathsf{par}, \mathcal{L})$ for the trapdoor Σ-protocol Π'.
2. Choose the description a one-time signature scheme $\mathsf{OTS} = (\mathcal{G}, \mathcal{S}, \mathcal{V})$ with verification keys in $\{0,1\}^L$, where $L \in \mathsf{poly}(\lambda)$.
3. Choose public parameters $\Gamma \leftarrow \Pi^{\mathsf{LPKE}}.\mathsf{Par\text{-}Gen}(1^\lambda, 1^L, 1^B)$ for an $\mathcal{R}_{\mathsf{NEQ}}$-lossy PKE scheme with tag space $\mathcal{K} = \mathcal{T} = \{0,1\}^L$. Then, generate lossy keys $(\mathsf{pk}_{\mathsf{LPKE}}, \mathsf{sk}_{\mathsf{LPKE}}, \mathsf{tk}_{\mathsf{LPKE}}) \leftarrow \Pi^{\mathsf{LPKE}}.\mathsf{LKeygen}(\Gamma, 0^L)$.
4. Generate a key $k \leftarrow \mathsf{Gen}(1^\lambda)$ for a correlation intractable hash function with output length $\kappa = \Theta(\lambda)$.

Output the language-dependent CRS $\mathsf{crs}_{\mathcal{L}} := (\mathsf{crs}'_{\mathcal{L}}, \mathsf{pk}_{\mathsf{LPKE}}, k)$ and the simulation trapdoor $\tau_{\mathsf{zk}} := \mathsf{sk}_{\mathsf{LPKE}}$. The global common reference string consists of $\mathsf{crs} = (\mathsf{par}, \mathsf{crs}_{\mathcal{L}}, \mathsf{pk}_{\mathsf{LPKE}}, \mathsf{OTS})$.

$\mathsf{P}(\mathsf{crs}, x, w, \mathsf{lbl})$: To prove a statement $x \in \mathcal{L}$ for a label $\mathsf{lbl} \in \{0,1\}^*$ using the witness w, generate a one-time signature key pair $(\mathsf{VK}, \mathsf{SK}) \leftarrow \mathcal{G}(1^\lambda)$. Then,

1. Compute $(a', st') \leftarrow \mathsf{P}'(\mathsf{crs}'_{\mathcal{L}}, x, w)$. Then, sample $r \hookleftarrow D_R^{\mathsf{LPKE}}$ in the randomness space R^{LPKE} of Π^{LPKE}. Using the tag $\mathsf{VK} \in \{0,1\}^L$, compute $a \leftarrow \Pi^{\mathsf{LPKE}}.\mathsf{Encrypt}(\mathsf{pk}_{\mathsf{LPKE}}, \mathsf{VK}, a'; r)$.
2. Compute $\mathsf{Chall} = \mathsf{Hash}(k, (x, a, \mathsf{VK}))$.
3. Compute $z' = \mathsf{P}'(\mathsf{crs}'_{\mathcal{L}}, x, w, a', \mathsf{Chall}, st')$ by executing the prover of Π'. Define $z = (z', a', r)$.
4. Generate $sig \leftarrow \mathcal{S}(\mathsf{SK}, (x, a, z, \mathsf{lbl}))$ and output $\boldsymbol{\pi} = \big(\mathsf{VK}, (a, z), sig\big)$.

$\mathbf{V}(\mathsf{crs}, x, \boldsymbol{\pi}, \mathsf{lbl})$: Given a statement x, a label lbl as well as a purported proof $\boldsymbol{\pi} = \big(\mathsf{VK}, (a, z), sig\big)$, return 0 if $\mathcal{V}(\mathsf{VK}, (x, a, z, \mathsf{lbl}), sig) = 0$. Otherwise,

1. Write $z = (z', a', r)$ and return 0 if any of these does not parse properly or if $a \neq \Pi^{\mathsf{LPKE}}.\mathsf{Encrypt}(\mathsf{pk}_{\mathsf{LPKE}}, \mathsf{VK}, a'; r)$.
2. Let $\mathsf{Chall} = \mathsf{Hash}\big(k, (x, a, \mathsf{VK})\big)$. If $\mathsf{V}'(\mathsf{crs}'_{\mathcal{L}}, x, a', \mathsf{Chall}, z')) = 1$, return 1. Otherwise, return 0.

Theorem 3.3. *The above argument is statistically (resp. computationally) zero-knowledge if: (i) Π^{LPKE} is statistically equivocable under lossy keys; (ii) The trapdoor Σ-protocol Π' is statistically (resp. computationally) special zero-knowledge.* (The proof is given in the full version of the paper.)

Theorem 3.4. *The above construction provides one-time simulation-soundness if: (i)* OTS *is a strongly unforgeable one-time signature; (ii) Π^{LPKE} is an $\mathcal{R}_{\mathsf{NEQ}}$-lossy PKE scheme; (iii) The hash function family $\mathcal{H}$ is correlation-intractable for all relations that are searchable within time T, where T denotes the maximal running time of algorithms* $\mathsf{BadChallenge}(\cdot,\cdot,\cdot,\cdot)$ *and* $\Pi^{\mathsf{LPKE}}.\mathsf{Decrypt}(\cdot,\cdot,\cdot)$. (The proof is given in the full version of the paper.)

4 An Adaptively Secure CCA2-Secure Threshold Encryption Scheme Based on Paillier and LWE

Our construction combines a one-time simulation-sound argument of composite residuosity with a threshold variant of an Elgamal-Paillier combination due to Camenisch and Shoup [20]. As in [66], we use a generalization of the Camenisch-Shoup system based on ideas from Damgård and Jurik [34].

For simplicity, we first present a non-robust version of the scheme. In the full version of the paper, we explain how to obtain robustness against malicious adversaries by having each server prove that its decryption share is consistent with some public commitment to its corresponding secret key share.

KeyGen$(1^\lambda, \mathbb{A})$**:** The dealer conducts the following steps:

1. Choose a safe-prime product $N = pq$, of which the prime factors are of the form $p = 2p' + 1$, $q = 2q' + 1$ for some primes primes $p', q' > 2^{l(\lambda)}$, where $l : \mathbb{N} \to \mathbb{N}$ is a polynomial. Choose an integer $\zeta \geq 1$ so as to define the message space as $\mathsf{MsgSp} = \mathbb{Z}_{N^\zeta}$. Then, define the language

$$\mathcal{L}^{\mathsf{DCR}} := \{x \in \mathbb{Z}^*_{N^{\zeta+1}} \mid \exists w \in \mathbb{Z}^\star_N : x = w^{N^\zeta} \bmod N^{\zeta+1}\}$$

and choose $g_0 \hookleftarrow U(\mathbb{Z}^*_N)$.

2. Generate a common reference string $\mathsf{crs} \leftarrow \mathsf{Setup}(1^\lambda)$ for the one-time simulation-sound argument system $\Pi^{\mathsf{OTSS}} = (\mathsf{Setup}, \mathsf{P}, \mathsf{V})$ of Sect. 3.
3. Let $\sigma > \sqrt{\lambda \cdot e} \cdot N^\zeta$ be a Gaussian parameter, where $e = \Omega(\ell^{(1+\sqrt{2})/2})$ is the dimension of the matrix $\mathbf{M}$ in Sect. 2.3. Sample a secret key $x \hookleftarrow D_{\mathbb{Z},\sigma}$ and compute $h = g_0^{4N^\zeta \cdot x} \bmod N^{\zeta+1}$. Define the public key $\mathsf{pk} := (N, \zeta, g_0, \mathsf{crs})$ whereas the centralized secret key $\mathsf{sk} := x \in \mathbb{Z}$.
4. Share sk using a LISS scheme. To this end, sample $\bar{\boldsymbol{\rho}} = (\rho_2, \ldots, \rho_e)^\top \hookleftarrow (D_{\mathbb{Z},\sigma})^{(e-1)}$, define $\boldsymbol{\rho} = [x \mid \bar{\boldsymbol{\rho}}^\top]^\top \in \mathbb{Z}^e$ and compute

$$\boldsymbol{s} = \begin{bmatrix} s_1 \\ \vdots \\ s_d \end{bmatrix} = \mathbf{M} \cdot \boldsymbol{\rho} \in \mathbb{Z}^d,$$

where $\mathbf{M} \in \mathbb{Z}^{d \times e}$ is the share-generating matrix of Sect. 2.3, which computes the Boolean formula associated with the threshold access structure $\mathbb{A}$. Then, define the private key shares as

$$\mathsf{sk}_i = \big(s_j\big)_{j \in \psi^{-1}(i)} = \big(\mathbf{M}_j \cdot \boldsymbol{\rho}\big)_{j \in \psi^{-1}(i)} \in \mathbb{Z}^{d_i} \qquad \forall i \in [\ell],$$

where $\mathbf{M}_j \in \mathbb{Z}^{1 \times e}$ denotes the j-th row of $\mathbf{M}$ while d_i stands for the number of rows assigned by the LISS scheme to server i.

Finally, output the public key $\mathsf{pk} = (N, \zeta, g_0, \mathsf{crs})$ and the vector of secret-key shares $(\mathsf{sk}_1, \mathsf{sk}_2, \ldots, \mathsf{sk}_\ell)$.

Encrypt$(\mathsf{pp}, \mathsf{pk}, \mathsf{Msg})$**:** To encrypt $\mathsf{Msg} \in \mathbb{Z}_{N^\zeta}$, choose $r \hookleftarrow U(\{0, \ldots, \lfloor N/4 \rfloor\})$ and compute

$$C_0 = {g_0}^{2N^\zeta \cdot r} \bmod N^{\zeta+1} \qquad C_1 = (1+N)^{\mathsf{Msg}} \cdot h^r \bmod N^{\zeta+1}$$

Then, using the witness $w = g_0^{2r} \bmod N$, compute a simulation-sound NIZK argument $\boldsymbol{\pi} \leftarrow \mathsf{P}\big(\mathsf{crs}, C_0, g_0^{2r} \bmod N, \mathsf{lbl}\big)$ that $C_0 \in \mathcal{L}^{\mathsf{DCR}}$ using the label $\mathsf{lbl} = C_1$. Then, return the ciphertext $\mathsf{ct} := (C_0, C_1, \boldsymbol{\pi})$.

PartDec$(\mathsf{pp}, \mathsf{sk}_i, \mathsf{ct})$**:** On input of its share $\mathsf{sk}_i = \{s_j = \mathbf{M}_j \cdot \boldsymbol{\rho}\}_{j \in \psi^{-1}(i)}$ and a ciphertext $\mathsf{ct} = (C_0, C_1, \boldsymbol{\pi})$, the i-th server does the following.

1. If $\mathsf{V}(\mathsf{crs}, C_0, \boldsymbol{\pi}, \mathsf{lbl}) = 0$, return $\perp$.
2. For each $j \in \psi^{-1}(i) = \{j_1, \ldots, j_{d_i}\}$, compute $\mu_{i,j} = C_0^{2 \cdot s_j} \bmod N^{\zeta+1}$ and return

$$\begin{aligned} \boldsymbol{\mu}_i &= (\mu_{i,j_1}, \ldots, \mu_{i,j_{d_i}}) \\ &= \big(C_0^{2 \cdot s_{j_1}} \bmod N^{\zeta+1}, \ \ldots, \ C_0^{2 \cdot s_{j_{d_i}}} \bmod N^{\zeta+1}\big) \in (\mathbb{Z}_{N^{\zeta+1}}^*)^{d_i}. \end{aligned}$$

Combine$\big(\mathsf{pp}, \mathcal{B} = (\mathcal{S} \in \mathbb{A}, \{\boldsymbol{\mu}_i\}_{i \in \mathcal{S}}), \mathsf{ct} = (C_0, C_1, \boldsymbol{\pi})\big)$**:** First, parse the set $\mathcal{S}$ as $\mathcal{S} = \{j_1, \ldots, j_t\}$ and find a vector $\boldsymbol{\lambda}_{\mathcal{S}} = [\boldsymbol{\lambda}_{j_1}^\top \mid \ldots \mid \boldsymbol{\lambda}_{j_t}^\top]^\top \in \{-1, 0, 1\}^{d_{\mathcal{S}}}$ such that $\boldsymbol{\lambda}_{\mathcal{S}} \cdot \mathbf{M}_{\psi^{-1}(\mathcal{S})} = (1, 0, \ldots, 0)$, where $d_{\mathcal{S}} = \sum_{i \in \mathcal{S}} d_i$ and $\boldsymbol{\lambda}_{j_i} = (\lambda_{j_i,1}, \ldots, \lambda_{j_i,d_{j_i}}) \in \{-1, 0, 1\}^{d_i}$ for all $i \in [t]$. Then, do the following:

1. Compute
$$\hat{\mu} \triangleq \prod_{i\in[t]} \prod_{k\in[d_{j_i}]} \mu_{j_i,k}^{\lambda_{j_i,k}} \bmod N^{\zeta+1}.$$
2. Compute $\hat{C}_1 = C_1/\hat{\mu} \bmod N^{\zeta+1}$ and return $\perp$ if $\hat{C}_1 \not\equiv 1 \pmod N$. Otherwise, return $\mathsf{Msg} = (\hat{C}_1 - 1)/N \in \mathbb{Z}_{N^\zeta}$.

In the dealing phase, the matrix $\mathbf{M} \in \mathbb{Z}^{d\times e}$ has $O(\log \ell)$ non-zero entries for threshold access structures. If we apply the LISS scheme based on the Benaloh-Leichter secret sharing [9] and the result of Hoory *et al.* [54], $\mathbf{M}$ has dimensions $d, e = O(\ell^{1+\sqrt{2}})$, so that its rows have norm $\|\mathbf{M}_j\| = O(\sqrt{e}\log \ell)$, which leads to share units of magnitude $|s_j| = O(\sigma e \cdot \log \ell)$.

The scheme thus provides compactness in the sense of Definition 2.13 since the size of ciphertexts and public keys only depends on λ. By increasing the exponent $\zeta > 1$, the ratio between ciphertext and plaintext sizes can approach 1, which was not possible in [62,65].[6] We now prove security in the sense of Definition 2.16.

Theorem 4.1. *The above scheme provides IND-CCA security in the adaptive corruption setting assuming that: (i) The* DCR *assumption holds; (ii) The argument system* Π^{OTSS} *provides one-time simulation-soundness.*

Proof. We consider a sequence of games where, for each i, we call W_i the event that the adversary wins in Game_i.

Game_0: This is the real IND-CCA game. The challenger faithfully answers all queries. In the challenge phase, the adversary $\mathcal{A}$ chooses two messages $\mathsf{Msg}_0, \mathsf{Msg}_1 \in \mathbb{Z}_{N^\zeta}$. The challenger flips a coin $b \hookleftarrow U(\{0,1\})$ and computes the challenge ciphertext $\mathsf{ct}^* = (C_0^*, C_1^*, \boldsymbol{\pi}^\star)$ by running the real encryption algorithm. When $\mathcal{A}$ halts, it outputs $b' \in \{0,1\}$ and we denote by W_0 the event that $b' = b$. By definition $\mathbf{Adv}^{\text{ind-cca}}(\mathcal{A}) := |\Pr[W_0] - 1/2|$.

Game_1: This game is identical to Game_0 except that we change the generation of the common reference string and the generation of $\boldsymbol{\pi}^\star$ in the challenge ciphertext. In the key generation phase, the challenger runs $(\mathsf{crs}, \tau_{\mathsf{zk}}) \leftarrow \mathsf{Sim}_0(1^\lambda, \mathcal{L}^{\mathsf{DCR}})$. In the challenge ciphertext $\mathsf{ct}^\star = (C_0^\star, C_1^\star, \boldsymbol{\pi}^\star)$, the NIZK argument $\boldsymbol{\pi}^\star$ is simulated as $\boldsymbol{\pi}^\star \leftarrow \mathsf{Sim}_1(\mathsf{crs}, \tau_{\mathsf{zk}}, C_0^\star, C_1^\star)$ without using the witness. From the perfect zero-knowledge property of Π^{OTSS}, Game_1 is indistinguishable from Game_0 and $\Pr[W_1] = \Pr[W_0]$.

Game_2: This game is identical to Game_1 except that we change the generation of the challenge ciphertext $\mathsf{ct}^\star = (C_0^\star, C_1^\star, \boldsymbol{\pi}^\star)$. Now, the challenger first samples $z_0 \hookleftarrow U(\mathbb{Z}_N^*)$, which is used to compute $z = z_0^{N^\zeta} \bmod N^{\zeta+1}$ and then
$$C_0^\star = z^2 \bmod N^{\zeta+1}, \qquad C_1^\star = (1+N)^{\mathsf{Msg}_b} \cdot C_0^{\star\,2x} \bmod N^{\zeta+1}, \tag{4}$$

[6] While the rate can be optimized via hybrid encryption, this would ruin the voting-friendly property of the scheme [12]. Moreover, the KEM/DEM framework does not immediately work in the threshold setting (see, e.g., [3]).

before simulating $\boldsymbol{\pi}^\star \leftarrow \mathsf{Sim}_1(\mathsf{crs}, \tau_{\mathsf{zk}}, C_0^\star, C_1^\star)$ as in Game_1. Since the subgroup of $2N^\zeta$-th residues is a cyclic group of order $p'q'$, the distribution of $(C_0^\star, C_1^\star)$ is statistically close to that of Game_1. Indeed, the distribution of $C_0^\star$ is now perfectly (instead of statistically) uniform in the subgroup of $2N^\zeta$-th residues. Hence, $|\Pr[W_2] - \Pr[W_1]| < 2^{-\Omega(\lambda)}$.

Game_3: This game is like Game_2 except that, in order to construct the challenge ciphertext, we now sample $z \hookleftarrow U(\mathbb{Z}_{N^{\zeta+1}}^*)$ uniformly in $\mathbb{Z}_{N^{\zeta+1}}^*$ instead of sampling it from the subgroup of N^ζ-th residues. Then, $(C_0^\star, C_1^\star)$ are still computed as per (4). Under the DCR assumption, this change goes unnoticed and a straightforward reduction shows that $|\Pr[W_3] - \Pr[W_2]| \leq \mathbf{Adv}^{\mathsf{DCR}}(\lambda)$.

At this point, we are done with the DCR assumption and we can henceforth use the factorization of N in subsequent games.

Game_4: In this game, the challenger rejects all pre-challenge partial decryption queries $\mathsf{ct} = (C_0, C_1, \boldsymbol{\pi})$ such that C_0 is not an N^ζ-th residue (note that this can be efficiently checked using the factorization of N). The soundness of the argument system (which is implied by its simulation-soundness) implies that the probability to reject a ciphertext that would not have been rejected in Game_3 is negligible: we have $|\Pr[W_4] - \Pr[W_3]| \leq \mathbf{Adv}^{\mathsf{OTSS}}(\lambda)$.

Game_5: We modify the partial decryption oracle and now reject post-challenge queries $\mathsf{ct} = (C_0, C_1, \boldsymbol{\pi})$ such that $(C_0, C_1, \boldsymbol{\pi}) \neq (C_0^\star, C_1^\star, \boldsymbol{\pi}^\star)$ and C_0 is not an N^ζ-th residue. By doing so, the challenger does not reject a ciphertext that would not have been rejected in Game_4 until the event F_5 that $\mathcal{A}$ queries the partial decryption of a ciphertext $\mathsf{ct} = (C_0, C_1, \boldsymbol{\pi}) \neq (C_0^\star, C_1^\star, \boldsymbol{\pi}^\star)$ such that $\mathsf{V}(\mathsf{crs}, C_0, \boldsymbol{\pi}, C_1) = 1$ although $C_0^{2p'q'} \bmod N^{\zeta+1} \neq 1$. Clearly, event F_5 would contradict the one-time simulation-soundness of the NIZK argument system Π^{OTSS}. We have $|\Pr[W_5] - \Pr[W_4]| \leq \mathbf{Adv}^{\mathsf{OTSS}}(\lambda)$.

Game_6: We finally modify the challenge ciphertext and now compute $(C_0^\star, C_1^\star)$ by sampling $C_0^\star \hookleftarrow \mathbb{QR}_{N^{\zeta+1}}$ as a random quadratic residue in $\mathbb{Z}_{N^{\zeta+1}}^*$ and computing $C_1^\star = (1+N)^{\mathsf{Msg}^\star} \cdot C_0^{\star 2x} \bmod N^{\zeta+1}$ for a random $\mathsf{Msg}^\star \hookleftarrow U(\mathbb{Z}_{N^\zeta})$. Lemma 4.2 shows that Game_6 and Game_5 are negligibly far apart in terms of statistical distance, so that $|\Pr[W_6] - \Pr[W_5]| \leq 2^{-\lambda}$.

In Game_6, we have $\Pr[W_6] = 1/2$ since $\mathsf{ct}^\star$ is completely independent of the challenger's bit $b \sim U(\{0,1\})$. □

Lemma 4.2. Game_6 *and* Game_5 *are statistically indistinguishable.*

Proof. The proof uses similar arguments to [4, Theorem 5]. In Game_5, the challenge ciphertext has components $(C_0^\star, C_1^\star)$ of the form

$$C_0^\star = (1+N)^{\alpha_z} \cdot g^{\beta_z} \bmod N^{\zeta+1},$$
$$C_1^\star = (1+N)^{\mathsf{Msg}_b + 2\alpha_z \cdot (x \bmod N^\zeta)} \cdot g^{2\beta_z \cdot (x \bmod p'q')} \bmod N^{\zeta+1},$$

with $g = g_0^{2N^\zeta} \bmod N^{\zeta+1}$ and for uniform $\alpha_z \sim U(\mathbb{Z}_{N^\zeta})$, $\beta_z \sim U(\mathbb{Z}_{p'q'})$. Since $\gcd(2\alpha_z, N^\zeta) = 1$ with overwhelming probability $\varphi(N)/N$, we only need to show that, from $\mathcal{A}$'s view, $x \bmod N^\zeta$ is statistically uniform over $\mathbb{Z}_{N^\zeta}$ in order to prove that the distribution of $(C_0^\star, C_1^\star)$ is statistically close to that of Game_6.

In Game_5, we note that the challenger rejects all ciphertexts $\mathsf{ct} = (C_0, C_1, \boldsymbol{\pi})$ such that $C_0 \notin \mathcal{L}^{\mathsf{DCR}}$ and $(C_0, C_1, \boldsymbol{\pi}) \neq (C_0^\star, C_1^\star, \boldsymbol{\pi}^\star)$. For each partial decryption query $(i, (C_0, C_1, \boldsymbol{\pi}))$ such that $C_0 \in \mathcal{L}^{\mathsf{DCR}}$, the adversary can only learn the information $\{\mathbf{M}_j \cdot \boldsymbol{\rho} \bmod p'q'\}_{j \in \psi^{-1}(i)}$. As for partial decryption queries involving the challenge ciphertext $\mathsf{ct}^\star = (C_0^\star, C_1^\star, \boldsymbol{\pi}^\star)$, we can handle them as if they were corruption queries since the latter reveal at least as much information as the former. Let $\mathcal{C}^\star$ the set of parties for which the adversary made either a corruption query or a decryption query on the challenge $\mathsf{ct}^\star = (C_0^\star, C_1^\star, \boldsymbol{\pi}^\star)$. Let $\mathbf{M}_{\mathcal{C}^\star}$ to be the sub-matrix of $\mathbf{M}$ obtained by stacking up the rows assigned to those parties.

Since $\mathcal{C}^\star$ is not authorized in $\mathbb{A}$, there exists $\boldsymbol{\kappa} \in \mathbb{Z}^e$ such that $\kappa_1 = 1$ and $\mathbf{M}_{\mathcal{C}^\star} \cdot \boldsymbol{\kappa} = \mathbf{0}^{d_{\mathcal{C}^\star}}$. Let a matrix $\mathbf{L}$ whose rows form a basis of the lattice $\{\mathbf{m} \in \mathbb{Z}^e, \langle \mathbf{m}, \boldsymbol{\kappa} \rangle = 0\}$, where the rows of $\mathbf{M}_{\mathcal{C}^\star}$ live. Note that $(\mathbf{L}, \mathbf{L} \cdot \boldsymbol{\rho})$ reveals at least as much information as $(\mathbf{M}_{\mathcal{C}^\star}, \mathbf{M}_{\mathcal{C}^\star} \cdot \boldsymbol{\rho})$, so that we may condition on $(\mathbf{L}, \mathbf{L} \cdot \boldsymbol{\rho})$. When we additionally condition on $(\mathbf{M}_{[\ell] \setminus \mathcal{C}^\star} \cdot \boldsymbol{\rho} \bmod p'q')$, we condition on something that reveals fewer information than $\boldsymbol{\rho} \bmod p'q'$.

Let an arbitrary vector $\boldsymbol{\rho}_0 \in \mathbb{Z}^e$ satisfying

$$\mathbf{L} \cdot \boldsymbol{\rho}_0 = \mathbf{L} \cdot \boldsymbol{\rho}, \qquad\qquad \boldsymbol{\rho}_0 \equiv \boldsymbol{\rho} \pmod{p'q'}.$$

The conditional distribution of $\boldsymbol{\rho}$ is $\boldsymbol{\rho}_0 + D_{\Lambda, \sigma, -\boldsymbol{\rho}_0}$, where

$$\Lambda = \{\boldsymbol{x} \in \mathbb{Z}^e \mid \mathbf{L} \cdot \boldsymbol{x} = 0 \quad \wedge \quad \boldsymbol{x} = \mathbf{0} \bmod p'q'\}$$

is the lattice $\Lambda = \boldsymbol{\kappa} \cdot \mathbb{Z} \cap (p'q' \cdot \mathbb{Z}^e) = (p'q' \cdot \mathbb{Z}) \cdot \boldsymbol{\kappa}$. Let us write $\boldsymbol{\rho}_0 = y \cdot \boldsymbol{\kappa} + (\boldsymbol{\rho}_0^\perp)$, where $y \in \mathbb{R}$ and $\boldsymbol{\rho}_0^\perp \in \mathbb{Z}^e$ is orthogonal to $\boldsymbol{\kappa}$. Conditionally on $\mathbf{L} \cdot \boldsymbol{\rho}$ and $\boldsymbol{\rho} \bmod p'q'$, the distribution of $\boldsymbol{\rho}$ can be written

$$\begin{aligned} \boldsymbol{\rho}_0 + D_{\Lambda, \sigma, -\boldsymbol{\rho}_0} &= (\boldsymbol{\rho}_0^\perp) + y \cdot \boldsymbol{\kappa} + D_{(p'q' \cdot \mathbb{Z}) \cdot \boldsymbol{\kappa}, \sigma, -(\boldsymbol{\rho}_0^\perp) - y \cdot \boldsymbol{\kappa}} \\ &= (\boldsymbol{\rho}_0^\perp) + y \cdot \boldsymbol{\kappa} + \boldsymbol{\kappa} \cdot D_{(p'q' \cdot \mathbb{Z}), \sigma / \|\boldsymbol{\kappa}\|, -y}. \end{aligned}$$

Since $\kappa_1 = 1$, the conditional distribution of $x = \langle (1, 0, \ldots, 0), \boldsymbol{\rho} \rangle$ is thus

$$c + D_{(p'q' \cdot \mathbb{Z}), \sigma / \|\boldsymbol{\kappa}\|, -y},$$

where $c = y + \langle (1, 0, \ldots, 0), \boldsymbol{\rho}_0^\perp \rangle$. We now consider the distribution obtained by reducing the distribution $D_{(p'q' \cdot \mathbb{Z}), \sigma / \|\boldsymbol{\kappa}\|, -y}$ over $\Lambda_0 = p'q' \cdot \mathbb{Z}$ modulo its sublattice $\Lambda_0' = (p'q') \cdot (N^\zeta \mathbb{Z})$. Since $p'q' \cdot N^\zeta < N^{\zeta+1}$, by Lemma 2.7, choosing the standard deviation $\sigma > \sqrt{\lambda \cdot e} \cdot N^{\zeta+1}$ suffices (by [51, Lemma 3.1] which implies $\eta_\epsilon(\Lambda_0') < \lambda^{1/2} N^{\zeta+1}$) to ensure that $x \bmod N^\zeta$ is within distance $2^{-\lambda}$ from $U(\Lambda_0 / \Lambda_0')$ conditionally on $\mathcal{A}$'s view. This completes the proof since $\gcd(p'q', N^\zeta) = 1$ implies $\Lambda_0 / \Lambda_0' \simeq \mathbb{Z}_{N^\zeta}$. □

In the full version of the paper, we show how to turn the scheme into a robust TPKE system. This is achieved by using trapdoor Σ-protocols to prove the validity of decryption shares. To this end, we need to first construct a standard Σ-protocol with binary challenges in order to apply the generic trapdoor

Σ-protocol construction of Ciampi *et al.* [26]. The disadvantage of this approach is that parallel repetitions incur a communication overhead $\Theta(\lambda)$. In applications to voting (where "non-malleable" ciphertext components are removed from ciphertexts before homomorphically processing them), this may be acceptable if proofs of correct partial decryptions are computed by trustees with higher computational resources than voters. It remains an interesting open problem to achieve robustness without parallel repetitions.

Acknowledgements. Part of this research was funded by the French ANR ALAMBIC project (ANR-16-CE39-0006). This work was also supported in part by the European Union PROMETHEUS project (Horizon 2020 Research and Innovation Program, grant 780701). Khoa Nguyen was supported in part by the Gopalakrishnan - NTU PPF 2018, by A*STAR, Singapore under research grant SERC A19E3b0099, and by Vietnam National University HoChiMinh City (VNU-HCM) under grant number NCM2019-18-01.

References

1. Abe, M.: Robust distributed multiplication without interaction. In: Wiener, M. (ed.) CRYPTO 1999. LNCS, vol. 1666, pp. 130–147. Springer, Heidelberg (1999). https://doi.org/10.1007/3-540-48405-1_9
2. Abe, M., Fehr, S.: Adaptively secure feldman vss and applications to universally-composable threshold cryptography. In: Franklin, M. (ed.) CRYPTO 2004. LNCS, vol. 3152, pp. 317–334. Springer, Heidelberg (2004). https://doi.org/10.1007/978-3-540-28628-8_20
3. Abe, M., Gennaro, R., Kurosawa, K., Shoup, V.: Tag-KEM/DEM: a new framework for hybrid encryption and a new analysis of Kurosawa-Desmedt KEM. In: Cramer, R. (ed.) EUROCRYPT 2005. LNCS, vol. 3494, pp. 128–146. Springer, Heidelberg (2005). https://doi.org/10.1007/11426639_8
4. Agrawal, S., Libert, B., Stehlé, D.: Fully secure functional encryption for inner products, from standard assumptions. In: Robshaw, M., Katz, J. (eds.) CRYPTO 2016. LNCS, vol. 9816, pp. 333–362. Springer, Heidelberg (2016). https://doi.org/10.1007/978-3-662-53015-3_12
5. Almansa, J.F., Damgård, I., Nielsen, J.B.: Simplified threshold RSA with adaptive and proactive security. In: Vaudenay, S. (ed.) EUROCRYPT 2006. LNCS, vol. 4004, pp. 593–611. Springer, Heidelberg (2006). https://doi.org/10.1007/11761679_35
6. Alperin-Sheriff, J., Peikert, C.: Circular and KDM security for identity-based encryption. In: PKC (2012)
7. Asharov, G., Jain, A., Wichs, D.: Multiparty computation with low communication, computation and interaction via threshold FHE. Cryptology ePrint Archive: Report 2011/613 (2012)
8. Bellare, M., Hofheinz, D., Yilek, S.: Possibility and impossibility results for encryption and commitment secure under selective opening. In: Joux, A. (ed.) EUROCRYPT 2009. LNCS, vol. 5479, pp. 1–35. Springer, Heidelberg (2009). https://doi.org/10.1007/978-3-642-01001-9_1
9. Benaloh, J., Leichter, J.: Generalized secret sharing and monotone functions. In: Goldwasser, S. (ed.) CRYPTO 1988. LNCS, vol. 403, pp. 27–35. Springer, New York (1990). https://doi.org/10.1007/0-387-34799-2_3

10. Bendlin, R., Damgård, I.: Threshold decryption and zero-knowledge proofs for lattice-based cryptosystems. In: Micciancio, D. (ed.) TCC 2010. LNCS, vol. 5978, pp. 201–218. Springer, Heidelberg (2010). https://doi.org/10.1007/978-3-642-11799-2_13
11. Bendlin, R., Krehbiel, S., Peikert, C.: How to share a lattice trapdoor: threshold protocols for signatures and (H)IBE. In: Jacobson, M., Locasto, M., Mohassel, P., Safavi-Naini, R. (eds.) ACNS 2013. LNCS, vol. 7954, pp. 218–236. Springer, Heidelberg (2013). https://doi.org/10.1007/978-3-642-38980-1_14
12. Bernhard, D., Cortier, V., Pereira, O., Smyth, B., Warinschi, B.: Adapting helios for provable ballot privacy. In: Atluri, V., Diaz, C. (eds.) ESORICS 2011. LNCS, vol. 6879, pp. 335–354. Springer, Heidelberg (2011). https://doi.org/10.1007/978-3-642-23822-2_19
13. Boneh, D., Boyen, X.: Secure identity based encryption without random oracles. In: Franklin, M. (ed.) CRYPTO 2004. LNCS, vol. 3152, pp. 443–459. Springer, Heidelberg (2004). https://doi.org/10.1007/978-3-540-28628-8_27
14. Boneh, D., Boyen, X., Halevi, S.: Chosen ciphertext secure public key threshold encryption without random oracles. In: Pointcheval, D. (ed.) CT-RSA 2006. LNCS, vol. 3860, pp. 226–243. Springer, Heidelberg (2006). https://doi.org/10.1007/11605805_15
15. Boneh, D., et al.: Threshold cryptosystems from threshold fully homomorphic encryption. In: Shacham, H., Boldyreva, A. (eds.) CRYPTO 2018. LNCS, vol. 10991, pp. 565–596. Springer, Cham (2018). https://doi.org/10.1007/978-3-319-96884-1_19
16. Boneh, D., Lewi, K., Montgomery, H., Raghunathan, A.: Key homomorphic PRFs and their applications. In: Canetti, R., Garay, J.A. (eds.) CRYPTO 2013. LNCS, vol. 8042, pp. 410–428. Springer, Heidelberg (2013). https://doi.org/10.1007/978-3-642-40041-4_23
17. Boyd, C.: Digital multisignatures. In: Cryptography and Coding (1989)
18. Boyen, X., Mei, Q., Waters, B.: Direct chosen-ciphertext security from identity-based techniques. In: ACM-CCS (2005)
19. Boyle, E., Segev, G., Wichs, D.: Fully leakage-resilient signatures. In: Paterson, K.G. (ed.) EUROCRYPT 2011. LNCS, vol. 6632, pp. 89–108. Springer, Heidelberg (2011). https://doi.org/10.1007/978-3-642-20465-4_7
20. Camenisch, J., Shoup, V.: Practical verifiable encryption and decryption of discrete logarithms. In: Boneh, D. (ed.) CRYPTO 2003. LNCS, vol. 2729, pp. 126–144. Springer, Heidelberg (2003). https://doi.org/10.1007/978-3-540-45146-4_8
21. Canetti, R., et al.: Fiat-Shamir: from practice to theory. In: STOC (2019)
22. Canetti, R., Gennaro, R., Jarecki, S., Krawczyk, H., Rabin, T.: Adaptive security for threshold cryptosystems. In: Wiener, M. (ed.) CRYPTO 1999. LNCS, vol. 1666, pp. 98–116. Springer, Heidelberg (1999). https://doi.org/10.1007/3-540-48405-1_7
23. Canetti, R., Goldwasser, S.: An efficient *threshold* public key cryptosystem secure against adaptive chosen ciphertext attack (extended abstract). In: Stern, J. (ed.) EUROCRYPT 1999. LNCS, vol. 1592, pp. 90–106. Springer, Heidelberg (1999). https://doi.org/10.1007/3-540-48910-X_7
24. Canetti, R., Halevi, S., Katz, J.: Chosen-ciphertext security from identity-based encryption. In: Cachin, C., Camenisch, J.L. (eds.) EUROCRYPT 2004. LNCS, vol. 3027, pp. 207–222. Springer, Heidelberg (2004). https://doi.org/10.1007/978-3-540-24676-3_13
25. Canetti, R., Lombardi, A., Wichs, D.: Fiat-shamir: from practice to theory, Part II (NIZK and correlation intractability from circular-secure FHE). Cryptology ePrint Archive: Report 2018/1248 (2018)

26. Ciampi, M., Parisella, R., Venturi, D.: On adaptive security of delayed-input sigma protocols and Fiat-Shamir NIZKs. In: Galdi, C., Kolesnikov, V. (eds.) SCN 2020. LNCS, vol. 12238, pp. 670–690. Springer, Cham (2020). https://doi.org/10.1007/978-3-030-57990-6_33
27. Cramer, R.: Modular design of secure, yet practical cryptographic protocols. Ph.D. thesis, University of Amsterdam (1996)
28. Cramer, R., Damgård, I., Ishai, Y.: Share conversion, pseudorandom secret-sharing and applications to secure computation. In: Kilian, J. (ed.) TCC 2005. LNCS, vol. 3378, pp. 342–362. Springer, Heidelberg (2005). https://doi.org/10.1007/978-3-540-30576-7_19
29. Cramer, R., Damgård, I., Schoenmakers, B.: Proofs of partial knowledge and simplified design of witness hiding protocols. In: Desmedt, Y.G. (ed.) CRYPTO 1994. LNCS, vol. 839, pp. 174–187. Springer, Heidelberg (1994). https://doi.org/10.1007/3-540-48658-5_19
30. Cramer, R., Fehr, S.: Optimal black-box secret sharing over arbitrary Abelian groups. In: Yung, M. (ed.) CRYPTO 2002. LNCS, vol. 2442, pp. 272–287. Springer, Heidelberg (2002). https://doi.org/10.1007/3-540-45708-9_18
31. Cramer, R., Shoup, V.: A practical public key cryptosystem provably secure against adaptive chosen ciphertext attack. In: Krawczyk, H. (ed.) CRYPTO 1998. LNCS, vol. 1462, pp. 13–25. Springer, Heidelberg (1998). https://doi.org/10.1007/BFb0055717
32. Cramer, R., Shoup, V.: Universal hash proofs and a paradigm for adaptive chosen ciphertext secure public-key encryption. In: Knudsen, L.R. (ed.) EUROCRYPT 2002. LNCS, vol. 2332, pp. 45–64. Springer, Heidelberg (2002). https://doi.org/10.1007/3-540-46035-7_4
33. Damgård, I.: Efficient concurrent zero-knowledge in the auxiliary string model. In: Preneel, B. (ed.) EUROCRYPT 2000. LNCS, vol. 1807, pp. 418–430. Springer, Heidelberg (2000). https://doi.org/10.1007/3-540-45539-6_30
34. Damgård, I., Jurik, M.: A generalisation, a simplification and some applications of Paillier's probabilistic public-key system. In: Kim, K. (ed.) PKC 2001. LNCS, vol. 1992, pp. 119–136. Springer, Heidelberg (2001). https://doi.org/10.1007/3-540-44586-2_9
35. Damgård, I., Thorbek, R.: Linear integer secret sharing and distributed exponentiation. In: Yung, M., Dodis, Y., Kiayias, A., Malkin, T. (eds.) PKC 2006. LNCS, vol. 3958, pp. 75–90. Springer, Heidelberg (2006). https://doi.org/10.1007/11745853_6
36. De Santis, A., Desmedt, Y., Frankel, Y., Yung, M.: How to share a function securely. In: STOC (1994)
37. De Santis, A., Di Crescenzo, G., Ostrovsky, R., Persiano, G., Sahai, A.: Robust non-interactive zero knowledge. In: Kilian, J. (ed.) CRYPTO 2001. LNCS, vol. 2139, pp. 566–598. Springer, Heidelberg (2001). https://doi.org/10.1007/3-540-44647-8_33
38. Desmedt, Y.: Society and group oriented cryptography: a new concept. In: Pomerance, C. (ed.) CRYPTO 1987. LNCS, vol. 293, pp. 120–127. Springer, Heidelberg (1988). https://doi.org/10.1007/3-540-48184-2_8
39. Desmedt, Y., Frankel, Y.: Threshold cryptosystems. In: Brassard, G. (ed.) CRYPTO 1989. LNCS, vol. 435, pp. 307–315. Springer, New York (1990). https://doi.org/10.1007/0-387-34805-0_28
40. Devevey, J., Libert, B., Nguyen, K., Peters, T., Yung, M.: Non-interactive CCA2-secure threshold cryptosystems: achieving adaptive security in the standard model without pairings. Full version, Cryptology ePrint Archive Report (2021)

41. Dodis, Y., Fazio, N.: Public Key trace and revoke scheme secure against adaptive chosen ciphertext attack. In: Desmedt, Y.G. (ed.) PKC 2003. LNCS, vol. 2567, pp. 100–115. Springer, Heidelberg (2003). https://doi.org/10.1007/3-540-36288-6_8
42. Dodis, Y., Katz, J.: Chosen-ciphertext security of multiple encryption. In: Kilian, J. (ed.) TCC 2005. LNCS, vol. 3378, pp. 188–209. Springer, Heidelberg (2005). https://doi.org/10.1007/978-3-540-30576-7_11
43. Faust, S., Kohlweiss, M., Marson, G.A., Venturi, D.: On the non-malleability of the fiat-shamir transform. In: Galbraith, S., Nandi, M. (eds.) INDOCRYPT 2012. LNCS, vol. 7668, pp. 60–79. Springer, Heidelberg (2012). https://doi.org/10.1007/978-3-642-34931-7_5
44. Feller, W.: An Introduction to Probability theory and Its Applications. Wiley, New York (1968)
45. Fiat, A., Shamir, A.: How to prove yourself: practical solutions to identification and signature problems. In: Odlyzko, A.M. (ed.) CRYPTO 1986. LNCS, vol. 263, pp. 186–194. Springer, Heidelberg (1987). https://doi.org/10.1007/3-540-47721-7_12
46. Fouque, P.-A., Pointcheval, D.: Threshold cryptosystems secure against chosen-ciphertext attacks. In: Boyd, C. (ed.) ASIACRYPT 2001. LNCS, vol. 2248, pp. 351–368. Springer, Heidelberg (2001). https://doi.org/10.1007/3-540-45682-1_21
47. Frankel, Y., Gemmell, P., MacKenzie, P., Yung, M.: Optimal-resilience proactive public-key cryptosystems. In: FOCS (1997)
48. Frankel, Y., MacKenzie, P., Yung, M.: Adaptively-secure distributed public-key systems. In: Nešetřil, J. (ed.) ESA 1999. LNCS, vol. 1643, pp. 4–27. Springer, Heidelberg (1999). https://doi.org/10.1007/3-540-48481-7_2
49. Garay, J.A., MacKenzie, P., Yang, K.: Strengthening zero-knowledge protocols using signatures. In: Biham, E. (ed.) EUROCRYPT 2003. LNCS, vol. 2656, pp. 177–194. Springer, Heidelberg (2003). https://doi.org/10.1007/3-540-39200-9_11
50. Gentry, C.: Fully homomorphic encryption using ideal lattices. In: STOC (2009)
51. Gentry, C., Peikert, C., Vaikuntanathan, V.: Trapdoors for hard lattices and new cryptographic constructions. In: STOC (2008)
52. Goldreich, O.: On (Valiant's) polynomial-size monotone formula for majority. In: Goldreich, O. (ed.) Computational Complexity and Property Testing. LNCS, vol. 12050, pp. 17–23. Springer, Cham (2020). https://doi.org/10.1007/978-3-030-43662-9_3
53. Groth, J., Sahai, A.: Efficient non-interactive proof systems for bilinear groups. In: Smart, N. (ed.) EUROCRYPT 2008. LNCS, vol. 4965, pp. 415–432. Springer, Heidelberg (2008). https://doi.org/10.1007/978-3-540-78967-3_24
54. Hoory, S., Magen, A., Pitassi, T.: Monotone circuits for the majority function. In: Díaz, J., Jansen, K., Rolim, J.D.P., Zwick, U. (eds.) APPROX/RANDOM -2006. LNCS, vol. 4110, pp. 410–425. Springer, Heidelberg (2006). https://doi.org/10.1007/11830924_38
55. Jarecki, S., Lysyanskaya, A.: Adaptively secure threshold cryptography: introducing concurrency, removing erasures. In: Preneel, B. (ed.) EUROCRYPT 2000. LNCS, vol. 1807, pp. 221–242. Springer, Heidelberg (2000). https://doi.org/10.1007/3-540-45539-6_16
56. Jutla, C.S., Roy, A.: Shorter quasi-adaptive NIZK proofs for linear subspaces. In: Sako, K., Sarkar, P. (eds.) ASIACRYPT 2013. LNCS, vol. 8269, pp. 1–20. Springer, Heidelberg (2013). https://doi.org/10.1007/978-3-642-42033-7_1
57. Katz, J., Vaikuntanathan, V.: Smooth projective hashing and password-based authenticated key exchange from lattices. In: Matsui, M. (ed.) ASIACRYPT 2009. LNCS, vol. 5912, pp. 636–652. Springer, Heidelberg (2009). https://doi.org/10.1007/978-3-642-10366-7_37

58. Kiltz, E.: Chosen-ciphertext security from tag-based encryption. In: Halevi, S., Rabin, T. (eds.) TCC 2006. LNCS, vol. 3876, pp. 581–600. Springer, Heidelberg (2006). https://doi.org/10.1007/11681878_30
59. Lewko, A., Waters, B.: Decentralizing attribute-based encryption. In: Paterson, K.G. (ed.) EUROCRYPT 2011. LNCS, vol. 6632, pp. 568–588. Springer, Heidelberg (2011). https://doi.org/10.1007/978-3-642-20465-4_31
60. Libert, B., Nguyen, K., Passelègue, A., Titiu, R.: Simulation-sound arguments for LWE and applications to KDM-CCA2 security. In: Moriai, S., Wang, H. (eds.) ASIACRYPT 2020. LNCS, vol. 12491, pp. 128–158. Springer, Cham (2020). https://doi.org/10.1007/978-3-030-64837-4_5
61. Libert, B., Nguyen, K., Peters, T., Yung, M.: One-shot fiat-shamir-based NIZK arguments of composite residuosity in the standard model. Cryptology ePrint Archive: Report 2020/1334 (2020)
62. Libert, B., Peters, T., Joye, M., Yung, M.: Non-malleability from malleability: simulation-sound quasi-adaptive NIZK proofs and CCA2-secure encryption from homomorphic signatures. In: Nguyen, P.Q., Oswald, E. (eds.) EUROCRYPT 2014. LNCS, vol. 8441, pp. 514–532. Springer, Heidelberg (2014). https://doi.org/10.1007/978-3-642-55220-5_29
63. Libert, B., Stehlé, D., Titiu, R.: Adaptively secure distributed PRFs from LWE. In: TCC (2018)
64. Libert, B., Yung, M.: Adaptively secure non-interactive threshold cryptosystems. In: Aceto, L., Henzinger, M., Sgall, J. (eds.) ICALP 2011. LNCS, vol. 6756, pp. 588–600. Springer, Heidelberg (2011). https://doi.org/10.1007/978-3-642-22012-8_47
65. Libert, B., Yung, M.: Non-interactive CCA-secure threshold cryptosystems with adaptive security: new framework and constructions. In: Cramer, R. (ed.) TCC 2012. LNCS, vol. 7194, pp. 75–93. Springer, Heidelberg (2012). https://doi.org/10.1007/978-3-642-28914-9_5
66. Miao, P., Patel, S., Raykova, M., Seth, K., Yung, M.: Two-sided malicious security for private intersection-sum with cardinality. In: Micciancio, D., Ristenpart, T. (eds.) CRYPTO 2020. LNCS, vol. 12172, pp. 3–33. Springer, Cham (2020). https://doi.org/10.1007/978-3-030-56877-1_1
67. Micciancio, D., Peikert, C.: Trapdoors for lattices: simpler, tighter, faster, smaller. In: Pointcheval, D., Johansson, T. (eds.) EUROCRYPT 2012. LNCS, vol. 7237, pp. 700–718. Springer, Heidelberg (2012). https://doi.org/10.1007/978-3-642-29011-4_41
68. Micciancio, D., Regev, O.: Worst-case to average-case reductions based on Gaussian measures. SIAM J. Comput. **37**(1), 267–302 (2007)
69. Naor, M., Yung, M.: Public-key cryptosystems provably secure against chosen ciphertext attacks. In: STOC (1990)
70. Ostrovsky, R., Yung, M.: How to withstand mobile virus attacks. In: PODC (1991)
71. Paillier, P.: Public-key cryptosystems based on composite degree residuosity classes. In: Stern, J. (ed.) EUROCRYPT 1999. LNCS, vol. 1592, pp. 223–238. Springer, Heidelberg (1999). https://doi.org/10.1007/3-540-48910-X_16
72. Peikert, C., Shiehian, S.: Noninteractive zero knowledge for NP from (Plain) learning with Errors. In: Boldyreva, A., Micciancio, D. (eds.) CRYPTO 2019. LNCS, vol. 11692, pp. 89–114. Springer, Cham (2019). https://doi.org/10.1007/978-3-030-26948-7_4
73. Rabin, T.: A simplified approach to threshold and proactive RSA. In: Krawczyk, H. (ed.) CRYPTO 1998. LNCS, vol. 1462, pp. 89–104. Springer, Heidelberg (1998). https://doi.org/10.1007/BFb0055722

74. Rackoff, C., Simon, D.R.: Non-interactive zero-knowledge proof of knowledge and chosen ciphertext attack. In: Feigenbaum, J. (ed.) CRYPTO 1991. LNCS, vol. 576, pp. 433–444. Springer, Heidelberg (1992). https://doi.org/10.1007/3-540-46766-1_35
75. Regev, O.: On lattices, learning with errors, random linear codes, and cryptography. In: STOC (2005)
76. Sahai, A.: Non-malleable non-interactive zero knowledge and adaptive chosen-ciphertext security. In: FOCS (1999)
77. Shoup, V., Gennaro, R.: Securing threshold cryptosystems against chosen ciphertext attack. In: Nyberg, K. (ed.) EUROCRYPT 1998. LNCS, vol. 1403, pp. 1–16. Springer, Heidelberg (1998). https://doi.org/10.1007/BFb0054113
78. Shoup, V., Gennaro, R.: Securing threshold cryptosystems against chosen ciphertext attack. J. Cryptol. **15**(2), 75–96 (2002)
79. Thorbek, R.: Linear integer secret sharing. Ph.D. thesis, Aarhus University (2009)
80. Valiant, L.G.: Short monotone formulae for the majority function, vol. 5, pp. 363–366. Elsevier (1984)
81. Wee, H.: Threshold and revocation cryptosystems via extractable hash proofs. In: Paterson, K.G. (ed.) EUROCRYPT 2011. LNCS, vol. 6632, pp. 589–609. Springer, Heidelberg (2011). https://doi.org/10.1007/978-3-642-20465-4_32
82. Wee, H.: Dual projective hashing and its applications — lossy trapdoor functions and more. In: Pointcheval, D., Johansson, T. (eds.) EUROCRYPT 2012. LNCS, vol. 7237, pp. 246–262. Springer, Heidelberg (2012). https://doi.org/10.1007/978-3-642-29011-4_16
83. Xie, X., Xue, R., Zhang, R.: Efficient threshold encryption from lossy trapdoor functions. In: Yang, B.-Y. (ed.) PQCrypto 2011. LNCS, vol. 7071, pp. 163–178. Springer, Heidelberg (2011). https://doi.org/10.1007/978-3-642-25405-5_11

Updatable Signatures and Message Authentication Codes

Valerio Cini[1(✉)], Sebastian Ramacher[1], Daniel Slamanig[1], Christoph Striecks[1], and Erkan Tairi[2]

[1] AIT Austrian Institute of Technology, Vienna, Austria
{valerio.cini,sebastian.ramacher,daniel.slamanig, christoph.striecks}@ait.ac.at
[2] TU Wien, Vienna, Austria
erkan.tairi@tuwien.ac.at

Abstract. Cryptographic objects with updating capabilities have been proposed by Bellare, Goldreich and Goldwasser (CRYPTO'94) under the umbrella of incremental cryptography. They have recently seen increased interest, motivated by theoretical questions (Ananth et al., EC'17) as well as concrete practical motivations (Lehmann et al., EC'18; Groth et al. CRYPTO'18; Klooß et al., EC'19). In this work, the form of updatability we are particularly interested in is that primitives are key-updatable *and* allow to update "old" cryptographic objects, e.g., signatures or message authentication codes, from the "old" key to the updated key at the same time without requiring full access to the new key (i.e., only via a so-called update token).

Inspired by the rigorous study of updatable encryption by Lehmann and Tackmann (EC'18) and Boyd et al. (CRYPTO'20), we introduce a definitional framework for updatable signatures (USs) and message authentication codes (UMACs). We discuss several applications demonstrating that such primitives can be useful in practical applications, especially around key rotation in various domains, as well as serve as building blocks in other cryptographic schemes. We then turn to constructions and our focus there is on ones that are secure and practically efficient. In particular, we provide generic constructions from key-homomorphic primitives (signatures and PRFs) as well as direct constructions. This allows us to instantiate these primitives from various assumptions such as DDH or CDH (latter in bilinear groups), or the (R)LWE and the SIS assumptions. As an example, we obtain highly practical US schemes from BLS signatures or UMAC schemes from the Naor-Pinkas-Reingold PRF.

1 Introduction

Updatable cryptographic primitives, initially introduced as incremental cryptography [10,11], support the transformation of one cryptographic object to a related one without recomputing it entirely and have been widely studied (cf. [6] for an overview). Recently, Ananth et al. in [2] studied a unified approach towards

J. A. Garay (Ed.): PKC 2021, LNCS 12710, pp. 691–723, 2021.
https://doi.org/10.1007/978-3-030-75245-3_25

adding updatability features to many cryptographic primitives such as attribute-based encryption, functional encryption or more generally cryptographic circuit compilers. Moreover, they study the updatability for classical protocols such as zero-knowledge proofs and secure multi-party computation. Their constructions thereby rely on a novel updatable version of randomized encodings [4,33]. Besides exploring such updatable primitives from a rather theoretical perspective, there have been various interesting lines of work on specific updatable primitives inspired by concrete practical applications. For instance, Groth et al. in [32] introduce the notion of an updatable common reference string (CRS) and apply it to zk-SNARKs (used within many real world protocols in the cryptocurrency and distributed ledger domain) to reduce the trust in the generator of the CRS and cope with malicious CRS generators. Later in [43] Lipmaa studied quasi-adaptive NIZK (QA-NIZK) proofs in an updatable CRS setting where in addition to CRS updates "old" valid proofs can be updated to be still valid under an updated CRS. Another such primitive that is strongly motivated by practical applications and has recently been studied quite intensively is updatable encryption (UE) [14,15,18,27,35,40,42]. An UE scheme is a symmetric encryption scheme that allows the key holder to update keys and to compute an update token, which can be given to a party storing ciphertexts, and can be used to update existing ciphertexts to ones under the new key. UE is motivated by the fact that it is a good key management practice to change encryption keys periodically and it avoids the cumbersome requirement to download, decrypt and re-encrypt and upload all the data again.

Motivation. Our work is now essentially motivated by this previous work on UE and the observation that it is equally important in context of signatures and message authentication codes (MACs) to follow good key management practices and to periodically switch keys. For instance, any kind of software distribution channels including App stores or operating system updates rely on signatures to ensure the authenticity of the software they distribute. Moreover, file systems or (outsourced) databases usually require signatures or MACs to ensure integrity of stored data (we discuss this in more detail later in this section). What we envision therefore are signatures and MACs that are updatable in a sense that, similar to UE, holders of a secret key can compute a token that allows some third party to update existing signatures and MACs to ones valid under the new key. Thereby, we want to guarantee unforgeability even if the adversary can see lots of different keys and tokens with the restriction that we exclude trivial forgeries (we discuss this possible leakage in more detail later).

Related and Previous Work. While there are notions of signatures that support updating keys or even guarantee unforgeability when allowing queries under (adversarially) updated keys, none of them rigorously covers what we have sketched above and in particular guaranteeing security even if signatures can be updated between different keys. Closest are updatable signatures by Klooß et al. [40] implicitly used in one of their UE constructions. But they do not treat their security in the updatable setting and rather sketch how they can be obtained from unforgeable signatures in combination with generic properties of the token generation. Key-updatable signatures by Jaeger and Stepanovs [34] or key-updating signatures by Jost et al. [38] proposed in context of secure messaging allow to update keys and obtain signatures under updated keys, but do not consider signature updates. Similarly, signatures with re-randomizable keys by Fleischhacker et al. [29] consider adversarially chosen updates of the secret key (and access to a signing oracle under updated keys), but do not consider updating existing signatures. Somewhat orthogonal, key-homomorphic signatures by Derler and Slamanig [25] consider updating keys as well as updating existing signatures (this concept is similar to key-homomorphic PRFs [15]). But they only study the required properties functional-wise and do not consider an unforgeability notion (rather they implicitly prove them for their respective applications). Nevertheless, as we will see these key-homomorphic signatures and key-homomorphic PRFs [8,15,39] can be used as the basis for some constructions of US and UMACs, respectively. Finally, there is a recent notion of updatable signatures by Abdolmaleki et al. [1], which however focuses on key-update tokens that serve as a proof of correct update and allow extractability of update keys in order to be used within zk-SNARKs with updatable CRS.

Our Framework for Updatable Signatures and MACs. Since none of the existing works cover updatable signatures with strong security guarantees (and there is to the best of our knowledge no work related to updatable MACs), our goal is to design a comprehensive framework and security model. Therefore, similar to models for UE [18,42], we use the concept of epochs, where each epoch e has an associated key-pair (sk_e, pk_e) of a signature scheme starting with an initial key-pair in epoch 1 (all the discussion below analogously applies to UMACs). An US scheme then provides the functionality that in epoch e given (sk_e, pk_e) we can compute a key-pair (sk_{e+1}, pk_{e+1}) for the next epoch together with an update token Δ_{e+1} that is capable of updating signatures under a key from epoch e to $e+1$. Our focus is on schemes where these update tokens are independent of the signature and so Δ_{e+1} can be used for any signature from epoch e. We want that the schemes support an arbitrary number of epochs (any polynomial in the security parameters) but to support schemes from lattice assumptions we also consider a bounded number of epochs (bounded US) with a concrete bound T that usually depends on some parameters of the scheme. The goal is now to achieve strong security guarantees, in particular, the US scheme stays secure even after signing keys are compromised (a feature which is called post-compromise secrecy) and also before signing keys get corrupted (a feature called forward secrecy). Furthermore, outside of our model, we consider as an additional practical feature of US and UMAC the so called message-independence. This means that the update functionality only requires the update token and a signature, but does not need to access the respective message.

For unforgeability, we allow the adversary to trigger arbitrary signature computations, computations of next keys and updates adaptively and also adaptively compromise tokens and signing keys. We thereby use the concept of leakage profiles originally defined in [42] and also used in [18] to capture key, token, and signature "leakage" that cannot be captured by the oracles in the security experiment. The reason is that due to the nature of updates, US schemes inherently allow for information leakage of updated message-signature pairs, keys, and tokens besides what is modeled in the security experiment. For instance, if the adversary compromises a secret key sk_e and a token Δ_{e+1} it might be possible to derive sk_{e+1} (or sk_e from key sk_{e+1} and token Δ_{e+1}). Also, a token Δ_e besides allowing to update signatures into the next epoch may also allow to switch signatures back to previous epochs. However, we stress that in contrast to UE, where no-directional UE schemes are highly desirable, for US it does not seem to be that useful. The reason is that upgrading old signatures is covered by correctness (and thus cannot be prevented) and preventing switching keys or signatures back to previous epochs is only required if old public keys are not considered revoked (and we currently do not see such applications).

In addition to the unforgeability notion, we also provide an unlinkability notion that essentially says that updated signatures cannot be distinguished from fresh signatures. More precisely, we require that an adversary even when given all signing keys, tokens as well as signatures is not able to distinguish a fresh signature from an updated version of the signature that it already holds. While this property does not seem essential to the practical applications discussed below, we discuss cryptographic applications where this notion is important.

Exploring Applications. We will now discuss practical as well as cryptographic applications of US and UMACs.

Key Rotation in Software Distributions with US. Software distribution channels including App stores such as Google Play [26,31,52], Apple's App Store [3], or Microsoft's Windows Apps [45] and Windows Updates, or Linux distributions such as Debian [41], Ubuntu, Red Hat [49] and Arch Linux [5] rely on signatures to ensure the authenticity of their software packages. In one way or another, they either sign indices including hashes of the software packages or sign the software packages directly. For the latter, packages are often signed by individual developers whose keys are either signed by some central party like the app store provider or are shipped to the user directly via keyring packages containing all trusted keys. In this setting, key rotation of individual developer keys becomes an issue, since, if keys are rotated, all software packages signed by the old key have to be re-signed with the new one. The same issue can also be observed in the context of signed boot loaders and kernels for secure boot [44]. When relying on US, key rotation of developer keys becomes less of a burden on the developer. Indeed, the developer would update the key and produce an update token which is then used to update all signatures from this developer. Thus, instead of the developer having to re-sign all their packages, the signature adaption can be outsourced to a service run by the app store. Note that the effort for certifying new or updated keys would be the same in both settings.

File System and (Outsourced) Database Integrity with UMACs. Modern file systems including zfs [54] ensure the on-disk data integrity by storing hashes of the data. Additionally, when replicating data from one storage pool to another, the digests ensure integrity during transport. Similarly, databases support integrity checks which are helpful for replication and backups. Especially interesting is the application to outsourced databases [46,53], where in case of key-rotation the use of an UMAC enables these updates to be performed without re-computing all the authentication tags from scratch and without giving the actual key to the third party hosting the database.

Malleable Signatures and Revocation in Privacy Protocols. Redactable signatures (RS) [37,51] and sanitizable signatures (SS) [7,19] are malleable signatures that allow to remove parts from signed messages or replace designated parts of signed messages by designated parties without invalidating the signatures. They have numerous applications, but due to their selective disclosure functionality are especially attractive to protect privacy in medical documents when shared with other parties. Replacing the conventional EUF-CMA secure signature scheme that typically serves as a building block in such schemes with an US can, similar to the above applications, help to reduce re-signing effort in case of a key-rotation. This is particularly interesting when large amounts of signed medical documents are involved. US providing unlinkability can firstly help if one requires unlinkability from the respective RS or SS scheme (cf. [20] for a discussion of the linkability problem when joining different versions of a document to derive additional information) even over different versions of one document under different (updated) keys. Secondly, unlinkable RS [21,50] serve as a building block to construct anonymous credentials (ACs). In this context, unlinkable US allow to realize credential revocation in the following way: the issuer can provide an update token to a service that receives signatures from users and only updates credentials of non-revoked users to the current issuer key. Unlinkability of the US thereby in particular guarantees that it is hard to distinguish between credentials of non-revoked users from that of newly joined users. The same revocation idea can also be applied to replace re-issuing based revocation [17] in group signatures that follow the sign-randomize-prove paradigm [12,24,48]. Moreover, UMACs seem to be suitable for the same purpose in keyed-verification ACs [22], i.e., ACs where issuer and verifier are the same entity, typically constructed from algebraic MACs instead of signatures. An in-depth study of these cryptographic applications of US and UMACs is considered as future work.

CCA-Secure UE with Ciphertext Integrity Using UMACs. Klooß et al. [40] showed how to achieve CCA security and ciphertext integrity for UE using the Encrypt-and-MAC transformation. Their transformation requires encryption and MAC schemes that support key-rotation. In [40] the key-rotatable MAC was instantiated using the DDH-based PRF (NPR) [47] using a key-switching akin to the proxy re-encryption approach due to Blaze et al. [13]. We note that a UMAC satisfies the key-rotatable property, and hence, can be directly plugged into the described transformation to obtain CCA-secure UE with ciphertext integrity by using a suitable encryption scheme and any UMAC.

Further Contributions. Besides the already discussed comprehensive framework for US and UMACs, we provide the following contributions:

US and UMAC from KH Primitives. We construct US from key-homomorphic (KH) signatures [25], which satisfy some additional requirement that all natural schemes provide. Due to the properties of KH signatures, they are unlinkable. With respect to provable security, we use a proof-technique that is inspired by the key-insulation technique due to Klooß et al. [40], where we essentially can use the unlinkability property of the underlying KH signature. Similarly, we obtain fixed-length UMACs from key-homomorphic PRFs [15], which we generically turn into variable-input UMACs and our proof technique essentially follows the ones for signatures. This allows us to instantiate US and UMACs from various assumptions such as DDH or CDH (latter in bilinear groups). For instance, we achieve instantiations for highly practical US schemes from BLS signatures [16] or UMAC schemes from the Naor-Pinkas-Reingold PRF [47]. Interestingly, by using some tricks, we can show how to generically construct UMACs from "almost" key-homomorphic PRFs [15] leading to constructions from the (R)LWE assumption, and thus, post-quantum UMACs. Unfortunately, there are no known key-homomorphic signatures with the required properties from post-quantum assumptions. Consequently, we investigate direct constructions of US from lattices. On the positive side we are able to provide a US construction based on the probabilistic GPV scheme [30] under the SIS assumption. On the negative side, we therefore have to weaken the adversarial capabilities to prove it secure. While we provide formal evidence that this does not seem to be too problematic in practice, we consider it as a challenging open issue to construct US schemes from post-quantum assumptions being provable secure without any such restrictions.

Message-Independent US and UMAC. We further discuss message-independent constructions of US and UMAC from the BLS signature scheme [16], from the Pointcheval-Sanders signature scheme [48], and from the Naor-Pinkas-Reingold PRF [47]. These overcome the limitations of the respective constructions directly obtained from them viewed as KH-signatures and -PRFs, which are message-dependent. Message-independence can be a desirable property in practical applications, as access to the message is not required for updating signatures and MACs, i.e., if they are verified and then stored and at a later point updated (in a batch) one does not need to access the respective messages and improves update performance.

2 Preliminaries

Notation. For $n \in \mathbb{N}$, let $[n] := \{1, \ldots, n\}$, and let $\lambda \in \mathbb{N}$ be the security parameter. For a finite set $\mathcal{S}$, we denote by $s \leftarrow \mathcal{S}$ the process of sampling s uniformly from $\mathcal{S}$. For an algorithm A, let $y \leftarrow A(\lambda, x)$ be the process of running A on input (λ, x) with access to uniformly random coins and assigning the result to y (we may omit to mention the λ-input explicitly and assume that all algorithms take λ as input). To make the random coins r explicit, we write $A(\lambda, x; r)$. We use $\perp$ to indicate that an algorithm terminates with an error and A^B when A has oracle access to B, where B may return $\top$ as a distinguished special symbol. We say an algorithm A is probabilistic polynomial time (PPT) if the running time of A is polynomial in λ. Given $\mathbf{x} \in \mathbb{Z}^n$, we denote by $||\mathbf{x}||$ its infinity norm, i.e., for $\mathbf{x} = (x_1, x_2, \ldots, x_n)$, we have $||\mathbf{x}|| := \max(|x_1|, \ldots, |x_n|)$. A function f is negligible if its absolute value is smaller than the inverse of any polynomial (i.e., if $\forall c \exists k_0 \forall \lambda \geq k_0 : |f(\lambda)| < 1/\lambda^c$). We may write $q = q(\lambda)$ if we mean that the value q depends polynomially on λ.

Basic Primitives. Due to the lack of space we recall PRFs, signature schemes and MACs in the full version.

Key-homomorphic Signatures. We recall relevant parts of the definitional framework of key-homomorphic signatures as introduced in [23,25]. Let $\Sigma = (\mathsf{KGen}, \mathsf{Sign}, \mathsf{Verify})$ be a signature scheme and the secret and public key elements live in groups $(\mathbb{H}, +)$ and $(\mathbb{E}, \cdot)$, respectively. For these two groups it is required that group operations, inversions, membership testing as well as sampling from the uniform distribution are efficient.

Definition 1 (Secret Key to Public Key Homomorphism [25]**).** *A signature scheme Σ provides a secret key to public key homomorphism, if there exists an efficiently computable map $\mu : \mathbb{H} \rightarrow \mathbb{E}$ such that for all $sk, sk' \in \mathbb{H}$ it holds that $\mu(sk + sk') = \mu(sk) \cdot \mu(sk')$, and for all $(sk, pk) \leftarrow \mathsf{Gen}(\lambda)$, it holds that $pk = \mu(sk)$.*

In the discrete logarithm setting, it is usually the case $sk \leftarrow \mathbb{Z}_p$ and $pk = g^{sk}$ with g being the generator of some group $\mathbb{G}$ of prime order p.

Definition 2 (Key-Homomorphic Signatures [23]**).** *A signature scheme is called key-homomorphic, if it provides a secret key to public key homomorphism and an additional PPT algorithm* Adapt*, defined as:*

$\mathsf{Adapt}(pk, M, \sigma, \Delta)$: *Given a public key pk, a message M, a signature σ, and a shift amount Δ outputs a public key pk' and a signature σ',*

such that for all $\Delta \in \mathbb{H}$ and all $(pk, sk) \leftarrow \mathsf{Gen}(\lambda)$, all messages $M \in \mathcal{M}$ and all σ with $\mathsf{Ver}(pk, M, \sigma) = 1$ and $(pk', \sigma') \leftarrow \mathsf{Adapt}(pk, M, \sigma, \Delta)$ it holds that

$$\Pr[\mathsf{Ver}(pk', M, \sigma') = 1] = 1 \quad \wedge \quad pk' = \mu(\Delta) \cdot pk.$$

The following notion covers whether adapted signatures look like freshly generated ones, *even* if the initial signature used in Adapt *is known.*

Definition 3 (Perfect Adaption [25]**).** *A key-homomorphic signature scheme provides perfect adaption, if for every $\kappa \in \mathbb{N}$, every message $M \in \mathcal{M}$, it holds that*

$$[\sigma, (sk, pk), \mathsf{Adapt}(pk, M, \sigma, \Delta)],$$

where $(sk, pk) \leftarrow \mathsf{Gen}(\lambda)$, $\sigma \leftarrow \mathsf{Sign}(sk, M)$, $\Delta \leftarrow \mathbb{H}$, and

$$[\sigma, (sk, \mu(sk)), (\mu(sk) \cdot \mu(\Delta), \mathsf{Sign}(sk + \Delta, M))],$$

where $sk \leftarrow \mathbb{H}$, $\sigma \leftarrow \mathsf{Sign}(sk, M)$, $\Delta \leftarrow \mathbb{H}$, are identically distributed.

Key-homomorphic PRFs. Key-homomorphic PRFs (KH-PRFs) are PRFs which satisfy additional algebraic properties. More precisely, the key space $\mathcal{K}$ and the range $\mathcal{Y}$ of the PRF exhibit certain group structures such that the evaluation of the PRF on any fixed input $x \in \mathcal{X}$ is homomorphic with the respect to these group structures. More precisely:

Definition 4 (Key-Homomorphic PRFs [15,47]**).** *Let* $(\mathcal{K}, \oplus), (\mathcal{Y}, +)$ *be groups. Then, a keyed function* $F\colon \mathcal{K} \times \mathcal{X} \to \mathcal{Y}$ *is a key-homomorphic PRF (KH-PRF) if* F *is a secure PRF and for every key* $k_1, k_2 \in \mathcal{K}$ *and every input* $x \in \mathcal{X}$*, we have*

$$F(k_1, x) + F(k_2, x) = F(k_1 \oplus k_2, x).$$

We note that KH-PRFs constructed from assumptions such as Learning with Errors (LWE) as proposed in [14,15,39] do not achieve the perfect homomorphism as described in the definition above, but are only "almost" key-homomorphic in that $F(k_1, x) + F(k_2, x) = F(k_1 \oplus k_2, x) + e$, where e is a small error term. For them one needs to bound the number of successive applications and provide T-time correctness for a pre-specified $T \geq 1$ (cf. [15,39] for a comprehensive treatment). Note also, that only achieving an "almost" key-homomorphic property allows to distinguish fresh evaluations of the PRF from ones obtained via the key-homomorphic property.

3 Updatable MACs and Signatures

In this section, we present our definitional framework of updatable MACs and signatures. In order to make the illustration compact and avoid redundancy, we try to unify the notation as much as possible and will, whenever necessary, point to the differences between the two primitives.

3.1 Updatable MACs

We define updatable message authentication codes (UMACs) next and their security model in Sect. 3.3. An UMAC scheme UMAC with message space $\mathcal{M}$ is a tuple of the PPT algorithms (Setup, Next, Sig, Update, Ver):

$\mathsf{Setup}(\lambda, n)$: On input security parameter $\lambda \in \mathbb{N}$ and the maximum number of epochs $n \in O(2^\lambda)$, the setup algorithm outputs a (secret) key k_1[1].

$\mathsf{Next}(k_e)$: On input key k_e for epoch $e \in [n-1]$, the key-update algorithm outputs an updated key k_{e+1} together with an update token Δ_{e+1}.

$\mathsf{Sig}(k_e, M)$: On input key k_e for epoch $e \in [n]$ and a message $M \in \mathcal{M}$, the signing algorithm outputs a tag σ_e[2].

[1] See that such large values of n allow for virtually unbounded number of epochs.

[2] We assume that from keys, tokens, and tags, the associated epoch is efficiently extractable.

$\mathsf{Update}(\Delta_{e+1}, M, \sigma_e)$: On input an update token Δ_{e+1}, a message M, and a tag σ_e for epoch $e < n$, the update algorithm outputs an updated message-tag pair (M, σ_{e+1}) or $\perp$.
$\mathsf{Ver}(k_e, M, \sigma_e)$: On input key k_e, a message M, and a tag σ_e for epoch $e \in [n]$, the verification algorithm outputs a verdict $b \in \{0, 1\}$.

Correctness of UMAC. Correctness ensures that an update of a valid tag σ_e (via Δ_{e+1}) from epoch e to $e+1$ yields a valid tag σ_{e+1} that can be verified under the epoch key k_{e+1} which is derived from k_e. More formally, we require that for all $\lambda, n \in \mathbb{N}$, for all $k_1 \leftarrow \mathsf{Setup}(\lambda, n)$, for all $e \in [n-1]$, for all $(k_{e+1}, \Delta_{e+1}) \leftarrow \mathsf{Next}(k_e)$, for all $M \in \mathcal{M}$, for all σ_e with $\mathsf{Ver}(k_e, M, \sigma_e) = 1$, for all $(M, \sigma_{e+1}) \leftarrow \mathsf{Update}(\Delta_{e+1}, M, \sigma_e)$, we have that $\Pr\left[\mathsf{Ver}(k_{e'}, M, \sigma_{e'}) \neq 1\right] \leq \varepsilon(\lambda)$ holds, for all $e' \in [n]$, where $\varepsilon(\lambda) = \mathsf{negl}(\lambda)$, and we call it perfectly correct if $\varepsilon(\lambda) = 0$.

3.2 Updatable Signatures

We define updatable signatures (US) next and their security model in Sect. 3.3. An US scheme US with message space $\mathcal{M}$ is a tuple of the PPT algorithms (Setup, Next, Sig, Update, Ver):

$\mathsf{Setup}(\lambda, n)$: On input security parameter λ and the maximum number of epochs $n \in O(2^\lambda)$, the setup algorithm outputs a public and secret key pair (pk_1, sk_1).[3]
$\mathsf{Next}(pk_e, sk_e)$: On input a public key pk_e and secret key sk_e for epoch $e \in [n-1]$, the key-update algorithm outputs an updated public key pk_{e+1}, an updated secret key sk_{e+1} and an update token Δ_{e+1}.
$\mathsf{Sig}(sk_e, M)$: On input secret key sk_e for epoch $e \in [n]$ and a message $M \in \mathcal{M}$, the signing algorithm outputs a signature σ_e.
$\mathsf{Update}(\Delta_{e+1}, M, \sigma_e)$: On input an update token Δ_{e+1}, a message M, and a signature σ_e for epoch $e < n$, the update algorithm outputs an updated message-signature pair (M, σ_{e+1}) or $\perp$.
$\mathsf{Ver}(pk_e, M, \sigma_e)$: On input public key pk_e, a message M, and a signature σ_e for epoch $e \in [n]$, the verification algorithm outputs a verdict $b \in \{0, 1\}$.

Correctness of US. For all $\lambda, n \in \mathbb{N}$, for all $(pk_1, sk_1) \leftarrow \mathsf{Setup}(\lambda, n)$, for all $e \in [n-1]$, for all $(pk_{e+1}, sk_{e+1}, \Delta_{e+1}) \leftarrow \mathsf{Next}(pk_e, sk_e)$, for all $M \in \mathcal{M}$, for all σ_e with $\mathsf{Ver}(pk_e, M, \sigma_e) = 1$, for all $(M, \sigma_{e+1}) \leftarrow \mathsf{Update}(\Delta_{e+1}, M, \sigma_e)$, we have that $\Pr\left[\mathsf{Ver}(pk_{e'}, M, \sigma_{e'}) \neq 1\right] \leq \varepsilon(\lambda)$ holds, for all $e' \in [n]$, where $\varepsilon(\lambda) = \mathsf{negl}(\lambda)$, and we call it perfectly correct if $\varepsilon(\lambda) = 0$.

3.3 Security of UMAC and US

We are now ready to define the security notions of UMAC and US where we will use UX with $\mathsf{X} \in \{\text{MAC, S}\}$ to distinguish between those two primitives. In order to make the description as compact as possible, we will use pk_e and

[3] As in UMACs, such large values of n allow for virtually unbounded number of epochs.

sk_e, for $e \in [n]$, as handles to the public and secret key, respectively; where for UMACs we have $pk_e := \bot$ and $sk_e := k_e$. Moreover, we will also call the tags in UMACs signatures henceforth.

We introduce security definitions for existential unforgeability under chosen-message attack (UX-EUF-CMA) and unlinkable updates under chosen-message attack (UX-UU-CMA). Loosely speaking, the UX-EUF-CMA notion ensures that signatures cannot be forged even when the PPT adversary sees many signatures of chosen messages while the UX-UU-CMA notion guarantees that signatures derived from Update are unlinkable even when the PPT adversary sees many (updated) signatures of chosen messages.

In our security experiments, let $q \in \mathbb{N}$ be the number of signature queries and e the current epoch. Furthermore, we introduce a global state $\mathbf{S} = (\mathcal{I}, \mathcal{K}, \mathcal{T}, \mathcal{S})$:

$\mathcal{I} = \{((pk_{e'}, sk_{e'}), \Delta_{e'})_{e' \in [e]}\}$: all keys and update tokens.
$\mathcal{K} = \{e' \in [e]\}$: all epochs where the adversary queried $\mathsf{Corrupt}(\mathsf{key}, e')$.
$\mathcal{T} = \{e' \in [e]\}$: all epochs where the adversary queried $\mathsf{Corrupt}(\mathsf{token}, e')$.
$\mathcal{S} = \{(e', M, \sigma_{e'})_{e' \in [e]}\}$: all tuples where the adversary queried $\mathsf{Sig}'(M, e')$ in epoch e' or $\mathsf{Update}'(M, \cdot)$ in epoch $e' - 1$;

When the experiment is initialized, we set $\mathcal{I} = \{((pk_1, sk_1), \Delta_1)\}$, for $(pk_1, sk_1) \leftarrow \mathsf{Setup}(\lambda, n)$ and $\Delta_1 := \bot$, and let $\mathcal{S}$, $\mathcal{K}$, and $\mathcal{T}$ be initially empty sets. Additionally, we require the following oracles which are eligible to change sets in $\mathbf{S}$ for any epoch $e' \in [e]$:

$\mathsf{Sig}'(M, e')$: on input message M and epoch $e' \in [e]$, compute signature $\sigma_{e'} \leftarrow \mathsf{Sig}(sk_{e'}, M)$, set $\mathcal{S} := \mathcal{S} \cup \{(e', M, \sigma_{e'})\}$, and return $\sigma_{e'}$. Else, return $\bot$.
Next' : find $(pk_e, sk_e) \in \mathcal{I}$, compute $(pk_{e+1}, sk_{e+1}, \Delta_{e+1}) \leftarrow \mathsf{Next}(pk_e, sk_e)$, update $\mathcal{I} := \mathcal{I} \cup \{((pk_{e+1}, sk_{e+1}), \Delta_{e+1})\}$, return pk_{e+1} and set $e := e + 1$.
$\mathsf{Update}'(M, \sigma_{e'})$: on input a message-signature pair $(M, \sigma_{e'})$, return $\bot$ if $\mathsf{Ver}'(M, \sigma_{e'}) \neq 1$; else, compute $(M, \sigma_{e'+1}) \leftarrow \mathsf{Update}(\Delta_{e'+1}, M, \sigma_{e'})$, set $\mathcal{S} := \mathcal{S} \cup \{(e'+1, M, \sigma_{e'+1})\}$ and return $\sigma_{e'+1}$.
$\mathsf{Corrupt}(\{\mathsf{token}, \mathsf{key}\}, e')$: on input handles token or key, and epoch $e' \in [e]$,
- return $\Delta_{e'+1}$ and set $\mathcal{T} := \mathcal{T} \cup \{e'\}$, if called with token and $e' < e$,
- return $sk_{e'}$ and set $\mathcal{K} := \mathcal{K} \cup \{e'\}$, if called with key. Else, return $\bot$.
$\mathsf{Ver}'(M, \sigma_{e'})$: on input a message-signature pair $(M, \sigma_{e'})$,
- return $b \leftarrow \mathsf{Ver}(sk_{e'}, M, \sigma_{e'})$ in the UMAC case,
- return $b \leftarrow \mathsf{Ver}(pk_{e'}, M, \sigma_{e'})$ in the US case.

Leakage Profile $(\mathcal{K}^*, \mathcal{T}^*, \mathcal{S}^*)$**.** We use the concept of a leakage profile originally defined in [42] to capture key, token, and signature "leakage" that cannot be directly captured via oracles. The reason is that due to the nature of signature updates, UX schemes inherently allow for information leakage of updated message-signature pairs, keys, and tokens besides what is modeled via the global state $\mathbf{S}$. For example, one token $\Delta_{e'+1}$ alone in such schemes is capable of updating polynomially many message-signature pairs $((M_1, \sigma_{1,e'}), \ldots, (M_\ell, \sigma_{\ell,e'}))$, for all $\ell = \ell(\lambda)$ and for each epoch $e' \in [n-1]$. As this is required by the correctness of the scheme, we cannot capture which particular signature σ' the adversary retrieves (via an update token) and, hence, cannot include it into $\mathcal{S}$.

Furthermore, signatures, keys, and tokens cannot only be "upgraded" but also potentially "downgraded", e.g., a token $\Delta_{e'}$ and key $sk_{e'}$ or a token $\Delta_{e'}$ and a message-signature pair $(M, \sigma_{e'})$ for epoch $e' \in [n]$ might be used to derive a key $sk_{e'-1}$ or message-signature pair $(M, \sigma_{e'-1})$ of the previous epoch $e' - 1$, respectively. Hence, we cannot capture which particular key sk' or signature σ' the adversary retrieves (via an update token) and, hence, cannot include those as well into $\mathcal{K}$ or $\mathcal{S}$, respectively.

We want to emphasize that the directionality of updates, i.e., either bidirectional or unidirectional, is subject to discussion in updatable encryption [36]. In context of US or UMACs, we observe that due to correctness one always can upgrade signatures (so leakage in this direction does not add anything), and stronger schemes could only prevent to derive keys or signatures "into the past". This, however, seems of limited interest in authentication primitives, where old keys are typically assumed to be invalidated. Consequently, we opted for the arguably simpler bidirectional setting.

When looking ahead, we will construct US from key-homomorphic (KH) signatures. Now, in [25], the authors also provide a number of constructions of KH signatures that provide a property being weaker than the one we are using and which is called adaption of signatures. Now, one could wonder why we do not support such schemes. Firstly, it would only allow to achieve a very weak notion of unlinkability. Secondly, and more importantly, all known KH signatures with this "weak" adaption (e.g., Schnorr or Guillou-Quisquater signatures) have the property that a signature and its updated version leak the update token. Consequently, an adversary who obtains a signing key in some old epoch and then sees a signature and its updated versions, can compute all the signing keys up to the epoch of the latest updated version it sees. As this results in very weak security guarantees, we decided that our framework should not support schemes with these weak security guarantees.

Now, let us consider an UX scheme with optimal leakage to be the one where we only have signature upgrade (but no downgrade) and tokens are not useful to upgrade or downgrade keys in any way. The leakage would be limited for such schemes, however, the model would still need to restrict the adversary to retrieve the update token in epoch $e^* - 1$, i.e., Δ_{e^*}, where e^* is the forgery epoch. The reason is that otherwise the adversary could trivially win the game by updating any signature computed under a corrupted key to epoch e^*. Hence, also such strong schemes with so-called no-directional key updates would not achieve any stronger security in our model; at least with the applications we have in mind.

Now we are ready to introduce the leakage profile. We model leakage via key-update, token, and signature-update inferences where the leakage profile

$(\mathcal{K}^*, \mathcal{T}^*, \mathcal{S}^*)$ of a concrete scheme is specified by the respective sets.

Key-Update Inferences. Key-update inferences of a specific UX scheme can be formally captured as $\mathcal{K}^*$ with corrupted-key set $\mathcal{K}$ and corrupted-token set $\mathcal{T}$ maintained by the oracles:

$$\mathcal{K}^* := \begin{cases} \{e \in [n] \mid \mathsf{corrupt\text{-}key}(e) = \mathsf{true}\} \text{ with } \mathsf{true} = \mathsf{corrupt\text{-}key}(e) \text{ iff:} \\ \quad (e \in \mathcal{K}) \vee (e-1 \in \mathcal{K} \wedge e \in \mathcal{T}) \vee (e+1 \in \mathcal{K} \wedge e+1 \in \mathcal{T}). \end{cases}$$

Token Inferences. Token inferences can be formally captured as $\mathcal{T}^*$ with corrupted-token set $\mathcal{T}$ and key-leakage set $\mathcal{K}^*$:

$$\mathcal{T}^* := \{e \in [n] \mid (e \in \mathcal{T}) \ \vee \ (e-1 \in \mathcal{K}^* \ \wedge \ e \in \mathcal{K}^*)\}.$$

Signature-Update Inferences. Signature-update inferences can be formally captured as $\mathcal{S}^*$ with corrupted-signature set $\mathcal{S}$ maintained by the oracles and sets $\mathcal{K}^*$ and $\mathcal{T}^*$ with $M \in \mathcal{M} \cup \{\top\}$[4]:

$$\mathcal{S}^* := \begin{cases} \{(e, M) \mid \mathsf{corrupt\text{-}sig}(e, M) = \mathsf{true}\} \text{ with } \mathsf{true} = \mathsf{corrupt\text{-}sig}(e, M) \text{ iff:} \\ \quad ((e, M, \cdot) \in \mathcal{S}) \ \vee \ ((e, M) \in \mathcal{K}^* \times \{\top\}) \ \vee \ (\mathsf{corrupt\text{-}sig}(e-1, M) \ \wedge \\ \quad e \in \mathcal{T}^*) \ \vee \ (\mathsf{corrupt\text{-}sig}(e+1, M) \ \wedge \ e+1 \in \mathcal{T}^*), \end{cases}$$

where $\mathsf{corrupt\text{-}sig}(0, M) = \mathsf{false}$.

In Fig. 1 we provide an example of potential leakage in UX schemes with our leakage profile.

epoch:	$e-5$	$e-4$	$e-3$	$e-2$	$e-1$	e	$e+1$	$e+2$	$e+3$	$e+4$
keys:	k_{e-5}	k_{e-4}	k_{e-3}	k_{e-2}	k_{e-1}	k_e	k_{e+1}	k_{e+2}	k_{e+3}	k_{e+4}
tokens:	Δ_{e-4}	Δ_{e-3}	Δ_{e-2}	Δ_{e-1}	Δ_e	Δ_{e+1}	Δ_{e+2}	Δ_{e+3}	Δ_{e+4}	Δ_{e+5}
signature:	σ_{e-5}	σ_{e-4}	σ_{e-3}	σ_{e-2}	σ_{e-1}	σ_e	σ_{e+1}	σ_{e+2}	σ_{e+3}	σ_{e+4}

Fig. 1. Example of directly obtained (green) and inferable information (blue) for UX schemes.

Existential Unforgeability Under Chosen-Message Attacks (UX-EUF-CMA). Informally, the UX-EUF-CMA notion ensures that no PPT adversary

[4] $M = \top$ is a placeholder for "all messages" in $\mathcal{M}$ and helps us to construct the set $\mathcal{S}^*$ efficiently.

can non-trivially forge signatures even when the adversary adaptively compromises a number of keys and tokens. We say that an UX scheme is UX-EUF-CMA-secure if any PPT adversary succeeds in the following experiment only with negligible probability. The experiment starts by computing the initial keys $(pk_1, sk_1) \leftarrow \mathsf{Setup}(\lambda, n)$. During the experiment, via the oracles, the adversary may query signatures for any epoch e' up to the current epoch e, iterate to the next epoch $e+1$, update signatures, and corrupt tokens or keys for any epoch e' up to the current epoch e (note that the global state $\mathbf{S}$ is changed by the oracles). Eventually, the adversary outputs a message-signature pair $(M^*, \sigma^*_{e^*})$, for epoch $e^* \in [n]$, and succeeds if $\mathsf{Ver}(pk_{e^*}, M^*, \sigma^*_{e^*}) = 1$ in the US case and $\mathsf{Ver}(sk_{e^*}, M^*, \sigma^*_{e^*}) = 1$ in the UMAC case, and the adversary is *valid* which we define in Definition 5.

Definition 5 Validity of $A$for UX-EUF-CMA). *Depending on $(\mathcal{S}^*, \mathcal{K}^*, \mathcal{T}^*)$, a PPT adversary A is valid in the UX-EUF-CMA experiment if*

$$\{\{(e^*, \top)\} \cup \{(e^*, M^*)\}\} \cap \mathcal{S}^* = \emptyset, \tag{1}$$

i.e., A has not learned any useful forgery-message information for epoch e^*.

Remark. Definition 5 essentially says that the adversary is not able to derive a valid message-signature pair for epoch e^* which excludes trivial wins. The leftmost term in Eq. (1) "checks" that A does not possess a valid (derived) secret key in e^* while the middle term "checks" that A is not able to derive a valid signature for M^* in epoch e^* via corrupted tokens.

See that the keys (pk_{e^*}, sk_{e^*}) for any $e^* \in [n]$ can be derived, i.e., if $e^* \leq e$, we have that $((pk_{e^*}, sk_{e^*}), \cdot) \in \mathcal{I}$, otherwise, if $e^* > e$, we can derive (pk_{e^*}, sk_{e^*}) iteratively by invoking Next' starting with (pk_e, sk_e). If $e^* \leq e$ we set $e_{\max} := e$, else $e_{\max} := e^*$. Figure 2 depicts the UX-EUF-CMA experiments.

Definition 6 (UX-EUF-CMA security of UX). *A UX scheme* UX *is UX-EUF-CMA-secure iff for any valid PPT adversary A the advantage function*

$$\mathsf{Adv}^{\mathsf{ux\text{-}euf\text{-}cma}}_{\mathsf{UX},A}(\lambda, n) := \Pr\left[\mathsf{Exp}^{\mathsf{ux\text{-}euf\text{-}cma}}_{\mathsf{UX},A}(\lambda, n) = 1\right],$$

is negligible in λ, where $\mathsf{Exp}^{\mathsf{ux\text{-}euf\text{-}cma}}_{\mathsf{US},A}(\lambda, n)$ is defined in Fig. 2.

Unlinkable Updates Under Chosen-Message Attacks (UX-UU-CMA). Informally, the UX-UU-CMA notion ensures that no PPT adversary can distinguish fresh signatures from updated signatures even seeing (all) keys, update tokens and signatures from the past. We say that an UX scheme is UX-UU-CMA-secure if any PPT adversary succeeds in the following experiment only with negligible probability. The experiment starts by computing the initial keys $(pk_1, sk_1) \leftarrow \mathsf{Setup}(\lambda, n)$. During the experiment, via the oracles, the adversary may query signatures for any epoch e' up to the current epoch e, iterate to the next epoch $e+1$, update signatures, and corrupt tokens or keys for any epoch e' up to the current epoch e, and has access to a verification oracle (note

Experiment $\mathsf{Exp}_{\mathsf{UX},A}^{\mathsf{ux\text{-}euf\text{-}cma}}(\lambda, n)$
$(pk_1, sk_1) \leftarrow \mathsf{Setup}(\lambda, n)$
$\mathbf{S} = (\mathcal{I}, \mathcal{K}, \mathcal{T}, \mathcal{S})$, for $\mathcal{I} := \{((pk_1, sk_1), \perp)\}, \mathcal{K} := \mathcal{T} := \mathcal{S} := \emptyset$
$(M^*, \sigma_{e^*}^*) \leftarrow A^{\mathsf{Sig}', \mathsf{Next}', \mathsf{Update}', \mathsf{Ver}', \mathsf{Corrupt}}(\lambda)$
if A is valid and $\mathsf{Ver}(\{pk_{e^*}, sk_{e^*}\}, M^*, \sigma_{e^*}^*) = 1$ then return 1 else return 0

Fig. 2. The UX-EUF-CMA security notions for UX. For US, we verify $\mathsf{Ver}(pk_{e^*}, M^*, \sigma_{e^*}^*) = 1$; for UMAC, we use $\mathsf{Ver}(sk_{e^*}, M^*, \sigma_{e^*}^*) = 1$ in the last step.

that the global state $\mathbf{S}$ is changed by the oracles). Then, the adversary outputs a message M^* and epoch e^* for which it queried Sig' in some epoch $e' < e^*$. It receives a challenge signature $\sigma^{(b)}$ which is either a fresh signature on M^*, $\sigma^{(0)}$, or the existing signature for M^* updated to epoch e^*, $\sigma^{(1)}$. For the latter case, we use the compact notation of $\mathsf{UpdateCh}(M^*)$ to denote the repeated application of Update' starting with $\sigma_{e'}$ for M^* and finally resulting in $\sigma^{(1)}$ as signature for M^* in epoch e^* (note that Update' implicitly checks the condition $\mathsf{Ver}(pk_{e'}, M^*, \sigma_{e'}) = 1$). In both cases, this might require calling repeatedly Next until (sk_{e^*}, pk_{e^*}) is defined. Eventually it outputs a bit b^* and wins if $b = b^*$. Note that the adversary can call $\mathsf{Corrupt}$ arbitrarily. We call an adversary valid if it queried M^* to Sig' in some epoch $e' < e^*$. Figure 3 depicts the UX-UU-CMA experiments.

Definition 7 (UX-UU-CMA security of UX). *A UX scheme* UX *is UX-UU-CMA-secure iff for any valid PPT adversary A the advantage function*

$$\mathsf{Adv}_{\mathsf{UX},A}^{\mathsf{ux\text{-}uu\text{-}cma}}(\lambda, n) := \left| \Pr\left[\mathsf{Exp}_{\mathsf{UX},A}^{\mathsf{ux\text{-}uu\text{-}cma}}(\lambda, n) = 1\right] - 1/2 \right|,$$

is negligible in λ, *where* $\mathsf{Exp}_{\mathsf{US},A}^{\mathsf{ux\text{-}uu\text{-}cma}}(\lambda, n)$ *is defined in Fig. 3.*

Experiment $\mathsf{Exp}_{\mathsf{UX},A}^{\mathsf{ux\text{-}uu\text{-}cma}}(\lambda, n)$
$(pk_1, sk_1) \leftarrow \mathsf{Setup}(\lambda, n)$
$\mathbf{S} = (\mathcal{I}, \mathcal{K}, \mathcal{T}, \mathcal{S})$, for $\mathcal{I} := \{((pk_1, sk_1), \perp)\}, \mathcal{K} =: \mathcal{T} =: \mathcal{S} := \emptyset$
$(M^*, e^*) \leftarrow A^{\mathsf{Sig}', \mathsf{Next}', \mathsf{Update}', \mathsf{Ver}', \mathsf{Corrupt}}(\lambda)$
$b \leftarrow \{0, 1\}$
$\sigma^{(0)} \leftarrow \mathsf{Sig}(sk_{e^*}, M^*)$, $\sigma^{(1)} \leftarrow \mathsf{UpdateCh}(M^*)$
$b^* \leftarrow A^{\mathsf{Sig}', \mathsf{Next}', \mathsf{Update}', \mathsf{Ver}', \mathsf{Corrupt}}(\sigma^{(b)})$
if $(e', M^*, \cdot) \in \mathcal{S}$, $e' < e^*$, and $b = b^*$ then return 1 else return 0

Fig. 3. The UX-UU-CMA security notions for UX.

4 Construction of Updatable Signatures

In this section, we will present different instantiations of updatable signatures from different assumptions (see Sect. 4.4 for an overview and discussion.)

4.1 Updatable Signatures from KH Signatures

Subsequently, we show how to generically construct US with polynomially many updates from key-homomorphic (KH) signatures. Let $\Sigma = (\mathsf{Gen}, \mathsf{Sig}, \mathsf{Adapt}, \mathsf{Ver})$ be a KH signature scheme providing perfect adaption, where we denote the secret key space by $\mathbb{H}$ and the secret key to public key homomorphism by μ. The so-obtained US scheme US is depicted in Fig. 4. Before discussing the security, we will note that correctness straightforwardly follows from inspection.

Theorem 1. *Let* $\Sigma = (\mathsf{Gen}, \mathsf{Sig}, \mathsf{Adapt}, \mathsf{Ver})$ *be a uniform-keys key-homomorphic signature scheme. If* Σ *is EUF-CMA secure and provides perfect adaption, then the updatable signature scheme* US *from Fig. 4 is US-EUF-CMA-secure and US-UU-CMA secure.*

In the above theorem, we require uniform-keys KH signatures, which we introduce now. This notion is satisfied by all natural schemes and in particular the ones discussed in [25]:

Definition 8 (Uniform-Keys Key-Homomorphic Signatures) . *A key-homomorphic signature scheme* Σ *is said to be uniform-keys if the distribution of* sk *with* $(sk, pk) \leftarrow \Sigma.\mathsf{Gen}(1^\lambda)$ *is the uniform distribution over the secret key space* $\mathbb{H}$.

$\mathsf{Setup}(1^\lambda, n)$:
- Return $(pk_1, sk_1) \leftarrow \Sigma.\mathsf{Gen}(1^\lambda)$.

$\mathsf{Next}(pk_e, sk_e)$:
- Choose random $sk' \in \mathbb{H}$ and set $\Delta'_{e+1} := sk'$ and $\Delta_{e+1} := (\Delta'_{e+1}, pk_e)$.
- Compute $pk_{e+1} = pk_e \cdot \mu(\Delta'_{e+1})$ and $sk_{e+1} = sk_e + \Delta'_{e+1}$.
- Return $(pk_{e+1}, sk_{e+1}, \Delta_{e+1})$.

$\mathsf{Sig}(sk_e, M)$:
- Return $\Sigma.\mathsf{Sig}(sk_e, M)$.

$\mathsf{Update}(\Delta_{e+1}, M, \sigma_e)$:
- Parse $\Delta_{e+1} = (\Delta'_{e+1}, pk_e)$
- Compute $\sigma_{e+1} := \Sigma.\mathsf{Adapt}(pk_e, M, \sigma_e, \Delta'_{e+1})$.
- Return (M, σ_{e+1}).

$\mathsf{Ver}(pk_e, M, \sigma_e)$:
- Return $\Sigma.\mathsf{Ver}(pk_e, M, \sigma_e)$.

Fig. 4. US from KH signatures.

Helper Lemmas. Notice that a valid adversary should not trivially forge signatures using the updatable property of the US scheme and the information provided by the leakage profile (e.g., produce a valid signature for epoch $e' \in \mathcal{K}^*$ using $sk_{e'}$ and update it to a valid signature for epoch e^* using the update tokens in $\mathcal{T}^*$) for epochs in an appropriate window containing epoch e^*. More formally, we can define

$$e^- := \max_{1 \le e \le e^*} \{e \mid e \notin \mathcal{T}^* \cup \mathcal{K}^* \text{ and } e' \notin \mathcal{K}^*,\ e' \in \mathcal{T}^* \quad \forall\, e < e' \le e^*\},$$
$$e^+ := \min_{e^* < e \le e_{\max}} \{e \mid e \notin \mathcal{T}^* \text{ and } e' \notin \mathcal{K}^*,\ e' \in \mathcal{T}^* \quad \forall\, e^* < e' < e\},$$

and let the interval $[e^-, e^+[$ denote such a window and notice that e^- is well-defined. Suppose on the contrary that the set

$$E := \{e \in [1, e^*] \mid e \notin \mathcal{T}^* \cup \mathcal{K}^* \ \wedge\ e' \notin \mathcal{K}^*,\ e' \in \mathcal{T}^* \quad \forall\, e < e' \le e^*\},$$

is empty (if it is not empty then it has a maximum element). We claim, by backward induction on the epoch number k and starting from e^*, that this implies that $[k, e^*] \subseteq \mathcal{T}^*$ for all $k \in [1, e^*]$ which is a contradiction as $1 \notin \mathcal{T}^*$ by construction of $\mathcal{T}^*$. The base case is $k = e^*$. Indeed if E is empty then $e^* \notin E$ which implies that $e^* \in \mathcal{T}^*$ as $\nexists e'$ with $e^* < e' \le e^*$ and it cannot be that $e^* \in \mathcal{K}^*$. Now assume by induction hypothesis that $[k, e^*] \subseteq \mathcal{T}^*$ for $k < e^*$. We deduce from it, using that $k-1 \notin E$, that $k-1 \in \mathcal{T}^*$ as $k-1$ cannot be in $\mathcal{K}^*$ by validity of the adversary when $[k, e^*] \subseteq \mathcal{T}^*$. Hence, $[k-1, e^*-1] \subseteq \mathcal{T}^*$ which concludes the proof. A similar argument also proves the well-definedness of e^+. We can summarize the above discussion in the following lemma.

Lemma 1. *Let A be a valid adversary that produces a forgery in epoch $0 < e^* \le e_{\max}$ in the US-EUF-CMA experiment, then there exists a maximum integer $0 < e^- \le e^*$ and a minimum integer $e^* < e^+ \le e_{\max}$ s.t. A*

1) does not obtain tokens Δ_{e^-} and Δ_{e^+},
2) obtains no secret key sk_e for all $e^- \le e < e^+$ and
3) can obtain all tokens Δ_e for $e^- < e < e^+$,

from the queries made to the oracles. Subsequently, we often denote the interval $[e^-, e^+[$ as the window.

From Definition 8, the following lemma easily follows.

Lemma 2. *Let Σ be a uniform-keys key-homomorphic signature scheme. Then the following hold:*

1) For every $(sk, pk) \leftarrow \Sigma.\mathsf{Gen}(1^\lambda)$ the distributions of $sk + \Delta$ with $\Delta \leftarrow \mathbb{H}$ and sk' with $(sk', pk') \leftarrow \Sigma.\mathsf{Gen}(1^\lambda)$ are identical.
2) For every $(sk, pk) \leftarrow \Sigma.\mathsf{Gen}(1^\lambda)$ and $\Delta \in \mathbb{H}$ we have that $(sk + \Delta, pk \cdot \mu(\Delta)) \in \Sigma.\mathsf{Gen}(1^\lambda)$.

Now we are ready for the proof of Theorem 1.

Proof. First we observe that correctness follows straightforwardly from inspection.

For US-UU-CMA security, we can observe that in the US-UU-CMA experiment all keys, signing operations, updates and token computations are performed honestly by the experiment. Any adversary A is given access to all keys, tokens and signatures and what we need to consider is the computation of the challenge signature $\sigma^{(b)}$. Now, due to the adaption property of Σ, the outputs of $\Sigma.\mathsf{Sig}$ and $\Sigma.\mathsf{Adapt}$ are identical and thus also the outputs of $\mathsf{US.Sig}$ and $\mathsf{US.Update}$. By repeatedly applying Definition 3 within $\mathsf{US.UpdateCh}$ for computing $\sigma^{(1)}$ and using Lemma 2 we are done. More formally, let us consider the sequence of games as outlined below:

Game 0. This is the experiment $\mathsf{Exp}_{\mathsf{US},A}^{\mathsf{us\text{-}uu\text{-}cma}}(\lambda, n)$ with $b = 0$, i.e., we always return $\sigma^{(0)} \leftarrow \mathsf{Sig}(sk_{e^*}, M^*)$.
Game 1. This is the experiment $\mathsf{Exp}_{\mathsf{US},A}^{\mathsf{us\text{-}uu\text{-}cma}}(\lambda, n)$ with $b = 1$, i.e., we always return $\sigma^{(1)} \leftarrow \mathsf{UpdateCh}(M^*)$.

Lemma 3 (Game 0 to Game 1). *For any adversary A it holds that*

$$|\Pr[S_{A,0}] - \Pr[S_{A,1}]| = 0.$$

Observe that in both games the adversary A is given access to all keys, tokens and signatures and outputs a message M^* and epoch e^* for which it queried Sig' in some epoch $e' \leq e^*$. Now, in **Game 0** we finally output $\sigma^{(0)} \leftarrow \mathsf{Sig}(sk_{e^*}, M^*)$, i.e., a fresh signature of M^* that verifies under pk_{e^*} to A. In **Game 1** let us denote by $\sigma_{e'}$ the signature for M^* under $(sk_{e'}, pk_{e'})$ that the adversary queried for message M^* during the experiment. Let us w.l.o.g. assume that (sk_{e^*}, pk_{e^*}) is already defined (otherwise repeatedly call Next until it is defined) and let $(sk_{e'+1}, pk_{e'+1}, \Delta_{e'+1}), \ldots, (sk_{e^*}, pk_{e^*}, \Delta_{e^*})$ be the sequence of keys and update tokens. Now, $\mathsf{UpdateCh}$ does the following:

- For $i = e', \ldots, e^* - 1$ compute $\sigma_{i+1} \leftarrow \mathsf{Update}(\Delta_{i+1}, M^*, \sigma_i)$, where Update parses $\Delta_{i+1} = (\Delta'_{i+1}, pk_i)$ and calls $\sigma_{i+1} \leftarrow \Sigma.\mathsf{Adapt}(pk_i, M^*, \sigma_i, \Delta'_{i+1})$.

By using Lemma 2, we know that every key pair in the sequence $(sk_{e'}, pk_{e'}), \ldots,$ (sk_{e^*}, pk_{e^*}) is distributed identical as one obtained from $\Sigma.\mathsf{Gen}$. Now, this allows us to repeatedly apply the perfect adaption notion to the output of the previous Update in this sequence to conclude that in the sequence of signatures $(\sigma_{e_i}, \ldots, \sigma_{e^*} =: \sigma^{(1)})$ the last signature $\sigma^{(1)}$ is distributed identically to a fresh signature computed as $\mathsf{Sig}(sk_{e^*}, M^*)$.

This lets us conclude that $\mathsf{Adv}_{\mathsf{US},A}^{\mathsf{us\text{-}uu\text{-}cma}}(\lambda, n) = 0$ for any adversary A, which concludes the proof of US-UU-CMA security. □

To prove US-EUF-CMA security, we reduce US-EUF-CMA security to the EUF-CMA security of Σ, where the challenger will be associated to period e^-. While we can use the Sig oracle of the EUF-CMA challenger for period e^-, we have to answer Sig queries for epoch e^* and adjacent ones, and Update queries from older epochs to e^* and from e^* to newer epochs. Moreover, we have to provide secret keys and tokens on $\mathsf{Corrupt}$ queries to the adversary. By Lemma 1 we know that in order for an adversary to be valid and to rule out a trivial forgery, there needs to be a maximum epoch $1 \leq e^- \leq e^*$ and a minimum epoch $e^* < e^+ \leq e_{\max}$ for which A does not query tokens Δ_{e^-} and Δ_{e^+} and consequently does not know any secret key but knows all tokens for the window of epochs $[e^-, e^+[$. We now can use the key insulation technique from Klooß et al. [40] for optimization, so that instead of guessing the challenge epoch e^* and the window to the left and to the right, we only guess the boundaries of this region e^- and e^+ (containing the challenge epoch somewhere) and we can just associate the EUF-CMA challenger of Σ to some epoch in this interval (lets say e^-). This reduces the overall reduction loss from $e_{\max}^2(e_{\max}+1)$ to $e_{\max}(e_{\max}+1)$.

Outside of the window, i.e., for epochs up to $e^- - 1$ and starting from e^+ upwards, we will behave in our simulation as in the original game and in particular choose and know all secret keys and update tokens (except Δ_{e^+}). For all epochs inside the window, our strategy will be as follows: we do not know the secret keys associated to the epochs, but they are implicitly set by choosing for every epoch e_i in the window a random token Δ_{e_i} as in the real Next algorithm. Then for every epoch e_i in the window starting from e^- we use the secret key to public key homomorphism of Σ and set the corresponding public key as $pk_{e_i} = pk_{e_{i-1}} \cdot \mu(\Delta_{e_i})$ (for $e^- < e_i < e^+$). Now for any signature query for message M and epoch e_i within the window, we query M to the EUF-CMA challenger of Σ associated to e^- and use the $\Sigma.\mathsf{Adapt}$ algorithm in the forwards direction to obtain the signature for M in epoch e_i within the window. Note that due to the adaption property of Σ and thus the identical distribution of signatures from $\Sigma.\mathsf{Sig}$ and $\Sigma.\mathsf{Adapt}$, this is indistinguishable for A. The Update' oracle is performed as in the original game for all those epochs where the update token is knows. For the remaining epochs, i.e., e^- and e^+, when asked to update $(M, \sigma_{e^- -1})$ (or $(M, \sigma_{e^+ -1})$, respectively), we query M to the EUF-CMA challenger of Σ associated to e^- (or produce a fresh signature using sk_{e^+}, respectively) and return it to the adversary. Again by the adaption property of Σ and thus the identical distribution of freshly generated signatures and updated ones, this is indistinguishable. Now if A outputs a valid forgery $(M^*, \sigma^*_{e^*})$ for epoch e^*, if $e^* = e^-$ we can directly output it. Otherwise we use $\Sigma.\mathsf{Adapt}$ to adapt the forgery backwards into epoch e^- and output it. Note that in any case a valid forgery output by A represents a valid forgery for Σ, as validity guarantees that we have never queried M^* throughout the game for any epoch inside the window.

More formally, let us consider the following sequence of games.

Game 0. This is the experiment $\mathsf{Exp}^{\mathsf{us\text{-}euf\text{-}cma}}_{\mathsf{US},A}(\lambda, n)$.

Game 1. This is identical to the previous game with the exception that we guess the window $[e^-, e^+[$ in which the epoch e^* for which A outputs the forgery is located and abort if our guess is incorrect.

Game 2. This is identical to the previous game up to the following differences:
- For call to Next' in epoch $e^- - 1$ we set $\Delta_{e^-} := \bot$ and run $(sk_{e^-}, pk_{e^-}) \leftarrow \Sigma.\mathsf{Gen}(1^\lambda)$ to obtain an independent key for epoch e^-. The same is done for a call to Next' in epoch $e^+ - 1$.
- For each call to the Next' oracle for epoch $e \in \{e^-, \ldots, e^+ - 2\}$, we run $\mathsf{Next}(pk_e, \bot)$ where we ignore the secret key and just set the key implicitly via the public-key, i.e., choose random $sk' \in \mathbb{H}$ and set $\Delta'_{e+1} := sk'$ and $\Delta_{e+1} := (\Delta'_{e+1}, pk_e)$, compute $pk_{e+1} := pk_e \cdot \mu(\Delta_{e+1})$, set $sk_{e+1} = \bot$.

- For each call to the Sig' oracle for message M in any epoch e within $[e^-, e^+[$, we compute $\sigma \leftarrow \Sigma.\mathsf{Sig}(sk_{e^-}, M)$ and then call $\Sigma.\mathsf{Adapt}$ using the respective public keys to adapt it to a signature σ_e valid under pk_e and add (e, M, σ_e) to $\mathcal{S}$.
- For each call to the Update' oracle for signature (M, σ_e) in epoch $e \in \{e^- - 1, e^+ - 1\}$, we compute $\sigma_{e+1} \leftarrow \Sigma.\mathsf{Sig}(sk_{e+1}, M)$. We then add $(e+1, M, \sigma_{e+1})$ to $\mathcal{S}$ and $\mathcal{U}$, and return σ_{e+1} to the adversary.

Now, let us analyze the transitions:

Lemma 4. *For any adversary A it holds that*

$$\left(\frac{1}{(e_{max}+1)e_{max}}\right) \Pr\left[S_{A,0}\right] \leq \Pr\left[S_{A,1}\right].$$

Proof. We guess the window by simply drawing $e^- \leftarrow \{0, ..., e_{max}\}$ and $e^+ \leftarrow \{e^- + 1, ..., e_{max}\}$ uniformly at random. Thus, this guess is correct with probability at least $\frac{1}{(e_{max}+1)e_{max}}$ and if the guess turns out to be wrong, we abort. Note that such a window always exists for a valid adversary A due to Lemma 1. □

Lemma 5. *For any adversary A it holds that*

$$|\Pr\left[S_{A,1}\right] - \Pr\left[S_{A,2}\right]| = 0.$$

Proof. We observe that due to having a valid adversary A w.r.t. window $[e^-, e^+[$ and due to Lemma 1 we recall that A

1) does not obtain tokens Δ_{e^-} and Δ_{e^+},
2) obtains no secret key sk_e for all $e^- \leq e < e^+$ and
3) can obtain all tokens Δ_e for $e^- < e < e^+$,

from the queries made to the oracles, given the leakage profile. Note that due to 1) we know that there implicitly exists a token mapping keys and signatures from $e^- - 1$ to e^- and from $e^+ - 1$ to e^+ (but we do not need to know them) and all (implicit) keys due to Lemma 2 are distributed as expected. Also, all the tokens Δ_e in this window that are given to A are distributed as expected. Finally, we can use the same argumentation as in the proof of Lemma 3 to show all signatures given to the adversary within the window in **Game 2** are distributed identical to the ones in **Game 1**. □

Lemma 6. *For any adversary A it holds* $\Pr\left[S_{A,2}\right] \leq \mathsf{Adv}_{\Sigma,A}^{\mathsf{euf\text{-}cma}}(\lambda)$.

Proof. Now we are at the point where we can associate an EUF-CMA challenger for Σ to the keys in time slot e^-. Now, for every signature query for message M and epoch e within the window to the Sig' oracle, we query M to the EUF-CMA challenger of Σ and then execute the remaining parts of the Sig' oracle to adapt the so obtained signature in the forwards direction to obtain the signature for M in epoch e within the window. Now if A eventually outputs a valid forgery

$(M^*, \sigma^*_{e^*})$ for epoch e^*, we know that in order to be valid, A did not query message M^* for any epoch within the window (otherwise, since it knows all tokens this would be a trivial forgery). In case $e^* = e^-$, we can directly output $(M^*, \sigma^*_{e^*})$ to the EUF-CMA challenger of Σ. Otherwise, we use Σ.Adapt to adapt the forgery backwards into epoch e^- and then output the message M^* and the adapted signature σ as forgery to the EUF-CMA challenger.

Taking all together this concludes the proof. □

4.2 Message-Independent US from the BLS Signature Scheme

Next, we discuss US schemes that do not require the message in order to update signatures, a feature which we call message-independence (MI). We prove that they are secure US in the conventional sense, i.e., in the model we always have access to the messages and verify their validity and we rather consider MI to be a practical feature in the following sense. In many practical applications, signatures can be verified offline at some point and then when performing (a batch of) updates at a later point in time, one does not need to access all the messages and verify the signatures. This helps to improve the performance of the updating procedure.

In Fig. 5, we provide a message-independent US scheme from the BLS signature. In contrast to BLS viewed as a KH signature scheme, where key updates are additive and the next public key is $pk' = pk \cdot \tilde{g}^{\Delta'} = \tilde{g}^{sk+\Delta'}$, we here consider a slight variation where the key update is multiplicative, i.e., $pk' = pk^{\Delta'} = \tilde{g}^{sk \cdot \Delta'}$. While this does not anymore yield a KH signature scheme in the framework of [25], due to the absence of the secret to public key homomorphism, it is easy to see that this variant provides an Adapt algorithm satisfying Definition 2, i.e., given a signature $\sigma = H(M)^{sk}$ the update is computed as $\sigma' = \sigma^{\Delta'} = H(M)^{sk \cdot \Delta'}$. It is also easy to see that the BLS scheme with this Adapt algorithm satisfies perfect adaption (cf. Definition 3), where in the definition $\mu(sk)$ is replaced by $\tilde{g}^{sk}$ and $\mu(sk) \cdot \mu(\Delta)$ is replaced by $\tilde{g}^{sk \cdot \Delta}$.

Consequently, we can exactly follow the proof of Theorem 1 with the only exception that we do not use μ for computing the pk's in the window, but choose $\Delta_{e_i} \leftarrow \mathbb{Z}_p$ and compute $pk_{e_i} = pk_{e_{i-1}}^{\Delta_{e_i}}$ (for all $e^- \leq e_i < e^+$). Moreover, it is easy to see that we adapt Lemma 2 with the same changes as discussed above. Checking correctness is straightforward. Hence, we obtain the following:

Corollary 1. *Let* $\Sigma = (\mathsf{Gen}, \mathsf{Sig}, \mathsf{Adapt}, \mathsf{Ver})$ *be the BLS signature scheme with the* Adapt *algorithm defined as* $\left(pk^{\Delta'}, \sigma^{\Delta'}\right) \leftarrow \mathsf{Adapt}(pk, M, \sigma, \Delta')$*, then the updatable signature scheme* US *from Fig. 5 is US-EUF-CMA secure and US-UU-CMA secure.*

MI US from PS Signatures. We note that the same technique (i.e., using multiplicative updates to obtain MI) can be applied to other KH signatures, such as Pointcheval-Sanders (PS) [48]. More precisely, for PS we can set the public key to $pk := (\tilde{X}, \tilde{Y}) = (\tilde{g}^x, \tilde{g}^y)$ for the secret key $sk := (x, y)$ with $x \leftarrow \mathbb{Z}_p$ and $y \leftarrow \mathbb{Z}_p^*$. The signature is computed by sampling $h \leftarrow \mathbb{G}_1^*$ and setting

$\mathsf{Setup}(1^\lambda, n)$:
- Run $\mathsf{BG} = (\mathbb{G}_1, \mathbb{G}_2, \mathbb{G}_T, g, \tilde{g}, e, p) \leftarrow \mathsf{BGGen}(1^\lambda)$, choose a hash function $H : \{0,1\}^* \rightarrow \mathbb{G}_1$ uniformly at random from hash function family $\{H_k\}_k$.
- Choose $x \leftarrow \mathbb{Z}_p^*$, and set $sk = x$ and $pk = \tilde{g}^x$.
- Return $(pk_1, sk_1) \leftarrow (pk, sk)$.

$\mathsf{Next}(pk_e, sk_e)$:
- Choose $x' \leftarrow \mathbb{Z}_p^*$ and set $\Delta'_{e+1} := x'$ and $\Delta_{e+1} := (\Delta'_{e+1}, pk_e)$.
- Compute $pk_{e+1} = pk_e^{\Delta_{e+1}}$ and $sk_{e+1} = sk_e \cdot \Delta'_{e+1}$.
- Return $(pk_{e+1}, sk_{e+1}, \Delta_{e+1})$.

$\mathsf{Sig}(sk_e, M)$:
- Return $\sigma = H(M)^{sk_e}$.

$\mathsf{Update}(\Delta_{e+1}, \sigma_e)$:
- Parse $\Delta_{e+1} = (\Delta'_{e+1}, pk_e)$.
- Compute $\sigma_{e+1} = \sigma_e^{\Delta'_{e+1}}$.
- Return σ_{e+1}.

$\mathsf{Ver}(pk_e, M, \sigma_e)$:
- Return $e(H(M), pk_e) = e(\sigma_e, \tilde{g})$.

Fig. 5. US with message-independent updates from BLS signatures.

$\sigma := (\sigma_1, \sigma_2) = (h, h^{x+y \cdot m})$. The verification holds for $e(\sigma_1, \tilde{X} \cdot \tilde{Y}^m) = e(\sigma_2, \tilde{g})$. In order to provide message-independent updates, we can sample $\Delta_1 \leftarrow \mathbb{Z}_p^*$ and $\Delta_2 \leftarrow \mathbb{Z}_p$, set the update token to $\Delta := (\Delta_1, \Delta_2)$, and compute the updated key pair as $sk' := (x \cdot \Delta_1 + \Delta_2, y \cdot \Delta_1)$ and $pk' := (\tilde{X}', \tilde{Y}') = (\tilde{X}^{\Delta_1} \cdot \tilde{g}^{\Delta_2}, \tilde{Y}^{\Delta_1})$. Then, the update procedure is performed by sampling a random $r \leftarrow \mathbb{Z}_p^*$ and computing $\sigma' := (\sigma'_1, \sigma'_2) = (\sigma_1^r, \sigma_2^{r \cdot \Delta_1} \cdot \sigma_1^{r \cdot \Delta_2})$.

4.3 Towards Updatable Signatures from Lattices

In this section, we aim to construct an US scheme from lattices. In particular, we start from the well-known GPV signature scheme [30] and, by using methods inspired by the lattice-based proxy re-signature approach in [28], we obtain an US scheme that we call $\mathsf{US}_{\mathsf{GPV}}$. In order to prove its US-EUF-CMA security, however, we have to restrict the capabilities of the adversary, but will provide evidence that this does not seem to make a huge difference in the practical use of the scheme compared to the original leakage profile.

Let us briefly recall the construction of the GPV signature scheme in its probabilistic full-domain hash (FDH) variant. For a recollection of lattice preliminaries we refer the reader to the full version. In the following let $H : \{0,1\}^* \rightarrow \mathbb{Z}_q^n$ be a hash function modeled as a random oracle. The GPV signature scheme consists of the following algorithms:

- $\mathsf{Gen}(1^n)$: Run $\mathsf{TrapGen}(n, m, q, s)$ to get pair $(\mathbf{A}, \mathbf{T_A})$ ($\mathbf{A}$ is an $n \times m$ matrix over $\mathbb{Z}_q$ and $\mathbf{T_A}$ is a short basis of $\Lambda^\perp(\mathbf{A})$). Output $(pk = \mathbf{A}, sk = \mathbf{T_A})$.
- $\mathsf{Sig}(M, sk = \mathbf{T_A})$: Sample $t \leftarrow \{0,1\}^n$, compute $\mathbf{y} = H(M||t)$, and output $(\mathbf{u}, t)$, where $\mathbf{u}$ is a short vector computed via $\mathbf{u} \leftarrow \mathsf{SamplePre}(\mathbf{A}, \mathbf{T_A}, s, \mathbf{y})$.

- $\mathsf{Ver}((\mathbf{u}, t), M, pk = \mathbf{A})$: Compute $\mathbf{y} = H(M||t)$. Output 1 if and only if $\mathbf{A} \cdot \mathbf{u} = \mathbf{y}$ and $||\mathbf{u}||$ is small enough, and 0 otherwise.

To transform this scheme into an updatable one, we can apply a method similar to the one used in [28] to generate the re-signing keys and re-sign signatures: given the secret key of epoch $e+1$, using the $\mathsf{SamplePre}$ algorithm, it is possible to compute a small norm matrix Δ_{e+1} (for the sake of conciseness, we do not include the old public key as part of the update token) that maps, by left multiplication, the current public key to the previous one, i.e., $pk_{e+1} \cdot \Delta_{e+1} = pk_e$. Then, we can use this matrix to map, by right multiplication, a signature valid in the previous epoch to a signature valid in the current one. The small norm of Δ_{e+1} ensures that, in the update process, the norm of the signature does not increase "too much". Figure 6 describes the so obtained lattice-based US scheme $\mathsf{US}_{\mathsf{GPV}}$.

Public parameters: security parameter λ, $T = \text{polylog}(\lambda)$ maximum allowed updates, $q = n^{O(T)}$, $n = \text{poly}(\lambda)$, $m = O(n \log q)$, $s = \omega(\sqrt{\log n})$ and $B = \omega(2^T)$.

$\mathsf{KeyGen}(1^\lambda)$:
- Let $(\mathbf{A}_1, \mathbf{T}_{\mathbf{A}_1}) \leftarrow \mathsf{TrapGen}(n, m, q, s)$.
- Return $(sk_1 := \mathbf{T}_{\mathbf{A}_1}, pk_1 := \mathbf{A}_1)$.

$\mathsf{Next}(pk_e, sk_e)$:
- Let $(\mathbf{A}_{e+1}, \mathbf{T}_{\mathbf{A}_{e+1}}) \leftarrow \mathsf{TrapGen}(n, m, q, s)$.
- Let $\Delta_{e+1} \leftarrow \mathsf{SamplePre}(\mathbf{A}_{e+1}, \mathbf{T}_{\mathbf{A}_{e+1}}, s, \mathbf{A}_e)$.
- Return $(sk_{e+1} := \mathbf{T}_{\mathbf{A}_{e+1}}, pk_{e+1} := \mathbf{A}_{e+1}, \Delta_{e+1})$.

$\mathsf{Sig}(sk_e, M)$:
- Sample $t \leftarrow \{0, 1\}^k$.
- Compute $\mathbf{y} = H(M||t)$, and $\tau_e \leftarrow \mathsf{SamplePre}(\mathbf{A}_e, \mathbf{T}_{\mathbf{A}_e}, s, \mathbf{y})$.
- Return $\sigma_e = (\tau_e, t)$.

$\mathsf{Update}(\Delta_{e+1}, \sigma_e)$:
- Parse $\sigma_e = (\tau_e, t)$.
- Compute $\tau_{e+1} = \Delta_{e+1} \cdot \tau_e$.
- Return $\sigma_{e+1} = (\tau_{e+1}, t)$.

$\mathsf{Ver}(pk_e, M, \sigma_e)$:
- Parse $\sigma_e = (\tau_e, t)$.
- Compute $\mathbf{y} = H(M||t)$.
- Return 1 if $||\tau_e|| < B$ and $pk_e \cdot \tau_e = \mathbf{y}$, otherwise return $\perp$.

Fig. 6. Message-independent unidirectional US from GPV.

Correctness and Leakage Profile. In the Next algorithm, the token Δ_e is computed by running $\mathsf{SamplePre}(\mathbf{A}_{e+1}, \mathbf{T}_{\mathbf{A}_{e+1}}, s, \mathbf{A}_e)$. In this way we obtain an $m \times m$ matrix Δ_{e+1} (of short norm) such that

$$\mathbf{A}_{e+1} \cdot \Delta_{e+1} = \mathbf{A}_e.$$

If $\sigma_e = (\tau_e, t)$ is a valid signature of M under the public key $\mathbf{A}_e$, we must have that $\mathbf{A}_e \cdot \tau_e = H(M||t)$, and that τ_e is of small norm. When we update the signature σ_e we get $\tau_{e+1} = \Delta_{e+1} \cdot \tau_e$. Since both Δ_e and τ_e are of small norm, so is τ_{e+1}. Moreover

$$\begin{aligned}\mathbf{A}_{e+1} \cdot \tau_{e+1} &= \mathbf{A}_{e+1} \cdot (\Delta_{e+1} \cdot \tau_e) = (\mathbf{A}_{e+1} \cdot \Delta_{e+1}) \cdot \tau_e \\ &= \mathbf{A}_e \cdot \tau_e = H(M||t),\end{aligned}$$

which proves correctness of the updated signature. As a signature produced by algorithm Sign has size $O(s\sqrt{m})$, and after each update, the size grows at the rate of $O(sm)$, as in [28], we set the parameter used in verification to be $B = \omega(2^T)$. The US construction can support $T = \text{polylog}(\lambda)$ updates using the subexponential SIS assumption.

Modified Leakage Profile. As far as the leakage profile is concerned, in order to be able to prove the US-EUF-CMA security of $\mathsf{US}_{\mathsf{GPV}}$, we need to add a restriction that the adversary is not allowed to query the update oracle at epoch $e^- - 1$ to obtain signatures at epoch e^-. We note that this restriction is needed to allow the challenger to simulate all responses to the oracle queries of the adversary. In the general case, this weakened model would allow to prove US schemes US-EUF-CMA which leak the token when seeing a signature and its updated version (such as Schnorr type signatures). However, as proven in Proposition 1 below, even updating a large but limited amount of signatures will not leak the token for the $\mathsf{US}_{\mathsf{GPV}}$ scheme. Consequently, weakening the model merely seems to be an artifact that results from our proof technique, but does not seem to represent a significant weakness in practice.

Moreover, as updated signatures are distinguishable from fresh ones, one has to keep track of the different signatures given to the adversary: for this reason, in the security proof we will split the set $\mathcal{S}$ into sets $\mathcal{S}'$ and $\mathcal{U}'$, which will consist of the fresh and updated signatures respectively. In addition to also supporting the feature of message-independence, interestingly, the $\mathsf{US}_{\mathsf{GPV}}$ scheme satisfies also unidirectional updates: by construction, the secret key of epoch e alone is required to produce the update token Δ_e. In particular this implies that the token cannot be used to backward adapt signatures, since this will contradict the unforgeability of the underlying signature scheme. This "feature" can be seen as one reason for the weakening of the model, as it is incompatible with the proof technique used for the other US constructions.

Security of $\mathsf{US}_{\mathsf{GPV}}$. For this construction, we can prove the following theorem:

Theorem 2. *Assuming the hardness of* $\mathsf{SIS}_{q,n,m,2B}$*, the US scheme* $\mathsf{US}_{\mathsf{GPV}}$ *from Fig. 6 is US-EUF-CMA secure, with the above discussed restriction on the adversary, in the random oracle model.*

Proof (Sketch). We can follow, here as well, the proof of Theorem 1: we guess the forgery period e^* and the window $[e^-, e^+[$ (by the above discussion regarding the uni-directionality of the US under consideration, the window will be, in this case, one-sided, i.e., we can even assume that A has access to Δ_{e^+}). Outside of the window, we will behave in our simulation as in the original game and will know all secret keys and update tokens. Inside the window, we start by embedding the SIS matrix $\mathbf{A}^*$ as public key of the forgery epoch e^*. We then have to distinguish the right part of the window, $e \in]e^*, e^+[$, from the left part, $e \in [e^-, e^*[$. For all epochs e in the right part, we can produce pk_e and Δ_e as in the real game (and thus we also have the corresponding secret key sk_e). For those in the left part, we start by sampling $\Delta_{e^*} \leftarrow \mathcal{D}_{\mathbb{Z}^{m \times m}, s}$ and set $pk_{e^*-1} := pk_{e^*} \cdot \Delta_{e^*}$. Since this distribution is statistically close to the one of the matrices output by the SamplePre algorithm, the adversary will not be able to distinguish the simulation from the real game. We then iterate this process till we obtain pk_{e^-}. In this way we can respond to all secret key and token corruption queries. As far as the signature queries are concerned, we rely on the programmability of the random oracle model: when the adversary queries the signature oracle, we first sample the short vector that will serve as signature and then program the random oracle H accordingly. The presence of the "salt" t guarantees us that, except with negligible probability, we will be able to reply to all signing queries (e.g., even if the adversary asks for signature of the same message in different epochs, which would not be possible if there was no "salt" involved in the signing algorithm). The update queries can be answered as in the real game as, by the restriction imposed on the adversary, we will know all the tokens require to run the allowed update queries. Since simulation and real game are computationally indistinguishable, the reduction can derive a SIS solution from the forgery tuple. □

We provide a full proof in the full version.

Remark 1. The above $\mathsf{US}_{\mathsf{GPV}}$ scheme does not achieve US-UU-CMA security: Firstly, the tag associated to a signature is not changed during the update and, secondly, the norm of the signature acts as distinguishing feature between fresh and updated signatures.

The following proposition shows that, under the parameter restriction required by the TrapGen algorithm, i.e., $m \geq 5n \log q$, we can update a large but limited amount of signatures, namely k, without leaking the update token Δ to the adversary.

Proposition 1. *Let $m \geq 5n \log q$ and $k \leq n$. For any PPT adversary $\mathcal{A}$, the probability that $\mathcal{A}$ on input (pk_e, sk_e, pk_{e+1}) and any k pairs of updated signatures $(\tau_{M_i,t_i,e}, \Delta_{e+1} \cdot \tau_{M_i,t_i,e})$ outputs the update token Δ_{e+1} is negligible.*

Proof. By the second claim of Lemma 5.2 from [30], Δ_{e+1} is distributed according to a discrete Gaussian over $\mathbb{Z}^{m \times m}$, which has, by Lemma 2.10 from [30], at least min-entropy $m(m-1)$. By the chain rule of min-entropy, every pair of updated signatures $(\tau_e, \Delta_{e+1} \cdot \tau_e)$ lowers the entropy of Δ_{e+1} by $m \log q$. Hence the min-entropy of Δ_{e+1} conditioned on the view of the adversary is at least $m(m-1) - k \cdot m \log q$, which is greater than n by our bounds on k and m. □

4.4 Overview and Discussion

We provide a compact overview of US schemes obtained from different KH signatures as well as our dedicated BLS-, PS- and GPV-based constructions in

Table 1. We present the scheme along with the required hardness assumption, whether it is in the standard model, in the generic group model (GGM) or require random oracles (RO), whether it is unlinkable (UU-CMA), whether it is message-dependent or -independent (MD/MI) and whether it supports an unbounded number of epochs (UB), i.e.,. at least polynomially many in the security parameter, or a concrete bound T on the number of updates.

Table 1. Overview of updatable signature schemes.

Scheme	Assumption	Model	UU-CMA	MD/MI	UB
BLS (Sect. 4.2)	co-CDH	RO	✓	MI	✓
BLS (Sect. 4.1)	co-CDH	RO	✓	MD	✓
PS (Sect. 4.2)	P-LRSW	GGM	✓	MI	✓
PS (Sect. 4.1)	P-LRSW	GGM	✓	MD	✓
Waters (Sect. 4.1)	co-CDH	SM	✓	MD	✓
GPV (Sect. 4.3)†	SIS	RO	✗	MI	T

† Provides US-EUF-CMA security only in a weakened model.

As far as efficiency is concerned (counting only expensive operations), and in order to provide some intuition, the BLS construction requires 1 exponentiation for the Next algorithm, while the Update algorithm needs 1 hash to group operation and 1 exponentiation. On the other hand, the message-independent BLS from Sect. 4.2 requires 1 exponentiation in the Next algorithm and only 1 exponentiation in the Update algorithm. PS requires 2 exponentiations for the Next algorithm, followed by 3 exponentiations in the Update algorithm. On the other hand, message-independent PS from Sect. 4.2 requires 3 exponentiations for the Next algorithm, followed by 3 exponentiations in Update.

5 Construction of Updatable MACs

In this section we present a generic constructions of UMACs from (almost) key-homomorphic PRFs and then present a dedicated construction of a UMAC from the Naor, Pinkas, and Reingold (NPR) PRF [47].

Before we start, we will discuss a well-known approach to turn a PRF $F : \mathcal{K} \times \mathcal{X} \rightarrow \mathcal{Y}$ into a MAC by setting $\sigma \leftarrow \Pi.\mathsf{Sig}(sk, M) := F(sk, M)$ with the canonical verification that recomputes the tag σ and compares it to the obtained one. Analogously, a KH-PRF gives a KH-MAC due to the key-homomorphism property and security of the PRF. However, if we use an "almost" KH-PRF, then the canonical verification needs to be replaced with an "approximate" canonical verification (i.e., noisy equality check), where the verification involves a metric function (e.g., Euclidean distance) that gives the distance between input tag and recomputed tag, and verification only succeeds if the distance is smaller than some bound δ.

Clearly, the above discussed approach only yields a fixed-length MAC with message space $\mathcal{X}$. If the message space is too small, however, we can use a collision-resistant hash function family (Gen_H, H) with $H : S \times \{0,1\}^* \to \mathcal{X}$ to obtain a variable-length MAC that supports arbitrary length messages by defining $\Pi'.\mathsf{Sig}(sk, M) := F(sk, H(s, M))$. For that construction we can show the following (cf. [9]):

Lemma 7. *If Π is a fixed-length EUF-CMA secure MAC for message space $\mathcal{X}$ and (Gen_H, H) a collision resistant hash function family, then Π' is a variable-length EUF-CMA secure MAC for messages of arbitrary length.*

Proof (Sketch). Let A be the adversary in the experiment $\mathsf{Exp}^{\mathsf{euf\text{-}cma}}_{\Pi,A}$ and let $(M_1, \ldots, M_q)$ be the messages queried by A to oracle Sig' and (M^*, σ^*) be the valid forgery output by the adversary. Now, we have two cases: In the first case *i)* we have that $H(s, M^*) = H(s, M_i)$ for some $i \in [q]$, which yields a collision pair (M^*, M_i) for H, contradicting collision-resistance of (Gen_H, H). In the second case *ii)* we have that $H(s, M^*) \neq H(s, M_i)$ for all $i \in [q]$. However, this means that $(H(s, M^*), \sigma^*)$ represents a valid tag (signature) for a new message $H(s, M^*)$ and thus a valid forgery for Π. □

Subsequently, in our generic construction we consider KH PRFs, which we can equivalently view as KH MACs for fixed-length inputs. We will not make it explicit in our construction, but straightforwardly applying Lemma 7 to our generic construction in Sect. 5.1 will yield UMACs for variable-length inputs.

5.1 UMACs from KH PRFs

Now we show how to obtain UMACs from (almost) KH-PRFs generically. For $\mathcal{K}$ we write $\oplus$ as the group operation and $-k$ as the inverse of k. For the group $\mathcal{Y}$, we use the common addition. The UMAC obtained from a KH-PRF can be seen in Fig. 7, where the text in blue color is only required when using "almost" KH-PRF and $\mathcal{D}_\chi$ represents the error distribution (e.g., error distribution used in lattice-based constructions).

We can show the following:

Theorem 3. *If $F : \mathcal{K} \times \mathcal{X} \to \mathcal{Y}$ is a secure (almost) key-homomorphic PRF (equivalently an EUF-CMA secure (approximate) MAC for message space $\mathcal{X}$), then the UMAC construction in Fig. 7 is UMAC-EUF-CMA secure and UMAC-UU-CMA secure.*

Setup($1^\lambda, n$):
- Sample a random key $k_1 \in \mathcal{K}$ and output k_1.

Next(k_e) :
- Sample a random key $k_{e+1} \in \mathcal{K}$.
- Compute $\Delta_{e+1} = k_{e+1} \oplus -k_e$ and (k_{e+1}, Δ_{e+1}).

Sig(k_e, M) :
- Sample $(\chi_2, \ldots, \chi_e) \leftarrow_\$ \mathcal{D}_\chi$.
- Compute $\sigma_e = F(k_e, M) + \sum_{i=2}^{e} \chi_i$ and output (M, σ_e).

Update($\Delta_{e+1}, M, \sigma_e$) :
- Compute $\sigma_{e+1} = \sigma_e + F(\Delta_{e+1}, M)$ and output (M, σ_{e+1}).

Ver(k_e, M, σ_e) :
- If $F(k_e, M) = \sigma_e$ ($\|\sigma_e - F(k_e, M)\| \leq \delta$) output 1, otherwise output 0.

Fig. 7. Bi-directional UMAC from (almost) KH-PRF. Blue parts correspond to the changes when using almost KH-PRF.

The proof of UMAC-EUF-CMA security follows exactly the strategy in the proof of Theorem 1 with the only exceptions that within the window we need to simulate the Ver$'$ oracle, and for the almost KH-PRF we need to account for the additional error terms. For completeness, we provide a sketch of the proof in the full version.

A Note on Almost KH-PRFs. In the notion of almost KH-PRFs such as those from the (R)LWE assumption [14,15,39] every homomorphic operations increases the error χ and thus the constructions are only T-time correct. This means, that UMACs constructed from such KH-PRFs by default will not satisfy the UMAC-UU-CMA notion, while the tags obtained from the Update algorithm will have higher error compared to fresh tags obtained from the Sig algorithm, thus making them trivially distinguishable. In order to circumvent this issue, in Fig. 7, we use the trick to make the error depend on the epoch e that we are in. Hence, freshly computed tags and updated ones have the same amount of error, which makes them indistinguishable, and allows us to achieve the UMAC-UU-CMA notion.

Another issue to consider is the effect of the approximate canonical verification on the security of the UMAC. Since we have a noisy equality check during the verification algorithm, we can consider that we have a ball centered around the tag σ, such that verification accepts any vector within this ball as a valid tag. This implies that an adversary can just change the low-order bits of a valid tag σ to produce another valid tag σ' that will be within this ball and pass the verification, and hence, break the strong unforgeability. However, since in this work we are only interested in conventional unforgeability of the MAC (i.e., do not require strongly unforgeable MACs), this approach is not useful to a valid adversary against our UMAC. The adversary in our case is required to come up with a valid tag that lies sufficiently far away from any tags that it was provided with. Though, the adversary cannot do this due to the security of the underlying

KH-PRF. Nevertheless, the security of the KH-MAC obtained from KH-PRF is correlated with the verification bound. If the verification bound is extremely large, then we have that the balls around the valid tags are overlapping (i.e., the balls are so large that they cover the entire space), and then with high probability any random vector is sufficiently close to a random tag. However, by setting the parameters appropriately we can bound this probability to be negligible. More precisely, when using lattice-based almost KH-PRFs as MACs, for a MAC verification bound δ, modulus q and lattice dimension n, we have that the ball around a valid tag σ takes up $(\delta/q)^n$ of the area, where the entire space has area of q^n. If the space taken by the ball is negligible, then it is hard for the adversary to forge a valid tag. Since this will depend on the instantiation and parameters of the almost KH-PRF, we leave it as an open problem to setup tighter bounds and compute exact parameters. For our construction in Fig. 7, we can set the verification bound to $\delta = T \cdot B$, for a constant T denoting the maximum number of epochs for our UMAC, and B the bound on the errors sampled from $\mathcal{D}_\chi$.

5.2 Message-Independent UMAC from the NPR PRF

Since UMACs from KH-PRFs are inherently message-dependent, we now present a dedicated construction of a variable-length UMAC scheme that is message-independent (MI) from the PRF due to Naor, Pinkas, and Reingold (NPR) [47]. Let us recall the NPR PRF and therefore let $\mathbb{G}$ be a cyclic group of prime oder p in which the DDH assumption holds and $H : \{0,1\}^* \rightarrow \mathbb{G}$ a hash function modeled as a random oracle, then the NPR PRF with $F : \mathbb{Z}_p^* \times \{0,1\}^* \rightarrow \mathbb{G}$ is defined as $F(k, M) := H(M)^k$. It is secure under the DDH assumption in the random oracle model. In contrast to the key-homomorphic variant of the NPR PRF which considers keys from the additive group $\mathbb{Z}_p$, we consider key updates multiplicatively with $\Delta \in \mathbb{Z}_p^*$, in the vein of the multiplicative variant of the US from the BLS scheme in Sect. 4.2. Note that as in Sect. 4.2 we consider MI to be a feature of UMACs for practical applications where one can assume that one operates on valid UMACs.

To show the security of this construction, we can exactly follow the proof of Theorem 3 with the only exception that we do not use the key-homomorphic property of the PRF in Update, but choose $\Delta_{e_i+1} \leftarrow \mathbb{Z}_p^*$ and compute $\sigma = \sigma^{\Delta_{e_i+1}^{-1}}$ or $\sigma = \sigma^{\Delta_{e_i+1}}$ if we have to switch PRF evaluations back (from epoch $e_i + 1$ to epoch e_i) or forth (from epoch e_i to epoch $e_i + 1$). Checking correctness is straightforward and we obtain the following:

$\mathsf{Setup}(1^\lambda, n)$:
- Run $\mathcal{G} = (\mathbb{G}, p, g) \leftarrow \mathsf{GGen}(1^\lambda)$, choose a hash function $H : \{0,1\}^* \rightarrow \mathbb{G}_1$ uniformly at random from hash function family $\{H_k\}_k$.
- Sample a random key $k_1 \in \mathbb{Z}_p^*$ and return $(\mathcal{G}, H, k_1)$.

$\mathsf{Next}(k_e)$:
- Choose $\Delta_{e+1} \leftarrow \mathbb{Z}_p^*$ and return $(k_{e+1} := (\mathcal{G}, H, k_e \cdot \Delta_{e+1}), \Delta_{e+1})$.

$\mathsf{Sig}(k_e, M)$:
- Compute $\sigma_e = H(M)^{k_e}$ and return (M, σ_e).

$\mathsf{Update}(\Delta_{e+1}, \sigma_e)$:
- Compute $\sigma_{e+1} = \sigma_e^{\Delta_{e+1}}$ and return σ_{e+1}.

$\mathsf{Ver}(k_e, M, \sigma_e)$:
- If $H(M)^{k_e} = \sigma_e$ return 1, otherwise return 0.

Fig. 8. Bi-directional variable-length UMAC from NPR PRF.

Corollary 2. *Let F be the NPR PRF, then the construction in Fig. 5 is an UMAC-EUF-CMA-secure and UMAC-UU-CMA secure UMAC.*

5.3 Overview and Discussion

We provide a compact overview of UMACs obtained from different KH-PRFs as well as our dedicated NPR-based construction in Table 2. We use the same criteria for comparison as in Sect. 4.4.

Table 2. Overview of updatable MACs.

Scheme	Assumption	Model	UU-CMA	MD/MI	UB
BLMR (NPR) [15]	DDH	RO	✓	MD	✓
NPR (Sect. 5.2)	DDH	RO	✓	MI	✓
BEKS [14]	RLWE	RO	✓	MD	T
Kim [39]	LWE	SM	✓	MD	T

Regarding efficiency (again only counting expensive operations), for the key-homomorphic NPR UMAC for instance Update requires 1 hashing to the group as well as 1 exponentiation and Next only cheap operations. The variant of the NPR UMAC from Sect. 5.2 requires instead 1 exponentiation for Update and Next also only cheap operations.

Acknowledgements. We thank the anonymous reviewers for their comments. This project has received funding from the European Union's Horizon 2020 research and innovation programme under grant agreements n°830929 (CyberSec4Europe) and n°871473 (KRAKEN), European Union's Horizon 2020 ECSEL Joint Undertaking project under grant agreement n°783119 (SECREDAS), by the Austrian Science Fund (FWF) and netidee SCIENCE grant P31621-N38 (PROFET) and FWF grant W1255-N23.

References

1. Abdolmaleki, B., Ramacher, S., Slamanig, D.: Lift-and-shift: obtaining simulation extractable subversion and updatable SNARKs generically. In: ACM CCS 20 (2020)
2. Ananth, P., Cohen, A., Jain, A.: Cryptography with updates. In: Coron, J.-S., Nielsen, J.B. (eds.) EUROCRYPT 2017. LNCS, vol. 10211, pp. 445–472. Springer, Cham (2017). https://doi.org/10.1007/978-3-319-56614-6_15
3. Apple: code signing. https://developer.apple.com/support/code-signing/
4. Applebaum, B.: Computationally private randomizing polynomials and their applications. In: Cryptography in Constant Parallel Time. ISC, pp. 79–106. Springer, Heidelberg (2014). https://doi.org/10.1007/978-3-642-17367-7_5
5. Arch Linux Wiki: pacman/package signing. https://wiki.archlinux.org/index.php/Pacman/Package_signing
6. Arte, V., Bellare, M., Khati, L.: Incremental cryptography revisited: PRFs, nonces and modular design. In: Bhargavan, K., Oswald, E., Prabhakaran, M. (eds.) INDOCRYPT 2020. LNCS, vol. 12578, pp. 576–598. Springer, Cham (2020). https://doi.org/10.1007/978-3-030-65277-7_26
7. Ateniese, G., Chou, D.H., de Medeiros, B., Tsudik, G.: Sanitizable signatures. In: di Vimercati, S.C., Syverson, P., Gollmann, D. (eds.) ESORICS 2005. LNCS, vol. 3679, pp. 159–177. Springer, Heidelberg (2005). https://doi.org/10.1007/11555827_10
8. Banerjee, A., Peikert, C.: New and improved key-homomorphic pseudorandom functions. In: Garay, J.A., Gennaro, R. (eds.) CRYPTO 2014. LNCS, vol. 8616, pp. 353–370. Springer, Heidelberg (2014). https://doi.org/10.1007/978-3-662-44371-2_20
9. Bellare, M.: New proofs for NMAC and HMAC: security without collision-resistance. In: Dwork, C. (ed.) CRYPTO 2006. LNCS, vol. 4117, pp. 602–619. Springer, Heidelberg (2006). https://doi.org/10.1007/11818175_36
10. Bellare, M., Goldreich, O., Goldwasser, S.: Incremental cryptography: the case of hashing and signing. In: Desmedt, Y.G. (ed.) CRYPTO 1994. LNCS, vol. 839, pp. 216–233. Springer, Heidelberg (1994). https://doi.org/10.1007/3-540-48658-5_22
11. Bellare, M., Goldreich, O., Goldwasser, S.: Incremental cryptography and application to virus protection. In: 27th ACM STOC (1995)
12. Bichsel, P., Camenisch, J., Neven, G., Smart, N.P., Warinschi, B.: Get shorty via group signatures without encryption. In: Garay, J.A., De Prisco, R. (eds.) SCN 2010. LNCS, vol. 6280, pp. 381–398. Springer, Heidelberg (2010). https://doi.org/10.1007/978-3-642-15317-4_24
13. Blaze, M., Bleumer, G., Strauss, M.: Divertible protocols and atomic proxy cryptography. In: Nyberg, K. (ed.) EUROCRYPT 1998. LNCS, vol. 1403, pp. 127–144. Springer, Heidelberg (1998). https://doi.org/10.1007/BFb0054122
14. Boneh, D., Eskandarian, S., Kim, S., Shih, M.: Improving speed and security in updatable encryption schemes. In: Moriai, S., Wang, H. (eds.) ASIACRYPT 2020. LNCS, vol. 12493, pp. 559–589. Springer, Cham (2020). https://doi.org/10.1007/978-3-030-64840-4_19
15. Boneh, D., Lewi, K., Montgomery, H., Raghunathan, A.: Key homomorphic PRFs and their applications. In: Canetti, R., Garay, J.A. (eds.) CRYPTO 2013. LNCS, vol. 8042, pp. 410–428. Springer, Heidelberg (2013). https://doi.org/10.1007/978-3-642-40041-4_23

16. Boneh, D., Lynn, B., Shacham, H.: Short signatures from the weil pairing. In: Boyd, C. (ed.) ASIACRYPT 2001. LNCS, vol. 2248, pp. 514–532. Springer, Heidelberg (2001). https://doi.org/10.1007/3-540-45682-1_30
17. Bootle, J., Cerulli, A., Chaidos, P., Ghadafi, E., Groth, J.: Foundations of fully dynamic group signatures. In: Manulis, M., Sadeghi, A.-R., Schneider, S. (eds.) ACNS 2016. LNCS, vol. 9696, pp. 117–136. Springer, Cham (2016). https://doi.org/10.1007/978-3-319-39555-5_7
18. Boyd, C., Davies, G.T., Gjøsteen, K., Jiang, Y.: Fast and secure updatable encryption. In: Micciancio, D., Ristenpart, T. (eds.) CRYPTO 2020. LNCS, vol. 12170, pp. 464–493. Springer, Cham (2020). https://doi.org/10.1007/978-3-030-56784-2_16
19. Brzuska, C., Fischlin, M., Freudenreich, T., Lehmann, A., Page, M., Schelbert, J., Schröder, D., Volk, F.: Security of sanitizable signatures revisited. In: Jarecki, S., Tsudik, G. (eds.) PKC 2009. LNCS, vol. 5443, pp. 317–336. Springer, Heidelberg (2009). https://doi.org/10.1007/978-3-642-00468-1_18
20. Brzuska, C., Fischlin, M., Lehmann, A., Schröder, D.: Unlinkability of sanitizable signatures. In: Nguyen, P.Q., Pointcheval, D. (eds.) PKC 2010. LNCS, vol. 6056, pp. 444–461. Springer, Heidelberg (2010). https://doi.org/10.1007/978-3-642-13013-7_26
21. Camenisch, J., Dubovitskaya, M., Haralambiev, K., Kohlweiss, M.: Composable and modular anonymous credentials: definitions and practical constructions. In: Iwata, T., Cheon, J.H. (eds.) ASIACRYPT 2015. LNCS, vol. 9453, pp. 262–288. Springer, Heidelberg (2015). https://doi.org/10.1007/978-3-662-48800-3_11
22. Chase, M., Meiklejohn, S., Zaverucha, G.: Algebraic MACs and keyed-verification anonymous credentials. In: ACM CCS 2014 (201)
23. Derler, D., Slamanig, D.: Key-homomorphic signatures: definitions and applications to multiparty signatures and non-interactive zero-knowledge. Cryptology ePrint Archive, Report 2016/792. https://eprint.iacr.org/2016/792
24. Derler, D., Slamanig, D.: Highly-efficient fully-anonymous dynamic group signatures. In: ASIACCS 18 (2018)
25. Derler, D., Slamanig, D.: Key-homomorphic signatures: definitions and applications to multiparty signatures and non-interactive zero-knowledge. Des. Codes Cryptogr. **87**, 1373–1413 (2019)
26. Elenkov, N.: Android Security Internals: An In-Depth Guide to Android's Security Architecture (2015)
27. Everspaugh, A., Paterson, K., Ristenpart, T., Scott, S.: Key rotation for authenticated encryption. In: Katz, J., Shacham, H. (eds.) CRYPTO 2017. LNCS, vol. 10403, pp. 98–129. Springer, Cham (2017). https://doi.org/10.1007/978-3-319-63697-9_4
28. Fan, X., Liu, F.-H.: Proxy re-encryption and re-signatures from lattices. In: Deng, R.H., Gauthier-Umaña, V., Ochoa, M., Yung, M. (eds.) ACNS 2019. LNCS, vol. 11464, pp. 363–382. Springer, Cham (2019). https://doi.org/10.1007/978-3-030-21568-2_18
29. Fleischhacker, N., Krupp, J., Malavolta, G., Schneider, J., Schröder, D., Simkin, M.: Efficient unlinkable sanitizable signatures from signatures with re-randomizable keys. In: Cheng, C.-M., Chung, K.-M., Persiano, G., Yang, B.-Y. (eds.) PKC 2016. LNCS, vol. 9614, pp. 301–330. Springer, Heidelberg (2016). https://doi.org/10.1007/978-3-662-49384-7_12
30. Gentry, C., Peikert, C., Vaikuntanathan, V.: Trapdoors for hard lattices and new cryptographic constructions. In: 40th ACM STOC (2008)
31. Google developers: sign your app. https://developer.android.com/studio/publish/app-signing

32. Groth, J., Kohlweiss, M., Maller, M., Meiklejohn, S., Miers, I.: Updatable and universal common reference strings with applications to ZK-SNARKs. In: Shacham, H., Boldyreva, A. (eds.) CRYPTO 2018. LNCS, vol. 10993, pp. 698–728. Springer, Cham (2018). https://doi.org/10.1007/978-3-319-96878-0_24
33. Ishai, Y., Kushilevitz, E.: Randomizing polynomials: a new representation with applications to round-efficient secure computation. In: 41st FOCS (2000)
34. Jaeger, J., Stepanovs, I.: Optimal channel security against fine-grained state compromise: the safety of messaging. In: Shacham, H., Boldyreva, A. (eds.) CRYPTO 2018. LNCS, vol. 10991, pp. 33–62. Springer, Cham (2018). https://doi.org/10.1007/978-3-319-96884-1_2
35. Jarecki, S., Krawczyk, H., Resch, J.K.: Updatable oblivious key management for storage systems. In: ACM CCS 2019)
36. Jiang, Y.: The direction of updatable encryption does not matter much. In: Moriai, S., Wang, H. (eds.) ASIACRYPT 2020. LNCS, vol. 12493, pp. 529–558. Springer, Cham (2020). https://doi.org/10.1007/978-3-030-64840-4_18
37. Johnson, R., Molnar, D., Song, D., Wagner, D.: Homomorphic signature schemes. In: Preneel, B. (ed.) CT-RSA 2002. LNCS, vol. 2271, pp. 244–262. Springer, Heidelberg (2002). https://doi.org/10.1007/3-540-45760-7_17
38. Jost, D., Maurer, U., Mularczyk, M.: Efficient ratcheting: almost-optimal guarantees for secure messaging. In: Ishai, Y., Rijmen, V. (eds.) EUROCRYPT 2019. LNCS, vol. 11476, pp. 159–188. Springer, Cham (2019). https://doi.org/10.1007/978-3-030-17653-2_6
39. Kim, S.: Key-homomorphic pseudorandom functions from LWE with small modulus. In: Canteaut, A., Ishai, Y. (eds.) EUROCRYPT 2020. LNCS, vol. 12106, pp. 576–607. Springer, Cham (2020). https://doi.org/10.1007/978-3-030-45724-2_20
40. Klooß, M., Lehmann, A., Rupp, A.: (R)CCA secure updatable encryption with integrity protection. In: Ishai, Y., Rijmen, V. (eds.) EUROCRYPT 2019. LNCS, vol. 11476, pp. 68–99. Springer, Cham (2019). https://doi.org/10.1007/978-3-030-17653-2_3
41. Krafft, M.F.: The Debian System: Concepts and Techniques. No Starch Press Series (2005)
42. Lehmann, A., Tackmann, B.: Updatable encryption with post-compromise security. In: Nielsen, J.B., Rijmen, V. (eds.) EUROCRYPT 2018. LNCS, vol. 10822, pp. 685–716. Springer, Cham (2018). https://doi.org/10.1007/978-3-319-78372-7_22
43. Lipmaa, H.: Key-and-argument-updatable QA-NIZKs. In: Galdi, C., Kolesnikov, V. (eds.) SCN 2020. LNCS, vol. 12238, pp. 645–669. Springer, Cham (2020). https://doi.org/10.1007/978-3-030-57990-6_32
44. Löhr, H., Sadeghi, A., Winandy, M.: Patterns for secure boot and secure storage in computer systems. In: ARES (2010)
45. Microsoft: sign a windows 10 app package. https://docs.microsoft.com/en-us/windows/msix/package/signing-package-overview
46. Mykletun, E., Narasimha, M., Tsudik, G.: Authentication and integrity in outsourced databases. TOS (2006)
47. Naor, M., Pinkas, B., Reingold, O.: Distributed pseudo-random functions and KDCs. In: Stern, J. (ed.) EUROCRYPT 1999. LNCS, vol. 1592, pp. 327–346. Springer, Heidelberg (1999). https://doi.org/10.1007/3-540-48910-X_23
48. Pointcheval, D., Sanders, O.: Short randomizable signatures. In: Sako, K. (ed.) CT-RSA 2016. LNCS, vol. 9610, pp. 111–126. Springer, Cham (2016). https://doi.org/10.1007/978-3-319-29485-8_7
49. Red hat: how to sign rpms with GPG. https://access.redhat.com/articles/3359321

50. Sanders, O.: Efficient redactable signature and application to anonymous credentials. In: Kiayias, A., Kohlweiss, M., Wallden, P., Zikas, V. (eds.) PKC 2020. LNCS, vol. 12111, pp. 628–656. Springer, Cham (2020). https://doi.org/10.1007/978-3-030-45388-6_22
51. Steinfeld, R., Bull, L., Zheng, Y.: Content extraction signatures. In: Kim, K. (ed.) ICISC 2001. LNCS, vol. 2288, pp. 285–304. Springer, Heidelberg (2002). https://doi.org/10.1007/3-540-45861-1_22
52. Wang, H., Liu, H., Xiao, X., Meng, G., Guo, Y.: Characterizing android app signing issues. In: ASE (2019)
53. Weintraub, G., Gudes, E.: Data integrity verification in column-oriented NoSQL databases. In: Kerschbaum, F., Paraboschi, S. (eds.) DBSec 2018. LNCS, vol. 10980, pp. 165–181. Springer, Cham (2018). https://doi.org/10.1007/978-3-319-95729-6_11
54. Zhang, Y., Rajimwale, A., Arpaci-Dusseau, A.C., Arpaci-Dusseau, R.H.: End-to-end data integrity for file systems: a ZFS case study. In: FAST (2010)

Multi-Client Functional Encryption for Separable Functions

Michele Ciampi[1], Luisa Siniscalchi[2], and Hendrik Waldner[1](✉)

[1] The University of Edinburgh, Edinburgh, UK
{michele.ciampi,hendrik.waldner}@ed.ac.uk
[2] Concordium Blockchain Research Center, Aarhus University, Aarhus, Denmark
lsiniscalchi@cs.au.dk

Abstract. In this work, we provide a compiler that transforms a *single-input functional encryption* scheme for the class of polynomially bounded circuits into a *multi-client functional encryption* (MCFE) scheme for the class of *separable functions*. An n-input function f is called separable if it can be described as a list of polynomially bounded circuits $f^1, \ldots, f^n$ s.t. $f(x_1, \ldots, x_n) = f^1(x_1) + \cdots + f^n(x_n)$ for all $x_1, \ldots, x_n$. Our compiler extends the works of Brakerski et al. [Eurocrypt 2016] and of Komargodski et al. [Eurocrypt 2017] in which a generic compiler is proposed to obtain *multi-input functional encryption* (MIFE) from single-input functional encryption. Our construction achieves the stronger notion of MCFE but for the less generic class of separable functions. Prior to our work, a long line of results has been proposed in the setting of MCFE for the inner-product functionality, which is a special case of a separable function. We also propose a modified version of the notion of *decentralized* MCFE introduced by Chotard et al. [Asiacrypt 2018] that we call *outsourceable mulit-client functional encryption* (OMCFE). Intuitively, the notion of OMCFE makes it possible to distribute the load of the decryption procedure among at most n different entities, which will return decryption shares that can be combined (e.g., additively) thus obtaining the output of the computation. This notion is especially useful in the case of a very resource consuming decryption procedure, while the combine algorithm is non-time consuming. We also show how to extend the presented MCFE protocol to obtain an OMCFE scheme for the same functionality class.

1 Introduction

Compared to traditional public-key encryption, functional encryption (FE) [10, 34] enables fine-grained access control of encrypted data. In more detail, a FE scheme is equipped with a key generation algorithm that allows the owner of a master secret key to generate a *functional key* sk_f associated with a function f. Using such a functional key sk_f for the decryption of a ciphertext $\mathsf{ct} = \mathsf{Enc}(\mathsf{sk}, x)$ yields *only* $f(x)$. Roughly speaking, the security of a functional encryption scheme guarantees that no other information except for $f(x)$ is leaked. In the

J. A. Garay (Ed.): PKC 2021, LNCS 12710, pp. 724–753, 2021.
https://doi.org/10.1007/978-3-030-75245-3_26

classical notion of FE, the decryption algorithm takes as input a single ciphertext and a functional key for a single-input (one-variable) function. The more general notion of *Multi-Input Functional Encryption (MIFE)* [25] allows the evaluation of an n-input function on n encrypted inputs. In more detail, the decryption algorithm takes as an input n ciphertexts $\mathsf{Enc}(\mathsf{sk}, x_1), \dots, \mathsf{Enc}(\mathsf{sk}, x_n)$ and a functional key for an n-input function f' and outputs $f'(x_1, \dots, x_n)$.

In this work we consider an even stronger notion than MIFE called *multi-client functional encryption (MCFE)* [25]. In the MCFE setting, each ciphertext $\mathsf{Enc}(\mathsf{sk}_i, x_i)$ is encrypted using a different secret key sk_i. Moreover, an arbitrary set of secret keys $\mathcal{I} = \{\mathsf{sk}_{i_1}, \dots, \mathsf{sk}_{i_m}\}$ can be leaked to the adversary. Intuitively, the notion of MCFE, says that the adversary cannot learn more about the ciphertexts generated using the disclosed keys than what it can learn by evaluating f'. Note that the adversary in this case can evaluate f' using any input that it chooses with respect to the positions $i_1, \dots, i_m$. In general, we can distinguish between two types of MCFE schemes: *labeled* and *unlabeled* [2,4]. In the labeled case every ciphertext is encrypted under a label ℓ. A valid decryption requries that the input ciphertexts have been encrypted under the same label (otherwise the decryption procedure generates an invalid output). Our results are proven secure under the stronger notion of security with labels, which also allows the adversary to obtain multiple ciphertexts under the same label. This additional security requirement has been considered since [2,18].

In this work we focus on MCFE for a specific functionality class called *separable functions* [32,33]. A separable function is an efficiently computable function f that can be separated into a list of efficiently computable functions $f^1, \dots, f^n$ s.t. $f(x_1, \dots, x_n) = f^1(x_1) + \dots + f^n(x_n)$ for all $x_1, \dots x_n$, with x_i contained in the domain of f^i. This is not restricted to addition but to any group operation, therefore also multiplication (i.e., $f(x_1, \dots, x_n) = f^1(x_1) \cdot \dots \cdot f^n(x_n)$ for all $x_1, \dots x_n$, with x_i contained in the domain of f^i). Separable functions are used in many real-world applications, and a MCFE scheme, covering such a functionality class, would enable privacy in these scenarios. For example, consider the problem of counting a specific word w in n different files, provided by n different parties, that contain sensitive information. In more detail, assume that we have n parties and each party P_i owns a file which is encrypted using a FE scheme under the secret key sk_i. Consider now an entity P_{w} that receives all the encrypted files and wants to count the number of times that the word w occurs in all these files. In addition, P_{w} receives a functional key $\mathsf{sk}_{f_{\mathsf{w}}}$ for the separable function $f_{\mathsf{w}} = f_{\mathsf{w}}^1, \dots, f_{\mathsf{w}}^n$, where each function f_{w}^i simply counts the number of occurrences of the word w in a file. Given all the encrypted files and $\mathsf{sk}_{f_{\mathsf{w}}}$, P_{w} can compute the number of occurrences of w over all the encrypted files. In addition, even if P_{w} manages to obtain some of the encryption keys, the content of the files remains partially hidden[1]. A second scenario where a MCFE scheme can be useful is the aggregation of *SQL-queries*. In this context, it would be

[1] For example in the worst case, where the adversary has all but the key sk_j, it should be able to compute the number of times that the word w appears in the i-th file, but nothing more than that.

possible to do the computation of sums, counting, and averages over multiple (n) encrypted tables held by different authorities. As already mentioned in [33] separable functions have several applications in sensor and peer-to-peer networks, where different functions are computed over the data of the different sensors (or resp. peers) and only the sum of evaluations should be learned by the decryptor, but nothing about the individual results of the sensors (resp. peers).

Decentralized MCFE. Both, the notions of MIFE and MCFE, assume the existence of a central trusted authority that generates and distributes the secret and functional keys. This is undesirable in some scenarios, given that an adversarial trusted authority can compromise the security of the MCFE scheme (note that the trusted authority can generate any functional key, hence also the functional key for the identity function). To remove the need for a trusted authority, Chotard et al. [17] introduced the notion of *decentralized multi-client functional encryption* (DMCFE), where the generation of the secret keys and the functional keys happens in a decentralized way. In this work, we consider DMCFE for the case of separable functions.

1.1 Our Contribution

In this paper we investigate the feasibility of constructing MCFE for separable functions starting from *any* general-purpose FE scheme. In more detail, we provide a compiler that takes as input any secret-key FE scheme and outputs a MCFE scheme for separable functions that is *selectively* secure[2] and supports an a priori bounded (but still polynomial) number of encryption and an unbounded number of n-input functional key queries (where n is polynomially related to the security parameter). We show how to extend the above scheme to the case of *adaptive* security[3] (where the adversary can request an a priori bounded number of encryptions and functional keys at any time). We now state our theorems informally.

Theorem 1 (informal). *Assuming the existence of any selective secure secret-key FE scheme that supports an a priori bounded number of encryption queries and an unbounded number of functional key queries, then there exists a selective secure MCFE scheme for separable functions that supports a bounded number of encryption queries and an ubounded number of functional key queries.*

Theorem 2 (informal). *Assuming the existence of any adaptive secure secret-key FE scheme that supports an a priori bounded number of encryption and functional key queries, then there exists an adaptive secure MCFE scheme for*

[2] We actually mean static-selective, i.e. the adversary has to submit all its message and corruption queries at the beginning of the game.

[3] We consider adaptive-adaptive security, which means that the adversary is allowed to query all the oracles, i.e. message and corruption oracles, throughout the whole game.

separable functions that supports a bounded number of encryption queries and functional key queries.

We prove our constructions for the so-called *pos*$^+$ security notion [1,18]. In a pos$^+$ security game an adversary is required to ask a left-or-right query under a specific label in either every or none position. A second notion called *any* security [1,18] allows the adversary to ask a left-or-right encryption query on as many positions as it wants without any restrictions. To achieve the notion of any security, we make use of a slightly modified version of a black-box compiler presented in [1] which amplifies any pos$^+$ secure MCFE scheme into an any secure MCFE scheme.

In the next step, we discuss how to modify our constructions in order to obtain a DMCFE scheme for separable functions and prove the following theorem.

Theorem 3 (informal). *Assuming the existence of any selective (adaptive) secure secret-key FE scheme that supports an a priori bounded number of encryptions queries (and a bounded number of functional key queries), then there exists a selective (adaptive) secure DMCFE scheme for separable functions that supports a bounded number of encryption queries (and a bounded number of functional key queries).*

Outsourceable MCFE. As an additional contribution, we introduce a new notion called outsourceable multi-client functional encryption (OMCFE). Intuitively, the notion of OMCFE makes it possible to outsource the load of the decryption procedure among n different entities. In more detail, let f be the n-input separable function that we want to evaluate, then the key-generation algorithm of an OMCFE scheme generates n partial functional keys $\mathsf{sk}_{f,1}, \ldots, \mathsf{sk}_{f,n}$ (one for each input-slot of f), instead of generating one functional key sk_f for f. Each of the functional keys $\mathsf{sk}_{f,i}$ can be applied on a ciphertext $\mathsf{ct}_{i,\ell}$ (a ciphertext under label ℓ that contains the i-th input of the function) to obtain a decryption share $\varphi_{i,\ell}$. An evaluator that obtains all the n share (one for each input slot), can compute the final output by running a *combine* algorithm taking the shares as an input.

This notion becomes important in the case where the combine algorithm is significantly more efficient than the *partial* decryption procedure. More formally, we require that the computational complexity of the combine algorithm is independent from the computational complexity of the function f.

Coming back to the word count example, it is possible to give $\mathsf{sk}_{f_{\mathsf{w}}^i}$ and an encryption of the i'th part of a huge file, to an entity P_i (for each $i \in [n]$) and let P_i generate the decryption share by executing the decryption procedure. In this way an evaluator P_{w}, would receive the decryption shares from $P_1, \ldots, P_n$, and execute the (light) combine algorithm to obtain the final output of the computation. The word count example can also be seen as a special case of a class of problems that can be parallelized using the *MapReduce* paradigm [21]. This parallelization paradigm consists of a *map* phase which divides the problem into sub-problems and a *reduce* phase which parallelizes the aggregation of the partial solutions. It is easy to see that if the reduce phase consists of addition/multiplication operations then our OMCFE scheme could be particularly useful to implement a layer of privacy on top of this parallelization paradigm.

The security definition of this notion is almost identical to the security definition of MCFE. They mainly differ in their correctness definition (since the key generation algorithm and the decryption algorithm are different). We show how to obtain an OMCFE for the class of separable functions. In particular, we have the following informal theorem.

Theorem 4 (informal). *Assuming the existence of any selective (adaptive) secure secret-key FE scheme that supports an a priori bounded number of encryptions queries (and a bounded number of functional key queries), then there exists a selective (adaptive) secure OMCFE scheme for separable functions that supports a bounded number of encryption queries (and a bounded number of functional key queries).*

Instantiations. Our constructions can be instantiated from various assumptions. There exists a general-purpose secret-key FE scheme from indistinguishability obfuscation or multilinear maps [13]. We can obtain our adaptive secure MCFE scheme (and the decentralized one) from learning with errors [26], one-way functions or low-depth pseudorandom generators [27]. In more detail, as already mentioned in [13], based on the results of Ananth et al. [8] and Brakerski et al. [15], it is possible to generically obtain a function-hiding scheme by relying on any selectively secure and message-private functional encryption scheme.[4] This implies that function-hiding schemes for any number of encryption and key-generation queries can be based on indistinguishability obfuscation [23,35], differing-input obfuscation [7,11], and multilinear maps [24]. Besides this, it is possible to construct function-hiding schemes for a polynomially bounded number, denoted by q, of encryption and key-generation queries by relying on the Learning with Errors (LWE) assumption (where the length of ciphertexts grows with q and with a bound on the depth of allowed functions) [26], or on pseudorandom generators computable by small-depth circuits (where the length of ciphertexts grows with q and with an upper bound on the circuit size of the functions) [27], and based on one-way functions (for $q = 1$) [27].

1.2 Overview of Our Techniques

Our Compiler. We present a compiler that transforms any selectively secure single-input FE scheme FE into a selectively secure MCFE scheme MCFE for the class of n-input separable functions. We provide an incremental description of how our compiler works.

In the setup procedure of MCFE we execute n times the setup of FE thus obtaining n master secret keys $\mathsf{msk}_1, \ldots, \mathsf{msk}_n$. We define the i'th secret key

[4] In the informal theorems above we actually require the underlying functional encryption scheme to be function-hiding, but since this property comes for free from any selectively secure and message-private functional encryption scheme, we do not state it specifically.

for MCFE as $\mathsf{sk}_i := \mathsf{msk}_i$ for $i = 1, \ldots, n$, whereas the master secret key of MCFE is represented by all the secret keys $\{\mathsf{sk}_1, \ldots, \mathsf{sk}_n\}$. To encrypt a message x_i for the position i we simply run the encryption algorithm of FE using the secret key sk_i and the message x_i thus obtaining the ciphertext ct_i. To generate a functional key for a separable function $f := \{f^1, \ldots, f^n\}$ the key generation algorithm randomly samples a secret sharing of 0: $r_1 + \cdots + r_n = 0$ (we refer to this values as r-values) and runs, using the master secret key msk_i (which corresponds to sk_i) of FE the key generation algorithms for FE to generate a functional key $\mathsf{sk}_{f^i_{r_i}}$ for $f^i_{r_i}$. The function $f^i_{r_i}$ takes as an input x_i and outputs $f^i(x_i) + r_i$. The output of the key generation algorithm is then represented by $\{\mathsf{sk}_{f^1_{r_1}}, \ldots, \mathsf{sk}_{f^n_{r_n}}\}$. The decryption algorithm of MCFE, on input the ciphertext $\mathsf{ct} := \{\mathsf{ct}_1, \ldots, \mathsf{ct}_n\}$ and the functional keys $\{\mathsf{sk}_{f^1_{r_1}}, \ldots, \mathsf{sk}_{f^n_{r_n}}\}$ runs the decryption algorithm for FE on input $\mathsf{sk}_{f^i_{r_i}}$ and ct_i thus obtaining φ_i for $i = 1, \ldots, n$. The output of the decryption procedure is then given by $\varphi_1 + \cdots + \varphi_n$ which is equal to $f(x_1, \ldots, x_n)$ due to the property of f and the way the values $r_1, \ldots, r_n$ are sampled. Intuitively, the security of this scheme comes from the fact that a functional key $\mathsf{sk}_{f^i_{r_i}}$ for FE hides the description of the function, hence it hides the value r_i. The fact that the value r_i is protected allows us to argue that φ_i encrypts the partial output $f^i(x_i)$ (that the adversary is not supposed to see). Indeed, φ_i can be seen as the one-time pad encryption of $f^i(x_i)$ using the key r_i.

We show that for the class of separable functions the described one-time pad encryption is sufficient for several encryption queries. This is possible by exploiting the fact that the security game for functional encryption requires that $f(x^0_1, \ldots, x^0_n) = f(x^1_1, \ldots, x^1_n)$ for all the challenge queries (x^0_i, x^1_i) and all the functional key queries f. This means, in the case of separable functions, that $\sum_{i \in [n]} f^i(x^0_i) = \sum_{i \in [n]} f^i(x^1_i)$, which is equivalent to $f^{i^*}(x^0_{i^*}) - f^{i^*}(x^1_{i^*}) = \sum_{i \in [n] \setminus \{i^*\}} f^i(x^1_i) - f^i(x^0_i)$. This restriction enforces the security of the information-theoretic encryption under many queries (we show this using a simple reduction).

To extend our scheme to the labeled setting, we modify it as follows: Assuming that we know a polynomial upper-bound on the number of labels q, during the setup phase, we generate q random secret sharings of 0: $t_{1,j} + \cdots + t_{n,j} := 0$, with $j \in [q]$ (we refer to this values as the t-values) and the i'th secret key now becomes $\mathsf{sk}_i := (\mathsf{msk}_i, \{t_{i,j}\})_{j \in [q]}$. To encrypt a message x_i under the label j the encryptor runs the encryption algorithm of FE on input sk_i and the concatenation of x_i with $t_{i,j}$, thus obtaining $\mathsf{ct}_{i,j}$.

To generate a functional key for the function f, a secret sharing of 0 is generated as before (i.e., $r_1 + \cdots + r_n = 0$), but this time we generate the functional key $\mathsf{sk}_{\tilde{f}^i_{r_i}}$ of FE for the function $\tilde{f}^i_{r_i}$. The function $\tilde{f}^i_{r_i}$ takes as input $(x_i, t_{i,j}, j)$ and outputs $f^i(x_i) + r_i + t_{i,j}$. The output of the key generation algorithm is then represented by $\{\mathsf{sk}_{\tilde{f}^1_{r_1}}, \ldots, \mathsf{sk}_{\tilde{f}^n_{r_n}}\}$. The decryption procedure for this new scheme works exactly as before. Let $\varphi_{i,j}$ be the output of the decryption algorithm of FE on input $\mathsf{ct}_{i,j}$ (the ciphertext computed with respect to the label j) and $\mathsf{sk}_{f^i_{r_i}}$.

Intuitively, our new scheme allows encrypting multiple messages under different labels, since the partial decryption $\varphi_{i,j}$ is now encrypted using a fresh one-time pad key which corresponds to the combination of the r-value r_i (hidden inside the function) and the t-value $t_{i,j}$ (hidden inside the ciphertext) for every label j. Note that even if new t-values are generated for each encryption we still need to rely on the r-values hidden inside the function. Otherwise an adversary could use the same ciphertext $\mathsf{ct}_{i,j}$ as the input of multiple functions, which would be the same as reusing a one-time pad key.

Even if this scheme is secure under the generation of multiple encryptions and functional keys it has the drawback that the size of each secret key growths with q (the upper-bound to the number of encryptions). To tackle this problem we borrow a technique from the work of Abdalla et al. [1][5], that allows multiple parties to generate a secret sharing of 0 non-interactively by agreeing on a set (of size n) of pseudo-random function (PRF) keys during the setup. We refer to Sect. 4 for more details. The adaptive q-message q-function bounded MCFE scheme works in a similar way, the main differences are regarding the size of the ciphertext and the size of the functional keys. For the selective scheme only the size of the functional keys depends on q, whereas in the adaptive scheme also the ciphtertexts grow with q. The details for this proof can be found in Sect. 5.

Decentralized Multi-Client Functional Encryption. In a DMCFE scheme, as introduced in [17], the key-generation phase is decentralized in the sense that each secret key owner should be able to compute a *partial functional key* for a function f, such that the combination of all these partial functional keys allows the generation of a valid functional key for f. Additionally, it is assumed that the setup procedure is a protocol between the different parties that allows for the generation of the different secret keys. This results in a completely decentralized setup that does not require a trusted authority. The MCFE scheme presented above seems to be easily translatable into the decentralized setting but there is an issue: the key generation phase of MCFE requires the computation of a new set of r-values such that $r_1 + \cdots + r_n = 0$ for each function f which needs to be computed without interaction between the parties. To do that, we adopt again the technique proposed in [1] to distributively generate a secret sharing of 0. The idea of decentralizing a MCFE scheme in this way has first been proposed in [2].

Outsourceable Multi-Client Functional Encryption. We show how to obtain, with minor modifications to the presented compiler, an OMCFE scheme. The proof works, as already mentioned in the previous sections, by relying on the fact that the values $\varphi_{i,\ell}$ do not reveal any information on the encrypted messages.

[5] This technique has previously been used in [16] to remove the central authority in the context of multi-authority attribute based encryption and in [30] in the context of privacy-friendly aggregation.

Remark 1.1. Without loss of generality, in the remainder of this paper, we only refer to the case of additive separability. However, our compiler also works for the case of multiplicative separability. To achieve multiplicative separability all the additive operators need to be replaced by its multiplicative counterparts (i.e. addition with multiplication and subtraction with division). Also the group we need to operate in needs to be changed from an additive group to a multiplicative group, e.g. from $\mathbb{Z}_p$ to $\mathbb{Z}_p^*$

1.3 Related Work

Multi-input/client Functional Encryption. Since the introduction of multi-input and multi-client functional encryption [25] several contributions have been made to provide constructions in these areas. In this work we follow the notation of [28], which means that we denote a scheme with a single encryption key that can be used to generate ciphertexts for every position as a MIFE scheme and a scheme where every position is associated with its own encryption key as multi-client functional encryption scheme. One of the main techniques that have been proposed to construct MIFE schemes are "liftings" from single-input functional encryption into the multi-input setting. The first foundational work that presents such a "lifting" in the secret-key setting is the work of Brakerski et al. [12]. In this work, the authors manage to transform a single-input selectively secure functional encryption scheme into an adaptive function-hiding multi-input functional encryption scheme which supports a constant number of inputs. In [29] the authors, among other results, improve the result of [12] by obtaining a MIFE scheme that supports functions with $2^t = (\log \lambda)^\delta$ inputs, where $0 < \delta < 1$. Both of these transformations require a single-input functional encryption scheme for the class of polynomially bounded circuits as an input. The schemes that cover the class of polynomially bounded circuits can be divided into two categories. The first category is only able to handle a bounded number of plaintexts (a so called message-bounded scheme) and (or) a bounded number of functional keys, whereas the second class is able to handle an unbounded number of queries and functional keys. A construction that falls into the first category is given by Gorbunov, Vaikuntanathan and Wee [27]. Their construction relies only on the existence of one-way functions. A second construction in this category has been proposed by Goldwasser et al. [26] and it is based on the Learning with Errors (LWE) assumption.

In the case of unbounded message security most of the known constructions are based on less standard assumptions like indistinguishable obfuscation [9,23,35], multilinear maps [24] and differing-input obfuscation [7,11]. All of the mentioned schemes are also covering the functionality class of polynomially bounded circuits.

Beside the class of polynomially bounded circuits, it is also possible to construct multi-input functional encryption schemes for more specific functionality classes, like inner-product. The first multi-input functional encryption scheme for inner-product functions has been provided by Abdalla et al. [5]. The construction they present relies on pairings. A follow up work [4] proposes a compiler

Table 1. Comparison with the most relevant compilers. λ: the security parameter, SK: secret key, PK: public key.

	Number of inputs	Functions	Setting	Assumptions
[12]	Constant	Generic	MIFE	SK Single-input FE
[29]	$\log(\lambda)^{\delta}$ $0 < \delta < 1$	Generic	MIFE	SK Single-input FE
[4]	poly(λ)	Inner-product	(D)MCFE (no labels)	SK Single-input FE for Inner-product
[1]	poly(λ)	Inner-product	(D)MCFE	PK Single-input FE for Inner-product
This work	poly(λ)	Separable functions	(D)MCFE	SK Single-input FE

that takes as input a single-input functional encryption scheme that fulfills some special properties and outputs a MIFE scheme for inner-product functions. This construction does not require pairings and can be instantiated using DDH, Paillier or LWE. It turns out that the construction of Abdalla et al. [4] also fulfills the stronger notion of multi-client functional encryption (without labels) which has been proven in [2]. In the case of multi-client functional encryption, it can be distinguished between two cases, the labeled and the unlabeled case. Labels enforce an additional restriction on the decryption procedure. Namely, it is only possible to decrypt tuples of ciphertexts that are encrypted under the same label, otherwise the decryption procedure outputs an invalid value. The first labeled scheme for the inner-product functionality has been proposed in [17]; its security is proven based on DDH in the random oracle model. Following, Abdalla et al. [1] and Libert and Titiu [31] show how to construct multi-client functional encryption with labels in the standard model. In more detail, Abdalla et al. [1] present a compiler that lifts a single-input public key functional encryption scheme, which can be instantiated using MDDH, DCR or LWE, into a MCFE scheme with labels. Whereas, Libert and Titiu [31] show how to directly construct a MCFE scheme with labels based on LWE. More recently, Abdalla et al. [3] show how to construct a MCFE scheme with labels in the random oracle model based on MDDH, DCR or LWE, which extends the results of Chotard et al. [17]. In Table 1 we provide a short comparison between the most relevant compilers that turn a single-input FE scheme into a MIFE or MCFE scheme.

Decentralization. The notion of DMCFE has been introduced in the work of Chotard et al. [17] in the context of inner product functional encryption. In their work, the authors also present a construction based on the symmetric external Diffie-Hellman assumption in the random oracle model that achieves security in the DMCFE setting. Since then, several compilers for inner product functional encryption have been proposed [1,2,18] that turn a MCFE scheme into a DMCFE scheme. In the works [1,2] the authors present decentralization compilers that purely rely on information theoretic arguments in the standard model and in the work of Chotard et al. [18] the authors present a compiler based on either the CDH assumption in the random oracle model or the DDH assumption in the standard model. The standard notion of DMCFE [17], with and without labels [2], has the main limitation that it is not possible to let parties join or leave adaptively after the setup procedure has been executed. This problems has been first considered in the work of Agrawal et al. [6], where the authors propose the notion of Ad Hoc Multi-Input Functional Encryption. In this setting every user generates its own public and secret key. Functional key shares are generated with respect to the public keys of other parties. Combining all the functional keys of the specified subset of parties yields the full functional key. This notion allows every party to join the system adaptively and to decide during the key generation which parties' data can be used in the decryption. The authors show how to realize this notion by bootstrapping standard MIFE to ad hoc MIFE without relying on additional assumptions. They also present a direct construction of an ad hoc MIFE for the inner product functionality based on the LWE assumption. In both constructions malicious security is achieved in the common reference string (CRS) model. The high level idea of these constructions is to combine standard MIFE and two-round secure multi-party computation. Another work that considers the above mentioned limitation is the work of Chotard et al. [19]. In their work, the authors introduce the notion of dynamic decentralized MCFE, which generalizes the notion of ad-hoc MIFE. The notion of dynamic DMCFE does not require a specified group of users for the generation of a functional key. Additionally, their notion also considers labels, to prevent certain mix and match attacks and leaks less information about the underlying plaintexts. The authors present a dynamic DMCFE scheme for the inner product functionality from standard assumptions in the random oracle model.

2 Preliminaries

Notation. We denote the security parameter with $\lambda \in \mathbb{N}$. A randomized algorithm $\mathcal{A}$ is running in *probabilistic polynomial time* (PPT) if there exists a polynomial $p(\cdot)$ such that for every input x the running time of $\mathcal{A}(x)$ is bounded by $p(|x|)$. We call a function $\mathrm{negl} : \mathbb{N} \to \mathbb{R}^+$ *negligible* if for every positive polynomial $p(\lambda)$ a $\lambda_0 \in \mathbb{N}$ exists, such that for all $\lambda > \lambda_0 : \epsilon(\lambda) < 1/p(\lambda)$. We denote by $[n]$ the set $\{1, \ldots, n\}$ for $n \in \mathbb{N}$. We use "=" to check equality of two different elements (i.e. $a = b$ then...) and ":=" as the assigning operator (e.g. to assign to a the value of b we write $a := b$). A randomized assignment is denoted with $a \leftarrow A$, where A is a randomized algorithm and the randomness used by A is not explicit. If the randomness is explicit we write $a := A(x; r)$ where x is the input and r is the randomness. We denote the winning probability of an adversary $\mathcal{A}$ in a game or experiment G as $\mathsf{Win}^{\mathsf{G}}_{\mathcal{A}}(\lambda, n)$, which is $\Pr[\mathsf{G}(\lambda, n, \mathcal{A}) = 1]$. The probability is taken over the random coins of G and $\mathcal{A}$. We define the distinguishing advantage between games G_0 and G_1 of an adversary $\mathcal{A}$ in the following way:

$\mathsf{Adv}^{\mathsf{G}}_{\mathcal{A}}(\lambda, n) = \left|\mathsf{Win}^{\mathsf{G}_0}_{\mathcal{A}}(\lambda, n) - \mathsf{Win}^{\mathsf{G}_1}_{\mathcal{A}}(\lambda, n)\right|$. The notation $(-1)^{j<i}$ denotes -1 if $j < i$ and 1 otherwise.

2.1 Secret-Key Functional Encryption

In this section, we define the notion of secret-key functional encryption (SK-FE) [14]. They are an adaption of the notion from [10,34].

Definition 2.1 (Secret-Key Functional Encryption). *Let $\mathcal{F} = \{\mathcal{F}_\lambda\}_{\lambda\in\mathbb{N}}$ be a collection of function families (indexed by λ), where every $f \in \mathcal{F}_\lambda$ is a polynomial time function $f\colon \mathcal{X}_\lambda \to \mathcal{Y}_\lambda$. A secret-key functional encryption scheme (SK-FE) for the function family $\mathcal{F}_\lambda$ is a tuple of four algorithms* $\mathsf{FE} = (\mathsf{Setup}, \mathsf{KeyGen}, \mathsf{Enc}, \mathsf{Dec})$*:*

$\mathsf{Setup}(1^\lambda)$: *Takes as input a unary representation of the security parameter λ and generates a master secret key* msk.
$\mathsf{KeyGen}(\mathsf{msk}, f)$: *Takes as input the master secret key* msk *and a function $f \in \mathcal{F}_\lambda$, and outputs a functional key* sk_f.
$\mathsf{Enc}(\mathsf{msk}, x)$: *Takes as input the master secret key* msk, *a message $x \in \mathcal{X}_\lambda$ to encrypt, and outputs a ciphertext* ct.
$\mathsf{Dec}(\mathsf{sk}_f, \mathsf{ct})$: *Takes as input a functional key* sk_f *and a ciphertext* ct *and outputs a value $y \in \mathcal{Y}_\lambda$.*

A scheme FE *is correct, if for all $\lambda \in \mathbb{N}$,* $\mathsf{msk} \leftarrow \mathsf{Setup}(1^\lambda)$, *$f \in \mathcal{F}_\lambda$, $x \in \mathcal{X}_\lambda$, when* $\mathsf{sk}_f \leftarrow \mathsf{KeyGen}(\mathsf{msk}, f)$, *we have*

$$\Pr\left[\mathsf{Dec}(\mathsf{sk}_f, \mathsf{Enc}(\mathsf{msk}, x)) = f(x)\right] = 1 \ .$$

We define the security of a SK-FE scheme using a left-or-right oracle. We distinguish between selective and adaptive submission of the encryption challenges. We consider a function-hiding secure SK-FE scheme, which, intuitively, means that the SK-FE scheme guarantees privacy for both, the description of the functions and the encrypted messages. We will recall now the formal definition.

Definition 2.2 (Function-Hiding of SK-FE). *Let* FE *be an SK-FE scheme, $\mathcal{F} = \{\mathcal{F}_\lambda\}_{\lambda\in\mathbb{N}}$ a collection of function families indexed by λ. For $\mathrm{xx} \in \{\mathrm{sel}, \mathrm{ad}\}$ and $\beta \in \{0, 1\}$, we define the experiment $\mathrm{xxFH}^{\mathsf{FE}}_\beta$ in Fig. 1, where the oracles are defined as:*

Left-or-Right oracle $\mathsf{QLeftRight}(x^0, x^1)$: *Outputs* $\mathsf{ct} \leftarrow \mathsf{Enc}(\mathsf{msk}, x^{\beta,j})$ *on a query (x^0, x^1). We denote by $Q_{\mathsf{LeftRight}}$ the set containing the queries (x^0, x^1).*
Key generation oracle $\mathsf{QKeyG}(f^0, f^1)$: *Outputs* $\mathsf{sk}_f \leftarrow \mathsf{KeyGen}(\mathsf{msk}, f^\beta)$ *on a query (f^0, f^1). We denote by Q_f the queries of the form* $\mathsf{QKeyG}(\cdot, \cdot)$.

and where Condition (*) *holds if all the following condition holds:*

- *For every query (f^0, f^1) to* QKeyG, *and every query $(x^0, x^1) \in Q_{\mathsf{LeftRight}}$, we require that:*

$$f^0(x^0) = f^1(x^1) \ .$$

$\text{sel-FH}_\beta^{\mathsf{FE}}(\lambda, \mathcal{A})$	$\text{ad-FH}_\beta^{\mathsf{FE}}(\lambda, \mathcal{A})$
$Q_{\mathsf{LeftRight}} \leftarrow \mathcal{A}(1^\lambda)$ $\mathsf{msk} \leftarrow \mathsf{Setup}(1^\lambda)$ $\mathsf{ct}^j \leftarrow \mathsf{QLeftRight}(x^{j,0}, x^{j,1})$, for all $(x^{j,0}, x^{j,1}) \in Q_{\mathsf{LeftRight}}$ $\alpha \leftarrow \mathcal{A}^{\mathsf{QKeyG}(\cdot,\cdot)}(\{\mathsf{ct}^j\}_{j\in[Q_{\mathsf{Enc}}]})$ Output: α if Condition (*) is satisfied, or a uniform bit otherwise	$\mathsf{msk} \leftarrow \mathsf{Setup}(1^\lambda)$ $\alpha \leftarrow \mathcal{A}^{\mathsf{QLeftRight}(\cdot,\cdot),\mathsf{QKeyG}(\cdot,\cdot)}(1^\lambda)$ Output: α if Condition (*) is satisfied, or a uniform bit otherwise

Fig. 1. Function-Hiding Games for SK-FE

We define the advantage of an adversary $\mathcal{A}$ *for* $\text{xx} \in \{\text{sel}, \text{ad}\}$ *in the following way:*

$$\mathsf{Adv}_{\mathsf{FE},\mathcal{A}}^{\text{xx-FH}}(\lambda) = |\Pr[\text{xx-FH}_0^{\mathsf{FE}}(\lambda, \mathcal{A}) = 1] - \Pr[\text{xx-FH}_1^{\mathsf{FE}}(\lambda, \mathcal{A}) = 1]| \ .$$

A secret-key functional encryption scheme FE *is* xx-FH *secure, if for any polynomial-time adversary* $\mathcal{A}$, *there exists a negligible function* negl *such that:* $\mathsf{Adv}_{\mathsf{FE},\mathcal{A}}^{\text{xx-FH}}(\lambda) \leq \text{negl}(\lambda)$. *In addition, we call a scheme q-message bounded, if* $|Q_{\mathsf{LeftRight}}| < q$ *and q-message-and-key bounded, if* $|Q_{\mathsf{LeftRight}}| < q$ *and* $|Q_f| < q$, *with* $q = \text{poly}(\lambda)$.

2.2 Multi-Client Functional Encryption

Now, we introduce multi-client functional encryption (MCFE) as in [1,2,25]. In a multi-client functional encryption scheme, every client can encrypt its own input (corresponding to a slot) and the evaluation of a functional key is executed over the ciphertexts of all the clients.

Definition 2.3 (Multi-Client Functional Encryption). *Let* $\mathcal{F} = \{\mathcal{F}_\lambda\}_{\lambda\in\mathbb{N}}$ *be a collection of function families (indexed by* λ*), where every* $f \in \mathcal{F}_\lambda$ *is a polynomial time function* $f\colon \mathcal{X}_{\lambda,1} \times \cdots \times \mathcal{X}_{\lambda,n} \rightarrow \mathcal{Y}_\lambda$. *Let* $\mathsf{Labels} = \{0,1\}^*$ *or* $\{\perp\}$ *be a set of labels. A multi-client functional encryption scheme (MCFE) for the function family* $\mathcal{F}_\lambda$ *supporting* n *users, is a tuple of four algorithms* $\mathsf{MCFE} = (\mathsf{Setup}, \mathsf{KeyGen}, \mathsf{Enc}, \mathsf{Dec})$*:*

$\mathsf{Setup}(1^\lambda, n)$: *Takes as input a unary representation of the security parameter* λ, *and the number of parties* n *and generates* n *secret keys* $\{\mathsf{sk}_i\}_{i\in[n]}$, *and a master secret key* msk.

$\mathsf{KeyGen}(\mathsf{msk}, f)$: *Takes as input the master secret key* msk *and a function* $f \in \mathcal{F}_\lambda$, *and outputs a functional key* sk_f.

$\mathsf{Enc}(\mathsf{sk}_i, x_i, \ell)$: *Takes as input a secret key* sk_i, *a message* $x_i \in \mathcal{X}_{\lambda,i}$ *to encrypt, a label* $\ell \in \mathsf{Labels}$, *and outputs a ciphertext* $\mathsf{ct}_{i,\ell}$.

$\mathsf{Dec}(\mathsf{sk}_f, \mathsf{ct}_{1,\ell}, \ldots, \mathsf{ct}_{n,\ell})$: *Takes as input a functional key* sk_f *and* n *ciphertexts under the same label* ℓ *and outputs a value* $y \in \mathcal{Y}_\lambda$.

A scheme MCFE *is correct, if for all* $\lambda, n \in \mathbb{N}$, $(\{\mathsf{sk}_i\}_{i\in[n]}, \mathsf{msk}) \leftarrow \mathsf{Setup}(1^\lambda, n)$, $f \in \mathcal{F}_\lambda$, $x_i \in \mathcal{X}_{\lambda,i}$, *when* $\mathsf{sk}_f \leftarrow \mathsf{KeyGen}(\mathsf{msk}, f)$, *we have*

$$\Pr\left[\mathsf{Dec}(\mathsf{sk}_f, \mathsf{Enc}(\mathsf{sk}_1, x_1, \ell), \ldots, \mathsf{Enc}(\mathsf{sk}_n, x_n, \ell)) = f(x_1, \ldots, x_n)\right] = 1 \ .$$

A scheme can either be *without labels*, in this case $\mathsf{Labels} = \{\perp\}$ or *with labels/labeled*, where $\mathsf{Labels} = \{0,1\}^*$. In this work, we only consider schemes that are labeled, i.e. $\mathsf{Labels} = \{0,1\}^*$. Where the latter case implies the former.

The security definition is the initial definition of Goldwasser et al. [25] (more specifically [28]), whereas we also allow the adversary to determine under which label it wants to query the left-or-right oracle and, in addition, we give the adversary access to an encryption oracle. Besides this, we also allow the adversary to query a single label several times. This security definition has initially been considered in [1,18]. As also noted in [1,2] the security model of multi-client functional encryption is similar to the security model of standard multi-input functional encryption, whereas in the latter only a single master secret key msk is used to generate encryptions for every slot i. In comparison to the standard multi-input functional encryption model, we also consider static and adaptive corruption of the different slots and selective and adaptive left-or-right and encryption oracle queries in the multi-client case. In more detail, in the selective case the adversary is required to ask all his left-or-right, encryption and corruption queries in the beginning of the game. In the adaptive case, the adversary is allowed to ask left-or-right, encryption and corruption queries throughout the whole game.

Definition 2.4 (Security of MCFE). *Let* MCFE *be an MCFE scheme,* $\mathcal{F} = \{\mathcal{F}_\lambda\}_{\lambda\in\mathbb{N}}$ *a collection of function families indexed by* λ *and* Labels *a label set. For* $\mathrm{xx} \in \{\mathrm{sel}, \mathrm{ad}\}$, $\mathrm{yy} \in \{\mathrm{pos}^+, \mathrm{any}\}$ *and* $\beta \in \{0,1\}$, *we define the experiment* $\text{sel-yy-IND}_\beta^{\mathsf{MCFE}}$ *in Fig. 2 and* $\text{ad-yy-IND}_\beta^{\mathsf{MCFE}}$ *in Fig. 3, where the oracles are defined as:*

Corruption Oracle $\mathsf{QCor}(i)$: *Outputs the encryption key* sk_i *of slot* i. *We denote by* $\mathcal{CS}$ *the set of corrupted slots at the end of the experiment.*

Left-or-Right Oracle $\mathsf{QLeftRight}(i, x_i^0, x_i^1, \ell)$: *Outputs* $\mathsf{ct}_{i,\ell} \leftarrow \mathsf{Enc}(\mathsf{sk}_i, x_i^\beta, \ell)$ *on a query* (i, x_i^0, x_i^1, ℓ). *We denote the queries of the form* $\mathsf{QLeftRight}(i, \cdot, \cdot, \ell)$ *by* $Q_{i,\ell}$ *and the set of queried labels by* QL.

Encryption Oracle $\mathsf{QEnc}(i, x_i, \ell)$ *Outputs* $\mathsf{ct}_{i,\ell} \leftarrow \mathsf{Enc}(\mathsf{sk}_i, x_i, \ell)$ *on a query* (i, x_i, ℓ). *We denote the queries of the form* $\mathsf{QEnc}(i, \cdot, \ell)$ *by* $Q'_{i,\ell}$ *and the set of queried labels by* QL'.

Key generation oracle $\mathsf{QKeyG}(f)$: *Outputs* $\mathsf{sk}_f \leftarrow \mathsf{KeyGen}(\mathsf{msk}, f)$ *on a query* f. *We denote by* Q_f *the queries of the form* $\mathsf{QKeyG}(\cdot)$.

and where Condition (*) *holds if all the following conditions hold:*

- *If* $i \in \mathcal{CS}$ *(i.e., slot* i *is corrupted): for any query* $\mathsf{QLeftRight}(i, x_i^0, x_i^1, \ell)$, $x_i^0 = x_i^1$.

- *For any label* $\ell \in \mathsf{Labels}$, *for any family of queries* $\{\mathsf{QLeftRight}(i, x_i^0, x_i^1, \ell)$ *or* $\mathsf{QEnc}(i, x_i, \ell)\}_{i \in [n] \setminus \mathcal{CS}}$, *for any family of inputs* $\{x_i \in \mathcal{X}_{\lambda,i}\}_{i \in \mathcal{CS}}$, *we define* $x_i^0 = x_i^1 = x_i$ *for any slot* $i \in \mathcal{CS}$ *and any slot queried to* $\mathsf{QEnc}(i, x_i, \ell)$, *and we require that for any query* $\mathsf{QKeyG}(f)$:

$$f(\boldsymbol{x}^0) = f(\boldsymbol{x}^1) \text{ where } \boldsymbol{x}^b = (x_1^b, \ldots, x_n^b) \text{ for } b \in \{0, 1\} .$$

- *When* $\mathrm{yy} = \mathrm{pos}^+$: *If there exists a slot* $i \in [n]$ *and a* $\ell \in \mathsf{Labels}$, *such that* $|Q_{i,\ell}| > 0$, *then for any slot* $k \in [n] \setminus \mathcal{CS}, |Q_{k,\ell}| > 0$. *In other words, for any label, either the adversary makes no left-or-right encryption query or makes at least one left-or-right encryption query for each slot* $i \in [n] \setminus \mathcal{CS}$.
- *When* $\mathrm{yy} = \mathrm{any}$: *there is no restriction in the left-or-right queries of the adversary.*

$\text{sel-yy-IND}_\beta^{\mathsf{MCFE}}(\lambda, n, \mathcal{A})$
$(\mathcal{CS}, \{Q_{i,\ell}\}_{i \in [n], \ell \in QL}, \{Q'_{i,\ell}\}_{i \in [n], \ell \in QL'}) \leftarrow \mathcal{A}(1^\lambda, n)$ $(\{\mathsf{sk}_i\}_{i \in [n]}, \mathsf{msk}) \leftarrow \mathsf{Setup}(1^\lambda, n)$ $\mathsf{ct}_{i,\ell}^j \leftarrow \mathsf{QLeftRight}(i, x_i^{j,0}, x_i^{j,1}, \ell)$, for all $(x_i^{j,0}, x_i^{j,1}) \in Q_{i,\ell}$, for all $i \in [n]$ and $\ell \in QL$. $\mathsf{ct}'^j_{i,\ell} \leftarrow \mathsf{QEnc}(i, x_i^j, \ell)$, for all $x_i^j \in Q'_{i,\ell}$, for all $i \in [n]$ and $\ell \in QL'$. $\alpha \leftarrow \mathcal{A}^{\mathsf{QKeyG}(\cdot)}(\{\mathsf{sk}_i\}_{i \in \mathcal{CS}}, \{\mathsf{ct}_{i,\ell}^j\}_{i \in [n], \ell \in QL, j \in [\lvert Q_{i,\ell} \rvert]}, \{\mathsf{ct}'^j_{i,\ell}\}_{i \in [n], \ell \in QL', j \in [\lvert Q'_{i,\ell} \rvert]})$ Output: α if Condition (*) is satisfied, or a uniform bit otherwise

Fig. 2. Selective security games for MCFE

We define the advantage of an adversary $\mathcal{A}$ *for* $\mathrm{xx} \in \{\mathrm{sel}, \mathrm{ad}\}$, $\mathrm{yy} \in \{\mathrm{pos}^+, \mathrm{any}\}$ *in the following way:*

$$\mathsf{Adv}_{\mathsf{MCFE},\mathcal{A}}^{\text{xx-yy-IND}}(\lambda, n) = |\Pr[\text{xx-yy-IND}_0^{\mathsf{MCFE}}(\lambda, n, \mathcal{A}) = 1] - \Pr[\text{xx-yy-IND}_1^{\mathsf{MCFE}}(\lambda, n, \mathcal{A}) = 1]| .$$

A multi-client functional encryption scheme MCFE *is* xx-yy-IND *secure, if for any polynomial-time adversary* $\mathcal{A}$, *there exists a negligible function* negl *such that:* $\mathsf{Adv}_{\mathsf{MCFE},\mathcal{A}}^{\text{xx-yy-IND}}(\lambda, n) \leq \mathrm{negl}(\lambda)$.

In addition, we call a scheme q-message bounded, *if* $\sum_{i \in [n]}(\sum_{\ell \in QL} |Q_{i,\ell}| + \sum_{\ell \in QL'} |Q'_{i,\ell}|) < q$ *and* q-message-and-key bounded, *if* $\sum_{i \in [n]}(\sum_{\ell \in QL} |Q_{i,\ell}| + \sum_{\ell \in QL'} |Q'_{i,\ell}|) < q$ *and* $|Q_f| < q$, *with* $q = \mathrm{poly}(\lambda)$.

$\text{ad-yy-IND}_\beta^{\mathsf{MCFE}}(\lambda, n, \mathcal{A})$
$(\{\mathsf{sk}_i\}_{i\in[n]}, \mathsf{msk}) \leftarrow \mathsf{Setup}(1^\lambda, n)$ $\alpha \leftarrow \mathcal{A}^{\mathsf{QCor}(\cdot),\mathsf{QKeyG}(\cdot),\mathsf{QEnc}(\cdot,\cdot,\cdot),\mathsf{QLeftRight}(\cdot,\cdot,\cdot,\cdot)}(1^\lambda)$ Output: α if Condition (*) is satisfied, or a uniform bit otherwise

Fig. 3. Adaptive security games for MCFE

We omit n when it is clear from the context. We also often omit $\mathcal{A}$ as a parameter of experiments or games when it is clear from the context.

Multi-input functional encryption (MIFE) and functional encryption (FE) are special cases of MCFE. MIFE is the same as MCFE without corruption, and FE is the special case of $n = 1$ (in which case, MIFE and MCFE coincide as there is no non-trivial corruption). In the case of single-input functional encryption, we only consider the two security definitions of sel-FH and ad-FH. For simplicity, in the notion of MCFE security, we denote by sel the case of static corruption, and selective left-or-right and encryption queries. By ad we denote the case in which all three, corruption, left-or-right and encryption queries, are adaptive.

2.3 Separable Functions

In this work, we focus on the class of additive separable functions. We recap the definition of a separable function and the corresponding functionality:

Definition 2.5 (Separable Functions [32]**).** *A function $f : \mathcal{X}_{\lambda,1} \times \cdots \times \mathcal{X}_{\lambda,n} \to \mathcal{Y}_\lambda$, is called separable, if there exists a function $f^i : \mathcal{X}_{\lambda,i} \to \mathcal{Y}_\lambda$ for all $i \in [n]$, such that*

$$f(x_1, \ldots, x_n) = \sum_{i\in[n]} f^i(x_i), \text{ with } x_i \in \mathcal{X}_{\lambda,i} \text{ for all } i \in [n] \ .$$

Functionality Class. We define the functionality class for separable functions as $\mathcal{F}_n^{\mathsf{sep}} := \{f(x_1, \ldots, x_n) = f^1(x_1) + \cdots + f^n(x_n), \text{ with } f^i : \mathcal{X}_{\lambda,i} \to \mathcal{Y}_\lambda\}$.

In this work, we consider the class of separable functions over the group $\mathbb{Z}_p$. Since the separability of a function f is not necessarily unique, we require the adversary to submit its functional key generation query as a set of the separated functions $\{f^i\}_{i\in[n]}$.

2.4 Security Compiler, Pseudorandom Functions (PRF), Symmetric Encryption and One-Time Pad Extension

The details of the security compiler presented in Abdalla et al. [1] and its adaptation to the bounded case as well as the details on pseudorandom functions and regarding symmetric encryption and the one-time pad extension can be found in the full version[20].

3 Multi-Client Functional Encryption for Separable Functions

In this section, we present our compiler, described in Fig. 4, that turns a single-input functional encryption scheme for class $\mathcal{F}_1^{\mathsf{sep}}$ into a multi-client functional encryption scheme MCFE with labels Labels for the class of separable functions $\mathcal{F}_n^{\mathsf{sep}}$, by relying on a PRF instantiated with the keyspace $\mathcal{K} := \{0,1\}^\lambda$, the domain $\mathcal{V} :=$ Labels and the range $\mathcal{W} := \mathcal{Y}_\lambda$, where $\mathcal{Y}_\lambda$ is the range of the functions $f \in \mathcal{F}_n^{\mathsf{sep}}$.

The construction works in the following way: In the setup procedure, n different instances of the single-input functional encryption scheme $\{\mathsf{msk}_i\}_{i\in[n]}$ and shared keys $\mathsf{K}_{i,j}$ (shared between slot i and j) for all $i, j \in [n], i \neq j$, with $\mathsf{K}_{i,j} = \mathsf{K}_{j,i}$ are generated. These keys are used as PRF keys in the encryption procedure. The setup procedure outputs a master secret key msk containing all the different master secret keys from the different single-input instances and a secret key $\mathsf{sk}_i := (\mathsf{msk}_i, \{\mathsf{K}_{i,j}\}_{j\in[n]})$ for every slot $i \in [n]$. We continue by describing the behavior of the remaining algorithms.

To encrypt a message for position i, the encryption algorithm takes as input the secret key sk_i, a message x_i and a label ℓ. In the first step, a padding $t_{i,\ell}$ will be generated using the PRF keys $\{\mathsf{K}_{i,j}\}_{j\in[n]}$ contained in the secret key sk_i. This padding is different for every label ℓ and ensures that ciphertexts created under different labels cannot be combined. In more detail, for every padding it holds that $\sum_{i\in[n]} t_{i,\ell} = 0$ for each label, but if paddings for different labels are combined they do not add up to 0. To generate the ciphertext $\mathsf{ct}_{i,\ell}$, the message x_i concatenated with the padding $t_{i,\ell}$ and the label ℓ is encrypted using msk_i.

The key generation procedure, takes as inputs the master secret key msk and a function $f \in \mathcal{F}_n^{\mathsf{sep}}$ separated into the functions $f^1, \ldots, f^n$ with $f^i \in \mathcal{F}_1^{\mathsf{sep}}$ for all $i \in [n]$. In the first step of the key generation, n different random values r_i are sampled in such a way that $\sum_{i\in[n]} r_i = 0$, these values are used to ensure that different functional keys cannot be combined. In the next step, a functional key $\mathsf{sk}_{f^i_{r_i}}$ for the function $f^i_{r_i}$ is generated for every single-input instance $i \in [n]$. The function $f^i_{r_i}$ takes as input the message x_i and the padding $t_{i,\ell}$ and outputs the addition of these values together with the hardcoded value r_i, i.e. $f^i_{r_i}(x_i, t_{i,\ell}, \ell) = f^i(x_i) + t_{i,\ell} + r_i$. The functional key sk_f is defined as the set of all the functional keys generated by the single-input instances $\{\mathsf{sk}_{f^i_{r_i}}\}_{i\in[n]}$.

To decrypt a set of ciphertexts $\{\mathsf{ct}_{i,\ell}\}_{i\in[n]}$ using a decryption key $\mathsf{sk}_f = \{\mathsf{sk}_{f^i_{r_i}}\}_{i\in[n]}$, the decryptions of all the instances are generated and the final output is computed by adding up all of the decryptions. In more detail, $\mathsf{Dec}(\mathsf{sk}_{f^i_{r_i}}, \mathsf{ct}_{i,\ell}) = f^i(x_i) + t_{i,\ell} + r_i$ is computed for all $i \in [n]$ and the final output $f(x_1, \ldots, x_n)$ is equal to $\sum_{i\in[n]} f^i(x_i) + t_{i,\ell} + r_i$.

The output of the decryption of a single-input instance, i.e. $f^i(x_i) + t_{i,\ell} + r_i$ ensures that it is not possible to combine ciphertexts encrypted under different labels or functional keys generated in different key generation procedures. If one of the ciphertexts in the decryption procedure is generated under a different label

$\mathsf{Setup}^{\mathsf{mc}}(1^\lambda, n)$:	$\mathsf{KeyGen}^{\mathsf{mc}}(\mathsf{msk}, \{f^i\}_{i\in[n]})$:
$\mathsf{msk}_i \leftarrow \mathsf{Setup}^{\mathsf{si}}(1^\lambda)$, for all $i \in [n]$	Parse $\mathsf{msk} := (\{\mathsf{msk}_i\}_{i\in[n]}, \{\mathsf{K}_{i,j}\}_{i,j\in[n],i\neq j})$
For $i \in [n], j > i$:	For all $i \in [n-1]$, $r_i \leftarrow \mathcal{Y}_\lambda$
$\mathsf{K}_{i,j} = \mathsf{K}_{j,i} \leftarrow \{0,1\}^\lambda$	$r_n := -\sum_{i\in[n-1]} r_i$
$\mathsf{msk} := (\{\mathsf{msk}_i\}_{i\in[n]}, \{\mathsf{K}_{i,j}\}_{i,j\in[n],i\neq j})$	$\mathsf{sk}_{f^i_{r_i}} \leftarrow \mathsf{KeyGen}^{\mathsf{si}}(\mathsf{msk}_i, f^i_{r_i})$,
$\mathsf{sk}_i := (\mathsf{msk}_i, \{\mathsf{K}_{i,j}\}_{j\in[n]})$	with $f^i_{r_i}$ as defined in Fig. 5a Fig. 5b.
Return $(\{\mathsf{sk}_i\}_{i\in[n]}, \mathsf{msk})$	Return $\mathsf{sk}_f := \{\mathsf{sk}_{f^i_{r_i}}\}_{i\in[n]}$
$\mathsf{Enc}^{\mathsf{mc}}(\mathsf{sk}_i, x_i, \ell)$:	$\mathsf{Dec}^{\mathsf{mc}}(\mathsf{sk}_f, \{\mathsf{ct}_{i,\ell}\}_{i\in[n]})$:
Parse $\mathsf{sk}_i := (\mathsf{msk}_i, \{\mathsf{K}_{i,j}\}_{j\in[n]})$	Parse $\mathsf{sk}_f := \{\mathsf{sk}_{f^i_{r_i}}\}_{i\in[n]}$
$t_{i,\ell} := \sum_{j\neq i}(-1)^{j<i}\mathsf{PRF}_{\mathsf{K}_{i,j}}(\ell)$	$\mathsf{Dec}^{\mathsf{si}}(\mathsf{sk}_{f^i_{r_i}}, \mathsf{ct}_{i,\ell}) = f^i(x_i) + t_{i,\ell} + r_i$
$\mathsf{ct}_{i,\ell} \leftarrow \mathsf{Enc}^{\mathsf{si}}(\mathsf{msk}_i, (x_i, \perp, t_{i,\ell}, \ell))$	Return $\sum_{i\in[n]} f^i(x_i) + t_{i,\ell} + r_i$
Return $\mathsf{ct}_{i,\ell}$	

Fig. 4. The generic construction of q-message bounded sel-pos$^+$-IND-secure MCFE and q-message-and-key bounded ad-pos$^+$-IND-secure MCFE multi-client functional encryption from single-input functional encryption. We note that "$\perp$" denotes a slot of size q.

$f^i_{r_i}(x, t_{i,\ell}, \ell)$:
Output: $f^i(x) + t_{i,\ell} + r_i$

(a) Selective Security

$f^i_{r_i}(x, \perp, t_{i,\ell}, \ell)$:
Output: $f^i(x) + t_{i,\ell} + r_i$

(b) Adaptive Security

Fig. 5. Description of the function that is used for the key generation under the different security definitions.(We note that the label ℓ of the plaintext is ignored by the functions and therefore not necessary for the correctness of the construction. However, it is needed in the security proof later.)

or a different partial functional key has been used the decryption procedure will not output the correct $f(x_1, \ldots, x_n)$.

Correctness. The correctness of the multi-client scheme follows from the correctness of the single input scheme and the fact that $\sum_{i\in[n]} t_{i,\ell} = 0$ and $\sum_{i\in[n]} r_i = 0$. Let us consider in more detail the decryption of the correctly generated ciphertexts $\mathsf{ct}_{1,\ell}, \ldots, \mathsf{ct}_{n,\ell}$ under a correctly generated functional key $\mathsf{sk}_f = \{\mathsf{sk}_{f^i_{r_i}}\}_{i\in[n]}$. Due to the correctness of the single-input scheme it holds that $f^i(x_i) + t_{i,\ell} + r_i = \mathsf{Dec}^{\mathsf{si}}(\mathsf{sk}_{f^i_{r_i}}, \mathsf{ct}_{i,\ell})$ and together with the properties of the $t_{i,\ell}$ values and the r_i values it follows that $\sum_{i\in[n]} f^i(x_i) + t_{i,\ell} + r_i = \sum_{i\in[n]} f^i(x_i)$. Together with the separability property of the function $\sum_{i\in[n]} f^i(x_i) = f(x_1, \ldots, x_n)$ correctness follows.

4 Selective Security

To prove the selective security of the proposed construction, we proceed via a hybrid argument. In the first hybrid, we replace the PRF's with random functions between a selected honest party i^* and all the remaining honest parties $i \in \mathcal{HS} \setminus i^*$ such that the padding values $t_{i,\ell}$ are randomly generated. Our goal is to encode all the function evaluations of the left submitted challenges, i.e. $f^i(x_i^0) + t_{i,\ell} + r_i$ inside the functional keys[6] and switch from encryptions of $(x_i^0, t_{i,\ell}, \ell)$ to encryptions of $(x_i^1, 0^\lambda, \ell)$[7]. Since, after this step, all the random values are part of the functional key, we can rely on an information theoretic argument and change the values encoded in the functional key from $f^i(x_i^0)+t_{i,\ell}+r_i$ to $f^i(x_i^1)+t_{i,\ell}+r_i$. In the next hybrid, we generate the functional key in the same way as before and change from encryptions of $(x_i^1, 0^\lambda, \ell)$ to encryptions of $(x_i^1, t_{i,\ell}, \ell)$. In the last hybrid, we replace the random functions again with pseudorandom functions and therefore security follows. We present the formal security proof:

Theorem 4.1 (q-message sel-pos$^+$-IND-security of MCFE). *Let* $\mathsf{FE} = (\mathsf{Setup}^{\mathsf{si}}, \mathsf{KeyGen}^{\mathsf{si}}, \mathsf{Enc}^{\mathsf{si}}, \mathsf{Dec}^{\mathsf{si}})$ *be a q-message bounded* sel-FH*-secure single-input functional encryption scheme for the functionality class* $\mathcal{F}_1^{\mathsf{sep}}$*, and* PRF *an* IND *secure pseudorandom function, then the MCFE scheme* $\mathsf{MCFE} = (\mathsf{Setup}^{\mathsf{mc}}, \mathsf{KeyGen}^{\mathsf{mc}}, \mathsf{Enc}^{\mathsf{mc}}, \mathsf{Dec}^{\mathsf{mc}})$ *described in Fig. 4 is a q-message bounded* sel-pos$^+$-IND*-secure for the functionality class* $\mathcal{F}_n^{\mathsf{sep}}$*. Namely, for any PPT adversary* $\mathcal{A}$*, there exists PPT adversaries* $\mathcal{B}$ *and* $\mathcal{B}'$ *such that:*

$$\mathsf{Adv}^{\text{sel-pos}^+\text{-IND}}_{\mathsf{MCFE},\mathcal{A}}(\lambda) \leq 2(n-1) \cdot \mathsf{Adv}^{\text{IND}}_{\mathsf{PRF},\mathcal{B}}(\lambda) + 2n \cdot \mathsf{Adv}^{\text{sel-FH}}_{\mathsf{FE},\mathcal{B}'}(\lambda) \ .$$

Proof. The arguments used for the generation of the values $t_{i,\ell}$ are based on the proof in [1] and we recap those parts here adapted to our construction. For the case with only one honest (non-corrupted) position, we can rely directly on the sel-FH security of the underlying single-input functional encryption scheme FE.

Namely, we build a PPT adversary $\mathcal{B}$ such that $\mathsf{Adv}^{\text{sel-pos}^+\text{-IND}}_{\mathsf{MCFE},\mathcal{A}}(\lambda, n) \leq \mathsf{Adv}^{\text{sel-pos}^+\text{-FH}}_{\mathsf{FE},\mathcal{B}}(\lambda)$. After $\mathcal{B}$ has received $\{Q_{i,\ell}\}_{i\in[n],\ell\in QL}$, $\{Q'_{i,\ell}\}_{i\in[n],\ell\in QL'}$ and $\mathcal{CS}$ from $\mathcal{A}$, it generates $\mathsf{msk}_i \leftarrow \mathsf{Setup}^{\mathsf{si}}(1^\lambda)$ for all $i \in [n] \setminus i^*$, where i^* denotes the honest slot, and samples $\mathsf{K}_{i,j}$ for all $i, j \in [n]$. Finally $\mathcal{B}$ sets $\mathsf{sk}_i := (\mathsf{msk}_i, \{\mathsf{K}_{i,j}\}_{j\in[n]})$ and sends $\{\mathsf{sk}_i\}_{i\in[n]\setminus\{i^*\}}$ to $\mathcal{A}$. It must hold for the queries $\{Q_{i,\ell}\}_{i\in[n],\ell\in QL}$, i.e. $\{(i, x_i^{j,0}, x_i^{j,1}, \ell)\}_{i\in[n],\ell\in QL,j\in[|Q_{i,\ell}|]}$, of $\mathcal{A}$ that $x_i^{j,0} = x_i^{j,1}$ for

[6] This encoding results in a functional key size that polynomially depends on the number of challenge and encryption queries. The security of our construction can therefore only been shown if the number of challenge and encryption queries is bounded such that the desired programming is possible.

[7] For our compiler to work, it is required that the underlying single-input functional encryption scheme allows for the desired programmability of the functional keys. Therefore every functional encryption scheme which allows for the desired programming can be used in our compiler and not only functional encryption schemes for a general functionality class, as stated in the formal theorem.

all $i \in [n] \setminus \{i^*\}$ and $j \in [|Q_{i,\ell}|]$. This results in the fact that $f^i_{r_i}(x^{j,0}_i) = f^i_{r_i}(x^{j,1}_i)$ in every slot $i \in [n] \setminus \{i^*\}$ and for all queries $j \in [|Q_{i,\ell}|]$, which implies that $f^{i^*}_{r_{i^*}}(x^{j,0}_{i^*}) = f^{i^*}_{r_{i^*}}(x^{j,1}_{i^*})$. The left-or-right queries $\{Q_{i,\ell}\}_{i\in[n]\setminus i^*,\ell\in QL}$ can directly be answered by $\mathcal{B}$, it submits $\{((x^{j,0}_{i^*}, t_{i^*,\ell}, \ell), (x^{j,1}_{i^*}, t_{i^*,\ell}, \ell))\}_{\ell\in QL, j\in[|Q_{i,\ell}|]}$, with $t_{i^*,\ell} := \mathsf{Gen}(\mathsf{sk}_{i^*}, i^*, \ell)$ for all $\ell \in QL$ computed by $\mathcal{B}$, as its own left-or-right queries to the experiment. It receives $\{\mathsf{ct}^j_{i^*,\ell}\}_{\ell\in QL, j\in[|Q_{i,\ell}|]}$ as an answer and sends $\{\mathsf{ct}^j_{i,\ell}\}_{i\in[n],\ell\in QL,j\in[|Q_{i,\ell}|]}$ as a reply to $\mathcal{A}$.

For the submitted queries $\{Q'_{i,\ell}\}_{i\in[n],\ell\in QL'}$, i.e. $\{(i, x^j_i, \ell)\}_{i\in[n],\ell\in QL',j\in|Q'_{i,\ell}|}$, to the encryption oracle QEnc, we distinguish between two different cases. In the case that $\mathcal{A}$ asks for an encryption for all positions $i \neq i^*$, $\mathcal{B}$ computes $t_{i,\ell} := \mathsf{Gen}(\mathsf{sk}_i, i, \ell)$ for all $\ell \in QL'$ and $\mathsf{ct}^j_{i,\ell} \leftarrow \mathsf{Enc}^{\mathsf{si}}(\mathsf{msk}_i, (x^j_i, t_{i,\ell}, \ell))$ for all $j \in [|Q'_{i,\ell}|]$ and $\ell \in QL'$. If $\mathcal{A}$ queries QEnc for the position i^*, i.e. it queries (i^*, x^j, ℓ), $\mathcal{B}$ computes $t_{i,\ell} := \sum_{j\neq i}(-1)^{j<i}\mathsf{PRF}_{\mathsf{K}_{i,j}}(\ell)$ for all $\ell \in QL'$, queries its own left-or-right encryption oracle on $((i^*, x^j, \ell), (i^*, x^j, \ell))$ for all $j \in [|Q'_{i,\ell}|]$ and $\ell \in QL'$. Finally, $\mathcal{B}$ sends the answer $\{\mathsf{ct}^j_{i,\ell}\}_{i\in[n],\ell\in QL',j\in[|Q'_{i,\ell}|]}$ to $\mathcal{A}$.

Whenever $\mathcal{A}$ asks a key generation query $\mathsf{QKeyG}(\{f^i\}_{i\in[n]})$, $\mathcal{B}$ samples $r_i \leftarrow \mathcal{Y}_\lambda$ for all $i \in [n-1]$, sets $r_n := -\sum_{i\in[n-1]} r_i$ and generates $\mathsf{sk}_{f^i_{r_i}} \leftarrow \mathsf{KeyGen}(\mathsf{msk}_i, f^i_{r_i})$ for all $i \in [n] \setminus \{i^*\}$. For the functional key $\mathsf{sk}_{f^{i^*}_{r_{i^*}}}$, $\mathcal{B}$ queries its own key generation oracle on $(f^{i^*}_{r_{i^*}}, f^{i^*}_{r_{i^*}})$. Finally it sends $\mathsf{sk}_f := \{\mathsf{sk}_{f^i_{r_i}}\}_{i\in[n]}$ as a reply to $\mathcal{A}$.

This results in the fact that $\mathsf{Adv}^{\text{sel-pos}^+\text{-IND}}_{\mathsf{MCFE},\mathcal{A}}(\lambda, n) \leq \mathsf{Adv}^{\text{sel-FH}}_{\mathsf{FE},\mathcal{B}}(\lambda)$.

For the cases with more than one honest position, we use a hybrid argument with the games defined below. More details on the description of the different games can be found in the full version [20]. Note that G_0 corresponds to the game sel-pos$^+$-IND$^{\mathsf{MCFE}}_0(\lambda, n, \mathcal{A})$, and G_5 corresponds to the game sel-pos$^+$-IND$^{\mathsf{MCFE}}_1(\lambda, n, \mathcal{A})$. This results in:

$$\mathsf{Adv}^{\text{sel-pos}^+\text{-IND}}_{\mathsf{MCFE},\mathcal{A}}(\lambda, n) = |\mathsf{Win}^{\mathsf{G}_0}_{\mathcal{A}}(\lambda, n) - \mathsf{Win}^{\mathsf{G}_5}_{\mathcal{A}}(\lambda, n)| \ .$$

We describe the different intermediate games in more detail:

Game G_1: We replace the PRF evaluation for the computation of the masking values $t_{i,\ell}$ for the left-or-right oracle QLeftRight and the encryption oracle QEnc in the non-corrupted positions $i \in [n] \setminus \mathcal{CS}$ with random function evaluations. In more detail, we switch from the PRF generated values $\mathsf{PRF}_{\mathsf{K}_{i_1,i_s}}$ to $\mathsf{RF}_s(\ell)$, for all $s \in \{2, \ldots, h\}$, where the set of honest users is denoted as $\mathcal{HS} := \{i_1, \ldots, i_h\}$, $h \leq n$ denotes the number of honest users, and RF denotes a random function (see the full version [20] for more details). The transition from G_0 to G_1 is justified by the security of the PRF. Namely, we exhibit a PPT adversary $\mathcal{B}_0$ such that:

$$|\mathsf{Win}^{\mathsf{G}_0}_{\mathcal{A}}(\lambda, n) - \mathsf{Win}^{\mathsf{G}_1}_{\mathcal{A}}(\lambda, n)| \leq (h-1) \cdot \mathsf{Adv}^{\text{IND}}_{\mathsf{PRF},\mathcal{B}_0}(\lambda).$$

Game G_2: We replace the encryptions of $(x^{j,0}_i, t_{i,\ell}, \ell)$ with the encryptions of $(x^{j,1}_i, 0^\lambda, \ell)$ for all $(x^{j,0}_i, x^{j,1}_i) \in Q_{i,\ell}$, all $\ell \in QL$ and all $i \in [n]$ in the left-or-right oracle and we replace the encryptions of $(x_i^j, t_{i,\ell}, \ell)$ with the encryptions of $(x_i^j, 0^\lambda, \ell)$ for all $x_i^j \in Q'_{i,\ell}$, all $\ell \in QL'$ and all $i \in [n]$ in the encryption oracle. The values $t_{i,\ell}$ in the left-or-right queries and the encryption queries are replaced with 0^λ to make the ciphertexts independent from the masking values $t_{i,\ell}$. We also replace the functional key $\mathsf{sk}_f := \{\mathsf{sk}_{f^i_{r_i}}\}_{i\in[n]}$ (see Fig. 5a for the function description) with $\mathsf{sk}_f := \{\mathsf{sk}_{f^i_{\mathcal{Q}_i, Y_i}}\}_{i\in[n]}$ (see Fig. 6 for the function description). The hardcoded values $y_{i,\ell}^{j,f^i} \in Y_i$ are generated using the random value r_i, the queries $(x_i^{j,0}, x_i^{j,1}) \in Q_{i,\ell}$ and by computing the masking values $t_{i,\ell}$, i.e. $y_{i,\ell}^{j,f^i} := f^i(x_i^{j,0}) + t_{i,\ell} + r_i$. The same holds for the hardcoded values $y'^{j,f^i}_{i,\ell} \in Y_i$. They are generated using the random value r_i, the queries $x_i^j \in Q'_{i,\ell}$ and by computing the masking values $t_{i,\ell}$, i.e. $y'^{j,f^i}_{i,\ell} := f^i(x_i^j) + t_{i,\ell} + r_i$. The transition from G_1 to G_2 is achieved using a hybrid argument with a sequence of games $\mathsf{G}_{1.k}$, for $k \in [n]$. It holds that $\mathsf{G}_1 = \mathsf{G}_{1.0}$ and $\mathsf{G}_2 = \mathsf{G}_{1.n}$. This results in

$$\mathsf{Win}_{\mathcal{A}}^{\mathsf{G}_1}(\lambda, n) - \mathsf{Win}_{\mathcal{A}}^{\mathsf{G}_2}(\lambda, n)| \le \sum_{k=1}^{n} |\mathsf{Win}_{\mathcal{A}}^{\mathsf{G}_{1.k-1}}(\lambda, n) - \mathsf{Win}_{\mathcal{A}}^{\mathsf{G}_{1.k}}(\lambda, n)|,$$

The transition from $\mathsf{G}_{1.k-1}$ to $\mathsf{G}_{1.k}$ is justified by the function-hiding security of FE. Namely, we exhibit a PPT adversary $\mathcal{B}_k$ for all $k \in [n]$ such that:

$$|\mathsf{Win}_{\mathcal{A}}^{\mathsf{G}_{1.k-1}}(\lambda, n) - \mathsf{Win}_{\mathcal{A}}^{\mathsf{G}_{1.k}}(\lambda, n)| \le \mathsf{Adv}_{\mathsf{FE},\mathcal{B}_k}^{\text{sel-FH}}(\lambda).$$

Combining both of the statements and noticing that a PPT adversary $\mathcal{B}_1$ can be obtained by picking $i \in [n]$ and running $\mathcal{B}_i$, we can justify the transition from G_1 to G_2. Namely, we exhibit a PPT adversary $\mathcal{B}_1$ such that:

$$|\mathsf{Win}_{\mathcal{A}}^{\mathsf{G}_1}(\lambda, n) - \mathsf{Win}_{\mathcal{A}}^{\mathsf{G}_2}(\lambda, n)| \le n \cdot \mathsf{Adv}_{\mathsf{FE},\mathcal{B}_1}^{\text{sel-FH}}(\lambda).$$

Game G_3: We change the generation of all the values $y_{i,\ell}^{j,f^i} \in Y_i$, which are computed using the random value r_i, the queries $(x_i^{j,0}, x_i^{j,1}) \in Q_{i,\ell}$ and the masking values $t_{i,\ell}$. We change the generation from $y_{i,\ell}^{j,f^i} := f^i(x_i^{j,0}) + t_{i,\ell} + r_i$ to $y_{i,\ell}^{j,f^i} := f^i(x_i^{j,1}) + t_{i,\ell} + r_i$. The transition from G_2 to G_3 is justified by an information theoretic argument and happens for all $i \in [n]$. In more detail, we prove the transition by relying on the conditioned perfect security of several instances of the one-time pad as shown in the full version [20]. Namely, we show that

$$|\mathsf{Win}_{\mathcal{A}}^{\mathsf{G}_2}(\lambda, n) - \mathsf{Win}_{\mathcal{A}}^{\mathsf{G}_3}(\lambda, n)| = 0.$$

Game G_4: We replace the encryptions of $(x_i^{j,1}, 0^\lambda, \ell)$ with the encryptions of $(x_i^{j,1}, t_{i,\ell}, \ell)$ for all $(x_i^{j,0}, x_i^{j,1}) \in Q_{i,\ell}$, all $\ell \in QL$ and all $i \in [n]$ in the left-or-right oracle and we replace the encryptions of $(x_i^j, 0^\lambda, \ell)$ with the encryptions of $(x_i^j, t_{i,\ell}, \ell)$ for all $x_i^j \in Q'_{i,\ell}$, all $\ell \in QL'$ and all $i \in [n]$ in the encryption oracle. The masking values $t_{i,\ell}$ are inserted back into the ciphertext and replace the 0^λ values. We also replace the functional key $\mathsf{sk}_f := \{\mathsf{sk}_{f^i_{\mathcal{Q}_i,Y_i}}\}_{i\in[n]}$ (see Fig. 6 for the function description) with $\mathsf{sk}_f := \{\mathsf{sk}_{f^i_{r_i}}\}_{i\in[n]}$ (see Fig. 5a for the function description). The transition from G_3 to G_4 is almost symmetric to the transition from G_1 to G_2, justified by the function-hiding security of FE applied on every slot $i \in [n]$. Namely, it can be proven that there exists a PPT adversary $\mathcal{B}_2$ such that:

$$|\mathsf{Win}_{\mathcal{A}}^{\mathsf{G}_3}(\lambda, n) - \mathsf{Win}_{\mathcal{A}}^{\mathsf{G}_4}(\lambda, n)| \leq n \cdot \mathsf{Adv}_{\mathsf{FE},\mathcal{B}_2}^{\text{sel-FH}}(\lambda).$$

Game G_5: This game is identical to sel-pos$^+$-$\text{IND}_1^{\mathsf{MCFE}}(\lambda, n, \mathcal{A})$. The transition from G_4 to G_5 is almost symmetric to the transition from G_0 to G_1, justified by the security of the PRF. Namely, it can be proven that there exists a PPT adversary $\mathcal{B}_3$ such that:

$$|\mathsf{Win}_{\mathcal{A}}^{\mathsf{G}_4}(\lambda, n) - \mathsf{Win}_{\mathcal{A}}^{\mathsf{G}_5}(\lambda, n)| \leq (h-1) \cdot \mathsf{Adv}_{\mathsf{PRF},\mathcal{B}_3}^{\text{IND}}(\lambda).$$

Putting everything together, we obtain the theorem. □

The detailed proof of the different game transitions can be found in the full version [20].

5 Adaptive Security

To prove the adaptive security of our construction, we face two main problems that do not occur in the case of selective security: First, we do not know all the honest slots in advance and therefore cannot directly replace the honest pseudorandom function evaluations with random function evaluations. The second problem is that we cannot encode all the function evaluations inside the functional keys since we do not know all the message queries in advance.

We overcome the first problem using a proof technique borrowed from [1]. We define an explicitly honest slots (as in [1]) as slots where the first left-or-right

$f^i_{\mathcal{Q}_i,Y_i}(x, t_{i,\ell}, \ell)$:

Parse $\mathcal{Q}_i := \{\{Q_{i,\ell}\}_{\ell\in QL}, \{Q'_{i,\ell}\}_{\ell\in QL'}\}$ and

$Y_i := \{\{y^{j,f^i}_{i,\ell}\}_{\ell\in QL, j\in[|Q_{i,\ell}|]}, \{y'^{j,f^i}_{i,\ell}\}_{\ell\in QL', j\in[|Q'_{i,\ell}|]}\}$

If $(\cdot, x) \in Q_{i,\ell}$

Output: $y^{j,f^i}_{i,\ell}$

If $x \in Q'_{i,\ell}$

Output: $y'^{j,f^i}_{i,\ell}$

Fig. 6. Description of the function that is used in the reduction for the selective security reduction.

oracle query happens for different messages x_i^0 and x_i^1, i.e. $x_i^{1,0} \neq x_i^{1,1}$. Notice that if a slot i is disclosed as explicitly honest it cannot be corrupted afterwards anymore and we can replace the pseudorandomness in this slot with real randomness (i.e. by relying on the security of the PRF). To know which slots are going to be explicitly honest, we will guess, at a very high level, the number of corrupted slots and the index of the first and the last slots that will be corrupted. This results only in a polynomial loss in the reduction instead of an exponential loss. To solve the second issue, we make use of the $\perp$ slot in the different encryptions. In more detail, we create a list that contains all the functions that have already been queried to the key generation oracle and whenever the adversary queries the left-or-right oracle or the encryption oracle on a new challenge, we place all the function evaluations for every previous queried functions inside the $\perp$ position of the ciphertext. Combining this with the approach from the selective security proof, we ensure that the function evaluation happens correctly no matter if the encryption or left-or-right oracle query happened before or after a functional key query. Since the ciphertext also contains function evaluations, we need to replace them together with function evaluations contained inside the functional key. This happens with the same information theoretic argument as in the selective security case extended to the ciphertexts. The formal proof of the theorem can be found in the full version [20].

Theorem 5.1 (q-message-and-key ad-pos$^+$-IND-security of MCFE). *Let* $\mathsf{FE} = (\mathsf{Setup}^{\mathsf{si}}, \mathsf{KeyGen}^{\mathsf{si}}, \mathsf{Enc}^{\mathsf{si}}, \mathsf{Dec}^{\mathsf{si}})$ *be a q-message-and-key bounded* ad-FH-*secure single-input functional encryption scheme for the functionality class* $\mathcal{F}_1^{\mathsf{sep}}$, *and* PRF *an* IND *secure pseudorandom function, then the MCFE scheme* MCFE *described in Fig. 4 is a q-message-and-key bounded* ad-pos$^+$-IND-*secure functional encryption scheme for the functionality class* $\mathcal{F}_n^{\mathsf{sep}}$. *Namely, for any PPT adversary $\mathcal{A}$, there exists PPT adversaries $\mathcal{B}$ and $\mathcal{B}'$ such that:*

$$\mathsf{Adv}^{\text{ad-IND}}_{\mathsf{MCFE},\mathcal{A}}(\lambda) \leq 2(n+1)n(n-1)^2 \cdot \mathsf{Adv}^{\text{IND}}_{\mathsf{PRF},\mathcal{B}}(\lambda) + 4(n+1)n \cdot \mathsf{Adv}^{\text{ad-FH}}_{\mathsf{FE},\mathcal{B}'}(\lambda) \ .$$

6 Decentralized Multi-Client Functional Encryption

6.1 Definition of Decentralized Multi-Client Functional Encryption

Here, we recap the definition of decentralized multi-client functional encryption (DMCFE) as introduced in [17].

Definition 6.1 (Decentralized Multi-Client Functional Encryption). *Let $\mathcal{F} = \{\mathcal{F}_\lambda\}_\lambda$ be a family (indexed by λ) of sets $\mathcal{F}_\lambda$ of functions $f\colon \mathcal{X}_{\lambda,1} \times \cdots \times \mathcal{X}_{\lambda,n} \to \mathcal{Y}_\lambda$. Let* $\mathsf{Labels} = \{0,1\}^*$ *or* $\{\perp\}$ *be a set of labels. A decentralized multi-client functional encryption scheme (DMCFE) for the function family $\mathcal{F}$ and the label set* Labels *is a tuple of six algorithms* $\mathsf{DMCFE} = (\mathsf{Setup}, \mathsf{KeyGenShare}, \mathsf{KeyGenComb}, \mathsf{Enc}, \mathsf{Dec})$:

$\mathsf{Setup} = (\mathcal{P}_1,\ldots,\mathcal{P}_n)$: *Is an interactive protocol between* n *PPT algorithms* $\mathcal{P}_1,\ldots,\mathcal{P}_n$, *s.t. for all* $i \in [n]$ $\mathcal{P}_i$ *on input* 1^λ *and interacting with* $\mathcal{P}_j$ *for all* $j \in [n]$ *with* $i \neq j$ *obtains the* i*-th secret key* sk_i.

$\mathsf{KeyGenShare}(\mathsf{sk}_i, f)$: *Takes a secret key* sk_i *from position* i *and a function* $f \in \mathcal{F}_\lambda$, *and outputs a partial functional key* $\mathsf{sk}_{i,f}$.

$\mathsf{KeyGenComb}(\mathsf{sk}_{1,f},\ldots,\mathsf{sk}_{n,f})$: *Takes as input* n *partial functional decryption keys* $\mathsf{sk}_{1,f},\ldots,\mathsf{sk}_{n,f}$ *and outputs the functional key* sk_f.

$\mathsf{Enc}(\mathsf{sk}_i, x_i, \ell)$ *is defined as for MCFE in Definition 2.3.*

$\mathsf{Dec}(\mathsf{sk}_f, \mathsf{ct}_{1,\ell},\ldots,\mathsf{ct}_{n,\ell})$ *is defined as for MCFE in Definition 2.3.*

A scheme DMCFE *is correct, if for all* $\lambda, n \in \mathbb{N}$, $\{\mathsf{sk}_i\}_{i\in[n]}$ *are the output of* $\mathsf{Setup} = (\mathcal{P}_1,\ldots,\mathcal{P}_n)$ *executed between* $\mathcal{P}_1,\ldots,\mathcal{P}_n$, $f \in \mathcal{F}_\lambda$, $\ell \in \mathsf{Labels}$, $x_i \in \mathcal{X}_{\lambda,i}$, *when* $\mathsf{sk}_{i,f} \leftarrow \mathsf{KeyGenShare}(\mathsf{sk}_i, f)$ *for* $i \in [n]$, *and* $\mathsf{sk}_f \leftarrow \mathsf{KeyGenComb}(\mathsf{sk}_{1,f},\ldots,\mathsf{sk}_{n,f})$, *we have*

$$\Pr\left[\mathsf{Dec}(\mathsf{sk}_f, \mathsf{Enc}(\mathsf{sk}_1, x_1, \ell),\ldots,\mathsf{Enc}(\mathsf{sk}_n, x_n, \ell)) = f(x_1,\ldots,x_n)\right] = 1 \ .$$

Definition 6.2 (Security of DMCFE). *The* xx-yy-IND *security notion of DMCFE (*$\text{xx} \in \{\text{sel}, \text{ad}\}$ *with* $\text{yy} \in \{\text{pos}^+, \text{any}\}$*) is similar to the notion of MCFE (Definition 2.4), except that the* Setup *is executed by* $\mathcal{P}_1,\ldots,\mathcal{P}_n$ *and the adversary* $\mathcal{A}$ *can corrupt a subset of them, namely* $\mathcal{P}_{j_1},\ldots,\mathcal{P}_{j_n}$ *s.t.* $j_i \in \mathcal{CS}$. *Moreover, there is no* msk *and the key generation oracle is now defined as:*

Key generation oracle $\mathsf{QKeyG}(f)$: *Computes* $\mathsf{sk}_{i,f} \leftarrow \mathsf{KeyGenShare}(\mathsf{sk}_i, f^i)$ *for all* $i \in [n]$ *and outputs* $\{\mathsf{sk}_{i,f}\}_{i\in[n]}$.

6.2 Construction of Decentralized Multi-Client Functional Encryption

In this section, we describe the necessary modifications to turn the presented MCFE of Fig. 4 into a decentralized MCFE scheme (DMCFE). In the decentralized setting, following Definition 6.1, the algorithm KeyGenShare is decentralized and non-interactive. Therefore we can not directly use KeyGen, as described in Fig. 4, since the r_i-values for a certain function f are required to be chosen in such a way that their sum is equal to 0, which requires a simultaneous generation of the functional keys. A way to work around this problem is to generate the r_i-values as a PRF output, in the same way as for the encryption procedure of the scheme described in Fig. 4. In more detail, for the position i the $r_{i,f}$-value for the function f is defined as $r_{i,f} := \sum_{j\neq i}(-1)^{j<i}\mathsf{PRF}_{\mathsf{K}^{\mathsf{F}}_{i,j}}(f)$. The idea of decentralizing a multi-client functional encryption scheme in this way has already been informally described in [2].

The PRF keys for KeyGenShare and Enc are generated during the setup phase, where the setup is executed between a set of players $\mathcal{P}_1,\ldots,\mathcal{P}_n$, (i.e., $\mathcal{P}_i$ is the i-th client of DMCFE scheme). Let $\Pi = (P_1,\ldots,P_n)$ be a n-party MPC protocol [36] that securely computes the function $F_\mathcal{K}$ which is defined as follows. $F_\mathcal{K}$ on input the indexes $1,\ldots n$ outputs for each index i the keys $\{\mathsf{K}_{i,j}, \mathsf{K}^{\mathsf{F}}_{i,j}\}_{j\in[n]}$. s.t. $j \in [n]$ with $j > i$: $\mathsf{K}_{i,j} = \mathsf{K}_{j,i} \leftarrow \{0,1\}^\lambda$ and $\mathsf{K}^{\mathsf{F}}_{i,j} = \mathsf{K}^{\mathsf{F}}_{j,i} \leftarrow \{0,1\}^\lambda$. In the setup phase $\mathcal{P}_i$ executes the player P_i of Π thus obtaining keys for the functional keys and for the encryption algorithm.

We formally describe the DMCFE scheme in Fig. 7.

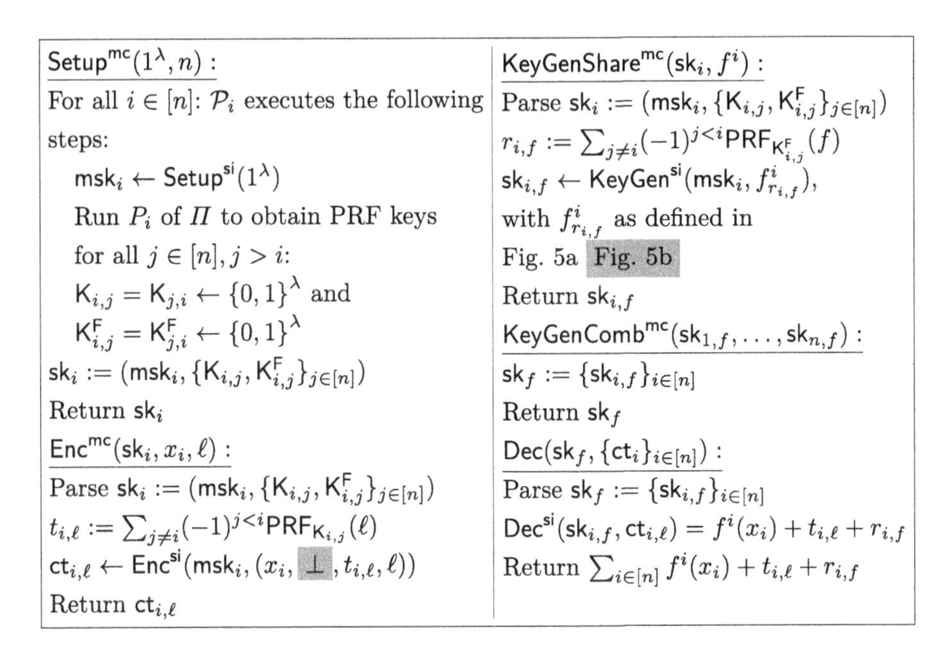

Fig. 7. The generic construction of q-message bounded sel-DMCFE and q-message-and-key bounded ad-DMCFE decentralized multi-client functional encryption from single-input functional encryption. We note that "$\perp$" denotes a slot of size q.

Following the approach of Sect. 5 we also obtain a decentralized MCFE scheme DMCFE that is ad-IND secure with a bounded number of message-and-functional key queries.

Correctness. The correctness of DMCFE follows from the correctness of FE, and the completeness of Π. We note that $\mathsf{Dec}(\mathsf{sk}_f, \mathsf{ct}_{1,\ell}, \ldots, \mathsf{ct}_{n,\ell})$ outputs the value $\sum_{i\in[n]} f^i(x_i) + t_{i,\ell} + r_{i,f} = \sum_{i\in[n]} f^i(x_i)$, where the equality follows from the fact that $\sum_{i\in[n]} t_{i,\ell} = 0$ and $\sum_{i\in[n]} r_{i,f} = 0$. This shows the correctness of the construction.

Theorem 6.3 (sel-pos$^+$-IND security). *Let* $\mathsf{FE} = (\mathsf{Setup}^{\mathsf{si}}, \mathsf{KeyGen}^{\mathsf{si}}, \mathsf{Enc}^{\mathsf{si}}, \mathsf{Dec}^{\mathsf{si}})$ *be a q-message bounded* sel-FH-*secure single-input functional encryption scheme for the functionality class* $\mathcal{F}^{\mathsf{sep}}_1$, PRF *an* IND *secure pseudorandom function, and Π secure realizes function $F_{\mathcal{K}}$, then* DMCFE *described in Fig. 7 is q-message bounded* sel-pos$^+$-IND-*secure for the functionality class* $\mathcal{F}^{\mathsf{sep}}_n$.

Proof (Sketch). The security proof proceeds very similar to the one of Theorem 4.1, with the following two differences:

1. We consider an initial game G_1^* where we switch to the simulator $\mathcal{S}_\Pi$ of Π in order to simulate $\mathcal{P}_{j_1}, \ldots, \mathcal{P}_{j_n}$ s.t. $j_i \in \mathcal{HS}$. The transition from G_1^* to G_1 follows from the security of Π.
2. The game G_1 is slightly modified and separated into two games, G_1' and G_1''. The game G_1' corresponds to G_1 and in game G_1'' we switch from the pseudo-random values $\mathsf{PRF}_{\mathsf{K}^{\mathsf{F}}_{i_1,i_s}}(f)$ to random values $\mathsf{RF}_s(f)$, for all $s \in \{2, \ldots, h\}$, where the set of honest users is denoted as $\mathcal{HS} := \{i_1, \ldots, i_h\}$, with $h \leq n$ as the number of honest users.

The transition from G_1' to G_1'' and from G_1'' to G_2 follows as in the transition from G_0 to G_1 in Theorem 4.1 with the observation that all the keys $\mathsf{K}_{j_i,j_k}, \mathsf{K}^{\mathsf{F}}_{j_i,j_k}$ with $j_i, j_k \in \mathcal{HS}$ are not visible to $\mathcal{A}$ since we are executing $\mathcal{S}_\Pi$ for $\mathcal{P}_{j_1}, \ldots, \mathcal{P}_{j_n}$ with $j_i \in \mathcal{HS}$ in Setup. □

Theorem 6.4 (ad-pos$^+$-IND security). *Let* $\mathsf{FE} = (\mathsf{Setup}^{\mathsf{si}}, \mathsf{KeyGen}^{\mathsf{si}}, \mathsf{Enc}^{\mathsf{si}}, \mathsf{Dec}^{\mathsf{si}})$ *be a q-message-and-key bounded* ad-FH*-secure single-input functional encryption scheme for the functionality class* $\mathcal{F}_1^{\mathsf{sep}}$, PRF *an* IND *secure pseudo-random function and* Π *secure realizes function* $F_{\mathcal{K}}$ *with security against adaptive corruption, then the* DMCFE *scheme described in Fig. 4 is a q-message-and-key bounded* ad-FH*-secure for the functionality class* $\mathcal{F}_n^{\mathsf{sep}}$.

The security proof proceeds very similar to the one of Theorem 5.1 with the argument described above. Moreover correctness of DMCFE follows from the same arguments as the correctness of DMCFE. A description on how to lift an pos$^+$ secure DMCFE scheme into an any secure DMCFE scheme can be found in the full version [20]

7 Outsourceable Multi-Client Functional Encryption

7.1 Definition of Outsourceable Multi-Client Functional Encryption

In addition to the definition of (decentralized) multi-client functional encryption, we present another definition called outsourceable multi-client functional encryption (OMCFE). The notion of OMCFE makes it possible to outsource the decryption procedure of the n different ciphertexts to at most n different entities. This notion is especially useful in the case of a very resource consuming decryption procedure. The different ciphertexts $\mathsf{ct}_{i,\ell}$ can be sent together with the corresponding partial functional key $\mathsf{sk}_{i,f}$ to the i-th entity. The partial decryption procedure applied on $\mathsf{ct}_{i,\ell}$ using $\mathsf{sk}_{i,f}$ generates a decryption share $s_{i,\ell}$. Finally, the shares $s_{i,\ell}$ for every position $i \in [n]$ can be used to reconstruct the final functional output $f(x_1, \ldots, x_n)$. We capture this notion formally:

Definition 7.1 (Outsourceable Multi-Client Functional Encryption). *Let* $\mathcal{F} = \{\mathcal{F}_\lambda\}_{\lambda \in \mathbb{N}}$ *be a collection of function families (indexed by* λ*), where every* $f \in \mathcal{F}_\lambda$ *is a polynomial time function* $f \colon \mathcal{X}_{\lambda,1} \times \cdots \times \mathcal{X}_{\lambda,n} \to \mathcal{Y}_\lambda$. *Let* $\mathsf{Labels} = \{0,1\}^*$ *or* $\{\bot\}$ *be a set of labels. A outsourceable multi-client functional encryption scheme (OMCFE) for the function family* $\mathcal{F}_\lambda$ *supporting* n *users, is a tuple of four algorithms* $\mathsf{OMCFE} = (\mathsf{Setup}, \mathsf{KeyGen}, \mathsf{Enc}, \mathsf{PartDec}, \mathsf{DecComb})$*:*

$\mathsf{Setup}(1^\lambda, n)$: *Takes as input a unary representation of the security parameter* λ *and the number of parties* n*, and generates* n *secret keys* $\{\mathsf{sk}_i\}_{i\in[n]}$ *and a master secret key* msk.

$\mathsf{KeyGen}(\mathsf{msk}, f)$: *Takes as input the master secret key* msk *and a function* $f \in \mathcal{F}_\lambda$*, and outputs* n *functional keys* $\mathsf{sk}_{1,f}, \dots \mathsf{sk}_{n,f}$.

$\mathsf{Enc}(\mathsf{sk}_i, x_i, \ell)$: *Takes as input a secret key* sk_i*, a message* $x_i \in \mathcal{X}_{\lambda,i}$ *to encrypt, a label* $\ell \in \mathsf{Labels}$*, and outputs a ciphertext* $\mathsf{ct}_{i,\ell}$.

$\mathsf{PartDec}(\mathsf{sk}_{i,f}, \mathsf{ct}_{i,\ell})$: *Takes as input a functional key* $\mathsf{sk}_{i,f}$ *and a ciphertext* $\mathsf{ct}_{i,\ell}$ *and outputs a decryption share* $s_{i,\ell} \in \mathcal{Y}_\lambda$.

$\mathsf{DecComb}(\{s_{i,\ell}\}_{i\in[n]})$ *Takes as input* n *decryption shares* $\{s_{i,\ell}\}_{i\in[n]}$ *under the same label* ℓ *and outputs a value* $y \in \mathcal{Y}_\lambda$.

We require that the computational complexity of $\mathsf{DecComb}$ *is independent from the computational complexity of the function* f*, where* $f \in \mathcal{F}_\lambda$.

A scheme OMCFE *is correct, if for all* $\lambda, n \in \mathbb{N}$*,* $(\{\mathsf{sk}_i\}_{i\in[n]}, \mathsf{msk}) \leftarrow \mathsf{Setup}(1^\lambda, n)$*,* $f \in \mathcal{F}_\lambda$*,* $x_i \in \mathcal{X}_{\lambda,i}$*, when* $\{\mathsf{sk}_{i,f}\}_{i\in[n]} \leftarrow \mathsf{KeyGen}(\mathsf{msk}, f)$*, we have*

$$\Pr[\mathsf{DecComb}(\mathsf{PartDec}(\mathsf{sk}_{1,f}, \mathsf{Enc}(\mathsf{sk}_1, x_1, \ell)), \dots, \mathsf{PartDec}(\mathsf{sk}_{n,f}, \mathsf{Enc}(\mathsf{sk}_n, x_n, \ell))) = f(x_1, \dots, x_n)] = 1 \ .$$

The security definition for this new notion is the same as for multi-client functional encryption (Definition 2.4). We remark that in [22] the authors describe a definition of distributed public key FE that has a similar syntax as our definition of OMCFE. Our main goal is to provide a notion of MCFE with an outsourceable decryption procedure, whereas Fan and Tang [22] try to construct a public-key functional encryption scheme that achieves a notion of function-hiding. In particular, our definition does not require any privacy w.r.t. the partial functional key.

Respectively, we can also define a decentralized version of OMCFE by decentralizing the key generation procedure and the setup as in Definition 6.1. This adaption is straightforward and we omit it here.

7.2 Construction of Outsourceable Multi-Client Functional Encryption

In our $\mathsf{OMCFE} = (\mathsf{Setup}, \mathsf{KeyGen}, \mathsf{Enc}, \mathsf{PartDec}, \mathsf{DecComb})$ scheme the algorithms $\mathsf{Setup}, \mathsf{KeyGen}$, and Enc are defined as for the MCFE scheme MCFE described in Fig. 4 and the algorithms $\mathsf{PartDec}$ and $\mathsf{DecComb}$ are defined as follows:

We observe that $\mathsf{DecComb}$ satisfies the efficiency requirement stated in Definition 7.1 since it only consists of a single addition of shares.

Correctness. The correctness of the OMCFE scheme follows from the correctness of FE. We note that the values $s_{i,\ell}$ correspond to $f^i(x_i) + t_{i,\ell} + r_i$ for $i \in [n]$, which in turns implies that $\mathsf{DecComb}(\{s_{i,\ell}\}_{i\in[n]})$ outputs the value $\sum_{i\in[n]} s_{i,\ell} = \sum_{i\in[n]} f^i(x_i) + t_{i,\ell} + r_i = \sum_{i\in[n]} f^i(x_i)$, where the equality follows from the fact that $\sum_{i\in[n]} t_{i,\ell} = 0$ and $\sum_{i\in[n]} r_i = 0$. This shows the correctness of the construction.

$\mathsf{PartDec}(\mathsf{sk}_{i,f}, \mathsf{ct}_{i,\ell})$:
Return $s_{i,\ell} = \mathsf{Dec}^{\mathsf{si}}(\mathsf{sk}_{i,f}, \mathsf{ct}_{i,\ell})$
$\mathsf{DecComb}(\{s_{i,\ell}\}_{i\in[n]})$:
Return $\sum_{i\in[n]} s_{i,\ell}$

Fig. 8. Description of PartDec and DecComb

Theorem 7.2. *Let* $\mathsf{FE} = (\mathsf{Setup}^{\mathsf{si}}, \mathsf{KeyGen}^{\mathsf{si}}, \mathsf{Enc}^{\mathsf{si}}, \mathsf{Dec}^{\mathsf{si}})$ *be a q-message bounded* sel-FH-*secure single-input functional encryption scheme for the functionality class* $\mathcal{F}_1^{\mathsf{sep}}$ *and* PRF *an* IND *secure pseudorandom function, then the* OMCFE *scheme described above is q-message bounded* ad-pos$^+$-IND-*secure scheme for the functionality class* $\mathcal{F}_n^{\mathsf{sep}}$.

We notice that the proof of Theorem 5.1 can be carried out in the same way for Theorem 7.2 with the only difference that the decryption phase is composed of the algorithms PartDec and DecComb.

Following the approach of Sect. 5 we also obtain an outsourceable MCFE scheme OMCFE that is ad-pos$^+$-IND-secure with a bounded number of message-and-key queries. In the adaptively secure scheme OMCFE = (Setup, KeyGen, Enc, PartDec, DecComb) the algorithms Setup, KeyGen, Enc correspond to the ones of the MCFE scheme MCFE as described in Fig. 4, whereas PartDec, DecComb are defined as described in Fig. 8.

Theorem 7.3. *Let* $\mathsf{FE} = (\mathsf{Setup}^{\mathsf{si}}, \mathsf{KeyGen}^{\mathsf{si}}, \mathsf{Enc}^{\mathsf{si}}, \mathsf{Dec}^{\mathsf{si}})$ *be a q-message-and-key bounded* ad-FH-*secure single-input functional encryption scheme for the functionality class* $\mathcal{F}_1^{\mathsf{sep}}$ *and* PRF *an* IND *secure pseudorandom function, then the* OMCFE *scheme described above is q-message-and-key bounded* ad-pos$^+$-IND-*secure scheme for the functionality class* $\mathcal{F}_n^{\mathsf{sep}}$.

The proof proceeds with the same arguments as the proof of Theorem 7.2.

We remark that we achieve sel-pos$^+$-IND and ad-pos$^+$-IND security for the schemes OMCFE and OMCFE respectively.

Acknowledgments. We thank Michel Abdalla for helpful discussions. This work was supported in part by the European Union's Horizon 2020 Research and Innovation Programme under grant agreement 780108 (FENTEC) and by the European Union's Horizon 2020 Research and Innovation Programme under grant agreement 780477 (PRIVILEDGE).

References

1. Abdalla, M., Benhamouda, F., Gay, R.: From single-input to multi-client inner-product functional encryption. In: Galbraith, S.D., Moriai, S. (eds.) ASIACRYPT 2019. LNCS, vol. 11923, pp. 552–582. Springer, Cham (2019). https://doi.org/10.1007/978-3-030-34618-8_19

2. Abdalla, M., Benhamouda, F., Kohlweiss, M., Waldner, H.: Decentralizing inner-product functional encryption. In: Lin, D., Sako, K. (eds.) PKC 2019. LNCS, vol. 11443, pp. 128–157. Springer, Cham (2019). https://doi.org/10.1007/978-3-030-17259-6_5
3. Abdalla, M., Bourse, F., Marival, H., Pointcheval, D., Soleimanian, A., Waldner, H.: Multi-Client inner-product functional encryption in the random-Oracle model. In: Galdi, C., Kolesnikov, V. (eds.) SCN 2020. LNCS, vol. 12238, pp. 525–545. Springer, Cham (2020). https://doi.org/10.1007/978-3-030-57990-6_26
4. Abdalla, M., Catalano, D., Fiore, D., Gay, R., Ursu, B.: Multi-input functional encryption for inner products: function-hiding realizations and constructions without pairings. In: Shacham, H., Boldyreva, A. (eds.) CRYPTO 2018. LNCS, vol. 10991, pp. 597–627. Springer, Cham (2018). https://doi.org/10.1007/978-3-319-96884-1_20
5. Abdalla, M., Gay, R., Raykova, M., Wee, H.: Multi-input inner-product functional encryption from pairings. In: Coron, J.-S., Nielsen, J.B. (eds.) EUROCRYPT 2017. LNCS, vol. 10210, pp. 601–626. Springer, Cham (2017). https://doi.org/10.1007/978-3-319-56620-7_21
6. Agrawal, S., Clear, M., Frieder, O., Garg, S., O'Neill, A., Thaler, J.: Ad hoc multi-input functional encryption. In: Vidick, T. (ed.) ITCS 2020, vol. 151, pp. 40:1–40:41. LIPIcs, January 2020. https://doi.org/10.4230/LIPIcs.ITCS.2020.40
7. Ananth, P., Boneh, D., Garg, S., Sahai, A., Zhandry, M.: Differing-inputs obfuscation and applications. Cryptology ePrint Archive, Report 2013/689 (2013). http://eprint.iacr.org/2013/689
8. Ananth, P., Brakerski, Z., Segev, G., Vaikuntanathan, V.: From selective to adaptive security in functional encryption. In: Gennaro, R., Robshaw, M. (eds.) CRYPTO 2015. LNCS, vol. 9216, pp. 657–677. Springer, Heidelberg (2015). https://doi.org/10.1007/978-3-662-48000-7_32
9. Badrinarayanan, S., Gupta, D., Jain, A., Sahai, A.: Multi-input functional encryption for unbounded arity functions. In: Iwata, T., Cheon, J.H. (eds.) ASIACRYPT 2015. LNCS, vol. 9452, pp. 27–51. Springer, Heidelberg (2015). https://doi.org/10.1007/978-3-662-48797-6_2
10. Boneh, D., Sahai, A., Waters, B.: Functional encryption: definitions and challenges. In: Ishai, Y. (ed.) TCC 2011. LNCS, vol. 6597, pp. 253–273. Springer, Heidelberg (2011). https://doi.org/10.1007/978-3-642-19571-6_16
11. Boyle, E., Chung, K.-M., Pass, R.: On extractability obfuscation. In: Lindell, Y. (ed.) TCC 2014. LNCS, vol. 8349, pp. 52–73. Springer, Heidelberg (2014). https://doi.org/10.1007/978-3-642-54242-8_3
12. Brakerski, Z., Komargodski, I., Segev, G.: Multi-input functional encryption in the private-key setting: stronger security from weaker assumptions. In: Fischlin, M., Coron, J.-S. (eds.) EUROCRYPT 2016. LNCS, vol. 9666, pp. 852–880. Springer, Heidelberg (2016). https://doi.org/10.1007/978-3-662-49896-5_30
13. Brakerski, Z., Komargodski, I., Segev, G.: Multi-input functional encryption in the private-key setting: stronger security from weaker assumptions. J. Cryptol. **31**(2), 434–520 (2017). https://doi.org/10.1007/s00145-017-9261-0
14. Brakerski, Z., Segev, G.: Function-private functional encryption in the private-key setting. In: Dodis, Y., Nielsen, J.B. (eds.) TCC 2015. LNCS, vol. 9015, pp. 306–324. Springer, Heidelberg (2015). https://doi.org/10.1007/978-3-662-46497-7_12
15. Brakerski, Z., Segev, G.: Function-private functional encryption in the private-key setting. J. Cryptol. **31**(1), 202–225 (2017). https://doi.org/10.1007/s00145-017-9255-y

16. Chase, M., Chow, S.S.M.: Improving privacy and security in multi-authority attribute-based encryption. In: Al-Shaer, E., Jha, S., Keromytis, A.D. (eds.) ACM CCS 2009, pp. 121–130. ACM Press, November 2009. https://doi.org/10.1145/1653662.1653678
17. Chotard, J., Dufour Sans, E., Gay, R., Phan, D.H., Pointcheval, D.: Decentralized multi-client functional encryption for inner product. In: Peyrin, T., Galbraith, S. (eds.) ASIACRYPT 2018. LNCS, vol. 11273, pp. 703–732. Springer, Cham (2018). https://doi.org/10.1007/978-3-030-03329-3_24
18. Chotard, J., Dufour Sans, E., Gay, R., Phan, D.H., Pointcheval, D.: Multi-Client functional encryption with repetition for inner product. Cryptology ePrint Archive, Report 2018/1021 (2018). https://eprint.iacr.org/2018/1021
19. Chotard, J., Dufour-Sans, E., Gay, R., Phan, D.H., Pointcheval, D.: Dynamic decentralized functional encryption. Cryptology ePrint Archive, Report 2020/197 (2020). https://eprint.iacr.org/2020/197
20. Ciampi, M., Siniscalchi, L., Waldner, H.: Multi-Client functional encryption for separable functions. Cryptology ePrint Archive, Report 2020/219 (2020). https://eprint.iacr.org/2020/219
21. Dean, J., Ghemawat, S.: Mapreduce: simplified data processing on large clusters. Commun. ACM **51**(1), 107–113 (2008). https://doi.org/10.1145/1327452.1327492
22. Fan, X., Tang, Q.: Making public key functional encryption function private, distributively. In: Abdalla, M., Dahab, R. (eds.) PKC 2018. LNCS, vol. 10770, pp. 218–244. Springer, Cham (2018). https://doi.org/10.1007/978-3-319-76581-5_8
23. Garg, S., Gentry, C., Halevi, S., Raykova, M., Sahai, A., Waters, B.: Candidate indistinguishability obfuscation and functional encryption for all circuits. In: 54th FOCS, pp. 40–49. IEEE Computer Society Press, October 2013. https://doi.org/10.1109/FOCS.2013.13
24. Garg, S., Gentry, C., Halevi, S., Zhandry, M.: Functional encryption without obfuscation. In: Kushilevitz, E., Malkin, T. (eds.) TCC 2016. LNCS, vol. 9563, pp. 480–511. Springer, Heidelberg (2016). https://doi.org/10.1007/978-3-662-49099-0_18
25. Goldwasser, S., et al.: Multi-input functional encryption. In: Nguyen, P.Q., Oswald, E. (eds.) EUROCRYPT 2014. LNCS, vol. 8441, pp. 578–602. Springer, Heidelberg (2014). https://doi.org/10.1007/978-3-642-55220-5_32
26. Goldwasser, S., Kalai, Y.T., Popa, R.A., Vaikuntanathan, V., Zeldovich, N.: Reusable garbled circuits and succinct functional encryption. In: Boneh, D., Roughgarden, T., Feigenbaum, J. (eds.) 45th ACM STOC, pp. 555–564. ACM Press, June 2013. https://doi.org/10.1145/2488608.2488678
27. Gorbunov, S., Vaikuntanathan, V., Wee, H.: Functional encryption with bounded collusions via multi-party computation. In: Safavi-Naini, R., Canetti, R. (eds.) CRYPTO 2012. LNCS, vol. 7417, pp. 162–179. Springer, Heidelberg (2012). https://doi.org/10.1007/978-3-642-32009-5_11
28. Gordon, S.D., Katz, J., Liu, F.H., Shi, E., Zhou, H.S.: Multi-input functional encryption. Cryptology ePrint Archive, Report 2013/774 (2013). http://eprint.iacr.org/2013/774
29. Komargodski, I., Segev, G.: From minicrypt to obfustopia via private-key functional encryption. In: Coron, J.-S., Nielsen, J.B. (eds.) EUROCRYPT 2017. LNCS, vol. 10210, pp. 122–151. Springer, Cham (2017). https://doi.org/10.1007/978-3-319-56620-7_5
30. Kursawe, K., Danezis, G., Kohlweiss, M.: Privacy-friendly aggregation for the smart-grid. In: Fischer-Hübner, S., Hopper, N. (eds.) PETS 2011. LNCS, vol. 6794, pp. 175–191. Springer, Heidelberg (2011). https://doi.org/10.1007/978-3-642-22263-4_10

31. Libert, B., Ţiţiu, R.: Multi-Client functional encryption for linear functions in the standard model from LWE. In: Galbraith, S.D., Moriai, S. (eds.) ASIACRYPT 2019. LNCS, vol. 11923, pp. 520–551. Springer, Cham (2019). https://doi.org/10.1007/978-3-030-34618-8_18
32. Mosk-Aoyama, D., Shah, D.: Computing separable functions via gossip. In: Ruppert, E., Malkhi, D. (eds.) 25th ACM PODC, pp. 113–122. ACM, July 2006. https://doi.org/10.1145/1146381.1146401
33. Mosk-Aoyama, D., Shah, D.: Fast distributed algorithms for computing separable functions. IEEE Trans. Inf. Theory **54**(7), 2997–3007 (2008). https://doi.org/10.1109/TIT.2008.924648
34. O'Neill, A.: Definitional issues in functional encryption. Cryptology ePrint Archive, Report 2010/556 (2010). http://eprint.iacr.org/2010/556
35. Waters, B.: A punctured programming approach to adaptively secure functional encryption. In: Gennaro, R., Robshaw, M. (eds.) CRYPTO 2015. LNCS, vol. 9216, pp. 678–697. Springer, Heidelberg (2015). https://doi.org/10.1007/978-3-662-48000-7_33
36. Yao, A.C.C.: How to generate and exchange secrets (extended abstract). In: 27th FOCS, pp. 162–167. IEEE Computer Society Press, October 1986. https://doi.org/10.1109/SFCS.1986.25

Author Index

Printed in the United States
by Baker & Taylor Publisher Services